Riding Lawn Mower

SERVICE MANUAL ■ 4TH EDITION

Intertec Publishing
P.O. Box 12901 ■ Overland Park, KS 66282-2901

© Copyright 1993 by Intertec Publishing   Printed in the United States of America.
Library of Congress Catalog Card Number 93-78504

This book can be recycled. Please remove cover.

Cover photo courtesy of:
John Deere

Riding Lawn Mower

SERVICE MANUAL ■ 4TH EDITION

Riding Lawn Mower Manufacturers:

- AGCO-ALLIS
- Allis-Chalmers
- AMF
- Ariens
- Bolens
- Case/Ingersoll
- Columbia
- Cub Cadet
- John Deere

- Deutz-Allis
- Dixon ZTR
- Dynamark
- Ford
- Gilson
- Gravely
- Homelite
- Homelite/Jacobsen
- Honda

- Hustler
- International Harvester
- Jacobsen
- Massey-Ferguson
- Maxim
- MTD
- Murray
- Mustang
- J.C. Penney

- Ride King
- Roper
- Sears-Craftsman
- Simplicity
- Snapper
- Wards
- Wheel Horse
- White
- Wizard

The following books and guides are published by Intertec Publishing.

CLYMER SHOP MANUALS
Boat Motors and Drives
Motorcycles and ATVs
Snowmobiles
Personal Watercraft

ABOS/INTERTEC BLUE BOOKS AND TRADE-IN GUIDES
Recreational Vehicles
Outdoor Power Equipment
Agricultural Tractors
Lawn and Garden Tractors
Motorcycles and ATVs
Snowmobiles and Personal Watercraft
Boats and Motors

AIRCRAFT BLUEBOOK-PRICE DIGEST
Airplanes
Helicopters

AC-U-KWIK DIRECTORIES
The Corporate Pilot's Airport/FBO Directory
International Manager's Edition
Jet Book

I&T SHOP SERVICE MANUALS
Tractors

INTERTEC SERVICE MANUALS
Snowmobiles
Outdoor Power Equipment
Personal Watercraft
Gasoline and Diesel Engines
Recreational Vehicles
Boat Motors and Drives
Motorcycles
Lawn and Garden Tractors

CONTENTS

CONTENTS (Cont.)

CONTENTS (Cont.)

FUNDAMENTALS

INTRODUCTION

Correct-fast-easy service may not be possible if the servicing mechanic does not have an understanding of how the machine is supposed to operate. Understanding these fundamentals will not, however, repair worn or damaged equipment. Knowledge of the machine design fundamentals, familiarity with standard accepted service procedures, specific repair information, proper tools and necessary new parts can be combined by service personnel to repair damaged equipment. The mechanic should also be aware that his safety and the safety of others is most important. **Do not take chances.** Be prepared to handle crises (such as spills, fires or run-away equipment) quickly and safely, even before an emergency occurs.

SAFETY INTERLOCK SYSTEMS

Riding lawn mowers may be equipped with two or more interlock safety switches which prevent the engine from starting if blade clutch or drive clutch is engaged or if transmission is in gear. Various types of interlock safety starting systems are used and safety switches may be located on blade clutch, main drive clutch, transmission, under mower seat or on recoil starter rope handle lock.

Always inspect the interlock safety starting system and make sure it is in good operating condition before checking the basic ignition system.

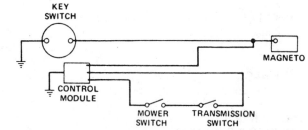

Fig. 2—Typical wiring diagram of interlock safety starting system used on some models equipped with recoil starter. Refer to text.

NOTE: Never return a mower to service with any safety interlock system switches bypassed. The switches are installed to encourage safe operation. Defeating any of the system will permit unsafe operation, which may result in injury.

The interlock safety starting system shown in Fig. 2 is equipped with an electronic control module. Before engine can be started, mower switch and transmission switch must be closed (mower blade clutch disengaged and transmission in neutral). When engine is operating, current feedback from engine magneto switches the control module, isolating the safety switch circuit. At this time, mower blade clutch can be engaged and transmission shifted from neutral without affecting engine operation. If engine will not start with blade clutch disengaged and transmission in neutral or if engine will start with blade clutch engaged or transmission in gear, check and repair safety starting system.

CAUTION: Use extreme care when checking the system as the interlock switches may be bypassed at times during tests.

If engine will not start with blade clutch disengaged and transmission in neutral, disconnect wires to safety switches at control module. Install a bypass wire on control module where switch wires were removed. If engine will start now, use a continuity light or ohmmeter and test for faulty safety switches or switch circuit wires. If engine will not start, disconnect control module wire from engine magneto terminal. If engine will start now, control module is faulty and must be renewed. If engine will still not start, check basic ignition system as trouble is not in safety starting system.

If engine will start with blade clutch engaged or transmission in gear, disconnect wires to safety switches at control module. If engine will not start, inspect safety switches and switch circuit wiring and renew as necessary. If engine will start with safety switch wires disconnected, but will not start with magneto terminal grounded to frame, control module is faulty and must be renewed.

NOTE: Always make certain that interlock safety starting system is in good condition and that all safety switches are connected before returning mower to service.

Another type of safety starting system is shown in Fig. 3. Safety switches

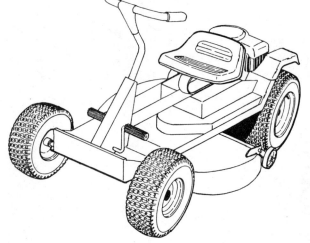

Fig. 1—Operate and service all power equipment carefully and safely.

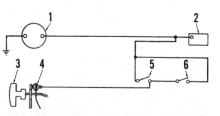

Fig. 3—Typical wiring diagram of interlock safety starting system used on some recoil starter models. Refer to text.

1. Key switch
2. Engine magneto
3. Recoil starter handle
4. Safety switch
5. Drive clutch pedal safety switch
6. Blade disengagement safety switch

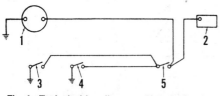

Fig. 4—Typical wiring diagram of interlock safety starting system used on some recoil starter models. Refer to text.

1. Key switch
2. Engine magneto
3. Drive clutch safety switch
4. Blade clutch safety switch
5. Seat safety switch

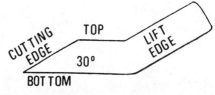

Fig. 6—Drawing of typical blade cross-section identifying parts of blade. The cutting edge should form approximately a 30° angle with bottom.

(5 and 6) must be open (drive clutch pedal locked in fully disengaged position and mower lift and blade disengagement lever in fully disengaged position) before engine can be started. When recoil starter handle (3) is unlocked, spring leaf type safety switch (4) moves to ground against frame. After engine is started, recoil starter handle must be locked in position in frame pushing safety switch (4) open, before blade or drive clutch is engaged. If engine will not start with drive clutch and blade fully disengaged, check for faulty switches (5 and 6) and grounded wires (safety switches to magneto) and renew as necessary.

If engine will start with drive clutch or blade engaged, check to see that safety switch (4) makes good ground contact when recoil starter handle is unlocked. Then, with handle unlocked, check safety switches (5 and 6) and wiring using a continuity light or ohmmeter. Renew faulty components as required.

NOTE: Always make certain that interlock safety starting system is in good condition and that all safety switches are connected before returning mower to service.

On models equipped with safety starting system shown in Fig. 4, safety switch (5) is located under the lawn mower seat. When operator is off the seat, switch (5) is closed. Before engine can be started, safety switches (3 and 4) must be open (mower blade clutch disengaged and drive clutch pedal locked in fully depressed position). After engine is started and operator is seated on the riding mower, the weight of operator on the seat (normally 100 pounds is required) pushes switch (5) to open

position. At this time, blade clutch and drive clutch can be engaged without affecting engine operation. However, if operator raises off the seat while blade clutch or drive clutch is engaged, engine will stop. If engine will not start when blade clutch and drive clutch are in disengaged position, use a continuity light or an ohmmeter and check for faulty safety switches (3 and 4) or grounded switch wires. Renew faulty switches and wiring as necessary.

If engine will start with mower blade clutch or drive clutch engaged, first check to see that seat safety switch (5) closes when operator is off the seat. Then, check to see that safety switches (3 and 4) are closed when clutches are engaged. Renew faulty switches as required.

NOTE: Always make certain that interlock safety starting system is in good condition and that all safety starting switches are connected before returning mower to service.

Many electric start models are equipped with the safety starting system shown in Fig. 5. On this system, safety switches are in the electric starter solenoid switch circuit instead of the magneto ignition circuit as on recoil start models. Transmission must be in neutral and mower blade clutch in disengaged position (both switches closed) before the key switch will operate the electric starter solenoid (magnetic) switch.

If electric starter will not operate when transmission is in neutral and blade clutch is disengaged or if starter will operate when transmission is in gear or blade is engaged, use a continuity light or an ohmmeter and check for faulty safety switches. Renew faulty switches as necessary.

NOTE: Always make certain that safety starting system is in good condition and that all safety starting switches are connected before returning mower to service.

MAINTENANCE

Normal maintenance should include a complete check of the equipment, making sure that equipment is adequately lubricated and adjusting com-

ponents/controls as required. These normal maintenance procedures can effectively reduce the amount of wear and damage that will require repair.

Encourage operators to check all systems as described in the operating instructions, each time the equipment is to be used. Additional regular inspections by service personnel should be encouraged, usually at the beginning and end of normal operating seasons.

Follow the manufacturer's lubrication recommendations. The manufacturer recommends type of lubricant and frequency of lubrication service to reduce damage to the equipment. Altering recommended lubrication intervals or changing type of lubricant may result in extensive damage.

Adjust drive belt (or chain) tension, tire pressure, controls, etc., as required. Checks may indicate the need for adjustments, repair or installation of new parts. Delaying needed adjustments or repairs may result in increased wear rate and/or extensive damage to otherwise usable parts.

CUTTING BLADES

INSPECTION. Mower blades should be inspected frequently for sharpness, balance and straightness. Dull blades will cause ragged grass cutting and can cause excessive load on

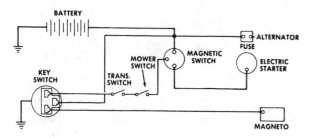

Fig. 5—Typical wiring diagram of interlock safety starting system used on some models equipped with electric starter. Refer to text.

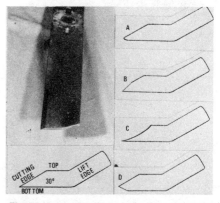

Fig. 7—Views of typical blade. View "A" shows typical cross-section of dull blade. View "B" is incorrect because of sharpening at too much angle. View "C" is sharpened at less than 30° angle. View "D" shows incorrect method of sharpening caused by grinding lower edge of blade.

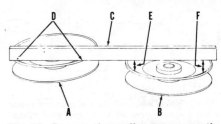

Fig. 8—View of a commonly used cone type balancer. Alignment of the two parts of cone indicate balanced blade.

Fig. 10—Be sure that pulleys are correctly aligned so that belt will move smoothly from one pulley to the other. Sometimes belt is used to drive pulleys that are not aligned, but special guides are employed to change direction of belt. Refer to text.

engine. Bent or out-of-balance blades cause excessive vibration.

CAUTION: Always remove wire from engine spark plug before performing any inspection or service of blades.

Dull blades can normally be sharpened, but bent or cracked blades must be renewed. Refer to the following paragraphs for blade servicing.

SHARPENING. Slightly dulled blades can normally be restored with a few strokes of a file. Badly dulled or nicked blades should be removed and sharpened on a grinder. Ideal cutting edge is sharpened at a 30° angle as shown in Fig. 6. Blades wear on the underside as shown at (A-Fig. 7). If blade is not worn excessively, the 30° angle cutting edge and flat underside can be obtained without excessive grinding. Do not sharpen bottom edge as shown at (D). Sharpen both ends of blade evenly so that blade remains bal-

anced. Always check blade for balance after sharpening.

BALANCING. An unbalanced blade can cause severe vibration resulting in damaged blade spindle bearings and cracked mower housing. Various types of blade balancers are available. A popular blade balancer is the cone type shown in Fig. 8. Before balancing blade, make sure blade is clean and properly sharpened. Place blade center mounting hole over cone balancer and check balance. Mark heavy end of blade. Resharpen blade to remove metal from heavy end. DO NOT grind away the lift edge to balance blade.

BLADE TRACKING. Mower blades should cut on a plane parallel to the level mower housing. With riding mower on a smooth floor, measure distance from end of blade to floor. Rotate blade 180° and measure distance from opposite end of blade to floor. Measurements should be the same within $\frac{1}{16}$ inch (1.6

mm). If not, blade or blade spindle (sometimes crankshaft) is bent and should be renewed.

DRIVE BELTS, BELT GUIDES AND PULLEYS

Drive belts should be checked periodically and adjusted if necessary to prevent slippage under normal operating conditions. Belts should be kept clean and dry. Wipe belts with a clean rag to remove any oil or dirt and carefully check condition of belts. Install new belt of correct size if old belt is stretched, worn or otherwise damaged. Refer to Fig. 9. Worn or damaged belt may be normal after much use, but quick wear or damage may be caused by other failure.

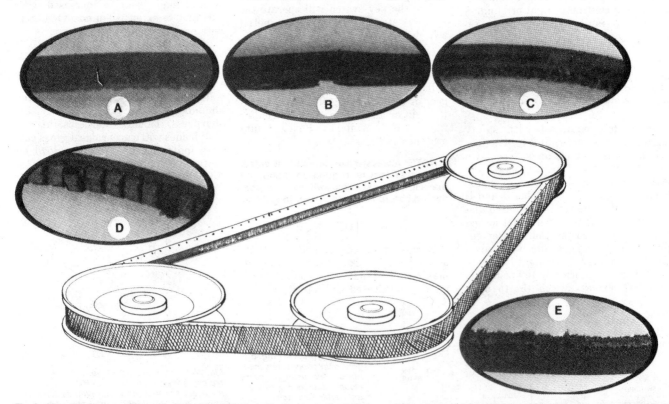

Fig. 9—Visually check condition of belt. Problems illustrated in the insets should be corrected and new belt installed. Inset "A" shows cracks or cuts in belt. Inset "B" shows localized burned section of belt caused by drive pulley turning with belt not moving. Inset "C" shows frayed and worn friction sides. Inset "D" shows notched belt with sections broken loose or out. Inset "E" shows frayed and worn backside of belt which is usually caused by incorrectly adjusted belt guard.

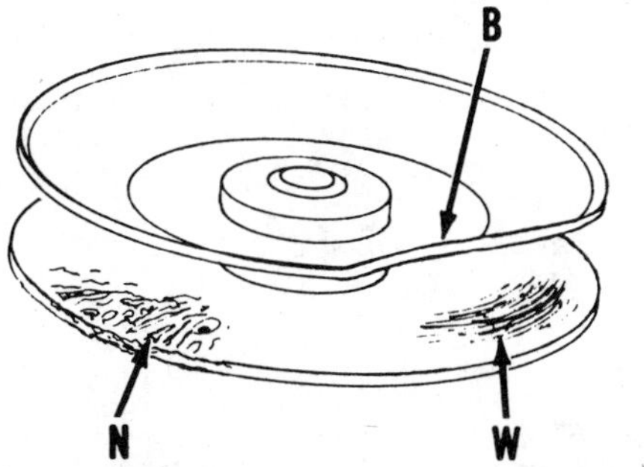

Fig. 11—Damage to pulley such as rough surface (N), cupped surface (W) or bent sides (B) will quickly wear belt out.

Pulleys should be aligned. Straight edge (C–Fig. 10) should indicate that all are in line. If side of pulley (A) is thicker than side of pulley (B), clearance (E & F) should be the same and equal to the difference in thickness of the sides when straight edge is touching at points (D). If the sides of pulleys are the same, clearance at (E & F) indicates that pulley (B) is lower than pulley (A). Method indicated in text for moving pulley should be employed to align pulleys. If clearance (E & F) are different, pulley may be bent or one of the shafts is not in line with the other shaft. Correct alignment to improve belt operation and increase operating life. Check pulleys and install new pulley and belt if nicked (N–Fig. 11), worn (W) or bent (B). Condition and alignment of pulleys is critical to life of belt.

Belt guides and belt stops must be positioned so they will be free of belt when clutch is engaged but will hold belt free of drive pulley when clutch is disengaged. If belt guide specified clearance is not available, position belt guides for ⅛-inch (3 mm) clearance (clutch engaged) and check operation. Be sure to reinstall all guards to prevent injury or belt damage.

DRIVE CHAIN

On models equipped with a drive chain, make certain that chain sprockets are aligned to prevent excessive wear on chain and sprockets. Drive chain should be adjusted so that chain has about ¼-inch (6.4 mm) slack. If chain is too tight, excessive wear and stretch will result. If chain is too loose, it may jump off the sprocket or ride into the sprocket teeth resulting in excessive wear on sprockets and chain. Under normal operating conditions, open drive chain should be lubricated with engine oil each 10 hours of operation.

Sprocket tooth profile (B–Fig. 12) is precisely ground to fit the roller diameter and chain pitch (A). When chain and sprocket are new, the chain moves around the sprocket smoothly with a minimum of friction, and the load is evenly distributed over several sprocket teeth. Wear on pins and bushings of a roller chain results in a lengthening or "stretch" of each individual chain pitch as well as lengthening of the complete chain. The worn chain, therefore, no longer perfectly fits the sprocket. Each roller contacts the sprocket tooth higher up on the bearing area (C) and that tooth bears the total load until the next tooth and roller make contact. Chain wear will therefore quickly result in increased sprocket wear.

As a rule of thumb, a new chain should be installed whenever chain stretch exceeds 2%, or ¼ inch (6.4 mm) for 1 foot (304.8 mm) of length. Renew #40 chain when a 24 pitch length of chain measures 12¼ inches (311.2 mm). Check sprockets carefully for wear if chain wear is substantially greater than 2%, and renew sprockets if in doubt. Sprocket wear usually shows up as a hooked tooth profile. A good test is to fit the sprocket to a new chain. Wear on sides of sprocket indicates misalignment. If sprockets must be renewed

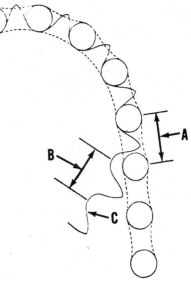

Fig. 12—Chain pitch (A) should be matched to the pitch and contour of sprocket tooth (B).

because of wear, always renew the chain. Early failure can be expected if a new chain is mated with worn sprockets or new sprockets with a worn chain.

REPAIR

Adjustment and repair information for the individual mower units is included within the MOWER SERVICE section. Engine application is listed in the MOWER SERVICE section; however, specific engine repair information is described in ENGINE REPAIR section. Transmission, transaxle and differential application is listed in the MOWER SERVICE section, but procedure for servicing the more common units is described in the TRANSMISSION REPAIR or DIFFERENTIAL REPAIR sections of this manual.

DRIVE BELTS

Make & Model	Mfg. Part No.	Dayco No.	Gates No.	Size (inches)
ARIENS				
927001 (RM728)				
Drive	072112	L335	6735	3/8x35
Mower	072113	L465	6865	1/2x65
927002 (RM626)				
Drive	072112	L335	6735	3/8x35
Mower	072115	L467	....	1/2x67
927003 (RM626)				
Drive	072112	L335	6735	3/8x35
Mower	072115	L467	....	1/2x67
927004 (RM830e)				
Drive	072112	L335	6735	3/8x35
Mower	072113	L465	6865	1/2x65
927005 (RM832)				
Drive	072112	L335	6735	3/8x35
Mower	072124	L465	6865	1/2x65
927006 (RM832e)				
Drive	072112	L335	6735	3/8x35
Mower	072124	L465	6865	1/2x65
927007 (RM1032)				
Drive	072112	L335	6735	3/8x35
Mower	072124	L465	6865	1/2x65
927008 (RM1032e)				
Drive	072112	L335	6735	3/8x35
Mower	072124	L465	6865	1/2x65
927009 (RM828)				
Drive	072112	L335	6735	3/8x35
Mower	072113	L465	6865	1/2x65
927010 (RM830)				
Drive	072112	L335	6735	3/8x35
Mower	072113	L465	6865	1/2x65
927011 (RM830e)				
Drive	072112	L335	6735	3/8x35
Mower	072113	L465	6865	1/2x65
927012 (RM832)				
Drive	072112	L335	6735	3/8x35
Mower	072124	L465	6865	1/2x65
927013 (RM832e)				
Drive	072112	L335	6735	3/8x35
Mower	072124	L465	6865	1/2x65
927014 (RM830)				
Drive	072112	L335	6735	3/8x35
Mower	072113	L465	6865	1/2x65
927015 (RM1032)				
Drive	072112	L335	6735	3/8x35
Mower	072124	L465	6865	1/2x65
927016 (RM1032e)				
Drive	072112	L335	6735	3/8x35
Mower	072124	L465	6865	1/2x65
927017 (SRM830)				
Drive	072112	L335	6735	3/8x35
Mower	072113	L465	6865	1/2x65
927018 (SRM626)				
Drive	072112	L335	6735	3/8x35
Mower	072115	L467	....	1/2x67
927020 (SRM1030)				
Drive	072112	L335	6735	3/8x35
Mower	072113	L465	6865	1/2x65

Make & Model	Mfg. Part No.	Dayco No.	Gates No.	Size (inches)
ARIENS (Cont.)				
927021 (RM828)				
Drive	072112	L335	6735	3/8x35
Mower	072113	L465	6865	1/2x65
927023 (RM1032e)				
Drive	072112	L335	6735	3/8x35
Mower	072155	L465	6865	1/2x65
927024 (RM830)				
Drive	072112	L335	6735	3/8x35
Mower	072113	L465	6865	1/2x65
927025 (RM830e)				
Drive	072112	L335	6735	3/8x35
Mower	072169	....	....	....
927026 (RM1032)				
Drive	072112	L335	6735	3/8x35
Mower	072124	L465	6865	1/2x65
927027 (SRM830)				
Drive	072112	L335	6735	3/8x35
Mower	072113	L465	6865	1/2x65
927028 (RM1032e)				
Drive	072112	L335	6735	3/8x35
Mower	072155	L465	6865	1/2x65
927029 (RM830e)				
Drive	072112	L335	6735	3/8x35
Mower	072113	L465	6865	1/2x65
927030 (RM1132e)				
Drive	072112	L335	6735	3/8x35
Mower	072155	L465	6865	1/2x65
927031 (RM828e)				
Drive	072112	L335	6735	3/8x35
Mower	072113	L465	6865	1/2x65
927032 (RM1130e)				
Drive	072112	L335	6735	3/8x35
Mower	072113	L465	6865	1/2x65
927033 (RM928e)				
Drive	072112	L335	6735	3/8x35
Mower	072162	L464	6864	1/2x64
927034 (RM1232e)				
Drive	072112	L335	6735	3/8x35
Mower	072163	L464	6864	1/2x64
927037 (RM830e)				
Drive	072112	L335	6735	3/8x35
Mower	072169	....	....	....
927039 (RM828e)				
Drive	072112	L335	6735	3/8x35
Mower	072169	....	....	....
927040 (RM1232e)				
Drive	072112	L335	6735	3/8x35
Mower	072163	L464	6864	1/2x64
927041 (RM1232e)				
Drive	072112	L335	6735	3/8x35
Mower	072155	L465	6865	1/2x65
927042 (RM928e)				
Drive	072112	L335	6735	3/8x35
Mower	072162	L464	6864	1/2x64
BOLENS				
528 (Serial Numbers 0200101-0299999)				
Drive	1731719	L451	6851	1/2x51
Mower	1736248	L464	6864	1/2x64
528 (Serial Numbers 0300101-0399999)				
Drive	1731719	L451	6851	1/2x51
Mower	1738406	....	....	5/8x65

Make & Model	Mfg. Part No.	Dayco No.	Gates No.	Size (inches)
BOLENS (Cont.)				
628				
Drive	1731719	L451	6851	½x51
Mower	1738496	L465	....	½x65
728				
Drive	1724261	L452	6851	½x52
Mower	1724035	L468	6868	½x68
828				
Drive	1724261	L452	6851	½x52
Mower	1724035	L468	6868	½x68
829				
Drive	1724261	L452	6851	½x52
Mower	1724035	L468	6868	½x68
830 & 831 (Serial Numbers 0200101-0299999)				
Drive	1731719	L451	6851	½x51
Mower	1731719	L451	6851	½x51
830 & 831 (Serial Numbers 0300101-0399999)				
Drive	1731719	L451	6851	½x51
Mower	1722238	L465	6865	½x65
830 & 831 (Serial Numbers 0400101-0499999)				
Drive	1731719	L451	6851	½x51
Mower	1738511	L466	6866	½x66
1130				
Drive	1731719	L451	6851	½x51
Mower	1722238	L465	6865	½x65
1134				
Drive	1731719	L451	6851	½x51
Mower	1741568	L495	6350	½x95
1136				
Drive	1731719	L451	6851	½x51
Mower	1747938	L496	6896	½x96
2027, 2028				
Drive	1731719	L451	6851	½x51
Mower	1738496	L465	....	½x65
2030				
Drive	1731719	L451	6851	½x51
Mower	1738511	L466	6866	½x66
2036, 2136, 2136A				
Drive	1731719	L451	6851	½x51
Mower	1747938	L496	6896	½x96
2128A				
Drive	1731719	L451	6851	½x51
Mower	1722238	L465	6865	½x65
CASE/INGERSOLL				
80, 80XC, 80XE, 80XM				
Traction Drive..................	C24342	L436	6836	½x36
Mower	C24349	L460	6860	½x60
COLUMBIA				
Refer to corresponding MTD model.				
CUB CADET				
136-511-100				
Traction Drive..................	754-0249	L530	....	⅝x30
Mower	754-0264	L452	6852	½x52
136-514-100, 136-518-100, 526, 800, 830, 1002, 1136, 1208				
Traction Drive (Primary)	754-0241	L535	6935	⅝x35
Traction Drive (Secondary)	754-0240	L538	6938	⅝x38

Make & Model	Mfg. Part No.	Dayco No.	Gates No.	Size (inches)
JOHN DEERE				
55, 56				
Transmission	M44483	....	6848	½x48
Mower	M44498	L460	A58	½x60
57				
Transmission	M44483	....	6848	½x48
Mower	M45863	L456	A54	½x56
Deck	M45862	L448	A45	½x47
66				
Transmission	M82167	L451	6851	½x51
or M49155	L452	6852	½x52
or M80652	L451	6851	½x51
or M81505	L451	6851	½x51
Mower	M80386	L464	6864	½x64
or M49920	L499	6899	21/32x99
68				
Transmission	M82167	L451	6851	½x51
or M49155	L452	6852	½x52
or M80652	L451	6851	½x51
or M81505	L451	6851	½x51
Mower, 30 in.	M80386	L464	6864	½x64
34 in.	M49920	L499	6899	½ or 21/32x99
GX70, GX75				
Transmission	M94020	....	....	....
Mower	M112006	....	....	....
R70, R72, R92				
Transmission	M86421	L453	....	½x53
Mower	M86422	....	....	....
S80, S82				
Transmission	M82167	L451	6851	½x51
Mower	M82538	L463	....	½x63
S92				
Transmission	M82167	L451	6851	½x51
Mower	M86248	....	....	....
SRX75				
Transmission:				
Primary	M94049	....	....	....
Secondary	M91470	....	....	....
Mower	M112006	....	....	....
SRX95				
Transmission:				
Primary	M94049	....	....	....
Secondary	M91470	....	....	....
Mower	M112490	....	....	....
RX63				
Transmission:				
Primary	M76054	....	....	....
Secondary	M91470	....	....	....
Mower	M72031	....	....	....
RX73, RX75, RX95, SX75				
Transmission:				
Primary	M76054	....	....	....
Secondary	M91470	....	....	....
Mower	M71529	....	6865	½x65
SX95				
Transmission:				
Primary	M76054	....	....	....
Secondary	M91470	....	....	....
Mower	M72683	...	6899	½x99
DEUTZ-ALLIS				
Scamp 5				
Transmission	2028241	L431	6831	½x31
Pto	2028217	L434	6834	½x34
Mower, 24 in.	2025893	L448	6848	½x48
26 in.	2029223	L444	6844	½x44

Make & Model	Mfg. Part No.	Dayco No.	Gates No.	Size (inches)
DEUTZ-ALLIS (Cont.)				
Scamp 8				
Main Drive....................	2025879	L463	6863	½x63
	or 2029660	L462	6862	½x62
Directional Drive................	2029451	L4293	....	½x29⁵⁄₁₆
Mower	2029582	AP133	A133	½x135
405				
Transmission...................	2028241	L431	6831	½x31
Pto	2028217	L434	6834	½x34
Mower	2929223	L444	6844	½x44
508				
Main Drive....................	2029660	L462	6862	½x62
Directional Drive................	2029451	L4293	....	½x29⁵⁄₁₆
Mower	2029582	AP133	A133	½x135
526				
Transmission...................	1665706	L439	6839	½x39
Mower	1664946	L457	6857	½x57
830				
Transmission...................	1665706	L439	6839	½x39
Mower	1665024	L454	6854	½x54
836				
Transmission...................	71678354	....	6842	½x42
Mower	71664644	....	....	....
1036				
Transmission...................	1665706	L439	6839	½x39
Mower	2087732	L478	6878	½x78
1236H				
Transmission...................	71700581	L452	....	½x52
Intermediate	71700362	....	....	....
Mower	71664644	....	....	....
1242				
Transmission...................	71678354	....	6842	½x42
Mower	71678241	....	....	....
1242H				
Transmission...................	71700581	L452	....	½x52
Intermediate	71700362	....	....	....
Mower	71678241	....	....	....
1312				
Transmission...................	71678354	....	6842	½x42
Mower	71703371	....	....	....
1312H				
Transmission...................	71704735	....	....	....
Intermediate	71700362	....	....	....
Mower	71703371	....	....	....
1316H				
Transmission...................	71704735	....	....	....
Intermediate	71700362	....	....	....
Mower	71703372	....	....	....
DIXON				
ZTR308				
Transmission...................	30-2426	4L440	3440	21⁄32x44
	....	L440	6944	21⁄32x44
Mower	....	....	3740	21⁄32x74
ZTR 424, 425, 426				
Transmission...................	1539	L541	6941	⅝ or 21⁄32x41
Mower Drive..................	6111	....	B75	21⁄32x78
Blade	6109	AP80	A80	½x82
ZTR 311				
Transmission...................	2469	....	....	....
Mower	2412	....	....	....
DYNAMARK				
826, 1260, 1269				
Transmission...................	43979	L456	6856	½x56
Mower	45187	L444	6844	½x44

Make & Model	Mfg. Part No.	Dayco No.	Gates No.	Size (inches)
DYNAMARK (Cont.)				
832, 1261				
Transmission	43979	L456	6856	½x56
Mower	45186	L463	6863	½x63
or 47390	or 47390	L471	6871	½x71
1281				
Transmission	39454	L488	6888	½x88
Mower	39456	L569	6969	⅝x69
or 42111	or 42111	L570	6970	⅝x70
or 43066	or 43066	L571	6971	⅝x71
1284				
Transmission	39454	L488	6888	½x88
Mower	46466	L483	6883	½x83
or 48044	or 48044	L582	6982	⅝x82
1288				
Transmission	39454	L488	6888	½x88
Pto	44313	L452	6852	½x52
or 45509	or 45509	L453	6853	½x53
Mower	44264	L498	6898	½x98
2650				
Transmission	55450	L442	....	½x42
Mower	55442	L458	....	½x58
3180, 3181				
Transmission	49405	L488	6888	½x88
3188				
Transmission	39454	L488	6888	½x88
	50737	L484	6884	½x84
Mower	43066	L571	6971	⅝x71
3189				
Transmission	43979	L456	6856	½x56
Mower	45186	L463	6863	½x63
3208				
Transmission	54758	L482	....	½x82
Mower	45186	L463	....	½x63
3280				
Transmission	55450	L442	....	½x42
Mower	47611	L488	....	½x88
3294				
Transmission	51855	L441	....	½x41
Mower	47611	L488	....	½x88
3610				
Transmission	54758	L482	....	½x82
Mower	43066	L571	6971	⅝x71
3611 (3611-0200, 3611-0400)				
Transmission	54758	L482	....	½x82
Mower	49878	....	....	....
3611 (3611-0300, 3611-0500, 3611-0700, 3611-0800, 3611-2101, 3611-2300, 3611-2700, 3611-2800, 3611-3100, 3611-3400)				
Transmission	54758	L482	....	½x82
Mower	43066	L571	6971	⅝x71
3611 (3611-2200, 3611-2400, 3611-3600)				
Transmission	54758	L482	....	½x82
Mower	48044	L582	....	⅝x82
3611 (3611-0600)				
Transmission:				
Primary	54829	L4305	....	½x30½
Secondary	54830	L471	....	½x71
Mower	49878	....	....	....

Make & Model	Mfg. Part No.	Dayco No.	Gates No.	Size (inches)
DYNAMARK (Cont.)				
3612				
Transmission	54758	L482	....	½x82
Mower	48044	L582	....	⅝x82
5180, 5181				
Transmission	49405	L488	6888	½x88
5184				
Transmission	43979	L456	6856	½x56
5188				
Transmission	39454	L488	6888	½x88
Mower	43066	L571	6971	⅝x71
5267				
Transmission	43979	L456	6856	½x56
Mower	44039	L444	6844	½x44
or 45187	L444	6844	½x44	
or 45186	L463	6863	½x63	
5282, 5285, 5288				
Transmission	39454	L488	6888	½x88
Mower	39456	L569	6969	⅝x69
or 42111	L570	6970	⅝x70	
or 43066	L571	6971	⅝x71	
or 48044	L582	6982	⅝x82	
5289				
Transmission	43979	L456	6856	½x56
Mower	44148	L463	6863	½x63
or 45186	L463	6863	½x63	
5294				
Transmission	44150	L441	6841	½x41
Mower	45186	L463	6863	½x63
or 47611	L488	6888	½x88	
5296				
Transmission	39454	L488	6888	½x88
Mower	43066	L571	6971	⅝x71
or 46466	L483	6883	½x83	
or 48044	L582	6982	⅝x82	
5297				
Transmission	39454	L488	6888	½x88
Pto	44313	L452	6852	½x52
or 45509	L453	6853	½x53	
Mower	44264	L498	6898	½x98
FORD				
51				
Transmission	308506	L331	6731	⅜x31
Mower	308494	L466	6866	½x66
60 (early), 65 (early)				
Transmission	308475	L431	6831	½x31
Mower	308476	L470	6870	½x70
60 (late), 61, 65 (late), 66				
Transmission	308491	L331	6731	⅜x31
or 308506	L331	6731	⅜x31	
Mower	308493	L470	6869	½x69 or 70
526				
Transmission	308511	L438	6838	½x38
Mower	308510	L456	6856	½x56
Early Belt Drive Models— 830, 830E				
Transmission	308491	L331	6731	⅜x31
Mower	308493	L470	6869	½x69 or 70
Late Belt Drive Models— 830, 830E, 1130E				
Transmission	308491	L331	6731	⅜x31
Mower	308522	L468	6867	½x67 or 68

Make & Model	Mfg. Part No.	Dayco No.	Gates No.	Size (inches)
FORD (Cont.)				
Friction Drive Models—				
830, 830E, 1130E				
Mower	392545	....	....	....
R8				
Transmission..................	231362	L345	....	3/8x45
Mower	240773	....	....	....
8E				
Transmission..................	231362	L345	....	3/8x45
Mower	240773	....	....	....
R11E				
Transmission..................	231362	L345	....	3/8x45
Mower	240773	....	....	....
GILSON				
52013, 52031, 52038				
Mower	14365	L451	....	1/2x51
52014, 52015				
Mower	17518	L460	....	1/2x60
52032, 52033,				
52039, 52040				
Mower	23472	L356	....	3/8x56
52051C				
Transmission..................	36750	....	....	....
Mower	11793	L590	....	5/8x90
....	or 36751	L488	....	1/2x88
52060				
Transmission..................	36750	....	....	....
Mower	210692	L496	....	1/2x96
52061				
Transmission:				
Primary.......................	210752	....	....	....
Secondary	210753	L4313	....	1/2x31 5/16
Mower	36751	L488	....	1/2x88
52064, 52065,				
52072, 52073				
Transmission..................	212931	....	....	....
Mower	213676	L485	....	1/2x85
52066, 52074				
Transmission..................	212931	....	....	....
Mower	210692	L496	....	1/2x96
52080, 52080-A, 52081,				
52081-A, 52081-B, 52081-C				
Transmission..................	212931	....	....	....
Mower	213676	L485	....	1/2x85
52082 & 52082-A				
Transmission..................	212931	....	....	....
Mower	210692	L496	....	1/2x96
52082-B				
Transmission..................	212931	....	....	....
Mower:				
Primary.......................	235955	L339	....	3/8x39
Secondary....................	235956	L488	....	1/2x88
52089, 52090, 52091				
Transmission..................	231362	L345	....	3/8x45
Mower	231511	....	....	....
52106, 52107, 52108				
Transmission..................	231362	L345	....	3/8x45
Mower	231511	....	....	....
52106-A, 52106-B, 52107-A,				
52107-B, 52108-A, 52120				
Transmission..................	231362	L345	....	3/8x45
Mower	240773	....	....	....
5213, 5213-A, 52117, 52118				
Transmission	212931	....	....	....
Mower.......................	237738	L486	....	1/2x86

Make & Model	Mfg. Part No.	Dayco No.	Gates No.	Size (inches)
GRAVELY				
830, 830-E, 1130-E				
Transmission	26137	L331	6731	⅜x31
Mower	26149	L468	6867	½x67 or 68
HOMELITE/JACOBSEN				
(also see Jacobsen)				
RE-5				
Transmission	158573	L431	6831	½x31
Mower	174911	L444	6844	½x44
Pto	121398	L434	6834	½x34
RE-8E				
Transmission	177452	L462	6862	½x62
Pto	176451	....	A133	½x135
RE-30				
Transmission	1651201	L473	A71	½x73
Pto	176451	....	A133	½x135
HR830, HR830E, HR1230E				
Transmission	99263-8	....	6839	½x39
Mower	99263-9	L465	6865	½x65
HR930E				
Transmission	99073-8	....	6852	½x52
Mower	99148-8	L473	6873	½x73
JR830, JR1030, JR1230				
Transmission	99073-8	....	6852	½x52
Mower	99148-8	L473	6873	½x73
RE830, RE830E, RE1030E, RE1230E				
Transmission	99073-8	....	6852	½x52
Mower	99148-8	L473	6873	½x73
MX8, RMX8E, RMX11E				
Transmission	99073-8	....	6852	½x52
Mower (early)	99095-9	....	....	....
Later	99148-8	L473	6873	½x73
INTERNATIONAL HARVESTER				
Cadet 55				
Forward	549108-R1	L438	6837	½x37-38
To Deck	549609-R1	L450	6850	½x50
or	62817-C1	L449	6849	½x49
Mower	488077-R1	L448	6848	½x48
Cadet 60				
Transmission:				
Forward	487994-R1	L437	6837	½x37
Reverse	487996-R1	L435	6835	½x35
Mower	488082-R1, -R2	L452	6852	½x52
Blade Spindle	488077-R1	L448	A46	½x48
Cadet 75				
Mower	488077-R1	L448	6848	½x48
Cadet 85				
Transmission	549107-R1	L439	6839	½x39
Mower	106991-C1	....	A53	½x55
Blade	106990-C1	L445	A43	½x45
Cadet 85 Special				
Transmission	549107-R1	L439	6839	½x39
Mower	106465-C1	L451	A49	½x51
Cadet 95 Electric				
Transmission	57842-C1	L433	6833	½x33
JACOBSEN				
42635				
Transmission	546341	L525	6925	⅝ or ²¹⁄₃₂x25
Variable	546342	L531	6931	⅝ or ²¹⁄₃₂x31
Mower	546343	L552	6852	½x52
Other 426 Models				
Mower	330463	L476	6876	½x76

Make & Model	Mfg. Part No.	Dayco No.	Gates No.	Size (inches)
JACOBSEN (Cont.)				
430 Models With				
30-in. Mower				
Mower	330463	L476	6876	½x76
RMX				
Mower	JA392545	....	....	....
MASSEY-FERGUSON				
MF5, MF6, MF626				
Transmission..................	523733M1	L436	6836	½x36
Mower	523734M1	L458	6858	½x58
MF8, MF832				
Transmission..................	530669M1	L437	6837	½x37
Mower	530756M1	L498	6898	½x98
MAXIM				
GL830, GL1230				
Transmission..................	272216	L431	6831	½x31
Mower	272217	....	A74	½x76
GL12F				
Transmission..................	272222			
Deck	272235	....	6967	⅝x67
	272236	L557	6957	⅝x57
Blade	272234	L588	6988	⅝x88
MTD				
400				
Transmission..................	754-101	L435	6835	½x35
Blade	754-188	L551	6951	⅝x51
402, 405, 406, 407				
Transmission				
Primary.....................	754-187	L524	3240	⅝x24
Secondary	754-136	L531	6931	⅝x31
Blade	754-188	L551	6951	⅝x51
410, 412				
Transmission..................	754-101	L435	6835	½x35
Blade	754-138	L550	6950	⅝x50
420 (early), 425 (early)				
Transmission..................	754-136	L531	6931	⅝x31
Variable Speed..............	754-135	L525	6925	⅝x25
Blade	754-127	L566	6966	⅝x66
420 (late), 425 (late)				
Transmission..................	754-135	L525	6925	⅝x25
	or 754-136	L531	6931	⅝x31
Blade	754-147	L552	6952	⅝x52
430, 435				
Transmission..................	754-135	L525	6925	⅝x25
	or 754-136	L531	6931	⅝x31
Blade	754-127	L566	6966	⅝x66
440 (early), 445 (early)				
Transmission..................	754-185	L449	6849	½x49
Blade	754-178	L582	6982	⅝x82
440 (late), 445 (late)				
Transmission..................	754-200	L448	6848	½x48
Blade	754-178	L582	6982	⅝x82
500, 501 (early),				
510 (early), 511 (early)				
Transmission..................	754-0249	L530	6930	21⁄32x30
Mower	754-0264	L452	....	½x52
501 (late), 502, 504,				
506, 510 (late), 511 (late),				
512, 514, 516, 518, 520,				
521, 530, 531, 550, 551				
Transmission:				
Primary.....................	754-0241	L535	6935	21⁄32x35
Secondary	754-0240	L538	6938	21⁄32x38

Make & Model	Mfg. Part No.	Dayco No.	Gates No.	Size (inches)
MTD (Cont.)				
501 (late), 502, 504, 506, 510 (late), 511 (late), 512, 514, 516, 518, 520, 521, 530, 531, 550, 551 (Cont.)				
Mower:				
26-, 30-in.	754-0264	L452	....	½x52
32-in.	754-0347	L463	6863	½x63
36-in.	754-0214	L450	6850	½x50
Blade:				
32-in.	754-0290	....	A45	½x47
36-in.	754-0250	L453	6853	½x53
796, 797				
Transmission	754-207	L442	6842	½x42
Blade	754-198	L463	6863	½x63
MURRAY				
2503, 2513				
Drive	20716	L437	6837	½x37
Mower	20717	L456	6856	½x56
3013, 3033, 3043, 3063 (with Cross Drive)				
Drive	20716	L437	6837	½x37
Mower	20556	L448	6848	½x48
Cross Drive	20555	L441	6841	½x41
3013, 3033 (without Cross Drive)				
Drive	20716	L437	6837	½x37
Mower	23496	L474	6874	½x74
	or 21649	L455	6855	½x55
3233				
Drive	20716	L437	6837	½x37
Mower	21058	L463	6863	½x63
Cross Drive	21059	L444	6844	½x44
3633				
Drive	20716	L437	6837	½x37
Mower	20558	L464	6864	½x64
Cross Drive	20557	L446	6846	½x46
25501, 25502				
Drive	37X38	....	....	....
Mower	37X36	L455	....	½x55
30501, 30502				
Drive	37X38	....	....	....
Mower	37X37	....	....	....
31501				
Drive	37X27	L483	....	½x83
Mower	37X34	L477	....	½x77
36503				
Drive	37X35	L490	....	½x90
Mower	37X39	L483	....	½x83
39001				
Drive	37X26	L488	....	½x88
Mower	37X39	L483	....	½x83
MUSTANG				
245, 248, 248E				
Drive	23	L431	6831	½x31
J.C. PENNEY				
1820				
Transmission	754-198	L463	6863	½x63
Blade	754-195	L454	6854	½x54
1824				
Transmission	21615	L495	6895	½x95
Mower	21649	L455	6855	½x55
Blade	20557	L446	6846	½x46

Make & Model	Mfg. Part No.	Dayco No.	Gates No.	Size (inches)
J.C. PENNEY (Cont.)				
1831				
Transmission	754-198	L463	6863	½x63
Blade	754-195	L454	6854	½x54
1832				
Transmission	754-936	L447	6847	½x47
Blade	754-107	L430	6830	½x30
1834				
Transmission	21615	L495	6895	½x95
Mower	23748	L462	6862	½x62
Blade	23749	L499	6899	½x99
1835				
Transmission	754-226	L482	6882	½x82
Blade	754-225	AP105	....	½x107$\frac{5}{16}$
1839				
Transmission	754-0198	L463	6863	½x63
Blade	754-0167	L564	6964	⅝x64
1840				
Transmission	754-0191	L465	6865	½x65
Blade	754-0151	L567	6967	⅝x67
1841, 1842				
Transmission	23347	L484	6884	½x84
Mower	23882	L459	6859	½x59
Blade	20557	L446	6846	½x46
1844				
Primary Drive	754-0245	L459	....	½x59
Secondary Drive	754-0244	L440	....	½x40
Blade	754-0246	1440-8M-20	6354	....
1845, 1846				
Transmission	754-0226	L482	6882	½x82
Blade	754-0145	L569	6969	⅝x69
1847				
Transmission	754-0248	L489	....	½x89
Blade	754-0246	1440-8M-20	6354	....
1848				
Transmission	754-0226	L482	....	½x82
Blade	754-0145	L569	....	$\frac{21}{32}$x69
1905, 1907, 1907A, 1908, 1909				
Transmission	20716	L437	6837	½x37
Blade	20717	L456	6856	½x56
1910				
Transmission	20716	L437	6837	½x37
Blade	21649	L455	6855	½x55
ROPER				
K511, K512, K522				
Transmission	67346	L439	6839	½x39
Mower	67438	L447	6847	½x47
K831, K832				
Transmission	67346	L439	6839	½x39
Mower	67398	L453	6853	½x53
K852—Belt information unavailable.				
L711, L721, L722				
Transmission	58406	L465	6865	½x65
Mower	70637	L440	6840	½x40
L821, L861, L863				
Transaxle	71240	L492	6892	½x92
SEARS-CRAFTSMAN				
502.256011, 502.256091				
Transmission	20716	L437	6837	½x37
Blade	20717	L456	6856	½x56

Make & Model	Mfg. Part No.	Dayco No.	Gates No.	Size (inches)
SEARS-CRAFTSMAN (Cont.)				
502.256020, 502.256030, 502.256040				
Transmission	20715	L437	6837	½x37
Blade	20717	L456	6856	½x56
502.256071				
Transmission	20715	L437	6837	½x37
Blade	23496	L474	6874	½x74
502.256080				
Transmission	20715	L437	6837	½x37
Blade	23536	L477	6877	½x77
502.256111, 502.256121, 502.256130, 502.256141				
Transmission	20715	L437	6837	½x37
Blade	21649	L455	6855	½x55
SIMPLICITY				
305, 315				
Transmission	158573	L431	6831	½x31
Mower	174911	L444	6844	½x44
or 108248	L448	6848	½x48	
Pto	121398	L4335	6834	½x33½ or 34
355				
Transmission	158573	L431	6831	½x31
Pto	164146	L434	6834	½x34
808				
Transmission	177452	L462	6862	½x62
Pto	176451	....	A133	½x135
3005				
Transmission	158573	L431	6831	½x31
Mower	174911	L444	6844	½x44
Pto	121398	L4335	6834	½x33½ or 34
3008-2, 3008-3				
Transmission	1651201	L473	A71	½x73
Pto	176451	....	A133	½x135
3105				
Transmission	1665706	....	6839	½x39
Mower	1664946	....	A55	½x57
3108				
Transmission	1665706	....	6839	½x39
Mower	1665024	....	6854	½x54
3110				
Transmission	1665706	....	6839	½x39
Mower	108505	....	A68	½x70
8GW6				
Transmission	1678354	....	6842	½x42
Mower	1664644	....	....	....
1036				
Transmission	1665706	L439	6839	½x39
Mower	2087732	L478	6878	½x78
12GW2				
Transmission	1678354	....	6842	½x42
Mower	1678241	....	....	....
12HW2				
Transmission	1700581	L452	....	½x52
Intermediate	1700362	....	....	....
Mower	1678241	....	....	....
12HW6				
Transmission	1700581	L452	....	½x52
Intermediate	1700362	....	....	....
Mower	1664644	....	....	....
12FC42				
Transmission	1678354	....	6842	½x42
Mower	1703371	....	....	....

Make & Model	Mfg. Part No.	Dayco No.	Gates No.	Size (inches)
SIMPLICITY (Cont.)				
12FCH42				
Transmission	1704735	....	....	....
Intermediate	1700362	....	....	....
Mower	1703371	....	....	....
16FCH48				
Transmission	1704735	....	....	....
Intermediate	1700362	....	....	....
Mower	1703372	....	....	....
SNAPPER				
Mower				
Prior to Series 7,				
except 33 & 41 in.	1-0749	AA68	6234	*
17T700				
33 in.	1-8236	....	6375	**
41 in.	1-4525	AA105	6399	
Series 7, 8 & 9	1-8236	....	6375	**

*Double ½-inch, 36 degree drive belt, 71⅜ inches long.
**Double ½-inch, 36 degree drive belt, 74¼ inches long.

Make & Model	Mfg. Part No.	Dayco No.	Gates No.	Size (inches)
WARDS				
33857A, 33857B				
Transmission	36750	8X1030	....	¹⁷/₃₂x104
Mower	36751	L488	....	¹⁷/₃₂x88¹¹/₁₆
33867A				
Primary	210752	....	....	....
Secondary	210753	L4313	....	½x31⁵/₁₆
Mower	36751	L488	....	¹⁷/₃₂x88¹¹/₁₆
33877A				
Transmission	36750	8X1030	....	¹⁷/₃₂x104
Mower	210692	L496	....	¹⁷/₃₂x96½
33887A, 33889A				
Transmission	212931	....	....	¹⁷/₃₂x100¾
Mower	210692	L496	....	¹⁷/₃₂x96½
WHEEL HORSE				
A-50 (30114)				
Transmission	103345	L325	6725	⅜x25
Mower	8430	L459	6859	½x59
A-51 (05BP01, 02)				
Transmission	9430	L436	6836	½x36⁵/₁₆
A-60 (05BF01)				
Transmission	225282	L441	....	....
A-70 (08BP01)				
Transmission	225187	....	....	....
A-81 (08BP01)				
Transmission	9430	L436	6836	½x36⁵/₁₆
A-111 (11BP01, 02)				
Transmission	9430	L436	6836	½x36⁵/₁₆
R-26				
Transmission	1597	L325	6725	⅜x25
Reverse	1597	L325	6725	⅜x25
Mower	8430	L459	6859	½x59
RR-532, RR-832				
Transmission	9430	L436	6836	½x36⁵/₁₆
Mower	108491	L467	....	½x67
26MS01 (Mower)	225360	L463	6863	½x63
32MS01 (Mower)	107298	L472	6872	½x72
	108491	L467	....	½x67
32XS01 (Mower)	107647	....	....	....
	108503	....	....	...
36MR01, 36MR02,				
36MS00, 36MS01 (Mower)				
Drive	102741	L497	6897	½ or ²¹/₃₂x97
	105477	L440	6840	½x40
Spindle	8411	L477	6877	½x77
	105476	L480	A78	½x80

Make & Model	Mfg. Part No.	Dayco No.	Gates No.	Size (inches)
WHEEL HORSE				
36XR00, 36XR01, 36XS00, 36XS01, 36XS02 (Mower)				
Drive	102741	L497	6897	$\frac{1}{2}$ or $\frac{21}{32}$x97
	105477	L440	6840	$\frac{1}{2}$x40
	106533	L440	A38	$\frac{1}{2}$x40
Spindle.....................	8411	L477	6877	$\frac{1}{2}$x77
	105476	L480	A78	$\frac{1}{2}$x80
	106751	L481	6880	$\frac{1}{2}$x80
36YR01, 36YR02 (Mower)				
Drive	107230	L460	6860	$\frac{1}{2}$x60
	108492	....	....	....
Spindle.....................	8411	L477	6877	$\frac{1}{2}$x77
108-R, 108-3, 108-5, 111-5				
Drive	110364	L433	....	$\frac{1}{2}$x33
Mower	110376	....	....	$\frac{1}{2}$x38$\frac{1}{2}$
WHITE				
R10				
Transmission:				
Primary.....................	754-0241	L535	6935	$\frac{21}{32}$x30
Secondary	754-0240	L538	....	$\frac{21}{32}$x38
Mower	754-0347	L463	6863	$\frac{1}{2}$x63
Blade	754-0290	....	A45	$\frac{1}{2}$x47
R50				
Engine to Variator...............	32-0021415	L524	6924	$\frac{21}{32}$x24
Variator to Trans.	32-0021407	L531	6931	$\frac{21}{32}$x31
Mower	32-0021253	L551	6951	$\frac{21}{32}$x51
R53				
Transmission...................	754-0249	L530	....	$\frac{21}{32}$x30
Mower	754-0264	L452	....	$\frac{1}{2}$x52
R80				
Transmission...................	32-0018635	L550	6950	$\frac{21}{32}$x50
Mower	32-0018910	L582	6982	$\frac{21}{32}$x82
R82				
Transmission...................	32-0055301	L442	6842	$\frac{1}{2}$x42
Mower	32-0024368	L462	6862	$\frac{1}{2}$x62
R86				
Transmission:				
Primary.....................	754-0241	L535	6935	$\frac{21}{32}$x35
Secondary	754-0240	....	6938	$\frac{21}{32}$x38
Mower	754-0328	L549	6949	$\frac{21}{32}$x49
WIZARD				
7110, 7115				
Transmission...................	212931	....	....	$\frac{17}{32}$x100$\frac{3}{4}$
Mower	212676	....	....	....
7380				
Transmission...................	36750	8X1030	6990	$\frac{17}{32}$x104
Mower	36751	L488	....	$\frac{17}{32}$x88

AGCO-ALLIS

AGCO-ALLIS
5295 Triangle Parkway
Norcross, GA 30092

NOTE: The models included in this section may have been marketed as Allis-Chalmers, Deutz-Allis or AGCO-ALLIS riding lawn mowers.

Model	Make	Engine Model	Horsepower	Cutting Width, In.
Scamp 5	B&S	130000	5	26
Scamp 8	B&S	190000	8	30
405	B&S	130000	5	26
508	B&S	190000	8	30
526	B&S	130000	5	26
830	B&S	190000	8	30
1036	B&S	220000	10	36

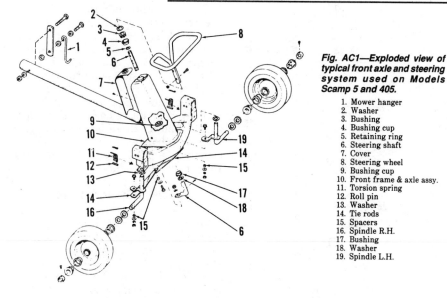

Fig. AC1—Exploded view of typical front axle and steering system used on Models Scamp 5 and 405.

1. Mower hanger
2. Washer
3. Bushing
4. Bushing cup
5. Retaining ring
6. Steering shaft
7. Cover
8. Steering wheel
9. Bushing cup
10. Front frame & axle assy.
11. Torsion spring
12. Roll pin
13. Washer
14. Tie rods
15. Spacers
16. Spindle R.H.
17. Bushing
18. Washer
19. Spindle L.H.

cotter pin from steering shaft. Withdraw steering shaft from bottom of frame and remove cup (9), bushing (17) and washer (18).

Clean and inspect all parts and renew any showing excessive wear or other damage. Reassemble by reversing the disassembly procedure. Lubricate spindles and steering shaft bushings with SAE 30 oil.

Models Scamp 8 and 508

REMOVE AND REINSTALL. The axle main member is also the front frame assembly (19-Fig. AC2). Pivot point is at joint of front and rear frame

STEERING SYSTEM

Models Scamp 5 and 405

REMOVE AND REINSTALL. The axle main member is also the front frame assembly (10-Fig. AC1). Pivot point is at joint of front and rear frame sections. To disassemble the steering system, support front of unit and remove front wheel assemblies. Unbolt and remove tie rods (14). Remove cotter pins from top of spindles (16 and 19), drive out roll pins (12) and remove both spindles with washers (13) and torsion springs (11). Unbolt and remove steering wheel (8) and cover (7). Remove washer (2), bushing (3), cup (4) and retaining ring (5) from upper end of steering shaft (6). Working through rear opening in front frame, remove

Fig. AC2—Exploded view of typical front axle and steering system used on Models Scamp 8 and 508.

1. Steering wheel
2. Washer
3. Bushing
4. Steering shaft & pinion
5. Washer
6. Bushing
7. Spacers
8. Quadrant gear
9. Bushing
10. Washer
11. Drag link
12. Retaining ring
13. Spindle R.H.
14. Spring
15. Shoulder bolt
16. Spindle bushings
17. Tie rod
18. Spindle L.H.
19. Front frame & axle assy.
20. Steering support
21. Support cover

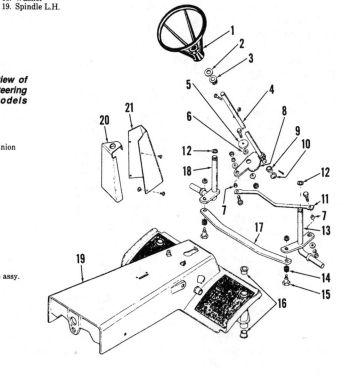

sections. To disassemble the steering system, support front of unit and remove front wheel assemblies. Unbolt and remove the tie rod (17) and drag link (11). Remove retaining rings (12) and remove spindles (13 and 18). Remove steering wheel (1), washer (2) and bushing (3). Unbolt and remove steering support and cover (20 and 21). Remove cotter pin and washer (10) from lower end of steering shaft (4), then withdraw steering shaft and pinion. Unbolt and remove quadrant gear (8), special washer (5) and bushing (6). Remove steering shaft bushing (9) and spindle bushing (16), if need for renewal is indicated.

Clean and inspect all parts and renew any showing excessive wear or other damage. Using Fig. AC2 as a guide, reassemble by reversing the disassembly procedure. Tighten flange nut on quadrant gear center bolt to a torque of 60 ft.-lbs. (81 N·m). Torque flange nuts on tie rod shoulder bolts (15) to 30 ft.-lbs. (40 N·m). Apply a light coat of lithium grease to pinion and quadrant gear teeth and lubricate tie rod, drag link and steering shaft bushings with SAE 30 oil. Spindle bushings (16) are nylon and require no lubrication.

Models 526, 830 and 1036

REMOVE AND REINSTALL. Remove mower deck as needed, refer to MOWER BLADE CLUTCH AND BELT section for removal. To remove front axle and steering parts, raise and securely block front portion of chassis.

Remove locking caps securing front wheels, then slide wheel assembly off spindles (31 and 32–Fig. AC3). Remove cotter key (12) securing drag link (28) in spindle arm (31), then lift drag link out of bushing (29) and swing clear of axle assembly. Remove nut (24) and washer (23) from pivot pin (22). While supporting axle assembly (25) withdraw pivot pin (22), then lower complete axle assembly and place to the side for inspection and repair.

With reference to Fig. AC3 disassemble and inspect spindles, axle tubes and control linkage for excessive wear, bending, cracks and any other damage. Inspect bushings (21 and 29) for excessive wear or any other damage and renew all parts as needed. Reassemble in reverse order of disassembly.

Inspect steering gear (17), pinion gear (10) and bushings (8) for excessive wear or any other damage and renew all parts as needed.

Reinstall and lubricate front wheel bushings, shouldered spindle bushings, steering shaft and wear points in linkage with SAE 30 engine oil. Wipe off excess to prevent dirt accumulation.

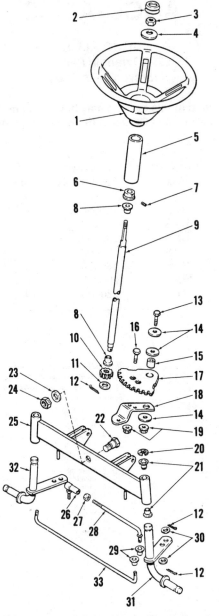

Fig. AC3—Exploded view of typical front axle and steering system used on Models 526, 830 and 1036.

1. Steering wheel	
2. Cap	18. Steering arm
3. Nut	19. Nut
4. Washer	20. "E" clip
5. Tube	21. Bushing
6. Collar	22. Pivot pin
7. Set screw	23. Washer
8. Bushing	24. Nut
9. Shaft	25. Axle assy.
10. Pinion gear	26. Ball joint
11. Washer	27. Jam nut
12. Cotter key	28. Drag link
13. Cap screw	29. Bushing
14. Washer	30. Washer
15. Spacer	31. Spindle (L.H.)
16. Cap screw	32. Spindle (R.H.)
17. Steering gear	33. Tie rod

ENGINE

All Models

Refer to appropriate engine section in this manual for tune-up specifications, engine overhaul procedures and engine

maintenance.

Refer to following paragraphs for removal and installation procedures.

Models Scamp 5 and 405

To remove the engine assembly, unbolt and remove engine hood on all models so equipped. On electric start models, disconnect battery cables and starter wires. On all models, disconnect ignition wire and throttle control cable. Unbolt and remove pulley and belt guard from left side and remove the belt guide. Place the blade clutch lever in disengaged position, depress clutch-brake pedal and remove belts from engine pulley. Unbolt and remove engine assembly. Reinstall engine by reversing the removal procedure.

Models Scamp 8 and 508

To remove the engine assembly, open the rear frame cover and on electric start models, disconnect battery cables and starter wires. On all models, disconnect throttle cable and ignition wire. Push transmission primary drive belt idler forward and remove belt from engine pulley. Place blade clutch control lever in disengaged position and remove mower drive belt from engine pulley. Unbolt and remove engine assembly. Reinstall engine by reversing the removal procedure.

Models 526, 830 and 1036

To remove engine assembly, open rear frame cover and on electric start models, disconnect battery cables and starter wires. On all models, disconnect throttle cable and ignition wire. For ease in repair, remove mower deck and drive belt assembly as outlined in MOWER BLADE CLUTCH AND BELT section. Loosen cap screws securing engine drive pulley belt guard, then slide clear of pulley. Loosen tension on traction drive belt idler as needed, then slip drive belt off engine drive pulley. Remove any parts that will obstruct in removal of engine, then unbolt and remove engine assembly. Reinstall engine by reversing the removal procedure. Clearance between engine drive pulley belt guard and lower pulley should be ⅛ inch (3 mm).

TRACTION DRIVE CLUTCH AND BRAKE

All Models

The traction drive clutch on all models is of belt idler type. Band and drum type brake is used on all models.

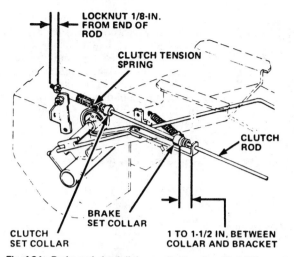

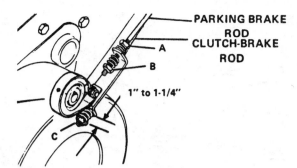

Fig. AC6—Brake adjustment on Models Scamp 8 and 508. Refer to text.

Fig. AC4—Brake and clutch linkage adjustment on Model Scamp 5.

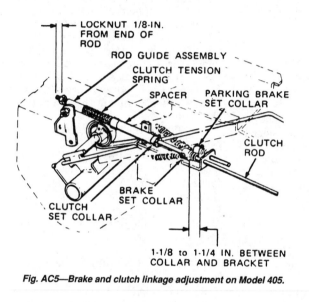

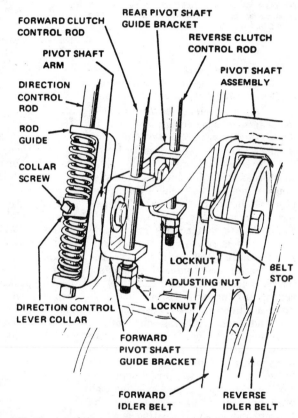

Fig. AC5—Brake and clutch linkage adjustment on Model 405.

Models Scamp 5 and 405

To adjust the clutch and brake linkage, remove rear hitch plate, refer to Figs. AC4 and AC5 and proceed as follows: With clutch-brake pedal in fully up (clutch engaged) position, adjust the brake set collar to a distance of 1 to 1½ inches (25.4-38.1 mm) (Scamp 5) or 1⅛ to 1¼ inches (28.6-31.7 mm) (405) from bracket as shown. On all models, adjust locknut to ⅛ inch (3 mm) from end of clutch rod. On Model Scamp 5 with clutch-brake pedal in up position, adjust the clutch set collar so that clutch tension spring is preloaded $\frac{1}{16}$ inch (1.6 mm). On Model 405 depress the clutch-brake pedal until brake is fully applied. Adjust clutch set collar so that spacer holds the clutch tension spring against the clutch rod guide. Spring should not be compressed when pedal is fully depressed.

Fig. AC7—View of clutch and forward-reverse drive linkage on Models Scamp 8 and 508. Refer to text for adjustment procedure.

Models Scamp 8 and 508

To adjust the clutch and brake linkage, refer to Fig. AC6 and turn nut (A) on parking brake rod to end of threads. Engage parking brake and tighten nut (B) until the spring against it is fully compressed. Adjust nut (C) to obtain a distance of 1 to 1¼ inches (25.4-31.7 mm) between flat washer and brake band bracket as shown. Disengage parking brake and check to see that spring by nut (A) pushes brake band free of brake drum. If not, adjust nut (A) as required.

Clutching occurs when the pivot shaft assembly is moved to neutral position and belt tension is released from both the forward and reverse idler belts. Depressing the clutch-brake pedal or moving the direction control lever to NEUTRAL position will place the pivot shaft in neutral. Refer to Fig. AC7 and loosen the set screw in directional control lever collar. Place directional control lever in NEUTRAL position. Rotate pivot shaft assembly to tighten forward idler belt, applying about five pounds pressure. Place a mark on directional control rod at front edge of rod guide. Rotate pivot shaft in opposite direction to tighten reverse idler belt, once again applying about five pounds (2.3 kg.) pressure. Place a second mark

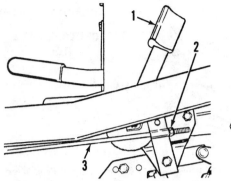

Fig. AC8—Adjust brake-clutch pedal (1) height by turning adjustment nut (2) on linkage rod (3) on Models 526, 830 and 1036. Clearance between brake pedal arm and front edge of slot should be 1/4-1/2 inch (6.4-12.7 mm).

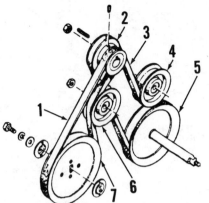

Fig. AC10—View showing traction drive belt, pto drive belt and pulleys used on Models Scamp 5 and 405.

1. Traction drive belt
2. Engine pulley
3. Pto drive belt
4. Pto (blade) clutch idler pulley
5. Pulley and jackshaft
6. Traction drive clutch idler pulley
7. Transmission input pulley

on directional control rod at front edge of rod guide. Distance between the two marks should be $^{11}/_{16}$ inch (17.5 mm). If this distance is incorrect, loosen the four cap screws securing pivot shaft in place. Move pivot shaft assembly forward or rearward as necessary to obtain the correct distance. Moving pivot shaft rearward will increase the distance. When the $^{11}/_{16}$-inch (17.5 mm) distance is obtained, tighten the four cap screws to a torque of 15 ft.-lbs. (20 N·m). Place a center mark on rod halfway between front and rear marks. Align front edge of rod guide with the center mark and tighten the collar set screw. Place the directional control lever in full forward position and pull pivot shaft downward. Loosen the locknut and turn adjusting nut until a clearance of ¼ inch (6.4 mm) exists between the adjusting nut and the forward pivot shaft guide bracket. Tighten the locknut. Move the directional control lever to full reverse position and push pivot shaft upward. Loosen the locknut and set the adjusting nut to a clearance of ¼ inch (6.4 mm) from the reverse pivot shaft guide bracket. Tighten the locknut.

Models 526, 830 and 1036

To adjust engagement and disengagement of traction brake and clutch proceed as follows. Fully depress brake-clutch pedal (1-Fig. AC8) using normal pressure, then measure clearance between pedal arm and front edge of frame slot. Clearance should be ¼-½ inch (6.4-12.7 mm). To adjust, turn adjustment nut (2) on linkage rod (3) until correct clearance is attained.

With pedal in released position measure length of spring (2-Fig. AC9). Spring should be 1-1¼ inches (25.4-31.7 mm) long. To adjust, loosen set screw in set collar (3), then slide collar on rod (1) until correct length is attained. Retighten set screw.

TRACTION DRIVE BELTS

Models Scamp 5 and 405

REMOVE AND RENEW. To remove the traction drive belt (1-Fig. AC10), unbolt and remove engine hood on all models so equipped. On electric start models, disconnect battery cables. On all models, disconnect spark plug

wire, then unbolt and remove pulley and belt guard from left side. Remove the belt guide and place blade clutch lever in disengaged position. Remove the pto belt (3) from engine pulley. Depress the clutch-brake pedal and remove the traction drive belt.

Install new belt by reversing the removal procedure. Adjust clutch and brake linkage as required.

Models Scamp 8 and 508

REMOVE AND RENEW. To remove the traction drive belts (3, 4 and 9-Fig. AC11), disconnect spark plug wire, open the rear frame cover and on electric start models, remove the battery. On all models, push the primary drive belt idler (1) forward until primary belt (3) can be removed from engine pulley (2). Remove primary belt from left side of transmission pulley. Note position of belt stops on the forward and reverse control idler pulleys and loosen the mounting bolts. Remove reverse drive belt (4) and forward drive belt (9), then complete the removal of the primary belt.

Install new belts by reversing the removal procedure. Refer to Fig. AC12 and adjust outer adjusting nut until the length of the idler tension spring is 1⅛ inches (28.6 mm). Adjust the inner elastic stop nut to a clearance of $^{1}/_{16}$ inch (1.6 mm) from frame bracket. Adjust clutch and brake linkage as outlined in previous paragraphs.

Models 526, 830 and 1036

REMOVE AND RENEW. Remove mower deck and drive belt as outlined in MOWER BLADE CLUTCH AND BELT section. Loosen drive belt finger on idler pulley and swing clear of belt. Loosen engine pulley drive belt guard securing nuts and slide belt guard away from drive pulley. Release tension on traction belt idler as needed, then slip drive belt off pulleys.

Inspect drive pulleys for excessive wear, cracks, looseness, burrs or any other damage and renew parts as

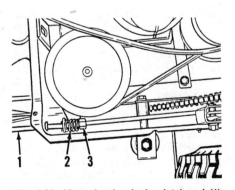

Fig. AC9—View showing brake-clutch rod (1), spring (2) and set collar (3) on Models 526, 830 and 1036. Spring released measured length should be 1 to 1-1/4 inches (25.4-31.7 mm) long.

Fig. AC11—View showing clutch and brake linkage and drive belt arrangement on Models Scamp 8 and 508.

1. Primary drive belt idler
2. Engine pulley
3. Primary drive belt
4. Reverse drive belt
5. Pivot shaft assy.
6. Parking brake lever
7. Directional control lever
8. Clutch-brake pedal
9. Forward drive belt
10. Brake assy.

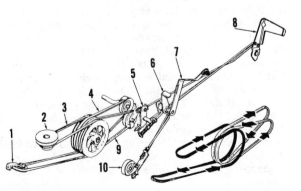

Illustrations Courtesy AGCO

needed. Renew drive belt, then reassemble in reverse order of disassembly.

TRANSMISSION

All Models

Transmission used on Models Scamp 5 and 405 are equipped with two forward gears and one reverse. The transmission used on Models Scamp 8 and 508 is equipped with two forward gears. No reverse gear is used in this transmission as forward-reverse drive belt arrangement allows for forward or reverse operation in either gear. All units are of the transaxle type with the transmission gears and shafts, differential and axle shafts contained in one case.

Transmission used on Models 526, 830 and 1036 is equipped with five forward gears and one reverse. Power is transmitted from transmission assembly to differential assembly by use of a chain and sprockets.

NOTE: On models so equipped, make certain that safety interlock switches are connected and are in good operating condition before returning mower to service.

Models Scamp 5 and 405

REMOVE AND REINSTALL. The transmission shafts, shifter shafts and left axle shaft extend through the rear frame. The following procedures will outline the removal of components necessary for removal of the transmission and differential. Actual removal of the shafts, gears and differential is outlined in the Simplicity portion of the TRANSMISSION REPAIR section of this manual.

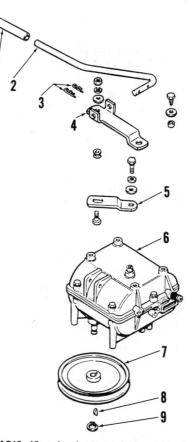

Fig. AC13—View showing transmission and associated parts on Models 526, 830 and 1036.

1. Handle grip	
2. Shift rod	6. Transmission assy.
3. Hairpin clip	7. Input pulley
4. Pivot lever	8. Woodruff key
5. Shift link	9. Retaining ring

Unbolt and remove engine hood on all models so equipped. On electric start models, disconnect battery cables and remove battery. On all models, disconnect spark plug wire. Unbolt and remove the pulley and belt guard from left side, then remove the belt guide.

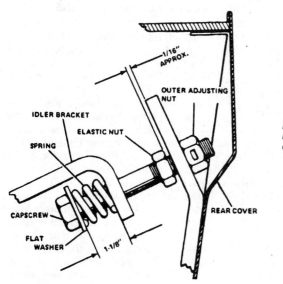

Fig. AC12—View showing primary drive belt idler adjustment on Models Scamp 8 and 508.

Place blade clutch control lever in disengaged position and remove the pto drive belt from engine pulley. Depress the clutch-brake pedal and remove the main drive belt. Unbolt and remove transmission input pulley, then remove the rear hitch plate. Loosen the set screw and remove brake drum and key from brake shaft. Support rear of unit and remove rear wheel assemblies. Remove shift links, retaining rings and springs from shifter shafts and the transmission case. All gears, shafts and differential assembly can now be removed.

Reassemble by reversing the disassembly procedure. Lubricate with general purpose lithium grease.

Models Scamp 8 and 508

REMOVE AND REINSTALL. To remove the transaxle assembly, disconnect spark plug wire, open rear frame cover and on electric start models, remove the battery. Push primary drive belt idler forward until primary belt can be removed from engine pulley. Remove primary belt from left side of transmission pulley. Remove reverse drive and forward drive belts from transmission pulley. Unbolt and remove brake band, loosen set screw and remove brake drum. Attach a hoist to rear frame, unbolt transmission and left axle housing from frame, then raise rear of unit to clear shift lever. Roll transaxle assembly from chassis.

Reinstall transaxle by reversing the removal procedure. Adjust clutch and brake as required.

Models 526, 830 and 1036

REMOVE AND REINSTALL. Remove mower deck and drive belt as outlined in MOWER BLADE CLUTCH AND BELT section. Raise hood covering engine and transmission assembly. On models equipped with electric start disconnect battery cables from battery. Unhook engine spark plug wire, then unplug transmission interlock switch. Remove transmission input pulley (7-Fig. AC13) retaining ring (9), then withdraw pulley from transmission input shaft. Remove Woodruff key (8) from input shaft groove and save. Remove hairpin clips (3) from shaft rod (2), then slide rod out of pivot lever (4). Loosen traction drive chain tensioner, then slide drive chain off transmission output shaft sprocket. Inspect and remove any part that will obstruct in removal of transmission. Remove transmission mounting bolts, then lift transmission assembly (6) out of chassis and set to the side for inspection and repair.

Reinstall transmission in reverse order of removal. Adjust traction drive chain and reconnect electrical components.

All Models

OVERHAUL. For Models Scamp 5, Scamp 8, 405 and 508 refer to the Simplicity paragraphs in the TRANSMISSION REPAIR section of this manual.

For Models 526, 830 and 1036 refer to the Peerless Series 700 paragraphs in the TRANSMISSION REPAIR section of this manual.

DIFFERENTIAL

Models Scamp 5, Scamp 8, 405 and 508

R&R AND OVERHAUL. Transmission gears, shafts, differential and axle shafts are contained in one case. To remove the transaxle assembly, refer to the R&R procedures outlined earlier in TRANSMISSION paragraphs.

For differential overhaul procedures, refer to the Simplicity paragraphs in the TRANSMISSION REPAIR section of this manual.

Models 526, 830 and 1036

REMOVE AND REINSTALL. Remove mower deck and drive belt as outlined in MOWER BLADE CLUTCH AND BELT section. Raise rear of chassis until rear wheels are clear of ground. Remove E-clips retaining rear wheel assemblies on axle shaft, then remove wheel assemblies. Release tension on drive chain, then slip chain off transmission output sprocket. Unhook ground brake actuating lever from brake band assembly. Remove screws securing axle shaft bearing flanges (12-Fig. AC14) to chassis axle support (10); left and right, then slide axle shafts out of support slots. Place differential as-

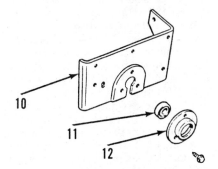

Fig. AC14—View showing axle support (10), bearing (11) and flange (12) used for differential mounting on Models 526, 830 and 1036.

Fig. AC15—On Models Scamp 5 and 405, when blade clutch control lever is in engaged position, clearance between set collar and rod bracket should be 1/2 inch (12.7 mm).

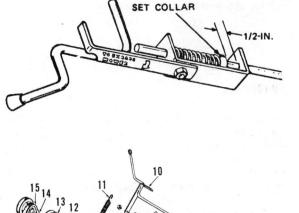

SET COLLAR

1/2-IN.

Fig. AC16—View of blade clutch (pto) linkage, pulleys and drive belts used on Models Scamp 5 and 405.

1. Mower pulley
2. Secondary mower belt
6. Clutch rod
7. Tension spring
8. Set collar
9. Rod bracket
10. Blade clutch (pto) control lever
11. Spring
12. Pulley & jackshaft
13. Blade clutch idler pulley
14. Mower clutch belt
15. Engine pulley
16. Transmission input pulley
17. Pto brake
18. Clutch idler arm
19. Jackshaft pulley bracket
20. Jackshaft pulley

Fig. AC17—On Models Scamp 8 and 508, when blade clutch control lever is in engaged position, clearance between set collar and rod bracket should be 3/4 inch (19 mm).

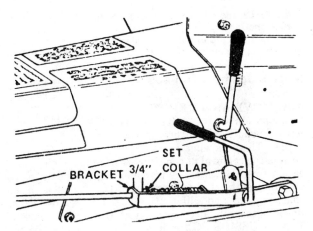

SET COLLAR

BRACKET 3/4"

---

sembly to the side for inspection and repair.

For differential overhaul procedures, refer to the Stewart paragraphs in the DIFFERENTIAL section of this manual.

MOWER BLADE CLUTCH AND BELT

All Models

Belt idler type blade clutch is used on all models. If the mower drive belt slips during normal operation, check and adjust the clutch tension on belt. If belt cannot be adjusted, due to excessive wear or stretching, renew the belt. On models equipped with two belts, R&R procedures will be given for both belts.

Models Scamp 5 and 405

To adjust the blade clutch, move the control lever to fully engaged position. Clearance between the set collar and bracket should be ½ inch (12.7 mm) as shown in Fig. AC15. If clearance is incorrect, disengage blade clutch, loosen set screw and reposition set collar. Engage clutch and recheck clearance.

To remove the mower clutch belt (14-Fig. AC16), unbolt and remove engine hood on models so equipped. Disconnect spark plug wire, then unbolt and remove pulley and belt guard from left side. Remove belt guide and place blade clutch lever (10) in disengaged position. On models so equipped, pull the pto brake (17) away from belt. Remove mower drive clutch belt. Pull jackshaft pulley bracket (19) forward and remove

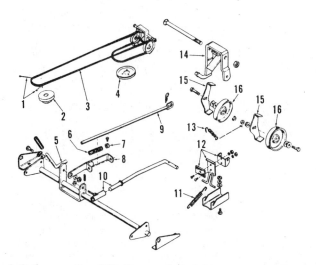

Illustrations Courtesy AGCO

Fig. AC18—View of blade clutch linkage, pulleys and mower drive belt used on Models Scamp 8 and 508.

1. Belt stops
2. Engine pulley
3. Mower drive belt
4. Mower pulley
5. Blade clutch control lever
6. Tension spring
7. Set collar
8. Rod bracket
9. Clutch rod
10. Blade brake rod
11. Brake spring
12. Blade brake
13. Spring
14. Blade clutch idler arm
15. Belt guides
16. Clutch idler pulleys

belt from pulley (20). Remove belt from mower.

Install new belts by reversing the removal procedure and adjust blade clutch as required.

Models Scamp 8 and 508

To adjust the blade clutch, move the control lever to fully engaged position. Clearance between the set collar and rod bracket should be ¾ inch (19 mm)

Fig. AC19—View showing procedure for adjusting pto control linkage. Adjust by loosening set screw (3) and sliding set collar (1). Distance is measured between set collar (1) and rod guide (2).

measured as shown in Fig. AC17. If clearance is not correct, disengage blade clutch, loosen set screw and reposition set collar on rod. Engage clutch and recheck clearance.

To remove the mower drive belt (3-Fig. AC18), first remove mower unit as follows: Disconnect spark plug wire and on electric start models, open rear frame cover and remove battery. Place blade clutch lever in disengaged position. Disconnect the mower lift link and blade clutch rod, then unpin front of mower from frame. Unbolt pulley and belt cover from mower housing. Remove mower drive belt from mower pulley and slide mower unit out from under left side.

Refer to Fig. AC11 and push primary drive belt idler (1) forward until primary (transmission drive) belt (3) can be removed from engine pulley (2). Loosen mounting bolts and move belt stops (1-Fig. AC18) away from engine pulley. Remove mower clutch belt (3) from engine pulley.

On all models, note position of belt guides (15-Fig. AC18) on idler pulleys (16) and loosen the mounting bolts. Move belt stops as required to remove the mower clutch belt (3).

Install new mower belt by reversing the removal procedure. Make certain that belt guides and belt stops are properly installed. Adjust blade clutch as necessary.

Models 526, 830 and 1036

To adjust blade clutch, move pto control lever to fully engaged position. Raise engine cover, then measure distance between set collar (1-Fig. AC19) and rod guide (2). Distance should be ½ inch (12.7 mm). If distance is incorrect, then disengage pto control lever. Loosen set collar (1) securing setscrew (3). Slide set collar on control rod, then retighten setscrew. Engage control lever, then recheck distance. Continue adjustment procedure until correct distance is attained.

To remove the mower drive belt, first remove mower deck unit as follows: Open engine cover, then disconnect spark plug wire and on electric start models, disconnect battery cable. Place pto control lever in disengaged position. Place mower height control lever in lowest cutting position. Unbolt rear mower bracket (6-Fig. AC20) on 26 and 30-inch models and (7-Fig AC21) on 36-inch models. Loosen cap screws securing engine pulley belt guard, then slide guard clear of pulley assembly. Loosen idler pulley belt stop finger securing hardware, then swing finger away from belt. Remove clips and pins securing front of chassis to mower deck hitch. Slip drive belt off engine drive pulley and idler pulley. Disconnect belt brake linkage and remove all other parts that will obstruct in removal of mower deck. Slide mower deck to one side. Push mower deck belt brake away from pulley(s), then slide belt off pulley(s).

Install new drive belt by reversing removal procedures. Reinstall mower

Fig. AC20—View showing 26 and 30-inch mower deck assembly used on Models 526 and 830.

1. Hitch
2. Lift rod flange
3. Belt brake
4. Pulley belt guard
5. Spacer
6. Mower bracket
7. Brake rod

Fig. AC21—View showing 36-inch mower deck assembly used on Model 1036.

1. Brake rod
2. Lift rod
3. Jam nut
4. Leveling rod
5. Cotter pin
6. Hitch
7. Mower bracket

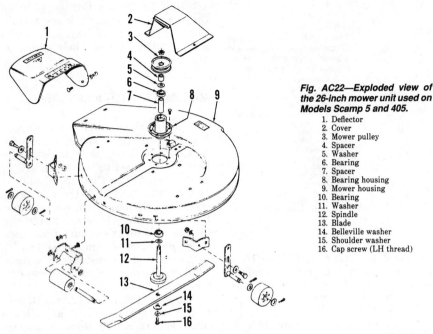

Fig. AC22—Exploded view of the 26-inch mower unit used on Models Scamp 5 and 405.

1. Deflector
2. Cover
3. Mower pulley
4. Spacer
5. Washer
6. Bearing
7. Spacer
8. Bearing housing
9. Mower housing
10. Bearing
11. Washer
12. Spindle
13. Blade
14. Belleville washer
15. Shoulder washer
16. Cap screw (LH thread)

damage. Reassemble by reversing disassembly procedure. Tighten mower pulley retaining nut to a torque of 70 ft.-lbs. (95 N·m) and left hand thread cap screw (16) to a torque of 80 ft.-lbs. (108 N·m).

Models Scamp 8 and 508

REMOVE AND REINSTALL. To remove the blade, spindle and bearings, remove mower unit as follows: Place blade clutch control lever in disengaged position. Disconnect blade clutch rod, then disconnect lift link and unpin front of mower from frame. Unbolt and remove covers (1–Fig. AC23) and remove mower drive belt from pulley (4). Slide mower unit from under left side. Remove cap screws (17) and blade (16). Unbolt mower pulley (4), then unbolt and remove bearing housing (10) from mower housing (6). Remove nut, hub (5) and spacer (7) from top of bearing housing. Remove spindle (15) and washers (12, 13 and 14). Separate bearings (8 and 11) and spacer (9) from bearing housing.

Clean and inspect all parts and renew any showing excessive wear or other damage. Reassemble by reversing the disassembly procedure. Tighten pulley hub retaining nut to a torque of 95 ft.-lbs. (129 N·m) and blade retaining cap screw (17) to 45 ft.-lbs. (61 N·m).

deck in reverse order of removal. Clearance between belt stop and drive belt should be ⅛ inch (3 mm) when pto control lever is engaged. Clearance between engine pulley belt guard and lower pulley should be ⅛ inch (3 mm).

MOWER BLADES AND SPINDLES

All Models

Models Scamp 5, 405, Scamp 8, 508, 526 and 830 are equipped with single blade rotary mowers. A twin blade rotary mower is used on Model 1036.

CAUTION: Always disconnect spark plug wire and on electric start models disconnect battery cable before performing any inspection, adjustment or other service on the mower.

Make certain that safety starting switches are connected and in good operting condition before returning unit to service.

Models Scamp 5 and 405

REMOVE AND REINSTALL. To remove the blade, spindle and bearings, remove mower unit as follows: Place blade clutch control lever in disengaged position. Pull jackshaft pulley housing (19–Fig. AC16) forward and remove mower belt (2) from pulley (20). Unhook rear of mower and unpin front of mower, then slide mower unit from under left side. Unbolt cover (2–Fig. AC22) and remove mower belt. Remove left

hand thread cap screw (16), washers (14 and 15) and blade (13). Remove nut, pulley (3), spacer (4) and washer (5) from above and spindle (12) and washer (11) from below. Unbolt bearing housing (8) and separate bearings (6 and 10) and spacer (7) from housing.

Clean and inspect all parts and renew any showing excessive wear or other

Fig. AC23—Exploded view of the 30-inch mower unit used on Models Scamp 8 and 508.

1. Covers
2. Deflector
3. Rock guard
4. Mower pulley
5. Hub
6. Mower housing
7. Spacer
8. Bearing
9. Spacer
10. Bearing housing
11. Bearing
12. Washers
13. Wave washer
14. Washer
15. Spindle
16. Blade
17. Cap screw

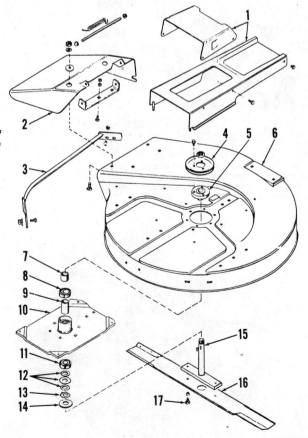

Models 526, 830 and 1036

REMOVE AND REINSTALL. To remove mower blade and associated drive parts, first remove mower deck assembly as outlined in appropriate paragraphs within the MOWER BLADE CLUTCH AND BELT section.

With reference to Fig. AC24 disassemble blade drive components as follows. Remove cap screw (14), spring washer (13) and washer (12), then withdraw blade assembly (11). Unbolt and withdraw mower pulley (1), then unbolt and remove top bearing housing (3). Withdraw lower drive assembly out bottom of mower unit. Separate bearings (4) from housings (3 and 6).

Clean and inspect all parts, renew any parts showing excessive wear or any other damage. Reassemble by reversing disassembly procedure. Tighten blade retaining cap screw to 50 ft.-lbs. (68 N·m) torque.

LUBRICATION

All Models

Lubricate all linkage pivot points with SAE 30 oil. Use multi-purpose lithium grease on all models equipped with lubrication fittings on bearing housings. Others are equipped with sealed bearings and require no additional lubrication.

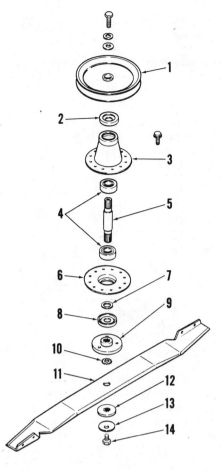

Fig. AC24—Exploded view showing mower blade and associated drive parts on 526 and 830 models. Model 1036 is similar.

1. Pulley
2. Shield
3. Top housing
4. Bearing
5. Shaft
6. Bottom housing
7. Shim
8. Shield
9. Blade adapter
10. Ring
11. Blade
12. Washer
13. Spring washer
14. Cap screw

AGCO-ALLIS

NOTE: Early models covered in this section were sold under the brand name of
Deutz-Allis.

Model	Make	Engine Model	Horsepower	Cutting Width, In.
836	B&S	190000	8	36
1236H	B&S	280000	12	36
1242	B&S	280000	12	42
1242H	B&S	280000	12	42
1312	B&S	283700	12	42
1312H	B&S	283700	12	42
1316H	B&S	303700	16	48

FRONT WHEELS

All Models

The front wheels are the drive wheels for the machine. A key (15—Fig. AC31) transfers power to each wheel from the axle. The wheel may be removed after supporting the machine and removing hub cap (18), snap ring (17) and washer (16). If so equipped, do not lose shims (14) behind wheel.

Before assembly, apply antiseize compound to wheel contact surface on axle. Be sure the snap ring is properly seated in groove on axle.

STEERING SYSTEM

Models 836, 1236H, 1242 and 1242H

LUBRICATION. Early models are equipped with a grease fitting at base of steering column so lower bushings may be lubricated. Remove rear cover on steering tower for access to grease fitting. Inject lithium based grease into grease fitting after every 25 hours of operation.

Later models are equipped with bearings that do not require periodic lubrication.

R&R AND OVERHAUL. Early models are equipped with a cable-actuated steering system that controls steering of the rear wheels. Cables should be inspected periodically and renewed if damaged.

To remove steering shaft, unscrew bolt (6—Fig. AC32) and remove steering wheel. Remove rear cover on steering tower and disconnect linkage inside tower that will prevent removal of tower. Unscrew and remove tower. Unscrew reel retaining nut (15) and withdraw steering shaft (9). If required, detach steering cables (11) from reel (12).

Reassemble steering components by reversing disassembly procedure. Coat spacers (36) with antiseize compound. Note that left steering cable attaches to upper reel groove and is wound around reel in counterclockwise direction viewed from bottom of reel. Right steering cable attaches to lower reel groove and is wound around reel in clockwise direction viewed from bottom of reel.

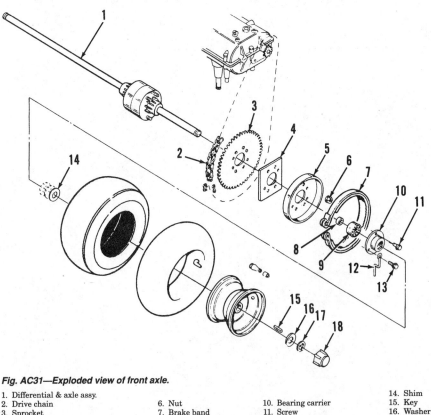

Fig. AC31—Exploded view of front axle.

1. Differential & axle assy.
2. Drive chain
3. Sprocket
4. Plate
5. Brake drum
6. Nut
7. Brake band
8. Spacer
9. Bearing
10. Bearing carrier
11. Screw
12. Brake band stop
13. Screw
14. Shim
15. Key
16. Washer
17. "E" ring
18. Hub cap

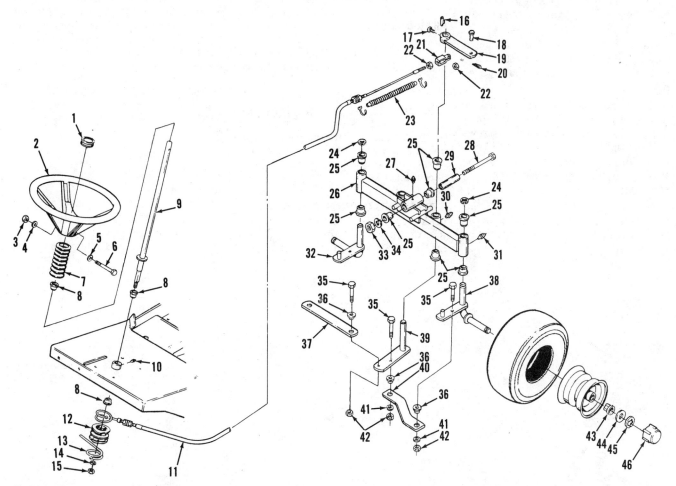

Fig. AC32—Exploded view of steering system and rear axle assembly used on Models 836, 1236H, 1242 and 1242H. Steering shaft on later models is supported by flange bearings in place of bushings shown.

1. Cap	9. Steering shaft			31. Grease fitting	39. Steering arm
2. Steering wheel	10. Grease fitting			32. Spindle (R.H.)	40. Steering link
3. Nut	11. Steering cable	17. Screw	24. "E" ring	33. Nut	41. Washer
4. Washer	12. Reel	18. Clevis pin	25. Bushing	34. Lockwasher	42. Locknut
5. Washer	13. Steering cable	19. Steering arm	26. Rear axle main member	35. Bolt	43. Bearing
6. Bolt	14. Washer	20. Cotter pin	27. Grease fitting	36. Spacer	44. Washer
7. Boot	15. Locknut	21. Clevis	28. Bolt	37. Steering link	45. "E" ring
8. Bushing	16. Key	22. Nuts	29. Pivot pin	38. Spindle (L.H.)	46. Hub cap
		23. Boot	30. Grease fitting		

After installing steering shaft assembly, steering wheel and steering cables, position steering wheel so cable ends (not clevis) are same length (measure from a similar reference point). Steering wheel should now be in centered, straight-ahead position. Place rear wheels in straight-ahead position. Rotate adjusting nuts (22) on each cable clevis so hole in clevis (21) aligns with hole on steering arm and insert clevis pin. Check steering operation.

Models 1312, 1312H and 1316H

LUBRICATION. All models are equipped with a grease fitting (F—Fig. AC33) on sector gear. Inject lithium based grease into grease fitting after every 25 hours of operation.

R&R AND OVERHAUL. Steering gear (15—Fig. AC34) may be removed

after withdrawing cotter pin (12). To remove sector gear (17), detach drag link end (26) and remove pivot screw (23). To remove steering shaft, unscrew

bolt (6) and remove steering wheel. Remove rear cover on steering tower and disconnect linkage inside tower as necessary to allow removal of tower. Re-

Fig. AC33—To adjust brake, push brake rod (R) as far forward as possible. Rotate nut (N) so there is a gap of 3/8 inch (9.5 mm) between nut and end of coupler (P).

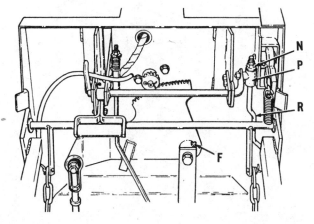

move tower mounting screws and remove tower. Withdraw steering shaft (11).

Refer to Fig. AC34 for an exploded view of steering components attached to rear axle and remove components as required.

Reassemble steering components by reversing disassembly procedure. Apply Loctite to steering arm retaining screws (33) and tighten to 72-84 in.-lbs. (8.1-9.5 N•m). Apply grease or oil to rubbing surfaces. Apply grease to steering shaft splines.

Adjust length of drag link (28) so rear wheels are pointing straight ahead when steering gear (15) is centered on sector gear (17).

GROUND DRIVE BRAKE

All Models

A band-type brake acts against a drum attached to the left side of the differential.

ADJUSTMENT. To adjust brake, release parking brake and push brake rod (R—Fig. AC33) as far forward as possible. Rotate nut (N) so there is a gap of 3/8 inch (9.5 mm) between nut and end of coupler (P).

R&R AND OVERHAUL. To remove brake band (7—Fig. AC35), remove mower unit as outlined in MOWER DECK section. Support front of ma-

chine and remove left front wheel. Remove cotter pin (4) and separate brake rod (11) from brake arm (6). Remove bolt (12) and pins (8), then remove brake band (7). Inspect brake band and renew if excessively worn or damaged.

Brake drum (5—Fig. AC31) is attached to differential, which must be removed as outlined in DIFFERENTIAL section before removing brake drum.

DRIVE CHAIN

All Models

LUBRICATION. The drive chain should be lubricated with a good quality chain oil after every 10 hours of opera-

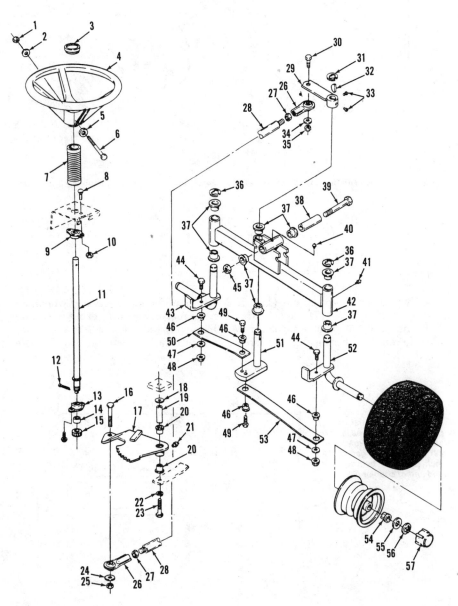

Fig. AC34—Exploded view of steering system and rear axle assembly used on Models 1312, 1312H and 1316H.

1. Nut
2. Washer
3. Cap
4. Steering wheel
5. Washer
6. Bolt
7. Boot
8. Screw
9. Bearing
10. Nut
11. Steering shaft
12. Cotter pin
13. Bearing
14. Spacer
15. Steering gear
16. Bolt
17. Sector gear
18. Washer
19. Pivot pin
20. Bushing
21. Grease fitting
22. Washer
23. Screw
24. Washer
25. Nut
26. Rod end
27. Nut
28. Drag link
29. Steering arm
30. Screw
31. "E" ring
32. Key
33. Screws
34. Washer
35. Nut
36. "E" ring
37. Bushing
38. Pivot pin
39. Grease fitting
40. Grease fitting
41. Grease fitting
42. Rear axle main member
43. Spindle (R.H.)
44. Bolt
45. Nut
46. Spacer
47. Washer
48. Locknut
49. Screw
50. Steering link
51. Steering arm
52. Spindle (L.H.)
53. Steering link
54. Bearing
55. Washer
56. "E" ring
57. Hub cap

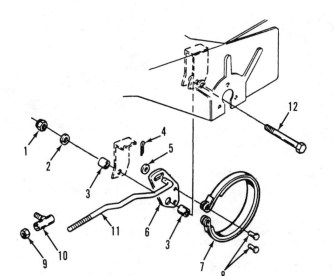

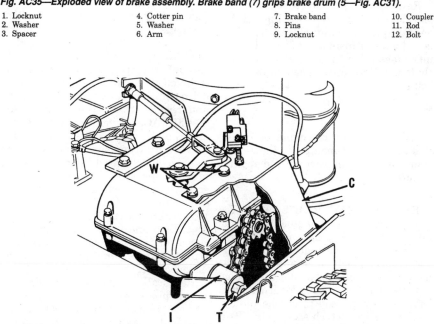

Fig. AC35—Exploded view of brake assembly. Brake band (7) grips brake drum (5—Fig. AC31).

1. Locknut	4. Cotter pin	7. Brake band	10. Coupler
2. Washer	5. Washer	8. Pins	11. Rod
3. Spacer	6. Arm	9. Locknut	12. Bolt

Fig. AC36—To adjust chain tension on models equipped with a gear transmission, loosen nut (T) and push idler (I) toward chain to remove chain slack.

tion, or more frequently during hot weather or under severe operating conditions.

ADJUSTMENT. Chain tension on models equipped with a hydrostatic transmission is determined by a spring-loaded idler. Adjustment is not required.

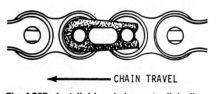

Fig. AC37—Install drive chain master link clip so closed end of clip is toward direction of chain travel in forward gears.

To adjust chain tension on models equipped with a gear transmission, remove screws (W—Fig. AC36) and remove cover (C). Loosen nut (T) and push idler (I) towards chain to remove chain slack. Tighten nut (T). Idler should remove slack from chain, but not produce tension in chain.

REMOVE AND REINSTALL. To remove chain on models with a gear transmission, remove screws (W—Fig. AC36) and cover (C). Loosen nut (T) and push idler (I) away from chain. Locate and disconnect master link in chain, then remove chain.

To remove chain on models equipped with a hydrostatic transmission, disconnect chain idler spring. Locate and dis-

connect master link in chain, then remove chain.

When installing chain, attach master link clip so closed end of clip is in direction of normal chain travel. See Fig. AC37.

DIFFERENTIAL

All Models

REMOVE AND REINSTALL. To remove differential, first remove mower unit as outlined in MOWER DECK section. Raise and support front of machine and remove front wheels. Remove brake band and drive chain as previously outlined. Remove screws attaching axle bearing carriers (10—Fig. AC31) to frame and remove differential and axle assembly (1). If required, unscrew nuts (6) and remove brake drum (5), plate (4) and sprocket (3).

Reverse removal procedure to reinstall differential assembly. Tighten brake drum retaining nuts (6) to 120-168 in.-lbs. (14-19 N•m). Install shims (14) as needed to remove axle end play.

OVERHAUL. All models are equipped with a Peerless Series 100 differential. Refer to DIFFERENTIAL REPAIR section for service information.

ENGINE

Models 836 and 1242

Refer to appropriate engine section in this manual for tune-up specifications, engine overhaul procedures and engine maintenance.

REMOVE AND REINSTALL. To remove engine, raise engine cover and disconnect spark plug wire. Loosen belt guide at mower belt idler and remove mower belt from engine pulley. Relocate belt guides as needed, then relieve spring pressure against traction drive belt idler and remove belt from idler and engine pulley. Unscrew retaining screw in end of engine crankshaft and remove engine pulley. Disconnect throttle cable from engine. Disconnect all wires from engine that will interfere with removal. Remove engine mounting bolts and remove engine.

Reinstall engine by reversing removal procedure.

Models 1236H and 1242H

Refer to appropriate engine section in this manual for tune-up specifications, engine overhaul procedures and engine maintenance.

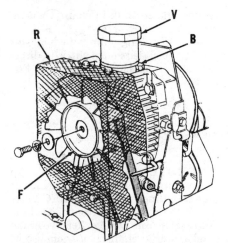

Fig. AC38—Remove cover (R) on hydrostatic transmission for access to fan (F). Bleed screw (B) is located adjacent to reservoir (V).

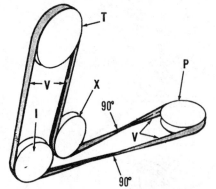

Fig. AC40—The traction drive belt on models equipped with a hydrostatic transmission. Note position of "V" side (V) of belt and that belt twists 90° between engine pulley (P) and idlers (I and X).

I. Spring-loaded idler   T. Transmission pulley
P. Engine pulley   X. Fixed idler

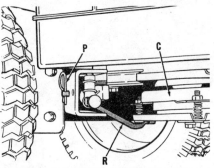

Fig. AC41—Detach spring clip (P) and push torque rod (R) out of frame before removing electric clutch (C).

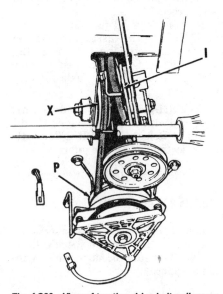

Fig. AC39—View of traction drive belt pulleys on underside of models equipped with a hydrostatic transmission. Refer to Fig. AC40 for belt routing diagram.

REMOVE AND REINSTALL. To remove engine, first raise engine cover and disconnect spark plug wire. Remove belt cover on mower deck, pull back spring-loaded belt idler and separate mower belt from idlers. Remove mower drive belt from engine pulley. Unscrew and remove transmission fan screen (R—Fig. AC38), remove fan (F) and remove belt from transmission pulley. Remove belt from spring-loaded idler (I—Fig. AC39), fixed idler (X) and engine pulley (P). Unscrew retaining screw in end of engine crankshaft and remove engine pulley. Disconnect throttle cable from engine. Disconnect all wires from engine that will interfere with removal. Remove engine mounting bolts and remove engine.

Reinstall engine by reversing removal procedure. Refer to Fig. AC40 and note proper routing of traction drive belt. Install transmission fan so tab on inner face of fan hub matches hole on shaft end. Gap between belt guides and belt should be $\frac{1}{16}$-$\frac{1}{8}$ inch (1.6-3.2 mm).

Model 1312

Refer to appropriate engine section in this manual for tune-up specifications, engine overhaul procedures and engine maintenance.

REMOVE AND REINSTALL. To remove engine, raise engine cover and disconnect spark plug wire. Remove belt cover on mower deck, pull back spring-loaded belt idler and separate mower belt from fixed idlers (do not remove belt from spring-loaded idler). Disconnect wire lead to engine pulley electric clutch. Detach spring clip (P—Fig. AC41), push the torque rod (R) through the frame and unscrew rod from electric clutch. Remove mower drive belt from electric clutch. Apply brake to provide slack in traction drive belt. Loosen or remove belt guides as needed and remove drive belt from engine pulley. Unscrew retaining screw in end of engine crankshaft and remove electric clutch and engine pulley. Disconnect throttle cable from engine. Disconnect all wires from engine that will interfere with removal. Remove engine mounting bolts and remove engine.

Reinstall engine by reversing removal procedure.

Models 1312H and 1316H

Refer to appropriate engine section in this manual for tune-up specifications, engine overhaul procedures and engine maintenance.

REMOVE AND REINSTALL. To remove engine, raise engine cover and disconnect spark plug wire. Remove belt cover on mower deck, pull back spring-loaded belt idler and separate mower belt from fixed idlers (do not remove belt from spring-loaded idler). Disconnect wire lead to engine pulley electric clutch. Detach spring clip (P— Fig. AC41), push the torque rod (R) through the frame and unscrew rod from electric clutch. Remove mower drive belt from electric clutch. Unscrew and remove transmission fan screen (R—Fig. AC38), remove fan (F) and remove belt from transmission pulley. Remove belt from spring-loaded idler (I—Fig. AC39), fixed idler (X) and engine pulley (P). Unscrew retaining screw in end of engine crankshaft and remove electric clutch and engine pulley. Disconnect throttle cable from engine. Disconnect all wires from engine that will interfere with removal. Remove engine mounting bolts and remove engine.

Reinstall engine by reversing removal procedure. Refer to Fig. AC40 and note proper routing of traction drive belt. Install transmission fan so tab on inner face of fan hub matches hole on shaft end. Gap between belt guides and belt should be $\frac{1}{16}$-$\frac{1}{8}$ inch (1.6-3.2 mm).

TRACTION DRIVE CLUTCH AND DRIVE BELT

Models 836, 1242 and 1312

The traction drive clutch is a spring-tensioned, belt idler-type operated by the clutch/brake pedal. When the pedal is depressed, belt tension is removed, allowing the engine drive pulley to rotate freely within the drive belt. After the pedal passes midpoint, the brake is applied.

LUBRICATION. Periodically lubricate all rubbing surfaces with engine oil.

ADJUSTMENT. With brake released, length of clutch rod spring (G—Fig. AC42) should be 2-2⅛ inches (51-54 mm). Rotate nut (N) at end of clutch rod to obtain desired spring length.

R&R DRIVE BELT. Models 836 and 1242. To remove drive belt, disconnect spark plug wire. Loosen belt guide at mower belt idler and remove mower belt from engine pulley. Relocate belt guides as needed, then relieve spring pressure against traction drive belt idler and remove belt from idler and engine pulley. Remove traction drive belt. Install belt by reversing removal procedure. Gap between belt guides and belt should be 1/16-1/8 inch (1.6-3.2 mm).

Model 1312. To remove drive belt, disconnect spark plug wire. Remove belt cover on mower deck, pull back spring-loaded belt idler and separate mower belt from fixed idlers (do not remove belt from spring-loaded idler). Disconnect wire lead to engine pulley electric clutch. Detach spring clip (P—Fig. AC41), push torque rod (R) through frame and unscrew rod from electric clutch. Remove mower drive belt from electric clutch. Apply brake to provide slack in traction drive belt. Loosen or remove belt guides as needed and remove drive belt from engine pulley. Remove belt. Reverse removal procedure to install drive belt. Gap between belt guides and belt should be 1/16-1/8 inch (1.6-3.2 mm).

Models 1236H, 1242H, 1312H and 1316H. The traction drive clutch is a spring-tensioned, belt idler-type operated by the clutch/brake pedal. When the pedal is depressed, belt tension is removed, allowing the engine drive pulley to rotate freely within the drive belt. After the pedal passes midpoint, the brake is applied.

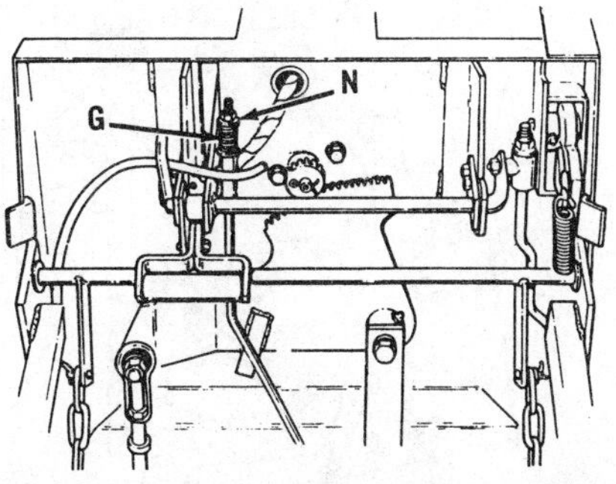

Fig. AC42—On Models 836, 1242 and 1312, clutch rod spring (G) length should be 2 to 2-1/8 inches (51-54 mm) when the brake is released. On Models 1236H, 1242H, 1312H and 1316H, spring length should be 13/16-15/16 inches (30-33 mm). Rotate nut (N) at end of clutch rod to obtain desired spring length.

LUBRICATION. Periodically lubricate all rubbing surfaces with engine oil.

ADJUSTMENT. With brake released, length of clutch rod spring (G—Fig. AC42) should be 1 3/16-1 5/16 inches (30-33 mm). Rotate nut (N) at end of clutch rod to obtain desired spring length.

R&R DRIVE BELT. Models 1236H and 1242H. To remove traction drive belt, raise engine cover and disconnect spark plug wire. Remove belt cover on mower deck, pull back spring-loaded belt idler and separate mower belt from idlers. Remove mower drive belt from engine pulley. Unscrew and remove transmission fan screen (R—Fig. AC38), remove fan (F) and remove belt from transmission pulley. Remove belt from spring-loaded idler (I—Fig. AC39), fixed idler (X) and engine pulley (P). Remove drive belt. Reverse removal procedure to install drive belt. Refer to Fig. AC40 and note proper routing of traction drive belt. Install transmission fan so tab on inner face of fan hub matches hole on shaft end. Gap between belt guides and belt should be 1/16-1/8 inch (1.6-3.2 mm).

Models 1312H and 1316H. To remove traction drive belt, raise engine cover and disconnect spark plug wire. Remove belt cover on mower deck, pull back spring-loaded belt idler and separate mower belt from fixed idlers (do not remove belt from spring-loaded idler). Disconnect wire lead to engine pulley electric clutch. Detach spring clip (P—Fig. AC41), push the torque rod (R) through the frame and unscrew rod from electric clutch. Remove mower drive belt from electric clutch. Unscrew and remove transmission fan screen (R—Fig. AC38), remove fan (F) and remove belt from transmission pulley. Remove belt from spring-loaded idler (I—Fig. AC39), fixed idler (X) and engine pulley (P). Remove drive belt. Reverse removal procedure to install drive belt. Refer to Fig. AC40 and note proper routing of traction drive belt. Install transmission fan so tab on inner face of fan hub matches hole on shaft end. Gap between belt guides and belt should be 1/16-1/8 inch (1.6-3.2 mm).

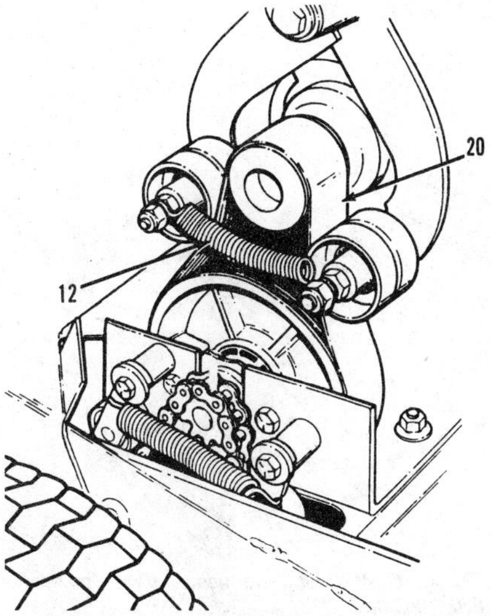

Fig. AC43—To remove intermediate drive belt (20) on Models 1236H, 1242H, 1312H and 1316H, disconnect idler spring (12) and refer to text.

INTERMEDIATE DRIVE BELT AND SHAFT

Models 1236H, 1242H, 1312H and 1316H

REMOVE AND REINSTALL. To remove intermediate drive belt (20—Fig. AC43), remove drive chain as previously outlined. Raise engine cover and disconnect idler spring (12). Unscrew bearing carrier (15—Fig. AC44) mounting screws. Lift out shaft, pulley and belt assembly, then disassemble as needed. Reassemble by reversing removal procedure. Be sure belt (20) ridges are properly aligned with grooves on pulleys.

SHIFT CONTROL LINKAGE

Models 836, 1242 and 1312

NEUTRAL ADJUSTMENT. The shift control lever and transmission shift lever must be synchronized. Raise engine cover and remove clevis pin (P—Fig. AC45). Shift transmission into neutral and place shift control lever in middle of neutral position on control panel. Rotate nuts at transmission end of shift cable so pin hole in clevis (V) aligns with pin hole in transmission shift lever (F) and install clevis pin (P). Additional adjustment is possible by rotating nuts at shift control lever end of shift cable. Tighten nuts and check adjustment.

Models 1236H, 1242H, 1312H and 1316H

NEUTRAL ADJUSTMENT. To adjust shift control linkage, raise machine so wheels are above ground and machine is supported securely. Loosen nuts (N—Fig. AC46) on shift rod so there is a 1/4-inch (6.4 mm) gap between each nut and coupler (P). Raise engine cover and loosen screws (S—Fig. AC47). Shift control lever must be in neutral position.

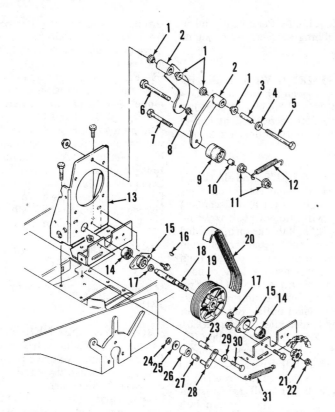

Fig. AC44—Exploded view of intermediate belt drive used on Models 1236H, 1242H, 1312H and 1316H.

1. Bushing	9. Idler	17. Snap ring	24. Snap ring
2. Idler arm	10. Spacer	18. Intermediate shaft	25. Washer
3. Pivot pin	11. Nuts	19. Pulley	26. Chain tension roller
4. Washer	12. Spring	20. Intermediate drive belt	27. Spacer
5. Bolt	13. Panel	21. Sprocket	28. Chain tension arm
6. Screw	14. Bearing	22. Snap ring	29. Washer
7. Screw	15. Bearing carrier	23. Spacer	30. Screw
8. Spacer	16. Key		31. Spring

Start engine and run at high speed. Loosen jam nut (J) and rotate inner nut (T) in either direction so pulley (Y) does not rotate. Tighten screws (S) and jam nut (J). Stop engine. Be sure shift control lever is still in neutral and tighten nuts (N—Fig. AC46) against coupler (P).

TRANSMISSION

Models 836, 1242 and 1312

REMOVE AND REINSTALL. To remove transmission, remove drive belt as previously outlined and remove transmission pulley. Raise engine cover, remove cover (C—Fig. AC45) and disconnect chain. Remove shift lever clevis pin (P) and detach shift cable bracket (B) from transmission. Disconnect wire lead to neutral switch (N). Unscrew transmission mounting screws (screws are different lengths and should be marked) and remove transmission.

NOTE: Some screws used on transmission are self-tapping and must be

installed carefully to prevent cross-threading.

Install transmission by reversing removal procedure. Tighten transmission mounting screws to 14-20 ft.-lbs. (19-27 N·m).

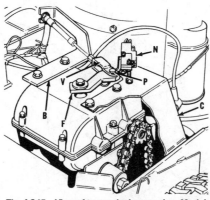

Fig. AC45—View of transmission used on Models 836, 1242 and 1312.

B. Bracket	N. Neutral switch
C. Cover	P. Pin
F. Shift arm	V. Clevis

OVERHAUL. Models 836, 1242 and 1312 are equipped with a Peerless Series 700 transmission. Refer to TRANSMISSION REPAIR section for service information.

Models 1236H, 1242H, 1312H and 1316H

LUBRICATION. To check transmission fluid level, unit must be at ambient temperature. Raise engine cover and note fluid level in reservoir (V—Fig. AC38). Fluid should be at "FULL COLD" mark.

NOTE: Due to close tolerances present in the hydrostatic transmission, particular care must be taken to prevent debris or other contaminants from entering transmission. Clean area around reservoir cap or any other opening to transmission.

Fill with Deutz-Allis hydrostatic transmission fluid or equivalent. If reservoir is empty, unscrew bleed screw (B) and add fluid to reservoir. With clutch/brake pedal depressed, move traction drive belt so fan on transmis-

Fig. AC46—On Models 1236H, 1242H, 1312H and 1316H, loosen nuts (N) on shift rod so there is a 1/4-inch (6.4 mm) gap between each nut and coupler (P) and adjust shift control linkage as outlined in text.

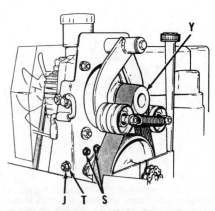

Fig. AC47—View of hydrostatic transmission used on Models 1236H, 1242H, 1312H and 1316H. Rotate adjustment nut (T) as outlined in text for neutral adjustment.

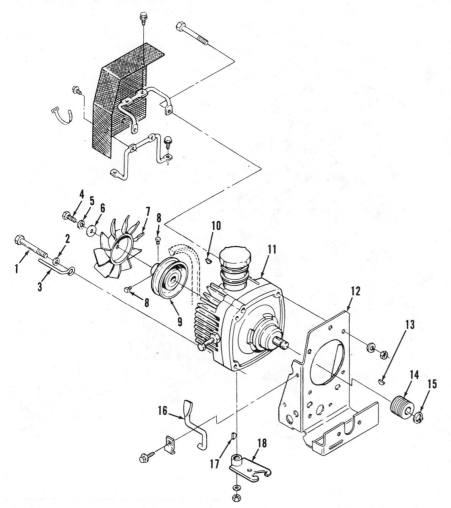

Fig. AC48—Exploded view of hydrostatic transmission and mounting components used on Models 1236H, 1242H, 1312H and 1316H.

1. Bolt	6. Washer	14. Pulley
2. Washer	7. Fan	15. Snap ring
3. Belt guide	8. Screws	16. Release lever
4. Screw	9. Pulley	17. Key
5. Lockwasher	10. Key	18. Control arm
	11. Hydrostatic transmission	
	12. Panel	
	13. Key	

REAR AXLE

All Models

LUBRICATION. The axle is fitted with grease fittings to lubricate the spindles, pivot pin and steering arm(s). See Figs. AC49 and AC50. Inject lithium based grease into grease fitting after every 25 hours of operation.

R&R AND OVERHAUL. To remove a rear spindle, raise and support side to be serviced. Remove hub cap (Figs. AC51 or AC52), "E" ring, wheel and tire. Disconnect steering link from spindle. Detach snap ring at top of spindle and remove spindle. Inspect components for excessive wear and damage. Install spindle by reversing removal procedure.

The rear axle on all models pivots on a center pin. To remove the rear axle, disconnect the drag link or steering control cables from the upper steering arm(s). Raise and support rear of machine, unscrew axle pivot bolt and separate axle assembly from machine. Refer to Figs. AC51 or AC52 and disassemble axle assembly as needed. Inspect components for excessive wear and damage. Install axle by reversing removal procedure.

MOWER BELT

Models 836, 1236H, 1242 and 1242H

REMOVE AND REINSTALL. To remove mower belt, raise engine cover and disconnect spark plug wire. Loosen belt guide near mower belt idler on machine and remove belt from engine pulley. Detach belt cover on mower deck. Remove belt from mower deck. Reverse removal procedure to install belt while referring to Figs. AC53 or AC54 for belt routing diagram. Be sure belt is routed between belt brake bracket (28—Fig. AC55) and brake rod (34). Gap between

sion rotates. Continue belt movement until only air-free fluid is expelled from bleed screw hole. Install bleed screw and fill reservoir. Start engine and operate machine while monitoring fluid level until level stabilizes.

REMOVE AND REINSTALL. To remove transmission, remove traction drive belt and intermediate drive belt as previously outlined. Detach shift control rod from shift arm (18—Fig. AC48). Unscrew transmission mounting bolts and remove transmission.

Install transmission by reversing removal procedure. If removed, install pulley (9) so long side of pulley hub is toward end of shaft and flush with end of shaft. Tighten pulley retaining screws (8) to 70 in.-lbs. (7.9 N•m). Tighten transmission mounting bolts to 20 ft.-lbs. (27 N•m).

REAR WHEELS

All Models

Each rear wheel hub is equipped with a grease fitting (F—Fig. AC49). Inject lithium based grease into grease fitting after every 25 hours of operation. Rear wheel bearings are renewable.

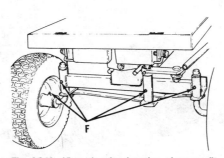

Fig. AC49—View showing location of grease fittings (F) on rear axle assembly.

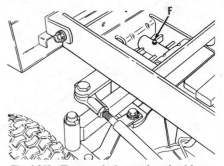

Fig. AC50—The rear deck must be raised for access to grease fitting (F) on rear axle pivot tube.

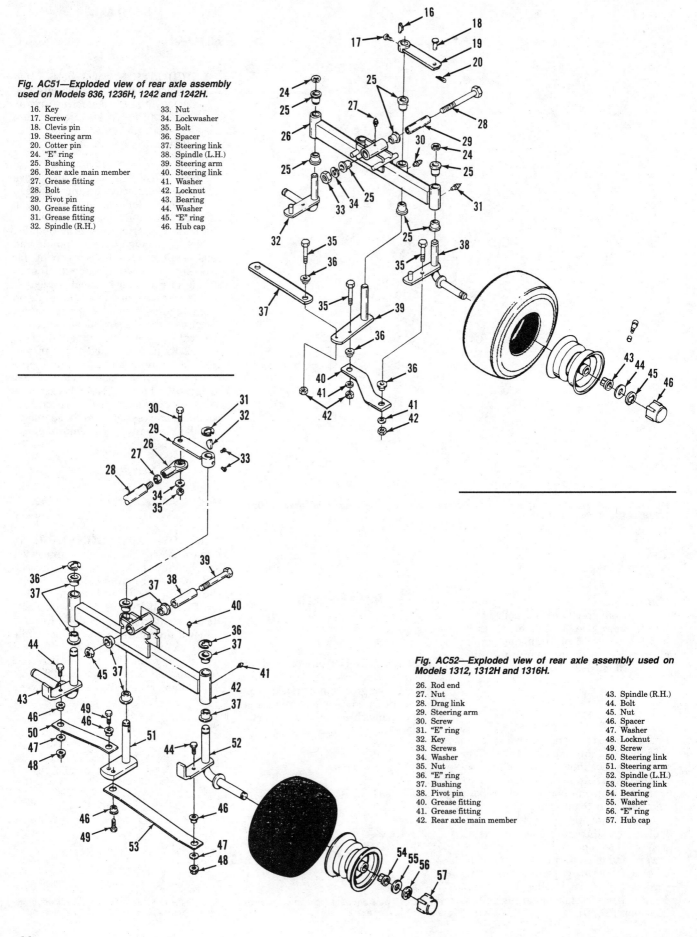

Fig. AC51—Exploded view of rear axle assembly used on Models 836, 1236H, 1242 and 1242H.

16. Key	33. Nut
17. Screw	34. Lockwasher
18. Clevis pin	35. Bolt
19. Steering arm	36. Spacer
20. Cotter pin	37. Steering link
24. "E" ring	38. Spindle (L.H.)
25. Bushing	39. Steering arm
26. Rear axle main member	40. Steering link
27. Grease fitting	41. Washer
28. Bolt	42. Locknut
29. Pivot pin	43. Bearing
30. Grease fitting	44. Washer
31. Grease fitting	45. "E" ring
32. Spindle (R.H.)	46. Hub cap

Fig. AC52—Exploded view of rear axle assembly used on Models 1312, 1312H and 1316H.

26. Rod end	
27. Nut	
28. Drag link	
29. Steering arm	43. Spindle (R.H.)
30. Screw	44. Bolt
31. "E" ring	45. Nut
32. Key	46. Spacer
33. Screws	47. Washer
34. Washer	48. Locknut
35. Nut	49. Screw
36. "E" ring	50. Steering link
37. Bushing	51. Steering arm
38. Pivot pin	52. Spindle (L.H.)
40. Grease fitting	53. Steering link
41. Grease fitting	54. Bearing
42. Rear axle main member	55. Washer
	56. "E" ring
	57. Hub cap

belt guides and belt should be $\frac{1}{16}$-$\frac{1}{8}$ inch (1.6-3.2 mm).

Models 1312, 1312H and 1316H

REMOVE AND REINSTALL. To remove mower belt, raise engine cover and disconnect spark plug wire. Remove belt cover on mower deck, pull back spring-loaded belt idler and separate mower belt from fixed idlers (do not remove belt from spring-loaded idler). Disconnect wire lead to engine pulley electric clutch. Detach spring clip (P—Fig. AC41), push torque rod (R) through the frame and unscrew rod from electric clutch. Remove mower drive belt from electric clutch. Detach belt cover on mower deck. Remove belt from mower deck. Reverse removal procedure to install belt while referring to Fig. AC54 for belt routing diagram. Gap between belt guides and belt should be $\frac{1}{16}$-$\frac{1}{8}$ inch (1.6-3.2 mm).

MOWER DECK

Models 836, 1236H, 1242 and 1242H

LUBRICATION. Each mower wheel spindle housing is equipped with a grease fitting. Inject lithium based grease into grease fitting after every 25 hours of operation. Lubricate all rubbing surfaces with engine oil.

HEIGHT ADJUSTMENT. All mower control linkage must be in good operating condition and tires properly

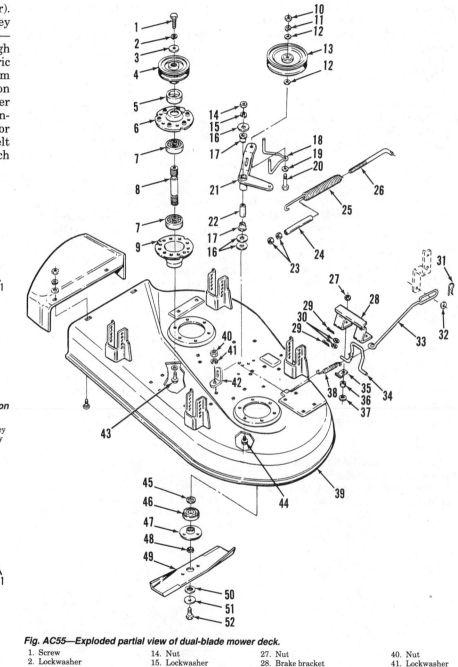

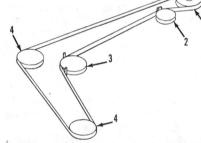

Fig. AC53—Diagram of mower belt routing on mower decks with dual blades.

1. Engine pulley
2. Fixed pulley
3. Movable pulley
4. Spindle pulley

Fig. AC55—Exploded partial view of dual-blade mower deck.

1. Screw	14. Nut	27. Nut	40. Nut
2. Lockwasher	15. Lockwasher	28. Brake bracket	41. Lockwasher
3. Washer	16. Washer	29. Cotter pin	42. Bracket
4. Spindle pulley	17. Bushing	30. Washer	43. Screw
5. Dust shield	18. Belt guide	31. Spring clip	44. Screw
6. Upper housing	19. Washer	32. Washer	45. Washer
7. Bearing	20. Bolt	33. Brake control rod	46. Shield
8. Spindle	21. Idler arm	34. Brake rod	47. Adapter
9. Lower housing	22. Spacer	35. Clamp	48. Collar
10. Nut	23. Nuts	36. Spacer	49. Blade
11. Lockwasher	24. Spacer	37. Nut	50. Spline washer
12. Washer	25. Spring	38. Spring	51. Washer
13. Movable pulley	26. Clutch rod	39. Mower deck	52. Screw

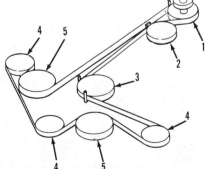

Fig. AC54—Diagram of mower belt routing on mower decks with three blades.

1. Engine pulley or electric clutch
2. Fixed pulley
3. Movable pulley
4. Spindle pulley
5. Fixed pulley

inflated. Park machine on a level surface with engine stopped and spark plug wire disconnected.

Front-to-rear height difference is determined by measuring height of blade above ground at front and rear. Height difference should be within 1/8 inch (3.2 mm). To adjust front-to-rear height difference, rotate leveling bolts at front and rear of mower deck.

Side-to-side height difference should be within 1/8 inch (3.2 mm). To adjust side-to-side dimension, rotate leveling bolts at front and rear on one side of mower deck.

CLUTCH ADJUSTMENT. When mower is engaged, clutch spring (25—Fig. AC55) length should be 4¾ inches (121 mm). Measure length as shown in Fig. AC56. To adjust spring length, disengage mower and rotate nuts (23).

REMOVE AND REINSTALL. To remove mower, raise engine cover and disconnect spark plug wire. Loosen belt guide near mower belt idler on machine and remove belt from engine pulley. Disconnect mower clutch rod and lift rod. Detach attachment pins at rear of mower frame and remove mower. Install mower by reversing removal procedure.

Models 1312, 1312H and 1316H

LUBRICATION. Mower wheel spindle housings and clutch idler arm are equipped with a grease fitting. Inject lithium based grease into grease fitting after every 25 hours of operation. Lubricate all rubbing surfaces with engine oil.

HEIGHT ADJUSTMENT. All mower control linkage must be in good operating condition and tires properly inflated. Park machine on a level sur-

face with engine stopped and spark plug wire disconnected.

Front-to-rear height difference is determined by measuring height of blade above ground at front and rear. Height difference should be zero. To adjust height, remove belt covers, detach spring clips (C—Fig. AC57) and remove pins in each adjustment rod. Loosen jam nuts (N) and rotate each clevis (L) equal turns to adjust height. Retighten nuts and install pins, spring clips and belt covers.

Side-to-side height difference should be zero. To adjust side-to-side height, loosen screw (S—Fig. AC58) and relocate roller bracket (B).

REMOVE AND REINSTALL. To remove mower belt, raise engine cover and disconnect spark plug wire. Remove belt cover on mower deck, pull back spring-loaded belt idler and separate mower belt from fixed idlers (do not remove belt from spring-loaded idler). Disconnect wire lead to engine pulley electric clutch. Detach spring clip (P—Fig. AC41), push torque rod (R) through frame and unscrew rod from electric clutch. Remove mower drive belt from electric clutch. Place mower in lowest position. Detach rear lift arms from lift chains. Detach rear mower frame arms from machine. Detach spring clip (C—Fig. AC59) from pin (P) and disconnect lift link. Roll mower away from machine.

Refer to Fig. AC60 for a exploded partial view of mower deck. Install mower by reversing removal procedure.

MOWER SPINDLE

All Models

LUBRICATION. Mower spindle housings on some models are equipped with a grease fitting on the bottom of the housing. If so equipped, inject lithium

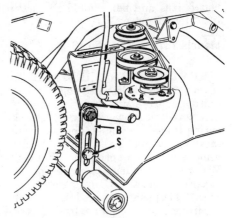

Fig. AC58—On Models 1312, 1312H and 1316H, loosen screw (S) and relocate bracket (B) to adjust side-to-side mower height.

based grease into grease fitting after every 25 hours of operation.

R&R AND OVERHAUL. Remove mower deck, belt and blade. Unscrew spindle housing mounting screws and remove spindle assembly. Disassembly is evident after inspection and referral to Figs. AC55 or AC60. During assembly, apply gasket forming compound to mating surfaces of top and lower spindle housings. Let gasket forming compound cure, then fill lower spindle housing with lithium based grease. If spindle pulley hub has a long end, install pulley so long end of hub is toward housing. Tighten pulley retaining screw to 50-70 ft.-lbs. (68-95 N•m). Tighten spindle housing retaining screws to 14-20 ft.-lbs. (19-27 N•m). Tighten blade retaining screw to 50-70 ft.-lbs. (68-95 N•m).

MOWER ELECTRIC CLUTCH

Models 1312, 1312H and 1316H

On Models 1312, 1312H and 1316H, the mower drive pulley is attached to an electric clutch.

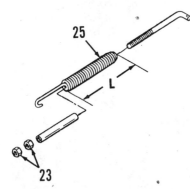

Fig. AC56—When mower on Models 836, 1236H, 1242 and 1242H is engaged, clutch spring (25) length (L) should be 4-3/4 inches (121 mm). Rotate nuts (23) to adjust spring length.

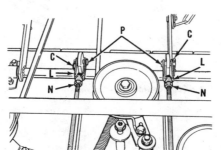

Fig. AC57—Refer to text to adjust mower height on Models 1312, 1312H and 1316H.

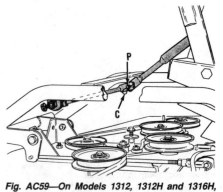

Fig. AC59—On Models 1312, 1312H and 1316H, detach spring clip (C) and disconnect lift rod from pin (P) to remove mower deck.

ADJUSTMENT. The clutch air gap must be set correctly so the clutch will engage properly. Desired air gap is 0.010-0.012 inch (0.25-0.30 mm). With the mower clutch switch in "OFF" position, insert a 0.010-0.012 inch (0.25-0.30 mm) feeler gauge through slots (S—Fig. AC61) in side of clutch. Check gap through all three of the slots. Rotate three nuts (N) as needed to obtain correct gap.

R&R AND OVERHAUL. Remove mower drive belt as previously outlined. Unscrew clutch retaining screw and remove clutch assembly. Refer to Fig. AC62 for an exploded view of mower clutch.

If installing a new clutch or components, adjust clutch air gap as previously outlined. Engage clutch several times after mower is installed to burnish clutch surfaces.

ELECTRICAL

All Models

Refer to Figs. AC63 through AC67 for wiring diagrams. Note the following points:

• Transmission must be in neutral, the mower must be disengaged and the operator must be in seat for engine to start.

• The engine should stop if the transmission is in gear or the mower is engaged and the operator leaves the seat.

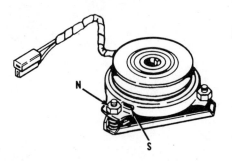

Fig. AC61—Turn each adjusting nut (N) of electric clutch so clearance between rotor and armature is 0.010-0.012 inch (0.25-0.30 mm).

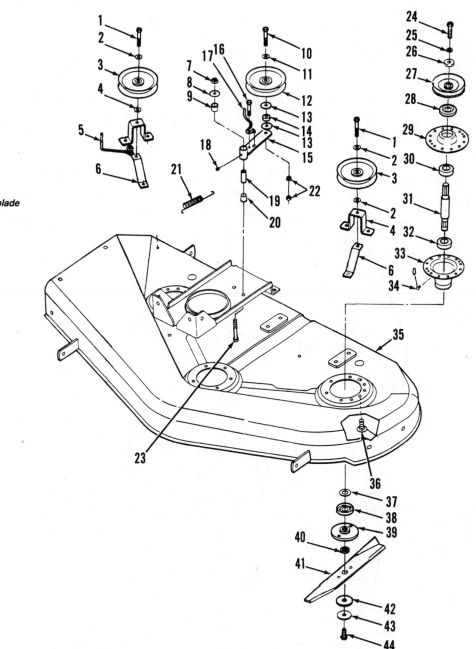

Fig. AC60—Exploded partial view of triple-blade mower deck.

1. Screw
2. Washer
3. Pulley
4. Bracket
5. Belt guide
6. Brace
7. Locknut
8. Washer
9. Bushing
10. Bolt
11. Washer
12. Movable pulley
13. Washer
14. Spacer
15. Idler arm
16. Screw
17. Belt guide
18. Grease fitting
19. Spacer
20. Bushing
21. Spring
22. Locknuts
23. Bolt
24. Screw
25. Lockwasher
26. Washer
27. Spindle pulley
28. Dust shield
29. Upper housing
30. Bearing
31. Spindle
32. Spacer
33. Lower housing
34. Grease fitting
35. Mower deck
36. Screw
37. Washer
38. Shield
39. Adapter
40. Collar
41. Blade
42. Spline washer
43. Washer
44. Screw

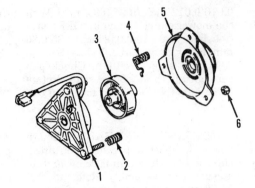

Fig. AC62—Exploded view of mower electric clutch.

1. Field coil
2. Spring
3. Rotor

4. Spring
5. Armature
6. Nut

Fig. AC63—Wiring diagram for early Models 836 and 1242.

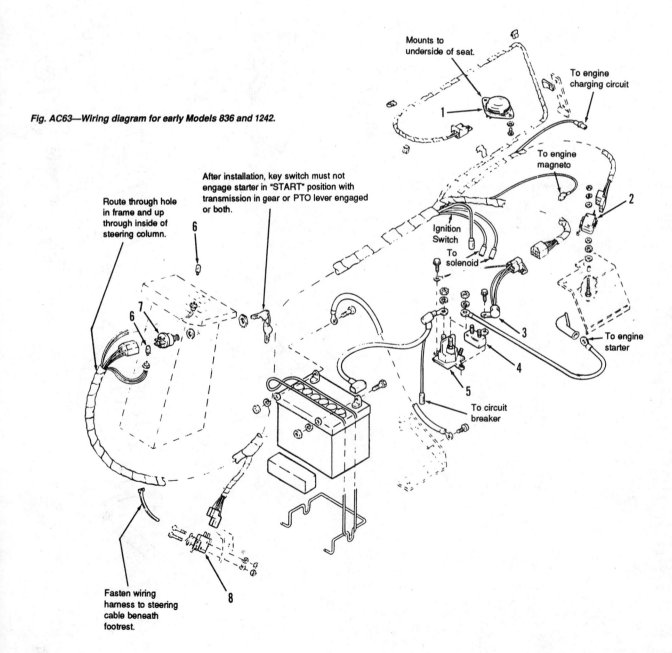

Illustrations Courtesy AGCO

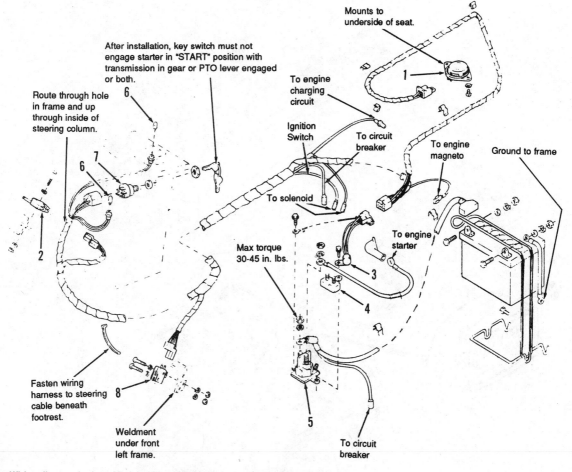

Mounts to
underside of seat.

After installation, key switch must not
engage starter in "START" position with
transmission in gear or PTO lever engaged
or both.

To engine
charging
circuit

Route through hole
in frame and up
through inside of
steering column.

6

Ignition
Switch

To circuit
breaker

To engine
magneto

Ground to frame

6   7

To solenoid

2

Max torque
30-45 in. lbs.

To engine
starter

3

4

Fasten wiring
harness to steering
cable beneath
footrest.

8

5

Weldment
under front
left frame.

To circuit
breaker

Fig. AC64—Wiring diagram for later Models 836 and 1242. Models 1236H and 1242H are similar.

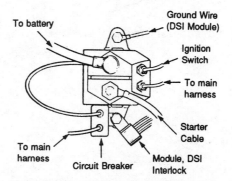

To battery

Ground Wire
(DSI Module)

Ignition
Switch

To main
harness

Starter
Cable

To main
harness

Circuit Breaker

Module, DSI
Interlock

Fig. AC65—Wiring diagram for solenoid on Models 836, 1236H, 1242 and 1242H.

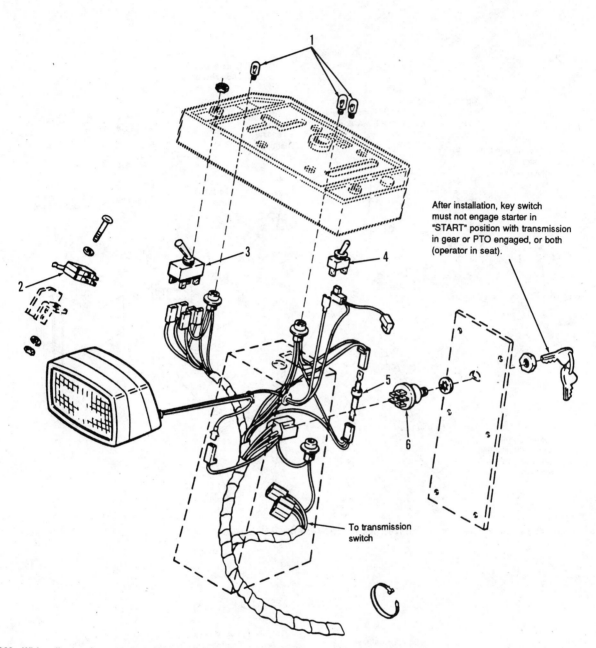

After installation, key switch must not engage starter in "START" position with transmission in gear or PTO engaged, or both (operator in seat).

To transmission switch

Fig. AC66—Wiring diagram for console on Models 1312, 1312H and 1316H. Refer to Fig. AC67 for wiring diagram of remainder of machine.

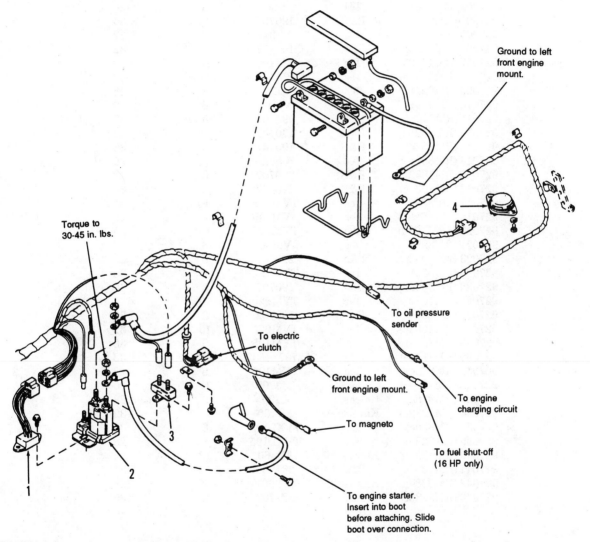

Ground to left
front engine
mount.

Torque to
30-45 in. lbs.

To electric
clutch

To oil pressure
sender

Ground to left
front engine
mount.

To engine
charging circuit

To magneto

To fuel shut-off
(16 HP only)

To engine starter.
Insert into boot
before attaching. Slide
boot over connection.

4

3

2

1

Fig. AC67—Wiring diagram for rear of machine on Models 1312, 1312H and 1316H. Refer to Fig. AC66 for wiring diagram of console.

ARIENS

ARIENS
655 West Ryan St.
Brillion, WI 54110

Model	Make	Engine Model	Horsepower	Cutting Width, In.
927001 (RM728)	Tec	VM70	7	28
927002 (RM626)	Tec	V60	6	26
927003 (RM626)	Tec	V60	6	26
927004 (RM830e)	B&S	190707	8	30
927005 (RM832)	Tec	VM80	8	32
927006 (RM832e)	B&S	190707	8	32
927007 (RM1032)	Tec	VM100	10	32
927008 (RM1032e)	Tec	VM100	10	32
927009 (RM828)	Tec	VM80	8	28
927010 (RM830)	Tec	VM80	8	30
927011 (RM830e)	B&S	190707	8	30
927012 (RM832)	B&S	190702	8	32
927013 (RM832e)	B&S	190707	8	32
927014 (RM830)	Tec	VM80	8	30
927015 (RM1032)	B&S	220702	8	32
927016 (RM1032e)	B&S	220707	8	32
927017 (SRM830)	Tec	TVM195	8	30
927018 (SRM626)	Tec	TVM140	6	26
927020 (SRM1030)	Tec	TVM220	10	30
927021 (RM828)	Tec	VM80	8	28
927023 (RM1032e)	B&S	220707	8	32
927024 (RM830)	Tec	TVM195	8	30
927025 (RM830e)	B&S	190707	8	30
927026 (RM1032)	Tec	TVM220	10	32
927027 (RM830)	B&S	190702	8	30
927028 (RM1032e)	Tec	TVM220	10	32
927029 (RM830e)	Tec	TVM195	8	30
927030 (RM1132e)	B&S	252707, 253707	11	32
927031 (RM828e)	Tec	TVM195	8	28
927032 (RM1130e)	B&S	253707	11	30
927033 (RM928e)	Kawasaki	FC290V	9	28
927034 (RM1232e)	Kawasaki	FB460	12	32
927037 (RM830e)	Tec	TVXL195	8	30
927039 (RM828e)	Tec	TVXL195	8	28
927040 (RM1232e)	Kawasaki	FB460	12	32
927041 (RM1232e)	B&S	281707	12	32
927042 (RM928e)	Kawasaki	FC290V	9	28
927043 (RM1230e)	B&S	281707	12	30

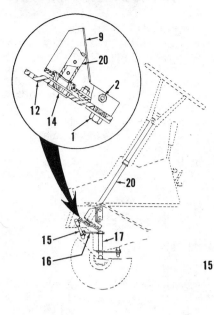

Fig. AR1—Views of typical steering system and front axle. Tighten axle pivot nut (19) to 35 ft.-lbs. (48 N·m).

1. Nut
2. Nut
9. Bracket
12. Steering gear
14. Pinion
15. Steering link
16. Arm
17. Spindle
18. Tie rod
19. Nut
20. Steering shaft

All Models

Refer to appropriate engine section in this manual for tune-up specifications, engine overhaul procedures and engine maintenance.

REMOVE AND REINSTALL. To remove engine, disconnect spark plug wire. On electric start models, disconnect and remove battery. Disconnect any interfering electrical wires from engine. Disconnect throttle cable from engine. Remove belts from engine pulley. Remove engine mounting bolts and remove engine.

Reinstall by reversing removal procedure.

FRONT AXLE

All Models

R&R AND OVERHAUL. Axle main member is center-pivoted in channel at front of chassis. Repair procedure will depend upon extent of service required. However, reference to Fig. AR1 will indicate correct assembly. Axle pivot nut (19—Fig. AR1) should be tightened to 35 ft.-lbs. (48 N·m).

STEERING GEAR

All Models

R&R, OVERHAUL AND ADJUST. If equipped with a rear service bar, drain fuel and operate engine until all fuel is removed from carburetor. Disconnect spark plug wire, remove battery, air cleaner and rear grass catcher. Raise front enough to tip unit back onto service bar. Be careful not to knock unit over while servicing.

If not equipped with service bar at rear, it is necessary to raise unit using sufficient blocks or hoist to permit access to steering gear from below. Be extremely careful to prevent unit from falling over while servicing. If unit is raised only at front remove fluids as described in preceding paragraph. Always disconnect spark plug wire when servicing to help prevent injury.

The steering gear assembly (Fig. AR2) can be removed after detaching link (15—Fig. AR1) from steering gear (12) and steering shaft (20) from pinion (14).

Adjustment to compensate for wear of pinion and steering gear teeth is possible without removing steering gear

assembly. To adjust, loosen nut (1—Figs. AR1 or AR2), then tighten nut (2) slightly. Tighten nut (1), then turn steering to be sure that steering does not bind anywhere in operating range. If binding is observed, loosen nut (1), loosen nut (2), retighten nut (1), then recheck steering for smoothness.

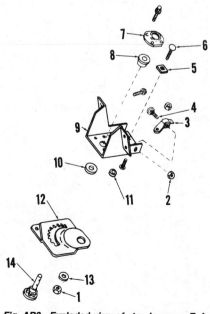

Fig. AR2—Exploded view of steering gear. Refer to Fig. AR1 for cross-sectional view.

1. Nut
2. Nut
3. Adjuster block
4. Screw
5. Pivot spacer
6. Screw
7. Retainer
8. Bushing
9. Bracket
10. Washer
11. Bushing
12. Steering gear
13. Washer
14. Pinion

TRACTION DRIVE BELT

All Models

REMOVE AND REINSTALL. To remove traction drive belt, it is first necessary to remove the mower drive belt, then remove friction wheel as described in FRICTION DRIVE section. Remove belt, then locate new belt in grooves of engine pulley, drive disc and idler pulley. Make sure belt is not twisted, then install and adjust friction wheel. Install and adjust mower drive belt as described in MOWER DRIVE BELT section.

TRACTION DRIVE CLUTCH

All Models

ADJUSTMENT. Clutch action is accomplished by raising drive disc (3—Fig. AR3) vertically away from the friction wheel (4). The clutch and brake are interactive and depressing the brake pedal also causes the clutch to release. Adjust the clutch linkage first, then check and, if necessary, adjust brake controls.

To adjust the clutch, tip unit back onto rear service bar (5) or raise unit sufficiently to provide access from below. Move speed control lever to neutral position, depress clutch pedal fully and engage parking brake (6). Turn nuts (2—Fig. AR4) until clearance between neutral stop (7) and carrier yoke (8) is ⅛-¼ inch (3-6 mm). Release parking brake and rotate rear wheels by hand. Wheels should rotate freely in neutral position, but not in any other position.

Brake is engaged by depressing brake pedal or by depressing clutch pedal past the clutch range. To adjust, move speed control to neutral, then

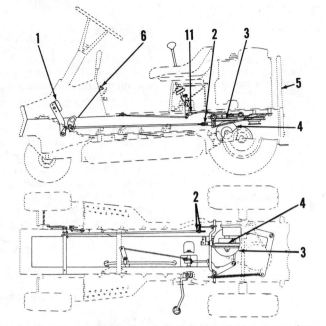

Fig. AR3—Drawing of clutch operating system. Refer to text for adjustment procedures.

1. Pedal
2. Adjusting nuts
3. Drive disc
4. Friction wheel
5. Rear service bar
6. Parking brake control
11. Link

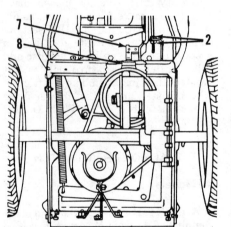

Fig. AR4—Refer to text for adjustment of traction drive clutch and friction drive. Linkage is interactive and must be adjusted correctly.

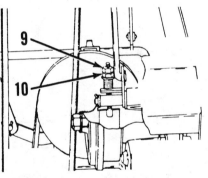

Fig. AR5—Refer to text for adjustment of brake linkage.

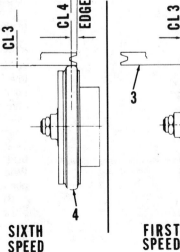

Fig. AR6—Views of drive disc (3) and friction wheel (4) showing relative location in first speed and sixth speed.

SIXTH SPEED

FIRST SPEED

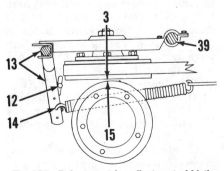

Fig. AR7—Refer to text for adjustment of friction drive.

loosen nuts (9 and 10—Fig. AR5). Be careful not to distort the brake band when loosening nuts. Tighten nut (10) until wheel just starts to bind, then loosen 1½ turns and tighten locknut (9). Recheck brake action using clutch pedal. The drive disc should just move away from friction wheel (clutch action) when clutch pedal is approximately ¾ inch (19 mm) from limit of travel. The final ¾ inch (19 mm) should be sufficient to engage brake. Be sure that brake band is not twisted.

FRICTION DRIVE

All Models

ADJUSTMENT. Disengagement of the clutch is accomplished by raising the drive disc (3—Fig. AR3) vertically away from the friction wheel (4). Refer to preceding TRACTION DRIVE CLUTCH paragraphs for adjustment procedures.

Speed control is accomplished by moving the drive disc (3) laterally across the friction surface of the friction wheel (4). Locating the center of the drive disc over the friction wheel provides a neutral position.

To adjust shift positions, proceed as follows: Move carrier yoke (8—Fig. AR4) until it is centered on neutral stop (7). Detach link (11—Fig. AR3) from speed control lever. Change length of link (11) if necessary so that it can be reattached with shift lever in neutral and carrier yoke centered. Connect link and shift to sixth speed. Check to be sure that rubber friction wheel (4—Fig. AR4) is still on drive disc (3). Shift to first and reverse speeds and check to be sure that the carrier yoke (8—Fig. AR4) moves off center in both directions. Distance between centerline of drive disc (CL3—Fig. AR6) and centerline of friction wheel (CL4) should be $^{11}/_{16}$-¾ inch (17.5-19 mm) in first speed.

The friction wheel must be removed to measure clearance between guard (15—Fig. AR7) and drive disc (3) when adjusting position of stop (12). Refer to the following R&R AND OVERHAUL paragraphs for removal of friction wheel and adjusting stop.

R&R AND OVERHAUL. The friction drive consists of friction wheel (4—Fig. AR8), drive disc (3) and related parts of spindle carrier (24 through 36). Some models are equipped with the die cast carrier (35) shown in Fig. AR8; other models are equipped with the stamped carrier frame (36) shown in Fig. AR9.

If friction wheel (4—Figs. AR8 or AR9) is damaged, careful analysis may indicate necessary repair. Refer to Fig. AR10. **View 1** shows small scuff marks and localized flat spot that could be caused by parking brake not releasing completely or by drive disc contacting friction wheel in neutral. **View 2** shows larger, chunked-out spot with cracks running around friction surface, which can be caused by drive disc contacting friction wheel in neutral. **View 3** shows normal deterioration after long period of normal use. If this occurs prematurely, however, cause is too much pressure on friction roller. **View 4** shows shiny friction surface with cracks across surface caused by not enough pressure or operator riding the clutch. **View 5** shows split indicating failure of friction surface seam. **View 6** shows radical failure that is usually caused by slippage even though pressure is too much (or at least enough). Overloading mower or operating on long inclines for extended time can result in damage shown in **View 6**. Improper bond may result in missing rubber friction surface as shown in **View 7**. **View 8** shows friction surface worn at an angle caused by bent or loose spindle or carrier frame. Rubber friction surface may be prematurely worn and roughened as shown in **View 9** if the drive disc surface is not smooth. Cuts in the friction surface as shown in **View 10** are usually caused by foreign objects caught in drive assembly.

To disassemble and adjust, proceed as follows: Remove battery, drain fuel, then raise machine or tip machine back onto service bar, if so equipped. Remove attaching screws (16—Figs. AR8 or AR9), remove guard (15) and friction wheel (4).

When reinstalling, assemble guard (15) without wheel (4), then adjust stop (12—Fig. AR7). Move speed control to a forward position, then check clearance between drive disc (3) and guard (15). Loosen the two nuts on clutch shaft stop screw (12), then reposition stop screw in slot so that only a small amount of clearance exists between guard (15) and disc (3). Move speed control back to neutral, then proceed with disassembly or reinstall friction wheel. Be sure that friction wheel is correctly located over shoulder of hub and that all five retaining screws are tightened upon final assembly.

To remove the carrier assembly (24 through 36—Fig. AR8) and drive disc (3), first remove friction wheel (4) as described in previous paragraph. Remove cotter pin from link (37) and detach from lever (38). Disconnect spring (14—Fig. AR7) from shaft and lever (13), then remove cotter pin and withdraw shaft (39). Disengage yoke from

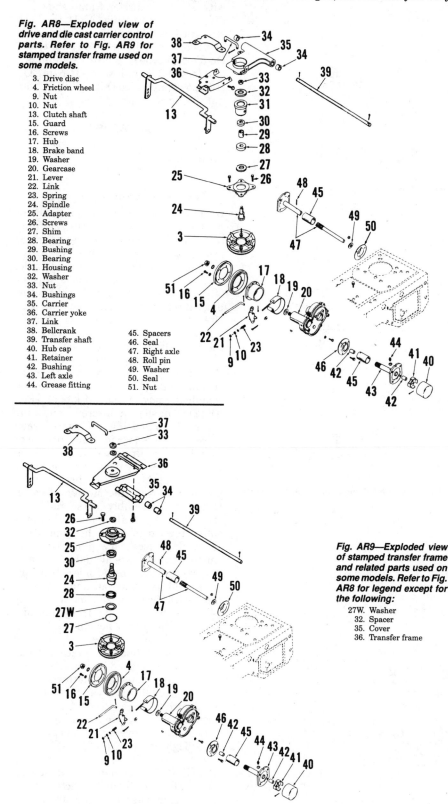

Fig. AR8—Exploded view of drive and die cast carrier control parts. Refer to Fig. AR9 for stamped transfer frame used on some models.

3. Drive disc
4. Friction wheel
9. Nut
10. Nut
13. Clutch shaft
15. Guard
16. Screws
17. Hub
18. Brake band
19. Washer
20. Gearcase
21. Lever
22. Link
23. Spring
24. Spindle
25. Adapter
26. Screws
27. Shim
28. Bearing
29. Bushing
30. Bearing
31. Housing
32. Washer
33. Nut
34. Bushings
35. Carrier
36. Carrier yoke
37. Link
38. Bellcrank
39. Transfer shaft
40. Hub cap
41. Retainer
42. Bushing
43. Left axle
44. Grease fitting
45. Spacers
46. Seal
47. Right axle
48. Roll pin
49. Washer
50. Seal
51. Nut

Fig. AR9—Exploded view of stamped transfer frame and related parts used on some models. Refer to Fig. AR8 for legend except for the following:

27W. Washer
32. Spacer
35. Cover
36. Transfer frame

Ariens

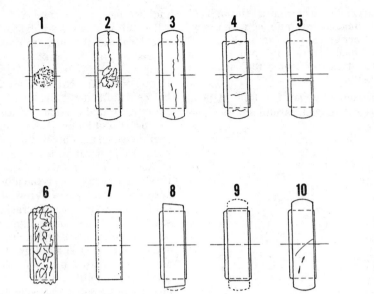

Fig. AR10—Drawings of some friction wheel failures. Refer to text for description of conditions shown.

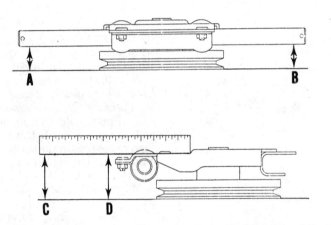

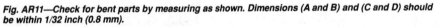

Fig. AR11—Check for bent parts by measuring as shown. Dimensions (A and B) and (C and D) should be within 1/32 inch (0.8 mm).

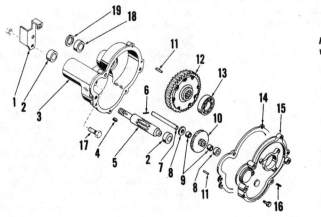

Fig. AR12—Exploded view of gearcase.

1. Brake bracket
2. Ball bearing
3. Housing
4. Woodruff key
5. Pinion shaft
6. Roll pin
7. Idler shaft
8. Washer
9. Needle bearings
10. Cluster gear
11. Groove pin
12. Differential assy.
13. Ball bearing
14. Gasket
15. Cover
16. Breather
17. Special screw
18. Bushing
19. Seal

clutch shaft (13) and withdraw carrier assembly.

On some models, carrier is die cast (35) as shown in Fig. AR8, while other models use stamped assembly as shown in Fig. AR9. Disassembly procedure will be self-evident after examining applicable Fig. AR8 or Fig. AR9. On models with stamped carrier frame shown in Fig. AR9, refer to Fig. AR11 to check straightness. Shims (27) are used to adjust bearings (28 and 30) on both types. On die cast type (Fig. AR8), tighten nut (33) to 250-275 in.-lbs. (28-31 N•m). On stamped frame type (Fig. AR9), tighten nut (33) to 45 ft.-lbs. (61 N•m).

GEARCASE

All Models

R&R AND OVERHAUL. To remove traction drive gearcase (20—Fig. AR8 or AR9), first remove hub cap retaining cotter pin, hub cap (40) and retainer (41) from the short left side axle (43). Drive roll pin (48) from long right side axle, then withdraw axle. Remove washer (49) from inside bearing. Remove cotter pin, then detach rod (22) from lever (21). Unbolt and remove seal (46). Remove screws attaching gearcase (20) to frame, then withdraw gearcase assembly.

To disassemble gearcase, remove nut (51), then slide friction wheel (4), guard (15) and hub (17) from shaft as an assembly. Remove Woodruff key (4—Fig. AR12) from shaft and screws retaining cover (15) to housing (3). Insert screwdrivers in slots provided and pry cover from housing. Breather (16) can be removed by pressing it out from the inside toward outside. Install breather by pressing in from the outside of cover. Differential assembly (12) should be installed with small inside diameter spline toward inside of housing (3). If renewal is necessary, pinion (5) and cluster gear (10) are available only as a matched set. Numbered side of bearings (9) should be facing out and should be flush with face of gear. Bushing (18) is removed by pressing from outside. Press bushing into housing until bottomed against shoulder in bore. Seal (19) should be flush with face of housing. Special ribbed screws (17) are pressed into housing to attach brake bracket (1). Gearcase cavity should be filled with 8 ounces (237 mL) of multipurpose grease before installing cover.

Reinstall by reversing removal procedure. Tighten nut (51—Fig. AR8) to 70 ft.-lbs. (95 N•m). Refer to TRACTION DRIVE CLUTCH adjustment section and to FRICTION DRIVE section while installing and assembling gearcase.

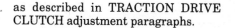
as described in TRACTION DRIVE CLUTCH adjustment paragraphs.

MOWER DRIVE BELT

All Models

ADJUSTMENT. During first hours of operation, new mower drive belt will stretch and will require adjustment as follows.

Set mower height in the middle notch. Hold mower clutch lever (2—Fig. AR14) so front edge of lever is aligned with rear edge of forward notch (detent) of quadrant as viewed through slot in left side of cowl. Turn adjustment screw (3) with ¾-inch socket. Press socket against spring clip when turning screw (3), then be sure that wire spring clip engages adjustment screw when released. The mower clutch lever will pull rearward slightly as tension is increased sufficiently. Mower clutch should begin to engage when front edge of lever is aligned with rear edge of forward notch in quadrant and should be fully locked in when lever is completely engaging notch. Do not overtighten as bearing and belt may fail prematurely due to increased wear.

If mower is usually operated in lowest cutting position, readjust belt tension with height set in this (lowest) position. On models equipped with a belt finger retaining the belt in idler pulley, belt slippage can also be caused by the finger being adjusted against belt. Correct adjustment is ⅛-inch (3 mm) clearance between retaining finger and back edge of belt. Blade attaching nut should be tightened to 50-55 ft.-lbs. (68-75 N•m).

REMOVE AND REINSTALL. If equipped with a rear service bar, drain fuel, remove battery and tip unit up onto rear service bar, If not equipped with a rear service bar, drain fuel, remove battery, then raise unit sufficiently to provide easy access to underside. On all models, use all possible precautions to prevent unit from falling while servicing. Move mower clutch lever to "OUT" (disengaged) position. Loosen three nuts (4—Fig. AR15) and move rear finger out of the way. Roll belt out of pulley groove. Renew drive belt, then reinstall in reverse order of disassembly.

MOWER SPINDLE

All Models

LUBRICATION. On all models, mower spindle bearings (7 and 11—Figs. AR16 and AR17) should be packed

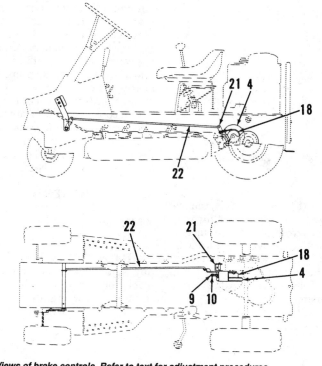

Fig. AR13—Views of brake controls. Refer to text for adjustment procedures.

4. Friction wheel
9. Nut
10. Nut
18. Brake band
21. Lever
22. Link

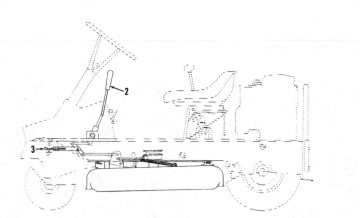

Fig. AR14—View of mower clutch adjustment screw (3), mower lever (2) and associated controls.

GROUND DRIVE BRAKE

All Models

ADJUSTMENT. Refer to Fig. AR13 for views of brake controls. The clutch and brake are interactive and depressing the brake pedal causes the clutch to release. Adjust clutch linkage first, then adjust brake controls. Refer to TRAC-

TION DRIVE CLUTCH adjustment paragraphs for procedures.

R&R AND OVERHAUL. The brake band (18—Fig. AR8) operates by contracting around hub (17). Refer to GEARCASE section to remove the gearcase and disassemble brake. When assembling, tighten hub retaining nut (51) to 70 ft.-lbs. (95 N•m). Adjust brake

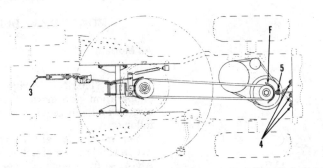

Fig. AR15—View of drive belt controls and belt guard (finger) for mower drive. Refer to text.

On models with two blades, center drive pulley (13—Fig. AR17) can be removed after removing cap (26), cotter pin and adjustment nut (15). Bearings (24) should be cleaned, inspected and renewed if necessary. Be sure that bearing cups are seated in pulley. Pack bearing cones before installing and be sure seal (23) is installed properly. Adjust bearings by tightening nut (15) until pulley rolls freely with no end play, then install cotter pin. Lubricate bearings by injecting grease into grease fitting (33).

On all models, tighten blade retaining nut (1—Fig. AR16 or Fig. AR17) to 50-55 ft.-lbs. (68-75 N•m).

MOWER DECK

All Models

ADJUSTMENT. Before attempting any adjustment, machine must be on level ground and tires must be properly inflated. Turn ingnition switch OFF,

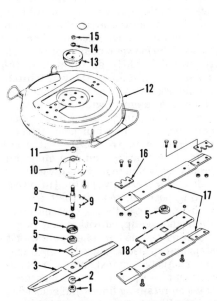

Woodruff key (9). On all models, remove hub (5—Figs. AR16 or AR17), slinger (6) and lower Woodruff key (9). On models with two blades, remove belt guards (34 and 35—Fig. AR17) and belt to mower spindle pulleys. On all models, bump spindle (8—Figs. AR16 or AR17) out of spindle housing (10).

Fig. AR16—Views of mower deck, spindle and three different blades used on most models.

1. Nut
2. Lockwasher
3. Blade
4. Blade tray
5. Retainer hub
6. Bearing slinger
7. Bearing
8. Spindle
9. Woodruff keys
10. Spindle housing
11. Bearing
12. Mower deck
13. Pulley
14. Washer
15. Nut
16. Vanes
17. Blade
18. Blade tray (late type)

with grease when assembling and should not require additional lubrication until disassembled for other service. On 38-inch mowers with two blades (3—Fig. AR17), bearings (24) for drive pulley (13) should be lubricated through grease fitting (33) after every 25 hours of operation.

R&R AND OVERHAUL. To remove spindle (8—Figs. AR16 or AR17), first remove mower deck as outlined in appropriate following paragraph. Remove blade retaining nut (1), lockwasher (2) and blade (3 or 17). On models with one cutting blade, remove nut (15—Fig. AR16), washer (14), pulley (13) and top

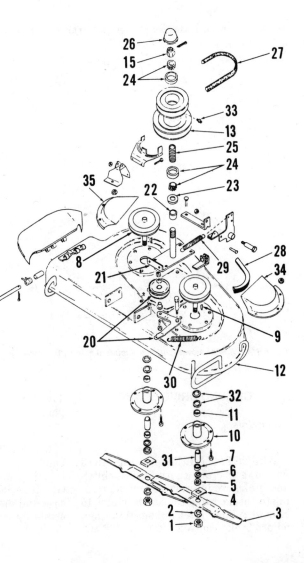

Fig. AR17—Exploded view of 38-inch mower deck with two blades.

1. Nut
2. Lockwasher
3. Blade
4. Blade tray
5. Retainer hub
6. Bearing slinger
7. Bearing
8. Spindle
9. Woodruff keys
10. Spindle housing
11. Bearing
12. Mower deck
13. Center drive pulley
14. Washer
15. Nut
20. Idler arm & pulley
21. Center spindle & bracket
22. Spacer
23. Seal
24. Taper bearings
25. Spring
26. Cap
27. Belt
28. Blade drive belt
29. Spring
30. Spring
31. Spring
32. Seals
33. Grease fitting
34. Belt guard
35. Belt guard

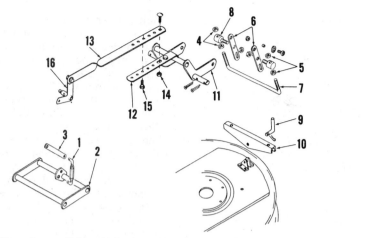

Fig. AR18—Views of mower linkage. Refer also to Figs. AR19 and AR20.

1. Link	5. Nuts	9. Pin	13. Lift strap
2. Front lift arm	6. Link plates	10. Swivel bracket	14. Nut
3. Strap	7. Link	11. Rear mower hanger	15. Cap screw
4. Nuts	8. Blocks	12. Adjusting strap	16. Lift arm

disconnect spark plug wire and tie it out of way to prevent accidental starting of the engine. Cutting height should be checked with clutch engaged.

Front-to-rear height difference is determined by measuring height of blade above ground at front and rear. Rear height should be ¼-⅜ inch (6.4-9.5 mm) higher. Adjust front height of mower by adjusting length of link (1—Fig. AR18 or Fig. AR19). To change link length, loosen locknuts, then turn center coupling of link. Rear height of mower is adjusted by turning nuts (4 and 5—Fig. AR18 or Fig. AR20). If specified front-to-rear height dimension cannot be obtained using preceding adjustment procedure, additional adjustment may be obtained by relocating screw (15—Fig. AR18) in lift straps. Moving straps apart will decrease rear mower height.

If mower deck side-to-side height is uneven, rotate nuts (4 or 5—Fig. AR18) on one side to correct unevenness. On some models, a screw adjuster adjacent to the front mower hanger (Fig. AR21) can be rotated to alter side-to-side height.

After mower deck height has been adjusted, runners should be spaced to correspond to the cutting height. If cutting height of mower blade is set to approximately 1 inch (25.4 mm), install two spacers as shown in view "L"—Fig. AR22. If cutting height is high, install all three spacers as shown in view "H". Incorrect installation of spacers for runners may cause scalping.

REMOVE AND REINSTALL. To remove mower deck, move mower control lever to disengaged position and lower mower to lowest setting. Remove

Fig. AR19—View of front link (1) installed.

Fig. AR21—On later models, loosen nut (N) and rotate screw (S) to alter side-to-side height.

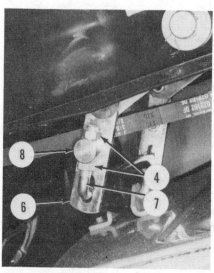

Fig. AR20—Refer to text for adjustment of rear links by turning nuts (4).

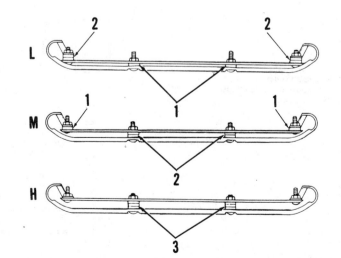

Fig. AR22—Views of runners set for low cutting height (L), medium (M) and high cutting height (H). Numbers indicate number of spacers at locations.

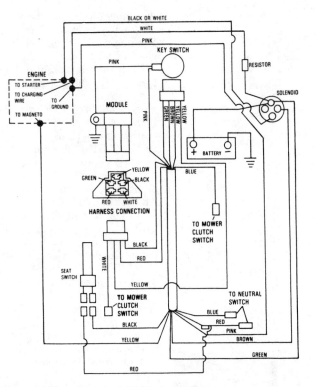

Fig. AR23—Wiring diagram of early models with electric start.

belt finger attaching nuts (4—Fig. AR15), remove finger assembly, then roll the blade drive belt out of rear pulley. On 32-inch mowers, disconnect clutch rod at front. On all models, remove clip from pin (9—Fig. AR18), then remove pin (9) and lower rear of mower. Remove clips from link (1), then remove link (1) and lower front of mower. On models so equipped, remove pins and detach positioning arms from mower deck.

Reinstall mower deck by reversing removal procedure. Be sure to check and adjust mower drive belt tension, belt finger clearance and deck height as previously outlined.

ELECTRICAL

All Models

Refer to Figs. AR23, AR24 and AR25 for wiring schematics. Note the following points:

- The transmission must be in neutral, the mower must be disengaged and the operator must be in the seat for engine to start.
- The engine should stop if the transmission is in gear or the mower is engaged and the operator leaves the seat.

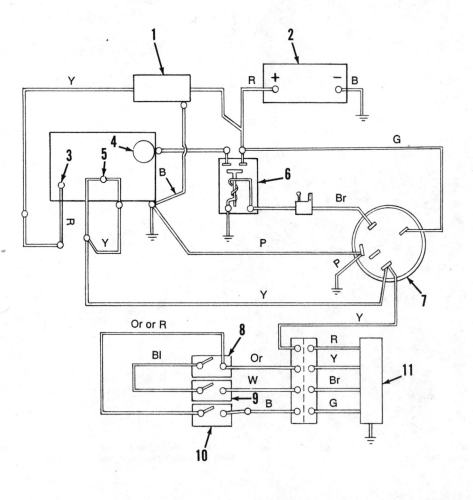

Fig. AR24—Wiring diagram of later models using Briggs & Stratton or Kawasaki engines with electric start.

B. Black
Bl. Blue
Br. Brown
G. Green
Or. Orange
P. Pink
R. Red
W. White
Y. Yellow
1. Regulator
2. Battery
3. Alternator
4. Starter
5. Engine magneto
6. Starter solenoid
7. Ignition switch
8. Neutral switch
9. Mower clutch switch
10. Seat switch
11. Module

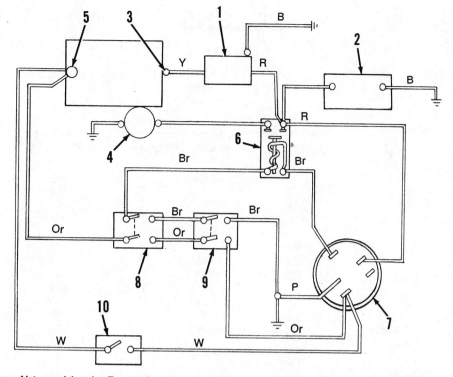

Fig. AR25—Wiring diagram of later models using Tecumseh engines with electric start. Refer to Fig. AR24 for parts identification and wire color codes.

BOLENS

BOLENS
102nd & 9th Avenue
Troy, NY 12180

Model	Make	Engine Model	Horsepower	Cutting Width, In.
528	B&S	130000	5	28
628	Tec	TVM140	6	28
728	Tec	V70	7	28
828	Tec	VM80	8	28
829*	Tec	VM80	8	28
830	B&S	190000	8	30
831	B&S	190000	8	30
1130	B&S	250000	11	30
1134	B&S	250000	11	34
1136	B&S	250000	11	36
2027	B&S	190000	8	28
2028	B&S	190000, 191000	8	28
2030	B&S	190000	8	30
2036	B&S	250000	11	36
2128A	B&S	281000	12	28
2136	B&S	281000	12	36
2136A	B&S	281000	12	36

*1978 Models 829-03 are equipped with B&S 190000 series, 8-hp engine and a 28-inch mower deck.

NOTE: Some models are equipped with rear support bars so the machine can be placed in an upright position, which allows easier access for servicing some components. Observe the following safety recommendations when raising machine to upright position:

1. Drain fuel tank or make certain that fuel level is low enough so that fuel will not drain out.

2. Close fuel shut-off valve if so equipped.

3. Remove battery if so equipped.

4. Disconnect spark plug wire and tie it out of way.

5. Although not absolutely essential, on models with spark plug at rear of machine, engine oil should be drained to prevent flooding the combustion chamber with oil when the engine is tilted.

6. Secure mower from tipping by lashing machine to a post or overhead beam.

FRONT AXLE

All Models

LUBRICATION. All models are equipped with a grease fitting (F—Fig. BN1) on top of the spindle or at the end of the axle to lubricate the spindle. Inject a good quality multipurpose grease into fitting after every 25 hours of operation.

R&R AND OVERHAUL. To remove a front spindle, raise and support side to be serviced. Remove wheel and tire. Disconnect tie rod end. On early models remove rubber cap (16—Fig. BN2 or 21—Fig. BN3) and drive out roll pin in spindle end. On later models, detach snap ring on spindle end. Withdraw spindle from axle. Install spindle by reversing removal procedure.

To remove axle main member, remove mower deck then raise and support

Fig. BN1—Lubricate spindles by injecting grease through fitting (F). Grease fitting on early models is located on axle.

front of machine. Remove front wheels. Disconnect outer tie rod ends from spindles. Support the axle assembly. Remove axle pivot bolt (14—Fig. BN2 or 17—Fig. BN3) and lower axle assembly from the machine.

Before assembly, lubricate bushing (if so equipped) and axle pivot bolt with multipurpose grease.

STEERING SYSTEM

Gear-Type Steering System

R&R AND OVERHAUL. To remove steering gear, drive out roll pin (5—Fig. BN2) and pull steering wheel off steering shaft (6). Unbolt inner ends of tie rods (12) from steering arm (11), then unbolt retainer (9) from column base (7) and parts (8, 9, 10 and 11) will separate as a unit. Remove retainer (2) at top end of steering shaft and pull shaft down and out of column (7). Do not lose thrust washers (3). Separate sector gear (8) from steering lever arm (11) by carefully driving out roll pin (10).

Inspect components for excessive wear and damage. Reassemble by reversing disassembly procedure. Lubricate bearing (4), shaft (6) and sector gear (8) with multipurpose grease.

Direct Link-Type Steering

R&R AND OVERHAUL. To remove steering shaft, disconnect steering rod (13—Fig. BN3) from steering arm at bottom end of steering shaft (8). Drive out roll pin (2) and pull steering wheel off steering shaft. Withdraw steering shaft from underside of machine.

Inspect components for excessive wear and damage. Reassemble by reversing disassembly procedure. Lubricate bearings and shaft with multipurpose grease.

ENGINE

All Models

Refer to appropriate engine section in this manual for tune-up specifications, engine overhaul procedures and engine maintenance.

REMOVE AND REINSTALL. To remove engine, disconnect spark plug wire and tie out of way. Disconnect battery cables. Raise and support rear of machine. With mower control lever in disengaged position, loosen belt guide adjacent to engine pulley and remove mower drive belt from engine pulley. Disconnect mower lift linkage, then pull mower unit out from either side. Loosen idler for traction drive belt to increase

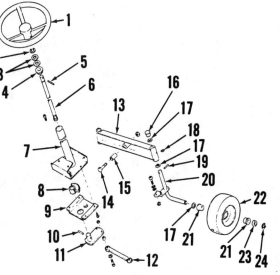

Fig. BN2—Exploded view of front axle and steering system used on models equipped with gear-type steering.

1. Steering wheel
2. Retainer
3. Thrust washer (2)
4. Shaft bearing
5. Roll pin
6. Shaft & pinion
7. Column & base
8. Sector gear
9. Retainer
10. Roll pin
11. Steering arm
12. Tie rod (2)
13. Front axle
14. Pivot bolt
15. Spacer
16. Rubber cap
17. Washer
18. Grease fitting
19. Roll pin
20. Spindle
21. Flange bearing
22. Wheel & tire
23. Spacer
24. Snap ring

Fig. BN3—Exploded view of front axle and steering system used on models with direct-link steering.

1. Steering wheel
2. Pin
3. Washer
4. Bushing
5. Column
6. Frame
7. Bushing
8. Steering shaft
9. Nut
10. Washer
11. Washer
12. Bolt
13. Steering rod
14. Tie rod
15. Pin
16. Washer
17. Pivot bolt
18. Bushing
19. Bushing
20. Nut
21. Rubber cap
22. Washer
23. Grease fitting
24. Pin
25. Spindle
26. Washer
27. Tire
28. Spacer (528/628)
29. Washer
30. Snap ring
31. Axle

Bolens

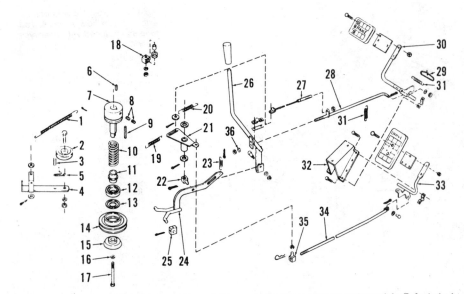

Fig. BN4—Exploded view of clutch, brake and drive control linkages used on early models. Refer to text for adjustment sequence and procedures.

1. Extension spring	10. Clutch spring	19. Clutch spring	28. Brake rod
2. Idler	11. Retainer	20. Brake spring	29. Link
3. Drive pin	12. Ball bearing	21. Cam	30. Brake lever
4. Clutch idler arm	13. Slinger	22. Pivot stud	31. Extension spring (2)
5. Belt guide	14. Clutch pulley	23. Extension spring	32. Linkage support
6. Crankshaft key	15. Clutch cone	24. Clutch-brake lever	33. Clutch-drive lever
7. Pulley & shaft	16. Pyramid washer	25. Brake block (2)	34. Clutch rod
8. Set screws	17. Cap screw	26. Blade control lever	35. Adjustment block
9. Key	18. Cable guide assy.	27. Brake cable	36. Pivot washer

traction drive belt slack and remove traction drive belt from engine pulley.

On early models with spring-loaded mower clutch on engine crankshaft (see Fig. BN4), proceed as follows: Fit a pin punch or small bar into clutch extension shaft as shown in Fig. BN5, then carefully back out clutch retaining screw to remove mower drive clutch assembly. Clutch unit is spring-loaded (see MOWER CLUTCH section) and must be handled with care. To remove clutch

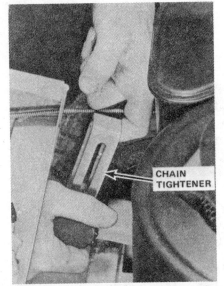

Fig. BN5—Insert a punch or bar as shown when removing mower clutch/brake. Unit is spring-loaded. Refer to text for removal procedure while noting caution statements.

extension, back out **both** socket-head set screws using a $7/32$-inch Allen wrench. Screws are located in upper pulley hub directly over the keyway. Use a suitable gear puller to remove extension shaft and/or main drive pulley from engine crankshaft lower end.

On later models with a conventional single-piece dual groove pulley on the engine crankshaft, unscrew set screw at top of pulley, unscrew lower retaining screw and use a suitable puller to remove pulley from engine crankshaft.

On Model 728, raise operator's seat, disengage spring wire retainer from groove in seat pivot shaft, then lift seat from side-to-side and separate from its brackets. Engine cover can now be unlatched at rear and tilted forward on its hinges, or hinge pins can be pulled for complete removal. On all other models equipped with an engine cover, remove operator's seat, then detach and remove engine cover/fender assembly. If desired, remove rear stand.

On all models, disconnect throttle cable from engine. Disconnect all wires from engine that will interfere with removal. On some models, it may be necessary to detach oil drain pipe. Remove engine mounting bolts and remove engine.

Reinstall engine by reversing removal procedure.

TRACTION DRIVE CLUTCH AND BRAKE

Early Models

ADJUSTMENT. Because of interaction of control linkages of main drive clutch, transmission disc brake and automatic disengagement of mower drive clutch/brake, adjustment of each element should be checked and performed, when necessary, in the following sequence:

DRIVE BELT AND CHAIN. Drive belt tension is correct when belt runs deep enough to remain in drive pulley of engine crankshaft and in driven pulley on transmission input shaft when belt idler (clutch) is disengaged. If main drive belt is too loose on sheaves, loosen drive chain tensioner (Fig. BN6) and transmission to chassis bolts and move transmission forward in slots to eliminate excessive slack in main drive belt. A correctly adjusted belt will remain in sheaves when tension on clutch idler is released and transmission pulley can rotate freely. If drive belt is worn or stretched to a point that such adjustment is not possible, renew belt. When belt is correctly adjusted, readjust chain tightener by hand only as shown in Fig. BN5 to remove slack from drive chain. If chain is damaged or defective, unbolt forward end of chain guard and swing guard out of the way. Disconnect master link and remove chain for repair or renewal.

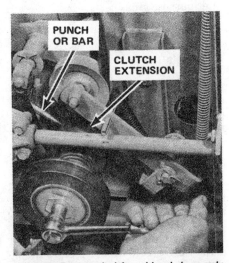

Fig. BN6—Remove slack from drive chain on early models, as shown, using hand pressure only. Some machines may have a T-handle on retaining nut instead of knob.

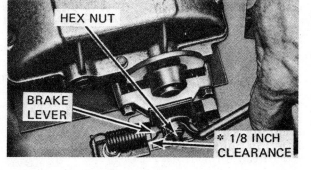

Fig. BN7—When adjusting brake on early models, clearance between brake lever and stop should be a minimum of 1/8 inch (3 mm) when brake is applied.

TRANSMISSION BRAKE. A properly adjusted disc brake should keep rear wheels from turning except when drive pedal is depressed 1 inch (25 mm) or more. When drive pedal is released during operation, there is controlled service braking for normal stopping. When brake pedal is sharply applied, mower blade clutch will disengage, and drive wheels will lock up for emergency stopping. Brake lock holds pedal down for parking.

NOTE: If drive belt tension has been adjusted by shifting transmission as covered under DRIVE BELT AND CHAIN, all linkages for transmission brake, drive pedal and brake pedal **must be checked and readjusted as necessary.**

Adjust transmission brake by these steps: Depress drive pedal 1 inch (25 mm) or more so that brake is released and brake lever shown in Fig. BN7 is vertical. Move stop against brake lever and lock, then turn adjusting nut in or out so that brake pads are just clear of brake disc. Now, allow drive pedal to retract so that brake is applied, and reset stop for minimum 1/8-inch (3 mm) clearance from brake lever. If brake does not release so brake disc rotates freely when drive pedal is depressed 1 inch (25 mm), recheck adjustment.

Brake spring (20—Fig. BN4) should be hooked into whichever hole in brake lever will hold drive pin (3) of clutch idler arm (4) 5/16-inch (8 mm) clear of rear axle. Remove clevis pin at forward end of clutch rod (34) while making this adjustment.

DRIVE PEDAL. Adjustment of drive pedal should always coincide with transmission brake adjustment. Proceed as follows:

When transmission brake adjustment has been checked or performed, remove clevis pin at forward end of drive pedal (clutch) rod (34—Fig. BN4). Now, rotate rod (34) in threaded adjustment block (35) as necessary for clevis pin to be slipped back easily to reconnect with lever (33). Be sure that 5/16-inch (8 mm) clearance between pin (3) and rear axle is not affected and there is no interference or binding of parts. Damaged or defective springs, keepers or pins should be renewed if performance is unsatisfactory or adjustments cannot be made.

BRAKE PEDAL. As previously indicated, service braking for routine slowing or stopping of machine is a function of drive pedal. Brake pedal is applied for emergency stops. When properly adjusted, its action will lock mower drive wheels, disengage mower drive clutch and halt blade rotation simultaneously.

When correctly adjusted, brake pedal should lock rear wheels when depressed half way. Adjust by use of locknut on brake cable (27—Fig. BN4). To do so, tighten nut against welded tab on brake rod (28) until brake engages solidly with pedal pushed down half of complete stroke. Be sure not to overtighten. If brake cable is drawn up too tightly, transmission brake will not be allowed to release. When brake cable adjustment is satisfactorily completed, press pedal down hard and engage brake lock. With mower blade clutch disengaged (handle to rear in "OFF" position), pivot washer (36) on brake rod (28) should contact welded tab on blade control lever (26). Turn locknut behind pivot washer (36) to adjust if necessary. Adjustment of mowing unit clutch-brake is covered in MOWER CLUTCH.

Late Models

ADJUSTMENT. Refer to following paragraphs for adjustment of traction drive belt, chain and brake components. Refer to Fig. BN8 for an exploded view of typical drive system control components used on late models.

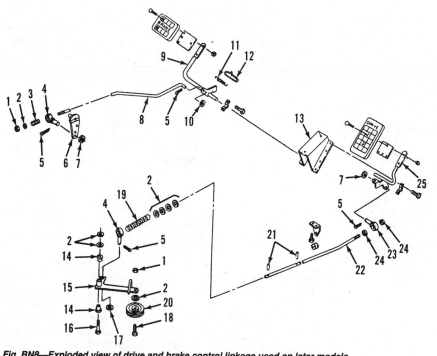

Fig. BN8—Exploded view of drive and brake control linkage used on later models.

1. Locknut
2. Washer
3. Spring
4. Swivel
5. Cotter pin
6. Brake lever
7. Washer
8. Brake rod
9. Brake lever
10. Washer
11. Spring
12. Spring link
13. Support
14. Bushing
15. Idler arm
16. Pivot bolt
17. Washer
18. Screw
19. Spring
20. Pulley
21. Pins
22. Clutch rod
23. Swivel
24. Nuts
25. Clutch lever

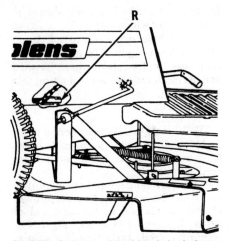

Fig. BN9—On later models, drive chain slack may be adjusted by relocating chain tensioner (R).

DRIVE BELT. Late models are equipped with a spring-loaded idler to maintain correct belt tension. Adjustment is not required. If drive belt slips, renew belt, as well as pulleys, if excessively worn.

DRIVE CHAIN. The drive chain on late models is adjusted by relocating chain tightener (R—Fig. BN9). Raise seat for access to chain tightener. Place tightener so there is a slight amount of slack in drive chain.

TRANSMISSION BRAKE. The transmission brake on Models 528-02, 628, 828-02, 830, 831, 1130, 1134, 1136, 2027, 2028, 2030, 2036, 2128A, 2136 and 2136A should be adjusted with brake lever (L—Fig. BN10) on transmission in a vertical position. With brake applied, brake lever should be vertical and distance (D) from lever to front of slot in frame should be approximately 3/16-1/4 inch (4.8-6.4 mm). Adjust lever position by rotating nuts (N) on lever shaft. Do not overtighten or brake will drag and overheat. Check brake operation after adjustment. Adjust

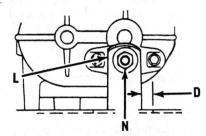

Fig. BN10—With brake applied, brake lever (L) should be vertical and distance (D) from lever to front of slot in frame should be approximately 3/16-1/4 inch (4.8-6.4 mm). Adjust lever position by rotating nuts (N).

safety switch, if so equipped, so it is activated when brake pedal is locked.

DRIVE PEDAL. The drive pedal on Models 528-02, 628, 828-02, 830, 831, 1130, 1134, 1136, 2027, 2028, 2030, 2036, 2128A, 2136 and 2136A should be adjusted by turning nuts (24—Figs. BN1 and BN8) at front end of drive pedal rod to compress spring 5½ inches (14.6 cm) when pedal is fully depressed. Locknut must be adjusted so spring can rotate freely when drive is engaged.

BRAKE PEDAL. The brake pedal on Models 828-02 and 829-02 is adjusted with brake pedal in released position and drive disengaged. Spring should be fully relaxed and is adjusted at the spring anchor. Do not preload spring.

The brake pedal on all other models is adjusted by turning nut (1—Fig. BN8) at end of control rod (8). Adjust position of nut so that brake operates properly when pedal is depressed, but brake does not drag when pedal is released.

GROUND DRIVE BRAKE

All Models

All models are equipped with a disc brake that is mounted on the transmission, which is located inside the seat tower.

R&R AND OVERHAUL. Detach control linkage and refer to Fig. BN11. Unscrew lever retaining nut (9) and unscrew caliper mounting screws (10). Disassemble brake components. Brake pad wear limit is ¼ inch (6.4 mm). When assembling brake, coat transaxle brake shaft with Lubriplate. Apply Lubriplate to ends of actuator pins (5) and

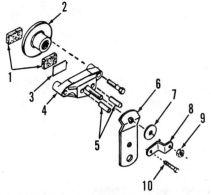

Fig. BN11—Exploded view of disc brake assembly.

1. Brake pads	6. Brake lever
2. Brake disc	7. Washer
3. Plate	8. Brace
4. Caliper half	9. Nut
5. Dowel pins	10. Screw

rubbing surfaces of brake lever and washer (7). Be sure actuator pins (5) are installed with rounded end toward brake lever (6). Adjust brake as outlined in previous section.

TRANSMISSION

All Models

REMOVE AND REINSTALL. To remove transmission, remove mower deck as outlined in MOWER DECK section. Loosen idler for traction drive belt to increase traction drive belt slack and remove traction drive belt from transmission pulley. Detach snap ring at end of transmission shaft and remove pulley from transmission shaft. Relieve chain tension and disconnect drive chain. On some models, it may be necessary to remove battery and fuel tank from seat pedestal compartment for access to transmission. Detach control linkage from transmission brake lever. Detach shift control from transmission shift shaft. On models so equipped, unscrew safety switch on transmission. Remove transmission mounting bolts and remove transmission.

Reinstall transmission by reversing removal procedure.

OVERHAUL. All models are equipped with a Peerless transmission. Early models are equipped with a 500 series transmission and later models are equipped with a 730 series transmission. Refer to TRANSMISSION REPAIR section for service information.

DIFFERENTIAL

All Models

R&R AND OVERHAUL. Raise rear of machine so rear wheels are clear of ground, then remove rear wheels. Release tension on drive chain, then disconnect chain. Clean axles, then remove screws securing axle bearing flanges to frame and slide bearing flanges off axles. Remove differential and axle assembly from frame. Reinstall differential and axle assembly by reversing removal procedure.

These models have been equipped with differentials manufactured by Indus Wheel (Mast Foos), Peerless and Stewart. Refer to appropriate paragraphs in the DIFFERENTIAL REPAIR section of this manual.

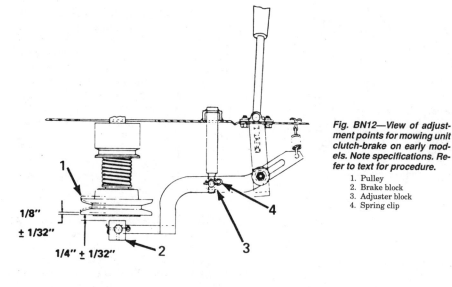

Fig. BN12—View of adjustment points for mowing unit clutch-brake on early models. Note specifications. Refer to text for procedure.

1. Pulley
2. Brake block
3. Adjuster block
4. Spring clip

MOWER CLUTCH

Early Models

ADJUSTMENT. For correct operation of mower clutch-brake, note adjustment specifications shown in Fig. BN12 and following adjustment procedure.

Place control lever in rear "OFF" position. Remove cotter pin (4—Fig. BN12) from adjuster (3) and slip lever off pivot stud. Turn adjuster block in or out on threaded mounting stud to obtain ¼ inch (6.4 mm) clearance between brake blocks (2) and friction surface of pulley (1). Move lever forward to "ON" position and measure upward movement of pulley when lifted by brake

blocks. This measurement should be ⅛ inch (3.2 mm), plus or minus ¹⁄₃₂ inch (0.8 mm). If not, cone clutch inside pulley will not disengage. If adjustment cannot be made by raising or lowering adjusting block (3), remove cotter pins from brake blocks (2) and rotate each block one-quarter turn to provide a new, unworn contact surface. If these procedures do not succeed, it may be necessary to dismantle and overhaul the clutch-brake assembly. See following section.

NOTE: Brake blocks should track on outer margin of pulley friction surface. If they are misaligned, loosen control handle mounting bolts and shift assembly from side-to-side to gain correct alignment.

R&R AND OVERHAUL. Remove mowing unit drive belt and disconnect mower lift chains, then remove four clevis pins that attach mower lift linkage to frame and remove mower deck. Position machine on its rear stand as previously outlined. Refer to Fig. BN4, insert a pin punch or bar into clutch extension shaft and remove clutch retainer screw as shown.

CAUTION: Clutch spring (12—Fig. BN13) is under compression, and when threads of cap screw (7) are released from engine crankshaft (1), a pad or cushion should be used to prevent accidental injury.

Parts of assembly are shown in exploded view in Fig. BN4 with sectional view in Fig. BN13 to show order of parts arrangement. All parts should be thoroughly cleaned in nonpetroleum base

solvent and carefully evaluated for wear and damage. Renew parts as needed.

Cone clutch (15—Fig. BN4 or 6—Fig. BN13) may be renewed completely or new clutch facing (9—Fig. BN13) can be installed using following procedure: Remove compression spring (12) and retainer (4). Carefully pull or press bearing (11) from hub of pulley (5) without damaging slinger (10). Place adhesive side of new clutch facing (9) on well-cleaned surface of clutch cone (6), then assemble cone into cup portion of pulley (5) while holding parts firmly together with a bolt and nut and large washers. After an oven reaches a temperature of 400° F (204° C), place clutch in oven for 20 minutes.

When reassembling cone clutch, note the following: Retainer (4) must slip freely on shaft extension. Renew if doubtful. Key (3) that locks clutch cone (6) to extension shaft must not ride up ramp in keyway during installation. Renew pyramid washer (8) if questionable. Tighten cap screw (7) to 15 ft.-lbs. (20 N•m). Reassemble and install clutch-brake assembly in reverse order of disassembly.

NOTE: A conventional gear puller may be used to remove extension shaft and/or main drive pulley from engine crankshaft. Be sure to remove set screws (8—Fig. BN4) in pulley hub before pulley removal. Do not damage threads in end of crankshaft.

Late Models

ADJUSTMENT. Late models are equipped with a spring-loaded idler to maintain correct mower belt tension. On single-blade mowers, rotate nuts (N—Fig. BN14) on lift rods so distance (D—Fig. BN15) between belt runs is 1½ inches (38 mm) with mower engaged. On dual-blade mowers, belt tension may be adjusted by unbolting fixed idler (F—Fig. BN16) and relocating idler bolt in mounting slot.

MOWER DECK

Early Models

HEIGHT ADJUSTMENT. Park machine on a level surface with tires properly inflated. Place spacers that are 2¼-inches (57 mm) thick under rear mower skirt as shown in Fig. BN17. Move lift lever down to its lowest position and loosen nuts of gauge wheel brackets (3). Use leveling nuts and studs (1) to adjust height of forward edge of cutting deck to 2⅞ inches (73 mm) above ground. Install square stud of gauge wheel axle in middle hole of

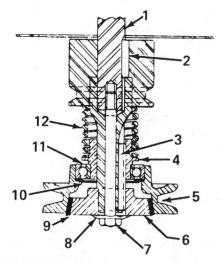

Fig. BN13—Sectional view of mower clutch-brake used on early models.

1. Engine crankshaft
2. Crankshaft key
3. Clutch key
4. Retainer
5. Pulley
6. Cone clutch
7. Clutch cap screw
8. Pyramid washer
9. Clutch facing
10. Slinger
11. Ball bearing
12. Clutch spring

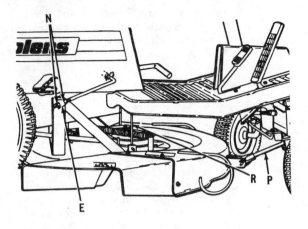

Fig. BN14—View of mower deck and linkage used on later models. Refer to text for mower height adjustment and removal procedure.

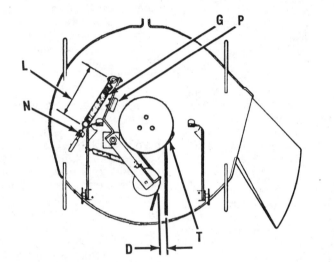

Fig. BN15—Length (L) of spring (G) on single-blade mower deck should be 5-3/4 inches (14.6 cm). Adjust spring length by turning nuts (N) on cable.

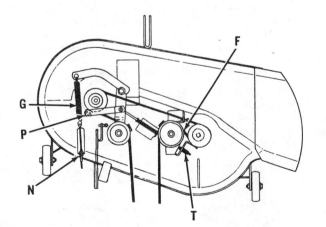

Fig. BN16—Spring (G) on dual-blade mower deck should have a small amount of slack. Rotate nuts (N) on cable end to adjust spring slack.

gauge wheel mounting brackets, and with gauge wheels in contact with ground, tighten both gauge wheel brackets. Pull out spacers from under rear edge of mower deck and set lift handle in fourth notch from bottom. Raise mower seat and adjust lift chain wing nuts to remove slack from chain. When mower cutting height is changed, square stud on gauge wheel axle should always be reset in proper hole (1 through 5) of gauge wheel bracket to correspond with whichever of five lever positions is chosen.

REMOVE AND REINSTALL. To remove mower deck, first remove drive belt from mower clutch/brake pulley. Disconnect mower lift chains, then remove four clevis pins that attach mower lift linkage to frame and remove mower deck. Reinstall mower deck by reversing removal procedure.

Late Models

HEIGHT ADJUSTMENT. Park machine on a level surface with tires properly inflated. The mower deck height should be adjusted so blade height at front and rear is equal. To adjust mower deck height, remove clevis pin in end of front hanger rod (P—Fig. BN14) and rotate rod, or rotate nut at upper end of each rear hanger rod (R).

Side-to-side height difference of blade should be zero. Adjust side-to-side blade height by rotating nuts at upper ends of rear hanger rods (R).

REMOVE AND REINSTALL. To remove mower deck, place mower lift lever in lowest position. Remove mower drive belt from engine pulley. Detach rear hanger rods (R—Fig. BN14) from mower deck. Detach lift rod ends (E) from mower deck bracket. Unscrew control cable retaining bracket from mower deck and detach cable end from spring. Remove clevis pin on front hanger rod (P). Remove mower deck. Reinstall mower deck by reversing removal procedure.

BLADE BRAKE

Early Models

Early models are equipped with a clutch-brake unit. Refer to MOWER CLUTCH section.

Late Models

ADJUSTMENT. On mowers with a single blade, place mower control lever in disengaged position. Length (L—Fig.

MOWER SPINDLE

Early Models

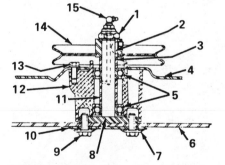

2-7/8 INCH

SPACER BLOCK

2-1/4 INCH

Fig. BN17—Refer to text for leveling procedure on mower decks on early models.

1. Leveling stud & nut   2. Gauge wheel   3. Gauge wheel bracket

LUBRICATION. Periodically inject a good quality multipurpose grease into grease fitting (15—Fig. BN18) at top of spindle.

R&R AND OVERHAUL. Remove mower deck and belt as previously outlined. Unscrew grease fitting (15—Fig. BN18), then unscrew locknut (1). Unscrew set screw over Woodruff key and remove pulley. Remove Woodruff key (2) and spacer (3), then pull spindle (8) down and out of housing (12). If necessary, detach spindle housing from mower deck. If required, tap bearings out of housing.

When assembling spindle components, install bearings so shielded sides are out. Be sure spacer (11) is installed between bearings. Tighten locknut (1) to 90 ft.-lbs. (122 N•m).

Fig. BN18—Sectional view of mower spindle assembly used on early models.

1. Locknut	
2. Woodruff key	9. Cap screw
3. Spacer	10. Plate stiffener
4. Mower deck	11. Bearing spacer
5. Ball bearings	12. Spindle housing
6. Blade	13. Flange set screw
7. Pyramid washer	14. Pulley
8. Spindle	15. Grease fitting

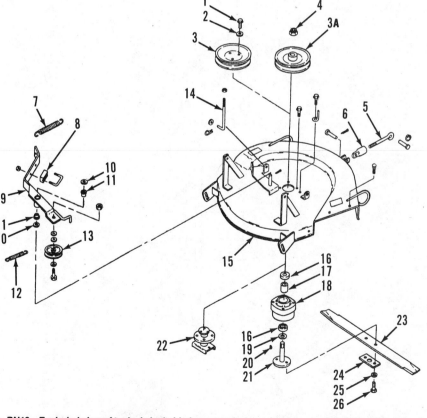

BN15) of spring (G) should be 5¾ inches (14.6 cm). Adjust spring length by turning nuts (N) on cable. Blade brake pad (P) should contact spindle pulley squarely. Relocate pad by loosening mounting bolts or clamp.

On dual-blade mower units, place mower control lever in disengaged position. Spring (G—Fig. BN16) should have a small amount of slack. Rotate nuts (N) on cable end to adjust spring slack. Blade brake pad (P) should contact spindle pulley squarely. Adjust pad position by rotating nut (T).

Fig. BN19—Exploded view of typical single-blade mower deck used on later models. Pulley (3) retained by three screws (1) is used with spindle assembly (22), which is available only as a unit. Pulley (3A) retained by nut (4) is attached to spindle (21).

1. Screw	7. Spring	14. Hanger rod	20. Key
2. Washer	8. Brake pad	15. Mower deck	21. Spindle
3. Pulley	9. Idler arm	16. Ball bearing	22. Spindle assy.
3A. Pulley	10. Washer	17. Spacer	23. Blade
4. Nut	11. Bushing	18. Spindle housing	24. Blade adapter
5. Hanger rod	12. Spring	19. Washer	25. Lockwasher
6. Rod end	13. Idler		26. Screw

Late Models

LUBRICATION. Spindle units are sealed and should not require periodic lubrication.

R&R AND OVERHAUL. Spindle assemblies are accessible after removing mower deck. On single-blade mowers, some spindle assemblies are available only as a unit assembly, while internal components are available on some units. See Fig. BN19.

Spindle unit on dual-blade mowers is shown in Fig. BN20. Disassembly is evident after inspection and referral to Fig. BN20. Use a suitable gasket forming compound on mating surfaces of top and lower spindle housings. Fill lower spindle housing with lithium based grease. Tighten pulley retaining screw to 50-70 ft.-lbs. (68-95 N•m). Tighten blade retaining screw on dual-blade mowers to 50-70 ft.-lbs. (68-95 N•m).

ELECTRICAL

All Models

Refer to Figs. BN21 and BN22 for wiring schematics. Early models were equipped with a transmission switch and later models are equipped with a brake switch. Note the following points:
• To start engine, the mower must be disengaged and the operator must be in seat. On early models, the transmission must also be in neutral. On later models, the brake pedal must be depressed.
• The engine should stop if the operator leaves the seat.

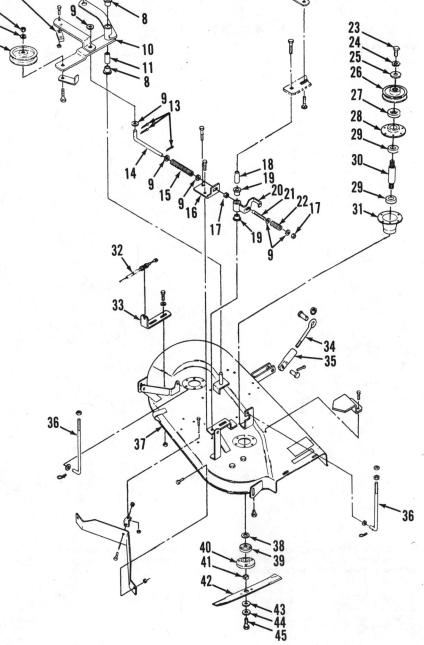

Fig. BN20—Exploded view of dual-blade mower deck used on later models.

1. Spring
2. Brake pad
3. Locknut
4. Washer
5. Idler
6. Cotter pin
7. Washer
8. Bushing
9. Washer
10. Idler arm
11. Spacer
12. Pulley
13. Cotter pin
14. Brake rod
15. Spring
16. Bracket
17. Locknut
18. Spacer
19. Bushing
20. Brake arm
21. Brake rod
22. Spring
23. Screw
24. Lockwasher
25. Washer
26. Pulley
27. Bearing shield
28. Upper spindle housing
29. Bearing
30. Spindle
31. Lower spindle housing
32. Cable
33. Bracket
34. Hanger rod
35. Rod end
36. Hanger rod
37. Mower deck
38. Washer
39. Grass shield
40. Blade adapter
41. Collar
42. Blade
43. Washer
44. Lockwasher
45. Screw

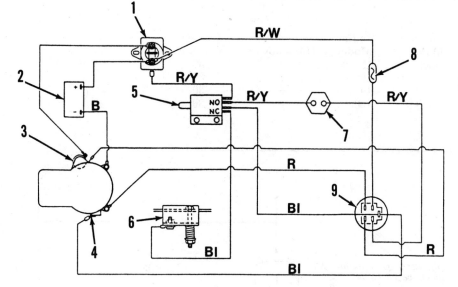

Fig. BN21—Typical wiring diagram for early models equipped with a transmission switch.

B. Black
Bl. Blue
R. Red
W. White
Y. Yellow
1. Solenoid
2. Battery
3. Electric starter motor
4. Magneto
5. Mower switch
6. Seat switch
7. Transmission switch
8. Fuse
9. Ignition switch

Fig. BN22—Typical wiring diagram for later models equipped with a brake switch. Refer to Fig. BN21 for wire codes and parts identification except for: 10. Brake switch.

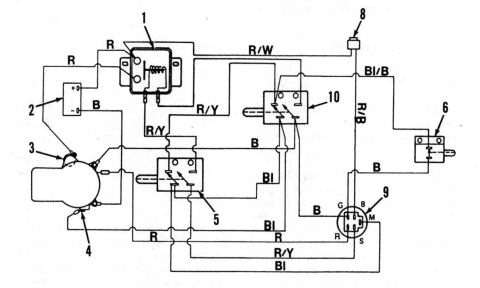

CASE/INGERSOLL

INGERSOLL EQUIPMENT CO., INC.
Winneconne, Wisconsin 54986-9576

Model	Make	Engine Model	Horsepower	Cutting Width, In.
80	B&S	190000	8	30
80XC	B&S	190000	8	30
80XE	B&S	190000	8	30
80XM	B&S	190000	8	30

FRONT AXLE

All Models

TOE-IN ADJUSTMENT. Position mower on a level surface with front wheels straight ahead and tire pressure 8 psi (55 kPa). Adjust tie-rod ends equally, as necessary, to obtain ⅛-⅜ inch (3.2-9.5 mm) toe-in. Refer to Fig. CI10.

R&R STEERING SHAFT AND SECTOR GEAR. Support hub and drive pin retaining steering wheel to steering shaft out. Remove screws at tower crown. Remove steering sector gear pivot pin and disengage sector gear from steering pinion gear. Remove lower end of shaft from bushing and pull through from bottom. To remove sector gear, remove tie-rod at sector gear. Remove cotter pin and sector gear pivot pin and remove sector gear. Reverse removal procedure for reassembly.

ENGINE

All Models

Refer to appropriate engine section in this manual for tune-up specifications, engine overhaul procedures and engine maintenance.

REMOVE AND REINSTALL. Engine is removed complete with drive pivot and sprocket housing. Remove rear chain guard bolt. Drain fuel tank and engine crankcase. Remove battery (as equipped). Disconnect spark plug and ground spark plug lead to engine. Stand mower on rear support bars and secure in this position by lashing unit to nearby post or overhead beam. Remove mower deck as outlined in MOW-ER DECK section. Remove chain guard and chain. Remove traction drive belt. Remove control rod from drive pivot and loosen engine pulley. Lower rider back on its wheels. Disconnect all necessary electrical wiring and throttle control from engine. Disconnect clutch

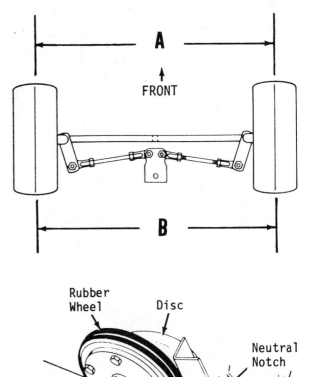

Fig. CI10—Dimension "A" should be 1/8-3/8 inch (3.2-9.5 mm) less than dimension "B" to provide correct toe-in. Adjust tie-rod ends to obtain proper toe-in.

Fig. CI11—View showing clutch link location.

link at sprocket housing (Fig. CI11). Remove the four bolts retaining engine mounting plate to chassis and lift engine, drive pivot and sprocket housing assembly from chassis allowing pulley to slip from engine crankshaft as engine is removed. Remove exhaust pipe

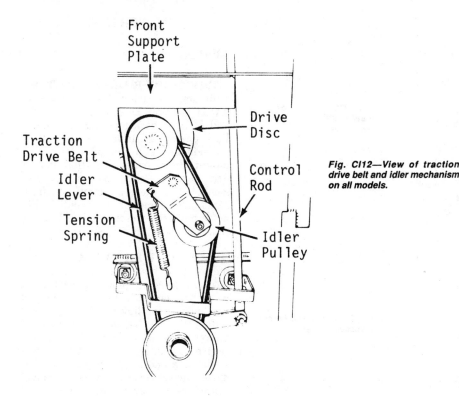

Front Support Plate

Drive Disc

Traction Drive Belt

Idler Lever

Tension Spring

Control Rod

Idler Pulley

Fig. CI12—View of traction drive belt and idler mechanism on all models.

and muffler. Remove the four bolts securing engine to mounting plate.

Reverse removal procedure for reinstallation. Tighten mounting plate bolts to 8 ft.-lbs. (11 N·m). Adjust clutch link as necessary.

TRACTION DRIVE

All Models

TRACTION DRIVE BELT ADJUSTMENT. Traction drive belt tension is controlled by a spring loaded idler and no adjustment is provided. If traction drive belt slips, renew belt.

NEUTRAL ADJUSTMENT. With travel control in neutral detent, roller (Fig. CI11) on sprocket housing should engage notch on drive pivot. To adjust, position roller on sprocket housing in notch on drive pivot and loosen ball joint jam nut on forward end of control rod (not pictured). Remove bolt retaining ball joint to travel control arm. Position travel control in neutral detent and turn ball joint until holes are in line and install bolt. Tighten jam nut.

CLUTCH LINK ADJUSTMENT. When properly adjusted, clutch link (Fig. CI11) should be loose (no tension or compression) and rubber wheel should contact disc with clutch pedal released. Rubber wheel should not contact disc when clutch/brake pedal is

depressed halfway. To adjust, loosen jam nut and remove bolt retaining ball joint to sprocket housing. Turn ball joint to obtain correct adjustment.

DISC/WHEEL CENTER LINE ADJUSTMENT. When properly adjusted, travel control will move with minimal effort but remains in selected speed range when rider is driven. To adjust, remove drive disc, rubber wheel and traction drive belt from disc pulley. Remove ball joint from chain and sprocket housing and loosen disc bearing flangettes. Move bearing flangettes as required to position drive disc $\frac{1}{16}$-$\frac{3}{32}$ inch (1.6-2.3 mm) forward of the centerline of the rubber wheel.

R&R TRACTION DRIVE BELT. Remove mower deck and mower drive belt as outlined in MOWER DECK section. Push in on traction drive belt idler pulley and lever (Fig. CI12) to relieve belt tension. Slip belt off pulleys and install new belt.

R&R DRIVE DISC. Remove engine complete with transmission drive pivot and sprocket housing as outlined in ENGINE section. Hold belt securely around pulley and tap rib on underside of disc with hammer and punch to loosen. NOTE—Disc has LEFT HAND threads. Remove drive disc.

R&R DRIVE PILOT. Remove mower deck as outlined in MOWER DECK section. Drain fuel tank and crankcase. Remove battery (as equipped). Discon-

nect spark plug and ground spark plug lead to engine. Stand rider on rear support bars and secure in this position by lashing unit to nearby post or overhead beam. Remove chain guard and final drive chain. Remove rear axle bearings. Raise and support rear of rider and roll rear axle away from rider. Remove belt and center bolt in pulley. Use care not to distort engine pulley and remove engine pulley. Remove pivot control rod (Fig. CI12) and front support plate. Remove snap ring (Fig. CI13) and pivot from engine mounting plate. Drive disc shaft and bearings are a press fit.

To reinstall, apply a light coating of grease to flange bushing and install pivot to engine mounting plate. Install snap ring. Install control rod to pivot and adjust neutral adjustment as previously outlined. Apply anti-seize compound to engine crankshaft and install pulley. Install traction drive belt. Install rear axle with spacers between bearings and rider chassis. Install chain with connector link inboard and closed end of link facing forward direction (Fig. CI14). Install chain guard. Adjust disc/wheel center line as previously outlined. Install drive disc.

R&R SPROCKET HOUSING. Mark large sprocket on intermediate shaft with an arrow to show direction of rotation (Fig. CI14) and remove final drive chain. Remove clutch link. Remove cotter pin retaining pivot pin. On early production models, pry pivot pin in outboard direction until it can be removed. On late production models, remove pivot pin. Remove sprocket housing from rider.

To disassemble sprocket housing, mark direction of rotation on rubber wheel with arrow. Loosen set screws on

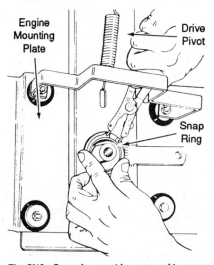

Engine Mounting Plate

Drive Pivot

Snap Ring

Fig. CI13—Snap ring must be removed to remove pivot. Refer to text.

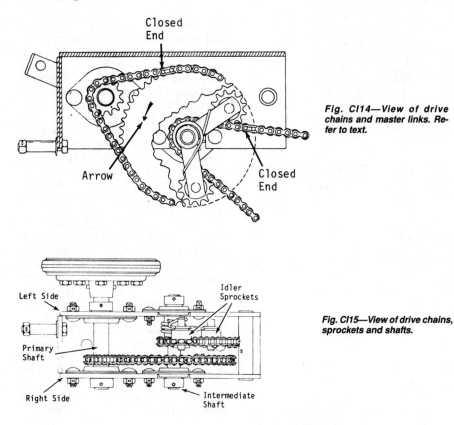

Fig. CI14—View of drive chains and master links. Refer to text.

Fig. CI15—View of drive chains, sprockets and shafts.

MOWER DECK

All Models

R&R MOWER DRIVE BELT. Position mower height control lever in lowest position. Disconnect spark plug and ground spark plug lead to engine. Position mower drive lever in "OFF" position and slip belt off left side of mower drive pulley. Position mower drive lever in "ON" position to disengaged belt brake and remove belt from right side of mower drive pulley. Remove belt from engine pulley. Reverse removal procedure for reinstallation.

R&R MOWER DECK. Positon mower height control lever in lowest position. Remove mower drive belt as previously outlined. Remove front and rear suspension link and height adjust link cotter pin, left side first. Remove mower drive clutch rod pin and brake return spring. Remove right-hand side suspension and height adjust link. Remove mower deck. Reverse removal procedure for reinstallation.

LEVELING MOWER DECK. Mower must be on level, hard surface and all tire pressures must be 8 psi (55 kPa). Disconnect spark plug lead and ground lead to engine. Position mower height control lever in mid-position. With blade at right angle to rider chassis, turn height adjust link adjusting nuts until blade tips are equal distance from floor. With blade parallel to rider chassis, turn front suspension link adjustment nuts equally until front tip of blade is ⅜-½ inch (10-12 mm) lower than rear if bagger is installed; ¼-⅜ inch (7-10 mm) lower than rear without bagger.

bearing locking collars. Remove intermediate chain, bearing flangettes and shafts.

To reassemble sprocket housing, loosely reassemble shafts, bearings and flangettes as shown in Fig. CI15. Assemble intermediate shaft idler sprockets as shown in Fig. CI15. Position intermediate shaft to idler sprocket side of housing. Align primary shaft sprocket to intermediate shaft sprocket. Position bearings, flangettes and locking collars. Install intermediate

drive chain with closed end of connector spring clip facing toward direction of chain travel. Tighten flangettes and locking collars. Tighten set screws.

To install sprocket housing, position sprocket housing between pivot tabs. Align cotter pin holes, insert pivot pin and secure with cotter pin. Connect clutch link and adjust as previously outlined. Install final drive chain with connector link plate and spring clip outboard and closed end of spring clip facing toward direction of chain travel.

COLUMBIA

Model	Make	Engine Model	Horsepower	Cutting Width, In.
380, 400	B&S	130000	5	25
455, 480, 485	B&S	190000	8	34
495	B&S	190000	8	38
497	B&S	230000	10	38
525	B&S	190000	8	26

For service information and procedures, use the following model cross reference and refer to the MTD section of this manual.

CUB CADET

CUB CADET CORP.
P.O. Box 36900
Cleveland, OH 44136

Model	Make	Engine Model	Horsepower	Cutting Width, In.
055132	B&S	130000	5	28
085132	B&S	190000	8	32
085133	B&S	190000	8	32
085134	B&S	190000	8	32
087132	B&S	190000	8	28
087133	B&S	190000	8	28
087134	B&S	190000	8	28
136-511-100	B&S	130000	5	28
136-514-100	B&S	190000	8	30
136-518-100	B&S	250000	11	36
526	B&S	130000	5	26
800	B&S	190000	8	30
830	B&S	190000	8	30
1002	B&S	250000	10	32
1136	B&S	250000	11	36
1208	B&S	280000	12	38

For service information on Model 055132, refer to International Harvester Model 55. For service information on Models 085132, 085133 and 085134, refer to International Harvester Model 85. For service information on Models 087132, 087133 and 087134, refer to International Harvester Model 85 Special. Service information on remaining models is outlined in the following sections.

FRONT AXLE AND STEERING SYSTEM

All Models

R&R AND OVERHAUL. To remove axle main member (20 or 20A—Fig. CC11), remove mower unit as outlined in MOWER DECK section. Remove steering shaft (5) as follows: Remove steering wheel cap, retaining nut and washer, then lift off steering wheel (4). Remove cover (31). On early models, unscrew nut at lower end of steering shaft, remove gear (36) and remove steering shaft. On later models, unscrew nut at lower end of steering shaft, remove gear (36), unscrew steering shaft bolt (7) and remove upper and lower steering shaft sections. Discon-nect tie rods (26) at spindles. Detach steering support plate (30) and sector gear (35). Raise and support the frame and remove front wheels. Remove cotter pins or speed nuts and washers, then lower spindles (25) from axle. Detach front axle support (28) from frame and remove axle main member (20).

Clean and inspect all parts and renew any showing excessive wear or damage. Reassemble by reversing the disassembly procedure and lubricate bushings and all pivot points with SAE 30 oil. Steering gear backlash on later models is adjusted by moving plate (29). After adjusting plate position, operate steering through full range of movement and check for binding. Check front wheel toe-in and, if necessary, adjust tie rods to obtain a toe-in of 1/8 inch (3 mm).

ENGINE

All Models

Refer to appropriate engine section in this manual for tune-up specifications, engine overhaul procedures and engine maintenance.

REMOVE AND REINSTALL. To remove engine, disconnect spark plug wire and remove engine cover. On electric start models, disconnect and remove battery. Disconnect any interfering electrical wires from engine. Disconnect throttle cable from engine. Detach exhaust pipe. Remove mower as outlined in MOWER DECK section. Remove traction drive belt from engine pulley as outlined in TRACTION DRIVE CLUTCH AND DRIVE BELTS section. Detach pulleys from the engine crankshaft. Remove engine mounting bolts, then remove engine.

Reinstall by reversing removal procedure.

TRACTION DRIVE CLUTCH AND DRIVE BELT

Model 136-511-100

The traction drive clutch is a spring-tensioned, belt idler-type operated by the clutch/brake pedal (Fig. CC12). When the pedal is depressed, belt tension is removed, allowing the engine drive pulley to rotate freely within the drive belt. After the pedal passes midpoint, the brake is applied.

No adjustment is required. If belt slippage occurs, and pulleys and linkage are in good operating condition, a new belt should be installed.

R&R DRIVE BELT. To remove drive belt, disconnect spark plug wire and tie out of way. Remove mower deck as outlined in MOWER DECK section. Disconnect traction drive idler spring and relocate or detach any interfering belt guides. Detach torque rod and support from transaxle, then pull drive belt out through the opening in frame just below the engine pulley and above the transaxle pulley.

Install drive belt by reversing removal procedure. Be sure belt guides are in position.

All Other Models

All models, except Model 136-511-100, are equipped with a drive system that uses two drive belts and a variable speed pulley to transfer power from the engine to the transaxle. The primary (lower) drive belt connects the engine to the variable speed pulley (23—Fig. CC13). The diameters of the pulley

grooves are determined by belt tension, which is regulated by the position of idlers (10 and 17). The idlers move when the speed control lever is operated. Ground speed changes when the pulley diameters change on the variable speed pulley.

ADJUSTMENT. The speed control lever and gear shift lever must be synchronized with the positions of the belt idlers. With engine running and gear shift lever in neutral position, place speed control lever in high-speed posi-

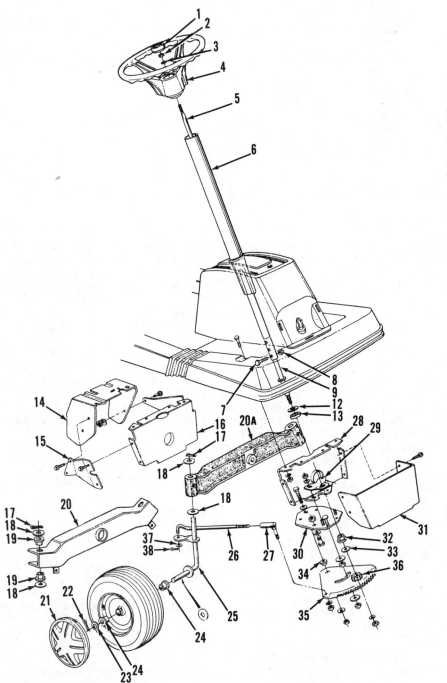

Fig. CC11—Exploded view of typical front axle and steering system. Axle (20) and bushings (19) are used on early models, and axle (20A) is used on later models. Early models use a single-piece steering shaft, and later models are equipped with the two-piece steering shaft shown. Early models are equipped with speed nuts in place of cotter pins (17).

  1. Cap
  2. Nut
  3. Washer
  4. Steering wheel
  5. Upper steering shaft
  6. Steering column
  7. Screw
  8. Nut
  9. Lower steering shaft
12. Washer
13. Spacer
14. Bracket
15. Plate
16. Axle support
17. Cotter pin
18. Washer
19. Bushing
20. Axle main member
20A. Axle main member
21. Hub cap
22. Cotter pin
23. Washer
24. Bushing
25. Spindle
26. Tie rod
27. Tie rod end
28. Axle support
29. Steering adjuster
30. Steering plate
31. Bracket
32. Bushing
33. Washer
34. Bushing
35. Sector gear
36. Steering gear

tion. Release the clutch/brake pedal, then slowly depress the pedal and hold it in the fully depressed position. Shut off engine and release clutch/brake pedal when engine stops. Move the speed control lever to third speed position. Detach adjuster end (A—Fig. CC13) of lower speed control rod (32). Pull down rod so it is in bottom of slot at upper end. Turn adjuster (A) so adjuster will just enter hole (H) and reattach rod.

Move gear shift lever to neutral slot on gear indicator panel. If machine does not move freely forward and backward, thereby indicating transaxle is in neutral, detach and rotate adjuster (R—Fig. CC13). Adjust rod (36) length by rotating adjuster as needed so transaxle is in neutral and shift lever is in center of neutral slot on control panel.

R&R DRIVE BELTS. Lower Belt.

To remove lower drive belt (25—Fig. CC13), disconnect spark plug wire and remove battery. Remove mower as outlined in MOWER DECK section. Disconnect idler spring (16). Detach torque rod bracket (34) from transaxle and torque rod (8) and remove the bracket. Disengage belt from pulleys and remove belt.

Install lower belt by reversing removal procedure.

Upper Belt. The lower belt must be removed as outlined in previous section before removing upper belt (22—Fig. CC13). Detach engine pulley belt guard (14), then unscrew retaining nut and remove idler (10). Remove upper belt.

Install upper belt by reversing removal procedure. Be sure hub side of idler (10) is next to idler arm (3). Install belt and idler simultaneously so belt is inside belt guide (9).

VARIABLE SPEED PULLEY

All Models So Equipped

R&R AND OVERHAUL. The variable speed pulley (23—Fig. CC13) is accessible after removing drive belts as previously outlined. Individual components of the variable speed pulley used on early models may be available, while the variable speed pulley on later models is available only as a unit assembly. Check for parts availability on early models. Bearings are sealed and do not require lubrication. Apply a dry lubricant to movable pulley half and sleeve if variable speed pulley on early models is disassembled.

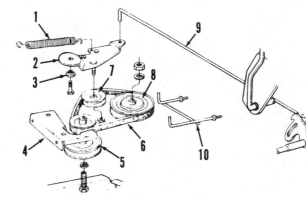

Fig. CC12—Exploded view of traction drive belt and pulley arrangement for Model 136-511-100.

1. Spring
2. Idler bracket
3. Spacer
4. Guard
5. Engine pulley
6. Belt
7. Idler
8. Transaxle pulley
9. Clutch rod
10. Guide

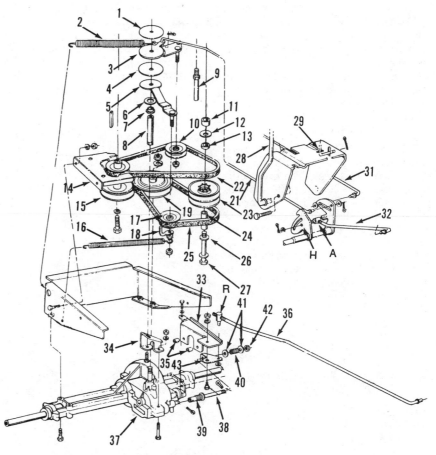

Fig. CC13—Exploded view of clutch and variable speed assembly.

1. Thrust washer	12. Belleville washer	23. Variable speed pulley	33. Bracket
2. Spring	13. Thrust washer	24. Spacer	34. Bracket
3. Idler arm	14. Belt guard	25. Lower drive belt	35. Spacers
4. Thrust washer	15. Engine pulley	26. Thrust washer	36. Shift lever rod
5. Idler arm	16. Spring	27. Cap screw	37. Transaxle
6. Washer	17. Idler	28. Pedal rod	38. Shift rod
7. Bushing	18. Belt guide	29. Park brake rod	39. Spring
8. Torque rod	19. Transaxle pulley	30. Ferrule	40. Spring
9. Belt guide	20. Spring switch	31. Brake rod	41. Washers
10. Idler	21. Clutch rod	32. Speed control rod	42. Nut
11. Spacer	22. Upper drive belt		43. Shift arm

TRANSAXLE

All Models

REMOVE AND REINSTALL. To remove transaxle (37—Fig. CC13), first remove drive belts as previously outlined. Disconnect brake linkage and shift linkage. Support rear of machine and remove transaxle mounting bolts. Raise rear of machine and roll transaxle assembly from under machine.

Reinstall by reversing removal procedure.

OVERHAUL. All models are equipped with a MTD Model 717 transaxle. Refer to TRANSMISSION REPAIR section for service information.

GROUND DRIVE BRAKE

All Models

ADJUSTMENT. Check brake operation by pushing brake pedal and attempting to move machine. If brake does not hold machine with pedal fully depressed, adjust brake. To adjust brake, release brake and turn nut (3—Fig. CC14) on cam lever until desired brake operation is obtained.

R&R AND OVERHAUL. To remove brake caliper assembly, disconnect brake spring and brake rod from actuating lever. Unbolt and remove brake pad carrier (8—Fig. CC14). Slide brake disc off transaxle shaft and remove inner brake pad from slot in transaxle housing.

Clean and inspect all parts for excessive wear and damage. Reassemble by reversing disassembly procedure.

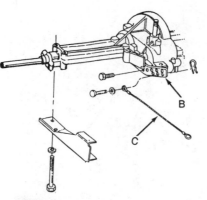

Fig. CC15—On models equipped with a single-blade mower, attach end of blade brake cable as outlined in text.

MOWER DRIVE BELTS

Models With Single Blade

REMOVE AND REINSTALL. To remove the mower drive belt on models with a single mower blade, proceed as follows: Disconnect spark plug wire. Place blade engagement lever in disengaged position. Locate outside engine belt guard at right rear side of machine and remove one retaining bolt while

loosening the other bolt. Pivot belt guard out and away from engine pulley. Disconnect blade brake cable from belt guard and remove belt guard. Disconnect mower deck links and remove belt guides on deck. Remove belt.

Install mower belt by reversing removal procedure.

Models With Dual Blades

REMOVE AND REINSTALL. To remove the mower drive belt on models with dual mower blades, proceed as follows: Disconnect spark plug wire. Move mower deck to lowest position. Place blade engagement lever in disengaged position. Locate outside engine belt guard at right rear side of machine and remove one retaining bolt while loosening the other bolt. Pivot belt guard out and away from engine pulley. Locate inside engine pulley belt guard, remove one bolt, loosen other bolt and pivot guard out of way. Separate drive belt from engine pulley. Detach blade brake spring, remove belt guard and remove upper belt. Detach mower belt idler spring and remove lower belt.

Install mower belts by reversing removal procedure.

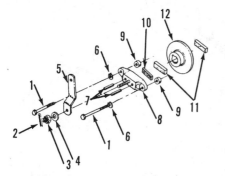

Fig. CC14—Exploded view of brake used on all models.

1. Cap screws		7. Pins	
2. Cotter pin		8. Carrier	
3. Adjusting nut		9. Spacer	
4. Washer		10. Backup plate	
5. Cam lever		11. Brake pads	
6. Washer		12. Brake disc	

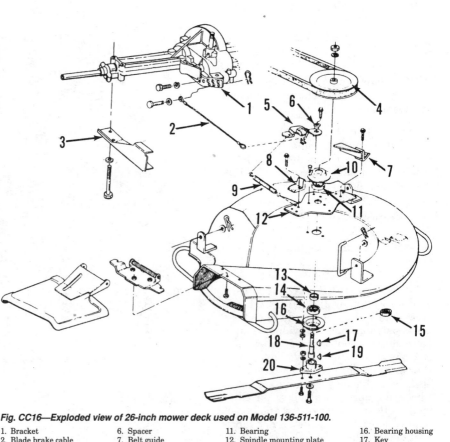

Fig. CC16—Exploded view of 26-inch mower deck used on Model 136-511-100.

1. Bracket	6. Spacer	11. Bearing	16. Bearing housing
2. Blade brake cable	7. Belt guide	12. Spindle mounting plate	17. Key
3. Bracket	8. Belt guide	13. Spacer	18. Spindle
4. Pulley	9. Spring	14. Bearing	19. Key
5. Blade brake	10. Bearing housing	15. Bearing shield	20. Blade adapter

MOWER DECK

All Models

HEIGHT ADJUSTMENT. Front of mower blade should be $\frac{1}{4}$-$\frac{3}{8}$ inch (6.4-9.5 mm) lower than rear of blade. Mower deck should be level from side-to-side. Adjust hanger lengths as needed to obtain desired height.

REMOVE AND REINSTALL. Disconnect spark plug wire. Move mower deck to lowest position. Place blade engagement lever in disengaged position. Locate outside engine belt guard at right rear side of machine and remove one retaining bolt while loosening the other bolt. Pivot belt guard out and away from engine pulley. On models with a single mower blade, disconnect blade brake cable from belt guard and remove belt guard. On models with dual mower blades, locate inside engine pulley belt guard, remove one bolt, loosen other bolt and pivot guard out of way. Separate drive belt from engine pulley. Disconnect safety switch wire on models so equipped. Detach lift linkage from mower deck and remove mower deck.

Reinstall by reversing removal procedure. On models equipped with a blade brake cable, adjust cable as outlined in BLADE BRAKE section.

BLADE BRAKE

Models With Single Blade

ADJUSTMENT. On models with a single-blade mower, adjust location of transaxle end of the brake cable as follows: Place mower deck in lowest position and move blade engagement lever to disengaged position. Attach cable (C—Fig. CC15) end to rearmost hole in bracket (B) so cable has least amount of slack but no tension.

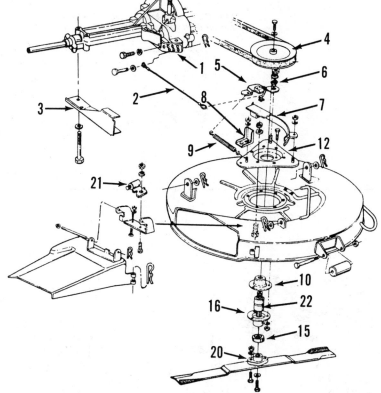

Fig. CC17—Exploded view of 30-inch mower deck used on Model 136-514-100.

1. Bracket	5. Blade brake	9. Spring	16. Bearing housing
2. Blade brake cable	6. Spacer	10. Bearing housing	20. Blade adapter
3. Bracket	7. Belt guide	12. Spindle mounting plate	21. Safety switch
4. Pulley	8. Belt guide	15. Bearing shield	22. Bearing & spindle assy.

MOWER SPINDLE

All Models

LUBRICATION. Periodic lubrication of mower spindle is not required.

R&R AND OVERHAUL. Remove mower deck, belt(s) and blade(s). Refer to Figs. CC16 through CC20 for exploded views of mower decks and spindle assemblies. Spindle assembly on later models is available only as a unit assembly. Disassembly of spindle assembly is evident after inspection of unit and referral to exploded view. Inspect components for excessive wear and damage.

ELECTRICAL

All Models

Refer to Figs. CC21 through CC23 for wiring schematics. All switches must be in good operating condition for machine to operate properly.

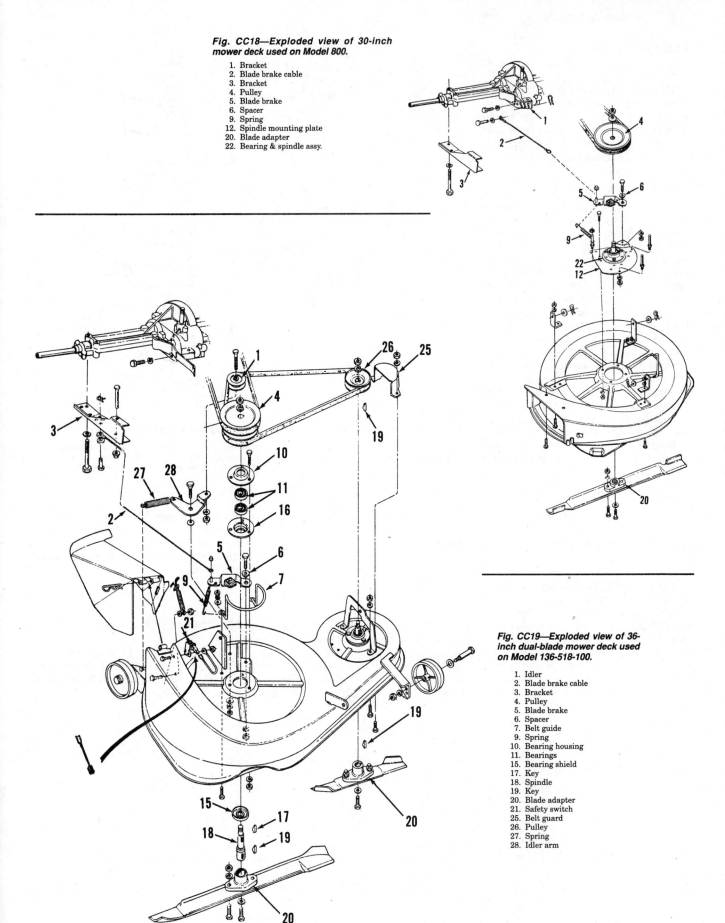

Fig. CC18—Exploded view of 30-inch mower deck used on Model 800.

1. Bracket
2. Blade brake cable
3. Bracket
4. Pulley
5. Blade brake
6. Spacer
9. Spring
12. Spindle mounting plate
20. Blade adapter
22. Bearing & spindle assy.

Fig. CC19—Exploded view of 36-inch dual-blade mower deck used on Model 136-518-100.

1. Idler
2. Blade brake cable
3. Bracket
4. Pulley
5. Blade brake
6. Spacer
7. Belt guide
9. Spring
10. Bearing housing
11. Bearings
15. Bearing shield
17. Key
18. Spindle
19. Key
20. Blade adapter
21. Safety switch
25. Belt guard
26. Pulley
27. Spring
28. Idler arm

Illustrations Courtesy Cub Cadet Corp.

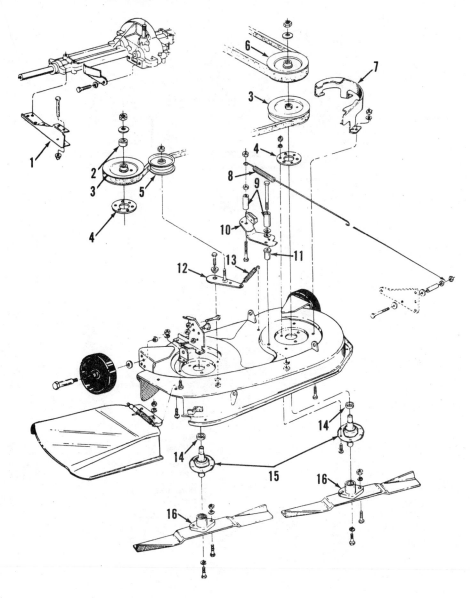

Illustrations Courtesy Cub Cadet Corp.

Fig. CC20—Exploded view of typical dual-blade mower used on Model 1002. Model 1208 is similar except spindle is mounted on top side of deck.

1. Bracket
2. Spacer
3. Pulley
4. Plate
5. Idler
6. Pulley
7. Belt guard
8. Spring
9. Spacers
10. Brake arm
11. Spacer
12. Idler arm
13. Spring
14. Spacer
15. Spindle assy.
16. Adapter

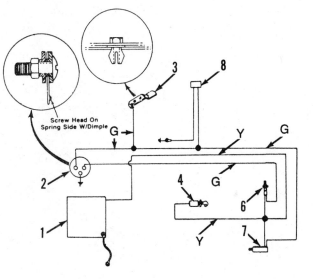

Fig. CC21—Typical wiring schematic for models with rewind starter and seat switch (8).

G. Green
Y. Yellow
1. Engine
2. Rewind starter switch
3. Reverse gear switch
4. Ignition switch
6. Clutch switch
7. Blade engagement switch
8. Seat switch

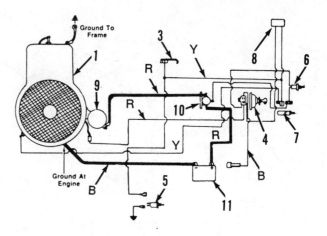

Fig. CC22—Typical wiring schematic for early models with electric start and chute deflector switch (5).

B. Black
G. Green
R. Red
Y. Yellow
1. Engine
3. Reverse gear switch
4. Ignition switch
5. Chute deflector switch
6. Clutch switch
7. Blade engagement switch
8. Seat switch
9. Starter
10. Starter solenoid
11. Battery

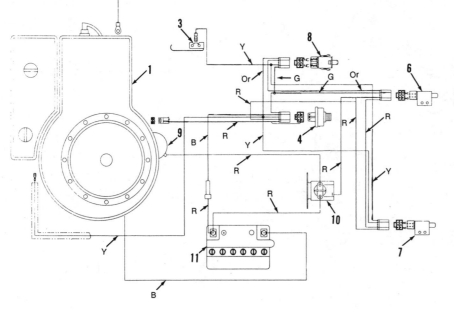

Fig. CC23—Typical wiring schematic for later models with electric start.

B. Black
G. Green
Or. Orange
R. Red
Y. Yellow
1. Engine
3. Reverse gear switch
4. Ignition switch
6. Clutch switch
7. Blade engagement switch
8. Seat switch
9. Starter
10. Starter solenoid
11. Battery

JOHN DEERE

DEERE & COMPANY
John Deere Road
Moline, IL 61265

Model	Make	Engine Model	Horsepower	Cutting Width, In.
55	Tecumseh	V50	5.0	26
56	Tecumseh	V60	6.0	28
57	Tecumseh	V70	7.0	34
66	Tecumseh	V60	6.0	30
68	B&S	191702	8.0	30/34
R70	B&S	190000	8	30
R72	B&S	190000	8	30
S80	B&S	190000	8	30
S82	B&S	190000	8	30
R92	B&S	250000	11	30
S92	B&S	250000	11	30

FRONT AXLE

All Models

REMOVE AND REINSTALL. Axle main member is center-pivoted in cross channel at forward end of chassis frame. Mowing unit is fitted to a clevis or to a draft rod (11–Fig. JD2) which is part of axle assembly. If removal of steering gear or front axle is planned, mower deck should first be separated from chassis. Removal of under-chassis items may be done with all wheels on the ground, however, these mowers are provided with a rear-mounted stand (optional on Models 66 and 68) designed for placing mower upright on its rear end. If this is done, observe the following:

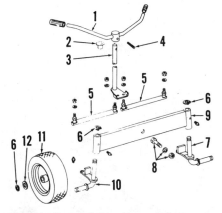

Fig. JD1—Exploded view of front axle and steering gear parts for Model 55.

1. Handlebar
2. Plastic bushing
3. Steering shaft & lever
4. Drive pin
5. Tie rod (2)
6. Snap ring (4)
7. Spindle, LH
8. Axle pivot bolt (1/2X1½)
9. Axle assy.
10. Spindle, RH
11. Wheel & tire
12. Spindle washer

CAUTION: Frequently, the performance of maintenance, adjustment or repair operations on a riding mower is more convenient if mower is standing on end. This procedure can be considered a recommended practice providing the following safety recommendations are performed:

1. Drain fuel tank or make certain that fuel level is low enough so that fuel will not drain out.
2. Close fuel shut-off valve if so equipped.
3. Remove battery on models so equipped.
4. Disconnect spark plug wire and tie out of way.
5. Although not absolutely essential, it is recommended that crankcase oil be drained to avoid flooding the combustion chamber with oil when engine is tilted.
6. Secure mower from tipping by lashing unit to a nearby post or overhead beam.

On models not equipped with a stand, cradle blocks made of scrap lumber can be fitted under rear wheels so that each tire is lifted about five inches clear of floor.

Remove mower unit as outlined in MOWER DECK paragraphs. Set machine up on rear stand as previously outlined.

Before disassembly of steering gear parts, check carefully for looseness, damage or wear through entire system with special attention to condition of non-adjustable tie rods (5–Fig. JD1) or gear sector (9–Fig. JD2) and steering shaft pinion.

To remove front axle, first remove wheels for weight reduction, then disconnect tie rods from steering spindles and remove pivot bolt from center of frame channel. With axle assembly sep-

arated from frame, remove snap rings (6– Fig. JD1 or 18–Fig. JD2) and remove spindles from axle ends.

STEERING GEAR

Model 55

REMOVE AND REINSTALL. To remove steering gear from Model 55, disconnect tie rods (5–Fig. JD1) from steering arm, carefully drive out pin (4) at hub of handlebar (1), pull handlebar off steering shaft (3) and lower steering shaft out of control console.

All Other Models

REMOVE AND REINSTALL. To remove steering gear from other models, disconnect tie rods (10–Fig. JD2) and remove gear sector (9) at lower end of steering shaft. Carefully drive out groove pin (5) from steering wheel hub, remove steering wheel and note number of shim washers (4) used to take up vertical play of steering shaft. Pull steering shaft (8) down and out of control console taking care not to damage bushing (6). Reassemble in reverse order. Lubricate at fittings using John Deere Multipurpose Lubricant No. TY2098. Tighten tie-rod end retaining nuts to 20 ft.-lbs. (28 N·m) torque.

ENGINE

Engine make and model are listed at the beginning of this section. Refer to appropriate engine section in this manual for tune-up specifications, engine overhaul procedures and engine maintenance.

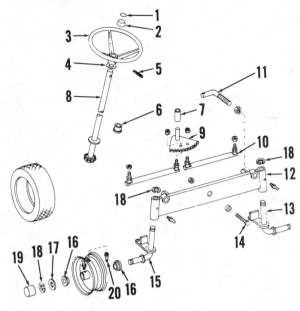

Fig. JD2—Exploded view of typical steering gear and front axle parts for Models 56, 57, 66 and 68. Model 68 shown. Models R70, R72, R92, S80, S82 and S92 are similar.

1. Logo
2. Cap
3. Wheel
4. Shim washer
5. Groove pin
6. Plastic bushing
7. Bronze bushing
8. Steering shaft & pinion
9. Gear sector
10. Tie rod
11. Draft rod
12. Axle
13. Spindle, LH
14. Pivot bolt
15. Spindle, RH
16. Wheel bearing (4)
17. Special washer (2)
18. Snap ring (4)
19. Cap
20. Valve stem

Refer to following paragraphs for removal and installation procedure.

All Models Except "R" And "S" Series

REMOVE AND REINSTALL. To remove engine, tip unit up to rest on its rear stand as previously outlined, and remove mowing deck and mower drive belt after first unbolting hitch and belt guide on Models 55, 56 and 57 or belt guide only on Models 66 and 68. Back out cap screw from end of engine crankshaft and use a puller to remove mower drive and traction drive pulleys. While chassis is up-ended, it is advisable to partially loosen seat pedestal cap screws (Models 55, 56 and 57) and engine mounting bolts from under side for convenience in later removal. Lower unit to rest on all wheels.

On Model 55, removal of seat pedestal to expose engine is optional. On Models 56 and 57, engine shroud and seat assembly are hinged to pedestal and may be tilted forward out of way. Access to engine is improved by complete removal of pedestal. Models 66 and 68 require only that seat assembly and shroud be tipped forward to uncover engine enclosure housing. Remove fuel tank vent tube at carburetor end, slide engine enclosure box forward to disengage latch pins at rear and lift front of enclosure simultaneously to expose engine.

On models equipped for electric starting, disconnect cable from starter terminal post. Disconnect key switch wire and safety interlock wire at engine end. Disconnect throttle control bowden cable at carburetor and on Models 66 and 68 disconnect fuel line at inlet fitting on carburetor. Remove mounting bolts and lift engine from frame.

Reverse removal sequence to reinstall engine.

NOTE: On Models 66 and 68, to prevent damage to muffler during engine removal, it may be advisable to back out manifold cap screws at valve cage in cylinder block so that muffler and exhaust pipe can remain in place.

Models R70, R72, R92

REMOVE AND REINSTALL. Disconnect battery (as equipped). Disconnect all necessary electrical wiring and throttle/choke cable at engine. Close fuel shut-off valve and remove fuel line. Remove the 3 nuts, washers and mower drive belt guard and slip mower drive belt off engine pulley. Remove the 4 engine mounting bolts and lift engine up, disengaging transmission drive belt as engine is lifted off rider.

Reverse removal procedure for reinstallation.

Models S80, S82 and S92

REMOVE AND REINSTALL. Disconnect battery (as equipped). Disconnect all necessary electrical wiring and throttle/choke cable at engine. Remove the 2 locknuts, washers and mower drive belt guard and slip mower drive belt off engine pulley. Remove the 2 nuts and rider transmission drive belt guide. Remove exhaust pipe shroud and right side shroud. Close fuel shut-off valve and disconnect fuel line at carburetor. Depress clutch to remove rider drive belt tension. Remove cap screw retaining engine drive pulley and install a 5/8 x 2 inch cap screw in its place. Tighten 5/8 x 2 inch cap screw to remove engine drive pulley. Remove the 2 cap screws and spacers and disconnect exhaust pipe. Remove muffler, exhaust pipe and gasket. Remove the 4 engine mounting bolts and remove engine.

Reverse removal procedure for reinstallation. Make certain all belt guides are properly positioned.

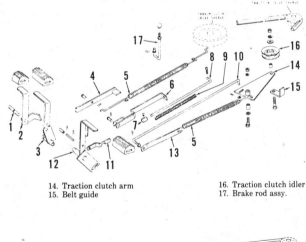

Fig. JD3—Exploded view of traction clutch-brake and mower clutch linkages used on early Model 55 (to Ser. No. 20950) and on early Model 56 (to Ser. No. 21750).

1. Clutch shaft
2. Mower drive throw-out pedal
3. Mower drive clutch pedal
4. Latch lever
5. Tension spring (2)
6. Clutch arm
7. Locking collar
8. Mower clutch rod
9. Mower clutch spring
10. Traction clutch rod
11. Brake lock
12. Clutch-brake pedal
13. Link

14. Traction clutch arm
15. Belt guide
16. Traction clutch idler
17. Brake rod assy.

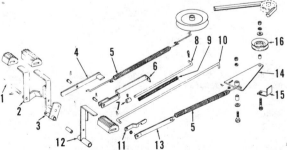

Fig. JD4—Exploded view of mower and traction control linkages used on Model 55 (Ser. No. 20951 and after), Model 56 (to Ser. No. 44000) and Model 57 (to Ser. No. 14000). Refer to Fig. JD3 for parts identification legend.

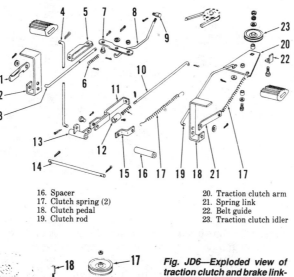

Fig. JD5—Exploded view of mower and traction control linkages as used on Model 56 (Ser. No. 44001 and after) and on Model 57 (Ser. No. 14001 and after).

1. Brake lock
2. Brake pedal
3. Brake rod (front)
4. Mower clutch rod
5. Retainer
6. Spring
7. Brake link
8. Brake rod (rear)
9. Brake adjuster
10. Mower clutch rod
11. Mower clutch arm
12. Locking collar
13. Throwout pivot
14. Pedal shaft
15. Spring link

16. Spacer
17. Clutch spring (2)
18. Clutch pedal
19. Clutch rod

20. Traction clutch arm
21. Spring link
22. Belt guide
23. Traction clutch idler

clutch pedal and wedge a piece of wood scrap between clutch arm and frame to hold clutch disengaged. Next, remove idler pulley from clutch arm. Belt will be completely loose, but it will be necessary to bend belt guides away from transmission pulley so belt can be lifted out of pulley. Slip belt to rear and between axle and driving pulley for removal. Proceed in reverse order to reinstall, and be sure to bend belt guides back toward transmission pulley, leaving ¼-inch (6.4 mm) clearance. After mower is reinstalled, adjust belt guides on hitch plate for 1/16 to 1/8-inch (1.6-3.2 mm) clearance from driving pulley.

Models 66-68

REMOVE AND REINSTALL. Remove mower deck as outlined in MOWER DECK section. Set unit up on its rear stand as previously outlined. Unbolt and remove frame reinforcement located next to transmission pulley, then remove pulley belt guide. Remove idler pulley and slip belt out between pulleys and rear axle. Reverse procedure to install new belt. Adjust belt guide to ⅛-inch (3.2 mm) clearance between guide and belt.

Models R70-R72-S80-S82-R92-S92

REMOVE AND REINSTALL. Lock park brake in depressed position. Remove mower deck and mower drive belt. Loosen all necessary belt guides and remove belt guards. Slip rider drive belt off pulleys and remove.

Reinstall by reversing removal procedure. Make certain all belt guides are properly positioned and belt guards are in place.

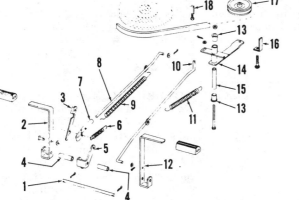

Fig. JD6—Exploded view of traction clutch and brake linkages used on Models 66 and 68.

1. Shaft
2. Brake pedal
3. Brake lock
4. Spacer (2)
5. Throwout pivot
6. Return spring
7. Brake tube
8. Brake rod
9. Brake spring
10. Clutch rod
11. Clutch spring
12. Clutch pedal
13. Nylon bushing (2)
14. Idler arm
15. Bushing
16. Belt guide
17. Clutch idler pulley
18. Belt guide

TRACTION DRIVE CLUTCH AND DRIVE BELT

All Models

ADJUSTMENT. The traction drive clutch consists of a spring-loaded idler with no special adjustment feature. Figs. JD3 through JD6 show typical linkages and parts arrangement of traction controls.

If performance is marginal or inadequate, with slippage an apparent problem, inspection of clutch idler, belt and linkage will probably disclose that belt is damaged, stretched or glazed, idler pulley or its bearing may be worn or defective, driving pulley (engine) or drive pulley (transmission) may be damaged or loose on shafts, or linkage rods, springs or cotters may be broken, bent, missing or disconnected. Refer to appropriate figures for parts identification and placement in reassembly.

Models 55-56-57

REMOVE AND REINSTALL. To change drive belt, remove mower deck as outlined in MOWER DECK section. Set unit up on its rear stand as previously outlined. Mower drive belt and

rear hitch will have been removed as a part of mowing deck removal task, which will leave underside open for full access to traction drive system.

Proceed as follows: On older units with a common pedal for drive clutch-brake, depress pedal and set brake lock. With newer production models, which have a separate clutch pedal, depress

Fig. JD7—Exploded view of chain case which also serves as differential housing for Models 66 and 68. Models S80, S82 and S92 are similar.

1. LH (fixed) side of case
2. Ball bearings (2)
3. Gasket
4. RH (outer) half of case
5. Tie bracket
6. Tensioner spring (2)
7. Tensioner arm (2)
8. Drive chain
9. Snap ring
10. Drive sprocket

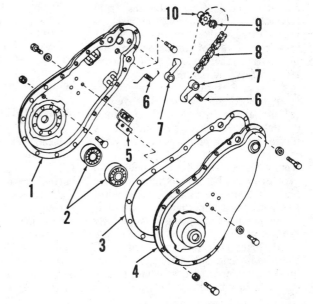

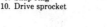

TRANSMISSION

Models 55-56-57

REMOVE AND REINSTALL. Transmissions on these models are located under operator's seat pedestal. Removal of pedestal is a matter of convenience and is a mechanic's option. Other removal steps are as follows:

Tip unit up on rear stand as previously outlined and remove mowing deck as outlined in MOWER DECK section. Relieve belt tension by depressing clutch. Use a wooden block against idler arm for convenience. Remove snap ring and washer from transmission input shaft and remove transmission pulley. Do not lose key from shaft or pulley hub. Disconnect return spring for disc brake and remove brake rod from brake lever. Disconnect leads from neutral-start safety switch when so equipped. Loosen drive chain tensioner and remove master link and drive chain. Back out the four mounting cap screws and remove transmission. Reverse this procedure to reinstall and reset tension on drive chain as outlined in DRIVE CHAIN paragraphs.

Models 66-68

REMOVE AND REINSTALL. To remove transmission, first remove mower deck as outlined in MOWER DECK section. Block idler arm in released position to relieve belt tension and remove snap ring, washer, input pulley and key from transmission input shaft. Slightly loosen each of the transmission mounting cap screws working from underside of unit, then set mower down on all four wheels. Raise and unbolt engine shroud at hinge pivots and remove shroud, then disconnect fuel line and remove fuel tank and its mounting bracket by unbolting from frame. With brake pedal relaxed, remove cotter pin and disconnect brake rod from lever of transmission disc brake. Disconnect wires from neutral-start safety switch. Raise and block under frame at right rear so wheel is clear, then remove wheel. Remove cotter pin and collar from inner (small diameter) axle shaft, then pull axle by its flange out of chain case. Note that inner end of axle will be disengaged from differential side gear inside chain case. See Fig. JD8. Wrap this end with a paper shop towel to keep it clean for reassembly. At upper end of chain case, disconnect lift arm spring and carefully remove groove pin which attaches hub of lift arm (bellcrank) to cross shaft, then pull arm off shaft end. Now, unbolt and remove outer cover, taking care not to damage gasket if reuse is

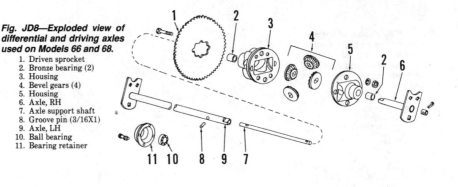

Fig. JD8—Exploded view of differential and driving axles used on Models 66 and 68.
1. Driven sprocket
2. Bronze bearing (2)
3. Housing
4. Bevel gears (4)
5. Housing
6. Axle, RH
7. Axle support shaft
8. Groove pin (3/16X1)
9. Axle, LH
10. Ball bearing
11. Bearing retainer

planned. When chain case is thus opened, remove snap ring from transmission input shaft and remove input sprocket and Woodruff key. Remove transmission mounting cap screws then move transmission inward so shaft end clears chain case half and lift out of mower.

NOTE: Take care not to lose or damage nylon bushing which supports lift shaft in flanges of chain case.

Reverse this procedure to reinstall transmission.

Models R70-R72-R92

REMOVE AND REINSTALL. Remove mower deck as outlined in MOWER DECK section. Remove deck lift rod. Disconnect spark plug and ground lead to engine. Lock park brake to remove transmission drive belt tension. Close fuel shut-off valve and disconnect fuel line, throttle/choke cable, seat safety switch and ignition switch. Remove seat and pedestal assembly. Remove snap ring from transmission drive pulley and remove pulley. Remove drive chain, safety-neutral switch and shift lever assembly. Remove the 4 cap screws, belt guide (mark belt guide location) and remove transmission.

Reverse removal procedure for reinstallation. Make certain safety-neutral switch operates properly and that all belt guides are properly positioned.

Models S80-S82-S92

REMOVE AND REINSTALL. Remove mower deck as outlined in MOWER DECK section. Remove battery, battery case and fuel tank. Remove right rear wheel and axle. Disconnect spring, turn lift arm and remove spring pin which will allow lift arm to be removed. Pull linkage shaft from chain case cover. Remove bushings as necessary. Remove cap screws, chain case cover and gasket. Remove drive chain, shift lever assembly and safety-neutral

switch. Disconnect brake linkage and remove transmission drive pulley. Remove the 4 cap screws and remove transmission.

Reverse removal procedure for reinstallation. Make certain safety-neutral switch operates properly.

All Models

OVERHAUL. Models 55, 56 and 57 are equipped with Foote transmission Model 2240-2 (JD #AM32670), Models 56 and 57 are equipped with Foote transmission Model 2500-6 (JD #AM34464), Models 66 and 68 are equipped with Foote transmission Model 2600-2 (JD #AM35523) and Models R70, R72, S80, S82, R92 and S92 are equipped with Peerless 700 series transmission. Refer to appropriate TRANSMISSION section in this manual.

DRIVE CHAIN

Models 55-56-57-R70-R72-R92

R&R AND ADJUSTMENT. Adjustment of chain tension is performed with seat and shroud assembly raised. There is no need for mower removal or other disassembly. Proceed as follows: Loosen axle bolt for idler sprocket and move idler bolt in its slot under transmission platform. Tension is correct when chain can be flexed ½ inch (12.7 mm) at a mid-point between drive and driven sprocket in top strand. If chain is defective, loosen adjusting sprocket and pull master link. Chain can then be removed for cleaning, lubrication, repair or renewal.

Models 66-68-S80-S82-S92

R&R AND ADJUSTMENT. These models are without external adjustment means for drive chain. If drive chain becomes noisy due to looseness within chain case, it is likely that spring-loaded automatic chain tensioner assembly (see Fig. JD7) is defective.

Refer to DIFFERENTIAL AND REAR AXLE paragraphs.

DIFFERENTIAL AND REAR AXLE

Model 55

REMOVE AND REINSTALL. Set mower up on rear stand as previously outlined, then release drive chain tensioner, disconnect master link and remove drive chain. Unbolt bearing blocks at each end of rear axle and withdraw entire rear axle, differential and rear wheels as a unit.

Models 56-57

NOTE: Some earlier production Models 56 and 57 (pre-1972) were equipped with same rear axle bearing block and mounting as used on Model 55.

REMOVE AND REINSTALL. Remove mower deck as outlined in MOWER DECK section. Set mower up on its rear stand as previously outlined. Remove cap screw from engine crankshaft which retains mower drive pulley. Use a suitable puller to remove pulley from shaft.

Remove rear wheels. In earlier pro-

duction, wheel hubs are directly bolted by through-bolt to axle shaft. Later, wheel is attached by lug bolts to a flanged hub which is cross-bolted to end of axle. Whichever design is used, strip all bushings, spacers, keys and washers from outer end of axle and unbolt axle bearing retainer from frame. Release tension on drive chain, then remove master link and lift chain off sprockets. Shift axle assembly from side to side to clear frame and lift out. Reverse these steps to reinstall.

Models 66-68

REMOVE AND REINSTALL. Remove mower deck as outlined in MOWER DECK paragraphs, and set unit on rear stand as previously outlined.

NOTE: If service to differential only is planned, remove only right rear wheel. If entire axle is to be serviced remove both rear wheels.

Mower lift linkage must be removed from lift shaft which passes through chain case flange. Disconnect lift arm spring, remove groove pin which attaches lift arm hub to shaft and pull arm from shaft. Remove cotter pin and retainer collar from axle support shaft

(7-Fig. JD8) and pull short right hand axle (6) out by its flanged end. Unbolt outer case half (4-Fig. JD7) and carefully separate from inner half of case (1). Remove chain tensioners (7) with springs (6) so chain will relax, then remove snap ring (9), transmission output shaft sprocket (10) and drive chain. At this point, entire assembly, driven sprocket (1-Fig. JD8) and differential (3, 4 and 5) can be slipped from left hand axle shaft (9) for further disassembly and overhaul as needed. Ball bearing sets (2-Fig. JD7) should be checked and evaluated for possible renewal. It is unlikely that inner half of chain case (1) will need to be unbolted from frame; procedure is apparent if this becomes necessary. Left side axle shaft (9-Fig. JD8) may readily be pulled out for inspection and evaluation of groove pin (8) and support shaft (7). Unbolt and remove bearing retainer (11) for access to left side axle bearing (10). Reinstall all parts in reverse of this sequence.

Models R70-R72-R92

REMOVE AND REINSTALL. Remove mower deck as outlined in MOWER DECK section. On early models, remove lug nuts and remove rear tire and wheel assemblies. Remove hub and key from axle shafts. On later models, remove "E" rings at outer axle ends and remove rear tire and wheel assemblies. Disconnect brake rod and loosen drive chain by loosening drive chain idler. Remove the 4 locknuts and separate brake drum and sprocket from differential. Remove bearings from frame and move differential toward left side of unit until brake drum and drive sprocket can be removed. Remove differential.

Reverse removal procedure for reinstallation. Adjust drive chain tension as previously outlined.

Models S80-S82-S92

REMOVE AND REINSTALL. Remove mower deck as outlined in MOWER DECK section. Disconnect battery. Remove rear wheels, axle and outer drive chain case cover. Remove sprocket and chain. Remove chain tensioners. Remove differential assembly.

Reverse removal procedure for reinstallation.

All Models

OVERHAUL. Peerless, Mast Foos and John Deere differentials are used. Refer to appropriate DIFFERENTIAL section in this manual for overhaul procedure.

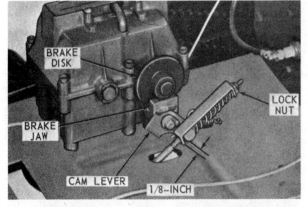

Fig. JD9—View of brake adjustment point for transmission disc brake on Foote two-speed model. Refer to text.

Fig. JD10—View of disc brake used on three-speed Foote transmission for Models 56 and 57 in 1973-74. See text for adjustment procedure.

Illustrations for Fig. JD9 & Fig. JD10 reproduced by permission of Deere & Company. Copyright Deere & Company

GROUND DRIVE BRAKE

Models 55-56-57-66-68

Disc brake which serves both as a service brake and as a parking brake when locked in applied position is cam-actuated with its disc (rotor) assembly keyed to inboard end of transmission output shaft.

ADJUSTMENT. Design of brake mechanisms varies somewhat dependent upon transmission model used. Brake shown in Fig. JD9 is found on two-speed transmissions on Models 55, 56 and 57. To adjust, set parking brake lock, tilt seat forward on pedestal and take up locknut on end of brake rod to set ⅛-inch (3.2 mm) gap as shown between spring retainer strap and threaded adjuster stud. If adjustment is unsatisfactory, check condition of brake pads and operating linkage, renewing parts which prove defective.

Brake shown in Fig. JD10 is used on mower Models 56 and 57 with three-speed transmissions in 1973 production and after. To adjust, tilt engine shroud and seat forward for access to transmission and brake. On these models, spring tension on brake rod must be

maintained so that cam lever just engages cam ramp on brake jaw, without causing brake pads to drag on disc, but providing good response to brake pedal. Pivot stud, threaded on brake rod, rotates inward to tighten, outward to release tension. If adjustment is ineffective, check condition of brake pads and linkage and renew damaged or defective parts.

On Models 66 and 68 which have a five-speed transmission, a set screw adjustment in brake jaw is provided to take up wear on brake pads. Tilt engine shroud and seat forward, then use a ⅛-inch (3.2 mm) Allen wrench on No. 8 socket head set screw to set clearance between brake pad and rotor disc at 0.022 inch (0.56 mm) working through opening in fuel tank support with brake pedal in relaxed position. Pads (friction pucks) and all brake parts are renewable, and should be checked for condition whenever adjustment is needed or when service to transmission is being performed.

R&R AND OVERHAUL. Tilt seat and engine shroud forward for access to transmission and brake. Disconnect brake rod from cam lever. Remove shoulder bolt and withdraw brake jaw with outer pad. Slide brake disc from transmission shaft and remove inner brake pad from transmission case. Clean and inspect parts for wear or other damage. Renew parts as required and reassemble by reversing removal procedure. Brake disc must slide freely on transmission shaft. Torque shoulder bolt to 275 in.-lbs. (31 N·m). Adjust brake as outlined in previous paragraphs.

Models R70-R72-R92

ADJUSTMENT. Band brake is adjusted by turning yoke on brake rod. Adjust to attain slight tension on brake band with no slack in brake rod.

R&R AND OVERHAUL. Disconnect brake rod and yoke. Remove the 2 nuts and carriage bolts retaining brake arm bracket to frame. Remove brake band from bracket pins and remove brake band from around drum. For drum removal, refer to DIFFERENTIAL section.

Reverse removal procedure for reinstallation. Adjust brake as previously outlined.

Models S80-S82-S92

ADJUSTMENT. Disc brake assembly is located on the side of transmission housing. To adjust, place an 0.010 inch (0.25 mm) feeler gage between

brake disc and brake pad. Tighten adjust nut at brake lever until feeler gage can just be removed.

R&R AND OVERHAUL. Remove battery and battery base. Remove fuel tank and disconnect brake rod from brake lever. Remove the 2 cap screws at caliper and remove caliper assembly. Slide brake disc off transmission brake shaft. Remove inner brake pad from pad depression in transmission housing. Remove outer pad, pad plate and the two actuating pins from brake caliper. Remove brake lever as necessary.

Reverse disassembly procedure for reassembly. Make certain actuating pins work freely in caliper bores and that pad plate is installed between actuating pins and outer brake pad. Adjust brake as previously outlined.

MOWER DRIVE BELTS

Models 55-56

REMOVE AND REINSTALL. Disconnect spark plug wire and remove mower as outlined in MOWER DECK paragraphs. Loosen and move belt guides as needed. Remove idler arm retaining pin and lift idler off pivot post. Unbolt and remove idler pulley from arm and remove belt. Renew drive belt in reverse order of removal. Adjust belt guides to ⅛-inch (3.2 mm) clearance from pulley.

NOTE: Be sure belt is installed with back side against idler pulley and idler is centered with blade pulley.

Model 57

REMOVE AND REINSTALL. To remove mower drive belt, disconnect spark plug wire and remove mower as outlined in MOWER DECK paragraphs. Remove belt shields from mower deck. Loosen idler pulley belt guide and slip belt out of pulley and remove from mower. Renew belt by reversing removal procedure.

Mower deck belt can be removed without removing drive belt. Remove belt shields from mower deck. Remove cotter pin from idler arm stud and slide idler arms upward on stud. Flex idler arm inward and slip belt from idler pulley and remove from mower. Renew belt by reversing removal procedure.

Models 66-68-R70-R72-R92-S80-S82-S92 With 30 Inch Mower

REMOVE AND REINSTALL. Disconnect spark plug wire and remove

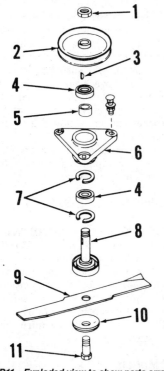

Fig. JD11—Exploded view to show parts arrangement of typical mower spindle assembly. Spindle for Model 68, 34-inch mower deck, is shown.

1. Locknut, ¾-inch
2. Sheave
3. Woodruff key (⅛X¾)
4. Bearing
5. Spacer
6. Hub flange
7. Snap ring (2)
8. Spindle
9. Blade
10. Drive washer
11. Cap screw (⅛X1)

mower as outlined in MOWER DECK paragraphs. Loosen belt guides and remove idler pulleys. Remove belt from mower. Renew belt by reversing removal procedure.

Model 68 With 34-Inch Mower

REMOVE AND REINSTALL. Disconnect spark plug wire and remove mower as outlined in MOWER DECK paragraphs. Remove shields from mower deck. Remove bolt and spacer from idler arms and remove belt from pulleys. Renew belt by reversing removal procedure.

MOWER SPINDLE

All Models

REMOVE AND REINSTALL. To remove blade spindle from mower deck, first separate mower from chassis as outlined in MOWER DECK paragraphs. Fit a scrap of wood under mower deck to prevent blade from turning, then remove locknut (1–Fig. JD11) at top of drive spindle. Use a carefully fitted puller and remove pulley (2).

NOTE: Sheaves are less likely to be crushed or distorted if a three-jaw gear puller is used. Remove Woodruff key (3) and pull spindle and blade down and out of hub/flange (6). Disassemble blade from spindle. Ball bearing (4) may be pulled or driven from hub/flange (6). However, note that snap ring (7) at bottom must be removed before lower bearing can be pulled or tapped from bearing bore.

IMPORTANT: Do not force, and use heat sparingly if its use becomes necessary.

Thoroughly clean all parts and renew any showing excessive wear or other damage. If hub flange has been removed from deck, torque bolts to 20-25 ft.-lbs. (34 N·m). Reassemble spindle and torque locknut (1) to 60-70 ft.-lbs. (81-95 N·m). Torque cap screw (11) to 80 ft.-lbs. (108 N·m).

MOWER DECK

Models 55-56-57

LEVEL ADJUSTMENT. Unit should be parked on a smooth, level surface such as a driveway or concrete garage floor. Tire pressures should be adjusted to specification shown in Operator's Manual for each particular model. Remove spark plug wire and disengage mower clutch. Set mower height control in lowest position, then measure height of blade tip above floor at four points, 90° apart, by rotating blade a quarter-turn for each measurement. All measurements should be equal within ⅛ inch (3.2 mm). Check of opposite end of blade will show if blade is bent, how much, and direction of bend. Damaged blade should be repaired or renewed.

For side-to-side leveling, loosen bolt (1–Fig. JD12) in right front draft link and tilt mower deck up or down laterally until blade is level; retighten adjuster.

To level deck from front-to-rear, remove cotter pin (2) at forward end of

Fig. JD12—View of mower deck level adjustment points typical for Models 55, 56 and 57. See text.
1. Draft arm adjuster bolt
2. Transfer rod

Fig. JD13—View of mower deck leveling points on Models 66 and 68. Refer to text for procedure.
A. Blade tip
B. Block for measurement
C. Lift link adjuster nuts

rod and rotate threaded end of rod inward to raise rear of mower deck or out to lower. Recheck level, reset cotter pin.

Models 66-68

LEVEL ADJUSTMENT. Check tires for proper inflation and park mower on level, smooth surface. Remove spark plug lead and disengage mower clutch. Lower mower height control lever, then rotate blade(s) by hand to point from side-to-side as shown in Fig. JD13. Then, measure height of each blade tip above surface. Make side-to-side adjustment by turning adjusting nuts (C–Fig. JD13) to raise or lower lift link on each side to equalize blade height.

To make front-to-rear adjustment, rotate mower blade to point straight ahead. Blade tip at rear should be ⅛ inch (3.2 mm) higher than in front. Adjust by turning nuts on draft rod (11–Fig. JD2) at each side of front axle.

Gage wheels should be set to just clear surface with mower at preferred cutting height.

Models R70-R72-R92-S80-S82-S92

LEVEL ADJUSTMENT. Check tires for proper inflation and park mower on level, smooth surface. Remove spark plug lead and disengage mower clutch. Lower mower height control lever, then rotate blade by hand so it points side-to-side. Raise seat shroud and turn adjustment nut on right lift link until blade ends are an equal distance from ground surface. Rotate blade by hand so it points straight ahead. Adjust both front attaching rods equally until front blade edge is ⅛-¼ inch (3.2-6.4 mm) higher than rear blade edge.

All Models

REMOVE AND INSTALL. Disconnect spark plug wire and place mower in lowest position. Pull spring pins and disconnect clutch rod and lift linkage. Unbolt rear hitch and slip blade drive belt off engine pulley. Remove lock pin from rear draft link. Disconnect lift helper spring on Models 66 and 68 only. On Models 55, 56 and 57, pull spring pins and disconnect front draft links at front axle. Remove mower deck from under chassis.

Reverse removal procedure to install mower. Adjust belt guide to ¹⁄₁₆-⅛ inch (1.6-3.2 mm) clearance from engine pulley.

John Deere

ELECTRICAL

Fig. JD14—Pictorial view of ignition and safety start circuits for Models 66 and 68 with manual start.

1. Engine terminal
2. Transmission terminal
3. Ignition switch/lock
4. Harness retainer (2)
5. Neutral-start switch
6. Wire loom bushing
7. Ignition interlock

All Models

Units are equipped with safety interlock starting systems to prevent starting engine with drives engaged. Refer to wiring diagrams JD14 through JD18.

Fig. JD15—Typical schematic for ignition and safety-start wiring for recoil-start Models 55, 56 and 57 in pre-1972 production.

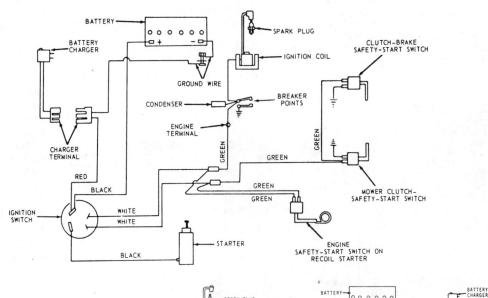

Fig. JD16—Typical schematic for ignition and safety-start systems for electric-start Models 56 and 57 in pre-1972 production.

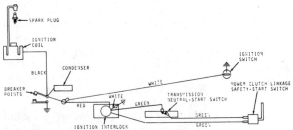

Fig. JD17—Typical schematic for ignition and safety-start wiring for recoil-start Models 56 (Ser. No. 44001 and after) and 57 (Ser. No. 14001 and after).

Fig. JD18—Typical schematic for ignition and safety-start systems for electric-start Models 56 (Ser. No. 44001 and after) and 57 (Ser. No. 14001 and after).

JOHN DEERE

Model	Make	Engine Model	Horsepower	Cutting Width, In.
RX63	Kawasaki	FA210V	6	26
RX73, RX75	Kawasaki	FC290V	9	30
RX95	Kawasaki	FB460V	12.5	30
SX75	Kawasaki	FC290V	9	30
SX95	Kawasaki	FB460V	12.5	38

FRONT WHEELS

All Models

The front wheels are equipped with renewable sealed bearings. No periodic lubrication is required.

Wheel (24—Fig. JD22) and bearings (23) may be removed after first removing hub cap (26) and retaining ring (25).

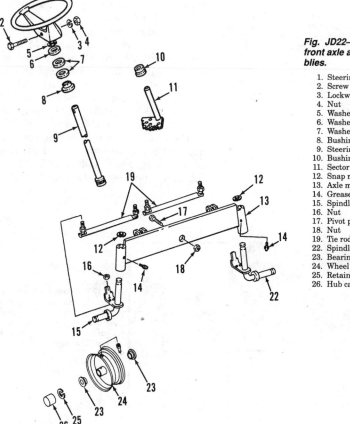

FRONT AXLE

All Models

LUBRICATION. The front wheel spindles should be lubricated after every 10 hours of operation. Apply grease to spindles through grease fitting (14—Fig. JD22) at each end of axle. One or two shots from a hand-held

Fig. JD22—Exploded view of front axle and steering assemblies.

1. Steering wheel
2. Screw
3. Lockwasher
4. Nut
5. Washer
6. Washer
7. Washer
8. Bushing
9. Steering shaft
10. Bushing
11. Sector gear
12. Snap ring
13. Axle main member
14. Grease fitting
15. Spindle (R.H.)
16. Nut
17. Pivot pin
18. Nut
19. Tie rod
22. Spindle (L.H.)
23. Bearings
24. Wheel
25. Retaining ring
26. Hub cap

grease gun should be sufficient. Use a good quality, multipurpose grease.

R&R AND OVERHAUL. To remove a front spindle, raise and support side to be serviced. Remove wheel and tire. Disconnect tie rod end. Detach snap ring (12—Fig. JD22) securing top of spindle and withdraw spindle from axle.

Check spindle for excessive wear and renew if necessary. Tighten tie rod retaining nut to 19-22 ft.-lbs. (26-30 N•m).

To remove axle main member, remove mower deck as outlined in MOWER DECK section. Remove the battery, then raise and support front of machine. Disconnect tie rod outer ends from spindles. Remove steering wheel and lower steering shaft and tie rod assembly from machine to gain clearance for removal of axle. Support the axle assembly. Unscrew pivot pin nut (18), withdraw pivot pin (17) and lower axle assembly from the machine.

Before assembly, lubricate pivot pin with multipurpose grease. Do not overtighten pivot pin nut (18) during assembly; axle must pivot freely.

STEERING SECTOR AND SHAFT

All Models

R&R AND OVERHAUL. Detach steering wheel by removing retaining bolt, then install a pin in steering shaft hole to hold shaft in position. Remove mower unit as outlined in MOWER DECK section. Remove battery, then raise and support front of machine. Disconnect tie rod (19—Fig. JD22) inner ends from steering sector (11). Remove pin at upper end of steering shaft and remove steering shaft (9) with steering sector (11).

Inspect components and renew if damaged or excessively worn. Reassem-

JD23) and belt should be 0.08-0.16 inch (2-4 mm). Clearance between belt guide (I) and belt should be 0.04 inch (1 mm).

VARIATOR AND DRIVE BELTS

All Models

All are equipped with a drive system that uses two drive belts and a variable diameter pulley (variator) to transfer power from the engine to the transaxle. The primary (lower) drive belt (20—Fig. JD27) connects the engine to the variator (23). The diameters of the variator pulley grooves are determined by primary belt tension. Primary belt tension changes according to pressure applied to the speed control lever. Moving the speed control lever forward increases primary belt tension and decreases the diameter of the lower pulley on the variator (23). When the lower variator pulley diameter decreases, the upper pulley diameter increases, thereby increasing ground speed. Moving the speed control lever rearward decreases primary belt tension and ground speed decreases. When the clutch pedal is in full up position, the primary belt idler (15) moves away from the belt and the drivetrain is in neutral. The secondary (upper) drive belt (2) connects the variator (23) to the transaxle pulley (1). A spring-loaded pulley (9) maintains secondary belt tension.

BELT GUIDES. The engine pulley belt guides must be positioned so there is a clearance of 0.08-0.16 inch (2-4 mm) between belt guide (G—Fig. JD23) and belt and a clearance of 0.04 inch (1 mm) between belt guide (I) and belt. Clearance between primary (lower) drive belt (20—Fig. JD28) and variator belt guide (28) should be 0.04-0.08 inch (1.0-2.0 mm).

ADJUSTMENT. Before performing belt adjustments, operate machine to warm belts. Operate machine in 7th speed, then depress clutch pedal and let the machine stop. Stop the engine, then release clutch pedal. Do not release clutch pedal until engine stops. Move speed control lever to 1st speed and note position of primary (lower) drive belt (20—Fig. JD28) in variator (23) groove. If belt is more than 1/8 inch (3.2 mm) from top of pulley, repeat procedure. Raise seat and loosen nut (N—Fig. JD29). Belt tension should relocate pivot arm, then retighten nut (N).

If reduced maximum ground speed is desired, move speed control lever to 2nd speed rather than 1st speed during procedure.

Clutch pedal pressure is increased if spring (S—Fig. JD30) end is attached to

hole (H) or reduced if attached to hole (L). Attaching spring end to hole (H) also decreases speed range.

Refer to TRANSAXLE section for adjustment of shift control lever.

R&R DRIVE BELTS. Primary Belt. To remove primary (lower) belt (20—Fig. JD31), disconnect spark plug wire and remove battery. Place shift lever in neutral position and mower deck in lowest position. Raise and support rear of machine. Loosen engine pul-

ley belt guides (G and I—Fig. JD32), then disconnect clutch spring (S). Loosen carriage bolt (29—Fig. JD31) that secures belt guide (28) and relocate guide. Remove mower belt from engine pulley, then remove primary drive belt from pulleys and withdraw past fixed idler (12) and transaxle pulley (1).

Install primary belt by reversing removal procedure. Adjust belt guides as previously outlined.

Fig. JD27—Drawing of drive system.

1. Transaxle pulley
2. Secondary belt
9. Secondary belt idler
12. Primary belt fixed idler
15. Primary belt idler
17. Engine pulley
20. Primary belt
23. Variator

Fig. JD28—Clearance between primary (lower) drive belt (20) and variator belt guide (28) should be 0.040-0.080 inch (1.0-2.0 mm).

Fig. JD29—Refer to text to adjust speed control linkage.

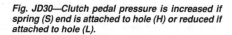

Fig. JD30—Clutch pedal pressure is increased if spring (S) end is attached to hole (H) or reduced if attached to hole (L).

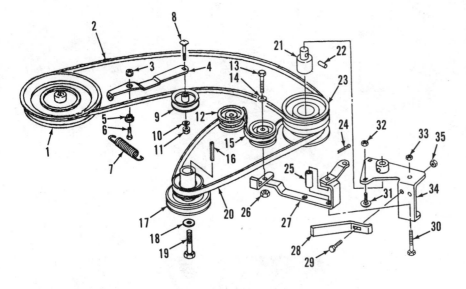

Fig. JD31—Exploded view of drive system.

1. Transaxle pulley	10. Washer	19. Bolt	27. Arm
2. Secondary belt	11. Nut	20. Primary belt	28. Belt guide
3. Nut	12. Primary belt fixed idler	21. Bearing assy.	29. Bolt
4. Idler arm	13. Bolt	22. Pin	30. Bolt
5. Bushing	14. Washer	23. Variator	31. Bolt
6. Bolt	15. Primary belt idler	24. Cotter pin	32. Nut
7. Spring	16. Key	25. Bushing	33. Nut
8. Bolt	17. Engine pulley	26. Nut	34. Bracket
9. Secondary belt idler	18. Washer		35. Nut

R&R AND OVERHAUL VARIATOR. The variator must be serviced as a unit assembly except for the bushing, which is available separately.

To remove variator, place shift lever in neutral position and mower deck in lowest position. Raise and support rear of machine. Remove bolt (30—Fig. JD28) and detach clutch arm (27). Remove primary (lower) belt from variator, then force secondary (upper) belt idler (9—Fig. JD34) against spring tension and remove the secondary belt from variator (23). Drive out pin (22—Fig. JD35) and remove variator.

To remove bushing in variator hub, force bushing towards top of variator. Install bushing so it bottoms against step in variator.

Install variator by reversing disassembly procedure.

GROUND DRIVE BRAKE

All Models

All models are equipped with a disc brake that is mounted on the transaxle.

Secondary Belt. To remove secondary (upper) belt (2—Fig. JD31), disconnect spark plug wire and remove battery. Place shift lever in neutral position and mower deck in lowest position. Raise and support rear of machine. Loosen engine pulley belt guides (G and I—Fig. JD32), then disconnect clutch spring (S). Loosen carriage bolt (29—Fig. JD31) that secures belt guide (28) and relocate guide. Remove primary (lower) and secondary (upper) belts from variator (23). Remove screw (S—Fig. JD33). Loosen transaxle retaining nut (N) and screws (W), move transaxle down slightly and remove secondary belt by passing over transaxle pulley.

Install secondary belt by reversing removal procedure. Adjust belt guides as previously outlined.

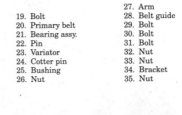

Fig. JD33—Unscrew nut (N), support screw (S) and outer screws (W) to lower or remove transaxle. See text.

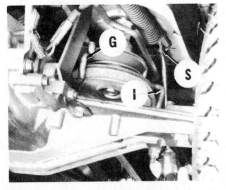

Fig. JD32—Belt guides (G and I) must be moved to remove belts from engine pulley. Refer to text for belt removal procedure.

Fig. JD34—To remove variator (23), remove primary (lower) belt from variator, then force secondary (upper) belt idler (9) against spring tension and remove the secondary belt from variator (23).

Fig. JD35—Drive out pin (22) before removing variator.

Refer to Fig. JD36 for view of brake operating components. No adjustment is required.

R&R AND OVERHAUL. Refer to Fig. JD36 and detach operating rod (23). Unscrew lever retaining nut (2—Fig. JD37) and unscrew caliper mounting screws (1). Disassemble brake components. Brake pad wear limit is ¼ inch (6.4 mm).

When assembling brake, coat transmission brake shaft with Lubriplate. Apply Lubriplate to ends of dowel pins (6) and rubbing surfaces of brake lever and washer (4). Tighten caliper screws (7) to 95 in.-lbs. (10.7 N•m).

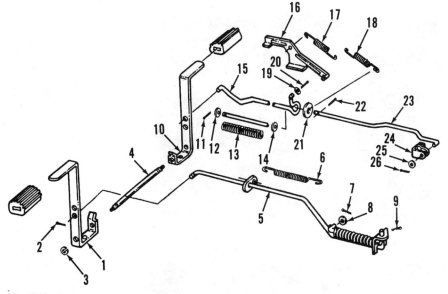

Fig. JD36—Exploded view of clutch and brake control linkage.

1. Clutch pedal
2. Cotter pin
3. Snap ring
4. Shaft
5. Clutch rod
6. Spring
7. Cotter pin
8. Washer
9. Cotter pin
10. Brake pedal
11. Cotter pin
12. Washer
13. Spring
14. Washer
15. Brake rod
16. Arm
17. Spring
18. Spring
19. Washer
20. Cotter pin
21. Washer
22. Cotter pin
23. Brake rod
24. Arm
25. Washer
26. Cotter pin

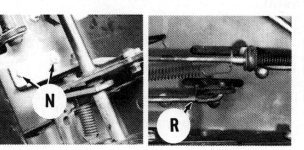

Fig. JD37—Exploded view of disc brake assembly.

1. Screw
2. Nut
3. Brace
4. Washer
5. Brake lever
6. Dowel pins
8. Caliper half
9. Plate
10. Brake pads
11. Brake disc

TRANSAXLE

All Models

ADJUSTMENT. To adjust shift linkage, engine must be stopped. Move shift control lever to any forward speed, raise seat and loosen nuts (N—Fig. JD38). Move shift rod (R) forward as far as possible and retighten nuts (N).

REMOVE AND REINSTALL. To remove transaxle, raise and support rear of machine, then remove rear wheels and secondary drive belt. Disconnect shift linkage, disconnect brake link and disconnect neutral switch wire from switch on transaxle. Detach rear and side transaxle mounts. Support transaxle then unscrew outer retaining screws (W—Fig. JD33). Lower transaxle away from machine towards rear so pulleys clear.

Install transaxle by reversing removal procedure.

OVERHAUL. All models are equipped with a Peerless transaxle. Refer to TRANSMISSION REPAIR section for service information.

MOWER CONTROL LINKAGE

All Models

ADJUSTMENT. All mower control linkage must be in good operating condition. With engine stopped and machine parked on level surface, place mower control in full forward position and place mower in "4" setting. Projections (P—Fig. JD39) should be pulled away from flange (F). Place mower control in full rearward position and place mower in "1" setting. Projections (P) should contact flange (F) and brake arm (A) should contact belt. To adjust mower control linkage, place mower control in full rearward position and place mower in "1" setting. Loosen nut (N—Fig. JD40) and push the rod (R—Fig. JD39) to front of slot (L), then retighten nut.

MOWER DECK

All Models

HEIGHT ADJUSTMENT. Position machine on a level surface, then disconnect spark plug wire. Measure distance from ground to blade from side to side. Maximum difference should be ⅛ inch

Fig. JD38—To adjust shift linkage, move shift control lever to any forward speed, raise seat and loosen nuts (N). Move shift rod (R) forward as far as possible and retighten nuts (N).

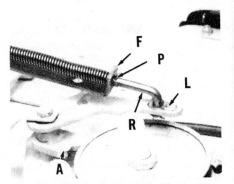

Fig. JD39—With mower control in disengaged position and mower in "1" setting, projections (P) should contact flange (F) and brake arm (A) should contact belt. Refer to text for adjustment.

A. Blade brake arm
F. Flange
P. Projections
R. Control rod
S. Slot

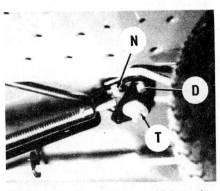

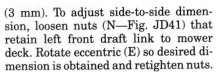

Fig. JD40—To adjust mower control linkage, place mower control in full rearward position and place mower in "1" setting. Loosen nut (N) and push the rod (R—Fig. JD39) to front of slot (L), then retighten nut.

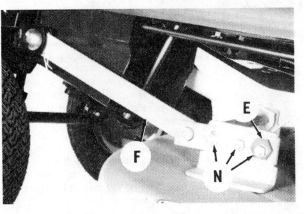

Fig. JD41—Refer to text for side-to-side blade adjustment procedure.

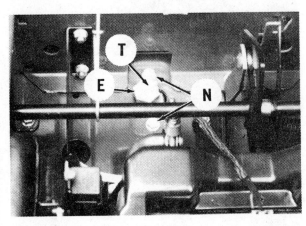

Fig. JD42—Refer to text for front-to-rear blade adjustment procedure.

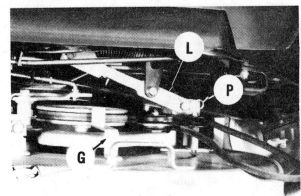

Fig. JD43—When removing mower deck, remove pin (P) and detach rear draft link (L). See text.

(3 mm). To adjust side-to-side dimension, loosen nuts (N—Fig. JD41) that retain left front draft link to mower deck. Rotate eccentric (E) so desired dimension is obtained and retighten nuts.

Measure distance from ground to blade from front to rear. Front of blade should be 0-¼ inch (0-6 mm) lower than rear of blade. To adjust front-to-rear dimension, first loosen nuts (N—Fig. JD42), then loosen nut (T) on eccentric (E). Rotate eccentric (E) so desired dimension is obtained and retighten nuts.

REMOVE AND REINSTALL. Move mower engagement lever to disengaged position. Loosen engine pulley belt guides (G and I—Fig. JD32), move guides and separate mower belt from engine pulley. On all models except SX95, loosen nut on mower idler. Remove pin (P—Fig. JD43) and separate rear draft link (L) from mower bracket. Remove nut (T—Fig. JD40) and detach rod (D). Detach front draft links (F—

Fig. JD41) from front axle main member and remove mower.

Reverse removal procedure to install mower deck. On later models, mower belt must be routed through "U" portion of engine belt guide as shown in Fig. JD26. Clearance between belt guide (G—Fig. JD23) and belt should be 0.080-0.160 inch (2-4 mm). Clearance between belt guide (I) and belt should be 0.040 inch (1 mm).

MOWER BELT

Model SX95

REMOVE AND REINSTALL. Remove mower deck as previously outlined. Remove belt shield. Loosen and relocate belt guides as necessary for belt removal, push back brake arms and remove belt.

Reverse removal procedure to install mower belt. After installing belt, push

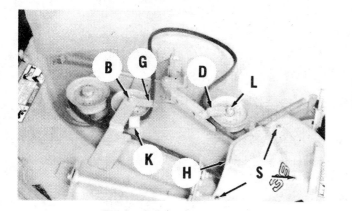

Fig. JD44—View of mower deck used on Model SX95.

B. Bolt
D. Belt Guide
G. Belt guide
H. Belt shield
K. Belt guide
L. Bolt
S. Screws

the belt guide (G—Fig. JD44) to the right so it fits in slot, then tighten bolt (B). Install mower deck.

All Other Models

REMOVE AND REINSTALL. Move mower engagement lever to disengaged position. Loosen engine pulley belt guides (G and I—Fig. JD32), move guides and separate mower belt from engine pulley. Remove pin (P—Fig. JD43) and separate rear draft link (L) from mower bracket. Loosen retaining nut and relocate belt guide (G). Move mower engagement lever to full forward position and remove belt.

Reverse removal procedure to install mower belt.

MOWER SPINDLE

Model SX95

LUBRICATION. Each mower spindle should be lubricated after every 10 hours of operation. Apply grease to mower spindles through grease fitting (9—Fig. JD45) in each spindle housing (7). One or two shots from a hand-held grease gun should be sufficient. Use a good quality, multipurpose grease.

R&R AND OVERHAUL. Remove mower deck and blade. Disengage belt from spindle pulley. Unscrew bolts securing spindle housing (7—Fig. JD45) and remove spindle assembly. Unscrew spindle nut (1) and disassemble spindle assembly components as needed. Inspect components for excessive wear and damage. When assembling spindle components, tighten spindle nut (1) to

103 ft.-lbs. (140 N·m). Tighten mower blade retaining screw to 55 ft.-lbs. (75 N·m).

All Other Models

LUBRICATION. Periodic lubrication of mower spindle is not required.

R&R AND OVERHAUL. Remove mower deck and blade. Disengage belt from spindle pulley. Unscrew pulley retaining nut (1—Fig. JD46) and remove pulley (2). Unscrew bolts securing plate (8) and spindle housing (7) and remove spindle assembly. Disassemble spindle assembly components as needed. Spin-

dle and bearings must be pressed out of housing. Inspect components for excessive wear and damage. During assembly fill spindle housing a little over half full with multipurpose grease. Press upper bearing (5) in until flush with top of spindle housing (7). Install inner snap ring (9) and spacer (5) and press lower bearing (10) in until bottomed against spacer. Install outer snap ring (9) and press spindle into bearings until bottoms. Install spindle assembly and tighten housing mounting bolts to 222 in.-lbs. (25 N·m). Tighten spindle nut (1) to 103 ft.-lbs. (140 N·m). Tighten mower blade retaining screw to 55 ft.-lbs. (75 N·m).

ELECTRICAL

All Models

Refer to Figs. JD47, JD48 and JD49 for wiring schematics. Note the following points:

• The transmission must be in neutral, the mower must be disengaged and the operator must be in the seat for engine to start.
• The engine should stop if the transmission is in gear or the mower is engaged and the operator leaves the seat.

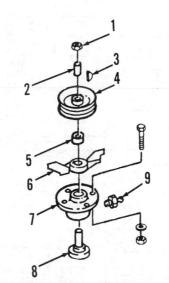

Fig. JD45—Exploded view of mower spindle assembly used on Model SX95.

1. Nut
2. Spacer
3. Key
4. Pulley
5. Bearing
6. Fan
7. Housing
8. Blade adapter
9. Grease fitting

Fig. JD46—Exploded view of mower spindle assembly used on all models except SX95.

1. Nut
2. Pulley
3. Spacer
4. Key
5. Bearing
6. Spacer
7. Housing
8. Plate
9. Snap ring
10. Bearing
11. Blade adapter

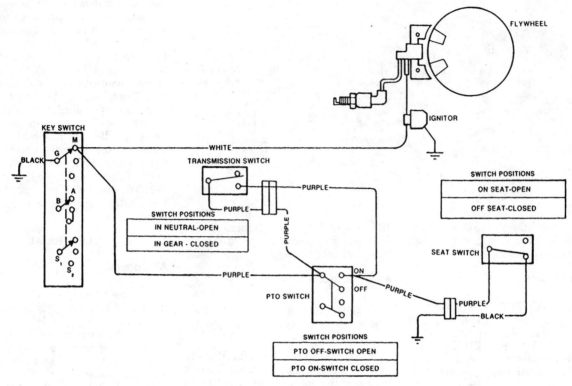

Fig. JD47—Wiring schematic for Models RX63 and RX73.

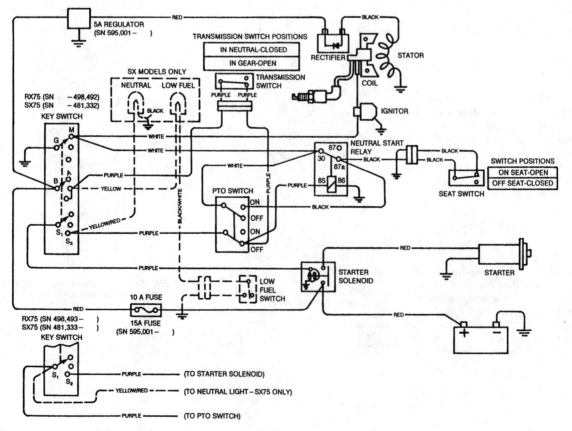

Fig. JD48—Wiring schematic for Models RX75 and SX75.

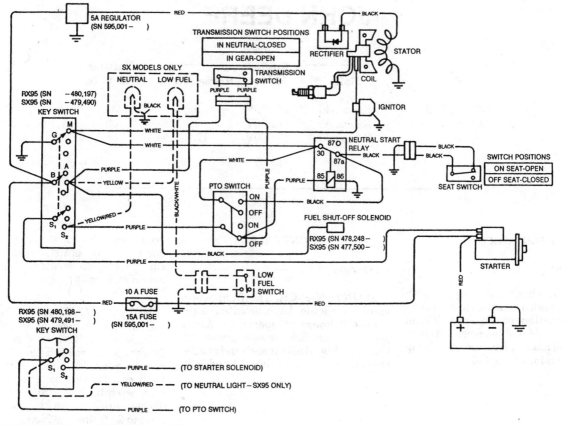

Fig. JD49—Wiring schematic for Models RX95 and SX95.

JOHN DEERE

Model	Make	Engine Model	Horsepower	Cutting Width, In.
GX70, GX75	Kawasaki	FC290V	9	30
SRX75	Kawasaki	FC290V	9	30
SRX95	Kawasaki	FB460V	12.5	38

FRONT WHEELS

All Models

The front wheels are equipped with renewable sealed bearings and no periodic lubrication is required. Wheel (24—Fig. JD60) and bearings (23) may be removed after first removing hub cap (26) and retaining ring (25).

FRONT AXLE

All Models

MAINTENANCE. The front wheel spindles should be lubricated after every 10 hours of operation. Apply grease to spindles through grease fitting (14—Fig. JD60) at each end of axle. One or two shots from a hand-held grease gun should be sufficient. Use a good quality, multipurpose grease. Check for looseness and binding in front axle components.

R&R AND OVERHAUL. To remove a front spindle, raise and support side to be serviced. Remove wheel and tire. Disconnect tie rod end (20—Fig. JD60), and if needed, drag link end (19). Detach snap ring (12) securing top of spindle and withdraw spindle from axle. Tighten drag link and tie rod retaining nuts to 22 ft.-lbs. (30 N•m).

To remove axle main member (13), remove mower deck as outlined in MOWER DECK section, then raise and support front of machine. Disconnect drag link end (19) from steering sector arm (11). Using a suitable jack, support axle assembly. Unscrew pivot pin nut (18), withdraw pivot pin (17) and lower the axle assembly from the machine.

Before assembly, lubricate pivot pin with multipurpose grease. Do not overtighten pivot pin nut (18) during assembly; axle must pivot freely.

STEERING SECTOR AND SHAFT

All Models

R&R AND OVERHAUL. Detach steering wheel by removing retaining bolt, then install a pin in steering shaft hole to hold shaft in position. Remove mower as outlined in MOWER DECK section. Raise and support front of machine. Remove tie rod (20—Fig. JD60) and disconnect drag link (19) from steering sector arm (11). Remove pin at upper end of steering shaft and remove steering shaft (9) with steering sector (11).

Inspect components and renew if damaged or excessively worn. Reassemble steering components by reversing disassembly procedure. Tighten drag link and tie rod retaining nuts to 22 ft.-lbs. (30 N•m).

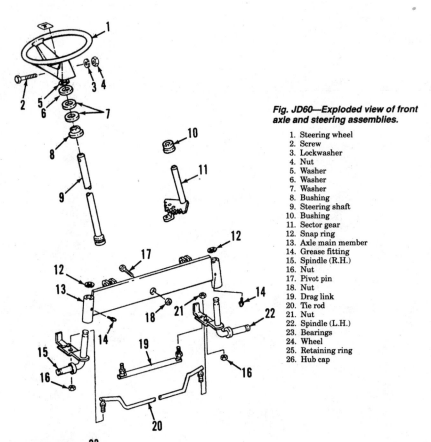

Fig. JD60—Exploded view of front axle and steering assemblies.

1. Steering wheel
2. Screw
3. Lockwasher
4. Nut
5. Washer
6. Washer
7. Washer
8. Bushing
9. Steering shaft
10. Bushing
11. Sector gear
12. Snap ring
13. Axle main member
14. Grease fitting
15. Spindle (R.H.)
16. Nut
17. Pivot pin
18. Nut
19. Drag link
20. Tie rod
21. Nut
22. Spindle (L.H.)
23. Bearings
24. Wheel
25. Retaining ring
26. Hub cap

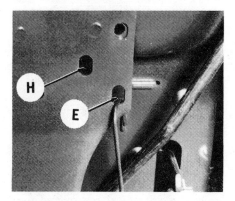

Fig. JD61—On Model GX70 and GX75, increase spring tension on the clutch pulley by relocating the spring end (E) to outermost hole (H).

ENGINE

Model SRX95

Refer to appropriate engine section in this manual for tune-up specifications, engine overhaul procedures and engine maintenance.

REMOVE AND REINSTALL. To remove engine, remove transaxle as outlined in TRANSAXLE section. Lift up seat and remove right-side control panel. Unscrew engine shroud mounting nuts so shroud can be moved to allow removal of seat pivot rod, then remove rod and seat. Detach throttle and mower control knobs. Push shift lever and mower control lever forward. Close fuel valve and detach fuel hose from valve. Unscrew any remaining engine shroud mounting nuts and remove engine shroud and fuel tank. Remove muffler heat shield and muffler. Disconnect throttle cable. Disconnect fuel solenoid wire and disconnect fuel line. Disconnect wires leading to engine. Remove screws securing engine. Remove engine.

To reinstall engine, reverse disassembly procedure. If engine pulley was removed, apply antiseize compound to crankshaft before installing pulley. Tighten pulley retaining screw to 54 ft.-lbs. (73 N•m). Tighten engine mounting screws to 80 in.-lbs. (9 N•m).

All Other Models

Refer to appropriate engine section in this manual for tune-up specifications, engine overhaul procedures and engine maintenance.

REMOVE AND REINSTALL. To remove engine, remove transaxle as outlined in TRANSAXLE section. Remove engine shroud on Model SRX75 using procedure outlined in engine removal section for Model SRX95. Close fuel valve and disconnect fuel line. Remove muffler heat shield. Disconnect throttle cable. Unscrew nut and screws securing engine. Move engine for access to red wire and white wire and disconnect wires. If equipped with electric starter, disconnect starter cable. Remove engine.

To reinstall engine, reverse disassembly procedure. If engine pulley was removed, apply antiseize compound to crankshaft before installing pulley. Tighten pulley retaining screw to 54 ft.-lbs. (73 N•m). Tighten engine mounting screws and nut to 80 in.-lbs. (9 N•m).

TRACTION DRIVE CLUTCH AND DRIVE BELT

Models GX70 And GX75

The traction drive clutch is a spring-tensioned, belt idler-type operated by the clutch pedal. When the clutch pedal is depressed, belt tension is removed, allowing the engine drive pulley to rotate freely within drive belt. When the brake pedal is depressed, the clutch pedal is also actuated so the drivetrain is disengaged when the brake is operated. Spring tension on the clutch pulley may be increased by relocating the spring end (E—Fig. JD61) to outermost hole (H). No other adjustment is available. If belt is worn or stretched so slippage occurs, belt must be renewed.

R&R DRIVE BELT. To remove drive belt, disconnect spark plug wire and, if so equipped, remove battery. Place shift lever in neutral position and mower deck in lowest position. Raise and support rear of machine. Loosen nuts securing transaxle and remove belt guide on transaxle and remove mower belt from engine pulley. Disconnect spring (7—Fig. JD62), remove belt guide (27) and loosen idler pulley retaining nut (19). Remove drive belt.

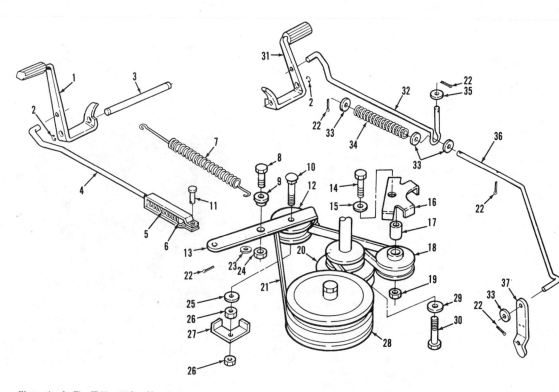

Fig. JD62—Exploded view of traction drive, brake and control components used on Models GX70 and GX75.

1. Clutch pedal
2. Snap ring
3. Shaft
4. Clutch rod
5. Spring
6. Washer
7. Spring
8. Bolt
9. Bushing
10. Spindle bolt
11. Clevis pin
12. Tension pulley
13. Clutch lever
14. Bolt
15. Washer
16. Belt guide
17. Spacer
18. Idler
19. Nut
20. Engine pulley
21. Belt
22. Cotter pin
23. Washer
24. Nut
25. Washer
26. Nut
27. Belt guide
28. Transaxle pulley
29. Washer
30. Screw
31. Brake pedal
32. Brake rod
33. Washer
34. Spring
35. Washer
36. Brake rod
37. Brake lever

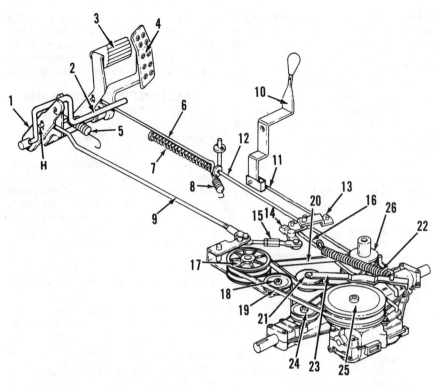

Fig. JD63—Drawing of drive system and control mechanism used on Models SRX75 and SRX95.

1. Speed control lever			20. Primary belt
2. Brake interlock rod	8. Spring	14. Interlock	21. Secondary belt idler
3. Brake pedal	9. Speed control rod	15. Adjuster	22. Spring
4. Speed control pedal	10. Shift control lever	16. Shift rod	23. Secondary belt idler arm
5. Spring	11. Shift rod	17. Variator	24. Primary belt fixed idler
6. Brake rod	12. Brake rod	18. Primary belt idler	25. Transaxle pulley
7. Spring	13. Shift lever	19. Secondary belt	26. Engine pulley

Reverse removal procedure to install drive belt. Tighten transaxle retaining nuts to 80 in.-lbs. (9 N•m). Belt guide (16) should be positioned so it does not interfere with belt. Install belt guide (27) so it contacts clutch arm (13) near pivot screw (8).

VARIATOR AND DRIVE BELTS

Models SRX75 And SRX95

Models SRX75 and SRX95 are equipped with a drive system that uses two drive belts and a variable diameter pulley (variator) to transfer power from the engine to the transaxle. The primary (lower) drive belt (20—Fig. JD63) connects the engine to the variator (17). The diameters of the variator pulley grooves are determined by primary belt tension. Primary belt tension changes according to pressure applied to the speed control pedal (4). Depressing the pedal increases primary belt tension and decreases the diameter of the lower pulley on the variator (17). When the lower variator pulley diameter decreases, the upper pulley diameter increases, thereby increasing ground speed. Releasing the pedal decreases primary belt tension and ground speed

decreases. When the pedal is in full up position, the primary belt idler (18) moves away from the belt and the drivetrain is in neutral. The secondary (upper) drive belt (19) connects the variator (17) to the transaxle pulley (25). A spring-loaded pulley (21) maintains secondary belt tension.

An interlock (14) prevents depression of the speed control pedal when the transaxle is in neutral or movement of the gear shift lever when the pedal is depressed.

BELT GUIDES. The belt guides must be positioned so there is a clearance of 0.064-0.128 inch (1.63-3.25 mm) at engine pulley and 0.04-0.08 inch (1.0-2.0 mm) at variator.

ADJUSTMENT. To adjust drive mechanism, proceed as follows: Speed control pedal must be in full up position. Engage park brake. Loosen locknut on adjuster (15—Fig. JD63) and rotate adjuster so clearance between interlock (14) and lever (13) is ¼ inch (6.4 mm). Detach pin from front end of control rod (9) and detach rod end from arm (1). Rotate rod (9) so primary belt idler (18) just touches belt, but variator is not loaded, and insert rod end in upper hole

on arm (1). Install pin in rod end. Move rear of interlock (14) towards engine pulley so play in linkage is removed, then turn adjuster so clearance between interlock (14) and lever (13) is 0.030-0.060 inch (0.76-1.52 mm). Retighten locknut on adjuster.

Control rod (9) should be adjusted to a slightly longer length if the machine does not stop moving when the speed control pedal is released, if drive is jerky when engaged, or if operator desires a slower maximum ground speed. If operator desires a faster maximum ground speed, adjust control rod to a slightly longer length, but be sure machine will stop when speed control pedal is released.

Additional adjustment is possible by relocating the position of primary belt idler arm. Prior to adjustment, move shift lever to forward position and measure distance (D—Fig. JD64) between bottom of speed control pedal and opening in floor. Depress pedal so free play is just removed. If distance (D) is not at least 1½ inches (38 mm), this adjustment procedure must not be performed as there is not sufficient free play in components. To perform adjustment, remove screw (S—Fig. JD65) and loosen screw (W). Push idler (I) toward belt (B) and reinstall screw in hole (H). Tighten screws and check operation. If machine does not stop when speed control pedal is released, return screw and arm to original positions.

Speed control pedal pressure may be reduced and maximum ground speed may be reduced if control rod (9—Fig. JD63) is inserted in lower hole (H) in arm (1).

R&R DRIVE BELTS. Primary Belt. To remove primary (lower) belt, disconnect spark plug wire and remove battery. Place shift lever in neutral position and mower deck in lowest posi-

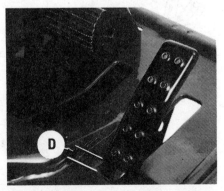

Fig. JD64—Depress speed control pedal on Models SRX75 and SRX95 so pedal free play is just removed. If distance (D) between bottom of speed control pedal and opening in floor is more than 1-1/2 inches (38 mm), adjust drive mechanism as outlined in text.

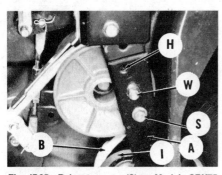

Fig. JD65—Relocate screw (S) on Models SRX75 and SRX95 to adjust drive mechanism as outlined in text.

A. Arm	M. Arm
B. Primary belt	R. Screw
H. Hole	S. Screw
I. Idler	W. Screw

tion. Raise and support rear of machine. Loosen innermost belt guide and remove outermost belt guide adjacent to engine pulley. Detach secondary (upper) belt idler spring (22—Fig. JD63). Remove mower drive belt from engine pulley. Loosen retaining nut for belt guide at variator (17) and push back belt guide. Loosen retaining nut on bottom of transaxle that secures fixed idler (24). Remove belt.

Install primary belt by reversing removal procedure. Adjust belt guides as previously outlined.

Secondary Belt. The primary (lower) belt must be removed as outlined in previous section before removing secondary (upper) belt. Loosen, but do not totally unscrew, four nuts (N—Fig. JD66) that retain transaxle so belt can pass over transaxle pulley. Remove belt.

Install secondary belt by reversing removal procedure. Tighten transaxle retaining nuts to 80 in.-lbs. (9 N•m).

R&R AND OVERHAUL VARIATOR. The variator must be serviced as a unit assembly except for the bushing, which is available separately.

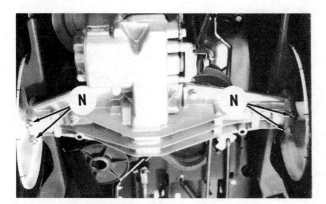

Fig. JD67—Drive out pin (P) before removing variator.

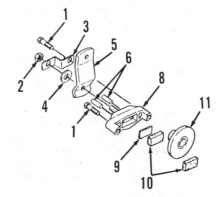

Fig. JD68—Exploded view of disc brake assembly used on Models SRX75 and SRX95.

1. Screw	6. Dowel pins
2. Nut	8. Caliper half
3. Brace	9. Plate
4. Washer	10. Brake pads
5. Brake lever	11. Brake disc

To remove variator, disconnect spark plug wire and remove battery. Place shift lever in neutral position and mower deck in lowest position. Raise and support rear of machine. Disconnect links from variator arm (M—Fig. JD65). Unscrew idler arm screw (R) and move arm away from variator bracket, then remove primary (lower) belt from

Fig. JD66—Tighten transaxle outer retaining nuts (N) on all models to 80 in.-lbs. (9 N•m).

variator. Move spring-loaded secondary (upper) belt idler back and remove secondary belt from variator. Drive out pin (P—Fig. JD67) and remove variator.

To remove bushing in variator hub, force bushing toward top of variator. Install bushing so it bottoms against step in variator.

Install variator by reversing disassembly procedure.

GROUND DRIVE BRAKE

All Models

All models are equipped with a disc brake that is mounted on the transaxle. Refer to Figs. JD62 and JD63 for views of brake operating components. No adjustment is required.

R&R AND OVERHAUL. Models GX70 And GX75. The transaxle must be disassembled for access to the brake on Models GX70 and GX75. Refer to TRANSMISSION REPAIR section for service information.

Models SRX75 And SRX95. Refer to Fig. JD68 and detach operating rod. Unscrew lever retaining nut (2) and unscrew caliper mounting screws (1). Disassemble brake components. Brake pad wear limit is 1/4 inch (6.4 mm).

When assembling brake, coat transmission brake shaft with Lubriplate. Apply Lubriplate to ends of dowel pins (6) and rubbing surfaces of brake lever and washer (4). Tighten caliper screws (7) to 95 in.-lbs. (10.7 N•m).

TRANSAXLE

Models GX70 And GX75

LUBRICATION. The outer ends of the transaxle are equipped with grease fittings (G—Fig. JD69) that should be injected with grease after every 25 hours of operation. One or two shots from a hand-held grease gun should be sufficient. Use a good quality, multipurpose grease. Refer to TRANSMISSION REPAIR section for internal lubrication information.

NEUTRAL ADJUSTMENT. The shift linkage should be adjusted so neutral positions in transaxle and at shift lever are synchronized. Raise and support rear of machine. Move shift lever so transaxle is in neutral, then loosen locknut (N—Fig. JD70) and rotate adjuster (A) so shift lever is aligned with neutral mark on shift control panel. Retighten locknut and check adjustment.

Fig. JD69—The transaxle on Models GX70 and GX75 is equipped with grease fittings (G) at outer ends.

Fig. JD70—On Model GX70 and GX75, loosen locknut (N) and rotate adjuster (A) to synchronize shift control lever and marks on control panel.

REMOVE AND REINSTALL. To remove transaxle, raise and support rear of machine, then remove rear wheels and drive belt. Disconnect shift linkage, disconnect brake link, detach wiring harness clamp and disconnect neutral switch wire from switch on transaxle. Detach upper transaxle mount. Support transaxle, then unscrew outer retaining nuts (N—Fig. JD66). Lower transaxle away from machine toward rear so pulleys clear.

Install transaxle by reversing removal procedure. Tighten transaxle retaining nuts to 80 in.-lbs. (9 N•m).

OVERHAUL. Models GX70 and GX75 are equipped with a Peerless transaxle. Refer to TRANSMISSION REPAIR section for service information.

Models SRX75 And SRX95

ADJUSTMENT. No adjustment is required, however, if faulty shifting is encountered, inspect shift linkage for excessive wear and damage.

The drive system uses an interlock (14—Fig. JD63) that prevents depression of the speed control pedal when the transaxle is in neutral or movement of

the gear shift lever when the pedal is depressed. Clearance between the interlock and shift lever (13) should be adjusted as outlined in VARIATOR AND DRIVE BELTS section.

REMOVE AND REINSTALL. To remove transaxle, raise and support rear of machine, then remove rear wheels and drive belts. Disconnect shift linkage, disconnect brake link and disconnect neutral switch wire from switch on transaxle. Detach rear and side transaxle mounts. Support transaxle then unscrew outer retaining nuts (N—Fig.

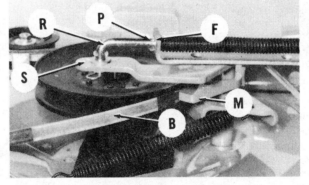

Fig. JD71—With mower control in disengaged position on Models GX70 and GX75, control rod (R) should not contact either end of slot (L) and brake arm (M) should contact mower belt. Refer to text for adjustment.

B. Belt
F. Flange
M. Blade brake arm
P. Projections
R. Control rod
S. Slot

JD66). Lower transaxle away from machine toward rear so pulleys clear.

Install transaxle by reversing removal procedure. Tighten transaxle retaining nuts to 80 in.-lbs. (9 N•m).

OVERHAUL. Models SRX75 and SRX95 are equipped with a Peerless transaxle. Refer to TRANSMISSION REPAIR section for service information.

MOWER CONTROL LINKAGE

All Models

ADJUSTMENT. All mower control linkage must be in good operating condition. With engine stopped and machine parked on level surface, place mower in lowest position. With mower control in disengaged position, control rod (R—Fig. JD71 or JD72) should not contact either end of slot (S), and brake arm (M) should contact mower belt. With mower control in engaged position, flange (F) on Models GX70, GX75 and SRX75 should be pulled away from projections (P) on rod, and brake arm (M) should not contact belt. On Model SRX95, bend (D) in rod should be pulled away from flange (F), and brake arm (M) should not contact belt. Place

Fig. JD72—With mower control in disengaged position on Models SRX75 and SRX95, control rod (R) should not contact either end of slot (L) and brake arm (M) should contact mower belt. Refer to text for adjustment.

B. Belt
D. Bend in rod
M. Blade brake arm
R. Control rod
S. Slot

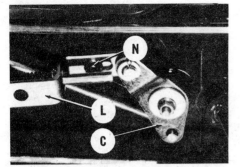

Fig. JD73—To adjust mower control mechanism, loosen nut (N) and relocate link (L).

against belt to remove belt slack. When blades are not engaged, spring-loaded blade brake arms (4) contact belt to prevent blade rotation. The control mechanism pushes the brake arms away from the belt when blade rotation is selected.

HEIGHT ADJUSTMENT. Position machine on a level surface, then disconnect spark plug wire. Measure distance from ground to blades from side to side. Maximum difference should be 1/8 inch (3.2 mm). To adjust side-to-side dimension, loosen front (F—Fig. JD75) and rear (R) nuts that retain left front draft

Fig. JD74—Drawing showing location of mower deck components on Model SRX95.

1. Drive pulleys
2. Pulley spindles
3. Fixed idler
4. Blade brake arm
5. Spring
6. Belt
7. Engine pulley
8. Brake rods
9. Engagement lever
10. Belt tension pulley
11. Blade
12. Mower deck
13. Front draft link
14. Bracket

REMOVE AND REINSTALL. Move mower engagement lever to full rear position. Place mower in highest position. Loosen nut (N—Fig. JD77) and move belt guide (G) away from engine pulley. Unscrew nut (T) and remove belt guide (D). Separate belt from engine pulley. Place mower in lowest position, then remove pin (P—Fig. JD78) and separate rear draft link (L) from mower bracket. Remove pin (N) and detach rod (R). Detach front draft links (13—Fig. JD74) from front axle main member (13—Fig. JD60) and remove mower from left side of machine.

Reverse removal procedure to install mower deck. The engine pulley belt guides must be positioned so there is a clearance of 0.064-0.128 inch (1.63-3.25 mm).

All Other Models

Refer to Fig. JD79 for drawing of mower deck components. The blade rotates when actuation of the mower control lever forces belt tension pulley (10) against belt to remove belt slack. When blade is not engaged, spring-loaded blade brake arm (4) contacts belt to prevent blade rotation. The control mechanism pushes the brake arm away from the belt when blade rotation is selected.

mower in highest position and repeat checking procedure. If components are out-of-position, loosen nut (N—Fig. JD73) and relocate link (L) as needed. Retighten nut and recheck adjustment.

MOWER DECK

Model SRX95

Refer to Fig. JD74 for drawing of mower deck components. The blades rotate when actuation of the mower control lever forces belt tension pulley (10)

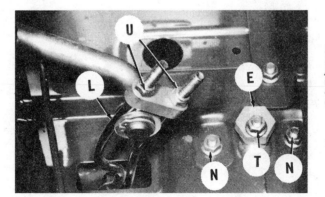

Fig. JD76—Refer to text for front-to-rear blade adjustment procedure. Additional adjustment is available by turning nuts (U) on lift link (L).

Fig. JD75—Refer to text for side-to-side blade adjustment procedure. Do not loosen center nut (M).

link to mower deck; do not loosen middle nut (M). Rotate eccentric (E) so desired dimension is obtained. Retighten front nut (F) first and then retighten rear nut (R).

Measure distance from ground to blades from front to rear. Front of blades should be 1/8-3/8 inch (3.2-9.5 mm) lower than rear of blades. To adjust front-to-rear dimension, loosen nuts (N—Fig. JD76) then loosen nut (T) on eccentric (E). Rotate eccentric (E) so desired dimension is obtained and retighten nuts. Additional height adjustment is available by turning nuts (U) on lift link (L).

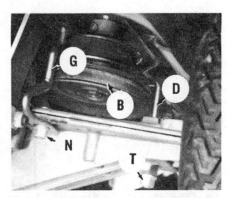

Fig. JD77—Refer to text to disengage belts from engine pulley.

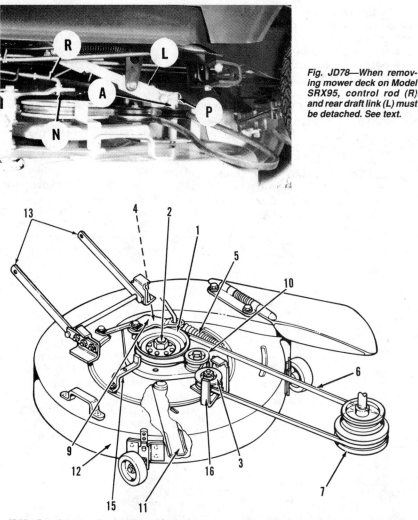

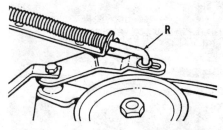

Fig. JD78—When removing mower deck on Model SRX95, control rod (R) and rear draft link (L) must be detached. See text.

Fig. JD81—When removing mower deck on Models GX70, GX75 and SRX75, detach control rod (R). See text.

MOWER BELT

Model SRX95

REMOVE AND REINSTALL. Remove mower deck as previously outlined. Remove belt shield. Loosen spindle nut or bolt on idler (3—Fig. JD74) and tension pulley (10) to reposition belt guides, push back brake arms (4) and remove belt.

Reverse removal procedure to install mower belt. Note belt routing in Fig. JD74. Push belt guide on tension pulley (10) against bracket (14) after installing belt. After installing belt and positioning belt guides, tighten spindle nut or bolt on idler (3) and tension pulley (10). Install mower deck.

All Other Models

REMOVE AND REINSTALL. Remove mower deck as previously outlined. Loosen spindle nut on idler (3—Fig. JD79) and move belt guide (16) away from belt. Loosen retaining screw of front belt guide (15) and move guide. Push back brake arm (4) and remove belt.

Reverse removal procedure to install mower belt. Position belt guides (15 and 16) 1/16 inch (1.6 mm) from belt and tighten fasteners. Install mower deck.

MOWER SPINDLE

Model SRX95

LUBRICATION. Each mower spindle should be lubricated after every 10 hours of operation. Apply grease to mower spindles through grease fitting (9—Fig. JD82) in each spindle housing (7). One or two shots from a hand-held grease gun should be sufficient. Use a good quality, multipurpose grease.

R&R AND OVERHAUL. Remove mower deck and blade. Disengage belt from spindle pulley. Unscrew bolts securing spindle housing (7—Fig. JD82) and remove spindle assembly. Unscrew

Fig. JD79—Drawing showing location of mower deck components on Models GX70, GX75 and SRX75. Refer to Fig. JD74 for parts identification except for: 15 and 16. Belt guides.

HEIGHT ADJUSTMENT. Follow procedure previously outlined for Model SRX95.

REMOVE AND REINSTALL. Move mower engagement lever to full rear position. Place mower in highest position. Loosen nut (N—Fig. JD77) and move belt guide (G) away from engine pulley. Unscrew nut (T) and remove belt guide (D). Separate belt from engine pulley. Place mower in lowest position, then remove pin (P—Fig. JD80) and separate rear draft link (L) from mower bracket. Remove pin and detach rod (R—Fig. JD81). Detach front draft links (13—Fig. JD79) from front axle main member (13—Fig. JD60) and remove mower from left side of machine.

Reverse removal procedure to install mower deck. The engine pulley belt guides must be positioned so there is a clearance of 0.064-0.128 inch (1.63-3.25 mm).

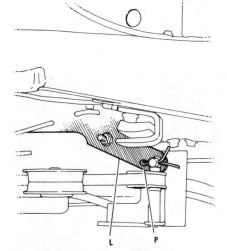

Fig. JD80—When removing mower deck on Models GX70, GX75 and SRX75, remove pin (P) and detach rear draft link (L). See text.

Illustrations for Fig. JD78, Fig. JD79, Fig. JD80 & Fig. JD81 reproduced by permission of Deere & Company. Copyright Deere & Company.

spindle nut (1) and disassemble spindle assembly components as needed. Inspect components for excessive wear and damage. When assembling spindle components, tighten spindle nut (1) to 103 ft.-lbs. (140 N•m). Tighten mower blade retaining screw to 55 ft.-lbs. (75 N•m).

All Other Models

LUBRICATION. Periodic lubrication of mower spindle is not required.

R&R AND OVERHAUL. Remove mower deck and blade. Disengage belt from spindle pulley. Unscrew pulley retaining nut (1—Fig. JD83) and remove

pulley (2). Unscrew bolts securing plate (8) and spindle housing (7) and remove spindle assembly. Disassemble spindle assembly components as needed. Spindle and bearings must be pressed out of housing. Inspect components for excessive wear and damage. During assembly fill spindle housing a little over half full with multipurpose grease. Press upper bearing (5) in until flush with top of spindle housing (7). Install inner snap ring (9) and spacer (5) and press lower bearing (10) in until bottomed against spacer. Install outer snap ring (9) and press spindle into bearings until it bottoms. Install spindle assembly and tighten housing mounting bolts to 222 in.-lbs. (25 N•m). Tighten spindle nut (1) to 103 ft.-lbs. (140 N•m). Tighten mower blade retaining screw to 55 ft.-lbs. (75 N•m).

ELECTRICAL

All Models

Refer to Figs. JD84, JD85 and JD86 for wiring schematics. Note the following points:

- The transmission must be in neutral, the mower must be disengaged and the operator must be in the seat for engine to start.
- The engine should stop if the transmission is in gear or the mower is engaged and the operator leaves the seat.
- Model SRX95 is equipped with a fuel shutoff solenoid that is closed if operator is not in seat.

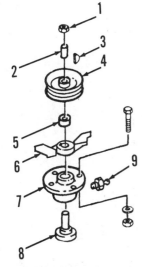

Fig. JD82—Exploded view of mower spindle assembly used on Model SRX95.

1. Nut
2. Spacer
3. Key
4. Pulley
5. Bearing
6. Fan
7. Housing
8. Blade adapter
9. Grease fitting

Fig. JD83—Exploded view of mower spindle assembly used on Models GX70, GX75 and SRX75.

1. Nut
2. Pulley
3. Spacer
4. Key
5. Bearing
6. Spacer
7. Housing
8. Plate
9. Snap ring
10. Bearing
11. Blade adapter

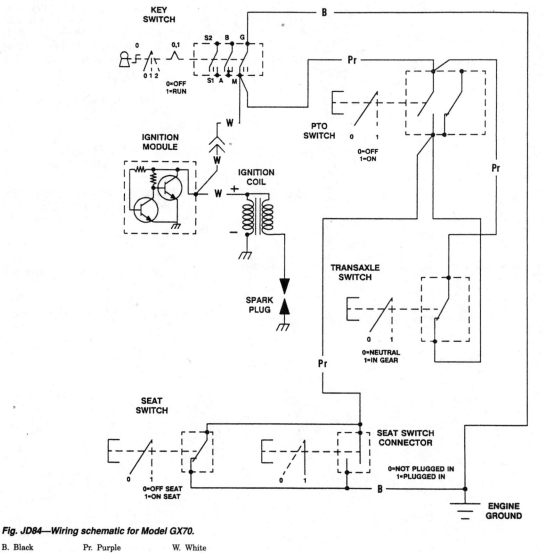

Fig. JD84—Wiring schematic for Model GX70.

B. Black   Pr. Purple   W. White

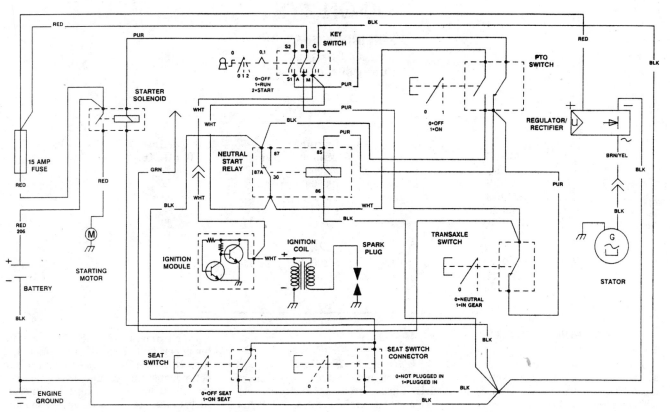

Fig. JD85—Wiring schematic for Models GX75 and SRX75.

Blk. Black   Grn. Green   Pur. Purple   Wht. White

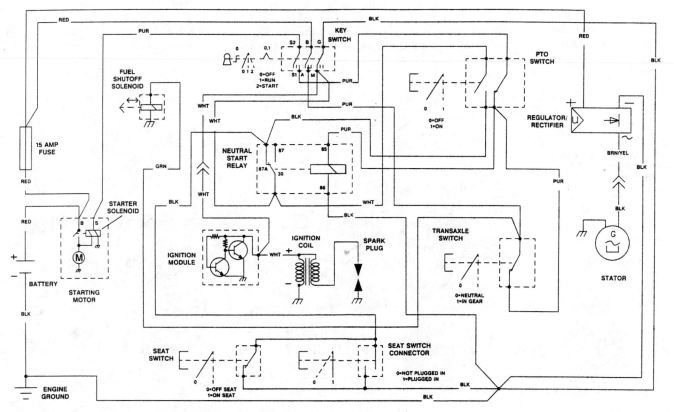

Fig. JD86—Wiring schematic for Model SRX95. Refer to Fig. JD85 for wire color code.

DIXON ZTR

DIXON INDUSTRIES, INC.
P.O. Box 1569
Coffeyville, KS 67337

Model	Make	Engine Model	Horsepower	Cutting Width, In.
ZTR-1	B&S	190000*	8	42
ZTR-2	B&S	190000*	8	42
ZTR-3	B&S	190000	8	42
ZTR-308	B&S	190000*	8	30
ZTR-311	B&S	250000*	11	30
ZTR-424	B&S	250000*	11	42
ZTR-425	B&S	250000*	11	42
ZTR-426	B&S	250000*	11	42
ZTR-427	Kawasaki	FB460V	12.5	42

*Synchrobalanced

STEERING SYSTEM

These units do not have a conventional front axle or steering system; instead, heavy-duty, rubber-tired caster wheels mounted on front corners of frame respond to steering effort of mower transaxle by swivel action in desired direction of turn. See TRANSAXLE section for details of steering adjustment and control.

ENGINE

Refer to appropriate engine section in this manual for tune-up specifications, engine overhaul procedures and engine maintenance.

All Models

REMOVE AND REINSTALL. To remove engine, first disengage mower drive then disconnect throttle control cable which extends from throttle hand control at right front of operator's seat and separate bowden cable from engine at carburetor.

On electric start models, disconnect battery ground cable and cable from starter solenoid to starter motor. Disconnect ignition switch (primary) wires.

Loosen engine mounting bolts (four) holding engine base to its platform on mower frame, loosen locknut of engine tensioner bolt, back off tensioner and remove mower deck and transaxle drive belts from pulleys under engine. Remove belt keeper (7–Fig. D1) if necessary. Completely remove engine mounting bolts from slotted openings in platform and lift engine from frame. Reverse procedure to reinstall engine.

CLUTCH

All Models

Clutch function is incorporated in drive unit of transaxle. There is no con-

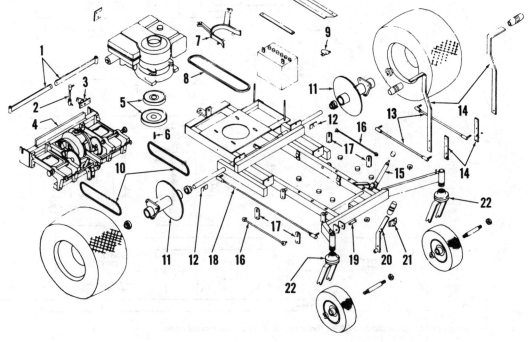

Fig. D1—Exploded view of mower chassis and frame assemblies.
1. Brake arms
2. Brake rod
3. Brake pivot
4. Transaxle assy.
5. Drive pulleys
6. Key
7. Belt keeper
8. Drive belt
9. Starter solenoid
10. Drive chains
11. Hub & sprocket
12. Shims
13. Control rod assemblies
14. Control lever assemblies
15. Lift lever
16. Lift tie rods
17. Lift links
18. Brake rod
19. Pivot pin
20. Brake lever
21. Pedal
22. Caster assy.

ventional, separate, belt-type master clutch. See TRANSAXLE section for clutch functions and adjustments.

BRAKES

All Models

These units do not have a service brake as such. Braking is accomplished by moving control levers opposite to direction of movement. Proper adjustment of transaxle will ensure that braking is effective for safe operation.

Parking brake, mounted at rear of transaxle frame, is an over-center, linkage design used to hold unit after motion is halted. If adjustment of parking brake becomes necessary, unbolt ball joint of linkage rod (18–Fig. D1) and shorten rod working length to tighten brake. If brake arms (1) exert excessive pressure against inner sidewalls of tires, readjust to decrease pressure. Test for holding by pushing mower by hand with parking brake applied.

TRANSAXLE

All Models

The friction-drive transaxle provides for all functions of clutch, brakes, steering, variable speed transmission and differential. Each of the rear (Driving) wheels rotates independently on its own axle shaft. If proper adjustments

are maintained among working parts, especially the friction drive components and control linkages, over-all operation will be satisfactory.

ADJUST. In order to gain sufficient access to make adjustments, body assembly should be removed from frame. To do so, proceed as follows:

Disconnect throttle control bowden cable from engine. Separate interfering electrical wires by disconnecting at looms and multiconnectors at front and rear of body pan. Pay particular attention to key switch on Model ZTR-1 and to seat safety switch wire on all models. Unbolt upper (handle) portion of control levers (14–Fig. D1) from lower section and set aside. Remove control handle (1–Fig. D3) by removing through-bolt which attaches handle to cutting deck control rod (2). Remove two bolts which attach brake pedal (21–Fig. D1) to brake lever arm (20). Now, remove two acorn style nuts at front of body floor and sheet metal screws which secure body to transaxle mount at rear. Note that brake arm clips are released at the same time. Body assembly can now be lifted clear of frame. Reverse these steps to reinstall body.

After body has been removed, a check for correct adjustments to drive train involves the following:

ENGINE TO TRANSAXLE DRIVE BELT. For operation without undue slippage or excess loading of shafts due to tightness, main drive belt should take ½-inch (12.7 mm) deflection by

hand between engine and transaxle pulley centers. To adjust, slightly loosen four engine mounting bolts and the locknut on tensioner bolt; screw tensioner in or out to gain proper belt flex. Retighten mounting bolts and locknut.

NOTE: Drive pulley for mower deck is also keyed to engine crankshaft.

DRIVE CHAINS. Two sets of drive chains should be checked for correct adjustment. Primary chain (20–Fig. D2) driven by 9-tooth sprocket (18) of cradle shaft (11) which is fitted directly to discup (3) drives 24-tooth intermediate sprocket (19) on support shaft (15). This chain must run loose so that cradle (10) can pivot freely. There is no provision for take-up of excessive slack on this chain; therefore, if extreme wear of sprockets or chain links develops, renewal of chain and/or sprockets will be necessary. Chains are fitted with master links for convenience.

Final drive chains (10–Fig. D1) drive 60-tooth axle sprockets (11) and are driven by 9-tooth output sprocket (17–Fig. D2) on support shaft (15). To adjust these chains, proceed as follows: Loosen four bolts which attach transaxle to main frame after providing support under rear of frame to relieve weight on drive wheels. Insert additional shims (12–Fig. D1) as needed to overcome wear and slack between drive sprockets and chain. It is not necessary to remove master link from chain when fitting shims. When correctly adjusted, a small deflection of $\frac{3}{16}$-$\frac{1}{4}$ inch (4.8-6.4

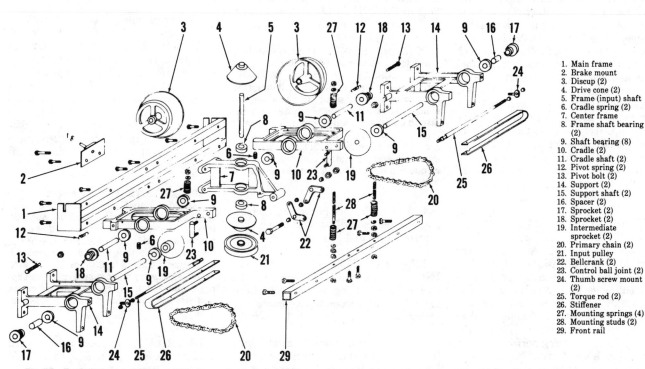

1. Main frame
2. Brake mount
3. Discup (2)
4. Drive cone (2)
5. Frame (input) shaft
6. Cradle spring (2)
7. Center frame
8. Frame shaft bearing (2)
9. Shaft bearing (8)
10. Cradle (2)
11. Cradle shaft (2)
12. Pivot spring (2)
13. Pivot bolt (2)
14. Support (2)
15. Support shaft (2)
16. Spacer (2)
17. Sprocket (2)
18. Sprocket (2)
19. Intermediate sprocket (2)
20. Primary chain (2)
21. Input pulley
22. Bellcrank (2)
23. Control ball joint (2)
24. Thumb screw mount (2)
25. Torque rod (2)
26. Stiffener
27. Mounting springs (4)
28. Mounting studs (2)
29. Front rail

Fig. D2—Exploded view of friction-drive transaxle. Refer to text for service procedures and parts functions. Shaft roll pin (12 used) are not shown.

mm) in chain at mid-point between sprocket centers will provide adequate slack to minimize both noise and tension strain and to prevent rapid wear. It is important that deflection be equal on each side of drive.

NOTE: When shims have been added, check and readjust engine to transaxle drive belt as well as control rod linkage which will have been affected.

POSITIVE NEUTRAL ADJUSTMENT. When in neutral, control levers should align, side by side, approximately 10 degrees (4 inches) to the rear of vertical, in easy reach of operator. Lever action should allow for free movement forward and back by operator and engagement (drive application) should be smooth and positive. There should be little or no side play in controls. All slack and looseness should be eliminated by careful check and tightening of all control linkage beginning with levers (14-Fig. D1) through lever pivots and control rods (13) to bell cranks (22-Fig. D2) and to ball joints (23) which deflect cradle assemblies (10). When control lever and linkage adjustments are correct, mower should not creep with controls in neutral. Because controls are spring-loaded for return to neutral whenever released, the term "positive neutral" is used.

To properly adjust for positive neutral, pressure must be equalized on springs (27) which are fitted above and below cradle (10) on mounting stud (28). Tighten or loosen adjustment nuts so that clearance between friction face of drive cone (4) and contact zone of steel discup (3) is as nearly equal as possible. Use feeler gage stock of 0.020 inch (0.51 mm) thickness. As a preliminary check of neutral adjustment, move levers forward and back until contact between cones and discups can be felt, noting if range of movement for each lever is not very nearly equal. After locknuts are drawn up, recheck with feeler gage to ensure that adjustment was not disturbed. Levers should spring back to neutral when released and mower should not creep after engine is started.

CRADLE/DISCUP ADJUSTMENT. This adjustment is made with transaxle controls in neutral. A preliminary check to determine if inner edge of discup (3-Fig. D2) is exactly parallel to adjacent edge of center frame (7) is important. If discup does not run true in relation to center frame, further adjustment is ineffective. This is normally a factory setting performed with production jigs and gages; however, satisfactory measurements can be achieved by using a good Vernier caliper, particularly one equipped with a "T" head. If mower is blocked under frame so that drive wheels can be rotated freely, objectionable excess runout is easily observed and measured while discup turns. If bad alignment is found, carefully check condition of cradle shaft (11) and shaft bearings (9). Damaged or defective parts must be renewed. When discups are parallel, use a 0.020-inch (0.51 mm) feeler gage to check clearance between discup and friction surface of upper and lower driving cones (4). Check at all four contact areas. If need for clearance adjustment is apparent, before proceeding, check condition of input (frame) shaft (5) and its bearings (8). Looseness due to wear or bearing failure can be corrected only by renewal of defective parts. To proceed with clearance adjustment, follow this sequence:

1. Determine direction in which discup must be moved to set required clearance between discup and drive cone.
2. To INCREASE clearance (that is, to move discup AWAY from cone) loosen nut on threaded torque rod (25) at inboard side of thumb screw mount (24), then tighten outer nut by same number of turns.
3. In order to keep cradle (10) and discup (3) parallel to center frame (7), pivot bolt (13) must be adjusted to correspond with changes in length of torque rod (25). This is accomplished by loosening locknut on pivot bolt without allowing bolt to turn, then screwing bolt in COUNTERCLOCKWISE direction to move discup AWAY from cone.

NOTE: Use opposite procedures and rotation to move discup TOWARD drive cone or to DECREASE clearance. Whenever torque rod length is adjusted, it must be kept in mind that pivot bolt will require simultaneous adjustment in order to keep discup parallel to center frame. Because of thread difference, the turn ratio of torque rod nuts to pivot bolt is 2:1. When adjusting, it should be noted that two turns of torque rod nuts will equal one turn of pivot bolt.

4. When clearance is correct, recheck positive neutral adjustment along with control levers and linkages.

TRANSAXLE TROUBLESHOOTING. Some problems which may be encountered during mower operation are listed with recommended corrective action.

Unit will not travel in straight line. Check for loose control lever, then for loose or damaged control rod to include all linkage to transaxle. Tighten, adjust or renew parts as necessary. If trouble is not corrected, remove body and check clearance adjustments between discups and drive cones. Be sure that all cradle springs (6, 12 and 27-Fig. D2) are in place and fully functional. If all items checked appear normal, it is possible that friction surfaces of drive cones are damaged or contaminated with foreign material such as oil. Repair or renew as necessary. Both cones must be renewed though only one may be defective.

Torque rods break during operation. This condition may be caused by excessive clearance between discup and drive cone. Check and correct as necessary. It is possible that some older models may not have torque rod stiffeners (26) installed. If this is the case, install the parts needed.

Mower travels only in a circle. Check for broken torque rod first, then check for possible broken pivot or broken shaft. If there is no evident problem here, block under frame so that wheels are clear and check carefully for possible broken roll pin. There is a total of twelve roll or spirol pins used to secure sprockets to support shafts, sprockets and discups to cradle shafts and bearings and drive cones to frame shaft. Any problem with a drive chain will be apparent–disengagement or breakage. It is advisable to check condition of sprocket teeth and for proper chain tension. Repair or adjust as necessary.

Mower creeps in neutral. Check for looseness in linkage first, then check for correct clearance between discups and cones. It is also possible that a cradle and its discup have slipped out of alignment with center frame. This condition can cause discup to contact drive cone away from proper friction zone so as to make correct clearance adjustment nearly impossible. Check measurement and correct condition. Readjust positive neutral.

SPECIAL NOTE: Correct clearance between drive cones and discups has been emphasized as being 0.020 inch (0.51 mm). Operation of transaxle will be acceptable at 0.005 inch (0.127 mm) more or less than this setting. However, excessive clearance such as 0.035 or 0.040 inch (0.89-1.02 mm) will cause excessive slippage and result in overheating of cones and discups leading to damage or destruction.

OVERHAUL. If previously covered adjustments and parts renewals do not suffice to restore transaxle perform-

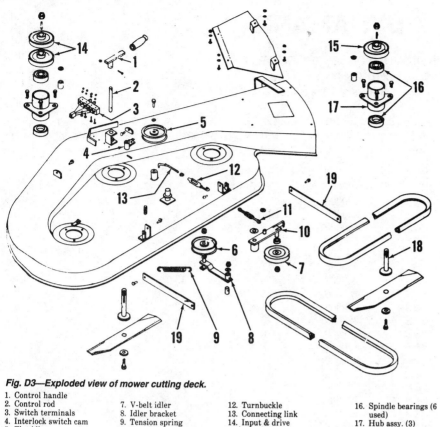

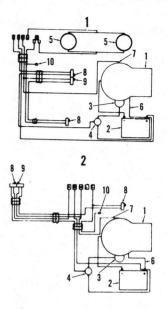

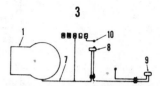

Fig. D3—Exploded view of mower cutting deck.

1. Control handle
2. Control rod
3. Switch terminals
4. Interlock switch cam
5. Flat idler
6. Flat idler
7. V-belt idler
8. Idler bracket
9. Tension spring
10. Engagement bracket
11. Engagement spring
12. Turnbuckle
13. Connecting link
14. Input & drive pulleys
15. Drive pulley
16. Spindle bearings (6 used)
17. Hub assy. (3)
18. Blade spindle (3)
19. Stabilizers (2)

Fig. D4—Electrical layout diagrams for all models. Wire color code: Green-Solenoid; Red-Battery (+); Black-Battery (–); Brown-Magneto; White-Ground.

1. Engine
2. Battery
3. Starter motor
4. Solenoid
5. Headlights
6. Alternator lead wire
7. Magneto lead wire
8. Microswitch (NC)
9. Microswitch (NO)
10. Switch ground

ance, disassembly, careful evaluation of all parts, thorough cleaning and careful reassembly with new parts will be necessary. To do so, first remove engine and body from frame as previously described. Disconnect control rods, then remove master links from drive chains (10-Fig. D1) and remove chains. Remove brake arms (1). Unbolt transaxle assembly (4) from main frame taking care not to lose adjustment shims (12). Remove the separated transaxle assembly. Refer to Fig. D2 for parts arrangement and identification.

Remove master links and drive chains (20-Fig. D2). Further disassembly procedures will be apparent. It is suggested that parts not be removed from transaxle unless there is a clear need to do so. Because transaxle, after drive chains are removed, is open to easy access, all shafts, anti-friction bearings, drive sprockets and roll pins can be carefully examined and checked by hand for looseness, wear or damage. Particular care should be taken with evaluation of discups and drive cones. Damage, due to heat of friction, especially if unit has been operated with excessive clearance between friction drive components should not be overlooked.

Reassemble, using necessary renewal parts and reinstall in reverse order of disassembly. Refer to preceding ADJUSTMENT section.

MOWER

All Models

ADJUST. Unsatisfactory cutting performance by mower unit, streaking or patchy finish on lawn, is frequently caused by slippage of drive belts.

Tension of main drive belt from engine pulley is increased by moving V-belt idler (7-Fig. D3) farther forward. Note that this idler also serves for clutch function to engage and disengage mower drive with its linkage connected to control handle (1). Adjustment, when needed, is made by rotation of turnbuckle (12) to shorten or lengthen control linkage and to increase or decrease tension on engagement spring (11). Properly adjusted control linkage will exert enough pressure upon the spring-loaded idler (7) to eliminate slippage and will disengage cleanly in response to movement of control handle (1).

NOTE: Be sure that interlock switch cam (4) which operates safety interlock micro switch on later models makes proper contact.

Drive belt for mower spindles is held under tension by spring (9) which is applied to belt flat side by flat idler pulley (6). Flat idler (5) serves mainly as a belt guide. There are no other service adjustments required for mower deck.

R&R AND OVERHAUL. To remove mowing unit from under mower frame, disconnect spark plug wire first to ensure that mower cannot be accidentally started, especially if jumpers or by-pass connectors have been used to override interlocks. Position control handle (1-Fig. D3) to disengage mower drive and relax drive belt. Remove belt keeper under engine platform and remove drive belt from sheaves. Disconnect wire loom at switch connectors and terminals (3). Unbolt control handle (1) from control rod (2), then remove pins from stabilizers (19). Now, remove pins which attach mower pan (deck) to lift links (17-Fig. D1) and lower cutting deck down away from frame. Be sure that control rod (2-Fig. D3) is clear of body and frame and slide cutting unit from under mower frame. It may be considered easier to lift front wheels and roll body and frame rearward on the drive wheels. Clean mower deck thoroughly to prepare for inspection of parts and necessary disassembly.

DYNAMARK

NOMA OUTDOOR PRODUCTS INC.
210 American Drive
Jackson, TN 38301

Model	Make	Engine Model	Horsepower	Cutting Width, In.
826	B&S	190000	8	26
832	B&S	190000	8	32
1260	B&S	190000	8	26
1261	B&S	190000	8	32
1269	B&S	130000	5	26
1274	B&S	220000	10	36
1281	B&S	190000	8	36
1284	B&S	190000	8	
		220000	10	
		250000	11	36
1288	B&S	220000	10	42
2650	B&S	130000	5	26
3180	B&S	250000	11	42
3181	B&S	326000	16	42
3184	B&S	220000	10	36
3188	B&S	190000	8	
		220000	10	
		250000	11	36
3189	B&S	190000	8	32
3208	B&S	190000	8	32
3280	B&S	190000	8	32
3294	B&S	190000	8	32
3610	B&S	220000	10	36
3611	B&S	250000	11	36
3612	Tecumseh	OVM120	12	36
5180	B&S	250000	11	42
5181	B&S	220000	10	
		326000	16	42
5184	B&S	250000	10	36
5188	Tecumseh	V100	10	
	B&S	250000	11	36 or 42
5267	B&S	130000	5	
		190000	8	26 or 32
5282	B&S	190000	8	36
5285	B&S	190000	8	36
5288	B&S	220000	10	
	B&S	250000	11	
	Tecumseh	V100	10	36 or 42
5289	B&S	190000	8	
	Tecumseh	V100	10	32
5294	B&S	130000	5	
		190000	8	32
5296	B&S	220000	10	
		250000	11	36
5297	B&S	220000	10	42

FRONT AXLE STEERING SYSTEM

Front Engine Models (Early)

REMOVE AND REINSTALL. To remove axle main member (24-Fig. DM1), place mower unit in lowest position and unpin mower from mower hanger. Support front of unit and remove front wheels. Disconnect drag link end (20) from steering arm (22) and tie rod ends (27) from spindles. Drive out roll pin (23), remove steering arm (22) and remove spindle (26) from axle. Remove "E" ring (15) and remove spindle (17). Remove pivot bolt (25), then lower axle main member (24) from frame. Inspect spindle bushings (16) for excessive wear and renew as necessary. Reassemble by reversing disassembly

Front Engine Models (Late)

REMOVE AND REINSTALL. To remove axle main member (19-Fig. DM2), unpin front of mower from mower hanger, then unbolt and remove mower hanger from front support (16). Support front of unit and remove front wheels. Disconnect drag link end (14) from steering arm (18) and tie rod ends (24) from spindles. Drive out roll pin, remove steering arm (18) and lower spindle (23) from axle. Remove "E" ring (20) and spindle (26). Remove pivot bolt (17) and lower axle main member (19) from frame. Inspect spindle bushings (21) for excessive wear and renew as necessary. Reassemble by reversing disassembly procedure. Check front wheel toe-in and adjust ends (24) on tie rod (25) as required to obtain ⅛-inch (3 mm) toe-in.

To remove steering gear, drive out roll pin (2) and remove steering wheel (1). Drive roll pin (6) from pinion gear (7) and remove "E" ring (13) from lower end of shaft (5). Withdraw steering shaft (5) and remove pinion gear (7).

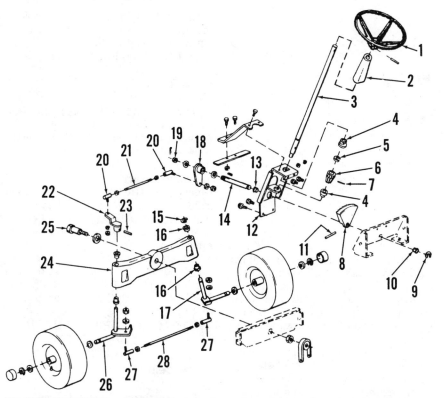

Fig. DM1—Exploded view of front axle and steering system used on early production models.

1. Steering wheel	8. Quadrant gear	15. "E" ring	22. Steering arm
2. Cover	9. "E" ring	16. Spindle bushings	23. Roll pin
3. Steering shaft	10. Bushing	17. Spindle R.H.	24. Axle main member
4. Bushings	11. Roll pin	18. Quadrant arm	25. Pivot bolt
5. "E" ring	12. Steering support	19. Adjusting nut	26. Spindle L.H.
6. Pinion gear	13. Bushing	20. Drag link ends	27. Tie rod ends
7. Roll pin	14. Quadrant shaft	21. Drag link	28. Tie rod

procedure. Check front wheel toe-in and adjust ends (27) on tie rod (28) to obtain a toe-in of ⅛ inch (3 mm).

To remove steering gears and shafts, drive out roll pin and remove steering wheel (1) and cover (2). Unbolt and remove console from around steering unit. Disconnect drag link end (20) from quadrant arm (18) and remove cotter pin, adjusting nut (19), quadrant arm and washers. Drive out roll pin (11) and remove "E" ring (9). Remove shaft (14) from front and lift out quadrant gear (8). Drive out roll pin (7) and remove "E" ring (5). Withdraw steering shaft (3) and remove pinion gear (6). Bushings (4, 10 and 13) can now be removed. Clean and inspect all parts for wear or other damage and renew as necessary. When reassembling, adjust steering gear free play as follows: Turn adjusting nut (19) clockwise to remove excessive play, then install cotter pin. Free play should be adjusted to a minimum but gears should not bind.

Lubricate all bushings and pivot points with SAE 30 oil. Apply a light coat of lithium grease to pinion gear and quadrant gear teeth.

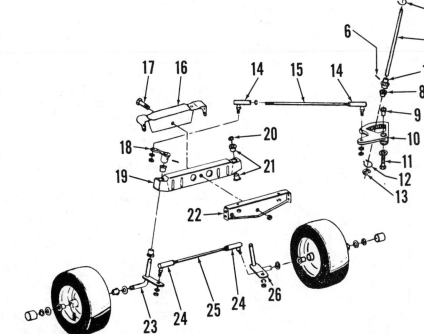

Fig. DM2—Exploded view of front axle and steering system used on late production models.

1. Steering wheel	8. Bushing	20. "E" ring
2. Roll pin	9. Eccentric adjuster	21. Spindle bushings
3. Bushing	10. Quadrant gear	22. Axle support
4. Retaining ring	11. Lock bolt	23. Spindle L.H.
5. Steering shaft	12. Retaining ring	24. Tie rod ends
6. Roll pin	13. "E" ring	25. Tie rod
7. Pinion gear	14. Drag link ends	26. Spindle R.H.
	15. Drag link	
	16. Front support	
	17. Pivot bolt	
	18. Steering arm	
	19. Axle main member	

Dynamark

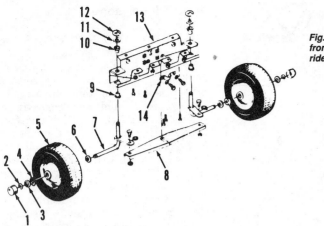

Fig. DM2A—Exploded view of front axle used on rear engine riders.

1. Cap
2. Retaining ring
3. Flat washer
4. Flat washer
5. Tire & wheel
6. Flat washer
7. Spindle
8. Steering link
9. Bushing
10. Bushing
11. Flat washer
12. Retaining ring
13. Axle main member
14. Steering bracket

Reinstall engine assembly by reversing removal procedure. Adjust belts as outlined in TRACTION DRIVE and MOWER DRIVE BELT paragraphs.

Rear Engine Models

REMOVE AND REINSTALL. Disconnect spark plug wire and remove mower as outlined in MOWER DECK paragraphs. Remove drive belt as outlined. Disconnect battery (as equipped) and all necessary electrical wiring. Disconnect throttle linkage. Remove seat support bracket at front of engine. Remove engine pulley and key. Remove engine retaining bolts and remove engine.

Reinstall engine assembly by reversing removal procedure. Adjust belts as outlined in TRACTION DRIVE and MOWER DRIVE BELT paragraphs.

TRACTION DRIVE CLUTCH AND DRIVE BELT

All Models

The traction drive clutch used on all models (except variable speed models) is a belt idler type. When clutch is disengaged, tension is relieved on drive belt and engine pulley turns freely within belt.

On models equipped with variable speed drive, the variable speed pulley is also the clutch idler. The variable speed pulley contains a movable center section which allows a change in diameter of pulleys for primary and secondary belts. Position of pulleys and belts in disengaged and engaged positions are shown in Fig. DM6.

Models With Transmission-Differential

ADJUSTMENT. Drive belt adjustment is made by moving transmission on early models or sliding idler pulley in mounting slot on later models. To adjust, remove mower as outlined in MOWER DECK paragraphs. Depress clutch-brake pedal to remove belt tension and engage park brake. Loosen transmission mounting bolts on early models and move transmission rearward to tighten belt and retighten bolts. On late models, loosen idler mounting bolt and slide idler in slot as necessary and tighten idler mounting bolt. On all models, release pedal and check adjustment, pedal should be approximately straight up and down when adjustment is correct. Check drive chain tension and adjust if needed as outlined in DRIVE CHAIN paragraphs.

Disconnect drag link end (14) from quadrant gear (10). Remove lock bolt (11) and eccentric adjuster (9), then lift out quadrant gear (10). Bushings (3 and 8) can be removed after first removing retaining rings (4 and 12). Reassemble be reversing disassembly procedure. To adjust steering gear free play, loosen lock bolt (11) slightly and rotate eccentric adjuster (9). When excessive play is removed, tighten lock bolt (11).

Lubricate all bushings and pivot points with SAE 30 oil. Apply a light coat of lithium grease to pinion gear and quadrant gear teeth.

Rear Engine Models

REMOVE AND REINSTALL. Rear engine rider models are equipped with a front axle assembly as shown in Fig. DM2A. To disassemble, raise and support front of rider. Remove wheel caps (1), retaining ring (2), washers (3 and 4) and tire and wheel assemblies (5). Remove washer (6). To remove spindles (7), disconnect steering link (8), remove retaining rings (12) and washers (11). Remove spindles (7). Inspect bushings (9 and 10) and renew as necessary.

To remove steering shaft, remove steering link (8). Remove steering bracket (14). Remove the ¼ inch roll pin from steering wheel and shaft and remove steering wheel. Slide decorative steering tube off steering shaft. Remove the ³⁄₁₆ inch roll pin from steering shaft and steering post and remove steering shaft.

Lubricate all bushings and pivot points with SAE 30 oil during reassembly.

ENGINE

All Models

Refer to appropriate engine section in this manual for tune-up specifications, engine overhaul procedures and engine maintenance.

Front Engine Models

REMOVE AND REINSTALL. Disconnect spark plug wire and remove mower as outlined in MOWER DECK paragraphs. Unbolt and remove hood, body panels and protective shields as necessary. Disconnect fuel line and drain fuel tank. On electric start models, disconnect battery cables, starter and alternator wires. On all models, disconnect ignition wiring, throttle cable and all other components as needed. Remove engine pulley belt guides and slip belts off pulley. For assistance in removal of belts refer to TRACTION DRIVE CLUTCH AND DRIVE BELT paragraphs. Remove engine mounting bolts and lift off engine.

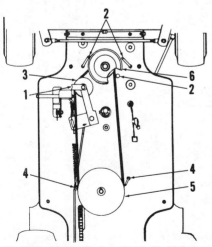

Fig. DM3—Underside view of typical belt idler traction drive clutch, belt and belt guides used on transmission equipped models.

1. Belt retainer
2. Belt guides
3. Clutch idler pulley
4. Belt guides
5. Transmission pulley
6. Engine pulley

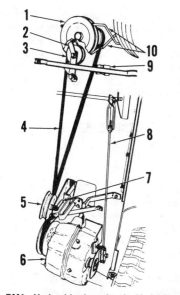

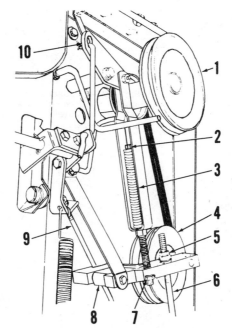

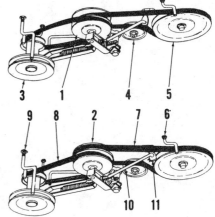

Fig. DM4—Underside view of typical belt idler traction drive clutch, belt and belt guides used on
transaxle equipped models.

1. Engine pulley
2. Belt retainer
3. Clutch idler pulley
4. Drive belt
5. Backside idler pulley
6. Transaxle assy.
7. Adjustment slot
8. Brake rod
9. Footrest bracket
10. Belt guides

Fig. DM5—Underside view of traction drive variable speed pulley and control linkage used on
some models.

1. Engine pulley
2. Adjustment screw
3. Tension spring
4. Variable speed pulley
5. Front jam nut
6. Variable speed adjustment rod
7. Adjustment nut
8. Control arm
9. Brake rod
10. Disengage lever

Fig. DM6—View of variable speed pulley (1) in
disengaged position and pulley (2) in fast position.

1. Variable speed pulley (disengaged position)
2. Variable speed pulley (fast position)
3. Engine pulley
4. Backside idler
5. Transmission pulley
6. Belt guide
7. Secondary drive belt
8. Primary drive belt
9. Belt guide
10. Adjustment rod
11. Control lever

REMOVE AND REINSTALL. Remove mower as outlined in MOWER DECK paragraphs. Depress clutch pedal and engage park brake. Note position of idler pulley belt retainer (1-Fig. DM3), then loosen idler pulley bolt. Loosen and move belt guides (2 and 4) away from pulleys. Slip belt off idler pulley then remove from transmission and engine pulleys.

Renew belt by reversing removal procedure. Hold idler pulley belt retainer in position while tightening idler pulley bolt. Adjust belt guides to 1/16-inch (1.6 mm) clearance from belt. Adjust belt tension as previously outlined.

Models With Transaxle

ADJUSTMENT. On transaxle equipped models, belt adjustment is made by moving backside idler (5-Fig. DM4) in its adjusting slot. Adjust idler until clutch-brake pedal is approximately straight up and down.

REMOVE AND REINSTALL. Remove mower as outlined in MOWER DECK paragraphs. Depress brake-clutch pedal and engage park brake. If unit has a footrest bracket (9-Fig. DM4) straddling drive belt, unbolt and remove bracket. Loosen belt guides and move them away from pulleys. Note position of idler pulley belt retainers, then loosen bolts on clutch idler (3) and backside idler (5) pulleys. Remove belt

from idlers, engine pulley and transaxle pulley. Remove belt from chassis by pushing it up through gear shift opening.

Renew belt by reversing removal procedure. Before installing footrest bracket, release brake-clutch pedal. Belt must be under tension to properly align belt and bracket. Adjust belt guides to 1/16-inch (1.6 mm) clearance from belt. Hold idler pulley belt retainers in place while tightening idler retainer bolts. Adjust belt as previously outlined.

Models With Variable Speed Pulley

ADJUSTMENTS. If unit moves when variable speed lever is in latched position, adjust as follows: Place lever in latched position and remove mower deck. Loosen front jam nut (5-Fig. DM5) on variable speed adjustment rod (6) two turns, then tighten rear jam nut two turns. Check operation and repeat adjustment as required.

If variable speed lever will not stay in selected speed position, adjust as follows: Place variable speed lever in latched position. Tighten friction adjustment nut, located inside console on right hand side behind engine, one turn. Check operation and repeat adjustment as needed.

To check and adjust brake, proceed as follows: Shift transmission to neutral, then depress brake pedal and engage park brake. Push unit forward or backward. If rear wheels are not locked, tighten adjusting nut on brake rod (9-Fig. DM5) two turns. Check operation and repeat adjustment as needed.

If variable speed does not return to disengaged position when brake is depressed and held, adjust as follows: With transmission in neutral, start engine and push speed lever to full forward position, then shut off engine. Adjustment nut (7-Fig. DM5) should be tight against pulley control arm (8) and all connecting parts should have tension against them. To adjust spring (3) hold adjustment screw (2) and tighten adjustment nut (7) until tight against support arm.

REMOVE AND REINSTALL. To remove secondary drive belt (7-Fig. DM6), first remove mower as outlined in MOWER DECK paragraphs. Unhook adjustment rod (10) from lower end of variable speed lever (11). Loosen belt guide (6) and move away from transmission pulley. Pull backside idler (4) away from belt and slip belt off underside of idler pulley. Roll belt off underside of transmission pulley, then remove belt from variable speed pulley. Belt can be removed over top of pulley by pushing toward front of unit and twisting belt sideways.

To remove primary belt (8-Fig. DM6) it is necessary to first remove secondary belt as previously outlined. Loosen engine pulley belt guide and move it

Dynamark

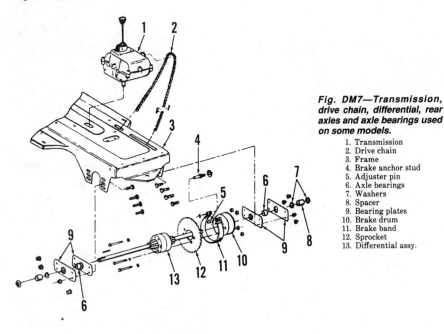

Fig. DM7—Transmission, drive chain, differential, rear axles and axle bearings used on some models.

1. Transmission
2. Drive chain
3. Frame
4. Brake anchor stud
5. Adjuster pin
6. Axle bearings
7. Washers
8. Spacer
9. Bearing plates
10. Brake drum
11. Brake band
12. Sprocket
13. Differential assy.

away from pulley. Remove belt from variable speed pulley by pushing pulley toward front of unit and twisting belt sideways. Remove belt from engine pulley.

Renew belts in reverse order of removal. Adjust belt guides to $\frac{1}{16}$-inch (1.6 mm) clearance from belts. Check and adjust if needed as previously outlined.

TRANSMISSION

All Models

The transmissions used on models so equipped are manufactured by J.B. Foote Foundry Co. or Peerless Division of Tecumseh Products Co. For overhaul and repair procedures refer to Foote or Peerless paragraphs in TRANSMISSION REPAIR section of this manual.

REMOVE AND REINSTALL. Disconnect spark plug wire and remove mower as outlined in MOWER DECK paragraphs. Depress brake-clutch pedal and engage park brake. Loosen belt guides, then slip traction drive belt off transmission pulley. Remove retaining ring and pulley from transmission shaft. Unbolt and remove body panels or protective shields as necessary to provide access to transmission. Disconnect drive chain and transmission safety starting switch wires. If unit is equipped with transmission mounted brake, disconnect brake rod from brake lever. Unbolt and remove shift lever. Unbolt and remove transmission from chassis. Reinstall in reverse order of removal procedure.

TRANSAXLE

All Models

The transaxles used on models so equipped are manufactured by J.B. Foote Foundry Co. or Peerless Division of Tecumseh Products Co. For overhaul and repair procedures, refer to Foote or Peerless paragraphs in TRANSMISSION REPAIR section of this manual.

REMOVE AND REINSTALL. Disconnect spark plug wire and remove mower as outlined in MOWER DECK paragraphs. Depress brake-clutch pedal and engage park brake. Loosen belt guides and roll belt out of idler pulley and transmission pulley. Disconnect brake rod from disc brake lever. Support rear of unit and remove rear wheels. Unbolt and remove transaxle from chassis. Reinstall by reversing removal procedures.

DRIVE CHAIN

All Models

R&R AND ADJUSTMENT. To remove chain, on models so equipped, rotate differential sprocket to locate master link. Disconnect master link and remove chain. Reinstall in reverse order of removal. Lubricate with a light coat of SAE 30 oil.

To adjust chain (2-Fig. DM7), loosen bolts securing rear axle to frame. On models with band brake, loosen brake anchor stud (4). Move axle rearward

(equal distance on both sides) to tighten chain. Chain should deflect approximately ¼ inch (6.4 mm). On band brake models, push anchor stud as close as possible to brake band (11) and tighten pin, then adjust brake rod to account for axle movement.

DIFFERENTIAL

All Models

The differential used on models so equipped is manufactured by Peerless Division of Tecumseh Products Co. For overhaul procedure refer to Peerless paragraphs in DIFFERENTIAL REPAIR section of this manual.

REMOVE AND REINSTALL. To remove differential assembly (13-Fig. DM7), raise rear of unit and support securely. Remove rear wheel assemblies, washers and spacers. On band brake models, disconnect front end of brake rod from clutch idler arm, then unscrew brake rod from adjuster pin (5) and pull brake band (11) from drum (10). Disconnect drive chain. Unbolt bearing retainers (9) from frame and remove differential assembly. Clean rust, paint and burrs from axle shafts and remove axle bearings (6). Remove nuts inside brake drum and remove drum and sprocket (12).

Reinstall by reversing removal procedure. Adjust drive chain as previously outlined. Lubricate axle bearings with SAE 30 oil.

GROUND DRIVE BRAKE

Models With Band Brake

ADJUSTMENT. To adjust brake, refer to Fig. DM8 and disconnect brake rod (11) from idler arm (6). Turn brake rod into adjuster pin (17) to tighten brake. Reconnect brake rod, fully depress clutch-brake pedal (5) and engage parking brake lock. Main drive belt (9) should be free from engine pulley (1) and rear wheels should be locked. Always make certain that drive belt tension is removed before brake is applied.

Models With Disc Brake

ADJUSTMENT. To adjust brake on transmission equipped models, brake-clutch pedal must be fully released. To tighten brake, loosen front nut on brake rod and tighten rear nut.

To adjust brake on models equipped with Peerless Model 639 transaxle, first release brake-clutch pedal. Loosen jam nut on brake actuating lever and turn adjusting nut until brake pads just clear brake disc. Hold adjusting nut and tighten jam nut against it.

To adjust brake on models equipped with all other transaxle models, release brake-clutch pedal. Disconnect and adjust length of brake rod to adjust brake. Do not turn rod more than one turn without reinstalling to check adjustment.

Models With Band Brake

R&R AND OVERHAUL. Normal overhaul consists of renewing brake band (15–Fig. DM8). To remove brake band, disconnect front of brake rod (11) from clutch idler arm (6). Unscrew brake rod adjuster pin (17). Remove band retaining "E" ring from anchor stud (12). Pull brake band from around brake drum (16) and remove band from anchor stud.

Install new brake band by reversing removal procedure and adjust brake as outlined previously.

NOTE: To remove brake drum (16), refer to R&R procedure in DIFFERENTIAL paragraphs.

Models With Disc Brake

R&R AND OVERHAUL. Normal overhaul of disc brake consists of renewing brake pads. To remove brake assembly, disconnect brake rod from brake lever. Unbolt and remove brake carrier, brake disc and brake pads.

Clean and inspect parts and renew as necessary. Reassemble by reversing removal procedure and adjust brake as previously outlined.

MOWER DRIVE BELT

Models With 26-Inch Mower

ADJUSTMENT. On early production models, adjust as follows: Raise and block front of mower deck and remove pull pin from deck front hitch. Loosen jam nut and turn deck hitch in or out to adjust belt tension. Check blade brake action when blade clutch is disengaged. Blade should stop and remain stopped. If blade does not stop, belt adjustment is too tight.

On late production models, adjust as follows: Loosen nut securing hitch bar in pivot bracket. Slide deck forward to loosen belt and rearward to tighten

belt. Retighten nut and check blade brake action. If blade does not stop when blade clutch is disengaged, belt adjustment is too tight.

REMOVE AND REINSTALL. Blade drive belt can be replaced without removing mower, but it is easier with mower removed. Note position of idler pulley belt retainer (4–Fig. DM9), then remove idler pulley (5). Loosen and move belt guides for clearance and remove belt from pulleys.

Renew belt in reverse order of removal. With blade clutch engaged, adjust belt guides to provide $\frac{1}{16}$-inch (1.6 mm) clearance between belt and guide. Check belt adjustment as previously outlined.

Models With 32-Inch Mower

ADJUSTMENT. On early style models, adjust belt as follows: Disengage blade clutch and loosen nut on bolt securing bar hitch (1–Fig. DM10) to pivot bracket (2). Loosen front jam nut and tighten rear nut on hitch adjustment screw to tighten belt. Check blade brake action. If blades do not stop or tend to creep with blade clutch disengaged, adjust nuts on brake rod (7) that connects to left brake bracket (8). There should be approximately $\frac{1}{16}$-inch (1.6 mm) clearance between nut and bracket with clutch disengaged.

On late style models, adjust belt as follows: Disengage blade clutch and remove bolt (4–Fig. DM11) from lock bracket (5). Loosen bolt (2) securing bar hitch (1) to pivot bracket (3) and slide bar hitch forward to tighten belt. Retighten bolt and check blade brake action. If blades do not stop or tend to creep, adjustment is too tight. When adjustment is correct, install bolt in lock bracket.

REMOVE AND REINSTALL. Disconnect spark plug wire and remove mower as outlined in MOWER DECK paragraphs. Note position of idler pulley belt retainer (4–Fig. DM10), and loosen idler pulley mounting bolt. Loosen belt guards (9) and remove belt.

Install new belt by reversing removal procedure. Hold idler pulley belt retainer in position and tighten mounting bolt. Adjust belt guides to $\frac{1}{16}$-inch (1.6 mm) clearance from belt. Check belt adjustment as previously outlined.

Models With 36-Inch Mower

ADJUSTMENT. On early production side discharge mowers, adjust as follows: Loosen jam nut on drive belt adjustment bolt and turn bolt counter-

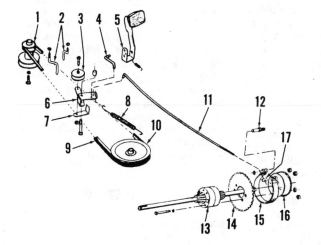

Fig. DM8—Exploded view of typical main drive clutch and band brake used on some models.

1. Engine pulley
2. Belt guides
3. Clutch idler pulley
4. Clutch link
5. Clutch-brake pedal
6. Idler arm
7. Belt retainer
8. Clutch tension spring
9. Main drive belt
10. Transmission input pulley
11. Brake rod
12. Brake anchor stud
13. Differential assy.
14. Sprocket
15. Brake band
16. Brake drum
17. Adjuster pin

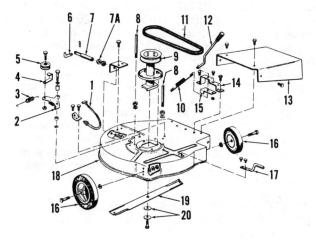

Fig. DM9—Exploded view of typical single spindle mower unit.

1. Safety starting switch
2. Clutch idler arm
3. Blade brake spring
4. Belt retainer
5. Clutch idler pulley
6. Pin
7. Mower mount
7A. Locknut
8. Belt retainers
9. Mower spindle assy.
10. Clutch tension spring
11. Mower belt
12. Blade clutch lever
13. Deflector
14. Lever bracket (upper)
15. Lever bracket (lower)
16. Gage wheels
17. Rear guide bar
18. Mower housing
19. Blade 26"
20. Belleville washers

Dynamark

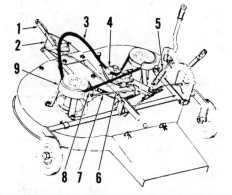

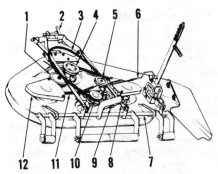

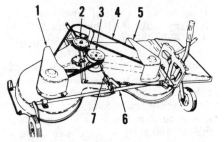

Fig. DM10—View of typical double spindle mower unit used on some models.

1. Bar hitch
2. Pivot bracket
3. Blade drive belt
4. Belt retainer
5. Blade engage spring
6. Lift cable & clevis
7. Blade brake rod
8. Left brake bracket
9. Belt guard

Fig. DM12—View of early style (prior to 1979) triple spindle mower unit. Unit uses a deck drive belt and a blade drive belt.

1. Front idler
2. Hitch pull pin
3. Deck drive belt
4. Center spindle assy.
5. Idler pulley & belt retainer
6. Blade clutch rod
7. Rear roller shaft
8. Eyebolt
9. Deck drive spring
10. Jackshaft pulley
11. Blade drive belt
12. Spindle shield

Fig. DM13—View of late style (1979 and on) triple spindle mower unit. Unit uses a single drive belt.

1. Spindle shield
2. Idler pulley & belt retainer
3. Center spindle
4. Drive belt
5. Spindle shield
6. Deck guide bar
7. Lift cable & clevis

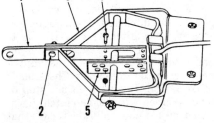

Fig. DM11—View of mower front hitch and pivot bracket.

1. Bar hitch
2. Bolt
3. Pivot bracket
4. Bolt
5. Lock bracket

clockwise to tighten belt. Hold bolt and tighten jam nut, then check blade brake action. If blades do not stop or tend to creep, belt adjustment is too tight.

On early production rear discharge and intermediate production side discharge models, adjust belt as follows: Disengage mower clutch and loosen bolt securing bar hitch (1-Fig. DM10) to pivot bracket (2), then loosen front and tighten rear nut on adjustment screw to tighten belt. Tighten bar hitch bolt and check blade brake action. If blades do not stop or tend to creep, adjust nuts on brake rod (7) that connects to left brake bracket (8). There should be approximately 1/16-inch (1.6 mm) clearance between nuts and bracket with mower clutch disengaged.

On late production side and rear discharge models, adjust belt as follows: Disengage blade clutch and loosen bar hitch bolt (2-Fig. DM11). Remove bolt (4) from lock bracket (5) and slide bar hitch (1) forward to tighten belt. Tighten bar hitch bolt and check blade brake action. If blades do not stop or tend to creep, belt adjustment is too tight.

When adjustment is correct, reinstall bolt in lock bracket.

REMOVE AND REINSTALL. Disconnect spark plug wire and remove mower as outlined in MOWER DECK paragraphs. Note position of idler pulley belt retainer (4-Fig. DM10), and loosen idler pulley mounting bolt. Loosen belt guards and remove belt.

Install new belt by reversing removal procedure. Hold idler pulley belt retainer in position and tighten bolt. Adjust belt guides to $1/16$-inch (1.6 mm) clearance from belt. Check belt adjustment as previously outlined.

Models With 42-Inch Mower

ADJUSTMENT. On early production models, two belts are used — a deck drive belt (3-Fig. DM12) and a blade drive belt (11). To adjust deck drive belt, disengage blade clutch and adjust clutch rod (6) to increase or decrease idler spring tension. Deck hanger clevis, mounted on front axle pivot bolt, should be positioned halfway between engine pulley and front axle. To adjust blade drive belt, loosen front idler pulley (1) and move pulley toward center of mower deck to tighten belt.

On late production models, adjust belt as follows: Disengage blade clutch and loosen bar hitch bolt (2-Fig. DM11). Remove bolt from lock bracket (5) and slide bar hitch (1) forward to tighten belt. Tighten bar hitch bolt and check blade brake action. If blades do not stop or tend to creep, belt adjustment is too tight. When adjustment is correct, reinstall bolt in lock bracket.

REMOVE AND REINSTALL. On early production models, remove drive belts as follows: Remove mower as outlined in MOWER DECK paragraphs. Remove belt shields and loosen and move belt guides away from pulleys. Note position of idler pulley belt retainer (5-Fig. DM12), then loosen idler pulley bolt. Note position of deck drive spring (9), then unhook spring. Remove belts from pulleys.

Install new belts by reversing removal procedure. Hold idler pulley belt retainer in position while tightening bolt. Adjust belt guides to 1/16-inch (1.6 mm) from belt. Adjust belts as previously outlined.

On late production models, remove drive belt as follows: Place mower in lowest position. Loosen and move belt guides away from pulleys. Note position of idler pulley belt retainer (2-Fig. DM13), then loosen retainer. Remove belt from pulleys.

Install new belt by reversing removal procedure. Hold idler pulley belt retainer in position while tightening bolt. Adjust belt guides to 1/16-inch (1.6 mm) from belt. Adjust belt as previously outlined.

MOWER SPINDLE

All Models

REMOVE AND REINSTALL. The spindle assemblies are similar on all models. The spindle, spindle housing and mower pulley are available only as an assembly. Refer to Fig. DM9 or DM14 and remove mower spindle assembly as follows: Remove mower unit and drive belt. Place wood block between blade and mower housing to prevent blade from turning. Remove retaining cap screw, washers and blade from spindle. Unbolt and remove spindle assembly from top of mower housing. Renew parts as necessary and reassemble by reversing removal procedure. Torque blade mounting cap screw to 30-35 ft.-lbs. (40-48 N·m).

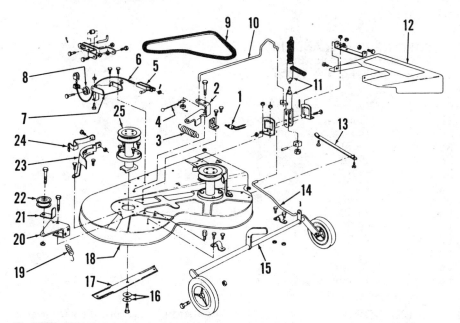

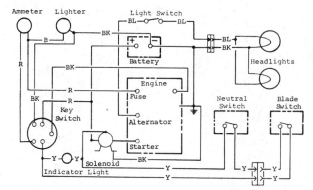

Fig. DM14—Exploded view of typical double spindle mower unit.

1. Safety starting switch
2. Bellcrank
3. Clutch tension spring
4. Brake cable
5. Clevis
6. Lift cable
7. Lift bracket
8. Pulley
9. Mower belt
10. Clutch rod
11. Lift and blade clutch lever
12. Deflector
13. Skid bar
14. Lift rod
15. Gage wheels assy.
16. Belleville washers
17. Blade 18"
18. Mower housing
19. Spring
20. Clutch idler arm
21. Belt retainer
22. Clutch idler pulley
23. Belt guard
24. Blade brake
25. Mower spindle assy.

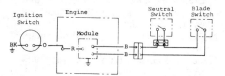

Fig. DM15—Wiring diagram for manual start models with safety interlock starting system.

1. BK-Black
2. O-Orange
3. R-Red
4. B-Brown

MOWER DECK

All Models

LEVEL ADJUSTMENT. With unit on level surface and tires properly inflated, measure height of blade from ground at front and rear of mower deck. Blade should be approximately ⅛-inch (3 mm) lower in front.

Fig. DM16—Wiring diagram for electric start models with safety interlock, headlights, indicator light, ammeter and lighter.

1. R-Red
2. B-Brown
3. Y-Yellow
4. BK-Black
5. BL-Blue

To level mowers equipped with lift cable (6-Fig. DM10), raise and block front of mower deck to remove weight of unit from lift cable. Remove clevis pin from cable rear clevis and turn clevis to raise or lower front of deck. Each 1½ turn of clevis changes front deck height approximately ⅛ inch (3 mm).

To level 26 inch mowers not equipped with lift cable, loosen front deck hanger mounting bolts and move hanger up or down to desired level position. Retighten hanger mounting bolts.

To level 42 inch mowers not equipped with lift cable, lower mower to lowest position and place block under rear of mower deck. Disconnect lift linkage eye bolts (8-Fig. DM12) from rear roller shaft (7). Turn eye bolts clockwise to lower rear of deck. Both eyebolts must be turned same number of turns. Reconnect eyebolts to roller shaft.

All Models

REMOVE AND REINSTALL. Place mower in lowest position and disengage blade clutch. Turn front wheels full left, and disconnect mower safety switch wires. Remove pull pin securing mower deck to front mounting bracket. Move mower deck forward to free rear deck guide bracket, then loosen belt guides on engine pulley and slip mower drive belt off pulley. Deck can now be slid out from under right side of unit. On some models removal will be easier if right front of unit is raised to provide clearance.

Reinstall deck by reversing removal procedure. Check deck level adjustment and blade drive belt adjustment.

ELECTRICAL

All Models

All models are equipped with safety interlock starting systems to prevent starting when drives are engaged. Refer to wiring diagrams Fig. DM15 and Fig. DM16.

FORD

FORD NEW HOLLAND, INC.
500 Diller Avenue
New Holland, PA 17557

Model	Make	Engine Model	Horsepower	Cutting Width, In.
51	B&S	130902	5	26
60	B&S	170702	7	30
61	B&S	190702	8	30
65	B&S	170705	7	30
66	B&S	190705	8	30
526	B&S	130902	5	26
830	B&S	190702	8	30
830E	B&S	190705	8	30
1130E	B&S	252707	11	30
R8	B&S	191702	8	30
R8E	B&S	191707	8	30
R11E	B&S	252707	11	30

For service information and procedures on **FRICTION-DRIVE** Models 830, 830E and 1130E, use the following model cross reference and refer to JACOBSEN section of this manual.

Ford Model	Jacobsen Model
830	RMX
830E	RMX
1130E	RMX

For **BELT-DRIVE** Models 830, 830E and 1130E, refer to the following service procedures.

FRONT AXLE

All Models

Axle main member is center-pivoted and mounts within cross channel at front of main frame. Removal of underchassis items may be aided by standing mower unit upright on its rear stand. If this is done, observe the following:

CAUTION: Frequently, the performance of maintenance, adjustment or repair operations on a riding mower is more convenient if mower is standing on end and these units are provided with a stand for this purpose. This procedure can be considered a recommended practice providing the following safety recommendations are performed:

1. Drain fuel tank or make certain that fuel level is low enough so that fuel will not drain out.
2. Close fuel shut-off valve if so equipped.
3. Remove battery on models so equipped.

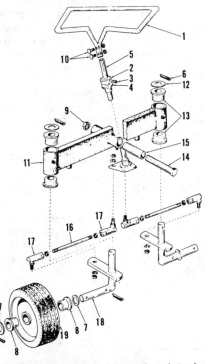

Fig. F1—Exploded view of front axle and steering assembly used on Models 51, 60 and 65.

1. Steering handle
2. Steering shaft collar
3. Set screw
4. Steering shaft bearing
5. Steering shaft
6. Pin
7. Washers
8. Wheel bushings
9. Nut
10. Screws
11. Axle
12. Washer
13. Spindle bushings
14. Axle pivot bolt
15. Axle spacer
16. Steering tie rod
17. Tie rod end
18. Spindle
19. Wheel

Fig. F2—Exploded view of front axle and steering gear used on Models 51, 61 and 66.

1. Steering wheel
2. Tube
3. Washers
4. Washer
5. Steering shaft
6. Roll pin
7. Steering gear
8. Bearing
9. Collar
10. Pinion gear
11. Axle
12. Washer
13. Spindle bushings
14. Axle pivot bolt
15. Spacer
16. Nut
17. Tie rod
18. Spindle
19. Pin
20. Washer
21. Wheel bushings
22. Wheel
23. Bolt
24. Washer
25. Spacer
26. Flanged bearing (in steering console)

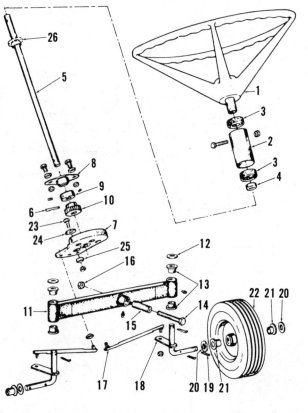

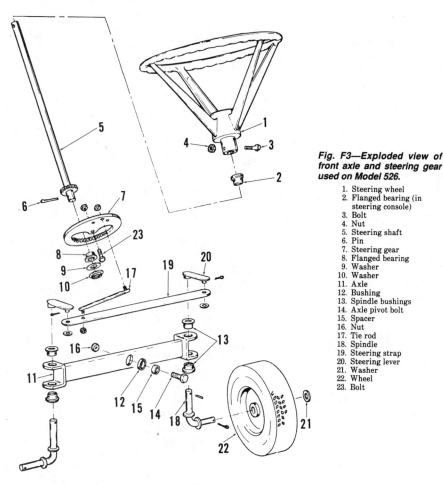

Models 51-60-65

REMOVE AND REINSTALL. To remove steering gear, first stand unit on end as previously outlined. Disconnect tie rod ends (17-Fig. F1) from bottom of steering shaft (5). Unbolt steering handle (1) from steering shaft. Loosen set screw (3) in steering shaft collar (2), then lower shaft out of steering support and remove collar (2) and bearing (4).

Reinstall in reverse order of removal. When installing steering shaft, remove all end play, then push collar (2) down against bearing (4) and tighten set screw to hold shaft in position.

Other Models

REMOVE AND REINSTALL. To remove steering gear, stand unit on end as previously outlined. On Model 526 only, remove steering console front cover and frame front plate. On all models remove steering wheel retaining bolt and pull steering wheel (1-Fig. F2, F3 or F4) from steering shaft (5). On all models except Model 526, remove steering tube (2) and washers (3 and 4), then unbolt and remove steering console and shaft upper bearing (26). Disconnect tie rods (17) from steering gear (7). On Models 51, 61 and 66, drive roll pin (6-Fig. F2) from pinion gear (10) and loos-

Fig. F3—Exploded view of front axle and steering gear used on Model 526.

1. Steering wheel
2. Flanged bearing (in steering console)
3. Bolt
4. Nut
5. Steering shaft
6. Pin
7. Steering gear
8. Flanged bearing
9. Washer
10. Washer
11. Axle
12. Bushing
13. Spindle bushings
14. Axle pivot bolt
15. Spacer
16. Nut
17. Tie rod
18. Spindle
19. Steering strap
20. Steering lever
21. Washer
22. Wheel
23. Bolt

4. Disconnect spark plug wire and tie out of way.
5. Although not absolutely essential, it is recommended that crankcase oil be drained to avoid flooding the combustion chamber with oil when engine is tilted.
6. Secure mower from tipping by lashing unit to a nearby post or overhead beam.

REMOVE AND REINSTALL. To remove front axle (11-Fig. F1, F2, F3 or F4), raise and block front of frame or stand unit on end. On all models except Model 526, unbolt outer ends of tie rods (17) from steering spindles (18). On Model 526, unbolt end of tie rod (17) from steering strap (19). On all models, remove front wheels from spindles, then remove pivot bolt (14) and spacer (15) from frame and withdraw axle member from frame channel. With axle assembly separated from frame, remove retaining pins and remove spindles (18) and bushings (13) from axle ends.

Clean and inspect parts for possible renewal. Reinstall in reverse order of removal. Lubricate at fittings using multi-purpose lithium base grease. Use SAE 30 oil at pivot points not having grease fittings.

Fig. F4—Exploded view of front axle and steering gear used on Models 830, 830E and 1130E. Models R8, R8E and R11E are similar.

1. Steering wheel
2. Tube
3. Washers
4. Spring washers
5. Steering shaft
6. Pin
7. Steering gear
8. Flanged bearing
9. Washer
10. Washer
11. Axle
12. Washer
13. Spindle bushings
14. Axle pivot bolt
15. Spacer
16. Nut
17. Tie rod
18. Spindle
19. Washer
20. Felt washer
21. Wheel bushing
22. Wheel
23. Bolt
24. Washer
25. Spacer
26. Flanged bearing (in steering console)

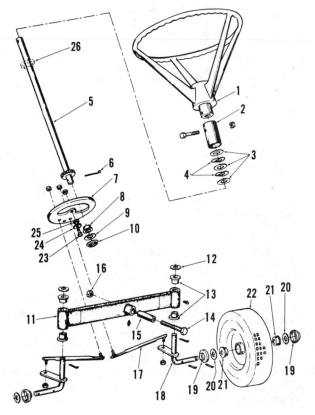

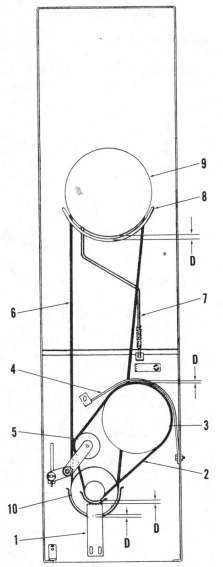

Fig. F5—Typical traction drive and blade drive belt installation. Note belt guide clearance "D" of 1/16 to 1/8 inch (1.6-3 mm) between guide and outside surface of belt or pulley.

1. Engine pulley belt guide
2. Traction drive belt
3. Transmission pulley
4. Transmission pulley belt guide
5. Idler pulley
6. Blade drive belt
7. Blade brake rod
8. Blade drive belt guide
9. Blade pulley
10. Engine pulley

en set screws in collar (9). Unbolt bearing (8) and remove steering shaft, bearing, collar and pinion gear. Remove bolt (23), washer (24) and spacer (25), then lift out steering gear (7). On Models 526, 830, 830E and 1130E, remove pin (6-Fig. F3 or F4) and withdraw steering shaft (5), bearing (8) and washers (9 and 10). Remove retaining bolt (23) and lift out steering gear (7). Clean and inspect parts for wear and renew as necessary.

Reinstall in reverse of removal procedure. Lubricate bushings and pivot points with SAE 30 oil. Apply light coat of multi-purpose grease to pinion gear and steering gear teeth.

ENGINE

Refer to appropriate engine section in this manual for tune-up specifications, engine overhaul procedures and engine maintenance.

Refer to the following paragraphs for removal and installation procedures.

All Models Except Models R8, R8E And R11E

REMOVE AND REINSTALL. To remove engine, disconnect spark plug wire, battery cables, throttle control cable and wiring harness from engine. Remove hitch plate from rear of frame. Place mower blade clutch control lever in disengaged position and mower height control lever in lowest position. Depress clutch pedal and engage pedal lock. Remove engine pulley belt guide and slip blade drive belt and traction drive belt off engine pulley. Remove engine mounting bolts and lift engine from frame.

Reinstall engine by reversing removal procedure. Make certain belt guides are reinstalled properly and all safety starting switches are connected and operating properly.

Models R8-R8E-R11E

REMOVE AND REINSTALL. To remove engine, set parking brake and disconnect spark plug. Disconnect and remove battery as equipped. Drain fuel tank and engine crankcase. Disconnect throttle cable and all necessary electrical connections. Raise front of rider and stand on rear support bars. Remove drive belt guide near engine pulley. Remove idler pulley. Lower front of rider back to the ground and remove the four bolts securing engine to main frame. Lift engine slightly and move engine forward. Reach under rear of main frame and remove drive belt from engine pulley. Remove engine noting location and quantity of engine mounting spacer washers for reinstallation.

Reinstall engine by reversing removal procedure. Make certain belt guides are reinstalled properly and all safety starting switches are connected and operating properly.

TRACTION DRIVE CLUTCH AND DRIVE BELT

All Models

All models use a pedal-operated, spring-loaded belt idler to apply or relieve tension on drive belt. No adjust-

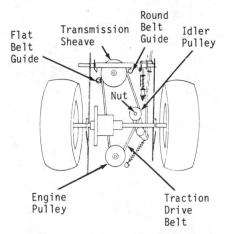

Fig. F5A—View showing location of belts and pulley arrangement on Models R8, R8E and R11E.

ment is provided. If belt slippage occurs during normal operation due to belt wear or stretching, belt must be renewed.

All Models Except Models R8, R8E And R11E

REMOVE AND REINSTALL. To remove traction drive belt (2-Fig. F5), disconnect spark plug wire, then place blade clutch control lever in disengaged position and height control lever in lowest position. Depress clutch pedal and engage pedal lock. Stand unit on end as previously outlined. Remove engine pulley belt guide (1) and slip mower drive belt (6) off engine pulley (10). Remove idler pulley (5). Loosen transmission pulley belt guide (8) and move guide away from pulley, then pull belt out between pulleys and frame.

Renew belt in reverse order of removal. Adjust belt guides to provide $\frac{1}{16}$ to $\frac{1}{8}$-inch (1.6-3mm) clearance between inside of guide and outer surface of belt.

Models R8-R8E-R11E

REMOVE AND REINSTALL. To remove traction drive belt (Fig. F5A), disconnect spark plug. Remove mower deck and set parking brake. Drain fuel from tank and engine oil from crankcase. Disconnect and remove battery as equipped. Raise front of rider and stand on rear support bars. Remove idler pulley. Loosen flat belt guide and rotate guide 90° clockwise. Remove round belt guide and then remove traction drive belt.

Renew belt in reverse order of removal. Manufacturer recommends applying talcum powder or soap stone powder to new belts and operating rider in first gear for at least 10 minutes at low speed to break-in new belts.

Illustrations Courtesy Ford New Holland Inc.

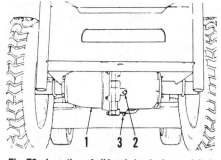

Fig. F6—Location of oil level check plug and drain plug on transaxle.

1. Transaxle
2. Oil level check plug
3. Drain plug

TRANSAXLE

All Models So Equipped

LUBRICATION. With unit on level surface, check rear axle oil by removing oil level plug (2-Fig. F6). If lubricant does not run out, add SAE 90 EP oil through oil level hole until it begins to run out. Do not overfill. The transaxle lubricant can be drained by removing drain plug (3) in bottom of housing.

REMOVE AND REINSTALL. To remove transaxle (18-Fig. F7), disengage mower blade clutch and place mower in lowest position. Depress clutch pedal and engage pedal lock, then stand unit on end as previously outlined. Disconnect brake rod (13) from brake lever (19). Remove retaining ring (17) from axle ends and remove wheels. Place temporary support under axle, then unbolt axle from mounting bracket (15) and frame. Slip traction drive belt (1) off transaxle pulley (10), and lower transaxle assembly from frame.
Reinstall in reverse order of removal.

OVERHAUL. The transaxles used are Peerless models. For overhaul procedures, refer to TRANSMISSION REPAIR service section of this manual.

TRANSMISSION

Model 526

REMOVE AND REINSTALL. To remove transmission, remove seat and seat bracket. Disconnect drive chain and safety switch. Remove throttle cable clamp from left side of transmission. Remove transmission mounting bolts and remove transmission.
Reinstall in reverse order of removal making certain throttle cable clamp is correctly positioned and safety switch is connected.

OVERHAUL. A Peerless transmission is used. For overhaul procedures, refer to TRANSMISSION REPAIR service section of this manual.

Models R8-R8E-R11E

REMOVE AND REINSTALL. To remove transmission, drain fuel tank and disconnect and remove battery (as equipped). Remove mower deck as required. Tilt seat up and remove cap screw and washers retaining transmission shift lever to top of transmission. Move lever out of the way. Remove the chain guard and unhook brake return spring from hole in transmission brake control arm. Stand mower on rear support bars. Use wire to lock battery box cover in open position. Locate drive chain master link and remove chain from sprocket (right rear wheel assembly may have to be removed to gain access to master link). Remove idler pulley, loosen locknut retaining flat belt guide and rotate belt guide 90° clockwise. Remove cap screw retaining round belt guide to main frame. Remove traction drive belt from transmission pulley. Disconnect transmission brake control arm at brake adjustment rod link. Remove transmission pulley and key from transmission input shaft. Remove the three remaining cap screws securing transmission to main frame and lift transmission out of battery access hole.
Reinstall transmission by reversing the removal procedure. Make certain brake is readjusted and all belt guides are in place.

OVERHAUL. For transmission overhaul procedure, refer to Peerless Series 700 paragraphs in the TRANSMISSION REPAIR section of this manual.

DRIVE CHAIN

Model 526

ADJUSTMENT. To adjust chain, loosen nuts securing axle bearing retainer plates to frame. Move plates rearward to tighten chain. Both plates must be moved equal distance to keep axle square with frame. Chain should have ⅛ to ¼-inch (3-6.4 mm) deflection. When tension is correct, tighten bearing plate nuts.

REMOVE AND REINSTALL. Remove chain guard, then rotate rear wheel to locate master link at transmission sprocket. Disconnect master link and remove chain. Clean and inspect

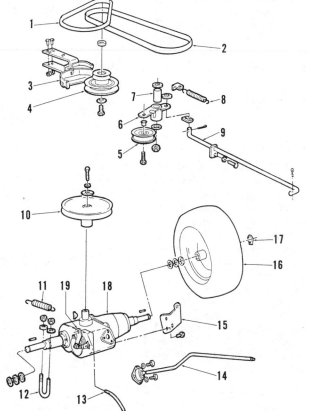

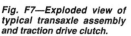

Fig. F7—Exploded view of typical transaxle assembly and traction drive clutch.

1. Traction drive belt
2. Blade drive belt
3. Engine pulley belt guide
4. Engine pulley
5. Idler pulley
6. Idler pivot bracket
7. Sleeve
8. Idler arm spring
9. Clutch rod
10. Transaxle pulley
11. Brake return spring
12. U-bolt
13. Brake rod
14. Shift lever
15. Mounting bracket
16. Wheel
17. Retaining ring
18. Transaxle
19. Brake lever

Ford

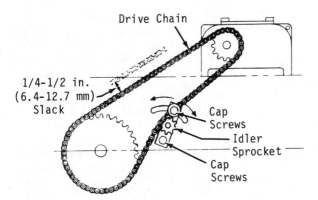

Fig. F7A—Drive chain on Models R8, R8E and R11E should be adjusted to provide 1/4-1/2 inch (6.4-12.7 mm) slack at point shown. Refer to text.

chain and renew if excessively worn.

Reinstall in reverse order of removal. Adjust chain tension and lubricate with light coat of SAE 30 oil.

Models R8-R8E-R11E

ADJUSTMENT. Drive chain tension should be adjusted to provide ¼ - ½ inch (6.4-12.7 mm) slack at point indicated in Fig. F7A. Chain tension may be increased or decreased by loosening cap screws and adjusting drive chain idler sprocket.

REMOVE AND REINSTALL. Raise and support rear of rider so drive wheels are off the ground. Remove the chain guard and rotate rear drive wheel until drive chain master link is accessible. Carefully remove master link while holding chain ends. Connect one end of new chain to master link and the old chain end and slowly pull chain out over transmission sprocket until master link and new chain appears again. Remove old chain section and install new master link. Adjust chain tension as necessary.

DIFFERENTIAL

Model 526

REMOVE AND REINSTALL. To remove differential, raise rear of unit and support securely. Disconnect master link and remove drive chain. Remove retaining ring from axle ends and remove rear wheels. Unbolt bearing retainer plates and withdraw differential assembly from chassis. Clean paint, rust and dirt from axle ends before removing bearings.

Reinstall in reverse order of removal. Adjust drive chain tension as outlined in previous paragraphs. Apply light coat of SAE 30 oil to chain. Lubricate axle bearings with multi-purpose lithium base grease.

OVERHAUL. A Peerless model differential is used. For differential over-

haul procedures, refer to DIFFERENTIAL REPAIR service section of this manual.

Models R8-R8E-R11E

REMOVE AND REINSTALL. To remove the differential assembly, raise rear of chassis and support securely. Remove snap rings, wheels, square keys and axle spacers from left and right sides of rear axle. Locate drive chain master link and remove master link and drive chain. Support differential and remove the two top nuts and carriage bolts at right side axle bearing plate. Slide axle bearing plate off axle. Slide differential out of left axle bearing plate.

OVERHAUL. All models are equipped with Peerless 100 series differential. Refer to the DIFFERENTIAL REPAIR section of this manual.

GROUND DRIVE BRAKE

All Models

The brake used on early Models 51, 60 and 65 is a band and drum type (Fig. F8). A caliper type disc brake (Fig. F9) is used on all other models.

ADJUSTMENT. To adjust brake, depress clutch pedal and brake pedal and engage pedal locks, then attempt to

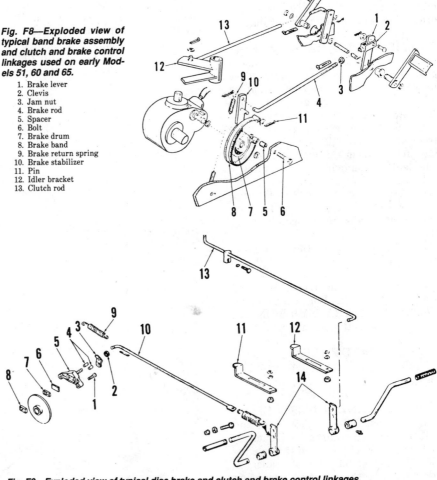

Fig. F8—Exploded view of typical band brake assembly and clutch and brake control linkages used on early Models 51, 60 and 65.

1. Brake lever
2. Clevis
3. Jam nut
4. Brake rod
5. Spacer
6. Bolt
7. Brake drum
8. Brake band
9. Brake return spring
10. Brake stabilizer
11. Pin
12. Idler bracket
13. Clutch rod

Fig. F9—Exploded view of typical disc brake and clutch and brake control linkages.

1. Bolt
2. Adjusting nut
3. Brake lever
4. Actuating pins
5. Carrier
6. Back-up plate
7. Outer brake pad
8. Inner brake pad
9. Brake return spring
10. Brake rod
11. Brake lock lever
12. Clutch lock lever
13. Clutch rod
14. Brake and clutch link

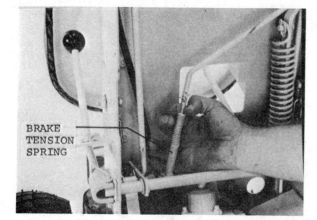

Illustrations Courtesy Ford New Holland Inc.

Fig. F10—View of brake tension spring and holes in brake rod used to adjust length of spring.

BRAKE TENSION SPRING

push unit. If rear wheels rotate, release brake pedal and tighten adjusting nut (2–Fig. F9) ½ turn on disc brake. On band brake, loosen jam nut (3–Fig. F8) on brake rod (4), then disconnect clevis (2) from brake lever (1). Turn clevis ½ turn onto brake rod to tighten brake band. Recheck brake operation and repeat adjustment as required.

REMOVE AND REINSTALL. To remove brake band (8–Fig. F8), remove pin (11) securing band to brake stabilizer (10). Remove anchor bolt (6) and spacer (5), then slide band off brake drum (7). Renew brake band by reversing removal procedure and adjust brake as outlined in previous paragraph.

SCREWS

HOUSING ADJUSTMENT STRAP

HOUSING ENGAGING STRAP

Fig. F11—View of adjustment strap and engaging strap. Linkage is lengthened to decrease belt tension or shortened to increase belt tension.

To remove disc brake, unhook brake return spring (9-Fig. F9), then disconnect brake rod (10) from brake cam lever (3). Unscrew cap screws (1), then remove brake parts (2 through 7). Remove adjusting nut (2) and separate cam lever (3), actuating pins (4), backup plate (6) and outer brake pad (7) from carrier (5). Slide brake disc from transmission shaft and remove inner brake pad (8) from holder slot in transmission case.

Clean and inspect all parts for excessive wear or damage. Renew parts as required and reassemble by reversing removal procedure. Adjust brake as previously outlined.

BLADE DRIVE BRAKE

Models 51-60-61-65-66

ADJUSTMENT. Disconnect spark plug wire and disengage blade clutch, then stand unit on rear as previously outlined. Compress brake tension spring (Fig. F10) and reposition retainer pin in blade brake rod to increase spring tension and shorten braking time. An additional adjustment can be

made as shown in Fig. F11. Loosen screws holding adjustment strap to engaging strap, and move adjustment strap to lengthen the linkage. Tighten screws in linkage, then recheck braking action and repeat adjustment as necessary.

Models 830-830E-1130E

ADJUSTMENT. Disconnect spark plug wire and disengage blade clutch. Loosen the three screws on both adjustment plates (3-Fig. F12). Moving adjustment plates rearward, to decrease tension on drive belt (1), will shorten braking time. When adjustment is correct, tighten adjustment plate screws and check mower deck level adjustment.

Models R8-R8E-R11E

ADJUSTMENT. Mower drive belt brake is controlled by mower drive belt adjustment on early models and by mower drive cable adjustment of late models. Refer to appropriate DRIVE BELT section. If mower drive belt or drive cable is correctly adjusted and mower drive belt still does not function properly, mower drive brake must be renewed.

MOWER DRIVE BELT

Models 51-60-61-65-66

ADJUSTMENT. Disconnect spark plug wire. Disengage blade drive clutch and set mower deck in highest position. Loosen screws (Fig. F11) securing housing adjustment strap to housing engaging strap, then move adjustment strap rearward to shorten linkage and increase belt tension. When adjustment is correct, tighten screws. Make sure

Fig. F12—View of mower deck mounting brackets and adjustment plates. Note locating stud on front mounting bracket must be inserted into hole in frame for proper mower deck alignment.

1. Blade drive belt
2. Mounting chain
3. Adjustment plates
4. Cam nuts
5. Mounting straps
6. Pins
7. Support shafts
8. Front mounting bracket
9. Locating stud
10. Rear mounting bracket

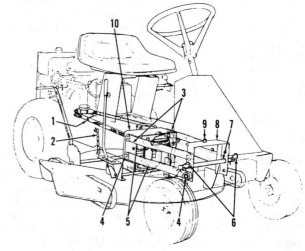

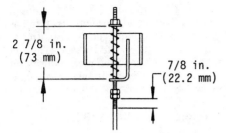

Fig. F12A—Spring measurements should be as shown. Refer to text.

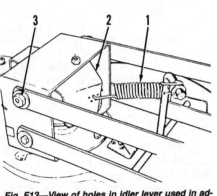

Fig. F13—View of holes in idler lever used in adjusting blade engage spring tension on Model 526.
1. Engaging spring
2. Idler lever
3. Cam nut

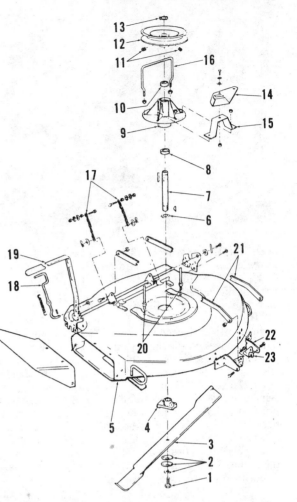

Fig. F14—Exploded view of mower deck with lift operating controls used on Model 51.

1. Bolt
2. Washers
3. Blade
4. Blade holder
5. Mower deck
6. Retaining ring
7. Spindle shaft
8. Bearing
9. Bearing retainer housing
10. Bearing
11. Set screws
12. Blade pulley
13. Retaining ring
14. Brake lever
15. Brake mounting bracket
16. Belt guide
17. Lift chains
18. Latch slide
19. Height adjusting shaft
20. Belt guides
21. Parallel bars
22. Mounting bracket
23. Pivot bracket

blade braking action is not slowed by having linkage too short. Refer to blade brake adjustment covered in previous paragraphs.

Model 526

ADJUSTMENT. Disconnect spark plug wire. Disengage blade drive clutch and set mower deck in lowest position. Remove engaging spring (1-Fig. F13) from idler lever (2) and relocate spring to hole which increases tension on spring.

Models 830-830E-1130E

ADJUSTMENT. Disconnect spark plug wire. Disengage blade drive clutch and set mower deck in lowest position. Loosen the three screws on both adjustment plates (3-Fig. F12). Move adjustment plates forward to increase tension on drive belt. Tighten adjustment plate screws and check mower deck position. Make sure blade braking action is not slowed by having blade drive belt too tight. Refer to blade brake adjustment covered in previous paragraphs.

Early Models R8-R8E-R11E

ADJUSTMENT. To adjust mower drive belt, engage mower drive lever. Remove plastic tray from frame in front of seat. Refer to Fig. F12A and adjust nuts on rod to obtain spring

measurements shown. Look at drive belt through slot in rear hitch plate. Mower drive belt sides must be more than 1 inch (25.4 mm) from each other at closest point. If less than 1 inch (25.4 mm) clearance is observed, disengage mower drive lever, loosen the two nuts on each of the three mower deck brackets and move mower deck bracket toward rear of mower deck. Tighten bracket retaining nuts and check measurements.

Late Models R8-R8E-R11E

ADJUSTMENT. To check mower drive cable tension, lift mower drive lever upward from its full engaged position (lever against back of footrest). There should be no more than ½-1 inch (12.7-25.4 mm) initial movement of lever before resistance in cable can be felt.

To adjust mower drive cable, place mower in lowest cutting position. Locate threaded adjusting end of mower drive cable attached to cable bracket behind right side of footrest, on underside of frame. Loosen and back off the jam nut from the cable bracket 4 or 5 turns. Take up cable slack and increase cable tension by turning the adjusting

nut (on opposite side of bracket) further onto cable end. Check mower drive cable tension as previously outlined.

If mower drive cable is over tensioned, mower drive belt cannot fully disengage from the blade pulley and the mower blade brake will not operate properly.

All Models

REMOVE AND REINSTALL. Disconnect spark plug wire and remove console tray. Disengage blade clutch and set mower height to lowest position. Stand unit on end as previously outlined. Remove engine pulley belt guide (1-Fig. F5) and slip belt off engine pulley (10). Move blade clutch control lever to engaged position. Disconnect blade brake rod (7) from brake lever at mower spindle on Models 51, 60, 61, 65 and 66. Remove or tilt remaining belt guides as necessary to slip drive belt out of blade pulley and idler pulley, then pull belt free of mower.

Renew belt by reversing removal procedures and adjust to proper tension as previously outlined. Adjust belt guides to provide clearance "D" 1/16 to ⅛ inch (1.6-3 mm) between guide and outside surface of belt or pulley.

Illustrations Courtesy Ford New Holland Inc.

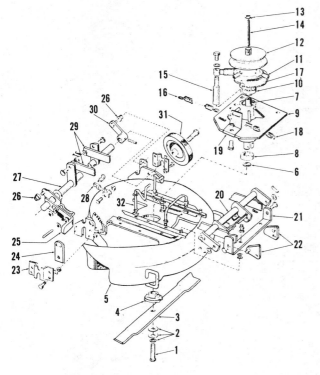

Fig. F15—Exploded view of mower deck and spindle assembly with lift operating controls used on early Models 60 and 65.

1. Bolt
2. Washers
3. Blade
4. Blade holder
5. Mower deck
6. Retaining ring
7. Spindle shaft
8. Bearing
9. Bearing retainer housing
10. Bearing
11. Set screws
12. Blade pulley
13. Retaining ring
14. Square key
15. Brake band spacer
16. Brake spring
17. Brake band
18. Brake release spring
19. Brake band bracket
20. Pivot shaft
21. Front support
22. Height adjusting plates
23. Height adjustment slide retainer
24. Height adjustment slide
25. Handle grip
26. Height adjustment slide bushings
27. Wheel adjustment shaft
28. Chain
29. Height adjustment straps
30. Height adjustment link
31. Height adjustment wheel
32. Belt guide

MOWER SPINDLE

Model 51

REMOVE AND REINSTALL. Remove mower deck as outlined in MOWER DECK paragraphs. Remove blade retaining bolt (1–Fig. 14) and remove washers (2), blade (3) and blade holder (4) from spindle shaft (7). Remove blade pulley retaining ring (13) and loosen set screws (11), then pull blade pulley (12) off spindle shaft. Unbolt and remove brake mounting bracket (15) and brake lever (14), belt guide (16) and bearing retainer housing (9) from mower deck. Remove snap ring (6) from bottom of spindle shaft and separate shaft and bearings (8 and 10) from retainer housing.

Clean and inspect all parts and renew any showing excessive wear or damage. Reinstall by reversing removal procedure. Spindle bearings are sealed and require no additional lubrication.

Models 60-65

REMOVE AND REINSTALL. Remove mower deck as outlined in MOWER DECK paragraphs. Remove blade retaining bolt (1–Fig. F15) and remove washers (2), blade (3) and blade holder (4) from spindle shaft (7). Unbolt brake band spacer (15) from brake band (17), then disconnect and remove brake drum from brake band bracket (19). Loosen set screws (11) and remove retaining ring (13) from blade pulley (12), then pull pulley off spindle shaft

(7). Unbolt and remove bearing retainer housing (9) from mower deck. Remove retaining ring (6) from bottom of spindle shaft, then separate shaft and bearings (8 and 10) from retainer housing.

Clean and inspect all parts and renew any showing excessive wear or damage. Reinstall by reversing removal procedure.

Models 60-61-65-66-830-830E

REMOVE AND REINSTALL. Remove mower deck as outlined in MOW-

Fig. F16—Exploded view of mower deck and spindle assembly with lift operating controls used on late Models 60 and 65, Models 61 and 66 and early Models 830 and 830E. Note on Models 830 and 830E the spindle is renewed as a complete assembly. All other models can be renewed as shown in inset.

1. Bolt
2. Washers
3. Blade
4. Holder
5. Mower deck
6. Retaining ring
7. Spindle shaft
8. Bearing
9. Bearing retainer housing
10. Bearing
11. Set screws
12. Blade pulley
13. Retaining ring
14. Blade brake lever
15. Blade spindle assy.
16. Clutch lever
17. Chains
18. Slide latch
19. Height adjust shaft
20. Blade brake rod
21. Height adjust straps
22. Height adjust plate
23. Front support
24. Stabilizer
25. Belt guide

ER DECK paragraphs. Remove blade retaining bolt (1–Fig. F16) and remove washers (2), blade (3) and blade holder (4) from spindle shaft (7). Remove retaining ring (13) and loosen set screws (11), then pull blade pulley (12) off spindle shaft (7). Unbolt and remove spindle bearing housing (9) from mower deck. Remove retaining ring (6) from bottom of spindle shaft and separate shaft and bearings (8 and 10) from retainer housing. On Models 830 and 830E, the pulley and spindle assembly (15) is renewed as complete unit.

Clean and inspect parts and renew any showing excessive wear or damage. Reinstall by reversing removal procedure. Spindle bearings are sealed and require no additional lubrication.

Models 526-830-830E-1130E

REMOVE AND REINSTALL. Remove mower deck as outlined in MOWER DECK paragraphs. Remove blade retaining bolt (1–Fig. F17) and remove washers (2) and blade (3) from spindle. Unbolt and remove idler pulley (9) and idler lever (11) and mounting bracket (13) from mower deck. Unbolt blade spindle assembly (8) and lift off mower deck. Blade spindle assembly is renewed as a complete unit.

Reinstall in reverse order of removal and check level adjustment.

Models R8-R8E-R11E

REMOVE AND REINSTALL. Remove mower deck as outlined in MOWER DECK paragraphs. Remove blade brake spring and mower drive belt.

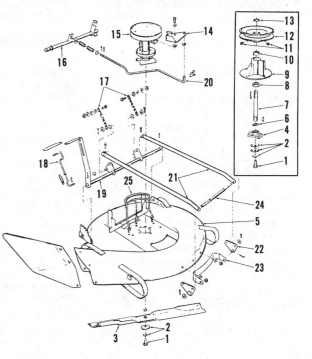

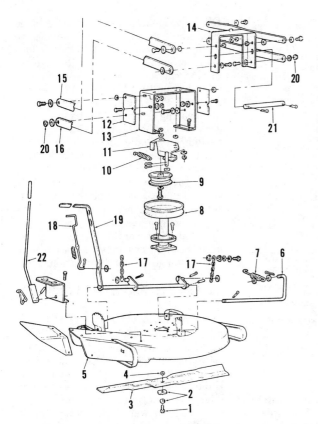

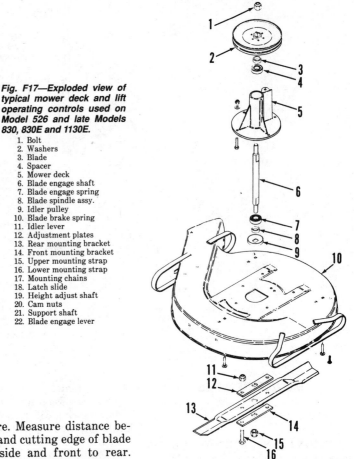

Fig. F17—Exploded view of typical mower deck and lift operating controls used on Model 526 and late Models 830, 830E and 1130E.

1. Bolt
2. Washers
3. Blade
4. Spacer
5. Mower deck
6. Blade engage shaft
7. Blade engage spring
8. Blade spindle assy.
9. Idler pulley
10. Blade brake spring
11. Idler lever
12. Adjustment plates
13. Rear mounting bracket
14. Front mounting bracket
15. Upper mounting strap
16. Lower mounting strap
17. Mounting chains
18. Latch slide
19. Height adjust shaft
20. Cam nuts
21. Support shaft
22. Blade engage lever

Fig. F17A—Exploded view of mower deck and spindle assembly on Models R8, R8E and R11E.

1. Nut	7. Bearing	12. Support bar
2. Pulley	8. Spacer	13. Blade
3. Spacer	9. Cap	14. Support bar
4. Bearing	10. Deck	15. Nut
5. Housing	11. Nut	16. Bolt
6. Spindle shaft		

Support mower deck in upright position and remove nut (15-Fig. F17A). Loosen, but do not remove, cap screws retaining blade support bars (14). Remove blade/support bar assembly, cap (9) and spacer (8). Remove nut (1), pulley (2) and spacer (3). Renew bearings (4) and (7) or shaft (6) as necessary.

Reverse disassembly procedure for reassembly. Tighten nut (1) to 100 ft.-lbs. (136 N·m). Tighten nut (15) to 50 ft.-lbs. (68 N·m), then tighten blade support bar bolts (16) to 60 ft.-lbs. (81 N·m) and then tighten nut (15) to 100 ft.-lbs. (136 N·m).

MOWER DECK

Models 51-60-61-65-66

LEVEL ADJUSTMENT. Position unit on level surface and disconnect spark plug wire. Measure distance between ground and cutting edge of blade from side to side and front to rear. Blade should be ¼ inch (6.4 mm) lower in front than at rear. Level mower deck using adjustment slots (Fig. F18) where mounting chains attach to frame. Some models also have slotted holes in front mounting plate for side to side adjustments.

Models 526-830-830E-1130E

LEVEL ADJUSTMENT. Position unit on level surface and disconnect

spark plug wire. Measure distance between ground and cutting edge of blade from side to side and front to rear. Blade should be ¼ inch (6.4 mm) lower in front than at rear. Adjust front to rear height by rotating cam nuts (4-Fig. F12). On Model 526, level deck from side to side by adjusting length of height adjust cables where cables attach to rear of mower deck. On Models 830, 830E and 1130E use adjustment slot where mounting chains (2-Fig. F12) attach to frame.

Models R8-R8E-R11E

LEVEL ADJUSTMENT. Position unit on level surface and disconnect spark plug wire. Make certain all four tires have the same amount of air pressure. Measure distance between ground and cutting edge of blade from side to side and front to rear. Blade should be ¼ inch (6.4 mm) lower in front than at rear. Adjust by turning clevis on lift rod. Mower deck slides must be with ¼ inch (6.4 mm) of being level. Reposition

lift assembly mounting brackets to obtain equal measurements.

Models 51-60-61-65-66

REMOVE AND REINSTALL. Disconnect spark plug wire. Disengage blade drive clutch and set mower height to lowest position. Stand unit on end as previously outlined. Remove blade pulley belt guide (Fig. F19) and disconnect blade brake rod from brake lever, then slip belt off blade pulley. Lower unit to operating position, then disconnect mounting chains from rear of mower deck. Disconnect clutch and brake

Fig. F18—View of deck mounting chains and adjustment slot.

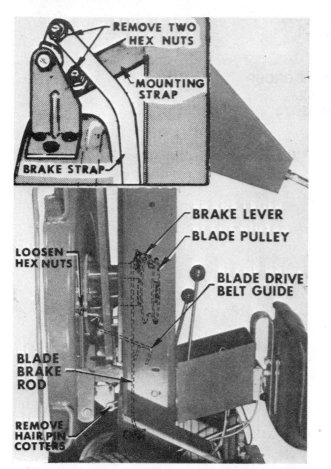

Fig. F19—Typical mower deck mounting on Models 51, 60, 61, 65 and 66.

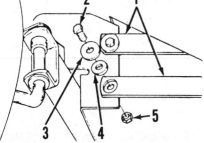

Fig. F20—Mower deck mounting straps attach to front of frame on Model 526.

1. Mounting straps
2. Bolt
3. Washer
4. Bushing
5. Nut

straps and mounting straps from the height adjust plates on front of mower deck, then remove mower deck.

Reinstall in reverse of removal and check deck level adjustment.

Model 526

REMOVE AND REINSTALL. Disconnect spark plug wire. Disengage blade drive clutch and set mower height to highest position. Stand unit on end as previously outlined. Slip blade drive belt off engine pulley. Disconnect wiring from blade clutch switch. Remove nuts from bottom side of deck which attach height adjust cables. Unbolt deck mounting straps (1-Fig. F20) at front of frame, then remove mower deck.

Reinstall in reverse order of removal. Check mower deck level adjustment.

Models 830-830E-1130E

REMOVE AND REINSTALL. Disconnect spark plug wire. Disengage blade drive clutch and set mower in highest position. Stand unit on end as previously outlined. Slip blade drive belt off engine pulley. Disconnect wiring harness. Remove pins (6–Fig. F12) from pivot shaft (7), then lower unit to operating position. Remove chains (2) from rear of mower deck. Drive pivot shaft (7) through the frame, then remove mower deck.

Reinstall in reverse order of removal. Locating stud (9) must be inserted into hole in frame first for proper mower deck alignment. Check mower deck level adjustment.

Models R8-R8E-R11E

REMOVE AND REINSTALL. Disconnect spark plug wire. Disengage

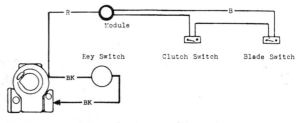

Fig. F21—Wiring schematic for manual start models.

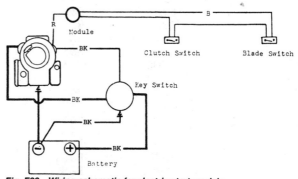

Fig. F22—Wiring schematic for electric start models.

1. R-Red
2. B-Brown
3. BK-Black

blade drive and set mower height to lowest position. Remove cotter pin and clevis pin retaining blade engagement link to mower drive lever. Remove cap screws retaining cross shaft assembly to front mower deck bracket. Remove cap screws, washers, bushings and nuts retaining left and right rear mower deck brackets to rear lift assembly. Loosen, but do not remove, the two nuts retaining engine pulley belt guide to frame. Slide engine pulley belt guide to rear, reach under rear of frame and remove drive belt from engine pulley. Rotate blade engagement rod to the left to clear cross shaft. Lift front of rider up and push rider backwards over mower deck.

Reinstall by reversing removal procedure. Make certain belt is routed above rear lift cross brace and differential when attaching belt to engine pulley and blade engagement rod is positioned above the cross shaft.

ELECTRICAL

All Models

All models are equipped with an interlock safety switch system. Safety switches are located on blade clutch control linkage and traction clutch control linkage (except on Model 526, switch is located on transmission shift linkage). The switches are connected in series to a control module mounted on the engine. Refer to wiring schematic Fig. F21 or F22.

GILSON

LAWN BOY PRODUCT GROUP
P.O. Box 152
Plymouth, WI 53073

Model	Make	Engine Model	Horsepower	Cutting Width, In.
52013	B&S	130000	5	25
52014	B&S	190000	8	34
52015	B&S	190000	8	34
52031	B&S	130000	5	25
52032	B&S	190000	8	30
52033	B&S	190000	8	30
52038	B&S	130000	5	25
52039	B&S	190000	8	30
52040	B&S	190000	8	30
52051C	B&S	250000	11	36
52060	B&S	250000	11	38
52061	B&S	250000	11	36
52064	B&S	190000	8	38
52065	B&S	250000	11	38
52066	B&S	250000	11	38
52072	B&S	190000	8	38
52073	B&S	250000	11	38
52074	B&S	250000	11	38
52080	B&S	190000	8	38
52081	B&S	250000	11	38
52082	B&S	250000	11	38
52089	B&S	190000	8	30
52090	B&S	190000	8	30
52091	B&S	250000	11	30
52106	B&S	190000	8	30
52107	B&S	190000	8	30
52108	B&S	250000	11	30
52113	B&S	190000	8	38
52117	B&S	250000	11	38
52118	B&S	250000	11	38
52120	B&S	280000	12	30

FRONT AXLE

Models 52013-52014-52015-52031-52032-52033-52038-52039-52040

R&R AND OVERHAUL. To remove the axle main member (22-Fig. G1), support front of unit and remove front wheels. Disconnect steering link (9) from steering arm (12). Remove pivot pin (11) and lower axle assembly from chassis. On models so equipped, remove stabilizer springs (19). On all models, remove tie rod assembly (13 through 15). Loosen clamp bolt, remove steering arm (12) and key, then remove spindle (17). Drive out roll pin (21), remove washer (23) and lower spindle (20) out of axle main member (22). Inspect spindle bushings (16) and pivot bushings (24) for excessive wear and

renew as necessary. Reassemble by reversing disassembly procedure and adjust tie rod as required for 0 to 1/16-inch (0-1.6 mm) toe-in.

To remove steering shaft (2), disconnect steering link (9). Unbolt or unpin and remove steering wheel (1). Remove steering column tube (3), then slide steering shaft (2) downward and out of frame. Clean and inspect all parts and renew any showing excessive wear or other damage. When reassembling, add washers (7) as required to remove excessive end play of steering shaft (2).

Models 52051C-52060-52061-52113-52117-52118

R&R AND OVERHAUL. Remove mower deck as needed, refer to MOWER BLADE CLUTCH AND BELT section for removal procedures. To remove

axle assembly (22-Fig. G2A) and steering parts, raise and securely block front portion of chassis.

Remove cap (34) and cotter key (30), then slide wheel assembly off spindles (24 and 29). Remove drag link end (14) from spindle steering arm (17) and swing clear of axle assembly. Remove nut and washer from pivot bolt (27). While supporting axle assembly withdraw pivot belt, then lower complete axle assembly and place to the side for inspection and repair.

With reference to Fig. G2A disassemble and inspect complete axle assembly. Inspect spindles, axle assembly and tie bar for excessive wear, bending or any other damage and renew all parts as needed. Reassemble in reverse order of disassembly.

Inspect steering shaft (4), steering gear (5), bearings (3 and 10), drag link

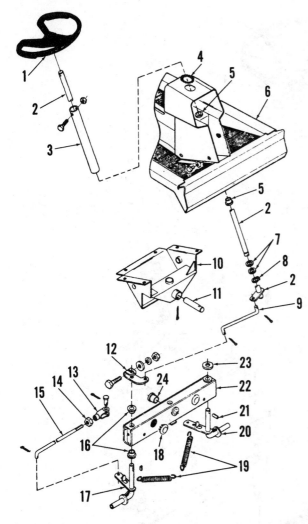

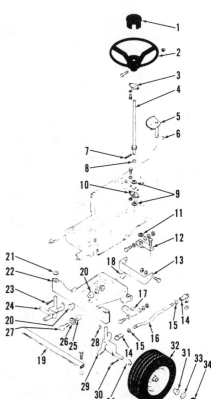

Fig. G1—Exploded view of typical front axle and steering system used on Models 52038, 52039 and 52040. Models 52013, 52014, 52015, 52031, 52032 and 52033 are similar, but are not equipped with stabilizer springs (19).

1. Steering wheel
2. Steering shaft
3. Column tube
4. Grommet
5. Flange bushing (2)
6. Frame
7. Washers
8. Snap ring
9. Steering link
10. Axle support
11. Pivot pin
12. Steering arm
13. Clevis
14. Jam nut
15. Tie rod
16. Flange bushings (4)
17. Spindle R.H.
18. Button plug
19. Stabilizer springs
20. Spindle L.H.
21. Roll pin
22. Axle main member
23. Washer
24. Axle pivot bushings (2)

Fig. G2A—Exploded view showing steering components and related parts for Models 52051C, 52060, 52061, 52113, 52117 and 52118.

1. Cap
2. Steering wheel
3. Upper flange bearing
4. Steering shaft
5. Steering gear
6. Woodruff key
7. Cotter key
8. Spacer
9. Spacer washer
10. Lower flange bearing
11. Spacer washer
12. Steering arm
13. Bracket
14. Drag link end
15. Jam nut
16. Drag link
17. Spindle steering arm
18. Bearing
19. Tie bar
20. Bushing
21. Washer
22. Axle assy.
23. Cotter key
24. Right spindle assy.
25. Sleeve
26. Washer
27. Axle pivot bolt
28. Woodruff key
29. Left spindle assy.
30. Cotter key
31. Bushing
32. Wheel assy.
33. Washer
34. Cap

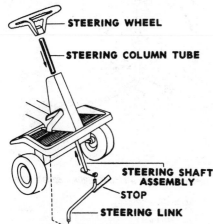

Fig. G2—On Models 52013, 52014, 52015, 52031, 52032 and 52033, install steering link so that stop is toward steering shaft.

arm (16) and ends (14) for excessive wear or any other damage and renew all parts as needed.

Reinstall and lubricate spindle bushings, steering shaft and wear points in linkage with SAE 30 engine oil. Wipe off excess to prevent dirt accumulation. As

provided, grease front wheel bushings using grease fittings on inside of front wheel assemblies with No. 2 wheel bearing grease.

To adjust steering gear mesh between steering shaft (4) and steering gear (5) proceed as follows: Loosen cap screws securing lower bearing flange (10) to frame. Slide bearing flange in slots as needed until gears mesh together evenly and steering is smooth, then retighten cap screws.

Models 52064-52065-52066-52072-52073-52074-52080-52081-52082

R&R AND OVERHAUL. Remove mower deck as needed, refer to MOWER BLADE CLUTCH AND BELT section for removal procedures. To remove axle assembly (22—Fig. G2B) and steering parts, raise and securely block front portion of chassis.

Remove cap (34) and cotter key (30), then slide wheel assembly off spindles (24 and 29). Remove drag link end (14) from spindle steering arm (17) and swing clear of axle assembly. Remove nut and washer from pivot bolt (27).

While supporting axle assembly withdraw pivot bolt, then lower complete axle assembly and place to the side for inspection and repair.

With reference to Fig. G2B disassemble and inspect complete axle assembly. Inspect spindles, axle assembly and tie bar for excessive wear, bending or any other damage and renew all parts as needed. Reassemble in reverse order of disassembly.

Inspect steering shaft (4), steering gear (5), bearings (3 and 10), drag link arm (16) and ends (14) for excessive wear or any other damage and renew all parts as needed.

Reinstall and lubricate spindle bushings, steering shaft and wear points in linkage with SAE 30 engine oil. Wipe off excess to prevent dirt accumulation. As provided, grease front wheel bushings using grease fittings on inside of front

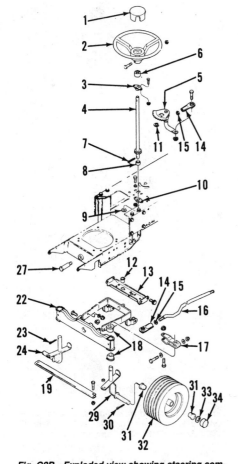

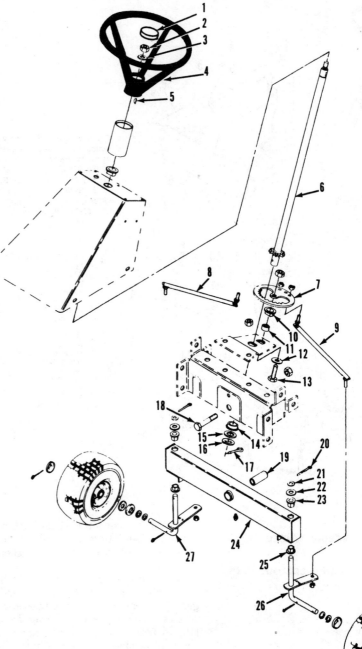

Fig. G2B—Exploded view showing steering components and related parts for Models 52064, 52065, 52066, 52072, 52073, 52074, 52080, 52081 and 52082. Refer to legend at Fig. G2A for identification of parts except for the following.

6. Sleeve	12. Bushing
11. "E" Clip	18. Spindle bushing

wheel assembly with No. 2 wheel bearing grease.

To adjust steering gear mesh between steering shaft (4) and steering gear (5) proceed as follows: Loosen cap screws securing lower bearing flange (10) to frame. Slide bearing flange in slots as needed until gears mesh together evenly and steering is smooth, then retighten cap screws.

Models 52089-52090-52091-52106-52107-52108-52120

R&R AND OVERHAUL. To remove the axle main member (24-Fig. G2C), support front of unit and remove front wheels. Disconnect left and right drag links (8 and 9) at spindles. Support axle main member (24) and remove pivot pin bolt (18). Remove axle main member.

Clean and inspect all parts. Renew any parts showing signs of wear, dam-

Fig. G2C—Exploded view of front axle and steering assembly used on Models 52089, 52090, 52091, 52106, 52107 and 52108.

1. Cap	8. Tie rod	15. Washer	22. Washer
2. Nut	9. Tie rod	16. Washer	23. Bushing
3. Washer	10. Bushing	17. Cotter pin	24. Axle
4. Steering wheel	11. Bushing	18. Pivot bolt	25. Bushing
5. Key	12. Washer	19. Bushing	26. Spindle
6. Steering shaft	13. Bolt	20. Cotter pin	27. Spindle
7. Gear	14. Bushing	21. Washer	

age or looseness. Reverse removal procedure for reinstallation and lubricate grease fittings with multi-purpose lithium base grease. Lubricate all pivot points which do not have grease fittings with SAE 30 oil.

ENGINE

All Models

Refer to appropriate engine section in this manual for tune-up specifications,

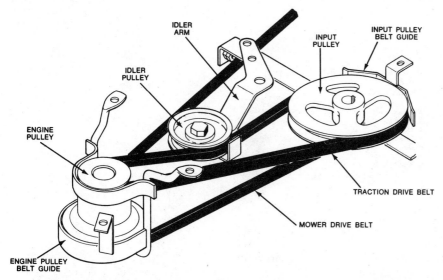

Fig. G3—View showing traction drive belt, clutch idler and pulley on Models 52013, 52014, 52015, 52031, 52032, 52033, 52038, 52039 and 52040. Note locations of belt guides.

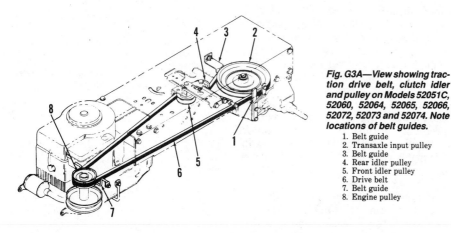

Fig. G3A—View showing traction drive belt, clutch idler and pulley on Models 52051C, 52060, 52064, 52065, 52066, 52072, 52073 and 52074. Note locations of belt guides.

1. Belt guide
2. Transaxle input pulley
3. Belt guide
4. Rear idler pulley
5. Front idler pulley
6. Drive belt
7. Belt guide
8. Engine pulley

move engine hood assembly. Remove drive belt from engine drive pulley. Disconnect engine throttle cable and ignition wiring as needed. Inspect and remove all parts that will obstruct in removal of engine assembly. Remove engine mounting bolts and lift engine assembly from frame.

Reinstall engine in reverse order of removal.

Models 52080-52081-52082-52089-52090-52091-52106-52107-52108-52120

REMOVE AND REINSTALL. Drain fuel from fuel tank, disconnect negative and positive battery cables and remove battery. Disconnect throttle cable at engine. Disconnect all necessary engine wiring harness. Stand mower on rear support bars. Remove carriage bolts, washers and locknuts retaining engine pulley belt guide and remove belt guide. Disengage mower drive lever and remove drive belt from engine pulley. Remove nut retaining traction drive idler pulley to idler bracket and remove pulley. Slip traction drive belt off engine pulley towards bottom of engine. Lower mower back to the ground. Remove the four bolts retaining engine to frame (note location and number of engine spacer washers under each mounting location) and move engine forward while lifting slightly. Reach under rear of main frame and remove traction drive belt from engine pulley and remove engine.

Reinstall engine in reverse order of removal.

TRACTION DRIVE CLUTCH

Models 52013-52014-52015-52031-52032-52033-52038-52039-52040

The traction drive clutch is a belt idler type operated by the clutch-brake pedal on right side. When pedal is depressed, belt tension is removed, allowing engine drive pulley to rotate freely within the drive belt. There is no adjustment on the traction drive clutch. If belt slippage occurs during normal operation due to excessive belt wear or stretching, a new belt should be installed.

REMOVE AND RENEW DRIVE BELT. To remove traction drive belt, depress clutch-brake pedal and engage brake lock. Place mower blade clutch control lever in disengaged position. Unbolt and remove engine pulley belt guide (Fig. G3) and remove mower drive belt from engine pulley. Loosen transmission input pulley belt guide

engine overhaul procedures and engine maintenance.

Refer to the following paragraphs for removal and installation procedures.

Models 52013-52014-52015-52031-52032-52033-52038-52039-52040

REMOVE AND REINSTALL. To remove the engine assembly, disconnect spark plug wire. On Models 52038, 52039 and 52040, unbolt and remove engine rear cover and side panels. On electric start models, disconnect battery cables. On all models disconnect ignition wires and throttle control cable. Place mower blade clutch control lever in disengaged position. Depress clutch-brake pedal and engage brake lock. Unbolt and remove engine pulley belt guide and remove mower drive belt from engine pulley. Loosen transmission input pulley belt guide and slip main drive belt

from transmission pulley. Remove main drive belt from engine pulley. Remove engine mounting bolts and lift engine assembly from frame.

Reinstall engine by reversing the removal procedure. With main drive clutch engaged (pedal up), there should be $\frac{1}{16}$-inch (1.6 mm) clearance between transmission input pulley belt guide and belt and a clearance of $\frac{1}{16}$ to $\frac{1}{8}$-inch (1.6-3 mm) between engine pulley and the engine pulley belt guide.

Models 52051-52060-52061-52064-52065-52066-52072-52073-52074-52080-52081-52082-52113-52117-52118

REMOVE AND REINSTALL. Remove mower deck as required. Disconnect battery ground cable from battery terminal (as equipped). Disconnect engine spark plug wire. Unbolt and re-

and slip traction drive belt from transmission pulley. Remove traction drive belt from idler and engine pulley.

Install new traction drive belt by reversing removal procedure and adjust belt guide clearances as follows: With main drive clutch engaged (pedal up), there should be $\frac{1}{16}$-inch (1.6 mm) clearance between transmission input pulley belt guide and belt and a clearance of $\frac{1}{16}$-$\frac{1}{8}$ inch (1.6-3mm) between engine pulley and engine pulley belt guide. Adjust brake as outlined in TRACTION DRIVE BRAKE paragraph.

Models 52051C-52060-52064-52065-52066-52072-52073-52074

The traction drive clutch is a belt idler type operated by the clutch-brake pedal on left side. When pedal is depressed, belt tension is removed, allowing engine drive pulley to rotate freely within the drive belt. There is no adjustment on the traction drive clutch. If belt slippage occurs during normal operation due to excessive belt wear or stretching, a new belt should be installed.

REMOVE AND RENEW DRIVE BELT. Remove mower deck as outlined in MOWER BLADE CLUTCH AND BELT section. Disconnect engine spark plug wire and set tractor parking brake. Disconnect battery ground cable from battery terminal. Loosen belt guide (3-Fig. G3A) mounting bolt. Slide drive belt off input pulley (2) and past belt guide (1). Loosen rear idler pulley (4) and belt finger mounting bolt, then slide drive belt off idler pulleys. Remove drive belt retainer (7), then slip drive belt off engine pulley (8). Inspect all drive pulleys for wear and renew as needed. Renew drive belt by reversing removal procedure. To adjust belt guide (3), release parking brake, then position belt guide $\frac{1}{16}$-$\frac{1}{8}$ inch (1.6-3 mm) from drive belt.

Model 52061

ADJUSTMENT. (Primary Drive Belt). Lift up seat support assembly to allow access to frame nut (9-Fig. G3B). Loosen nut (10) on underside of frame, then turn top nut clockwise $\frac{1}{2}$ turn to tighten belt and $\frac{1}{2}$ turn counterclockwise to loosen belt. Retighten underside nut, then check drive belt deflection at midpoint of belt. Drive belt deflection should be one inch. Repeat adjustment procedure until correct deflection is attained.

(Secondary Drive Belt). There is no adjustment required on secondary

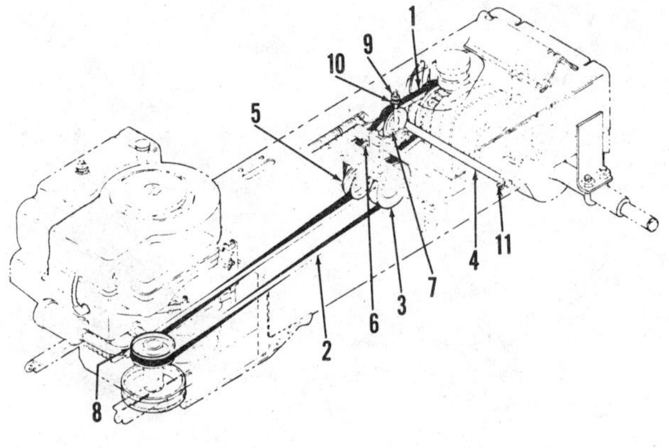

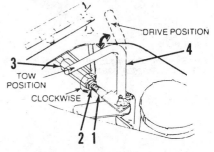

Fig. G3B—View showing primary and secondary traction drive belt and associated components for Model 52061.

1. Secondary drive belt
2. Primary drive belt
3. Inner jackshaft pulley
4. Lift shaft
5. Fixed idler pulley
6. Outer jackshaft pulley
7. Spring loaded idler
8. Engine pulley
9. Frame top nut
10. Frame underside nut
11. Roll pin

drive belt. Idler pulley is spring loaded, check pulley arm periodically for freedom of movement and for providing correct belt tension.

REMOVE AND RENEW. (Primary Drive Belt). Remove bolts and nuts attaching engine pulley belt cover to chassis. Remove mower deck as outlined in MOWER BLADE CLUTCH AND BELT section. Lift up seat support assembly to allow access to frame nut (9-Fig. G3B). Loosen nut (9), then remove belt from inner jackshaft pulley (3). Slip belt off engine pulley (8), then withdraw belt. Inspect all drive pulleys for excessive wear and renew as needed. Renew drive belt by reversing removal procedure. Adjust drive belt tension as outlined in ADJUSTMENT paragraph. Complete reassembly in reverse order of disassembly.

(Secondary Drive Belt). Remove bolts and nuts attaching engine pulley belt cover to chassis. Remove mower deck as outlined in MOWER BLADE CLUTCH AND BELT section. Remove roll pin (11-Fig. G3B), then withdraw lift shaft (4). Push idler pulley (7) down to loosen belt tension, then slip drive belt off outer jackshaft pulley (6). Slip drive belt off transmission pulley, then withdraw drive belt. Inspect all drive pulleys for excessive wear and renew as needed. Renew drive belt by reversing removal procedure. Reassemble in reverse order of disassembly.

Models 52080-52081-52082-52113-52117-52118

The traction drive clutch is a spring loaded, belt idler type operated by the clutch-brake pedal on left side of mower. When pedal is depressed, belt tension is removed, allowing engine drive pulley to rotate freely within the drive belt. There is no adjustment on the traction drive clutch. If belt slippage occurs during normal operation due to excessive belt wear or stretching, a new belt should be installed.

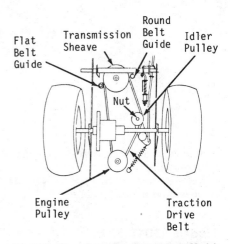

Fig. G3C—View showing position of control lever (4) for normal operation and for moving tractor when engine is inoperative. Adjust hydrostatic pump control linkage by loosening locknut (2) and turning turnbuckle (3) on control rod (1).

Fig. G3D—View of traction drive belt on Models 52089, 52090 and 52091.

REMOVE AND RENEW TRANSAXLE DRIVE BELT. To remove transaxle drive belt, remove mower deck and set parking brake. Note placement of belt guides and remove the flat idler pulley, "V" idler pulley and belt guides from pivot bracket. Disconnect shift rod at gear select lever. Loosen, but do not remove, left and right input pulley belt guides and swing guides out of the way. Remove traction belt from input pulley. Remove upper belt guide. Remove transaxle drive belt from engine pulley.

Reverse removal procedure to install new belt. Make certain belt guides are positioned correctly.

Models 52089-52090-52091

The traction drive clutch is a spring loaded, belt idler type operated by the clutch-brake pedal on left side of mower. When pedal is depressed, belt tension is removed, allowing engine drive pulley to rotate freely within the drive belt. There is no adjustment on the traction drive clutch. If belt slippage occurs during normal operation due to excessive belt wear or stretching, a new belt should be installed.

REMOVE AND RENEW TRANSMISSION DRIVE BELT. To remove transmission drive belt, remove mower deck, set parking brake, drain fuel tank and disconnect and remove battery (as equipped). Stand rider on rear support bars. Remove locknut retaining idler pulley to idler lever and remove idler pulley (Fig. G3D). Loosen flat belt guide and rotate guide 90° clockwise. Remove the $\frac{5}{16}$ inch bolt and remove transmission drive belt.

Reverse removal procedure to install new belt. Manufacturer recommends applying talcum or soap stone powder to new belt and operating mower in low gear for a 10 minute break-in period.

Models 52106-52107-52108-52120

The traction drive clutch is a spring loaded, belt idler type operated by the clutch-brake pedal on left side of mower. When pedal is depressed, belt tension is removed, allowing engine drive pulley to rotate freely within the drive belt. There is no adjustment on the traction drive clutch. If belt slippage occurs during normal operation due to excessive belt wear or stretching, a new belt should be installed.

REMOVE AND RENEW TRANSMISSION DRIVE BELT. Disengage mower drive lever and position mower in lowest position. Set parking brake, drain fuel tank and disconnect and remove battery (as equipped). Stand rider on rear support bars. Remove engine pulley belt guide and remove mower drive belt and transmission drive belt from engine pulley. Remove idler pulley at clutch idler arm and remove long belt guide next to transmission pulley. Remove transmission drive belt. Reverse removal procedure to install new belt.

HYDROSTATIC PUMP CONTROL LINKAGE

Model 52061

Tractor can be moved a short distance without engine running by lifting seat and turning control lever (4-Fig. G3C) counterclockwise. Lift lever to lock in place. Do not move tractor faster than walking speed. To release control lever, push lever down and turn clockwise.

Periodically check oil reservoir on top of transmission and fill to indicated level with SAE 20W High Detergent oil as necessary.

LINKAGE ADJUSTMENT. Linkage adjustment is correct when tractor does not move with engine running, clutch engaged and control lever in neutral.

To adjust linkage, raise both rear wheels and securely block. Loosen locknut (2-Fig. G3C) on control rod (1) and turn turnbuckle (3) clockwise if tractor creeps forward and counterclockwise if tractor creeps backward. Retighten locknut, then recheck tractor for creeping. Continue adjustment procedure until correct adjustment is attained.

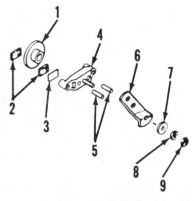

Fig. G4A—Exploded view showing a typical disc brake assembly used on transaxle models.

1. Disc	
2. Pads	6. Lever
3. Plate	7. Flat washer
4. Carrier assy.	8. Adjuster nut
5. Dowel pins	9. Locknut

TRACTION DRIVE BRAKE

Differential Models

The brake is a band and drum type and is operated by the clutch-brake pedal. The brake drum is secured to the differential sprocket.

ADJUSTMENT. To adjust the brake, refer to Fig. G4 and turn the locknut clockwise to tighten brake. Tighten locknut about 2½ turns and test brake. If necessary, repeat the adjustment until braking action is satisfactory.

CAUTION: Do not overtighten brake. Make certain that brake does not drag when clutch is engaged.

OVERHAUL. Normal overhaul of the brake consists of renewing the band and lining assembly. The procedure is obvious after examination of the unit and reference to Fig. G6.

Transaxle/Transmission Models

The brake is a disc type brake that is mounted on the transaxle or transmission. Shown in Fig. G4A is a view of a typical disc brake assembly used, other models are similar.

ADJUSTMENT. Loosen locknut (9-Fig. G4A), then turn adjuster nut (8) so that brake is fully applied when foot pedal is completely engaged. Be sure brake disc (1) revolves freely when foot pedal is in released position. Retighten locknut.

OVERHAUL. Remove brake return spring, then disconnect brake rod from lever (6-Fig. G4A). Remove mounting cap screws from carrier and pad assembly (4). Withdraw brake disc (1), then

TURN THIS
HEX. LOCK NUT

BRAKE SHOE
AND LINING

Fig. G4—View showing brake adjusting nut typical of all models. Refer to text for adjustment procedure.

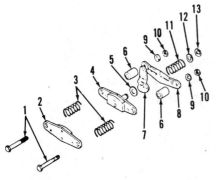

Fig. G4B—Exploded view showing disc brake assembly used on Model 52061.

1. Bolt
2. Pad
3. Spring
4. Pad
5. Flat washer
6. Spacer
7. Lever
8. Plate
9. Lockwasher
10. Nut
11. Spring
12. Flat washer
13. Snap ring

remove old brake pads. Renew brake pads, then reassemble in reverse order of disassembly. If brake adjustment is needed, refer to previous paragraph.

Model 52061

The brake is a disc type brake that is mounted on the differential assembly.

ADJUSTMENT. Adjust brake by turning adjuster nut on brake rod. Turn nut clockwise to reduce clearance between brake disc and brake pad. Brake should fully apply when foot pedal is completely engaged. After adjustment and foot pedal is released, check to be sure brake is not overtightened by placing control lever to tow position and rolling tractor back and forth.

OVERHAUL. Disconnect brake rod from lever (7–Fig. G4B). Remove nut and lockwasher (10 and 9), then remove pad (4), flat washer (5), lever (7), plate (8), spring (11), flat washer (12) and snap ring (13) as an assembly. Withdraw spacers (6), springs (3), brake disc and inner brake pad (2). Remove ring (13) from outer brake pad assembly, then disassemble with reference to Fig. G4B. Renew brake pads, then reassemble·in reverse order of disassembly. If brake adjustment is needed, refer to previous paragraph.

TRANSMISSION

Models 52013, 52014 and 52015 are equipped with a 3-speed Model 2010-13 transmission manufactured by the J. B. Foote Foundry Company. All other models are equipped with either a 3-speed Model 505 or a 5-speed Model 782 transmission manufactured by Peerless Division of Tecumseh Products Company.

All 3-Speed Transmission Models

REMOVE AND REINSTALL. To remove the transmission assembly, disconnect spark plug wire and on electric start models disconnect battery cables. On Models 52038, 52039 and 52040, unbolt and remove right side panel. On all models unbolt and remove drive chain guard. Locate connecting link, then disconnect drive chain. On Models 52013, 52014 and 52015, remove transmission shift handle. Disconnect safety starting switch wires from transmission on Models 52038, 52039 and 52040. On all models, depress clutch-brake pedal and engage brake lock. Unbolt and remove frame cross brace. See Fig. G5. Loosen transmission input pulley belt guide and remove main drive belt from input pulley. Remove the snap ring from transmission input shaft and the two socket head set screws from input pulley. Remove the pulley from transmission input shaft. Unbolt and remove transmission assembly.

Reinstall transmission by reversing the removal procedure. Adjust transmission input pulley belt guide so there is 1/16-inch (1.6 mm) clearance between belt guide and main drive belt when clutch is engaged. On Models 52038, 52039 and 52040, make certain that safety starting switches are connected and in good condition before returning mower to service.

OVERHAUL. For transmission overhaul procedures, refer to Foote Model 2010-13 on Models 52013, 52014 and 52015 and Peerless Model 505 or 782 on all other models in the TRANSMISSION REPAIR section of this manual.

All 5-Speed Transmission Models

REMOVE AND REINSTALL. To remove transmission, drain fuel tank and disconnect and remove battery (as

equipped). Remove mower deck as required. Tilt seat up and remove cap screw and washers retaining transmission shift lever to top of transmission. Move lever out of the way. Remove the chain guard and unhook brake return spring from hole in transmission brake control arm. Stand mower on rear support bars. Use wire to lock battery box cover in open position. Locate drive chain master link and remove chain from sprocket (right rear wheel assembly may have to be removed to gain access to master link). Remove idler pulley, loosen locknut retaining flat belt guide and rotate belt guide 90° clockwise. Remove cap screw retaining round belt guide to main frame. Remove traction drive belt from transmission pulley. Disconnect transmission brake control arm at brake adjustment rod link. Remove transmission pulley and key from transmission input shaft. Remove the three remaining cap screws securing transmission to main frame and lift transmission out of battery access hole.

Reinstall transmission by reversing the removal procedure. Make certain brake is readjusted and all belt guides are in place.

OVERHAUL. For transmission overhaul procedure, refer to Peerless Series 700 paragraphs in the TRANSMISSION REPAIR section of this manual.

TRANSAXLE

All Models So Equipped

The transaxles used are manufactured by Peerless Division of Tecumseh Products Company. Models 52051C, 52060, 52064, 52065 and 52066 use a 3-speed Series 600. Models 52072, 52073, 52074, 52080, 52081, 52082, 52113, 52117 and 52118 use a 5-speed Series 800.

Fig. G5—Underneath view of a typical rear engine rider with mower unit removed.

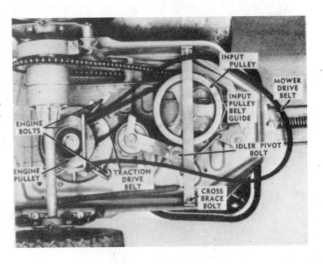

REMOVE AND REINSTALL. To remove the transaxle assembly, disconnect spark plug wire and battery ground cable from battery terminal. Loosen belt guide bolts and slide belt guides away from belt. Remove traction drive belt from transaxle input pulley. Disconnect brake linkage. Remove cap screws retaining transaxle to frame and remove "U" bolts securing axle housings to frame. Raise rear of tractor and remove transaxle assembly from tractor.

Reinstall by reversing the removal procedure. Adjust clutch and brake linkage as required.

OVERHAUL. For overhaul procedures, refer to Peerless transaxle Series 600 on Models 52051C, 52060, 52064, 52065 and 52066 and Series 800 on Models 52072, 52073, 52074, 52080, 52081, 52082, 52113, 52117 and 52118 in the TRANSMISSION REPAIR section of this manual.

HYDROSTATIC TRANSMISSION

Model 52061

Model 52061 is equipped with a Model 7 hydrostatic transmission manufactured by Eaton Corporation.

REMOVE AND REINSTALL. To remove transmission and differential, disconnect hydrostatic control rod at transmission. Disconnect brake linkage and remove rear drive belt. Raise rear wheels clear of ground and securely block. Remove axle housing mounting nuts and "U" bolts securing axle housings to frame, then remove transmission and differential assembly from tractor. Separate transmission and differential.

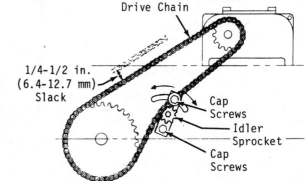

Fig. G6A—View of Models 52106, 52107, 52108 and 52120 drive chain.

Reinstall by reversing the removal procedure. Adjust linkage rods as needed.

OVERHAUL. For hydrostatic pump overhaul procedures, refer to Eaton Hydrostatic section in the TRANSMISSION REPAIR section of this manual.

DIFFERENTIAL

Models Equipped With 3-Speed Transmission

REMOVE AND REINSTALL. To remove the rear axle and differential assembly, raise rear of chassis and support securely. Disconnect brake rod from brake lever (8–Fig. G6). Locate connecting link and disconnect drive chain. Remove rear wheels, spacer washers (1), spacers (2) and thin washers (3). Unbolt mounting brackets (7 and 16) from frame and remove the rear axle assembly. Clean all rust or paint from axles and slide axle bearing and bracket assemblies from axles. Brake band (9) and lever (8) will be removed with bracket (7). Brake drum

(12) and sprocket (13) can be removed after removal of nuts from the four differential through-bolts. Unbolt bearing clamps (4) and remove bearings (6) if necessary. Clean and inspect all parts and renew any showing excessive wear or other damage.

Reassemble by reversing the disassembly procedure. Adjust drive chain and brake as necessary. Lubricate axle bearings with automotive type wheel bearing grease and drive chain with SAE 30 oil.

OVERHAUL. Peerless differentials are used on all models. Model 1523 differential is used on Models 52038, 52039 and 52040. Model 100 differential is used on all other models. For overhaul procedures, refer to the DIFFERENTIAL REPAIR section of this manual.

Models Equipped With 5-Speed Transmission

REMOVE AND REINSTALL. To remove the differential assembly, raise rear of chassis and support securely. Remove snap rings, wheels, square keys and axle spacers from left and right sides of rear axle. Locate drive chain master link and remove master link and drive chain. Support differential and remove the two top nuts and carriage bolts at right side axle bearing plate. Slide axle bearing plate off axle. Slide differential out of left axle bearing plate.

OVERHAUL. All models are equipped with Peerless 100 series differential. Refer to the DIFFERENTIAL REPAIR section of this manual.

Model 52061

Refer to HYDROSTATIC TRANSMISSION section for removal of differential assembly. For overhaul procedures, refer to Peerless Series 1300 in the DIFFERENTIAL REPAIR section of this manual.

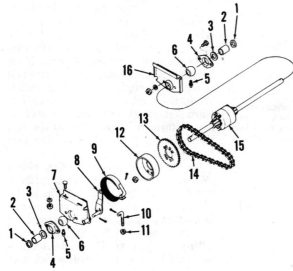

Fig. G6—Exploded view of rear axle mounting bracket assemblies.

1. Spacer washer
2. Spacer
3. Washer (thin)
4. Bearing clamp
5. Lube fitting
6. Axle bearing
7. Mounting bracket R.H.
8. Brake lever
9. Brake band
10. Link
11. Adjusting nut
12. Brake drum
13. Sprocket
14. Drive chain
15. Axle & differential assy.
16. Mounting bracket L.H.

DRIVE CHAIN

Models 52106-52107-52108-52120

ADJUSTMENT. Drive chain tension should be adjusted to provide ¼ - ½ inch (6.4-12.7 mm) slack. Chain tension may be increased or decreased by loosening cap screws and adjusting drive chain idler sprocket (Fig. G6A).

REMOVE AND REINSTALL. Raise and support rear of mower so drive wheels are off the ground. Remove the chain guard and rotate rear drive wheel until drive chain master link is accessible. Carefully remove master link while holding chain ends. Connect one end of new chain to master link and slowly pull chain out over transmission sprocket until master link appears again. Remove old chain section and install new master link. Adjust chain tension as necessary.

All Remaining Models So Equipped

ADJUSTMENT. To adjust drive chain, refer to Fig. G7 and loosen the hex nuts on bolts securing axle mounting brackets to the frame. Move brackets rearward or tighten axle adjustment nuts (as equipped) to tighten chain. Both brackets must be moved the same distance to keep the axle and sprocket square with frame. The chain should have a slight amount of slack, approximately ¼ - ⅜ inch (6.4-9.5 mm). Tighten the hex nuts securely when chain adjustment is correct.

REMOVE AND REINSTALL. To remove the drive chain, remove the right side panel on Models 52038, 52039

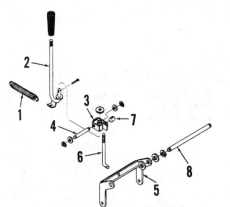

Fig. G7—To adjust drive chain, loosen nuts on axle mounting bracket bolts and move brackets equally as necessary.

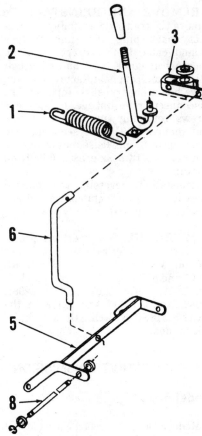

Fig. G8—Exploded view of blade clutch linkage used on Models 52038, 52039 and 52040.

1. Clutch tension spring
2. Blade clutch control lever
3. Pivot bracket
4. Pivot pin
5. Hanger arm assy.
6. Clutch link
7. Link pivot
8. Hanger pivot shaft

and 52040, then unbolt and remove the chain guard from all models. Locate and disconnect the drive chain master link making certain chain ends do not fall through rear chain hole in main frame. Connect one end of new chain to master link and slowly pull end of old chain out over transmission sprocket until master link appears. It may be necessary to adjust chain tension as outlined previously to install new master link. Lubricate chain with a light coat of SAE 30 oil.

MOWER BLADE CLUTCH AND BELT

All Models

CAUTION: Always disconnect spark plug wire before performing any inspection, adjustment or other service on the mower unit.

Fig. G9—Exploded view of blade clutch linkage used on Models 52013, 52014, 52015, 52031, 52032 and 52033. Clutch link (6) is nonadjustable on these models. Refer to Fig. G8 for legend.

The mower unit on all rear engine models is attached to the hanger arm assembly (5–Fig. G8 or G9). The blade clutch is operated by control lever (2) and the linkage which moves mower unit forward or rearward, tightening or loosening mower drive belt. When control lever (2) is moved rearward and locked in disengaged position, mower assembly is moved rearward, loosening the belt. The idler spring (10–Fig. G12, G13 and G14) pulls the idler and brake arm (8) around until brake shoe (9) contacts the mower pulley, stopping blade rotation. At this time, mower drive belt is free from engine crankshaft pulley. When the control lever is moved forward (engaged position), mower is moved forward. This tightens the belt and pulls the brake shoe on idler arm free from the mower pulley.

On late model rear engine riders (Models 52080, 52081, 52082, 52089, 52090, 52091, 52106, 52107, 52108, 52113, 52117, 52118 and 52120), mower deck is attached by a hanger strap assembly at the front and by a lift cable assembly or lift rod at the rear. The blade clutch is operated by a control lever which uses

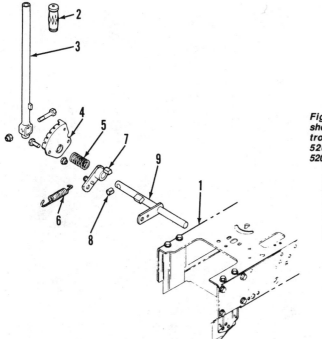

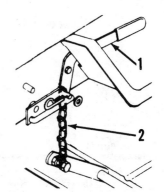

Fig. G9A—Exploded view showing mower deck lift control assembly for Models 52064, 52065, 52072 and 52073.

1. Frame
2. Grip
3. Handle
4. Quadrant
5. Spring
6. Spring
7. Lift arm
8. Spacer
9. Lift shaft

Fig. G9B—View showing lift control lever (1) and chain (2) used in raising and lowering mower deck on Models 52051C, 52060, 52061, 52066 and 52074.

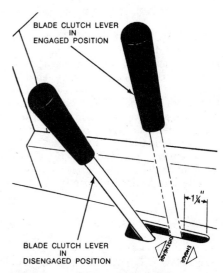

Fig. G10—On Models 52038, 52039 and 52040, adjust blade clutch linkage so that a distance of 1-1/4 inches (31.8 mm) exists between clutch lever and end of slot when blade clutch is engaged.

spring tension to pivot an idler pulley to tighten drive belt.

The mower unit on all front engine tractors is attached to the hanger bracket located at the front of the chassis. On Models 52064, 52065, 52072 and 52073 mower deck is raised and lowered by a chain attached to a lift arm which is operated by a cable attached to a lift control lever located on right-hand side of frame, typical of the one shown in Fig. G9A. On Models 52051C, 52060, 52061, 52066 and 52074 mower deck is raised and lowered by a chain attached to a lift control lever located on right-hand side of frame, typical of the one shown in Fig. G9B. Mower engagement lever is located on left side of instrument panel. When mower control lever is moved to engaged position, idler pulley should tighten tension on drive belt and blade brake should move away from pulleys. When control lever is moved to disengaged position, idler pulley should move away from drive belt and blade brake should come in contact with pulleys. Refer to the following paragraphs for adjustment of mower engagement clutch and renewing drive belt.

Models 52038-52039-52040

ADJUSTMENT. If blade clutch does not disengage when blade clutch lever is in disengaged position (Fig. G10), adjust linkage as follows: Disconnect mower from hanger arm assembly. Turn the link clockwise one complete turn into pivot (7–Fig. G8) and reconnect link to hanger arm assembly.

Reattach mower and recheck clutch operation. Repeat the adjustment if necessary.

If the clutch control lever contacts front end of slot before the clutch is engaged, adjust link (6) counter-clockwise until clutch lever is approximately 1¼ inches (31.8 mm) from end of slot when clutch is engaged. See Fig. G10.

R&R MOWER BELT. To remove the mower belt, place blade clutch lever in disengaged position. Unbolt and remove engine pulley belt guide. Remove belt from engine pulley. Unbolt and remove belt cover and guide (15–Fig. G14 or 11 and 13–Fig. G12), then remove belt from mower pulley (16–Fig. G14 or 14–Fig. G12) and idler.

Install new belt by reversing the removal procedure and adjust clutch linkage as outlined in the preceding paragraph. With clutch engaged, adjust engine pulley belt guide to a clearance of ¹⁄₁₆ to ⅛-inch (1.6-3 mm) pulley and guide.

Models 52013-52031-52032-52033

ADJUSTMENT. Clutch link (6–Fig. G9) is non-adjustable. If the mower belt is worn or stretched to a point where blade clutch will not engage, a new belt must be installed.

R&R MOWER BELT. To remove the mower belt, place blade clutch lever in disengaged position. Unbolt and remove the engine pulley belt guide. Remove belt from engine pulley. On Mod-

els 52013 and 52031, unbolt and remove belt cover (13–Fig. G12) and belt guide (11). Remove belt (12) from mower pulley (14) and idler (7). On Models 52032 and 52033, refer to Fig. G14 and unbolt and remove belt cover and guide (15–Fig. G14). Remove belt (13) from mower pulley (16) and idler (7).

On all models, install new belt by reversing the removal procedure. With clutch engaged, adjust engine pulley belt guide until a clearance of ¹⁄₁₆ to ⅛ inch (1.6-3 mm) exists between the pulley and guide.

Models 52014-52015

ADJUSTMENT. Clutch link (6–Fig. G9) is non-adjustable. If the mower drive belt is worn or stretched to a point where blade clutch will not engage, a new drive belt must be installed.

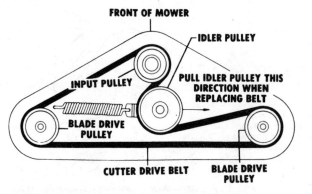

FRONT OF MOWER
IDLER PULLEY
INPUT PULLEY
PULL IDLER PULLEY THIS DIRECTION WHEN REPLACING BELT
BLADE DRIVE PULLEY
CUTTER DRIVE BELT
BLADE DRIVE PULLEY

Fig. G11—View showing correct installation of blade belt on Models 52014 and 52015.

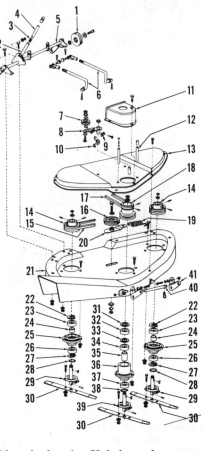

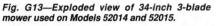

Fig. G13—Exploded view of 34-inch 3-blade mower used on Models 52014 and 52015.

1. Cutting height gage wheels	22. Retaining ring
2. Lever	23. Bearing
3. Spring	24. Spacer
4. Rod	25. Spindle housing
5. Pivot shaft & support assy.	26. Bearing
6. Leveler links	27. Retaining ring
7. Idler pulley	28. Spacer
8. Idler & brake arm	29. Spindle
9. Brake shoe	30. Blades (3)
10. Spring	31. Washer
11. Belt cover	32. Bearing
12. Belt guides (2)	33. Washer
13. Blade belt cover	34. Bearing
14. Blade pulleys	35. Spacer
15. Blade belt	36. Spindle housing
16. Blade belt idler	37. Bearing
17. Mower drive belt	38. Spacer
18. Input (center spindle) pulley	39. Spindle
19. Spring	40. Mower attaching pin
20. Idler arm	41. Bellcranks (2)
21. Mower housing	

The blade belt (Fig. G11) is under constant tension of the spring loaded idler and no adjustment is required.

R&R MOWER BELTS. To remove the mower drive belt and the blade belt, place blade clutch lever in disengaged position. Unbolt and remove engine pulley belt guide. Remove mower drive belt from engine pulley. Unbolt and remove belt cover (11-Fig. G13), then remove belt (17) from center spindle pulley (18) and idler (7).

To remove the blade belt (15), unpin front of mower from hanger arm assembly and remove mower from right

side of chassis. Unbolt and remove blade belt cover (13). Refer to Fig. G11 and pull idler pulley in direction shown and remove the belt.

Install new belts by reversing the removal procedure. With mower attached, engage the clutch and adjust engine pulley belt guide until a clearance of 1/16 to 1/8 inch (1.6-3 mm) exists between the pulley and guide.

Models 52051C-52061

ADJUSTMENT. Move mower engagement lever to engaged position. Turn adjustment nut (1-Fig. G15) until tension spring (2) measured length is 2⅝ inches (66.7 mm) as shown in Fig. G15. If correct adjustment can not be attained, then disengage mower engagement lever. Unbolt idler pulley (1-Fig. G16) from idler arm (5), then reposition idler pulley in back hole (2) on idler arm. Engage mower lever and measure length of tension spring. Readjust adjustment nut (1-Fig. G15) until correct length is attained. Clearance between belt retainer (3-Fig. G16) and drive belt should be 1/16 to 1/8 inch (1.6-3 mm). If drive belt still slips on drive pulleys, then drive belt must be renewed.

R&R MOWER BELT. Move mower engagement lever to disengaged posi-

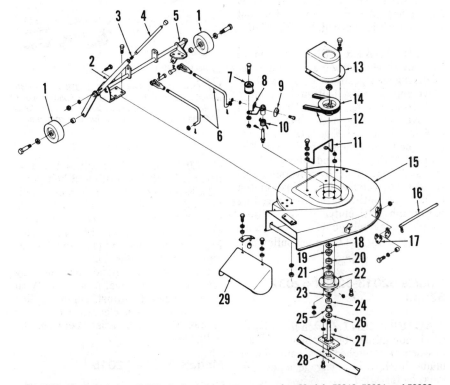

Fig. G12—Exploded view of 25-inch single blade mower used on Models 52013, 52031 and 52038.

1. Cutting height gage wheels	7. Idler pulley	14. Mower pulley	22. Spindle housing
2. Lever	8. Idler & brake arm	15. Mower housing	23. Retaining ring
3. Spring	9. Brake shoe	16. Mower attaching pin	24. Bearing cup
4. Rod	10. Spring	17. Bell cranks (2)	25. Bearing cone
5. Pivot shaft & support assy.	11. Belt guide	18. Seal	26. Seal
6. Leveler links	12. Mower drive belt	19. Bearing cone	27. Spindle
	13. Belt cover	20. Bearing cup	28. Blade 25"
		21. Retaining ring	29. Deflector

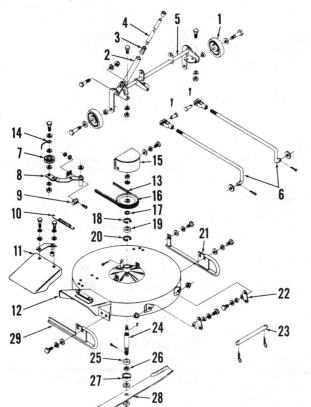

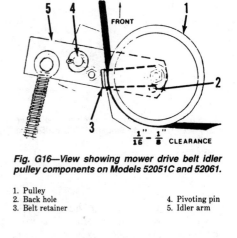

Fig. G16—View showing mower drive belt idler pulley components on Models 52051C and 52061.

1. Pulley
2. Back hole
3. Belt retainer
4. Pivoting pin
5. Idler arm

Fig. G14—Exploded view of 30-inch single blade mower used on Models 52032, 52033, 52039 and 52040.

1. Cutting height gage wheels
2. Lever
3. Spring
4. Rod
5. Pivot shaft & support assy.
6. Leveler links
7. Idler pulley
8. Idler & brake arm
9. Brake shoe
10. Spring
11. Deflector
12. Mower housing
13. Mower drive belt
14. Belt finger
15. Belt cover & guide
16. Mower pulley
17. Snap ring
18. Retaining ring
19. Bearing
20. Retaining ring
21. Mower runner L.H.
22. Bellcranks (2)
23. Mower attaching pin
24. Spindle
25. Bearing
26. Jam nut
27. Dust cup
28. Blade 30″
29. Mower runner R.H.

Models 52060-52066-52074

ADJUSTMENT. Move mower engagement lever to engaged position. Turn adjustment nut (1-Fig. G17) until tension spring (2) measured length is 2⅝ inches (66.7 mm) as shown in Fig. G18. If correct adjustment can not be attained, then disengage mower engagement lever. Unbolt idler pulley (1) from idler arm (5), then reposition idler pulley in a slot (2) closer to rear of mower deck. There are four possible adjustment slots. Engage mower lever and measure length of tension spring. Readjust adjustment nut (1-Fig. G17) until correct length is attained. Clearance between belt retainer (3-Fig. G18) and drive belt should be 1/16 to 1/8 inch (1.6-3 mm). If drive belt still slips on drive pulleys and idler pulley has been adjusted as far toward rear of mower as possible, then drive belt must be renewed.

R&R MOWER BELT. Move mower engagement lever to disengaged position. Remove engine drive belt cover, then slip drive belt off engine pulley. Unhook mower deck lift chain, then remove pins securing mower deck front

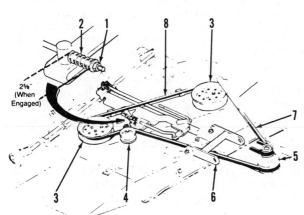

Fig. G15—View showing mower drive belt routing and associated components on Models 52051C and 52061. Refer to text for adjustment procedure.

1. Adjustment nut
2. Tension spring
3. Spindle drive pulley
4. Idler pulley
5. Engine pulley
6. Front hanger
7. Belt guard
8. Drive belt

tion. Remove engine drive belt cover, then slip drive belt off engine pulley. Unhook mower deck lift chain, then remove pins securing mower deck front hanger to tractor frame hanger. Remove any other components that will obstruct mower deck removal, then withdraw mower deck. Remove mower deck front hanger (6-Fig. G15), idler pulley (4) and belt guard (7). Slip drive belt off pulleys. Inspect all pulleys for excessive wear or any other damage and renew as needed. Renew drive belt.

Reassemble in reverse order of disassembly. Refer to previous ADJUSTMENT section for drive belt adjustment procedure.

Fig. G17—View showing mower drive belt routing and associated components on Models 52060, 52066 and 52074. Refer to text for adjustment procedure.

1. Adjustment nut
2. Tension spring
3. Spindle drive pulley
4. Idler pulley
5. Engine pulley
6. Front hanger
7. Belt guard
8. Drive belt

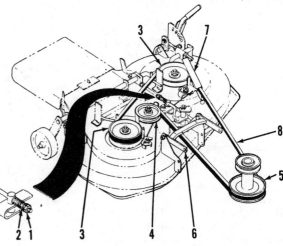

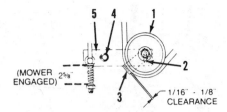

Fig. G18—View showing mower drive belt idler pulley components on Models 52060, 52066 and 52074.

1. Idler pulley
2. Adjustment slots
3. Belt retainer
4. Pivoting pin
5. Idler arm

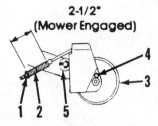

Fig. G19—View showing mower drive belt idler pulley components on Models 52064, 52065, 52072 and 52073.

1. Adjustment nut
2. Tension spring
3. Idler pulley
4. Front hole
5. Idler arm

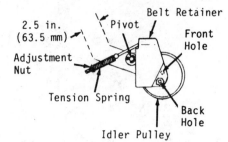

Fig. G20A—View showing location of tension spring and adjustment nut on Models 52080 and 52081.

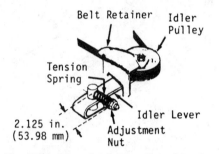

Fig. G20B—View showing location of tension spring and adjustment nut on Model 52082.

hanger to tractor frame hanger. Remove any other components that will obstruct mower deck removal, then withdraw mower deck front hanger (6-Fig. G17), idler pulley (4) and belt guard (7). Slip drive belt off pulleys. Inspect all pulleys for excessive wear or any other damage and renew as needed. Renew drive belt.

Reassemble in reverse order of disassembly. Refer to previous ADJUSTMENT section for drive belt adjustment procedure.

Models 52064-52065-52072-52073

ADJUSTMENT. Move mower engagement lever to engaged position. Turn adjustment nut (1-Fig. G19) until tension spring (2) measured length is 2½ inches (63.5 mm) as shown in Fig. G19. If belt still slips after adjustment, then disengage mower engagement lever. Unbolt idler pulley (3) from idler arm (5), then reposition idler in back hole as shown in Fig. G19. Front hole (4) is shown open in Fig. G19. Engage mower lever and measure length of tension spring. Readjust adjustment nut (1) until correct length is attained. Clearance between idler pulley belt retainer and drive belt should be 1/16 to 1/8 inch (1.6-3 mm). If drive belt still slips on drive pulleys, then drive belt must be renewed.

R&R MOWER BELT. Move mower engagement lever to disengaged position. Remove engine drive belt guide, then slip drive belt off engine pulley. Unhook mower deck lift chain, then remove pins securing mower deck front hanger to tractor frame hanger. Remove any other components that will obstruct mower deck removal, then withdraw mower deck. Remove mower deck front hanger (6-Fig. G20), idler pulley belt retainer and belt guard (7). Turn pivot assembly (9) completely counterclockwise, then slip drive belt off pulleys. USE CAUTION when sliding belt between pulleys and brake pads. Inspect all pulleys for excessive

wear or any other damage and renew as needed. Renew drive belt.

Reassemble in reverse order of disassembly. Refer to previous ADJUSTMENT section for drive belt adjustment procedure.

Models 52080-52081

ADJUSTMENT. Place mower drive lever in engaged position. Locate adjustment nut (Fig. G20A) and turn nut to obtain spring measurement of 2.5 inches (63.5 mm). Turn nut clockwise to decrease spring measurement or counterclockwise to decrease spring measurement. If belt still slips, place idler pulley in back hole of idler bracket. If belt slips with idler pulley in back hole of idler bracket and correct spring tension, renew belt.

R&R MOWER BELT. Remove mower deck from rider. Remove front hanger assembly and belt retainer. Remove left belt guard. Rotate pivot assembly counterclockwise as far as possible and remove old belt. Reinstall in reverse order of disassembly. Refer to previous ADJUSTMENT section for drive belt adjustment procedure.

Model 52082

ADJUSTMENT. Place mower drive lever in engaged position. Locate adjustment nut (Fig. G20B) and turn nut to obtain spring measurement of 2.125 inches (53.98 mm). If unable to obtain correct spring measurement or if belt still slips, reposition idler pulley on idler pulley lever. Lever has four different pulley mounting positions (holes). If idler pulley is located in last hole and spring tension cannot be correctly adjusted, renew belt.

R&R MOWER BELT. Remove mower deck from rider. Remove front hanger assembly and belt retainer from

Fig. G20—View showing mower drive belt routing and associated components on Models 52064, 52065, 52072 and 52073.

1. Belt guide
2. Brake strap
3. Spindle drive pulley
4. Idler pulley
5. Engine pulley
6. Front hanger
7. Belt guard
8. Drive belt
9. Pivot assy.

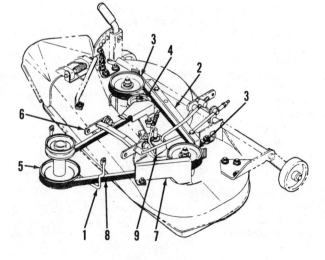

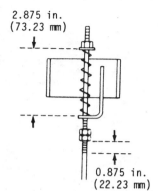

2.875 in.
(73.23 mm)

0.875 in.
(22.23 mm)

Fig. G20C—Models 52089, 52090 and 52091 mower drive clutch adjustment dimensions. Refer to text.

mower deck. Remove belt guard and belt. Reinstall in reverse order of disassembly. Refer to previous ADJUSTMENT section for drive belt adjustment procedure.

Models 52089-52090-52091

ADJUSTMENT. Place mower drive lever in engaged position. Remove plastic tray from frame in front of seat. Refer to Fig. G20C and adjust clutch spring to obtain dimensions shown. Looking through slot in rear hitch plate toward front of rider, make certain there is a minimum clearance between the two sides of the mower drive belt (at idler pulley) of 1 inch (25.4 mm). To adjust clearance, disengage mower drive lever, loosen the two nuts on each of the three mower deck brackets and move mower deck brackets toward rear of mower deck. Tighten nuts and check belt adjustment.

R&R MOWER BELT. Remove mower deck from rider. Disconnect blade brake spring at mower deck. Remove locknut holding idler pulley on idler lever. Lift pulley and remove mower drive belt. Install new belt. Adjust mower belt as previously outlined.

Models 52106-52107-52108

ADJUSTMENT. Place mower drive lever in engaged position. Looking through slot in rear hitch plate, check clearance between the two sides of the mower drive belt at idler pulley. If clearance is less than 1.5 inches (38.1 mm), disengage mower drive lever. Loosen the nuts on all three mower deck hanger brackets (on some models, removal of plastic tray in front of seat will be necessary). Pull one side of mower deck as far toward front of rider as possible and tighten hanger bracket nuts on that side. Repeat sequence on opposite side. Check clearance between belt sides at idler as previously outlined. To check mower drive cable spring tension, lower mower deck to lowest position. Locate threaded adjusting end of mower drive cable just behind right side of footrest, on underside of rider frame. Adjust spring tension so there is ½-1 inch (12.7-25.4 mm) free play in mower drive lever before lever begins engaging mower drive belt.

R&R MOWER BELT. Drain fuel tank and crankcase. Remove battery (as equipped). Stand rider on rear support bars. Remove clevis pin at front pivoting lift arm and allow mower deck to drop downward. Make certain thick spacer washer between lift arm is not lost. Remove belt guide at engine pulley. Pull mower drive belt back and over lower engine pulley. Slip belt between blade pulley and belt guide tab on idler plate (it may be necessary to loosen idler pulley). Pull belt forward and out.

Reassemble in reverse order of disassembly. Refer to previous ADJUSTMENT section for drive belt adjustment procedure.

Models 52113-52117-52118

ADJUSTMENT. Place mower lift lever so mower is at its lowest position. Place mower drive lever in engaged position. Locate tension spring on mower clutch cable at mower deck. Spring should measure 4.375 inches (111.13 mm) from curved portion of spring hook to cable/spring joint. To adjust spring length, locate clevis at opposite cable end, loosen jam nut, remove clevis pin and thread clevis on or off cable end as necessary. If belt slips with mower clutch cable spring correctly adjusted, idler pulley may be positioned in an alternate notch in pivot bracket.

R&R MOWER BELT. Loosen nut on idler pulley and tilt idler away from belt guide. Push brake shoe away from right side blade pulley and remove belt from pulley. Loosen nuts on belt guard and tilt belt guard away from left blade pulley and remove belt from pulley. Remove belt.

Reassemble in reverse order of disassembly. Refer to previous ADJUSTMENT section for drive belt adjustment procedure.

Model 52120

ADJUSTMENT. Place mower deck in lowest cutting position. Locate threaded adjusting end of mower drive clutch cable just behind right side of footrest, on underside of frame. Loosen jam nut and adjust adjusting nut so there is ½-1 inch (12.7-25.4 mm) free play in mower drive lever before mower begins to engage. Lock adjustment nut in position with jam nut. Place mower drive lever in disengaged position. Loosen the hex nuts on all three mower deck hanger brackets (if equipped with plastic tray in front of seat, tray may be removed to gain access). Pull one side of mower deck as far as possible toward front of rider and tighten hanger brackets on that side. Repeat procedure for opposite side. Check mower clutch cable tension spring adjustment.

R&R MOWER BELT. Drain fuel tank and crankcase. Remove battery (as equipped). Stand rider on rear support bars. Remove clevis pin at front pivoting lift arm and allow mower deck to drop downward. Make certain thick spacer washer between lift arm is not lost. Remove belt guide at engine pulley. Pull mower drive belt back and over lower engine pulley. Slip belt between blade pulley and belt guide tab on idler plate (it may be necessary to loosen idler pulley). Pull belt forward and out.

Reassemble in reverse order of disassembly. Refer to previous ADJUSTMENT section for drive belt adjustment procedure.

MOWER BLADES AND SPINDLES

All Models

Models 52013, 52031, 52032, 52033, 52038, 52039, 52040, 52089, 52090, 52091, 52106, 52107, 52108 and 52120 are equipped with single blade rotary mowers. Models 52113, 52117, 52118, 52051C, 52060, 52061, 52064, 52065, 52066, 52072, 52073, 52074, 52080, 52081 and 52082 are equipped with dual blade rotary mowers. Models 52014 and 52015 are equipped with three blade rotary mowers.

CAUTION: Always disconnect spark plug wire before performing any inspection, adjustment or other service on the mower.

On models so equipped, make certain that safety starting switches are connected and are in good working condition before returning mower to service.

The following paragraphs contain procedures for removing blades, spindles and renewing spindle bearings.

Models 52013-52031-52038

REMOVE AND REINSTALL. To remove the blade and blade spindle, first remove mower assembly as follows: Place blade clutch control lever in disengaged position. Unbolt and remove engine pulley belt guide and remove mower belt from engine pulley. Unpin front of mower from hanger arm assembly. Remove mower from right side of chassis. Unbolt and remove belt cover (13–Fig. G12) and belt guide (11). Remove belt (12) from pulley (14) and idler (7). Remove nut and mower pulley (14), then unbolt blade (28) from spindle (27). Unbolt and remove spindle housing assembly (18 through 27) from mower housing (15). Remove spindle (27), then remove seals (18 & 26), bearing cones (19 & 25), bearing cups (20 & 24) and retaining rings (21 & 23).

Clean and inspect all parts and renew any showing excessive wear or other damage. Reassembly is the reverse of disassembly procedure. Reinstall mower, engage clutch and adjust engine pulley belt guide for a clearance of $\frac{1}{16}$ to $\frac{1}{8}$ inch (1.6-3 mm) between the pulley and belt guide.

Models 52014-52015

REMOVE AND REINSTALL. To remove the blades and spindles, first remove mower assembly as follows: Place blade clutch control lever in disengaged position. Unbolt and remove engine pulley belt guide and remove mower drive belt from engine pulley. Unpin front of mower from hanger arm assembly. Remove mower unit out from under right side. Unbolt and remove belt cover (11-Fig. G13), then remove mower drive belt (17) from center spindle pulley (18) and idler pulley (7). Unbolt and remove blade belt cover (13). Refer to Fig. G11 and pull idler pulley in direction shown, then remove blade belt.

Remove nut, lock washer and two set screws, then lift off center pulley (18-Fig. G13). Remove blade (30), then unbolt and remove center spindle housing assembly (31 through 39) from mower housing (21). Remove spindle (39), spacer (38) and bearing (37) from bottom of spindle housing (36) and washers (31 & 33), bearings (32 & 34) and spacer (35) from top of spindle housing. Clean and inspect all parts and renew any showing excessive wear or other damage. Reassemble center spindle by reversing disassembly procedure.

Left and right spindle assemblies are identical. To remove either left or right spindle, remove nut, lockwasher and two set screws, then lift off pulley (14). Remove blade (30), then unbolt and remove spindle housing assembly (22 through 29) from mower housing (21). Withdraw spindle (29) and spacer (28) from spindle housing (25). Remove retaining rings (22 & 28), bearings (23 & 26) and spacer (24) from spindle hous-

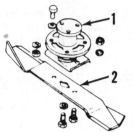

Fig. G21—View showing spindle assembly (1) and mower blade (2) used on Models 52051C and 52061.

ing. Clean and inspect all parts and renew any showing excessive wear or other damage. Reassemble by reversing disassembly procedure.

Complete the balance of mower reassembly and reinstall the mower assembly. Engage clutch and adjust engine pulley belt guide for a clearance of $\frac{1}{16}$ to $\frac{1}{8}$ inch (1.6-3 mm) between the pulley and belt guide.

Models 52032-52033-52039-52040

REMOVE AND REINSTALL. To remove the blade and blade spindle, first remove mower assembly as follows: Place blade clutch control lever in disengaged position. Unbolt and remove engine pulley belt guide and remove mower belt from engine pulley. Unpin front of mower from hanger arm assembly. Remove mower unit out from right side. Unbolt and remove belt cover and guide (15-Fig. G14), then remove mower belt (13) from mower pulley (16) and idler pulley (7). Remove nut, lock washer, pulley (16) and snap ring (17) from upper end of spindle. Remove blade and spindle assembly (24 through 28) from bottom of mower housing (12). Clamp center of spindle (24) in a vise and remove nut, washers, blade (28) and dust cup (27), then remove nut (26) and bearing (25) from spindle (24). Remove retaining rings (18 & 20) and bearing (19) from mower housing.

Clean and inspect all parts and renew any showing excessive wear or other damage. Reassemble by reversing disassembly procedure. Reinstall mower unit, engage clutch and adjust engine pulley belt guide for a clearance of 1/16 to 1/8 inch (1.6-3 mm) between the pulley and belt guide.

Models 52051C-52061-52080-52081-52113-52117-52118

REMOVE AND REINSTALL. To remove mower blade and blade spindle, first remove mower deck. Remove drive belt from pulleys. Unbolt and remove spindle drive pulley. Remove spindle

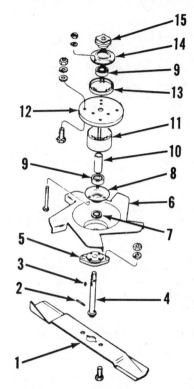

Fig. G22—Exploded view showing mower spindle unit used on Models 52060, 52066, 52074 and 52082.

1. Blade
2. Pin
3. Key
4. Shaft
5. Adapter
6. Fan
7. Spacer
8. Bearing cup

9. Bearing
10. Spacer
11. Housing
12. Flange
13. Housing
14. Bearing cup
15. Pulley hub

assembly (1-Fig. G21) mounting bolts, then withdraw spindle and blade as a unit. Separate blade from spindle assembly.

Clean and inspect spindle assembly for excessive wear or any other damage. Spindle assembly must be renewed as a complete unit. Reassemble by reversing disassembly procedure. Reinstall mower unit, then adjust drive belt as outlined in MOWER BLADE CLUTCH AND BELT section.

Models 52060-52066-52074-52082

REMOVE AND REINSTALL. To remove mower blade and blade spindle, first remove mower deck as outlined in MOWER BLADE CLUTCH AND BELT section. Remove drive belt from pulleys. Remove nut, lockwasher and flat washer securing drive pulley to pulley hub (15-Fig. G22), then withdraw drive pulley. Remove spindle assembly mounting bolts, then withdraw spindle assembly and blade as a unit. Separate blade from spindle assembly. Disassemble spindle assembly with reference to Fig. G22.

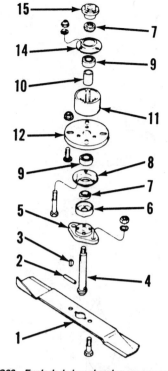

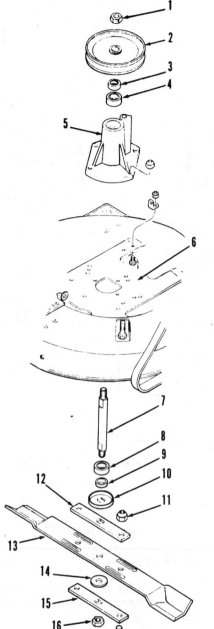

Fig. G23—Exploded view showing mower spindle unit used on Models 52064, 52065, 52072 and 52073.

1. Blade	8. Bearing cup
2. Pin	9. Bearing
3. Key	10. Spacer
4. Shaft	11. Housing
5. Adapter	12. Flange
6. Shield	14. Bearing cup
7. Spacer	15. Pulley hub

Fig. G24—Exploded view of mower spindle used on Models 52089, 52090, 52091, 52106, 52107, 52108 and 52120.

1. Nut	
2. Pulley	10. Cover
3. Spacer	11. Nut
4. Bearing	12. Blade support
5. Housing	13. Blade
6. Mower deck	14. Special washer
7. Shaft	15. Blade support
8. Bearing	16. Nut
9. Spacer	17. Bolt

Clean and inspect all parts for excessive wear or any other damage and renew as needed. Reassemble by reversing disassembly procedure. Reinstall mower unit, then adjust drive belt as outlined in MOWER BLADE CLUTCH AND BELT section.

Models 52064-52065-52072-52073

REMOVE AND REINSTALL. To remove mower blade and blade spindle, first remove mower deck as outlined in MOWER BLADE CLUTCH AND BELT section. Remove drive belt from pulleys. Remove nut, lockwasher and flat washer securing drive pulley to pulley hub (15–Fig. G23), then withdraw drive pulley. Remove spindle assembly mounting bolts, then withdraw spindle assembly and blade as a unit. Separate blade from spindle assembly. Disassemble spindle assembly with reference to Fig. G23.

Clean and inspect all parts for excessive wear or any other damage and renew as needed. Reassemble by reversing disassembly procedure. Reinstall mower unit, then adjust drive belt as outlined in MOWER BLADE CLUTCH AND BELT section.

Models 52089-52090-52091-52106-52107-52108-52120

REMOVE AND REINSTALL. Remove mower deck assembly and mower drive belt. Remove nut (1–Fig. G24), pulley (2) and spacer (3). Remove nut (16), blade assembly (13), cover (10), and spacer (9). Press shaft (7) out of bearing housing (5) and remove bearings (4 and 8).

Clean and inspect all parts for wear or damage. Reassemble by reversing disassembly procedure.

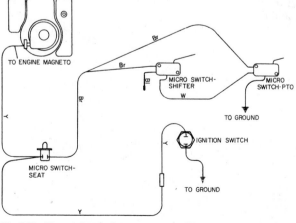

Fig. G25—View of electrical components and their adjoining wires on rear engine riders with recoil start.

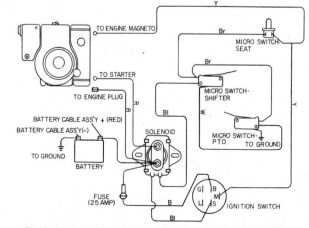

Fig. G26—View of electrical components and their adjoining wires on rear engine riders with electric start.

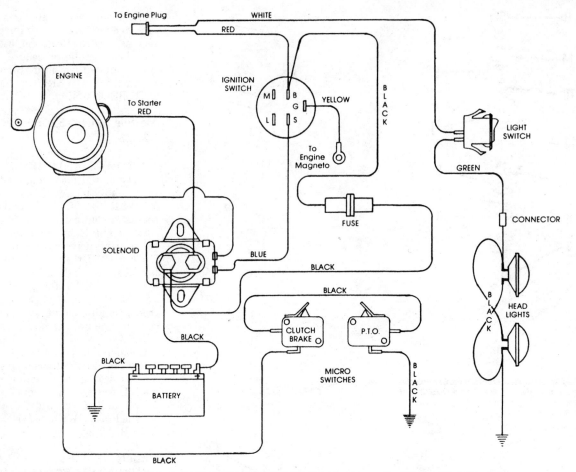

Fig. G27—Diagram showing electrical components and their adjoining wires on Front Engine Model Tractors.

ELECTRICAL

Rear Engine Rider

Refer to Figs. G25 and G26 for electrical components and their adjoining wires.

Front Engine Tractors

Shown in electrical diagram Fig. G27 are electrical components and their adjoining wires.

GRAVELY

GRAVELY CORPORATION
One Gravely Lane
Clemmons, NC 27012

Model	Make	Engine Model	Horsepower	Cutting Width, In.
830	B&S	191702	8	30
830-E	B&S	191707	8	30
1130-E	B&S	252707	11	30

FRONT AXLE

All Models

REMOVE AND REINSTALL. The axle member (20-Fig. GR1) mounts within steering channel (15) and is center-pivoted on its mounting bolt (19). To remove axle, raise and securely block front of unit. Remove front wheel assemblies and unbolt outer end of tie rods (9) from spindles (21). Remove retaining pins and washers from top of spindles, then remove spindles. Remove pivot bolt (19) and spacer (16), then remove axle from steering channel. Remove nylon spindle bushings (18) if renewal is required.

Clean and inspect all parts and renew as necessary. Reassemble by reversing removal procedure. Lubricate wheel bearings and axle pivot with multipurpose lithium base grease.

STEERING GEAR

All Models

REMOVE AND REINSTALL. To remove steering gear, remove nut (2-Fig. GR1) and pull steering wheel (1) from shaft (6). Remove cotter pin (14) and special washers (13) from bottom of steering shaft. Remove screws securing steering stand (5) to frame and disconnect pto linkage, then lift off steering stand and remove steering shaft. Remove nut (7) from below to remove steering gear (8).

CAUTION: Frequently, the performance of maintenance, adjustment or repair operations on a riding mower is more convenient if mower is standing on end and these units are provided with a stand for this purpose. This procedure can be considered a recommended practice providing the fol-

lowing safety recommendations are performed:

1. **Drain fuel tank or make certain that fuel level is low enough so that fuel will not drain out.**
2. **Close fuel shut-off valve if so equipped.**
3. **Remove battery on models so equipped.**
4. **Disconnect spark plug wire and tie out of way.**
5. **Although not absolutely essential, it is recommended that crankcase oil be drained to avoid flooding the combustion chamber with oil when engine is tilted.**
6. **Secure mower from tipping by lashing unit to a nearby post or overhead beam.**

Clean and inspect all parts. Renew any that are excessively worn or otherwise damaged. Lubricate bearings and

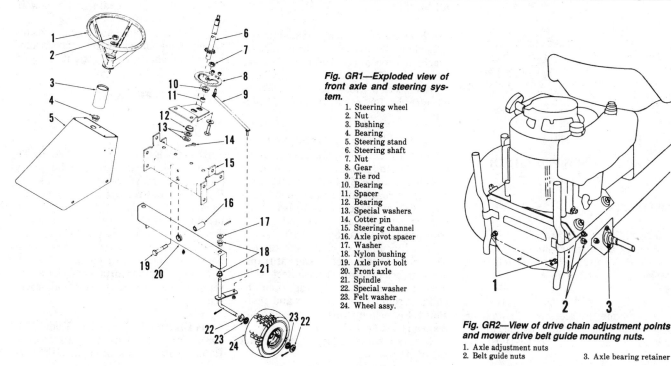

Fig. GR1—Exploded view of front axle and steering system.

1. Steering wheel
2. Nut
3. Bushing
4. Bearing
5. Steering stand
6. Steering shaft
7. Nut
8. Gear
9. Tie rod
10. Bearing
11. Spacer
12. Bearing
13. Special washers
14. Cotter pin
15. Steering channel
16. Axle pivot spacer
17. Washer
18. Nylon bushing
19. Axle pivot bolt
20. Front axle
21. Spindle
22. Special washer
23. Felt washer
24. Wheel assy.

Fig. GR2—View of drive chain adjustment points and mower drive belt guide mounting nuts.

1. Axle adjustment nuts
2. Belt guide nuts
3. Axle bearing retainer

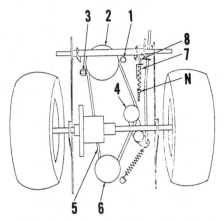

Fig. GR3—View of traction drive belt and brake adjustment rod.

1. Round belt guide	5. Traction drive belt
2. Transmission pulley	6. Engine pulley
3. Flat belt guide	7. Spring
4. Idler pulley	8. Brake adjustment rod

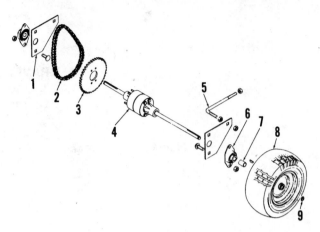

Fig. GR4—Differential and rear axle assembly.
1. Axle bearing retainer
2. Chain
3. Sprocket
4. Differential
5. Axle adjustment rod
6. Bearing
7. Spacer
8. Wheel assy.
9. Retaining ring

steering gear with SAE 30 oil. Reassemble in reverse order of removal.

ENGINE

All Models

Refer to appropriate engine section in this manual for tune-up specifications, engine overhaul procedures and engine maintenance.

REMOVE AND REINSTALL. To remove engine, disconnect spark plug wire, throttle cable and electrical wiring as needed. Move pto lever to "OFF" position. Loosen two nuts (2–Fig. GR2) on mower belt guide and slide guide to rear. Remove mower drive belt from engine pulley. Depress clutch-brake pedal and set park lock to release spring tension on traction drive belt, then remove belt from engine pulley. Remove engine mounting bolts and lift off engine.

Reinstall in reverse order of removal. Adjust mower belt as outlined in MOWER DRIVE BELT section.

TRACTION DRIVE CLUTCH AND BELT DRIVE

All Models

The main drive clutch consists of a non-adjustable, spring-loaded idler (4–Fig. GR3) when the clutch pedal is fully depressed, tension is removed from drive belt (5) and engine pulley (6) rotates freely within the belt. If drive belt slips due to excessive belt wear or stretching, renew belt as outlined under the following REMOVE AND REINSTALL paragraphs.

REMOVE AND REINSTALL. To remove the traction drive belt (5–Fig. GR3), disconnect spark plug wire and remove mower deck as outlined under MOWER DECK paragraphs. Depress clutch-brake pedal and set park brake lock. Set unit up on its rear stand as previously outlined. Loosen nut on flat belt guide (3) and turn guide 90° clockwise. Remove round belt guide (1), then remove drive belt from pulleys.

Renew drive belt by reversing removal procedure.

TRANSMISSION

All Models

A Peerless Model 706-A transmission is used on all models. For transmission overhaul procedures, refer to Peerless section in TRANSMISSION REPAIR service section. Refer to the following paragraphs for removal and installation.

REMOVE AND REINSTALL. To remove transmission, disconnect spark plug wire and remove mower unit as outlined in MOWER DECK section. Set unit up on rear stand as previously outlined. Remove traction drive belt, then remove retaining ring and pull pulley from transmission input shaft. Locate master link in drive chain and disconnect chain. Disconnect linkage at transmission brake lever. Disconnect shift linkage and necessary wiring, then unbolt and remove seat support and chain guard. Remove mounting bolts and lift transmission from frame.

Reinstall transmission by reversing removal procedure.

DRIVE CHAIN

All Models

ADJUSTMENT. To adjust drive chain, loosen nuts securing rear axle bearing retainers (3–Fig. GR2) on each side of frame. To tighten chain, move axle assembly rearward (equal distance on both sides) by turning adjusting nuts (1) clockwise. Drive chain should deflect approximately ½ inch (12.7 mm) when about five pounds (2.7 kg) pressure is applied on chain. When chain tension is correct, tighten bearing retainer nuts.

REMOVE AND REINSTALL. To remove drive chain, rotate differential sprocket to locate master link. Disconnect master link and remove chain. Clean and inspect chain and renew if excessively worn.

Install drive chain and adjust tension as outlined in preceding paragraph. Lubricate chain with a light coat of SAE 30 oil.

DIFFERENTIAL

All Models

REMOVE AND REINSTALL. To remove, raise rear of unit and support securely. Remove retaining rings (9–Fig. GR4) and remove rear wheels (8). Remove drive chain (2). Unbolt axle bearing retainers (1), then remove differential and axle assembly. Clean rust, dirt and paint off axle ends, then slide bearings (6) from axle ends.

Reinstall differential and axle assembly by reversing the removal procedure.

OVERHAUL. A Peerless Model 100-008 differential is used on all models. Refer to Peerless section in DIFFER-

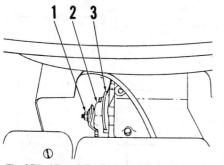

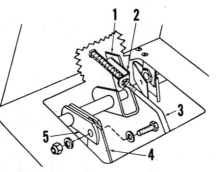

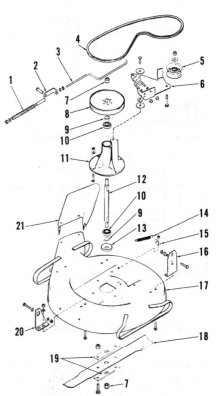

Fig. GR5—View of disc brake carrier and adjusting nut.
1. Adjusting nut
2. Carrier
3. Brake disc

Fig. GR7—View of mower linkage located beneath steering console.
1. Pto crank
2. Blade engagement link
3. Blade engagement rod
4. Front deck bracket
5. Cross shaft

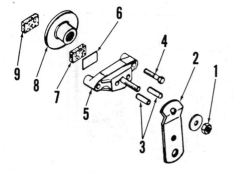

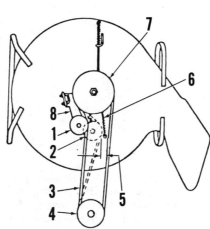

Fig. GR6—Exploded view of disc brake assembly.
1. Adjusting nut
2. Brake actuating lever
3. Actuating pins
4. Cap screw
5. Carrier
6. Back-up plate
7. Brake pad (outer)
8. Brake disc
9. Brake pad (inner)

Fig. GR8—View of mower drive belt and idler.
1. Idler pulley disengaged
2. Idler pulley engaged
3. Drive belt
4. Engine pulley
5. Correct distance is one inch minimum
6. Blade brake spring
7. Blade pulley
8. Idler pulley bracket

Fig. GR9—Exploded view of mower unit.
1. Blade engagement spring
2. Blade engagement link
3. Blade engagement rod
4. Drive belt
5. Idler pulley
6. Idler bracket
7. Nut
8. Blade pulley
9. Spacer
10. Bearing
11. Spindle housing
12. Spindle shaft
13. Spinner cap
14. Blade brake spring
15. Spring bracket
16. Rear deck bracket
17. Mower deck
18. Blade
19. Support bar
20. Front deck bracket
21. Deflector chute

ENTIAL REPAIR service section for overhaul procedures.

GROUND DRIVE BRAKE

All Models

The brake is applied by depressing either of the foot pedals. Brake disc is mounted on transmission output shaft at end opposite drive sprocket.

ADJUSTMENT. To adjust brake, set unit up on rear stand as previously outlined. Tighten nut (N–Fig. GR3) on brake adjustment rod (8) to compress spring (7) to length of 10 inches (254 mm). Put unit back on its wheels and shift transmission to neutral. Depress clutch-brake pedal and engage pedal lock. If rear wheels turn when pushing unit, release brake and tighten adjusting nut (1–Fig. GR5) on disc brake carrier (2) 1/2-turn. Recheck and repeat adjustment if necessary.

REMOVE AND REINSTALL. To remove disc brake, disconnect return spring and brake rod from actuating lever (2–Fig. GR6). Remove cap screws

(4) and remove pad carrier assembly. Slide brake disc (8) from shaft and remove inner brake pad (9) from holder slot in transmission case. Remove adjusting nut (1) and separate brake lever (2), actuating pins (3), back-up plate (6) and outer brake pad (7) from pad carrier (5). Renew parts as required and reassemble by reversing the removal procedure. Adjust brake as outlined in previous paragraph.

MOWER DECK

All Models

LEVEL ADJUSTMENT. To adjust gage wheels on mower, position unit on level ground, then remove pins from gage wheel spindles letting wheels touch ground. Align one hole in left hand support with hole in the spindle and reinstall pin. Reinstall pin in corresponding holes in right hand support and spindle. If mower height is changed, readjust gage wheels.

REMOVE AND REINSTALL. To remove mower, disconnect spark plug wire, disengage pto and remove console tray. Disconnect blade engagement link (2-Fig. GR7) from pto crank (1) and cross shaft (5) from mower deck front bracket (4). Disconnect mower deck rear brackets from rear lift shaft. Loosen the two belt guide nuts (2-Fig. GR2), then slide guide rearward and remove drive belt from engine pulley. Move unit forward until blade engagement rod (3-Fig. GR7) clears cross shaft (5), then lift front wheels over mower.

Reinstall by reversing removal procedure. Be sure blade engagement rod goes over cross shaft. Torque belt guide nuts to 25 ft.-lbs (34 N·m). Check belt adjustment.

MOWER DRIVE BELT

All Models

ADJUSTMENT. To adjust belt, put pto lever in ""OFF" position and loosen nuts on the three mower deck brackets.

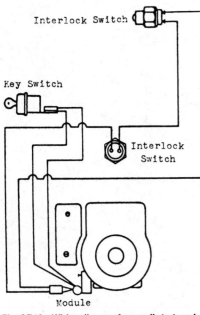

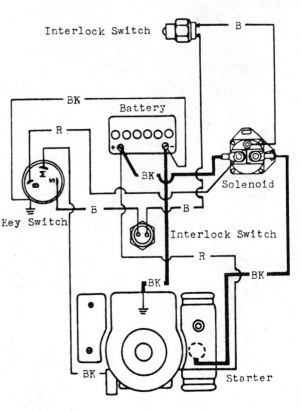

Fig. GR10—Wiring diagram for recoil start models.

Fig. GR11—Wiring diagram for electric start models.
1. BK-Black
2. B-Brown
3. R-Red

Move each bracket rearward to take slack out of belt. Check belt adjustment by looking through slot in hitch plate. With pto engaged, there must be a minimum clearance of one inch (5–Fig. GR8) between sides of drive belt measured at idler pulley (2).

REMOVE AND REINSTALL. To remove belt, disconnect spark plug wire and remove mower deck. Disconnect blade brake spring (6–Fig. GR8) from deck. Remove idler pulley (1) from idler bracket (8). Remove drive belt (3) from blade pulley (7).

Reinstall in reverse of removal. Torque idler pulley nut to 25 ft.-lbs. (34 N·m).

MOWER SPINDLE

All Models

REMOVE AND REINSTALL. Remove mower deck as previously outlined. Block mower blade (18–Fig. GR9) from turning. Loosen bolts in blade support bars (19), then remove lower nut (7) from spindle shaft to remove blade. Disconnect blade brake spring (14) from mower deck. Remove idler pulley (5) and drive belt (4). Remove retaining nut and pull blade pulley (8)

from spindle shaft (12). Remove idler bracket (6) and spindle housing (11) from mower deck, then remove spindle shaft (12), bearings (10) and spacers (9) from housing.

Clean and inspect all parts. Reassemble by reversing removal procedure. Spindle bearings are sealed and require no additional lubrication. When installing blade, torque spindle nuts (7) to 50 ft.-lbs. (67 N·m), then torque blade support bar nuts to 60 ft.-lbs (81 N·m). Finish tightening spindle nuts to 100 ft.-lbs. (136 N·m) torque.

ELECTRICAL

All Models

All units are equipped with safety interlock switches (Fig. GR10 and Fig. GR11) on transmission shift linkage and pto linkage. The transmission must be in neutral and pto disengaged before the unit will start.

ADJUSTMENT. To adjust the pto interlock switch (3–Fig. GR12) remove

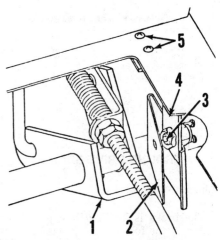

Fig. GR12—View of pto interlock switch.
1. Pto crank
2. Interlock spring
3. Interlock switch
4. Interlock bracket
5. Screws

the console tray and move pto lever to "OFF" position. Pto crank (1) should compress interlock spring (2) against interlock switch (3), closing the switch. If not, loosen screws (5) holding interlock bracket (4), reposition bracket, then tighten screws (5).

HOMELITE

HOMELITE DIVISION OF TEXTRON INC.
P.O. Box 7047
Charlotte, North Carolina 28241

Model	Make	Engine Model	Horsepower	Cutting Width, In.
RE-5	B&S	130202	5	26
RE-8E	B&S	190707	8	30
RE-30	B&S	190402	8	30

For service information and procedures, use the following model cross reference and refer to the SIMPLICITY section of this manual.

Homelite Models	Simplicity Models
RE-5	3005
RE-8E	808
RE-30	3008-2

HOMELITE/JACOBSEN

HOMELITE DIVISION OF TEXTRON INC.
P.O. Box 7047
Charlotte, NC 28241

This section contains information on later Homelite and Jacobsen models. For information on earlier models, refer to the Homelite and Jacobsen sections in this manual.

Model	Make	Engine Model	Horsepower	Cutting Width, In.
HR830	B&S	191702	8	30½
HR830E	B&S	191707	8	30½
HR930E	Kawasaki	FC290V	9	30½
HR1230E	B&S	281707	12	30½
JR830	B&S	191702	8	30½
JR1030	B&S	256707	10	30½
JR1230	B&S	281707	12	30½
RE830	B&S	191702	8	30½
RE830E	B&S	191707	8	30½
RE1030E	B&S	256707	10	30½
RE1230E	B&S	281707	12	30½
RMX8	B&S	191702	8	30½
RMX8E	B&S	191707	8	30½
RMX11E	B&S	252707	11	30½

NOTE: Some operations may be performed more easily if the machine is standing upright. Observe the following safety recommendations when raising machine to upright position:

1. Drain fuel tank or make certain that fuel level is low enough so that fuel will not drain out.
2. Close fuel shut-off valve if so equipped.
3. Remove battery if so equipped.
4. Disconnect spark plug wire and tie it out of way.
5. Although not absolutely essential, on models with spark plug at rear of machine, engine oil should be drained to prevent flooding the combustion chamber with oil when the engine is tilted.
6. Secure mower from tipping by lashing machine to a post or overhead beam.

FRONT WHEELS

All Models

Each front wheel hub is equipped with a grease fitting. Periodically inject a good quality multipurpose grease into grease fitting. Wheel must be serviced as a unit assembly.

FRONT AXLE

All Models

R&R AND OVERHAUL. To remove a front spindle, raise and support side to be serviced. Remove hub cap (35—Fig. HM11 or HM12), pin (31), wheel and tire. Disconnect steering link from spindle. Remove bolts attaching spindle bearing (30) to axle and remove spindle (32). Inspect components for excessive wear and damage. Install spindle by reversing removal procedure.

The front axle on all models except HR830 and HR830E pivots on a center pin (the front axle on Models HR830 and HR830E is bolted to the frame).

To remove front axle (29—Fig. HM11) on Models HR830 and HR830E, drive out pin (2) and remove steering wheel. Raise and support front of machine. Detach steering links (41 and 43) from spindles. Remove pin (4) and withdraw steering shaft (3) out bottom of machine. Detach axle braces (24). Remove axle mounting bolts and remove axle from machine.

To remove the front axle on all models except HR830 and HR830E, detach axle braces (24—Fig. HM12). Detach steer-

ing link (23) from the spindles. Raise and support front of machine, remove retaining bolts from axle pivot bearings (28) and separate axle assembly (29) from machine. Inspect components for excessive wear and damage. Install axle by reversing removal procedure.

STEERING SYSTEM

Models HR830 And HR830E

R&R AND OVERHAUL. To remove steering shaft, drive out pin (2—Fig. HM11) and remove steering wheel. Remove cotter pin at steering link end of steering shaft (3). Raise and support front of machine. Remove pin (4) and withdraw steering shaft out bottom of machine. Inspect components for excessive wear and damage. Install steering shaft by reversing removal procedure. Apply a suitable lubricant to all wear points.

All Other Models

R&R AND OVERHAUL. To remove steering shaft, remove cover (21—Fig. HM12). Drive out pin (2) and remove

Illustrations Courtesy Homelite Div. of Textron, Inc.

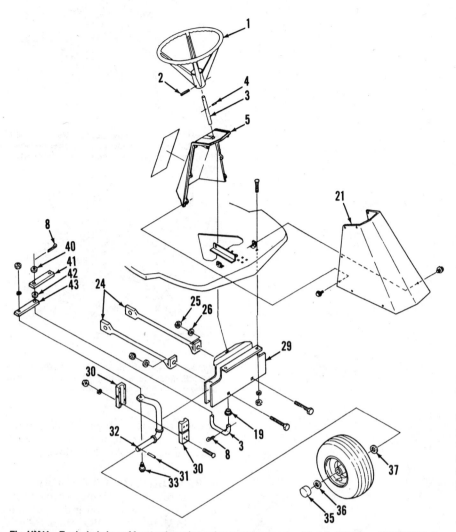

Fig. HM11—Exploded view of front axle and steering systems used on Models HR830 and HR830E. Refer to Fig. HM12 for parts identification except for:

40. Washer	41. Steering link	42. Washer	43. Steering link

steering wheel. Drive out pins (11 and 12) and withdraw steering shaft (3). Remove steering gear (13). Unscrew steering stud (14) from steering link (23). Unscrew ring gear pivot pin (15) and remove ring gear (16). Inspect components for excessive wear and damage. Install steering shaft by reversing removal procedure. Apply a suitable lubricant to all wear points.

ENGINE

Models HR830 And HR830E

Refer to appropriate engine section in this manual for tune-up specifications, engine overhaul procedures and engine maintenance.

REMOVE AND REINSTALL. To remove engine, disconnect spark plug wire and tie out of way. Detach access

panels on underside of machine as needed. Position mower deck at lowest setting. Remove belt guard on mower deck and loosen bolt that secures belt idler (I—Fig. HM13). Move mower engagement lever (L) to a midpoint position, remove belt from mower pulley, then remove mower belt from engine pulley. Disconnect traction drive idler spring and remove drive belt from engine pulley. Unscrew retaining screw and remove mower drive pulley and traction drive pulley from engine crankshaft. Disconnect throttle cable from engine. Disconnect all wires from engine that will interfere with removal. Remove engine mounting bolts and remove engine.

Reinstall engine by reversing removal procedure. Tighten pulley retaining cap screw in end of engine crankshaft to 50 ft.-lbs. (68 N•m).

All Other Models

Refer to appropriate engine section in this manual for tune-up specifications, engine overhaul procedures and engine maintenance.

REMOVE AND REINSTALL. To remove engine, disconnect spark plug wire and tie out of way. Detach access panels on underside of machine as needed. Position mower deck at lowest setting. Disconnect mower belt idler spring (S—Fig. HM14), remove belt from mower pulley, then remove mower belt from engine pulley. If necessary, relocate or detach belt guides for traction drive belt. Relieve spring tension against traction belt idler (16—Fig. HM15) and remove traction drive belt from transmission pulley, then remove belt from engine pulley. Disconnect electrical lead to mower drive clutch (20). Unscrew retaining screw and remove mower clutch unit and traction drive pulley from engine crankshaft. Disconnect throttle cable from engine. Disconnect all wires from engine that will interfere with removal. Remove engine mounting bolts and remove engine.

Reinstall engine by reversing removal procedure. When installing mower drive clutch (20), be sure stud (19) engages slot in upper plate of clutch. Tighten pulley retaining cap screw in end of engine crankshaft to 50 ft.-lbs. (68 N•m).

TRACTION DRIVE CLUTCH AND DRIVE BELT

Models HR830 And HR830E

The traction drive clutch is a spring-tensioned, belt idler-type operated by the clutch/brake pedal (24—Fig. HM16). When the pedal is depressed, belt tension is removed, allowing the engine drive pulley to rotate freely within the drive belt. After the pedal passes midpoint, the brake is applied.

LUBRICATION. After every 25 hours of operation, lubricate pedal shaft bushings (22—Fig. HM16) and clutch idler arm (4—Fig. HM17) pivot surfaces with SAE 30 engine oil.

R&R DRIVE BELT. To remove drive belt, disconnect spark plug wire and tie out of way. Remove mower deck as outlined in MOWER DECK section. Detach access panels on underside of machine as needed. Disconnect traction drive idler spring and relocate or detach any interfering belt guides. Remove drive belt from pulleys.

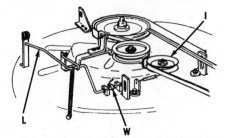

Fig. HM13—View of mower used on Models HR830 and HR830E showing location of mower belt idler (I), mower engagement lever (L) and safety switch (W).

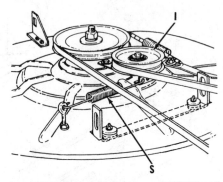

Fig. HM14—On all models except HR830 and HR830E, detach idler spring (S) and move idler (I) so the mower belt can be removed.

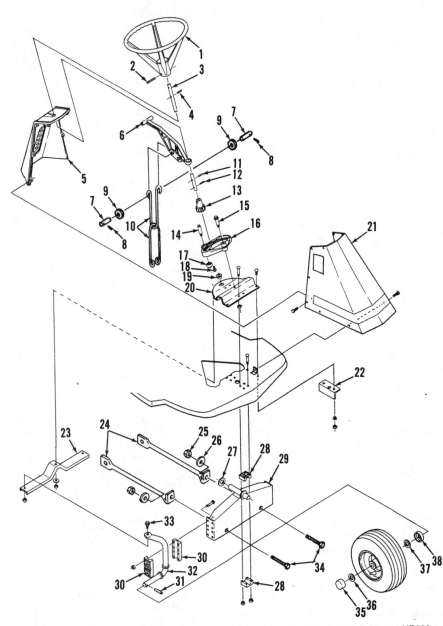

Fig. HM12—Exploded view of front axle and steering systems used on all models except HR830 and HR830E.

1. Steering wheel	11. Pin	20. Bracket
2. Pin	12. Pin	21. Cover
3. Steering shaft	13. Steering gear	22. Bracket
4. Pin	14. Steering stud	23. Steering link
5. Pedestal	15. Pivot pin	24. Axle braces
6. Mower lift handle	16. Ring gear	25. Nut
7. Pin	17. Ball bushing	26. Washer
8. Cotter pin	18. Screw	27. Washer
9. Washer	19. Bushing	28. Pivot bearing
10. Mower lift links		

29. Axle main member	
30. Spindle bearing	
31. Pin	
32. Spindle	
33. Screw	
34. Screw	
35. Hubcap	
36. Washer	
37. Washer	
38. Dust cap	

of operation, inject a good quality multipurpose grease into grease fitting on clutch idler arm (25—Fig. HM15).

R&R DRIVE BELT. To remove drive belt, disconnect spark plug wire and tie out of way. Remove mower deck as outlined in MOWER DECK section. Detach access panels on underside of machine as needed. Disconnect traction drive idler spring and relocate or detach any interfering belt guides. Unscrew idler pivot bolt nuts (27—Fig. HM15) and remove spacer (26). Remove drive belt from pulleys.

Install drive belt by reversing removal procedure. No adjustment of drive belt is required.

GROUND DRIVE BRAKE

All Models

ADJUSTMENT. All models are equipped with a disc brake that is mounted on the transmission, which is located inside the seat tower. To adjust brake, position machine on a level surface with the brakes released and the transmission in neutral. Roll machine back and forth while turning nut (N—Fig. HM19) clockwise. Stop turning nut when resistance is felt when moving machine. Turning nut in too far will cause excessive brake pad wear. Check brake action after adjustment.

Install drive belt by reversing removal procedure. No adjustment of drive belt is required.

All Other Models

The traction drive clutch is a spring-tensioned, belt idler-type. The clutch is operated either by a single clutch pedal (23—Fig. HM18) on early models or by a clutch/brake pedal on later models.

When the pedal is depressed, belt tension is removed, allowing the engine drive pulley to rotate freely within the drive belt. On later models, after the pedal passes midpoint, the brake is applied.

LUBRICATION. After every 25 hours of operation, lubricate pedal shaft bushings (16 and 24—Fig. HM18) with SAE 30 engine oil. After every 25 hours

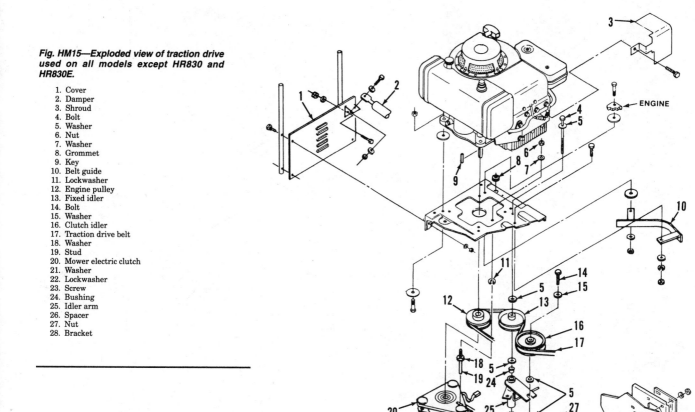

Fig. HM15—Exploded view of traction drive used on all models except HR830 and HR830E.

1. Cover
2. Damper
3. Shroud
4. Bolt
5. Washer
6. Nut
7. Washer
8. Grommet
9. Key
10. Belt guide
11. Lockwasher
12. Engine pulley
13. Fixed idler
14. Bolt
15. Washer
16. Clutch idler
17. Traction drive belt
18. Washer
19. Stud
20. Mower electric clutch
21. Washer
22. Lockwasher
23. Screw
24. Bushing
25. Idler arm
26. Spacer
27. Nut
28. Bracket

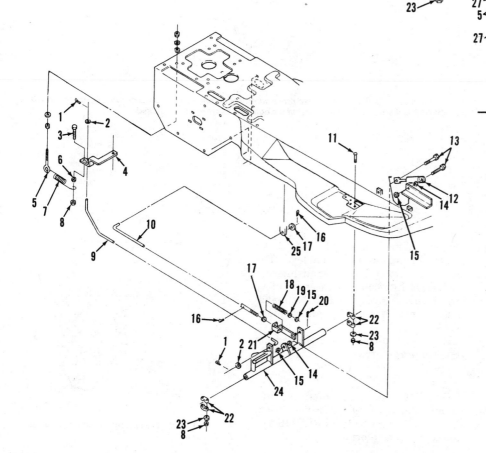

Fig. HM16—Exploded view of clutch and brake control components used on Models HR830 and HR830E.

1. Cotter pin
2. Washer
3. Screw
4. Idler arm
5. Eyebolt
6. Washer
7. Spring
8. Washer
9. Clutch rod
10. Brake rod
11. Carriage bolt
12. Damper
13. Bolt
14. Nut
15. Nut
16. Cotter pin
17. Washer
18. Spring
19. Washer
20. Cotter pin
21. Bracket
22. Bushings
23. Washer
24. Pedal & shaft assy.

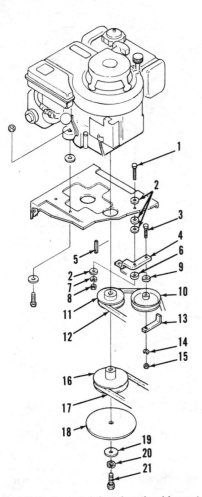

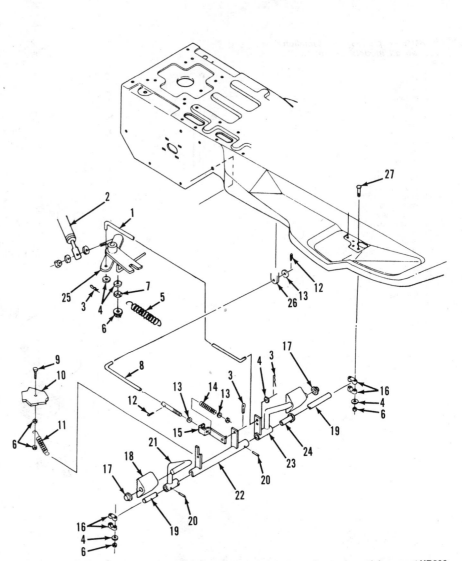

Fig. HM17—Exploded view of traction drive system on Models HR830 and HR830E.

1. Screw
2. Washers
3. Screw
4. Idler arm
5. Key
6. Washer
7. Lockwasher
8. Nut
9. Washer
10. Idler
11. Engine pulley
12. Traction drive belt
13. Belt guide
14. Lockwasher
15. Nut
16. Mower drive pulley
17. Mower drive belt
18. Belt guide disc
19. Washer
20. Lockwasher
21. Screw

Fig. HM18—Exploded view of clutch and brake control components used on early models, except HR830 and HR830E. Later models are similar, but a single clutch/brake pedal is used.

1. Clutch rod
2. Damper
3. Cotter pin
4. Washer
5. Lockwasher
6. Nut
7. Spring
8. Brake rod
9. Screw
10. Frame
11. Spring
12. Cotter pin
13. Washer
14. Spring
15. Bracket
16. Bushings
17. Push nut
18. Brake footpad
19. Shaft
20. Pin
21. Brake pedal
22. Brake control shaft
23. Clutch pedal
24. Bushing
25. Idler arm
26. Brake arm
27. Carriage bolt

OVERHAUL. To renew brake pads, unscrew carrier screws (S—Fig. HM19) and remove carrier assembly. Slide brake disc (D) off shaft. Inspect brake pads in carrier and side of transmission case. Renew brake pads if excessively worn, damaged or contaminated by oil or grease. Inspect brake disc. Reassemble brake components and adjust brake as outlined in previous section.

TRANSMISSION

All Models

REMOVE AND REINSTALL. To remove transmission, remove traction drive belt as previously outlined. Remove pulley from transmission shaft.

Disconnect drive chain. Detach brake rod from transmission brake lever. Detach shift control from transmission shift shaft. Lift seat and unscrew safety switch on transmission. Remove transmission mounting bolts and remove transmission.

Reinstall transmission by reversing removal procedure.

OVERHAUL. All models are equipped with a Peerless transmission. Refer to TRANSMISSION REPAIR section for service information.

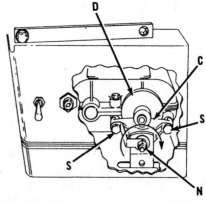

Fig. HM19—Adjust brake by turning nut (N) as outlined in text.

Illustrations Courtesy Homelite Div. of Textron, Inc.

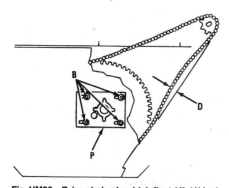

Fig. HM20—Drive chain should deflect 1/8-1/4 inch (3.2-6.4 mm) when pushed at midpoint (D) between sprockets. See text for adjustment.

DRIVE CHAIN

All Models

LUBRICATION. The drive chain should be lubricated after every 10 hours of operation with a good quality chain oil or SAE 30 engine oil.

ADJUSTMENT. To adjust chain tension, remove rear wheels. Loosen bolts (B—Fig. HM20) securing axle bearing retainer plates and slide axle rearward to tighten chain. Move each side equally to maintain alignment. Adjust chain tension so chain deflects 1/8-1/4 inch (3.2-6.4 mm) when pushed at midpoint between sprockets. See Fig. HM20. Tighten bolts to 115-130 in.-lbs. (13.0-14.7 N•m) and recheck adjustment.

REAR AXLE BEARING

All Models

LUBRICATION. Some models are equipped with rear axle bearings that have a grease fitting. Periodically inject a good quality multipurpose grease into grease fitting. Other models are equipped with sealed bearings that do not require periodic lubrication.

REMOVE AND REINSTALL. Rear axle bearings are accessible after removing rear wheels. Unscrew retaining bolts (B—Fig. HM20) and remove bearing plate. Bearing and plate are available only as a unit assembly. Tighten bolts to 115-130 in.-lbs. (13.0-14.7 N•m). Adjust drive chain after installing bearing plate.

DIFFERENTIAL

All Models

REMOVE AND REINSTALL. To remove differential and axle assembly, raise and support rear of machine. Disconnect drive chain. Remove rear wheels and bearing plates (P—Fig. HM20). Remove differential and axle unit from machine.

Reinstall differential and axle unit by reversing removal procedure.

OVERHAUL. All models are equipped with either a Peerless or a Stewart differential. Refer to DIFFERENTIAL REPAIR section for service information.

MOWER BELT

All Models

REMOVE AND REINSTALL. To remove mower drive belt, disconnect spark plug wire and tie out of way. Detach idler spring (9—Fig. HM21 or 3—Fig. HM22) and remove belt from idler, spindle pulley and engine clutch pulley. Install belt by reversing removal procedure. On later models, belt tension may be increased to compensate for a stretched belt by engaging idler spring in inner hole (H—Fig. HM22).

MOWER DECK

All Models

LUBRICATION. On Models RMX8, RMX8E and RMX11E, the belt idler arm should be lubricated after every 25 hours of operation. Apply grease to idler arm through grease fitting (F—Fig. HM23) in idler arm (8). Use a good quality, multipurpose grease.

HEIGHT ADJUSTMENT. All mower control linkage must be in good operating condition and tires properly inflated. Park machine on a level surface with engine stopped and spark plug wire disconnected.

Front-to-rear height difference is determined by measuring height of blade above ground at front (F—HM24) and rear (R). Rear height should be 1/4-3/8 inch (6.4-9.5 mm) higher. To adjust front-to-rear height difference, loosen carriage bolts (B—Fig. HM25) on left and right front mower deck hangers, then slide brackets forward (F) to raise front of blade or backward (R) to lower front of deck. Make sure sides are adjusted evenly, then retighten bolts. Recheck height measurements.

If mower deck side-to-side height is uneven, add washers between rear lift bracket (15—Fig. HM23 or HM26) and mower deck or support bracket until even.

REMOVE AND REINSTALL. Remove mower drive belt as previously outlined. On early RMX8, RMX8E and RMX11E models, disconnect mower deck cover switch (18—Fig. HM23). On Models HR830 and HR830E, disconnect safety switch (W—Fig. HM13). Detach mower deck from front and rear hanger links and remove mower deck.

Refer to Fig. HM23 or HM26 and disassemble mower deck as needed. Inspect components and renew if damaged or excessively worn. Reverse removal procedure to install mower deck.

MOWER SPINDLE

Early Models RMX8, RMX8E And RMX11E

LUBRICATION. Periodic lubrication of mower spindle is not required.

R&R AND OVERHAUL. Remove mower deck and blade. Unscrew spindle pulley retaining screw and remove pulley (1—Fig. HM23). Remove drive key and withdraw spindle (26). Unscrew bearing housings (2 and 25) for access to

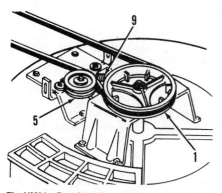

Fig. HM21—Drawing of mower deck used on early RMX8, RMX8E and RMX11E models.

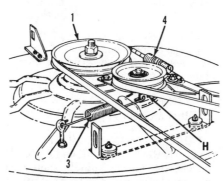

Fig. HM22—Drawing of mower deck used on all models except early RMX8, RMX8E and RMX11E models.

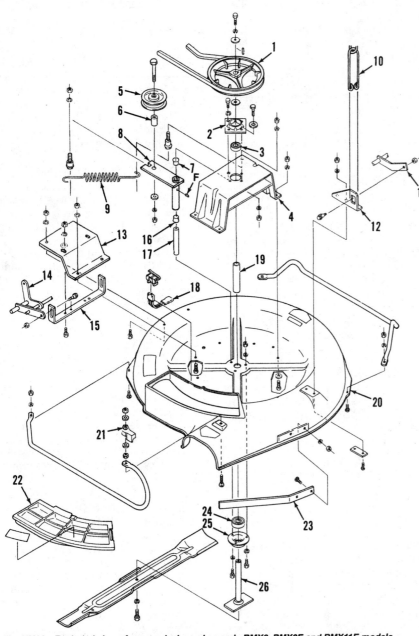

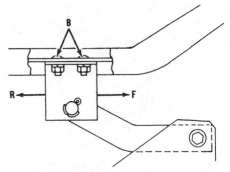

Fig. HM25—Adjust mower front-to-rear height difference by loosening carriage bolts (B) on left and right front mower deck hangers and sliding brackets forward (F) to raise front of blade or backward (R) to lower front of deck.

Fig. HM23—Exploded view of mower deck used on early RMX8, RMX8E and RMX11E models.

1. Pulley	8. Idler arm	14. Rear hanger
2. Bearing housing	9. Spring	15. Rear lift bracket
3. Bearing	10. Lift links	16. Bushing
4. Support	11. Lift handle	17. Spacer
5. Idler	12. Bracket	18. Safety switch
6. Spacer	13. Bracket	19. Spacer
7. Bushing		

20. Mower deck
21. Latch
22. Cover
23. Belt guide
24. Bearing
25. Bearing housing
26. Spindle

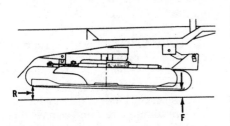

Fig. HM24—Mower front-to-rear height difference measured at front (F) and rear (R) should be 1/4-3/8 inch (6.4-9.5 mm).

bearings. Inspect components for excessive wear and damage. Tighten mower blade retaining screw to 35-40 ft.-lbs. (48-54 N•m).

All Other Models

LUBRICATION. On all models except early RMX8, RMX8E and RMX11E models, the mower spindle should be lubricated after every 25 hours of operation. Apply grease to mower spindle through grease fitting (F—Fig. HM26)

in spindle housing (18). Use a good quality, multipurpose grease.

R&R AND OVERHAUL. Remove mower deck and blade. Unscrew spindle pulley retaining nut and remove pulley (1—Fig. HM26). Remove drive key and withdraw spindle (21). If bearings are excessively worn or damaged, use a suitable tool to remove bearings from spindle housing (18). Inspect components for excessive wear and damage. Tighten mower blade retaining bolts to 80-90 ft.-lbs. (109-122 N•m).

MOWER CLUTCH

All Models Except HR830 And HR830E

On all models, the mower drive pulley is attached to an electric clutch.

ADJUSTMENT. The clutch air gap must be set correctly so the clutch will engage properly. Desired air gap is 0.010 inch (0.25 mm). With the clutch switch in "OFF" position, insert a 0.010 inch (0.25 mm) feeler gauge through slots in side of clutch (Fig. HM27). Check gap through all three of the slots. Rotate the three adjustment nuts as needed to obtain correct gap at each position.

R&R AND OVERHAUL. Remove mower drive belt as previously outlined. Disconnect electrical lead to mower drive clutch (20—Fig. HM15). Unscrew clutch retaining screw (23) and remove clutch assembly. Clutch is available only as a unit assembly. Reinstall clutch by reversing removal procedure. When installing clutch, be sure stud (19) engages slot in upper plate of clutch. Tighten pulley retaining cap screw in end of engine crankshaft to 50 ft.-lbs. (68 N•m).

Illustrations Courtesy Homelite Div. of Textron, Inc.

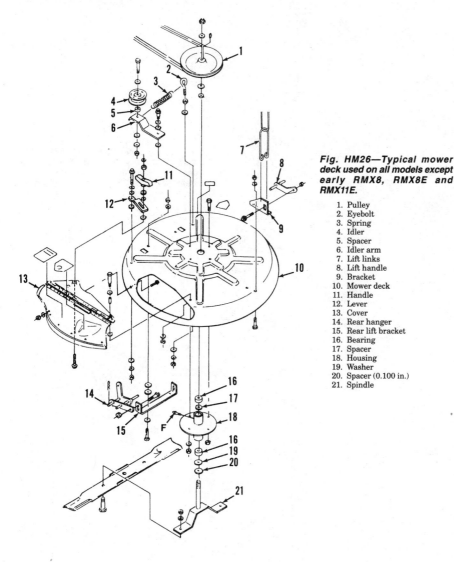

Fig. HM26—Typical mower deck used on all models except early RMX8, RMX8E and RMX11E.

1. Pulley
2. Eyebolt
3. Spring
4. Idler
5. Spacer
6. Idler arm
7. Lift links
8. Lift handle
9. Bracket
10. Mower deck
11. Handle
12. Lever
13. Cover
14. Rear hanger
15. Rear lift bracket
16. Bearing
17. Spacer
18. Housing
19. Washer
20. Spacer (0.100 in.)
21. Spindle

ELECTRICAL

All Models

Refer to Figs. HM28 through HM32 for wiring schematics. Note the following points:

- The transmission must be in neutral, the mower must be disengaged and the operator must be in seat for engine to start.
- The engine should stop if the transmission is in gear or the mower is engaged and the operator leaves the seat.

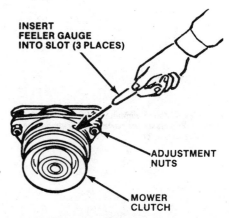

Fig. HM27—Insert a 0.010 inch (0.25 mm) feeler gauge through each of the three slots in side of clutch to measure air gap. Rotate three nuts as needed to obtain correct gap.

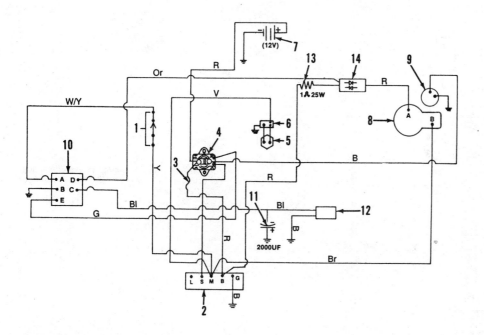

Fig. HM28—Wiring schematic for Models JR1030E, JR1230E, RE830E, RE1030E, RE1230E, RMX8E and RMX11E. Early Model RMX11E is equipped with a deck switch similar to Model HR830E (Fig. HM31).

B. Black	
Bl. Blue	4. Solenoid
Br. Brown	5. Neutral switch
G. Green	6. Safety module
Or. Orange	7. Battery
R. Red	8. Engine
V. Violet	9. Starter motor
W. White	10. Mower switch
Y. Yellow	11. Capacitor
1. Seat switch	12. Mower drive clutch
2. Ignition switch	13. Resistor
3. Fuse	14. Rectifier

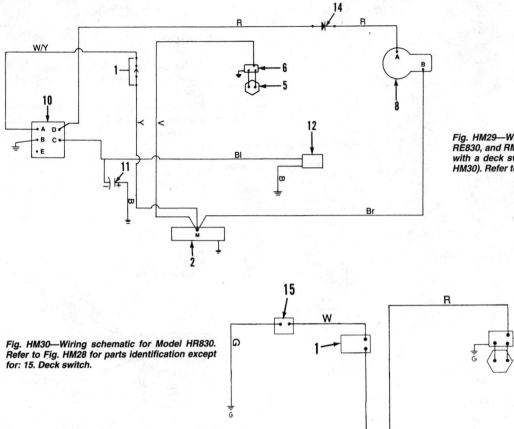

Fig. HM29—Wiring schematic for Models JR830, RE830, and RMX8. Early Model RMX8 is equipped with a deck switch similar to Model HR830 (Fig. HM30). Refer to Fig. HM28 for parts identification.

Fig. HM30—Wiring schematic for Model HR830. Refer to Fig. HM28 for parts identification except for: 15. Deck switch.

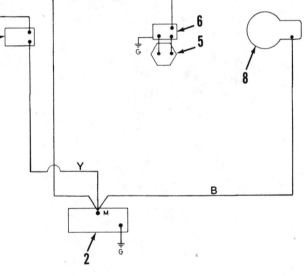

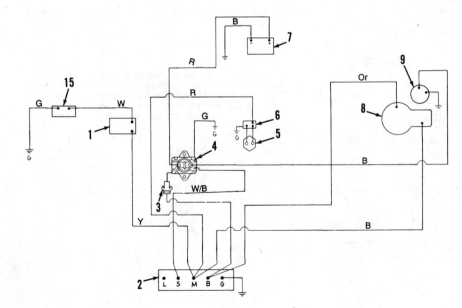

Fig. HM31—Wiring schematic for Model HR830E. Refer to Fig. HM28 for parts identification except for: 15. Deck switch.

Illustrations Courtesy Homelite Div. of Textron, Inc.

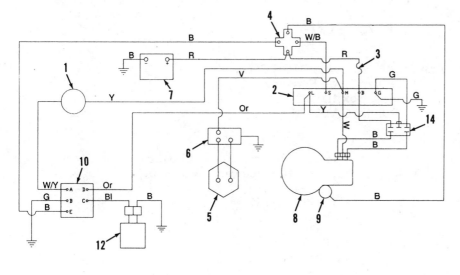

Fig. HM32—Wiring schematic for Model HR930E. Refer to Fig. HM28 for parts identification.

HONDA

AMERICAN HONDA MOTOR CO.
4475 River Green Parkway
P.O. Box 100020
Duluth, GA 30136

Model	Make	Engine Model	Horsepower	Cutting Width, In.
H3011	Honda	GXV340	11	30
H3011H	Honda	GXV340	11	30
H3013H	Honda	GXV390	13	38
HTR3009	Honda	GXV270	8½	30
HTR3811	Honda	GXV340	11	38

NOTE: Honda special tools may be required for some procedures and are indicated in text. Read text completely before attempting procedure.

FRONT WHEELS

All Models

Front wheel bearings do not require periodic lubrication. All models except HTR3009 use a nut to secure the wheel on the spindle (the wheel on Model HTR3009 is retained by a snap ring). Tighten the nut to 55 N•m (40 ft.-lbs.) then continue turning the nut until the cotter pin can be inserted. Do not exceed 65 N•m (48 ft.-lbs.) torque. Do not loosen the nut to insert the cotter pin.

FRONT AXLE

All Models

LUBRICATION. The axle is fitted with grease fittings (F—Fig. HN11) at each end to lubricate the spindles. Inject good quality grease into grease fitting annually or after every 100 hours of operation.

TOE-IN SETTING. Before checking toe-in setting, inspect front steering assembly and renew or repair any loose or damaged components.

To check toe-in, tires must be inflated to proper pressure. Position machine on a flat, smooth surface and set steering wheel in straight forward position. Use a suitable measuring tool and measure distance (B—Fig. HN12) at spindle height between the center of the tires on the rear sides. Locate the same tire centerline points on front side of tires and measure front distance (F). The toe-in distance on the front side (F) should be shorter than the measured distance on the rear side (B). Toe-in should be 2-10 mm (0.08-0.39 in.). Loosen locknuts at both ends of the tie rod (13—Fig. HN13) and rotate tie rod to adjust toe-in. Note that locknut next to ball joint marked with an "L" has left-hand threads. Retighten locknuts to 22 N•m (16 ft.-lbs.). After adjusting toe-in setting, check steering adjustment as outlined in STEERING SYSTEM section.

R&R AND OVERHAUL. To remove a front spindle (21 or 22—Fig. HN13), raise and support side to be serviced. Remove wheel and tire. Detach tie rod end from spindle, and on left spindle, detach drag link end. Remove snap ring (16) from top of spindle and remove spindle. Inspect components for excessive wear and damage. Install spindle by reversing removal procedure.

To remove axle, detach front mower deck links from axle and mower engagement rod from actuating arm on deck. Raise and support front of machine. Detach drag link (25—Fig. HN13). On Models H3011, H3011H and H3013H, remove steering gear (5) from steering shaft then remove steering base (3). On all models, unscrew axle pivot bolt and roll axle assembly away from machine. Disassemble axle assembly as needed. Note that ball joint ends marked with "L" have left-hand female threads.

Reassemble by reversing disassembly procedure. Tighten axle pivot bolt to 55 N•m (40 ft.-lbs.). On Model HTR3009 with 8 mm tie rod and drag link retaining nuts, tighten nuts to 20-24 N•m (15-

Fig. HN11—To lubricate spindles, inject good quality grease into grease fitting (F) at each end of axle annually or after every 100 hours of operation.

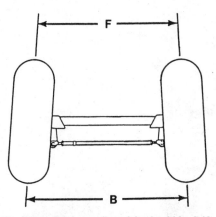

Fig. HN12—Toe-in on all models should be 2-10 mm (0.08-0.39 in.). Refer to text for measuring procedure and adjustment.

18 ft.-lbs.). On Model HTR3009 with 10 mm tie rod and drag link retaining nuts, and all other models, tighten nuts to 40 N•m (29 ft.-lbs.). On Models H3011, H3011H and H3013H, tighten steering base (3) retaining screws to 40 N•m (29 ft.-lbs.). On Models H3011, H3011H and H3013H, assemble steering gear (5) so lip portion of flanges (5 and 7) is away from gear and tighten retaining nut to 40 N•m (29 ft.-lbs.). After assembly, check toe-in setting and steering adjustment as outlined in previous section and STEERING SYSTEM section.

STEERING SYSTEM

All Models

ADJUSTMENT. Before adjusting steering, adjust toe-in setting as previously outlined. To adjust steering linkage, detach front mower deck links from axle and mower engagement rod from actuating arm on deck. Raise and support front of machine. Loosen locknuts on drag link (25—Fig. HN13); locknut adjacent to ball joint marked "L" has left-hand threads. Turn steering wheel to full left position. Rotate drag link (25) so steering gear (6) contacts stop on sector gear (4) just ahead or at same time steering spindle contacts stop on axle. Turn steering wheel to full right and repeat adjustment. With steering gear against stop on sector gear, clearance between steering spindle and axle stop should be 0-2 mm (0.00-0.08 in.). Tighten drag link locknuts to 22 N•m (16 ft.-lbs.).

R&R AND OVERHAUL. To remove steering shaft, remove steering wheel cover and unscrew steering wheel retaining nut. Remove steering wheel. Unscrew steering gear nut (9—Fig. HN13) and remove steering gear (6). Detach front and rear steering column covers. Force out upper bushing in steering column by pushing against projections on bushing. Withdraw steering shaft. Detach drag link (25) from sector gear (4). On Models H3011, H3011H and H3013H, remove steering base (3). On all models, detach cotter pin (1) and remove sector gear.

Reassemble by reversing disassembly procedure. Apply grease to sector gear spindle before installation. On Model HTR3009 with 8 mm drag link retaining nut, tighten nut to 20-24 N•m (15-18 ft.-lbs.). On Model HTR3009 with 10 mm drag link retaining nut and all other models, tighten nut to 40 N•m (29 ft.-lbs.). On Models H3011, H3011H and H3013H, tighten steering base (3) retaining screws to 40 N•m (29 ft.-lbs.). On all models, assemble steering gear (6) so lip portion of flanges (5 and 7) is away from gear and tighten retaining nut to 40 N•m (29 ft.-lbs.). Tighten steering wheel retaining nut to 60 N•m (44 ft.-lbs.). After assembly, check steering adjustment as outlined in previous section.

ENGINE

All Models

All models are equipped with a four-stroke, overhead valve, single-cylinder, air-cooled engine with a vertical crankshaft.

Horsepower ratings at 3600 rpm are as follows: engine Model GXV270—6.3 kW (8½ hp); Model GXV340—8.2 kW (11 hp); Model GXV390—9.7 kW (13 hp).

Engine model information appears on side of crankcase as shown in Fig. HN14.

REMOVE AND REINSTALL. To remove engine, raise seat unit and detach seat switch wire. On Models H3011, H3011H and H3013H, unscrew

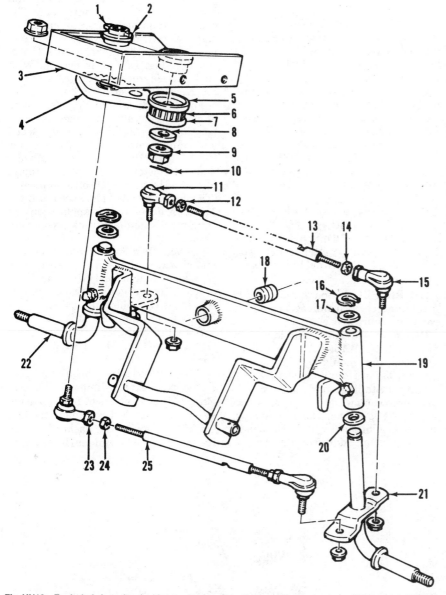

Fig. HN13—Exploded view of typical front axle assembly. Removable steering base (3) is used on Models H3011, H3011H and H3013H. Steering gear on all other models is mounted on frame. Ball joints marked "L" have left-hand female threads as do adjacent locknuts.

1. Cotter pin	8. Washer	14. Nut
2. Washer	9. Nut	15. Tie rod end
3. Base	10. Cotter pin	16. Snap ring
4. Sector gear	11. Tie rod end	17. Thrust washer
5. Cup washer	12. Nut	18. Bushing
6. Steering gear	13. Tie rod	19. Axle main member
7. Cup washer		

20. Thrust washer	23. Drag link end (L.H.)
21. Spindle (left)	24. Nut (L.H.)
22. Spindle (right)	25. Drag link

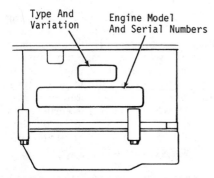

Fig. HN14—Engine model information is located on engine as shown.

Fig. HN15—Adjust low-speed mixture screw (LS) and throttle stop screw (TS) as outlined in text.

seat adjuster. On all models, unscrew seat retaining nuts then remove seat. Unscrew and remove engine cover. Remove mower deck as outlined in MOWER DECK section. Remove battery and drain engine oil. On Models HTR3009 and HTR3811 detach oil drain tube from engine. Mark, then disconnect all interfering electrical wires from engine. Remove fuel tank and disconnect throttle cable from engine. On Models HTR3009 and HTR3811 disconnect overflow fuel hose from carburetor. Detach heat shield on underside of machine and unscrew exhaust pipe retaining nuts from engine cylinder. Push idler away from engine drive belt and remove drive belt from engine pulley. Remove engine mounting screws and remove engine.

Reinstall engine by reversing removal procedure. If removed, install engine pulley so long end of hub is toward retaining screw and tighten screw to 50 N•m (37 ft.-lbs.). Tighten engine retaining bolts to 22 N•m (16 ft.-lbs.). Tighten exhaust pipe to cylinder retaining nuts to 24 N•m (18 ft.-lbs.). The spring washer under the seat adjuster knob must be installed so "OUT" on washer is toward knob.

ENGINE MAINTENANCE

All Models

AIR CLEANER. Engine is equipped with a dry-type air filter that should be cleaned and inspected after every 50 hours of operation.

Remove foam and paper air filter elements from air filter housing. Foam element should be washed in a mild detergent and water solution, rinsed in clean water and allowed to air dry. Soak foam element in clean engine oil. Squeeze out excess oil.

Paper element may be cleaned by directing low-pressure compressed air stream from inside the filter toward the outside. Reinstall elements.

LUBRICATION. Engine oil level should be checked prior to operating engine. Check oil level with oil cap not screwed in, but just touching first threads.

Oil should be changed after the first 20 hours of engine operation and after every 100 hours thereafter or once a year, whichever comes first.

Manufacturer recommends oil with an API service classification SF or SG. Use SAE 10W-30 or 10W-40 oil; use SAE 10W-40 if temperature is above 90° F (32° C).

Crankcase capacity is 1.1 L (1.16 qt.) for all models. Tighten oil drain plug on early models with 12 mm plug to 24 Nm (212 in.-lbs.) and on later models with 10 mm plug to 17.5 N•m (155 in.-lbs.).

SPARK PLUG. Spark plug should be removed, cleaned and inspected after every 100 hours of use.

Recommended spark plug is a NGK BPR5ES or ND W16EPR-U. Spark plug electrode gap should be 0.7-0.8 mm (0.028-0.031 in.) for all models.

When installing spark plug, manufacturer recommends installing spark plug fingertight, then, for a new plug, tighten an additional ½ turn. For a used plug, tighten an additional ¼ turn.

CARBURETOR. All models are equipped with a Keihin float-type carburetor with a fixed main fuel jet and an adjustable low-speed fuel mixture needle.

Initial adjustment of low-speed fuel mixture screw (LS—Fig. HN15) from a lightly seated position is 2¼ turns open for Model GXV270 and 2½ turns open for all other models.

To adjust throttle cable, disconnect spark plug wire and detach fuel tank. When throttle is in wide-open position, gap (G—Fig. HN16) between control lever (L) and choke lever (C) must be 0-1.0 mm (0.0-0.4 in.). To obtain correct gap, loosen locknut (N—Fig. HN17) and rotate adjuster (A) in throttle cable. The choke plate in the carburetor should be closed when throttle lever is in "START" position. If not, bend choke rod at U-section (U—Fig. HN16) as needed. With choke closed, rotate screw (S) so it just touches choke lever (C).

For final adjustment, engine must be at normal operating temperature and running. Operate engine at idle speed and adjust low-speed mixture screw (LS—Fig. HN15) to obtain a smooth idle and satisfactory acceleration. Adjust idle speed by turning throttle stop screw (TS). Recommended idle speed is 1550-1750 rpm depending on application and equipment manufacturer's recommendation.

To check float level, remove fuel bowl and invert carburetor. Measure from top edge of float to fuel bowl mating edge of carburetor body. Measurement should be 11.9-14.5 mm (0.47-0.57 in.). Renew float if float height is incorrect.

Standard main jet is #85 for Model GXV270, #88 for Model GXV340 and #98 for Model GXV390.

When reinstalling carburetor, note that gasket next to cylinder head has an outer hole or is notched. Install gasket so hole or notch is down and to the left. On some engines, the gasket between insulator block and carburetor is

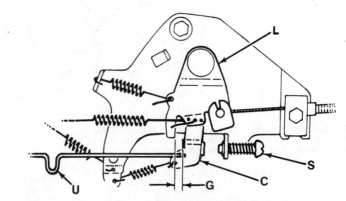

Fig. HN16—When throttle is in wide-open position, gap (G) between control lever (L) and choke lever (C) must be 0-1.0 mm (0.0-0.4 in.). Refer to text for adjustment.

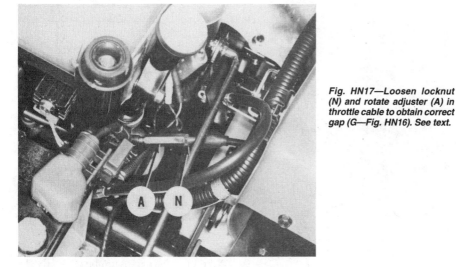

Fig. HN17—Loosen locknut (N) and rotate adjuster (A) in throttle cable to obtain correct gap (G—Fig. HN16). See text.

Fig. HN19—Valve clearance should be 0.13-0.17 mm (0.005-0.007 in.) for intake and 0.18-0.22 mm (0.007-0.009 in.) for exhaust. Loosen rocker arm jam nut (1) and turn adjusting nut (2) to obtain desired clearance.

1. Jam nut
2. Adjustment nut
3. Rocker arm
4. Valve stem clearance
5. Push rod

notched and must be installed so notch is down and to the left.

GOVERNOR. The mechanical fly-weight-type governor is located inside engine crankcase. To adjust external linkage, detach fuel tank and make certain all linkage is in good condition and tension spring (5—Fig. HN18) is not stretched or damaged. Loosen clamp bolt (7) and move governor lever (3) so throttle is completely open. Hold governor lever in this position and rotate governor shaft (6) in the same direction until it stops. Tighten clamp bolt.

Start engine and operate at an idle until operating temperature has been reached. Attach a tachometer to engine and move throttle so engine is operating at maximum speed. Maximum speed should be 3150-3450 rpm on Models H3011, HTR3009 and HTR3811, and 3200-3300 rpm on Models H3011H and H3013H. Adjust maximum speed by relocating end of governor-to-carburetor rod (1) to another hole in the governor

lever (3). Engine rpm will decrease when rod is moved to a lower hole.

IGNITION SYSTEM. The breaker-less ignition system requires no regular maintenance. Ignition coil unit is mounted outside the flywheel. Air gap between flywheel and coil should be 0.2-0.6 mm (0.008-0.024 in.).

To check ignition coil primary side, connect one ohmmeter lead to primary (black) coil lead and touch iron coil laminations with remaining lead. Ohmmeter should register 0.7-0.9 ohm.

To check ignition coil secondary side, connect one ohmmeter lead to the spark plug lead wire and remaining lead to the iron core laminations. Ohmmeter should read 6.3k-7.7k ohms. If ohmmeter readings are not as specified, renew ignition coil.

VALVE ADJUSTMENT. Valve-to-rocker arm clearance should be checked and adjusted after five years or after every 500 hours of operation.

To adjust valve clearance, refer to Fig. HN19 and remove rocker arm cover.

Rotate crankshaft so piston is at top dead center (TDC) on compression stroke. Insert a feeler gauge between rocker arm (3) and end of valve stem. Loosen rocker arm jam nut (1) and turn adjusting nut (2) to obtain desired clearance. Specified clearance (engine cold) is 0.13-0.17 mm (0.005-0.007 in.) for intake and 0.18-0.22 mm (0.007-0.009 in.) for exhaust. Tighten jam nut and recheck clearance. Install rocker arm cover.

ENGINE REPAIRS

All Models

TIGHTENING TORQUES. Recommended tightening torque specifications are as follows:

Connecting rod	14 N•m (124 in.-lbs.)
Cylinder head	35 N•m (26 ft.-lbs.)
Flywheel nut	115 N•m (85 ft.-lbs.)
Oil drain plug:	
10 mm	17.5 N•m (155 in.-lbs.)
12 mm	24 N•m (212 in.-lbs.)
Oil pan	24 N•m (212 in.-lbs.)
Rocker arm cover	8.5 N•m (75 in.-lbs.)
Rocker arm jam nut	10 N•m (88 in.-lbs.)
Rocker arm pivot stud	24 N•m (212 in.-lbs.)

CYLINDER HEAD. To remove cylinder head, remove cooling shroud and fuel tank. Disconnect and remove carburetor linkage and carburetor. Remove muffler. Remove rocker arm cover and the four head bolts. Remove cylinder head. Use care not to lose push rods.

Remove rocker arms, compress valve springs and remove valve retainers. Note that exhaust valve is equipped

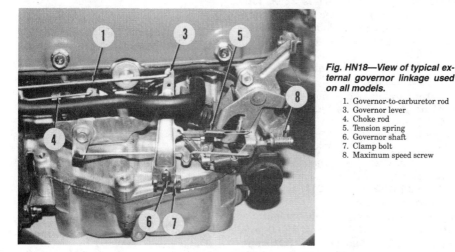

Fig. HN18—View of typical external governor linkage used on all models.

1. Governor-to-carburetor rod
3. Governor lever
4. Choke rod
5. Tension spring
6. Governor shaft
7. Clamp bolt
8. Maximum speed screw

with a valve rotator on valve stem. Remove valves and springs. Remove push rod guide plate if necessary.

When assembling valve system, note that intake and exhaust valve spring retainers are different. The exhaust valve spring retainer has a larger indentation than the intake valve spring retainer to accommodate the exhaust valve rotator.

Valve face and seat angles are 45° for intake and exhaust. Standard valve seat width is 1.1 mm (0.043 in.). Narrow the seat if seat width is greater than 2.0 mm (0.079).

Standard valve spring free length is 39.0 mm (1.54 in.). Renew valve spring if free length is less than 37.5 mm (1.48 in.).

Standard valve guide inside diameter for intake and exhaust is 6.60 mm (0.260 in.). Renew guide if inside diameter is greater than 6.66 mm (0.262 in.).

Valve stem-to-guide clearance should be 0.010-0.037 mm (0.0004-0.0015 in.) for intake valve and 0.050-0.077 mm (0.002-0.003 in.) for exhaust valve. Renew valve guide and/or valve if clearance is greater than 0.10 mm (0.004 in.) for intake valve or greater than 0.12 mm (0.005 in.) for exhaust valve.

To renew valve guides, heat entire cylinder head to 150° C (300° F) and use valve guide driver 07942-6570100 to remove and install guides. DO NOT heat head above recommended temperature as valve seats may loosen. Drive guides out toward rocker arm end of head. Chill valve guides in a freezer for approximately one hour prior to installation. Note if valve guide has a locating clip around the top. If there is NO clip, drive guide into cylinder head until guide is 24.5 mm (0.964 in.) below valve seat surface. If there is a clip around the valve guide, drive in the valve guide so the clip is bottomed against the head. Valve guides must be reamed after installation.

When installing cylinder head on all models, tighten head bolts to 35 N•m (26 ft.-lbs.) in a crossing pattern. Adjust valves as outlined in VALVE ADJUST-MENT paragraph.

OIL PUMP. The engine is equipped with a rotor-type oil pump that is located in the oil pan and driven by the camshaft. The oil pump is accessible by removing the pump cover on the outside of the oil pan.

Specified inner rotor-to-outer rotor clearance is 0.18 mm (0.007 in.) with a wear limit of 0.30 mm (0.012 in.). Specified outer rotor-to-bore clearance is 0.15-0.20 mm (0.006-0.008 in.) with a wear limit of 0.26 mm (0.010 in.). Minimum allowable outer rotor height is

Fig. HN20—Compression release spring and weight are installed on camshaft gear.

7.45 mm (0.293 in.). Maximum allowable pump bore depth is 7.56 mm (0.298 in.). Specified rotor-to-body end clearance is 0.02-0.09 mm (0.0008-0.0040 in.) with a wear limit of 0.11 mm (0.004 in.). Pump bore wear limit is 29.21 mm (1.150 in.).

CAMSHAFT AND CAM FOLLOW-ERS. Camshaft and camshaft gear are an integral casting equipped with a compression release mechanism (Fig. HN20). To remove camshaft, drain oil and remove engine as previously outlined. Remove rocker arm cover, rocker arms and push rods. Remove engine pulley. Clean crankshaft and remove any rust or burrs. Unscrew oil pan retaining screws and remove oil pan. Withdraw camshaft assembly and remove cam followers from cylinder block.

Standard camshaft bearing journal diameter is 15.984 mm (0.6293 in.). Renew camshaft if journal diameter is less than 15.916 mm (0.6266 in.).

Standard camshaft lobe height for engine Models GXV270 and GXV340 used on mower Models H3011, HTR3009 and HTR3811 is 33.00 mm (1.299 in.) for intake lobe and 32.60 mm (1.283 in.) for exhaust lobe (Fig. HN21). If intake lobe measures less than 32.75 mm (1.289 in.), or exhaust lobe measures less than 32.35 mm (1.274 in.), renew camshaft.

Standard camshaft lobe height for engine Model GXV340 used on mower Model H3011H is 32.05 mm (1.262 in.) for intake lobe and 31.77 mm (1.251 in.) for exhaust lobe (Fig. HN21). If intake lobe measures less than 31.80 mm (1.252 in.), or exhaust lobe measures less than 31.52 mm (1.241 in.), renew camshaft.

Standard camshaft lobe height for engine Model GXV390 is 32.60 mm (1.283 in.) for intake lobe and 32.09 mm

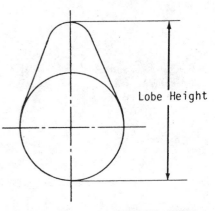

Fig. HN21—Measure camshaft lobe height as shown.

(1.263 in.) for exhaust lobe (Fig. HN21). If intake lobe measures less than 32.35 mm (1.274 in.), or exhaust lobe measures less than 31.84 mm (1.254 in.), renew camshaft.

Inspect cam followers for pitting, flaking or excessive wear. Cam followers should be renewed whenever new camshaft is installed.

Inspect compression release mechanism for damage. Spring must pull weight tightly against camshaft so decompressor lobe holds exhaust valve slightly open. When the engine is running, centrifugal forces causes the weight to overcome spring tension and moves decompressor lobe away from cam lobe to release exhaust valve.

When installing camshaft, make certain camshaft and crankshaft gear timing marks are aligned as shown in Fig. HN22. Be sure slot in end of camshaft aligns with oil pump rotor when installing oil pan. Tighten oil pan screws to 24 N•m (212 in.-lbs.). Adjust valves as outlined in VALVE ADJUSTMENT paragraph.

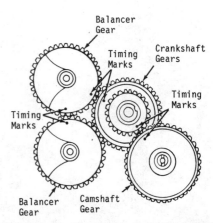

Fig. HN22—Drawing showing correct alignment of timing marks on crankshaft, camshaft and balancer shaft gears.

BALANCER SHAFTS. The engine is equipped with two balancer shafts that are accessible after removing oil pan (see previous section for oil pan removal procedure). Each balancer shaft rides in ball bearings at both ends that are a press fit in the crankcase and oil pan. Crankcase or oil pan must be renewed if ball bearing is loose in bore. Timing marks must be aligned as shown in Fig. HN22 during installation of shafts.

PISTON, PIN AND RINGS. Piston and connecting rod are removed as an assembly. To remove piston and connecting rod, drain oil and remove engine as previously outlined. Remove engine pulley. Clean crankshaft and remove any rust or burrs. Remove cylinder head. Unscrew oil pan retaining screws and remove oil pan. Remove balancer shafts. Remove connecting rod cap screws and cap. Push connecting rod and piston assembly out of cylinder. Remove piston pin retaining rings and separate piston from connecting rod.

Standard piston diameter measured at lower edge of skirt and 90° from piston pin is listed in the following table:

Piston Model	Diameter
GXV270	76.985 mm (3.0309 in.)
GXV340	81.985 mm (3.2277 in.)
GXV390	87.985 mm (3.4640 in.)

Reject piston if piston diameter is less than listed below:

Piston Reject

Model	Diameter
GXV270	76.85 mm (3.026 in.)
GXV340	81.85 mm (3.222 in.)
GXV390	87.85 mm (3.459 in.)

Piston oversizes are available for some models.

Standard piston pin bore diameter for Model GXV270 is 18.002 mm (0.7087 in.) with a wear limit of 18.048 mm (0.7105 in.). Standard piston pin bore diameter for Models GXV340 and GXV390 is 20.002 mm (0.7875 in.) with a wear limit of 20.042 mm (0.7890 in.). Standard piston pin diameter for Model GXV270 is 18.000 mm (0.7087 in.) with a wear limit of 17.954 mm (0.7068 in.). Standard piston pin diameter for Models GXV340 and GXV390 is 20.000 mm (0.7874 in.) with a wear limit of 19.95 mm (0.7854 in.). Standard clearance be-

tween piston pin and pin bore in piston is 0.002-0.014 mm (0.0001-0.0006 in.) for all models. If clearance is greater than 0.08 mm (0.003 in.), renew piston and/or pin.

Ring side clearance should be 0.015-0.045 mm (0.0006-0.0018 in.) for Model GXV270 and 0.030-0.060 mm (0.0012-0.0024 in.) for all other models. Ring end gap for compression rings on all models should be 0.2-0.4 mm (0.008-0.016 in.). Maximum allowable piston ring end gap is 1.0 mm (0.040 in.). Oversize piston rings are available for some models.

Note that top piston ring (1—Fig. HN23) is chrome plated and is not interchangeable with the second piston ring (2). Install marked piston rings with

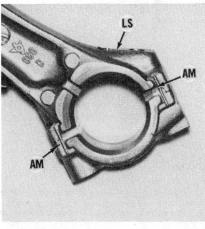

Fig. HN23—Long side of connecting rod and arrowhead (triangle) on top of piston must be on same side and facing push rod side of engine after installation. Refer to text.

A. Arrowhead
1. Top ring
2. Second ring
3. Oil control ring
4. Retaining ring
5. Piston pin
6. Piston
7. Connecting rod
8. Rod cap

Fig. HN24—View of connecting rod. Match marks (AM) on rod and cap must be aligned.

marked side toward piston crown and stagger ring end gaps equally around piston.

When reassembling piston on connecting rod, long side (LS—Fig. HN24) of connecting rod and arrowhead on piston crown (A—Fig. HN23) must be on the same side.

When reinstalling piston and connecting rod assembly in cylinder, arrowhead on piston crown must be on push rod side of engine. Align connecting rod cap and connecting rod match marks (AM—Fig. HN24), install connecting rod screws and tighten to 14 N•m (124 in.-lbs.).

CONNECTING ROD. The aluminum alloy connecting rod rides directly on crankpin journal of all models. To remove connecting rod, follow procedure outlined for piston removal in previous section. Standard piston pin bore diameter in connecting rod for Model GXV270 is 18.005 mm (0.7089 in.) with a wear limit of 18.07 mm (0.711 in.). Standard piston pin bore diameter in connecting rod for Models GXV340 and GXV390 is 20.005 mm (0.7876 in.) with a wear limit of 20.07 mm (0.790 in.).

Standard connecting rod bearing bore-to-crankpin clearance is 0.040-0.066 mm (0.0015-0.0026 in.) for all models. Renew connecting rod and/or crankshaft if clearance is 0.12 mm (0.0047 in.) or more. An undersize connecting rod is available for some models.

Connecting rod side play on crankpin should be 0.1-0.7 mm (0.004-0.028 in.) for all models. Renew connecting rod if side play is 1.1 mm (0.043 in.) or more.

Install connecting rod by following installation procedure for piston as outlined in previous section.

CRANKSHAFT, MAIN BEARINGS AND SEALS. The crankshaft is supported at each end in ball bearing-type main bearings. The crankshaft may be removed after removing piston as previously outlined.

Standard crankpin journal diameter for Model GXV270 is 32.985 mm (1.2986 in.) with a wear limit of 32.92 mm (1.296 in.). Standard crankpin journal diameter for Models GXV340 and GXV390 is 35.985 mm (1.4167 in.) with a wear limit of 35.93 mm (1.4146 in.).

The timing gears are a press fit on the crankshaft. Prior to removal of timing gears, mark position of gears on crankshaft using the timing marks on the gears as a reference point. Transfer marks to new timing gears so they can be installed in same position as old gears.

Ball bearing main bearings are a press fit on flywheel end of crankshaft and in bearing bore of oil pan. Renew bearings if damaged or rough. Renew oil pan if bearing bore is excessively worn.

Seals should be pressed into seal bores until outer edge of seal is flush with seal bore.

When installing crankshaft, make certain timing marks on crankshaft gear, camshaft gear and balancer gears are aligned as shown in Fig. HN22.

CYLINDER AND CRANKCASE. Cylinder and crankcase are an integral casting. Refer to following table for standard cylinder bore size:

Cylinder Model	Diameter
GXV270	77.000 mm
	(3.0315 in.)
GXV340	82.000 mm
	(3.2283 in.)
GXV390	88.000 mm
	(3.4646 in.)

Rebore or renew cylinder if cylinder bore diameter exceeds following specification:

Bore Model	Limit
GXV270	77.17 mm
	(3.038 in.)
GXV340	82.17 mm
	(3.235 in.)
GXV390	88.17 mm
	(3.471 in.)

Oversize pistons are available for some models.

GOVERNOR. The centrifugal flyweight-type governor, located in the oil pan, controls engine rpm via external linkage. Refer to GOVERNOR paragraphs in MAINTENANCE section for adjustment procedure.

To remove governor, drain oil and remove engine as previously outlined. Remove engine pulley. Clean crankshaft and remove any rust or burrs. Unscrew oil pan retaining screws and remove oil pan.

Reinstall governor assembly by reversing removal procedure. Adjust external linkage as outlined under GOVERNOR in MAINTENANCE section.

ELECTRIC STARTER. All models are equipped with an electric starter. Minimum brush length is 9.0 mm (0.35 in.). Cranking voltage should be 8.5 VDC under load and 11.5 VDC under no load. Cranking current should be below 165 amps under load and below 20 amps under no load. Align tabs and grooves when assembling brush plate, frame and drive-end housing.

DRIVE BELT

All Models

A spring-loaded idler maintains tension on the drive belt between the engine pulley and transmission pulley. Tension is not adjustable. If belt slippage occurs and all components are in good operating condition, a new belt must be installed.

REMOVE AND REINSTALL. To remove drive belt, remove mower deck as outlined in MOWER DECK section. Push idler away from belt and remove belt from pulleys. If idler arm is removed, apply grease to shaft before assembly. Tighten idler arm retaining screw to 40 N•m (29 ft.-lbs.).

GROUND DRIVE BRAKE

All Models

INSPECTION AND ADJUSTMENT. A wear indicator is attached to the brake camshaft. To determine thickness of brake shoes, apply brake fully and note position of brake indicator pointer. If pointer aligns with or passes

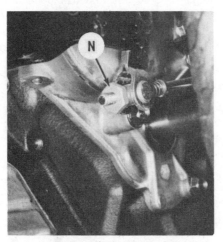

Fig. HN25—Rotate nut (N) at end of brake rod to adjust brake.

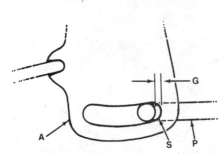

Fig. HN26—With park brake lever in disengaged position or brake pedal released, there should be a gap (G) of 0-1 mm (0.00-0.04 in.) between end of parking brake rod or brake pedal rod (P) and front of slot (S) in brake arm (A). Adjust park brake cable or brake rod as outlined in text.

wear mark on brake housing, the brake shoes are worn excessively and must be replaced.

To adjust brake, rotate adjuster nut (N—Fig. HN25) at brake end of brake actuating rod so there is 3-6 mm (0.12-0.24 in.) free play at brake arm with brake disengaged. With park brake lever in disengaged position, there should be a gap (G—Fig. HN26) of 0-1 mm (0.00-0.04 in.) between end of parking brake rod (P) and front of slot in brake arm (A). Gap width is adjusted by turning adjuster nuts at either end of parking brake cable. With brake pedal released, there should be a gap (G—Fig. HN26) of 0-1 mm (0.00-0.04 in.) between end of brake pedal rod (P) and front of slot in brake arm (A). To adjust gap width, detach rod from brake arm, loosen locknut on brake pedal rod near spring coupler and rotate rod.

R&R AND OVERHAUL. The brake assembly is accessible after removing right rear wheel, detaching brake actuating rod and removing brake housing. Minimum allowable brake shoe lining thickness is 1.00 mm (0.039 in.). Maximum allowable brake drum diameter is 81 mm (3.19 in.).

During assembly, apply grease to shaft and cam surface of brake cam. Do not allow grease on brake lining surfaces. Be sure that punch mark on end of brake cam aligns with the mark on brake arm and brake arm is positioned downward. Tighten brake drum bolt to 22 N•m (16 ft.-lbs.). Tighten rear wheel retaining nut to 80 N•m (59 ft.-lbs.) on Models HTR3009 and HTR3811 and to 65 N•m (48 ft.-lbs.) on Models H3011, H3011H and H3013H. Adjust brake as previously outlined.

CLUTCH

Models H3011, HTR3009 And HTR3811

The clutch on Models H3011, HTR3009 and HTR3811 is a multiple-disc-type that is actuated by cables connected to the transaxle shift mechanism and brake pedal. The clutch is disengaged when the transaxle is shifted or when the brake is applied. A hydraulic cylinder (damper) attached to the clutch arm regulates clutch engagement speed.

ADJUSTMENT. Shift transmission to second gear and raise engine cover. Loosen locknut (N—Fig. HN27) and back out adjusting screw (S). Rotate adjusting screw (S) clockwise until resistance is felt. Move clutch lever (L) forward so it contacts stop, then rotate

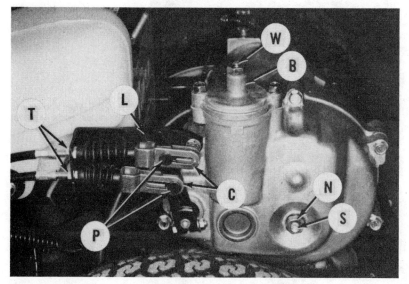

Fig. HN27—See text for adjustment of clutch screw (S) and cables.

adjusting screw (S) counterclockwise so the distance between point of lever (L) and edge of stop is 28 mm (1.1 in.). Tighten locknut (N) while holding adjusting screw (S).

Adjust clutch cables by rotating nuts (T) on cables. With clutch disengaged, clevis pins (P) should be aligned with index marks in center of slots in clevises (C). If pins will not align with index marks and control mechanism is operating properly, then clutch plates are worn and should be renewed.

Top of damper adjusting screw (W) must be 8-14 mm (0.31-0.55 in.) from top of boss on damper. Loosen locknut and turn screw as needed. Damper action can be adjusted by turning adjusting screw (W). Clutch engagement time is decreased when screw is turned in. After adjustment, the top of the screw must be within 8-14 mm (0.31-0.55 in.) of boss.

R&R AND OVERHAUL. Remove transaxle as outlined in TRANSAXLE section for access to clutch. Remove cover (8—Fig. HN28). Remove clutch arm (14) and cam lever (17). Remove bearing plate (19). Secure clutch drum (32) with Honda tool 07HGB-001000A, or equivalent suitable tool, and unscrew center nut (21) using Honda tool 07716-0020100 or equivalent suitable tool. Refer to Fig. HN28 and disassemble remainder of clutch. Do not interchange washer (31) and shim (33). The transaxle bevel gear is attached to back side of clutch drum (32) and original shim (33) must be reinstalled to maintain gear backlash.

Friction plate (28) wear limit is 2.20 mm (0.087 in.). Renew steel plate (26) if warped more than 0.10 mm (0.004 in.). Standard length of clutch springs (20) is 46.5 mm (1.83 in.) with a minimum allowable length of 43.5 mm (1.71 in.).

To check damper (4), remove damper from cover and suspend a 3.5 kg (7.7 lb.) weight from clevis and measure time

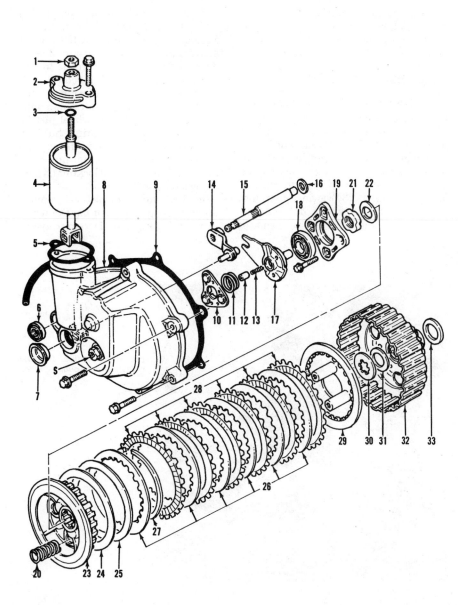

Fig. HN28—Exploded view of clutch used on Models H3011, HTR3009 and HTR3811. Components (24, 25 and 27) are not used on HTR3009 and HTR3811 and only five steel plates (26) are used (the first steel plate shown is absent).

1. Locknut	18. Bearing
2. Cover	19. Bearing plate
3. "O" ring	20. Springs
4. Damper	21. Nut
5. Gasket	22. Belleville washer
6. Seal	23. Clutch hub
7. Plug	24. Spring plate
8. Cover	25. Plate
9. Gasket	26. Steel plates
10. Ball plate	27. Ring
11. Spring	28. Friction plates
12. Sleeve	29. Pressure plate
13. Spring	30. Splined washer
14. Clutch arm	31. Shim
15. Shaft	32. Clutch drum
16. Thrust washer	33. Shim
17. Cam lever	

required for weight to drop from 19.5 mm (0.76 in.) to 28.4 mm (1.11 in.) below bottom of damper cylinder. If time is not within 2.0 to 3.5 seconds, renew damper.

Reassemble clutch by reversing removal procedure and referring to Fig. HN28 while noting the following: If clutch drum (32) is discarded, refer to TRANSAXLE section for gear backlash measuring procedure. Plug (7) must not be installed in cover prior to assembly. Install splined washer (30) so rounded face is out. On Model H3011, install plate (25) so tapered edge is toward spring plate (24). Install Belleville washer (22) so face marked "OUT" is toward nut (21). Install nut (21) so rounded side is toward Belleville washer (22) and tighten nut (21) to 60 N·m (44 ft.-lbs.). Tighten bearing plate (19) retaining screws in a crossing pattern to 11 N·m (97 in.-lbs.). Install clutch arm (14) on shaft (15) so punch marks are aligned. Install ball plate (10) on cam lever (17) so curved side (C) is toward clutch arm (14). Back out adjusting screw (S) before installing cover. Guide clevis of damper (4) onto clutch arm (14) through hole in cover for plug (7), then install plug. Tighten cover retaining screws to 10 N·m (88 in.-lbs.). Perform clutch adjustment procedures as previously outlined after installing transaxle.

SHIFT CONTROL LINKAGE

Models H3011, HTR3009 And HTR3811

ADJUSTMENT. The operator gearshift lever and transaxle gear selector arm must be synchronized for proper gear selection. Detach end of shift rod (E—Fig. HN29), loosen jam nut (N) on

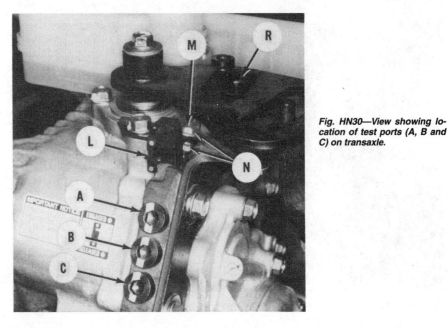

Fig. HN30—View showing location of test ports (A, B and C) on transaxle.

rod and rotate rod end to adjust length of rod. Adjust shift rod length so gear indicated by position of gearshift lever is same as gear engaged in transaxle.

Models H3011H And H3013H

ADJUSTMENT. To adjust shift control linkage, place blocks against front wheels to prevent movement and support rear of machine so rear wheels are off the ground. Place shift lever in center of neutral position, then raise engine cover and be sure transaxle release lever (L—Fig. HN30) is in uppermost position, next to green dot. Loosen locknuts (N—Fig. HN31) at both ends of

shift rod (D); locknut adjacent to ball joint marked "L" has left-hand threads. Disconnect seat safety switch and attach a jumper wire to main circuit leads. Start engine and move throttle to halfway position. Rotate shift rod (D) until rear wheel just begins to rotate. While counting turns, rotate shift rod in opposite direction until rear wheel just begins to rotate. Determine half the number of turns and rotate the shift rod in the original direction that number of turns. Tighten shift rod locknut (N). Reconnect seat safety switch.

Be sure shift control lever remains centered in neutral position. Detach return rod (R—Fig. HN31) from transaxle

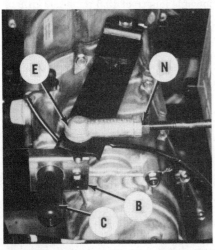

Fig. HN29—Loosen nut (N), detach shift rod end (E) from shift arm and adjust shift rod as outlined in text. Detach bracket (B) to remove shift shaft protector cap (C).

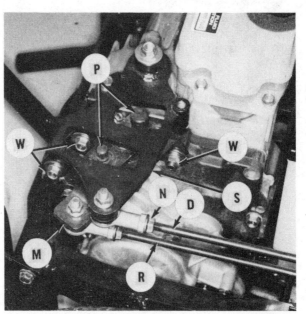

Fig. HN31—Adjust transaxle shift linkage as outlined in text.

return arm (M). Push return arm (M) forward, toward engine, until pins (P) contact ends of slots in shift arm (S). If pins do not contact slot ends, loosen bracket screws (W) and relocate bracket as needed so pins contact slot ends simultaneously. Tighten bracket screws. Reattach return rod (R) to return arm (M). When the brake pedal is depressed, pins (P) should contact end of slots just as brake pedal contacts stop. If not, loosen locknuts at both ends of return rod (R) and rotate rod as needed; locknut adjacent to ball joint marked "L" has left-hand threads. Reconnect seat safety switch.

TRANSAXLE

Models H3011, HTR3009 And HTR3811

LUBRICATION. Transmission oil level should be checked annually or after every 100 hours of operation, whichever occurs first. Transmission oil should be level with bottom edge of fill cap opening. Be sure machine is on level surface when checking oil level. Oil capacity is 2.8 L (3.0 qt.). Recommended oil is SAE 10W-30 engine oil.

REMOVE AND REINSTALL. To remove transaxle, remove mower unit as outlined in MOWER DECK section. Support rear of machine and remove rear wheels. Remove drive belt as previously outlined and drain oil from transaxle by unscrewing drain screw. Detach brake actuating rod at brake. Raise engine cover, disconnect neutral switch and ground wires, detach transaxle shift arm from transaxle shift shaft and remove battery. Move shift control lever to reverse position and detach clutch lever (L—Fig. HN27) from shaft. Detach right transmission bracket (B—Fig. HN29) and remove shaft protector cap (C). Unscrew three retaining screws at rear of frame. Support transaxle and remove axle mounting brackets. Tilt transaxle down and to the right and remove from frame.

To install transaxle, reverse removal procedure while noting the following: Be sure brake actuating rod is above rear axle before attaching rear axle bracket. Axle brackets must be installed so side with snap ring is toward transaxle. Hand-tighten axle bracket screws and the three screws on the rear of the frame, then tighten axle bracket screws to 38 N·m (28 ft.-lbs.) on Model H3011 and to 8-12 N·m (71-106 in.-lbs.) on Models HTR3009 and HTR3811. Tighten the three rear frame screws on all models to 24 N·m (18 ft.-lbs.). Be sure axles rotate freely, if not, loosen retain-

ing screws and retighten. Apply grease to shift fork shaft, then install protector cap (C—Fig. HN29) and attach bracket (B). Align punch marks on transaxle shift arm and end of shift shaft. Align punch marks on clutch lever (L—Fig. HN27) and shaft end. Tighten rear wheel retaining nut to 80 N·m (59 ft.-lbs.) on Models HTR3009 and HTR3811 and to 65 N·m (48 ft.-lbs.) on Model H3011. Adjust brake and clutch as previously outlined.

OVERHAUL. To disassemble transaxle, remove brake and clutch assemblies as previously outlined. Unscrew pulley retaining screw and remove pulleys (58 and 59—Fig. HN32). Unscrew and remove input shaft bearing housing (55). Using Honda tool 07916-7500000 with attachment 07FPA-7510110, unscrew nut (52) and remove input shaft (48). If bearing (50) must be removed, grind away staked area and use Honda tool 07916-7500000 to unscrew nut (51). Old nut should be discarded. Unscrew and separate transaxle case halves (41 and 107). Remove shift detent ball components (44 through 47) being careful not to lose detent ball (47). Refer to Fig. HN32 and remove components as needed.

To reassemble transaxle, proceed as follows: Press bearing (67) onto mainshaft (69) and install mainshaft in left transaxle case half (41). Tighten retainer (68) screw to 11 N·m (97 in.-lbs.). Install reverse idler gear assembly (62 through 65) and tighten retaining nut (40) to 38 N·m (28 ft.-lbs.). Install change shaft (95) and components (85 through 94)—grooved side of gears should be toward left case half (41). Note that washers (87) are 2 mm (0.080 in.) thick and washer (94) is 1 mm (0.039 in.) thick. Install gears (70 through 73), washer (74) and snap ring (75) on mainshaft (69). Rounded face of snap ring must be toward washer. Install shift fork (98), shaft (97) and gear selector (96). Install shift detent ball components (44 through 47) and tighten screw (44) to 22 N·m (195 in.-lbs.). Remainder of assembly is evident after inspection and referral to Fig. HN32 while noting the following: Install Belleville washer (80) so cup side is toward shift fork (78). Tighten final driven gear (113) retaining screws to 55 N·m (40 ft.-lbs.). Install shims (118) with a thickness that permits smooth axle rotation without excessive play. Shims (118) must be of equal thickness. Tighten case retaining screws to 10 N·m (88 in.-lbs.). Tighten input shaft bearing nut (51) to 75 N·m (55 ft.-lbs.) and stake nut to shaft at notch on shaft. Tighten nut (52) to 90 N·m (66 ft.-lbs.). Tighten input shaft

bearing housing (55) retaining screws to 22 N·m (195 in.-lbs.).

Input shaft gear and clutch gear contact pattern and backlash must be checked if the clutch drum, input shaft, input shaft bearing, shims or left transaxle case half have been renewed or changed. After the transaxle has been assembled with original shims, but before the clutch is installed, coat the input gear (48) and the bevel gear on the back of clutch drum (32—Fig. HN28) with Prussian Blue or other suitable compound. Install clutch components (21 through 33). Rotate input shaft in normal direction then check contact pattern on input gear teeth. Contact area should be centered on tooth surface. If contact area is toward edge of tooth, install a thinner shim (49—Fig. HN32). If contact area is toward base of tooth, install a thicker shim (49). If a proper contact area is not obtainable by shimming input shaft, change thickness of shim (33—Fig. HN28) and repeat procedure. Check gear backlash by reading movement of clutch drum (32). Hold input shaft, push in against clutch drum then rotate clutch drum. Backlash should be 0.12-0.20 mm (0.005-0.008 in.). If backlash is insufficient, increase thickness of shim (33). If backlash is excessive, decrease thickness of shim (33).

HYDROSTATIC TRANSAXLE

Models H3011H And H3013H

OPERATION. The hydrostatic transaxle provides infinitely variable selection of forward and reverse speed from stopped to full speed. The transaxle uses a hydraulic pump that is driven through a set of bevel gears from the input shaft, which is belt-driven from the engine. A control lever, which is linked to the operator's speed control panel on the side of the transaxle, determines pump output, thereby setting machine speed. Pressurized oil is directed from the pump to a hydraulic motor that is connected to the differential through a set of gears. Both pump and motor are a multiple-piston-type that uses a swashplate to vary the stroke of the pistons. Pump and motor assemblies are constructed to close tolerances and clean oil is a requirement to obtain a long service life.

LUBRICATION. Transmission oil level should be checked prior to use of machine. Transmission oil is contained in a reservoir on top of the transaxle. Oil level should be maintained between marks on reservoir. Recommended oil is Honda Hydrostatic Transmission Fluid.

NOTE: Due to close tolerances present in the hydrostatic transaxle, particular care must be taken to prevent debris or other contaminants from entering transaxle.

Transmission oil should be changed after every five years or 500 hours of operation, whichever occurs first. To change oil, unscrew drain plug on bottom of transaxle and drain oil. Tighten drain plug to 23 N·m (203 in.-lbs.). Fill reservoir to proper level. Transaxle oil capacity is 4.6 L (4.9 qt.).

BLEEDING. When transmission oil is drained and refilled, air must be bled from system as follows: Remove mower deck and drive belt as outlined in

MOWER DECK section. Place blocks at front wheels and support rear of machine so rear wheels are off the ground. Place blocks against left rear wheel so it cannot rotate. Raise engine cover and be sure transaxle release lever (L—Fig. HN30) is in uppermost position, next to green dot. Unscrew plug in port (B—Fig. HN30) and install Honda adapter 07KPJ-VD6010A and a hose fitting. Attach a clear hose to fitting and direct hose end into a container. Rotate transmission pulley counterclockwise until air-free fluid passes through hose. Reinstall port plug (B) and tighten to 17 N·m (150 in.-lbs.).

Attach a clear hose to port (C) using same procedure as just outlined for port (B). Attach another clear hose to port (A)

with a reservoir (funnel or similar container) at end of hose. Fill reservoir with Honda hydrostatic transmission fluid and hold reservoir above port so fluid will flow into transaxle. Fluid must flow without interruption during procedure (no air bubbles). Slowly rotate right rear wheel counterclockwise until air-free fluid flows from port (C). Place shift control lever in "TRANSPORT" position and rotate transmission pulley counterclockwise until air-free fluid flows from port (C). Remove hoses, install port plugs and tighten plugs to 17 N·m (150 in.-lbs.).

With shift control lever in "TRANSPORT" position, the right rear wheel should rotate clockwise when the trans-

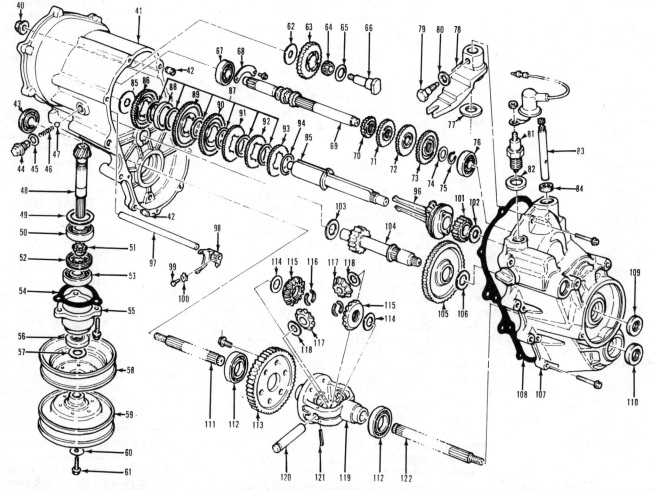

Fig. HN32—Exploded view of transaxle used on Models H3011, HTR3009 and HTR3811. Drive pulley (58) height is 58.5 mm (2.303 in.) and colored gold, while mower drive pulley (59) height is 62.5 mm (2.461 in.) and colored silver.

40. Locknut	54. Gasket	68. Retainer	82. Washer	96. Gear selector	109. Seal
41. Left case half	55. Bearing housing	69. Mainshaft	83. Shaft	97. Shift shaft	110. Seal
42. Dowel pin	56. Seal	70. Second drive gear	84. Seal	98. Shift fork	111. Left axle
43. Seal	57. Washer	71. Third drive gear	85. Thrust washer	99. Screw	112. Bearing
44. Screw	58. Drive pulley	72. Fourth drive gear	86. Reverse gear	100. Tab washer	113. Final driven gear
45. Washer	59. Mower drive pulley	73. Fifth drive gear	87. Washers	101. Countershaft drive gear	114. Thrust washer
46. Spring	60. Washer	74. Thrust washer	88. Spacer	102. Thrust washer	115. Side gear
47. Detent ball	61. Screw	75. Snap ring	89. First driven gear	103. Thrust washer	116. Split retainer ring
48. Input shaft	62. Washer	76. Bearing	90. Second driven gear	104. Countershaft	117. Pinion gear
49. Shim	63. Reverse idler gear	77. Washer	91. Third driven gear	105. Countershaft driven gear	118. Shim
50. Bearing	64. Bearing	78. Shift arm	92. Fourth driven gear	106. Thrust washer	119. Differential carrier
51. Nut	65. Washer	79. Screw	93. Fifth driven gear	107. Right case half	120. Pin
52. Nut	66. Shaft	80. Washer	94. Washer	108. Gasket	121. Roll pin
53. Bearing	67. Bearing	81. Neutral switch	95. Change shaft		122. Right axle

SERVICE MANUAL

Honda

Fig. HN33—Adjust maximum speed screw (S) as outlined in text.

mission pulley is rotated counterclockwise. With shift control lever in "REVERSE" position, the right rear wheel should rotate counterclockwise when the transmission pulley is rotated counterclockwise. If not, repeat bleeding procedure.

Reinstall drive belt and mower deck.

MAXIMUM SPEED ADJUSTMENT. Maximum speed may be adjusted on the transaxle. To correctly adjust maximum speed, tire pressures must be at recommended level (front—14 psi, rear—10 psi), tires must be original size, and maximum engine speed must be adjusted properly (see GOVERNOR section in ENGINE MAINTENANCE). Machine should traverse a distance of 15 m (49.2 ft.) on a level, hard surface in 7.0-7.9 seconds. To adjust maximum speed, raise engine cover, loosen nut (N—Fig. HN33) and turn adjusting screw (S). Rotating screw (S) clockwise will decrease maximum speed.

PRESSURE TESTS. To check charge pump pressure, first be sure transaxle fluid level is full. Raise engine cover and be sure transaxle release lever (L—Fig. HN30) is in released position, next to red dot. Unscrew plug in port (B) and install Honda adapter 07KPJ-VD6010A and a 0-700 kPa (0-100 psi) gauge. With shift control lever in neutral, run engine at full throttle. Charge pump pressure should be 196-392 kPa (29-57 psi).

To check line pressure, first be sure transaxle fluid level is full and engine maximum speed is adjusted correctly. Transaxle should be at normal operating temperature. Position machine so front end of frame abuts an immovable object so the rear wheels can spin without moving the machine. Raise engine cover and be sure transaxle release lever (L—Fig. HN30) is in uppermost

position, next to green dot. Unscrew plug in port (B) and install Honda adapter 07KPJ-VD6010A and a gauge that will read at least 20,000 kPa (3000 psi). Run engine at maximum speed with speed control lever in neutral. Slowly move speed control lever toward mowing position. Note location on control panel when rear wheels begin to spin and observe reading on gauge. Shift control lever should be approximately 45 mm (1.77 in) from neutral when rear wheels slip. Gauge reading should be 11,760 kPa (1700 psi) if operator weighs 70-90 kg (150-200 lbs.). Add 980 kPa (140 psi) for each 23 kg (50 lbs.) of additional operator weight, or subtract a like amount for less operator weight.

R&R AND OVERHAUL. Raise engine cover and remove battery, battery tray and cover over drive belt. Remove mower deck and drive belt as previously outlined. Support rear of machine, remove rear wheels and remove brake drum as previously outlined. Drain transaxle fluid. Detach shift rods (D and R—Fig. HN31) from transaxle. Support transaxle under left transaxle case half. Unscrew three retaining screws at rear of frame and remove axle mounting brackets. Remove transaxle from frame while turning to left and tilting top of transaxle down.

To disassemble transaxle, proceed as follows: Unscrew and remove fluid reservoir. Unscrew control shaft mounting flange (6—Fig. HN34) screws and withdraw control shaft assembly. Disassemble control shaft assembly after driving out roll pin (9). Remove pulleys (22 and 23) from input shaft. Unscrew and remove input shaft bearing housing (19). Using Honda tool 07916-7500000 with attachment 07FPA-7510110, unscrew nut (15) and remove input shaft (12). If bearing (13) must be removed, grind away staked area and use Honda tool 07916-7500000 to unscrew nut (14). Old nut should be discarded.

Unscrew retaining screws from backplate (92), position transaxle so backplate is facing down, remove retaining screws from transaxle case and lift off transaxle case (10). Remove rear axle and differential assembly. Remove countershaft gear (71) and shaft (72). Remove filter assembly components (74 through 79). Detach charge pump housing (122) from backplate (92). Remove bevel gear (28) and shim (29) from pump shaft. Remove pin (31) from end of pump shaft (30). Remove retaining screws and lift off pump housing (43). Remainder of disassembly is evident with inspection of unit and referral to Fig. HN34 while noting the following:

Pins (47) must be driven out to release ring (52) and bearing plate (51). To remove needle bearing (38), detach snap ring (37) and drive out bearing; bearing will be damaged during disassembly and must be discarded. Remove bushing and bearing (45) before removing swashplate (48) through gaps in pump housing (43).

Inspect components for excessive wear and damage. Pump and motor cylinder assemblies must be renewed as sets. To reassemble transaxle, install bearings, bushings, seals and dowel pins in cases and housings as required. Do not install bushing (110) yet. Lubricate components with Honda hydrostatic transmission oil prior to assembly.

Install check valve assembly (93 through 96) and tighten screw (93) to 33 N·m (24 ft.-lbs.). Install release valve assembly (97 through 103), but leave nuts (97) loose. Install return shaft (104), spring (105), washer and locknut on backplate (92). Shaft must slide freely. Install special screw (62) and washer (63). Install dowel pins (61), pump plate (60) and motor plate (68) on backplate. Install plates so side with arrow is up and points away from bearing (73). Install piston assembly in pump cylinder (58), then install cylinder assembly on backplate. Install bearing plate (57) and roller bearing (56) on cylinder.

Install bearing plate (51) and ring (52) in swashplate (48), then insert roll pins (47) so split in pin is away from ring (52) and inner end of pin does not extend past inside diameter of ring. Install washer (50) on swashplate trunnion that is near projection (P) on swashplate. Install swashplate in pump housing (43) so projection (P) is near wall of housing. Install bushing in housing and around swashplate trunnion with two holes in end so cutout in bushing is toward gap in housing. Install bearing (45) and snap ring (46). Install motor shaft (69), washer (36), gear (35) and snap ring (34) in pump housing (43). Note that inner bearing plate (64A) has a thicker inner ridge than outer bearing plate (64B). Ball bearing plate (65) must be installed so extruded side is toward inner bearing plate (64A). Install piston assembly in motor cylinder (66), then install cylinder assembly (64A through 66) on motor shaft in pump housing (43). Thread a suitable tool onto end of motor shaft (69) that will hold cylinder (66) in place, but is smaller than shaft bore in backplate (92). Tool holds cylinder while installing pump housing assembly on backplate. Install pump housing on backplate and tighten retaining screws loosely. Install bearing

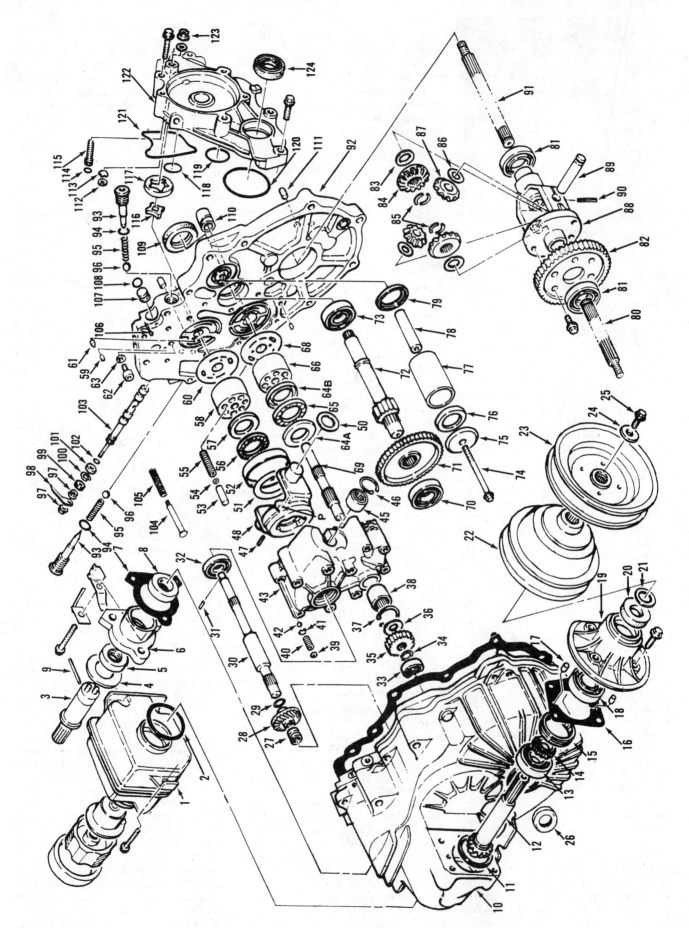

(32) on pump shaft (30) and install shaft. Rotate shafts and check for binding. Tighten pump housing screws in a crossing pattern to 25 N·m (18 ft.-lbs.). Look through check hole in side of pump housing and check for correct positioning of motor bearing plates (64A and 64B) and bearing (65). Remove special tool from motor shaft end and install bushing (110). Install relief valve assembly (38 through 42) with flat side of guide (41) next to spring (40) and secure with cotter pin.

Assemble remainder of transaxle by reversing disassembly and referral to Fig. HN34 while noting the following: Install seat (113) so concave side is toward snap ring (112). Tighten charge pump housing (122) retaining screws to 25 N·m (18 ft.-lbs.). Install countershaft gear (71) so long end of hub is toward

Fig. HN34—Exploded view of hydrostatic transaxle used on Models H3011H and H3013H.

  1. Fluid reservoir
  2. "O" ring
  3. Control shaft
  4. Washer
  5. Seal
  6. Flange
  7. Gasket
  8. Collar
  9. Roll pin
 10. Case
 11. Shim
 12. Input shaft
 13. Bearing
 14. Nut
 15. Nut
 16. Gasket
 17. Dowel pin
 18. Bearing
 19. Bearing housing
 20. Seal
 21. Washer
 22. Transaxle drive pulley
 23. Mower drive pulley
 24. Washer
 25. Screw
 26. Seal
 27. Bearing
 28. Bevel gear
 29. Shim
 30. Pump shaft
 31. Pin
 32. Bearing
 33. Bearing
 34. Snap ring
 35. Countershaft drive gear
 36. Thrust washer
 37. Snap ring
 38. Bearing
 39. Washer
 40. Spring
 41. Spring guide
 42. Relief valve ball
 43. Pump housing
 45. Bearing
 46. Snap ring
 47. Roll pin
 48. Swashplate
 50. Washer
 51. Bearing plate
 52. Ring
 53. Piston
 54. Washer
 55. Spring
 56. Roller bearing
 57. Bearing plate
 58. Pump cylinder
 59. Dowel pin
 60. Pump plate
 61. Dowel pin
 62. Screw
 63. Washer
 64A. Bearing plate
 64B. Bearing plate
 65. Bearing plate
 66. Motor cylinder
 68. Motor plate
 69. Motor shaft
 70. Bearing
 71. Gear
 72. Countershaft
 73. Bearing
 74. Screw
 75. Washer
 76. Collar
 77. Filter
 78. Spacer
 79. Collar
 80. Left axle
 81. Bearing
 82. Final driven gear
 83. Thrust washer
 84. Side gear
 85. Split retainer ring
 86. Shim
 87. Pinion gear
 88. Differential carrier
 89. Pin
 90. Roll pin
 91. Right axle
 92. Backplate
 93. Screw
 94. "O" ring
 95. Spring
 96. Check valve ball
 97. Nut
 98. Release lever
 99. Dust seal
100. Snap ring
101. Spacer
102. "O" ring
103. Release valve
104. Return shaft
105. Spring
106. Cotter pin
107. Plug
108. "O" ring
109. Seal
110. Bushing
111. Dowel pin
112. Snap ring
113. Seat
114. "O" ring
115. Adjusting screw
116. Charge pump inner rotor
117. Charge pump outer rotor
118. "O" ring
119. "O" ring
120. "O" ring
121. "O" ring
122. Charge pump housing
123. Flange nut
124. Seal

gear on countershaft (72). Tighten final driven gear (82) retaining screws to 55 N·m (40 ft.-lbs.). Install shims (86) with a thickness that permits smooth axle rotation without excessive play. Shims (86) must be equal thickness. Tighten transaxle case (10) retaining screws to 25 N·m (18 ft.-lbs.). Tighten input shaft bearing nut (14) to 75 N·m (55 ft.-lbs.) and stake nut to shaft at notch on shaft. Install nut (15) so stepped side is toward gear and tighten to 90 N·m (66 ft.-lbs.). Tighten input shaft bearing housing (19) retaining screws to 22 N·m (195 in.-lbs.). Lubricate control shaft (3) with lithium grease before inserting in holder (6). Install control shaft assembly so punch mark at splined end of control shaft (3) is on opposite side of shaft from reservoir after installation. Tighten control shaft holder (6) retaining screws to 21 N·m (186 in.-lbs.). Install control arm on control shaft (3) so punch mark on shaft end and mark on control arm (R—Fig. HN30) are aligned. When control arm is rotated counterclockwise, then released, arm should swing back to starting position. Apply thread locking compound to pulley retaining screw (25—Fig. HN34). Pull out release valve stem (M—Fig. HN30) and adjust nuts (N) so lever (L) is against upper stop.

To install transaxle, reverse removal procedure while noting the following: Be sure brake actuating rod is above rear axle before attaching rear axle bracket. Axle brackets must be installed so side with snap ring is toward transaxle. Hand-tighten axle bracket screws and the three screws on the rear of the frame, then tighten axle bracket screws to 38 N·m (28 ft.-lbs.). Tighten the three rear frame screws to 24 N·m (18 ft.-lbs.). Be sure axles rotate freely. If not, loosen retaining screws and retighten. Install brake assembly and attach brake rod. Install rear wheels and adjust brake as previously outlined. Tighten rear wheel retaining nut to 65 N·m (48 ft.-lbs.). Attach shift rods and tighten shift rod retaining nuts to 22 N·m (195 in.-lbs.). Adjust shift control linkage as previously outlined. Bleed transaxle as previously outlined. Install drive belt and mower deck.

MOWER BELT

All Models

BELT TENSION. Model HTR3811. To adjust mower drive belt (lower belt) tension on Model HTR3811, position machine on a level surface with wheels pointing straight ahead. Mower must be in highest position. Move mower control to engaged position. Belt tension must

be adjusted if index mark on tensioner arm aligns with or passes index mark on mower deck. Move mower deck to lowest position with mower control in engaged position. Loosen 8 mm flange screw on stationary idler plate and pull out stationary idler. If proper position of wear index marks cannot be attained by moving stationary idler, then belt is excessively worn and must be renewed.

All Other Models. Belt tension is provided by a spring-loaded idler and is not adjustable. Belt must be renewed if slippage is noted.

REMOVE AND REINSTALL. To remove the mower belt, remove mower unit as outlined in MOWER DECK section. Remove belt guides, remove belt shields (if so equipped) push idler away from belt and remove belt.

Model HTR3811 is equipped with two belts, each of which may be removed by following preceding procedure.

Reinstall belt by reversing removal procedure.

MOWER DECK

All Models

HEIGHT ADJUSTMENT. All mower control linkage must be in good operating condition and tires properly inflated. Park machine on a level surface with engine stopped and spark plug wire disconnected.

Front-to-rear height difference is determined by measuring height of blade above ground at front and rear. Height difference should be 6-9 mm (0.24-0.35 in.). To adjust front-to-rear height difference, adjust length of left and right front mower deck links as follows: Support front of mower deck, detach front end of link, loosen locknut (N—Fig. HN35) and rotate link to change length.

Fig. HN35—Loosen locknuts (N) and rotate mower hanger links to adjust mower deck height.

Honda

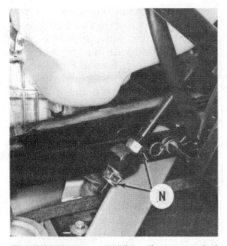

Fig. HN36—Loosen nuts (N) to adjust mower deck side-to-side height.

Make sure sides are adjusted evenly. Recheck height measurements.

If mower deck side-to-side height is uneven, rotate adjustment nuts (N—Fig. HN36) on side mower hanger rods as needed. On early models, detach ferrule and rotate ferrule to adjust height.

REMOVE AND REINSTALL. To remove mower deck, disconnect spark plug wire, place mower control lever in disengaged position and place mower deck in lowest position. Remove belt guide around mower belt pulley on transaxle shaft and separate belt from pulley. Detach control rod from idler arm. Detach mower deck links and carefully remove mower deck from left side of machine on Model H3013H or right side of machine on all other models. Reinstall mower deck by reversing removal procedure.

MOWER SPINDLE

All Models

LUBRICATION. Periodic lubrication of mower spindle is not required.

R&R AND OVERHAUL. Remove mower deck, blade and blade holder. Unscrew spindle pulley retaining screw and remove pulley. Unscrew bearing housing and remove spindle assembly. Remove drive key on early Model HTR3009. Remove spindle by withdrawing toward pulley end of shaft. Inspect components for excessive wear and damage. Tighten bearing housing retaining screws to 35-45 N•m (26-33 ft.-lbs.) on Model HTR3811 and to 60 N•m (44 ft.-lbs.) on all other models. Tighten pulley retaining screw on early Model HTR3009 (12 mm screw) to 85 N•m (62 ft.-lbs.) and to 38 N•m (28 ft.-lbs.) on all other models. On Models H3011 and H3011H, tighten center blade retaining screw to 50 N•m (37 ft.-lbs.) and outer blade retaining screws to 85 N•m (62 ft.-lbs.). On Models H3013H and HTR3811, tighten mower blade retaining screw to 50 N•m (37 ft.-lbs.). On Model HTR3009 with three blade retaining screws, tighten blade retaining screws to 85 N•m (62 ft.-lbs.). On Model HTR3009 with a single blade retaining screw, tighten blade retaining screw to 50 N•m (37 ft.-lbs.).

ELECTRICAL

All Models

Refer to Figs. HN37 and HN38 for wiring schematics and Fig. HN39 for a view of control relay, rectifier and fuse on Models H3011, H3011H and H3013H. Note the following points:

The transmission must be in neutral, the mower must be disengaged and the operator must be in seat for engine to start.

The engine should stop if the transmission is in gear or the mower is engaged and the operator leaves the seat.

The circuit is protected by a 5 amp main fuse.

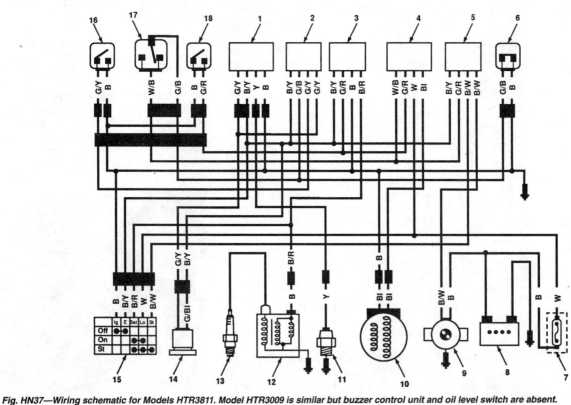

Fig. HN37—Wiring schematic for Models HTR3811. Model HTR3009 is similar but buzzer control unit and oil level switch are absent.

B. Black	W. White	3. Control relay	7. Fuse (5 amp)	11. Oil level switch	15. Ignition switch
Bl. Blue	Y. Yellow	4. Rectifier	8. Battery	12. Ignition coil	16. Parking brake switch
G. Green	1. Buzzer control unit	5. Starter relay	9. Starter	13. Spark plug	17. Blade engagement switch
R. Red	2. Buzzer relay	6. Neutral switch	10. Engine charge coil	14. Buzzer	18. Seat switch

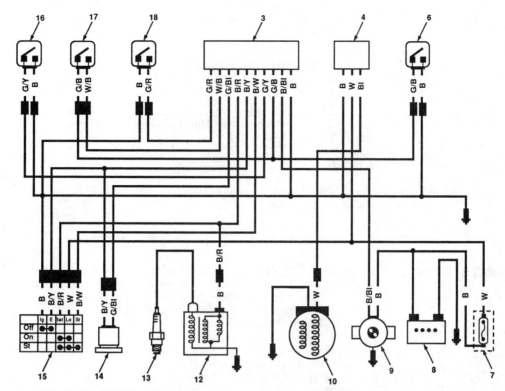

Fig. HN38—Wiring schematic for Models H3011H and H3013H. Model H3011 is similar. Refer to Fig. HN37 for parts identification and wiring color code.

Fig. HN39—View showing location of control relay (Y), rectifier (R) and fuse (F) on Models H3011, H3011H and H3013H.

HUSTLER

EXCEL INDUSTRIES
200 South Ridge Road
Heston, KS 67062

Model	Make	Engine Model	Horsepower	Cutting Width, In.
261	B&S	420000	18	60
275	Kohler	K532*	20	54**
295	Continental	TC-56	25	54**

*An optional K-582 (23 horsepower) engine is available.
**Optional mower decks are available.

STEERING SYSTEM

All Models

These units do not have a conventional front axle or steering system; instead two steering control levers control two Sundstrand hydrostatic pumps which control oil flow to a left and right Ross hydraulic wheel motor. Increasing oil flow to motors will increase traction speed. When oil flow decreases, traction speed decreases. Stopping oil flow will cause tractor to stop. Reversing oil flow to motor will cause tractor to move in reverse. If oil flows faster to one motor than the other, tractor will turn. If oil flow goes in one direction to one motor and in the opposite direction to the other motor, tractor will rotate on its axis. Figure HU1 shows positioning of control levers for making directional maneuvers.

ENGINE

All Models

Refer to appropriate engine section in this manual for tune-up specifications, engine overhaul procedures and engine maintenance on Briggs & Stratton or Kohler engines. For repair specifications on Continental TC-56 engine, refer to the following section.

Model Continental TC-56

Engine is of L-head design. All valves, valve lifters, cam and all other working components are contained in cylinder block assembly. Manufacturer does not recommend using fuel with an octane rating below 85.

To check ignition timing, connect timing light as instructed by manufacturer to No. 1 spark plug. Start engine and allow to warm up, then set idle speed at 400-500 rpm. Point timing light at marks located on either crankshaft dampener or flywheel ring. Timing is correct if timing pointer aligns with TDC mark on crankshaft dampener or flywheel ring. To adjust, loosen distributor securing cap screw, then turn distributor assembly until correct timing is attained. Retighten securing cap screw.

For engine specifications refer to the following chart.

Model TC-56
No. of cylinders 2
Bore . . . . 3 $\frac{3}{16}$ in.
  (81 mm)
Stroke . . . . .3½ in.
  (88.9 mm)
Displacement . . . . .56 cu. in.
  (917.6 cc)
Compression ratio 8:1
Maximum oil pressure . . . . 30-40 psi
Minimum oil pressure (idling) . .7 psi
Firing order 1-2
Breaker point gap . . . . . . .0.020 in.
  (0.51 mm)
Spark plug gap . . . . .0.025 in.
  (0.64 mm)
Ignition timing at
  400-500 rpm . . . . .TDC
Maximum cylinder taper . . .0.008 in.
  (0.20 mm)

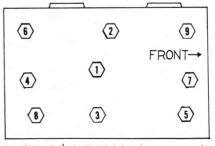

Fig. HU2—Cylinder head tightening sequence for engine Model Continental TC-56.

Valve clearance
  Intake . . . . .0.012 in.
    (0.30 mm)
  Exhaust . . . . .0.020 in.
    (0.51 mm)
Valve seat angle
  Intake . . . . .30°
  Exhaust . . . . .45°
Oil capacity
  Crankcase . . . . .2 qt.
    (1.8 L)
  Filter . . . . ½ qt.
    (0.47L)
Water capacity (engine) . . . . .2½ qt.
    (2.4L)

For torque values refer to the following chart. Cylinder head tightening sequence is shown in Fig. HU2.

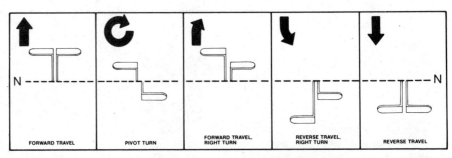

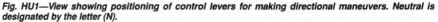

Fig. HU1—View showing positioning of control levers for making directional maneuvers. Neutral is designated by the letter (N).

Cylinder head . . . . 45-48 ft.-lbs.
(61-65 N·m)
Main bearing cap screws
⅜ inch . . . . 35-40 ft.-lbs.
(48-54 N·m)
7/16 inch . . . . 70-75 ft.-lbs.
(95-102 N·m)
Connecting rods
5⁄16 inch . . . . 25-30 ft.-lbs.
(34-40 N·m)
⅜ inch . . . . 45-50 ft.-lbs.
(61-68 N·m)
Flywheel
5⁄16 inch . . . . 20-25 ft.-lbs.
(27-34 N·m)
⅜ inch . . . . 35-40 ft.-lbs.
(48-54 N·m)
Manifolds (Intake and Exhaust)
5⁄16 inch . . . . 15-20 ft.-lbs.
(20-27 N·m)
⅜ inch . . . . 35-40 ft.-lbs.
(48-54 N·m)

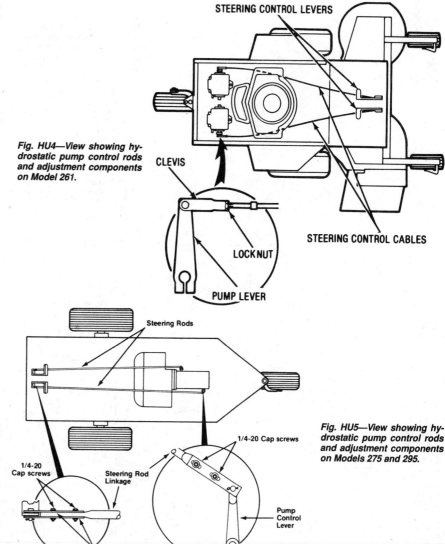

Fig. HU4—View showing hydrostatic pump control rods and adjustment components on Model 261.

Fig. HU5—View showing hydrostatic pump control rods and adjustment components on Models 275 and 295.

CONTROL LEVER ADJUSTMENT

All Models

Tractor should not creep in either direction when control levers are placed in neutral position. Rear stop lever as shown in Fig. HU3 is used to stop control levers from going past neutral position into reverse position when released from forward drive position. Rear stop lever must be raised up in order to pull control levers back into reverse drive position. Rear stop lever should return to the down position when control levers are released from reverse position. For engine to start, front lock lever must be in the forward position as shown in Fig. HU3 to engage neutral start switch. Raise front lock lever after engine starts to allow movement of control levers.

Should tractor creep when control levers are placed in neutral position adjust as follows:

CAUTION: If adjustment is made with engine running, use extreme caution to keep hands and feet clear of moving parts as severe personal injury could occur.

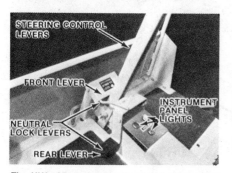

Fig. HU3—View showing front and rear control lever locks on all models.

Model 261

Raise traction drive wheels clear of ground and securely block. Start engine and allow to run until hydraulic oil is warm. Move control levers back and forth, then release levers to neutral position. Lock levers into position by use of front lock lever. If drive wheels are turning, adjust clevis (Fig. HU4) located on either end of control rod until pump lever is adjusted to neutral position. To adjust clevis, remove clevis pin, then loosen locknut on control rod and turn clevis on rod. Retighten locknut and reinstall clevis on pump rod. Recheck for traction wheel creep, repeat adjustment procedure until correct adjustment is attained.

Models 275 and 295

Raise traction drive wheels clear of ground and securely block. Start engine and allow to run until hydraulic oil is warm. Move control levers back and forth, then release levers to neutral position. Lock levers into position by use of front lock lever. If drive wheels are turning, loosen cap screws securing linkage straps to steering rod as shown in Fig. HU5, then slide steering rod until pump lever is adjusted to neutral position. Retighten cap screws.

BRAKE

All Models

If control levers are adjusted correctly, tractor should stop when levers are returned to neutral position as hydrostatic pump oil flow should be stopped to drive wheel motors.

To adjust parking brake, turn knob on top of brake lever clockwise to increase brake application. Parking

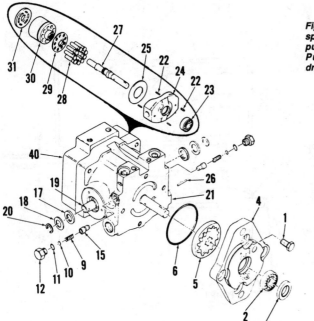

Fig. HU6—Exploded view of split Sundstrand hydrostatic pump used on Model 261. Pumps are individually driven.

1. Cap screw
2. Bearing
3. Seal
4. Charge pump housing
5. Charge pump (gerotor set)
6. "O" ring
9. Spring
10. Shim pack
11. "O" ring
12. Plug
15. Relief valve cone
17. Seal
18. Washer
19. Control shaft
20. Retaining ring
21. Pump housing
22. Roll pins
23. Bearing
24. Pump swash plate
25. Thrust plate
26. Pin
27. Pump shaft
28. Piston
29. Shoe plate
30. Cylinder block
31. Motor valve plate
40. Pump end cap

brake should retain tractor from moving when brake is applied and control levers are moved forward approximately one inch.

HYDROSTATIC PUMP

All Models

Model 261 uses two split Sundstrand hydrostatic pumps as shown in Fig. HU6, each pump is individually driven. Models 275 and 295 use two inline Sundstrand hydrostatic pumps (Fig. HU7) mounted back-to-back with a common drive shaft. Each pump operates independently with its own complete circuit and is connected in a closed loop to a traction drive motor.

R&R AND OVERHAUL. To remove hydrostatic drive pump, first unlatch an lift engine hood, then tilt seat assembly forward against steering con-

1. Cap screw
2. Bearing
3. Seal
4. Charge pump housing
5. Charge pump (gerotor set)
6. "O" ring
7. Plugs
8. Check ball
9. Spring
10. Shim pack
11. "O" ring
12. Plug
13. Gasket
14. Plug
15. Relief valve cone
16. Bearing
17. Seal
18. Washer
19. Control shaft
20. Retaining ring
21. Pump housing
22. Roll pins
23. Bearing
24. Pump swash plate
25. Thrust plate
26. Pin
27. Pump shaft
28. Piston
29. Shoe plate
30. Cylinder block
31. Motor valve plate
32. Locator pin
33. Gasket
34. Bearing
35. "O" ring
36. Check ball
37. Spring
38. "O" ring
39. Check valve plug
40. Pump end cap
41. Coupling
42. Retaining ring
43. Insert
44. Gasket
45. Pump assy. (Right motor drive)

FRONT

Fig. HU7—Exploded view of in-line Sundstrand hydrostatic pump used on Models 275 and 295. Pumps are mounted back-to-back with a common drive shaft.

trol levers. Disconnect battery ground cable from battery. Thoroughly clean exterior of pump assembly. Disconnect control arm on control shaft (19–Fig. HU6 and HU7), then withdraw arm from shaft.

CAUTION: Use safety precautions when working with hydraulic fluid as personal injuries can occur.

Place a suitable pan under tractor, then remove reservoir drain plug and drain oil. Disconnect hydraulic hoses from pump ssembly. Plug or cap all openings to prevent dirt or other foreign material from entering system. On Model 261 remove as needed all components used to drive hydrostatic pumps. On all models remove as needed all components and shields that will obstruct pump removal. Remove pump mounting cap screws, then withdraw pump assembly.

Hydrostatic pump on Models 275 and 295 can be separated into two individual pump sections with the removal of pump end caps (40–Fig. HU7) securing nuts to mounting studs. If pumps do not separate with removal of nuts use a soft mallet to tap housing. For assistance during overhaul refer to Fig. HU6 for exploded view of pump used on Model 261 and Fig. HU7 for exploded view of pump used on Models 275 and 295.

To disassemble the hydrostatic drive unit, first place a scribe mark across charge pump housing (4) and pump housing (21), pump housing and pump end cap (40) for aid in reassembly. Remove all rust, paint or burrs from end of pump shaft (27). Unbolt and remove charge pump housing (4), then remove charge pump (5) and withdraw

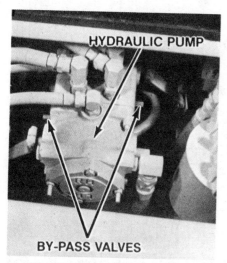

BY-PASS VALVES

Fig. HU8—View showing location of bypass valves on hydrostatic pumps for Models 275 and 295.

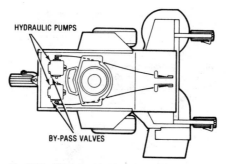

Fig. HU9—View showing location of bypass valves on hydrostatic pumps for Model 261.

drive pin (26) from pump shaft. Remove oil seal (3) from housing. Remove relief valve assemblies (9 through 12 and 15) and (8 through 12).

CAUTION: Keep valve assemblies separated. Do not mix the components.

Separate pump end cap (40) from pump housing (21). Valve plate (31) may stick to cylinder block (30). Use care when handling plates. Remove pump cylinder block and piston assembly (28 through 30) and lay aside for later disassembly. Remove thrust plate (25), drive out roll pins (22), then withdraw shafts (19) with snap ring (20) and washer (18). Lift out swashplate (24). Bearing (23) and input shaft (27) may be pressed from housing (21) as an assembly. Press bearing from input shaft. Oil seals (17) and needle bearings (16) can now be removed from housing (21). Remove check valve assemblies (36 through 39). Needle bearing (34) can be removed from end cap (40).

Carefully remove shoe plate (29) and pistons (28) from cylinder block (30). Inspect pistons and bores in cylinder blocks for excessive wear or scoring. Light scratches on piston shoes can be removed by lapping. Inspect valve plate (31) and valve plate contacting surfaces of cylinder block (30) for excessive wear or scoring and renew as needed. Check thrust plate (25) for excessive wear or any other damage. Inspect charge pump (5) for wear, pitting or scoring.

Renew all oil seals, "O" rings and gaskets, lubricate all internal parts with new engine oil as specified and reassemble in reverse order of disassembly. Refill hydraulic system reservior using only SAE 10W-40, 10W-30 or 5W-30 engine oil.

NOTE: Should tractor need to be moved when engine is inoperative, use a small screwdriver or punch through hole in bypass valve on hydrostatic pump as shown in Fig. HU8 for Models 275 and 295 and Fig. HU9 for Model 261. Turn valve one complete turn counterclockwise on Models 275 and

295 and one complete turn clockwise on Model 261. Oil will be allowed to flow through system enabling tractor to be moved.

HYDRAULIC WHEEL MOTOR

All Models

R&R AND OVERHAUL. Using a suitable jack, place it under the torsion bar which is located behind wheel motor and extends from one side of tractor frame to the other. Lift drive wheel clear of ground surface and remove lug bolts, then withdraw drive wheel. Disconnect hydraulic lines from hydraulic drive motor and plug or cap all openings. Remove motor mounting bolts, then withdraw motor.

To disassemble the hydraulic drive motor, clamp motor body port boss in a padded jaw vise with output shaft pointing downward. Remove the seven cap screws (24–Fig. HU10) and remove end cover (23), seal ring (22), commutator (19) and commutator ring (18). Remove sleeve (21), manifold (17) and manifold plate (16). Lift drive link (11), wear plate (12), rotor (13), rollers (14) and stator (15) off the body (5). Remove output shaft (10), then remove snap ring (1), spacer (2), shim (3) and oil seal (4). Remove seal ring (9). Do not remove needle bearing (8), thrust bearing (7) or

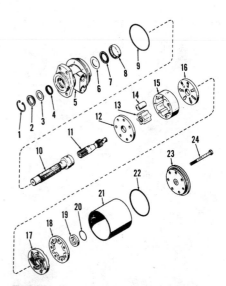

Fig. HU10—Exploded view of Ross hydraulic drive motor.

1. Snap ring	13. Rotor
2. Spacer	14. Roller (6)
3. Shim washer (0.010)	15. Stator
4. Oil seal	16. Manifold plate
5. Body	17. Manifold
6. Thrust washer	18. Commutator ring
7. Thrust bearing	19. Commutator
8. Needle bearing	20. Seal ring
9. Seal ring	21. Sleeve
10. Output shaft	22. Seal ring
11. Drive link	23. End cover
12. Wear plate	24. Cap screw (7)

Hustler

RIDING LAWN MOWER

thrust washer (6) from body (5) as these parts are not serviced separately.

Clean and inspect all parts for excessive wear or other damage and renew as needed. A seal ring and seal kit (items 2, 3, 4, 9, 20 and 22) is available for resealing the motor. To reassemble the motor, clamp body port boss in a padded vise with the seven tapped holes upward. Insert shaft (10) and drive link (11). Install new seal ring (9) in groove on body (5). Place stator (15) on wear plate (12) and install rotor and rollers (13 and 14) with counterbore in rotor facing upward. Place wear plate and rotor assembly over the drive link and on the body.

NOTE: Two cap screws, ⅜-24x4½" with heads removed, can be used to align bolt holes in body (5) with holes in wear plate (12), stator (15), manifold plate (16), manifold (17), commutator plate (18) and end cover (23).

Install manifold plate (16) with slots toward the rotor. Install manifold (17) with swirl grooves toward the rotor and the diamond shaped holes upward. Place commutator ring (18) and commutator (19) on the manifold with the bronze ring groove facing upward. Place bronze seal ring (20) into the groove with the rubber side downward. Lubricate seal ring (9) and install

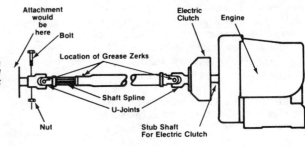

Fig. HU12—View showing pto drive shaft and operational components for Model 275 and 295.

sleeve (21) over the assembled components. Install new seal ring (22) on end cover (23), lubricate seal ring and install end cover. Remove line up bolts and install the seven cap screws (24). Tighten the cap screws evenly to a torque of 50 ft.-lbs. (67 N·m).

Remove motor from vise and place it on bench with output shaft pointing upward. Lubricate and install new oil seal (4), shim (3), spacer (2) and snap ring (1). Lubricate motor by pouring new engine oil as specified in one port and rotating output shaft until oil is expelled from other port. Reinstall motor in reverse order of removal. Tighten lug bolts in a criss-cross pattern to 45-55 ft.-lbs. (61-75 N·m).

ELECTRICAL

All Models

Shown in electrical diagrams Figs. HU13 through HU15 are electrical components and their adjoining wires. For component and wire identification refer to Fig. HU13 for Model 261, Fig. HU14 for Model 275 and Fig. HU15 for Model 295.

MOWER DECK DRIVE

Model 261

Install tractor tool bar arms through openings in mower deck until arms are fully inserted in deck openings. Install clevis pins through holes in tool bar arms and mower deck, then lock clevis pins into place using hair pin clips. Deck weight is balanced by hooking deck balance spring on left side of deck, then attaching spring to appropriate chain link on chain under drivers seat until deck weight is evenly distributed.

To install mower deck drive belt proceed as follows. Disengage pto clutch lever, then remove hair pin clip (6–Fig. HU11) from frame slot and slide belt guide (2) out of slot. Position drive belt over clutch cable and route belt to left side of adjustment idler (8), between

clutch idler (7) and brake post (5). Slip belt onto engine drive pulley (1). Reinstall belt guide and hair pin clip. Engage pto clutch lever and measure distance between belt as shown in Fig. HU11. Distance should be 1½ inches. To adjust, loosen bolt on adjustment idler (8) and slide idler until correct distance is attained, then retighten bolt.

Drive belt tension can also be changed by repositioning clutch cable in holes on pto lever.

Models 275 and 295

Tractors use a telescoping pto shaft to power mower deck gear box as shown in Fig. HU12. Yoke on shaft slides over splines on gear box input shaft and is secured by a bolt and nut. Pto shaft is engaged and disengaged by use of an electric clutch.

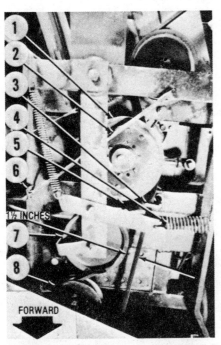

Fig. HU11—View showing mower deck drive belt components for Model 261.

1. Engine pulley
2. Removable belt guide
3. Belt guide
4. Clutch spring
5. Brake post
6. Hair pin
7. Clutch idler pulley
8. Adjustment idler pulley

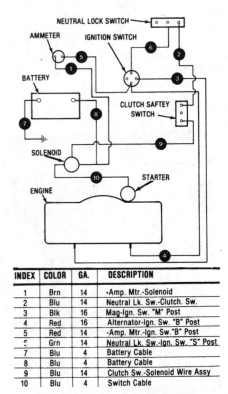

INDEX	COLOR	GA.	DESCRIPTION
1	Brn	14	+Amp. Mtr.-Solenoid
2	Blu	14	Neutral Lk. Sw.-Clutch. Sw.
3	Blk	16	Mag-Ign. Sw. "M" Post
4	Red	16	Alternator-Ign. Sw. "B" Post
5	Red	14	-Amp. Mtr.-Ign. Sw. "B" Post
6	Grn	14	Neutral Lk. Sw.-Ign. Sw. "S" Post
7	Blu	4	Battery Cable
8	Blu	4	Battery Cable
9	Blu	14	Clutch Sw.-Solenoid Wire Assy
10	Blu	4	Switch Cable

Fig. HU13—Wiring diagram for Model 261.

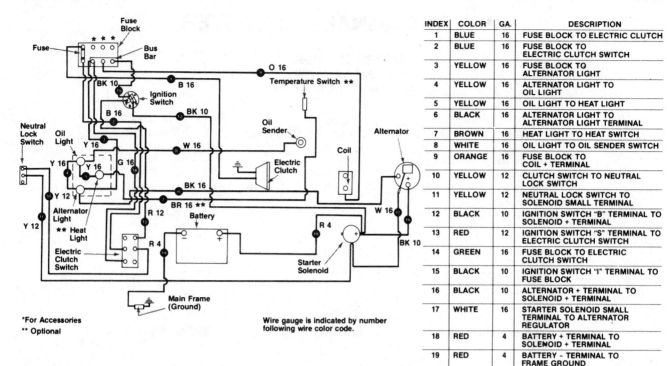

INDEX	COLOR	GA.	DESCRIPTION
1	BLUE	16	FUSE BLOCK TO ELECTRIC CLUTCH
2	BLUE	16	FUSE BLOCK TO ELECTRIC CLUTCH SWITCH
3	YELLOW	16	FUSE BLOCK TO ALTERNATOR LIGHT
4	YELLOW	16	ALTERNATOR LIGHT TO OIL LIGHT
5	YELLOW	16	OIL LIGHT TO HEAT LIGHT
6	BLACK	16	ALTERNATOR LIGHT TO ALTERNATOR TERMINAL
7	BROWN	16	HEAT LIGHT TO HEAT SWITCH
8	WHITE	16	OIL LIGHT TO OIL SENDER SWITCH
9	ORANGE	16	FUSE BLOCK TO COIL + TERMINAL
10	YELLOW	12	CLUTCH SWITCH TO NEUTRAL LOCK SWITCH
11	YELLOW	12	NEUTRAL LOCK SWITCH TO SOLENOID SMALL TERMINAL
12	BLACK	10	IGNITION SWITCH "B" TERMINAL TO SOLENOID + TERMINAL
13	RED	12	IGNITION SWITCH "S" TERMINAL TO ELECTRIC CLUTCH SWITCH
14	GREEN	16	FUSE BLOCK TO ELECTRIC CLUTCH SWITCH
15	BLACK	10	IGNITION SWITCH "I" TERMINAL TO FUSE BLOCK
16	BLACK	10	ALTERNATOR + TERMINAL TO SOLENOID + TERMINAL
17	WHITE	16	STARTER SOLENOID SMALL TERMINAL TO ALTERNATOR REGULATOR
18	RED	4	BATTERY + TERMINAL TO SOLENOID + TERMINAL
19	RED	4	BATTERY - TERMINAL TO FRAME GROUND

*For Accessories
** Optional

Fig. HU14—Wiring diagram for Model 275.

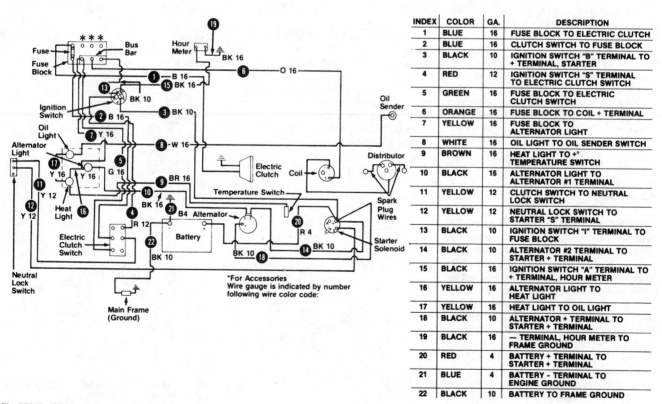

INDEX	COLOR	GA.	DESCRIPTION
1	BLUE	16	FUSE BLOCK TO ELECTRIC CLUTCH
2	BLUE	16	CLUTCH SWITCH TO FUSE BLOCK
3	BLACK	10	IGNITION SWITCH "B" TERMINAL TO + TERMINAL, STARTER
4	RED	12	IGNITION SWITCH "S" TERMINAL TO ELECTRIC CLUTCH SWITCH
5	GREEN	16	FUSE BLOCK TO ELECTRIC CLUTCH SWITCH
6	ORANGE	16	FUSE BLOCK TO COIL + TERMINAL
7	YELLOW	16	FUSE BLOCK TO ALTERNATOR LIGHT
8	WHITE	16	OIL LIGHT TO OIL SENDER SWITCH
9	BROWN	16	HEAT LIGHT TO +° TEMPERATURE SWITCH
10	BLACK	16	ALTERNATOR LIGHT TO ALTERNATOR #1 TERMINAL
11	YELLOW	12	CLUTCH SWITCH TO NEUTRAL LOCK SWITCH
12	YELLOW	12	NEUTRAL LOCK SWITCH TO STARTER "S" TERMINAL
13	BLACK	10	IGNITION SWITCH "I" TERMINAL TO FUSE BLOCK
14	BLACK	10	ALTERNATOR #2 TERMINAL TO STARTER + TERMINAL
15	BLACK	16	IGNITION SWITCH "A" TERMINAL TO + TERMINAL, HOUR METER
16	YELLOW	16	ALTERNATOR LIGHT TO HEAT LIGHT
17	YELLOW	16	HEAT LIGHT TO OIL LIGHT
18	BLACK	10	ALTERNATOR + TERMINAL TO STARTER + TERMINAL
19	BLACK	16	— TERMINAL, HOUR METER TO FRAME GROUND
20	RED	4	BATTERY + TERMINAL TO STARTER + TERMINAL
21	BLUE	4	BATTERY - TERMINAL TO ENGINE GROUND
22	BLACK	10	BATTERY TO FRAME GROUND

*For Accessories
Wire gauge is indicated by number following wire color code:

Fig. HU15—Wiring diagram for Model 295.

INTERNATIONAL HARVESTER

CUB CADET CORP.
P.O. Box 36900
Cleveland, Ohio 44136

Model	Make	Engine Model	Horsepower	Cutting Width, In.
Cadet 55	B&S	130902	5	28
Cadet 60	Tecumseh	V60	6	32
Cadet 75	B&S	170702	7	32
Cadet 85	B&S	191707	8	32
Cadet 85 Special	B&S	191707	8	28

FRONT AXLE

All Models

REMOVE AND REINSTALL. To remove axle main member (5–Fig. IH1), raise front of unit and securely block, then remove front wheels. Disconnect drag link (8–Fig. IH2) from right spindle (7–Fig. IH1). Remove axle center pivot bolt and lower axle assembly from chassis. Remove tie rod assembly, then unbolt and remove spindle (1 and 7). Inspect nylon bushings (2 and 4) and spacers (3 and 6) for excessive wear and renew as necessary. Reassemble by reversing disassembly procedure and adjust tie rod for 0 to $\frac{1}{16}$-inch (0-1.6 mm) toe-in.

STEERING GEAR

All Models

REMOVE AND REINSTALL. To remove the steering gear assembly (Fig. IH2), remove cotter pin and washer from lower end of steering shaft (12). Remove the three cap screws and withdraw covers (9 and 10) and quadrant gear (6). Drive out roll pin and remove upper shaft (14) and steering wheel (1) from steering shaft (12). Raise front of unit and withdraw steering shaft and pinion. Remove drag link end (7) from quadrant gear. Clean and inspect all parts and renew any showing excessive wear or other damage. When reassembling, lubricate steering gears and bushings with No. 2 multi-purpose lithium grease. With steering wheel and front wheels in straight ahead position, center teeth of quadrant gear (6) should be engaged with pinion on shaft (12).

ENGINE

All Models

Refer to appropriate engine section in this manual for tune-up specifications, engine overhaul procedures and engine maintenance.

Refer to the following paragraph for removal and installation procedure.

REMOVE AND REINSTALL. To remove engine assembly, disconnect spark plug wire and on electric start models, disconnect battery cables, starter wire and charging lead. On all models, disconnect throttle control cable. Lower mower housing and remove drive belts from engine. Unbolt and lift engine assembly from the chassis.

Reinstall engine by reversing the removal procedure.

Fig. IH1—Exploded view of front axle assembly used on all models.

1. Spindle L.H.
2. Nylon bushing
3. Spacer
4. Nylon bushing
5. Axle main member
6. Spacer
7. Spindle R.H.
8. Ball joint end (2 used)
9. Tie rod

TRACTION DRIVE CLUTCH AND DRIVE BELT

Models 55-75-85-85 Special

The traction drive clutch is a spring-tensioned, belt idler type operated by the clutch-brake pedal on left side. When pedal is depressed, belt tension is removed, allowing engine drive pulley to rotate freely within drive belt. No adjustment is required; if belt is worn or stretched to a point where slippage occurs, belt must be renewed.

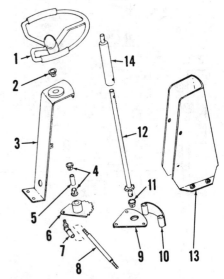

Fig. IH2—Exploded view of typical steering gear assembly used on all models.

1. Steering wheel
2. Nylon bushing
3. Steering support
4. Nylon bushing
5. Spacer
6. Quadrant gear
7. Ball joint end (2 used)
8. Drag link
9. Bottom cover
10. Front cover
11. Nylon bushing
12. Steering shaft & pinion
13. Shroud
14. Upper shaft

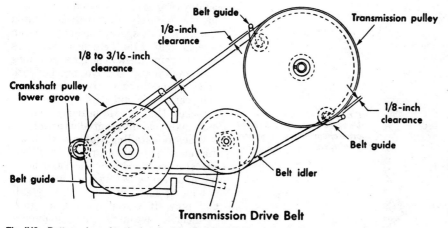

Fig. IH3—Bottom view of typical main drive belt installation on Models 55, 75, 85 and 85 Special. With clutch engaged, adjust belt guides to clearances shown.

REMOVE AND REINSTALL. To remove the main drive belt, disconnect spark plug wire and place mower clutch control in disengaged position. Lower mower and disconnect attaching pins. Slide mower rearward and remove mower drive belt from engine crankshaft pulley. Loosen belt guides around transmission input pulley and engine crankshaft pulley. Lock clutch-brake pedal in fully depressed position, then remove traction drive belt.

Install new belt and with clutch-brake pedal in up (clutch engaged) position, adjust belt guides to clearances shown in Fig. IH3. Reinstall mower by reversing the removal procedure. Check and adjust brake as outlined in BRAKE paragraph.

Model 60

A forward-reverse type drive is used on the Model 60. Two drive belts and a single idler pulley are used on this drive. One belt is driven by the engine crankshaft pulley (forward drive) and the other belt is driven by the engine camshaft pulley (reverse drive). The idler is located between the two drive belts. See Fig. IH4. The idler applies tension to only one belt at a time, depending on which foot pedal is depressed. Left foot pedal is for reverse drive and right foot pedal is forward drive. When neither pedal is depressed, tension is removed from both drive belts and the transmission input pulley stops rotating allowing transmission to be shifted to any of the four speeds. No adjustment is required on the forward-reverse drive belts. If belt slippage occurs due to excessive wear or stretching, renew the belts.

REMOVE AND REINSTALL. To remove the forward and reverse traction drive belts, disconnect spark plug wire and place mower clutch control lever in disengaged position. Lower mower and remove attaching pins at front lift arms. Slide mower rearward and remove mower drive belt from engine crankshaft pulley. Unbolt and remove drive belt guides. Remove forward drive belt and then reverse drive belt.

Install new belts and bolt belt guides in position. Reinstall mower by reversing the removal procedure.

TRANSMISSION

All Models

The transmissions used on all models are manufactured by the J.B. Foote Foundry Company. The transmission used on Models 55, 75, 85 and 85 Special is equipped with three forward gears and one reverse. Model 60 is equipped with a 4-speed transmission. A reverse gear is not required on this model since the forward-reverse drive allows operation in forward or reverse in any of the four gears.

Fig. IH4—Bottom view of forward and reverse main drive belts installed on Model 60.

REMOVE AND REINSTALL. To remove the transmission, disconnect spark plug wire and on electric start models, disconnect battery cables. Remove mower as outlined in MOWER DECK paragraphs and remove riding mower body as follows: Remove steering wheel, upper steering shaft and seat. Remove transmission shift lever knob, mower clutch lever and throttle control knob. Unbolt throttle control from body and disconnect ignition switch. Remove mower lift lever grip, then unscrew spring loaded cap screw and remove lift lever. Remove clutch-brake pedal (Models 55, 75, 85 and 85 Special) or forward and reverse pedals (Model 60) and when necessary, remove exhaust muffler. Remove body mounting bolts and note location of body mounting spacers. Tilt body slightly rearward and lift body from chassis.

Unbolt and remove chain guard and transmission belt guides. On Model 60, loosen chain idler and remove chain from transmission output sprocket. On Models 55, 75, 85 and 85 Special loosen rear axle bearing mounting bolts to loosen drive chain and remove chain from transmission output sprocket. Disconnect brake rod and transmission neutral start switch. On all models, remove drive belt(s) from transmission input pulley, then remove snap ring and pulley from input shaft. Unbolt and remove transmission assembly.

Reinstall by reversing the removal procedure. Adjust drive chain, belts and belt guides as required.

NOTE: On Models 55, 75, 85 and 85 Special, make certain safety starting switches are connected and in good condition before returning mower to service.

OVERHAUL. Foote transmissions are used on all models. For overhaul procedure refer to the Foote paragraphs in the TRANSMISSION REPAIR section of this manual.

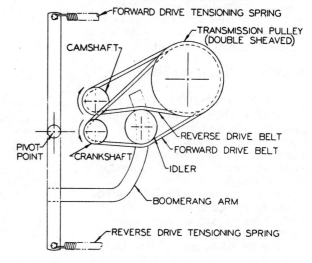

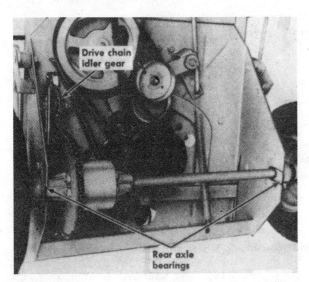

Fig. IH5—Bottom view of Model 60 showing location of drive chain idler and rear axle bearings.

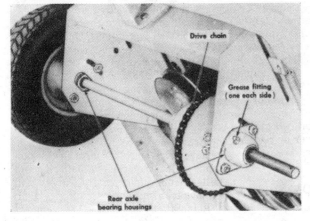

Fig. IH6—On Models 55, 75, 85 and 85 Special, rear axle assembly is pivoted rearward to tighten the drive chain.

DRIVE CHAIN

Model 60

R&R AND ADJUST. To remove chain, rotate differential sprocket to locate master link. Disconnect master link and remove chain. Clean and inspect chain and renew if excessively worn. Reinstall in reverse order of removal.

Adjust chain idler (Fig. IH5) until ⅛ to ¼-inch (3.2-6.4 mm) slack exists in chain on side opposite idler. Lubricate with light coat of SAE 30 oil.

Models 55-75-85-85 Special

R&R AND ADJUST. To remove chain (Fig. IH6), rotate differential sprocket to locate master link. Disconnect master link and remove chain. Clean and inspect chain and renew if excessively worn. Reinstall in reverse order of removal.

The rear axle bearing mounting plates are slotted so axle assembly can be pivoted to adjust chain tension. Loosen axle bearing mounting bolts and move both sides equally until drive chain has ⅛ to ¼-inch (3.2-6.4 mm) slack, then tighten mounting bolts. Lubricate with light coat of SAE 30 oil.

DIFFERENTIAL

Model 60

REMOVE AND REINSTALL. To remove rear axle and differential assembly (Fig. IH5), raise rear of unit and support securely. Remove rear wheels and keys. Note spacer washers between wheels and axle bearings. Washers must be reinstalled in original positions to align differential drive sprocket with drive chain. Loosen drive chain idler and remove chain from differential sprocket. Unbolt axle bearings and remove axle and differential assembly.

When reinstalling, tighten axle bearing retaining bolts securely. Install four spacer washers between each axle bearing and rear wheel and one washer on outside of each wheel. Check rear axle end play. If end play is more than ⅛ inch, add washers equally to outside of rear wheels, starting with right side, until end play is less than ⅛ inch. Secure rear wheels with new cotter pins. Adjust drive chain idler until ⅛ to ¼ inch (3.2-6.4 mm) slack exists in chain. Lubricate axle bearings with No. 2 multi-purpose lithium base grease and apply light coat of SAE 30 oil to drive chain.

Models 55-75-85-85 Special

REMOVE AND REINSTALL. To remove rear axle and differential assembly (Fig. IH6), raise rear of unit and support securely. Remove rear wheels and washers. Note location of washers. They must be reinstalled in original positions to maintain proper drive chain alignment. Unbolt and remove both rear axle bearings, then remove drive chain from differential sprocket. Remove four bolts from differential housing and slide sprocket off housing. Separate differential housing and carefully remove the two halves from main frame.

Lubricate differential with No. 2 multi-purpose lithium base grease and reinstall by reversing removal procedure. When installing wheels and washers, be sure washers are assembled in original order to maintain drive chain

Fig. IH7—View showing disc brake adjustment on Model 60. Refer to text.

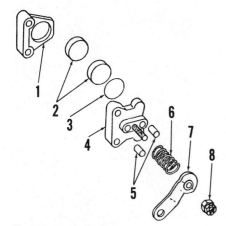

Fig. IH8—Exploded view of disc brake caliper assembly used on Model 60.

1. Brake pad carrier (inner)
2. Brake pads
3. Back-up plates
4. Brake pad carrier (outer)
5. Actuating pins
6. Spring
7. Cam lever
8. Adjusting nut

alignment. Check rear axle end play. If end play is more than ⅛ inch, (3.2 mm) add washers to outside of wheels, starting with right side, until end play is less than ⅛ inch (3.2 mm). Rear axle bearing mounting holes are slotted so axle can be pivoted to adjust drive chain. Adjust both sides equally until chain has ⅛ to ¼-inch (3.2-6.4 mm) slack, then tighten mounting. Lubricate axle bearings with No. 2 multi-purpose lithium base grease and apply light coat of SAE 30 oil to chain.

OVERHAUL. Peerless Series 100 differentials are used on all models. For overhaul procedures, refer to the DIFFERENTIAL REPAIR section of this manual.

GROUND DRIVE BRAKE

Model 60

The hand lever applied caliper type disc brake is used primarily as a parking brake. It can also be used as an emergency type brake. Normal braking is accomplished by lightly depressing opposite direction (forward or reverse) pedal. The brake disc is pinned to transmission output shaft.

ADJUSTMENT. To adjust disc brake, place brake hand lever in disengaged position. Remove cotter pin from brake adjustment nut and insert a 0.020-inch (0.51 mm) feeler gage between outer brake pad and brake disc. See Fig. IH7. Turn adjustment nut clockwise until a slight drag is felt on feeler gage. Install cotter pin to secure nut.

R&R AND OVERHAUL. To remove disc brake, disconnect brake return spring. Remove cap screws securing brake lever bracket and brake caliper bracket to the chassis, then lift out caliper assembly. To disassemble brake caliper, remove the two through-bolts and adjusting nut (8-Fig. IH8), then separate the parts. Clean and inspect all parts and renew any showing excessive wear or other damage. Check to see that brake disc is free to float axially on transmission shaft. Reinstall brake and adjust as outlined in the preceding paragraph.

Models 55-75-85-85 Special

The brake used is a caliper type disc brake located on output shaft of transmission. Brake is operated by the clutch-brake pedal located on left side.

ADJUSTMENT. To adjust brake, lock clutch-brake pedal in fully depressed position. On underside (near

Fig. IH9—Bottom view showing brake adjustment on Models 55, 75, 85 and 85 Special.

Fig. IH10—Disc brake assembly on transmission of Models 55, 75, 85 or 85 Special. Brake disc (1) should be free to move axially on transmission shaft.

1. Brake disc
2. Shoulder bolt
3. Cam lever

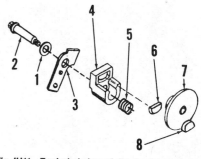

Fig. IH11—Exploded view of disc brake assembly used on Models 55, 75, 85 and 85 Special.

1. Washer
2. Shoulder bolt
3. Cam lever
4. Caliper
5. Spring
6. Brake pad (outer)
7. Brake disc
8. Brake pad (inner)

differential), adjust jam nuts on brake rod until spring length is 1½ inches (38.1 mm) measured as shown in Fig. IH9.

R&R AND OVERHAUL. To remove disc brake, disconnect brake rod from cam actuating lever (3-Fig. IH10). Remove shoulder bolt (2) and remove brake parts (1 through 6-Fig. IH11). Slide disc (7) from transmission shaft and remove inner brake pad (8) from holder slot in transmission housing. Clean and inspect all parts for excessive wear or other damage. Renew parts as required and reassemble by reversing the removal procedure. Adjust brake as outlined in the preceding paragraph.

MOWER DRIVE BELTS

All Models

Models 55 and 85 Special are equipped with single blade rotary mowers while the mowers used on Models 60, 75 and 85 are equipped with twin blades.

CAUTION: Always disconnect spark plug wire before performing any inspection, adjustments or other service on the mower.

Models 55-85 Special

ADJUSTMENT. The mower blade clutch is a belt idler type. When clutch is disengaged, a spring loaded brake arm comes into contact with drive belt at mower spindle pulley to stop blade rotation. A cable connected to brake arm and clutch control linkage pulls brake arm free from belt when clutch is engaged. No adjustment is required on blade brake. When mower drive belt has worn or stretched to a point where slippage occurs, a new belt should be installed as no adjustment can be made on clutch idler.

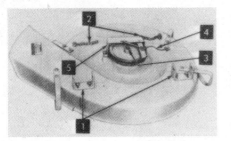

Fig. IH12—Mower unit used on Models 55 and 85 Special.

1. Front mounting brackets
2. Rear hanger chains
3. Blade spindle
4. Blade brake cable
5. Belt guide & blade brake bracket

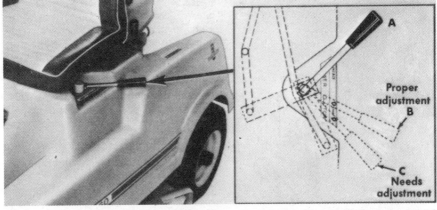

Fig. IH15—On Model 60, mower clutch control lever is in disengaged position at "A". When mower clutch belt is properly adjusted, position "B" is engaged position. Belt adjustment is required when lever moves to position "C" when clutch is engaged.

REMOVE AND REINSTALL. To remove mower drive belt, place mower clutch control lever in disengaged position. Set mower lift lever in lowest position and disconnect blade brake cable (4-Fig. IH12). Unpin front of mower and unhook chains at rear of mower. Move mower rearward and remove belt from crankshaft pulley. Place mower lift lever in highest position and slide mower out right side. Unbolt blade brake bracket (5) and remove belt.

Renew belt and reinstall mower by reversing removal procedure. Make certain that belt is correctly installed in belt guides as shown in Fig. IH13.

Models 60-75-85

ADJUSTMENT. The mower clutch is belt idler type. On Models 75 and 85, if mower clutch belt slips under normal operation, adjust belt as follows: Place mower lift lever in lowest position and engage mower clutch. Mark a pencil line on mower housing at front of each mounting bracket. Loosen front mounting bracket bolts (C-Fig. IH14) and move mower forward until a distance (D) of 1½ inches (38.1 mm) exists between inner sides of belt at idler pulley. Mower should be moved forward an equal distance on each side. Tighten mounting bracket bolts. Start engine and with mower lift lever in third position from bottom, check to see that mower clutch will engage and disengage properly.

On Model 60, when mower clutch control lever moves to position (C-Fig. IH15) when clutch is engaged, mower clutch belt should be adjusted. Position (C) is over front diamond on decal. To adjust clutch belt, move clutch control lever to the proper engaged position (B). Position (B) is directly over second diamond from front on decal. A wooden block may be used to hold lever in this position. With mower lift lever set in lowest position, loosen front mounting bracket bolts and move mower forward until belt tension will hold lever in position (B) when block is removed. Mower should be moved forward an equal distance on each side. Tighten mounting bracket bolts. Start engine and check to see that mower clutch will engage and disengage properly.

REMOVE AND REINSTALL. To remove mower clutch belt and blade spindle belt on Models 60, 75 or 85, place mower clutch control lever in disengaged position and set mower lift lever in lowest position. Unpin front of mower from lift arms and slide mower rearward so mower drive belt can be removed from engine crankshaft pulley. Remove belt from mower drive pulley. To remove blade spindle belt, unhook idler tension spring and move idler out of the way. Remove belt from spindle pulleys.

Install new blade spindle belt and attach idler tension spring. See Fig.

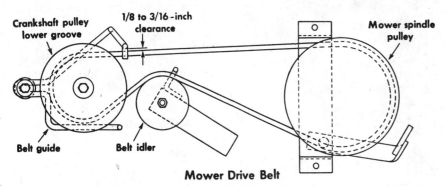

Fig. IH13—Mower drive belt installation on Models 55 and 85 Special. Note belt guide clearance.

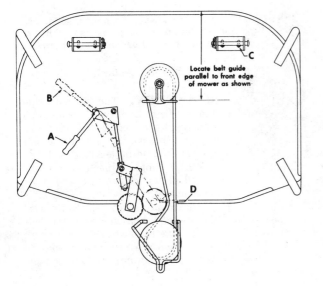

Fig. IH14—Mower drive clutch belt adjustment on Models 75 and 85.

A. Clutch disengaged
B. Clutch engaged
C. Front mounting bracket bolts
D. Correct distance is 1½ inches (38.1 mm)

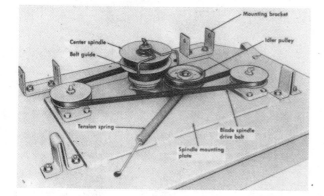

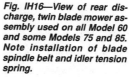

Fig. IH16—View of rear discharge, twin blade mower assembly used on all Model 60 and some Models 75 and 85. Note installation of blade spindle belt and idler tension spring.

IH16 or IH17. Install new mower drive clutch belt and reinstall mower on lift arms. Make certain belt is correctly installed on belt guides as shown in Fig. IH18. Adjust mower clutch belt as outlined in preceding ADJUSTMENT paragraph.

MOWER SPINDLE

All Models

LUBRICATION. Blade and center spindle bearings should be lubricated with No. 2 multi-purpose lithium grease when mower is disassembled and after each 10 hours of operation.

Models 55-85 Special

R&R AND OVERHAUL. To remove the single blade and blade spindle, first remove mower assembly as follows: Place mower blade clutch control lever in disengaged position. Set mower lift lever in lowest position and disconnect blade brake cable. Unpin front of mower and unhook chains at rear of mower. Move mower rearward and remove mower drive belt from crankshaft pulley. Place mower lift lever in highest position and slide mower out right side. Unbolt and remove blade brake bracket and belt. Place a wood block between blade and housing, then remove pulley retaining nut and mower pulley. Invert mower housing assembly, block the blade, then remove blade retaining nut, blade and spindle cup. See Fig. IH19. Unbolt and remove spindle assembly. Remove spindle housing (4-Fig. IH20) and spindle cap (2). Spindle shaft and bearing are available only as an assembly (3). Clean and inspect all parts and renew any showing excessive wear or other damage.

Reassemble mower by reversing disassembly. Tighten blade spindle nut to a torque of 55-60 ft.-lbs. (75-81 N·m). Reinstall mower and make certain mower drive belt is correctly installed in belt guides as shown in Fig. IH13.

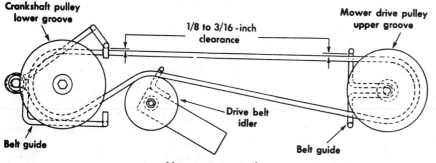

Fig. IH17—View of side discharge, twin blade mower assembly used on some 75 and 85 models.

1. Spindle cap
2. Pulley nut
3. Blade spindle drive belt
4. Belt guide
5. Idler tension spring

Crankshaft pulley lower groove

1/8 to 3/16 -inch clearance

Mower drive pulley upper groove

Drive belt idler

Belt guide

Belt guide

Mower Drive Belt

Fig. IH18—Mower drive clutch belt installation on Model 60, 75 or 85. Note belt guide clearance.

Models 60-75-85

R&R AND OVERHAUL. To remove the blades and spindles, first remove mower assembly as follows: Place mower blade clutch control lever in disengaged position and move mower lift lever to lowest position. Unpin front of mower from lift arms and slide mower rearward until lift arms are free of rear lift brackets. Remove mower clutch belt from mower drive pulley. Raise mower lift lever to highest position and slide mower out right side.

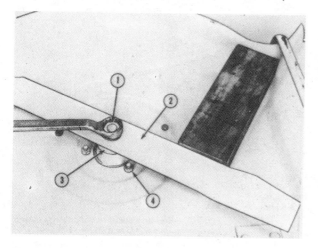

Fig. IH19—On Models 55 and 85 Special, place a wood block between blade and housing and remove blade retaining nut.

1. Blade retaining nut
2. Blade
3. Spindle cup
4. Spindle retaining nuts

On rear discharge mowers, unhook idler tension spring (18-Fig. IH21) and remove belt (15). Refer to Fig. IH23 and remove shaft bolt from center of each blade. Remove blades (14-Fig. IH21) and blade adapters (13). Unbolt and remove blade spindle assemblies from mower housing. Remove snap ring (11), washer (10) and withdraw pulley (3) and shaft (8). Remove lube fitting (1) and snap ring (2), then press shaft out of pulley. Remove thrust washers (4) and thrust bearing (5). Needle bearings (6) and oil seal (9) can now be pressed from spindle housing (7). When reassembling blade spindles, install oil seal (9) with lip towards washer (10). Torque blade shaft bolts to 57 ft.-lbs. (77 N·m).

To remove the center spindle assembly, refer to Fig. IH23 and remove center spindle jam nut. Lift center spindle assembly from mower. On Models 75 and 85, refer to Fig. IH22 and remove lube fitting (1), end bolt (3) and belt guide (2). Remove snap rings (4) and press shaft and bearing assembly (5) from pulley (6). If bearing is to be reused, press only on outer race. Shaft and bearing is available only as an assembly. On Model 60, refer to Fig. IH21 and remove lube fitting (31), end bolt (30) and belt guide (32). Remove pulley (29) with bearings from shaft (22). Remove spacers (24), oil seals (23), bearing cones (33), cups (28) and spacers (25, 26 and 27) from pulley. Renew parts as necessary and reassemble by reversing disassembly procedure. Install oil seals (23) with lips toward outside of pulley. Tighten center spindle jam nut to a torque of 185 ft.-lbs. (251 N·m). Reinstall blade spindle belt (15)

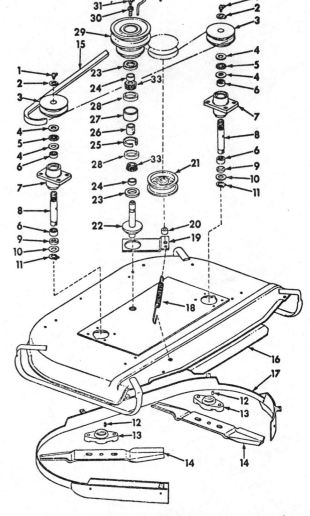

Fig. IH21—Exploded view of rear discharge mower assembly used on Model 60. Rear discharge mower used on Models 75 and 85 is similar. Refer to Fig. IH22.

1. Lube fitting
2. Snap ring
3. Blade pulley
4. Thrust washer
5. Thrust bearing
6. Needle bearing
7. Spindle housing
8. Blade spindle shaft
9. Oil seal
10. Thrust washer
11. Snap ring
12. Key
13. Blade adapter
14. Blade
15. Blade spindle belt
16. Mower housing
17. Shroud
18. Idler tension spring
19. Idler arm
20. Spacer
21. Idler pulley
22. Center spindle shaft
23. Oil seal
24. Spacer
25. Split outer spacer
26. Bearing spacer (inner)
27. Bearing spacer (outer)
28. Bearing cup
29. Center spindle pulley
30. End bolt
31. Lube fitting
32. Belt guide
33. Bearing cone

and hook idler tension spring (18) in hole in mower housing.

On side discharge mowers used on Models 75 and 85, unhook idler tension spring (14-Fig. IH24) and remove belt. Place a wood block between blades and mower housing, then remove pulley retaining nuts and pulleys (1). Invert mower housing assembly, block the blades (Fig. IH25) and remove blade retaining nuts (1), blades (19-Fig.

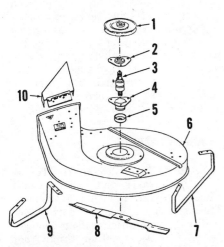

Fig. IH20—Exploded view of mower unit used on Models 55 and 85 Special.

1. Mower pulley
2. Spindle cap
3. Spindle shaft & bearing assy.
4. Spindle housing
5. Spindle cup
6. Mower housing
7. Mower runner L.H.
8. Blade 28"
9. Mower runner R.H.
10. Deflector

Fig. IH22—Center spindle assembly used on Models 75 and 85 rear discharge mower. Refer to Fig. IH21 for the balance of mower components.

1. Lube fitting
2. Belt guide
3. End bolt
4. Retaining ring
5. Shaft & bearing assy.
6. Center spindle pulley
7. Spacer
8. Idler arm

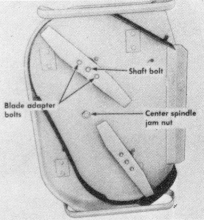

Fig. IH23—Bottom view of rear discharge mower used on Models 60, 75 and 85.

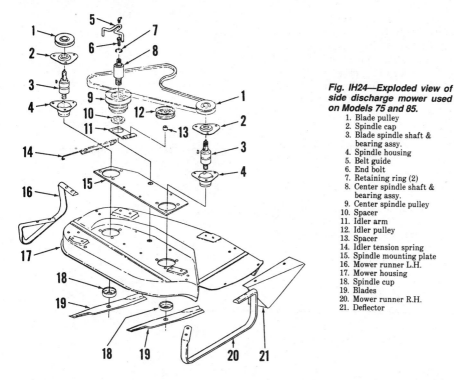

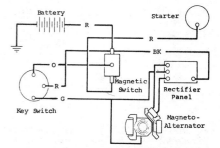

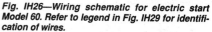

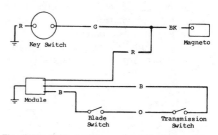

Fig. IH24—Exploded view of side discharge mower used on Models 75 and 85.

1. Blade pulley
2. Spindle cap
3. Blade spindle shaft & bearing assy.
4. Spindle housing
5. Belt guide
6. End bolt
7. Retaining ring (2)
8. Center spindle shaft & bearing assy.
9. Center spindle pulley
10. Spacer
11. Idler arm
12. Idler pulley
13. Spacer
14. Idler tension spring
15. Spindle mounting plate
16. Mower runner L.H.
17. Mower housing
18. Spindle cup
19. Blades
20. Mower runner R.H.
21. Deflector

Fig. IH26—Wiring schematic for electric start Model 60. Refer to legend in Fig. IH29 for identification of wires.

Fig. IH27—Typical wiring schematic for models with recoil start only. Refer to legend in Fig. IH29 for identification of wires.

IH24) and spindle cups (18). Unbolt and remove the blade spindle assemblies. Remove spindle caps (2) and spindle housings (4). Spindle shafts and bearings are available only as assemblies (3). Clean and inspect all parts and renew any showing excessive wear or other damage. When reassembling, tighten blade spindle nuts to a torque of 55-60 ft.-lbs. (75-81 N·m).

To remove the center spindle assembly, refer to Fig. IH25 and remove center spindle nut (4). Lift center spindle assembly from mower. Refer to Fig. IH24 and remove lube fitting, end bolt (6) and belt guide (5). Remove the two snap rings (7) and press shaft and bearing assembly (8) from pulley (9). Press only on outer race of bearing to prevent damage to bearing. Shaft and bearing are available only as an assembly (8). When reassembling, tighten center spindle jam nut (4-Fig. IH25) to a

torque of 185 ft.-lbs. (251 N·m). Reinstall blade spindle belt and hook idler tension spring (14-Fig. IH24) in hole in mower housing.

On all models, reinstall mower and make certain mower drive clutch belt is correctly installed in belt guides as shown in Fig. IH18.

MOWER DECK

Models 55-85 Special

LEVER ADJUSTMENT. Position unit on level surface, then disconnect spark plug wire. Measure distance from ground to blade from side to side and front to rear. Blade should be approximately ⅛-inch (3.2 mm) lower in front. Adjust front to rear by hooking rear hanger chains (2-Fig. IH12) in differ-

ent links or add 11/32-inch flat washers between mower deck and hanger chains. To adjust side to side, add washers between mower deck and front mounting bracket (1) and rear hanger chain (2) on side that measures high.

REMOVE AND REINSTALL. Place mower blade clutch control lever in disengaged position. Set mower lift lever in lowest position and disconnect blade brake cable. Unpin front of mower and unhook chains at rear of mower. Move mower rearward and remove mower drive belt from crankshaft pulley. Place mower lift lever in highest position and slide mower out right side.

Reinstall in reverse order of removal and make certain drive belt is correctly installed in belt guides as shown in Fig. IH13.

Models 60-75-85

LEVEL ADJUSTMENT. Position unit on level surface, then disconnect spark plug wire. Measure distance from ground to blade from side to side and front to rear. Blade should be approximately ⅛-inch (3.2 mm) lower in front. To adjust front to rear, add 11/32-inch washers between mower deck and front mounting brackets (Fig. IH16) or rear mounting brackets depending on which measures high. Note that front mounting brackets must be reinstalled in original positions to maintain proper drive belt adjustment. To adjust side to side, add washers between mower deck and front and rear mounting bracket on side that measures high.

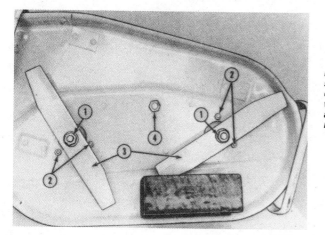

Fig. IH25—Bottom view of side discharge mower used on Models 75 and 85. Place a wood block between blade and mower housing when removing blade nut.

1. Blade retaining nut
2. Spindle retaining nuts
3. Blades
4. Center spindle nut

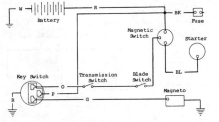

Fig. IH28—Typical wiring schematic for models with electric start only. Refer to legend in Fig. IH29 for identification of wires.

REMOVE AND REINSTALL.

Place mower blade clutch control lever in disengaged position and move mower lift lever to lowest position. Unpin front of mower from lift arms and slide mower rearward until lift arms are free of rear lift brackets. Remove mower clutch belt from mower drive pulley. Raise mower lift lever to highest position and slide mower out right side.

Reinstall in reverse order of removal and make certain drive belt is correctly installed in belt guides as shown in Fig. IH18.

ELECTRICAL

All Models

Some models are equipped with safety interlock switches on transmission shift linkage and blade clutch control linkage. The transmission must be in neutral and blade clutch disengaged be-

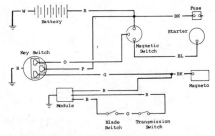

Fig. IH29—Typical wiring schematic for models with electric and recoil start.

1. G-Green
2. R-Red
3. O-Orange
4. P-Purple
5. W-White
6. B-Brown
7. BL-Blue
8. BK-Black

fore unit will start. Refer to Fig. IH26, IH27, IH28 or IH29.

INTERNATIONAL HARVESTER

Model	Engine		Cutting
	Make	Horsepower	Width, In.
Cadet 95	Electric Motor	1	32

FRONT AXLE

REMOVE AND REINSTALL. To remove axle main member (5–Fig. IH40), support front of unit and remove front wheels. Disconnect drag link (8–Fig. IH41) from right spindle (7–Fig. IH40). Remove axle center pivot bolt and lower axle assembly from chassis. Remove tie rod assembly, then unbolt and remove spindle (1 and 7). Inspect nylon bushings (2 and 4) and spacers (3 and 6) for excessive wear and renew as necessary. Reassemble by reversing disassembly procedure and adjust tie rod for 0 to 1/16-inch (0-1.6 mm) toe-in.

STEERING GEAR

REMOVE AND REINSTALL. To remove the steering gear assembly (Fig. IH41), remove cotter pin and washer from lower end of steering shaft (12). Remove the three cap screws and withdraw covers (9 and 10) and quadrant gear (6). Drive out roll pin and remove upper shaft (14) and steering wheel (1) from steering shaft (12). Raise front of unit and withdraw steering shaft and pinion (12). Remove drag link end (7) from quadrant gear. Clean and inspect all parts and renew any showing excessive wear or other damage. When reassembling, lubricate steering gears and bushings with No. 2 multi-purpose lithium grease. With steering wheel and front wheels in straight ahead position, center teeth of quadrant gear (6) should be engaged with pinion gear.

TRACTION DRIVE ELECTRIC MOTOR

Three 12 volt batteries (Fig. IH43) connected in series provide 36 volts D.C. for operation of traction and blade motors. The traction motor is protected from overload by a thermal switch in brush holder assembly and a 100 amp circuit fuse. Refer to Fig. IH42 and IH43.

REMOVE AND REINSTALL. Remove mower as outlined in MOWER DECK paragraphs and remove mower body as follows: Lift off battery cover shroud and disconnect and remove batteries and mounting plate. Drive out roll pin and remove steering wheel and upper steering shaft. Disconnect and remove clutch-brake pedal. Remove gear shift knob. Remove body mounting bolts and note location of body spacers. Raise body and disconnect wiring harness from traction motor and blade motor switches. Move mower lift handle to highest position, then raise body clear of handle and remove body.

Loosen drive pulley belt guide and slip drive belt off pulley. Remove snap ring and drive pulley from motor shaft. Remove motor end cover and disconnect wires from terminals. Unbolt and remove motor.

Reinstall by reversing removal procedure. Refer to Fig. IH44 for location of wires.

OVERHAUL. Clamp flat portion of armature in a vise. Remove through bolts and pry end frame off armature end bearing. Pull motor housing off armature with a quick upward thrust. Press armature and bearing from drive end frame. Clean and inspect all parts and renew any showing excessive wear or damage. Check armature for open or short circuits.

NOTE: When installing motor housing, hold housing by sides only. The magnets will pull motor housing down sharply against end plate as it goes over the armature.

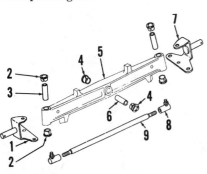

Fig. IH40—Exploded view of front axle assembly.

1. Spindle L.H.	6. Spacer
2. Nylon bushing	7. Spindle R.H.
3. Spacer	8. Ball joint end
4. Nylon bushing	(2 used)
5. Axle main member	9. Tie rod

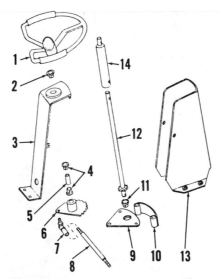

Fig. IH41—Exploded view of typical steering gear assembly.

1. Steering wheel	8. Drag link
2. Nylon bushing	9. Bottom cover
3. Steering support	10. Front cover
4. Nylon bushing	11. Nylon bushing
5. Spacer	12. Steering shaft &
6. Quadrant gear	pinion
7. Ball joint end	13. Shroud
(2 used)	14. Upper shaft

COMPONENTS MOUNTED ON TRACTOR

TRACTION MOTOR SWITCH

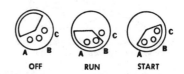

OFF   RUN   START

BLADE MOTORS SWITCH

OFF   RUN   START

Fig. IH42—View of switches showing operating positions.

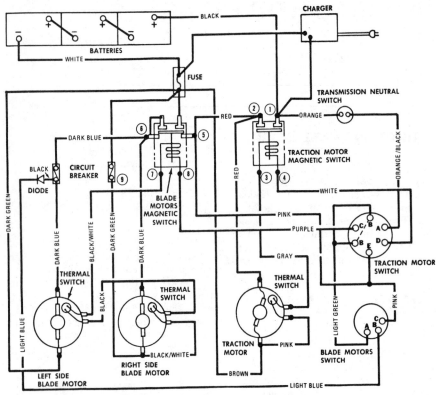

Fig. IH43—Schematic of electrical system for traction motor and blade motors.

mower control switch off. Remove mower deck as outlined in MOWER DECK paragraphs. Remove traction motor pulley belt guide (3–Fig. IH45) and loosen transmission pulley belt guides (1). Remove idler pulley (5) and remove drive belt (6).

Renew belt by reversing removal procedure and adjust belt guides to clearance ""B" shown in Fig. IH45.

TRANSMISSION

REMOVE AND REINSTALL. Remove the mower as outlined in MOWER DECK paragraphs and remove mower body as follows: Lift off battery cover shroud and disconnect and remove batteries and mounting plate. Drive out roll pin and remove steering wheel and upper steering shaft. Disconnect and remove clutch-brake pedal. Remove gear shift knob. Remove body mounting bolts and note location of body spacers. Raise body and disconnect wiring harness from traction motor and blade motor switches. Move mower lift handle to highest position, then raise body clear of handle and remove body.

Remove the traction drive belt as previously outlined and remove snap ring and drive pulley from transmission shaft. Loosen rear axle bearing mounting bolts to loosen drive chain and remove chain from transmission sprocket. Disconnect transmission neutral start switch wiring. Disconnect

Reassemble in reverse order of disassembly. Push brushes back into holder and rest spring against brush to hold in position. Install commutator end plate part way, then use a small screwdriver to push the brushes in against the commutator.

freely within drive belt. No adjustment is required; if belt is worn or stretched to a point where slippage occurs, belt must be renewed.

REMOVE AND REINSTALL. Turn traction motor key switch and

TRACTION DRIVE CLUTCH AND DRIVE BELT

The traction drive clutch is spring-tensioned, belt idler type operated by clutch-brake pedal on left side. When pedal is depressed, belt tension is removed, allowing drive pulley to rotate

Fig. IH45—Top view of traction drive belt installation. Note belt guide clearance "B" of 1/8 to 3/16 inch between guide and outside surface of belt or pulley.

1. Belt guides
2. Traction motor drive pulley
3. Belt guide
4. Belt guide
5. Idler pulley
6. Drive belt
7. Transmission pulley

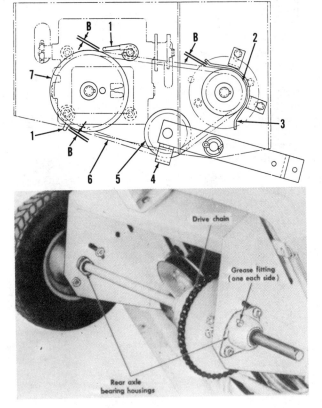

Fig. IH46—Rear axle assembly is pivoted rearward to tighten drive chain.

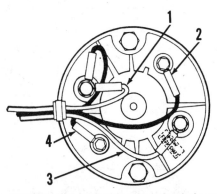

Fig. IH44—View of traction motor electrical connections. Note red wire is attached to post marked +CCW.

1. Brown wire to 100 amp fuse
2. Gray wire to magnetic switch
3. Red wire to post marked +CCW
4. Pink wire to brown wire on post No. 1

brake rod and return spring from brake actuating lever. Unbolt and remove transmission.

OVERHAUL. A Foote model transmission is used. For overhaul procedure refer to Foote paragraphs in TRANSMISSION REPAIR section of this manual.

DRIVE CHAIN

R&R AND ADJUST. To remove chain (Fig. IH46), rotate differential sprocket to locate master link. Disconnect master link and remove chain. Clean and inspect chain and renew if excessively worn. Reinstall in reverse order of removal.

The rear axle bearing mounting plates are slotted so axle assembly can be pivoted to adjust chain tension. Loosen axle bearing mounting bolts and move both sides equally until chain has ⅛ to ¼-inch (3.2-6.4 mm) slack, then tighten mounting bolts. Lubricate with light coat of SAE 30 oil.

DIFFERENTIAL

REMOVE AND REINSTALL. To remove rear axle and differential assembly (Fig. IH46), raise rear of unit and support securely. Remove rear

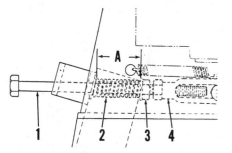

Fig. IH47—Brake adjusting bolt located near traction drive idler pulley. Adjust bolt until spring length "A" is 1-1/2 inches (38.1 mm).
1. Adjusting bolt
2. Spring
3. Jam nut
4. Clevis

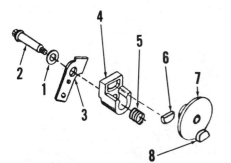

Fig. IH48—Exploded view of disc brake assembly.
1. Washer
2. Shoulder bolt
3. Cam lever
4. Caliper
5. Spring
6. Brake pad (outer)
7. Brake disc
8. Brake pad (inner)

wheels and washers. Note location of washers. They must be reinstalled in original positions to maintain proper drive chain alignment. Unbolt and remove axle bearings. Remove drive chain from differential sprocket and remove differential and axle from frame.

Reinstall by reversing removal procedure. When installing wheels and washers, be sure washers are assembled in original order to maintain drive chain alignment. Check rear axle end play. If end play is more than ⅛ inch (3.2 mm), add washers to outside of wheels, starting with right side, until end play is less than ⅛ inch (3.2 mm). Rear axle bearing mounting holes are slotted so axle can be pivoted to adjust drive chain. Adjust both sides equally until chain has ⅛ to ¼ inch (3.2-6.4 mm) slack, then tighten mounting bolts. Lubricate axle bearings with No. 2 multi-purpose lithium base grease and apply light coat of SAE 30 oil to chain.

GROUND DRIVE BRAKE

The brake is a caliper type disc brake located on output shaft of transmission. The brake is operated by clutch-brake pedal located on left side.

ADJUSTMENT. To adjust brake, lock clutch-brake pedal in fully depressed position. Loosen jam nut on clevis (4-Fig. IH47), located near drive belt idler pulley, and adjust brake adjusting bolt (1) until spring length "A" is 1½ inches (38.1 mm). Tighten jam nut on clevis and recheck brake operation.

R&R AND OVERHAUL. To remove the disc brake, disconnect brake rod from cam actuating lever (3-Fig. IH48). Remove the shoulder bolt (2) and remove brake parts (1 through 6). Slide disc (7) from transmission shaft and remove inner brake pad (8) from holder slot in transmission housing. Clean and inspect all parts for excessive wear or other damage. Renew parts as required

Fig. IH49—Twin blade mower and lift linkage.
1. Front mower bracket
2. Lift arm
3. Rear hanger bracket
4. Blade motors
5. Lift chains
6. Eyebolt
7. Lift linkage

and reassemble by reversing the removal procedure. Adjust brake as outlined in the preceding paragraph.

MOWER DECK

LEVEL ADJUSTMENT. Position unit on level surface and turn traction and blade motor switches off. Measure distance from ground to blade from side to side and front to rear. Blade should be approximately ⅛-inch (3.2 mm) lower in front. To adjust front to rear, loosen clevis jam nuts on leveling arms (2-Fig. IH49). Remove pin from one clevis at a time and adjust as needed. To adjust side to side, loosen nut securing lift chain eyebolt (6) to mower deck, depending on which side measures high, and adjust bolt as necessary.

REMOVE AND REINSTALL. Turn traction and blade motor off and lower mower to lowest position. Disconnect electrical connectors at each motor (4- Fig. IH49). Disconnect lift chains (5) and remove pin from front mower bracket (1). Disconnect lift arms (2) from rear hanger brackets (3), and slide mower out.

Reinstall in reverse order of removal. Place height control lever in lowest position. Be sure electrical connectors are properly installed.

BLADE DRIVE ELECTRIC MOTORS

Two electric motors (Fig. IH43) are used on the twin blade mower with the blades bolted directly to motor shaft. The blade motors are protected by circuit breakers and thermal switches. If either switch opens, the blade motor magnetic switch contact points open by spring action and short circuit blade motors providing a braking action.

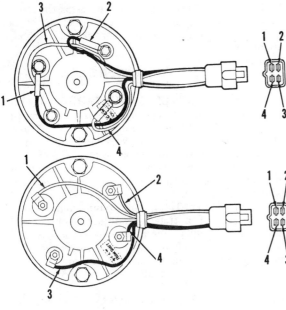

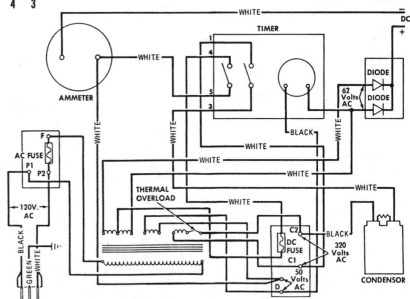

Fig. IH50—Blade motor electrical connections. Note blue wire connects to terminal marked +CCW.
1. Green wire
2. Black w/white tracer wire
3. Black wire
4. Blue wire

R&R BATTERY CHARGER. Remove the mower body as follows: Lift off battery cover shroud and disconnect and remove batteries and mounting plate. Drive out roll pin and remove steering wheel and upper steering shaft. Disconnect and remove clutch-brake pedal. Remove gear shift knob. Remove body mounting bolts and note location of body spacers. Raise body and disconnect wiring harness from traction motor and blade motor switches. Move mower lift handle to highest position, then raise body clear of handle and remove body.

Disconnect the D.C. leads to the circuit and remove the charger. Reinstall in reverse of removal.

REMOVE AND REINSTALL.
Remove mower as outlined in MOWER DECK paragraphs. Remove mower blades. Remove mounting bolts and slide motor out bottom of mower deck.

Reinstall motor by reversing removal procedure. Be sure motor is wired correctly. Refer to Fig. IH50. Torque blade nut to 45-55 ft.-lbs. (61-75 N·m).

ELECTRICAL

TESTING ELECTRICAL SYSTEM. Refer to Fig. IH42 and IH43. If traction motor fails to run, check the following: Check batteries and cable connections. Check continuity of 100 amp fuse. Traction motor magnetic switch should "click" when key switch is turned to start position. If click is not heard, check continuity of transmission neutral switch, key switch, magnetic switch and thermal switch. If click is heard, magnetic switch is defective or traction motor has internal damage. If motor starts but will not continue to run when switch is released to on position, the key switch is defective.

If blade motors fail to run, check the following: Traction motor circuit must be functional before blade motors will operate. Blade motor magnetic switch should "click" when blade motor switch is turned to start position. If click is not heard, check continuity of blade motor switch, blade magnetic switch, motor thermal switches and circuit breakers. If click is heard, magnetic switch is defective or blade motors have internal damage. If motors start but do not continue to run when switch is released to run position, the diode or blade motor switch is defective.

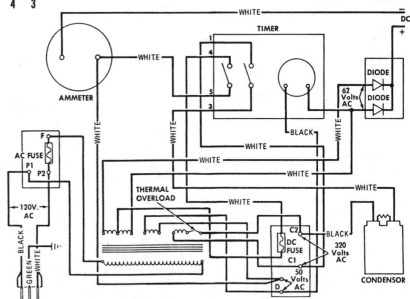

Fig. IH51—Wiring schematic for battery charger used on units with serial number 8921 and below.

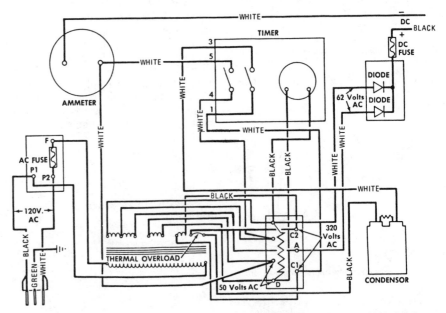

Fig. IH52—Wiring schematic for battery charger used on units with serial number 8922 and above.

JACOBSEN

JACOBSEN DIVISION OF TEXTRON INC.
1721 Packard Avenue
Racine, WI 53403-9988

Model	Make	Engine Model	Horsepower	Cutting Width, In.
42635*	B&S	130000	5	25
42636(526)	B&S	130000	5	26
42638	B&S	130000	5	26
42641	B&S	130000	5	26
42642	B&S	130000	5	26
Mark II				
43010	B&S	140000	6	30
43015	B&S	170000	7	30
43020	B&S	170000	7	30
Mark III				
43025	B&S	190000	8	30
43026	B&S	190000	8	30
43027	B&S	190000	8	30
43030	B&S	190000	8	30
43031	B&S	190000	8	30
43032	B&S	190000	8	30
43036	B&S	190000	8	30
43037	B&S	190000	8	30
43042	B&S	190000	8	30
43043	B&S	190000	8	30
RMX8	B&S	190000	8	30
RMX11	B&S	250000	11	30

*Gear drive model—all others, friction drive.

STEERING SYSTEM

All Models

For all models except RMX models steering is conventional and nonadjustable, with a center-mounted, lever-type steering shaft. Most models are fitted with a steering wheel (1–Fig. J1); however, Models 42636 and 42638 are equipped with a steering handle (2). Model 43635 (not shown) has a center-pivoted front axle. All others have their steering spindles (14) mounted in front support (10) with steering shaft (12). Pivot action of front end to allow for side-to-side twist is by rotation of frame tube in bushings (37). Single steering link (13) serves as a tie rod between spindles (14).

Lubrication of front wheel bushings, shouldered spindle bushings, steering shaft and wear points in linkage calls for use of SAE 30 engine oil. Wipe off excess to prevent dirt accumulation.

For RMX models Fig. J1A shows complete view of front steering components. By turning steering wheel, pinion gear (1–Fig. J1B) will rotate steering sector outer ring (2) on center bolt from side-to-side. Steering bracket (3) will move causing steering spindles (44–Fig. J1A) to pivot front wheels.

Periodically lubricate front wheel assemblies through grease fittings on inside of each wheel hub with a general purpose grease.

CAUTION: On some models the performance of maintenance, adjustment or repair operations is more convenient if mower is standing upright. This procedure can be considered a recommended practice providing the following safety recommendations are performed:

1. Drain fuel tank or make certain that fuel level is low enough so that fuel will not drain out.
2. Close fuel shut-off valve if so equipped.
3. Remove battery on models so equipped.
4. Disconnect spark plug wire and tie out of way.
5. Although not absolutely essential, it is recommended that crankcase oil be drained to avoid flooding the combustion chamber with oil when engine is tilted.
6. Secure mower from tipping by lashing unit to a nearby post or overhead beam.

For repair procedures refer to the following paragraphs.

R&R AND OVERHAUL (All Models Except RMX Models). With mower on its rear stand, carefully inspect for wear or damage to parts of steering gear, then disassemble as follows:

Remove hub caps (17–Fig. J1), cotter pins and wheels. Set wheel washers (16) and dust shields (15) aside with wheels. Clean thoroughly and determine need for renewal of any parts, especially wheel bearings (bushing type) or dust shields. Steering link assembly (13) can be removed after cotter pins are pulled at spindle ends. Use a small pin punch to drive out roll pins at top of steering spindles (14). Lower spindles out of place and carefully check condition of shouldered bushings (19 and 21) for possible renewal.

On models with steering wheel, drive out roll pin for removal. Unbolt steering handle of models so equipped. Lower steering shaft (12) out of front platform and check bushings (6).

NOTE: On Model 42635, disassembly is similar except that an axle is used, and the unit must be raised and blocked for service, not set up on a rear stand.

Renew all damaged or defective parts and reassemble by reversal of disassembly procedure. Lubricate, using SAE 30 engine oil.

(RMX Models). Remove eight lock nuts retaining front axle pivot shaft and bearing halves (45-Fig. J1A). Remove ball bushing retaining bolt securing steering sector outer ring (2-Fig. J1B) to steering bracket (3). Remove axle assembly (46-Fig. J1A), spindles (44) and steering bracket (42) as a complete unit.

Complete disassembly and inspect all parts for excessive wear or any other damage. Renew all parts as needed and reassemble in reverse order of disassembly. Reinstall front steering unit and lubricate all pivoting joints with a suitable lubricant.

ENGINE

All Models

Refer to appropriate engine section in this manual for tune-up specifications, engine overhaul procedures and engine maintenance.

Refer to the following paragraphs for removal and installation procedures.

All Models Except 42635 and RMX

REMOVE AND REINSTALL. To remove engine, disconnect spark plug lead, and disconnect battery cables on electric start models. Remove cover plate (6-Fig. J10) after mower engagement lever (4) is set in OFF position. Remove idler arm belt guide bolt (15) from idler arm (17) and release belt from idler pulley (13). Manually release cutter brake (7 and 8) so that brake pad (10) will clear sheave and remove belt from cutter spindle pulley. Remove belt by pulling to the rear.

Now, remove rear panel (19-Fig. J2). It will be noted that during removal of this panel that one of the bolts also serves to anchor top end of chain case support spring. Prior to unbolting, it is advisable to release this spring from chain case bearing shaft. Take care not to lose the damper tube fitted over this spring on most models. Also, remove lock nut (68-Fig. J4) from rear end of brake shaft (71) which is likewise fitted through rear panel. After rear panel has been removed, slip mower drive belt rearward and clear of the drive disc on engine crankshaft. Remove stiffener (29-Fig. J2) which reinforces and blocks

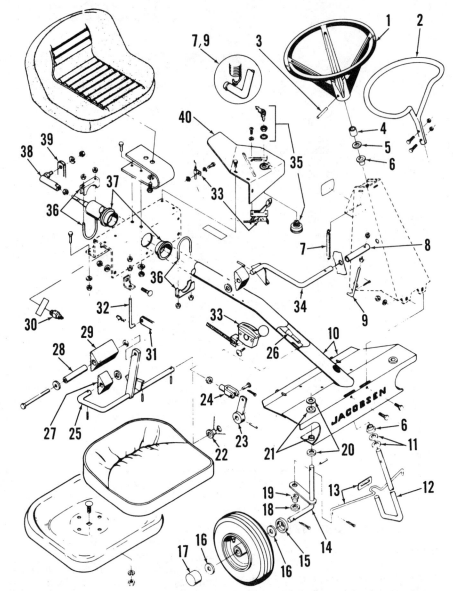

Fig. J1—Exploded view of steering system with drive, brake and operating controls, typical of all models except 42635.

1. Steering wheel	12. Steering shaft	22. Treadle bushing (2)	32. Support rod
2. Steering handle	13. Steering link assy.	23. Drive treadle lever	33. Throttle control
3. Roll pin (¼ X2)	14. Spindle RH	24. Push rod clevis	34. Neutral brake pedal
4. Spacer	15. Dust shield (2)	25. Treadle assy.	35. Ignition switch**
5. Washer	16. Wheel washer (4)	26. Push rod	36. Tube clamp (2)
6. Shaft bushing (2)	17. Hub cap	27. Reverse/brake pedal	37. Tube bushing (2)
7. Brake return spring	18. Washer, ⅜ (2)	28. Spacer bushing	38. Control ball joint
8. Brake tube	19. Steering link	29. Forward control	39. Control lever
9. Brake rod	bushing (2)	pedal	40. Control panel
10. Frame tube/	20. Spindle washer (2)	30. Ignition switch*	
front support	21. Spindle bushings (2)	31. Deck lift arm	*Manual start
11. Washers (2)			**Electric start

rear of crankshaft slot in rear platform (7).

Carefully check all other items connected to engine. Disconnect safety interlock module (1) at engine and the black cable from starter solenoid to engine starting motor on models so equipped. Disconnect throttle control cable (33-Fig. J1) at carburetor and be sure that ignition and interlock grounding wires are disconnected at engine end.

Unbolt engine from rear platform (7-Fig. J2) then slide rearward and out of

crankshaft slot in platform. Note assembly order of eight mounting washers (30) and placement of belt guide (23).

Reinstall engine by reversing removal procedure. Check control adjustments before returning mower to operation.

Model 42635

REMOVE AND REINSTALL. To remove engine, unbolt and remove operator's seat for easier access to en-

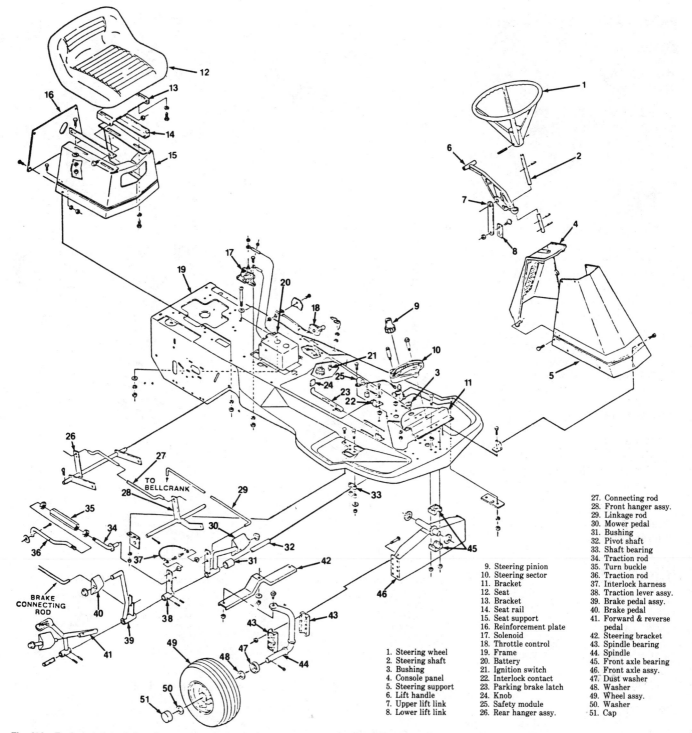

Fig. J1A—Exploded view of chassis, steering and linkage components for RMX models. Parts 17 and 20 are used only on electric start models.

1. Steering wheel
2. Steering shaft
3. Bushing
4. Console panel
5. Steering support
6. Lift handle
7. Upper lift link
8. Lower lift link
9. Steering pinion
10. Steering sector
11. Bracket
12. Seat
13. Bracket
14. Seat rail
15. Seat support
16. Reinforcement plate
17. Solenoid
18. Throttle control
19. Frame
20. Battery
21. Ignition switch
22. Interlock contact
23. Parking brake latch
24. Knob
25. Safety module
26. Rear hanger assy.
27. Connecting rod
28. Front hanger assy.
29. Linkage rod
30. Mower pedal
31. Bushing
32. Pivot shaft
33. Shaft bearing
34. Traction rod
35. Turn buckle
36. Traction rod
37. Interlock harness
38. Traction lever assy.
39. Brake pedal assy.
40. Brake pedal
41. Forward & reverse pedal
42. Steering bracket
43. Spindle bearing
44. Spindle
45. Front axle bearing
46. Front axle assy.
47. Dust washer
48. Washer
49. Wheel assy.
50. Washer
51. Cap

gine compartment. Pull starter cord out and, while extended, remove T-handle. Then, carefully allow cord to retract under cover and tie a knot to prevent wind-up of cord into manual starter. Remove rear cover from engine housing. Disconnect spark plug lead. Unbolt engine brace (1–Fig. J3) and disconnect throttle cable at carburetor. Remove

safety interlock grounding wires from engine.

Remove all belts, as follows: Set mower lift lever in ENGAGED position, and lock parking brake; then, remove belt keeper from right side of engine belt guard (30) and remove nut which retains mower clutch idler support (42) on left side. Remove belt keep-

ers and shoulder bolt from mower deck, disengage lift lever and remove belt from spindle pulley (39). Unbolt and remove belt guard (30). Back off nut from variable speed pulley shaft, then nut from transmission input shaft. Take care not to lose key or washers. Remove cap screw from end of engine crankshaft, then carefully remove belts

Fig. J1B—View of front steering sector components for RMX models.
1. Pinion gear
2. Outer ring
3. Steering bracket

and pulleys together. Take care not to lose engine pulley-to-crankshaft key. Unbolt and remove engine.

Reverse removal procedure to reinstall engine in mower chassis.

Model RMX

REMOVE AND REINSTALL. Stand unit upright and remove mower drive belt as follows: Disconnect counterbalance spring (2–Fig. J2A) from bottom cover (3). Move lift handle selector to lowest position. Remove front hanger bracket shoulder bolt and lower mower deck until rear portion rests on rear wheels. Loosen two spindle pulley belt guides (1–Fig. J2B), then remove belt from idler pulley. Rotate clutch arm (2) away from spindle pulley, then lift belt off pulley. Depress forward pedal until drive wheel (1–Fig. J2C) clears edge of retainer (2) on drive disc. Remove belt from engine drive pulley and slip belt between drive wheel and disc.

Remove crankshaft bolt and washers securing engine drive disc (3) and pulley (4) assembly. Withdraw drive assembly from engine crankshaft. Lower mower unit, then remove all engine attaching cables, wires and any other component that will obstruct engine removal. Remove engine mounting bolts and nuts, then lift engine clear of unit.

After repair of engine, reassemble in reverse order of disassembly.

FRICTION–DRIVE CLUTCH

Function of the friction drive clutch is to essentially place friction drive parts in a neutral or no-drive attitude

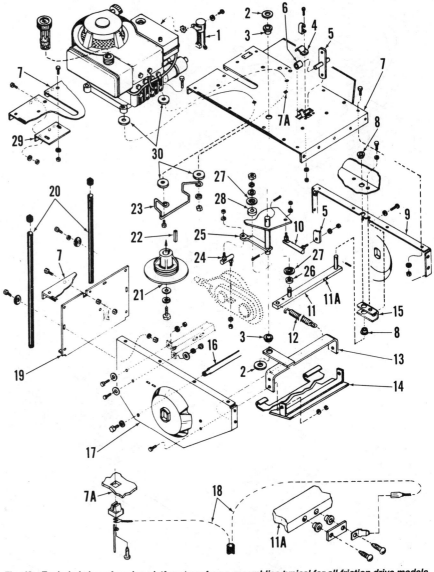

Fig. J2—Exploded view of engine platform/rear frame assemblies typical for all friction drive models.

1. Safety interlock module	7. Rear platform	15. Pivot bracket	23. Belt guide
2. Washer	8. Support bushing (2)	16. Tie rod	24. Ball joint link (180°)
3. Control cam bushing	9. Side plate LH	17. Side plate RH	25. Control cam assy.
4. Bushing clamp	10. Ball joint link (90°)	18. Interlock leads	26. Spacer
5. Control lever	11. Roller support assy.	19. Rear panel	27. Cam follower guide
6. Control lever bushing (2)	12. Drive cam spring	20. Rear stand tubes	28. Roller bearing
	13. Cross brace	21. Pulley/drive disc	29. Stiffener
	14. Drive shield	22. Crankshaft key	30. Mounting washer (8)

when not in drive-forward or drive-reverse.

All Models Except RMX

ADJUSTMENT. If slippage occurs and it becomes evident that forward or reverse drive is ineffective, or if there is noise chatter or drag in neutral, place unit on rear stand as previously outlined and proceed as follows:

Block or lash forward-reverse pedal in full FORWARD position which will shift and hold chain case and driven roller at right. Check for ⅜-inch (9.5 mm) clearance between chain case roller (59–Fig. J4) and angle-iron rail which supports neutral cam (60). Also

see Fig. J5. If clearance is not correct, loosen rail mounting screws in right hand side plate to adjust, then retighten. Now, depress reverse-drive pedal

Fig. J2A—View showing rear mower deck hanger assembly (1), counterbalance spring (2) and bottom plate (3) on RMX models.

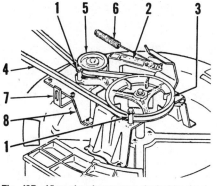

Fig. J2B—View showing mower deck drive components for RMX models.

1. Belt guide
2. Clutch arm
3. Spindle pulley
4. Drive belt
5. Idler pulley
6. Spring
7. Rear lift bracket
8. Support bracket

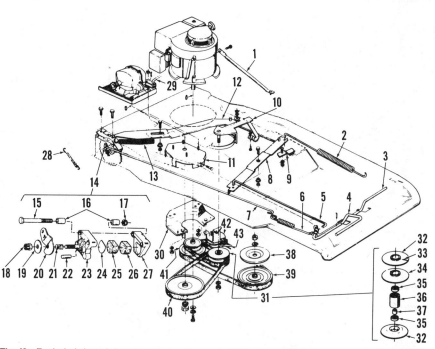

Fig. J3—Exploded view of chassis parts, traction control linkages, and belt arrangement for Model 42635.

1. Engine brace
2. Spring ¾ X11
3. Clutch pedal rod
4. Brake pedal rod
5. Link rod
6. Brake spring
7. Brake rod
8. Clutch bar
9. Blade brake
10. Guide bracket
11. Transmission belt guard
12. Variable drive arm
13. Variable drive spring
14. Disc brake assy.
15. Bridge bolt - 2½ (2)
16. Spacer (2)
17. Lock nut 5/16- 18
18. Lock nut ⅜-24
19. Washer
20. Brake cam lever
21. Cam spring
22. Push pin
23. Casting cam side
24. Back-up disc
25. Brake pad (0.450)
26. Brake pad (0.250)
27. Casting - inner
28. Brake return spring
29. Shift lever
30. Belt guard assy.
31. Variable speed pulley
32. Sheave half (2)
33. Spirol pin 5/32
34. Movable sheave
35. Ball bearing (2)
36. Steel tube
37. Spacer
38. Mower brake disc
39. Blade spindle pulley
40. Transmission pulley
41. Two-step engine pulley
42. Idler support
43. Idler

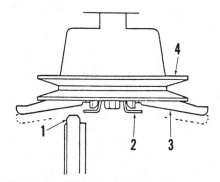

Fig. J2C—View showing drive wheel (1), retainer disc (2), drive disc (3) and drive pulley (4) on RMX models.

and secure by blocking at full RE-VERSE, then check for ⅜-inch (9.5 mm) clearance between chain case roller and rail at left hand side and adjust at left side mounting bolts if required. Release pedal to allow chain case to return to neutral position with case bearing centered on neutral cam. When in neutral, there must be 0.030-inch (0.76 mm) clearance between friction face of drive disc (21-Fig. J2) and rubber tread of driven disc (49-Fig. J4). Use feeler gage to measure. Rotate driven disc while checking to determine clearance at several points around disc circumference. To set required 0.030-inch (0.76 mm) clearance, loosen mounting bolts which attach neutral cam (60) to support rail, then shift cam plate for correct setting.

NOTE: Support rail is slotted at right angles to slots in cam plate. This will permit proper neutral centering (side-to-side) at the same time that vertical clearance of driven disc is being adjusted.

IMPORTANT: When making traction drive adjustment, carefully evaluate friction drive parts for condition. Drive disc on engine crankshaft must be smooth, clean and dry. Be especially watchful for oily film or a

slick, burnished surface. Clean thoroughly with a non-contaminating solvent, mineral spirits or denatured alcohol. Check driven disc on chain case for excessive wear, damaged rubber tread or flat spots. If driven disc is defective, unbolt drive wheel (49) from its hub (50) and renew; then, follow adjustment procedure outlined previously. Be sure to observe chain case and its neutral cam roller for wear, misalignment or lubricant leakage. Not if operating linkage functions without binding or excessive looseness. Do not return mower to service if there is an apparent problem in drive system.

R&R AND OVERHAUL (Sliding Chain Case). To remove chain case proceed as follows:

For convenience and to eliminate weight from up-ended mower, unbolt housing cover from cutting deck, remove mower drive belt, pull mower deck hanger shaft and suspension pins and remove mower from under chassis. Partially loosen bolts for right hand stand tube as this tube will be removed when right hand side plate is unbolted. Set unit up on stands as previously outlined, use some extra blocking (scrap 2 X 4 lumber will do) under rear panel to provide clearance above floor and lash

upper end so as to hold unit securely with most weight on left hand stand tube.

With freewheeling hub engaged (driving position) press inward on spring keeper (2-Fig. J4) to compress freewheeling lock spring (3) and remove snap ring (1) from axle end. Unbolt and remove wheel. When wheel has been removed so as to expose end of axle (13), carefully drive out roll pin (7) and remove hub (6), hub sleeve (8) and dust cap (9).

Disengage drive cam spring (12-Fig. J2) at its top end by reaching through frame and lifting upper hooked end from the hole which it engages in right hand side plate (17).

Now unbolt side plate (17) from rear platform (7) and from cross brace (13) which supports drive cam and roller support assembly (11), then unbolt right hand end of neutral cam support rail (7-Fig. J5). Back out screw from end of tie rod (16-Fig. J2), then loosen boot clamps (46-Fig. J4) on each side of chain case to release bellows (47). Disconnect spring (67) from chain case. Remove nut from ball joint link (24-Fig. J2) and swing ball joint away from chain case. Carefully lift off right hand

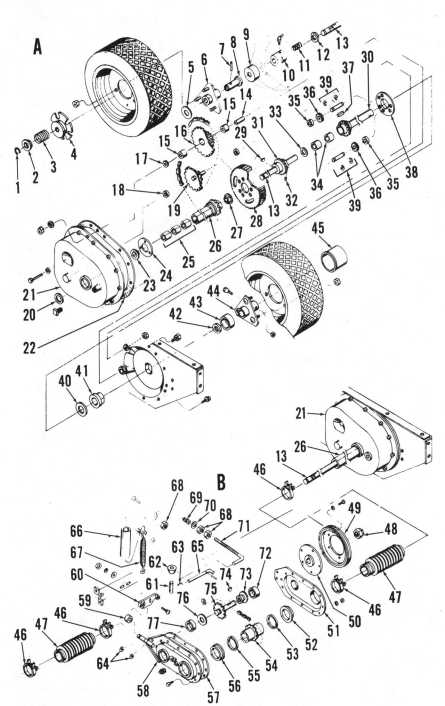

side plate, exposing chain case for removal.

NOTE: When side plate is being lifted away, hub seal spring (11—Fig. J4) and seal (12) with hex tube thrust washer (23) will usually remain inside bellows (47); however, they may fall out. Do not lose.

Chain case can now be slipped off right hand end of axle and hex sleeve (26). A light pull outward on axle will help chain case to clear linkage parts during removal.

Set chain case up in a well-padded vise with case roller bearing shaft secured in vise jaws. Use a strap wrench to hold rubber tread of driven disc against turning and back off flexloc nut from shaft. If no strap wrench (Jacobsen No. 545286) is on hand, a scrap of fabric or leather belt can be clamped in heavy pliers or vice grips to serve the purpose. After driven disc (49) and hub (50) are removed, pry Woodruff key (74) from recess in sprocket shaft (75). Unbolt case halves (51 and 58), noting that heads of all twelve assembly bolts are on driven disc side of chain case. Keep this in mind for reassembly. Because No. 3 Permatex is used on chain case gasket (57), case halves will not separate readily. Case halves may be forced apart by careful driving with a light hammer and drift on input shaft (75). However, the use of a strong, broad-bladed putty knife inserted into case joint will be less likely to damage parts. Carefully support case halves when separated and press or bump input shaft (75) lightly and remove chain, drive hex and sprocket (54), along with shaft.

Use clean solvent to thoroughly wash parts and case halves and carefully

Fig. J4—Exploded view of rear axle and JACOBSEN friction drive. View A shows differential, reduction gearing, axles and hub assemblies. View B shows differential case assembled and in place on left hand side plate with exploded view of variable drive chain case and parts.

1. Snap ring	21. Differential case	39. Pinion shaft/snap rings (6)
2. Spring keeper	22. Gasket	40. Thrust washer
3. Compression spring	23. Thrust washer	41. Axle bearing LH
4. Freewheeling hub	24. Sprocket thrust washer	42. Felt ring gasket
5. Hub washer	25. Bushing (3)	43. Dust cap LH
6. Rear hub, RH	26. Hex. sleeve & sprocket	44. Rear hub LH
7. Roll pin, 3/16X1¼	27. Thrust washer	45. Hub cap LH
8. Hub sleeve, RH	28. Differential gear	46. Boot clamp (4)
9. Dust cap	29. Woodruff key	47. Axle bellows (boot)
10. Axle hub w/grease fitting	30. Differential sleeve & gear	48. Lock nut ⅝-18
11. Hub seal spring	31. Sun gear	49. Drive wheel
12. Hub seal	32. Allen set screw	50. Hub
13. Axle shaft	33. Shim washer	51. Chain case, left half
14. Spacer bushing	34. Bushing (2)	52. Bushing
15. Bushing (2)	35. Pinion spacer (6)	53. Thrust washer
16. Gear & sprocket	36. Pinion gear (6)	54. Drive hex & sprocket
17. Thrust washer	37. Drive gear key	55. Thrust washer
18. Bushing	38. Differential plate	56. Bushing
19. Double sprocket		57. Chain case gasket
20. Case seal		

58. Chain case, right half	68. Nuts ¼ -20 (3)
59. Chain case roller	69. Brake rod spring
60. Neutral cam	70. Washer
61. Brake shaft	71. Brake rod
62. Brake	72. Drive wheel bearing
63. Roll pin ⅛ × ¾	73. Spacer/slinger
64. Snap rings	74. Woodruff key ⅛ × ½
65. Brake pivot shaft	75. Shaft & sprocket
66. Damper	76. Slinger
67. Spring	77. Drive wheel bearing

Fig. J5—View of adjustment points for friction drive. When in neutral, as shown, clearance between driven disc (3) and drive disc (4) on crankshaft must be 0.030 inch (0.76 mm). Refer to text for adjustment procedure.

1. Chain case roller	5. Neutral cam
2. Chain case	6. Mounting bolts
3. Driven disc	7. Cam support rail
4. Drive disc	

Illustrations Courtesy Jacobsen Division of Textron, Inc.

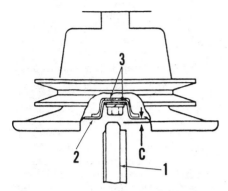

Fig. J5A—View showing drive clutch components on RMX models. clearance (C) distance between drive wheel 91) and retainer disc (2) should be between 0.02-0.04 inch (0.51-1 mm), adjust by washers (3).

examine all bearings, spacers, washers, slingers, chain and flanged bushings to determine if renewal is called for. If breakage, wear or dry galling of parts is evident, or if wear appears inside chain case, consider renewal of chain or sprockets. A new case gasket (57) must always be used.

Note parts arrangement in Fig. J4 and reassemble chain case as follows:

Apply gasket sealer to gasket flange of each chain case half, and position new gasket (57) on left side of chain case (51). Coat inside of each bearing boss with Loctite so that outer race of each drive wheel bearing (72 and 77) will be secure. Inner race of each bearing must also be coated to adhere to input shaft (75). Be sure that spacer is located on left side (keyway end) of shaft.

NOTE: Some earlier production models may not be equipped with grease slingers (73 and 76). In such cases, obtain JACOBSEN part number 351566 from parts outlet for installation.

Set shouldered bushing (52) in place, and assemble continuous chain on sprockets (54 and 75). Do not overlook thrust washer (53). Install complete assembly on left hand case half (51). Be sure that slinger (76) and thrust washer (55) are in place, then fit right hand case half over shaft ends, pressing carefully by hand until case flanges meet. DO NOT FORCE. Test by hand for freedom of movement of sprockets in bearings and bushings. Install case assembly bolts with heads on drive wheel side and tighten nuts alternately in a crisscross pattern to 55-85 inch-pounds (7-10 N·m). Again, check freedom of shaft rotation.

Lubricate with **no more** than 1½ ounces (0.04 kg.) of Fibrex grease through filler hole and install plug.

Reinstall driven disc and its bolt-on hub on input shaft, noting that Wood-

ruff key must be angled in its keyway to correspond with taper (slant) of keyway in hub. Torque retainer nut to 18-22 ft.-lbs. (24-30 N·m).

Chain case assembly can now be reinstalled in reverse of removal order.

(Differential Gear Case). If checkout of drive train indicates that drive problem is located in differential/final drive assembly, follow this order for gear case removal:

Remove mowing deck, and loosen left hand stand tube screws in preparation for removal. Raise mower up on rear stand as previously outlined, place extra blocking under rear panel and lash upper end so as to hold unit securely with most weight on right hand stand tube.

With freewheeling hub in drive position, press inward on spring keeper (2-Fig. J4), remove snap ring (1) and balance of freewheeling hub parts. Remove right rear wheel and when hub (6) is exposed, check condition of roll pin (7). If this roll pin has been sheared in axle (13), a no-drive condition will result. Renewal of pin may be a solution to a breakdown problem.

Now, remove left rear wheel from hub (44) and the bolt which attaches hub to differential sleeve (30) and remove hub.

Loosen outer boot clamps (46) so that hex shaft cover bellows (47) will be loose at each outboard end. Unbolt left hand side plate from rear platform (7-Fig. J2).

IMPORTANT: Loosen but DO NOT REMOVE bolt which holds pivot bracket (15) beneath engine platform, so that bracket will remain attached to platform when side plate (9) is unbolted and removed. Unbolt left side plate (9) from rear panel (19) and stand tube (20) at left side.

Unbolt left side plate (9) from cross brace (13) and back out cap screw from

left end of tie rod (16), then remove two bolts at left end of neutral cam support rail (7-Fig. J5). Differential case (21-Fig. J4) and left hand side plate with hex sleeve (26) and axle (13) can now be withdrawn outward and separated from bellows and chain case. Check inside right side bellows for loose parts from axle when withdrawn.

Disassemble chain case from left side plate as follows:

Secure hex sleeve in a well-padded vise so that side plate is horizontal, then unbolt from differential case (21). Gasket (22) will not be reusable. Remove through-bolt for bushing (14) and lift off side plate. Axle bearing (41) will remain with left side plate. Differential gears and reduction sprockets and chains will now be open for further service.

Lift thrust washer (40) from differential sleeve (30), then lift complete axle and differential assembly out of gear case and hex drive tube. Release hex tube from vise, and remove reduction sprocket (26) all together from differential gear case. Thoroughly wash all parts in solvent and clean fragments of gasket (22) from inner surface of side plate and from flange of case (21), then carefully check all parts for wear or damage.

If axle-differential assembly appears to be in good operating condition, further disassembly of its parts may be unnecessary; however, if there is any roughness in mesh of pinions or if there is a possibility that set screw (32) is loose in hub of sun gear (31) or that key (29 or 37) is damaged, further disassembly must be performed.

Set long axle (13) up in padded vise jaws with differential sleeve (30) upward as in Fig. J6. Remove retainers from each of six pinion shafts, then lift off differential sleeve (30-Fig. J4), followed by six pinions (36) and six spacers (35). Push pinion shafts (39) out and remove from under differential ring

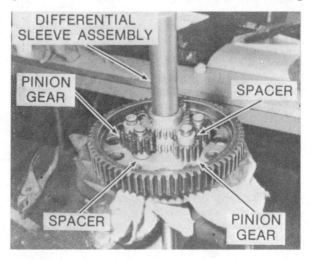

Fig. J6—View of axle-differential assembly removed from differential case. Note alternating arrangement of pinions and spacers. Refer to text for details.

gear (28). Remove gear (28) from hub of sun gear (31) and separate from axle (13).

When reassembling, check bushings (34) for wear and do not re-use if excessively loose on axle (13). Check condition of shim washer (33). If pinion shafts must be renewed, **press** new shafts into their six bores in ring gear (28). Carefully locate sun gear (31) on axle shaft (13), being sure that Woodruff key (29) is in place. Use Loctite on threads, and torque set screw (32) to 9-14 ft.-lbs. (12-19 N·m). Be sure that this (Allen) set screw does not extend above outer circumference of hub of sun gear (31). If set screw (32) is renewed, do not substitute a longer screw. When installing pinion gears (36) on pinion shafts (39), be sure that spacers (35) are arranged as shown in Fig. J6, in alternating order, with a pinion over spacer on every other shaft. ·

VERY IMPORTANT: When shim washer (33–Fig. J4) is reinstalled between sun gear (31) on axle (13) and sun gear of differential sleeve (30), ONE shim washer is usually sufficient. However, if both sun gears can contact teeth of the same pinion, differential will be locked up and not function. In such a case, use two shim washers during assembly to ensure that each sun gear contacts only three of the six pinion gears, alternate and opposite. Use Moly-grease on all differential gears, washers, spacers and shims during reassembly. After differential plate (38) is reinstalled over pinion shafts, differential sleeve and its sun gear (30), reinstall all six retainers on pinion shafts and set differential-axle assembly aside.

Reassemble differential gear case and reduction sprockets as follows:

Renew gear case seal (20) and use Loctite on its outer circumference to secure seal in shaft boss. Set differential sprocket thrust washer (24) in place inside case. Remove grease screw from hex sleeve and use a hand grease gun to preload hex sleeve with grease, then assemble drive chains on hex sleeve sprocket and reduction sprockets in this order: Longer of two continuous chains connects hex sleeve sprocket (26) to larger side of double sprocket (19). Shorter continuous chain runs between smaller side of double sprocket (19) and the sprocket portion of gear and sprocket (16). Install complete chain and sprocket assemblies with hex sleeve into gear case. Do not lose three bushings (25) and be sure that thrust washer (23) is in place at bottom of hex sleeve after fitting into case. Bushings (15) should be in place inside gear and sprocket (16) and bushing (14) and thrust washer (17) must be in place. Insert gear and sprocket mounting screw up through bushing (14) from

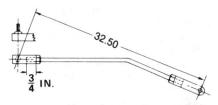

under gear case. Be sure that double sprocket (19) has its shaft portion squarely into bushing (18) in wall of gear case. Check for free movement of chains and sprockets, then carefully insert long axle (13) down through hex sleeve (26) and engage teeth of ring gear (28) with gear portion of gear and sprocket assembly (16). Again, check rotation by turning shaft slightly. Pour one pint (0.47L) of JACOBSEN gear lube, Part No. 500650, into open side of gear case. Install thrust washer (40) over shaft of differential sleeve and gear (30).

Now, apply No. 3 Permatex to gasket flange of gear case (21), install gasket (22), then coat face of gasket with Permatex.

Carefully align left hand side plate with differential case, and lower side plate into place over shaft of differential sleeve (30). Thread gear and sprocket mounting screw upwards through well in side plate and reinstall jam nut. Be sure that shaft of double sprocket is properly fitted into side plate. Reinstall all assembly bolts, check rotation of all exposed shafts for freedom of movement and tighten all case to side plate assembly bolts to 7-9 ft.-lbs. (10-12 N·m). torque in an alternating criss-cross pattern.

Before reinstalling side plate/gear case assembly on chassis, coat outer surface of hex sleeve with Molygrease along its entire length. This will ensure lubrication for easy side-to-side movement of sliding chain case.

Complete installation of side plate and differential case in reverse of removal order, then check adjustments as outlined in appropriate sections.

(Control Push Rod and Linkage). Drive controls are not adjustable, except as previously covered under CLUTCH. If it should occur that clutch adjustment cannot be made, even with a new rubber-faced driven disc and other parts apparently in order, a careful check should be made of all linkage parts as shown in Figs. J1 and J2. Pay particular attention to ball joints (10 and 24–Fig. J2), to bushings (3, 6 and 8)

and to cam roller bearing (28). If worn, loose or damaged,these items can cause trouble. Renew any which are defective.

If it is determined that control push rod (26–Fig. J1) is at fault, proceed as follows:

Remove cutting deck from under mower. At rear end of push rod, under operator's seat, remove nut from stud of ball joint (38) and separate rod from top end of control lever (39). Remove roll pin from hub of drive treadle lever (23) to release shaft of treadle assembly (25).

NOTE: Later Mark III models may have a set screw at this point. If so, loosen.

Slip pedal shaft out of treadle lever (23). Place mower on rear stand, as previously outlined. To gain access to push rod, front chassis tube will have to be removed from rear platform. On most models, if rearmost tube clamp (36) is removed, front of mower can be lifted clear of rear platform for removal. Some Mark III models require that seat bracket be unbolted and that a front end mounting plate be unbolted from rear platform. These same models must also have control panel unbolted from front console at steering column so that throttle cable and ignition switch wiring can be disconnected.

After front chassis tube is separated from rear platform, pull push rod from rear end of tube, then carefully measure working length of push rod from center of clevis yoke pin bore to center of ball joint stud as shown in Fig. J7. This length should be 32½ inches (825.5 mm). If a new push rod is installed, it is particularly important that this length be present before installing in chassis tube.

Reverse disassembly order to reinstall forward section of mower chassis, then check drive adjustments before returning unit to service.

Model RMX

ADJUSTMENT. Place forward-reverse pedal in "Neutral" position. Stand mower unit in upright position, observe safety precautions as outlined in earlier section. With a feeler gage measure clearance between top of rubber drive wheel (1–Fig. J5A) and bottom of retainer disc (2). Recommended clearance is between 0.02-0.04 inch (0.51-1 mm).

To change clearance distance, remove cap screw in crankshaft end. Reposition or add washers (3) above or below retainer (2) until correct clearance distance is attained. Retighten cap screw and lower unit.

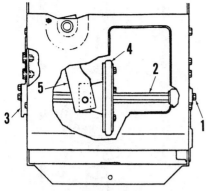

Fig. J7A—View showing clutch drive wheel and associated parts for RMX models.
1. Cap screw
2. Hex shaft
3. Traction arm
4. Drive wheel
5. Pivot shaft

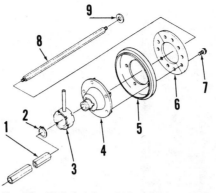

Fig. J7B—Exploded view of drive wheel assembly used on RMX models.
1. Hex slide
2. Snap ring
3. Sleeve & bearing assy.
4. Driven hub
5. Drive wheel
6. Plate
7. Cap screw
8. Hex shaft
9. Thrust washer

R&R AND OVERHAUL (Drive Wheel and Hex Shaft). While observing safety precautions as outlined in earlier section stand unit upright. Remove right rear wheel assembly, then remove cap screw (1–Fig. J7A) securing hex shaft assembly (2) on left side. Remove cap screws, lockwashers and nuts retaining traction arm (3) on right side. Withdraw traction arm, hex sleeve and shaft from right side of frame as an assembly. Be sure to note thrust washer located between hex sleeve and gear reducer housing. Disconnect and remove drive wheel assembly (4) from pivot shaft (5). Withdraw drive wheel assembly through access hole located in bottom plate.

With reference to Fig. J7B inspect and renew all parts that are excessively worn or damaged in any way. Inspect left frame bearing and traction arm bearing for binding or excessive wear, renew as needed. Reassemble in reverse order of disassembly. Refer to ADJUSTMENT section for adjustment procedures after reassembly.

(Gear Reducer). While observing safety precautions as outlined in earlier section stand unit upright. Remove drive wheel and hex shaft assembly as outlined in previous section. Locate and remove master link in drive chain (9–Fig. J7C), then remove chain from drive sprockets. Noting their location remove five cap screws securing gear housing to frame. Withdraw gear reduction assembly from mower unit.

With reference to Fig. J7C inspect parts 10 through 16 for excessive wear, roughness, broken teeth or any other damage. Renew all parts as needed and reassemble in reverse order of disassembly. Recommended gear box lubricant is two ounces of Kendall Kenlube L424 or a suitable Moly E.P. No. 2 Lithium grease.

(Differential). While observing safety precautions as outlined in earlier section stand unit upright, then remove both rear wheels. Disconnect rear hanger (1–Fig. J2A) counterbalance spring (2) and remove bottom cover (3). Remove two cap screws, washers and nuts securing right tube assembly and withdraw tube from axle shaft. Loosen cap screws and nuts retaining right bearing strap (18–Fig. J7C), then remove right differential bearing assembly (3) from frame. For reassembly, be sure to note location of spacer washers (2). Locate and remove master link in drive chain (9), then remove chain from drive sprockets. Remove cap screws and nuts retaining left bearing strap (18). Remove bolts securing left differential bearing to frame. Remove cap screws securing frame support (25), then withdraw support from mower frame. Lift differential assembly out left frame slot and slide shaft out right side.

Complete differential disassembly with reference to Fig. J7C. Remove four

bolts, washers and nuts securing differential hub to sprocket. Note alignment marks on differential hub and sprocket, marks must be aligned during reassembly to ensure proper alignment.

Separate hub and sprocket assembly. For reassembly, be sure to note location of shim washers installed between pinion gears and differential sprocket.

Inspect sprocket and gears for worn, chipped or missing teeth. Inspect all bushings, bearings and shafts for excessive wear or any other damage. Renew all parts as needed and reassemble in reverse order of disassembly. Lubricate drive chain with a good grade SAE 30 weight oil. Caution should be used not to get oil on traction drive wheel or disc. Refer to DRIVE CHAIN ADJUSTMENT AND ALIGNMENT section after reassembly.

(Drive Disc and Pulley). While observing safety precautions as outlined in earlier section stand unit upright and remove drive wheel and hex shaft as outlined in earlier section.

Disconnect traction drive brake rod (1–Fig. J7D), then remove retainer plate (2) cap screw and withdraw traction brake assembly. Remove cap screw (15–Fig. J7E) securing disc and pulley assembly to crankshaft. Be sure to note spacer washers (12) installed above and below disc retainer (13). Move pivot rod clear of disc, then lift disc and pulley assembly off crankshaft. Account for all shims installed between pulley and crankshaft end.

Complete disassembly of drive disc and pulley assembly with reference to Fig. J7E. Inspect all bushings for excessive wear or any other damage. Inspect disc and pulley for roughness, scoring, excessive wear or any other damage.

Reassemble in reverse order of disassembly. It is recommended to lubricate

Fig. J7C—Exploded view of differential and gear reduction unit on RMX models.
1. Right tube assy.
2. Spacer washers
3. Bearing assy.
4. Differential sprocket
5. Spacer
6. Pinion gears
7. Gear & shaft assy.
8. Left tube, bearing, hub & gear assy.
9. Drive chain
10. Sprocket shaft assy.
11. Gear reduction housing
12. Pinion bushing
13. Bearing
14. Primary drive pinion
15. Primary drive gear
16. Pin
17. Spacer
18. Strap
19. Bushing
20. Spacer
21. Pin
22. Bearing
23. Bearing
24. Housing cover
25. Frame support

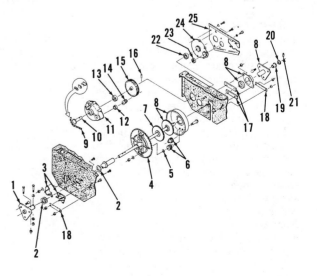

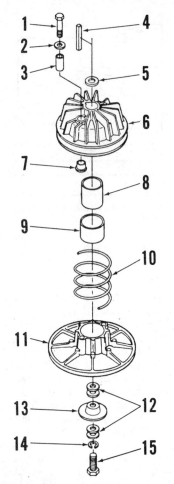

Fig. J7D—View showing traction drive brake rod (1) and retainer plate (2) used on RMX models.

Fig. J7E—Exploded view of drive disc and pulley assembly used on RMX models.

1. Cap screw	
2. Washer	9. Bushing
3. Spacer	10. Spring
4. Square key	11. Disc
5. Spacer washer	12. Spacer washer
6. Pulley	13. Disc retainer
7. Bushing	14. Lockwasher
8. Bushing	15. Cap screw

bushings (8) and (9) with camshaft oil or a suitable equivalent to prevent binding during operation.

TRACTION DRIVE CLUTCH

Model 42635

ADJUSTMENT. There is no actual adjustment of the clutch mechanism on this gear drive model. Clutch pedal (3–Fig. J3) operates through rod (5) and pivot bar (8) against tension of springs (2 and 13) to shift variable speed pulley (31), breaking drive contact between engine pulley (41) and transmission pulley (40). If clutch operation becomes unsatisfactory, check belts for glazing, wear or stretching, check for worn or damaged rods, examine springs for loss of tension or breakage and make sure there is no damage or binding in linkage. Worn or damaged parts should be renewed.

TRANSMISSION

Model 42635

R&R AND OVERHAUL. To remove transmission, proceed as follows:

Relieve drive chain adjustment by backing off chain tensioner bolt, then separate and remove drive chain. Remove rear cover from engine compartment and unbolt and remove operator's seat from its mounting bracket.

Block clutch pedal or linkage in disengaged position to release belt tension, then back off nut and remove pulley (40-Fig. J3) from transmission input shaft. When pulley is lowered from shaft end, take care not to lose Woodruff key. Disconnect control lever (29) from transmission shift arm, then remove four nuts at transmission mounting flanges on platform which are

threaded on through-bolts from transmission belt guard (11). Lift transmission from chassis.

NOTE: Procedure above is for removal of transmission only. If extensive work is planned for mower chassis, mower deck should also be removed along with all belts and pulleys as covered under R&R–ENGINE.

Reverse removal steps to reinstall transmission.

For complete disassembly and detailed repair service to this transmission refer to TRANSMISSION REPAIR section under FOOTE.

DIFFERENTIAL AND REAR AXLE

Model 42635

R&R AND OVERHAUL. To remove differential and rear axle, first release drive chain tensioner, pull out master link and remove chain. Disconnect brake rod from disc brake cam lever, then unbolt and remove disc brake mounting bracket.

Raise and block up rear frame and remove each rear wheel, then remove hub flanges from axle shaft ends by driving out 5/16 X 1⅜-inch spirol pins. Unbolt rear axle support (8–Fig. J8)

under chassis, then slip axle assembly to left to disengage short axle (2) from right side flange bearing (3) and remove axle assembly from frame. Check axles and bearings (3, 6 and 10) for wear or damage. Renew as necessary. Reinstall axle/differential assembly in reverse of removal order.

For disassembly and complete overhaul of differential, see DIFFERENTIAL REPAIRS section of this manual.

Fig. J8—View of differential and rear axle with bearings as used in Model 42635.

1. Wheel washer
2. Axle RH
3. Axle bearing RH
4. Differential assy.
5. Differential assy.
6. Axle bearing, center
7. Bearing bracket
8. Axle support
10. Axle bearing LH
11. Axle LH
12. Wheel washer

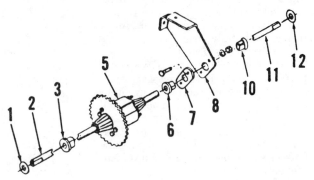

This differential unit is covered under MTD Products.

DRIVE CHAIN

RMX Models

ALIGNMENT. A misaligned drive chain may cause premature chain and sprocket wear or cause chain to jump off sprockets. To align sprockets proceed as follows: While observing safety precautions as outlined in earlier section, stand unit upright. Remove right rear wheel, then remove cap screws, flat washers and nuts securing right tube assembly (1-Fig. J7C) to axle shaft. Loosen bolt retaining right adjustment strap (18), then remove right bearing assembly (3) and spacer washers (2). Realign sprockets and reposition or add washers as needed to maintain correct alignment. Reassemble in reverse order of disassembly. Refer to ADJUSTMENT section for chain tension adjustment.

ADJUSTMENT. While observing safety precautions as outlined in earlier section, stand unit upright. Check chain deflection at center of reducer sprocket (1-Fig. J8A) and differential sprocket (2). Recommended deflection is ⅛ inch (3 mm) as shown by arrows.

To adjust proceed as follows: Remove both rear wheels, then loosen left and right differential bearing (3) and strap (4) retaining bolts. Slide differential in adjustment slots until ⅛ inch (3 mm) deflection is attained, then retighten retaining bolts. Lubricate drive chain with a good grade SAE 30 weight oil. Caution should be used as not to get oil on traction drive wheel or disc.

GROUND DRIVE BRAKES

Friction-Drive Models
Except RMX

The single brake system which operates both as service brake and parking brake is applied automatically whenever drive is in neutral.

CAUTION: Never park unit with free wheeling hub of right rear wheel disengaged. Brake is designed to lock the drive by preventing rotation of chain case driven disc and with it, the entire rear axle. If a rear wheel is unlocked from its axle, then opposite wheel is also free to rotate due to differential action, and parking brake will be ineffective.

When adjustment to brake is apparently needed, simple procedure is to be

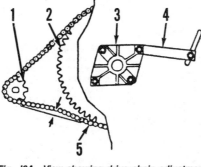

Fig. J8A—View showing drive chain adjustment components for RMX models.

1. Gear reducer sprocket
2. Differential sprocket
3. Bearing assy.
4. Strap
5. Chain

sure that brake rod spring (69-Fig. J4) is under compression when drive is in neutral and brake is applied. As a quick check, inner face of outside nut (68) on brake rod (71) should have a clearance of 1/32 to 1/16 inch (0.8-1.6 mm) from outer surface of rear panel. If there is no clearance, set mower up on rear stand as previously outlined and with drive in neutral, adjust inner nuts on brake rod (71) so that brake (62) is in solid contact with rubber tread of driven disc (49). Outer nut must be clear of rear panel so as not to restrict movement of brake rod. Adjust outer nut, if necessary, for minimum 1/32-inch (0.8 mm) clearance, then operate mower to test brake.

RMX Models

There is no adjustment provided on ground drive brake. If brake slips when applied, check condition of drive wheel and check brake linkage for binding or insufficient application. Make sure brake rod (1-Fig. J7D) is not bent or excessively worn. Renew all parts as needed in order to restore good working operation.

To apply parking brake, first push brake pedal down. Pull parking brake latch (23-Fig. J1A) rearward, then release foot from brake pedal.

Model 42635

This gear-drive model is equipped with a disc brake which engages axle sprocket inboard of right rear wheel. If operation is not satisfactory, adjust as follows:

Tighten locknut (18-Fig. J3) against cam lever (20) one-half turn at a time until brake action is suitable to operator.

If brake parts are worn to such extent that adjustment is no longer possible, uncouple brake rod (7) from

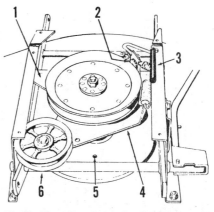

Fig. J9—View of mowing deck pulley housing with top cover removed. Note that blade brake (2) contacts spindle pulley rim when control handle (3) is in "OFF" position.

1. Stiffener plate
2. Blade brake
3. Control lever
4. Idler arm
5. Belt guide mounting hole
6. Idler pulley

brake spring (6), remove brake rod from brake cam lever (20), then unbolt disc brake bracket from frame.

When two bridge bolts (15) are removed, followed by locknut (18), all brake internal parts can be checked for condition and possible renewal. Brake pads (25 and 26) cannot be interchanged. Note difference in thickness. Be sure that rounded end of push pin (22) is installed toward cam lever (20), and reassemble in order shown in exploded view of Fig. J3.

BLADE DRIVE BRAKE

Friction-Drive Models

Non-adjustable blade brake is applied whenever cutting control lever is in "OFF" position. For all models except RMX refer to Fig. J9. If brake pad (10-Fig. J10) is badly worn it can be renewed or complete new brake bracket assembly (8) is available. For RMX models refer to Fig. J10A. If brake bracket (4) should become excessively worn or broken, bracket may be replaced separately or as an assembly with clutch arm (3).

Model 42635

On this model, blade brake (9-Fig. J3) contacts brake disc (38) when mower is disengaged. If blade brake is worn to the point of being ineffective, renew parts as needed.

NOTE: Components of mower cutting decks are usually conventional in design. Refer to applicable illustrations for assembly order of parts should it become necessary to renew a spindle shaft, a bearing or other part which fails in service.

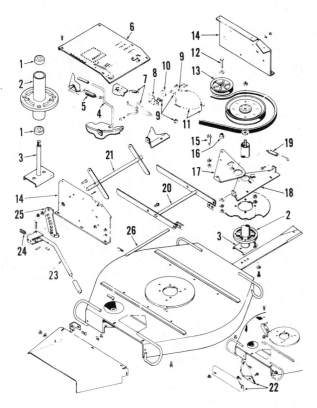

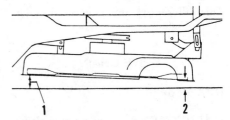

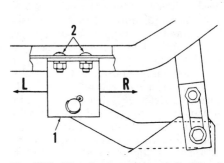

Fig. J10—Exploded view of friction drive mower cutting deck assembly to show parts arrangement.

1. Spindle bearing (2)
2. Spindle housing
3. Spindle shaft/blade saddle
4. Off-On control lever
5. Idler tension spring
6. Cover plate
7. Brake rod & spring
8. Brake bracket
9. Blade safety switch parts
10. Blade brake pad
11. Interlock switch wires
12. Idler bolt ⅜-16×1¾
13. Idler pulley
14. Side bracket (2)
15. Idler arm belt guide
16. Idler pulley spacer
17. Idler arm
18. Support plate
19. Idler return spring
20. Front lift arm
21. Rear lift arm
22. Rear discharge conversion parts
23. Lift handle
24. Compression spring
25. Height setting quadrant
26. Hanger shaft

Fig. J10B—View showing procedure for checking mower deck height on RMX models. Rear deck height (1) should be 1/4-3/8 inch (6.4-9.5 mm) higher than front (2).

Fig. J10C—View showing carriage bolts (2) and mower deck hanger (1) used to adjust mower deck height. Refer to text for adjustment procedures.

LEVEL MOWING DECK

Friction-Drive Models

Except RMX

Park mower on a level floor for all deck level measurements. Disconnect spark plug wire and set control lever to "OFF". Rotate blade so that tip is toward front. Adjust height control lever for **low cut,** then measure blade height at front and rear blade tips. Rear of blade should be ¼ to ⅜-inch (6.4-9.5 mm) higher than front. If adjustment is required, use adjusting nuts on threaded portion of support rod (32-Fig. J1) to set angle of cutting deck. When front-to-rear adjustment is correct, be sure that mower deck is level, side-to-side, by adjusting one or the other support rod (32), then recheck front-to-rear adjustment. Repair or renew all parts of mowing deck suspension or controls which are damaged or defective.

RMX Model

Place mower unit on level ground. Disconnect spark plug wire and tie out of way. Check tire pressure, recommended tire pressure is 10-12 lbs. per square inch. Measure rear mower deck height (1-Fig. J10B) and front mower deck height (2). Rear deck height (1) should be ¼ to ⅜ inch (6.4-9.5 mm) higher than front (2).

To adjust mower deck height proceed as follows: Loosen carriage bolts (2-Fig. J10C) on left and right front mower deck hanger (1), then slide brackets forward (R) to raise front and backward (L) to lower front. Make sure sides are adjusted evenly, then retighten carriage bolts. Remeasure front and rear deck height and readjust as needed.

If mower deck side-to-side height is uneven, then add washers between rear lift bracket (7-Fig. J2B) and support bracket (8) until even.

Model 42635

This gear model has no provision for leveling the deck in relation to mower chassis. Only gage wheels at rear of deck are adjustable and these should be set just clear of floor when lift and disengagement lever is in low position.

MOWER DRIVE BELT

Model RMX

REMOVE AND REINSTALL. Stand unit upright and remove mower drive belt as follows: Disconnect counterbalance spring (2-Fig. J2A) from bottom cover (3). Move lift handle selector to lowest position. Remove front hanger bracket shoulder bolt and lower mower deck until rear portion rests on rear wheels. Loosen two spindle pulley belt guides (1-Fig. J2B), then remove belt from idler pulley. Rotate clutch arm (2) away from spindle pulley, then lift belt off pulley. Depress forward pedal until drive wheel (1-Fig. J2C) clears edge of retainer (2) on drive disc. Remove belt from engine drive pulley and slip belt between drive wheel and disc.

Fig. J10A—View showing mower drive components for RMX models.

1. Mower drive pulley
2. Idler pulley
3. Clutch arm
4. Brake bracket

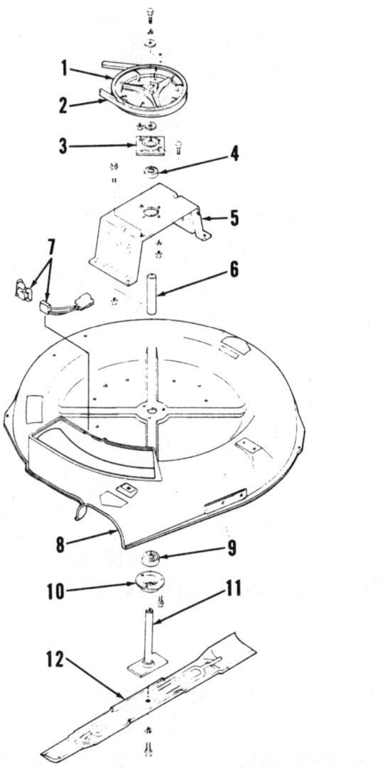

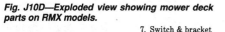

Fig. J10D—*Exploded view showing mower deck parts on RMX models.*

1. Pulley
2. Drive belt
3. Retainer
4. Bearing
5. Bracket assy.
6. Spindle spacer
7. Switch & bracket assy.
8. Mower deck
9. Bearing
10. Retainer
11. Spindle
12. Blade

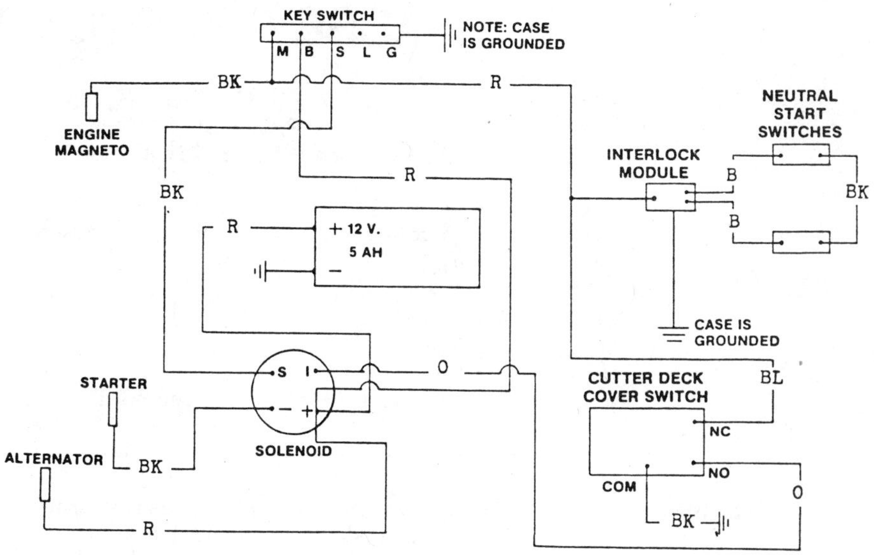

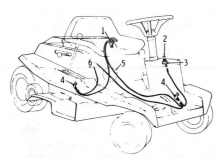

Fig. J11—*View to show placement of safety switches in Model 42635 interlock system.*

1. Starter safety switch
2. Ignition switch key
3. Ignition switch
4. Safety switches NC (2)
5. Wiring harness
6. Engine magneto connection

Fig. J12—*Wiring diagram for RMX models.*

1. BK-Black
2. BL-Blue
3. B-Brown
4. O-Orange
5. R-Red

Inspect all pulleys and renew if damaged or excessively worn. Renew drive belt and reassemble in reverse order of disassembly.

MOWER DECK

Model RMX

R&R AND OVERHAUL. Raise front of mower unit high enough to allow access to underneath side. First remove mower drive belt, proceed as follows: Disconnect counterbalance spring (2-Fig. J2A) from bottom cover (3). Move lift handle selector to lowest position. Remove front hanger bracket shoulder bolt and lower mower deck. Loosen two spindle pulley belt guides (1-Fig. J2B), then remove belt from idler pulley. Rotate clutch arm (2) away from spindle pulley, then lift belt off pulley. Depress forward pedal until drive wheel (1-Fig. J2C) clears edge of retainer (2) on drive disc. Remove belt from engine drive pulley and slip belt between drive wheel and disc. Discon-

nect clutch arm spring (6), then remove shoulder bolts retaining rear lift bracket to hanger assemblies and lower deck unit. Withdraw deck assembly from mower unit.

Complete disassembly of mower deck with reference to Fig. J10D. Inspect and renew pulleys if damaged or excessively worn. Inspect bearings for excessive wear, binding or any other damage. Check spindle shaft for straightness, excessive wear or any other damage. Renew all parts as needed and reassemble in reverse order of disassembly.

ELECTRICAL

Model RMX

Shown in electrical diagram Fig. J12 are electrical components and their adjoining wires. Shown is a diagram for an electric start model, recoil starter models are not equipped with a battery, alternator, starter or adjoining wiring harnesses.

MASSEY–FERGUSON

**MASSEY-FERGUSON, INC.
P.O. Box 1813
Des Moines, Iowa 50306**

Model	Make	Engine Model	Horsepower	Cutting Width, In.
MF5	Tecumseh	V50	5	26
MF6*	Tecumseh	V60	6	32
MF626	Tecumseh	V60	6	26
MF8*	Tecumseh	V80	8	32
MF832*	Tecumseh	V80	8	32

*Electric starting optional. All others are equipped for manual recoil start.

STEERING SYSTEM

Rigid front axle is center-pivoted under frame and steering linkage includes a steering arm at base of steering shaft which is connected by threaded ball joints at drag ink ends to arm portion of left wheel spindle. Steering spindles are connected by a single tie rod with counter-threaded ball joints at each end.

All Models

ADJUSTMENT. Steering adjustment is limited to setting of front wheel toe-in, and calls for adjusting lengths of drag link (15-Fig. MF1) and tie rod (13), measuring center-to-center on ball joint studs (9 and 12). To do so, set front wheels straight ahead, then loosen jam nut at right hand end of each rod and rotate rod (13 or 15) to set length. On Models MF5, MF6 and MF626, drag link (15) should measure 9-1/32 inch (229.5 mm) and tie rod (13) should measure 16 inches (406.4 mm). On Models MF8 and MF832, drag link (15) should measure 10-15/16 inches (277.8 mm) and tie rod (13) should measure 19-15/16 inches (506.4 mm). Be sure threads are engaged the same depth at each end.

R&R AND OVERHAUL. To remove front axle, suspension and steering parts, raise and securely block forward portion of chassis.

Remove "X" lockwasher (17-Fig. MF1) and washer (19), then remove each front wheel (23). Remove nuts from ball joint studs (9 and 12) and separate tie rod (13) and drag link (15) from steering arm of spindles (20 and 22) and from arm (11). Loosen set screw (14), remove steering arm (11), and pull steering shaft (8) out of tube (6) and support shaft. Need for further disassembly is based on determination of condition of parts at wear points, particularly bushing sets (7, 18 and 24),

ball joints (9 and 12), steering arm (11) and shaft (8). If looseness or heavy wear is apparent, parts should be renewed. To reinstall, reverse order of disassembly. Steering wheel retainer nut (3) should be torqued to 30-35 ft.-lbs. (40-48 N·m). Lubricate reassem-

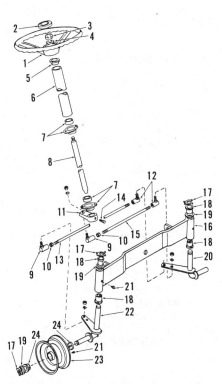

Fig. MF1—Exploded view of steering and front suspension parts typical of all models. On models MF5, MF6 and MF626, two washers (5) are used, one at top and one at bottom of tube (6). Models MF8 and MF832 are assembled as shown.

1. Steering wheel
2. Cap/logo
3. Nut (⅝-18)
4. Washer, flat
5. Washer, special
6. Tube
7. Bushing set (2)
8. Shaft
9. Ball joint (RH thread)
10. Nut (⅝-24)
11. Arm
12. Ball joint (LH thread)
13. Tie rod
14. Set screw
15. Drag link
16. Axle assy.
17. "X" lockwasher
18. Spindle bushing (4)
19. Washer (4)
20. Spindle, LH
21. Grease fitting
22. Spindle, RH
23. Wheel & rim
24. Wheel bushing (4)

bled front system with Multi-Purpose lithium base grease (MF Spec. M-1105).

ENGINE

All Models

Refer to appropriate engine section in this manual for tune-up specifications, engine overhaul procedures and engine maintenance.

Refer to the following paragraphs for removal and installation procedures.

REMOVE AND REINSTALL. Set mower engagement lever in "OFF" position and lower mower by height control handle to low position. Disconnect blade brake cable from brake band. Remove front pivot bolts and pins. Remove rear lift pin, shift cutting deck to rear for maximum slack in mower drive belt, then disengage belt from engine pulley and mower clutch idler. Slide mower out at right side of chassis. Depress and lock mower drive clutch-brake pedal to allow slack in main drive belt. For easier access to underside of chassis, it may be desirable to place mower up on its rear stand.

CAUTION: Frequently, the performance of maintenance, adjustment or repair operations on a riding mower is more convenient if mower is standing on end. This procedure can be considered a recommended practice providing the following safety recommendations are performed:

1. Drain fuel tank or make certain that fuel level is low enough so that fuel will not drain out.
2. Close fuel shut-off valve if so equipped.
3. Remove battery on models so equipped.
4. Disconnect spark plug wire and tie out of way.
5. Although not absolutely essential, it is recommended that crankcase oil be drained to avoid flooding the combus-

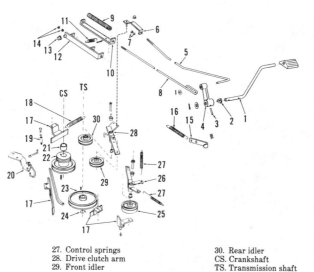

Fig. MF2—Exploded view of riding mower clutch-brake linkage and controls.

1. Clutch-brake pedal
2. Bushing
3. Spirol pin (3/16)
4. Pedal arm
5. Clutch rod
6. Clutch clevis
7. Adjustment nuts (5/16)
8. Brake rod
9. Brake spring
10. Spring retainer
11. Return spring
12. Brake link
13. Fastener
14. Adjustment nuts (5/16)
15. Pedal latch
16. Latch spring
17. Belt keepers
18. Clutch spring
19. Spring anchor
20. Support
21. Spacer
22. Crankshaft pulley
23. Transmission pulley
24. Snap ring
25. Mower clutch idler
26. Mower clutch arm
27. Control springs
28. Drive clutch arm
29. Front idler
30. Rear idler
CS. Crankshaft
TS. Transmission shaft

tion chamber with oil when engine is tilted.

6. **Secure mower from tipping by lashing unit to a nearby post or overhead beam.**

Loosen belt keeper bolts to allow greater clearance and work belt off transmission and engine pulleys. Loosen engine mounting bolts slightly and remove any belt keepers or supports which may be in the way. Lower mower to rest on all four wheels, then disconnect throttle control bowden cable at carburetor, magneto lead wire from ignition switch connector, and if so equipped, remove red cable from electric starter. Remove four bolts which attach rear stand to frame, then complete unbolting of engine base and lift engine from mower for further service. Be sure to check for possible interference from wiring for safety interlock systems, battery charger or other supplemental equipment. Observe circuitry and disconnect with care.

To reinstall engine, reverse order used for removal, and torque engine mounting bolts as follows: ¼ inch, 12-14 ft.-lbs. (16-19 N·m); 5/16 inch, 22-24 ft.-lbs. (30-33 N·m).

TRACTION DRIVE CLUTCH

All Models

ADJUSTMENT. Clutch-brake pedal (1–Fig. MF2) should be depressed to its limit and locked down by parking latch (15). Tip unit up on rear stand as previously outlined.

Make traction clutch adjustment by turning nuts (7), at rear of clutch rod (5), against clevis (6) to set distance between circumferences of front idler pulley (29) and smaller (2¼ inch diameter) sheave of crankshaft pulley (22). Correct clearance between pulleys should be from 15/16 to 1-1/16 inches (23.8-27 mm). If adjustment cannot be

made satisfactorily, carefully check condition of all parts of clutch system. Bent or binding control rod, stripped fasteners, defective or damaged springs, worn, damaged pulleys or bushings or frayed, worn belts must be renewed or repaired for satisfactory operation of unit.

Test before returning to service.

TRANSMISSION

All Models

REMOVE AND REINSTALL. To remove transmission, raise operator's seat, and if unit is equipped for electric starting, disconnect and remove battery. Detach safety start switch connector plug. If unit is so equipped, remove chain guard. Disconnect brake rod from disc brake assembly on transmission.

NOTE: As a matter of convenience, operator's seat support (1 and 2–Fig. MF6) and shroud (4) can be removed. Remove master link from drive chain, separate and remove chain. On Models 8 and 832 only, drain and remove fuel tank.

Release clutch and remove drive belt. Then extract snap ring from bottom end of transmission input shaft and remove transmission pulley. Take care not to lose Woodruff key. Remove shift lever which on Model MF5, requires removal of cam plate cover first. When lever has been removed, take care not to lose detent springs or balls. Remove retaining cap screws and lift transmission from frame.

To reinstall transmission, observe the reverse of this procedure. Readjust drive chain tension as covered in preceding section and torque the mounting

Fig. MF3—Underside view of drive system and mower clutch assembled. As shown, drive clutch is engaged, mower idler is disengaged. Note mounting of axle shaft bearings. See text for cautions regarding use of rear stand.

Fig. MF4—View of transmission disc brake adjustment points. Follow procedure in text.

Fig. MF5—View of traction chain adjustment points. Refer to text for tension adjustment procedure.
1. Shaft bolt
2. Roller
3. Chain

cap screws evenly to 18-20 ft.-lbs. (24-27 N·m). Adjust transmission brake.

OVERHAUL. After transmission is removed, refer to FOOTE TRANSMISSION REPAIR section of this manual for detailed service procedures.

DRIVE CHAIN

All Models

To set chain tension, loosen nut at outer end of roller bolt (1–Fig. MF5) and shift roller in its slot so there will be ½-inch (12.7 mm) slack in chain, measured at center of top strand. When adjustment is made, retighten nut to a torque of 40-45 ft.-lbs. (54-61 N·m). Be sure that inner nut on shaft allows roller to turn freely.

To remove chain for renewal or cleaning or in preparation for removal of transmission or rear axle, loosen tension adjustment roller, disconnect master link and withdraw chain. Easiest position for removal of master link is next to transmission sprocket under operator's seat. If a new chain is installed, tension should be adjusted during installation and rechecked after two or three hours operation.

DIFFERENTIAL AND REAR AXLE

All Models

REMOVE AND REINSTALL. Tip unit up on rear stand as previously outlined.

Loosen drive chain tensioner bolt so chain will go slack, extract master link and remove chain. Remove through-bolt at each rear wheel hub and remove both rear wheels. Remove nuts from carriage bolts which retain flange portion of rear wheel bearings to frame and lift axle-differential assembly from its "U" notches in frame rails. Thoroughly clean ends of axles before loosening set screws and removing bearings from axles. Reverse this procedure to reinstall. Tighten nuts on carriage bolts to 8-10 ft.-lbs. (11-13 N·m) torque.

OVERHAUL. Refer to DIFFERENTIAL REPAIR section of this manual under PEERLESS for overhaul procedures.

GROUND DRIVE BRAKE

All Models

ADJUSTMENT. Service brakes operate from a single clutch-brake pedal, with linkage designed to release traction clutch just before brake is applied. Disc brake is mounted on transmission output shaft at opposite end from drive sprocket.

Depress clutch-brake pedal to its limit and engage locking latch. Raise operator's seat for access, and use nuts (14-Fig. MF2) at rear end of brake rod (8) to

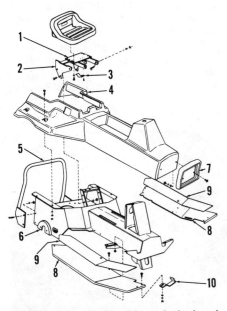

Fig. MF6—Exploded view of frame, body shroud removed, to show assembly details.

1. Seat plate & hinge	6. Frame
2. Support	7. Cap
3. Spring	8. Plate (2)
4. Shroud	9. Tread (2)
5. Rear stand	10. Clip (2)

Fig. MF7—Exploded view of typical mowing deck with lift operating controls and linkages. Two-spindle type shown is used on MF6, MF8 and MF832. See text for service.

1. Blade brake cable (2)
2. Blade brake band (2)
3. Shield
4. Lift lever assy.
5. Latch
6. Latch spring
7. Quadrant
8. Latch rod
9. Lift straps
10. Support bar
11. Link rod
12. Crank assy.
13. Spindle pulley (2)
14. Spacer
15. Guide pulley
16. Belt guide
17. Spacer
18. Stud (2)
19. Deck
20. Spindle bearing
21. Spacer
22. Spindle housing
23. Snap ring
24. Bearing
25. Snap ring
26. Spindle shaft
27. Blade
28. Spring cup washer

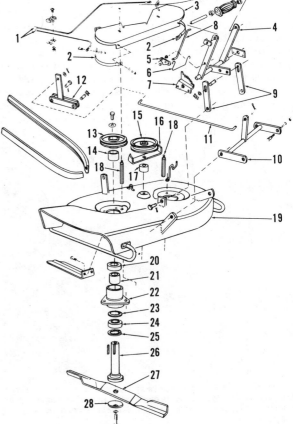

compress brake spring (9) to a length of 3⅞ to 4 inches (98.6-101.6 mm) on Models 5, 6 and 8, or 4⅛ inches (104.6 mm) on Models 626 and 832.

Carefully inspect all brake components paying particular attention to condition of disc brake pads and operating linkage, especially rod (8), to note if threads are damaged or if elongated loop at forward end of rod is sprung or distorted. Repair or renew parts as necessary. Brake parts for disc assembly will be found in FOOTE portion of TRANSMISSION REPAIR section of this manual.

NOTE: Mower blade brake is covered under MOWER SERVICE.

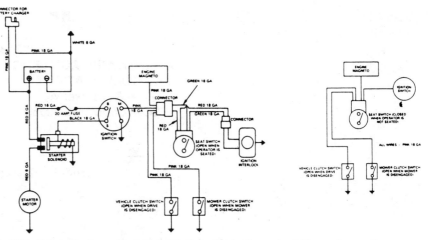

Fig. MF8—Schematic views of typical electrical circuitry to show color coding and connector arrangement. Diagram for electric start models is at left, manual start models at right.

MOWER BLADE BRAKE

Single Spindle Models

ADJUSTMENT. During routine operation, an occasional visual check should be made to determine if proper clearance exists between brake band and drive belt at left hand side of mower pulley. If clearance is insufficient (band dragging) or if braking is ineffective, adjust as follows:

Engage mower clutch control by setting handle in "ON" position. Adjust brake bracket (fixed end of brake band) for 1/32 to 1/16-inch (0.8-1.6 mm) clearance between brake band and drive belt. Measure at bracket end. Move control handle to "OFF" position. Now, manually swing idler pulley to a midpoint between "ON" and "OFF" positions, take up slack in cable with stop on brake band against stop post on mower deck and tighten cable set screw. Allow idler pulley to swing back

to "OFF" position and check tension of drive belt which should be relaxed at engine drive pulley. Observe blade brake action during normal mower operation.

Double Spindle Models

ADJUSTMENT. On these models there is a separate blade brake band on each spindle pulley. If band clearance is incorrect, set control handle in "ON" position, then loosen two nuts which hold shield (3–Fig. MF7) to mounting studs (18) on mower deck. Shift shield (3) in its slotted holes to obtain 1/32 to 1/16-inch (0.8-1.6 mm) clearance between each brake band and drive belt. Retighten nuts. Move control handle to "OFF". Swing mower clutch idler pulley to a mid-point between "ON" and "OFF" positions and adjust cable to remove slack but leaving running clearance between brake bands and belt.

Tighten cable clips and set screw. Let idler pulley return to "OFF" position and check drive belt tension. Belt should be relaxed at engine drive pulley. Check function of blade brake during normal mower operation.

LEVEL MOWER

All Models

Because the mowing deck is attached to the center-pivoted front axle and not suspended from rigid frame member only, it is imperative that unit be parked on a hard, level surface such as a concrete floor before attempting to level the cutting deck. Level deck by means of pivot bolts which attach support bar (10–Fig. MF7) to deck (19). When mower is leveled properly, tighten pivot bolts to 30-35 ft.-lbs. (40-48 N·m) torque.

MAXIM

MAXIM MANUFACTURING
CORPORATION
P.O. Drawer A
Sebastopol, MS 39359

Model	Make	Engine Model	Horsepower	Cutting Width, In.
GL830B	B&S	195702	8	30
GL830BHP	B&S	195702	8	30
GL830BEIC	B&S	196707	8	30
GL830BEICHP	B&S	196707	8	30
GL1230BEIC	B&S	283707	12	30
GL1230BEICHP	B&S	283707	12	30
GL1430BVE	B&S	303777	14	30

NOTE: Some operations may be performed more easily if the machine is standing upright. Observe the following safety recommendations when raising machine to upright position:

1. **Drain fuel tank or make certain that fuel level is low enough so that fuel will not drain out.**
2. **Close fuel shut-off valve (if so equipped).**
3. **Remove battery (if so equipped).**
4. **Disconnect spark plug wire and tie it out of way.**
5. **Although not absolutely essential, on models with spark plug at rear of machine, engine oil should be drained to prevent flooding the combustion chamber with oil when the engine is tilted.**
6. **Secure mower from tipping by lashing machine to a post or overhead beam.**

FRONT WHEELS

All Models

LUBRICATION. Each front wheel hub is equipped with a grease fitting. Front wheels should be injected with a good quality multipurpose grease after every 25 hours of operation.

FRONT SPINDLES

All Models

LUBRICATION. The front wheel spindles should be lubricated after every 25 hours of operation. Apply grease to spindles through grease fitting at each end of axle. Use a good quality, multipurpose grease.

R&R AND OVERHAUL. To remove a front spindle (14 and 16—Fig. MX11), raise and support side to be serviced. Remove hub cap (10), "E" ring (11), wheel and tire. Disconnect tie rod (15) from spindle. Detach "E" ring (7) and remove spindle. Inspect components for excessive wear and damage. Install spindle by reversing removal procedure.

STEERING SYSTEM

All Models

LUBRICATION. A grease fitting is located at bottom of steering shaft so bushings may be lubricated. Inject multipurpose grease into grease fitting after every 25 hours of operation.

R&R AND OVERHAUL. To remove steering shaft (9—Fig. MX11), raise front of machine and detach tie rods (15) from steering arm. Drive out steering shaft extension retaining pins (5) and separate steering wheel with extension (4) from steering shaft (some models may have handlebars). Withdraw steering shaft from bottom of machine.

Inspect components for excessive wear and damage. Bushings (6) are renewable. Reassemble steering shaft by reversing disassembly procedure.

ENGINE

All Models

Refer to appropriate engine section in this manual for tune-up specifications, engine overhaul procedures and engine maintenance.

REMOVE AND REINSTALL. To remove engine, disconnect spark plug wire. If engine is equipped with an electric starter, disconnect cable from starter motor. Depress clutch/brake pedal and remove traction drive belt from engine pulley. Shift mower control lever to disengaged position. Remove belt guide at engine pulley and separate mower drive belt from engine pulley. Detach throttle cable from carburetor. Disconnect all interfering wiring from engine. Remove engine mounting screws and remove engine.

Reinstall engine by reversing removal procedure.

TRACTION DRIVE CLUTCH
AND DRIVE BELT

All Models

The traction drive clutch is a spring-tensioned, belt idler-type operated by the clutch/brake pedal. When the pedal is depressed, belt tension is removed, allowing the engine drive pulley to rotate freely within the drive belt. After the pedal passes midpoint, the brake is applied.

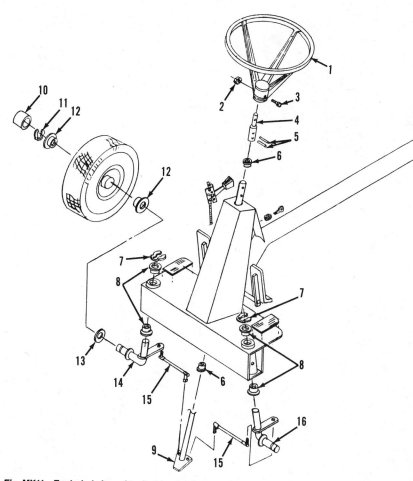

Fig. MX11—Exploded view of typical front axle assembly.

1. Steering wheel	5. Pins	9. Steering shaft	13. Washer
2. Nut	6. Bushing	10. Hub cap	14. Spindle (R.H.)
3. Screw	7. "E" ring	11. "E" ring	15. Tie rod
4. Steering shaft extension	8. Bushing	12. Bushing	16. Spindle (L.H.)

screw brake lever retaining nut (2) and unscrew caliper mounting screws (1). Disassemble brake components. Brake pad wear limit is ¼ inch (6.4 mm). When assembling brake, coat transaxle brake shaft with Lubriplate. Apply Lubriplate to ends of actuator pins (6) and rubbing surfaces of brake lever and washer (4). Be sure actuator pins (6) are installed with rounded end towards brake lever (5).

TRANSAXLE

All Models

REMOVE AND REINSTALL. To remove transaxle, disconnect spark plug wire and stand machine upright on rear stand as previously outlined or raise and support rear of machine. Remove rear belt guide (20—Fig. MX12). Depress clutch/brake pedal and remove traction drive belt from engine pulley. Remove traction drive belt from transaxle pulley. Remove rear wheels. Disconnect neutral safety switch, if so equipped. Detach shift rod (10—Fig. MX12) from transaxle shift arm (11). Detach brake rod (32) from brake lever (37). Unscrew transaxle retaining fasteners and remove transaxle.

Reinstall transaxle by reversing removal procedure.

OVERHAUL. All models are equipped with a Peerless 800 series transaxle. Refer to TRANSMISSION REPAIR section for service information.

MOWER BELT

All Models

ADJUSTMENT. Mower drive belt tension is determined by measuring distance between opposite runs of belt at closest point with mower engaged (see Fig. MX15). Remove mower belt cover and measure the distance (D) between belt runs, which should be 1 inch (25 mm). To adjust belt tension, loosen tube clamp (17—Fig. MX12) around main frame tube and move tube in or out as needed to obtain correct distance (D). Retighten clamp. Recheck clutch/brake cable adjustment as previously outlined.

Idler belt guide (B—Fig. MX16) should be perpendicular to belt when mower is disengaged.

REMOVE AND REINSTALL. To remove mower drive belt, remove rear belt guide (20—Fig. MX12). Depress clutch/brake pedal and remove traction drive belt from engine pulley. Detach

No periodic adjustment of the clutch is required. If belt slippage occurs due to a worn or stretched belt, the belt should be renewed.

R&R DRIVE BELT. To remove drive belt, disconnect spark plug wire. Remove rear belt guide (20—Fig. MX12). Depress clutch/brake pedal and remove traction drive belt from engine pulley. Remove traction drive belt from transaxle pulley.

Install drive belt by reversing removal procedure.

CLUTCH/BRAKE CABLE

All Models

All models are equipped with a cable-operated clutch/brake. The cable extends from a keyhole slot in the clutch/brake pedal through the main frame tube to the actuating lever (5—Fig. MX12). Movement of the actuating

lever results in movement of the belt idler (38) and brake lever (37).

ADJUSTMENT. A slight amount of slack should be present in clutch/brake cable with pedal released. To adjust cable slack, relocate end of cable in pedal slot so another ferrule in cable is engaged. Be sure brake operates properly after adjustment.

GROUND DRIVE BRAKE

All Models

ADJUSTMENT. Check brake operation by pushing brake pedal and attempting to move machine. If brake does not hold machine with pedal fully depressed, adjust brake. To adjust brake, release brake and turn nut (N—Fig. MX13) on brake cam lever until desired brake operation is obtained.

R&R AND OVERHAUL. Detach operating rod and refer to Fig. MX14. Un-

mower deck cover, and loosen belt guide bolt. Place mower control in disengaged position to increase belt slack. Remove mower drive belt.

Install mower drive belt by reversing removal procedure. Position belt guides so that clearance between belt and guides is ⅛ inch (3 mm). Adjust mower belt tension as outlined in ADJUST-MENT section.

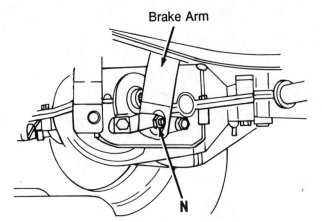

Fig. MX13—Turn nut (N) to adjust ground drive brake. Refer to text.

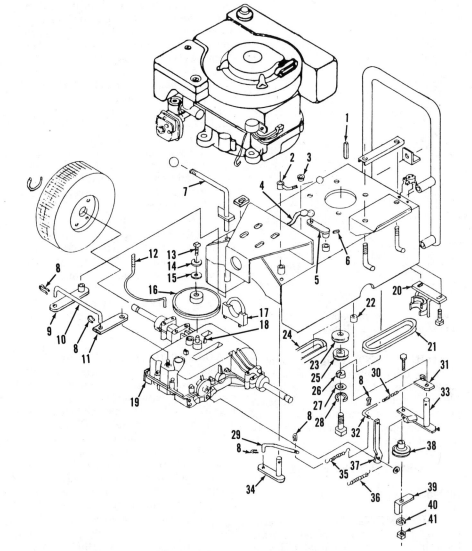

Fig. MX12—Exploded view of typical rear frame and drive assembly.

1. Key	12. Belt guide	22. Bushing	32. Brake rod
2. Parking brake lever	13. Screw	23. Mower drive pulley	33. Idler arm
3. Plug	14. Lockwasher	24. Mower drive belt	34. Parking brake arm
4. Clutch/brake cable	15. Washer	25. Traction drive pulley	35. Spring
5. Clutch/brake arm	16. Pulley	26. Spacer	36. Spring
6. Roll pin	17. Clamp	27. Washer	37. Brake lever
7. Shift control lever	18. Key	28. Lockwasher	38. Idler
8. Spring clip	19. Transaxle	29. Parking brake rod	39. Belt guide
9. Shift arm	20. Belt guide	30. Spring	40. Lockwasher
10. Shift rod	21. Traction drive belt	31. Brake arm	41. Nut
11. Transaxle shift arm			

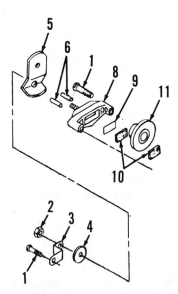

Fig. MX14—Exploded view of disc brake assembly.

1. Screw	6. Dowel pins
2. Nut	8. Caliper half
3. Brace	9. Plate
4. Washer	10. Brake pads
5. Brake lever	11. Brake disc

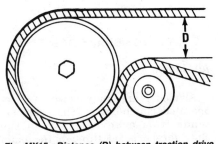

Fig. MX15—Distance (D) between traction drive belt runs should be 1 inch (25 mm). See text for adjustment.

MOWER DECK

All Models

HEIGHT ADJUSTMENT. All mower control linkage must be in good operating condition and tires properly inflated. Park machine on a level surface with engine stopped and spark plug wire disconnected.

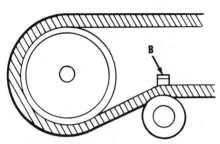

Fig. MX16—Belt guide on idler should be perpendicular to belt as shown.

Front-to-rear height difference is determined by measuring height of blade above ground at front and rear. Rear height should be ¼ inch (6 mm) higher than front height.

To adjust deck rear height, turn nuts (23—Fig. MX17) on hanger rods (27) at rear of deck. Maximum difference side-to-side should be ⅛ inch (3 mm). To adjust deck front height, remove mower cover (55). Remove clevis pin from lift link clevis (36—Fig. MX17) and rotate clevis. Turning the clevis clockwise will raise the deck. One complete turn of the clevis will change the deck height approximately ⅛ inch (3 mm).

REMOVE AND REINSTALL. To remove mower deck, remove mower belt as previously outlined. Disconnect mower safety switch. Remove mower blade brake band (2—Fig. MX17) and mower drive pulley (6). Detach mower deck rear hanger rods (27) from hanger arms (29). Detach front hanger arms from front axle main member. Remove mower deck. Reinstall mower deck by reversing removal procedure.

BLADE BRAKE

All models are equipped with a band-type brake (2—Fig. MX17) that stops rotation of the blade spindle. The blade brake is actuated by the mower engagement lever. The blade brake is spring-loaded and does not require adjustment.

MOWER SPINDLE

All Models

R&R AND OVERHAUL. Refer to Fig. MX17 for exploded view of spindle assembly. To remove spindle, remove mower deck as previously outlined. Removal and disassembly of spindle assembly is evident after inspection of unit and referral to Fig. MX17. Note that spindle bearings (38) are equipped

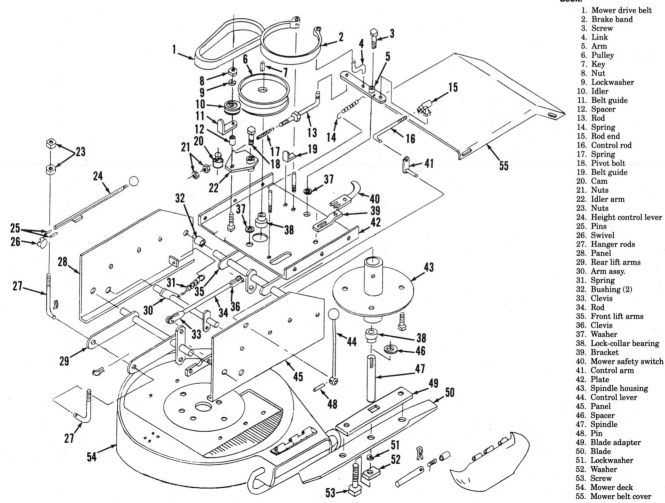

Fig. MX17—Exploded view of typical mower deck.

1. Mower drive belt
2. Brake band
3. Screw
4. Link
5. Arm
6. Pulley
7. Key
8. Nut
9. Lockwasher
10. Idler
11. Belt guide
12. Spacer
13. Rod
14. Spring
15. Rod end
16. Control rod
17. Spring
18. Pivot bolt
19. Belt guide
20. Cam
21. Nuts
22. Idler arm
23. Nuts
24. Height control lever
25. Pins
26. Swivel
27. Hanger rods
28. Panel
29. Rear lift arms
30. Arm assy.
31. Spring
32. Bushing (2)
33. Clevis
34. Rod
35. Front lift arms
36. Clevis
37. Washer
38. Lock-collar bearing
39. Bracket
40. Mower safety switch
41. Control arm
42. Plate
43. Spindle housing
44. Control lever
45. Panel
46. Spacer
47. Spindle
48. Pin
49. Blade adapter
50. Blade
51. Lockwasher
52. Washer
53. Screw
54. Mower deck
55. Mower belt cover

with a lock collar that must be rotated in opposite direction of normal spindle rotation to unlock the collar.

Tighten blade retaining screw to 70-80 ft.-lbs. (95-108 N m). Rotate bearing locking collars in direction of normal spindle rotation to lock the bearings to the spindle.

ELECTRICAL

All Models

Refer to Fig. MX18 for a typical wiring schematic. Note the following points:

The transmission must be in neutral, the mower must be disengaged and the operator must be in seat for engine to start.

The engine should stop if the transmission is in gear or the mower is engaged and the operator leaves the seat.

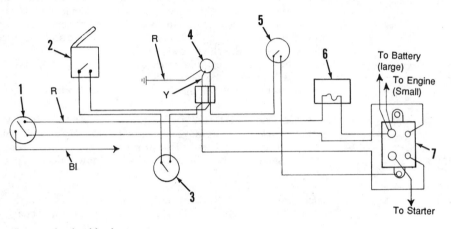

Fig. MX18—Typical wiring diagram of main wiring harness.

1. Ignition switch
2. Mower safety switch
3. Transaxle neutral switch
4. Engine
5. Seat safety switch
6. Fuse
7. Solenoid
Bl. Blue
R. Red
Y. Yellow

Illustrations Courtesy Maxim Manufacturing Corp.

MAXIM

Model	Make	Engine Model	Horsepower	Cutting Width, In.
GL8F30	B&S	196707	8	30
GL12F30	B&S	283707	12	30
GL12F42	B&S	283707	12	42
GL14F42	B&S	261777	14	42
GL15F42	B&S	303777	15	42

FRONT WHEELS

All Models

The front wheels are the drive wheels for the machine. A key transfers power to each wheel from the axle. The wheel may be removed after supporting the machine and removing the snap ring that retains the wheel on the axle. Before assembly, apply antiseize compound to wheel contact surface on axle. Be sure the snap ring is properly seated in groove on axle.

STEERING SYSTEM

All Models

R&R AND OVERHAUL. All models are equipped with a cable-actuated steering system that controls steering of the rear steering wheel. The cables are attached to a roller chain that contacts the sprocket on the steering shaft. Cables, chain and sprocket should be inspected periodically.

To remove steering shaft, remove mower deck as outlined in MOWER DECK section. Detach steering cable at rear steering wheel to provide slack in steering cable. Drive out pins (6—Fig. MX31) and remove steering wheel with steering shaft extension (5). Separate chain (11) from steering shaft sprocket. Detach bracket (10) and remove steering shaft (9).

Reassemble steering components by reversing disassembly procedure. Note that when rear steering wheel is in straight-ahead position, steering sprocket should be at midpoint of chain (11).

GROUND DRIVE BRAKE

All Models

ADJUSTMENT. Check brake operation by pushing brake pedal and attempting to move machine. If brake does not hold machine with pedal fully depressed, adjust brake. To adjust brake, release brake and turn nut (9—Fig. MX32) on cam lever until desired brake operation is obtained.

R&R AND OVERHAUL. Detach brake operating rod and refer to Fig. MX32. Unscrew lever retaining nut (9) and unscrew caliper mounting screws (10). Disassemble brake components. Brake pad wear limit is 1/4 inch (6.4 mm). When assembling brake, coat transaxle brake shaft with Lubriplate. Apply Lubriplate to ends of actuator pins (5) and rubbing surfaces of brake lever (6) and washer (7). Be sure actuator pins (5) are installed with rounded end toward brake lever (6).

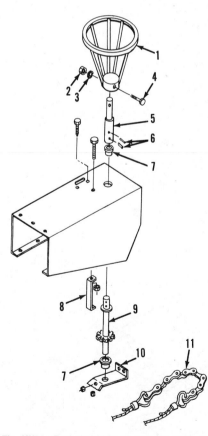

Fig. MX31—Exploded view of steering shaft assembly used on all models.

1. Steering wheel	7. Bushing
2. Nut	8. Bracket
3. Lockwasher	9. Steering sprocket & shaft
4. Bolt	10. Bracket
5. Steering shaft extension	11. Chain & cables
6. Roll pins	

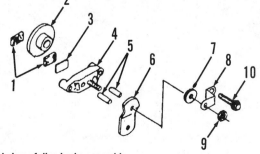

Fig. MX32—Exploded view of disc brake assembly.

1. Brake pads		8. Brace
2. Brake disc	4. Caliper half	6. Brake lever	9. Nut
3. Plate	5. Dowel pins	7. Washer	10. Screw

ENGINE

All Models

Refer to appropriate engine section in this manual for tune-up specifications, engine overhaul procedures and engine maintenance.

REMOVE AND REINSTALL. To remove engine, disconnect spark plug wire and remove seat. If engine is equipped with an electric starter, disconnect cable from starter motor. If necessary, loosen engine mounting bolts securing belt guide and reposition belt guide. Disconnect belt idler pulley spring. Depress clutch/brake pedal and remove traction drive belt from engine pulley. Shift mower control lever to disengaged position and separate mower drive belt from engine pulley. Disconnect fuel hose and detach throttle cable from carburetor. Disconnect all interfering wiring from engine. Remove engine mounting screws and remove engine.

Reinstall engine by reversing removal procedure.

TRACTION DRIVE CLUTCH AND DRIVE BELT

All Models

The traction drive clutch is a spring-tensioned, belt idler-type operated by the clutch/brake pedal. When the pedal is depressed, belt tension is relieved, allowing the engine drive pulley to rotate freely within the drive belt. After the pedal passes the midpoint, the brake is applied.

R&R DRIVE BELT. To remove drive belt, disconnect spark plug wire. If necessary, loosen engine mounting bolts securing belt guide and reposition belt guide. Depress clutch/brake pedal to relieve belt tension, then slip traction drive belt from engine pulley. Remove transmission belt keeper (7—Fig. MX33) and remove traction drive belt from transaxle pulley (8).

Install drive belt by reversing removal procedure.

TRANSAXLE

All Models

REMOVE AND REINSTALL. To remove transaxle (9—Fig. MX33), disconnect spark plug wire and remove mower deck as outlined in MOWER DECK section. Support front of machine. Remove traction drive belt as previously outlined. Disconnect neutral safety switch, if so equipped. Detach shift rod (17) from transaxle shift arm

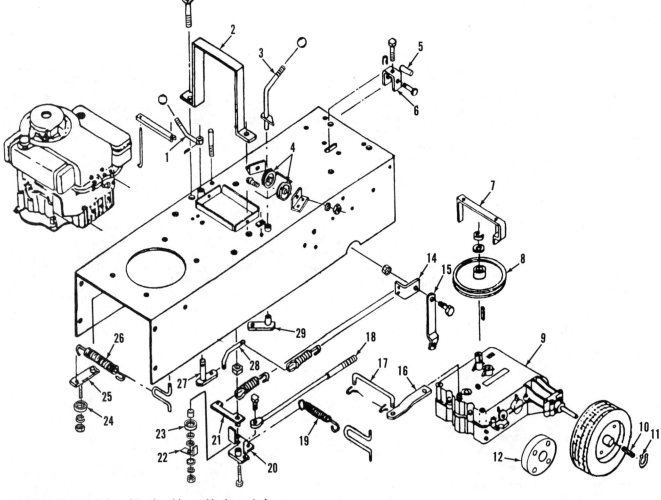

Fig. MX33—Exploded view of traction drive and brake controls.

1. Park brake lever	6. Roller bracket		
2. Seat support	7. Belt keeper	11. Retaining ring	16. Shift rod
3. Shift lever	8. Transaxle pulley	12. Spacer	17. Shift link
4. Idler pulleys	9. Transaxle	14. Brake spring bracket	18. Clutch/brake rod
5. Cable roller	10. Key	15. Brake lever	19. Traction clutch spring

20. Idler plate	25. Idler plate
21. Brake arm	26. Mower belt tension spring
22. Belt keeper	27. Brake arm
23. Idler pulley	28. Park brake link
24. Idler pulley	29. Shift arm

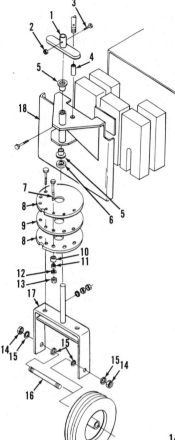

(15). Detach brake springs from brake lever bracket (14). Unscrew transaxle retaining fasteners and remove transaxle.

Reinstall transaxle by reversing removal procedure.

OVERHAUL. All models are equipped with a Peerless 800 series transaxle. Refer to TRANSMISSION REPAIR section for service information.

REAR WHEEL STEERING SYSTEM

All Models

LUBRICATION. A grease fitting is located on steering spindle tube. Inject multipurpose grease into grease fitting after every 25 hours of operation.

R&R AND OVERHAUL. To disassemble rear wheel steering system, detach steering cables from steering discs (8 and 9—Fig. MX34). Raise and support rear of machine. If additional clearance is needed when withdrawing spindle from housing, remove axle and wheel. Unscrew steering stop bolt (3), remove stop (1) and slide spindle (17) out of spindle support tube (18).

Inspect components for excessive wear and damage. Bushings (5) and thrust bearing (6) are renewable. Install spindle by reversing removal procedure. Check steering operation after assembly.

MOWER BELTS

All Models

Two drive belts transfer power from the engine pulley to the mower deck. An intermediate pulley (33—Fig. MX35) connects the two drive belts (26 and 32). Another drive belt (18) transfers power

Fig. MX34—Exploded view of rear wheel steering assembly.

1. Stop		10. Tube	
2. Nut		11. Washer	
3. Bolt		12. Lockwasher	
4. Tube		13. Nut	
5. Bushing		14. Nut	
6. Thrust bearing		15. Washer	
7. Bolt		16. Axle	
8. Disc		17. Wheel yoke & spindle	
9. Disc		18. Spindle support	

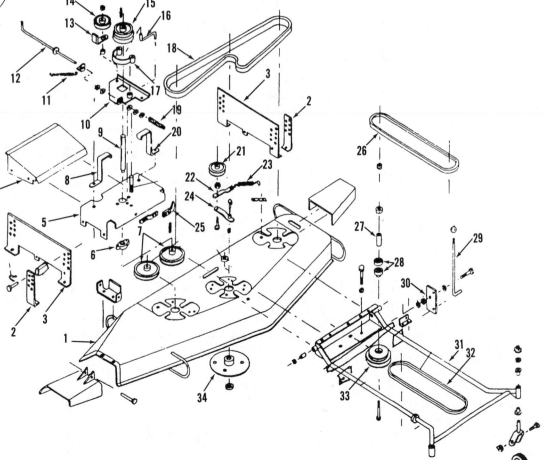

Fig. MX35—Exploded view of mower deck and related components.

1. Mower deck
2. Deck hanger, outside
3. Deck hanger, inside
4. Belt cover
5. Center plate
6. Bearing
7. Spindle pulleys
8. Belt keeper
9. Center spindle shaft
10. Idler plate
11. Spring
12. Blade brake rod
13. Belt keeper
14. Idler pulley
15. Center pulley
16. Brake link
17. Brake band
18. Mower deck belt
19. Brake spring
20. Belt keeper
21. Idler pulley
22. Spring hanger
23. Idler spring
24. Idler arm
25. Blade switch
26. Engine-to-intermediate pulley belt
27. Spacer
28. Bearing
29. Blade control rod
30. Bellcrank
31. Mower stub frame
32. Intermediate pulley-to-mower belt
33. Intermediate pulley
34. Spindle hub

to the three blade spindle pulleys (7 and 15). A band-type brake (17) acts against the upper pulley of the center blade spindle.

REMOVE AND REINSTALL. To remove the front intermediate mower drive belt (26—Fig. MX35) (from intermediate pulley to blade spindle pulley), remove belt cover from mower deck. Detach idler spring for rear intermediate mower drive belt and slip belt off intermediate mower belt pulley (33) (pulley has two grooves). Remove intermediate pulley mounting bolt and relocate pulley to increase slack in front intermediate mower drive belt, then remove the belt. Install belt by reversing removal procedure.

To remove rear intermediate mower drive belt (32) (from engine pulley to intermediate pulley), remove belt cover from mower deck. Disconnect spark plug wire. Loosen engine mounting bolts securing belt guide and reposition belt guide. Depress clutch/brake pedal and remove traction drive belt from engine pulley. Detach idler spring of mower belt idler and slip mower belt off intermediate mower belt pulley (pulley has two grooves). Remove mower belt

from engine pulley. Reinstall belt by reversing removal procedure.

To remove spindle belt (18—Fig. MX35) from mower deck, remove all belt covers. Remove front intermediate mower drive belt as previously outlined. Remove upper pulley (15) from center mower spindle, then remove center plate (5) and idler assembly from mower deck. Push against mower belt idler and remove belt from spindle pulleys. Reinstall belt by reversing removal procedure. Belt guides should be 1/8 inch (3.2 mm) from belt.

MOWER DECK

All Models

R&R AND OVERHAUL. To remove mower deck, detach idler spring of rear mower belt idler and slip rear mower drive belt off intermediate mower belt pulley (pulley has two grooves). Disconnect mower safety switch. Detach mower control rod from bellcrank. Remove mower deck retaining bolts and remove mower deck. Reinstall deck by reversing removal procedure.

Note that intermediate belt pulley (33—Fig. MX35) is equipped with bearings (28) that have lock collars. When

installing bearings on shaft, be sure that ends of shaft extend from each of the bearings approximately 0.020 inch (0.51 mm). Tighten blade retaining screw to 70-80 ft.-lbs. (95-108 N·m).

BLADE BRAKE

All models are equipped with a band-type brake (17—Fig. MX35) that stops rotation of the center blade spindle. The blade brake is actuated by the mower engagement lever. The blade brake is spring-loaded and does not require adjustment.

ELECTRICAL

All Models

Refer to Fig. MX36 for a typical wiring schematic. Note the following points:
- The transmission must be in neutral, the mower must be disengaged and the operator must be in the seat for engine to start.
- The engine should stop if the transmission is in gear or the mower is engaged and the operator leaves the seat.

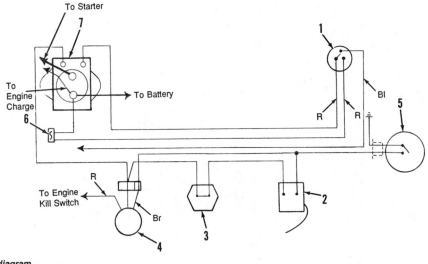

Fig. MX36—Typical wiring diagram.

1. Ignition switch	3. Transaxle neutral switch	7. Solenoid
2. Mower safety switch	4. Engine	Br. Brown
	5. Seat safety switch	Bl. Blue
	6. Fuse	R. Red

MTD

MTD PRODUCTS, INC.
P.O. Box 36900
Cleveland, OH 44136

MODELS COVERED

The MTD models covered in this section are rear-engine 400, 500 or 700 series models. Due to the large number of MTD models and the wide variety of engines installed, an accurate cross-reference table is not available. Determine the manufacturer and model number of the engine being serviced and refer to the appropriate engine section in the rear of this manual for service information.

FRONT AXLE AND STEERING SYSTEM

Models 410 (Early), 420, 425, 430 and 435

R&R AND OVERHAUL. To remove axle main member (8—Fig. MT11), first remove steering shaft (7) as follows: Remove steering wheel cap, retaining nut and washer, then remove steering wheel (1) and spacer tube (4). Drive out roll pin (5) and remove shaft extension (2). Raise and support front of machine. Remove tie rods (10), then withdraw steering shaft (7) from bottom of axle support (11). Remove front wheel assemblies and spindles (9 and 13). Unbolt axle support from frame and remove front axle and support assembly. Remove axle pivot bolt and separate axle main member from support. Remove flange bushings (3) and spindle bushings (14).

Clean and inspect all parts and renew any showing excessive wear or other damage. Reassemble by reversing the disassembly procedure and lubricate bushings and all pivot points with SAE 30 oil.

Models 440 and 445

R&R AND OVERHAUL. To remove axle main member (15—Fig. MT12), support front of machine and remove front wheels. Disconnect tie rods (14) from spindles. Remove cotter pins and washers, then lower spindles (12 and 18) from axle main member. Remove pivot bolt (17) and unhook mower springs from axle support (16). Unbolt axle support from frame (9) and separate axle main member (15) from axle support.

Inspect spindle bushings (13) for excessive wear and renew as needed. Reassemble by reversing the disassembly procedure.

To check front wheel toe-in, measure the distance between front wheels at spindle height at front and rear of wheels. Measured distance at front should be ⅛ inch (3 mm) smaller (toed-

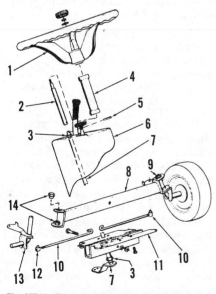

Fig. MT11—Exploded view of front axle and steering system used on Models 410 (early production), 420, 425, 430 and 435.

1. Steering wheel	8. Axle main member
2. Shaft extension	9. Spindle (L.H.)
3. Flange bushings	10. Tie rods
4. Spacer tube	11. Axle support
5. Roll pin	12. Tie rod end
6. Console	13. Spindle (R.H.)
7. Steering shaft	14. Spindle bushings

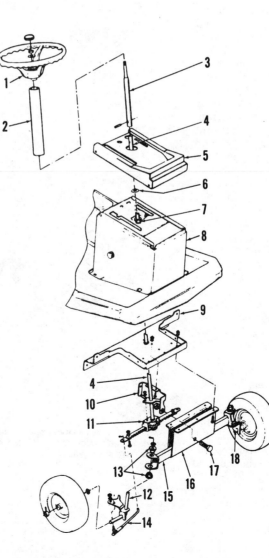

Fig. MT12—Exploded view of front axle and steering system used on Models 440 and 445.

1. Steering wheel
2. Spacer tube
3. Shaft extension
4. Steering shaft
5. Cover
6. Washer
7. Flange bushing
8. Console
9. Frame
10. Support
11. Rack & pinion
12. Spindle (R.H.)
13. Spindle bushings
14. Tie rods
15. Axle main member
16. Axle support
17. Pivot bolt
18. Spindle (L.H.)

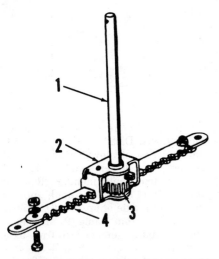

Fig. MT13—Steering rack and pinion assembly used on Models 440 and 445. Models 796 and 797 are similar.

1. Steering shaft	3. Pinion
2. Steering housing	4. Rack (2 pieces)

in) than distance at rear. If necessary, adjust length of tie rods (14) to obtain a toe-in of ⅛ inch (3 mm). Be sure tie rods are adjusted equally.

To remove steering gear, remove steering wheel cap, retaining nut and washer, then lift off steering wheel (1). Remove spacer tube (2), drive out roll pin and remove shaft extension (3) and washer (6). Raise front of machine and support securely. Disconnect tie rods (14) from ends of rack. Unbolt steering rack and pinion housing (11) from support (10) and withdraw steering unit from bottom. Refer to Fig. MT13 and drive out roll pin securing pinion (3) to steering shaft (1). Withdraw shaft and remove pinion. Remove bolt from one end of two-piece rack (4) and slide rack out of housing (2).

Clean and inspect all parts and renew any showing excessive wear or other damage. Flange bushing (7—Fig. MT12) can be removed and a new bushing installed if needed. Reassemble by reversing disassembly procedure. Lubricate rack and pinion with multipurpose lithium grease. Lubricate flange bushing (7), spindle bushings (13), pivot bolt (17) and front wheels with SAE 30 oil.

All Other 400 Series Models

R&R AND OVERHAUL. To remove axle main member (15—Fig. MT14), first remove steering shaft (4) as follows: Remove steering wheel cap, retaining nut and washer, then lift off steering wheel (1) and cover (2). Unbolt and remove shaft extension (3), speed nut (5) and washer (6). Disconnect tie rods (11) from spindles (10 and 13), raise front of machine and withdraw steering

shaft (4) from bottom of axle main member. Support frame and remove front wheels. Remove cotter pins and washers, then lower spindles (10 and 13) from axle. Unbolt and remove axle main member (15) from frame (9). Flange bushings (7 and 12) and spindle bushings (14) can now be removed if necessary.

Clean and inspect all parts and renew any showing excessive wear or damage. Reassemble by reversing the disassembly procedure and lubricate bushings and all pivot points with SAE 30 oil. Tie rods are not adjustable.

All 500 Series Models

R&R AND OVERHAUL. To remove axle main member (20—Fig. MT15), remove mower unit. Remove steering shaft (5) as follows: Remove steering wheel cap, retaining nut and washer, then lift off steering wheel (4). On Models 502, 504, 506, 510, 520, 530 and 550 remove sleeve (6). On all models, remove cover (31), unscrew nut at lower end of steering shaft and remove steer-

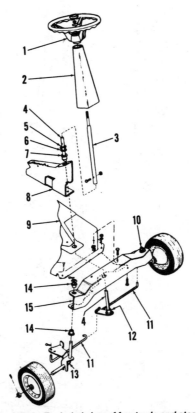

Fig. MT14—Exploded view of front axle and steering system used on Models 400, 402, 405, 406, 407, 410 (late production) and 412.

1. Steering wheel	
2. Cover	
3. Shaft extension	9. Frame
4. Steering shaft	10. Spindle (L.H.)
5. Retainer	11. Tie rods
6. Washer	12. Flange bushing
7. Flange bushing	13. Spindle (R.H.)
8. Support	14. Spindle bushings
	15. Axle main member

ing gear (36). Remove steering shaft. Disconnect tie rods (26) at spindles (25). Detach steering support plate (30) and sector gear (35). Raise and support the frame and remove front wheels. Remove cotter pins or speed nuts and washers, then lower spindles (25) from axle. Detach front axle support (28) from frame and remove axle main member (20).

Clean and inspect all parts and renew any showing excessive wear or damage. Reassemble by reversing the disassembly procedure and lubricate bushings and all pivot points with SAE 30 oil. Steering gear backlash is adjusted by moving adjuster plate (29) in the slotted mounting holes. After adjusting plate position, operate steering through full range of movement and check for binding.

To check front wheel toe-in, measure the distance between front wheels at spindle height at front and rear of wheels. Measured distance at front should be ⅛ inch (3 mm) smaller (toed-in) than distance at rear. If necessary, adjust length of tie rods (26) to obtain a toe-in of ⅛ inch (3 mm). Be sure tie rods are adjusted equally.

Models 796 and 797

R&R AND OVERHAUL. To remove axle main member (6—Fig. MT16), support front of machine and remove front wheels. Disconnect tie rods (9) from spindles (8). Remove cotter pins and washers, then withdraw spindles and bushings (7) from axle ends. Unbolt and remove axle from frame.

Inspect for excessive wear and renew if needed. Reassemble by reversing removal procedure and lubricate spindle bushings and front wheels with SAE 30 oil. Adjust tie rods to obtain a toe-in setting of ⅛ inch (3 mm).

To remove steering gear, remove steering wheel cap, retaining nut and washer, then lift off steering wheel (1—Fig. MT16) and cover (2). Drive out roll pin and remove shaft extension (3) and flange bushing (4). Disconnect tie rods (9) from rack (10). Unbolt mounting bracket (11) and withdraw steering unit from bottom. Drive out roll pin and withdraw shaft (1—Fig. MT13) and pinion (3). Remove bolt from end of two-piece rack and slide rack (4) out of housing (2).

Clean and inspect parts and renew if needed. Reassemble by reversing removal procedure. Lubricate rack and pinion with multipurpose lithium grease and flange bushings with SAE 30 oil.

SERVICE MANUAL

ENGINE

Models 440 and 445

Refer to appropriate engine section in this manual for tune-up specifications, engine overhaul procedures and engine maintenance.

REMOVE AND REINSTALL. To remove engine, raise engine cover and disconnect spark plug wire. Disconnect battery cables, ignition wire from mag-

neto, cable from starter and throttle control cable. Unbolt exhaust pipe from engine. Place lift and blade clutch lever in disengage position. Remove belt guides at engine pulley. Remove mower drive belt from engine pulley. Move lift and blade clutch lever to lowest notch. Unbolt and remove engine pulley belt guard. Unhook main drive belt clutch idler springs. Remove shoulder bolt near transmission input pulley. Remove main drive belt from transmission pulley first, then from engine pulley. Unbolt and remove the engine pulley.

Remove engine mounting bolts, then lift engine from frame.

Reinstall engine by reversing removal procedure. Make certain belt guard and guides are properly installed.

Models 796 and 797

Refer to appropriate engine section in this manual for tune-up specifications, engine overhaul procedures and engine maintenance.

REMOVE AND REINSTALL. To remove engine, disconnect spark plug wire, battery cables, ignition wire from magneto, cable from starter and throttle control cable at engine. Engage blade clutch lever. Loosen mower deck front mounting bolts and remove rear mounting bolts. Raise mower and slip mower drive belt off engine pulley. Remove engine pulley belt guard and shoulder bolts at transmission pulley. Slip traction drive belt off transmission pulley first, then off engine pulley. Remove en-

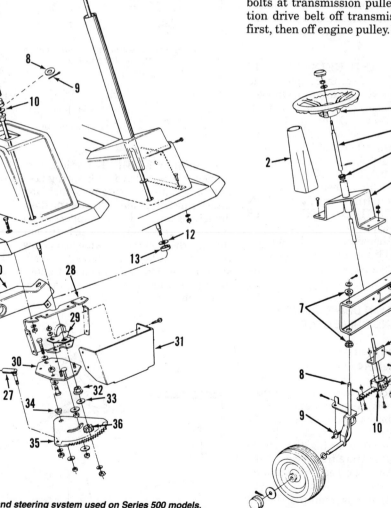

Fig. MT15—Exploded view of typical front axle and steering system used on Series 500 models.

1. Cap	10. Washer	19. Bushing	28. Axle support
2. Nut	11. Bushing	20. Axle main member	29. Steering adjuster
3. Washer	12. Washer	21. Hub cap	30. Steering plate
4. Steering wheel	13. Spacer	22. Cotter pin	31. Bracket
5. Steering shaft	14. Bracket	23. Washer	32. Bushing
6. Steering column	15. Plate	24. Bushing	33. Washer
7. Spacer	16. Axle support	25. Spindle	34. Bushing
8. Washer	17. Cotter pin	26. Tie rod	35. Sector gear
9. Cotter pin	18. Washer	27. Tie rod end	36. Steering gear

Fig. MT16—Exploded view of front axle and steering system used on Models 796 and 797.

1. Steering wheel
2. Cover
3. Shaft extension
4. Flange bushing
5. Steering support
6. Axle
7. Spindle bushing
8. Spindles
9. Tie rods
10. Steering rack
11. Mounting bracket

Illustrations Courtesy MTD Products, Inc.

227

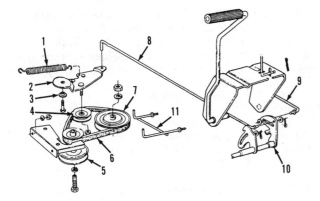

gine mounting bolts and lift engine from frame.

Reinstall by reversing removal procedure.

All Other Models

Refer to appropriate engine section in this manual for tune-up specifications, engine overhaul procedures and engine maintenance.

REMOVE AND REINSTALL. To remove engine, disconnect spark plug wire and remove engine cover. On electric start models, disconnect and remove battery. Disconnect any interfering electrical wires from engine. Disconnect throttle cable from engine. Detach exhaust pipe. Remove mower as outlined in MOWER DECK section. Remove traction drive belt from engine pulley as outlined in TRACTION DRIVE CLUTCH AND DRIVE BELTS section. Detach pulleys from the engine crankshaft, then remove engine mounting bolts and lift engine from frame.

Reinstall by reversing removal procedure.

TRACTION DRIVE CLUTCH AND DRIVE BELT

Single-Speed Models Except Models 440-445

The traction drive clutch is a spring-tensioned, belt idler-type operated by the clutch/brake pedal (Fig. MT17). When the pedal is depressed, belt tension is removed, allowing the engine drive pulley to rotate freely within the drive belt. After the pedal passes midpoint, the brake is applied.

No adjustment is required. If belt slippage occurs and pulleys and linkage are in good operating condition, a new belt should be installed.

R&R DRIVE BELT. To remove drive belt, disconnect spark plug wire and tie out of way. Remove mower deck as out-

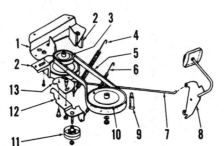

Fig. MT17—Exploded view of traction drive assembly used on later models with single-speed drive. Early models are similar.

1. Spring
2. Idler clutch arm
3. Bushing
4. Idler
5. Engine pulley
6. Drive belt
7. Transaxle pulley
8. Clutch rod
9. Brake rod
10. Clutch/brake pedal assy.
11. Belt guides

Fig. MT18—Exploded view of traction drive clutch assembly used on Models 440 and 445.

1. Engine pulley belt guard
2. Belt guides
3. Engine pulley
4. Clutch spring (heavy)
5. Main drive belt
6. Clutch spring (light)
7. Clutch rod
8. Clutch pedal
9. Shoulder bolt
10. Transmission pulley
11. Idler pulley
12. Idler arm
13. Idler pivot plate

lined in MOWER DECK section. Disconnect traction drive idler spring (1—Fig. MT17) and relocate or detach any interfering belt guides. On later models, detach torque rod and support from transaxle, then pull drive belt (6) out through the opening in frame just below the engine pulley and above the transaxle pulley. On early models, remove idler and transmission pulley and remove belt.

Install drive belt by reversing removal procedure. Be sure belt guides are in position.

Models 440-445

The traction drive clutch is a spring-tensioned, belt idler-type operated by the clutch pedal (Fig. MT18). When the pedal is depressed, belt tension is removed, allowing the engine drive pulley to rotate freely within the drive belt.

No adjustment is required. If belt slippage occurs and pulleys and linkage are in good operating condition, a new belt should be installed.

REMOVE AND REINSTALL. To remove traction drive belt, raise engine cover and disconnect spark plug wire. Place lift and blade clutch lever in disengaged position. Remove belt guides (2—Fig. MT18) at engine pulley and slip mower drive belt from engine pulley. Move lift and blade clutch lever to lowest notch. Unbolt and remove engine pulley guard (1), then unhook clutch idler springs (4 and 6). Remove shoulder bolt (9) near transmission input pulley. Remove traction drive belt (5) from transmission pulley first, then from engine pulley.

Install new belt by reversing removal procedure. Make certain belt guard and belt guides are properly installed.

Early Variable-Speed Models

Early models may be equipped with a drive system that uses two drive belts and a variable speed pulley to transfer power from the engine to the transaxle. The primary (lower) drive belt connects the engine to the variable speed pulley (7—Fig. MT19). The variable speed pulley also serves as the clutch idler. The

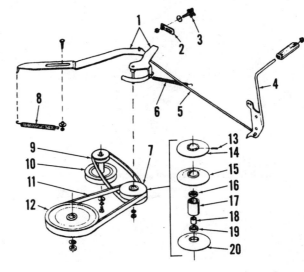

Fig. MT19—Exploded view of clutch and variable speed assembly used on early models.

1. Clutch and variable speed bracket
2. Speed control stop
3. Knob
4. Clutch pedal
5. Clutch rod
6. Clutch spring
7. Variable speed pulley
8. Variable speed spring
9. Primary drive belt
10. Engine pulley
11. Secondary drive belt
12. Transmission input pulley
13. Roll pin (2 used)
14. Pulley half (top)
15. Movable pulley half
16. Bearing
17. Sleeve
18. Spacer
19. Bearing
20. Pulley half (bottom)

Illustrations Courtesy MTD Products, Inc.

diameters of the pulley grooves are determined by spring tension, which is regulated by the position of the speed control. Ground speed changes when the pulley diameters change on the variable speed pulley.

R&R DRIVE BELTS. To remove traction drive belts (9 and 11—Fig. MT19), remove mower deck as outlined in MOWER DECK section. Depress clutch pedal and engage pedal lock. Remove engine pulley belt guide and un-

hook clutch tension springs. Remove retaining nuts from variable speed pulley and transmission pulley, then slide pulleys off shafts and remove drive belts.

Install new belts by reversing removal procedure. When reassembling transmission pulley (12), install hub side up.

Later Variable-Speed Models

Later models are equipped with a drive system that uses two drive belts

and a variable speed pulley to transfer power from the engine to the transaxle. The primary (lower) drive belt (25—Fig. MT20) connects the engine to the variable speed pulley (23). The diameters of the pulley grooves are determined by belt tension, which is regulated by the position of idlers (10 and 17). The idlers move when the speed control lever is operated. Ground speed changes when the pulley diameters change on the variable speed pulley.

ADJUSTMENT. The speed control lever (39—Fig. MT20) and gear shift lever (36) must be synchronized with the positions of the belt idlers. With engine running and gear shift lever in neutral position, place speed control lever in high-speed position. Release then slowly depress fully the clutch/brake pedal and hold down pedal. Shut off engine and release pedal when engine stops. Move the speed control lever to second speed position. Detach bent end of lower speed control rod (32—Fig. MT20) and turn rod so end of rod will just enter forward end of slot (S). Reattach rod.

Move gear shift lever to neutral slot on gear indicator panel. If machine does not move freely forward and backward thereby indicating transaxle is in neutral, loosen screw (W—Fig. MT20). Move shift lever (36) as needed so transaxle is in neutral and shift lever is in center of neutral slot on control panel. Retighten screw (W) to 13 ft.-lbs. (18 N•m).

R&R DRIVE BELTS. Lower Belt. To remove lower drive belt (25—Fig. MT20), disconnect spark plug wire and remove battery. Remove mower as outlined in MOWER DECK section. Disconnect idler spring (16). Detach torque rod bracket (34) from transaxle and torque rod (8) and remove bracket. Separate belt from pulleys and remove belt.

Install lower belt by reversing removal procedure.

Upper Belt. The lower belt must be removed as outlined in previous section before removing upper belt (22—Fig. MT20). Detach engine pulley belt guide (14), then unscrew retaining nut and remove idler (10). Remove upper belt.

Install upper belt by reversing removal procedure. Be sure hub side of idler (10) is next to idler arm (3). Install belt and idler simultaneously so belt is inside belt guide (9).

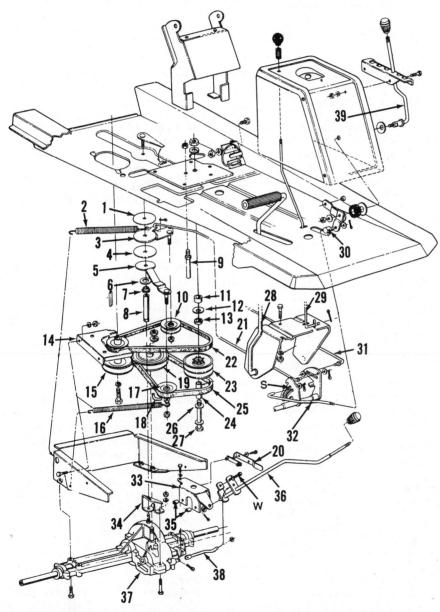

Fig. MT20—Exploded view of clutch and variable speed assembly used on later models.

1. Thrust washer	11. Spacer	21. Clutch rod	30. Ferrule
2. Spring	12. Belleville washer	22. Upper drive belt	31. Brake rod
3. Idler arm	13. Thrust washer	23. Variable speed pulley	32. Speed control rod
4. Thrust washer	14. Belt guard	24. Spacer	33. Bracket
5. Idler arm	15. Engine pulley	25. Lower drive belt	34. Bracket
6. Washer	16. Spring	26. Thrust washer	35. Spacers
7. Bushing	17. Idler	27. Cap screw	36. Shift lever
8. Torque rod	18. Belt guide	28. Pedal rod	37. Transaxle
9. Belt guide	19. Transaxle pulley	29. Park brake rod	38. Shift rod
10. Idler	20. Safety switch		39. Speed control lever

Illustrations Courtesy MTD Products, Inc.

VARIABLE SPEED PULLEY

All Models So Equipped

R&R AND OVERHAUL. The variable speed pulley is accessible after removing drive belts as previously outlined. Individual components of the variable speed pulley used on early models are available, while the variable speed pulley on later models is available only as a unit assembly. Refer to Fig. MT19 for an exploded view of early model variable speed pulley. Bearings are sealed and do not require lubrication. Apply a dry lubricant to movable pulley half and sleeve.

Fig. MT21—Exploded view of differential assembly, rear axles and axle bearings used on Models 400, 402, 405, 406, 407, 410 (late production) and 412.

1. Washer	4. Bearing bracket	7. Bearing plate	10. Axle bearing (outer)
2. Axle shaft (R.H.)	5. Differential assy.	8. Bearing bracket	11. Axle shaft (L.H.)
3. Axle bearing (outer)	6. Axle bearing (center)	9. Bearing bracket	12. Washer

TRANSMISSION/TRANSAXLE

Models With Chain Drive

REMOVE AND REINSTALL. Early models are equipped with a transmission that is coupled to the differential by a chain. To remove transmission, first remove mower as outlined in MOWER DECK section and remove traction drive belt as outlined in previous section. Unbolt and remove transmission pulley. Disconnect transmission shift linkage, then unbolt and remove engine cover. Disconnect drive chain at master link. Unbolt transmission from frame and remove transmission.

Reinstall by reversing removal procedure.

OVERHAUL. All models are equipped with either a Foote or Peerless transmission. Refer to TRANSMISSION REPAIR section for service information.

Models Without Chain Drive

REMOVE AND REINSTALL. To remove transaxle, first remove drive belts as previously outlined. Disconnect brake linkage and shift linkage. Support rear of machine and remove transaxle mounting bolts. Raise rear of machine and roll transaxle assembly from under machine.

Reinstall by reversing removal procedure.

OVERHAUL. All models are equipped with an MTD Model 717 transaxle. Refer to TRANSMISSION REPAIR section for service information.

DRIVE CHAIN

Models 440, 445, 796 and 797

ADJUSTMENT. Drive chain tension should be checked periodically. The chain should deflect approximately ½ inch (13 mm) when depressed with thumb midway between sprockets. To adjust drive chain, loosen chain idler mounting nuts and slide chain idler rearward to tighten or forward to loosen drive chain. When chain tension is correct, retighten idler mounting nuts.

REMOVE AND REINSTALL. To remove drive chain, rotate driven sprocket to locate master link. Disconnect master link and remove drive chain. Clean and inspect chain and sprockets and renew if excessively worn.

Install drive chain and adjust chain tension as outlined in previous paragraph. Lubricate chain with a light coat of SAE 30 oil.

All Other Models So Equipped

ADJUSTMENT. Drive chain tension should be checked periodically. The chain should deflect approximately ½ inch (13 mm) when depressed with thumb midway between sprockets. To adjust drive chain, loosen transmission mounting nuts slightly. Turn draw bolt, located under right side of main frame, clockwise to tighten or counterclockwise to loosen drive chain. When chain tension is correct, retighten transmission mounting nuts.

REMOVE AND REINSTALL. To remove drive chain, rotate driven sprocket to locate master link. Disconnect master link and remove drive chain. Clean and inspect chain and

sprockets and renew if excessively worn.

Install drive chain and adjust chain tension as outlined in previous paragraph. Lubricate chain with a light coat of SAE 30 oil.

DIFFERENTIAL, DRIVE SPROCKET AND REAR AXLE

Models 400, 402, 405, 406, 407, 410 (Late Production) and 412

REMOVE AND REINSTALL. To remove differential and rear axle assembly, raise and support rear of machine. Locate master link in drive chain and disconnect chain. Remove rear wheel assemblies. Refer to Fig. MT21 and unbolt axle bearing brackets (4, 8 and 9) from frame. Remove differential and axle assembly, being careful not to damage brake caliper assembly. Clean all paint, rust or burrs from axle shafts and remove axle bearings and brackets.

Clean and inspect axle bearings and renew as necessary. When reinstalling, flanges on outer axle bearings (3 and 10) must face outward (against wheel hubs). Flange on inner axle bearing (6) must be toward differential housing. Lubricate axle bearings and drive chain with SAE 30 oil. If drive chain requires adjustment, refer to DRIVE CHAIN section.

OVERHAUL. All models are equipped with a MTD differential. Refer to DIFFERENTIAL REPAIR section for service information.

Early Model 410

REMOVE AND REINSTALL. To remove differential and rear axle assembly, raise and support rear of machine. Locate master link in drive chain and disconnect chain. Remove rear wheel assemblies. Disconnect brake rod, then unbolt and remove brake caliper assembly. Withdraw axle bearings from each side of frame. Remove axle and sprocket assembly by sliding unit first to the left and then to the right until free of frame.

Clean and inspect all parts for excessive wear and damage. Drive sprocket and axle is serviced only as an assembly. Reassemble by reversing disassembly procedure. Lubricate axle bearings and drive chain with SAE 30 oil. If drive chain requires adjustment, refer to DRIVE CHAIN section.

OVERHAUL. Early Model 410 is equipped with an MTD differential. Refer to DIFFERENTIAL REPAIR section for service information.

Models 420, 425, 430 and 435

REMOVE AND REINSTALL. To remove differential and rear axle assembly, raise and support rear of machine. Locate master link in drive chain and disconnect chain. Remove rear wheel assemblies. Disconnect brake rod, then unbolt and remove brake caliper assembly. Remove washers (1 and 12—Fig. MT22) and outer axle bearings (3 and 10) from axles and frame. Unbolt bearing bracket (8) from frame, then remove differential and rear axle assembly by sliding unit first to the left and then to the right out of the frame. Clean all paint, rust or burrs from left axle shaft (11) and slide center bearing (6) and bearing bracket from axle.

Clean and inspect axle bearings and renew if necessary. During assembly, note that flanges on outer axle bearings (3 and 10) must face outward (against wheel hubs). Flange on center axle bearing (6) must be toward differential housing. Lubricate axle bearings and drive chain with SAE 30 oil. If drive chain requires adjustment, refer to DRIVE CHAIN section.

OVERHAUL. All models are equipped with an MTD differential. Refer to DIFFERENTIAL REPAIR section for service information.

Models 440 and 445

REMOVE AND REINSTALL. To remove differential and rear axle assembly, place mower lift and blade clutch lever in disengaged position. Remove belt keepers at engine pulley and slip mower drive belt from engine pulley. Raise rear of unit and support se-

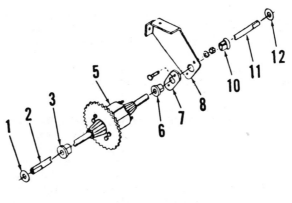

Fig. MT22—Exploded view of differential assembly, rear axles and axle bearings used on Models 420, 425, 430 and 435. Refer to Fig. MT21 for parts identification.

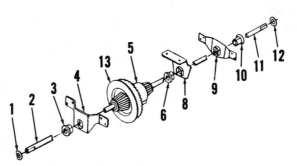

Fig. MT23—Exploded view of differential assembly, rear axles and axle bearings used on Models 440 and 445.

1. Washer
2. Axle shaft (R.H.)
3. Axle bearing (outer)
4. Bearing bracket
5. Differential assy.
6. Axle bearing (center)
8. Bearing bracket
9. Bearing bracket
10. Axle bearing (outer)
11. Axle shaft (L.H.)
12. Washer
13. Brake disc

curely. Locate master link in drive chain and disconnect chain. Remove rear wheel assemblies and disconnect brake rod. Unbolt and remove left axle bearing and bracket. See Fig. MT23. Unbolt right and center axle bearing brackets from main frame, move differential assembly forward to clear the brake caliper unit, then remove differential and rear axle assembly out toward right side. Clean all rust paint or burrs from axle shafts and remove axle bearings and brackets.

Clean and inspect axle bearings and renew as needed. When reinstalling, flanges on outer axle bearings must face outward (against wheel hubs). Flange on inner axle bearing must be toward differential housing. Remainder of reassembly is reverse of disassembly procedure. Lubricate axle bearings with SAE 30 oil.

Models 796 and 797

REMOVE AND REINSTALL. To remove differential and rear axle assembly (5—Fig. MT24), raise rear of unit and support securely. Disconnect drive chain at master link. Unbolt axle support bracket (8). Unbolt axle bearing brackets (2) and lower and remove differential assembly from frame. Remove rear wheels and spacers (1). Remove paint, rust or burrs from axle and slide bearings off axle.

Reinstall in reverse order of removal.

GROUND DRIVE BRAKE

Models With Chain Drive

ADJUSTMENT. Check brake operation by pushing brake pedal and attempting to move machine. If brake does not hold machine with pedal fully depressed, adjust brake. To adjust brake, release brake and turn nut (6—Fig. MT25) on cam lever until desired brake operation is obtained. Make certain brake does not drag when pedal is released.

R&R AND OVERHAUL. To remove brake caliper assembly, disconnect re-

Fig. MT24—Differential, rear axles and bearings used on Models 796 and 797.

1. Spacer
2. Axle bracket
3. Axle bushing (outer)
4. Washer
5. Differential & axle assy.
6. Disc brake
7. Axle bushing (inner)
8. Support bracket
9. Brake rod
10. Drive chain
11. Idler
12. Idler arm

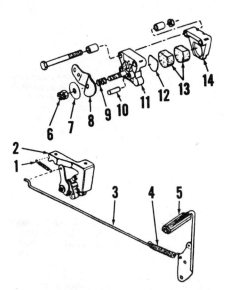

Fig. MT25—Exploded view of typical caliper brake used on models with chain drive. Drive chain sprocket is also brake disc.

1. Return spring
2. Caliper assy.
3. Brake rod
4. Brake tension spring
5. Brake pedal
6. Adjusting nut
7. Washer
8. Cam lever
9. Spring
10. Actuating pin (2)
11. Carrier (outer)
12. Backup plate
13. Brake pads
14. Carrier (inner)

turn spring (1—Fig. MT25) and brake rod (3). Unbolt mounting bracket from frame and remove caliper assembly (2). Remove adjusting nut (6), washer (7), cam lever (8), spring (9) and actuating pins (10). Remove through-bolts and separate brake pads (13) and backup plate (12) from carriers (11 and 14).

Clean and inspect all parts for excessive wear and damage. Reassemble by reversing disassembly procedure. Be sure actuator pins (10) are installed with rounded end toward cam lever (8).

Models Without Chain Drive

ADJUSTMENT. Check brake operation by pushing brake pedal and at-

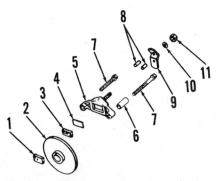

Fig. MT26—Exploded view of typical caliper brake used on models not equipped with a chain drive.

1. Brake pad (inner)
2. Brake disc
3. Brake pad (outer)
4. Backup plate
5. Carrier
6. Spacer
7. Cap screws
8. Adjusting pins
9. Cam lever
10. Washer
11. Adjusting nut

tempting to move machine. If brake does not hold machine with pedal fully depressed, adjust brake. To adjust brake, release brake and turn nut (11—Fig. MT26) on cam lever until desired brake operation is obtained.

R&R AND OVERHAUL. To remove brake caliper assembly, disconnect brake spring and brake rod from actuating lever. Unbolt and remove brake pad carrier (5—Fig. MT26). Slide brake disc off transaxle shaft and remove inner brake pad from slot in transaxle housing.

Clean and inspect all parts for excessive wear and damage. Reassemble by reversing disassembly procedure.

MOWER DRIVE BELTS

Models 420 and 425

REMOVE AND REINSTALL. Before removing mower drive belt (2—Fig. MT27), disconnect spark plug wire. Place lift and blade clutch lever in disengaged position. Remove belt guide and shoulder bolt at engine pulley, then slip mower drive belt from engine pulley. Move lift and blade clutch lever fully forward in engaged position and unhook both tension springs from mower deck. Unpin lift arms from mower deck and remove mower unit from under right side. Unbolt and remove shoulder bolt (8) and belt keepers (9) from mower housing and remove mower drive belt.

Install new belt by reversing removal procedure. Make certain belt guides and shoulder bolts are properly installed.

Models 400, 402, 405, 406, 407 and 410 (Early Production)

REMOVE AND REINSTALL. Before removing mower drive belt, disconnect spark plug wire. Place lift and blade clutch lever in engaged position. Unbolt and remove belt guides at engine pulley. Unbolt and remove belt guards, belt guides or shoulder bolts at mower pulleys. Move lift and blade clutch to disengaged position and remove belt from pulleys.

Install new belt by reversing removal procedure. Make certain belt guides, belt guards and shoulder bolts are properly installed.

Models 410 (Later Production) and 412

REMOVE AND REINSTALL. Before removing mower drive belt (1—Fig. MT28), disconnect spark plug wire. Place lift and blade clutch lever in disengaged position. Unbolt and remove belt guides or shoulder bolts at engine pulley. Remove blade pulley belt guide (5). Unbolt and remove idler pulley (3), then remove belt from mower.

Install new belt by reversing removal procedure. Make certain belt guides, belt guards and shoulder bolts are properly installed.

Models 440 and 445

REMOVE AND REINSTALL. To remove mower drive belt (4—Fig. MT29), place lift and blade clutch lever in disengaged position. Remove belt guides at engine pulley and slip mower drive belt from engine pulley. Move lift

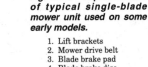

Fig. MT27—Exploded view of typical single-blade mower unit used on some early models.

1. Lift brackets
2. Mower drive belt
3. Blade brake pad
4. Blade brake disc
5. Mower pulley
6. Bearing housing
7. Ball bearing
8. Shoulder bolt
9. Belt guides
10. Spindle mounting plate
11. Mower tension springs
12. Spacer
13. Ball bearing
14. Bearing housing
15. Blade spindle
16. Adapter
17. Blade
18. Mower deck
19. Deflector bracket
20. Deflector

                 Illustrations Courtesy MTD Products, Inc.

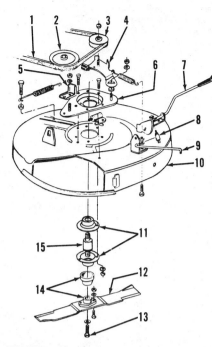

Fig. MT28—Exploded view of typical single-blade mower unit used on some early models.

1. Blade belt
2. Blade pulley
3. Idler
4. Idler & brake arm
5. Belt guide
6. Spindle mounting plate
7. Clutch lever
8. Safety switch
9. Stabilizer rod
10. Mower deck
11. Bearing housings
12. Blade
13. Center bolt
14. Blade adapter
15. Spindle & bearing assy.

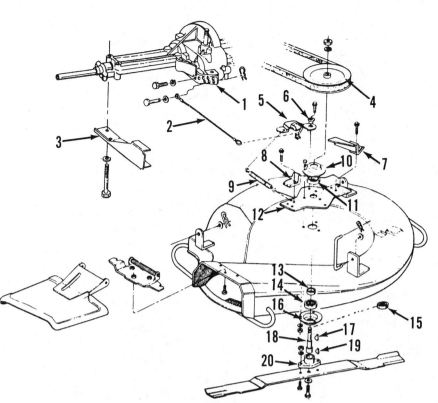

Fig. MT30—Exploded view of 26-inch mower deck used on some Series 500 models. Spindle components are available only as a unit assembly on later models.

1. Bracket
2. Blade brake cable
3. Bracket
4. Pulley
5. Blade brake
6. Spacer
7. Belt guide
8. Belt guide
9. Spring
10. Bearing housing
11. Bearing
12. Spindle mounting plate
13. Spacer
14. Bearing
15. Bearing shield
16. Bearing housing
17. Key
18. Spindle
19. Key
20. Blade adapter

and blade clutch lever to lowest notch. Unbolt and remove belt guide (7) at left mower pulley, then remove mower belt.

Install new belt by reversing removal procedure. Make certain belt guides are properly installed.

500 Series With Single Blade

REMOVE AND REINSTALL. To remove the mower drive belt on Series 500 models with a single mower blade, refer to appropriate Fig. MT30 through MT33 and proceed as follows: Disconnect spark plug wire. Place blade engagement lever in disengaged position. Locate outside engine belt guard at right rear side of machine and remove one retaining bolt while loosening the other bolt. Pivot belt guard out and away from engine pulley. Disconnect blade brake cable from belt guard and remove belt guard. Disconnect mower deck links and remove belt guides from deck. Remove belt.

Install mower belt by reversing removal procedure.

500 Series With Dual Blades

REMOVE AND REINSTALL. To remove the mower drive belt on Series 500 models with dual mower blades, refer to Fig. MT34 or Fig. MT35 and proceed as follows: Disconnect spark plug wire. Move mower deck to lowest position. Place blade engagement lever in disengaged position. Locate outside engine belt guard at right rear side of machine and remove one retaining bolt while loosening the other bolt. Pivot belt guard out and away from engine pulley. Locate inside engine pulley belt guard, remove one bolt, loosen other bolt and pivot guard out of way. Separate drive belt from engine pulley. Detach blade brake spring), remove belt guard and remove upper belt. Detach mower belt idler spring and remove lower belt.

Install mower belts by reversing removal procedure.

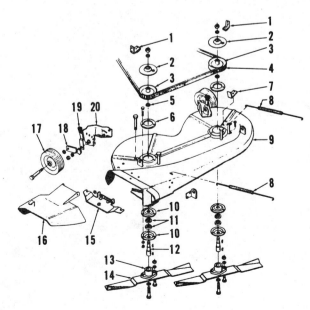

Fig. MT29—Exploded view of dual-blade mower unit used on Models 440 and 445.

1. Blade brake pad
2. Brake disc
3. Mower pulley
4. Mower belt
5. Washer
6. Plate
7. Belt guide
8. Mower tension springs
9. Mower housing
10. Bearing retainers
11. Ball bearings
12. Blade spindle
14. Blade adapter
14. Blade
15. Deflector bracket
16. Deflector
17. Gage wheel
18. Pivot bar
19. Adjusting lever
20. Wheel bracket

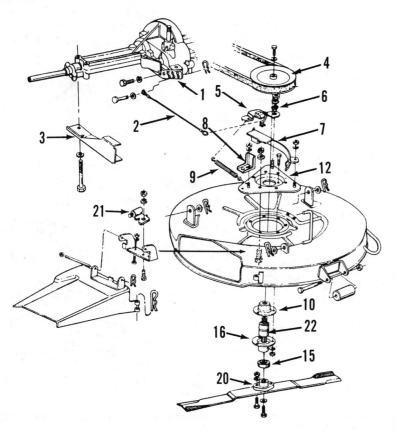

Fig. MT31—Exploded view of 30-inch mower deck used on some Series 500 models. Spindle components are available only as a unit assembly on later models.

1. Bracket
2. Blade brake cable
3. Bracket
4. Pulley
5. Blade brake
6. Spacer
7. Belt guide
8. Belt guide
9. Spring
10. Bearing housing
12. Spindle mounting plate
15. Bearing shield
16. Bearing housing
20. Blade adapter
21. Safety switch
22. Bearing & spindle assy.

Models 796 and 797

REMOVE AND REINSTALL. To remove the mower drive belt, proceed as follows: Disconnect spark plug wire. Place blade engagement lever in disengaged position. Locate outside engine belt guard at right rear side of machine and remove one retaining bolt while loosening the other bolt. Pivot belt guard out and away from engine pulley. Disconnect blade brake cable from belt guard and remove belt guard. Disconnect mower deck links and remove belt guides from deck. Remove belt.

Install mower belt by reversing removal procedure.

MOWER DECK

All Models

HEIGHT ADJUSTMENT. Front of mower blade should be $\frac{1}{4}$-$\frac{3}{8}$ inch (6.4-9.5 mm) lower than rear of blade. Mower deck should be level from side to side. Adjust mower deck hanger lengths as needed to obtain desired height.

REMOVE AND REINSTALL. Disconnect spark plug wire. Move mower deck to lowest position. Place blade engagement lever in disengaged position. Locate outside engine belt guard at right rear side of machine and remove

Fig. MT32—Exploded view of 30-inch mower deck used on some Series 500 models. Spindle components are available only as a unit assembly on later models.

1. Bracket
2. Blade brake cable
3. Bracket
4. Pulley
5. Blade brake
6. Spacer
9. Spring
12. Spindle mounting plate
20. Blade adapter
22. Bearing & spindle assy.

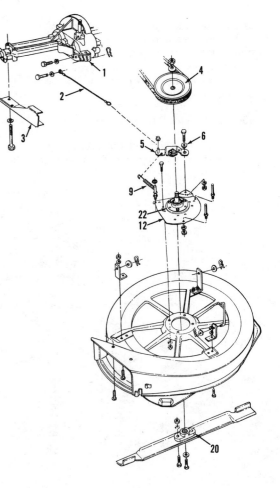

Illustrations Courtesy MTD Products, Inc.

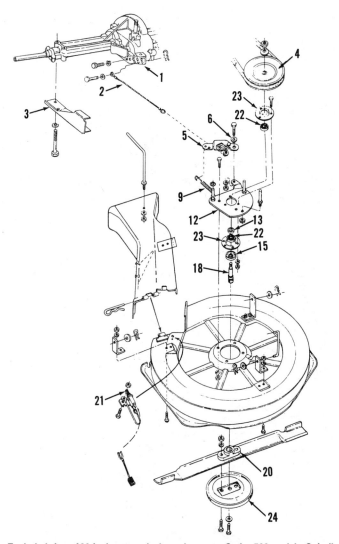

Fig. MT33—Exploded view of 30-inch mower deck used on some Series 500 models. Spindle components are available only as a unit assembly on later models.

1. Bracket
2. Blade brake cable
3. Bracket
4. Pulley
5. Blade brake
6. Spacer
9. Spring
12. Spindle mounting plate
13. Spacer
15. Bearing shield
18. Spindle
20. Blade adapter
21. Safety switch
24. Scalp plate

one retaining bolt while loosening the other bolt. Pivot belt guard out and away from engine pulley. On models with a single mower blade, disconnect blade brake cable from belt guard and remove belt guard. On models with dual mower blades, locate inside engine pulley belt guard, remove one bolt, loosen other bolt and pivot guard out of way. Separate drive belt from engine pulley.

Disconnect safety switch wire on models so equipped. Detach lift linkage from mower deck and remove mower deck.

Reinstall by reversing removal procedure. On models equipped with a blade brake cable, adjust cable as outlined in BLADE BRAKE section.

BLADE BRAKE

Series 500 Models

ADJUSTMENT. On Series 500 models with a blade brake cable, adjust location of transaxle end of the brake cable as follows: Place mower deck in lowest position and move blade engagement lever to disengaged position. Attach cable (C—Fig. MT36) end to rearmost hole in bracket (B) so cable has least amount of slack but no tension.

MOWER SPINDLE

All Models

LUBRICATION. Periodic lubrication of mower spindle is not required.

R&R AND OVERHAUL. Remove mower deck, belt(s) and blade(s). Refer to Figs. MT27 through MT35 for exploded views of mower decks and spindle assemblies. Spindle assembly on later models is available only as a unit assembly. Disassembly of spindle assembly is evident after inspection of unit and referral to exploded view. Inspect components for excessive wear and damage.

ELECTRICAL

All Models

Refer to Figs. MT37 through MT42 for wiring schematics. All switches must be in good operating condition for machine to operate properly.

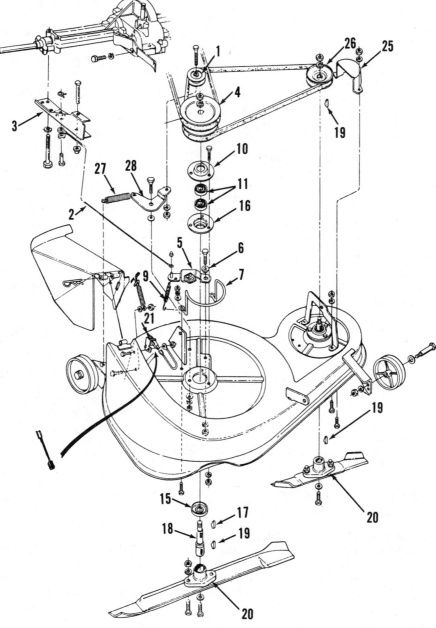

Fig. MT34—Exploded view of 36-inch dual-blade mower deck used on some Series 500 models.

1. Idler
2. Blade brake cable
3. Bracket
4. Pulley
5. Blade brake
6. Spacer
7. Belt guide
9. Spring
10. Bearing housing
11. Bearing
15. Bearing shield
17. Key
18. Spindle
19. Key
20. Blade adapter
21. Safety switch
25. Belt guard
26. Pulley
27. Spring
28. Idler arm

Illustrations Courtesy MTD Products, Inc.

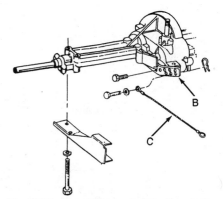

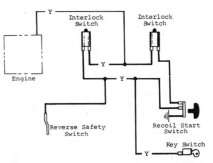

Fig. MT36—On models equipped with a brake cable, attach end of blade brake cable as outlined in text.

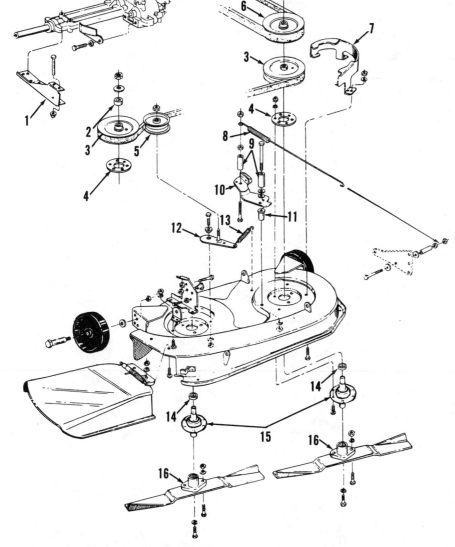

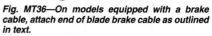

Fig. MT37—Typical wiring schematic for early models with rewind starter. Wires marked "Y" are yellow.

Fig. MT35—Exploded view of typical dual-blade mower used on some later models.

1. Bracket	5. Idler	9. Spacers	13. Spring
2. Spacer	6. Pulley	10. Brake arm	14. Spacer
3. Pulley	7. Belt guard	11. Spacer	15. Spindle assy.
4. Plate	8. Spring	12. Idler arm	16. Adapter

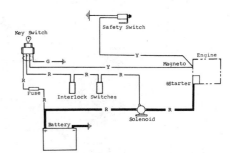

Fig. MT38—Typical wiring schematic for early models with electric start. Wire color codes are : G. Green; R. Red; Y. Yellow.

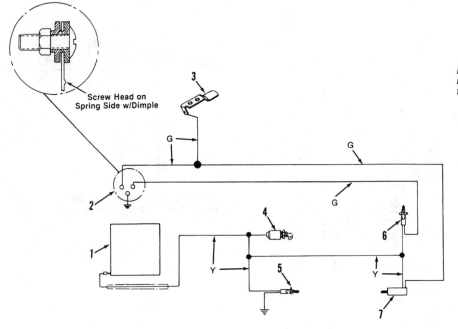

Screw Head on
Spring Side w/Dimple

Fig. MT39—Typical wiring schematic for early Series 500 models with rewind starter and chute deflector switch (5).

G. Green
Y. Yellow
1. Engine
2. Rewind starter switch
3. Reverse gear switch
4. Ignition switch
5. Chute deflector switch
6. Clutch switch
7. Blade engagement switch

Fig. MT40—Typical wiring schematic for later Series 500 models with rewind starter and seat switch (8).

G. Green
Y. Yellow
1. Engine
2. Rewind starter switch
3. Reverse gear switch
4. Ignition switch
6. Clutch switch
7. Blade engagement switch
8. Seat switch

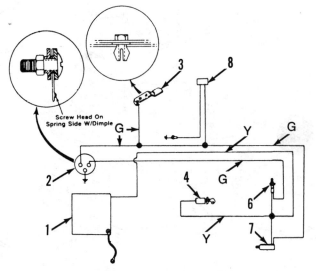

Screw Head On
Spring Side W/Dimple

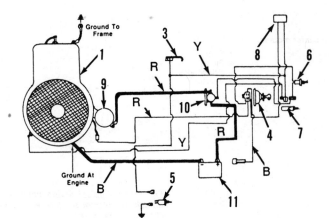

Ground To
Frame

Ground At
Engine

Fig. MT41—Typical wiring schematic for early Series 500 models with electric start and chute deflector switch (5).

B. Black
G. Green
R. Red
Y. Yellow
1. Engine
3. Reverse gear switch
4. Ignition switch
5. Chute deflector switch
6. Clutch switch
7. Blade engagement switch
8. Seat switch
9. Starter
10. Starter solenoid
11. Battery

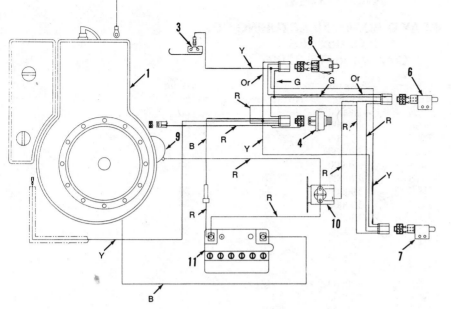

Fig. MT42—Typical wiring schematic for later Series 500 models with electric start.

B. Black
G. Green
Or. Orange
R. Red
Y. Yellow
1. Engine
3. Reverse gear switch
4. Ignition switch
6. Clutch switch
7. Blade engagement switch
8. Seat switch
9. Starter
10. Starter solenoid
11. Battery

MURRAY

MURRAY OHIO MANUFACTURING CO.
P.O. Box 268
Brentwood, TN 37027

Model	Make	Engine Model	Horsepower	Cutting Width, In.
2503	B&S	130000	5	25
2513	B&S	170000	7	25
25501	B&S	130000	5	25
25502	B&S	170000	7	25
3013	B&S	170000	7	30
3033	B&S	170000	7	30
3043	B&S	190000	8	30
3063	B&S	190000	8	30
3233	B&S	190000	8	32
3235	B&S	190000	8	32
3633	B&S	190000	8	36
30501	B&S	170000	7	30
30502	B&S	190000	8	30
31501	B&S	190000	8	31
36503	B&S	250000	11	36
39001	B&S	250000	11	39

FRONT AXLE

Models 2503-2513-3013-3033-3043-3063

The axle member (18–Fig. M1) is of the non-pivoting type and is also the front frame member. To remove the axle member, raise front of unit and block securely. Remove front wheel assemblies and unbolt and remove tie rod (21). Remove cotter pins and washers from top of spindles (20 and 22), then remove the spindles. On electric start models, disconnect battery cables. On all models, loosen locknut and unscrew clutch and brake pedal pad(s). Unbolt and raise console, then unbolt and remove front apron on Models 2503, 2513, 3013 and 3033. On all models, disconnect clutch and brake rod(s), then unbolt and remove axle member.

Clean and inspect all parts and renew as necessary. Reassemble by reversing the disassembly procedure.

To remove the steering shafts, disconnect battery cables on electric start models. On Models 3043 and 3063, remove the lower bolt through sleeve (4–Fig. M1) and withdraw steering wheel, upper shaft, sleeve and coupling (1 through 5) as an assembly. Remove second bolt through sleeve and separate sleeve and coupling from upper shaft. Drive out roll pin (2) and remove steering wheel from shaft. On Models 2503, 2513, 3013 and 3033, remove the screw from collar (8). Slide collar downward on sleeve (9) and remove the bolt through upper end of sleeve. Remove steering wheel (6) and sleeve (9) with collar (8) from upper shaft (7). Drive

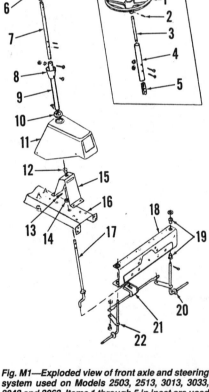

Fig. M1—Exploded view of front axle and steering system used on Models 2503, 2513, 3013, 3033, 3043 and 3063. Items 1 through 5 in inset are used on Models 3043 and 3063.

1. Steering wheel
2. Roll pin
3. Steering shaft (upper)
4. Sleeve
5. Coupling
6. Steering wheel
7. Steering shaft (upper)
8. Collar
9. Sleeve
10. Nylon bearing
11. Console
12. Nylon bearing
13. Cotter pin
14. Washer
15. Steering support
16. Frame
17. Steering shaft (lower)
18. Axle (front frame) member
19. Nylon bearings
20. Spindle L.H.
21. Tie rod
22. Spindle R.H.

out the two roll pins and remove the upper shaft. On all models, unbolt and remove tie rod (21). Unbolt and raise console (11), remove cotter pin (13), raise front of unit and withdraw lower steering shaft (17).

Clean and inspect all parts for excessive wear or other damage. Remove nylon bearings (10 and 12) and renew if necessary. Lubricate bearings with SAE 30 oil. Reassemble by reversing the disassembly procedure.

Models 3233-3235-3633

To remove the axle main member (24–Fig. M2), support front of unit and remove front wheel assemblies. Disconnect tie rod ends (19) from arms on spindles (22 and 25). Remove cotter pins and washers from top of spindles, then remove the spindles. Remove axle pivot bolt (23) and slide axle main member out from under side.

Clean and inspect all parts and renew any showing excessive wear or other damage. Reinstall by reversing the removal procedure. Lubricate pivot bolt and nylon spindle bearings with SAE 30 oil.

To remove the steering shafts and gears, first disconnect battery cables. Remove the lower bolt through sleeve (5) and withdraw steering wheel (1), collar (3), upper shaft (4), sleeve (5) and coupling (6) as an assembly. Remove screw from collar, slide collar downward on sleeve, drive out roll pin (2) and remove steering wheel. Remove the remaining bolt through sleeve and separate sleeve, shaft and coupling. Disconnect tie rods from lower steering shaft

Illustrations Courtesy Murray Ohio Manufacturing Co.

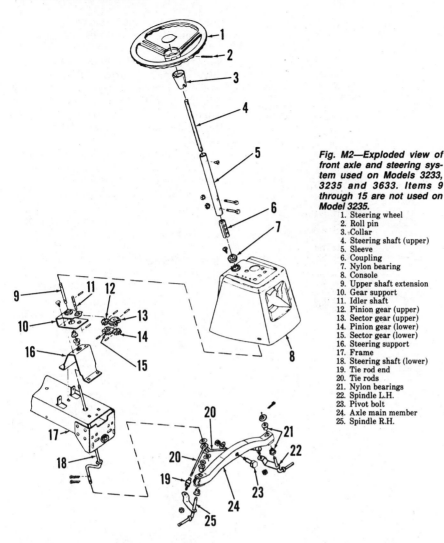

Fig. M2—Exploded view of front axle and steering system used on Models 3233, 3235 and 3633. Items 9 through 15 are not used on Model 3235.

1. Steering wheel
2. Roll pin
3. Collar
4. Steering shaft (upper)
5. Sleeve
6. Coupling
7. Nylon bearing
8. Console
9. Upper shaft extension
10. Gear support
11. Idler shaft
12. Pinion gear (upper)
13. Sector gear (upper)
14. Pinion gear (lower)
15. Sector gear (lower)
16. Steering support
17. Frame
18. Steering shaft (lower)
19. Tie rod end
20. Tie rods
21. Nylon bearings
22. Spindle L.H.
23. Pivot bolt
24. Axle main member
25. Spindle R.H.

Models 25501, 25502, 30501 and 30502

To remove axle main member (10–Fig. M2A), support front of unit and remove front wheel assemblies (19). Disconnect tie rod ends (16) and linkage rod (7) from arms on spindles (15 and 17). Remove cotter pins from top of spindles, then remove spindles. Remove axle pivot bolt (20) and slide axle main member out from under side.

Clean and inspect all parts for excessive wear or any other damage and renew as needed. Reinstall by reversing the removal procedure. Lubricate pivot bolt and nylon spindle bearings with SAE 30 oil.

To remove the steering shafts and sector assembly, first disconnect battery cables on Model 30502. Remove lower bolt through steering shaft (2) and pinion shaft (4) and withdraw steering wheel (1) and steering shaft (2) as an assembly. Unbolt sector assembly (6) from axle mounting hanger (9) and axle support assembly (11), then withdraw unit.

Clean and inspect all parts for excessive wear or any other damage and renew as needed. Reassemble by revers-

(18). Unbolt console (8) and lay console to the side, taking care not to damage electrical wiring. On Model 3235, remove cotter pin from lower steering shaft above frame. Raise front of unit and withdraw steering shaft (18) from bottom of frame (17). On Models 3233 and 3633, drive roll pin from pinion gear (12) and remove extension shaft (9) and gear (12). Drive roll pin from sector gear (15), raise front of unit and withdraw steering shaft (18) from bottom of frame (17). Remove sector gear (15). Sector gear (13), pinion gear (14) and idler shaft (11) can be removed after driving out the remaining roll pins. Unbolt gear support (10) and remove nylon bearings from gear support and steering support (16).

Clean and inspect all parts and renew any showing excessive wear or other damage. Reassemble by reversing the disassembly procedure. Lubricate nylon bearings and lower steering shaft pivot points with SAE 30 oil. Apply a light coat of lithium grease to pinion gears (12 and 14) and sector gears (13 and 15).

Fig. M2A—Exploded view of front axle and steering system used on Models 25501, 25502, 30501 and 30502.

1. Steering wheel
2. Steering shaft
3. Frame assy.
4. Pinion shaft
5. Bearing
6. Sector assy.
7. Linkage rod
8. Steering ball joint
9. Axle mounting hanger
10. Front axle assy.
11. Axle support assy.
12. Left suspension plate
13. Right suspension plate
14. Bearing
15. Left spindle assy.
16. Tie rod
17. Right spindle assy.
18. Bearing
19. Wheel assy.
20. Axle pivot bolt

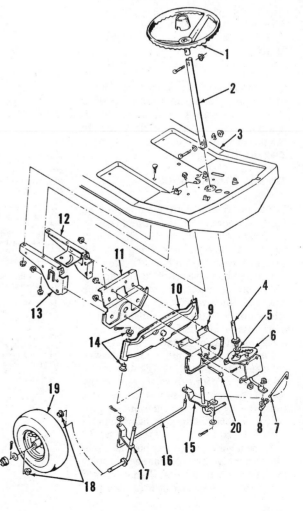

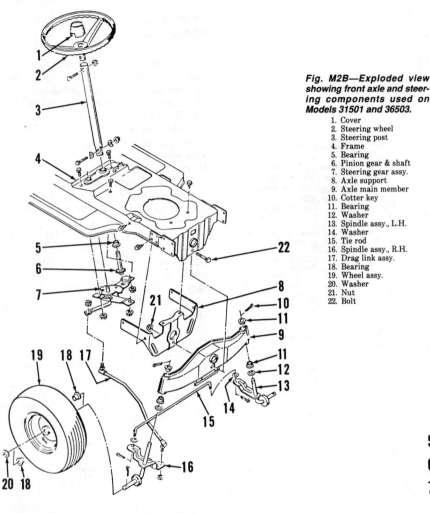

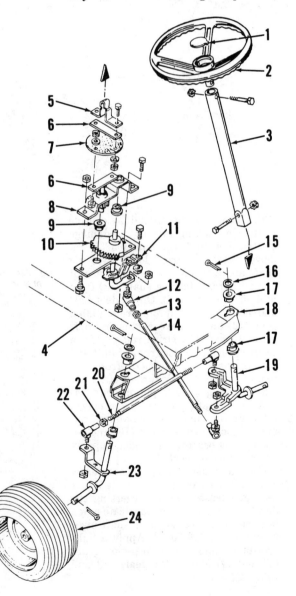

Fig. M2B—Exploded view showing front axle and steering components used on Models 31501 and 36503.

1. Cover
2. Steering wheel
3. Steering post
4. Frame
5. Bearing
6. Pinion gear & shaft
7. Steering gear assy.
8. Axle support
9. Axle main member
10. Cotter key
11. Bearing
12. Washer
13. Spindle assy., L.H.
14. Washer
15. Tie rod
16. Spindle assy., R.H.
17. Drag link assy.
18. Bearing
19. Wheel assy.
20. Washer
21. Nut
22. Bolt

ion shaft (6), then remove any other components that will obstruct steering post removal. Lift steering wheel (2) and steering post (3) out as an assembly. Disconnect drag link (17) from steering arm on steering gear assembly (7). Remove three mounting bolts securing steering gear assembly (7) to frame assembly (4), then withdraw assembly.

Clean and inspect all parts for excessive wear or any other damage and renew as needed. Reassemble by reversing the disassembly procedure. Lubricate bearing (5) with SAE 30 oil. Apply a light coat of lithium grease to pinion gear (6) and steering gear (7).

Model 39001

Front axle frame (18–Fig. M2C) can be removed as a complete unit with removal of front axle hanger. Steering components may be removed individually. To remove steering components,

Fig. M2C—Exploded view showing front axle and steering components used on Model 39001.

1. Cover
2. Steering wheel
3. Steering post
4. Frame
5. Upper steering coupling
6. Coupling plate
7. Steering disc
8. Steering gear bracket assy.
9. Bearing
10. Steering gear assy.
11. Steering bracket
12. Ball joint
13. Locknut
14. Drag link sleeve
15. Cotter key
16. Washer
17. Bearing
18. Axle frame
19. Spindle assy., L.H.
20. Tie rod sleeve
21. Locknut
22. Ball joint
23. Spindle assy., R.H.
24. Wheel assy.

ing the disassembly procedure. Lubricate nylon bearings and lower steering shaft pivot points with SAE 30 oil. Apply a light coat of lithium grease to pinion gear (4) and sector assembly gear (6).

Models 31501-36503

To remove axle main member (9–Fig. M2B), support front of unit and remove front wheel assemblies (19). Disconnect drag link (17) from steering arm on steering gear assembly (7). Remove mounting bolts securing axle support (8). Remove nut (21) from mounting bolt (22). Remove axle support (8), then while supporting axle member (9) withdraw mounting bolt (22). Lower axle assembly clear of tractor frame.

Complete disassembly of unit with reference to Fig. M2B. Clean and inspect all parts for excessive wear or any other damage and renew as needed. Reinstall by reversing the removal procedure. Lubricate spindle bearings (11) with SAE 30 oil.

To remove the steering post and sector assembly, first disconnect battery cables from battery post. Remove lower bolt through steering post (3) and pin-

raise front of unit and securely block. Remove front wheel assemblies (24). Remove nuts securing steering linkage rod ball joints (12 and 22) to steering gear arm (10) and spindle arms (19 and 23), then withdraw linkage rods. Remove cotter keys (15), then slide steering spindles (19 and 23) from axle frame (18). Remove front axle hanger mounting bolts to withdraw axle frame (18).

Clean and inspect all parts for excessive wear or any other damage and renew as needed. Reinstall by reversing the removal procedure. Lubricate spindle bearings (17) with SAE 30 oil.

To remove the steering post and sector assembly, first disconnect battery cables from battery post. Remove lower bolt through steering post (3) and upper steering coupling (5), then remove any other components that will obstruct in steering post removal. Lift steering wheel (2) and steering post (3) out as an assembly. Disconnect drag link arm (14) from steering arm on steering gear assembly (10). Remove mounting bolts securing steering gear assembly (10) and steering gear bracket assembly (8) to frame assembly (4), then withdraw assembly.

Clean and inspect all parts for excessive wear or any other damage and renew as needed. Reassemble by reversing the disassembly procedure. Lubricate bearings (9) with SAE 30 oil. Apply a light coat of lithium grease to pinion gear and steering gear (10).

ENGINE

All Models

Refer to appropriate engine section in this manual for tune-up specifications, engine overhaul procedures and engine maintenance.

Refer to the following paragraphs for removal and installation procedures.

Models 2503-2513-3013-3033

REMOVE AND REINSTALL. To remove the engine assembly, disconnect spark plug wire, ignition wire and throttle control cable. On Model 3033, disconnect battery cables, starter cable and alternator wires. On all models, place mower unit in lowest position and move blade clutch lever to disengaged (stop) position. Disconnect lift chains and unpin upper ends of scissor arms from mower hangers. Remove mower belt from engine pulley and disconnect blade clutch safety starting switch wires. Remove mower unit from under right side. Unhook main drive clutch tension spring and remove main drive belt from transmission input pulley

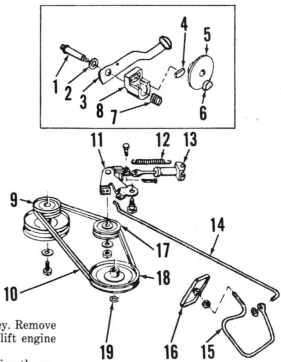

Fig. M3—Exploded view of typical main drive clutch and brake system used on Models 2503, 2513, 3013 and 3033.

1. Shoulder bolt
2. Washer
3. Parking brake cam lever
4. Brake pad (outer)
5. Brake disc
6. Brake pad (inner)
7. Spring
8. Carrier
9. Engine pulley
10. Traction drive belt
11. Clutch idler arm
12. Clutch tension spring
13. Air cylinder
14. Clutch rod
15. Pedal
16. Pedal pad
17. Clutch idler pulley
18. Transmission input pulley
19. Retaining ring

first, then from engine pulley. Remove engine mounting bolts and lift engine assembly from frame.

Reinstall engine by reversing the removal procedure. Make certain that blade clutch safety starting switch is connected and in good operating condition.

Models 3043-3063

REMOVE AND REINSTALL. To remove the engine assembly, disconnect spark plug wire and proceed as follows: On Model 3043, unbolt and remove the seat. On Model 3063, tilt seat forward and disconnect battery cables, starter cable and alternator wires. On both models, disconnect ignition wire and throttle control cable. Place mower unit in lowest position and move blade clutch lever to disengaged (stop) position. Unpin upper ends of scissor arms from mower hangers. Remove mower belt from engine pulley and disconnect blade clutch safety starting switch wires. Remove mower unit from under right side. Unhook main drive clutch tension spring and remove main drive belt from transmission input pulley first, then from engine pulley. Remove engine mounting bolts and lift engine from frame.

Reinstall engine by reversing the removal procedure. Make certain that blade clutch safety starting switch is connected and in good operating condition.

Models 3233-3235-3633

REMOVE AND REINSTALL. To remove the engine assembly, disconnect spark plug wire and proceed as follows: Tilt seat forward and disconnect bat-

tery cables, starter cable, alternator wires, ignition wire and throttle control cable. Unbolt and remove rear shroud crossbrace. Place mower unit in lowest position and move blade clutch lever to disengaged (stop) position. Disconnect lift chains and unpin upper ends of scissor arms from mower hangers. Remove mower belt from engine pulley and blade clutch idler pulley, then remove mower unit from under right side. Unhook main drive clutch tension spring and remove main drive belt from transmission input pulley first, then from engine pulley. Unbolt and remove engine assembly from frame.

Reinstall engine by reversing the removal procedure.

Models 25501, 25502, 30501 and 30502

REMOVE AND REINSTALL. To remove engine assembly, first remove all protective shields and obstructing parts as needed. Disconnect spark plug wire and throttle cable. On Model 30502, disconnect battery cables and on all models disconnect engine wiring. Mark engine wiring as needed for reassembly. Lower mower deck as needed to allow access to drive belts. Remove traction drive belt and blade drive belt. Unbolt engine from frame mounting assembly, then withdraw engine.

Reinstall engine by reversing the removal procedure. Reattach linkage and cables and check for correct operation. Complete reassembly in reverse order of disassembly.

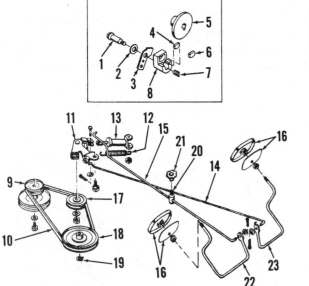

Fig. M4—Exploded view of typical main drive clutch and brake system used on Models 3043, 3063, 3233, 3235 and 3633.

1. Shoulder bolt
2. Washer
3. Cam lever
4. Brake pad (outer)
5. Brake disc
6. Brake pad (inner)
7. Spring
8. Carrier
9. Engine pulley
10. Traction drive belt
11. Clutch idler arm
12. Clutch tension spring
13. Air cylinder
14. Clutch rod
15. Brake rod
16. Pedal pad
17. Clutch idler pulley
18. Transmission input pulley
19. Retaining ring
20. Park brake lock
21. Knob
22. Brake pedal
23. Clutch pedal

Models 31501-36503-39001

REMOVE AND REINSTALL. To remove engine assembly, disconnect spark plug wire and proceed as follows: Remove engine cover assembly. Disconnect battery cables, starter cable, alternator wires, ignition wire and throttle control cable. Mark engine wiring as needed for reassembly. Lower mower deck as needed to allow access to drive belts. Remove traction drive belt and blade drive belt. Unbolt engine from frame mounting assembly, then withdraw engine.

Reinstall engine by reversing the removal procedure. Reconnect electrical wires and throttle cable, then check for correct operation. Complete reassembly in reverse order of disassembly.

TRACTION DRIVE CLUTCH AND DRIVE BELT

Rear Engine Models

The traction drive clutch used on all models is of the belt idler type. On Models 2503, 2513, 3013 and 3033 clutch is operated by a pedal on right side. On all other models, the clutch pedal is on the left side. On all models when clutch pedal is fully depressed, all tension is removed from drive belt (10–Fig. M3, M4 or M4A) and engine pulley (9) is allowed to rotate freely within the belt. At this time, on models so equipped a brake pad on clutch idler arm contacts the transmission input pulley. This transmission braking action will assist in stopping.

CAUTION: This brake is ineffective when transmission is in neutral position.

On Models 25501, 25502, 30501 and 30502 adjust drive clutch by turning adjustment nut (11-Fig. M4A). If complete adjustment is used and belt slippage still occurs, then belt must be renewed. On all other models there is no adjustment on the traction drive clutch. If the drive belt slips during normal operation due to excessive belt wear or stretching, renew the belt as outlined under the following REMOVE AND RENEW paragraphs.

Models 2503-2513-3013-3033-3043-3063

REMOVE AND RENEW. To remove the traction drive belt (10-Fig.

Fig. M4A—Exploded view of traction drive parts used on Models 25501, 25502, 30501 and 30502.

1. Knob
2. Shift lever
3. Spring
4. Transmission assy.
5. Pedal
6. Spring
7. Lever assy.
8. Spring
9. Engine pulley assy.
10. Drive belt
11. Adjustment nut
12. Spring
13. Idler arm assy.
14. Belt guide assy.
15. Axle bearing
16. Axle mounting bracket
17. Linkage rod
18. Spring
19. Idler pulley
20. Transmission drive pulley
21. Differential
22. Chain
23. Roller
24. Chain adjustment bracket
25. Sprocket
26. Axle mounting bracket
27. Wheel assy.

M3 or M4), disconnect spark plug wire and proceed as follows: Place mower unit in lowest position and move blade clutch lever to disengaged (stop) position. On Models 2503, 2513, 3013 and 3033, disconnect the lift chains. On all models, unpin upper ends of scissor arms from mower hangers. Remove mower belt from engine pulley and disconnect blade clutch safety starting switch wires. Remove mower unit from under right side. Unhook main drive clutch tension spring (12) and remove clutch idler pulley (17). Remove traction drive belt from transmission input pulley (18) first, then from engine pulley (9).

Install new belt by reversing the removal procedure. Make certain that blade clutch safety starting switch is connected and in good operating condition.

Models 3233-3235-3633

REMOVE AND RENEW. To remove the traction drive belt (10-Fig. M4), disconnect spark plug wire and proceed as follows: Place mower unit in lowest position and move blade clutch lever to disengaged (stop) position. Disconnect lift chains and unpin upper ends of scissor arms from mower hangers. Remove the blade clutch idler pulley, slip mower belt from engine pulley and remove mower unit from under right side. Unhook main drive clutch tension spring (12) and remove clutch idler pulley (17). Remove traction drive

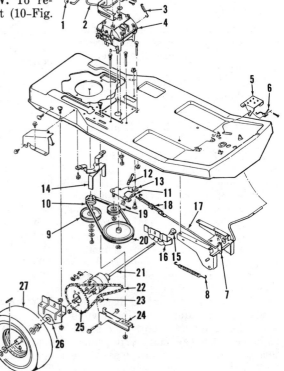

Illustrations Courtesy Murray Ohio Manufacturing Co.

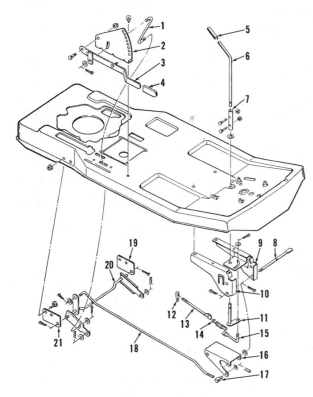

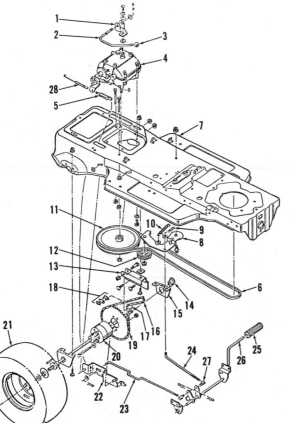

Fig. M4C—Exploded view of traction drive parts used on Model 31501.

1. Shift yoke	11. Transmission input pulley	20. Differential assy.
2. Shift lever	12. Idler pulley	21. Wheel assy.
3. Knob	13. Chain idler bracket	22. Brake link assy.
4. Transmission assy.	14. Axle bearing	23. Brake rod
5. Spring	15. Bearing plate	24. Clutch rod
6. Drive belt	16. Chain	25. Clutch & brake pedal
7. Frame	17. Roller	26. Lever assy.
8. Idler bracket assy.	18. Master chain link	27. Adjusting nut
9. Hairpin clip	19. Sprocket	28. Spring
10. Spring		

Fig. M4B—Exploded view of mower deck control components and blade engagement components for Models 25501, 25502, 30501 and 30502.

1. Lift rod
2. Index plate
3. Lift lever
4. Grip
5. Grip
6. Blade lever
7. Tube
8. Pin
9. Left suspension plate
10. Right suspension plate
11. Rod and arm assy.
12. Adjustment nut
13. Linkage rod
14. Spring
15. Front link
16. Front suspension bracket
17. Adjustment nut
18. Linkage rod
19. Left mounting plate
20. Deck lifter assy.
21. Right mounting plate

belt from transmission pulley (18) first, then from engine pulley (9).

Install new belt and reinstall mower unit by reversing the removal procedure.

Models 25501, 25502, 30501 and 30502

REMOVE AND RENEW. To remove the traction drive belt (10–Fig. M4A), disconnect spark plug wire and proceed as follows: Place mower unit in lowest position and move blade clutch lever to disengaged (stop) position. Disconnect mower deck hangers from deck lifter assembly (20–Fig. M4B) and front suspension plates. Disconnect adjustment nut (12), then remove mower belt from engine pulley and remove mower unit from under right side. Unhook main drive clutch tension spring (12–Fig. M4A) and remove clutch idler pulley (19). Remove traction drive belt from transmission pulley (20) first, then from engine pulley (9).

Install new belt and reinstall mower unit by reversing the removal procedure.

Front Engine Models

The traction drive clutch used on all models is of the belt idler type. On all

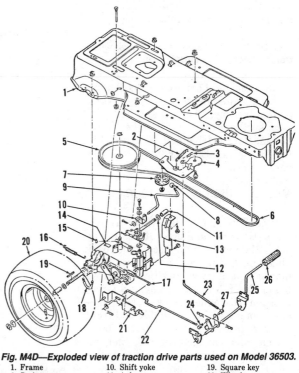

Fig. M4D—Exploded view of traction drive parts used on Model 36503.

1. Frame	10. Shift yoke	19. Square key
2. Spring	11. Axle spacer	20. Wheel assy.
3. Hairpin clip	12. Washer	21. Brake link assy.
4. Idler bracket assy.	13. Transaxle support	22. Brake rod
5. Transaxle input pulley	14. Transaxle assy.	23. Clutch rod
6. Drive belt	15. Woodruff key	24. Adjusting nut
7. Idler pulley	16. Spring	25. Lever assy.
8. Knob	17. Spring	26. Clutch & brake pedal
9. Shift lever	18. "U" bolt	27. Adjusting nut

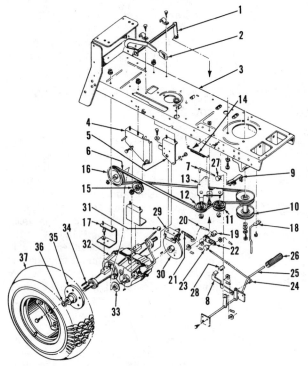

Fig. M4E—Exploded view of traction drive parts used on Model 39001.

1. Handle assy.
2. Grip
3. Frame
4. Idler bracket assy.
5. Transaxle bracket
6. Drive belt
7. Clutch rod
8. Parking brake arm
9. Belt guide
10. Engine pulley
11. Idler pulley
12. Clutch idler pulley
13. Idler bracket
14. Spring
15. Backside idler pulley
16. Pulley
17. Transaxle bracket
18. Belt guide
19. Adjusting nut
20. Adjusting rod
21. Spring
22. Link plate
23. Adjusting nut
24. Brake rod
25. Lever assy.
26. Clutch & brake pedal
27. Adjusting nut
28. Grip
29. Disc brake assy.
30. Brake disc
31. Knob
32. Transaxle assy.
33. Extruded washer
34. Square key
35. Wheel hub
36. "E" clip
37. Wheel assy.

blade rotary mowers. All other models are equipped with twin blades.

CAUTION: Always disconnect spark plug wire before performing any inspection, adjustment or other service on the mower.

Make certain that safety starting switches are connected and in good operating condition before returning mower to service.

On all models a belt idler type blade clutch is used. On Models 25501, 25502, 30501 and 30502 adjust drive clutch by turning adjustment nut (12-Fig. M4B). If complete adjustment is used and belt slippage still occurs, then belt must be renewed. On all other models the clutch idler is spring loaded and requires no adjustment. If mower drive belt slips during normal operation, due to excessive belt wear or stretching, renew belt as outlined in the following paragraphs.

Models 2503-2513

REMOVE AND RENEW. To remove the mower drive belt (1-Fig. M6),

models the clutch pedal is on the left side. On all models when clutch pedal is fully depressed, all tension is removed from drive belt (6-Fig. M4C, M4D and M4E) and engine pulley is allowed to rotate freely within the belt. At this time, brake pads come into contact with brake disc located on either transmission or transaxle assembly. This braking action will assist in stopping.

CAUTION: This brake is ineffective when transmission is in neutral position.

Adjustment of drive clutch is done by turning adjustment nut (27). If complete adjustment is used and belt slippage still occurs, then belt must be renewed. Renew drive belt as outlined in the following REMOVE AND RENEW paragraphs.

Models 31501-36503-39001

REMOVE AND RENEW. To remove the traction drive belt (6-Fig. M4C, M4D and M4E), disconnect spark plug wire and proceed as follows: Place mower unit in lowest position and move blade clutch lever to disengaged (stop) position. Disconnect mower deck hangers from deck lifter assembly and front hanger bracket. Disconnect mower clutch idler engagement rod, then remove mower belt from engine pulley and remove mower unit. Loosen tension on traction drive belt idler pulley and remove all belt guides and protective shields as needed to allow access to drive belt. Remove drive belt from drive pulleys.

Inspect all drive pulleys for excessive wear or any other damage and renew as needed. Install new drive belt and reinstall mower unit by reversing the removal procedure.

MOWER CLUTCH AND DRIVE BELT

Rear Engine Models

Models 2503, 2513, 25501, 25502, 30501 and 30502 are equipped with single

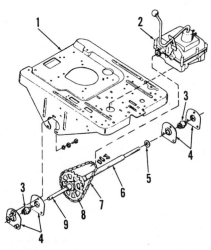

Fig. M5—View of typical transmission, drive chain, differential, rear axles and axle bearings used on all models.

1. Rear frame section
2. Transmission
3. Axle bearings
4. Bearing retainers
5. Washer
6. Sleeve
7. Drive chain
8. Sprocket
9. Rear axle & differential assy.

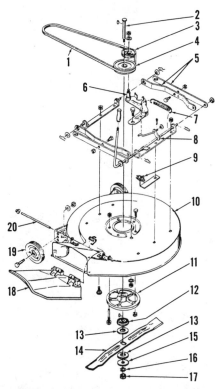

Fig. M6—Exploded view of mower unit used on Models 2503 and 2513.

1. Mower drive belt
2. Blade shaft
3. Clutch idler pulley
4. Mower pulley
5. Scissor arms
6. Blade clutch idler arm
7. Clutch tension spring
8. Clutch lever & linkage
9. Safety starting switch
10. Mower housing
11. Bearing & housing assy.
12. Blade adapter
13. Cushion washers
14. Blade
15. Flat washer
16. Lockwasher
17. Nut
18. Deflector
19. Gage wheel
20. Pin

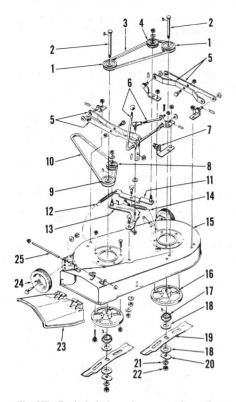

Fig. M7—Exploded view of mower unit used on Models 3013 and 3033.

1. Mower pulleys
2. Blade shafts
3. Blade cross belt
4. Idler pulley
5. Scissor arms
6. Clutch lever & linkage
7. Safety starting switch
8. Clutch idler pulley
9. Mower drive pulley
10. Mower drive belt
11. Idler arm
12. Idler spring
13. Blade clutch idler arm
14. Clutch tension spring
15. Mower housing
16. Bearing & housing assy.
17. Blade adapter
18. Cushion washers
19. Blade
20. Flat washer
21. Lockwasher
22. Nut
23. Deflector
24. Gage wheel
25. Pin

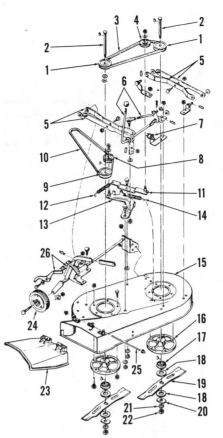

Fig. M8—Exploded view of mower unit used on Models 3043 and 3063.

1. Mower pulleys
2. Blade shafts
3. Blade cross belt
4. Idler pulley
5. Scissor arms
6. Clutch lever & linkage
7. Safety starting switch
8. Clutch idler pulley
9. Mower drive pulley
10. Mower drive belt
11. Idler arm
12. Idler spring
13. Blade clutch idler arm
14. Clutch tension spring
15. Mower housing
16. Bearing & housing assy.
17. Blade adapter
18. Cushion washers
19. Blade
20. Flat washer
21. Lockwasher
22. Nut
23. Deflector
24. Gage wheel
25. Pin
26. Mower height adjuster

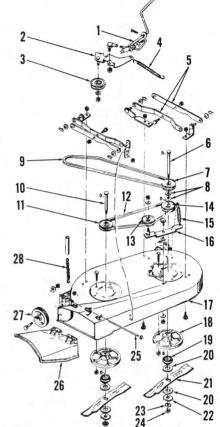

Fig. M9—Exploded view of mower unit used on Models 3233, 3235 and 3633.

1. Clutch lever & linkage
2. Blade clutch idler arm
3. Clutch idler pulley
4. Clutch tension spring
5. Scissor arms
6. Blade shaft
7. Mower drive pulley
8. Spacer washers
9. Mower drive belt
10. Blade shaft
11. Mower pulley
12. Blade cross belt
13. Idler pulley
14. Mower pulley
15. Idler spring
16. Idler arm
17. Mower housing
18. Bearing & housing assy.
19. Blade adapter
20. Cushion washers
21. Blade
22. Flat washer
23. Lockwasher
24. Nut
25. Pin
26. Deflector
27. Gage wheel
28. Lift chain

disconnect spark plug wire and remove mower unit as follows: Place mower in lowest position and move blade clutch lever to disengaged position and move blade clutch lever to disengaged (stop) position. Disconnect lift chains and un-pin upper ends of scissor arms (5) from mower hangers. Remove mower drive belt (1) from engine pulley and disconnect wires from blade clutch safety starting switch (9). Remove mower unit from under right side. Unbolt and remove idler pulley (3) from clutch idler arm (6). Move idler arm away from mower pulley (4) and remove belt (1).

Install new belt by reversing the removal procedure. Make certain that blade clutch safety starting switch is connected and in good operating condition.

Models 3013-3033-3043-3063

REMOVE AND RENEW. To remove the mower drive belt (10-Fig. M7 or M8) and blade cross belt (3), discon-

nect spark plug wire and remove mower unit as follows: Place mower in lowest position and move blade clutch lever to disengaged (stop) position. On Models 3013 and 3033, disconnect lift chains. On all models, unpin scissor arms (5) from mower hangers. Remove mower drive belt (10) from engine pulley and disconnect wires from blade clutch safety starting switch (7). Remove mower unit from under right side. Unhook idler spring (12) and remove blade cross belt (3). Remove nut, washer and idler pulley (8) from clutch idler arm (11). Remove mower drive belt (10).

Install new belts by reversing the removal procedure. Make certain that blade clutch safety starting switch is connected and in good operating condition.

Models 3233-3235-3633

REMOVE AND RENEW. To remove the mower drive belt (9-Fig. M9) and blade cross belt (12), disconnect spark plug wire and remove mower unit as follows: Place mower unit in lowest position and move blade clutch lever to disengaged (stop) position. Disconnect lift chains (28) and unpin upper ends of scissor arms (5) from mower hangers. Remove nut, washer and idler pulley (3) from clutch idler arm (2). Slip mower drive belt (9) from engine pulley and remove mower unit from under right side. Remove mower drive belt, unhook idler spring (15) and remove blade cross belt (12).

Install new belts by reversing the removal procedure.

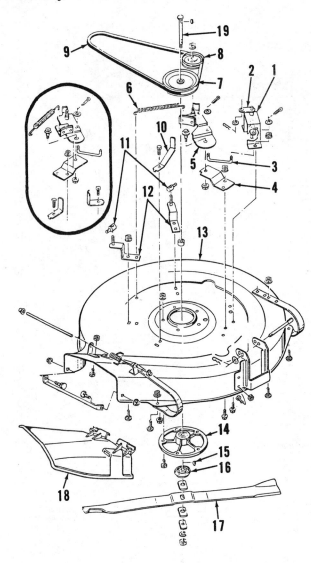

Make certain that safety starting switches are connected and in good operating condition before returning mower to service.

On all models a belt idler type blade clutch is used. Adjust drive clutch by turning adjustment nut (11-Fig. M10A and M10B). If adjustment limit is reached and belt slippage still occurs, then belt must be renewed. Renew drive belt as outlined under the following REMOVE AND RENEW paragraphs.

Models 31501-36503-39001

To remove mower drive belt (9-Fig. M10A and M10B), disconnect spark plug wire and proceed as follows: Place mower unit in lowest position and move blade clutch lever to disengaged (stop) position. Disconnect mower deck hangers from deck lifter assembly and front hanger bracket. Disconnect mower clutch idler engagement rod, then remove mower belt from engine pulley and remove mower unit.

Fig. M10—Exploded view of mower unit and operating components on Models 25501, 25502, 30501 and 30502. Parts shown in inset apply to Models 25501 and 25502.

1. Bracket assy.
2. Pivot rod
3. Idler link
4. Idler support bracket
5. Idler assy.
6. Spring
7. Pulley
8. Idler pulley
9. Drive belt
10. Belt guide
11. Adjustment nut
12. Rear bracket
13. Deck assy.
14. Bearing & housing assy.
15. Woodruff key
16. Blade adapter
17. Blade
18. Deflector chute
19. Blade shaft

Models 25501, 25502, 30501 and 30502

REMOVE AND RENEW. To remove mower drive belt (9-Fig. M10), disconnect spark plug wire and proceed as follows: Place mower unit in lowest position and move blade clutch lever to disengaged (stop) position. As needed disconnect mower deck hangers from deck lifter assembly (20-Fig. M4B) and front suspension plates. Disconnect adjustment nut (12), then remove mower belt from engine pulley, idler pulley and mower pulley.

Install new belt and reinstall mower unit by reversing the removal procedure.

Front Engine Models

Model 31501 is equipped with a single blade rotary mower. Models 36503 and 39001 are equipped with twin blade rotary mowers.

Fig. M10A—Exploded view of mower unit and operating components used on Model 31501.

1. Adjusting rod
2. Adjusting nut
3. Lifter bracket
4. Pulley cover
5. Jackshaft
6. Pulley
7. Pulley
8. Idler pulley
9. Drive belt
10. Control rod
11. Adjusting nut
12. Pivot lever
13. Spring
14. Spacer
15. Rear support bracket
16. Adjusting nut
17. Deck link
18. Belt guide
19. Link retainer
20. Brake & idler assy.
21. Spring
22. Belt guide
23. Skid flat stock, R.H.
24. Skid flat stock, L.H.
25. Idler mount assy.
26. Housing assy.
27. Chute deflector
28. Jackshaft housing assy.
29. Woodruff key
30. Blade adapter
31. Washer
32. Blade
33. Washer
34. Blade washer
35. Lockwasher
36. Nut

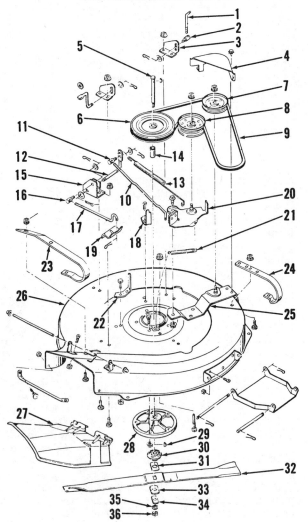

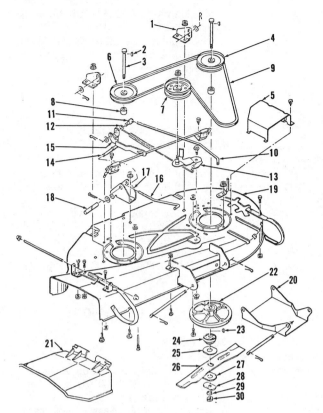

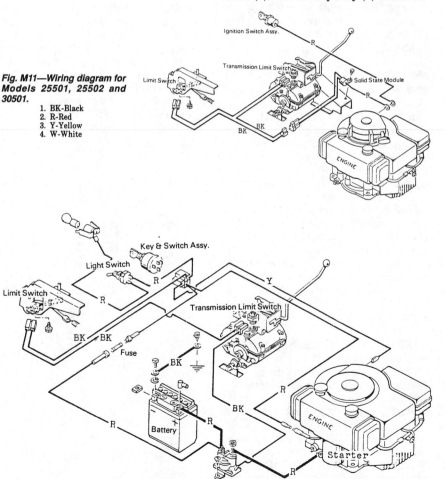

Models 3013-3033-3043-3063

REMOVE AND REINSTALL. Remove mower unit and mower belts (3 and 10–Fig. M7 or M8) as outlined in previous section. Remove nuts (22), washers (20 and 21), cushion washers (18), blades (19) and blade adapters (17) from bottom of shafts (2). Withdraw shafts (2) with mower pulleys (1) and drive pulley (9) from above. Note location of belt guide bolt, then unbolt and remove bearing and housing assemblies (16).

Clean and inspect all parts for excessive wear or other damage and renew as necessary. Reassemble by reversing the disassembly procedure. Tighten blade retaining nuts (22) to a torque of 15-18 ft.-lbs. (20-24 N·m).

Models 3233-3235-3633

REMOVE AND REINSTALL. Remove mower unit and mower belts (9 and 12–Fig. M9) as outlined in previous section. Remove nuts (24), washers (22 and 23), cushion washers (20), blades (21) and blade adapters (19) from bottom of shafts (6 and 10). Withdraw shaft (6) with drive pulley (7) and mow-

Fig. M10B—Exploded view of mower unit and operating components used on Models 36503 and 39001.

1. Lifter bracket
2. Woodruff key
3. Jackshaft
4. Pulley
5. Pulley cover
6. Pulley
7. Idler pulley
8. Spacer
9. Drive belt
10. Control rod
11. Adjusting nut
12. Spring
13. Idler bracket assy.
14. Pivot lever
15. Brake bar
16. Link rod
17. Rear hanger bracket
18. Adjusting bar
19. Housing assy.
20. Front hanger
21. Chute deflector
22. Jackshaft housing assy.
23. Woodruff key
24. Blade adapter
25. Blade washer
26. Blade
27. Blade washer
28. Washer
29. Lockwasher
30. Nut

Inspect all drive pulleys for excessive wear or any other damage and renew as needed. Install new drive belt and reinstall mower unit by reversing the removal procedure.

MOWER DECK

All Models

The following paragraphs outline the procedures for removing the blades, blade shafts and bearing and housing assemblies. Bearings and housings are available only as assemblies.

Lubricate all linkage pivot points with SAE 30 oil. All idler pulley bearings and blade shaft bearings are prelubricated and require no lubrication.

Models 2503-2513

REMOVE AND REINSTALL. Remove mower unit and mower drive belt (1–Fig. M6) as outlined in previous section. Remove nut (17), washers (15 and 16) cushion washers (13), blade (14) and adapter (12) from bottom of shaft (2). Withdraw shaft (2) with mower pulley (4) from above. Note location of belt guide bolt, then unbolt and remove bearing and housing assembly (11).

Clean and inspect all parts and renew as necessary. Reassemble by reversing the disassembly procedure. Tighten blade retaining nut (17) to a torque of 15-18 ft.-lbs. (20-24 N·m).

Fig. M11—Wiring diagram for Models 25501, 25502 and 30501.
1. BK-Black
2. R-Red
3. Y-Yellow
4. W-White

Fig. M12—Wiring diagram for Model 30502. Refer to legend in Fig. M11 for wire color codes.

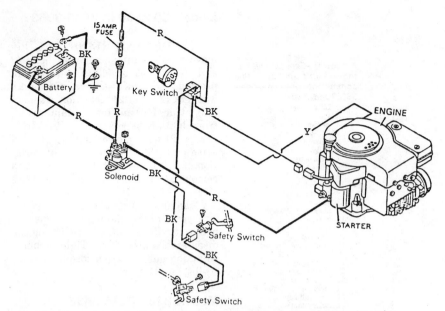

Fig. M13—Wiring diagram for Model 31501. Refer to legend in Fig. M11 for wire color codes.

and remove bearing and housing assembly (22).

Clean and inspect all parts and renew as needed. Reassemble by reversing the disassembly procedure.

ELECTRICAL

Models 25501-25502-30501-30502-31501-36503-39001

Shown in electrical diagrams Figs. M11, M12, M13, M14 and M15 are electrical components and their connecting wires. For component and wire identification refer to Fig. M11 for Models 25501, 25502 and 30501, Fig. M12 for Model 30502, Fig. M13 for Model 31501, Fig. M14 for Model 36503 and Fig. M15 for Model 39001.

TRANSMISSION

All Models

The transmission used on all models except 25501, 25502, 30501, 30502 and 31501 is manufactured by the J.B. Foote Foundry Co. A Peerless model transmission is used on Models 25501, 25502, 30501, 30502 and 31501. A Peerless model transaxle is used on Models 36503 and 39001.

For transmission or transaxle overhaul procedures, refer to the Foote or Peerless section in the TRANSMISSION REPAIR service section.

Refer to the following paragraphs for removal and installation of transmission or transaxle.

er pulley (14), then shaft (10) with mower pulley (11) from above. Unbolt and remove bearing and housing assemblies (18).

Clean and inspect all parts and renew any showing excessive wear or other damage. Reassemble by reversing the disassembly procedure. Tighten blade retaining nuts (24) to a torque of 15-18 ft.-lbs. (20-24 N·m).

Models 25501, 25502, 30501 and 30502

REMOVE AND REINSTALL. Remove mower unit and mower drive belt (9–Fig. M10) as outlined in previous section. Remove blade shaft (19) retaining nut, lockwasher, washers, blade (17), and adapter (16) from bottom of deck. Withdraw shaft (19) with mower pulley (7) from above. Be sure not to lose Woodruff keys located in shaft (19). Unbolt and remove bearing and housing assembly (14).

Clean and inspect all parts and renew as needed. Reassemble by reversing the disassembly procedure.

Model 31501

REMOVE AND REINSTALL. Remove mower unit and mower drive belt (9–Fig. M10A) as outlined in previous section. Remove jackshaft (5) retaining nut (36), lockwasher (35), washers (34 and 33), blade (32), washer (31) and adapter (30) from bottom of deck. Withdraw jackshaft (5) with mower pulley (6) from above. Be sure not to lose Woodruff keys located in shaft. Unbolt and remove bearing and housing assembly (28).

Clean and inspect all parts and renew as needed. Reassemble by reversing the disassembly procedure.

Models 36503-39001

REMOVE AND REINSTALL. Remove mower unit and mower drive belt (9-Fig. M10B) as outlined in previous section. Remove jackshaft (3) retaining nut (30), lockwasher (29), washers (28 and 27), blade (26), washer (25) and adapter (24) from bottom of deck. Withdraw jackshaft (3) with mower pulley (4 or 6) from above. Be sure not to lose Woodruff keys located in shaft. Unbolt

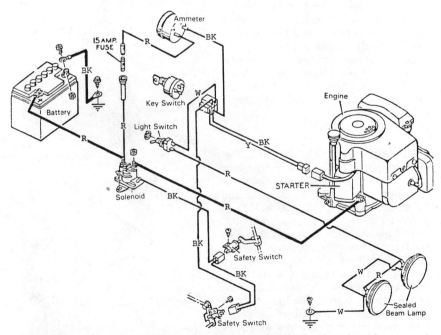

Fig. M14—Wiring diagram for Model 36503. Refer to legend in Fig. M11 for wire color codes.

Illustrations Courtesy Murray Ohio Manufacturing Co.

Models 2503-2513-3013-3033

REMOVE AND REINSTALL. To remove Foote 2010 transmission, disconnect spark plug wire and remove the mower unit as follows: Place mower unit in lowest position and move blade clutch lever to disengaged (stop) position. Disconnect lift chains and unpin upper ends of scissor arms from mower hangers. Remove mower belt from engine pulley and disconnect blade safety starting switch wires. Remove mower unit from under right side. Unhook main drive clutch tension spring (12-Fig. M3) and remove main drive belt (10) from transmission input pulley (18). Remove retaining ring (19) and pulley from transmission input shaft. Locate master link in drive chain and disconnect drive chain. Unbolt and remove seat assembly and engine shroud. Disconnect transmission safety starting switch wires and unhook brake lever spring. Remove mounting bolts and lift transmission from frame.

Reinstall transmission by reversing the removal procedure. Make certain that transmission and blade clutch safety starting switches are connected and in good operating condition.

Models 3043-3063

REMOVE AND REINSTALL. To remove Foote 2010 transmission, disconnect spark plug wire and proceed as follows: Place mower unit in lowest position and move blade clutch lever to disengaged (stop) position. Unpin upper ends of scissor arms from mower hangers. Remove mower belt from engine pulley and disconnect blade clutch safety starting switch wires. Remove mower unit from under right side. Unhook main drive clutch tension spring (12-Fig. M4) and remove main drive belt (10) from transmission pulley (18). Remove retaining ring (19) and pulley from transmission input shaft. Disconnect brake rod (15) from brake cam lever (3). Locate master link in drive chain and disconnect drive chain. Unbolt and remove seat assembly and engine shroud assembly. Disconnect transmission safety starting switch wires, then unbolt and remove transmission assembly.

Reinstall transmission by reversing the removal procedure. Make certain that transmission and blade clutch safety starting switches are connected and in good operating condition.

Models 3233-3235-3633

REMOVE AND REINSTALL. To remove Foote 2010 (Models 3233 and 3633) or Foote 2600 (Model 3235) trans-

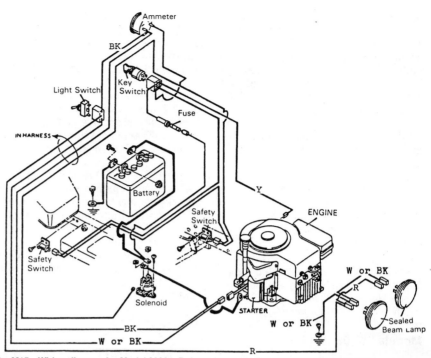

Fig. M15—Wiring diagram for Model 39001. Refer to legend in Fig. M11 for wire color codes.

mission, disconnect spark plug wire and proceed as follows: Place mower unit in lowest position and move blade clutch lever to disengaged (stop) position. Disconnect lift chains and unpin upper ends of scissor arms from mower hangers. Remove the blade clutch idler pulley, slip mower belt from engine pulley and remove mower unit from under right side. Unhook main drive clutch tension spring (12-Fig. M4) and remove main drive belt (10) from transmission pulley (18). Remove retaining ring (19) and pulley from transmission input shaft. Disconnect brake rod (15) from brake cam lever (3). Locate master link in drive chain and disconnect drive chain. Unbolt and remove seat assembly and engine shroud. Disconnect transmission safety starting switch wires, then unbolt and remove transmission assembly.

Reinstall transmission by reversing the removal procedure. Make certain that transmission safety starting switch is connected and in good operating condition.

Models 25501, 25502, 30501 and 30502

REMOVE AND REINSTALL. To remove Peerless 500 (Model 25501) or Peerless 700 (Models 25502, 30501 and 30502) transmission, disconnect spark plug wire and proceed as follows: Place mower unit in lowest position and move blade clutch lever to disengaged (stop) position. Disconnect mower deck hangers from deck lifter assembly (20- Fig. M4B) and front suspension plates. Disconnect adjustment nut (12), then remove mower belt from engine pulley and remove mower unit from under right side. Unhook main drive clutch tension spring (12-Fig. M4A) and remove clutch idler pulley (19). Remove traction drive belt from transmission pulley (20) first, then from engine pulley (9). Remove retaining ring and pulley from transmission input shaft. Locate master link in drive chain and disconnect drive chain. Unbolt and remove seat assembly and engine shroud. Disconnect transmission safety starting switch wires and unhook brake lever spring. Remove mounting bolts and lift transmission from frame.

Reinstall transmission by reversing the removal procedure. Make certain that transmission and blade clutch safety starting switches are connected and in good operating condition.

Model 31501

REMOVE AND REINSTALL. To remove the transmission, disconnect spark plug wire and proceed as follows: Place mower unit in lowest position and move blade clutch lever to disengaged (stop) position. Disconnect mower deck hangers from deck lifter assembly and front hanger bracket. Disconnect mower clutch idler engagement rod, then remove mower belt from engine pulley and remove mower unit. Loosen tension on traction drive belt idler pulley and remove all belt guides and protective shields as needed to allow access to drive belt. Remove drive belt from drive pulleys. Remove retaining ring and pulley from transmission input shaft. Locate master link in drive chain and disconnect drive chain. Remove seat deck and seat assembly. Disconnect transmission safety starting switch wires and unhook brake lever spring. Remove mounting bolts and lift transmission assembly from frame.

Reinstall transmission by reversing the removal procedure. Make certain that transmission and blade clutch safety starting switches are connected and in good operating condition.

OVERHAUL. For overhaul procedures, refer to Peerless transmission Series 700 in the TRANSMISSION REPAIR section of this manual.

Models 36503-39001

REMOVE AND REINSTALL. To remove the transaxle assembly, disconnect spark plug wire and battery ground cable from battery terminal. Remove mower deck and drive belt as outlined in MOWER DECK section. Remove traction drive belt from transaxle input pulley. Disconnect brake linkage. Remove cap screws retaining transaxle to frame, then on Model 36503 remove "U" bolts securing axle housings to frame and on Model 39001 remove cap screws securing frame brackets to axle housings. Raise rear of tractor and remove shift lever as needed, then remove transaxle assembly from tractor.

Reinstall by reversing the removal procedure. Adjust clutch and brake linkage as required.

OVERHAUL. For overhaul procedures, refer to Peerless transaxle Series 800 on Model 36503 and Series 2300 on Model 39001.

DRIVE CHAIN

Rear Engine Models

ADJUSTMENT. On all models except 25501, 25502, 30501 and 30502 adjust drive chain (7-Fig. M5) as follows: Loosen the three cap screws on each side of frame securing bearing retainers (4) to frame (1). Move rear axle assembly rearward (equal distance on both sides) to tighten drive chain. Drive chain should deflect approximately ½ inch (12.7 mm) when about five pounds (2.3 kg.) pressure is applied on chain. When chain tension is correct, tighten

bearing retainer mounting cap screws. On Models 25501, 25502, 30501 and 30502 drive chain is adjusted by sliding adjustment bracket (24-Fig. M4A) in slots on frame assembly. To adjust, loosen securing nut and slide bracket until approximately ½-inch (12.7 mm) deflection is attained at center of drive chain when about five pounds (2.3 kg.) pressure is applied. When chain tension is correct, retighten securing nut.

REMOVE AND REINSTALL. To remove drive chain, rotate differential sprocket to locate master link. Disconnect master link and remove chain. Clean and inspect drive chain and renew if excessively worn.

Install drive chain and adjust chain tension as outlined in the preceding paragraph. Lubricate chain with a light coat of SAE 30 oil.

Model 31501

ADJUSTMENT. Drive chain is adjusted by sliding adjustment bracket (13-Fig. M4C) in slots on frame assembly. To adjust, loosen securing nuts and slide bracket until approximately ½-inch (12.7 mm) deflection is attained at center of drive chain when about five pounds (2.3 kg.) pressure is applied. When chain tension is correct, retighten securing nuts.

REMOVE AND REINSTALL. To remove drive chain, rotate differential sprocket to locate master link. Disconnect master link and remove chain. Clean and inspect drive chain and renew if excessively worn.

Install drive chain and adjust chain tension as outlined in the preceding paragraph. Lubricate chain with a light coat of SAE 30 oil.

DIFFERENTIAL

Rear Engine Models

REMOVE AND REINSTALL. For assistance in removal of differential and rear axle assembly refer to Fig. M4A for Models 25501, 25502, 30501 and 30502 and Fig. M5 for all other models. To remove, raise rear of unit and securely support. Remove rear wheel assemblies. Rotate differential sprocket to locate the master link in drive chain, then disconnect the chain. Unbolt axle mounting brackets and remove differential assembly.

Reinstall differential and rear axle assembly by reversing the removal procedure. Adjust drive chain tension as outlined in previous section. Lubricate axle bearings with SAE 30 oil.

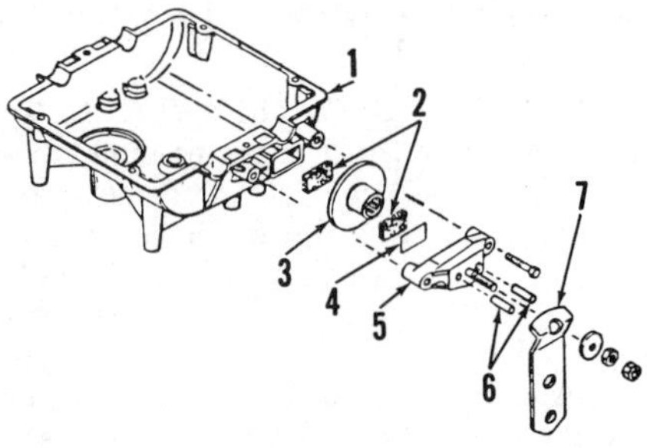

Fig. M16—Exploded view of traction brake assembly used on Models 25501, 25502, 30501 and 30502.

1. Lower case housing
2. Pads
3. Disc
4. Pad plate
5. Pad holder
6. Dowel pin
7. Lever

OVERHAUL. The differential used on all models except 25501, 25502, 30501 and 30502 is manufactured by Indus Wheel Company, Division of Carlisle Corp. A Peerless model differential is used on Models 25501, 25502, 30501 and 30502.

For differential overhaul procedures, refer to the Indus or Peerless section in the DIFFERENTIAL REPAIR service section.

Model 31501

REMOVE AND REINSTALL. For assistance in removal of differential and rear axle assembly refer to Fig. M4C. To remove, raise and securely support rear of unit. Remove rear wheel assemblies. Rotate differential sprocket to locate the master link in drive chain, then disconnect the chain. Unbolt axle mounting brackets and remove differential assembly.

Reinstall differential and rear axle assembly by reversing the removal procedure. Adjust drive chain tension as outlined in previous section. Lubricate axle bearings with SAE 30 oil.

OVERHAUL. A Peerless model differential is used. For overhaul procedures, refer to the Peerless section in the DIFFERENTIAL REPAIR service section.

GROUND DRIVE BRAKE

All Models

Traction drive brake is applied by depressing clutch/brake pedal on single pedal models or by depressing brake pedal on dual pedal models. All models except Models 25501, 25502, 30501, 30502, 31501, 36503 and 39001 are equipped with a brake pad on clutch idler arm (11-Fig. M3 or M4) which contacts the transmission input pulley (18) and assists in stopping.

Illustrations Courtesy Murray Ohio Manufacturing Co.

CAUTION: This brake is ineffective when transmission is in neutral position.

Models 2503, 2513, 3013 and 3033 are also equipped with a hand operated disc brake located on the transmission output shaft. See items (1 through 8-Fig. M3). This brake can be used as an emergency brake, parking brake or in conjunction with the brake on clutch idler.

Models 3043, 3063, 3233, 3235 and 3633 are equipped with a foot operated disc brake. Brake disc (5-Fig. M4) is located on the transmission output shaft. Use this brake in conjunction with the brake on clutch idler, or as an emergency brake or parking brake.

Models 25501, 25502, 30501, 30502, 31501, 36503 and 39001 are equipped with a foot operated disc brake. Brake disc is located on the transmission output shaft on Models 25501, 25502, 30501, 30502 and 31501 and transaxle brake shaft on Models 36503 and 39001.

On models equipped with clutch idler brake pad, depress clutch pedal before fully applying the disc brake. There is no adjustment on the disc brakes. When applying, the disc brake and brake lever travels the full length of its slot, brake pads must be renewed. Refer to the following paragraphs for procedures.

Models 2503-2513-3013-3033

REMOVE AND RENEW. To renew the brake pads (4 and 6-Fig. M3), disconnect the brake spring and remove knob from brake lever (3). Remove shoulder bolt (1) with washer (2), cam lever (3), carrier (8), outer pad (4) and spring (7). Slide brake disc (5) outward on transmission shaft and remove inner brake pad (6) from holding slot in transmission housing. Install new

brake pads and reassemble by reversing the disassembly procedure.

Models 3043-3063-3233-3235-3633

REMOVE AND RENEW. To renew the brake pads (4 and 6-Fig. M4), disconnect the brake rod (15) from cam lever (3). Tilt seat forward and unscrew shoulder bolt (1). Remove shoulder bolt with washer (2), cam lever (3), carrier (8), outer brake pad (4) and spring (7). Slide brake disc (5) outward on transmission shaft and remove inner brake pad (6) from holding slot in transmission housing. Install new brake pads and reassemble by reversing the disassembly procedure.

Models 25501-25502-30501-30502-31501

REMOVE AND RENEW. To renew brake pads (2-Fig. M16), remove all parts as needed to attain access to disc brake components. Remove jam nut, nut and washer from pad holder stud (5), then withdraw lever (7). Remove pad holder mounting bolts, then withdraw pad holder, pads and brake disc.

Install new brake pads and reassemble by reversing the disassembly procedure.

Model 36503

REMOVE AND RENEW. Disc brake assembly on Model 36503 is similar to type shown in Fig. M16, except unit is mounted on brake shaft and secured to transaxle housing.

To renew brake pads, remove all parts as needed to attain access to disc brake components. With reference to

components shown in Fig. M16, remove jam nut, nut and washer from pad holder stud (5), then withdraw lever (7). Remove pad holder mounting bolts, then withdraw pad holder, pads and brake disc.

Install new pads and reassemble by reversing the disassembly procedure.

Model 39001

REMOVE AND RENEW. To renew brake pads (7-Fig. M17), remove all parts as needed to attain access to disc brake components. Unhook actuating spring from lever (4), then remove bracket assembly (1) mounting cap screws. Remove locknuts (5), then withdraw bolts (3) and slide pads (7) out of bracket (6).

Install new brake pads and reassemble by reversing the disassembly procedure.

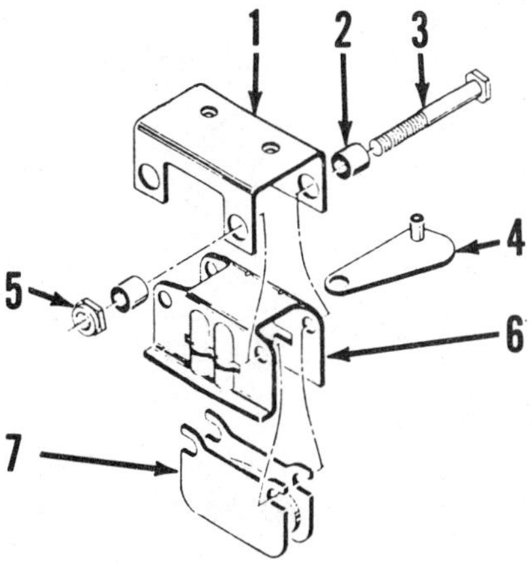

Fig. M17—Exploded view of traction brake assembly used on Model 39001.

1. Bracket assy.
2. Spacer
3. Bolt
4. Lever
5. Locknut
6. Bracket
7. Pads

MUSTANG

MOWETT SALES CO., INC.
110 W. Mason
P.O. Box 218
Odessa, MO 64076

Model	Make	Engine Model	Horsepower	Cutting Width, In.
245	B&S	130000	5	24
248	B&S	190000	8	24
248E	B&S	190707	8	24

FRONT AXLE

All Models

R&R AND OVERHAUL. Front end assembly (11-Fig. MU1) is secured to frame rails (7 and 8). To remove, raise front of unit until front wheel assemblies (10) are clear of ground. Loosen four bolts retaining mounting plate over steering shaft. Remove two bolts securing steering wheel shaft (2) to steering post, then lift steering wheel and shaft assembly from unit. Unbolt front end assembly from frame rails, then withdraw assembly from mower unit.

Complete disassembly and inspect all components for excessive wear or any other damage. Renew all parts as needed, then reassemble in reverse order of disassembly. After installation, if steering is too tight, loosen four bolts holding metal plate over steering post. If steering is too loose, tighten bolts as needed. Nylon bearings in front spindles and oil impregnated bearings in front wheel assemblies do not require lubrication.

ENGINE

All Models

Refer to appropriate engine section in this manual for tune-up specifications, engine overhaul procedures and engine maintenance.

Refer to the following paragraphs for removal and installation procedures.

REMOVE AND REINSTALL. To remove engine, first raise unit to allow access to underneath side. Unbolt blade retaining bolt and withdraw washers, spacers (26-Fig. MU1) and blade (30). Remove four bolts securing mower deck (22) to frame rails (7 and 8), then withdraw deck clear of unit. Remove drive belt (23) from pulleys, then withdraw clutch (25) from engine crankshaft. Be sure not to lose square key used between crankshaft keyway and clutch keyway.

Loosen four bolts retaining mounting plate over steering shaft. Remove two bolts securing steering wheel shaft (2) to steering post, then lift steering wheel and shaft assembly from unit.

Remove all bolts as needed to withdraw hood (3) from frame rails. Remove wiring, cables and any obstructing components to allow removal of engine assembly. Remove engine mounting bolts, then lift engine assembly from mower unit.

After repair of engine reverse removal procedure to reinstall engine.

TRACTION DRIVE CLUTCH

All Models

Figure MU2 shows a view of traction drive clutch components. Actuating

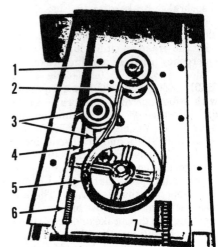

Fig. MU2—View of traction drive assembly.

1. Clutch assy.
2. Belt
3. Idler assy.
4. Idler rod
5. Transmission pulley
6. Spring
7. Chain

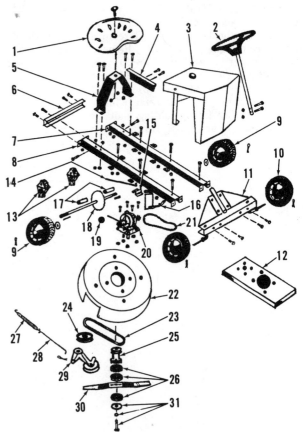

Fig. MU1—Exploded view of complete mower unit.

1. Seat
2. Steering wheel & shaft
3. Hood
4. Chain guard
5. Seat support
6. Rear channel
7. Left frame rail
8. Right frame rail
9. Rear wheel assy.
10. Front wheel assy.
11. Front end assy.
12. Mounting plate
13. Rear axle bearing assy.
14. Idler rod
15. Foot pedal bearing
16. Foot pedal
17. Axle spacer
18. Rear axle assy.
19. Knob
20. Transmission assy.
21. Chain
22. Mower deck
23. Belt
24. Pulley
25. Clutch
26. Spacers
27. Spring
28. Idler rod
29. Idler assy.
30. Blade
31. Bolt and washers

foot pedal will tighten idler pressure on drive belt which will engage traction power train. Excessive pressure on foot pedal will cause drive belt to over-stretch and slip on pulleys. If slippage occurs during engagement, then belt must be renewed. Unit speed is regulated by throttle control.

To renew clutch idler or drive belt refer to the following paragraphs.

REMOVE AND RENEW. Unhook ignition wire from spark plug, then invert mower assembly to where it is resting on the rear wheels and seat. Unbolt blade retaining bolt and withdraw washers, spacers and blade. Remove four bolts securing mower deck to frame rails, then withdraw deck clear of unit. Unhook spring (6–Fig. MU2) and idler rod (4) from idler assembly (3), then remove drive belt from pulleys. Remove snap ring retaining transmission input pulley on shaft, then withdraw pulley from shaft. Remove bolt holding idler assembly to mounting plate, then remove idler assembly.

Inspect and renew all parts as needed. Reassemble in reverse order of disassembly. Check pulley alignment during reassembly, misaligned pulleys will cause premature damage to drive belt.

TRANSMISSION

All Models

REMOVE AND REINSTALL. Unhook ignition wire from spark plug, then invert mower assembly to where it is resting on the rear wheels and seat. Unbolt blade retaining bolt and with-draw washers, spacers and blade. Remove four bolts securing mower deck to frame rails, then withdraw deck clear of unit. Unhook spring (6–Fig. MU2) and idler rod (4) from idler assembly (3), then remove drive belt from pulleys. Remove snap ring retaining transmission input pulley on shaft, then withdraw pulley from shaft.

Loosen all bolts that extend through left and right frame rails. Loosen bolt that extends through steering post support bracket and engine mounting plate. Push mounting plate assembly downward to release tension on chain, then remove chain from transmission sprocket. Remove transmission mounting bolts and lift transmission assembly from mounting plate.

After repair, reassemble in reverse order of disassembly. Pry upward on engine mounting plate to tighten chain tension. Check chain alignment after installation. If chain tries to jump off rear axle sprocket, then axle position must be changed to correct alignment. Move washers on outside of rear wheels from side to side to change axle position.

OVERHAUL. After transmission is removed, refer to FOOTE TRANSMISSION REPAIR section of this manual for detailed service procedures.

CHAIN

All Models

ADJUSTMENT. Loosen all bolts that extend through left and right frame rails. Loosen bolt that extends through steering post support bracket and engine mounting plate. Pry upward on mounting plate until correct chain tension is reached, then retighten all bolts. Chain is equipped with one half link that may be removed to provide additional chain adjustment.

REMOVE AND RENEW. Loosen all bolts that extend through left and right frame rails. Loosen bolt that extends through steering post support bracket and engine mounting plate. Push mounting plate assembly downward to release tension on chain, then remove chain from transmission sprocket.

Lower mower unit, then raise rear wheel assembly clear of ground. Unbolt rear axle bearing assembly (13–Fig. MU1) from frame rails, then withdraw rear axle assembly from mower unit.

Inspect and renew all components as needed. Reassemble in reverse order of disassembly. Adjust chain tension as outlined in ADJUSTMENT section. Lubricate chain with a good grade of oil after installation.

MOWER CUTTING HEIGHT

All Models

Mower blade cutting height may vary from 1½-3½ inches (38-89 mm) off the ground.

ADJUSTMENT. Unbolt blade retaining bolt and reposition spacers (26–Fig. MU1) to raise or lower blade height. Reinstall blade retaining bolt and washer after adjustment.

J. C. PENNEY

J. C. PENNEY CO., INC.
11800 West Burleigh Street
Milwaukee, Wisconsin 53201

The following J. C. Penney riding mowers were manufactured for J. C. Penney Co., Inc., by Murray Ohio Manufacturing, Brentwood, Tennessee and by MTD Products, Cleveland, Ohio. Service procedures for these J. C. Penney models will not differ greatly from those given for similar Murray and MTD models. However, parts are not necessarily interchangeable and should be obtained from J. C. Penney Co., Inc.

J.C. Penney Model	Murray Model	MTD Model
1905	2503	....
1907	2503	....

J.C. Penney Model	Murray Model	MTD Model
1907A	2503	....
1908	2513	....
1909	2513	....
1910	2513	....
1824	39001	....
1834*	36503	....
1841**	31501	....
1842**	31501	....
1820	....	525
1831	....	520
1832	....	362
1835***	....	498
1839†	....	495
1840††	....	495
1844	....	820

J.C. Penney Model	Murray Model	MTD Model
1845	....	497
1846	....	497
1847	....	498
1848	....	497

   * Model 1834 uses a four spindle mower.

  ** Models 1841 and 1842 use a two spindle mower.

 *** Model 1835 uses a three spindle mower and a Foote Series 4000 transaxle.

   † Model 1839 uses a Foote Series 2010 transmission.

  †† Model 1840 uses a Peerless Series 700 transmission.

RIDE KING

SWISHER MOWER & MACHINE CO.
P.O. Box 67
333 East Gay St.
Warrensburg, MO 64093

Model	Make	Engine Model	Horsepower	Cutting Width, In.
A-32	Tecumseh	V60	6	32
R-32	Tecumseh	V60	6	32

STEERING SYSTEM

Model A-32

Steering is controlled by turning steering wheel (1–Fig. RK1) which rotates steering shaft and sprocket (20). Steering shaft sprocket meshes with steering gear (21) located on gearbox. Steering gear (21) will allow front wheel to pivot 360°. For reference in disassembly and repair refer to Fig. RK1.

Model R-32

Steering is controlled by turning steering wheel (1–Fig. RK2) which rotates steering shaft and sprocket (20). Steering shaft sprocket rotates steering gear (21) by use of chain (37). Front wheel assembly has a 360° turning radius. For reference in disassembly and repair refer to Fig. RK2.

ENGINE

All Models

Refer to appropriate engine section in this manual for tune-up specifications, engine overhaul procedures and engine maintenance.

Refer to the following paragraphs for removal and installation procedures.

REMOVE AND REINSTALL. Disconnect spark plug lead from spark plug. Remove front hood assembly. On Model A-32 use caution as fuel tank is removed with hood assembly. Remove traction drive belt cover, then withdraw drive belt(s) from pulleys. Remove mower drive belt inspection covers, then loosen tension on belt and slip drive belt off pulleys. Remove steering wheel (1–Fig. RK1 and RK2). Inspect and remove as needed any part or parts that will obstruct in removal of engine assembly. Loosen and remove engine securing bolts and nuts, then lift engine assembly clear of mounting plate and

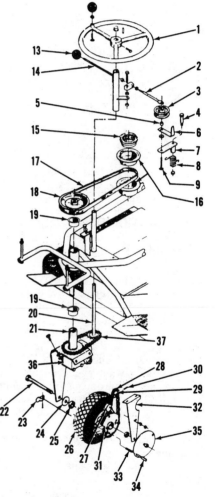

Fig. RK1—Exploded view showing steering and traction drive components for Model A-32.

1. Steering wheel	20. Steering shaft & sprocket
2. Idler spring	21. Steering gear
3. Pulley	22. Axle bolt
4. Shoulder bolt	23. Lockpin lever
5. Spacer	24. Spacer washer
6. Belt release finger	25. Bearing
7. Idler arm	26. Wheel assy.
8. Spring	27. Chain idler
9. Bolt	28. Chain
10. Key	29. Sprocket
11. Hub	30. Pin
12. Set screw	31. Drive sprocket & hub assy.
13. Knob	32. Bracket
14. Idler control assy.	33. Spring
15. Starter cup	34. Lockpin
16. Pulley	35. Chain guard
17. Drive belt	36. Gearbox assy.
18. Pulley	
19. Bearing	

mower unit. Place engine assembly to the side for inspection and repair.

After repair, reinstall in reverse order of disassembly.

Fig. RK2—Exploded view showing steering and traction components for Model R-32.

1. Steering wheel	21. Steering gear
2. Control rod	22. Axle bolt
3. Pulley	23. Lockpin lever
4. Shoulder bolt	24. Spacer washer
5. Spacer	25. Bearing
6. Belt release finger	26. Wheel assy.
7. Idler arm	27. Chain idler
8. Spring	28. Chain
9. Bolt	29. Sprocket
13. Knob	30. Pin
14. Idler control assy.	31. Drive sprocket & hub assy.
15. Starter cup	32. Bracket
16. Pulley	33. Spring
17. Drive belt	34. Lockpin
18. Pulley	35. Chain guard
19. Bearing	36. Gearbox assy.
20. Steering shaft & sprocket	37. Chain

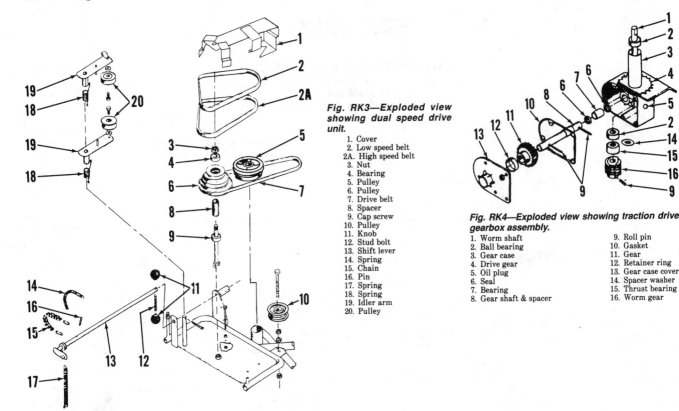

Fig. RK3—Exploded view showing dual speed drive unit.

1. Cover
2. Low speed belt
2A. High speed belt
3. Nut
4. Bearing
5. Pulley
6. Pulley
7. Drive belt
8. Spacer
9. Cap screw
10. Pulley
11. Knob
12. Stud bolt
13. Shift lever
14. Spring
15. Chain
16. Pin
17. Spring
18. Spring
19. Idler arm
20. Pulley

Fig. RK4—Exploded view showing traction drive gearbox assembly.

1. Worm shaft
2. Ball bearing
3. Gear case
4. Drive gear
5. Oil plug
6. Seal
7. Bearing
8. Gear shaft & spacer
9. Roll pin
10. Gasket
11. Gear
12. Retainer ring
13. Gear case cover
14. Spacer washer
15. Thrust bearing
16. Worm gear

TRACTION DRIVE BELT

Single Speed

Single traction drive belt (17-Fig. RK1 and RK2) is engaged and disengaged by control lever (14) which controls the operation of idler pulley (3). Moving control lever (14) forward will engage drive belt and pulling lever rearward will disengage drive belt. If drive belt slips when engaged on Model A-32 inspect condition of idler spring (2-Fig. RK1) and drive belt (17). Renew idler spring if excessively stretched or damaged in any way. Renew drive belt if frayed, cracked, excessively stretched or damaged in any way. Check for correct operation after repair and reassembly.

Dual Speed

Figure RK3 shows an exploded view of a dual speed drive unit. Turning idler control lever (13-Fig. RK3) forward will engage low speed belt (2) and turning lever rearward will engage high speed belt (2A). Center position is disengaged or neutral position. If drive belt slips when engaged check for correct operation of idler system. Idler pulley should fully engage drive belt when control lever is turned to engaged

position. Renew drive belts if frayed, cracked, excessively stretched or damaged in any way. Inspect all pulleys, springs and levers for excessive wear or any other damage and renew as needed. After repair and reassembly check for correct operation.

TRACTION DRIVE GEARBOX

All Models

Shown in Fig. RK4 is an exploded view of a traction drive gearbox assembly. To remove gearbox for disassembly proceed as follows: Raise and support front end of mower unit. Loosen chain tensioner (27-Fig. RK1 and RK2). Remove locknut from axle bolt (22), then withdraw chain guard (35). Unbolt and remove left hand support bracket (32). Remove lockpins (34), then lift drive sprocket and hub assembly (31) from wheel assembly (26) along with drive chain (28). Remove axle bolt (22) and wheel assembly (26). Remove front hood assembly. On Model A-32 use caution as fuel tank is removed with hood assembly. Slip traction drive belt (17) off pulley (18), then withdraw pulley (18) off gearbox worm shaft (1-Fig. RK4). Slide gearbox assembly out of frame housing, then place gearbox assembly to the side for disassembly and

repair.

Inspect bearings (19 and 25—Fig. RK1 and RK2) for roughness, binding or any other damage. Inspect all other parts for excessive wear or any other damage and renew parts as needed.

Disassemble gearbox assembly with reference to Fig. RK4. Inspect all parts for excessive wear, binding or any other damage. Inspect drive gears for chipped or missing teeth and renew all parts as needed. Reassemble in reverse order of disassembly. Manufacturer recommends using a high pressure gear oil with a high lead content in gearbox. Add gearbox oil until level is even with bottom of plug hole (5).

Reinstall gearbox assembly in mower unit and reassemble in reverse order of disassembly.

MOWER DRIVE BELT

All Models

REMOVE AND RENEW. Remove left and right mower deck inspection plate securing nuts. Lift inspection plates off mower deck and place to the side. Release tension on idler control arm as needed, then slip drive belt off engine and blade drive pulleys. Install new drive belt, then adjust idler control rod (17-Fig. RK5) as needed. Drive belt

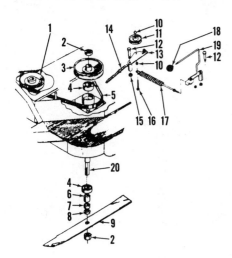

should not slip on pulleys when idler control rod is engaged and mower blades should not turn when control rod is in disengaged position. Reinstall inspection plates after completing adjustment.

Fig. RK5—Exploded view showing mower blade drive unit and drive belt engagement system.

1. Engine pulley
2. Locknut
3. Blade pulley
4. Bearing
5. Drive belt
6. Spacer (1-inch)
7. Spacer (1/2-inch)
8. Spacer (1/4-inch)
9. Blade
10. Nut
11. Idler pulley
12. Shoulder bolt
13. Control arm
14. Spring
15. Nut
16. Bolt
17. Idler control rod & spring
18. Knob
19. Idler control assy.
20. Shaft

MOWER BLADE DRIVE

All Models

Mower blade is belt driven, for renewing or adjusting tension on drive belt refer to previous section. Figure RK5 shows an exploded view of mower blade drive unit and drive belt engagement system. Periodically inspect all parts for excessive wear or any other damage and renew all parts as needed. To adjust mower blade cutting height, remove blade locknut (2) and blade (9). Reposition spacers (6, 7 and 8) above or below mower blade until desired cutting height is attained.

ROPER

YARD PRO
12052 Middleground Road
Savannah, GA 31419

Model	Make	Engine Model	Horsepower	Cutting Width, In.
K511	B&S	130902	5	26
K521	B&S	130902	5	26
K522	B&S	130905E	5	26
K831	B&S	190702	8	32
K832	B&S	190705E	8	32
K852	B&S	190705E	8	32
L711	Tecumseh	V70	7	26
L721	Tecumseh	V70E	7	26
L722	Tecumseh	V70E	7	26
L821	B&S	191707E	8	36
L861	Tecumseh	VM80	8	36
L863	B&S	191707E	8	36

K-prefix models: Rear engine, "Sprint" riders
L-prefix models: Tractor-style, "Mini-Brute", "Rally" riders

STEERING SYSTEM

Models K-511, K-521, K-522, K-831, K-832 and K-852

REMOVE AND REINSTALL. These models are fitted with a non-adjustable steering system as shown in Fig. R1. Tube portion of steering column may be shifted to a high or low position for comfort and convenience of operator.

If front system shows evidence of wear, hard turning or stiff operation, raise and block up under frame just forward of cutting deck so that wheels are clear of surface. Unbolt and lower axle cross member (16-Fig. R1) from frame without separate removal of king pins (13), wheels or tie bar (14). Slot in steering plate (15) will disengage from arm of steering shaft (6) when assembly is lowered. Thoroughly examine all parts and renew any which are damaged or worn.

If condition of steering column is questionable, unbolt steering shaft tube (3) with steering wheel and remove upward from steering shaft (6), then lower steering shaft out of support bracket and evaluate grommets which support shaft at wear points. Renew as needed.

If equipped with headlight and electric start, it is advisable to remove control console cover (four self-tapping metal screws) for access to steering shaft after steering column tube has been removed.

When reassembly is complete, lubricate steering linkage, shaft grommets, bushings and wheel bearings with SAE

30 engine oil. Wipe off excess to prevent dirt accumulation.

Models L-711, L-721, L-722, L-821, L-861 and L-863

REMOVE AND REINSTALL. All front engine riders are equipped with automotive type, gear sector and pinion steering as shown in Figs. R2 and R3.

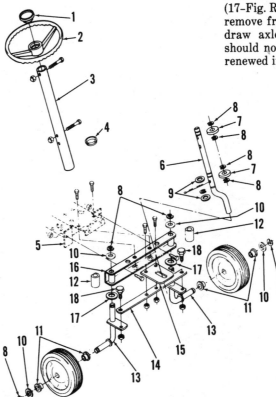

Raise and block unit under frame between front edge of cutting deck and steering tie rod so that wheels are clear of work surface. On Models L-711, L-721 and L-722, remove cotter pins from ends of steering link (13-Fig. R2) then unbolt front member from chassis platform and roll steering assembly forward from under unit for inspection and further disassembly as needed. On Models L-821, L-861 and L-863, remove nuts from ball joint studs of drag link (17-Fig. R3) and remove drag link, then remove front pivot bolt (24) and withdraw axle. Parts of steering system should now be carefully inspected and renewed if damaged or worn.

Fig. R1—Exploded view of steering system typical of Models K-511, K-521, K-522, K-831, K-832 and K-852. Shaft support not shown.

1. Logo cap
2. Steering wheel
3. Shaft tube & bolts
4. Grommet
5. Frame channel
6. Steering shaft
7. Shaft ring (2)
8. "E" ring, ⅜-in. (9)
9. Flat washer, 0.64 (2)
10. Flat washer 0.63 (4)
11. Wheel bearings
12. Spindle bearings
13. Kingpin/spindle, RH, LH
14. Tie bar
15. Steering plate
16. Cross member
17. Special washer (2)
18. Shoulder bolt, 5/16-24 (2)

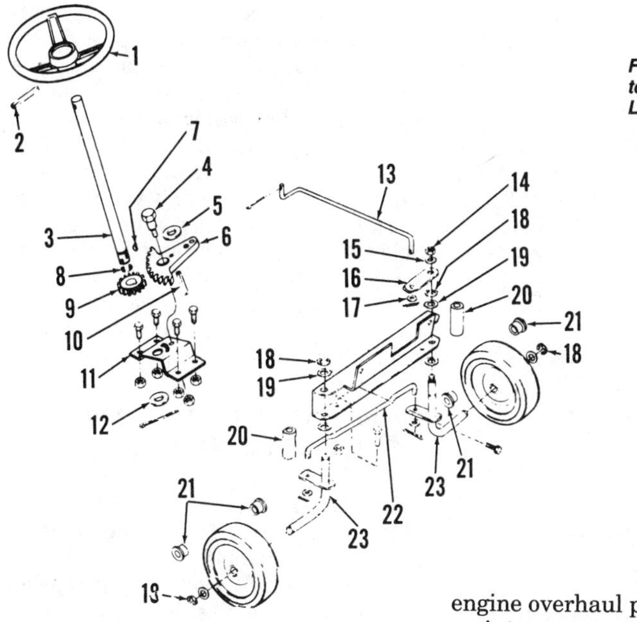

Fig. R2—View of steering system parts as used on Models L-711, L-721 and L-722.

1. Steering wheel
2. Lock pin ¼ X1½
3. Steering shaft
4. Shoulder bolt (spec.)
5. Flat washer, 0.515 bore
6. Gear sector
7. Woodruff key, #61
8. "E" ring, ¾-inch
9. Pinion gear
10. Roll pin, 3/16X1
11. Steering shaft mount
12. Flat washer, 0.765
13. Steering link
14. Nylok nut, ⅜-24
15. Flat washer, 0.40 bore
16. Steering arm
17. Flat washer, 0.515 bore
18. "E" ring, ⅝-inch (2)
19. Flat washer, 0.640 bore (4)
20. Spindle sleeve (2)
21. Wheel bearings (4)
22. Tie rod
23. Kingpin/spindle RH, LH

Before proceeding with disassembly of steering shaft, pinion or sector, front axle should be reinstalled and unit lowered to rest on all wheels. Drag link is left disconnected.

On Models L-711, L-721 and L-722, remove hood, then unbolt and remove dash panel from chassis cover. Unbolt steering shaft mount (11-Fig. R2) from chassis, withdraw the unit and disassemble as needed. Thoroughly clean all parts and renew any which are damaged or worn. Pay special attention to condition of shoulder bolt (4) and key (7). Renew steering shaft mount (11) if it shows any signs of wear. Lubricate all parts during reassembly.

On Models L-821, L-861 and L-863, swing hood forward to uncover engine compartment and unbolt steering bracket (9-Fig. R3) from frame. Clean, inspect and determine need for further disassembly and renewal of parts.

NOTE: If it is necessary to remove pinion gear (5) from steering shaft (4) or gear sector (11) from steering rod (10), use caution and buck shafts when driving out pins.

Pay particular attention to bushings (3, 8 and 16).

When damaged parts are renewed, lubricate with chassis grease and reassemble. Use SAE 30 engine oil at all wear points in steering linkage before returning unit to service.

ENGINE

All Models

Refer to appropriate engine section in this manual for tune-up specifications, engine overhaul procedures and engine maintenance.

Refer to the following paragraphs for removal and installation procedures.

Models K-511, K-521, K-522, K-831, K-832 and K-852

REMOVE AND REINSTALL. To remove engine, disconnect spark plug lead and on electric start models, disconnect battery cables from starter motor and battery.

Remove operator's seat and disconnect bowden cable (throttle control wire) at carburetor end.

Disengage blade clutch. At front of cutting deck, remove cotter pins from suspension rod, drive out rod at one end and remove spacers. Back off nut, washer and spring at rear of blade brake rod, then remove rod from cutting deck. Disconnect sway chains at rear of cutting deck on Models K-511, K-521 and K-522 or unbolt housing retainer on Models K-831, K-832 and K-852, then slip deck rearward to relieve pressure on drive belt and work belt from lower sheave of engine pulley. Pull cutting deck from under chassis.

Unhook clutch idler spring (16-Fig. R4) at end which is anchored to frame. Remove bolt (18) and idler pulley (19) from idler arm (17). Remove traction drive belt from sheaves of engine and transmission pulleys, then unbolt engine from rear pan (1) and lift out of chassis. Reverse this sequence to reinstall.

Models L-711, L-721 and L-722

REMOVE AND REINSTALL. To remove engine, unbolt and remove hood. Remove spark plug lead, then disconnect battery cables (L-721 and L-722) and remove cable from starter motor. Disconnect leads from ignition switch and throttle control (bowden cable) from carburetor.

Disengage blade drive clutch lever. Remove blade brake rod, and cotter pins from ends of pivot shaft. Pull out shaft to release cutting deck from hanger and take care not to lose spacers. Shift cutting deck forward to relieve belt tension and work blade drive belt from engine pulley. Remove cutting deck from under chassis.

Unhook clutch idler spring, then remove idler pulley from idler bracket for maximum belt slack and slip drive belt off engine pulley. Unbolt and lift engine from chassis.

Models L-821, L-861 and L-863

REMOVE AND REINSTALL. To remove engine, unlatch and tilt hood forward. Disconnect spark plug cable and battery cables, and on Models L-821

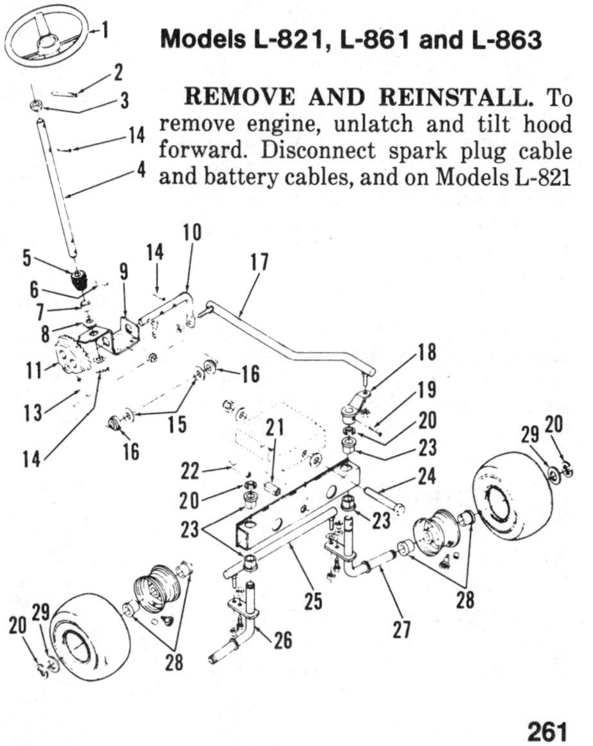

Fig. R3—Exploded view of steering system typical of that used on Models L-821, L-861 and L-863. Upper end of steering shaft is supported by console.

1. Steering wheel
2. Lock pin ¼ X1½
3. Bushing
4. Steering shaft
5. Pinion gear
6. Spring pin, ¼ X1½
7. Shaft spacer
8. Bushing
9. Steering bracket
10. Steering rod
11. Gear sector
13. Lock pin, ¼ x1½
14. Spring pin, 3/16X1 (2)
15. Flat washer, 0.656 (2)
16. Bushing
17. Drag link
18. Steering arm
19. Spring pin, ¼ X1¼
20. "E" ring, ¾-inch (4)
21. Rocker pivot
22. Pivot spacer
23. Kingpin bearing (4)
24. Bolt, ½-13X3
25. Tie rod
26. Kingpin/spindle, RH
27. Kingpin/spindle, LH
28. Wheel bearings (4)
29. Flat washer, 0.765 bore (2)

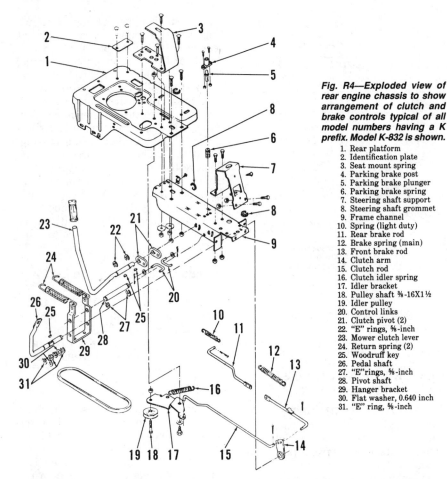

Fig. R4—Exploded view of rear engine chassis to show arrangement of clutch and brake controls typical of all model numbers having a K prefix. Model K-832 is shown.

1. Rear platform
2. Identification plate
3. Seat mount spring
4. Parking brake post
5. Parking brake plunger
6. Parking brake spring
7. Steering shaft support
8. Steering shaft grommet
9. Frame channel
10. Spring (light duty)
11. Rear brake rod
12. Brake spring (main)
13. Front brake rod
14. Clutch arm
15. Clutch rod
16. Clutch idler spring
17. Idler bracket
18. Pulley shaft ⅜-16X1½
19. Idler pulley
20. Control links
21. Clutch pivot (2)
22. "E" rings, ⅝-inch
23. Mower clutch lever
24. Return spring (2)
25. Woodruff key
26. Pedal shaft
27. "E"rings, ⅝-inch
28. Pivot shaft
29. Hanger bracket
30. Flat washer, 0.640 inch
31. "E" ring, ⅝-inch

from under chassis, as previously outlined. Disconnect spark plug lead as a safety precaution. Unhook idler spring (16-Fig. R4) from chassis, then remove nut from idler pulley shaft (18) and remove pulley (19) and drive belt. Pulley and its bearing should be very carefully checked for condition such as worn or cracked sheaves and rough or noisy bearing. Pulley and bearing are serviced as an assembly.

Reverse procedure to reinstall belt and idler. Be sure that long side of idler pulley bearing is upward.

Models L-711, L-721, L-722, L-821, L-861 and L-863

REMOVE AND REINSTALL. Remove mower deck from under unit as previously outlined, and disconnect spark plug lead. Disconnect idler spring (1-Fig. R5 or 16-Fig. R6) from frame. Unbolt and remove idler pulley for thorough examination and carefully check condition of idler bracket and all linkage. Note that idler pulley and bearing are serviced as an assembly. When removing belt from transaxle equipped models (L-821, L-861 and L-863) it will be necessary to remove shift lever plate and to insert a loop of drive belt through shift lever opening. Belt guides (11-Fig. R6) can be loosened so their positions can be shifted to make room for belt to clear sheaves. This also applies to snubbers under chassis.

Reverse procedure to reinstall belt and idler pulley.

and L-863, remove cable from starter motor. Disconnect ignition primary wires from engine, then unclamp and separate fuel line at filter. Plug or cap open line. Disconnect throttle cable.

Disengage blade drive clutch lever and remove blade brake rods from brackets on chassis. Now, remove cotter pins which secure parallel links to clutch arm assembly at each side, shift mower deck forward to ease tension on drive belt, slip belt from engine pulley, then slide mower from beneath unit.

Unhook clutch idler spring at chassis end, back off nut on pulley shaft and remove pulley. Work drive belt off engine pulley. Recheck for any interfering connections, then unbolt and remove engine.

IMPORTANT NOTE: Design of muffler may vary and on some TECUMSEH engines an exhaust tube may extend through front grille just below hood hinge; in which case, remove muffler before removing engine.

TRACTION DRIVE CLUTCH

All Models

All models use a conventional, pedal-operated, spring-loaded belt idler to apply or relieve belt tension between out-

put pulley of engine and input pulley of transmission or transaxle. No adjustment is provided. If belt becomes worn, stretched or glazed to the point that operation is unsatisfactory, a new belt must be installed.

To renew drive belt or clutch components refer to the following paragraphs for procedures.

Models K-511, K-521, K-522, K-831, K-832 and K-852

REMOVE AND REINSTALL. To remove drive belt, remove mower deck

Fig. R5—Exploded view of drive clutch and mower clutch controls typical of Models L-711, L-721 and L-722.

1. Idler spring
2. Idler arm
3. Clutch rod
4. Idler pulley
5. Pivot bolt, 5/16-24
6. Pedal sleeve
7. Pedal/shaft
8. Woodruff keys
9. Springs
10. Clutch-brake levers
11. "E" ring, ⅝-inch
12. Corner gussets
13. Hanger
14. Shoulder bolt, 5/16-18
15. Link bar
16. Pivot bolt 5/16-18
17. Clutch pivot lever
18. Shoulder bolt 5/16-18
19. Mower control handle
20. Grip

TRANSMISSION

All Models

Single-speed transmission for Model K-511 is covered in this section. Refer to TRANSMISSION REPAIR section for service details on other models:

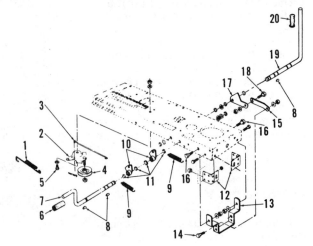

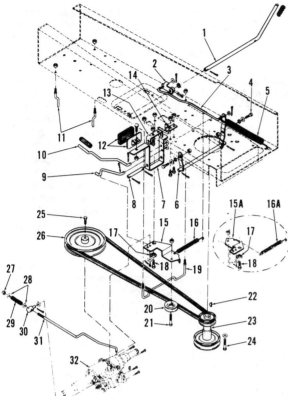

Fig. R6—Exploded view of drive clutch, brake and mower clutch controls typical of Models L-821, L-861 and L-863. Inset view shows different idler bracket for Models L-861 and L-863.

1. Blade clutch control handle
2. Blade clutch arm
3. Blade clutch rod
4. Pivot bolt, 5/16-18X¾
5. Spring
6. Clutch arm assy.
7. Pedal arm
8. Pedal shaft
9. Drive clutch rod
10. Park brake rod
11. Belt guides
12. Pedal & pad
13. Pedal bracket
14. Switch bracket
15/15A. Idler bracket
16/16A. Idler spring
17. Bushing
18. Pivot bolt, 5/16-18X¾
19. Belt guide
20. Idler pulley
21. Shaft bolt (⅜-16X1½)
22. Woodruff key (crankshaft)
23. Engine pulley
24. Cap screw ⅜-24X1⅜ w/Nylon washer
25. Cap screw, ¼-20X¾
26. Transaxle pulley
27. Locknut ⅜-16
28. Flat washer, 0.406 (2)
29. Brake spring
30. Trunnion
31. Brake rod
32. Transaxle assy.

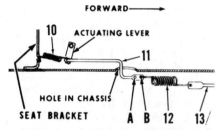

Fig. R7—When service brake performance is unsatisfactory on rear-engine (K) models, shift spring (12) from hole A to hole B in brake rod (11) to increase tension. Model K-511 linkage is shown. See text.

10. Light duty spring
11. Rear brake rod
12. Main brake spring
13. Forward brake rod
A. Forward hole
B. Rearward hole

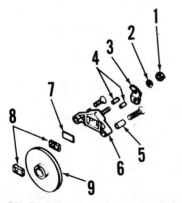

Fig. R8—Exploded view of transaxle-mounted disc brake assembly as used on Models L-821, L-861 and L-863.

1. Locknut
2. Flat washer
3. Brake lever
4. Dowel pins
5. Spacer
6. Pad holder
7. Brake pad plate
8. Brake pads
9. Brake disc

FOOTE Model 2010 transmission is used on Models K-521, K-522, K-831, K-832, L-711, L-721 and L-722. FOOTE 2600 type is used on Model K-852. Model 649 PEERLESS transaxle (600 series) is used on Models L-821, L-861 and L-863.

Model K-511

R&R AND OVERHAUL. To remove transmission, remove operator's seat and seat mount. Disconnect safety interlock leads at transmission. Disconnect light duty spring and brake rod from brake lever. Raise and block rear of unit so rear wheels can roll, disconnect master link and remove drive chain from transmission output sprocket. Disconnect clutch idler spring from frame, remove idler pulley and pull main drive belt clear of transmission pulley. Remove snap ring at bottom of

transmission input shaft and remove pulley. Unbolt transmission from chassis and remove.

Reverse procedure to reinstall. Check adjustment of drive chain before returning unit to service.

To disassemble removed transmission, back out seven cap screws which hold front case half (6-Fig. R9) to rear case half (19). Brake assembly (parts 1 through 5) will remain with front case half (6) when cases are separated. Shafts, gears and shifter will remain in rear case half (19). Note that there are no spring-loaded parts to pop out of place. Lift output shaft assembly from case half. Use a light-duty puller and remove brake disc (10) from shaft, taking care not to lose key (16). Remove "E" ring (11) at brake disc end of shaft and slip off thrust washer (12), bearing (13) and a bevel gear (14). Clutch (15) is a sliding fit over key (18). When clutch is bumped from shaft and key (18) is removed, balance of parts can be slipped off shaft end. Separate input shaft and pinion from bearing (8). Soak removed parts in solvent for thorough cleaning and easier inspection. Peel old gasket set (7) from case and prepare a new gasket by coating with a nonhardening sealer, Hi-Tack or light grade of Permatex. Clean flange surfaces thoroughly.

Check teeth of bevel gears (14) and pinion (9) for undue wear or damage. Inspect shaft (17), input shaft (9) and bearings (8 and 13) for signs of heavy wear, dry galling or severe wear. Renew as needed.

Inspect clutch (15) with care, paying special attention to its keyway and engagement teeth. Key (18) should be renewed.

If clutch yoke (22) is undamaged, there is no need for removal, however, if it is cracked or broken, use a pin punch to tap pins (21) out part way, then grasp pins with small pliers to pull clear.

Reassemble parts in reverse of disassembly order, lubricating all wear surfaces and contact points of shafts, bear-

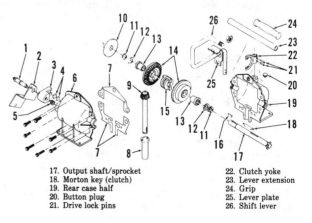

Fig. R9—Exploded view of single-speed, reversible transmission used on Model K-511. Brake assembly included.

1. Brake bolt (special)
2. Brake lever
3. Brake jaw
4. Brake pads
5. Spring
6. Front case half
7. Gasket set
8. Input shaft bearing
9. Input shaft & pinion
10. Brake disc
11. "E" ring ⅝-inch
12. Thrust washer
13. Bearing
14. Bevel gears
15. Clutch
16. Woodruff key
17. Output shaft/sprocket
18. Morton key (clutch)
19. Rear case half
20. Button plug
21. Drive lock pins
22. Clutch yoke
23. Lever extension
24. Grip
25. Lever plate
26. Shift lever

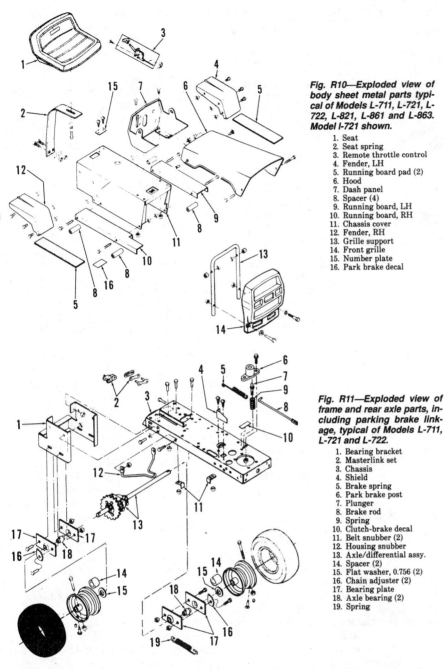

Fig. R10—Exploded view of body sheet metal parts typical of Models L-711, L-721, L-722, L-821, L-861 and L-863. Model I-721 shown.

1. Seat
2. Seat spring
3. Remote throttle control
4. Fender, LH
5. Running board pad (2)
6. Hood
7. Dash panel
8. Spacer (4)
9. Running board, LH
10. Running board, RH
11. Chassis cover
12. Fender, RH
13. Grille support
14. Front grille
15. Number plate
16. Park brake decal

Fig. R11—Exploded view of frame and rear axle parts, including parking brake linkage, typical of Models L-711, L-721 and L-722.

1. Bearing bracket
2. Masterlink set
3. Chassis
4. Shield
5. Brake spring
6. Park brake post
7. Plunger
8. Brake rod
9. Spring
10. Clutch-brake decal
11. Belt snubber (2)
12. Housing snubber
13. Axle/differential assy.
14. Spacer (2)
15. Flat washer, 0.756 (2)
16. Chain adjuster (2)
17. Bearing plate
18. Axle bearing (2)
19. Spring

volved because of its placement beneath operator's seat under sheet metal chassis cover (11–Fig. R10); however, transmission can be removed WITHOUT dismantling chassis cover, as follows:

Remove cutting deck as previously outlined. Disconnect lead from spark plug and, on electric-start models, disconnect battery leads. Unhook anchored end of clutch idler spring (1-Fig. R5) from frame and remove idler pulley (4). Pull drive belt off transmission pulley. Remove snap ring at bottom end of transmission input shaft and remove transmission pulley. Now, unbolt seat spring (2-Fig. R10) from rear of chassis and lift off seat and spring together. Disconnect safety interlock leads and rear brake rod from brake lever on transmission; then raise one rear wheel, disconnect master link and remove drive chain. Unbolt and remove transmission from chassis.

To reinstall, reverse order of removal.

DRIVE CHAIN

All Models So Equipped

To adjust drive chain, raise unit at rear, block up with wheels clear and remove rear wheels. Loosen retainer bolts at each rear axle bearing plate (17-Fig. R11) and shift axle rearward, using chain adjuster (16) on each side to keep axle square with frame. Proper chain tension calls for about ¼ to ⅜-inch (6.4-9.5 mm) slack between sprockets. Before retightening bolts, be sure that adjusters (16) are engaged in the same corresponding notches.

When adjustment is satisfactory, lubricate drive chain with SAE 30 engine oil. If drive chain fails due to wear, renew chain; do not attempt to repair.

TRANSAXLE

Models L-821, L-831 and L-863

REMOVE AND REINSTALL. To remove transaxle assembly, proceed as follows: Disconnect spark plug lead and remove cutting deck from under unit. Unscrew knob from shift lever, then back out four cap screws and lift off chassis cover plate (30-Fig. R12). Disconnect battery on electric start models, release clutch idler spring (16-Fig. R6) from chassis and remove idler pulley (26). Slip drive belt off transaxle pulley and work forward out of the way. Remove cotter pin from trunnion (30) and release brake rod from brake lever on transaxle.

ings and gear bores and teeth with a stable, medium weight grease. Manufacturer specifies Shell Darina AX.

Torque all assembly cap screws in an even criss-cross pattern to 6-7 ft.-lbs. (8-10 N·m). Reinstall transmission.

Models K-521, K-522, K-831, K-832 and K-852

REMOVE AND REINSTALL. To remove transmission, first remove operator's seat and on electric start models, disconnect and remove battery. Unbolt and remove seat mount spring. Disconnect electrical connections for safety interlock switch at transmission. Disconnect light duty spring and rear brake rod from lever on brake assem-

bly. Release clutch idler spring from frame, then unbolt and remove idler pulley and work main belt off and clear of transmission pulley. Remove snap ring at low end of transmission input shaft and remove pulley. With transmission in neutral and one wheel raised, disconnect master link and separate chain from output sprocket of transmission. Unbolt and lift out transmission.

Reverse these steps to reinstall. Check drive chain adjustment before operating unit.

Models L-711, L-721 and L-722

REMOVE AND REINSTALL. Removal of transmission is somewhat in-

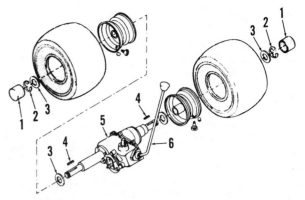

Fig. R13—Transaxle and rear wheels of Models L-821, L-831 and L-863. Transaxle is PEERLESS Model 649.

1. Hub cap	3. Washer, 0.765	5. Transaxle assy.
2. "E" ring, ¾-inch	4. Axle key, 3/16X2	6. Shift lever

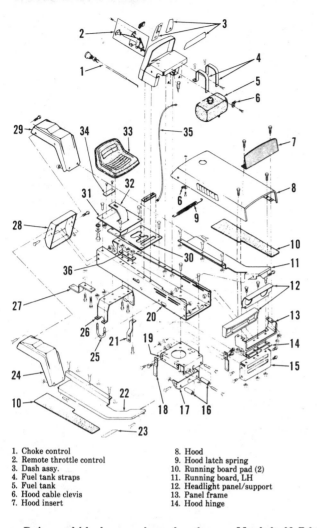

Fig. R12—Exploded view of chassis and body sheet metal parts typical of Models L-821, L-831 and L-863.

15. Lower grille
16. Spacer (2)
17. Axle support
18. Brake rod bracket (2)
19. Engine base
20. Chassis
21. Axle strap
22. Running board, RH
23. Clutch-brake decal
24. Fender, RH
25. Axle clamp
26. Transaxle support
27. Hitch plate
28. Rear cover
29. Fender, LH
30. Chassis cover
31. Cover plate
32. Seat spring
33. Seat
34. Identification plate
35. Hood cable
36. Support

1. Choke control
2. Remote throttle control
3. Dash assy.
4. Fuel tank straps
5. Fuel tank
6. Hood cable clevis
7. Hood insert
8. Hood
9. Hood latch spring
10. Running board pad (2)
11. Running board, LH
12. Headlight panel/support
13. Panel frame
14. Hood hinge

Raise and block securely under chassis just forward or rear wheels so that wheels are clear then remove nuts from axle clamp (25-Fig. R12) and remove two cap screws which hold transaxle housing in transaxle support (26). Roll transaxle out from under unit on its wheels for further service as needed.

DIFFERENTIAL AND REAR AXLE

All Models

Model K-511 is not equipped with a differential. Final drive sprocket and rear axle are integral.

Models K-521, K-522, K-831, K-832, K-852, L-711 and L-721 are equipped with a conventional gear-type differential identified as INDUS WHEEL type 73 DP. Refer to DIFFERENTIAL REPAIR section for details.

Limited slip differential, used in Model L-722 only, is covered in this section.

Models L-821, L-831 and L-863 are fitted with PEERLESS transaxle Model 649 which includes differential. Refer to TRANSMISSION REPAIR section.

Models K-511, K-521, K-522, K-831, K-832, K-852, L-711, L-721 and L-722

REMOVE AND REINSTALL. To remove axle and differential, disconnect spark plug lead and remove cutting deck from under unit.

Raise under frame just forward of rear wheels and block securely with wheels just clear.

With transmission in neutral, disconnect master link and remove drive chain. Removal of rear wheels is optional. Unbolt rear axle bearing plates (17-Fig. R11) from bearing bracket (1) or from frame. Lower axle, wheels and differential out of frame for further assembly.

Reverse procedure to reinstall.

Model L-722

OVERHAUL. This differential uses friction blocks (pucks) (6-Fig. R14) which are held by spring pressure against a drive disc within housing (4). To disassemble, after wheels and bearing plates have been removed, set axle and sprocket (8) up in a padded vise and

carefully unbolt housing (4), releasing spring pressure gradually. When case is opened, inspect all parts for undue wear, paying particular attention to condition of drive disc (7), friction blocks (6) and pressure springs (5).

Set up slip axle (1) in vise so that springs (5) can easily be inserted into their sockets in housing (4) and reassemble.

IMPORTANT: DO NOT LUBRICATE. Bearing in housing (4) is pre-lubricated, and no other lubricant should be introduced.

Torque case bolts to 20-24 ft.-lbs. (27-33 N·m) in alternating sequence. Reinstall axle bearings, bearing plates and wheels and reassemble. Adjust chain.

GROUND DRIVE BRAKE

Construction details on each disc brake appear in illustrations in applicable TRANSMISSION sections. Parking brakes are essentially a locking device to keep service brakes applied.

Models K-511, K-521, K-522, K-831, K-832 and K-852

ADJUSTMENT. Refer to Fig. R7 and/or to Fig. R4. Unhook light duty spring (10-Fig. R4) at frame, then remove brake rod (11) from actuating lever on brake. Shift main brake spring (12) to engage rearmost hole in brake rod, then reattach brake rod and light duty spring (10). If this does not satisfactorily restore service braking, check condition of brake disc which may be contaminated with oil or grease, and consider renewal of friction pads, ROPER part numbers 364259 or 370104.

If parking brake does not hold, check condition of plunger (5), spring (6) and parking brake tang on forward brake rod (13). Renew as necessary.

Roper

Models L-711, L-721 and L-722

Brake adjustment is similar to that outlined for K models in preceding paragraph.

Models L-821, L-861 and L-863

ADJUSTMENT. Brake linkage is shown in Fig. R6. To determine if service brake needs adjustment, observe if brake holds properly when clutch-brake pedal is fully depressed. If stopping force is ineffective, proceed as follows:

Be sure parking brake rod (10–Fig. R6) is unlocked, then turn locknut (27) on brake rod (31) until about ⅛-inch (3.2 mm) play can be measured between rearmost flat washer (28) and spring (29). If this adjustment alone does not restore braking, due to wear on brake pads, take up locknut (1–Fig. R8) against brake lever (3) so that brake pads (8) are closer to brake disc (9) but with no drag when brake is not applied. Recheck brake rod adjustment.

If these procedures do not restore braking, remove brake rod assembly, then unbolt and remove brake caliper assembly (6); install new brake pads (8). Reinstall over brake disc (9). Readjust.

MOWER CLUTCH AND DRIVE BELT

All Models

Blade clutch is designed to shift mower deck and blade spindle pulley(s) into firm contact with drive belt from engine by positive movement of a spring-loaded, over-center type linkage. There are no engagement adjustments. If blade drive becomes unsatisfactory, possible causes such as severely worn drive belt or worn, bent or damaged linkage parts will be immediately apparent upon inspection. Entire mower deck control assemblies are open for easy manual check and visual examination. Restore mower performance by repair or renewal of defective parts.

MOWER BLADE BRAKE

All Models

Blade brake(s) consists of a rod anchored to a frame member so as to engage and operate a brake shoe against blade pulley sheave. There is no brake shoe adjustment to compensate for wear. However, on Models K-831, K-832, K-852, L-711, L-721 and L-722 brake shoe end of rod is threaded to take up brake spring tension and pre-

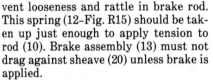

Fig. R14—Exploded view of Stewart limited slip differential used on Model L-722. See text.

1. Slip axle
2. Thrust washer, 0.751
3. Snap ring, ¾-inch
4. Housing w/bearing
5. Springs (4)
6. Friction blocks (8)
7. Drive disc
8. Axle & sprocket assy.

vent looseness and rattle in brake rod. This spring (12–Fig. R15) should be taken up just enough to apply tension to rod (10). Brake assembly (13) must not drag against sheave (20) unless brake is applied.

Brake pad alone is not renewable. If blade brake fails, renew entire assembly.

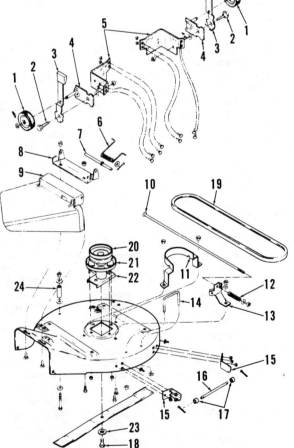

Fig. R15—Exploded view of cutting deck used on Models L-711, L-721 and L-722. NOTE: Items 20, 21 and 22 are furnished only as a complete "jackshaft assembly." Design is typical of that used on rear engine models.

1. Gage wheels, 5 in.
2. Shoulder bolt, ⅜-16
3. Spring lever assy.
4. Wheel bracket & axle
5. Gage wheel bracket
6. Guard spring
7. Hinge pin
8. Hinge bracket
9. Discharge guard
10. Blade brake rod
11. Belt snubber
12. Spring
13. Brake assy.
14. Belt keeper
15. Housing bracket (2)
16. Lower pivot shaft
17. Spacers (2)
18. Lockscrew, ⅜-24X⅞
19. Belt
20. Pulley
21. Jackshaft plate
22. Blade saddle
23. Washer, special
24. Spacer

MOWER CUTTING HEIGHT

Model K-511

ADJUSTMENT. On this model, a series of holes at front and rear of cutting deck allow for three positions of pivot shaft at front and gage wheels at rear. Cutting height levels are: 1¾, 2⅜ and 3 inches (44.5, 60.3 and 76.2 mm).

Models K-521, K-522, K-831, K-832 and K-852

ADJUSTMENT. Height adjustment is of the quick adjust type. A single lift handle rotates gage wheel axle through five positions for cutting heights which range from 1½ to 3 inches (65.3-76.2 mm).

Models L-711, L-721 and L-722

ADJUSTMENT. On these models, cutting height is set by manually changing setting of each of the individual selector levers (3-Fig. R15) to raise or lower gage wheels (1). There is no adjustment for front edge of cutting deck.

Models L-821, L-861 and L-863

ADJUSTMENT. Cutting height is controlled by a single lift handle which raises or lowers both gage wheels simultaneously through a choice of five height positions from 1½ to 3½ inches (65.3-76.2 mm).

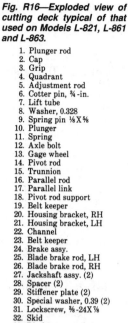

Fig. R16—Exploded view of cutting deck typical of that used on Models L-821, L-861 and L-863.

1. Plunger rod
2. Cap
3. Grip
4. Quadrant
5. Adjustment rod
6. Cotter pin, ¾-in.
7. Lift tube
8. Washer, 0.328
9. Spring pin ⅛ X ⅝
10. Plunger
11. Spring
12. Axle bolt
13. Gage wheel
14. Pivot rod
15. Trunnion
16. Parallel rod
17. Parallel link
18. Pivot rod support
19. Belt keeper
20. Housing bracket, RH
21. Housing bracket, LH
22. Channel
23. Belt keeper
24. Brake assy.
25. Blade brake rod, LH
26. Blade brake rod, RH
27. Jackshaft assy. (2)
28. Spacer (2)
29. Stiffener plate (2)
30. Special washer, 0.39 (2)
31. Lockscrew, ⅜-24X⅞
32. Skid
33. Discharge guard
34. Guard bracket
35. Hinge spring
36. Hinge rod

Provision is made for adjusting forward slope of the cutting deck. Measured from a level surface, forward tip of leading blade should be from ⅛ to ¼-inch (3.2-6.4 mm) lower than rearmost tip of rear blade. To adjust, remove cotter pin from stud of trunnion (15-Fig. R16) and turn trunnion clockwise to lower or counterclockwise to raise rear of deck. Check condition of parallel link (17) and rod assembly (16) and connections at clutch arm. Be sure cutter blades are straight.

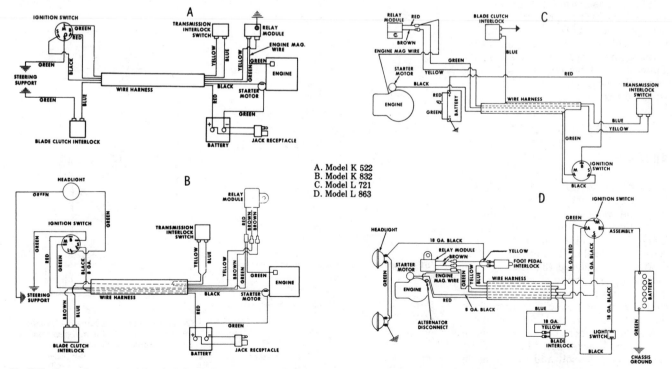

A. Model K 522
B. Model K 832
C. Model L 721
D. Model L 863

Fig. R17—Convenience views of typical circuit diagrams for electric-start mowers. Units without electric starting and/or lights are basically similar.

SEARS-CRAFTSMAN

SEARS, ROEBUCK & CO.
Sears Tower
Chicago, IL 60684

Model	Make	Engine Model	Horsepower	Cutting Width, In.
502.256011	Tecumseh	V50	5	25
502.256020	Tecumseh	V60	6	25
502.256030	Tecumseh	V70	7	25
502.256040	Tecumseh	V80	8	25
502.256071	Tecumseh	V80	8	30
502.256080	Tecumseh	V100	10	36
502.256091	Tecumseh	V60	6	25
502.256111	Tecumseh	V80	8	30
502.256121	Tecumseh	V80	8	30
502.256130	Tecumseh	V100	10	30
502.256141	B&S	250000	11	30

FRONT AXLE

All Models

REMOVE AND REINSTALL. The axle member (17-Fig. SE1) is non-pivoting type and is also the front frame member. To remove axle member, raise and block front of unit. Remove front wheels, unbolt and remove tie rod and bracket assembly (20) from spindles (19). Remove cotter pins and washers from top of spindles, then remove spindles and bushings (18) from axle ends. Loosen jam nut (8) and unscrew clutch-brake pedal pad (9). Unbolt and raise console (7), then unbolt and remove front apron (22). Disconnect clutch and brake rods (14 and 15), then unbolt and remove axle member.

Clean and inspect all parts and renew as necessary. Reassemble by reversing removal procedure. Lubricate bearings with light coat of SAE 30 oil.

STEERING SHAFT

All Models

REMOVE AND REINSTALL. On Models 502.256011 and 502.256091 unbolt and remove steering handlebar from lower steering shaft (13-Fig. SE1). On all other models, remove screw from collar (2) and slide collar downward on sleeve (3), then remove bolt through upper end of sleeve. Remove steering wheel and sleeve with collar from upper shaft (4), then drive out roll pins (5) and remove upper shaft. On all models, unbolt and remove tie rod and bracket assembly (20) from spindles (19). Unbolt and raise console (7) and remove cotter pin (12) from low-

er steering shaft (13). Raise front of unit and withdraw steering shaft.

Clean and inspect all parts for excessive wear or any other damage and renew as necessary. Lubricate bearings

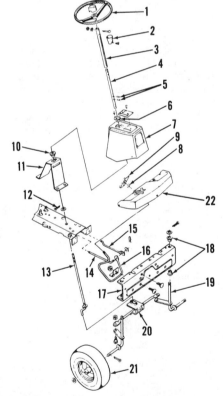

Fig. SE1—Exploded view of front axle and steering system.

1. Steering wheel	12. Cotter pin
2. Collar	13. Lower steering shaft
3. Sleeve	14. Clutch-brake rod
4. Upper steering shaft	15. Brake rod
5. Roll pins	16. Clutch-brake lever
6. Nylon bearing	17. Axle member
7. Console	18. Spindle bearings
8. Jam nut	19. Spindle
9. Clutch-brake pedal	20. Tie rod & bracket assy.
10. Nylon bearing	21. Wheel
11. Steering support	22. Front apron

with SAE 30 oil. Reassemble by reversing removal procedure.

ENGINE

All Models

Refer to appropriate engine section in this manual for tune-up specifications, engine overhaul procedures and engine maintenance.

Refer to the following paragraphs for removal and installation procedures.

REMOVE AND REINSTALL. Disconnect spark plug wire, ignition wires

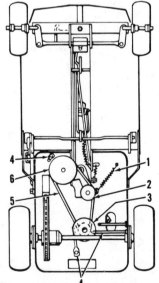

Fig. SE2—View of typical traction drive clutch and belt. Adjust belt guides to 1/8-inch clearance between guide and belt or pulley.

1. Idler spring	4. Belt guides
2. Idler pulley	5. Drive belt
3. Engine pulley	6. Transmission pulley

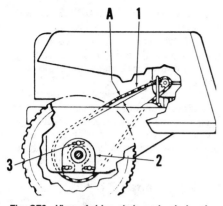

Fig. SE3—View of drive chain and axle bearing retainer. Chain should deflect approximately 1/2 inch (A) under light finger pressure.

1. Drive chain
2. Axle bearing retainer
3. Slotted holes

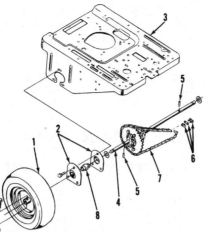

Fig. SE4—View of typical rear axle assembly used on all models.

1. Rear wheel
2. Bearing retainers
3. Rear frame section
4. Rear axle
5. Roll pins
6. Master link
7. Drive chain
8. Bearing

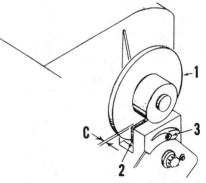

Fig. SE5—Exploded view of limited slip differential used on Model 502.256011.

1. Slip axle
2. Housing w/bearing
3. Friction block & spring assy.
4. Friction block
5. Axle & sprocket assy.
6. Drive disc
7. Retaining ring
8. Thrust washer

and throttle control cable. On recoil start models, unbolt and remove seat. On electric start models, tilt seat forward and disconnect battery cables and starter cables. On all models, remove mower as outlined in MOWER DECK paragraphs. Unhook traction drive idler spring and slip drive belt off transmission pulley first, then off engine pulley. Remove engine mounting bolts and lift engine from frame.

Reinstall engine by reversing removal procedure.

TRACTION DRIVE CLUTCH AND BELT DRIVE

All Models

All models use a pedal-operated, spring-loaded belt idler to apply or relieve tension on drive belt. No adjustment is provided. If belt slippage occurs during normal operation due to belt wear or stretching, belt must be renewed.

REMOVE AND REINSTALL. Disconnect spark plug wire and remove mower as outlined in MOWER DECK paragraphs. Unhook idler spring (1-Fig. SE2) and unbolt and remove idler pulley (2). Loosen or remove belt guides as needed, and slip drive belt off transmission pulley (6) first, then off engine pulley (3).

Renew belt by reversing removal procedure. Adjust belt guides to ⅛-inch (3.2 mm) clearance between guide and belt or pulley.

TRANSMISSION

All Models

Models 502.256011 and 502.256091 are equipped with single speed Foote trans-

missions. All other models are equipped with Peerless model transmissions. For overhaul procedures on all models, refer to TRANSMISSION REPAIR section of this manual.

REMOVE AND REINSTALL. Disconnect spark plug wire and remove mower as outlined in MOWER DECK paragraphs. Unhook traction drive idler spring (1-Fig. SE2). Loosen or remove belt guides as needed, and slip drive belt (5) off transmission pulley (6). Remove retaining ring and pulley from transmission shaft. On Models 502.256011 and 502.256091, remove chain guard and disconnect drive chain. On all other models, remove rear shroud assembly and seat and disconnect drive chain. Disconnect transmission safety switch wires and unhook brake spring and linkage from transmission brake. Remove mounting bolts and lift transmission from frame. Reinstall by reversing removal procedure.

DRIVE CHAIN

All Models

R&R AND ADJUSTMENT. To remove chain (1-Fig. SE3), rotate differential sprocket to locate master link. Disconnect master link and remove chain. Reinstall in reverse order of removal.

To adjust chain tension, loosen bolts securing axle bearing retainer plates (2) and slide axle rearward to tighten chain. Move each side of axle equally to maintain alignment. When tension is correct, chain can be depressed approximately ½ inch (12.7 mm) with light finger pressure, tighten bearing plate

bolts. Lubricate with light coat of SAE 30 oil.

DIFFERENTIAL

All Models

The differential used on all models except Model 502.256011 is manufactured by Indus Wheel Company. For overhaul procedure, refer to DIFFERENTIAL REPAIR section of this manual. Overhaul procedure for limited slip differential, used in Model 502.256011, is covered in this section.

REMOVE AND REINSTALL. Disconnect spark plug wire and raise and block rear of unit. Remove rear wheels (1-Fig. SE4). Disconnect master link (6) and remove drive chain (7). Unbolt axle bearing plates (2) from rear frame section (3) and lower differential and axle out of frame. Remove bearings (8) from axle ends. Reinstall by reversing removal procedure.

Model 502.256011

OVERHAUL. The differential uses friction blocks (3 and 4-Fig. SE5) which are held by spring pressure against a

Fig. SE6—View of typical brake assembly used on Models 502.256011 and 502.256091. Pad to disc clearance (C) should be 0.012-0.020 inch (0.30-0.50 mm).

1. Brake disc
2. Brake pad
3. Adjustment screw

drive disc (6) within housing (2). To disassemble, carefully unbolt housing from sprocket releasing spring pressure gradually. Separate housing and remove retaining ring (7) and thrust washer (8), then withdraw slip axle (1) from housing.

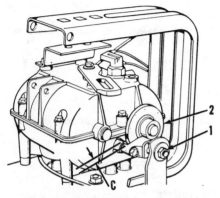

Fig. SE7—View of typical brake assembly used on all models except 502.256011 and 502.256091. Pad to disc (2) clearance (C) should be 0.010-0.015 inch (0.25-0.38 mm) and is adjusted by turning nut (1).

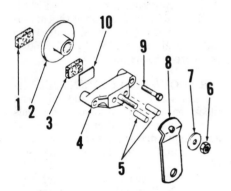

Fig. SE8—Exploded view of brake assembly used on all models except 502.256011 and 502.256091.

1. Inner brake pad	6. Adjusting nut
2. Brake disc	7. Washer
3. Outer brake pad	8. Actuating lever
4. Pad holder	9. Retaining bolts
5. Dowel pins	10. Back plate

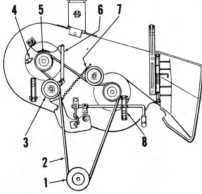

Fig. SE9—View of typical drive belt and clutch used on twin blade mowers.

1. Engine pulley	5. Blade brake
2. Drive belt	6. Blade brake rod
3. Idler pulley	7. Idler spring
4. Belt guide	8. Rear hanger bracket

Inspect all parts for wear or damage and renew as necessary. Reassemble in reverse order of disassembly. Torque case bolts to 20-24 ft.-lbs. (27-33 N·m)

NOTE: DO NOT LUBRICATE. Bearing in housing (2) is pre-lubricated and no other lubricant should be used.

GROUND DRIVE BRAKE

Models 502.256011-502.256091

ADJUSTMENT. To adjust brake, disengage parking brake lever. Turn brake adjustment screw (3–Fig. SE6) to adjust pads for 0.012-0.020 inch (0.30-0.51 mm) clearance between pad (2) and brake disc (1).

All Other Models

ADJUSTMENT. To adjust brake, disengage parking brake lever. Turn brake adjusting nut (1–Fig. SE7) to adjust pads for 0.010-0.015 inch (0.25-0.38 mm) clearance between pad and brake disc (2).

Fig. SE10—View of typical drive belt and clutch used on single blade mowers.

1. Idler spring	4. Engine pulley
2. Idler pulley	5. Belt guide
3. Drive belt	6. Guide arm

Fig. SE11—Exploded view of typical single blade mower.

1. Nut
2. Lockwasher
3. Blade washer
4. Washer
5. Blade
6. Washer
7. Blade adapter
8. Mower deck
9. Spindle bearing housing assy.
10. Front slotted bracket
11. Clutch lever & linkage
12. Idler spring
13. Blade clutch idler arm
14. Idler pulley
15. Spindle shaft
16. Drive belt
17. Blade pulley
18. Belt guide
19. Rear slotted bracket

Models 502.256011-502.256091

R&R AND OVERHAUL. Disconnect brake linkage from actuating lever. Remove shoulder bolt, brake pad holder and outer brake pad. Slide brake disc from shaft and remove inner brake pad from transmission case. Clean and inspect parts for wear or other damage. Renew parts as required and reassemble by reversing removal procedure. Adjust brake as previously outlined.

All Other Models

R&R AND OVERHAUL. Disconnect brake linkage from actuating lever (8–Fig. SE8). Unscrew retaining bolts (9) and remove parts (3 through 10). Remove adjusting nut (6) and separate lever (8), actuating pins (5), back-up plate (10) and outer brake pad (3) from carrier (4). Slide brake disc (2) off shaft and remove inner brake pad (1) from transmission case. Clean and inspect parts for excessive wear or any other damage. Renew parts as required and reassemble by reversing removal procedure. Adjust brake as previously outlined.

MOWER DRIVE BELT

Models 502.256071-502.256080

REMOVE AND REINSTALL. Disconnect spark plug wire and remove

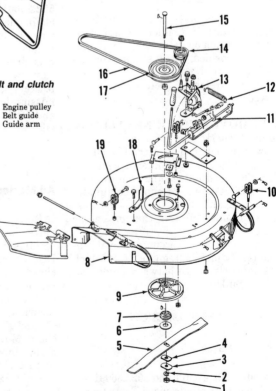

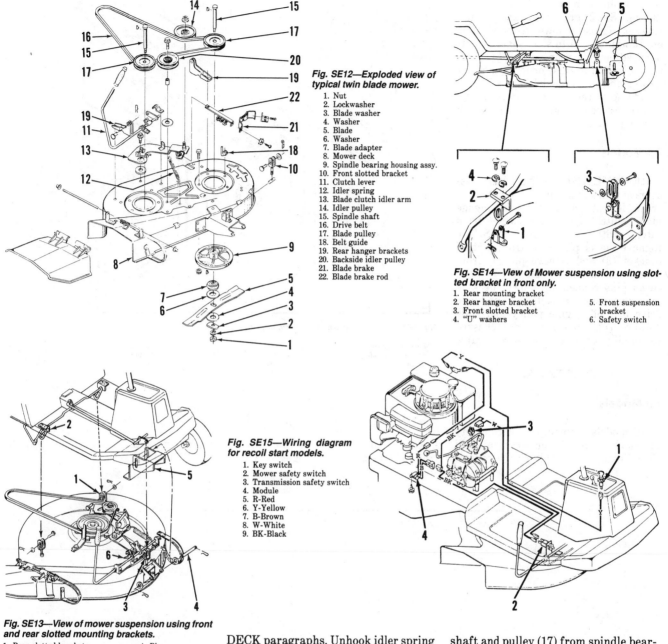

Fig. SE12—Exploded view of typical twin blade mower.

1. Nut
2. Lockwasher
3. Blade washer
4. Washer
5. Blade
6. Washer
7. Blade adapter
8. Mower deck
9. Spindle bearing housing assy.
10. Front slotted bracket
11. Clutch lever
12. Idler spring
13. Blade clutch idler arm
14. Idler pulley
15. Spindle shaft
16. Drive belt
17. Blade pulley
18. Belt guide
19. Rear hanger brackets
20. Backside idler pulley
21. Blade brake
22. Blade brake rod

Fig. SE14—View of Mower suspension using slotted bracket in front only.

1. Rear mounting bracket
2. Rear hanger bracket
3. Front slotted bracket
4. "U" washers
5. Front suspension bracket
6. Safety switch

Fig. SE15—Wiring diagram for recoil start models.

1. Key switch
2. Mower safety switch
3. Transmission safety switch
4. Module
5. R-Red
6. Y-Yellow
7. B-Brown
8. W-White
9. BK-Black

Fig. SE13—View of mower suspension using front and rear slotted mounting brackets.

1. Rear slotted brackets
2. Rear suspension bracket
3. Front slotted bracket
4. Pin
5. Front suspension bracket
6. Safety switch

mower unit as outlined in MOWER DECK paragraphs. On Model 502.256071, remove blade brake rod (6–Fig. SE9). On Model 502.256080, remove right hanger bracket (8). On both models, unhook idler spring (7) and unbolt and remove idler pulley (3), then remove drive belt (2).

Renew belt in reverse order of removal. Be sure belt is inside belt guides.

All Other Models

REMOVE AND REINSTALL. Disconnect spark plug wire and remove mower unit as outlined in MOWER

DECK paragraphs. Unhook idler spring (1–Fig. SE10) and unbolt and remove idler pulley (2), then remove drive belt (3).

Renew belt in reverse order of removal. Be sure belt is inside belt guide (5) and guide arm (6).

MOWER SPINDLE

All Models

REMOVE AND REINSTALL. Disconnect spark plug wire and remove mower and drive belt as outlined in MOWER DRIVE BELT paragraphs. Remove blade retainer nut (1–Fig. SE11 or SE12) and remove blade (5), washers, blade holder (7) and Woodruff key from spindle shaft (15). Remove spindle

shaft and pulley (17) from spindle bearing housing (9). Unbolt and remove spindle bearing housing from bottom of mower deck.

Clean and inspect parts for excessive wear or any other damage. Renew parts as required and reinstall in reverse order of removal. Torque blade retainer nut to 30 ft.-lbs. (40 N·m).

MOWER DECK

All Models

LEVEL ADJUSTMENT. With unit on level surface, measure distance from blade to ground from side to side and front to rear. Mower should be approximately ⅛-inch (3.2 mm) lower in front than in back. To adjust front to rear, remove pin from front slotted bracket (3-Fig. SE13 or SE14) and adjust bracket to raise or lower front of mower. To adjust side to side, some models have adjustable rear slotted brackets (1-Fig. SE13) to raise or lower sides of mower and other models are adjusted by adding or removing washers (4-Fig. SE14) between hanger bracket (2) and running board.

All Models

REMOVE AND REINSTALL. Disconnect spark plug wire and place mower in lowest position and disengage blade clutch. Disconnect wires from safety switch (6-Fig. SE13 or SE14). Remove clevis pin from front slotted bracket (3) and remove pin (4) from front suspension bracket (5). Remove clevis pins connecting mower deck to rear suspension brackets (1). Slip blade drive belt off engine pulley and slide mower deck out from under chassis. Reinstall in reverse order of removal.

ELECTRICAL

All Models

All models are equipped with safety interlock switches on transmission shift linkage and blade clutch control

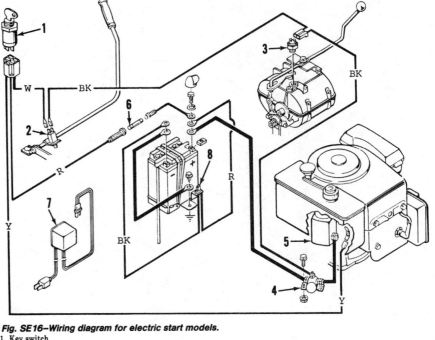

Fig. SE16–Wiring diagram for electric start models.

1. Key switch
2. Mower safety switch
3. Transmission safety switch
4. Solenoid
5. Starter
6. Fuse
7. Battery charger
8. Charger plug
9. R-Red
10. Y-Yellow
11. W-White
12. BK-Black

linkage. Transmission must be in neutral and blade clutch disengaged before engine will start. Refer to Fig. SE15 or Fig. SE16.

SIMPLICITY

SIMPLICITY MFG. CO., INC.
500 North Spring St.
Port Washington, WI 53074

Model	Make	Engine Model	Horsepower	Cutting Width, In.
305	B&S	130202	5	24
315	B&S	130202*	5	26
355	B&S	130202	5	28
808	B&S	190702**	8	30
3005	B&S	130202	5	26
3008-2	B&S	190402	8	30
3008-3	B&S	190707	8	30
3105	B&S	130902	5	26
3108	B&S	190702**	8	30
3110	B&S	220707, 255707 or 256707	8	36

*130207 on electric start models.
**190707 on electric start models.

LUBRICATION

All Models

Lubricate all linkage pivot points with SAE 30 oil. Use multipurpose lithium grease on all models equipped with lubrication fittings on bearing housings. Others are equipped with sealed bearings and require no additional lubrication.

FRONT AXLE AND STEERING SYSTEM

Models 305, 315, 355, 3005 and 3008-2

REMOVE AND REINSTALL. The axle main member is also the front frame assembly (10—Fig. S1). Pivot point is at joint of front and rear frame sections. To disassemble the steering system, support front of machine and remove front wheel assemblies. Unbolt and remove tie rods (14). Remove cotter pins from top of spindles (16 and 19), drive out roll pins (12) and remove both spindles with washers (13) and torsion springs (11). Unbolt and remove steering wheel (8) and cover (7). Remove washer (2), bushing (3), cup (4) and retaining ring (5) from upper end of steering shaft (6). Working through rear opening in front frame, remove cotter pin from steering shaft. Withdraw steering shaft from bottom of frame and remove cup (9), bushing (17) and washer (18).

Clean and inspect all parts and renew any showing excessive wear or other damage. Reassemble by reversing the disassembly procedure. Lubricate spindles and steering shaft bushings with SAE 30 oil.

Models 808 and 3008-3

REMOVE AND REINSTALL. The axle main member is also the front frame assembly (19—Fig. S2). Pivot point is at joint of front and rear frame sections. To disassemble the steering system, support front of unit and remove front wheel assemblies. Unbolt and remove the tie rod (17) and drag link (11). Remove retaining rings (12) and remove spindles (13 and 18). Remove steering wheel (1), washer (2) and bushing (3). Unbolt and remove steering support and cover (20 and 21). Remove cotter pin and washer (10) from lower end of steering shaft (4), then

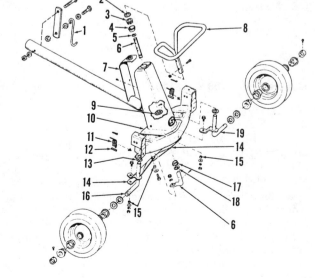

Fig. S1—Exploded view of typical front axle and steering system used on Models 305, 315 and 355. Models 3005 and 3008-2 are similar.

1. Mower hanger
2. Washer
3. Bushing
4. Bushing cup
5. Retaining ring
6. Steering shaft
7. Cover
8. Steering wheel
9. Bushing cup
10. Front frame & axle assy.
11. Torsion spring
12. Roll pin
13. Washer
14. Tie rods
15. Spacers
16. Spindle (R.H.)
17. Bushing
18. Washer
19. Spindle (L.H.)

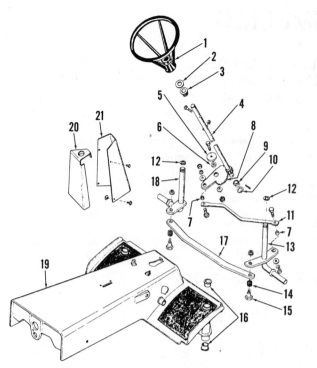

Fig. S2—Exploded view of typical front axle and steering system used on Models 808 and 3008-3.

1. Steering wheel			
2. Washer	7. Spacers	12. Retaining ring	17. Tie rod
3. Bushing	8. Quadrant gear	13. Spindle (R.H.)	18. Spindle (L.H.)
4. Steering shaft & pinion	9. Bushing	14. Spring	19. Front frame & axle assy.
5. Washer	10. Washer	15. Shoulder bolt	20. Steering support
6. Bushing	11. Drag link	16. Spindle bushings	21. Support cover

withdraw steering shaft and pinion. Unbolt and remove quadrant gear (8), special washer (5) and bushing (6). Remove steering shaft bushing (9) and spindle bushings (16), if renewal is required.

Clean and inspect all parts and renew any showing excessive wear or other damage. Using Fig. S2 as a guide, reassemble by reversing the disassembly procedure. Tighten flange nut on quadrant gear center bolt to a torque of 60 ft.-lbs. (81 N•m). Tighten flange nuts on tie rod shoulder bolts (15) to 30 ft.-lbs. (40 N•m). Apply a light coat of lithium grease to pinion and quadrant gear teeth and lubricate tie rod, drag link and steering shaft bushings with SAE 30 oil.

Models 3105, 3108 and 3110

REMOVE AND REINSTALL. Remove mower deck as outlined in MOWER BLADE CLUTCH AND BELT section. To remove front axle and steering parts, raise and securely block front portion of chassis.

Remove locking caps securing front wheels, then slide wheel assembly off spindles (31 and 32—Fig. S3). Remove cotter pin (12) securing drag link (28) in spindle arm (31), then lift drag link out of bushing (29) and swing clear of axle

assembly. Remove nut (24) and washer (23) from pivot pin (22). While supporting axle assembly (25), withdraw pivot pin (22), then lower complete axle assembly.

Refer to Fig. S3 and disassemble remainder of axle assembly. Inspect components and renew if excessively worn or damaged. Reassemble by reversing disassembly procedure. Lubricate bushings and wear points with SAE 30 engine oil.

ENGINE

Refer to appropriate engine section in this manual for tune-up specifications, engine overhaul procedures and engine maintenance.

Models 305, 315, 355, 3005 and 3008-2

REMOVE AND REINSTALL. To remove engine, unbolt and remove engine hood on all models so equipped. On electric start models, disconnect battery cables and starter wires. On all models, disconnect ignition wire and throttle control cable. Unbolt and remove pulley and belt guard from left side and remove the belt guide. Place the blade clutch lever in disengaged position, depress clutch-brake pedal and remove belts

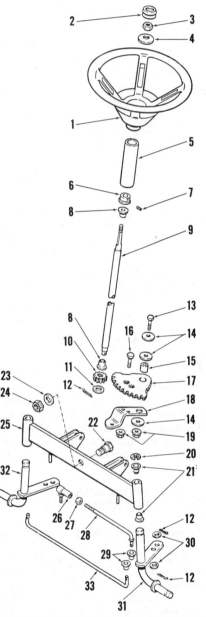

Fig. S3—Exploded view of typical front axle and steering system used on Models 3105, 3108 and 3110.

1. Steering wheel		
2. Cap	18. Steering arm	
3. Nut	19. Nut	
4. Washer	20. "E" ring	
5. Tube	21. Bushing	
6. Collar	22. Pivot pin	
7. Set screw	23. Washer	
8. Bushing	24. Nut	
9. Shaft	25. Axle assy.	
10. Pinion gear	26. Ball joint	
11. Washer	27. Jam nut	
12. Cotter pin	28. Drag link	
13. Cap screw	29. Bushing	
14. Washer	30. Washer	
15. Spacer	31. Spindle (L.H.)	
16. Cap screw	32. Spindle (R.H.)	
17. Steering gear	33. Tie rod	

from engine pulley. Remove engine mounting bolts and lift engine assembly from frame. Reinstall engine by reversing the removal procedure.

Models 808 and 3008-3

REMOVE AND REINSTALL. To remove the engine assembly, open the rear frame cover and, on electric start models, disconnect battery cables and starter wires. On all models, disconnect throttle cable and ignition wire. On Model 808, push transmission primary drive belt idler forward and remove belt from engine pulley. On Model 3008-3, depress clutch-brake pedal and remove transmission belt from engine pulley. On all models, place blade clutch control lever in disengaged position and remove mower drive belt from engine pulley. Remove engine mounting bolts and lift engine assembly from frame. Reinstall engine by reversing the removal procedure.

Models 3105, 3108 and 3110

REMOVE AND REINSTALL. To remove engine assembly, open rear frame cover and on electric start models, disconnect battery cables and starter wires. On all models, disconnect throttle cable and ignition wire. To ease removal, remove mower deck and drive belt assembly as outlined in MOWER BLADE CLUTCH AND BELT section. Loosen cap screws securing engine drive pulley belt guard, then slide clear of pulley. Loosen tension on traction drive belt idler as needed, then slip drive belt off engine drive pulley. Remove any parts that will obstruct in engine removal, then unbolt and remove engine assembly.

Reinstall engine by reversing removal procedure. Clearance between engine drive pulley belt guard and lower pulley should be $\frac{1}{8}$ inch (3 mm).

TRACTION DRIVE CLUTCH AND BRAKE

All models are equipped with a belt idler-type clutch and band-type brake.

Models 305, 315, 355, 3005 and 3008-2

ADJUSTMENT. To adjust the clutch and brake linkage, remove rear hitch plate, refer to Figs. S4 and S5 and proceed as follows: With clutch-brake pedal in fully up (clutch engaged) position, adjust the brake set collar so the distance from the bracket is 1 to 1½ inches (25.4-38.1 mm) on Models 305, 315 and 355, or 1⅛-1¼ inches (28.6-31.8 mm)

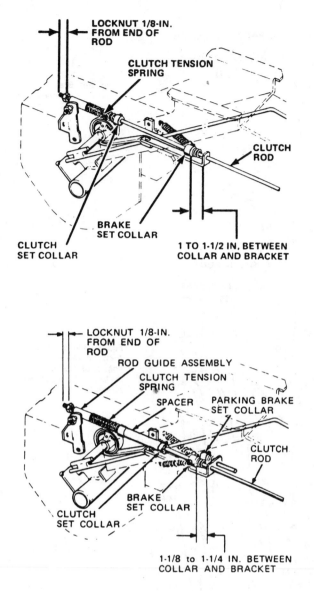

Fig. S4—Brake and clutch linkage adjustment on Models 305, 315 and 355.

Fig. S5—Brake and clutch linkage adjustment on Models 3005 and 3008-2.

on Models 3005-3008-2. On all models, adjust locknut to ⅛ inch (3.2 mm) from end of clutch rod. On Models 305, 315 and 355, with clutch-brake pedal in up position, adjust the clutch set collar so that clutch tension spring is preloaded ¹⁄₁₆ inch (1.6 mm). On Models 3005 and 3008-2, depress the clutch-brake pedal until brake is fully applied. Adjust clutch set collar so spacer holds the clutch tension spring against the clutch rod guide. Spring should not be compressed when pedal is fully depressed.

Model 808

ADJUSTMENT. To adjust the clutch and brake linkage, refer to Fig. S6 and turn nut (A) on parking brake rod to end of threads. Engage parking brake and tighten nut (B) until the spring against it is fully compressed. Adjust nut (C) to obtain a distance of 1 to 1¼ inches (25.4-31.8 mm) between flat washer and

brake band bracket as shown. Disengage parking brake and check to see that spring by nut (A) pushes brake band free of brake drum. If not, adjust nut (A) as required.

Clutching occurs when the pivot shaft assembly is moved to neutral position and belt tension is released from both the forward and reverse idler belts. Depressing the clutch-brake pedal or moving the direction control lever to NEUTRAL position will place the pivot shaft in neutral. Refer to Fig. S7 and loosen the set screw in directional control lever collar. Place directional control lever in NEUTRAL position. Rotate pivot shaft assembly to tighten forward idler belt, applying about 5 pounds (2.2 kg) pressure. Place a mark on directional control rod at front edge of rod guide. Rotate pivot shaft in opposite direction to tighten reverse idler belt, once again applying about 5 pounds (2.2 kg)

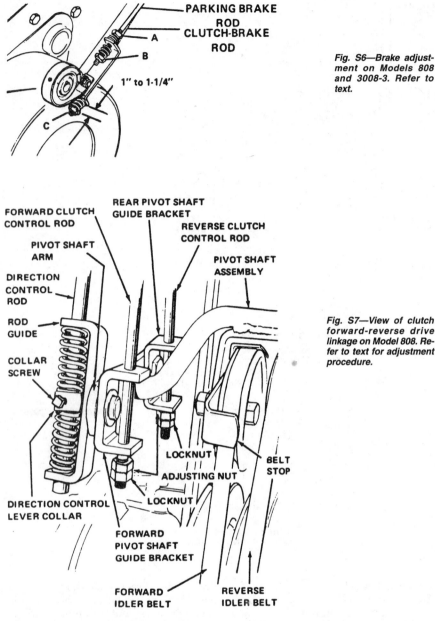

PARKING BRAKE ROD
CLUTCH-BRAKE ROD
A
B
1" to 1-1/4"
C

Fig. S6—Brake adjustment on Models 808 and 3008-3. Refer to text.

FORWARD CLUTCH CONTROL ROD
REAR PIVOT SHAFT GUIDE BRACKET
REVERSE CLUTCH CONTROL ROD
PIVOT SHAFT ARM
PIVOT SHAFT ASSEMBLY
DIRECTION CONTROL ROD
ROD GUIDE
COLLAR SCREW
DIRECTION CONTROL LEVER COLLAR
LOCKNUT
ADJUSTING NUT
LOCKNUT
BELT STOP
FORWARD PIVOT SHAFT GUIDE BRACKET
FORWARD IDLER BELT
REVERSE IDLER BELT

Fig. S7—View of clutch forward-reverse drive linkage on Model 808. Refer to text for adjustment procedure.

pressure. Place a second mark on directional control rod at front edge of rod guide. Distance between the two marks should be $^{11}/_{16}$ inch (17.5 mm). If this distance is incorrect, loosen the four cap screws securing pivot shaft in place. Move pivot shaft assembly forward or rearward as necessary to obtain the correct distance. Moving pivot shaft rearward will increase the distance. When the $^{11}/_{16}$-inch (17.5 mm) distance is obtained, tighten the four cap screws to a torque of 15 ft.-lbs. (20 N•m). Place a center mark on rod halfway between front and rear marks. Align front edge of rod guide with the center mark and tighten the collar set screw. Place the directional control lever in full forward position and pull pivot shaft downward. Loosen the locknut and turn adjusting

nut until a clearance of $^{1}/_{4}$ inch (6.4 mm) exists between the adjusting nut and the forward pivot shaft guide bracket. Tighten the locknut. Move the directional control lever to full reverse position and push pivot shaft upward. Loosen the locknut and set the adjusting nut to a clearance of $^{1}/_{4}$ inch (6.4 mm) from the reverse pivot shaft guide bracket. Tighten the locknut.

Model 3008-3

ADJUSTMENT. To adjust the brake linkage, refer to Fig. S6 and turn nut (A) on parking brake rod to end of threads. Engage parking brake and tighten nut (B) until the spring against it is fully compressed. Then, adjust nut (C) on clutch-brake rod to obtain a distance of

1 to $1^{1}/_{4}$ inches (25.4-31.8 mm) between flat washer and brake band bracket as shown. Disengage parking brake and check to see that front spring by nut (A) pushes brake band free of brake drum. If not, adjust nut (A) as required.

Clutching should occur when clutch-brake pedal is depressed approximately midway in pedal travel. If not, refer to Fig. S8 and loosen set screw in the set collar on clutch rod. Move set collar against or away from the compression spring as necessary, then retighten set screw. If clutch occurs too soon (before midpoint of pedal travel), move set collar away from spring. If clutching occurs too late (pedal too far down) move set collar against the spring. Move set collar at $^{1}/_{4}$-inch (6.4 mm) increments until correct pedal travel is obtained.

Models 3105, 3108 and 3110

To adjust engagement and disengagement of traction brake and clutch, proceed as follows. Fully depress brake-clutch pedal (1—Fig. S9) using normal pressure, then measure clearance between pedal arm and front edge of frame slot. Clearance should be $^{1}/_{4}$-$^{1}/_{2}$ inch (6.4-12.7 mm). To adjust, turn adjustment nut (2) on linkage rod (3) until correct clearance is attained.

With pedal in released position measure length of spring (2—Fig. S10). Spring should be 1-$1^{1}/_{4}$ inches (25.4-31.7 mm) long. To adjust, loosen set screw in set collar (3), then slide collar on rod (1) until correct length is attained. Retighten set screw.

TRACTION DRIVE BELTS

Models 305, 315, 355, 3005 and 3008-2

REMOVE AND REINSTALL. To remove the traction drive belt (1—Fig. S11), unbolt and remove engine hood on all models so equipped. On electric start models, disconnect battery cables. On all models, disconnect spark plug wire, then unbolt and remove pulley and belt guard from left side. Remove the belt guide and place blade clutch lever in disengage position. Remove the pto belt (3) from engine pulley. Depress the clutch-brake pedal and remove the traction drive belt.

Install new belt by reversing the removal procedure. Adjust clutch and brake linkage as required.

Model 808

REMOVE AND REINSTALL. To remove the traction drive belts (3, 4 and 9—Fig. S12), disconnect spark plug

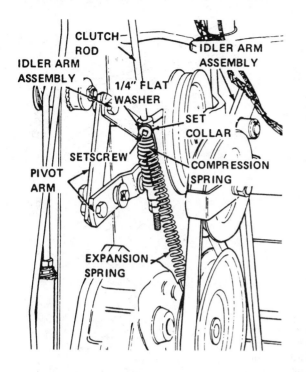

Fig. S8—Clutch linkage on Model 3008-3. Refer to text for adjustment procedure.

wire, open the rear frame cover and on electric start models, remove the battery. On all models, push the primary drive belt idler (1) forward until primary belt (3) can be removed from engine pulley (2). Remove primary belt from left side of transmission pulley. Note position of belt stops on the forward and reverse control idler pulleys and loosen the mounting bolts. Remove reverse drive belt (4) and forward drive belt (9), then complete the removal of the primary belt.

Install new belts by reversing the removal procedure. Refer to Fig. S13 and adjust outer adjusting nut until the length of the idler tension spring is $1\frac{1}{8}$ inches (28.6 mm). Adjust the inner elastic stop nut to a clearance of $\frac{1}{16}$ inch (1.6 mm) from frame bracket. Adjust clutch and brake linkage as outlined in previous paragraphs.

Model 3008-3

REMOVE AND REINSTALL. To remove the traction drive belt (2—Fig. S14), tie the clutch-brake pedal in fully depressed position. Disconnect spark plug wire and open rear frame cover. Working through rear opening, remove traction drive belt from engine pulley. Remove the belt from transmission input pulley (5), flat idler pulley (4) and clutch idler pulley (3). If necessary, loosen clutch idler pulley mounting bolt to provide clearance to remove belt from under belt stop.

Install belt by reversing removal procedure. Adjust clutch and brake linkage as required.

Models 3105, 3108 and 3110

REMOVE AND REINSTALL. Remove mower deck and drive belt as outlined in MOWER BLADE CLUTCH AND BELT section. Loosen drive belt

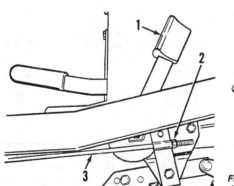

Fig. S9—On Models 3105, 3108 and 3110, adjust brake-clutch pedal (1) height by turning adjustment nut (2) on linkage rod (3). Clearance between brake pedal arm and front edge of slot should be 1/4-1/2 inch (6.4-12.7 mm).

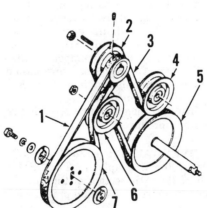

Fig. S11—View showing traction drive belt, pto drive belt and pulleys used on Models 305, 315, 355, 3005 and 3008-2.

1. Traction drive belt
2. Engine pulley
3. Pto drive belt
4. Pto (blade) clutch idler
5. Pulley & jackshaft
6. Traction drive clutch idler
7. Transmission input pulley

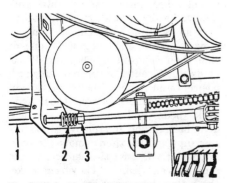

Fig. S10—On Models 3105, 3108 and 3110, when spring (2) on brake-clutch rod (1) is released, spring length should be 1 to 1-1/4 inches (25.4-31.7 mm). Adjust spring length by relocating set collar (3).

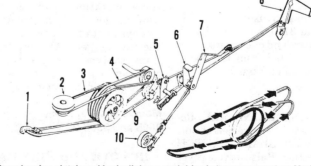

Fig. S12—View showing clutch and brake linkage, and drive belt arrangement on Model 808.

1. Primary drive belt idler
2. Engine pulley
3. Primary drive belt
4. Reverse drive belt
5. Pivot shaft assy.
6. Parking brake lever
7. Directional control lever
8. Clutch-brake pedal
9. Forward drive belt
10. Brake assy.

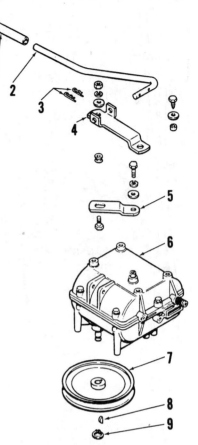

Fig. S13—View showing primary drive belt idler adjustment on Model 808.

Fig. S15—Exploded view of transmission and associated parts used on Models 3105, 3108 and 3110.

1. Handle grip
2. Shift rod
3. Spring clip
4. Pivot lever
5. Shift link
6. Transmission
7. Input pulley
8. Woodruff key
9. Snap ring

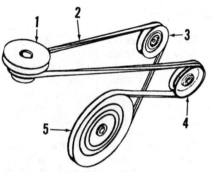

Fig. S14—Traction drive belt and pulleys used on Model 3008-3.

1. Engine pulley
2. Traction drive belt
3. Clutch idler
4. Flat idler
5. Transmission input pulley

finger on idler and swing clear of belt. Loosen engine pulley drive belt guard securing nuts and slide belt guard away from drive pulley. Release tension on traction belt idler as needed, then slip drive belt off pulleys. Install belt by reversing removal procedure.

TRANSMISSION

Models 3105, 3108 and 3110

The transmission used on Models 3105, 3108 and 3110 is equipped with five forward gears and one reverse gear. Power is transmitted from the transmission to the differential by a drive chain.

REMOVE AND REINSTALL. Remove mower deck and drive belt as outlined in MOWER BLADE CLUTCH AND BELT section. Raise engine cover and on models equipped with electric start, disconnect battery cables from battery. Disconnect spark plug wire,

then disconnect transmission neutral switch. Remove transmission input pulley (7—Fig. S15) retaining ring (9), then withdraw pulley from transmission input shaft. Detach spring clips (3) and slide rod (2) out of pivot lever (4). Loosen traction drive chain tensioner, then slide drive chain off transmission sprocket. Remove any components that will obstruct removal of transmission, remove transmission mounting bolts and remove transmission.

Install transmission by reversing removal procedure.

OVERHAUL. Refer to Peerless Series 700 paragraphs in TRANSMISSION REPAIR section of this manual for transmission overhaul procedure.

TRANSAXLE

The transaxle used on Models 305, 315, 355, 3005 and 3008-2 is equipped with two forward gears and one reverse gear. The transmission used on Model 808 is equipped with two forward gears. No reverse gear is used in this transmission as the forward-reverse drive belt arrangement allows for forward or reverse operation in either gear. The transmission used on Model 3008-3 is equipped with three forward gears and one reverse gear. All units are of the transaxle-type with the transmission gears and shafts, differential and axle shafts contained in one case.

Models 305, 315, 355, 3005 and 3008-2

REMOVE AND REINSTALL. The transmission shafts, shifter shafts and left axle shaft extend through the rear frame. The following procedures will

outline the removal of components necessary for removal of the transmission and differential. Actual removal of the shafts, gears and differential is outlined in the Simplicity portion of the TRANSMISSION REPAIR section of this manual.

Unbolt and remove engine hood on all models so equipped. On electric start models, disconnect battery cables and remove battery. On all models, disconnect spark plug wire. Unbolt and remove the pulley and belt guard from left side, then remove the belt guide. Place blade clutch control lever in disengaged position and remove the pto drive belt from engine pulley. Depress the clutch-brake pedal and remove the traction drive belt. Unbolt and remove transmission input pulley, then remove the rear hitch plate. Loosen the set screw and remove brake drum and key from brake shaft. Support rear of machine and remove rear wheel assemblies. Remove shift links, retaining rings and springs from shifter shaft and the transmission case. All gears, shaft and differential assembly can now be removed.

Reassemble by reversing disassembly procedure. Lubricate with general purpose lithium grease.

OVERHAUL. All models are equipped with a Simplicity transmission. Refer to TRANSMISSION REPAIR section for service information.

Models 808 and 3008-3

REMOVE AND REINSTALL. To remove the transaxle assembly, disconnect spark plug wire, open rear frame cover, and on electric start models, remove the battery. On Model 808, push primary drive belt idler forward until primary belt can be removed from engine pulley. Remove primary belt from left side of transmission pulley. Remove reverse drive and forward drive belts from transmission pulley. On Model 3008-3, tie the clutch-brake pedal in fully depressed position and remove traction drive belt from engine pulley first, then from transmission input pulley. On both models, unbolt and remove brake band, loosen set screw and remove brake drum. Attach a hoist to rear frame, unbolt transmission and left axle housing from frame, then raise rear of unit to clear shift lever. Roll transaxle assembly from chassis.

Reinstall transaxle by reversing the removal procedure. Adjust clutch and brake as required.

OVERHAUL. Both models are equipped with a Simplicity transmission. Refer to TRANSMISSION REPAIR section for service information.

DIFFERENTIAL

Models 3105, 3108 and 3110

R&R AND OVERHAUL. Remove mower deck and drive belt as outlined in MOWER BLADE CLUTCH AND BELT section. Raise rear of chassis so rear wheels are clear of ground. Remove "E" rings that secure wheels on axles, then remove wheels. Release tension on drive chain, then slip chain off transmission sprocket. Unhook ground brake actuating lever from brake band assembly. Remove screws securing axle bearing flanges (12—Fig. S16) to chassis axle support (10), then slide axles out of support slots. Reinstall differential and axle assembly by reversing removal procedure.

Differential overhaul procedures are outlined in the Stewart paragraphs in the DIFFERENTIAL REPAIR section of this manual.

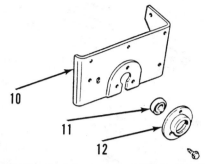

Fig. S16—View of axle support (10), bearing (11) and flange (12) used on Models 3105, 3108 and 3110.

All Other Models

R&R AND OVERHAUL. Transmission gears, shafts, differential and axle shafts are contained in one case. To remove the transaxle assembly, refer to the R&R procedures outlined previously in TRANSAXLE paragraphs.

Differential overhaul procedures are outlined in the Simplicity paragraphs in the TRANSMISSION REPAIR section of this manual.

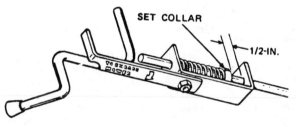

Fig. S17—On Models 305, 315, 355, 3005 and 3008-2, when blade clutch control lever is in engaged position, clearance between set collar and rod bracket should be 1/2 inch (13 mm).

MOWER BLADE CLUTCH AND BELT

All Models

A belt idler-type blade clutch is used on all models. If the mower drive belt slips during normal operation, check and adjust the clutch tension spring. If belt cannot be adjusted due to excessive wear or stretching, renew the belt. On models equipped with two belts, R&R procedures will be given for both belts.

Models 305, 315, 355, 3005 and 3008-2

To adjust the blade clutch, move the control lever to the fully engaged position. Clearance between the set collar and bracket should be 1/2 inch (13 mm) as shown in Fig. S17. If clearance is incorrect, disengage blade clutch, loosen set screw and reposition set collar. Engage clutch and recheck clearance.

To remove the mower clutch belt (14—Fig. S18), unbolt and remove engine hood on models so equipped. Disconnect spark plug wire, then unbolt and remove pulley and belt guard from left side. Remove belt guide and place

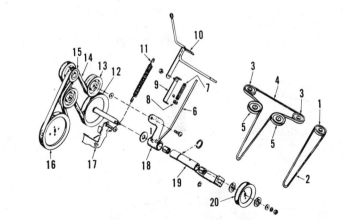

Fig. S18—View of blade clutch (pto) linkage, pulleys and drive belts used on Models 305, 315, 355, 3005 and 3008-2. Belt (4) and pulleys (3 and 5) are used on Model 355 dual-blade mower.

1. Mower pulley	7. Tension spring	11. Spring	16. Transmission input pulley
2. Secondary mower belt	8. Set collar	12. Pulley & jackshaft	17. Pto brake (3005 & 3005-2)
3. Mower pulleys (355)	9. Rod bracket	13. Blade clutch idler pulley	18. Clutch idler arm
4. Secondary mower belt (355)	10. Blade clutch (pto)	14. Mower clutch belt	19. Jackshaft pulley bracket
5. Flat idlers (355)	control lever	15. Engine pulley	20. Jackshaft pulley
6. Clutch rod			

blade clutch lever (10) in disengaged position. On models so equipped, pull the pto brake (17) away from belt. Remove the mower drive clutch belt. To remove the secondary mower belt (2 or 5), unbolt and remove pulley and belt cover from mower housing. Pull the jackshaft pulley bracket (19) forward and remove the belt from pulley (20). Remove belt from mower.

Install belts by reversing the removal procedure and adjust blade clutch as required.

Models 808 and 3008-3

To adjust the blade clutch, move the control lever to fully engaged position. Clearance between the set collar and rod bracket should be ¾ inch (19 mm) measured as shown in Fig. S19. If clearance is not correct, disengage blade clutch, loosen set screw and reposition set collar on rod. Engage clutch and recheck clearance.

To remove the mower drive belt (3—Fig. S20), first remove mower unit as follows: Disconnect spark plug wire and, on electric start models, open rear frame cover and remove battery. Place blade clutch lever in disengaged position. Disconnect the mower lift link and blade clutch rod, then unpin front of mower from frame. Unbolt pulley and belt cover from mower housing. Remove mower drive belt from mower pulley and slide mower unit out from under left side.

On Model 808, refer to Fig. S12 and push primary drive belt idler (1) forward until primary (transmission drive) belt (3) can be removed from engine pulley (2). Loosen mounting bolts and move belt stops (1—Fig. S20) away from engine pulley. Remove mower drive belt (3) from engine pulley.

On Model 3008-3, tie the clutch-brake pedal in fully depressed position. Working through rear frame opening, remove

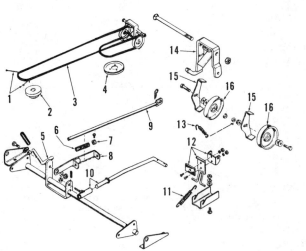

Fig. S20—View of blade clutch linkage, pulleys and mower drive belt used on Models 808 and 3008-3.

1. Belt stops
2. Engine pulley
3. Mower drive belt
4. Mower pulley
5. Blade clutch control lever
6. Tension spring
7. Set collar
8. Rod bracket
9. Clutch rod
10. Blade brake rod
11. Brake spring
12. Blade brake
13. Spring
14. Blade clutch idler arm
15. Belt guides
16. Clutch idler pulleys

transmission drive belt (2—Fig. S14) from engine pulley (1). Loosen mounting bolts and move belt stops (1—Fig. S20) away from engine pulley. Remove mower drive belt (3) from engine pulley.

On all models, note position of belt guides (15—Fig. S20) on idler pulleys (16) and loosen the mounting bolts. Move belt stops as required to remove the mower drive belt (3).

Install new mower belt by reversing the removal procedure. Make certain that belt guides and belt stops are properly installed. Adjust blade clutch as needed.

Models 3105, 3108 and 3110

To adjust blade clutch, move control lever to fully engaged position. Raise engine cover, then measure distance between set collar (1—Fig. S21) and rod guide (2). Distance should be ½ inch (13 mm). If distance is incorrect, disengage control lever and loosen set screw (3) in set collar (1). Slide set collar as needed and retighten set screw. Engage control lever and recheck distance.

To remove the mower drive belt, first remove mower deck as follows: Open

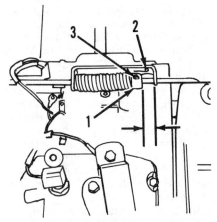

Fig. S21—On Models 3105, 3108 and 3110, adjust mower control linkage by loosening set screw (3) and relocating set collar (1). Refer to text.

engine cover, then disconnect spark plug wire. On electric start models, disconnect battery cables. Place mower control lever in disengage position. Place mower height control lever in lowest cutting position. Unbolt rear mower bracket (6—Fig. S22) on 26-inch, 30-inch and (7—Fig. S23) 36-inch mowers. Loosen cap screws securing engine pulley belt guard, then slide guard clear of pulley assembly. Loosen idler belt stop finger securing hardware, then swing finger away from belt. Remove clips and pins securing front of chassis to mower deck hitch. Slip drive belt off engine drive pulley and idler. Disconnect belt brake linkage and remove all other parts that will obstruct mower deck removal. Slide mower deck to one side. Push mower deck belt brake away from pulley(s), then slide belt off pulley(s).

Install belt and mower deck by reversing removal procedure. Clearance between belt stop and belt should be ⅛ inch (3 mm) when mower control lever is engaged. Clearance between en-

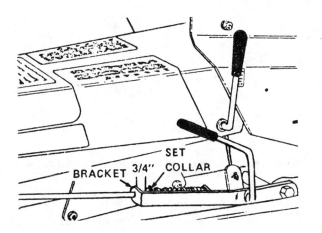

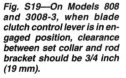

Fig. S19—On Models 808 and 3008-3, when blade clutch control lever is in engaged position, clearance between set collar and rod bracket should be 3/4 inch (19 mm).

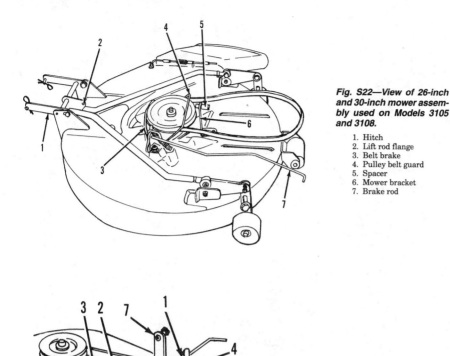

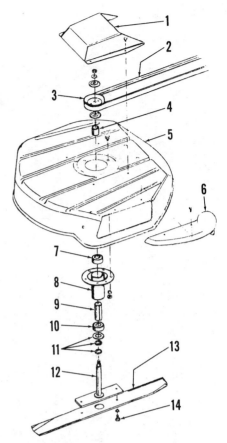

Fig. S22—View of 26-inch and 30-inch mower assembly used on Models 3105 and 3108.

1. Hitch
2. Lift rod flange
3. Belt brake
4. Pulley belt guard
5. Spacer
6. Mower bracket
7. Brake rod

Fig. S23—View showing 36-inch mower deck assembly used on Model 3110.

1. Brake rod
2. Lift rod
3. Jam nut
4. Leveling rod
5. Cotter pin
6. Hitch
7. Mower bracket

Fig. S24—Exploded view of the 24-inch mower unit used on Model 305.

1. Cover	8. Bearing housing
2. Mower drive belt	9. Spacer
3. Mower pulley	10. Bearing
4. Spacer	11. Washers
5. Mower housing	12. Spindle
6. Deflector	13. Blade
7. Bearing	14. Cap screw

gine pulley belt guard and lower pulley should be $\frac{1}{8}$ inch (3 mm).

MOWER BLADES AND SPINDLES

Model 355 is equipped with a dual-blade mower. All other models are equipped with a single-blade mower.

Model 305

REMOVE AND REINSTALL. Remove the mower unit as follows: Unbolt and remove cover (1—Fig. S24). Place blade clutch control lever in disengaged position. Pull jackshaft pulley bracket forward and remove mower drive belt from mower pulley (3). Unhook rear of mower and unpin front of mower, then slide mower unit from under left side. Remove the two cap screws (14) and remove blade (13). Remove nut, washers, pulley (3) and spacer (4) from above mower housing. Unbolt and remove bearing housing (8), then separate bear-

ings (7 and 10), spacer (9), washers (11) and spindle (12) from bearing housing.

Clean and inspect all parts and renew any showing excessive wear or other damage. Reassemble by reversing the disassembly procedure. Tighten mower pulley retaining nut to a torque of 25 ft.-lbs. (34 N•m). Tighten blade cap screws (14) to a torque of 30 ft.-lbs. (40 N•m).

Model 355

REMOVE AND REINSTALL. To remove the blades, spindles and bearings, first remove mower unit as follows: Place blade clutch control lever in disengaged position. Pull jackshaft pulley bracket (19—Fig. S18) forward and remove mower drive belt (4) from pulley (20). Unhook rear of mower and unpin front of mower, then slide mower from under left side. Refer to Fig. S25 and unbolt and remove cover (1). Remove mower drive belt (6). Remove cap screws (18) and remove blades (17). Remove nuts,

mower pulleys (5) and washers (9) from above mower housing (8). Unbolt bearing housings (12), then separate bearings (10 and 14), backing rings (11), spacers (13), washers (15) and spindles (16) from bearing housings. Unbolt and remove flat idler pulleys, if required.

Clean and inspect all parts and renew any showing excessive wear or other damage. Reassemble by reversing the disassembly procedure. Tighten mower pulley retaining nuts to a torque of 45 ft.-lbs. (61 N•m). Tighten blade cap screws (18) to a torque of 30 ft.-lbs. (40 N•m).

Models 315 and 3005

REMOVE AND REINSTALL. To remove the blade, spindle and bearings, remove mower unit as follows: Place blade clutch control lever in disengaged position. Pull jackshaft pulley housing (19—Fig. S18) forward and remove mower belt (2) from pulley (20). Unhook

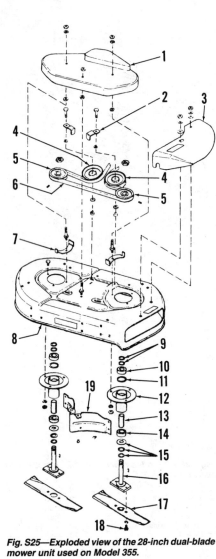

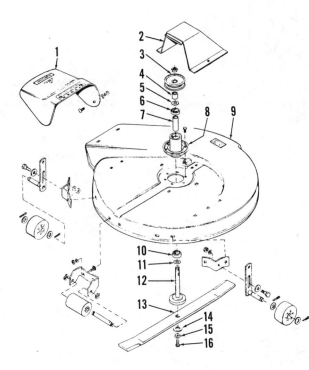

Fig. S26—Exploded view of the 26-inch mower unit used on Models 315 and 3005.

1. Deflector
2. Cover
3. Mower pulley
4. Spacer
5. Washer
6. Bearing
7. Spacer
8. Bearing housing
9. Mower housing
10. Bearing
11. Washer
12. Spindle
13. Blade
14. Belleville washer
15. Shoulder washer
16. Cap screw (L.H.)

Fig. S25—Exploded view of the 28-inch dual-blade mower unit used on Model 355.

1. Cover
2. Belt stops
3. Deflector
4. Flat idler pulleys
5. Mower pulleys
6. Mower drive belt
7. Belt guides
8. Mower housing
9. Washers
10. Bearing
11. Backing ring
12. Bearing housing
13. Spacer
14. Bearing
15. Washers
16. Spindle
17. Blade
18. Cap screw
19. Baffle plate

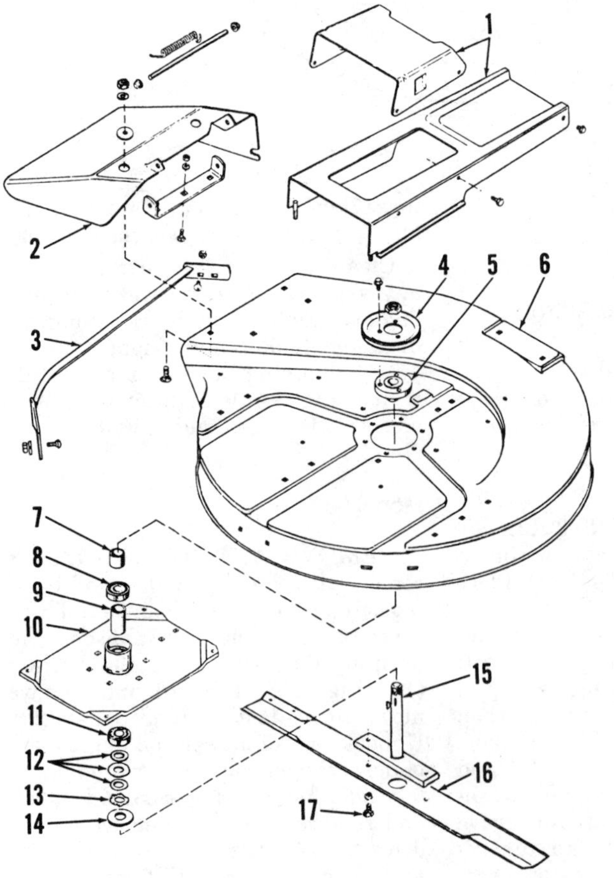

Fig. S27—Exploded view of the 30-inch mower unit used on Models 808, 3008-2 and 3008-3.

1. Covers
2. Deflector
3. Rock guard
4. Mower pulley
5. Hub
6. Mower housing
7. Spacer
8. Bearing
9. Spacer
10. Bearing housing
11. Bearing
12. Washers
13. Wave washer
14. Washer
15. Spindle
16. Blade
17. Cap screw

rear of mower and unpin front of mower, then slide mower unit from under left side. Unbolt cover (2—Fig. S26) and remove mower belt. Remove left-hand thread cap screw (16), washers (14 and 15) and blade (13). Remove nut, pulley (3), spacer (4) and washer (5) from above and spindle (12) and washer (11) from below. Unbolt bearing housing (8) and separate bearings (6 and 10) and spacer (7) from the housing.

Clean and inspect all parts and renew any showing excessive wear or other damage. Reassemble by reversing the disassembly procedure. Tighten mower pulley retaining nut to a torque of 70 ft.-lbs. (95 N•m) and left-hand thread

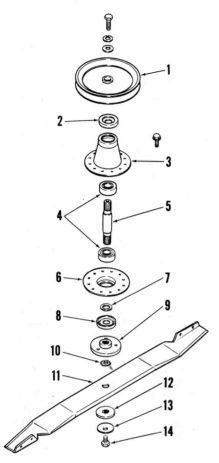

cap screw (16) to a torque of 80 ft.-lbs. (108 N•m).

Models 808, 3008-2 and 3008-3

REMOVE AND REINSTALL. To remove the blade, spindle and bearings, remove mower unit as follows: Place blade clutch control lever in disengage position. On Models 808 and 3008-3, disconnect blade clutch rod, then on all models, disconnect lift link and unpin front of mower from frame. Unbolt and remove covers (1—Fig. S27) and remove mower drive belt from pulley (4). Slide mower unit from under left side. Remove cap screws (17) and blade (16). Unbolt mower pulley (4), then unbolt and remove bearing housing (10) from mower housing (6). Remove nut, hub (5) and spacer (7) from top of bearing housing. Remove spindle (15) and washers

(12, 13 and 14). Separate bearings (8 and 11) and spacer (9) from bearing housing.

Clean and inspect all parts and renew any showing excessive wear or other damage. Reassemble by reversing the disassembly procedure. Tighten pulley hub retaining nut to a torque of 95 ft.-lbs. (129 N•m) and blade retaining cap screw (17) to 45 ft.-lbs. (61 N•m).

Models 3105, 3108 and 3110

REMOVE AND REINSTALL. To remove mower blade and associated drive parts, first remove mower deck assembly as outlined in MOWER BLADE CLUTCH AND BELT section.

Refer to Fig. S28 and disassemble blade drive components as follows: Remove cap screw (14), spring washer (13) and washer (12), then withdraw blade assembly (11). Unbolt and withdraw mower pulley (1), then unbolt and remove top bearing housing (3). Withdraw lower drive assembly out bottom of mower unit. Separate bearings (4) from housings (3 and 6).

Inspect components for excessive wear and damage. Reassemble by reversing disassembly procedure. Tighten blade retaining cap screw to 50 ft.-lbs. (68 N•m).

Fig. S28—Exploded view of mower blade and associated drive parts used on Models 3105, 3108 and 3110.

1. Pulley	8. Shield
2. Shield	9. Blade adapter
3. Top housing	10. Ring
4. Bearing	11. Blade
5. Shaft	12. Washer
6. Bottom housing	13. Spring washer
7. Shim	14. Cap screw

SIMPLICITY

Model	Make	Engine Model	Horsepower	Cutting Width, In.
8GW6	B&S	190000	8	36
12FC42	B&S	283700	12	42
12FCH42	B&S	283700	12	42
12GW2	B&S	280000	12	42
12HW2	B&S	280000	12	42
12HW6	B&S	280000	12	36
16FCH48	B&S	303700	16	48

FRONT WHEELS

All Models

The front wheels are the drive wheels for the machine. A key (15—Fig. S31) transfers power to each wheel from the axle. The wheel may be removed after supporting the machine and removing hub cap (18), snap ring (17) and washer (16). If so equipped, do not lose shims (14) behind wheel. Before assembly, apply antiseize compound to wheel contact surface on axle. Be sure the snap ring is properly seated in groove on axle.

STEERING SYSTEM

Models 8GW6, 12GW2, 12HW2 and 12HW6

LUBRICATION. Early models are equipped with a grease fitting at base of steering column so lower bushings may be lubricated. Remove rear cover on steering tower for access to grease fitting. Inject lithium based grease into grease fitting after every 25 hours of operation.

Later models are equipped with bearings that do not require periodic lubrication.

R&R AND OVERHAUL. Early models are equipped with a cable-actuated steering system that controls steering of the rear wheels. Cables should be inspected periodically and renewed if damaged.

To remove steering shaft, unscrew steering wheel retaining bolt and remove steering wheel. Remove rear cover on steering tower and disconnect linkage inside tower that will prevent removal of tower. Unscrew and remove tower. Unscrew reel retaining nut at bottom end of shaft and withdraw steering shaft. If required, detach steering cables from reel.

Reassemble steering components by reversing disassembly procedure. Coat flanged spacers in steering links with antiseize compound. Note that left steering cable attaches to upper reel groove and is wound around reel in counterclockwise direction viewed from bottom of reel. Right steering cable attaches to lower reel groove and is wound around reel in clockwise direction viewed from bottom of reel. After installing steering shaft assembly, steering wheel and steering cables, position steering wheel so cable ends (not clevis) are same length (measure from a similar reference point). Steering wheel should now be in centered, straight-ahead position. Place rear wheels in straight-ahead position. Rotate adjusting nuts (N—Fig. S32) on each cable clevis so hole in clevis aligns with hole on steering arm and insert clevis pin. Check steering operation.

Models 12FC42, 12FCH42 And 16FCH48

LUBRICATION. All models are equipped with a grease fitting on sector

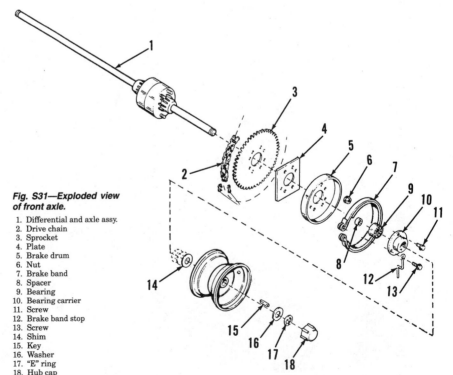

Fig. S31—Exploded view of front axle.

1. Differential and axle assy.
2. Drive chain
3. Sprocket
4. Plate
5. Brake drum
6. Nut
7. Brake band
8. Spacer
9. Bearing
10. Bearing carrier
11. Screw
12. Brake band stop
13. Screw
14. Shim
15. Key
16. Washer
17. "E" ring
18. Hub cap

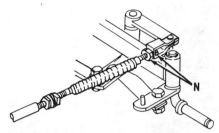

Fig. S32—View of rear-wheel steering cable adjustment point on Models 8GW6, 12GW2, 12HW2 and 12HW6. Refer to text for adjustment procedure.

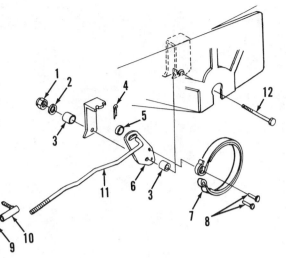

Fig. S34—Exploded view of brake assembly. Brake band (7) grips brake drum (5—Fig. S31).

1. Locknut
2. Washer
3. Spacer
4. Cotter pin
5. Washer
6. Arm
7. Brake band
8. Pins
9. Locknut
10. Coupler
11. Rod
12. Bolt

gear hub. Inject lithium based grease into grease fitting after every 25 hours of operation.

R&R AND OVERHAUL. Steering gear at bottom of steering shaft may be removed after withdrawing cotter pin. To remove sector gear, detach drag link end and remove sector gear pivot screw. To remove steering shaft, unscrew steering wheel retaining bolt and remove steering wheel. Remove rear cover on steering tower and disconnect linkage inside tower that will prevent removal of tower. Unscrew and remove tower. Withdraw steering shaft. Disassemble remainder of steering system as needed.

Reassemble steering components by reversing disassembly procedure. Coat flanged spacers in steering links with antiseize compound. Apply Loctite to steering arm retaining screws (W—Fig. S33) and tighten to 72-84 in.-lbs. (8.1-9.5 N•m). Apply grease or oil to rubbing surfaces. Apply grease to steering shaft splines.

Adjust length of drag link (D) so rear wheels are pointing straight ahead when steering gear is centered on sector gear.

GROUND DRIVE BRAKE

All Models

A band-type brake acts against a drum attached to the left side of the differential.

ADJUSTMENT. To adjust brake, push brake rod (11—Fig. S34) as far forward as possible. Rotate nut (9) so there is a gap of $\frac{3}{8}$ inch (9.5 mm) between nut and end of coupler (10).

R&R AND OVERHAUL. To remove brake band (7—Fig. S34), remove mower unit as outlined in MOWER DECK section. Support front of machine and remove left front wheel. Remove cotter pin (4) and separate brake rod (11) from brake arm (6). Remove bolt (12) and pins (8), then remove brake band (7). Inspect brake band and renew if excessively worn or damaged.

Brake drum (5—Fig. S31) is attached to differential, which must be removed

as outlined in DIFFERENTIAL section before removing brake drum.

DRIVE CHAIN

All Models

LUBRICATION. The drive chain should be lubricated with a good quality chain oil after every 10 hours of operation, or more frequently during hot weather or under severe operating conditions.

ADJUSTMENT. Chain tension on models equipped with a hydrostatic transmission is determined by a spring-loaded idler. Adjustment is not required.

To adjust chain tension on models equipped with a gear transmission, remove cover over transmission chain sprocket. Loosen nut (T—Fig. S35) and push idler (I) towards chain to remove chain slack. Tighten nut (T). Idler should remove slack from chain, but not produce tension in chain.

REMOVE AND REINSTALL. To remove chain on models with a gear

Fig. S33—To adjust rear-wheel steering on Models 12FC42, 12FCH42 and 16FCH48, refer to text. Apply Loctite to threads of set screws (W) and tighten to 72-84 in.-lbs. (8.1-9.5 N•m).

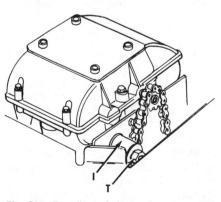

Fig. S35—To adjust chain tension on models equipped with a gear transmission, loosen nut (T) and push idler (I) toward chain to remove chain slack.

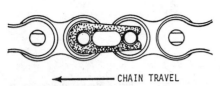

Fig. S36—Install drive chain master link clip so closed end of clip is toward direction of chain travel in forward gears.

Fig. S37—Remove cover (R) on hydrostatic transmission for access to fan (F). Bleed screw (B) is located adjacent to reservoir (V).

transmission, remove cover over transmission chain sprocket. Loosen nut (T—Fig. S35) and push idler (I) away from chain. Locate and disconnect master link in chain, then remove chain.

To remove chain on models equipped with a hydrostatic transmission, disconnect chain idler spring. Locate and disconnect master link in chain, then remove chain.

When installing chain, attach master link clip so closed end of clip is in direction of normal chain travel. See Fig. S36.

DIFFERENTIAL

All Models

REMOVE AND REINSTALL. To remove differential, remove mower unit as outlined in MOWER DECK section. Raise and support front of machine and remove front wheels. Remove brake band and drive chain as previously outlined. Unscrew axle bearing carrier (10—Fig. S31) and remove differential assembly. If required, unscrew nuts (6) and remove brake drum (5), plate (4) and sprocket (3).

Reverse removal procedure to reinstall differential assembly. Tighten brake drum retaining nuts (6) to 120-168 in.-lbs. (14-19 N·m). Install shims (14) as needed to remove axle end play.

OVERHAUL. All models are equipped with a Peerless Series 100 differential. Refer to DIFFERENTIAL REPAIR section for service information.

ENGINE

Models 8GW6 And 12GW2

Refer to appropriate engine section in this manual for tune-up specifications, engine overhaul procedures and engine maintenance.

REMOVE AND REINSTALL. To remove engine, raise engine cover and disconnect spark plug wire. Loosen belt guide at mower belt idler and remove mower belt from engine pulley. Relocate belt guides as needed, then relieve spring pressure against traction drive

belt idler and remove belt from idler and engine pulley. Unscrew retaining screw in end of engine crankshaft and remove engine pulley. Disconnect throttle cable from engine. Disconnect all wires from engine that will interfere with removal. Remove engine mounting bolts and remove engine.

Reinstall engine by reversing removal procedure.

Models 12HW2 And 12HW6

Refer to appropriate engine section in this manual for tune-up specifications, engine overhaul procedures and engine maintenance.

REMOVE AND REINSTALL. To remove engine, raise engine cover and disconnect spark plug wire. Remove belt cover on mower deck, pull back spring-loaded belt idler and separate mower belt from idlers. Remove mower drive belt from engine pulley. Unscrew and remove transmission fan screen (R—Fig. S37), remove fan (F) and re-

move belt from transmission pulley. Remove belt from spring-loaded idler, fixed idler and engine pulley. Unscrew retaining screw in end of engine crankshaft and remove engine pulley. Disconnect throttle cable from engine. Disconnect all wires from engine that will interfere with removal. Remove engine mounting bolts and remove engine.

Reinstall engine by reversing removal procedure. Refer to Fig. S38 and note proper routing of traction drive belt. Install transmission fan so tab on inner face of fan hub matches hole on shaft end. Gap between belt guides and belt should be $\frac{1}{16}$-$\frac{1}{8}$ inch (1.6-3.2 mm).

Model 12FC42

Refer to appropriate engine section in this manual for tune-up specifications, engine overhaul procedures and engine maintenance.

REMOVE AND REINSTALL. To remove engine, raise engine cover and

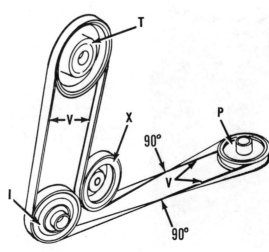

Fig. S38—The traction drive belt on models equipped with a hydrostatic transmission. Note position of "V" side (V) of belt and that belt twists 90° between engine pulley (P) and idlers (I and X).

I. Spring-loaded idler
P. Engine pulley
T. Transmission pulley
X. Fixed idler

Fig. S39—Detach spring clip (P) and push rod (R) out of frame before removing electric clutch (C).

disconnect spark plug wire. Remove belt cover on mower deck, pull back spring-loaded belt idler and separate mower belt from fixed idlers (do not remove belt from spring-loaded idler). Disconnect wire lead to engine pulley electric clutch. Detach spring clip (P—Fig. S39), push torque rod (R) through frame and unscrew rod from electric clutch. Remove mower drive belt from electric clutch. Apply brake to provide slack in traction drive belt. Loosen or remove belt guides as needed and remove drive belt from engine pulley. Unscrew retaining screw in end of engine crankshaft and remove electric clutch and engine pulley. Disconnect throttle cable from engine. Disconnect all wires from engine that will interfere with removal. Remove engine mounting bolts and remove engine.

Reinstall engine by reversing removal procedure.

Models 12FCH42 And 16FCH48

Refer to appropriate engine section in this manual for tune-up specifications, engine overhaul procedures and engine maintenance.

REMOVE AND REINSTALL. To remove engine, raise engine cover and disconnect spark plug wire. Remove belt cover on mower deck, pull back spring-loaded belt idler and separate mower belt from fixed idlers (do not remove belt from spring-loaded idler). Disconnect wire lead to electric engine pulley clutch. Detach spring clip (P—Fig. S39), push torque rod (R) through frame and unscrew rod from electric clutch. Remove mower drive belt from electric clutch. Unscrew and remove transmission fan screen (R—Fig. S37),

remove fan (F) and remove belt from transmission pulley. Remove belt from spring-loaded idle, fixed idler and engine pulley. Unscrew retaining screw in end of engine crankshaft and remove electric clutch and engine pulley. Disconnect throttle cable from engine. Disconnect all wires from engine that will interfere with removal. Remove engine mounting bolts and remove engine.

Reinstall engine by reversing removal procedure. Refer to Fig. S38 and note proper routing of traction drive belt. Install transmission fan so tab on inner face of fan hub matches hole on shaft end. Gap between belt guides and belt should be $\frac{1}{16}$-$\frac{1}{8}$ inch (1.6-3.2 mm).

TRACTION DRIVE CLUTCH AND DRIVE BELT

Models 8GW6, 12FC42 And 12GW2

The traction drive clutch is a spring-tensioned, belt idler-type operated by the clutch/brake pedal. When the pedal is depressed, belt tension is removed, allowing the engine drive pulley to rotate freely within the drive belt. After the pedal passes midpoint, the brake is applied.

LUBRICATION. Periodically lubricate all rubbing surfaces with engine oil.

ADJUSTMENT. With brake released, length of clutch rod spring (G—Fig. S40) should be 2-2$\frac{1}{8}$ inches (51-54 mm). Rotate nut (N) at end of clutch rod to obtain desired spring length.

R&R DRIVE BELT. Models 8GW6 and 12GW2. To remove drive belt, disconnect spark plug wire. Loosen belt

guide at mower belt idler and remove mower belt from engine pulley. Relocate belt guides as needed, then relieve spring pressure against traction drive belt idler and remove belt from idler and engine pulley. Remove traction drive belt. Install belt by reversing removal procedure. Gap between belt guides and belt should be $\frac{1}{16}$-$\frac{1}{8}$ inch (1.6-3.2 mm).

Model 12FC42. To remove drive belt, disconnect spark plug wire. Remove belt cover on mower deck, pull back spring-loaded belt idler and separate mower belt from fixed idlers (do not remove belt from spring-loaded idler). Disconnect wire lead to engine pulley electric clutch. Detach spring clip (P—Fig. S39), push torque rod (R) through frame and unscrew rod from electric clutch. Remove mower drive belt from electric clutch. Apply brake to provide slack in traction drive belt. Loosen or remove belt guides as needed and remove drive belt from engine pulley. Remove belt. Reverse removal procedure to install drive belt. Gap between belt guides and belt should be $\frac{1}{16}$-$\frac{1}{8}$ inch (1.6-3.2 mm).

Models 12FCH42, 12HW2, 12HW6 And 16FCH48

The traction drive clutch is a spring-tensioned, belt idler-type operated by the clutch/brake pedal. When the pedal is depressed, belt tension is removed, allowing the engine drive pulley to rotate freely within the drive belt. After the pedal passes midpoint, the brake is applied.

LUBRICATION. Periodically lubricate all rubbing surfaces with engine oil.

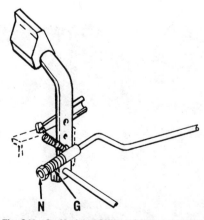

Fig. S40—On Models 8GW6, 12FC42 and 12GW2, clutch rod spring (G) length should be 2 to 2-1/8 inches (51-54 mm) when the brake is released. On Models 12FCH42, 12HW2, 12HW6 and 16FCH48, spring length should be 1-3/16 to 1-5/16 inches (30-33 mm). Rotate nut (N) at end of clutch rod to obtain desired spring length.

ADJUSTMENT. With brake released, length of clutch rod spring (G—Fig. S40) should be $1\frac{3}{16}$-$1\frac{5}{16}$ inches (30-33 mm). Rotate nut (N) at end of clutch rod to obtain desired spring length.

R&R DRIVE BELT. Models 12HW2 and 12HW6. To remove traction drive belt, raise engine cover and disconnect spark plug wire. Remove belt cover on mower deck, pull back spring-loaded belt idler and separate mower belt from idlers. Remove mower drive belt from engine pulley. Unscrew and remove transmission fan screen (R—Fig. S37), remove fan (F) and remove belt from transmission pulley. Remove belt from spring-loaded idler, fixed idler and engine pulley. Remove drive belt. Reverse removal procedure to install drive belt. Refer to Fig. S38 and note proper routing of traction drive belt. Install transmission fan so tab on inner face of fan hub matches hole on shaft end. Gap between belt guides and belt should be $\frac{1}{16}$-$\frac{1}{8}$ inch (1.6-3.2 mm).

Models 12FCH42 And 16FCH48. To remove traction drive belt, raise engine cover and disconnect spark plug wire. Remove belt cover on mower deck, pull back spring-loaded belt idler and separate mower belt from fixed idlers (do not remove belt from spring-loaded idler). Disconnect wire lead to engine pulley electric clutch. Detach spring clip (P—Fig. S39), push torque rod (R) through frame and unscrew rod from electric clutch. Remove mower drive belt from electric clutch. Unscrew and remove transmission fan screen (R—Fig. S37), remove fan (F) and remove belt from transmission pulley. Remove belt from spring-loaded idler, fixed idler and engine pulley. Remove drive belt.

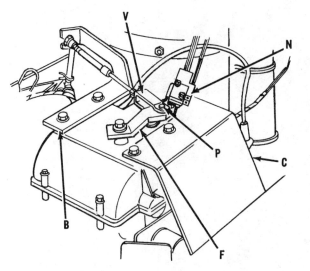

Fig. S42—View of transmission used on Models 8GW6, 12FC42 and 12GW2.

B. Bracket
C. Cover
F. Shift arm
N. Neutral switch
P. Pin
V. Clevis

Reverse removal procedure to install drive belt. Refer to Fig. S38 and note proper routing of traction drive belt. Install transmission fan so tab on inner face of fan hub matches hole on shaft end. Gap between belt guides and belt should be $\frac{1}{16}$-$\frac{1}{8}$ inch (1.6-3.2 mm).

INTERMEDIATE DRIVE BELT AND SHAFT

Models 12FCH42, 12HW2, 12HW6 And 16FCH48

REMOVE AND REINSTALL. To remove intermediate drive belt (B—Fig. S41), remove drive chain as previously outlined. Raise engine cover and disconnect idler spring (G). Unscrew bearing carrier mounting screws. Lift out shaft, pulley and belt assembly, then disassemble as needed. Reassemble by reversing removal procedure. Be sure belt ridges are properly aligned with grooves on pulleys.

SHIFT CONTROL LINKAGE

Models 8GW6, 12FC42 And 12GW2

NEUTRAL ADJUSTMENT. The shift control lever and transmission shift lever must be synchronized. Raise engine cover and remove clevis pin (P—Fig. S42). Shift transmission into neutral and place shift control lever in middle of neutral position on control panel. Rotate nuts at transmission end of shift cable so pin hole in clevis (V) aligns with pin hole in transmission shift lever (F) and install clevis pin (P). Additional adjustment is possible by rotating nuts at shift control lever end of shift cable. Tighten nuts and check adjustment.

Models 12FCH42, 12HW2, 12HW6 And 16FCH48

NEUTRAL ADJUSTMENT. To adjust shift control linkage, raise machine so wheels are above ground and machine is supported securely. Loosen nuts (N—Fig. S43) on shift rod so there is a $\frac{1}{4}$ inch (6.4 mm) gap between each nut and coupler (P). Raise engine cover and loosen screws (S—Fig. S44). Shift control lever must be in neutral position. Start engine and run at high speed. Loosen jam nut (J) and rotate inner nut (T) in either direction so pulley (Y) does not rotate. Tighten screws (S) and jam nut (J). Stop engine. Be sure shift control lever is still in neutral and tighten nuts (N—Fig. S43) against coupler (P).

TRANSMISSION

Models 8GW6, 12FC42 And 12GW2

REMOVE AND REINSTALL. To remove transmission, remove drive belt as previously outlined and remove

Fig. S41—To remove intermediate drive belt (B) on Models 12FCH42, 12HW2, 12HW6 and 16FCH48, disconnect idler spring (G) and refer to text.

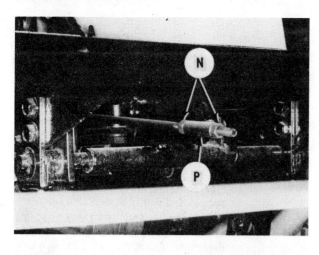

Fig. S43—On Models 12FCH42, 12HW2, 12HW6 and 16FCH48, loosen nuts (N) on shift rod so there is a 1/4-inch (6.4 mm) gap between each nut and coupler (P). Adjust shift control linkage as outlined in text.

Fig. S44—View of hydrostatic transmission used on Models 12FCH42, 12HW2, 12HW6 and 16FCH48. Rotate adjustment nut (T) as outlined in text for neutral adjustment.

transmission pulley. Raise engine cover, remove cover (C—Fig. S42) and disconnect chain. Remove shift lever clevis pin (P) and detach shift cable bracket (B) from transmission. Disconnect wire lead to neutral switch (N). Unscrew transmission mounting screws (screws are different lengths and should be marked) and remove transmission.

NOTE: Some screws used on transmission are self-tapping and must be installed carefully to prevent cross-threading.

Install transmission by reversing removal procedure. Tighten transmission mounting screws to 14-20 ft.-lbs. (19-27 N·m).

OVERHAUL. Models 8GW6, 12FC42 and 12GW2 are equipped with a Peerless Series 700 transmission. Refer to TRANSMISSION REPAIR section for service information.

Models 12FCH42, 12HW2, 12HW6 And 16FCH48

LUBRICATION. To check transmission fluid level, unit must be at ambient temperature. Raise engine cover and note fluid level in reservoir (V—Fig. S37). Fluid should be at "FULL COLD" mark.

NOTE: Due to close tolerances present in the hydrostatic transmission, particular care must be taken to prevent debris or other contaminants from entering transmission. Clean area around reservoir cap or any other opening to transmission.

Fill with multipurpose hydraulic/transmission fluid. If reservoir is empty, unscrew bleed screw (B) and add fluid to reservoir. With clutch/brake pedal depressed, move traction drive belt so fan on transmission rotates. Continue belt movement until only air-free fluid is expelled from bleed screw hole. Install bleed screw and fill reservoir. Operate machine while monitoring fluid level until level stabilizes.

REMOVE AND REINSTALL. To remove transmission, remove traction drive belt and intermediate drive belt as previously outlined. Detach shift control rod from transmission shift arm. Unscrew transmission mounting bolts and remove transmission.

Install transmission by reversing removal procedure. If removed, install transmission pulley so long side of pulley hub is towards end of shaft and flush with end of shaft. Tighten pulley retaining screws to 70 in.-lbs. (7.9 N·m). Tighten transmission mounting bolts to 20 ft.-lbs. (27.2 N·m).

REAR WHEELS

All Models

Each rear wheel hub is equipped with a grease fitting (F—Fig. S45). Inject lithium based grease into grease fitting after every 25 hours of operation. Rear wheel bearings are renewable.

REAR AXLE

All Models

LUBRICATION. The axle is fitted with grease fittings to lubricate the spindles, pivot pin and steering arm(s). See Figs. S45 and S46. Inject lithium based grease into grease fitting after every 25 hours of operation.

R&R AND OVERHAUL. To remove a rear spindle, raise and support side to be serviced. Remove hub cap, "E" ring, wheel and tire. Disconnect steering link from spindle. Detach snap ring at top of spindle and remove spindle. Inspect components for excessive wear and damage. Install spindle by reversing removal procedure.

The rear axle on all models pivots on a center pin. To remove the rear axle, disconnect the drag link or steering control cables from the upper steering arm(s). Raise and support front of machine, unscrew axle pivot bolt and separate axle assembly from machine. Disassemble remainder of axle assembly as needed. Inspect components for excessive wear and damage. Install axle by reversing removal procedure.

Fig. S45—View showing location of grease fittings (F) on rear axle assembly.

Fig. S46—The rear deck must be raised for access to grease fitting (F) on rear axle pivot tube.

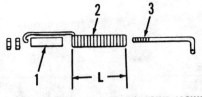

Fig. S47—When mower on Models 8GW6, 12GW2, 12HW2 and 12HW6 is engaged, clutch spring (2) length (L) should be 4-3/4 inches (121 mm). Rotate nuts on clutch rod (3) to adjust spring length.

MOWER BELT

Models 8GW6, 12GW2, 12HW2 And 12HW6

REMOVE AND REINSTALL. To remove mower belt, raise engine cover and disconnect spark plug wire. Loosen belt guide near mower belt idler on machine and remove belt from engine pulley. Detach belt cover on mower deck. Remove belt from mower deck. Reverse removal procedure to install belt. Be sure belt is routed between belt brake bracket and brake rod. Gap between belt guides and belt should be 1/16-1/8 inch (1.6-3.2 mm).

Models 12FC42, 12FCH42 And 16FCH48

REMOVE AND REINSTALL. To remove mower belt, raise engine cover and disconnect spark plug wire. Remove belt cover on mower deck, pull back spring-loaded belt idler and separate mower belt from fixed idlers (do not remove belt from spring-loaded idler). Disconnect wire lead to electric engine pulley clutch. Detach spring clip (P— Fig. S39), push torque rod (R) through frame and unscrew rod from electric clutch. Remove mower drive belt from electric clutch. Detach belt cover on mower deck. Remove belt from mower deck. Reverse removal procedure to install belt. Gap between belt guides and belt should be 1/16-1/8 inch (1.6-3.2 mm).

MOWER DECK

Models 8GW6, 12GW2, 12HW2 And 12HW6

LUBRICATION. Each mower wheel spindle housing is equipped with a grease fitting. Inject lithium based grease into grease fitting after every 25 hours of operation. Lubricate all rubbing surfaces with engine oil.

HEIGHT ADJUSTMENT. All mower control linkage must be in good operating condition and tires properly inflated. Park machine on a level surface with engine stopped and spark plug wire disconnected.

Front-to-rear height difference is determined by measuring height of blade above ground at front and rear. Height difference should be within 1/8 inch (3.2 mm). To adjust front-to-rear height difference, rotate leveling bolts at front and rear of mower deck.

Side-to-side height difference should be 1/8 inch (3.2 mm). To adjust side-to-side dimension, rotate leveling bolts at front and rear on one side of mower deck.

CLUTCH ADJUSTMENT. When mower is engaged, clutch spring length should be 4 3/4 inches (121 mm) measured between coil ends as shown in Fig.

S47. To adjust spring length, disengage mower and rotate nuts.

REMOVE AND REINSTALL. To remove mower, raise engine cover and disconnect spark plug wire. Loosen belt guide near mower belt idler on machine and remove belt from engine pulley. Disconnect mower clutch rod and lift rod. Detach attachment pins at rear of mower frame and remove mower. Install mower by reversing removal procedure.

Models 12FC42, 12FCH42 And 16FCH48

LUBRICATION. Mower wheel spindle housings and clutch idler arm are equipped with a grease fitting. Inject lithium based grease into grease fitting after every 25 hours of operation. Lubricate all rubbing surfaces with engine oil.

HEIGHT ADJUSTMENT. All mower control linkage must be in good operating condition and tires properly inflated. Park machine on a level surface with engine stopped and spark plug wire disconnected.

Front-to-rear height difference is determined by measuring height of blade above ground at front and rear. Height difference should be zero. To adjust height, remove belt covers, detach spring clips (C—Fig. S48) and remove pins in each adjustment rod. Loosen jam nuts (N) and rotate each clevis (L) equal turns to adjust height. Retighten nuts and install pins, spring clips and belt covers.

Side-to-side height difference should be zero. To adjust side-to-side height, loosen screw (S—Fig. S49) and relocate roller bracket (B).

REMOVE AND REINSTALL. To remove mower belt, raise engine cover and disconnect spark plug wire. Remove belt cover on mower deck, pull back spring-loaded belt idler and separate mower belt from fixed idlers (do not remove belt from spring-loaded idler). Disconnect wire lead to engine pulley electric clutch. Detach spring clip (P— Fig. S39), push torque rod (R) through frame and unscrew rod from electric

Fig. S48—Refer to text to adjust mower height on Models 12FC42, 12FCH42 and 16FCH48.

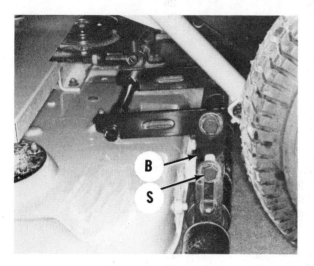

Fig. S49—On Models 12FC42, 12FCH42 and 16FCH48, loosen screw (S) and relocate bracket (B) so adjust side-to-side mower height.

clutch. Remove mower drive belt from electric clutch. Place mower in lowest position. Detach rear lift arms from lift chains. Detach rear mower frame arms from machine. Detach spring clip (C—Fig. S50) from pin (P) and disconnect lift link. Roll mower away from machine.

Install mower by reversing removal procedure.

MOWER SPINDLE

All Models

LUBRICATION. Mower spindle housings on some models are equipped with a grease fitting on the bottom of the housing. If so equipped, inject lithium based grease into grease fitting after every 25 hours of operation.

R&R AND OVERHAUL. Remove mower deck, belt and blade. Unscrew

spindle housing mounting screws and remove spindle assembly. Disassembly is evident after inspection of unit. During assembly, apply gasket forming compound to mating surfaces of top and lower spindle housings. Let gasket forming compound cure, then fill lower spindle housing with lithium based grease. If spindle pulley hub has a long end, install pulley so long end of hub is towards housing. Tighten pulley retaining screw to 50-70 ft.-lbs. (68-95 N·m). Tighten spindle housing retaining screws to 14-20 ft.-lbs. (19-27 N·m). Tighten blade retaining screw to 50-70 ft.-lbs. (68-95 N·m).

ELECTRIC MOWER CLUTCH

Models 12FC42, 12FCH42 And 16FCH48

On Models 12FC42, 12FCH42 and 16FCH48, the mower drive pulley is attached to an electric clutch.

ADJUSTMENT. The clutch air gap must be set correctly so the clutch will engage properly. Desired air gap is 0.010-0.012 inch (0.25-0.30 mm). With the mower clutch switch in "OFF" position, insert a 0.010-0.012 inch (0.25-0.30 mm) feeler gauge through slots (S—Fig. S51) in side of clutch. Check gap through all three of the slots. Rotate nut (N) at each of the three slots as needed to obtain correct gap.

R&R AND OVERHAUL. Remove mower drive belt as previously outlined. Unscrew clutch retaining screw and remove clutch assembly. Unscrew clutch nuts (N—Fig. S51) to disassemble clutch.

If installing a new clutch or components, adjust clutch air gap as previously outlined. Engage clutch several times after mower is installed to burnish clutch surfaces.

Fig. S50—On Models 12FC42, 12FCH42 and 16FCH48, detach spring clip (C) and disconnect lift rod from pin (P) to remove mower deck.

Fig. S51—Turn each adjusting nut (N) of electric clutch so clearance between rotor and armature is 0.010-0.012 inch (0.25-0.30 mm).

SNAPPER

McDONOUGH POWER EQUIPMENT CO.
P.O. Box 777
McDonough, GA 30253

Model	Make	Engine Model	Horsepower	Cutting Width, In.
265X/XS	Tec.	V50	5	26
266X/XS	B&S	140000	6	26
267X/XS	B&S	170000	7	26
268X/XS	B&S	190000	8	26
305X/XS	Tec.	V50	5	30
306X/XS	Tec.	VH60	6	30
307X/XS	B&S	170000	7	30
308X/XS	B&S	190000	8	30
417X/XS	B&S	170000	7	41
418X/XS	Wisc.	HS8D	8	41
2550/S	B&S/Tec.	130000/V50	5	25
2650/S	Tec.	V50	5	26
2651/S	Tec.	V50	5	26
2652/S	B&S/Tec.	130000/V50	5	26
2680/S	B&S/Tec.	190000/VM80	8	26
2681/S	B&S/Tec.	190000/VM80	8	26
2681/S/W/WS	B&S/Tec.	190000/VM80	8	26
2810/W/WS	B&S	250000	11	28
2811X5/S	B&S	250000	11	28
2811X6S	B&S	250000	11	28
2812X6S	B&S	281707	12	28
2812X6SR	Robin	WI-450V	12	28
2812X6SR	Robin	WI-450V	12	28
2812X6ST	Tec.	OVXL120	12	28
2880/W/WS	B&S/Tec.	190000/VM80	8	28
3010/WS	B&S/Tec.	250000/VM110	11	30
3011X5/S	B&S	250000	11	30
3011X6S	B&S	250000	11	30
3012X6S	B&S	281707	12	30
3012X6SR	Robin	WI-450V	12	30
3012X6SR	Robin	WI-450V	12	30
3012X6ST	Tec.	OVXL120	12	30
3080/S	B&S/Tec.	190000/VM80	8	30
3081/S/W/WS	B&S/Tec.	190000/VM80	8	30
3311X5/S	B&S	250000	11	33
3311X6S	B&S	250000	11	33
3312X6S	B&S	281707	12	33
3312X6SR	Robin	WI-450V	12	33
3312X6SR	Robin	WI-450V	12	33
3312X6ST	Tec.	OVXL120	12	33
4111X5/S	B&S	250000	11	41
4111X6S	B&S	250000	11	41
4112X6S	B&S	281707	12	41
41126BE	B&S	281707	12	41
4112X6SR	Robin	WI-450V	12	41
4112X6ST	Tec.	OVXL-120	12	41
4210/W/WS	B&S	250000	11	28
25063/S	B&S/Tec.	140000/VM60	6	25
25064/S	Tec.	VM60	6	25
25065/S	Tec.	VM60	6	25
25066/S	Tec.	VM60	6	25
25069T	Tec.	TVM140	6	25

Model	Make	Engine Model	Horsepower	Cutting Width, In.
25083/S	B&S/Tec.	190000/VM80	8	25
25084/S	B&S/Tec.	190000/VM80	8	25
25085/S	B&S/Tec.	190000/VM80	8	25
25086/S/ST/T	B&S/Tec.	190000/VM80	8	25
25657B/BE	B&S	170702, 170707	6½	25
25659BE	B&S	170707	6½	25
26062/S	B&S/Tec.	140000/VM60	6	26
26063/S	B&S/Tec.	190000/VM80	8	26
26064/S	Tec.	VM60	6	26
26065/S	Tec.	VM60	6	26
26069T	Tec.	TVM140	6	26
26083/S	B&S/Tec.	190000/VM80	8	26
26084/S	B&S/Tec.	190000/VM80	8	26
26085/S	B&S/Tec.	190000/VM80	8	26
26086/S/ST/T	B&S/Tec.	190000/VM80	8	26
26657B/BE	B&S	170702, 170707	6½	26
26659BE	B&S	170707	6½	26
28083/S	B&S/Tec.	190000/VM80	8	28
28085/S	B&S/Tec.	190000/VM80	8	28
28086/S/ST/T	B&S/Tec.	190000/VM80	8	28
28087B/BE	B&S	191702, 191707	8	28
28088T/TE	Tec.	TVXL195	8	28
28106S	B&S	255707	10	28
28108BE	B&S	255707	10	28
28113/S	B&S	250000	11	28
28114/S	B&S	250000	11	28
28115/S	B&S	250000	11	28
28127BE	B&S	281707	12	28
28128BE	B&S	281707	12	28
28128TVE	Tec.	OVXL120	12	28
30083/S	B&S/Tec.	190000/VM80	8	30
30085/S	B&S/Tec.	190000/VM80	8	30
30086/S/ST/T	B&S/Tec.	190000/VM80	8	30
30087B/BE	B&S	191702, 191707	8	30
30088T/TE	Tec.	TVXL195	8	30
30106S	Tec.	255707	10	30
30108BE	B&S	255707	10	30
30113/S	B&S	250000	11	30
30114/S	B&S	250000	11	30
30115/S	B&S	250000	11	30
30126BE	B&S	281707	12	30
30127BE	B&S	281707	12	30
30128BE	B&S	281707	12	30
30148KVE	Kohler	CV14	14	30
33113/S	B&S	250000	11	33
33114/S	B&S	250000	11	33
33115/S	B&S	250000	11	33
33127BE	B&S	281707	12	33
33128BE	B&S	281707	12	33
33128RE	Robin	WI-450V	12	33
33128TVE	Tec.	OVXL120	12	33
33147BVE	B&S	261777	14	33
33148KVE	Kohler	CV14	14	33
41085/S	B&S/Tec.	190000/VM80	8	41
41147BVE	B&S	261707	14	41
42113/S	B&S	250000	11	42
R25089TE	Tec.	TVXL195	8	25
R28128BE	B&S	281707	12	28

NOTE: Some operations may be performed more easily if the machine is standing upright. Observe the following safety recommendations when raising machine to upright position:

1. Drain fuel tank or make certain that fuel level is low enough so that fuel will not drain out.

2. Close fuel shut-off valve if so equipped.

3. Remove battery if so equipped.

4. Disconnect spark plug wire and tie it out of way.

5. Although not absolutely essential, on models with spark plug at rear of machine, engine oil should be drained to prevent flooding the combustion chamber with oil when the engine is tilted.

6. Secure mower from tipping by lashing machine to a post or overhead beam.

MODEL IDENTIFICATION

Snapper models are categorized by series numbers that indicate design differences. The series number of a particular model is the last numeral in the model number. For instance, Model 28127BE is a Series 7 model and Model 3012X6S is a Series 6 model. Some service procedures in this section are directed to models of a specific series.

FRONT WHEELS

All Models

LUBRICATION. Each front wheel hub is equipped with a grease fitting. Front wheels should be injected with a good quality multipurpose grease after every 25 hours of operation. Two shots should be sufficient, however, ten shots may be required if hub assembly is clean and new bearings are installed.

FRONT SPINDLES

All Models

R&R AND OVERHAUL. Refer to Figs. SN1 and SN2 for exploded view of spindle assembly. To remove a front spindle, raise and support side to be serviced. Remove hub cap, cotter pin, wheel and tire. Disconnect tie rod from spindle. Detach snap ring and remove spindle. Inspect components for excessive wear and damage. Install spindle by reversing removal procedure.

STEERING SYSTEM

All Models

TOE-IN SETTING. Front wheel toe-in setting on all models, except 12 and 14-hp models, is not adjustable. Adjustable tie rods (17—Fig. SN1 and 25—Fig. SN2) are used on 12 and 14-hp models. To check toe-in, tires must be inflated to proper pressure. Position machine on a flat, smooth surface and set steering wheel in straight forward position. Use a suitable measuring tool and measure distance at spindle height between the center of the tires on the rear sides. Locate the same tire centerline points on front side of tires and measure front distance. The distance on the front side should be $\frac{3}{8}$-$\frac{1}{2}$ inch (9.5-12.7 mm) shorter (toed-in) than the measured distance on the rear side. To adjust toe-in, adjust tie rod length as follows: Detach tie rod end, loosen jam nut and turn tie rod end as necessary. Retighten jam nut after completing adjustment.

R&R AND OVERHAUL. To remove steering shaft, raise front of machine and detach tie rods from steering arm.

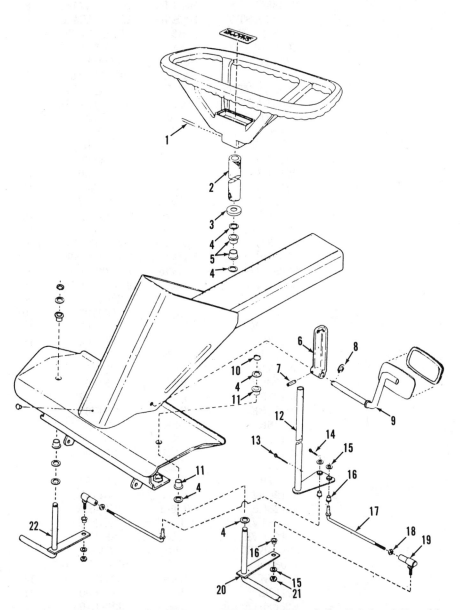

Fig. SN1—Exploded view of typical front steering system used on Series 7, 8, 9 and 11 models. Adjustable tie rod shown is used on 12 and 14-hp models. Tie rod is not adjustable on other models.

1. Pin	7. Roll pin	12. Steering shaft	17. Tie rod
2. Steering column	8. Snap ring	13. Cotter pin	18. Jam nut
3. Cover	9. Clutch/brake pedal	14. Cotter pin	19. Tie rod end
4. Washer	10. Snap ring	15. Washer	20. Spindle (L.H.)
5. Bushings	11. Bushing	16. Bushing	21. Locknut
6. Clutch/brake arm			22. Spindle (R.H.)

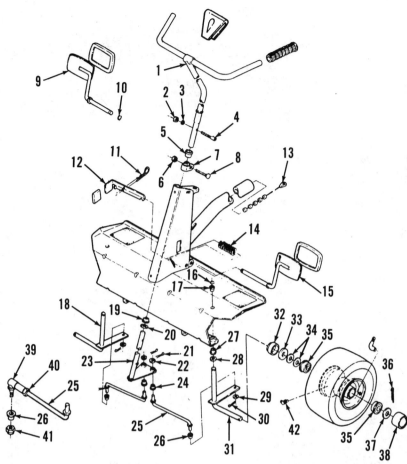

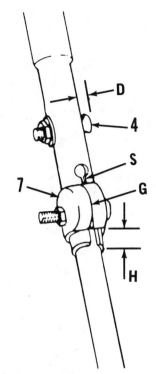

Fig. SN3—Tapered head of bolt (4) should be tightened until head is a distance (D) of 1/8 inch (3.2 mm) from shaft. Position clamp (7) so clamp gap (G) is aligned with tube slot (S) and bottom of clamp is a distance (H) of 1/4 inch (6.4 mm) from bottom of tube.

Fig. SN2—Exploded view of typical front steering system used on all models except Series 7, 8, 9 and 11. Adjustable tie rod shown in box is used on 12 and 14-hp models. Right pedal (9) for an auxiliary brake is absent on later models.

1. Handlebar
2. Nut
3. Lockwasher
4. Tapered screw
5. Bushing
6. Nut
7. Clamp
8. Carriage bolt
9. Auxiliary brake pedal
10. Snap ring
11. Spring clip
12. Parking brake latch
13. Clutch/brake cable
14. Parking brake spring
15. Clutch/brake pedal
16. Snap ring
17. Bushing
18. Spindle (R.H.)
19. Bushing
20. Washer
21. Cotter pin
22. Washer
23. Steering arm
24. Bushing
25. Tie rod
26. Bushing
27. Bushing
28. Washer
29. Washer
30. Cotter pin
31. Spindle (L.H.)
32. Boot
33. Felt seal
34. Washers
35. Bearing
36. Cotter pin
37. Washer
38. Hub cap
39. Tie rod end
40. Nut
41. Nut

On Series 7, 8, 9 and 11, drive out pin (1—Fig. SN1) and remove steering wheel. On all other models, separate handlebar (1—Fig. SN2) from upper end of steering shaft and clamp (7), if so equipped. Withdraw steering shaft (12—Fig. SN1 or 23—Fig. SN2) from bottom of machine. Steering shaft bushings are renewable.

Reassemble steering shaft by reversing disassembly procedure. On all models except Series 7, 8, 9 and 11 models, if equipped with two bolts (4—Fig. SN2), install bolts so bolt heads are on opposite sides of shaft. Bolts have a tapered head and should be tightened until head is a distance (D—Fig. SN3) of 1/8 inch (3.2 mm) from shaft. On models equipped with clamp (7) and a slotted steering tube, position clamp so clamp gap (G) is aligned with tube slot

(S) and bottom of clamp is a distance (H) of 1/4 inch (6.4 mm) from bottom of tube.

ENGINE

All Models

Refer to appropriate engine section in this manual for tune-up specifications, engine overhaul procedures and engine maintenance.

REMOVE AND REINSTALL. To remove engine, disconnect spark plug wire. If engine is equipped with an electric starter, disconnect cable from starter motor. Shift mower drive control lever to "OUT" position then unbolt and remove spindle cover from mower deck. Relieve tension from idler, then slip belt off mower spindle pulley (or pulleys).

Remove belt from driving disc hub pulley. On machines with a separate fuel tank, disconnect fuel hose from engine. Detach throttle cable from carburetor. Disconnect all interfering wiring from engine. Remove engine mounting screws and remove engine.

Reinstall engine by reversing removal procedure.

CLUTCH/BRAKE CABLE

All Models

Machine may be equipped with a single clutch/brake pedal or separate pedals to operate clutch and brake. Refer to BRAKE section for adjustment of brake on models equipped with a separate brake pedal.

NOTE: If location of frame tube is changed, for instance, to adjust mower belt tension, always check clutch/brake operating cable for proper adjustment.

All models are equipped with a cable-operated clutch. The cable extends from a keyhole slot in the clutch/brake pedal or control arm through the main frame tube to the lever arm portion of lift yoke (5—Fig. SN4, SN5 and SN10). Pulling

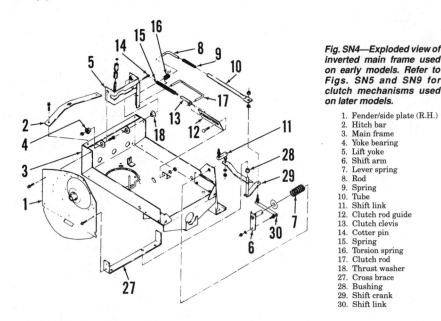

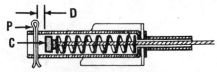

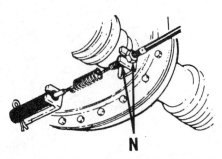

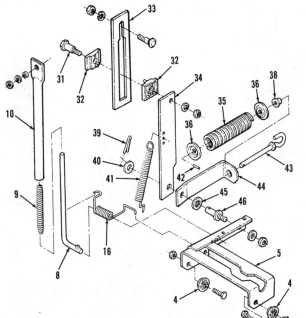

Fig. SN4—Exploded view of inverted main frame used on early models. Refer to Figs. SN5 and SN9 for clutch mechanisms used on later models.

1. Fender/side plate (R.H.)
2. Hitch bar
3. Main frame
4. Yoke bearing
5. Lift yoke
6. Shift arm
7. Lever spring
8. Rod
9. Spring
10. Tube
11. Shift link
12. Clutch rod guide
13. Clutch clevis
14. Cotter pin
15. Spring
16. Torsion spring
17. Clutch rod
18. Thrust washer
27. Cross brace
28. Bushing
29. Shift crank
30. Shift link

Fig. SN6—On Series 7, 8, 9, 10 and 11 models, distance (D) from cotter pin (P) to rear end of cable (C) should be 3/16-7/16 inch (4.8-11.1 mm). Rotate nuts (N—Fig. SN7) to obtain desired distance.

Fig. SN7—Rotate nuts (N) to obtain desired distance (D—Fig. SN6) at cable end on Series 7, 8, 9, 10 and 11 models.

Fig. SN5—Exploded view of clutch mechanism used on Series 4, 5, 6, 7 and 8 models.

4. Yoke bearing
5. Lift yoke
8. Rod
9. Spring
10. Tube
16. Torsion spring
31. Shoulder bolt
32. Slide half
33. Guide
34. Link
35. Spring
36. Spring seat
38. Flange washer
39. Cotter pin
40. Washer
41. Spring
42. Pin
43. Rod
44. Bracket
45. Lockwasher
46. Stud

Fig. SN8—Clutch link guide (33) on Series 4, 5, 6, 7 and 8 models must be positioned so top of slot (S) is flush with top of tab (T) on shift crank (29).

the lift yoke by depressing the clutch pedal moves the chain case and driven disc away from the drive disc attached to the engine.

Series 7, 8, 9, 10 And 11. To adjust clutch/brake cable, engage parking brake and place shift control lever in reverse position. Measure gap between drive disc and driven disc rubber ring. Gap should be 1/16-1/8 inch (1.6-3.2 mm). If gap is not correct, disengage parking brake and relocate front end of clutch/brake cable in control arm slot so another ferrule on cable is engaged. Recheck gap between discs.

Engage parking brake and measure distance (D—Fig. SN6) from cotter pin (P) to rear end of cable (C). Distance

should be 3/16-7/16 inch (4.8-11.1 mm). Rotate nuts (N—Fig. SN7) to obtain desired distance.

All Other Models. A slight amount of slack should be present in clutch/brake cable with pedal released and shift control lever in neutral or freewheel position. To adjust cable slack, relocate end of cable in pedal slot so another ferrule on cable is engaged. Be sure brake operates properly after adjustment.

TRACTION DRIVE CLUTCH

All Models

ADJUSTMENT. Adjustment is not possible on early models.

On Series 4, 5, 6, 7 and 8 models, clutch link guide (33—Fig. SN8) must be positioned so top of slot (S) is flush with top of tab (T) on shift crank (29). If traction is insufficient, additional traction may be obtained by relocating lift yoke spring (41—Fig. SN5) end. Reattach either end of spring to outer holes in clutch link (34—Fig. SN9) or lift yoke (5).

On Series 9, 10 and 11 models, normal spring (G—Fig. SN10) end location in clutch lever (L) is second hole from end. If unit stutters or hops during clutch engagement, move spring end to an inner hole. If traction is insufficient, move spring end to outermost hole in lever.

DISCS. Series 9, 10 And 11. Renew driven disc if rubber is worn to less than 1/16 inch (1.6 mm) as shown in Fig. SN11. To check disc contact, install a driven disc that has half the rubber ring re-

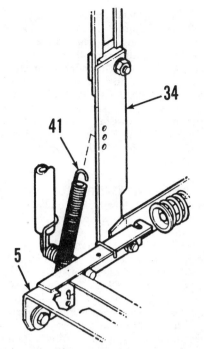

Fig. SN9—Additional traction on Series 4, 5, 6, 7 and 8 models may be obtained by attaching lift yoke spring (41) ends to outer holes in clutch link (34) or lift yoke (5).

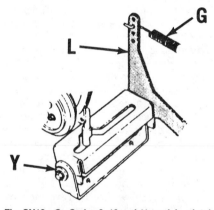

Fig. SN10—On Series 9, 10 and 11 models, clutch lever (L) is bolted to lift yoke (Y). Clutch traction is changed by relocating spring (G) end in holes in clutch lever. See text.

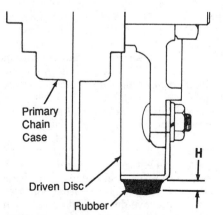

Fig. SN11—If height (H) of rubber ring on driven disc is 1/16 inch (1.6 mm) or less, disc must be renewed.

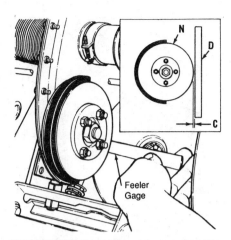

Fig. SN12—With the clutch pedal released and the shift control lever in any forward gear, clearance (C) between metal of driven disc gauge (N) and drive disc (D) should be 0.005-0.010 inch (0.13-0.25 mm).

moved so the metal is showing (if modification of an old driven disc is not possible, a test disc may be fabricated using the dimensions of the metal portion of the existing driven disc). With the clutch pedal released and the shift control lever in any forward gear, clearance (C—Fig. SN12) between metal of driven disc gauge (N) and drive disc (D) should be 0.005-0.010 inch (0.13-0.25 mm). To obtain desired clearance, adjust position of drive disc on engine crankshaft.

All Other Models. Before checking disc contact, be sure face of drive disc (D—Fig. SN13) is 3¾ inches (95.25 mm) from underside of frame on early models and 3¹³⁄₁₆ inches (96.8 mm) on models with smooth clutch (all models after 1984). If necessary, loosen set screws (S) and relocate drive disc on engine crankshaft. Renew driven disc if rubber is worn to less than ¹⁄₁₆ inch (1.6 mm) as shown in Fig. SN11.

To check disc contact, install a driven disc that has half the rubber ring removed so the metal is showing (if modification of an old driven disc is not possible, a test disc may be fabricated using the dimensions of the metal portion of the existing driven disc). With the clutch pedal released and the shift

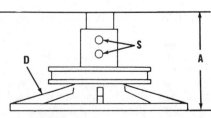

Fig. SN13—Distance (A) from face of drive disc (D) to underside of frame must be 3-3/4 inches (95.25 mm) on early models and 3-13/16 inches (96.8 mm) on models with smooth clutch (all models after 1984), except on Series 9, 10 and 11 models.

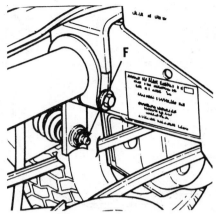

Fig. SN14—The shift lever grease fitting (F) should be injected with good quality multipurpose grease after every 25 hours of operation.

control lever in any forward gear, clearance (C—Fig. SN12) between metal of driven disc gauge (N) and drive disc (D) should be 0.005-0.010 inch (0.13-0.25 mm). To obtain desired clearance, loosen clutch rod guide (12—Fig. SN4) or clutch link guide (33—Fig. SN5) mounting bolt and relocate guide. Rotate driven disc gauge so rubber ring is near drive disc and fully depress clutch pedal and measure clearance between rubber ring on driven disc and drive disc. Clearance should be at least ¹⁄₃₂ inch (0.8 mm) with sliding chain case lightly contacting lift yoke.

SHIFT CONTROL LINKAGE

All Models

LUBRICATION. The shift lever grease fitting (F—Fig. SN14) should be injected with good quality multipurpose grease after every 25 hours of operation. Two shots should be sufficient.

ADJUSTMENT. The shift lever should be synchronized with the position of the driven disc against the drive disc. Refer to Fig. SN15 and note position of driven disc against drive disc at related ground speed. Note that first speed position of driven disc is approximately ¹⁄₁₆ inch (1.6 mm) from outer diameter of hole in drive disc. Loosen mounting screws (S—Fig. SN16) and relocate shift quadrant as needed so shift lever and driven disc positions are synchronized.

FRICTION DRIVE TRANSMISSION AND FINAL DRIVE

All Models

Power for the machine is transmitted through two discs, a drive disc and a

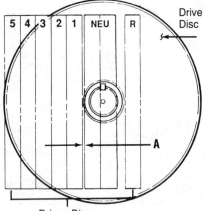

Fig. SN15—The driven disc should be positioned against drive disc (D) as shown for transmission speed shown. Distance (A) from outer diameter of drive disc hole to first speed position is 1/16 inch (1.6 mm).

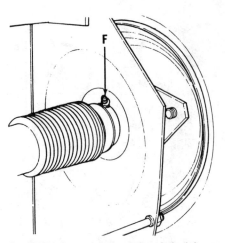

Fig. SN18—On models so equipped, the left rear axle grease fitting (F) should be injected with good quality multipurpose grease after every 25 hours of operation.

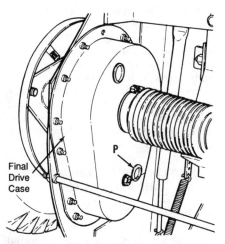

Fig. SN16—To synchronize shift lever and driven disc, loosen mounting screws (S) and relocate shift quadrant.

Fig. SN17—Level of grease in final drive case should be even with opening for plug (P).

observed. Check for normal action of differential pinions. Jamming, locking or noise in final drive case can be caused by damaged differential parts or a broken drive chain. Undue noise or abnormal operation in final drive case or in primary chain case will determine which assemblies should be remove for inspection and/or repair. Refer to DRIVE SYSTEM TROUBLESHOOTING GUIDE for additional service information.

R&R AND OVERHAUL. Refer to appropriate following section for service information on assembly requiring service.

Driven Disc. Driven disc rubber ring must not be worn to less than $\frac{1}{16}$ inch (1.6 mm), otherwise, renew driven disc (see Fig. SN11). If driven disc is excessively worn or damaged and requires service, place machine in upright position on rear stand as previously outlined. Unscrew disc retaining nuts and remove disc (20—Fig. SN19). When installing disc on models equipped with fiber thrust washer (21), be sure fiber washer is centered on hub (19) and is free-floating.

Drive Disc. Maximum allowable drive disc warpage is 0.020 inch (0.51 mm). To remove drive disc, remove driven disc as previously outlined as well as driven disc hub (19—Fig. SN19). Separate mower drive belt from idler and remove mower drive belt from drive disc pulley. Place shift control lever in fifth speed position. Unscrew set screws (S—Fig. SN13) and carefully pull drive disc off crankshaft. It may be necessary to move lift yoke aside during removal. To separate disc from hub, secure hub in a vise and unscrew disc from hub.

Reinstall drive disc by reversing removal procedure. On Series 9, 10 and 11 models, see TRACTION DRIVE CLUTCH section for procedure to position drive disc on engine crankshaft. On early models, be sure face of drive disc (D—Fig. SN13) is 3¾ inches (95.25 mm) from underside of frame. On models with smooth clutch (all models after 1984 except Series 9, 10 and 11), face of drive disc (D—Fig. SN13) must be 3¹³⁄₁₆ inches (96.8 mm) from underside of frame.

Left Side (Primary Chain Case). Place machine in upright position on rear stand as previously outlined then proceed as follows:

Remove left rear wheel, unscrew hub retaining screw and remove hub using Snapper tool 60237 or other suitable puller. Remove dust shield on axle. On 12 and 14-hp machines, remove lock collar (33—Fig. SN19) by rotating in clockwise direction after loosening set

driven disc. The drive disc is attached to the engine's crankshaft and the driven disc is attached to the primary chain case input shaft. As the primary chain case is moved from side to side through the shift mechanism, the driven friction disc contacts a different spot on the drive disc to change ground speed. Moving the driven disc to the opposite side of the drive disc reverses direction. The final drive case contains the reduction gear, differential and axle assemblies.

LUBRICATION. Position machine so it is upright as previously outlined. Annually fill final drive case so level of grease in case is even with opening for plug (P—Fig. SN17). Recommended lubricant is Snapper 0 grease or equivalent.

Annually add 1 oz. (30 mL) of Snapper 0 grease to primary chain case, but do not overfill. Primary chain case capacity is 2 oz. (60 mL).

On models so equipped, the left rear axle grease fitting (F—Fig. SN18) should be injected with good quality multipurpose grease after every 25 hours of operation. Two shots should be sufficient.

Periodically lubricate lift yoke pivot points.

INSPECTION AND TROUBLESHOOTING. If a malfunction in the drive system is suspected, raise machine so it is upright as previously outlined. Check for leaks at flanges of primary chain case, final drive case and shaft seals. Disengage mower deck drive and roll rear wheels by hand with clutch both depressed and released and with shift control lever in neutral and also when shifted into drive. Loosen clamps on drive tube boots and pull back so rotation of hex drive tube can be

DRIVE SYSTEM TROUBLESHOOTING GUIDE

PROBLEM	POSSIBLE CAUSE	CORRECTIVE ACTION
No drive–mower will not move in either direction.	Oil or grease on drive or driven disc.	Clean with solvent and wipe dry.
	Excessive clearance between drive and driven discs.	Check clutch adjustment. Check speed selector lever linkage and lift yoke for jamming or damage. Repair or renew.
	Rubber tread of driven disc damaged or worn out.	Renew driven disc.
	Breakage in primary chain case or final drive case.	Use check procedure to locate trouble. Disassemble and repair.
Selector hard to move when shifting through speed range.	Hex shaft dry-galled or burred.	Remove burrs, polish hex surface lightly, check shifting action.
	Jammed or damaged control linkage.	Disassemble linkage only, clean, lube and renew parts as needed.
Noisy drive.	Damaged driven chain or bearings.	Use check procedure to locate problem. Repair as needed.
Overheating of final drive case or primary chain case.	Insufficient lubrication.	Lubricate as required.
	Grease leaks from case.	Disassemble leaky case and renew gasket. Check for other possible damage.

screw. Detach boot (29). Unscrew tie rod (34) nut. Unscrew fasteners securing left fender plate (32) and remove left fender plate. Disconnect shift link from chain case half (8), and if so equipped, auxiliary brake band (4). On early models, detach brake cable from chain case. Detach boot from chain case half (8). Separate chain case rod from lift yoke and slide chain case off hex tube.

Secure driven disc hub (19) and unscrew brake drum retaining screw (1) and remove brake drum (3). Remove driven disc and hub assembly. Unscrew chain case bolts and separate chain case halves (8 and 18). Remove, clean and inspect chain case components. Remove needle bearings (10) and ball bearings (12) by pressing to inside of case half.

Reassemble primary chain case by reversing disassembly procedure. Press

ball bearings (12) into case halves until locating ring around outside of bearing seats against case. Press against lettered side of needle bearings (10) so lettered side is to inside of case half and bearing is flush with inner surface of case half. Cup side of Belleville washers (11) must be away from bearings (12).

After assembly, check end play between hex tube (T—Fig. SN20) and bearing (B). Desired end play is 3/32 inch (2.4 mm) and is adjusted by installing nylon split shims (S) between tube and bearing. Fill primary chain case with 2 oz. (60 mL) of Snapper 0 grease. A new plug (7—Fig. SN19) should be installed.

Right Side (Final Drive Case). Place machine in upright position on rear stand as previously outlined then proceed as follows:

Remove rear wheels, unscrew hub retaining screws and remove both wheel hubs using Snapper tool 60237 or other suitable puller. Remove dust shields on axles. On 12 and 14-hp machines, remove lock collars (33—Fig. SN19) on each axle by loosening set screw then rotating collar in direction opposite to forward wheel rotation. Unscrew tie rod nut. Detach boot (29) from final drive case. Unscrew fasteners securing right fender plate (5—Fig. SN21) to frame and remove right fender plate with final drive case (27). Place assembly on workbench so axle protrudes downward through a hole in the workbench and the fender plate is on top. Unscrew fender plate retaining screws and nuts and remove fender plate from final drive case. Prevent hex shaft (33) from moving and withdraw final drive gear (16) and axle assembly from case. Remove idler and sprocket components (17 through 26). Remove hex tube components (32 through 34). Bushings in hex tube (33) are not renewable.

To disassemble differential, unscrew cap screws securing differential plate (9). Discard cap screws—threads on screws are locking type that lose their locking capability when unscrewed. Disassemble differential components. Renew nylon spacer (12) if worn. Bushings in short axle (11) are not renewable. Be sure nylon spacer (12) fits over weld on long axle (15). Assemble pinions (14), spacers (13) and short axle (11) as shown in Figs. SN22 and SN23. Lubricate bushings in short axle before assembly. Install differential plate (9—Fig. SN21) using new cap screws (Snapper part 12333).

Reassemble final drive assembly and fender plate by reversing disassembly procedure while noting the following: Be sure thrust washers (32 and 34) are installed; absence of thrust washers will cause rapid wear. Install nylon hex washer with lip towards sprocket on hex tube. Lubricate bushings in hex tube (33) prior to assembly. Make sure lubrication hole in idler (19) is open. Install Belleville washers (18 and 24) so cupped side is towards "O" rings (17 and 26). Idler, sprocket, hex tube and chain must be installed as a unit. Lubricate outside of short axle (11). After placing fender plate on final drive case, tighten case retaining screws and nuts, then tighten idler bolt retaining locknut (N) to 18-20 ft.-lbs. (25-27 N•m). Locknut must be tightened properly as loosening of nut may allow chain to jump from sprockets due to sprocket misalignment. Lubricate outside of hex tube (33) before inserting in primary chain case. On 12 and 14-hp models, rotate lock collars in

Fig. SN19—Exploded view of primary chain case assembly. Spacer (30) and lock collar (33) are used only on 12 and 14-hp models.

1. Screw	10. Needle bearing	19. Driven disc hub	28. Clamp
2. Washers	11. Belleville washer	20. Driven disc	29. Boot
3. Brake drum	12. Bearing	21. Fiber washer	30. Spacer
4. Brake band	13. Key	22. Plate	31. Bearing
5. Snap ring	14. Sprocket shaft	23. Locknut	32. Fender plate (L.H.)
6. Roller	15. Thrust washer	24. Belleville washer	33. Lock collar
7. Plug	16. Sprocket & hub	25. Locknut	34. Tie rod
8. Chain case half	17. Chain	26. Hex thrust washer	35. Brake arm
9. Gasket	18. Chain case half	27. Nylon thrust washer	36. Bushing

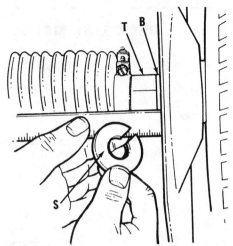

Fig. SN20—End play between hex tube (T) and bearing (B) should be 3/32 inch (2.4 mm).

Fig. SN19) rotates so its lined shoe contacts the inner rim of driven hub (19). Pressure on upper end of brake lever is exerted by lift yoke when actuated by tension on clutch/brake cable.

To adjust brake on models with a clutch/brake pedal, refer to CLUTCH/BRAKE CABLE section.

AUXILIARY BRAKE. On some models, an auxiliary band type brake (3 and 4—Fig. SN19) is mounted on opposite end of sprocket shaft (14). The auxiliary brake is actuated by a pedal on the right side of the machine. Adjustment of brake is limited to take-up of free play at pedal. When cable requires tightening, usually if pedal at full stroke reaches about $\frac{1}{2}$ inch (12.7 mm) from its bottom limit, take up cable by shifting ferrules on cable end through pedal key hole to underside of pedal to eliminate slack.

MOWER BELT

All Models

ADJUSTMENT. Mower drive belt tension is determined by measuring distance between opposite runs of belt at closest point with mower engaged. See Fig. SN24. On multiblade units, measure between idlers. Distance between belt runs should be 1 inch (25 mm) on single-blade units and $1\frac{1}{2}$ inches (38 mm) on multiblade units.

To adjust belt tension on all models except Series 10 and 11 models, loosen bolt (B—Fig. SN25) securing tube clamp (C) around main frame tube (T) and move tube in or out as needed. Retighten clamp bolt.

To adjust belt tension on Series 10 and 11 models, remove shoulder bolt (B—Fig. SN26) and relocate spacer

same direction as forward wheel rotation. Fill final drive case with Snapper 0 grease or equivalent so level of grease in case is even with opening for plug (P—Fig. SN17). New plugs (28 and 31—Fig. SN21) should be installed.

GROUND DRIVE BRAKE

All Models

Early models may be equipped with a clutch/brake pedal as well as an auxiliary brake operated by a pedal to the right of the steering column. Early models may also be equipped with brakes noted in the following paragraphs. Series 6 models are equipped with a clutch/brake pedal and a foot-operated parking brake latch. Series 7, 8, 9, 10 and 11 are equipped with a clutch/brake pedal and a hand-operated parking brake latch on the console.

NOTE: If location of frame tube is changed, for instance, to adjust mower belt tension, always check brake operating cable for proper adjustment.

MAIN BRAKE. All models are equipped with a combination clutch/brake pedal on left side of machine. The brake is applied when clutch/brake pedal is pressed down to its limit. At this point, brake lever (35—

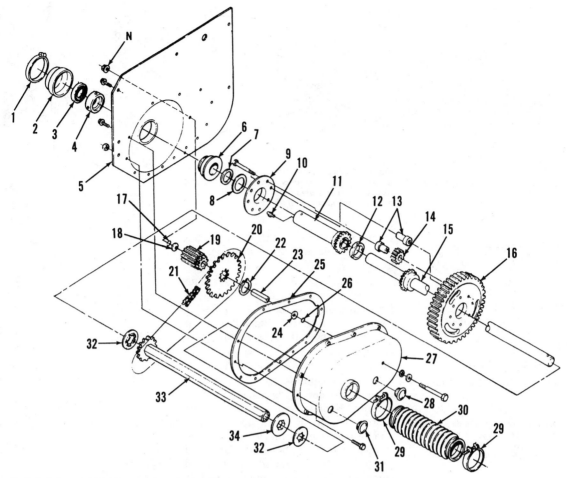

Fig. SN21—Exploded view of final drive assembly. Lock collar (4) is only used on 12- and 14-hp models.

1. Clamp	7. Spacer	13. Pinion spacers	19. Gear
2. Dust cover	8. Thrust washer	14. Pinions	20. Sprocket
3. Seal	9. Plate	15. Long axle	21. Chain
4. Lock collar	10. Grease fitting	16. Final drive gear	22. Snap ring
5. Fender plate (R.H.)	11. Short axle	17. "O" ring	23. Spacer
6. Bearing	12. Nylon spacer	18. Belleville washer	24. Belleville washer

25. Gasket	30. Boot
26. "O" ring	31. Plug
27. Case	32. Hex thrust washer
28. Plug	33. Hex drive tube
29. Clamp	34. Nylon thrust washer

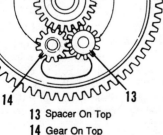

13 Spacer On Top
14 Gear On Top

Fig. SN22—When installing pinion spacers and pinions on final drive gear on all except 12 and 14-hp models, alternate top positions of pinion spacers (13) and pinions (14) so they appear as shown.

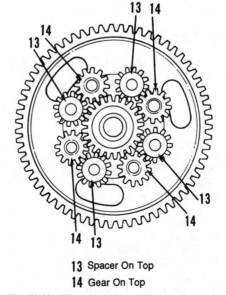

13 Spacer On Top
14 Gear On Top

Fig. SN23—When installing pinion spacers and pinions on final drive gear of 12 and 14-hp models, alternate top positions of pinion spacers (13) and pinions (14) so they appear as shown.

plates (R) in front or behind bracket (T) as needed. Reinstall and tighten shoulder bolt.

On triple-blade units with a separate drive belt on deck that connects spindles, check belt tension of spindle drive belt by applying a 5 pounds (11 kg.) pull at midpoint of longest run in belt. Belt should deflect 3/4-7/8 inch (19-22 mm). Adjust tension by loosening belt idler bolt and relocating belt idler. Retighten idler bolt.

Belt guides should be positioned at least 1/8 inch (3.2 mm) from belt.

REMOVE AND REINSTALL. To remove mower drive belt, detach mower deck cover, loosen belt idler and move idler away from belt to increase belt slack. Place machine in upright position on rear stand as previously outlined. Move clutch lift yoke so driven disc is moved away from drive disc and a gap exists. Separate mower drive belt from

Single Blade

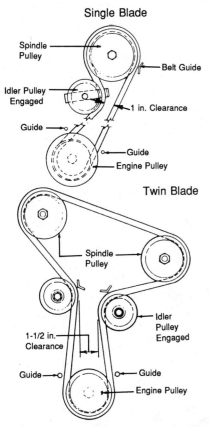

Twin Blade

Fig. SN24—Mower drive belt clearance should be 1 inch (25 mm) at idler pulley for single blade mowers and 1-1/2 inch (38 mm) for twin blade mowers as shown. Refer to text for adjustment procedure.

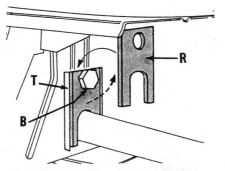

Fig. SN26—To adjust mower drive belt tension on Series 10 and 11 models, remove bolt (B) and relocate spacer plates (R) next to bracket (T) to extend or withdraw main frame tube.

engine pulley and feed through gap between driven and drive discs for removal.

Install mower drive belt by reversing removal procedure. The belt can be forced around drive disc by moving shift control lever to fifth speed position thereby forcing belt out towards edge of drive disc. Adjust belt tension as outlined in ADJUSTMENT section.

To remove spindle drive belt on later triple-blade models, detach covers from deck and remove mower drive belt from center spindle. Remove upper pulley and brake drum from center spindle. Detach snap ring above idler arm and rotate idler arm rearward. Unscrew and remove upper spindle housing (3—Fig. SN27). Loosen screw on idler and move idler to increase belt slack then remove belt. Install belt by reversing removal procedure. Adjust belt tension as outlined in ADJUSTMENT section.

MOWER DECK

All Models

HEIGHT ADJUSTMENT. All mower control linkage must be in good operating condition and tires properly inflated. Park machine on a level surface with engine stopped and spark plug wire disconnected.

The blade adapter bar on some models is equipped with adjusting screws to aid blade alignment. Distance (D—Fig. SN28) from mower deck to blade tip should be $\frac{3}{8}$ inch (9.5 mm) on 33-inch mower decks and $\frac{1}{4}$ inch (6.4 mm) on all other models. To adjust distance, loosen blade bar locknuts and turn blade adjusting screws (S) in or out as necessary. Be sure all fasteners are secure.

Front-to-rear height difference is determined by measuring height of blade above ground at front and rear. Rear height should be $\frac{5}{8}$ inch (15.9 mm) higher than front on all models except

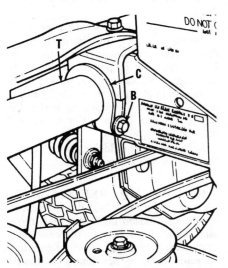

Fig. SN25—To adjust mower drive belt tension on all models except Series 10 and 11 models, loosen bolt (B) securing tube clamp (C) around main frame tube (T) and move tube in or out as needed.

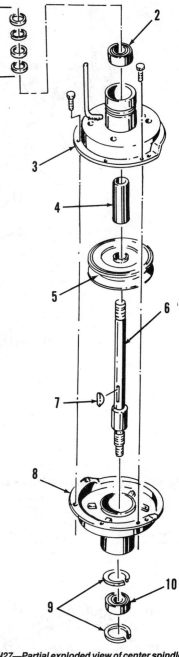

Fig. SN27—Partial exploded view of center spindle on later triple-blade mower deck.

1. Spacers
2. Bearing
3. Upper spindle housing
4. Spacer
5. Pulley
6. Spindle
7. Key
8. Lower spindle housing
9. Snap rings
10. Bearing

Hi-Vac mowers, which should have a zero height difference. To adjust height on early models, rotate chain hanger (20—Fig. SN29) bolts at rear of mower deck. To adjust height on later models, relocate ferrules on mower deck hanger cables.

Side-to-side height is adjustable on dual-blade and triple-blade mower decks. Maximum difference side-to-side should be $\frac{1}{8}$ inch (3.2 mm). To adjust

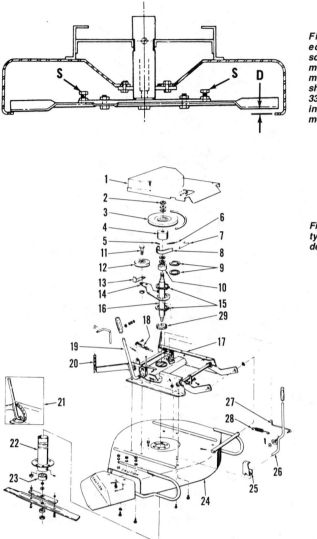

Fig. SN28—On models equipped with adjusting screws (S) to aid blade alignment, distance (D) from mower deck to blade tip should be 3/8 inch (9.5 mm) on 33-inch mower decks and 1/4 inch (6.4 mm) on all other models.

Fig. SN29—Exploded view of typical single-blade mower deck assembly.

1. Spindle cover
2. Locknut
3. Driven pulley
4. Brake drum
5. Cotter pin
6. Return spring
7. Wire link
8. Brake assy.
9. Snap rings
10. Upper spindle bearing
11. Idler shaft bolt
12. Idler pulley
13. Keeper
14. Idler arm
15. Retainer rings
16. Spindle shaft
17. Deck rail assy.
18. Timing link & rod
19. Lift handle
20. Suspension chain (2)
21. Height indicator
22. Spindle housing
23. Bearing
24. Deck
25. Handle mount
26. Blade control handle
27. Idler control rod
28. Idler spring
29. Tolerance ring

"OUT" position. If time required for blade to stop is not satisfactory, adjust blade brake as follows: Disconnect wire link (7—Fig. SN29) from spindle brake band (8) and reconnect link in another, closer hole to increase brake band tension. Perform test again. If wire link is connected to last adjustment hole and blade brake engagement time is unsatisfactory, renewal of brake components may be necessary.

R&R AND OVERHAUL. Blade brake components are accessible after removing mower belt and spindle pulley. Renew brake band if excessively worn or contaminated by oil or grease. Be sure all components are in good operating condition. Adjust blade brake as outlined in previous section.

Models With Blade Pedals

ADJUSTMENT. To check blade brake operation, remove mower deck cover so spindle pulley is visible. Run mower so blade is rotating at normal speed, then release blade stop pedal. If time required for blade to stop is not satisfactory, adjust blade brake as follows: Shut off the engine. Lower mower deck and remove belt cover. While holding mower engagement lever to rear, loosen jam nut (N—Fig. SN33). Move mower engagement lever to "ON" position and turn flange nut (F) clockwise to increase brake band tension. Be sure flange fits over bracket (B). Release blade stop pedal, move mower engagement lever to "OFF" position, then depress blade stop pedal. Rotate flange nut (F) so clearance (C—Fig. SN34) between front of mower engagement lever (L) and rear edge of latch plate (P) is ⅛-¼ inch (3.2-6.4 mm). Tighten jam nut (N—Fig. SN32) and recheck blade brake operation. If blade brake engagement time is unsatisfactory, renewal of brake components may be necessary.

R&R AND OVERHAUL. Blade brake components (see Fig. SN35) are accessible after removing mower belt and spindle pulley. Renew brake band (10) if excessively worn or contaminated by oil or grease. Be sure all components are in good operating condition. Adjust blade brake as outlined in previous section.

MOWER SPINDLE

All Models

LUBRICATION. The mower spindle should be lubricated annually. Apply grease to mower spindle through grease

side-to-side dimension on early models, unscrew locknut on set screw (13—Figs. SN30 and SN31) and turn screw so desired dimension is obtained then retighten locknut. To adjust side-to-side dimension on later models, loosen cap screw and rotate eccentric (E—Fig. SN32) on left front lift arm so desired dimension is obtained and retighten nuts. Rotate eccentric counterclockwise to raise right side of deck or clockwise to raise left side of deck.

REMOVE AND REINSTALL. To remove mower deck, detach mower deck cover, loosen belt idler and move idler away from belt to increase belt slack. Place machine in upright position on rear stand as previously outlined. Move clutch lift yoke so driven disc is moved away from drive disc and a gap exists. Separate mower drive belt from engine pulley and feed through gap between driven and drive discs. Place machine on all four wheels. Disconnect interlock

switch wire, if so equipped. Detach front and rear lift arms and links and remove mower deck. Reinstall mower deck by reversing removal procedure.

BLADE BRAKE

Models may be equipped with a band-type brake that stops rotation of the blade spindle within 3-5 seconds. The blade brake on early models is actuated by the mower engagement lever. On later models the mower engagement lever is held in position by pedals. When either pedal is released, the mower engagement lever snaps into disengaged position and the blade brake is actuated.

Models Without Blade Pedals

ADJUSTMENT. To check blade brake operation, remove mower deck cover so spindle pulley is visible. Run mower so blade is rotating at normal speed, then move operating handle to

Fig. SN30—Exploded view of typical dual-blade mower deck assembly.

1. Snap ring
2. Washer
3. Idler support
4. Idler arm
5. Washer
6. Snap ring
7. Blade brake eye-bolt
8. Bracket
9. Flange nut
10. Nut
11. Lift handle
12. Snap ring
13. Adjusting screw & nut
14. Spring
15. Idler rod
16. Engagement lever
17. Spring
18. Blade stop pedal
19. Push nut
20. Spring
21. Washers
22. Washer
23. Shoulder bolt
24. Spacer
25. Tolerance ring
26. Spindle assy.
27. Belleville washers
28. Screw

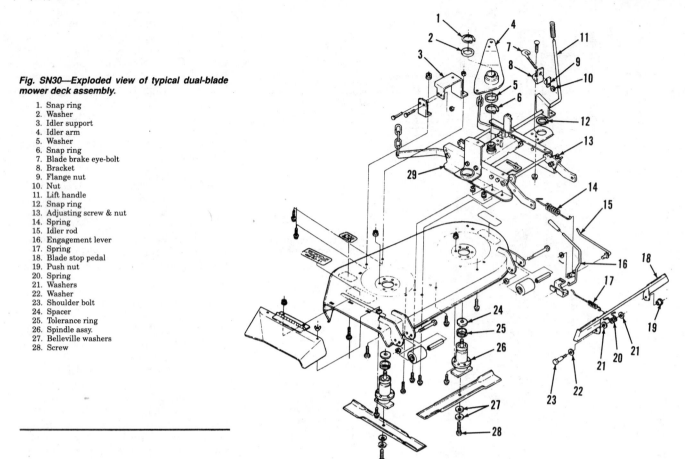

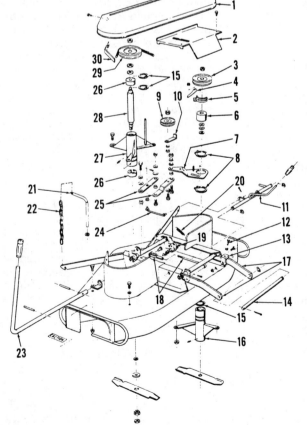

Fig. SN31—Exploded view of early triple-blade mower deck assembly.

1. Spindle cover
2. Front cover
3. Spindle pulley
4. Link
5. Spindle brake
6. Brake drum
7. Idler arm
8. Snap rings
9. Idler
10. Keeper
11. Idler control handle
12. Set screw
13. Level adjuster
14. Suspension bar
15. Snap rings
16. Spindle housing
17. Front lift arms
18. Timing rod & clevis
19. Lift cams
20. Cam spring
21. Chain arm
22. Deck chain
23. Lift handle
24. Idler link rod
25. Idler link arms
26. Spindle bearings
27. Center spindle housing
28. Spindle
29. Spindle pulley
30. Belt guard

fitting on underside of spindle housing. Two shots should be sufficient. Use a good quality, multipurpose grease.

R&R AND OVERHAUL. Refer to Figs. SN29, SN30 and SN31 for exploded views of spindle assembly. To remove spindle on all models except later triple-blade mowers, remove blade, spindle pulley and blade brake components. Unscrew spindle housing and remove from deck. Note location of

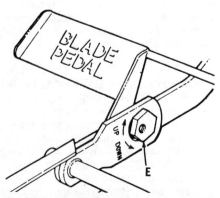

Fig. SN32—Loosen cap screw and rotate eccentric (E) on left front lift arm to adjust side-to-side dimension on later models with dual-blade and triple-blade mower decks.

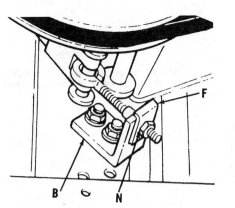

Fig. SN33—Loosen nut (N) and rotate flange nut (F) as outlined in text to adjust blade brake.

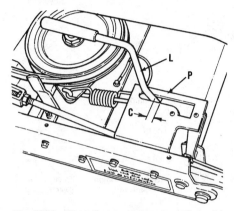

Fig. SN34—Front of mower engagement lever (L) should be 1/8-1/4 inch (3.2-6.4 mm) from rear edge of latch plate (P) when blade brake is properly adjusted. See text.

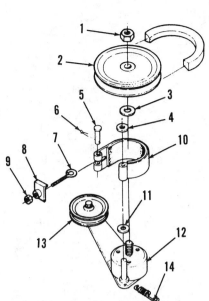

Fig. SN35—Exploded view of typical blade brake mechanism used on later models.

1. Nut	8. Flange nut
2. Pulley	9. Jam nut
3. Washer	10. Brake band
4. Washer	11. Spacer
5. Clevis pin	12. Brake drum
6. Cotter pin	13. Idler
7. Eye-bolt	14. Spring

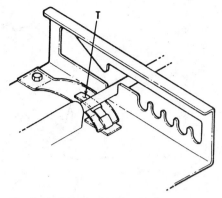

Fig. SN36—To adjust detent switch engagement on models prior to 1986, bend tongue (T) so switch is engaged sooner.

any spacers during disassembly and mark them so they can be installed in original position. Unscrew blade adapter, and if so equipped, detach snap ring at bottom of spindle housing. Drive or press spindle with lower bearing out bottom of spindle housing. Detach snap ring in upper end of spindle housing and press or drive out upper bearing. Reassemble by reversing disassembly procedure. When installing spindle housing on deck, position mounting bolts so there is not a bolt in front of grease fitting.

To remove outer spindles on later triple-blade mower decks, follow previous procedure for other models. To remove center spindle on later triple-blade models, remove blade, then remove mower drive belt from center spindle. Note lo-

cation of any spacers during disassembly and mark them so they can be installed in original position. Remove upper pulley and brake drum from center spindle. Detach snap ring above idler arm and rotate idler arm rearward. Unscrew and remove upper spindle housing (3—Fig. SN27). Loosen screw on idler and move idler to increase belt slack then remove belt. Withdraw spindle (6) from housing. Detach snap rings (9) and drive or press bearing from lower housing (8). Reassemble by reversing disassembly procedure.

The mounting holes on some spindle housings are oversized to allow the spindle to be centered in the mower deck.

The blade adapter bar on some models is equipped with adjusting screws (S—Fig. SN28) to aid blade alignment. Distance (D) from mower deck to blade tip should be $\frac{3}{8}$ inch (9.5 mm) on 33-inch mower decks and $\frac{1}{4}$ inch (6.4 mm)

on all other models. Be sure all fasteners are secure.

ELECTRICAL

All Models

Refer to Figs. SN37 through SN39 for wiring schematics.

The shift control lever must be in PARK and the mower must be disengaged for engine to start. The shift detent switch prevents engine starting unless the shift control lever is in PARK position. To adjust detent switch engagement on models prior to 1986, bend tongue (T—Fig. SN36) so switch is engaged sooner. On models after 1985, loosen screws (S—Fig. SN16) an reposition shift quadrant so switch is fully engaged with shift control lever in PARK.

On models prior to 1986, protective insulation on shift detent switch may wear through, grounding the system when the shift control lever is in PARK preventing engine starting. Inspect switch and renew if defective.

The interlock module should be considered faulty only after all other wiring and devices have been tested or checked. The interlock module may malfunction when subjected to heat and function normally when cold. Modules are designed for operation with specific engine brands and must not be interchanged. Use of improper module may result in unsafe operation.

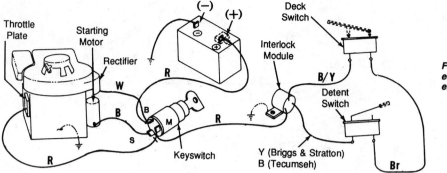

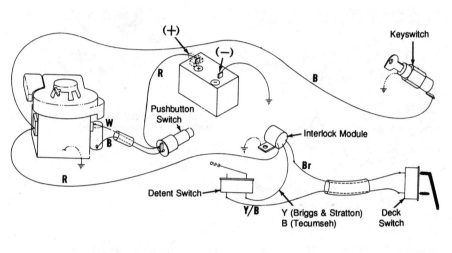

Fig. SN37—Wiring diagram for early models equipped with three-terminal ignition switch and electric starter.

    B. Black
    Br. Brown
    R. Red
    W. White
    Y. Yellow

Fig. SN38—Wiring diagram for early models equipped with push button ignition switch and electric starter.

    B. Black
    Br. Brown
    R. Red
    W. White
    Y. Yellow

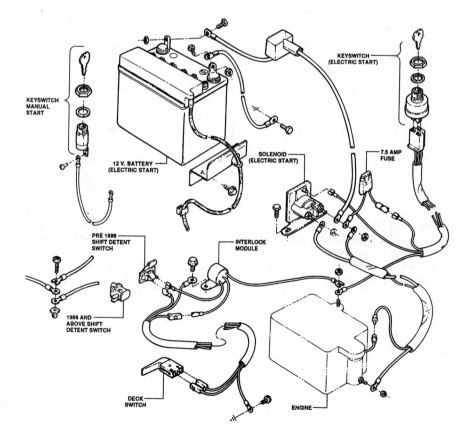

Fig. SN39—Wiring diagram for later models equipped with an electric starter.

Illustrations Courtesy Snapper Power Equipment

WARDS

MONTGOMERY WARD
Montgomery Ward Plaza
Chicago, IL 60671

Model	Make	Engine Model	Horsepower	Cutting Width, In.
33857A	B&S	250000	11	36
33857B	B&S	250000	11	36
33867A	B&S	250000	11	36
33877A	B&S	250000	11	38
33887A	B&S	250000	11	38
33889A	B&S	250000	11	38

For service information and procedures, use the following model cross reference and refer to the GILSON section of this manual. Parts are not necessarily interchangeable and should be obtained from Montgomery Ward Co.

Wards Models	Gilson Models
33857A	52051C
33857B	52051C
33867A	52061
33877A	52060
33887A	52066
33889A	52074

WHEEL HORSE

WHEEL HORSE PRODUCTS, INC.
515 West Ireland Road
P.O. Box 2649
South Bend, IN 46680

Model	Make	Engine Model	Horsepower	Cutting Width, In.
R-26	Tecumseh	V70	7	26
A-50	Tecumseh	V70	7	26
A-51	B&S	130000	5	32
A-60	B&S	130000	5	26
A-70	B&S	191000	8	32
A-81	B&S	191000	8	32/36
A-111	B&S	252000	11	32/36
RR-532	B&S	130000	5	32
RR-832	B&S	191000	8	32
108-R	B&S	190702	8	30
108-3	B&S	190707	8	30
108-5	B&S	193707	8	30
111-5	B&S	253707	11	30

FRONT AXLE AND STEERING SYSTEM

Models R-26 and A-50

These mowers are fitted with a non-adjustable, center control, gear and sector steering system. There is no front axle as such and steering spindles are set into bushed holes in front body support.

R&R AND OVERHAUL. Raise front of unit, block up under body frame to support front wheels clear of surface and lock parking brake. Remove hub cap (22–Fig. WH1), "E" ring retainer (20) and wheel and tire assemblies (21). Remove tie rods (18), disengage "E" ring from slot at top of spindles (19) and lower each spindle out of bushings (7). Thoroughly clean spindles (19), bushings (7), and wheel hub bores. Carefully inspect all parts for excessive wear or any other damage and renew as needed.

Drive out roll pin (5) at bottom of steering shaft assembly tube (6) and separate from lower shaft and pinion assembly (12). Unbolt and remove two plates which make up steering support (10), then perform a thorough cleaning and inspection of shaft and pinion (12), all bearings (7), washers (11 and 13), retainer (9) and spacers (16). Renew all defective parts and reassemble, observing parts arrangement in Fig. WH1. Lubricate, using a good grade of chassis grease, by hand on spindles (19) and bearings (7) and with a pressure gun on each front wheel hub and at fitting (15).

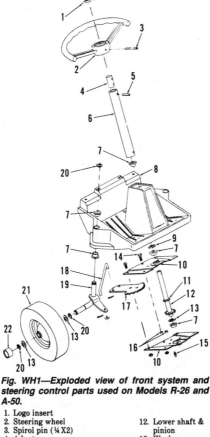

Fig. WH1—Exploded view of front system and steering control parts used on Models R-26 and A-50.
1. Logo insert
2. Steering wheel
3. Spirol pin (¼ X2)
4. Adapter
5. Roll pin (¼ X1½) (2)
6. Assembly tube
7. Sintered iron bearing
8. Body support
9. Retainer
10. Steering support (2 pc.)
11. Washer
12. Lower shaft & pinion
13. Washer
14. Pivot bolt
15. Lube fitting
16. Spacers (3)
17. Steering sector
18. Tie rod (2)
19. Steering spindle
20. "E" ring
21. Wheel & tire
22. Hub cap

Model A-60

R&R AND OVERHAUL. To remove and disassemble axle main member (9–Fig. WH2), remove pull pin to disconnect front of mower from hanger bracket (8). Raise and block front of unit. Remove hub cap (15), "E" ring retainer (14) and front wheel assemblies. Unbolt and remove steering link (12) from spindles (10).

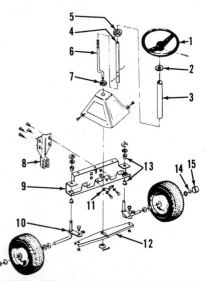

Fig. WH2—Exploded view of front axle and steering system used on Model A-60.
1. Steering wheel
2. Plastic washer
3. Steering tube housing
4. Steering tube
5. Speed nut
6. Steering shaft
7. Flange bushing
8. Deck hanger bracket
9. Front axle
10. Spindle
11. "U" bracket
12. Steering link
13. Spindle bushings
14. "E" ring
15. Hub cap

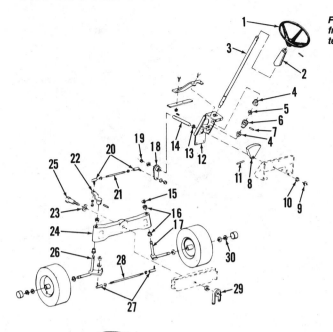

Fig. WH3—Exploded view of front axle and steering system used on Model A-70.

1. Steering wheel
2. Cover
3. Steering shaft
4. Bushings
5. "E" ring
6. Pinion gear
7. Roll pin
8. Sector gear
9. "E" ring
10. Bushing
11. Roll pin
12. Steering support
13. Bushing
14. Sector shaft
15. "E" ring
16. Spindle bushings
17. Spindle R.H.
18. Sector arm
19. Adjusting nut
20. Drag link ends
21. Drag link
22. Spindle arm
23. Spacer
24. Axle
25. Pivot bolt
26. Spindle L.H.
27. Tie rod ends
28. Tie rod
29. "U" bracket
30. "E" ring

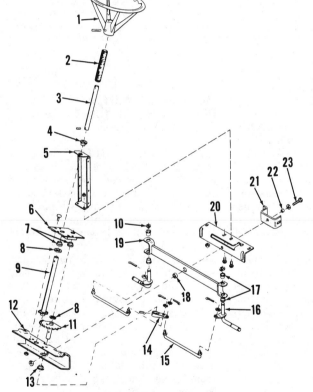

Fig. WH4—Exploded view of front axle and steering system used on Models A-51, A-81, A-111, RR-532, RR-832, 108-R, 108-3, 108-5 and 111-5.

1. Steering wheel
2. Cover
3. Steering shaft extension
4. Bushing
5. Steering support
6. Reinforcing plate
7. Bushings
8. Shim washer
9. Steering shaft
10. Retaining ring
11. Steering sector
12. Axle support
13. Bushing
14. Steering bar
15. Tie rod
16. Spindle
17. Bushings
18. Bushing
19. Axle
20. Rear support
21. Pivot bracket
22. Bushing
23. Pivot bolt

Remove "E" rings and washers, then lower spindles from axle and remove spindle bushings (13) from axle ends. Unbolt "U" bracket (11) securing steering shaft (6) to axle. Unbolt clutch and brake pedal brackets from axle. Unbolt and remove axle from frame. Reassemble by reversing removal procedure. Lubricate bushings, front wheel hubs and steering pivot points with SAE 30 oil.

To remove steering shaft (6-Fig. WH2), drive out roll pin and remove steering wheel from steering tube (4), then pull steering tube housing (3) out of flanged bushing (7). Drive out bottom roll pins and remove steering tube. Unbolt steering link (12) from spindles (10), then raise front of unit and withdraw steering shaft. Reinstall by reversing removal procedure.

Model A-70

R&R AND OVERHAUL. To remove axle main member (24-Fig. WH3), place mower unit in lowest position and unpin mower from mower hanger. Support front of unit and remove front wheels. Disconnect drag link end (20) from steering arm (22) and tie rod ends (27) from spindles. Drive out roll pin, remove steering arm (22) and remove spindle (26) from axle. Remove "E" ring (15) and remove spindle (17). Remove pivot bolt (25), then lower axle main member from frame. Inspect spindle bushings (16) for excessive wear and renew as necessary. Reassemble by reversing disassembly procedure. Check front wheel toe-in and adjust ends (27) on tie rod (28) to obtain a toe-in of ⅛ inch.

To remove steering gears and shafts, drive out roll pin and remove steering wheel (1) and cover (2). Unbolt and remove console from around steering unit. Disconnect drag link end (20) from quadrant arm (18) and remove cotter pin, adjusting nut (19), quadrant arm and washers. Drive out roll pin (11) and remove "E" ring (9), then remove shaft (14) from front and lift out sector gear (8). Drive out roll pin (7) and remove "E" ring (5). Withdraw steering shaft (3) and remove pinion gear (6). Bushings (4, 10 and 13) can now be removed. Clean and inspect all parts for wear or other damage and renew as necessary. When reassembling, adjust steering gear free play as follows: Turn adjusting nut (19) clockwise to remove excessive play, then install cotter pin. Free play should be adjusted to a minimum but gears should not bind.

Lubricate all bushings and pivot points with SAE 30 oil. Apply a light coat of lithium grease to pinion gear and quadrant gear teeth.

Models A-51, A-81, A-111, RR-532, RR-832, 108-R, 108-3, 108-5 and 111-5

R&R AND OVERHAUL. To remove axle main member (19-Fig. WH4), place mower unit in lowest position and unpin mower from front hanger. Raise and block front of unit and remove front wheel assemblies. Disconnect tie rods (15) from spindles (16). Remove retaining rings (10) and withdraw spindles and bushings (17) from axle ends. Remove pivot bolt (23), then lower axle from frame. Inspect bushings for excessive wear and renew as necessary. Reassemble by reversing disassembly procedure.

To remove steering gears and shafts, drive out roll pin and remove steering wheel (1-Fig. WH4) and steering shaft cover (2). Drive out roll pin and remove steering shaft extension (3) and flanged bushing (4). Remove steering column shroud, then unbolt and remove reinforcing plate (6), bushings (7) and shim washers (8). Raise front of unit and withdraw steering shaft (9). Disconnect tie rods from steering bar (14). Drive out roll pin and remove steering bar, steering sector (11) and bushing (13). Clean and inspect all parts and renew as necessary. Reassemble by reversing disassembly procedure. Use shim washers (8) as required to adjust end play of steering shaft and sector. Apply light coat of lithium base grease to gear teeth. Lubricate bushings and pivot points with SAE 30 oil.

ENGINE

All Models

Refer to appropriate engine section in this manual for tune-up specifications, engine overhaul procedures and engine maintenance.

Models R-26 and A-50

REMOVE AND REINSTALL. Remove mower as outlined in MOWER DECK paragraphs. Disconnect throttle control cable at carburetor. Disconnect switch lead and solenoid cable from terminals on engine ends, then disconnect solenoid cable from post on starter motor. Set transmission shift lever in neutral and place traction clutch lever in its neutral notch. Slip forward traction belt from lower sheave of transmission pulley and work it up against transmission input shaft for slack, then remove from engine pulley and through belt guide. Release traction clutch lever from neutral notch and allow it to move forward, then, slip reverse traction belt from its sheave in transmission pulley and off reverse engine pulley (camshaft). Work both belts up through access hole in deck. Unbolt engine mounts and lift engine clear of frame. Reverse this procedure to reinstall engine.

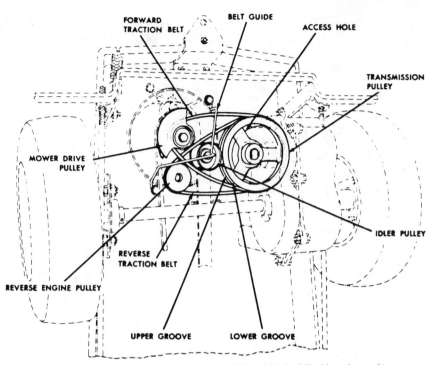

Fig. WH6—View to show traction clutch belts, pulleys and idler which is shifted from forward to reverse traction belts to change direction of transmission input pulley. Idler is shown in neutral.

Models A-60 and A-70

REMOVE AND REINSTALL. Loosen engine pulley belt guides, then remove mower as outlined in MOWER DECK paragraphs. On Model A-70, unbolt and remove engine cover and air intake duct. Shut off fuel at tank and disconnect fuel hose. On all models disconnect throttle control cable and ignition wires. On Model A-70 disconnect starter cable, alternator wire and unbolt muffler from engine. On all models, remove main clutch idler tension spring, then remove drive belt from engine pulley. Remove engine mounting bolts and lift off engine. Reinstall engine by reversing removal procedure.

Models A-51, A-81, A-111, RR-532, RR-832, 108-R, 108-3, 108-5 and 111-5

REMOVE AND REINSTALL. Unbolt rear of body, then raise body and support with support rod. On electric start models, disconnect battery cable and starter and alternator wires. On all models disconnect ignition wires and throttle control cable. On Model A-111 unbolt muffler. Remove mower as outlined in MOWER DECK paragraphs. Remove lower nuts, washer, spacer and clevis pin securing pto clutch-brake plate, then remove pto pulley (Fig. WH5). Unhook traction clutch idler spring and remove belt from transmission pulley and engine pulley. Unbolt and remove engine pulley. Remove engine mounting bolts and lift engine from frame. Reinstall engine by reversing removal procedure.

TRACTION DRIVE CLUTCH AND BELT

All Models

All models use belt idler type clutch. On Models R-26 and A-50, idler shifts between forward drive belt (engine crankshaft pulley to transmission pulley) and reverse drive belt (engine camshaft pulley to transmission pulley). See Fig. WH6. All other models use a single belt and idler arrangement.

Fig. WH5—Underside view of pto pulley and clutch-brake plate.

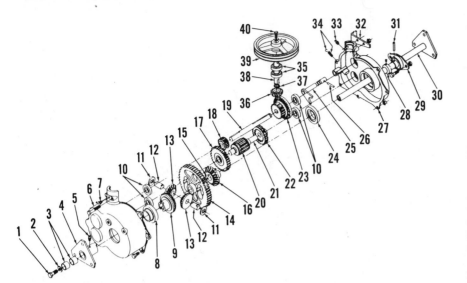

Fig. WH7—Exploded view of Model 5056 Wheel Horse transaxle. Note double-sheave driven pulley (39) for forward or reverse operation.

1. Cap screw	11. Thrust washer (2)
2. Washer	12. Differential pin (2)
3. Bronze bushings (3)	13. Differential pinion (2)
4. Hub & flange	14. Final drive gear
5. Grease fitting	15. Woodruff key
6. Gear case RH	16. Side gear LH
7. Grease fitting	17. Low gear
8. Ball bearing RH	18. Low gear pinion
9. Side gear RH	19. Pinion shaft
10. Ball bearing (4)	20. Sliding gear

21. Sliding gear shaft	31. Roll pin
22. High gear	32. Shift rod bracket
23. Combination gear	33. Grease fitting
24. Ball bearing LH	34. Detent ball & spring
25. Shift fork & shaft	35. Ball bearing (2)
26. Roll pin	36. Input pinion
27. Gear case LH	37. Snap ring
28. Collar & set screw	38. Input shaft
29. Flanged ball bearing	39. Transmission pulley
30. Rear axle	40. Bolt, nylok

Models R-26 and A-50

REMOVE AND REINSTALL. To remove drive belts, disengage mower clutch and traction clutch. Remove mower drive belt from crankshaft pulley, then slip traction drive belts (Fig. WH6) off transaxle pulley and engine pulleys. Renew belts by reversing removal procedure.

IMPORTANT: Brake has a clutch override feature for automatic application. See BRAKE paragraphs for adjustment procedure.

All Other Models

R&R AND ADJUST. Remove mower as outlined in MOWER DECK paragraphs. Disconnect spring from idler bracket and remove idler pulley. On Model A-60, disconnect clutch rod from idler bracket. Loosen belt guides as needed and slip belt out of pulleys. Install new belt by reversing removal procedure. Belt guides should be $\frac{1}{16}$ to $\frac{1}{8}$ inch (1.6-3 mm) from belt with belt under tension.

TRANSAXLE

Models R-26 and A-50

REMOVE AND REINSTALL. Disconnect spark plug lead and positive cable from battery if unit is equipped

for electric start. Remove mower deck as outlined in MOWER DECK paragraphs, and block front wheels securely. Raise and block under chassis and remove rear wheels. Disconnect transaxle shift lever from fork (25–Fig. WH7). For convenience, also unbolt shift lever hanger and grommet at forward end and move lever forward out of way. Set traction clutch lever in neutral and remove traction drive belts from drive pulleys on engine. Now, unbolt flanged bearing (29) from axle support on frame, place a temporary support under axle and remove cap screws which hold gear case to right hand axle support. Lower and remove entire transaxle assembly from frame. Reverse these steps to reinstall transaxle.

OVERHAUL. With transaxle removed and thoroughly cleaned, remove cap screw (1-Fig. WH7) and withdraw hub and flange (4). Remove cap screw (40) and, using a puller, remove input pulley (39) from input shaft (38). Set assembly up securely in shop vise with axle (30) pointed down. Remove the eight bolts which hold case halves together, then separate case halves part way and remove input shaft (38) along with bearings (35) and input pinion (36). Take care shift fork and shaft (25) do not slip from bore in left case (27) as detent ball and spring (34) may be dropped. Continue to carefully separate case halves and lift off case (6), expos-

ing all internal gears. Bearings (8 and 10) should remain in bores in case. Differential side gear (9) may lift out of place. Lift off side gear (9) and final drive gear (14) with differential pinions (13) and their pins (12). Left hand side gear (16) is keyed to axle (30) by Woodruff key (15) and its removal may call for use of a small gear puller. After side gear (16) is removed, lift gear case (27) from axle, then lift off low gear pinion (18), pull shaft (19) out of bearing (10) and remove combination gear (23). Lift low gear (17) from sliding gear shaft (21), then pull shaft out of sliding gear (20) and disengage shift collar on sliding gear from shift fork (25). High gear (22) will be released at the same time.

If there is no need to remove shift fork and shaft (25), leave it in place in its bore in gear case (27); however, if it must be removed, take care not to lose detent ball and spring (34).

Remove ball bearings (8, 10 and 24) with care so as not to damage case halves. Install new bearings and reassemble gears and shafts in reverse order in which they were removed. Lubricate wear surfaces of shafts and bores of gears during reassembly, then coat gear teeth by hand with a good grade of lithium base chassis grease. Torque case bolts to 18-20 ft.-lbs. (24-27 N·m). Use a grease gun at fittings (7 and 33) before reinstalling transaxle assembly.

Models 108-R, 108-3, 108-5 and 111-5

REMOVE AND REINSTALL. Disconnect spark plug lead and ground to engine. Disconnect battery (as equip-

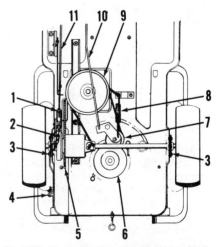

Fig. WH8—Underside view of traction drive clutch, brake linkage and differential assembly used on Model A-60.

1. Brake rod clevis	6. Engine pulley
2. Return spring	7. Clutch idler pulley
3. Axle bearing plates	8. Tension spring
4. Chain adjustment bracket	9. Transmission pulley
5. Chain	10. Clutch rod
	11. Brake rod

ped). Remove mower deck. Disconnect brake linkage and shift linkage at transaxle. Remove drive belt from transaxle pulley. Disconnect safety switches as equipped. Support rear of rider and unbolt transaxle mounting bolts. Raise rear of rider and roll transaxle assembly from under rider.

Reverse removal procedure for reinstallation and make certain brake is properly adjusted.

OVERHAUL. Models 108-R and 108-3 are equipped with Peerless 900 series transaxle and Models 108-5 and 111-5 are equipped with Peerless 800 series transaxle. Refer to appropriate PEERLESS TRANSAXLE section of this manual for overhaul procedure.

TRANSMISSION

All Models

Models A-60 and A-70 use Peerless 500 series transmissions. Models A-51, A-81, A-111, RR-532 and RR-832 are equipped with Peerless 700 series transmissions. For overhaul procedures, refer to Peerless paragraphs in TRANSMISSION REPAIR section of this manual.

REMOVE AND REINSTALL. Unbolt and raise or remove body components as needed for access to transmission. Disconnect wiring to transmission safety switch. Remove master link from drive chain and disconnect chain. Remove mower as outlined in MOWER DECK paragraphs. Slip drive belt off transmission pulley. Remove retaining ring from transmission input shaft and pull transmission pulley off shaft. Unbolt transmission and withdraw from chassis.

Reinstall by reversing removal procedure. Adjust drive belt and drive chain as needed.

DRIVE CHAIN

Models A-60 and A-70

R&R AND ADJUST. To remove chain (5-Fig. WH8), rotate differential sprocket to locate master link. Disconnect master link and remove chain. Inspect chain and sprockets for excessive wear and renew as needed. Lubricate chain with light coat of SAE 30 oil.

To adjust chain, raise and block rear of unit. Loosen bolts in rear axle bearing mounting brackets (3-Fig. WH8). On Model A-60, loosen brake bracket bolts, disconnect brake return spring (2) and disconnect clevis (1) from park-

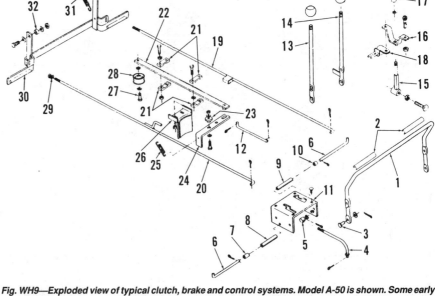

Fig. WH9—Exploded view of typical clutch, brake and control systems. Model A-50 is shown. Some early models have coil springs compressed on control bracket rods (6) as well as spacers shown.

1. Brake pedal
2. Surface material
3. Clevis pin
4. Mower clutch link
5. Trunnion stud
6. Control bracket rod (2)
7. Spacer, 1.82-inch
8. Spacer, 4.32-inch
9. Spacer, 5.46-inch
10. Spacer, 0.46X0.62X0.70
11. Control bracket
12. Traction clutch link
13. Traction clutch lever
14. Mower clutch lever
15. Parking brake stem
16. Parking brake bracket
17. Knob
18. Ignition interlock module
19. Brake rod, LH
20. Brake rod, RH
21. Guide blocks (4)
22. Traction clutch bar
23. Bushing
24. Clutch-brake pivot bar
25. Traction clutch spring
26. Blade brake/lining
27. Hex bolt
28. Forward-reverse idler
29. Elastic stop nut
30. Brake arm assembly
31. Return spring
32. Spacer

ing brake arm. On both models, tighten chain by tightening bolt in chain adjustment bracket (4). Move other end of axle equal amount to maintain axle to frame alignment. When adjustment is correct, chain deflects approximately ½ to ¾ inch (12.7-19 mm) with light finger pressure, retighten axle mounting bolts. On Model A-60, reconnect brake linkage components and check brake operation.

Models A-51, A-81, A-111, RR-532 and RR-832

R&R AND ADJUST. To remove chain, rotate differential sprocket to locate master link. Disconnect master link and remove chain. Inspect chain and sprockets for excessive wear and renew as needed. Lubricate chain with light coat of SAE 30 oil.

Adjust chain tension, by adjusting position of rear idler sprocket (idler mounting plate is slotted for this purpose).

DIFFERENTIAL

All Models

Models A-60, A-70 and early production A-51, A-81, A-111, RR-532 and RR-832 are equipped with Peerless Se-

ries 100 differential. Late production Models A-51, A-81, A-111, RR-532 and RR-832 are equipped with Stewart Model 9500 differential. For overhaul procedures, refer to DIFFERENTIAL REPAIR section of this manual.

Models A-60 and A-70

REMOVE AND REINSTALL. Raise and block rear of unit. Remove hub cap, retaining ring and rear wheel assemblies. On Model A-60, unhook brake return spring (2-Fig. WH8) and disconnect brake rod clevis (1) from brake lever. On all models, disconnect drive chain at master link. Unbolt bearing plates (3) and remove differential assembly. Clean rust, paint or burrs from axle shaft and remove bearings. On Model A-60, remove nuts from inside brake drum and remove drum and sprocket.

Reinstall differential assembly by reversing removal procedure. Lubricate axle bearings with SAE 30 oil.

Models A-51, A-81, A-111, RR-532 and RR-832

REMOVE AND REINSTALL. Raise and block rear of unit. Remove hub cap and retaining ring and remove wheel assemblies. Disconnect drive chain at master link. Loosen set screw

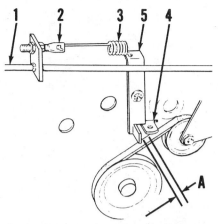

Fig. WH10—Underside view of brake linkage. Gap "A" should be 1/8 inch (3 mm). Hold pivot lever to front and brake lever to rear when checking gap.

1. Clutch-brake rod
2. Adjustment bolt
3. Brake spring
4. Transmission brake lever
5. Brake pivot lever

in axle lock collar and unbolt bearings from axle brackets. Remove differential and axle assembly from chassis (note location of spacers and washers).

Reinstall by reversing removal procedure.

GROUND DRIVE BRAKE

Models R-26 and A-50

ADJUSTMENT. Adjustment is performed on elastic stop nuts (29-Fig. WH9) at threaded rear end of brake rods (19 and 20). With brake relaxed (brake bars not contacting rear tires), nuts should be positioned so slack is equal on each rod.

To adjust so traction clutch will disengage automatically when brakes are applied, set traction clutch lever in **FORWARD** position and depress brake pedal, observing if traction clutch lever (13) moves to about ¾ inch (19 mm) from neutral notch just before brake bars contact rear tires. Turn nuts (29) an equal amount on each rod so braking will be balanced. Start engine and put mower in motion; then, observe action of traction clutch lever as brake is applied. If lever does not move to neutral notch, readjust nuts (29). If no declutching action occurs, check under chassis for condition of brake rod (20), especially hook portion welded to middle section of rod, spring (25) and pivot bar (24). While observing beneath deck, reach up and operate lever (13) and check for proper action of link (12), pivot bar (24) and its bushing (23) and traction clutch bar (22). Take steps to correct any binding or blockage found, and if parts are broken or defective, renew as necessary.

ADJUST PARKING LOCK. If parking brake does not hold when lock is engaged after brake pedal is applied, adjust as follows: Increase length of carriage-type bolt by backing out of parking brake stem (15-Fig. WH9) until it contacts welded block at middle of left hand brake rod (19) and holds brake arm (30) securely against rear tires. Test for holding by pushing mower by hand. Retighten locknut on adjuster.

Model A-60

ADJUSTMENT. To adjust brake, raise and block rear of unit and remove right rear wheel. Unhook brake return spring (2-Fig. WH8) and disconnect brake rod clevis (1) from brake lever. Loosen jam nut and turn clevis clockwise to tighten brake adjustment. Reconnect and check adjustment.

R&R AND OVERHAUL. Normal overhaul consists of renewing brake band. To remove brake assembly, raise and block rear of unit and remove right rear wheel. Unhook brake return spring and disconnect brake rod clevis from brake lever. Unbolt brake cam bracket and remove brake band roll pins, then remove brake band and cam bracket. Inspect for excessive wear and renew as needed. Reassemble by reversing removal procedure.

Models A-70, A-51, A-81, A-111, RR-532 and RR-832

ADJUSTMENT. To adjust disc brake, first unbolt and raise body. With brake released, loosen jam nut and tighten adjusting nut on brake lever until brake pads just clear brake disc. Lock adjusting nut with jam nut and recheck brake operation.

On all models except A-70, adjust clutch-brake rod (1-Fig. WH10) as follows: Disconnect idler plate spring. With clutch-brake pedal fully forward, idler plate should clear engine pulley by 1/16 to 1/8 inch (1.6-3 mm). Adjust length of rod with threaded trunnion at front of rod to obtain correct clearance. Reinstall idler spring and check for 1/8-inch (3 mm) clearance "A" between transmission brake lever (4) and brake pivot lever (5). Reposition jam nuts on adjustment bolt (2) to obtain clearance.

R&R AND OVERHAUL. Normal overhaul consists of renewing brake pads. To remove brake assembly, unbolt and raise body. On Model A-70, disconnect brake rod from disc brake lever. Unbolt brake pad holder from transmission and remove holder and outer brake pad, then remove brake disc and inner brake pad. Inspect parts for ex-

cessive wear and renew as needed. Reassemble in reverse order of removal and adjust brake as previously outlined.

Models 108-R, 108-3, 108-5 and 111-5

ADJUSTMENT. Brake rod spring must be adjusted before adjusting brake at caliper. With brake pedal released, turn brake rod spring adjustment nut to remove all clearance between spring seat and washer without compressing spring. Make certain transmission brake lever is contacting back stop rod with brake pedal in released position. Pull brake rod spring forward with moderate force. Clearance between rear end of spring and spring seat should be ⅜-½ inch (9.5-1.3 mm). Turn adjustment nut at brake caliper as required to obtain this clearance.

R&R AND OVERHAUL. Disconnect brake rod at brake caliper. Remove caliper adjusting nut, brake lever, caliper and outer brake pad assembly. Remove brake disc and inner brake pad.

Reverse removal procedure for reassembly. Make certain brake actuator pins move freely in outer caliper assembly before reinstallation.

PTO DRIVE BRAKE

Models A-51, A-81, A-111, RR-532 and RR-832

ADJUSTMENT. Check and adjust pto clutch and brake as follows: With pto engaged, there should be 0.010 inch (0.25 mm) clearance between brake pad (Fig. WH5) and pulley and 1/8-inch (3 mm) clearance between hex head of threaded spacer and clutch-brake plate. To adjust brake, adjust position of adjustment nuts on clutch bracket stud. To adjust pto cable, loosen locknut and turn threaded spacer as required, then tighten locknut.

Models 108-R, 108-3, 108-5 and 111-5

ADJUSTMENT. Tilt seat forward and engage pto. Turn adjustment nut until spring end is within silver area of adjustment bracket decal.

MOWER DRIVE BELT

Models R-26 and A-50

ADJUSTMENT. To adjust mower drive belt tension, disconnect trunnion

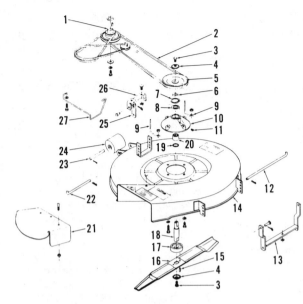

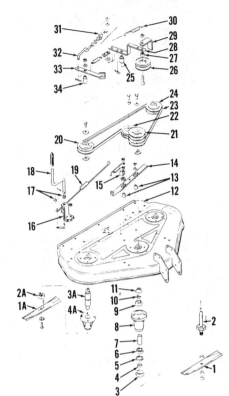

Fig. WH11—Exploded view of typical single spindle mower deck to show parts identification and arrangement.

1. Engine pulley
2. Mower drive belt
3. Nylok bolt
4. Dome washer (2)
5. Blade drive pulley
6. Spacer
7. Snap ring
8. Ball bearing
9. Belt guide (2)
10. Spindle housing
11. Grease fitting
12. Front support rod
13. Front hanger
14. Cutting deck
15. Roll pin
16. Blade
17. Blade driver
18. Spindle
19. Seal
20. Needle bearing
21. Deflector
22. Rear support rod
23. Roller shaft
24. Roller
25. Rear lift link (2)
26. Rear lift bracket
27. Belt retainer

stud (5–Fig. WH9) from mower clutch lever (14), then swing mower clutch link (4) to one side and back off threaded trunnion to increase length of clutch link. Check adjustment by reconnecting trunnion stud to clutch lever and move lever to engaged position. Tension of drive belt should be felt as lever reaches locking notch and a slight extra effort should be needed to set lever into engaged position.

To adjust blade brake (26), loosen brake adjusting nuts on floor under operator's seat and push mower clutch lever forward and hold beside disengage hooking notch of control panel; then, slide blade brake (26) forward so lining is in contact with edge of pulley and tighten adjusting nuts. Now, when lever is pushed and set firmly into blade disengage notch, positive stop of blade rotation should result. If blade brake lining is worn to the point of metal-to-metal contact, renew parts to prevent damage to mower drive pulley.

Models A-60 and A-70

ADJUSTMENT. Remove mower front hitch pull pin. On Model A-60 loosen front hitch jam nut and turn hitch clockwise to tighten belt. On Model A-70, turn leveling rod clevis clockwise to tighten belt. Check adjustment of belt by running at fast throttle setting, then disengage clutch. Blade should stop in short period of time. Repeat adjustment as needed.

Models A-51, A-81, A-111, RR-532 and RR-832

ADJUSTMENT. On 32 inch mowers, idler pulley is mounted on slotted bracket and is used to adjust belt tension. Move pulley rearward to increase belt tension. When properly adjusted,

Fig. WH12—Exploded view of typical double spindle mower to show parts location and arrangement.

1. Blade pulley
2. Spacer
3. Snap ring
4. Ball bearing
5. Spindle housing
6. Needle bearing
7. Seal
8. Clutch idler pulley
9. Spacer
10. Washers
11. Belt retainer
12. Idler return spring
13. Idler arm
14. Pivot bushing
15. Clutch tension spring
16. Idler pulley
17. Bushings
18. Clutch lever
19. Pivot bracket
20. Mower deck
21. Spindle shaft
22. Spindle cup
23. Blade
24. Dome washer
25. Retainer bolt

Fig. WH13—Exploded view of typical triple spindle mower to show parts location and arrangement. Two different styles of spindles are shown.

1A. Blade	16. Pivot bracket
2A. Spindle cup	17. Bushings
3A. Spindle shaft & bearing	18. Clutch lever
4A. Spindle housing	19. Tension spring
1. Blade	20. Blade pulley
2. Spindle shaft	21. Center pulley
3. Spindle cup	22. Belt tension idler
4. Spacer	23. Spindle belt
5. Snap ring	24. Blade pulley
6. Bearing	25. Bushing
7. Spacer	26. Clutch idler pulley
8. Spindle housing	27. Spacer
9. Bearing	28. Idler arm
10. Spacer	29. Belt retainer
11. Seal	30. Return spring
12. Deck	31. Trunnion
13. Bushing	32. Brake rod
14. Idler support bar	33. Brake lever
15. Belt guard	34. Bushing

belt should deflect one inch, under light finger pressure, at mid point between left spindle pulley and pto pulley.

On 36 inch mowers, adjust belt tension as follows: On early production

mowers, mower hanger bracket has slotted mounting holes. Mower can be moved forward or rearward to increase or decrease tension. On late production mowers, belt tension is adjusted by tightening two adjusting bolts evenly against front mounting "J" pin, until belt deflects approximately one inch under finger pressure, at mid point between pulleys. Tighten jam nuts on adjusting bolts when adjustment is correct.

Models R-26, A-50, A-60 and A-70

REMOVE AND REINSTALL. Place mower in lowest position and disengage blade clutch. Loosen belt guides as needed to remove belt from pulleys. Loosen idler pulley mounting bolt and slip belt between pulley and belt retainer and remove belt.

Renew belt by reversing removal procedure. Adjust belt guides to 1/16-inch clearance from belt. Position idler pulley belt retainer at right angle with idler arm.

Models A-51, A-81, A-111, RR-532, 108-R, 108-3, 108-5 and 111-5

REMOVE AND REINSTALL. Remove mower unit as outlined in MOWER DECK paragraphs. Remove shields and loosen belt guides as necessary to remove belt from pulleys.

Renew drive belt by reversing removal procedure. Adjust belt guides to $1/16$-inch (1.6 mm) clearance from belt.

MOWER SPINDLE

All Models

R&R AND OVERHAUL. Refer to Fig. WH11, WH12, or WH13 for parts identification and arrangement. Remove mower unit as outlined in MOWER DECK paragraphs. Place wood block between blade and housing and unbolt and remove blade and drive pulley. Unbolt and remove spindle housing from deck. Push spindle out of housing. Remove retaining ring and press bearings out of housing.

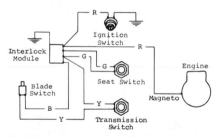

Fig. WH14—Typical wiring schematic for Models A-60, A-51 and A-81 with recoil start. Seat switch not used on all models.

1. BK-Black
2. O-Orange
3. R-Red
4. B-Brown
5. W-White
6. Y-Yellow
7. BL-Blue
8. G-Green

Reassemble in reverse order of removal. When installing new bearings, press on outer race only. On mowers equipped with blade retainer bolt, torque to 22 ft.-lbs. (30 N·m). If equipped with blade retainer nut, torque to 60-70 ft.-lbs. (81-95 N·m). Lubricate with No. 2 multi-purpose lithium base grease.

MOWER DECK

Models A-51, A-60, A-70, A-81, A-111, RR-532 and RR-832

LEVEL ADJUSTMENT. With unit on level surface and tires properly inflated, measure height of blade at front and rear of deck. Blade should be level to ⅛-inch (3 mm) lower in front. To adjust, loosen bolts and move front deck hanger bracket up or down on Model A-60. On Model A-70, block front of mower to remove weight and disconnect leveling rod clevis at front of mower. Turn clevis clockwise to lower front of mower. Each 1½ turns of clevis will change front deck height approximately ⅛ inch (3 mm). On all other models equipped with leveling cable, place wood block under front of mower and disconnect cable trunnion at rear of mower. Turn trunnion clockwise to raise front of mower. On models not equipped with leveling cable, adjustment is made with a jam bolt at front hanger bracket. With front of mower setting at specified height, turn jam bolt until head of bolt just contacts front hanger bracket. Tighten jam nut to lock adjustment.

Models R-26 and A-50

REMOVE AND REINSTALL. Disconnect wiring from mower safety switch. Disengage blade clutch and remove front and rear support rods from hanger brackets. Move mower to rear, remove belt from engine pulley and slip belt out of belt guard. Turn front wheels full left and pull mower deck out right side. Reinstall by reversing removal procedure.

Models A-60 and A-70

REMOVE AND REINSTALL. Disengage blade clutch and place mower in lowest position. Disconnect wiring from mower safety switch. Remove pull pin from front of mower. Loosen engine pulley belt guides, then move deck rearward and slip belt off pulley. Turn front wheels full left, then move deck forward to disengage rear deck guide and pull deck out right side of unit. Reinstall by reversing removal procedure.

Models A-51, A-81, A-111, RR-532 and RR-832

REMOVE AND REINSTALL. Place wood block under front of mower and lower mower onto block. If mower is equipped with leveling cable, disconnect cable trunnion at rear of mower. Disconnect wiring to mower safety switch. Loosen idler pulley to relieve belt tension and remove "J" bolts from front yoke, then slip drive belt out of mower pulleys. Remove lower nuts, washer and spacer from clutch-brake bracket stud (Fig. WH5). Hold pto pul-

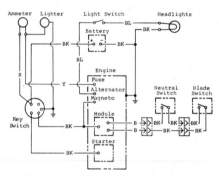

Fig WH17—Wiring diagram for Model A-70. Refer to Fig. WH14 legend for wiring color code.

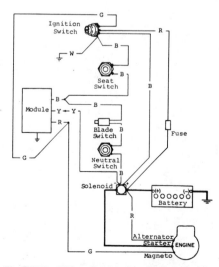

Fig. WH18—Wiring diagram for all other electric start models. Refer to Fig. WH14 legend for wiring color code.

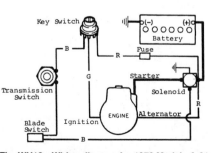

Fig. WH16—Wiring diagram for 1979 Models A-81 and A-111 with electric start. Refer to Fig. WH14 legend for wiring color code.

Fig. WH15—Wiring schematic for 1982 Model A-51 and RR-532.

ley and remove clevis pin, then lower clutch-brake plate and remove belt. Turn front wheels full left and pull mower out from right side. Reinstall by reversing removal procedure.

Models 108-R, 108-3, 108-5 and 111-5

REMOVE AND REINSTALL. Remove drive belt and support front of mower deck with wood blocks. Remove clip pin, washer and clevis pin from each side cable. Disconnect wiring to mower safety switch. Remove clip pin, washer and spring rod from front arm. Remove the two bolts, washers, spacers and nuts from front mower mounting brackets. Lift front of rider and swing away from mower.

Reverse removal procedure for reinstallation. Make certain mower safety switch wiring is properly routed and switch is connected and working.

ELECTRICAL

All Models

All units are equipped with safety interlock starting system to prevent starting with drives engaged. Refer to Fig. WH14 through WH18.

WHITE

WHITE OUTDOOR PRODUCTS
P.O. Box 361131
Cleveland, OH 44136

Model	Make	Engine Model	Horsepower	Cutting Width, In.
R10	B&S	250000	10	32
R50	B&S	130000	5	26
R53	B&S	130000	5	26
R80	B&S	190000	8	34
R82	B&S	190000	8	30
R86	B&S	190000	8	30

FRONT AXLE AND STEERING SYSTEM

Models R10-R53-R86

R&R AND OVERHAUL. To remove axle main member (20—Fig. W11), remove mower unit as outlined in MOWER DECK section. Remove steering shaft (5) as follows: Remove steering wheel cap, retaining nut and washer, then lift off steering wheel (4). Remove cover (31), unscrew nut at lower end of steering shaft and remove gear (36). Remove steering shaft. Disconnect tie rods (26) at spindles (25). Detach steering support plate (30) and sector gear (35). Support frame and remove front wheels. Remove speed nuts (17) and washers, then lower spindles (25) from axle. Detach front axle support (28) from frame and remove axle main member (20).

Clean and inspect all parts and renew any showing excessive wear or damage. Reassemble by reversing the disassembly procedure and lubricate bushings and all pivot points with SAE 30 oil. Steering gear backlash is adjusted by moving plate (29) in slotted mounting holes. After adjusting plate position, operate steering through full range of movement and check for binding.

Model R50

R&R AND OVERHAUL. To remove axle main member (15—Fig. W12), first remove steering shaft (4) as follows: Remove steering wheel cap, retaining nut and washer, then lift off steering wheel (1) and cover (2). Unbolt and remove shaft extension (3), speed nut (5) and washer (6). Disconnect tie rods (11) from spindles (10 and 13), raise front of machine and withdraw steering shaft (4) from bottom of axle main member. Support frame and remove front wheels. Remove cotter pins and washers, then lower spindles (10 and 13) from axle. Unbolt and remove axle main member (15) from frame (9). Flange bushings (7 and 12) and spindle bushings (14) can now be removed if necessary.

Clean and inspect all parts and renew any showing excessive wear or damage. Reassemble by reversing the disassembly procedure and lubricate bushings and all pivot points with SAE 30 oil. Tie rods are not adjustable.

Model R80

R&R AND OVERHAUL. To remove axle main member (15—Fig. W13), support front of machine and remove front wheels. Disconnect tie rods (14) from spindles. Remove cotter pins and washers, then lower spindles (12 and 18) from axle main member. Remove pivot bolt (17) and unhook mower springs form axle support (16). Unbolt axle support from frame (9) and separate axle main member (15) from axle support. Inspect spindle bushings (13) for excessive wear and renew as needed. Reassemble by reversing the disassembly procedure. Adjust tie rods to obtain front wheel toe-in setting of $1/8$ inch (3 mm).

To remove steering gear, remove steering wheel cap, retaining nut and washer, then lift off steering wheel (1). Remove spacer tube (2), drive out roll pin and remove shaft extension (3) and washer (6). Raise front of machine and support securely. Disconnect tie rods from ends of steering rack. Unbolt steering housing (2—Fig. W14) from support (10—Fig. W13) and withdraw steering unit from bottom. Refer to Fig. W14 and drive out roll pin securing pinion (3) to steering shaft (1). Withdraw shaft and remove pinion. Remove bolt from one end of two-piece rack (4) and slide rack out of housing (2). Clean and inspect all parts and renew any showing excessive wear or other damage. Flange bushing (7—Fig. W13) can be removed and a new bushing installed if needed. Reassemble by reversing disassembly procedure. Lubricate rack and pinion with multipurpose lithium grease. Lubricate flange bushing (7), spindle bushings (13), pivot bolt (17) and front wheels with SAE 30 oil.

Model R82

R&R AND OVERHAUL. To remove axle main member (6—Fig. W15), support front of machine and remove front wheels. Disconnect tie rods (9) from spindles (8). Remove cotter pins and washers, then withdraw spindles and bushings (7) from axle ends. Unbolt and remove axle from frame.

Inspect for excessive wear and renew if needed. Reassemble by reversing removal procedure and lubricate spindle bushings and front wheels with SAE 30 oil. Adjust tie rods to obtain front wheel toe-in setting of $1/8$ inch (3 mm).

To remove steering gear, remove steering wheel cap, retaining nut and washer, then lift off steering wheel (1—

Fig. W15) and cover (2). Drive out roll pin and remove shaft extension (3) and flange bushing (4). Disconnect tie rods (9) from rack (10). Unbolt mounting bracket (11) and withdraw steering unit from bottom. Drive out roll pin and withdraw shaft (1—Fig. W14) and pinion (3). Remove bolt from end of two-piece rack and slide rack (4) out of housing (2).

Clean and inspect parts and renew if needed. Reassembly by reversing removal procedure. Lubricate rack and pinion with multipurpose lithium grease and flange bushings with SAE 30 oil.

ENGINE

Model R80

REMOVE AND REINSTALL. To remove engine, raise engine cover and disconnect spark plug wire. Disconnect battery cables, ignition wire from magneto, cable from starter and throttle control cable. Unbolt exhaust pipe from engine. Plate lift and blade clutch lever in disengage position. Remove belt guides at engine pulley. Remove mower drive belt from engine pulley. Move lift and blade clutch lever to lowest notch. Unbolt and remove engine pulley belt guard. Refer to Fig. W16 and unhook

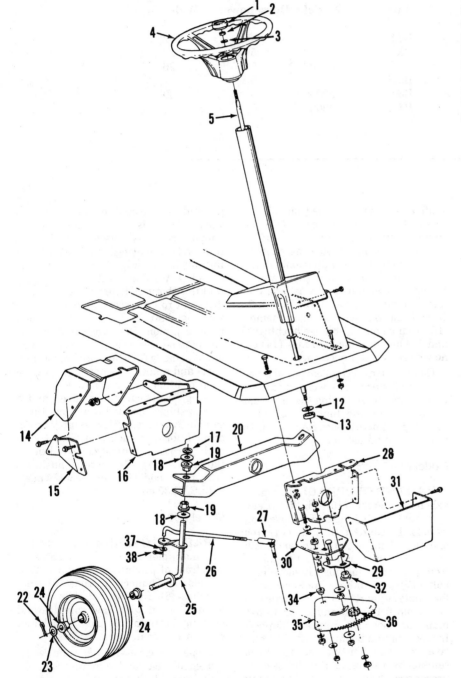

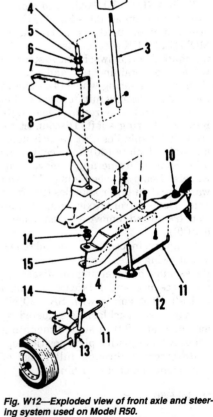

Fig. W12—Exploded view of front axle and steering system used on Model R50.

Fig. W11—Exploded view of typical front axle and steering system used on Models R10, R53 and R86.

1. Cap	15. Plate	23. Washer	30. Steering plate
2. Nut	16. Axle support	24. Bushing	31. Bracket
3. Washer	17. Push nut	25. Spindle	32. Bushing
4. Steering wheel	18. Washer	26. Tie rod	34. Bushing
5. Steering shaft	19. Bushing	27. Tie rod end	35. Sector gear
12. Washer	20. Axle main member	28. Axle support	36. Steering gear
13. Spacer	22. Cotter pin	29. Steering adjuster	37. Washer
14. Bracket			38. Cotter pin

1. Steering wheel	9. Frame
2. Cover	10. Spindle (L.H.)
3. Shaft extension	11. Tie rods
4. Steering shaft	12. Flange bushing
5. Retainer	13. Spindle (R.H.)
6. Washer	14. Spindle bushings
7. Flange bushing	15. Axle main member
8. Support	

main drive belt clutch idler springs. Remove shoulder bolt near transmission input pulley. Remove main drive belt from transmission pulley first, then from engine pulley. Unbolt and remove the engine pulley. Remove engine mounting bolts, then lift engine from frame.

Reinstall engine by reversing removal procedure. Make certain belt guard and guides are properly installed.

OVERHAUL. Refer to appropriate engine section in this manual for tune-up specifications, engine overhaul procedures and engine maintenance.

Model R82

REMOVE AND REINSTALL. To remove engine, disconnect spark plug wire, battery cables, ignition wire from magneto, cable from starter and throttle control cable at engine. Engage blade clutch lever. Loosen mower deck front mounting bolts and remove rear mounting bolts. Raise mower and slip mower drive belt off engine pulley. Remove en-

gine pulley belt guard and shoulder bolts at transmission pulley. Slip traction drive belt off transmission pulley first, then off engine pulley. Remove engine mounting bolts and lift engine from frame.

Reinstall by reversing removal procedure.

OVERHAUL. Refer to appropriate engine section in this manual for tune-up specifications, engine overhaul procedures and engine maintenance.

All Other Models

REMOVE AND REINSTALL. To remove engine, disconnect spark plug wire and remove engine cover. On electric start models, disconnect and remove battery. Disconnect any interfering electrical wires from engine. Disconnect throttle cable from engine. Detach exhaust pipe. Remove mower as outlined in MOWER DECK section. Remove traction drive belt from engine pulley as outlined in TRACTION DRIVE CLUTCH AND DRIVE BELTS

section. Detach pulleys from the engine crankshaft. Remove engine mounting bolts and lift engine from frame.

Reinstall by reversing removal procedure.

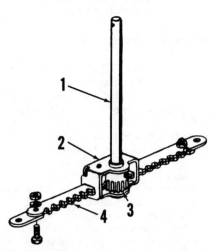

Fig. W14—Steering rack and pinion assembly used on Model R80. Model R82 is similar.

1. Steering shaft 3. Pinion
2. Steering housing 4. Rack (2 pieces)

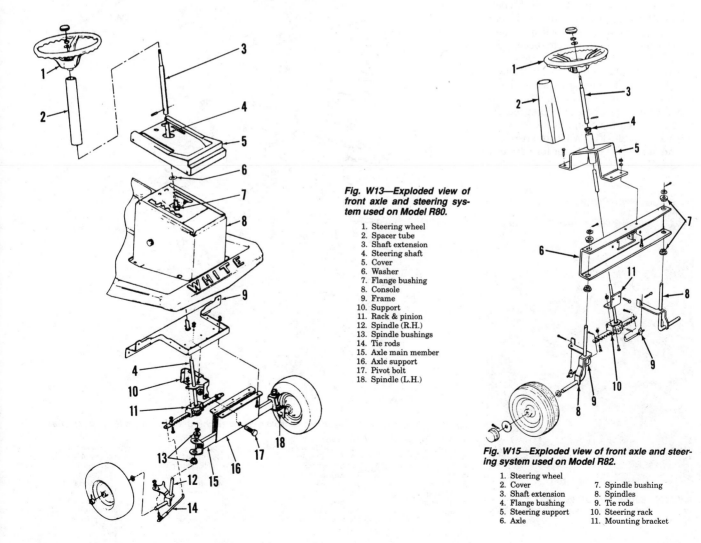

Fig. W13—Exploded view of front axle and steering system used on Model R80.

1. Steering wheel
2. Spacer tube
3. Shaft extension
4. Steering shaft
5. Cover
6. Washer
7. Flange bushing
8. Console
9. Frame
10. Support
11. Rack & pinion
12. Spindle (R.H.)
13. Spindle bushings
14. Tie rods
15. Axle main member
16. Axle support
17. Pivot bolt
18. Spindle (L.H.)

Fig. W15—Exploded view of front axle and steering system used on Model R82.

1. Steering wheel
2. Cover
3. Shaft extension
4. Flange bushing
5. Steering support
6. Axle
7. Spindle bushing
8. Spindles
9. Tie rods
10. Steering rack
11. Mounting bracket

OVERHAUL. Refer to appropriate engine section in this manual for tune-up specifications, engine overhaul procedures and engine maintenance.

TRACTION DRIVE CLUTCH AND DRIVE BELT

Models R10, R53 and R86

Models R10, R53 and R86 are equipped with a drive system that uses two drive belts and a variable speed pulley to transfer power from the engine to the transaxle. The primary (lower) drive belt connects the engine to the variable speed pulley (23—Fig. W17). The diameters of the pulley grooves are determined by belt tension, which is regulated by the position of idlers (10 and 17). The idlers move when the speed control lever is operated. Ground speed changes when the pulley diameters change on the variable speed pulley.

ADJUSTMENT. The speed control lever and gear shift lever must be synchronized with the positions of the belt idlers. With engine running and gear shift lever in neutral position, place speed control lever in high speed position. Release, then slowly depress fully the clutch/brake pedal and hold down pedal. Shut off the engine and release pedal when engine stops. Move the speed control lever to second speed position. Detach bent end of lower speed control rod (32—Fig. W17) and turn rod so end of rod will just enter forward end of slot (S). Reattach rod.

Fig. W16—Bottom view of Model R80, with mower unit removed. Note the heavy and light clutch idler springs.

Move gear shift lever to neutral slot on gear indicator panel. If machine does not move freely forward and backward thereby indicating transaxle is in neutral, loosen screw (W—Fig. W17). Move shift lever (36) as needed so transaxle is in neutral and shift lever is in center of neutral slot on control panel. Retighten screw (W) to 13 ft.-lbs. (18 N·m).

R&R DRIVE BELTS. Lower Belt. To remove lower drive belt (25—Fig. W17), disconnect spark plug wire and remove battery. Remove mower as outlined in MOWER DECK section. Disconnect idler spring (16). Detach torque rod bracket (34) from transaxle and torque rod (8) and remove bracket. Separate belt from pulleys and remove belt.

Install lower belt by reversing removal procedure.

Upper Belt. The lower belt must be removed as outlined in previous section before removing upper belt. Detach engine pulley belt guide (14—Fig. W17),

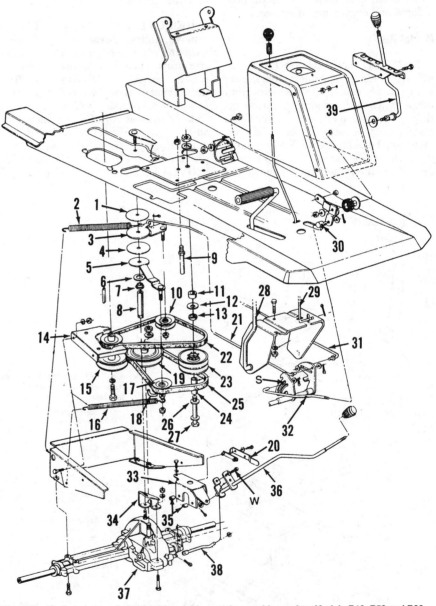

Fig. W17—Exploded view of clutch and variable speed assembly used on Models R10, R53 and R86.

1. Thrust washer	11. Spacer	30. Ferrule
2. Spring	12. Belleville washer	31. Brake rod
3. Idler arm	13. Thrust washer	32. Speed control rod
4. Thrust washer	14. Belt guard	33. Bracket
5. Idler arm	15. Engine pulley	34. Bracket
6. Washer	16. Spring	35. Spacers
7. Bushing	17. Idler	36. Shift lever
8. Torque rod	18. Belt guide	37. Transaxle
9. Belt guide	19. Transaxle pulley	38. Shift rod
10. Idler	20. Safety switch	39. Speed control lever
	21. Clutch rod	
	22. Upper drive belt	
	23. Variable speed pulley	
	24. Spacer	
	25. Lower drive belt	
	26. Thrust washer	
	27. Cap screw	
	28. Pedal rod	
	29. Park brake rod	

Illustrations Courtesy White Outdoor Products

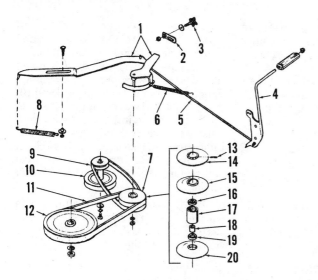

Fig. W18—View of traction drive belts, variable speed and clutch linkage and variable speed pulley used on Model R50.

1. Variable speed & clutch idler arms
2. Speed control bracket
3. Locking knob
4. Clutch pedal
5. Clutch rod
6. Spring
7. Variable speed pulley
8. Variable speed spring
9. Primary drive belt
10. Engine pulley
11. Secondary drive belt
12. Transmission pulley
13. Roll pin
14. Upper pulley half
15. Movable pulley half
16. Ball bearing
17. Sleeve
18. Spacer
19. Ball bearing
20. Lower pulley half

then unscrew retaining nut and remove idler (10). Remove upper belt (22).

Install upper belt by reversing removal procedure. Be sure hub side of idler (14) is next to idler arm (3). Install belt and idler simultaneously so belt is inside belt guide (9).

Model R50

Model R50 is equipped with a drive system that uses two drive belts and a variable speed pulley to transfer power from the engine to the transaxle. The primary (lower) drive belt connects the engine to the variable speed pulley (7—Fig. W18). The variable speed pulley also serves as the clutch idler. The diameters of the pulley grooves are determined by spring tension, which is regulated by the position of the speed control. Ground speed changes when the pulley diameters change on the variable speed pulley.

R&R DRIVE BELTS. To remove traction drive belts (9 and 11—Fig. W18), remove mower deck as outlined in MOWER DECK section. Depress clutch pedal and engage pedal lock. Remove engine pulley belt guide and unhook clutch tension springs. Remove retaining nuts from variable speed pulley and transmission pulley, then slide pulleys off shafts and remove drive belts.

Install new belts by reversing removal procedure. When reassembling transmission pulley, install hub side up.

Model R80

REMOVE AND REINSTALL. To remove traction drive belt, raise engine cover and disconnect spark plug wire. Place lift and blade clutch lever in disengaged position. Remove belt guides

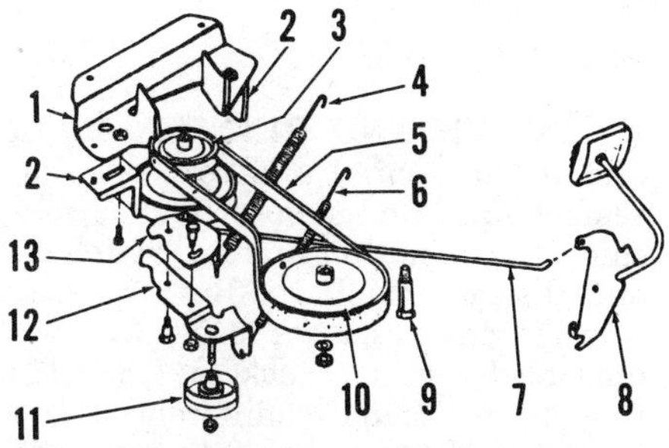

Fig. W19—Exploded view of traction drive clutch assembly used on Model R80.

1. Engine pulley belt guard
2. Belt guides
3. Engine pulley
4. Clutch spring (heavy)
5. Main drive belt
6. Clutch spring (light)
7. Clutch rod
8. Clutch pedal
9. Shoulder bolt
10. Transmission pulley
11. Idler pulley
12. Idler arm
13. Idler pivot plate

(2—Fig. W19) at engine pulley and slip mower drive belt from engine pulley. Move lift and blade clutch lever to lowest notch. Unbolt and remove engine pulley guard (1), then unhook clutch idler springs (4 and 6). Remove shoulder bolt (9) near transmission input pulley. Remove traction drive belt (5) from transmission pulley first, then from engine pulley.

Install new belt by reversing removal procedure. Make certain belt guard and belt guides are properly installed.

Model R82

REMOVE AND REINSTALL. To remove traction drive belt, disconnect spark plug wire and proceed as follows: Engage blade clutch lever. Loosen mower deck front mounting bolts and remove rear mounting bolts. Unbolt rear axle center bearing support bracket. Loosen engine mounting bolts, then raise engine for clearance and slide support bracket and bearing away from engine pulley. Raise mower deck and slip mower drive belt off engine pulley. Remove engine pulley belt guard (1—Fig. W20) and transmission pulley shoulder bolts (11). Unbolt and remove idler pulley (3). Slip belt (13) off transmission pulley first, then off engine pulley.

Install belt by reversing removal procedure. Make certain belt guard and guides are properly installed.

VARIABLE SPEED PULLEY

All Models So Equipped

R&R AND OVERHAUL. The variable speed pulley is accessible after removing drive belts as previously outlined. Individual components of the variable speed pulley used on Model R50 are available, while the variable speed pulley on later models is available only as a unit assembly. Refer to Fig. W18 for an exploded view of Model R50 variable speed pulley. Bearings are sealed and do not require lubrication. Apply a dry lubricant to movable pulley half and sleeve.

TRANSMISSION/TRANSAXLE

Models R50, R80 and R82

REMOVE AND REINSTALL. Early models are equipped with a transmission that is coupled to the differential by a chain. To remove transmission, first remove mower as outlined in MOWER DECK section and remove traction drive belt as outlined in previous

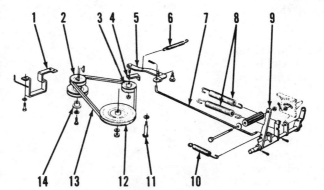

Fig. W20—Exploded view of traction drive belt and clutch linkage used on Model R82.

1. Engine belt guide
2. Engine pulley
3. Clutch idler pulley
4. Belt guide
5. Idler arm bracket
6. Idler spring
7. Clutch rod
8. Traction springs
9. Clutch-brake pedal assy.
10. Brake spring
11. Shoulder bolt
12. Transmission pulley
13. Traction drive belt
14. Step washer

section. Unbolt and remove transmission pulley. Disconnect transmission shift linkage, then unbolt and remove engine cover. Disconnect drive chain at master link. Unbolt transmission from frame and remove transmission.

Reinstall by reversing removal procedure.

OVERHAUL. Model 50 is equipped with a Foote transmission, Model R80 is equipped with a Peerless Model 515 transmission and Model R82 is equipped with a Peerless Model 701 transmission. Refer to TRANSMISSION REPAIR section for service information.

Models R10, R53 and R86

REMOVE AND REINSTALL. To remove transaxle, first remove drive belts as previously outlined. Disconnect brake linkage and shift linkage. Support rear of machine and remove transaxle mounting bolts. Raise rear of machine and roll transaxle assembly from under machine.

Reinstall by reversing removal procedure.

OVERHAUL. All models are equipped with a MTD Model 717 transaxle. Refer to TRANSMISSION REPAIR section for service information.

DRIVE CHAIN

Model R50

ADJUSTMENT. Drive chain tension should be checked periodically. The chain should deflect approximately ½ inch (13 mm) when depressed with thumb midway between sprockets. To adjust drive chain, loosen transmission mounting nuts slightly. Turn draw bolt, located under right side of main frame, clockwise to tighten or counterclockwise to loosen drive chain. When chain tension is correct, retighten transmission mounting nuts.

REMOVE AND REINSTALL. To remove drive chain, rotate driven sprocket to locate master link. Disconnect master link and remove drive chain. Clean and inspect chain and sprockets and renew if excessively worn.

Install drive chain and adjust chain tension as outlined in previous paragraph. Lubricate chain with a light coat of SAE 30 oil.

Models R80 and R82

ADJUSTMENT. Drive chain tension should be checked periodically. The chain should deflect approximately ½ inch (13 mm) when depressed with thumb midway between sprockets. To adjust drive chain, loosen chain idler mounting nuts and slide chain idler rearward to tighten or forward to loosen drive chain. When chain tension is correct, retighten idler mounting nuts.

REMOVE AND REINSTALL. To remove drive chain, rotate driven sprocket to locate master link. Disconnect master link and remove drive chain. Clean and inspect chain and sprockets and renew if excessively worn.

Install drive chain and adjust chain tension as outlined in previous paragraph. Lubricate chain with a light coat of SAE 30 oil.

DIFFERENTIAL, DRIVE SPROCKET AND REAR AXLE

Model R50

REMOVE AND REINSTALL. To remove differential and rear axle assembly, raise and support rear of machine. Locate master link in drive chain and disconnect chain. Remove rear wheel assemblies. Refer to Fig. W21 and unbolt axle bearing brackets (4, 8 and 9) from frame. Remove differential and axle assembly, being careful not to dam-

age brake caliper assembly. Clean all paint, rust or burrs from axle shafts and remove axle bearings and brackets.

Clean and inspect axle bearings and renew as necessary. When reinstalling, flanges on outer axle bearings (3 and 10) must face outward (against wheel hubs). Flange on inner axle bearing (6) must be toward differential housing. Lubricate axle bearings and drive chain with SAE 30 oil. If drive chain requires adjustment, refer to DRIVE CHAIN section.

OVERHAUL. All models are equipped with a MTD differential. Refer to DIFFERENTIAL REPAIR section for service information.

Model R80

REMOVE AND REINSTALL. To remove differential and rear axle assembly, place mower lift and blade clutch lever in disengaged position. Remove belt keepers at engine pulley and slip mower drive belt from engine pulley. Raise rear of unit and support securely. Locate master link in drive chain and disconnect chain. Remove rear wheel assemblies and disconnect brake rod. Unbolt and remove left axle bearing and bracket. See Fig. W22. Unbolt right

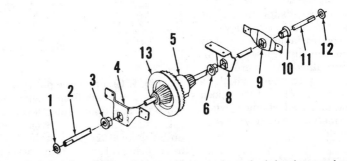

Fig. W21—Exploded view of differential assembly, rear axles and axle bearings used on Model R50.

1. Washer	4. Bearing bracket	7. Bearing plate	10. Axle bearing (outer)
2. Axle shaft (R.H.)	5. Differential assy.	8. Bearing bracket	11. Axle shaft (L.H.)
3. Axle bearing (outer)	6. Axle bearing (center)	9. Bearing bracket	12. Washer

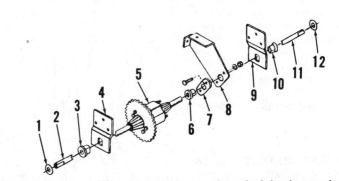

Fig. W22—Exploded view of differential assembly, rear axles and axle bearings used on Model R80.

1. Washer	4. Bearing bracket	8. Bearing bracket	11. Axle shaft (L.H.)
2. Axle shaft (R.H.)	5. Differential assy.	9. Bearing bracket	12. Washer
3. Axle bearing (outer)	6. Axle bearing (center)	10. Axle bearing (outer)	13. Brake disc

and center axle bearing brackets from main frame, move differential assembly forward to clear the brake caliper unit, then remove differential and rear axle assembly out toward right side. Clean all rust paint or burrs from axle shafts and remove axle bearings and brackets.

Clean and inspect axle bearings and renew as needed. When reinstalling, flanges on outer axle bearings must face outward (against wheel hubs). Flange on inner axle bearing must be toward differential housing. Remainder of reassembly is reverse of disassembly procedure. Lubricate axle bearings with SAE 30 oil.

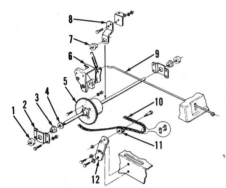

Fig. W23—Differential, rear axles and bearings used on Model R82.

1. Spacer
2. Axle bracket
3. Axle bushing (outer)
4. Washer
5. Differential & axle assy.
6. Disc brake
7. Axle bushing (inner)
8. Support bracket
9. Brake rod
10. Drive chain
11. Idler
12. Idler arm

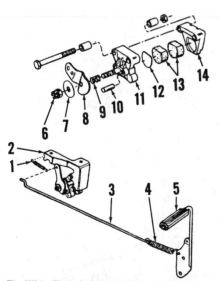

Fig. W24—Exploded view of typical caliper brake used on models with chain drive. Drive chain sprocket is also brake disc.

1. Return spring
2. Caliper assy.
3. Brake rod
4. Brake tension spring
5. Brake pedal
6. Adjusting nut
7. Washer
8. Cam lever
9. Spring
10. Actuating pin (2)
11. Carrier (outer)
12. Backup plate
13. Brake pads
14. Carrier (inner)

Model R82

REMOVE AND REINSTALL. To remove differential and rear axle assembly (5—Fig. W23), raise rear of unit and support securely. Disconnect drive chain at master link. Unbolt axle support bracket (8). Unbolt axle bearing brackets (2) and lower and remove differential assembly from frame. Remove rear wheels and spacers (1). Remove paint, rust or burrs from axle and slide bearings off axle.

Reinstall in reverse order of removal.

GROUND DRIVE BRAKE

Models With Chain Drive

ADJUSTMENT. Check brake operation by pushing brake pedal and attempting to move machine. If brake does not hold machine with pedal fully depressed, adjust brake. To adjust brake, release brake and turn nut (6—Fig. W24) on cam lever until desired brake operation is obtained.

R&R AND OVERHAUL. To remove brake caliper assembly, disconnect return spring (1—Fig. W24) and brake rod (3). Unbolt mounting bracket from frame and remove caliper assembly. Remove adjusting nut (6), washer (7), cam lever (8), spring (9) and actuating pins (10). Remove through-bolts and separate brake pads (13) and backup washer (12) from carriers (11 and 14).

Clean and inspect all parts for excessive wear and damage. Reassemble by reversing disassembly procedure. Be sure actuator pins (10) are installed with rounded end toward cam lever (8).

Models Without Chain Drive

ADJUSTMENT. Check brake operation by pushing brake pedal and attempting to move machine. If brake does not hold machine with pedal fully

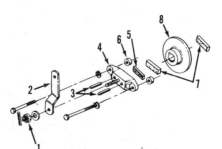

Fig. W25—Exploded view of typical caliper brake used on models not equipped with a chain drive.

1. Adjusting nut
2. Brake lever
3. Actuating pins
4. Brake carrier
5. Backup plate
6. Spacer
7. Brake pads
8. Brake disc

depressed, adjust brake. To adjust brake, release brake and turn nut (1—Fig. W25) on brake lever until desired brake operation is obtained.

R&R AND OVERHAUL. To remove brake caliper assembly, disconnect brake spring and brake rod from actuating lever. Unbolt and remove brake pad carrier (4—Fig. W25). Slide brake disc (8) off transaxle shaft and remove inner brake pad from slot in transaxle housing.

Clean and inspect all parts for excessive wear and damage. Reassemble by reversing disassembly procedure.

MOWER BELTS

Model R10

REMOVE AND REINSTALL. To remove the mower drive belt on Model R10, proceed as follows: Disconnect spark plug wire. Move mower deck to lowest position. Place blade engagement lever in disengaged position. Locate outside engine belt guard at right rear side of machine and remove one retaining bolt while loosening the other bolt. Pivot belt guard out and away from engine pulley. Locate inside engine pulley belt guard, remove one bolt, loosen other bolt and pivot guard out of way. Separate drive belt from engine pulley. Detach blade brake spring (8—Fig. W26), remove belt guard (7) and remove upper belt. Detach mower belt idler spring (13) and remove lower belt.

Install mower belts by reversing removal procedure.

Models R50 and R53

REMOVE AND REINSTALL. Before removing mower drive belt (5—Fig. W27), disconnect spark plug wire. Place lift and blade clutch lever in engaged position. Unbolt and remove belt guides at engine pulley. Unbolt and remove belt guards, belt guides or shoulder bolts at mower pulleys. Move lift and blade clutches to disengage position and remove belt from pulleys.

Install new belt by reversing removal procedure. Make certain belt guides, belt guards and shoulder bolts are properly installed.

Model R80

REMOVE AND REINSTALL. To remove mower drive belt (4—Fig. W28), place lift and blade clutch lever in disengaged position. Remove belt guides at engine pulley and slip mower drive belt from engine pulley. Move lift and blade

White

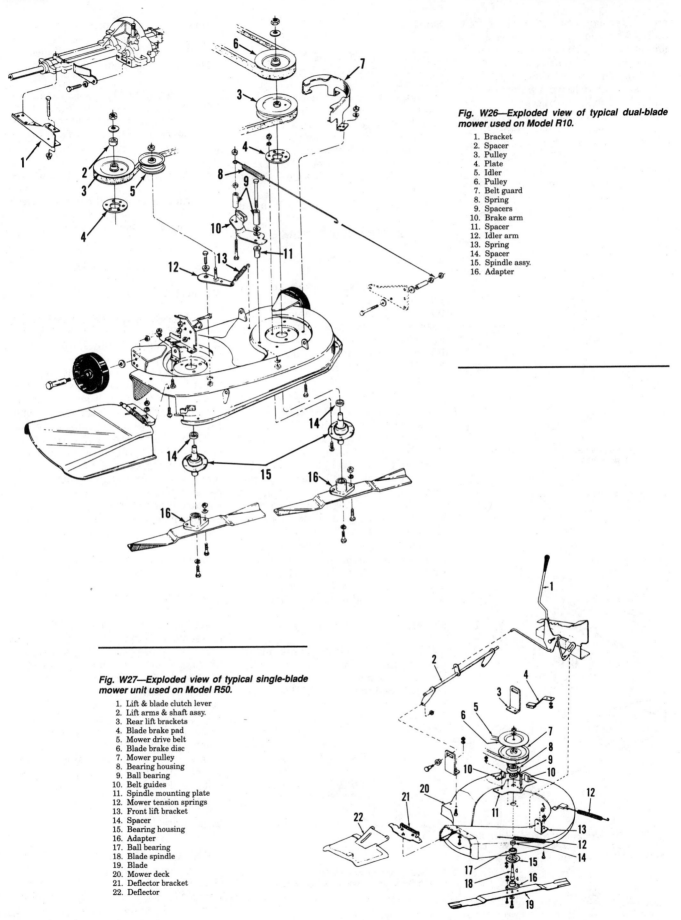

Fig. W26—Exploded view of typical dual-blade mower used on Model R10.

1. Bracket
2. Spacer
3. Pulley
4. Plate
5. Idler
6. Pulley
7. Belt guard
8. Spring
9. Spacers
10. Brake arm
11. Spacer
12. Idler arm
13. Spring
14. Spacer
15. Spindle assy.
16. Adapter

Fig. W27—Exploded view of typical single-blade mower unit used on Model R50.

1. Lift & blade clutch lever
2. Lift arms & shaft assy.
3. Rear lift brackets
4. Blade brake pad
5. Mower drive belt
6. Blade brake disc
7. Mower pulley
8. Bearing housing
9. Ball bearing
10. Belt guides
11. Spindle mounting plate
12. Mower tension springs
13. Front lift bracket
14. Spacer
15. Bearing housing
16. Adapter
17. Ball bearing
18. Blade spindle
19. Blade
20. Mower deck
21. Deflector bracket
22. Deflector

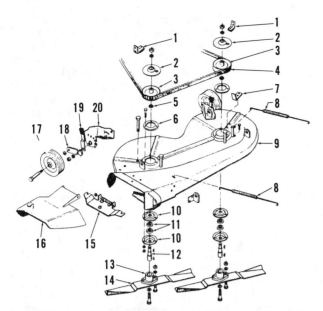

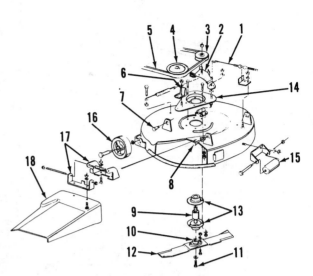

Fig. W28—Exploded view of dual-blade mower unit used on Model R80.

1. Blade brake pad
2. Brake disc
3. Mower pulley
4. Mower belt
5. Washer
6. Plate
7. Belt guide
8. Mower tension springs
9. Mower housing
10. Bearing retainers
11. Ball bearings
12. Blade spindle
13. Blade adapter
14. Blade
15. Deflector bracket
16. Deflector
17. Gauge wheel
18. Pivot bar
19. Adjusting lever
20. Wheel bracket

Fig. W29—Exploded view of typical single-blade mower unit used on Model R82.

1. Clutch cable
2. Idler & brake arm
3. Idler
4. Blade pulley
5. Blade belt
6. Belt guide
7. Rear mounting bolt
8. Front mounting bolt
9. Spindle & bearing assy.
10. Blade adapter
11. Center bolt
12. Blade
13. Bearing housings
14. Spindle mounting plate
15. Roller
16. Gauge wheel
17. Deflector hinge assy.
18. Deflector

clutch lever to lowest notch. Unbolt and remove belt guide (7) and belt keeper shoulder bolts from mower deck, then remove mower belt.

Install new belt by reversing removal procedure. Make certain belt guides are properly installed.

Models R82 and R86

REMOVE AND REINSTALL. To remove the mower drive belt (5—Fig. W29, Fig. W30 or Fig. W31) on Models R82 and R86, proceed as follows: Disconnect spark plug wire. Place blade engagement lever in disengaged position. Locate outside engine belt guard at right rear side of machine and remove one retaining bolt while loosening the other bolt. Pivot belt guard out and away from engine pulley. Disconnect blade brake cable from belt guide and remove belt guide. Disconnect mower deck links and remove belt guides from deck. Remove belt.

Install mower belt by reversing removal procedure.

MOWER DECK

All Models

REMOVE AND REINSTALL. Disconnect spark plug wire. Move mower deck to lowest position. Place blade engagement lever in disengaged position. Locate outside engine belt guard at right rear side of machine and remove one retaining bolt while loosening the

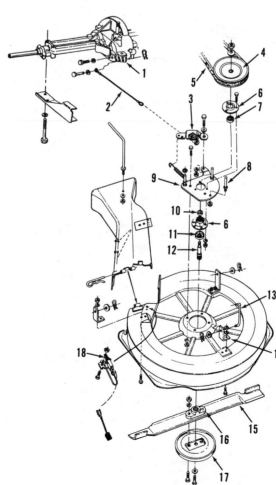

Fig. W30—Exploded view of mower deck used on some R86 models. Spindle components are available only as a unit assembly on later models.

1. Bracket
2. Blade brake cable
3. Blade brake assy.
4. Pulley
5. Mower belt
6. Bearing housing
7. Bearing
8. Belt keeper stud
9. Spindle plate
10. Spacer
11. Bearing shield
12. Blade spindle
13. Deck link
14. Hanger bracket
15. Blade
16. Blade adapter
17. Plate
18. Safety switch

other bolt. Pivot belt guard out and away from engine pulley. On models with a single mower blade, disconnect blade brake cable from belt guard and remove belt guard. On models with dual mower blades, locate inside engine pulley belt guard, remove one bolt, loosen other bolt and pivot guard out of way. Separate drive belt from engine pulley. Disconnect safety switch wire on models

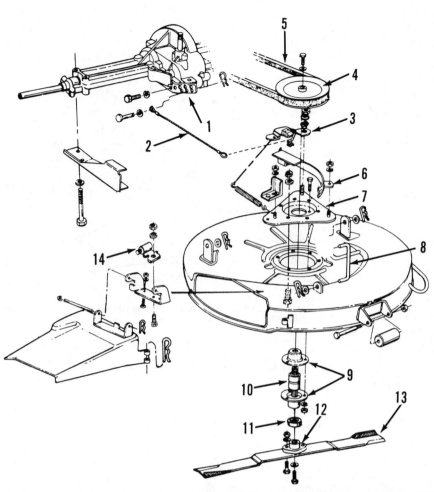

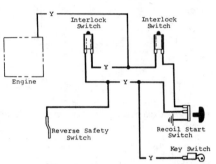

Fig. W33—Typical wiring schematic for Models R50 and R53. Wires marked "Y" are yellow.

Fig. W31—Exploded view of mower deck used on some R86 models. Spindle components are available only as a unit assembly on later models.

1. Bracket
2. Blade brake cable
3. Blade brake assy.
4. Pulley
5. Mower belt
6. Belt guard
7. Spindle mounting plate
8. Deck link
9. Bearing housing
10. Blade spindle assy.
11. Bearing shield
12. Blade adapter
13. Blade
14. Safety switch
24. Scalp plate

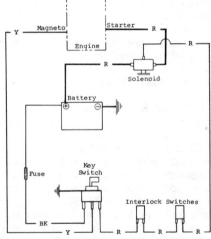

Fig. W34—Wiring diagram for Model R80. Wires marked "BK" are black, "R" are red and "Y" are yellow.

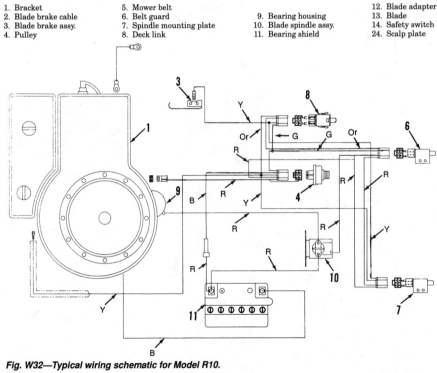

Fig. W32—Typical wiring schematic for Model R10.

B. Black
G. Green
Or. Orange
R. Red
Y. Yellow
1. Engine
3. Reverse gear switch
4. Ignition switch
6. Clutch switch
7. Blade engagement switch
8. Seat switch
9. Starter
10. Starter solenoid
11. Battery

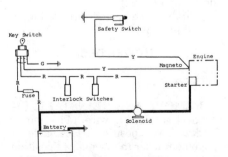

Fig. W35—Wiring diagram for Model R82. Wires marked "G" are green, "R" are red and "Y" are yellow.

Illustrations Courtesy White Outdoor Products

so equipped. Detach lift linkage from mower deck and remove mower deck.

Reinstall by reversing removal procedure. On models equipped with a blade brake cable, adjust cable as outlined in BLADE BRAKE section.

BLADE BRAKE

All Models So Equipped

ADJUSTMENT. On models equipped with a blade brake cable, adjust location of transaxle end of the brake cable as follows: Place mower deck in lowest position and move blade engagement lever to disengaged position. Attach cable (2—W31) end to rearmost hole in bracket (1) so cable has least amount of slack but no tension.

MOWER SPINDLE

All Models

LUBRICATION. Periodic lubrication of mower spindle is not required.

R&R AND OVERHAUL. Remove mower deck, belt(s) and blade(s). Refer to Figs. W26 through W31 for exploded views of mower decks and spindle assemblies. Spindle assembly on later models is available only as a unit assembly. Disassembly of spindle assembly is evident after inspection of unit and referral to exploded view. Inspect components for excessive wear and damage.

ELECTRICAL

All Models

Refer to Figs. W32 through W35 for wiring schematics. All switches must be in good operating condition for machine to operate properly.

WIZARD

WESTERN AUTO SUPPLY CO.
2107 Grand Avenue
Kansas City, MO 64108

Model	Make	Engine Model	Horsepower	Cutting Width, In.
7110	Tecumseh	TVM-220	10	38
7115	B&S	250000	11	38
7380	B&S	250000	10	36

For service information and procedures, use the following model cross reference and refer to the GILSON section of this manual. Parts are not necessarily interchangeable and should be obtained from Western Auto Co.

Wizard Models	Gilson Models
7110	52064
7115	52073
7380	52051C

TRANSMISSION REPAIR

The transmissions covered in this section are used in one or more makes and models of riding mowers. This section outlines the transmission overhaul procedures. Refer to the individual riding mower section for transmission R&R procedures.

Eaton transmissions are manufactured by the Eaton Corporation. Foote transmissions are manufactured by the J.B. Foote Foundry Co. Indus Wheel transmissions are manufactured by the Indus Wheel Co., Division of Carlisle Corporation. MTD transaxle is manufactured by MTD Products Inc. Peerless transmissions are manufactured by the Peerless Division of Tecumseh Products Co. Simplicity transmissions are manufactured by Simplicity Manufacturing Co.

EATON HYDROSTATIC

Model 7

OVERHAUL. The Model 7 transmission uses a ball piston type pump and motor as shown in flow diagram (Fig. E1). Two directional valves are used to maintain hydraulic pressure by allowing oil from the reservoir to enter the system. Transmission operation is as follows:

The ball piston pump is reversible and direction of high pressure oil to the ball piston motor is determined by location of shift lever. The ball piston motor will rotate according to the high pressure oil from the pump and transfer power to the reduction gears and differential. When the shift lever is in the neutral position, oil pressure is equal on both sides of motor and it will not turn. Directional valves open and close to allow oil from the reservoir to enter the low pressure line to replace oil which is lost from the system due to oil seepage or excess pressure. If direction valve

(V2) is forced to close due to high pressure in the adjoining oil line, then directional valve (V1) can open if low pressure in the adjoining line is not sufficient to keep valve (V1) closed and oil from reservoir can enter the system. If pump rotation is reversed, directional valve (V1) will be the high pressure valve and directional valve (V2) will be the low pressure valve.

CAUTION: If oil expansion reservoir is removed, precautions should be taken to prevent the entrance of dirt or other foreign material into transmission.

Before disassembling the transmission, thoroughly clean exterior of unit. Remove venting plug, invert assembly and drain fluid from unit. Remove transmission housing cap screws and place unit (output shaft downward) in a holding fixture similar to the one shown in Fig. E2. Remove aluminum housing (9—Fig. E3) with control shaft and input shaft assemblies.

CAUTION: Do not allow pump and cam ring assemblies (24 through 27) to lift with housing. If pump rotor is raised with housing, ball pistons may fall out of rotor.

The ball pistons (25) are selective fitted to rotor bores to a clearance of 0.0002-0.0006 inch (0.003-0.015 mm) and are not interchangeable. Place a wide rubber band around pump rotor (24) to prevent balls (25) from falling out of rotor. Remove cam ring (27) and pump race (26). Hold motor rotor (31) down and remove pintle assembly (30). Remove free wheeling valve bracket (18) and spring (19). Place a wide rubber band around motor rotor (31) to prevent balls (33) and spring (32) from falling

out of rotor. Remove motor assembly and motor race (39).

Remove snap ring (47), gear (46), spacer (45), retainer (44), snap ring (43) and key (38). Support body (40) and press output shaft (37) out of bearing (42) and oil seal (41). Ball bearing (42) and oil seal (41) can now be removed from body (40).

Remove retainer (1) and withdraw ball bearing (3) and input shaft (4). Bearing can be pressed from input shaft after removal of snap ring (2). Oil seal (5) can be removed from outside of housing. To remove the control shaft (22), drill an $\frac{11}{32}$-inch hole through aluminum housing (9) directly in line with center line of dowel pin. Press dowel pin from control shaft, remove snap ring (13) and washer (14) and withdraw control shaft. Remove oil seal (21). Thread the drilled hole with a $\frac{1}{8}$-inch pipe tap.

To remove the directional check valves from pintle (30), drill through the pintle with a drill bit that will pass freely through roll pins. Redrill the holes from the opposite side with a $\frac{1}{4}$-inch drill bit. Press roll pins from pintle. Using a $\frac{5}{16}$-18 tap, thread the inside of check valve bodies (36) and remove valve bodies using a draw bolt or a slide hammer puller. Remove check valve balls (35) and snap rings (34).

Number the piston bores (1 through 5) on pump rotor and on motor rotor. Use a plastic ice cube tray or equivalent and mark the cavities 1P-5P for the pump and 1M-5M, for the motor. Remove ball pistons (25) one at a time from pump rotor and place each ball in the correct cavity in the tray. Remove ball pistons (33) and springs (32) from motor rotor in the same manner.

Clean and inspect all parts and renew any showing excessive wear or any

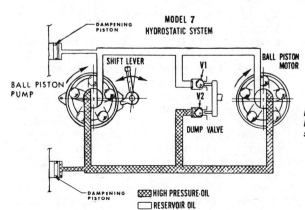

Fig. E1—Flow diagram of Eaton Model 7 hydrostatic transmission.

MODEL 7
HYDROSTATIC SYSTEM

DAMPENING PISTON

SHIFT LEVER

BALL PISTON PUMP

V1

V2

BALL PISTON MOTOR

DUMP VALVE

DAMPENING PISTON

▨ HIGH PRESSURE-OIL
☐ RESERVOIR OIL

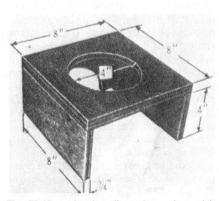

Fig. E2—View showing dimensions of wooden stand which may be used to disassemble and reassemble Eaton Model 7 hydrostatic transmission.

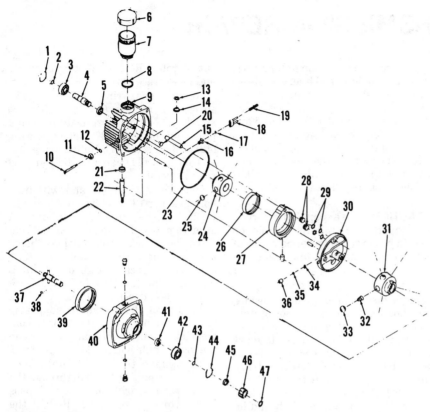

Fig. E3–Exploded view of Eaton Model 7 hydrostatic transmission.

1. Retainer	13. Retaining ring	24. Pump rotor	36. Check valve body
2. Snap ring	14. Control shaft	25. Pump ball pistons	37. Output shaft
3. Ball earing	washer	26. Pump race	38. Key
4. Input shaft	15. Pivot pin	27. Pump cam ring	39. Motor race
5. Oil seal	16. Guide	28. Dampening pistons	40. Body
6. Reservoir cap	17. "O" ring	29. "O" ring	41. Oil seal
7. Reservoir	18. Bracket	30. Pintle	42. Ball bearing
8. Gasket	19. Spring	31. Motor rotor	43. Snap ring
9. Housing	20. Dowel pin	32. Spring	44. Retainer
10. Free wheeling valve	21. Oil seal	33. Motor ball pistons	45. Spacer
11. Nut	22. Control shaft	34. Retaining ring	46. Drive gear
12. "O" ring	23. Square cut seal ring	35. Ball, Grade 200	47. Snap ring

other damage. Ball pistons are selective fitted to 0.0002-0.0006 inch (0.003-0.015 mm) clearance and must be reinstalled in their original bores. If rotor bushings are scored or badly worn, 0.002 inch (0.51 mm) or more clearance on pintle journals, renew pump rotor or motor rotor assemblies. Install ball pistons (25) in pump rotor (24) and ball pistons (33) and springs (32) in motor rotor (31) and use wide rubber bands to hold pistons in their bores. Install snap rings (34), check valve balls (35) and valve bodies (36) in pintle (30) and secure with new roll pins. Renew oil seals (5 and 21) and reinstall control shaft and input shaft in housing (9) by reversing the removal procedure. When installing oil seals (5, 21 or 41), apply a thin coat of Loctite grade #271 to a ⅛-inch pipe plug and install plug in the drilled and tapped disassembly hole. Tighten plug until snug. Do not overtighten. Renew oil seal (41) and reinstall output shaft (37), bearing (42),

snap rings, retainer, spacer and gear in body (40).

All components must be clean and dry before assembly. Place the aluminum housing assembly in the holding fixture with input shaft (4) pointing downward. Install pump cam ring (27) and race (26) on pivot pin (15) and dowel pin. Cam ring insert must be installed in cam ring with the hole to the outside. If insert is installed upside down, it will contact housing and interfere with assembly. Cam ring must move freely from stop to stop. Install the pump rotor assembly and remove the rubber band used to retain pistons. Install free-wheeling valve components (11, 12, 16 and 17). Install free-wheeling valve bracket (18) and springs (19). Install pintle assembly over cam pivot pin and into pump rotor. Place new "O" ring (23) in position on housing. Lay housing assembly on its side on a clean surface. Place the body assembly in the holding fixture with output shaft pointing

downward. Install motor race (39) in body, then install motor rotor assembly aligning the rotor slot with drive pin on output shaft. Remove rubber band used to retain pistons in rotor. Place body and motor assembly on its side so that motor rotor is facing pintle in housing assembly. Slide the assemblies together and align the two assembly bolt holes. Install the two transmission housing cap screws and tighten them to a torque of 15 ft.-lbs. (20 N•m). Rotate input shaft and output shaft. Both shafts should rotate freely. If not, disassemble the unit and correct as needed.

Screw free wheeling valve into transmission and install transmission in tractor. Fill reservoir to level indicated on reservoir. Check and adjust linkage as needed.

FOOTE

Models 35-3500

OVERHAUL. To disassemble the forward-reverse single speed transmissions, refer to Fig. FT1 and remove retaining ring (5), output sprocket (4) and key (3). Unbolt and remove case half (7). Remove bevel gear (8) and input shaft assembly (18 through 23). Remove retaining ring (14) and washer (15), then withdraw output shaft (2) and key (1). Remove shift dog (9) and shift fork (10), being careful not to lose detent ball and spring (12 and 13). Bevel gear (17) can now be removed. Remove snap ring (18), input bevel pinion (19) and flanged bushings (20) from input shaft (21). If necessary, flanged bushings (6 and 16) can be removed from case halves (7 and 11).

Clean and inspect all parts and renew any showing excessive wear or other damage. Lubricate shafts, gears and bushings and reassemble by reversing the disassembly procedure. Fill case halves with approximately 5 oz. (0.14 kg) of Shell Darina "AX" (35) or "O" (3500) or equivalent grease. Install housing bolts and tighten securely.

Models 2140-2240

OVERHAUL. To disassemble the 2-speed transmissions, refer to Fig. FT2, then unbolt and remove the cover and shifter assembly (1 through 10). Lift drive shaft and output shaft assemblies straight upward out of case (35). Remove retaining ring (11), washer (12), flanged bushing (13), bevel spur gear (19) and shift dog (18) from drive shaft (14). Then, remove retaining ring (11), washer (12), flanged bushing (13), spur gear (15), Woodruff key, washer (16) and bevel gear (17) from opposite end of

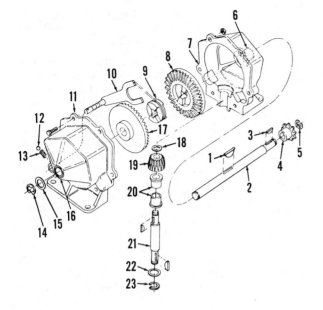

Fig. FT1–Exploded view of typical Models 35 and 3500 Foote single speed, forward-reverse transmissions.

1. Hi-pro key
2. Output shaft
3. Woodruff key
4. Output sprocket
5. Retaining ring
6. Flanged bushing
7. Case half
8. Bevel gear
9. Shift dog
10. Shift fork
11. Case half
12. Detent ball
13. Spring
14. Retaining ring
15. Washer
16. Flanged bushing
17. Bevel gear
18. Snap ring
19. Input bevel pinion
20. Flanged bushings
21. Input shaft
22. Washer
23. Snap ring

drive sprocket (13) can be removed from drive shaft (11) and chain (33). Remove the chain to separate the shafts. Remove shift dog (14) and its hi-pro key, first drive gear (15) and washer (16). From opposite end of shaft, remove bushing (25), washer (24), retaining ring (23), third drive gear (22), shift dog (21) and its hi-pro key, second drive gear (20), snap ring (19), washer (18) and bevel gear (17). Remove retaining ring (23), output sprocket (35), washer (24), bushing (25), reverse driven sprocket (32) and spring (31) from output shaft (34). From opposite end of shaft, remove brake disc (43), retaining ring (23), washer (24), bushing (25) third speed gear (26), spring (27), second speed gear (28), spacer (29) and first speed gear (30). Remove snap ring (41) and washer (40), then withdraw input shaft and bevel pinion assembly (37). Remove snap ring (36) and press input pinion from input shaft. If necessary, remove bushings (38 and 39) from case (42). Unbolt and remove brake assembly (44 through 51). To disassemble the cover and shifter assembly, remove the four screws and carefully raise shifter cover (2). Remove shift lever (1), cover (2), nylon insert (3), wave washer (6) and detent balls and springs (4 and 5) from

shaft. Remove brake disc (20), retaining ring (11), washer (12), flanged bushing (13), gear (21) and shift dog (22) from output shaft (26). Remove retaining ring (11), output sprocket (27), washer (12), flanged bushing (13), gear (25), Woodruff key and washer (24). Remove snap ring (28) and bevel pinion (29) and withdraw input shaft (32) from bottom of case (35). Unbolt and remove brake assembly (36 through 43). To disassemble the cover and shifter assembly, remove the five shoulder screws (10), shift forks (6), detent balls, springs and washer (7, 8 and 9). Remove the four screws and lift off shifter cover (1), shift lever (3) and cam plate (4) with nylon slides (2).

Clean and inspect all parts and renew any showing excessive wear or other damage. Lubricate all gears, shafts and bushings and reassemble by reversing the disassembly procedure. Make certain that locator tangs on flanged bushings (13) are seated in notches in case (35). Backlash between input bevel pinion (29) and bevel gears (17 and 19) should be 0.001-0.015 inch (0.03-0.38 mm). End play should be 0.001-0.015 inch (0.03-0.38 mm) for drive shaft (14) and 0.001-0.012 inch (0.03-0.30 mm) for output shaft (26). Fill case and cover the gears with approximately 14 oz. (0.40 kg) of Shell Darina "O" grease or equivalent lithium grease. Install cover (5) and tighten cap screws to a torque of 80-90 in.lbs. (9-10 N·m). Renew brake pads (36) as necessary and reinstall brake assembly.

Models 2010-2210

OVERHAUL. To disassemble the 3-speed transmission, refer to Fig. FT3

and place shift lever in neutral position. Unbolt and remove transmission cover and shifter assembly (1 through 10). Lift drive shaft and output shaft assemblies straight upward out of case (42). Move sprocket end of shafts together until flanged bushing (12) and reverse

Fig. FT2–Exploded view of typical Models 2140 and 2240 Foote 2-speed transmission.

1. Shifter cover
2. Nylon slide (2)
3. Shift lever
4. Cam plate
5. Transmission cover
6. Shift forks
7. Detent ball (2)
8. Spring (2)
9. Washer
10. Shoulder screw
11. Retaining ring
12. Washer
13. Flanged bushing
14. Drive shaft
15. Spur gear (22T)
16. Washer
17. Bevel gear
18. Shift dog
19. Bevel spur gear
20. Brake disc
21. Spur gear (22T)
22. Shift dog
23. Snap ring
24. Washer
25. Spur gear (28T)
26. Output shaft
27. Output sprocket
28. Snap ring
29. Input bevel pinion
30. Flanged bushing
31. Straight bushing
32. Input shaft
33. Washer
34. Snap ring
35. Transmission case
36. Brake pads
37. Back plate
38. Adjusting screw
39. Shoulder bolt
40. Washer
41. Brake lever
42. Brake caliper
43. Spring

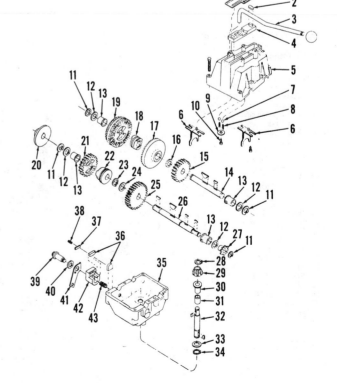

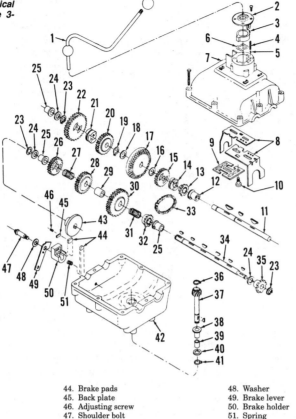

Fig. FT3—Exploded view of typical Models 2010 and 2210 Foote 3-speed transmission.

1. Shift lever
2. Shifter cover
3. Nylon insert
4. Spring (2)
5. Detent ball (2)
6. Wave washer
7. Transmission cover
8. Shift forks
9. Interlock plate
10. Shoulder bolt (4)
11. Drive shaft
12. Flanged bushing
13. Reverse drive sprocket
14. First & Rev. shift dog
15. First drive gear
16. Washer
17. Bevel gear
18. Washer
19. Snap ring
20. Second drive gear
21. Second & third shift dog
22. Third drive gear
23. Retaining ring
24. Washer
25. Flanged bushing
26. Third speed gear
27. Spring
28. Second speed gear
29. Spacer
30. First speed gear
31. Spring
32. Reverse driven sprocket
33. Chain
34. Output shaft
35. Output sprocket
36. Snap ring
37. Input shaft & bevel pinion
38. Flanged bushing
39. Straight bushing
40. Washer
41. Snap ring
42. Transmission case
43. Brake disc
44. Brake pads
45. Back plate
46. Adjusting screw
47. Shoulder bolt
48. Washer
49. Brake lever
50. Brake holder
51. Spring

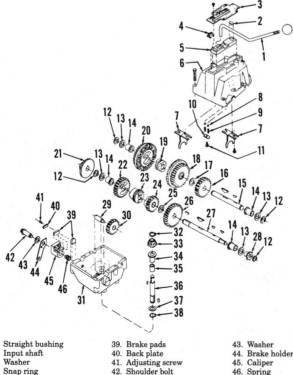

Fig. FT4—Exploded view of typical Model 2500 Foote 3-speed transmission.

1. Shift lever
2. Nylon slide (2)
3. Shifter cover
4. Safety starting switch
5. Cam plate
6. Transmission cover
7. Shift forks
8. Detent ball
9. Spring
10. Retaining plate
11. Shoulder screw
12. Retaining ring
13. Washer
14. Flanged bushing
15. Drive shaft
16. Spur gear
17. Washer
18. Bevel spur gear
19. Shift dog
20. Bevel & spur gear
21. Brake disc
22. Spur gear (25T)
23. Shift dog
24. Spur gear (17T)
25. Washer
26. Spur gear (28T)
27. Output shaft
28. Output sprocket
29. Idler shaft
30. Idler gear
31. Transmission case
32. Snap ring
33. Input bevel pinion
34. Flanged bushing
35. Straight bushing
36. Input shaft
37. Washer
38. Snap ring
39. Brake pads
40. Back plate
41. Adjusting screw
42. Shoulder bolt
43. Washer
44. Brake holder
45. Caliper
46. Spring

top of cover (7). Remove the four shoulder bolts (10), interlock plate (9) and shift forks (8) from bottom of cover.

Clean and inspect all parts and renew any showing excessive wear or other damage. Lubricate all gears, shafts and bushings and reassemble by reversing the disassembly procedure. Make certain that shift dogs (14 and 21) slide freely on the hi-pro keys. When installing drive shaft and output shaft assemblies, locator tangs on flanged bushings (12 and 25) must be seated in notches in case (42). Backlash between input bevel pinion and bevel gear (17) should be 0.001-0.015 inch (0.03-0.38 mm). End play should be 0.001-0.015 inch (0.03-0.38 mm) for the drive shaft (11) and 0.001-0.012 inch (0.03-0.30 mm) for the output shaft (34). Fill case and cover the gears, reverse sprockets and chain with approximately 14 oz. (0.40 kg) of Shell Darina "O" grease or equivalent No. 2 lithium grease. Install cover and shifter assembly, making certain that shift forks (8) engage slots in shift dogs (14 and 21). Tighten transmission cover cap screws to a torque of 80-90 in.-lbs. (9-10 N•m). Renew brake pads (44) as necessary and reinstall brake assembly.

Model 2500

OVERHAUL. To disassemble the 3-speed transmission, refer to Fig. FT4, then unbolt and remove transmission cover and shifter assembly (1 through 11). Lift drive shaft and output shaft assemblies straight upward out of case (31). Remove retaining ring (12), washer (13), flanged bushing (14), gear (16) and its Woodruff key, washer (17) and bevel spur gear (18) from drive shaft (15). Then, remove retaining ring (12), washer (13), flanged bushing (14), bevel spur gear (20) and shift dog (19) from opposite end of drive shaft. Remove retaining ring (12), output sprocket (28), washer (13), flanged bushing (14), gear (26), Woodruff key, washer (25) and gear (24 from output shaft. Remove brake disc (21), retaining ring (12), washer (13), flanged bushing (14), gear (22) and shift dog (23) from opposite end of shaft. Remove idler gear (30) and shaft (29). Remove snap ring (32), input bevel pinion (33) and key from input shaft (36), then withdraw input shaft from bottom of case. If necessary, remove bushings (34 and 35). Unbolt and remove brake assembly (39 through 46). To disassemble the cover and shifter assembly, remove the five shoulder screws (11), shift forks (7), detent balls (8), springs (9) and retaining plate (10). Remove the four screws and lift off shifter cover (3), shift lever (1) and cam plate (5) with nylon slides (2).

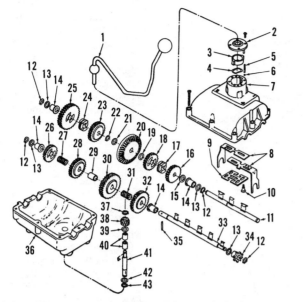

Fig. FT5–Exploded view of Foote 4-speed transmission. This transmission is not equipped with reverse gears.

1. Shift lever	12. Snap ring	23. Third drive gear	33. Output shaft
2. Shifter cover	13. Washer	24. Shift dog	34. Output sprocket
3. Nylon insert	14. Flanged bearing	25. Fourth drive gear	35. Roll pin
4. Wave washer	15. Thrust washer	26. Fourth speed gear	36. Transmission case
5. Spring (2)	16. Second drive gear	27. Spring	37. Snap ring
6. Detent ball (2)	17. Shift dog	28. Third speed gear	38. Input bevel pinion
7. Transmission cover	18. First drive gear	29. Spacer	39. Thrust washer
8. Shifter forks	19. Washer	30. First speed gear	40. Needle bearings
9. Interlock plate	20. Bevel gear	31. Spring	41. Input shaft
10. Shoulder bolt (4)	21. Washer	32. Second speed gear	42. Washer
11. Drive shaft	22. Snap ring		43. Snap ring

Clean and inspect all parts and renew any showing excessive wear or other damage. Lubricate all gears, shafts and bushings and reassemble by reversing the disassembly procedure. Make certain that shift dogs (19 and 23) slide freely on the hi-pro keys. When installing drive shaft and output shaft assemblies, locator tangs on flanged bushings (14) must be seated in notches in case (31). Backlash between input bevel pinion (33) and bevel spur gears (18 and 20) should be 0.001-0.015 inch (0.03-0.38 mm). End play should be 0.001-0.015 inch (0.03-0.38 mm) for the drive shaft (15) and 0.001-0.012 inch (0.03-0.30 mm) for the output shaft (27). Fill case and cover the gears, reverse sprockets and chain with approximately 12 oz. (0.34 kg) of Shell Darina "O" grease or equivalent No. 2 lithium grease. Install cover and shifter assembly, making certain that shift forks (7) engage slots in shift dogs (19 and 23). Tighten transmission cover cap screws to a torque of 80-90 in.-lbs. (9-10 N•m). Renew brake pads (39) as necessary and reinstall brake assembly.

Model 4-Speed W/No Reverse

OVERHAUL. To disassemble the 4-speed transmission, refer to Fig. FT5

and place shift lever in neutral position. Unbolt and remove transmission cover and shifter assembly (1 through 10). Lift drive shaft and output shaft assemblies straight upward out of case (36). Remove snap ring (12), washer (13), flanged bushing (14), thrust washer (15), second drive gear (16), shift dog (17) and its hi-pro key, first drive gear (18) and washer (19) from drive shaft (11). Then, remove snap ring (12), washer (13), flanged bushing (14), fourth drive gear (23), snap ring (22), washer (21) and bevel gear (20). Remove snap ring (12), output sprocket (34), washer (13), flanged bushing (14), second speed gear (32), spring (31) and first speed gear (30) from output shaft (33). From opposite end of shaft, remove snap ring (12), washer (13), flanged bushing (14), fourth speed gear (26), spring (27), third speed gear (28) and spacer (29). Remove snap ring (37), input bevel pinion (38) and thrust washer (39), then withdraw input shaft (41) from bottom of case (36). If necessary, press needle bearing (40) from case. To disassemble the cover and shifter assembly, remove the four screws and carefully raise shifter cover (2). Remove shift lever (1), cover (2), nylon insert (3), wave washer (4) and detent balls and spring (5 and 6) from top of cover (7). Remove the four

shoulder bolts (10), interlock plate (9) and shift forks (8) from bottom of cover.

Clean and inspect all parts and renew any showing excessive wear or other damage. lubricate all gears, shafts, needle bearings and bushings and reassemble by reversing the disassembly procedure. Keep the following points in mind: Shift dogs (17 and 24) must slide freely on the hi-pro keys. Locator tangs on flanged bushings (14) must be seated in notches in case (36). Backlash between input bevel pinion (38) and bevel gear (20) should be 0.001-0.015 inch (0.03-0.38 mm). End play should be 0.001-0.015 inch (0.03-0.38 mm) for the drive shaft (11) and 0.001-0.012 inch (0.03-0.30 mm) for the output shaft (33).

Fill case and cover the gears with approximately 10 oz. (0.28 kg) of Shell Darina "O" grease or equivalent No. 2 lithium grease. Install cover and shifter assembly, making certain that shift forks (8) engage slots in shift dogs (17 and 24). Tighten transmission cover cap screws to a torque of 80-90 in.-lbs. (9-10 N•m).

Model 2600

OVERHAUL. To disassemble the 5-speed transmission, refer to Fig. FT6 and unbolt and remove transmission cover and shifter assembly (1 through 16). Raise output shaft (30) slightly and remove shift fork, fork pivot and pivot bushing (52 through 55). Lift drive shaft and output shaft assemblies straight upward out of case (56). Move sprocket end of shafts together until flanged bushing (17) and reverse drive sprocket (26) can be removed from drive shaft (27) and chain (31). Remove the chain to separate the shafts. Remove first and second drive gear (25), spacer (24) and bevel gear (23) from drive shaft (27). Then, remove flanged bushing (17), fifth drive gear (18), fourth drive gear (19), third drive gear (20), washer (21) and spacer (22). Remove snap ring (28), output sprocket (29), flanged bushing (17), reverse driven sprocket (32), first speed gear (33) and second speed gear (34). From opposite end of output shaft, remove brake disc (43), flanged bushing (17), washer (42), fifth speed gear (41), fourth speed gear (40) and third speed gear (39). Carefully slide driving hubs (36) from output shaft. Identify and remove driving key assemblies (35), retaining washers (37) and collar (38). Right side driving key assemblies (1st, 2nd and reverse) have shortest distance between the key drive lugs. Do not interchange with left side key assemblies (3rd, 4th and 5th). Remove snap ring

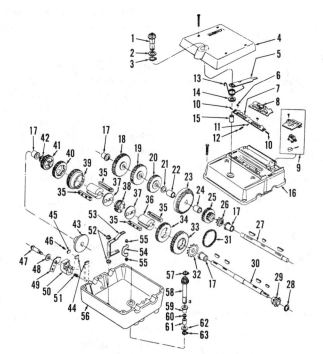

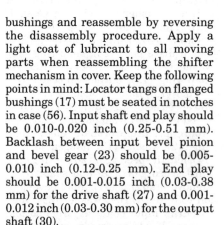

Fig. FT6–Exploded view of typical Model 2600 Foote 5-speed transmission.

1. Pivot shaft	17. Flanged bushing	33. First speed gear	48. Washer
2. Washer	18. Fifth drive gear	34. Second speed gear	49. Brake lever
3. Snap ring	19. Fourth drive gear	35. Driving key assemblies	50. Brake holder
4. Shifter cover	20. Third drive gear	36. Driving hubs	51. Spring
5. Actuator cover	21. Washer	37. Key retaining washers	52. Pivot bushings
6. Retaining clips	22. Spacer (short)	38. Collar	53. Shift fork
7. Interlock plate	23. Bevel gear	39. Third speed gear	54. Fork pivot
8. Interlock pawl & carrier	24. Spacer (long)	40. Fourth speed gear	55. Pivot bushings
9. Safety starting switch	25. First & second drive gear	41. Fifth speed gear	56. Transmission case
10. Springs	26. Reverse drive sprocket	42. Washer	57. Snap ring
11. Detent pin	27. Drive shaft	43. Brake disc	58. Input shaft & pinion
12. Detent spring	28. Snap ring	44. Brake pads	59. Flanged bushing
13. Torsion spring	29. Output sprocket	45. Back plate	60. "O" ring
14. Washer	30. Output shaft	46. Adjusting screw	61. Straight bushing
15. Sleeve bushing	31. Chain	47. Shoulder bolt	62. Washer
16. Transmission cover	32. Reverse driven sprocket		63. Snap ring

(63) and washer (62), then withdraw input shaft assembly from case. Remove snap ring (57) and bevel pinion from input shaft (58). Bushings (59 and 61) and "O" ring (60) can now be removed from case (56). Unbolt and remove brake assembly (43 through 51). To disassemble the cover and shifter assembly, remove shift lever, then unbolt and remove shifter cover (4). Remove snap ring (3) and washer (2) from bottom of cover (16) and remove pivot shaft (1), actuator lever (5), torsion spring (13) and washer (14) from top of cover. Remove clips (6) and lift out interlock plate (7) and springs (10). Remove pawl and carrier (8), detent pin (11) and spring (12). Press sleeve bushing (15) from cover. If necessary, remove safety starting switch (9).

Clean and inspect all parts and renew any showing excessive wear or other damage. Lubricate all gears, shafts and

bushings and reassemble by reversing the disassembly procedure. Apply a light coat of lubricant to all moving parts when reassembling the shifter mechanism in cover. Keep the following points in mind: Locator tangs on flanged bushings (17) must be seated in notches in case (56). Input shaft end play should be 0.010-0.020 inch (0.25-0.51 mm). Backlash between input bevel pinion and bevel gear (23) should be 0.005-0.010 inch (0.12-0.25 mm). End play should be 0.001-0.015 inch (0.03-0.38 mm) for the drive shaft (27) and 0.001-0.012 inch (0.03-0.30 mm) for the output shaft (30).

Fill case to centerline of shafts (27 and 30) with Shell Darina "O" grease or equivalent No. 2 lithium grease. Install transmission cover and shifter assembly as follows: Place lever end of shift fork (53) directly over bevel gear (23). Center the actuator lever (5) and inter-

lock pawl (8) in cover (16). Carefully set cover assembly on the case. Make certain that top pivot bushing (52) is seated properly in cover and that pin on interlock pawl (8) is engaged in slot in shift fork (53). Tighten transmission cover cap screws to a torque of 80-90 in.-lbs. (9-10 N•m). Renew brake pads (44) as necessary and reinstall brake assembly.

Model 4000

OVERHAUL. To disassemble transaxle, place shift lever in neutral and remove drive pulley. Remove shoulder bolt from brake assembly and remove brake caliper (69—Fig. FT7), spring (70), brake pads (71), brake disc (72) and Woodruff key. Unbolt and remove shift lever and cover. Remove the two set screws (10 and 12) from case, turn transmission over and catch detent spring (13) and balls.

With transmission upside down, remove case bolts and separate case halves with a plastic hammer or rubber mallet. Lift drive shaft assembly (44) out. All parts on drive shaft are a slip fit. Lift intermediate shaft assembly out and remove "E" ring (20) from one end. Slide parts off shaft, being careful to keep parts in order. Push axles together as differential assembly is removed. Axle bevel gears are a press fit; all other parts are slip fit. Further disassembly is evident after examination.

Clean and inspect all parts and renew any showing excessive wear or damage. Before installing input shaft, pack needle bearings with grease. Install Hi-Lo shift mechanism and check for free action. Apply a light coating of grease to reverse idler shaft and gear and torque mounting bolt to 80-90 in.-lbs (9-10 N•m). Assemble intermediate shaft with light coating of grease and new "E" rings (20). Intermediate and drive shaft end play is 0.020-0.030 inch (0.51-0.76 mm). End play is adjusted by changing shim thickness as shown in Fig. FT8. Input shaft end play is 0.010-0.020 inch (0.25-0.51 mm). End play is adjusted by changing shim washer (21—Fig. FT7) under snap ring (36). When installing detent balls, springs and set screws, tighten set screws until heads are flush with top of case.

Pack axle cavities in both case halves with grease. Use 24 oz. (0.68 kg) of Shell Darina "O" or equivalent grease spread equally in main part of gearcase. Tighten 14 case bolts to 80-90 in.-lbs. (9-10 N•m). Tighten center bolt to 100-110 in.-lbs. (11-12 N•m). Adjust brake assembly as previously described.

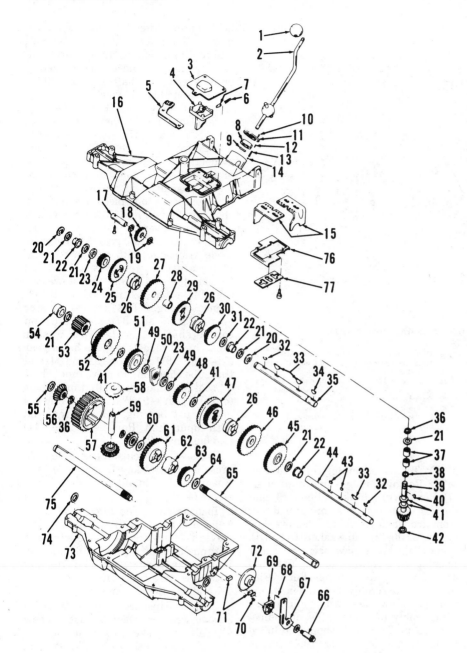

Fig. FT7–Exploded view of Foote Model 4000 sliding gear transmission.

1. Knob		41. Shim washer	
2. Shift lever		42. Snap ring	
3. Cover plate		43. Woodruff key #3	
4. Shift fork		special	
5. Hi-Lo shift lever		44. Drive shaft	
6. Detent spring		45. Gear (20T)	
7. Pin		46. Gear (33T)	
8. Nylon insert		47. Bevel gear assy.	
9. Wave washer		48. Gear (20T)	
10. Set screw		49. Shim washer	
11. Nylon cover		50. Shaft support assy.	
12. Set screw		51. Gear (25T)	
13. Spring		52. Gear (37T)	
14. Detent ball		53. Gear assy. (12T)	
15. Shift fork		54. Bearing	
16. Case half		55. Shim	
17. Idler shaft		56. Bevel gear (15T)	
18. Reverse idler gear		splined	
19. Washer		57. Spur gear (32T)	
20. "E" ring		58. Bevel gears	
21. Shim washer		59. Cross shaft	
22. Bearing		60. Shim	
23. Spacer		61. Spur gear (35T)	
24. Spur gear (13T)		62. Gear lock	
25. Spur gear (25T)		63. Spur gear (22T)	
26. Clutch collar		64. Shim	
27. Spur gear (30T)		65. Axle shaft R.H.	
28. Spacer		66. Shoulder bolt	
29. Spur gear (25T)		67. Brake lever	
30. Spur gear (20T)		68. Set screw	
31. Shim washer		69. Brake caliper	
32. Woodruff key #3		70. Spring	
33. Hi-pro key		71. Brake pads	
34. Woodruff key #61		72. Brake disc	
35. Intermediate shaft		73. Case half	
36. Snap ring		74. Felt seal	
37. Needle bearings		75. Axle shaft L.H.	
38. "O" ring		76. Support plate	
39. Input shaft		77. Lock-out plate	
40. Key			

INDUS WHEEL

Model 1138

OVERHAUL. To disassemble the transmission, refer to Fig. IWT1 and remove the eight cap screws (4). Remove cover and shifter assembly (1 through 11) and gasket (12). Lift drive shaft assembly from case (32) and separate bearings (13) and reverse drive gear (15) from drive shaft and gear assembly (14). Remove the output shaft assembly and remove snap ring (16), brake drum (17), thrust washers (18), bearing (13) and third speed gear (19). Remove snap ring (20), thrust washer (18), second and third shift dog (21), flat key (25) and thrust washer (18). Remove snap ring

(20), second speed gear (22), spacer (23) and first speed gear (24). Remove snap ring (20), thrust washer (18), first and reverse shift dog (28), flat key (25) and thrust washer (18). Remove snap ring (20), reverse gear (27), bearing (13), thrust washers (18) and last snap ring (20) from output shaft (26). Remove snap ring (34) and thrust washer (33), then withdraw input shaft and pinion assembly (29). Flanged bushing (30) and seal ring (31) can now be removed from bore in case.

To disassemble the cover and shifter assembly, hold downward on plate (2) and remove the four retaining screws (1). Carefully raise plate (2) and shift lever (3) so that springs (7) do not fly out. Invert the cover (6) and remove

Fig. FT8–View showing shim location in Foote Model 4000 transmission.

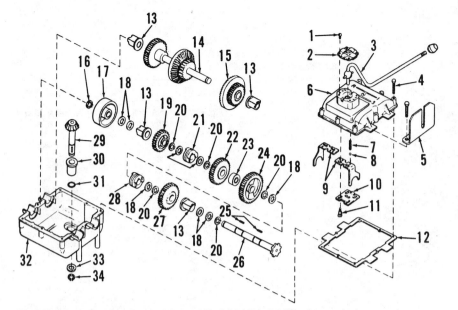

Fig. IWT1–Exploded view of typical 3-speed Model 11385 Indus Wheel transmission.

1. Screw (4)
2. Plate
3. Shift lever
4. Cap screw (8)
5. Shift bracket
6. Transmission cover
7. Spring
8. Detent ball
9. Shift forks
10. Backing plate
11. Shoulder bolt (4)
12. Gasket
13. Bearing
14. Drive shaft & gears assy.
15. Bevel spur gear (rev. drive)
16. Snap ring
17. Brake drum
18. Thrust washers
19. Third speed gear
20. Snap ring
21. Shift dog (2nd & 3rd)
22. Second speed gear
23. Spacer
24. First speed gear
25. Flat keys
26. Output shaft
27. Reverse gear
28. Shift dog (1st & Rev.)
29. Input shaft & pinion
30. Flanged bushing
31. Seal ring
32. Transmission case
33. Thrust washer
34. Snap ring

springs and detent balls (8). Remove the four shoulder bolts (11), backing plate (10) and shift forks (9).

Clean and inspect all parts and renew any showing excessive wear or other damage. When reassembling, install new seal ring (31) and install bushing (30). Lubricate bushing and input shaft (29), then install input shaft, thrust washer (33) and snap ring (34). Place approximately 7 oz. (0.20 kg) of Shell EPRO #71030 grease or equivalent in the case (32). Lubricate all gears, bearings and shafts, then using Fig. IWT1 as a guide, reassemble both shaft assemblies. Place shaft assemblies in case and apply approximately 3.5 oz. (0.10 kg) of the recommended grease over all gears. Make certain the flats on bearings (13) are level with case surface and install new gasket (12). Reassemble cover and shifter assembly by reversing the disassembly procedure. Reinstall cover and shifter assembly, making certain that shift forks (9) engage slots in shift dogs (21 and 28). Install shift bracket (5) and tighten cover retaining cap screws (4) securely.

MTD

Model 717-0775 Transaxle

OVERHAUL. Model 717-0775 is a single speed transaxle manufactured by

MTD. To disassemble, refer to Fig. MTD. Remove pulley from input shaft (7). Remove disc brake caliper (49) and disc (15). Remove inner brake pad (53) from transaxle housing. Remove key (1), snap ring (2) and washers (3 and 4). Remove the cap screws securing upper housing (5) to lower housing (54) and carefully separate housings. Remove input shaft assembly (7). Refer to exploded view for any necessary disassembly or reassembly of component parts. Transaxle should be lubricated by packing 10 oz. (0.28 kg) of grease (Part #737-0148) prior to joining housings.

PEERLESS

Series 600 Transaxle

OVERHAUL. To disassemble the transaxle, remove drain plug and drain lubricant. Remove brake assembly, input pulley and rear wheel assemblies. Place shift lever in neutral position, then unbolt and remove shift lever and housing assembly. Unbolt and remove axle housings (16 and 52—Fig. PT1). Place unit in a vise so that heads of socket head cap screws are pointing upward. Drive dowel pins out of case and cover. Unscrew socket head cap screws and lift off cover (55). Install two or three socket head screws into case to

hold center plate (76) down while removing the differential assembly. Pull differential assembly straight up out of case. It may be necessary to gently bump lower axle shaft to loosen differential assembly. Remove center plate (76). Hold shift rods (19) together and lift out shifter rods, forks (20), shifter stop (23), shaft (27), sliding gears (25 and 26) and spur gear (24). On early model transaxle, remove idler shaft (29) and gear (30) as individual parts. On late model transaxle, remove idler shaft and gear as a one-piece assembly as shown in 29A—Fig. PT3A. On all models, remove reverse idler shaft (79—Fig. PT1), spacer (80) and gear (81). On early model transaxle, with reference to Fig. PT1, remove cluster gears (35, 36 and 37) on sleeve (41) and thrust washer (42). On late model transaxle, with reference to Fig. PT3A, remove cluster gears (35, 36 and 37), spacers (S) on countershaft (C) and thrust washer (42). On all models remove bevel gear (31—Fig. PT1), washers (32 and 34) and thrust bearing (33). Remove input shaft oil seal (9), snap ring (10), input shaft (48) and gear (49). Washers (45 and 47) and thrust bearing (46) are removed with input shaft. Remove bearing (11) and bushing (12).

To disassemble cluster gear assembly, press gears and key from sleeve (41). Bushings (38 and 40) are renewable in sleeve (41).

To disassemble the differential, drive roll pin (71) out of drive pin (74). Remove drive pin, thrust washers (63 and 66) and differential pinions (64 and 65). Remove snap rings (56 and 70) and withdraw axle shafts from side gears (57 and 69). Remove side gears.

Clean and inspect components for excessive wear or other damage. Renew all seals and gaskets. Check for binding of shift forks on shift rods. When reassembling, position shift forks in neutral position by aligning notches on shift rods with notch in shifter stop. See Fig. PT2. Install input shaft assembly by reversing the removal procedure. Position case so that open side is up. Install needle bearing (13—Fig. PT1) and oil seal (14), then install idler shaft (29) and gear (30) on early model transaxle, or on late model transaxle install one-piece idler shaft and gear (29A—Fig. PT3A). On all models, install bevel gear (31—Fig. PT1), washers (32 and 34) and thrust bearing (33). Be sure thrust bearing is positioned between washers. Reverse idler shaft (79) may be used to temporarily hold idler gear assembly in position. On early model transaxle, place cluster gear (35, 36 and 37) on key (39) so that bevel on gears (35 and 36) is toward large gear (37) and short section of key (39) is between middle gear (36) and large gear (37) as shown in Fig. PT3. Press gears and key on sleeve (41—Fig. PT1). On late model transaxle, install thrust washer (42—Fig. PT3A), countershaft (C), cluster gears (35, 36 and 37) and spacers (S). On all models, install shifter assembly (18 through 27—Fig. PT1) in case, making certain that shifter rods are properly seated. Install reverse idler shaft (79), gear (81) and spacer (80). Beveled edge

of gear should be up. Install gasket (75), center plate (76), then second gasket (75) on case. Assemble differential by reversing disassembly procedure. Install differential assembly in case with longer axle pointing downward. Install locating dowel pins and secure cover (55) to case. Install oil seals (15 and 53), axle housings (16 and 52) and shift lever assembly (1 through 8).

Fill transaxle housing after unit is installed to level plug opening with SAE

90 EP gear oil. Capacity is approximately 1½ pints (0.71L).

Series 800 Transaxle

OVERHAUL. To disassemble the transaxle, first remove drain plug and drain lubricant. Place shift lever in neutral and remove shift lever. Remove setscrew (2—Fig PT4), spring (3) and index ball (4). Unbolt cover (5) and push shift

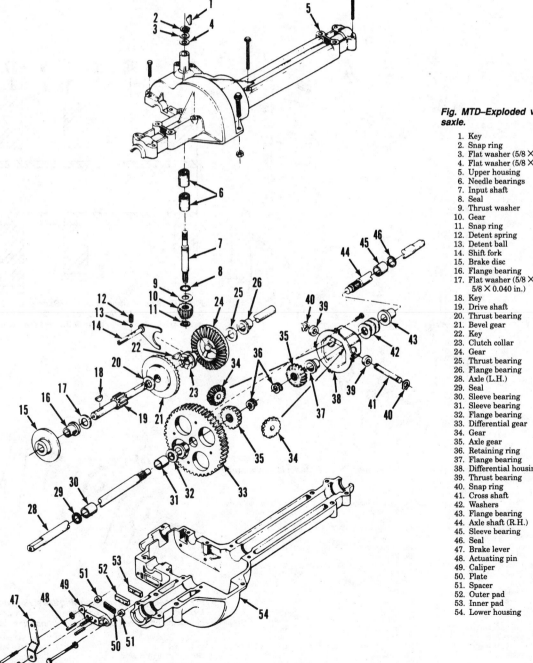

Fig. MTD—Exploded view of MTD 717-0775 transaxle.

1. Key
2. Snap ring
3. Flat washer (5/8 × 0.040 in.)
4. Flat washer (5/8 × 0.030 in.)
5. Upper housing
6. Needle bearings
7. Input shaft
8. Seal
9. Thrust washer
10. Gear
11. Snap ring
12. Detent spring
13. Detent ball
14. Shift fork
15. Brake disc
16. Flange bearing
17. Flat washer (5/8 × 0.030 or 5/8 × 0.040 in.)
18. Key
19. Drive shaft
20. Thrust bearing
21. Bevel gear
22. Key
23. Clutch collar
24. Gear
25. Thrust bearing
26. Flange bearing
28. Axle (L.H.)
29. Seal
30. Sleeve bearing
31. Sleeve bearing
32. Flange bearing
33. Differential gear
34. Gear
35. Axle gear
36. Retaining ring
37. Flange bearing
38. Differential housing
39. Thrust bearing
40. Snap ring
41. Cross shaft
42. Washers
43. Flange bearing
44. Axle shaft (R.H.)
45. Sleeve bearing
46. Seal
47. Brake lever
48. Actuating pin
49. Caliper
50. Plate
51. Spacer
52. Outer pad
53. Inner pad
54. Lower housing

Transmission Repair

fork assembly (12) in while removing cover. Before removing gear shaft assemblies, shift fork (12) may be removed. It will be difficult to keep parts from falling off. Note position of parts before removal. Remove gear and shaft assemblies from case taking care not to disturb drive chain (34). Remove needle bearing (43), flat washer (41), square cut seals (42), output gear (40) and output pinion (39) from the countershaft. Angle the two shafts together (Fig. PT5). Mark the position of chain on

sprocket collars and remove chain. Remove sprocket (35—Fig. PT4), bevel gear (32), spur gears (27, 28, 29, 30 and 31), thrust washer (9) and flange bushing (14). All gears are splined to the countershaft. Disassembly of brake shaft is self-evident from observation. Remove snap ring (11), input bevel gear (10) and pull input shaft (78) through cover.

To disassemble the differential, drive roll pin out of drive pin (58) and remove drive pin. Remove pinion gears (60) by

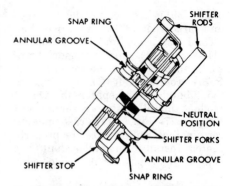

Fig. PT2–To position shifter assembly in neutral for reassembly, align notches in shifter forks with notch in shifter stop.

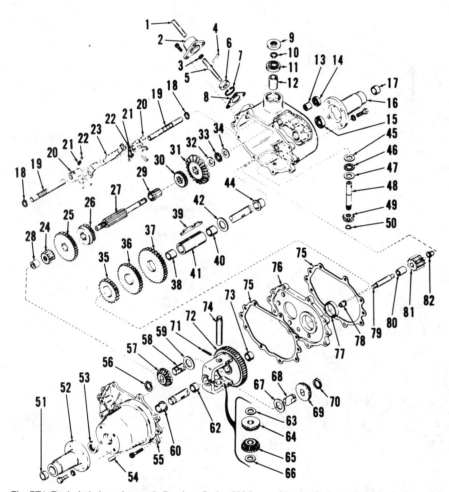

Fig. PT1–Exploded view of an early Peerless Series 600 3-speed transaxle. Late model is similar, refer to Fig. PT3A for internal parts difference.

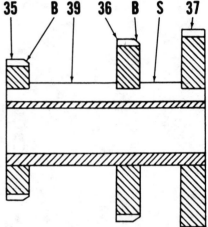

Fig. PT3–Note position of bevels (B) on gears (35 & 36) and short section (S) of key (39) between gears (36 & 37) used on early 600 series transaxle.

Fig. PT3A–Exploded view showing late style countershaft assembly and one-piece idler shaft and gear assembly used on 600 series transaxles.

1. Shift lever
2. Lever housing
3. Quad ring
4. Roll pin
5. Shift lever
6. Retainer
7. Snap ring
8. Gasket
9. Oil seal
10. Snap ring
11. Ball bearing
12. Bushing
13. Needle bearing
14. Oil seal
15. Oil seal
16. Axle housing
17. Bushing
18. Snap ring
19. Shift rod
20. Shift fork
21. Spring
22. Detent ball
23. Shifter stop
24. Spur gear
25. Sliding gear (1st & reverse)
26. Sliding gear (2nd & 3rd)
27. Shift & brake shaft
28. Needle bearing
29. Idler shaft
30. Gear
31. Bevel gear
32. Washer
33. Thrust bearing
34. Washer
35. Gear (25 teeth)
36. Gear (34 teeth)
37. Gear (39 teeth)
38. Bushing
39. Key
40. Bushing
41. Sleeve
42. Thrust washer
44. Bushing
45. Washer
46. Thrust bearing
47. Washer
48. Input shaft
49. Pinion gear
50. Snap ring
51. Bushing
52. Axle housing
53. Oil seal
54. Dowel pin
55. Cover
56. Snap ring
57. Side gear
58. Axle shaft
59. Thrust washer
60. Bushing
62. Bushing
63. Thrust washer
64. Differential pinion
65. Differential pinion
66. Thrust washer
67. Thrust washer
68. Axle shaft
69. Side gear
70. Snap ring
71. Roll pin
72. Differential carrier & gear
73. Bushing
74. Drive pin
75. Gasket
76. Center plate
77. Bushing
78. Bushing
79. Reverse idler shaft
80. Spacer
81. Reverse idler gear
82. Bushing

C. Countershaft
S. Spacer
29A. Idler shaft & gear assy.
35. Gear (25 teeth)
36. Gear (34 teeth)
37. Gear (39 teeth)
38. Bushing
40. Bushing
42. Thrust washer

Illustrations Courtesy Tecumseh Products Co.

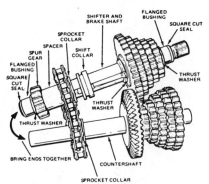

Fig. PT5–Mark position of chain on sprocket collars, angle shafts together and remove chain.

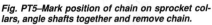

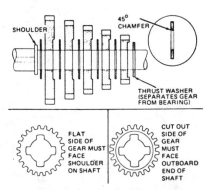

Fig. PT6–When installing thrust washers and gears on brake shaft, 45° chamfer on inside diameter of thrust washers must face shoulder on brake shaft.

Fig PT4–Exploded view of Series 800 Transaxle.

1. Plug	16. Spacer	32. Bevel gear (42 teeth)
2. Set screw	17. Sprocket (18 teeth)	33. Countershaft
3. Spring	18. Shift collar	34. Roller chain
4. Ball	19. Key	35. Sprocket (9 teeth)
5. Cover	20. Brake shaft	36. Flat washer
6. Needle bearing	21. Thrust washer	37. Square cut ring
7. Input shaft	22. Spur gear (35 teeth)	38. Needle bearing
8. Square cut ring	23. Spur gear (30 teeth)	39. Output pinion
9. Thrust washer	24. Spur gear (25 teeth)	40. Output gear
10. Input pinion	25. Spur gear (22 teeth)	41. Flat washer
11. Snap ring	26. Spur gear (20 teeth)	42. Needle bearing
12. Shift fork assy.	27. Gear (30 teeth)	43. Needle bearing
13. Square cut ring	28. Gear (28 teeth)	44. Spacer
14. Bushing	29. Gear (25 teeth)	45. Oil seal
15. Spur gear (12 or 15 teeth)	30. Gear (20 teeth)	46. Needle bearing
	31. Spur gear (12 or 15 teeth)	47. Spacer

48. Axle shaft (13 3/4 inches)	
49. Bushing	
50. Washer	
51. Bushing	
52. Pin	
53. Thrust washer	
54. Snap ring	
55. Bevel gear	
56. Axle shaft (14 7/8 inches)	
57. Differential gear assy.	
58. Drive pin	
59. Thrust washer	
60. Bevel pinion	
61. Case	

rotating gears in opposite directions. Remove snap rings (54), side gears (55), thrust washers (53) and slide axles out.

Clean and inspect all parts and renew any showing excessive wear or other damage. When installing new inner input shaft needle bearings, press bearing in to a depth of 0.135-0.150 inches (3.4-3.8 mm) below flush. When installing thrust washers and shifting gears on brake shaft, the 45° chamfer on inside diameter of thrust washers must face shoulder on brake shaft (Fig. PT6). The flat side of gears must face shoulder on

shaft. Complete assembly and torque case to cover cap screws to 80-100 in.-lbs. (9-11 N·m).

Reinstall transaxle by reversing removal procedure and pack transaxle with 24 oz. (0.68 kg) of E.P. lithium grease. Adjust brake and drive belt tension as required.

Series 910 Transaxle

OVERHAUL. To disassemble transaxle, first remove wheel assemblies and brake components as outlined in

equipment section and drain lubricant. Remove pulley from input shaft. Move shift lever to neutral position and remove shift lever from shift shaft. Remove neutral switch, if so equipped, and remove any brackets attached to cases. Remove disc brake assembly. Remove mounting bolts and separate upper case (6—Fig. PT6A) from lower case (40).

Disassembly of transaxle is evident after inspection and referral to Fig. PT6A. Note position of parts before removal. Lift shaft and gear assemblies from case. Do not lose detent ball (5) and spring (4) when removing shift arm (17). Note that two snap rings (34) are used to secure side gears (33) on axles. Detach snap ring (1) to remove input shaft (8) assembly. Detach snap ring (12) and separate pinion gear (11) from shaft.

Input shaft needle bearings (7) are renewable. Install upper bearing so it is flush with outer case surface and install lower bearing so it is 0.150 inch (3.81 mm) from inside case surface. Use a suitable tool to drive bearings (30) out of bearing sleeves (29). Install new bearings so they are centered in sleeves.

Inspect components for excessive wear and damage. Lubricate all internal components before assembly with Bentonite or other suitable grease.

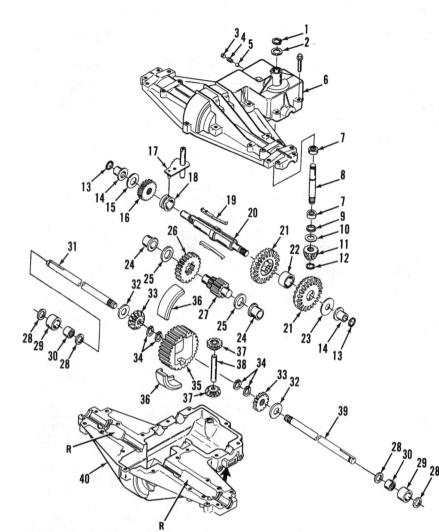

Fig. PT6A—Exploded view of Peerless Model 910 transaxle. Note that brake assembly may be located on either side of transaxle.

1. Snap ring	11. Pinion gear
2. Washer	12. Snap ring
3. Plug	13. Quad ring
4. Detent spring	14. Bushing
5. Detent ball	15. Thrust washer
6. Upper case half	16. Gear
7. Needle bearing	17. Shift arm
8. Input shaft	18. Shift collar
9. Quad ring	19. Shift key
10. Thrust washer	20. Shift/brake shaft

21. Bevel gear	31. Axle
22. Spacer	32. Thrust washer
23. Thrust washer	33. Side gear
24. Bushing	34. Snap rings
25. Thrust washer	35. Ring gear
26. Gear	36. Bearing block
27. Pinion shaft	37. Pinion gear
28. Quad ring	38. Pinion shaft
29. Sleeve	39. Axle
30. Bearing	40. Lower case half

Assemble unit by reversing disassembly procedure while noting the following: Be sure bushings and quad rings fit in case properly. With gear assemblies in lower case half, pack lower case half around gears and shafts with 18 oz. (533 mL) of Bentonite or equivalent grease. Grease should be present in recesses (R) of case, but there should not be grease between bearing blocks (36) and case. Install upper case half and tighten screws to 100 in.-lbs. (11.3 N•m).

Series 915 Transaxle

OVERHAUL. To disassemble transaxle, first remove wheel assemblies and brake components as outlined in equipment section and drain lubricant. Remove pulley from input shaft. Move shift lever to neutral position and remove shift lever from shift shaft. Remove neutral switch, if so equipped, and remove any brackets attached to cases. Remove mounting screws and separate upper case (4—Fig. PT6B) from lower case (57).

Remove differential and axle assembly from case and disassemble as needed. Note that two snap rings (51) are used to secure side gears (50) on axles.

Remove shift/brake shaft (27) assembly. Remove brake disc, then refer to Fig. PT6B and separate remainder of components from the shaft. Needle bearing (41) in bevel gear (40) is renewable. Install new bearing so it is flush with small gear side of gear.

Remove countershaft (13) assembly. Refer to Fig. PT6B and disassemble components. Withdraw shift fork (21) while being careful not to lose detent ball (23) and spring (22). Detach snap ring (2) and remove input shaft (6) assembly. Detach snap ring (10) and separate pinion gear (9) from shaft. Input shaft needle bearings (5) are renewable. Install upper bearing so it is flush with outer case surface and install lower bearing so it is 0.135-0.150 inch (3.43-3.81 mm) from inside case surface.

Inspect components for excessive wear and damage. Lubricate all internal components before assembly with Bentonite or other suitable grease.

Assemble unit by reversing disassembly procedure while noting the following: Washer (11) is thicker than washer (19). When assembling gears (33, 35, 36 and 38) on shift/brake shaft (27), place rounded side of thrust washers next to cutout side of gears as shown in Fig. PT6C. Coat brake disc splines on shift/brake shaft (27—Fig. PT6B) with Lubriplate before installing brake disc (59) on shaft. Install brake pads (58) and backup plate (60) in case before installing shift/brake shaft assembly. Be sure bushing (45) and quad ring (46) fit in case properly.

With gear assemblies in lower case half, pack lower case half around gears and shafts with 18 ounces (533 mL) of Bentonite or equivalent grease. Install upper case half and tighten screws to 100 in.-lbs. (11.3 N•m). Using a hand-held grease gun, inject one or two shots of grease into grease fittings (56) at outer axle ends.

Series 2300 Transaxle

OVERHAUL. To disassemble the transaxle, first remove drain plug and drain lubricant. Place shift lever in neutral position, then unbolt and remove shift lever assembly. Remove axle housings (14 and 64—Fig. PT6D). Remove seal retainers (11) with oil seals (12) and "O" rings (13) by pulling each axle shaft out of case and cover as far as possible. Place transaxle unit on the edge of a bench with left axle pointing downward. Remove cap screws securing case (16) to cover (66) and drive aligning dowel pins out of case. Lift case (16) up 1½ to 2 inches (38-50 mm), tilt case about 45°, rotate case clockwise and remove it from the assembly. Input shaft (32) and input gear (33) will be removed with the case. Withdraw differential and axle shaft assembly and lay aside for later

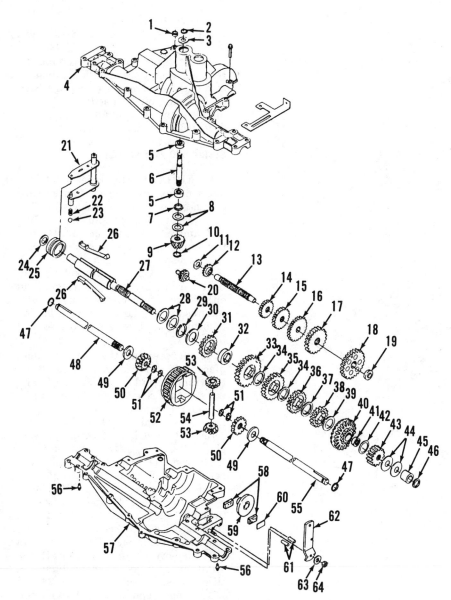

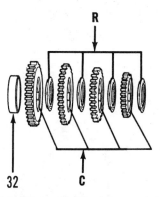

Fig. PT6C—When assembling gears and thrust washers on shift/brake shaft, note location of spacer (32), cutout (C) side of gears and rounded side (R) of thrust washers.

CAUTION: Do not allow cover or low reduction gear bearing boss to support any part of the pressure required to press brake shaft from gear.

Remove input shaft (32) with input gear (33) and thrust washer (34) from case (16).

To disassembly the differential, remove the our cap screws and separate axle shaft and carrier assemblies from ring gear (79). Drive blocks (78), bevel pinion gears (77) and drive pin (76) can now be removed from ring gear. Remove snap rings (59) and withdraw axle shafts (63 and 67) from axle gears (61) and carriers (62 and 72).

Clean and inspect all parts and renew any showing excessive war or other damage. When installing new needle bearings, press bearing (29) in spline shaft (28) to a depth of 0.010 inch (0.25 mm) below end of shaft and low reduction shaft bearings (54 and 58) 0.010 inch (0.25 mm) below thrust surfaces of bearing bosses. Carrier bearings (10) should be pressed in from inside of case and cover until bearings are 0.290 inch (7.37 mm) below face of axle housing mounting surface. All other needle bearings are to be pressed in from inside of case and cover to a depth of 0.015-0.020 inch (0.38-0.51 mm) below the thrust surfaces.

Renew all seals and gaskets and reassemble by reversing the disassembly procedure, keeping the following points in mind: When installing brake shaft (39) and idler gear (38), beveled edge of gear teeth must be up away from cover. Install reverse idler shaft (23), spacer (24) and reverse idler gear (25) with rounded end of teeth facing spacer. Install input gear (33) and shaft (32) so that chamfered side of input gear is facing case (16).

Fig. PT6B—Exploded view of Peerless Model 915 transaxle.

1. Quad ring	17. Gear	33. Gear	49. Thrust washer
2. Snap ring	18. Bevel gear	34. Thrust washer	50. Side gear
3. Washer	19. Thrust washer	35. Gear	51. Snap rings
4. Upper case half	20. Reverse idler	36. Gear	52. Ring gear
5. Needle bearing	21. Shift fork	37. Thrust washer	53. Pinion gear
6. Input shaft	22. Detent spring	38. Gear	54. Pinion shaft
7. "O" ring	23. Detent ball	39. Thrust washer	55. Axle
8. Thrust washer	24. Thrust washer	40. Bevel gear	56. Grease fitting
9. Pinion gear	25. Shift collar	41. Needle bearing	57. Lower case half
10. Snap ring	26. Shift key	42. Thrust washer	58. Brake pads
11. Thrust washer	27. Shift/brake shaft	43. Gear	59. Brake disc
12. Gear	28. Thrust washer	44. Thrust washer	60. Backup plate
13. Countershaft	29. Snap ring	45. Bushing	61. Pins
14. Gear	30. Washer	46. Quad ring	62. Brake lever
15. Gear	31. Gear	47. Quad ring	63. Washer
16. Gear	32. Spacer	48. Axle	64. Nut

disassembly. Remove the 3-cluster gear (44) with its thrust washer (46) and spacer (42). Lift out reverse idler gear (25), spacer (24) and shaft (23). Hold upper ends of shifter rods together and lift out shifter rods, forks, shifter stop (21), sliding gears (30 and 31) and shaft (28) as an assembly. Remove low reduction gear (57), reduction shaft (56) and thrust washer (55), then remove 2-cluster gear (40) from brake shaft. Lift out the output gear (50), shaft (51) and thrust washers (49 and 52). To remove brake shaft (39) and gear (38) from cover (66), block up under gear (38) and press shaft out of gear.

Shift lever housing
cap screws .... 8-10 ft.-lbs.
(11-13 N·m)

Reinstall transaxle by reversing the removal procedure and fill transaxle unit to the level plug opening with SAE 90 EP gear oil. Capacity is approximately 4 pints (1.9L). Adjust brake and drive belt tension as required.

Series 500 Transmission

OVERHAUL. The Series 500 transmission may have three or four forward speeds and one reverse. Models 503, 505 and 509 are 3-speed and Models 501, 508 and 515 are 4-speed units. The transmissions are very similar except that on 3-speed units, gear (13-Fig. PT7) is not used. Output sprocket (7) and brake assembly may be located on either side of transmission. Service procedures are similar for all models. The following procedures are for the 4-speed unit.

To disassemble the transmission, place shift lever in neutral position, then remove shift lever and safety starting switch if so equipped. Refer to Fig. PT7 and remove set screw (5), spring (4) and detent ball (3). Remove six cap screws (1) and lift off cover (2). Pull shifter assembly (21) upward and remove from case. See Fig. PT8. Lift both gear and shaft assemblies straight upward out of case (30-Fig. PT7). Move reverse sprockets (17 and 20) together until bushing (8), thrust washer (9) and reverse drive sprocket (20) can be removed from countershaft (22) and chain (19). Remove chain and separate the shaft assemblies. Remove bushing, thrust washer, spur gears (23, 24 and 25) and bevel spur gear (26) from countershaft (22). Remove snap ring (6), output sprocket (7), bushing (8), thrust washer (9) and spur gears (10, 11, 12, and 13) from output and brake shaft (14). Then, remove brake disc (18), bushing (8), thrust washer (9) and reverse driven sprocket (17) from opposite end of the shaft. Slide shifter collar (16) and shifter (drive) keys (15) from shaft. Remove snap ring (27), input bevel gear (28) and thrust washer (29), then withdraw input shaft (32) from case. Unbolt and remove brake assembly (35 through 41).

Clean and inspect all parts and renew any showing excessive wear or other damage. If needle bearings (31) are being renewed, press bearing in until they are flush to 0.005 inch (0.13 mm) below case surfaces. See Fig. PT9. Apply a light coat of E.P. lithium grease to bearings, shafts and gears, then reassemble by reversing the disassembly procedure. When installing gears (10 through

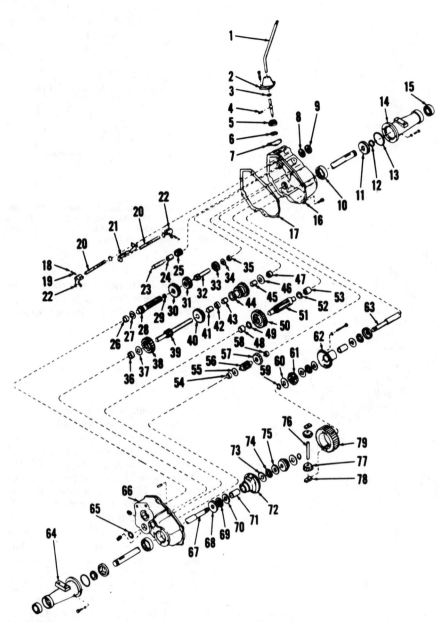

Fig. PT6D–Exploded view of Peerless Model 2300 4-speed transaxle.

1. Shift lever	22. Shifter fork	40. 2-cluster gear	60. Thrust washer
2. Shift lever housing	23. Reverse idler shaft	41. Bushing	61. Axle gear
3. Seal ring	24. Spacer	42. Spacer	62. Differential carrier
4. Roll pin	25. Reverse idler gear	43. Bushing	63. Axle shaft R.H.
5. Retainer	26. Needle bearing	44. 3-clster gear	64. Axle housing L.H.
6. Snap ring	27. Thrust washer	45. Bushing	65. Oil seal
7. Gasket	28. Shifter shaft	46. Thrust washer	66. Transaxle cover
8. Ball bearing	29. Needle bearing	47. Needle bearing	67. Axle shaft L.H.
9. Oil seal	30. 1st, 2nd & reverse	48. Needle bearing	68. Thrust washer
10. Carrier bearing	gear	49. Thrust washer	69. Thrust bearing
11. Seal retainer	31. 3rd & 4th gear	50. Output gear	70. Thrust washer
12. Oil seal	32. Input shaft	51. Output shaft	71. Bushing
13. "O" ring	33. Input gear	52. Thrust washer	72. Differential carrier
14. Axle housing R.H.	34. Thrust washer	53. Needle bearing	73. Thrust washer
15. Axle outer bearing	35. Needle bearing	54. Needle bearing	74. Thrust bearing
16. Transaxle case	36. Needle bearing	55. Thrust washer	75. Thrust washer
17. Gasket	37. Thrust washer	56. Low reduction shaft	76. Drive pin
18. Detent ball	38. Idler gear	57. Low reduction gear	77. Bevel pinion gear
19. Spring	39. Brake & cluster	58. Needle bearing	78. Drive block
20. Shifter rod	shaft	59. Snap ring	79. Ring gear
21. Shifter stop			

Tighten transaxle cap screws to the following torque:

Differential cap screws ... 7-10 ft.-lbs.
(10.13 N·m)

Case to cover cap screws .. 8-10 ft.-lbs.
(11-13 N·m)

Axle housing cap screws . 15-18 ft.-lbs.
(20-24 N·m)

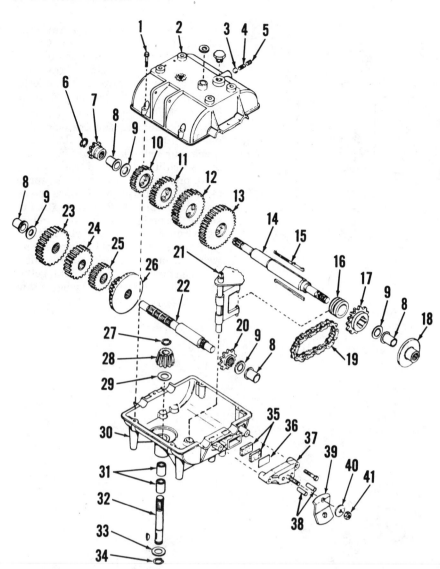

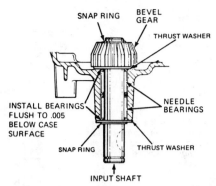

Fig. PT9–Input shaft needle bearings must be installed flush to 0.005 inch (0.13 mm) below case surfaces.

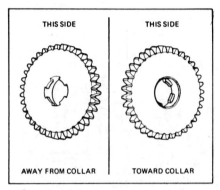

Fig. PT10–Install speed gears (10 through 13—Fig. PT7) with flat side away from shift collar.

Fig. PT7–Exploded view of typical 4-speed Series 500 Peerless transmission. Series 500 3-speed transmission is similar. Refer to text.

1. Cap screw (6)
2. Cover
3. Detent ball
4. Spring
5. Set screw
6. Snap ring
7. Output sprocket
8. Flanged bushing
9. Thrust washer
10. Fourth speed gear
11. Third speed gear
12. Second speed gear
13. First speed gear
14. Output & brake shaft
15. Shifter (drive) keys
16. Shifter collar
17. Reverse driven sprocket
18. Brake disc
19. Chain
20. Reverse drive sprocket
21. Shifter assy.
22. Countershaft
23. Fourth drive gear
24. Third drive gear
25. Second drive gear
26. Bevel & spur (first drive) gear
27. Snap ring
28. Input bevel gear
29. Thrust washer
30. Transmission case
31. Needle bearings
32. Input shaft
33. Thrust washer
34. Snap ring
35. Brake pads
36. Back-up plate
37. Brake caliper
38. Actuating pins
39. Brake lever
40. Washer
41. Adjusting nut

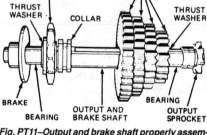

Fig. PT11–Output and brake shaft properly assembled for installation.

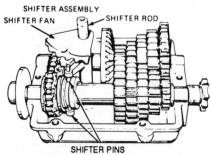

Fig. PT8–Series 500 transmission with cover removed. Shifter rod, fan, fork and pins are removed as an assembly.

13-Fig. PT7), refer to Fig. PT10 and install gears with flat side away from shifting collar. Reverse drive sprocket (20-Fig. PT7) must be installed with large hub side of sprocket facing away from bevel spur gear (26). Make certain that thrust washers are in positions shown in Fig. PT13 and that bearing locator tangs are seated in notches in case. Install shifter assembly, then cover gears, shafts, reverse sprockets and chain with 12 oz. (0.34 kg) of E.P. lithium grease. Install cover (2-Fig. PT7) and tighten cap screws (1) to a torque of 90-100 in.-lbs. (10-11 N•m).

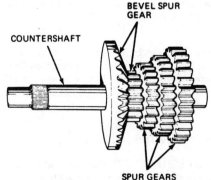

Fig. PT12–View showing correct installation of bevel spur gear and spur gears on countershaft.

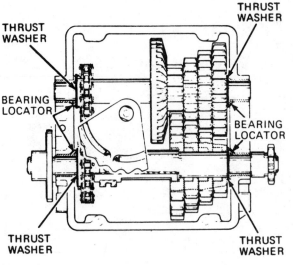

Fig. PT13–Make certain that thrust washers are in position shown and that bearing locator tangs are seated in notches in case.

THRUST WASHER

THRUST WASHER

BEARING LOCATOR

BEARING LOCATOR

THRUST WASHER

THRUST WASHER

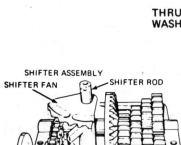

SHIFTER ASSEMBLY
SHIFTER FAN
SHIFTER ROD

SHIFTER PINS

Fig. PT14–Series 700 transmission with cover removed. Shifter rod, fan, fork and pins are removed as an assembly.

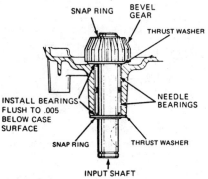

SNAP RING
BEVEL GEAR
THRUST WASHER
INSTALL BEARINGS FLUSH TO .005 BELOW CASE SURFACE
NEEDLE BEARINGS
SNAP RING
THRUST WASHER
INPUT SHAFT

Fig. PT15–Input shaft needle bearings must be installed flush to 0.005 inch (0.13 mm) below case surfaces.

Install detent ball (3), spring (4) and set screw (5) and tighten set screw two full turns below flush. Renew brake pads (35) as necessary and reinstall brake assembly.

Series 700 Transmission

OVERHAUL. The Series 700 transmission may be equipped with four or five speeds forward and one reverse. The transmissions are very similar ex-

cept that on 4-speed units, gears (11 and 32-Fig. PT16) are not used. Output sprockets (19) and brake assembly may be located on either side of transmission. Service procedures are similar for all models. The following procedures are for the 5-speed unit.

To disassemble the transmission, place shift lever in neutral position, then remove shift lever and safety starting switch if so equipped. Refer to Fig. PT16 and remove set screw (5), spring (4) and detent ball (3). Remove the six cap screws (1) and lift off cover (2). Pull shifter assembly (27) upward and remove from case. See Fig. PT14. Lift both gear and shaft assemblies straight upward out of case (23-Fig. PT16). Move reverse sprockets (18 and 22) together until bushing (7), thrust washer (8) and reverse drive sprocket (22) can be re-

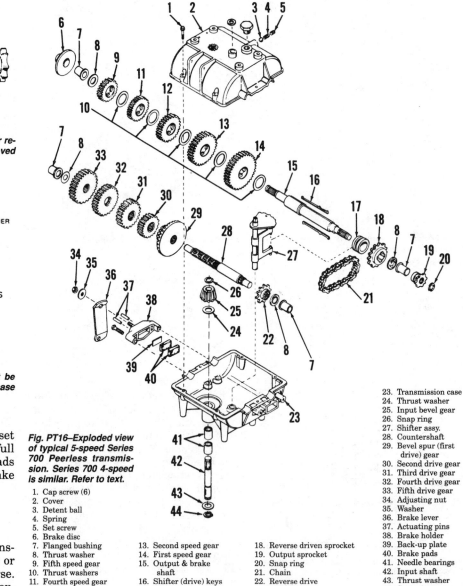

Fig. PT16–Exploded view of typical 5-speed Series 700 Peerless transmission. Series 700 4-speed is similar. Refer to text.

1. Cap screw (6)
2. Cover
3. Detent ball
4. Spring
5. Set screw
6. Brake disc
7. Flanged bushing
8. Thrust washer
9. Fifth speed gear
10. Thrust washers
11. Fourth speed gear
12. Third speed gear
13. Second speed gear
14. First speed gear
15. Output & brake shaft
16. Shifter (drive) keys
17. Shifter collar
18. Reverse driven sprocket
19. Output sprocket
20. Snap ring
21. Chain
22. Reverse drive sprocket
23. Transmission case
24. Thrust washer
25. Input bevel gear
26. Snap ring
27. Shifter assy.
28. Countershaft
29. Bevel spur (first drive) gear
30. Second drive gear
31. Third drive gear
32. Fourth drive gear
33. Fifth drive gear
34. Adjusting nut
35. Washer
36. Brake lever
37. Actuating pins
38. Brake holder
39. Back-up plate
40. Brake pads
41. Needle bearings
42. Input shaft
43. Thrust washer
44. Snap ring

Illustrations Courtesy Tecumseh Products Co.

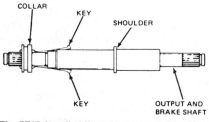

Fig. PT17–Install shifter collar and shifter (drive) keys on output shaft as shown. Thick side of collar must face shoulder on shaft.

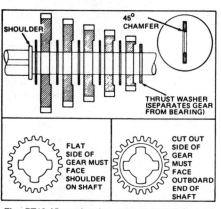

Fig. PT18–View showing correct installation of thrust washers and gears on output shaft. The 45 degree inside chamfer on thrust washers must face the shoulder on the shaft.

ers (9 through 14-Fig. PT16), flat side of gears and the 45° inside chamfer on thrust washers must face the shoulder on shaft. See Fig. PT18. Reverse drive sprocket (22-Fig. PT16) must be installed with large hub side of sprocket facing towards bevel spur gear (29).

Make certain that thrust washers are installed in positions shown in Fig. PT13 and that bearing locator tangs are seated in notches in case. Install shifter assembly, then cover gears, shafts, reverse sprocket and chain with 12 oz. (0.34 kg) of E.P. lithium grease. Install cover (2-Fig. PT16) and tighten cap screws (1) to a torque of 90-100 in.-lbs. (10-11 N•m). Install detent ball (3),

spring (4) and set screw (5) and tighten set screw two full turns below flush. Renew brake pads (40) as necessary and reinstall brake assembly.

SIMPLICITY

2-Speed W/Reverse

OVERHAUL. With transmission case (14-Fig. ST1), shift links (10, 17 and 20), retaining rings (7) and springs (8) removed as outlined in the riding mower section, proceed as follows: remove shaft and gear assemblies (W, X, Y and V), then remove set collar (23) and withdraw differential and axle assem-

moved from countershaft (28) and chain (21). Remove chain and separate shaft assemblies. Remove bushing, thrust washer, spur gears (33, 32, 31 and 30) and bevel spur gear (29) from countershaft (28). Remove brake disc (6), bushing (7), thrust washer (8), spur gears (9, 11, 12, 13 and 14) and thrust washers (10) from output and brake shaft (15). Then, remove snap ring (20), output sprocket (19), bushing (7), thrust washer (8) and reverse driven sprocket (18) from opposite end of shaft. Slide shifter collar (17) and shifter (drive) keys (16) from shaft. Remove snap ring (26), input bevel gear (25) and thrust washer (24), then withdraw input shaft (42) from bottom of case. Unbolt and remove brake assembly (34 through 40).

Clean and inspect all parts and renew any showing excessive wear or other damage. If needle bearings (41) are being renewed, press bearings in until they are flush to 0.005 inch (0.13 mm) below case surfaces. See Fig. PT15. Apply a light coat of E.P. lithium grease to bearings, shafts and gears, then reassemble by reversing the disassembly procedure. Refer to Fig. PT17 and install shifter collar and shifter keys on output and brake shaft. Thick side of collar must face shoulder on shaft. When installing gears and thrust wash-

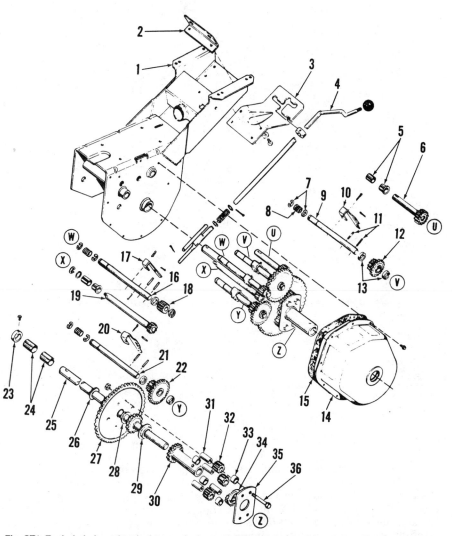

Fig. ST1–Exploded view of typical transmission and differential assembly used on Simplicity Models 305, 315, 355, 3005 and 3008-2.

1. Rear frame	11. Roll pin	19. Input shaft & gear
2. Shift rod guide	12. Low speed gear	20. Shift link
3. Shift quadrant	13. Thrust collars	21. Shifter shaft (Hi)
4. Shift rod	14. Gear case	22. High speed gear
5. Bronze bushings	15. Gasket	23. Set collar
6. Brake shaft	16. Shifter shaft (Reverse)	24. Bushings
7. Retaining rings	17. Shift link	25. Axle shaft L.H.
8. Spring	18. Reverse gear	26. Washer
9. Shifter shaft (low)		27. Drive gear
10. Shift link		28. Bushing
		29. Thrust cap
		30. Axle shaft R.H.
		31. Pinion spindle (4)
		32. Differential pinion (4)
		33. Spacer (4)
		34. Bushing
		35. Differential plate
		36. Through-bolt (4)

Illustrations for Fig. PT17 & Fig. PT18 Courtesy Tecumseh Products Co.

assemblies. Place the transaxle in a vise with left axle housing (37-Fig. ST2) pointing downward. Unbolt and remove transaxle cover (3). Remove right axle (31) with spacer (34), then withdraw left axle (32) from differential right side. Tilt drive gear (33) and remove drive gear and differential assembly and second spacer (34). Remove washer (21), withdraw brake shaft (18) and remove cluster gear (22) and washer (23). Remove shift lever assembly (2). Remove nut and lockwasher from shift rail (8), then remove rail, shift fork (5), input shaft (15) and sliding gear (13) as an assembly. Remove either snap ring (12) and slide gear (13) from input shaft. If necessary, remove shift fork from rail after first removing cap screw, detent ball (6) and spring (7). Remove the four through-bolts and separate differential plate (26), spindles (27), pinions (28), spacers (29) and springs (30) from drive gear (33). Unbolt and remove axle housing (37) from transaxle case (1).

Clean and inspect all parts and renew any showing excessive wear or other damage. Do not remove needle bearing (10) or bushings (16, 20, 24, 36 and 38) unless need for renewal is indicated. Renew gasket (4), seal ring (35) and all oil seals and reassemble by reversing the disassembly procedure. Fill transaxle housing, after unit is installed, to level plug opening with SAE 90 gear oil. Capacity is approximately 2½ pints (1.18L).

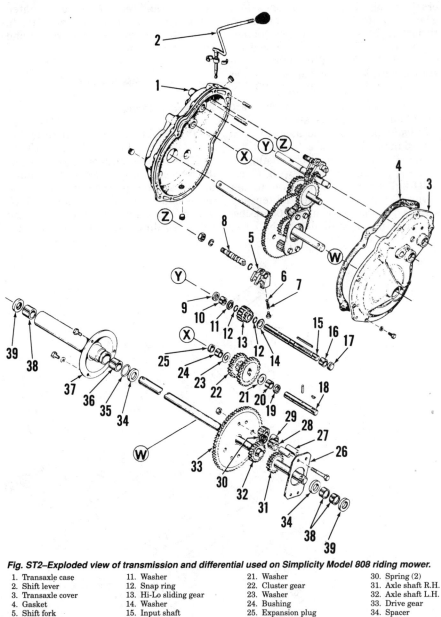

Fig. ST2–Exploded view of transmission and differential used on Simplicity Model 808 riding mower.

1. Transaxle case	11. Washer	21. Washer	30. Spring (2)
2. Shift lever	12. Snap ring	22. Cluster gear	31. Axle shaft R.H.
3. Transaxle cover	13. Hi-Lo sliding gear	23. Washer	32. Axle shaft L.H.
4. Gasket	14. Washer	24. Bushing	33. Drive gear
5. Shift fork	15. Input shaft	25. Expansion plug	34. Spacer
6. Detent ball	16. Bushing	26. Differential plate	35. Seal ring
7. Spring	17. Expansion plug	27. Pinion spindle	36. Bushing
8. Shift rail	18. Brake shaft	28. Differential pinion	37. Axle housing
9. Oil seal	19. Oil seal	(4)	38. Bushings
10. Needle bearing	20. Bushing	29. Spacer (2)	39. Oil seal

3-Speed

OVERHAUL. To disassemble either 3-speed transaxle (Fig. ST3 or ST4), first remove rear wheel and hub assemblies, brake drum (1) and input pulley (20). Unbolt and remove side plates on models so equipped. Remove plug and drain lubricant. Remove cap screws securing transaxle cover (2) to case (26). Drive out the alignment roll pins at edge of cover and using a screwdriver, pry the cover off the case. Remove left axle shaft (34). Align differential pinion teeth and remove right axle shaft (33) out left side of differential. Lift out drive gear (28) and differential assembly. Remove brake shaft and cluster gear (36 and 37) and low reduction gear and shaft (18). Remove the nuts from shift rails (11 and 39) and reverse shaft (14). Remove shift rod and lever assembly. Withdraw shift fork (38), shift rail (39), sliding gear (35) and input shaft (40). Shift fork (8), shift rail (11), reverse gear (13) and shaft (14) can now be removed. Note location of springs (29) and spacers (44) and remove the four through-bolts. Separate differential pinions, spacers, springs

bly (Z). Remove brake shaft and gear assembly (U). Drive roll pins (11) from shaft (9, 16 and 21) and slide off thrust collars (13) and gears (12, 18 and 22). Remove the four through-bolts (36) and carefully separate differential pinions (32), spacers (33) and pinion spindles (31) from drive gear (27) and differential plate (35). Note location of washer (26), bushing (28), thrust cup (29) and bushing (34) and remove right axle (30) and drive gear (27) from left axle (25).

Clean and inspect all parts and renew any showing excessive wear or other

damage. Inspect bushings in rear frame and renew as necessary. Reassemble by reversing the disassembly procedure. Lubricate all gears, shafts and bushings with general purpose lithium grease during assembly. Additional lubrication should be pumped through grease zerk in case (14) each 10 hours of operation.

2-Speed W/No Reverse

OVERHAUL. To disassemble the 2-speed transaxle, drain gear oil from unit and remove input pulley and rear wheel

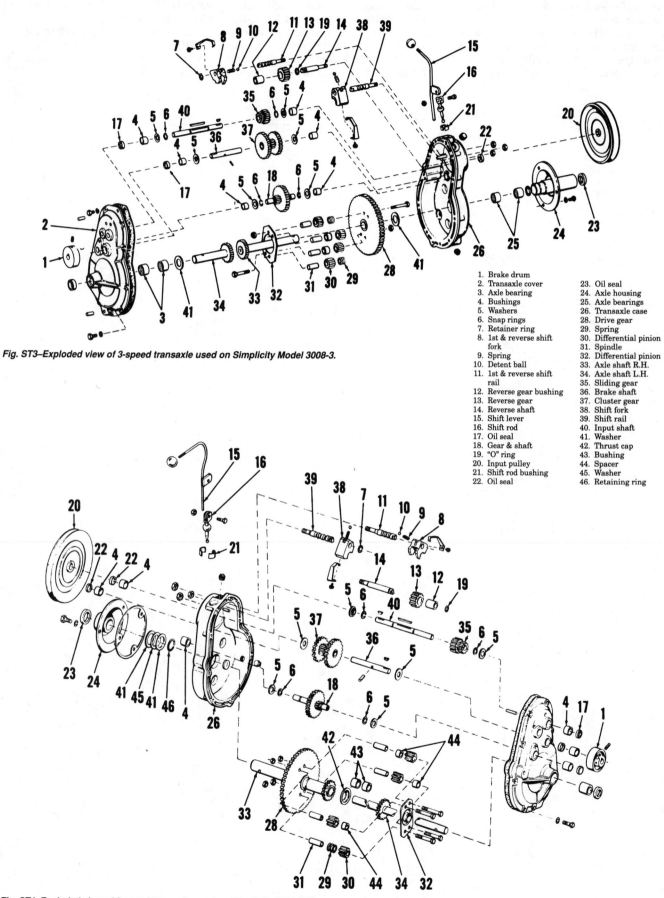

Fig. ST3–Exploded view of 3-speed transaxle used on Simplicity Model 3008-3.

1. Brake drum
2. Transaxle cover
3. Axle bearing
4. Bushings
5. Washers
6. Snap rings
7. Retainer ring
8. 1st & reverse shift fork
9. Spring
10. Detent ball
11. 1st & reverse shift rail
12. Reverse gear bushing
13. Reverse gear
14. Reverse shaft
15. Shift lever
16. Shift rod
17. Oil seal
18. Gear & shaft
19. "O" ring
20. Input pulley
21. Shift rod bushing
22. Oil seal

23. Oil seal
24. Axle housing
25. Axle bearings
26. Transaxle case
28. Drive gear
29. Spring
30. Differential pinion
31. Spindle
32. Differential pinion
33. Axle shaft R.H.
34. Axle shaft L.H.
35. Sliding gear
36. Brake shaft
37. Cluster gear
38. Shift fork
39. Shift rail
40. Input shaft
41. Washer
42. Thrust cap
43. Bushing
44. Spacer
45. Washer
46. Retaining ring

Fig. ST4–Exploded view of 3-speed transaxle used on Simplicity 3008-FE3.

and spindles from differential plate (32) and drive gear (28).

Clean and inspect all parts and renew any showing excessive wear or other damage. Renew oil seals and gaskets and reassemble by reversing the disas-

sembly procedure. Tighten differential through-bolts to a torque of 20 ft.-lbs. (27 N•m) and nuts securing reverse shaft and shift rails to case to a torque of 50 ft.-lbs. (68 N•m). Install shims (45-Fig. ST4) as required to obtain

0.010-0.040 inch (0.25-1.02 mm) end play on axle shaft (33).

Fill transaxle housing, after unit is installed, to level plug opening with SAE 90 gear oil. Capacity is approximately 2½ pints (1.18L).

DIFFERENTIAL REPAIR

Differentials used in most riding mowers are manufactured by other than OEM plant. Exceptions are noted as they occur. The differential and axle shaft suppliers normally provide axle ends of custom design and in lengths to match hub and wheel designs specified by the base manufacturer.

Differentials are identified by make and models, according to latest available information, in each riding mower section of this manual.

Removal and reinstallation procedures are covered in each unit manufacturer's section. Also see manufacturer's section for such external adjustments as axle alignment and correct setting of drive chain tension.

DEERE AND COMPANY

OVERHAUL. NOTE: Complete differential assembly is not identified by a model number; therefore, if parts are needed, be sure to specify mower model number.

When rear axle-differential assembly has been removed, clean exterior thoroughly, then remove cotter pin from retainer collar (9-Fig. JD1) and back off four nuts (7) from housing cap screws (1). This will allow separation of housing halves (4) and removal of all

Fig. IW1—Exploded view of Indus Wheel Company's Model 73DP differential. This model is also referred to as a Mast-Foos differential.

1. Bolt, 5/16 NF X 1 1/4 (4)
2. Bolt, 5/16 NF X 2 5/8 (2)
3. Housing half (2)
4. Pinion gear (2)
5. Long axle and bevel gear
6. Short axle and bevel gear
7. Sprocket
8. Cap screw, 5/16 X 1 (4)
9. Flange nut, 5/16 NF (6)

internal gears. Clean housings, gears and shafts and renew as necessary.

If axle support shaft (10) is damaged or badly worn, drive out groove pin (11)

to separate support shaft (10) from left side axle shaft (12).

During reassembly, lubricate parts with a generous coating of JOHN DEERE No. AT30408 High Temperature grease or an equivalent quality EP lithium grease. Add a little excess to each case half.

Tighten assembly bolts to 13-16 ft.-lbs. (18-22 N·m) to complete reassembly.

FOOTE

Model 2260

OVERHAUL. Disassemble removed axle-differential after exterior clean-up by removing four locknuts (5—Fig. FD1). Separate case halves (7) and remove all internal parts for cleaning and inspection. Renew any parts which show signs of extensive wear or damage. Sleeve bearing (12) may have to be pressed from its bore in center of idler shaft (11) if renewal is necessary. If bushed axle bosses of housing halves (7) are worn excessively, housing will require renewal as bushings are not serviced separately. Do not overlook condition of four flat thrust washers (8). If worn badly (original thickness—0.062 inch), these should be renewed to pre-

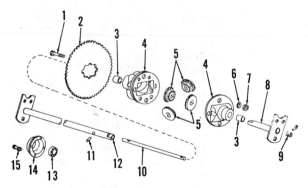

Fig. JD1—Exploded view of differential assembly manufactured by John Deere for riding mower Models 66 and 68.

1. Cap screw 5/16 X 1 1/4 (4)
2. Sprocket
3. Bronze bearing (2)
4. Housing half (2)
5. Bevel gear (4)
6. Washer, 0.048 (4)
7. Elastic locknut (4)
8. Axle, RH
9. Retainer collar
10. Axle support shaft
11. Groove pin, 3/16
12. Axle, LH
13. Ball bearing
14. Axle bearing retainer
15. Cap screw 1/4 X 1/2 (4)

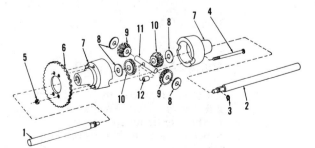

Fig. FD1—Exploded view of Foote Model 2260 differential.

1. Short axle shaft
2. Long axle shaft
3. Snap ring (2)
4. Bolt, 5/16-18 X 3 3/4 (4)
5. Locknut, 5/16-18 (NC)
6. Sprocket
7. Housing half (2)
8. Flat washer 0.062 (4)
9. Pinion gear (2)
10. Miter (side) gear (2)
11. Idler shaft
12. Sleeve bearing

vent excessive looseness when differential is reassembled.

Coat all gear teeth and wear surfaces of shafts liberally with a good grade of EP lithium grease during reassembly and torque assembly bolts and nuts (4 and 5) to 12-15 ft.-lbs. (16-20 N·m).

INDUS WHEEL
(Mast-Foos)

Model 73DP

OVERHAUL. With rear axle differential removed and thoroughly cleaned, unbolt and remove axle sprocket (7-Fig. IW1). Unbolt and separate cast housings (3) then withdraw pinions (4) and axle gears (5 and 6).

Use solvent to clean up all parts, then inspect carefully for undue wear or damage.

Torque assembly bolts to 115-140 in.-lbs. (13-16 N·m).

LUBRICATION. Use ¾ to 1¼ ounces (0.02-0.04 kg) of grease applied to gear teeth and to wear surfaces of axle shafts and castings. Shell EPRO 71030 (Alrania) is recommended by Indus Wheel Company. John Deere recommends use of their number AT30408 High Temperature or equivalent EP lithium grease. Lawn Boy (OMC) specifies use of Lubriplate number 630-AA. Roper recommends Shell Darina type AX. Do not substitute inexpensive lead soap greases or other lubricants of unknown quality or performance characteristics.

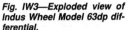

Fig. IW3—Exploded view of Indus Wheel Model 63dp differential.
1. Flanged axle bearing (2)
2. Wheel hub key (2)
3. Short axle shaft
4. Locknut (4)
5. Housing halves (2)
6. Bevel gear (2)
7. Snap ring (2)
8. Bevel pinion (2)
9. Cross
10. Pinion shaft
11. Long axle shaft
12. Assembly bolt (4)

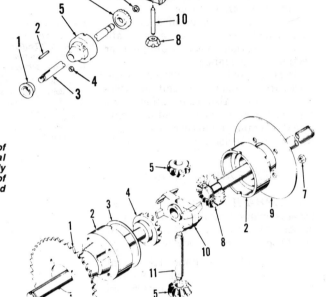

Fig. IW4—Exploded view of Indus Wheel differential known by Murray assembly number 21402. It is typical of Models 21000, 21179 and 20685.
1. Sprocket
2. Housing half (2)
3. Gasket
4. Gear & short axle
5. Bevel pinion (2)
6. Bolt, 5/16-24 (3¼)
7. Locknut, 5/16-24 (NF)
8. Gear & long axle
9. Brake disc*
10. Differential cross
11. Pinion shaft
*Selected models only

Model 63DP

OVERHAUL. With axle-differential assembly removed, thoroughly clean exterior of axle, differential housing and sprocket with a suitable solvent. Pay particular attention to axle shaft ends, threads and keyways. Remove burrs from axle.

Remove locknuts (4–Fig. IW3) from assembly bolts (12) and pull bolts out as sprocket is removed. Separate housing halves and withdraw internal differential parts. To remove gears (6) from axles (3 and 11), first remove snap rings (7).

Renew all defective parts and reassemble in reverse of disassembly order.

During reassembly, lubricate all wear surfaces with a minimum of three ounces of Shell EPRO 71030 grease or equivalent.

Torque locknuts (4) in an even cross-pattern to 13-15 ft.-lbs. (18-20 N·m). Heads of bolts (12) are on sprocket side.

Murray Assembly 21402

Overhaul procedure for differential unit shown in Fig. IW4 is very similar to that for Indus Wheel Model 63DP, which is described in the preceding section.

Fig. IW2—Exploded view of Indus Wheel Model 73DP differential with sprocket installed (View A) and partially disassembled (View B). See text.

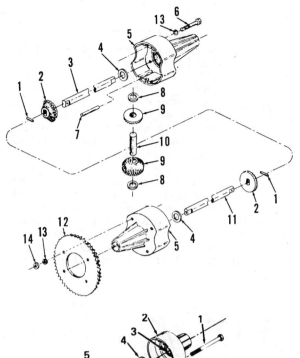

Fig. MTD1—Exploded view of MTD Products differential.

1. Spring pin
2. Bevel gear
3. Long axle
4. Washer, 0.76X1.49
5. Housing half (2)
6. Screw, $5/16$-24X4 (4)
7. Dowel, $3/16$
8. Flat washer 0.64 ID
9. Pinion gear (2)
10. Drive pin
11. Short axle
12. Sprocket
13. Lockwasher, $5/16$ (8)
14. Locknut, $5/16$-24 (NF)

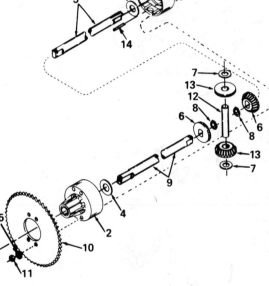

Fig. MTD2—Exploded view of MTD Products differential No. 10483, identified also by Jacobsen No. 501062.

1. Bolt $5/16$-24X4 (4)
2. Housing half (2)
3. Sleeve bearing
4. Flat washer (2)
5. Long axle
6. Bevel gear
7. Flat washer (2)
8. Snap ring, $3/4$-in.
9. Short axle
10. Sprocket
11. Locknut, $5/16$-24
12. Drive pin
13. Pinion gear (2)
14. Dowel pin, $3/16$-in.
15. Lockwasher (4)

MTD PRODUCTS

All Models

OVERHAUL. Differential models shown in Fig. MTD1 and MTD2 are very similar in design and appearance and many internal parts can be interchanged from one model to the other. Side and pinion gears, drive pins, assembly dowels, spacer washers and assembly bolts and nuts for each model bear identical part numbers. Obviously, housings used are different and axle lengths and sprockets will vary among different riding mower models. The outstanding difference to be noted is that in Fig. MTD1, bevel gears (2) are attached to axles (3 and 11) by spring

Fig. PD1—Exploded view of 100 Series PEERLESS differential.

1. Sprocket
2. Differential housing (2)
3. Bushing (2)
4. Thrust washer (2)
5. Axle shaft (long)
6. Through-bolt (4) $5/16$-inch
7. Flat washer (4)
8. Bevel gear (2)
9. Thrust washer (2)
10. Pinion gear (2)
12. Drive pin
13. Snap ring (2)
14. Axle shaft (short)

pins (1); whereas, as shown in Fig. MTD2, snap rings (8) are used. Housings (2-Fig. MTD2) also have renewable bushings (3) while flanged bearings are used in housing half assemblies (5-Fig. MTD1). On both models, the overhaul procedure will be obvious after removing the assembly bolts.

Approximately two ounces of high temperature EP lithium grease applied to friction surfaces during reassembly is required for lubrication.

Torque all four assembly bolts evenly to 13-15 ft.-lbs. (18-20 N·m) in a cross pattern with locknut fitted on sprocket side of differential.

PEERLESS

Series 100

OVERHAUL. The 100 Series PEERLESS differentials, when TECUMSEH-PEERLESS assembly numbers are used, may be identified by numbers 101 through 199, sometimes with a letter suffix. Number variations specify particular differences in axle shaft lengths and configuration of shaft ends for matching to various hub styles.

Before disassembly of removed axle differential, thoroughly clean outside. Clear keyways and/or pin bores and carefully remove burrs from axle surfaces. Hardened shaft metals call for use of a stone to smooth finish.

Remove four locknuts which hold sprocket (1-Fig. PD1) to differential housing (2), then back out through-bolts (6) and separate housing halves. Lift out drive pin (12) together with pinion gears (10) and thrust washers (9). Remove snap ring (13), then bevel gears (8) and thrust washers (4). Examine all parts for wear, cracks, chips or galling after thorough clean-up with solvent.

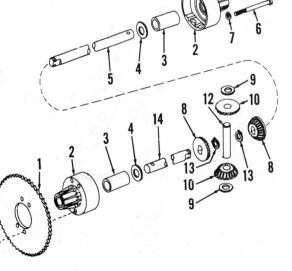

Differential Repair

Fig. PD2—Partially disassembled view of PEERLESS 100 Series differential. Through-bolts are threaded into left housing.

Series 1300

OVERHAUL. Unscrew cap screws and drive out dowel pins in cover (29-Fig. PD3). Lift cover off case and axle shaft. Withdraw brake shaft (5), idler gear (4) and thrust washers (3 and 6) from case. Remove output shaft (11), output gear (10), spacer (9), thrust washer (8) and differential assembly from case. Axle shaft housings (20 and 22) must be pressed from case and cover.

To disassemble differential, unscrew four cap screws (17) and separate axle shaft and carrier assemblies from ring gear (28). Drive blocks (25), bevel pinion gears (26) and drive pin (27) can now be removed from ring gear. Remove snap rings (12) and slide axle shafts (18 and

Bushings (3) can be pressed from housing halves (2). PEERLESS bushing tool No. 670204 is available for reinstallation of bushings.

Renew all defective parts and reassemble differential in reverse of disassembly order. It will be noted that sprocket (1), threaded side of differential housing (2) and assembly nuts are all assembled on short axle side.

During assembly, lubricate differential using one ounce of EP (Extreme Pressure) lithium grease on wear points and gear teeth, apply grease to bushings (3) before inserting axles, and grease drive pin and gears. No seals, sealer compounds or gaskets are used.

Observe these torque values in checking final assembly:

Housing through-bolts 250-300 in.-lbs.
(28-34 N·m)
Sprocket locknuts . . .120-150 in.-lbs.
(13-17 N·m)

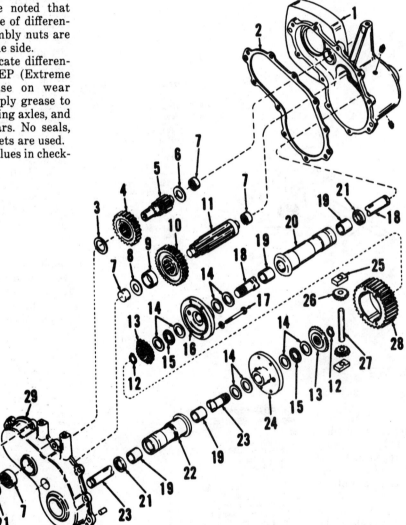

Fig. PD3—Exploded view of Peerless Series 1300 gear reduction and differential unit.

1. Case	6. Washer	11. Output shaft	16. Differential carrier
2. Gasket	7. Bearing	12. Snap ring	17. Bolt
3. Washer	8. Washer	13. Side gears	18. Axle shaft R.H.
4. Idler gear	9. Spacer	14. Thrust washers	19. Bushing
5. Brake shaft	10. Output gear	15. Thrust bearing	20. Axle housing

21. Oil seal	25. Drive block
22. Axle housing	26. Drive pinion
23. Axle shaft L.H.	27. Drive pin
24. Differential carrier	28. Ring gear
	29. Cover

Illustrations Courtesy Tecumseh Products Co.

Fig. SW1—Exploded view of Stewart Model 9500 differential.

5. End cap, L.H.
6. Axle shaft, L.H.
7. Housing and spider gears
8. Axle shaft, R.H.
9. End cap, R.H.

23) from axle gears (13) and carriers (16 and 24.)

Clean and inspect all parts and renew any parts damaged or excessively worn. When installing needle bearings, press bearings in from inside of case or cover until bearings are 0.015-0.020 inch (0.38-0.51 mm) below thrust surfaces. Be sure heads of differential cap screws (17) and right axle shaft (18) are installed in right carrier housing (16). Right axle shaft is installed through case (1). Tighten differential cap screws to 7 ft.-lbs. (10 N·m) and cover cap screws to 10 ft.-lbs. (13 N·m). Differential assembly and output shaft (11) must be installed in case at same time. Remainder of assembly is reverse of disassembly procedure.

STEWART

Model 9500

OVERHAUL. To disassemble differential, remove bolts and nuts securing end caps (5 and 7—Fig. SW1) to housing assembly (7). Separate end caps from housing, then clean and inspect all parts and renew any showing excessive wear or any other damage. Reassemble by reversing the disassembly procedure. Fill differential housing with ¾-1¼ ounces (0.02-0.04 kg) of multipurpose EP grease.

ENGINE REPAIR

BRIGGS & STRATTON

BRIGGS & STRATTON CORPORATION
Milwaukee, Wisconsin 53201

BRIGGS & STRATTON ENGINE IDENTIFICATION INFORMATION

In order to obtain correct service parts for Briggs & Stratton engines it is necessary to correctly identify engine model or series and provide engine serial number.

Briggs & Stratton model or series number also provides information concerning important mechanical features or optional equipment.

Refer to the table below for an explanation of each digit in relation to engine identification or description of mechanical features and options.

As an example, a 401417 series model number is broken down in the following manner:

40 – Designates 40 cubic inch displacement.
 1 – Designates design series 1.
 4 – Designates horizontal shaft, Flo-Jet carburetor and mechanical governor.
 1 – Designates flange mounting with plain bearings.
 7 – Designates electric starter, 12 volt gear drive with alternator.

	FIRST DIGIT AFTER DISPLACEMENT		SECOND DIGIT AFTER DISPLACEMENT	THIRD DIGIT AFTER DISPLACEMENT	FOURTH DIGIT AFTER DISPLACEMENT
CUBIC INCH DISPLACEMENT	BASIC DESIGN SERIES		CRANKSHAFT, CARBURETOR GOVERNOR	BEARINGS, REDUCTION GEARS & AUXILIARY DRIVES	TYPE OF STARTER
6	0		0 -	0 - Plain Bearing	0 - Without Starter
8	1		1 - Horizontal Vacu-Jet	1 - Flange Mounting Plain Bearing	1 - Rope Starter
9	2		2 - Horizontal Pulsa-Jet	2 - Ball Bearing	2 - Rewind Starter
10	3		3 - Horizontal Flo-Jet	3 - Flange Mounting Ball Bearing	3 - Elecric - 110 Volt, Gear Drive
11	4		4 - Horizontal Flo-Jet	4 -	4 - Electric Starter-Generator - 12 Volt, Belt Drive
13	5				
14	6		5 - Vertical Vacu-Jet	5 - Gear Reduction (6 to 1) Gear Drive	5 - Electric Starter Only - 12 Volt,
17	7				
19	8		6 -	6 - Gear Reduction (6 to 1) Reverse Rotation	6 - Alternator Only*
20	9				
23			7 - Vertical Flo-Jet	7 -	7 - Electric Starter, 12 Volt Gear Drive, with Alternator
24					
25			8 -	8 - Auxiliary Drive Perpendicular to Crankshaft	8 - Vertical-pull Starter
30					
32			9 - Vertical Pulsa-Jet	9 - Auxiliary Drive Parallel to Crankshaft	*Digit 6 formerly used for "Wind-Up" Starter on 60000, 80000 and 92000 Series

Explanation of model or series number of Briggs & Stratton engines.

A. First one or two digits indicate CUBIC INCH DISPLACEMENT.
B. First digit after displacement indicates BASIC DESIGN SERIES, relating to cylinder construction, ignition, general configuration, etc.
C. Second digit after displacement indicates POSITION OF CRANKSHAFT AND TYPE OF CARBURETOR.
D. Third digit after displacement indicates TYPE OF BEARINGS and whether or not engine is equipped with REDUCTION GEAR or AUXILIARY DRIVE.
E. Last digit indicates TYPE OF STARTER.

BRIGGS & STRATTON

4-STROKE ENGINES (except Quantum & Vanguard)

Model Series	Bore	Stroke	Displacement
6B, Early 60000, Early 61000	2.3125 in. (58.7 mm)	1.500 in. (38.1 mm)	6.3 cu.in. (103 cc)
Late 60000, Late 61000	2.375 in. (60.3 mm)	1.500 in. (38.1 mm)	6.7 cu.in. (109 cc)
8B, 80000, 81000, 82000	2.375 in. (60.3 mm)	1.750 in. (44.5 mm)	7.8 cu.in. (127 cc)
90000, 91000, 92000, 93000, 94000, 95000	2.5625 in. (65.1 mm)	1.750 in. (44.5 mm)	9.0 cu.in. (148 cc)
100000	2.500 in. (63.5 mm)	2.125 in. (54.0 mm)	10.4 cu.in. (169 cc)
110000, 111000, 112000, 113000, 114000	2.7812 in. (70.6 mm)	1.875 in. (47.6 mm)	11.4 cu.in. (186 cc)
130000, 131000, 132000	2.5625 in. (65.1 mm)	2.438 in. (60.9 mm)	12.6 cu.in. (203 cc)
140000	2.750 in. (69.9 mm)	2.375 in. (60.3 mm)	14.1 cu.in. (231 cc)

ENGINE IDENTIFICATION

Engines covered in this section have aluminum cylinder blocks with either plain aluminum cylinder bore or with a cast iron sleeve integrally cast into the block.

Early production of the 60000 and 61000 model engine were of the same bore and stroke as the 6B model engine. The bore on 60000 and 61000 engine was changed from 2.3125 inches (58.7 mm) to 2.375 inches (60.3 mm) at serial number 5810060 on engines with plain aluminum bore, and at serial number 5810030 on engines with a cast iron sleeve.

Refer to BRIGGS & STRATTON ENGINE IDENTIFICATION INFORMATION section for engine identification. Always furnish correct engine model and serial number when ordering parts.

MAINTENANCE

SPARK PLUG. Recommended spark plug for all models is Champion J-8C if a 2 inch plug is desired, or CJ-8 if a 1½ inch plug is required. Use an RJ-8C or RCJ-8 if a resistor plug is needed to decrease radio interference. Spark plug electrode gap for all models is 0.030 inch (0.76 mm).

CAUTION: Briggs & Stratton does not recommend using abrasive blasting method to clean spark plugs as this may introduce some abrasive material into the engine which could cause extensive damage.

FLOAT TYPE (FLO-JET) CARBURETORS. Walbro Type. Some 83000, 90000, 91000, 110000, 111000, 112000, 114000, 1300000 and 131000 models may be equipped with the Walbro type carburetor shown in Fig. B59. The carburetor may be equipped with a fixed main jet or the adjustable high speed mixture screw shown.

Initial setting of idle mixture screw (10) and high-speed mixture screw (23), if so equipped, is 1¼ turns out. With engine at normal operating temperature and equipment control lever in "SLOW" position, adjust idle speed screw (8) so engine idles at 1750 rpm. With engine running at idle speed, turn idle mixture screw clockwise until engine speed just starts to drop. Note screw position. Turn idle mixture screw counterclockwise until engine speed just starts to drop again. Note screw position, then turn screw to midpoint between the noted screw positions. If equipped with high speed mixture screw, set control to "FAST" and adjust high speed screw using same procedure. If engine will not accelerate cleanly, slightly enrichen mixture by turning idle mixture screw counterclockwise. If necessary, readjust idle speed screw. If engine does not run properly at high altitude, remove main air jet (13) and adjust mixture for smooth operation.

Overhaul of carburetor is evident after inspection of carburetor and referral to exploded view in Fig. B59. A ⁵⁄₃₂ inch punch ground flat at the end makes a suitable tool for removing Welch plug (9). Clean and inspect components and discard any parts which are damaged or excessively worn.

When reassembling carburetor, note the following: Do not deform Welch plug (9) during installation; it should be flat. Seal outer edges of plug with non-hardening sealer. Install choke and throttle plates so numbers are on outer face when choke or throttle plate is in closed position. Install fuel inlet seat using B&S drive 19057 or a suitable tool so grooved face of seat is down. Float height is not adjustable. Tighten fuel bowl retaining nut to 50 in.-lbs. (5.6 N·m). Tighten carburetor mounting nuts to 90 in.-lbs. (10.2 N·m).

B&S Flo-Jet Carburetors. Three different B&S Flo-Jet carburetors are used. They are called a "two-piece" (Fig. B60), a small "one-piece" (Fig. B64) or a large "one-piece" (Fig. B66) carburetor depending upon the type of construction.

Float type carburetors are equipped with adjusting needles for both idle and power fuel mixtures. Counterclockwise rotation of the adjusting needles richens the mixture. For initial starting adjustment, open the main needle valve (power fuel mixture) 1½ turns on the two-piece carburetor and 2½ turns on the small one-piece carburetor. Open the idle needle ½ to ¾ turn on the two-piece carburetor and 1½ turns on the small one-piece carburetor. On the large one-piece carburetor, open both needle valves 1⅛ turns.

Make final adjustments with engine at operating temperature and running. Set the speed control for desired operating speed, turn main needle clockwise until engine misses, and then turn it counterclockwise just past the smooth operating point until the engine begins to run unevenly. Return the speed control to idle position and adjust the idle speed

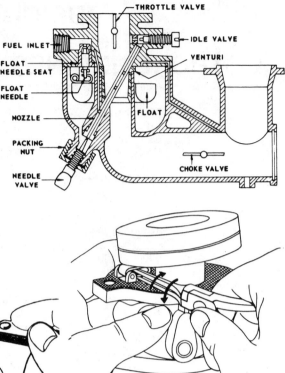

Fig. B60—Cross-sectional view of typical B&S "two-piece" carburetor. Before separating upper and lower body sections, loosen packing nut and unscrew nut and needle valve as a unit. Then, using special screwdriver, remove nozzle. Refer to text.

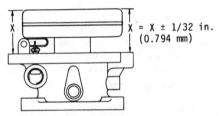

Fig. B61—Checking upper body of "two-piece" carburetor for warpage. Refer to text.

Fig. B63—Bending tang with needlenose pliers to adjust float setting. Refer to Fig. B62 for method of checking float setting.

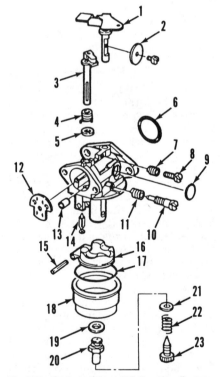

Fig. B59—Exploded view of Walbro type float carburetor. The carburetor may be equipped with fixed main jet or adjustable high speed mixture screw as shown.

1. Throttle shaft
2. Throttle plate
3. Choke shaft
4. Spring
5. Seal
6. Gasket
7. Spring
8. Idle speed screw
9. Welch plug
10. Idle mixture screw
11. Spring
12. Choke plate
13. Air jet
14. Fuel inlet valve
15. Float pin
16. Float
17. Gasket
18. Fuel bowl
19. Washer
20. Bowl retainer
21. "O" ring
22. Spring
23. Main fuel mixture screw

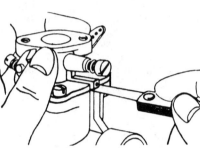

$X = X \pm 1/32$ in. (0.794 mm)

Fig. B62—Carburetor float setting should be within specifications shown. To adjust float setting, bend tang with needlenose pliers as shown in Fig. B63.

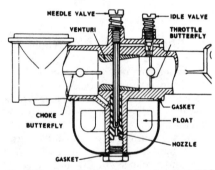

Fig. B64—Cross-sectional view of typical B&S small "one-piece" float type carburetor. Refer to Fig. B65 for disassembly views.

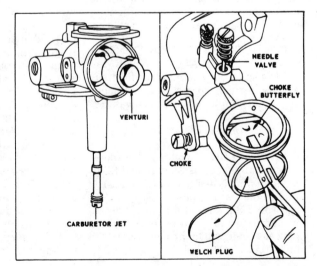

Fig. B65—To disassemble the small "one-piece" float type carburetor, pry out welch plug, remove choke butterfly (disc), remove choke shaft and needle valve; venturi can then be removed as shown in left view.

Illustrations Courtesy Briggs & Stratton Corp.

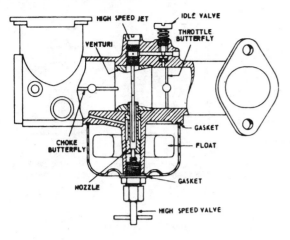

Fig. B66—Cross-sectional view of B&S large "one-piece" float type carburetor.

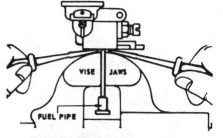

Fig. B68—Removing brass fuel feed pipe from suction-type carburetor. Press new brass pipe into carburetor until it projects 2-9/32 to 2-5/16 inches (57.9-58.7 mm) from carburetor face. Nylon fuel feed pipe is threaded into carburetor.

stop screw until the engine idles at 1750 rpm. Adjust the idle needle valve until the engine runs smoothly. Reset the idle speed stop screw if necessary. The engine should then accelerate without hesitation. If engine does not accelerate properly, turn the main needle valve counterclockwise slightly to provide a richer fuel mixture.

The float setting on all float type carburetors should be within dimensions shown in Fig. B62. If not, bend the tang on float as shown in Fig. B63 to adjust float setting. If any wear is visible on the inlet valve or the inlet valve seat, install a new valve and seat assembly. On large one-piece carburetors, the renewable inlet valve seat is pressed into the carburetor body until flush with the body.

NOTE: The upper and lower bodies of the two-piece float type carburetor are locked together by the main nozzle. Refer to cross-sectional view of carburetor in Fig. B60. Before attempting to separate the upper body from the lower body, loosen packing nut and unscrew nut and needle valve. Then, using special screwdriver (B&S tool 19061 or 19062), remove nozzle.

If a 0.002 inch (0.05 mm) feeler gage can be inserted between upper and lower bodies of the two-piece carburetor as shown in Fig. B61, the upper body is warped and should be renewed.

Check the throttle shaft for wear on all float type carburetors. If 0.010 inch (0.25 mm) or more free play (shaft-to-bushing clearance) is noted, install new throttle shaft and/or throttle shaft bushings. To remove worn bushings, turn a ¼ inch × 20 tap into bushing and pull bushing from body casting with the tap. Press new bushings into casting by using a vise and, if necessary, ream bushings with a 7/32 inch drill bit.

SUCTION TYPE (VACU-JET) CARBURETORS. A typical suction type (Vacu-Jet) carburetor is shown in Fig. B67. This type carburetor has only one fuel mixture adjusting needle. Turning the needle clockwise leans the air:fuel mixture. Adjust suction type carburetors with fuel tank approximately one-half full and with the engine at operating temperature and running at approximately 3000 rpm, no-load. Turn needle valve clockwise until engine begins to run unevenly from a too rich air:fuel mixture. This should result in a correct adjustment for full load operation. Adjust idle speed to 1750 rpm.

To remove the suction type carburetor, first remove carburetor and fuel tank as an assembly, then remove carburetor from fuel tank. When reinstalling carburetor on fuel tank, use a new gasket and tighten retaining screws evenly.

The suction type carburetor has a fuel feed pipe extending into fuel tank. The pipe has a check valve to allow fuel to feed up into the carburetor but prevents fuel from flowing back into the tank. If check valve is inoperative and cleaning in alcohol or acetone will not free the check valve, renew the fuel feed pipe. If feed pipe is made of brass, remove as shown in Fig. B68. Using a vise, press new pipe into carburetor so it extends from 2⁹/₃₂ to 2⁵/₁₆ inches (57.9-58.7 mm) from carburetor body. If pipe is made of nylon (plastic), screw pipe out of carburetor body with wrench. When installing new nylon feed pipe, be careful not to overtighten.

NOTE: If soaking carburetor in cleaner for more than one-half hour, be sure to remove all nylon parts and "O" ring, if used, before placing the carburetor in cleaning solvent.

PUMP TYPE (PULSA-JET) CARBURETORS. The pump type (Pulsa-Jet) carburetor is basically a suction type carburetor incorporating a fuel

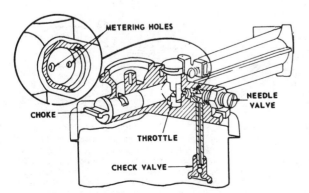

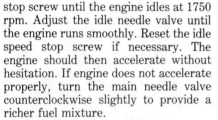

Fig. B67—Cutaway view of typical suction type (Vacu-Jet) carburetor. Inset shows fuel metering holes which are accessible for cleaning after removing needle valve. Be careful not to enlarge the holes when cleaning them.

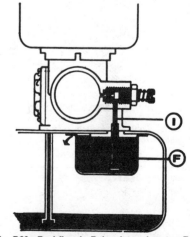

Fig. B69—Fuel flow in Pulsa-Jet carburetor. Fuel pump incorporated in carburetor fills constant level sump (F) below carburetor and excess fuel flows back into tank. Fuel is drawn from sump through inlet (I) past fuel mixture adjusting needle by vacuum in carburetor.

Illustrations Courtesy Briggs & Stratton Corp.

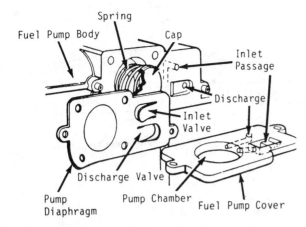

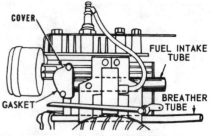

Fig. B70—Exploded view of fuel pump that is incorporated in Pulsa-Jet carburetor except those used on 82900, 92900, 94900, 110900, 111900, 112200 and 113900 models; refer to Fig. B71.

Fig. B74—On 82000 Models, intake tube is threaded into intake port of engine; a gasket is placed between intake port cover and intake port.

pump to fill a constant level fuel sump in top of fuel tank. Refer to schematic view in Fig. B69. This makes a constant air:fuel mixture available to engine regardless of fuel level in tank. Adjustment of the pump type carburetor fuel mixture needle valve is the same as outlined for suction type carburetors in previous paragraph, except that fuel level in tank is not important.

To remove the pump type carburetor, first remove the carburetor and fuel tank as an assembly; then, remove carburetor from fuel tank. When reinstalling carburetor on fuel tank, use a new gasket or pump diaphragm as required and tighten retaining screws evenly.

Fig. B70 shows an exploded view of the pump unit used on all carburetors except those for Models 82900, 92900, 94900, 110900, 111900, 112200 and 113900 the pump diaphragm is placed between the carburetor and fuel tank as shown in Fig. B71.

The pump type carburetor has two fuel feed pipes. The long pipe feeds fuel into the pump portion of the carburetor from which fuel then flows to the constant level fuel sump. The short pipe extends into the constant level sump and feeds fuel into the carburetor venturi via fuel mixture needle valve.

As check valves are incorporated in the pump diaphragm, fuel feed pipes on pump type carburetors do not have a check valve. However, if the fuel screen in lower end of pipe is broken or clogged and cannot be cleaned, the pipe or screen housing can be renewed. If pipe is made of nylon, pipe snaps into place and considerable force is required to remove or install pipe. Be careful to not damage new pipe. If pipe is made of brass, clamp pipe lightly in a vise and drive old screen housing from pipe with a screwdriver or small chisel as shown in Fig. B72. Drive a new screen housing onto pipe with a soft faced hammer.

NOTE: If soaking carburetor in cleaner for more than one-half hour, be sure to remove all nylon parts and "O" ring, if used, before placing carburetor in cleaning solvent.

NOTE: On engine Models 82900, 92900, 94900, 95500, 110900, 111900 and 113900, be sure air cleaner retaining screw is in place if engine is being operated (during tests) without air cleaner installed. If screw is not in place, fuel will lift up

through the screw hole and enter carburetor throat as the screw hole leads directly into the constant level fuel sump.

INTAKE TUBE. Models 82000, 92000, 93500, 94500, 94900, 95500, 100900, 110900, 111900, 113900, 130900 and 131900 have an intake tube between carburetor and engine intake port. Carburetor is sealed to intake tube with an "O" ring as shown in Fig. B73.

On Model 82000 engines, the intake tube is threaded into the engine intake port. A gasket is used between the engine intake port cover and engine casting. Refer to Fig. B74.

On Models 92000, 93500, 94500, 94900, 95500, 110900, 111900 and 113900 engines, the intake tube is bolted to the engine intake port and gasket is used between the intake tube and engine casting. Refer to Fig. B75. On Models 100900, 130900 and 131900 intake tubes are attached to engine in similar manner.

CHOKE-A-MATIC CARBURETOR CONTROLS. Engines equipped with float, suction or pump type carburetors may be equipped with a control unit with which the carburetor choke, throttle and magneto grounding switch are operated from a single lever (Choke-A-Matic carburetors). Refer to Figs. B76 through B82 for views showing the different

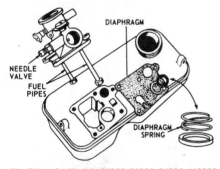

Fig. B71—On Models 82900, 92900, 94900, 110900, 111900, 112200 and 113900, pump type (Pulsa-Jet) carburetor diaphragm is installed between carburetor and fuel tank.

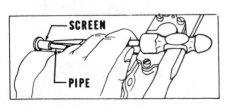

Fig. B72—To renew screen housing on pump type carburetor with brass feed pipes, drive old screen housing from pipe as shown. To hold pipe, clamp lightly in a vise.

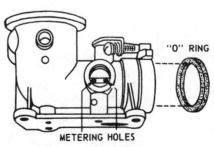

Fig. B73—Metering holes in pump type carburetors are accessible for cleaning after removing fuel mixture needle valve. On models with intake pipe, carburetor is sealed to pipe with "O" ring.

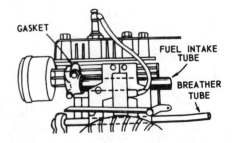

Fig. B75—On 92000, 93500, 94500, 94900, 95500, 110900, 111900 and 113900 models, fuel intake tube is bolted to engine intake port and a gasket is placed between tube and engine. On 100900, 130900 and 131900 vertical crankshaft models, intake tube and gasket are similar.

Illustrations Courtesy Briggs & Stratton Corp.

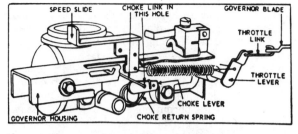

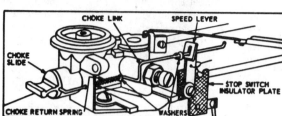

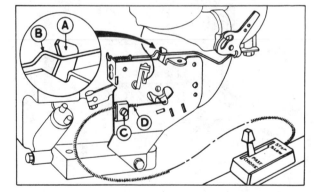

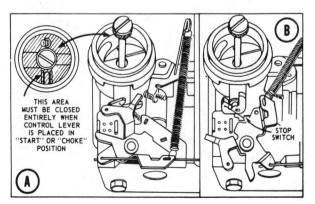

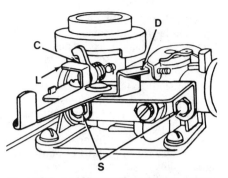

Fig. B76—Choke-A-Matic control on float type carburetor. Remote control can be attached to speed slide.

Fig. B77—Typical Choke-A-Matic control on suction type carburetor. Remote control can be attached to speed lever.

Fig. B78—Choke-A-Matic control in choke and stop positions on float carburetor.

Fig. B79—Choke-A-Matic controls in choke and stop positions on suction carburetor. Bend choke link if necessary to adjust control.

Fig. B80—On Choke-A-Matic control shown, choke actuating lever (A) should just contact choke link or shaft (B) when control is at "FAST" position. If not, loosen screw (C) and move control wire housing (D) as required.

Fig. B81—When Choke-A-Matic control is in "START" or "CHOKE" position, choke must be completely closed as shown in view A. When control is in "STOP" position, arm should contact stop switch (view B).

Fig. B81A—On Models 100900, 130900, 131900, and 132900 with Choke-A-Matic linkage, lever (L) should just touch choke lever (C) when lever (D) is in "FAST" detent. Loosen screws (S) and reposition control plate as needed.

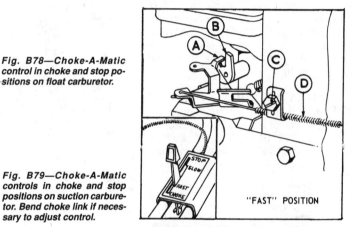

Fig. B82—On Choke-A-Matic controls shown, lever (A) should just contact choke shaft arm (B) when control is in "FAST" position. If not, loosen screw (C) and move control wire housing (D) as required, then tighten screw.

types of Choke-A-Matic carburetor controls.

To check operation of Choke-A-Matic carburetor controls, move control lever to "CHOKE" position. Carburetor choke slide or plate must be completely closed. Then, move control lever to "STOP" position. Magneto grounding switch should be making contact. With the control lever in "RUN", "FAST" or "SLOW" position, carburetor choke should be completely open. On units with remote controls, synchronize movement of remote lever to carburetor control lever by loosening screw (C – Fig. B80 or Fig. B82) and moving control wire housing (D) as required; then, tighten screw to clamp the housing securely. Refer to Fig. B83 to check remote control wire movement.

AUTOMATIC CHOKE (THERMOSTAT TYPE). A thermostat operated choke is used on some models equipped with the two-piece carburetor. To adjust choke linkage, hold choke shaft so thermostat lever is free. At room temperature, stop screw in thermostat collar should be located midway between thermostat stops. If not, loosen stop screw, adjust the collar and tighten stop screw. Loosen set screw (S – Fig. B84) on thermostat lever. Then, slide lever on shaft to ensure free movement of choke unit. Turn thermostat shaft clockwise until stop screw contacts thermostat stop. While holding shaft in this position, move shaft lever until choke is open exactly $\frac{1}{8}$ inch (3.17 mm) and tighten lever set screw. Turn thermostat shaft counterclockwise until stop screw contacts thermostat stop as shown in Fig. B85. Manually open choke valve until it stops against top of choke link opening. At this time, choke valve should be open at least $\frac{3}{32}$ inch (2.38 mm), but not more than $\frac{5}{32}$ inch (3.97 mm). Hold choke valve in wide open position and check position of counterweight lever. Lever should be in a horizontal position with free end towards right.

AUTOMATIC CHOKE (VACUUM TYPE). A spring and vacuum operated automatic choke is used on some 92000, 93500, 94500, 94900, 95500, 110900, 111900 and 113900 vertical crankshaft

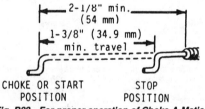

Fig. B83—For proper operation of Choke-A-Matic controls, remote control wire must extend to dimension shown and have a minimum travel of 1-3/8 inches (34.9 mm).

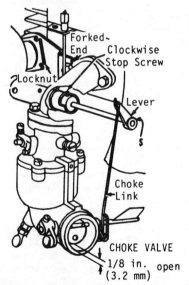

Fig. B84—Automatic choke used on some models equipped with "two-piece" Flo-Jet carburetor showing unit in "HOT" position.

engines. A diaphragm under carburetor is connected to the choke shaft by a link. The compression spring works against the diaphragm, holding choke in closed position when engine is not running. See Fig. B86. As engine starts, increased

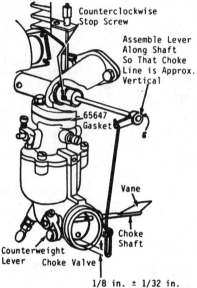

Fig. B85—Automatic choke on "two-piece" Flo-Jet carburetor in "COLD" position.

Fig. B86—Diagram showing vacuum operated automatic choke used on some 92000, 93500, 94500, 94900, 95500, 110900, 111900 and 113900 model vertical crankshaft engines in closed (engine not running) position.

Fig. B87—Diagram showing vacuum operated automatic choke in open (engine running) position.

vacuum works against the spring and pulls the diaphragm and choke link down, holding choke in open (running) position shown in Fig. B87.

During operation, if a sudden load is applied to engine or a lugging condition develops, a drop in intake vacuum occurs, permitting choke to close partially. This provides a richer fuel mixture to meet the condition and keeps the engine running smoothly. When the load condition has been met, increased vacuum returns choke valve to normal running (fully open) position.

ALL-TEMPERATURE/AUTOMATIC CHOKE. Some Pulsa-Jet and Vacu-Jet carburetors may be equipped with a choke that is controlled by a bimetallic spring located on the side of the carburetor body (Fig. B88). The spring reacts to air carried in the breather tube. Bimetallic spring and shaft may be detached by prying against shaft from inside the carburetor bore so the shaft is forced toward the outside of the carburetor.

FUEL TANK OUTLET. Small models with float type carburetors are equipped with a fuel tank outlet having a filter screen. On larger engines, a fuel sediment bowl is incorporated with

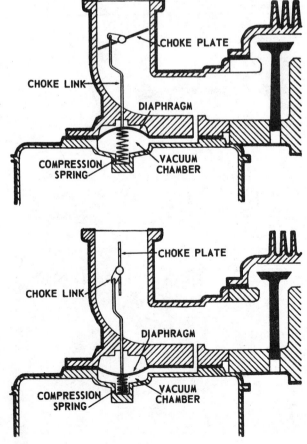

Illustrations Courtesy Briggs & Stratton Corp.

the fuel tank outlet. Clean any lint and dirt from tank outlet screens with a brush. Varnish or other gasoline deposits may be removed by using a suitable solvent. Tighten packing nut or remove nut and shut-off valve, then renew packing if leakage occurs around shut-off valve stem.

FUEL PUMP. A fuel pump is available as optional equipment on some models. Refer to SERVICING BRIGGS & STRATTON ACCESSORIES section in this manual for fuel pump service information.

GOVERNOR. All models are equipped with either a mechanical (flyweight type) or an air vane (pneumatic) governor. Refer to the appropriate paragraph for model being serviced.

Mechanical Governor. Three different designs of mechanical governors are used.

On all engines except 100000, 112200, 130000, 131000 and all late 140000 models, a governor unit as shown in Fig. B90 is used. An exploded view of this governor unit is shown in Fig. B91. The governor housing is attached to inner

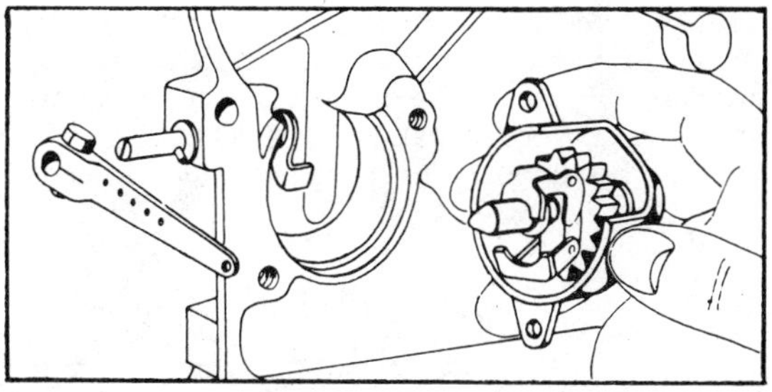

Fig. B90—Removing governor unit (except on 100000, 112200, 130000, 131000 and late 140000 models) from inside crankcase cover on horizontal crankshaft models. Refer to Fig. B91 for exploded view of governor.

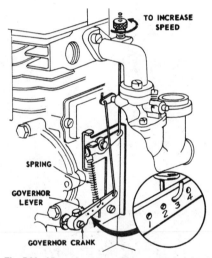

side of crankcase cover, and the governor gear is driven from the engine camshaft gear. Use Figs. B90 and B91 as a disassembly and assembly guide. Renew any parts that bind or show excessive wear. After governor is assembled, refer to Fig. B92 and adjust linkage by loosening screw clamping governor lever to governor crank. Turn governor lever counterclockwise so carburetor throttle is in wide open position. Hold lever and turn governor crank as far counterclockwise as possible, then tighten screw clamping lever to crank. Governor crank can be turned with a screwdriver. Check linkage to be sure it is free and that the carburetor throttle will move from idle to wide open position.

On 100000, 112200, 130000, 131000 and late 140000 horizontal crankshaft models, the governor gear and weight unit (G—Fig. B93) is supported on a pin in engine crankcase cover and the governor crank is installed in a bore in the engine crankcase. A thrust washer (W) is placed between governor gear and crankcase cover. When assembling

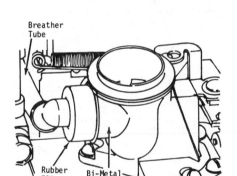

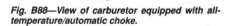

Fig. B88—View of carburetor equipped with all-temperature/automatic choke.

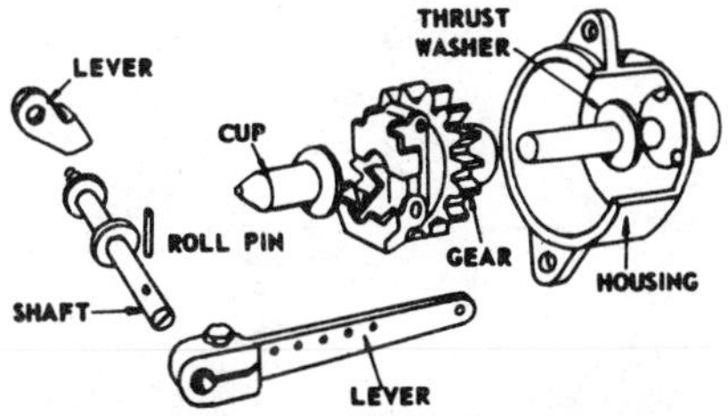

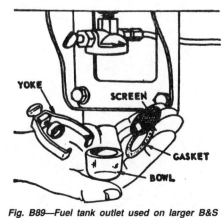

Fig. B91—Exploded view of governor unit used on all horizontal crankshaft models (except 100000, 112200, 130000, 131000 and late 140000 models) with mechanical governor. Refer also to Figs. B90 and B92.

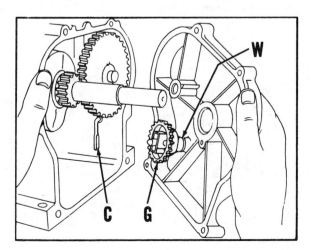

Fig. B92—View of governor linkage used on horizontal crankshaft mechanical governor models except 100000, 112200, 130000, 131000 and late 140000 models. Governor spring should be hooked in governor lever as shown in inset.

Fig. B89—Fuel tank outlet used on larger B&S engines.

Fig. B93—Installing crankcase cover on 100000, 112200, 130000, 131000 and late 140000 models with mechanical governor. Governor crank (C) must be in position shown. A thrust washer (W) is placed between governor (G) and crankcase cover.

crankcase cover to crankcase, be sure governor crank (C) is in position shown in Fig. B93. After governor unit and crankcase cover is installed, refer to Fig. B94 for installation of linkage. Before at-

tempting to start engine, refer to Fig. B95 and adjust linkage by loosening bolt clamping governor lever to governor crank. Set control lever in high speed position. Using a screwdriver, turn

governor crank as far clockwise as possible and tighten governor lever clamp bolt. Check to be sure carburetor throttle can be moved from idle to wide open position and that linkage is free.

On vertical crankshaft 95500, 100000, 113900, 130000, 131000 and 140000 with mechanical governor, the governor weight unit is integral with the lubricating oil slinger and is mounted on lower end of camshaft gear as shown in Fig. B96. With engine upside down, place governor and slinger unit on camshaft gear as shown, place spring washer (100000, 130900 and 131900 models only) on camshaft gear and install engine base on crankcase. Assemble linkage as shown in Fig. B97; then, refer to Fig. B98 and adjust linkage by loosening governor lever to governor crank clamp bolt, place control lever in high speed position, turn governor crank with screwdriver as far as possible and tighten governor lever clamping bolt.

Air Vane (Pneumatic) Governor. Refer to Fig. B99 for views showing typical air vane governor operation.

The vane should stop ⅛ to ¼ inch (3.17-6.35 mm) from the magneto coil (Fig. B100, illustration 2) when the linkage is assembled and attached to carburetor throttle shaft. If necessary to adjust, spring the vane while holding the shaft. With wide open throttle, the link from the air vane arm to the carburetor throttle should be in a vertical position on horizontal crankshaft models and in a horizontal position on vertical crankshaft models. (Fig. B100, illustration 3 and 4.) Check linkage for binding. If binding condition exists, bend links slightly to correct. Refer to Fig. B100, illustration 5.

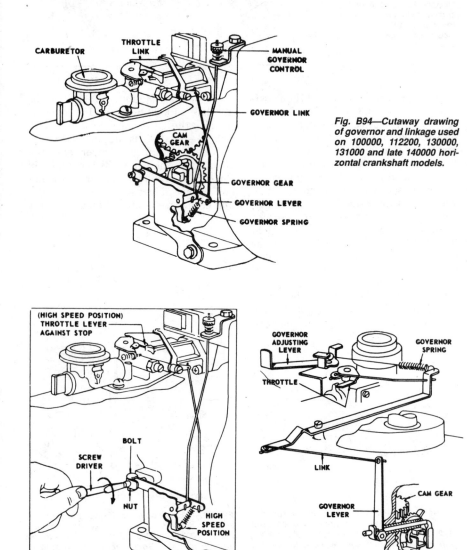

Fig. B94—Cutaway drawing of governor and linkage used on 100000, 112200, 130000, 131000 and late 140000 horizontal crankshaft models.

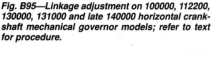

Fig. B95—Linkage adjustment on 100000, 112200, 130000, 131000 and late 140000 horizontal crankshaft mechanical governor models; refer to text for procedure.

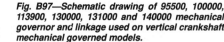

Fig. B97—Schematic drawing of 95500, 100000, 113900, 130000, 131000 and 140000 mechanical governor and linkage used on vertical crankshaft mechanical governed models.

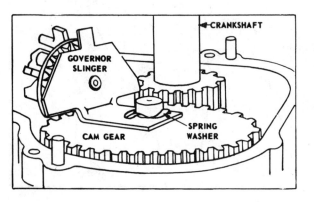

Fig. B96—View showing 95500, 100000, 113900, 130000, 131000 and 140000 vertical crankshaft model mechanical governor unit. Drawing is of lower side of engine with oil sump (engine base) removed; note spring washer location used on 100000, 130000 and 131000 models only.

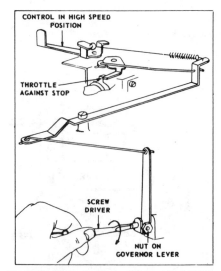

Fig. B98—View showing adjustment of 95500, 100000, 113900, 130000, 131000 and 140000 vertical crankshaft mechanical governor; refer to text for procedure.

NOTE: Some engines are equipped with a nylon governor vane which does not require adjustment.

MAGNETO. Breaker contact gap on all models with magneto type ignition is 0.020 inch (0.51 mm). On all models except "Sonoduct" (vertical crankshaft with flywheel below engine), breaker points and condenser are accessible after removing engine flywheel and breaker cover. On "Sonoduct" models, breaker points are located below breaker cover on top side of engine.

On some models, one breaker contact point is an integral part of the ignition condenser and the breaker arm pivots on a knife edge retained by a slot in pivot post. On these models, breaker contact gap is adjusted by moving the condenser as shown in Fig. B101. On other models, breaker contact gap is adjusted by relocating position of breaker contact bracket. Refer to Fig. B102.

On all models, breaker contact arm is actuated by a plunger held in a bore in engine crankcase and rides against a cam on engine crankshaft. Plunger can

be removed after removing breaker points. Renew plunger if worn to a length of 0.870 inch (22.1 mm) or less. Plunger must be installed with grooved end to the top to prevent oil seepage (Fig. B102A). Check breaker point plunger bore wear in crankcase with B&S plug gage 19055. If plug gage will enter bore ¼ inch (6.35 mm) or more, bore should be reamed and a bushing installed. Refer to Fig. B103 for method of checking bore and to Fig. B104 for steps in reaming bore and installing bushing if bore is worn. To ream bore and install bushing, it is necessary that the breaker points, armature and ignition coil and the crankshaft be removed.

On "Sonoduct" models, armature and ignition coil are inside flywheel on bottom side of engine. Armature air gap is correct if armature is installed flush with mounting boss as shown in Fig. B105. On all other models, armature and ignition coil are located outside flywheel. Armature air gap should be

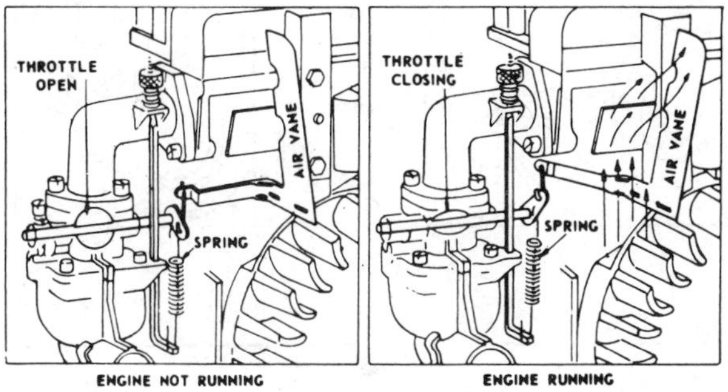

Fig. B99—Views showing operating principle of air vane (pneumatic) governor. Air from flywheel fan acts against air vane to overcome tension of governor spring; speed is adjusted by changing spring tension.

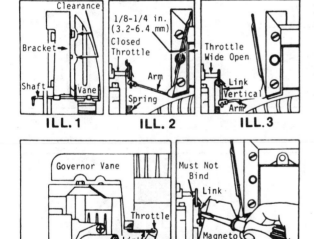

Fig. B100—Air vane governors and linkage. ILL. 1; the governor vane should be checked for clearance in all positions. ILL. 2; the vane should stop 1/8 to 1/4 inch (3.175-6.35 mm) from the magneto coil. ILL. 3; with wide open throttle, the link connecting vane arm to throttle lever should be in a vertical position on vertical cylinder engines and in a horizontal position (ILL. 4) on horizontal cylinder engines. Bend link slightly (ILL. 5) to remove any binding condition in linkage.

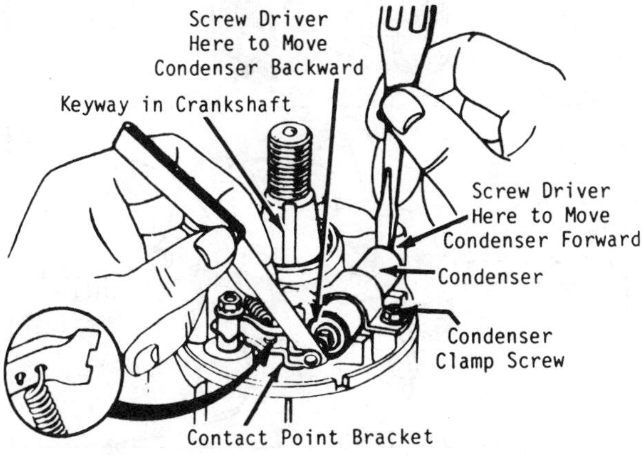

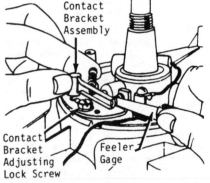

Fig. B102—Adjustment of breaker point gap on models having breaker point separate from condenser.

Fig. B101—View showing breaker point adjustment on models having breaker point integral with condenser. Move condenser to adjust point gap.

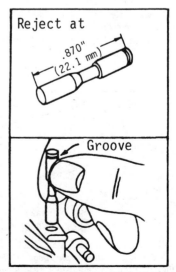

Fig. B102A—Insert plunger into bore with groove toward top. Refer to text.

0.012-0.016 inch (0.30-0.41 mm) for models with a three-leg armature. On models with a two-leg armature, the air gap should be 0.010-0.014 inch (0.25-0.36 mm) for Models 100000, 130000, 131000, 132000 and 140000, or 0.006-0.010 inch (0.15-0.25 mm) for all other models with a two-leg armature.

MAGNETRON IGNITION. Magnetron ignition is a self-contained breakerless ignition system. Flywheel does not need to be removed except to check or service keyways or crankshaft key.

To check spark, remove spark plug. Connect spark plug cable to B&S tester, part 19051, and ground remaining tester lead to cylinder head. Spin engine at 350 rpm or more. If spark jumps 0.165 inch (4.2 mm) tester gap, system is functioning properly.

Armature and module have been manufactured as either one-piece units or as a separable two-piece assembly. Two-piece units are identified by the large rivet heads on one side of the armature laminations. To remove armature and Magnetron module, remove flywheel shroud and armature retaining screws. On one-piece units, disconnect stop switch wire at spade connector. On two-piece units, use a $^3/_{16}$ inch (4.8 mm) diameter pin punch to release stop switch wire from module. To remove module on two-piece units, unsolder wires, push module retainer away from laminations and remove module. See Fig. B105A.

Armature air gap should be 0.010-0.014 inch (0.25-0.36 mm) for 100000 and 130000 models and 0.006-0.010 inch (0.15-0.25 mm) for all other models.

LUBRICATION. Vertical crankshaft engines are lubricated by an oil slinger wheel driven by the cam gear. On early 6B and 8B models, the oil slinger wheel was mounted on a bracket attached to the crankcase. Renew the bracket if pin on which gear rotates is worn to 0.490 inch (12.45 mm). Renew steel bushing

in hub or gear if worn. On later model vertical crankshaft engines, the oil slinger wheel, pin and bracket are an integral unit with the bracket being retained by the lower end of the engine camshaft.

On 100000, 130000 and 131000 models, a spring washer is placed on lower end of camshaft between bracket and oil sump boss. Renew the oil slinger assembly if teeth are worn on slinger gear or if gear is loose on brack-

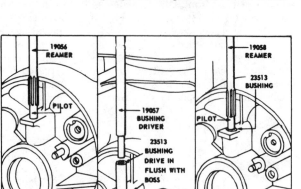

Fig. B104—Views showing reaming plunger bore to accept bushing (left view), installing bushing (center) and finish reaming bore (right) of bushing.

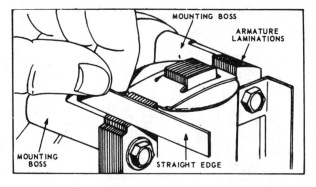

Fig. B105—On "Sonoduct" models, align armature core with mounting boss for proper magneto air gap.

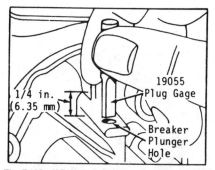

Fig. B103—If Briggs & Stratton plug gage #19055 can be inserted in breaker plunger bore a distance of 1/4 inch (6.35 mm) or more, bore is worn and must be rebushed.

Fig. B105A—Wires must be unsoldered to remove Magnetron ignition module. Refer to text.

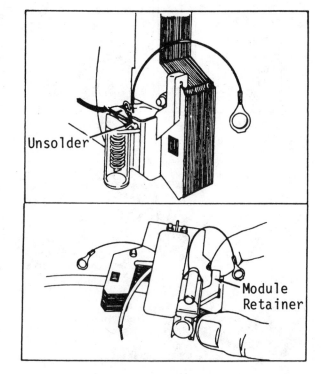

et. On horizontal crankshaft engines, a splash system (oil dipper on connecting rod) is used for engine lubrication.

Check engine oil level at five hour intervals and maintain at bottom edge of filler plug or to FULL mark on dipstick.

Change oil after first eight hours of operation and after every 50 hours of operation or at least once each operating season. Change oil weekly or after every 25 hours of operation if equipment undergoes severe usage.

Manufacturer recommends using oil with an API service classification of SF or SG. Use SAE 30 oil for temperatures above 40° F (4° C); use SAE 10W-30 oil for temperatures between 0° F (−18° C) and 100° F (38° C).

Crankcase capacity for all aluminum cylinder engines with displacement of 9 cubic inches (147 cc) or below is 1¼ pint (0.6 L).

Crankcase capacity of vertical crankshaft aluminum cylinder engines with displacement of 11 cubic inches (186 cc) is 1¼ pint (0.6 L).

Crankcase capacity for all 10 and 13 cubic inch (169 and 203 cc), vertical crankshaft, aluminum cylinder engines is 1¾ pint (0.8 L).

Crankcase capacity for all 10 and 13 cubic inch (169 and 203 cc), horizontal crankshaft, aluminum cylinder engines is 1¼ pint (0.6 L).

Crankcase capacity for 14 cubic inch (231 cc), vertical crankshaft, aluminum cylinder engines is 2¼ pint (1.1 L).

Crankcase capacity for 14 cubic inch (231 cc), horizontal crankshaft, aluminum cylinder engines is 2¾ pint (1.3 L).

Crankcase capacity for all engines with cast iron cylinder liner is 3 pints (1.4 L).

CRANKCASE BREATHER. The crankcase breather is built into the engine valve cover. The mounting holes are offset so the breather can only be installed one way. Rinse breather in solvent and allow to drain. A vent tube connects the breather to the carburetor air horn on certain model engines for extra protection against dusty conditions.

REPAIRS

CYLINDER HEAD. When removing cylinder head, be sure to note the position from which each of the different length screws was removed. If screws are not reinstalled in the same holes when installing the head, it will result in screws bottoming in some holes and not enough thread contact in others.

Lubricate the cylinder head screws with graphite grease before installation. Do not use sealer on head gasket. When installing cylinder head, tighten screws in

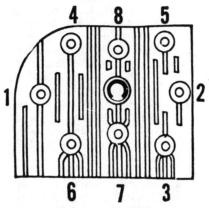

Fig. B106—Cylinder head screw tightening sequence. Long screws are used in positions 2, 3 and 7.

Fig. B107—Exploded view of typical vertical crankshaft model with air vane (pneumatic) governor. To remove flywheel, remove blower housing and starter unit; then, unscrew starter clutch housing (5). Flywheel can then be pulled from crankshaft.

1. Snap ring
2. Washer
3. Ratchet
4. Steel balls
5. Starter clutch
6. Washer
7. Flywheel
8. Breaker cover
9. Breaker point spring
10. Breaker arm & pivot
11. Breaker plunger
12. Condenser clamp
13. Coil spring (primary wire retainer)
14. Condenser
15. Governor air vane & bracket assy.
16. Spark plug wire
17. Armature & coil assy.
18. Air baffle
19. Spark plug grounding switch
20. Cylinder head
21. Cylinder head gasket
22. Cylinder block
23. Crankshaft oil seal
24. Cylinder shield
25. Flywheel key
26. Gasket
27. Breather & tappet chamber cover
28. Breather tube assy.
29. Coil spring
30. Crankshaft
31. Cam gear & shaft
32. Piston rings
33. Piston
34. Connecting rod
35. Rod bolt lock
36. Piston pin retaining rings
37. Piston pin
38. Intake valve
39. Valve springs
40. Valve spring keepers
41. Tappets
42. Exhaust valve
43. Gasket
44. Oil slinger assy.
45. Oil sump (engine base)
46. Crankshaft oil seal

several steps in sequence shown in Fig. B106 to a final torque of 165 in.-lbs. (19 N·m) on 140000 models and to 140 in.-lbs. (16 N·m) on all other models. Run the engine for about 5 minutes to allow it to reach operating temperature, then retighten the head screws following sequence shown in Fig. B106 to the torque specified above.

OIL SUMP REMOVAL, AUXILIARY PTO MODELS. On models equipped with an auxiliary pto, one of the oil sump (engine base) to cylinder retaining screws is installed in the recess in the sump for the pto auxiliary drive gear. To remove the oil sump, refer to Fig. B108 and remove the cover plate (upper view) and then remove the shaft stop (lower left view). The gear and shaft can then be moved as shown in lower right view to allow removal of the retaining screws. Reverse procedure to reassemble.

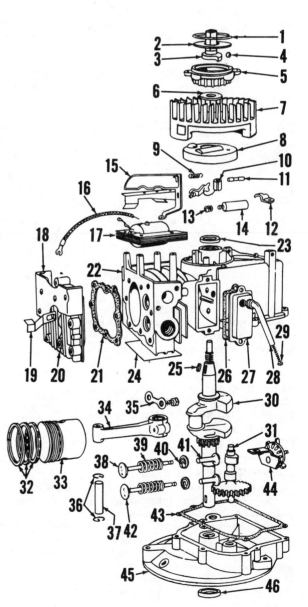

OIL BAFFLE PLATE. Model 140000 engines with mechanical governor have a baffle located in the cylinder block (crankcase). When servicing these engines, it is important that the baffle be correctly installed. The baffle must fit tightly against the valve tappet boss in the crankcase. Check for this before installing oil sump (vertical crankshaft models) or crankcase cover (horizontal crankshaft models).

CONNECTING ROD. The connecting rod and piston are removed from cylinder head end of block as an assembly. The aluminum alloy connecting rod rides directly on the induction hardened crankpin. The rod should be renewed if the crankpin hole or piston pin hole is scored. Renew connecting rod if crankpin hole is out-of-round more than 0.0007 inch (0.018 mm) or if piston pin hole is out-of-round more than 0.0005 inch (0.013 mm). Wear limit sizes are given in the following chart. Renew the connecting rod if either the crankpin or piston pin hole exceeds specified diameters.

REJECT SIZES FOR CONNECTING ROD

Model	Bearing Bore	Pin Bore
6B, 60000 61000	0.876 in. (22.25 mm)	0.492 in. (12.50 mm)
100200, 100900	1.001 in. (25.43 mm)	0.555 in. (14.10 mm)
140000	1.095 in. (27.81 mm)	0.674 in. (17.12 mm)
All Other Models	1.001 in. (25.43 mm)	0.492 in. (12.50 mm)

NOTE: Piston pins of 0.005 inch (0.13 mm) oversize are available for service. Piston pin hole in rod can be reamed to this size if crankpin hole in rod is within specifications.

Connecting rod must be reassembled so match marks on rod and cap are aligned. Tighten connecting rod bolts to 165 in.-lbs. (19 N·m) for 140000 models and to 100 in.-lbs. (11 N·m) for all other models.

PISTON, PIN AND RINGS. Pistons for use in engines having aluminum bore ("Kool Bore") are not interchangeable with those for use in cylinder having cast iron sleeve. Pistons may be identified as follows: Those for use in cast iron sleeve cylinders have a plain, dull aluminum finish, have an "L" stamped on top and use an oil ring expander. Those for use in aluminum bore cylinders are chrome plated (shiny finish), do not have an identifying letter and do not use an oil ring expander.

Renew piston showing visible signs of wear, scoring or scuffing. If, after cleaning carbon fom top ring groove, a new top ring has a side clearance of 0.009 inch (0.23 mm) on Model 140000 or 0.007 inch (0.18 mm) on all other models, renew the piston. Renew piston or hone piston pin hole to 0.005 inch (0.13 mm) oversize if pin hole is 0.0005 inch (0.013 mm) or more out-of-round, or is worn to a diameter of 0.554 inch (14.07 mm) or more on 100200 and 100900 engines, 0.673 inch (17.09 mm) or more on 140000 engines, or 0.491 inch (12.47 mm) or more on all other engines.

If the piston pn is 0.0005 inch (0.013 mm) or more out-of-round, or is worn to a diameter of 0.552 inch (14.02 mm) or smaller on 100200 and 100900 engines, 0.671 inch (17.04 mm) or smaller on 140000 engines, or 0.489 ich (12.42 mm) or smaller on all other models, renew the pin.

On aluminum bore engines, maximum allowable end gap for compression rings is 0.035 inch (0.90 mm) and maximum end gap for oil ring is 0.045 inch (1.14 mm). On cast iron bore engines, maximum allowable end gap for compression rings is 0.030 inch (0.75 mm) or more and maximum end gap for oil ring is 0.035 inch (0.90 mm).

Pistons and rings are available in several oversizes as well as standard. Refer to Fig. B109 for correct installation of piston rings.

CYLINDER. If cylinder bore wear is 0.003 inch (0.08 mm) or more or is 0.0025 inch (0.06 mm) or more out-of-round, cylinder must be rebored to next larger oversize.

The standard cylinder bore sizes for each model are given in the following table.

STANDARD CYLINDER BORE SIZES

Model	Cylinder Diameter
6B, Early 60000, Early 61000	2.3115-2.3125 in. (58.71-58.74 mm)
Late 60000, Late 61000	2.3740-2.3750 in. (60.30-60.33 mm)
8B, 80000, 81000, 82000	2.3740-2.3750 in. (60.30-60.33 mm)
90000, 91000, 92000, 93000, 94000, 95000	2.5615-2.5625 in. (65.06-65.09 mm)
100000	2.4990-2.5000 in. (63.47-63.5 mm)
110000, 111000, 112000, 113000, 114000	2.7802-2.7812 in. (70.62-70.64 mm)
130000, 131000, 132000	2.5615-2.5625 in. (65.06-65.09 mm)
140000	2.7490-2.7500 in. (69.82-69.85 mm)

A hone is recommended for resizing cylinders. Operate hone at 300-700 rpm and with an up and down movement that will produce a 45 degree crosshatch pattern. Clean cylinder after honing with oil or hot soapy water. Always check availability of oversize piston and ring sets before honing cylinder.

NOTE: A chrome piston ring set is available for slightly worn standard bore cylinders. No honing or cylinder deglazing is required for these rings. The cylinder bore can be a maximum of 0.005 inch (0.01 mm) oversize when using chrome rings.

CRANKSHAFT AND MAIN BEARINGS. Except where equipped with ball bearings, the main bearings are an in-

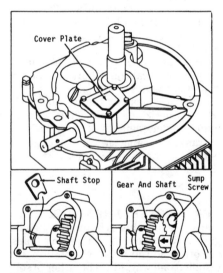

Fig. B108—To remove oil sump (engine base) on 92000, 93500, 94900, 95500, 110900 or 113900 models with auxiliary pto, remove cover plate, shaft stop and retaining screw as shown.

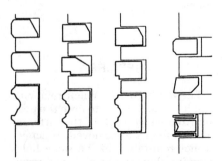

Fig. B109—View showing correct location of piston rings for typical ring sets used on engines in this section.

tegral part of the crankcase and cover or sump. The bearings are renewable by reaming out the crankcase and cover or sump bearing bores and installing service bushings. The tools for reaming the crankcase and cover or sump, and for installing the service bushings are available from Briggs & Stratton. If the bearings are scored, out-of-round 0.0007 inch (0.018 mm) or more, or are worn larger than the reject sizes in the following table, ream the bearings and install service bushings.

MAIN BEARING REJECT SIZES

Model	Magneto Bearing	Pto Bearing
6B, 60000, 61000	0.878 in. (22.30 mm)	0.878 in.* (22.30 mm)*
8B, 80000, 81000, 82000	0.878 in. (22.30 mm)	0.878 in.* (22.30 mm)*
90000, 91000, 92000, 93000, 94000, 95000	0.878 in. (22.30 mm)	0.878 in.* (22.30 mm)*
100700	0.878 in. (22.30 mm)	1.065 in. (27.05 mm)
100200, 100900 . . .	0.878 in. (22.30 mm)	1.003 in. (25.48 mm)
110000, 111000, 112000, 113000, 114000	0.878 in. (22.30 mm)	0.878 in.* (22.30 mm)*
130000, 131000, 132000 . . .	0.878 in. (22.30 mm)	1.003 in. (25.48 mm)
140000 . . .	1.004 in. (25.50 mm)	1.185 in. (30.10 mm)

*All models equipped with auxiliary drive unit have a main bearing rejection size for main bearing at pto side of 1.003 inch (25.48 mm).

Bushings are not available for all models; therefore, on some models the sump must be renewed if main bearing bore is worn beyond specified limits.

Install steel-backed aluminum service bushing as follows. Prior to installing bushing, use a chisel to make an indentation in inside edge of bearing bore in crankcase. Install bushing so oil notches are properly aligned and bushing is

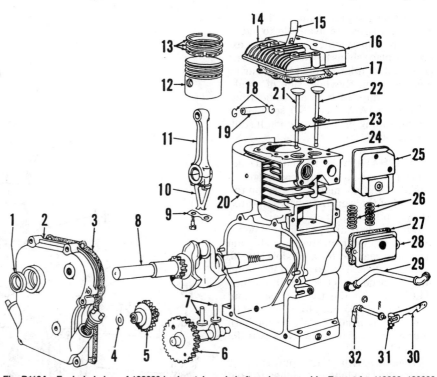

Fig. B110A—Exploded view of 100000 horizontal crankshaft engine assembly. Except for 112200, 130000 and late 140000 models, other horizontal crankshaft models with mechanical governor will have governor unit as shown in Fig. B90; otherwise, construction of all other horizontal crankshaft models is similar.

1. Crankshaft oil seal
2. Crankcase cover
3. Gasket
4. Thrust washer
5. Governor assy.
6. Cam gear & shaft
7. Tappets
8. Crankshaft
9. Rod bolt lock
10. Oil slinger
11. Connecting rod
12. Piston
13. Piston rings
14. Cylinder head
15. Spark plug ground switch
16. Air baffle
17. Cylinder head gasket
18. Piston pin retaining rings
19. Piston pin
20. Air baffle
21. Exhaust valve
22. Intake valve
23. Valve spring retainers
24. Cylinder block
25. Muffler
26. Valve springs
27. Gaskets
28. Breather & tappet chamber cover
29. Breather pipe
30. Governor lever
31. Clamping bolt
32. Governor crank

flush with outer face of bore. Stake bushing into previously made indentation and finish ream bushing. Do not stake where bushing is split.

When installing "DU" type bushing, stake bushing at oil notches in crankcase, but locate bushing so bushing split is not aligned with an oil notch. Bushing should be $\frac{1}{32}$ inch (0.8 mm) below face of crankcase bore except for 140000 model flywheel side bushing, which should be $\frac{3}{32}$ inch (2.4 mm) deep.

Ball bearing mains are a press fit on the crankshaft and must be removed by pressing the crankshaft out of the bearing. Reject ball bearing if worn or rough. Expand new bearing by heating it in oil, then install it on crankshaft with seal side toward crankpin journal.

Crankshaft main journal diameter reject size is 0.873 inch (22.17 mm) for flywheel and pto side main bearing journals on all standard models with plain bearings except Models 100200, 100700, 100900, 130000, 131000, 132000 and 140000. Main bearing journal diameter reject size for Models 100200, 100900, 130000, 131000 and 132000 is 0.873 inch

(22.17 mm) for flywheel side and 0.998 inch (25.35 mm) for pto side. Main bearing journal diameter reject size for model 100700 is 0.873 inch (22.17 mm) for flywheel side and 1.060 inch (26.92 mm) for pto side. Main bearing journal diameter reject size for Model 140000 is 0.997 inch (25.32 mm) for flywheel side and 1.179 inch (29.95 mm) for pto side. On models equipped with auxiliary drive unit, pto side main bearing journal diameter reject size is 0.998 inch (25.35 mm).

Crankpin journal rejection size for 6B, 60000 and 61000 models is 0.870 inch (22.10 mm), crankpin journal rejection size for 140000 models is 1.090 inch (27.69 mm) and crankpin journal rejection size for all other models is 0.996 inch (25.30 mm).

Crankshaft end play is 0.002-0.030 inch (0.05-0.76 mm) on all 100700 models and 92500 and 92900 models with a next-to-last digit of "5" in the code number. Crankshaft end play is 0.002-0.008 inch (0.05-0.20 mm) for all other models. At least one 0.015 inch crankcase gasket must be in place when measuring end play. Additional gaskets in several sizes are available to aid in end play adjustment. If end play is excessive, place shims between crankshaft gear and crankcase on plain bearing models, or on flywheel side of crankshaft if equipped with a ball bearing.

Refer to VALVE TIMING section for proper timing procedure when installing crankshaft.

CAMSHAFT. The camshaft and camshaft gear are an integral casting on all models. On some models, a gear on the pto end of the camshaft drives the auxiliary pto shaft.

The camshaft and gear should be inspected for wear on the journals, cam lobes and gear teeth. On Models 110000, 111000, 112000, 113000 and 114000 camshaft journal reject size is 0.436 inch (11.07 mm) for the flywheel side and 0.498 inch (12.65 mm) for the pto side. Camshaft journal reject size for both journals for all other models is 0.498 inch (12.65 mm).

On models with "Easy-Spin" starting, the intake cam lobe is designed to hold the intake valve slightly open on part of the compression stroke. Therefore, to check compression, the crankshaft must be turned backward.

"Easy-Spin" camshafts (cam gears) can be identified by two holes drilled in the web of the gear. Where part number of an older cam gear and an "Easy-Spin" cam gear are the same (except for an "E" following the "Easy-Spin" part number), the gears are interchangeable.

Some "Easy-Spin" camshafts are also equipped with a mechanically operated compression release on the exhaust lobe. With engine stopped or at cranking speed, the spring holds the actuator cam weight inward against the rocker cam. See Fig. B111. The rocker cam is held slightly above the exhaust cam surface which in turn holds the exhaust valve open slightly during the compression stroke. This compression release greatly reduces the power needed for cranking.

When the engine starts and rpm is increased, the actuator cam weight moves outward overcoming the spring pressure. See Fig. B111A. The rocker cam is rotated below the cam surface to provide normal exhaust valve operation.

Refer to VALVE TIMING section for proper timing procedure when installing camshaft.

Note that on models with an auxiliary pto shaft, a thrust washer is used to accommodate additional axial thrust of camshaft. Thrust washer is located at flywheel end of camshaft if pto shaft rotation is clockwise, while thrust washer is located at gear end of camshaft if pto shaft rotation is counterclockwise.

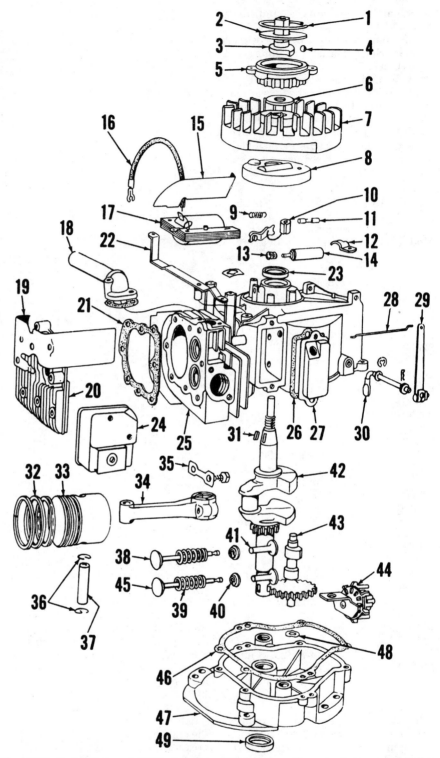

Fig. B110B—Exploded view of 100000 vertical crankshaft engine with mechanical governor. Models 130000, 131000 and 140000 vertical crankshaft models with mechanical governor are similar. Refer to Fig. B107 for typical vertical crankshaft models with air vane governor.

1. Snap ring
2. Washer
3. Starter ratchet
4. Steel balls
5. Starter clutch
6. Washer
7. Flywheel
8. Breaker cover
9. Breaker arm spring
10. Breaker arm & pivot
11. Breaker plunger
12. Condenser clamp
13. Primary wire retainer spring
14. Condenser
15. Air baffle
16. Spark plug wire
17. Armature & coil assy.
18. Intake pipe
19. Air baffle
20. Cylinder head
21. Cylinder head gasket
22. Linkage lever
23. Crankshaft oil seal
24. Muffler
25. Cylinder block
26. Gasket
27. Breather & tappet chamber cover
28. Governor link
29. Governor lever
30. Governor crank
31. Flywheel key
32. Piston rings
33. Piston
34. Connecting rod
35. Rod bolt lock
36. Piston pin retaining rings
37. Piston pin
38. Intake valve
39. Valve springs
40. Valve spring retainers
41. Tappets
42. Crankshaft
43. Cam gear
44. Governor & oil slinger assy.
45. Exhaust valve
46. Gasket
47. Oil sump (engine base)
48. Thrust washer
49. Crankshaft oil seal

Illustration Courtesy Briggs & Stratton Corp.

VALVE SYSTEM. Valve tappet clearance (engine cold) for intake valve is 0.005-0.007 inch (0.13-0.18 mm) for all models. Exhaust valve clearance for Models 130000, 131000, 132000 and 140000 is 0.009-0.011 inch (0.23-0.28 mm). Exhaust valve clearance for all other models is 0.007-0.009 inch (0.18-0.23 mm), except on models which have a clearance of 0.005-0.007 inch (0.13-0.18 mm) stamped on inside of breather cover.

To correctly set tappet clearance, remove spark plug and using a suitable measuring tool, rotate crankshaft in normal direction (clockwise at flywheel) so piston is at top dead center on compression stroke. Continue to rotate crankshaft so piston is $\frac{1}{4}$ inch (6.4 mm) down from top dead center. This position places the tappets away from the compression release device on the exhaust cam lobe.

Valve tappet clearance is adjusted on all models by carefully grinding end of valve stem to increase clearance or by grinding valve seats deeper and/or renewing valve or lifter to decrease clearance.

Valve face and seat angle should be ground at 45 degrees for intake and exhaust. Renew valve if margin is $\frac{1}{64}$ inch (0.4 mm) or less. Seat width should be $\frac{3}{64}$ to $\frac{1}{16}$ inch (1.2-1.6 mm). All models are equipped with seat inserts. Peen around insert after installing new insert.

The original valve guides on all engines with aluminum cylinder blocks are an integral part of the block. To repair worn guides, they must be reamed out and a bushing installed.

On all models except 140000 model, ream guide out first with B&S reamer 19064 approximately $\frac{1}{16}$ inch (1.6 mm) deeper than length of bushing. Press in bushing with driver 19065 until bushing is flush with top of guide bore. Finish ream the bushing with finish reamer 19066.

On 140000 model, ream guide out with B&S reamer 19231 approximately $\frac{1}{16}$ inch (1.6 mm) deeper than length of bushing. Using tool 19204 press in bushing so bushing is flush with top of guide bore. Finish ream the bushing with finish reamer 19233.

Some engines may be equipped with a "Cobalite" exhaust valve and exhaust seat insert as well as a rotocoil on the exhaust valve stem. These components are offered as replacement parts for engines used in severe engine service.

VALVE TIMING. On engines equipped with ball bearing mains, align the timing mark on the cam gear with the timing mark on the crankshaft counterweight as shown in Fig. B112. On

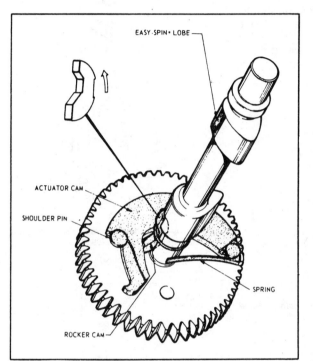

Fig. B111—Compression release camshaft used on 111200, 111900 and 112200 engines. At cranking speed, spring holds actuator cam inward against the rocker cam and rocker cam is forced above exhaust cam surface.

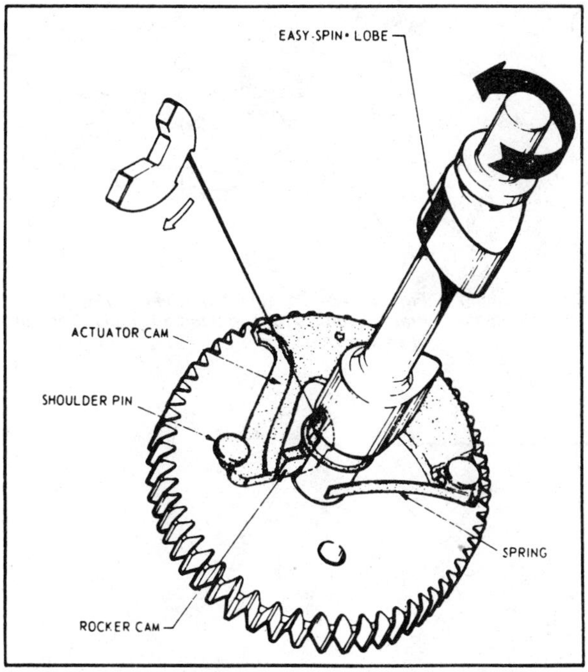

Fig. B111A—When engine starts and rpm is increased, actuator cam weight moves outward allowing rocker cam to rotate below exhaust cam surface.

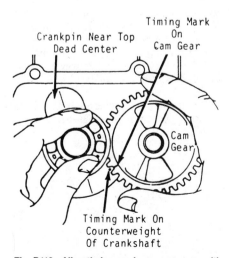

Fig. B112—Align timing marks on cam gear with mark on crankshaft counterweight on ball bearing equipped models.

engines with plain bearings, align the timing marks on the camshaft gear with the timing mark on the crankshaft gear as shown in Fig. B113. If the timing mark is not visible on the crankshaft gear, align the timing mark on the camshaft gear with the second tooth to the left of the crankshaft counterweight parting line as shown in Fig. B114.

AUXILIARY PTO. To remove auxiliary pto shaft and gear, refer to Fig. B108 and remove shaft stop. Drive pin out of gear and shaft then withdraw shaft.

Model 110980 is equipped with a clutch mechanism on the camshaft to engage the pto shaft assembly. When spring tang of clutch sleeve (4—Fig. B114A) is pushed, worm should lock. With spring released, worm should rotate freely in both directions. When assembling clutch and worm, upper end of spring (3) must engage hole in camshaft while lower end of spring must engage hole in clutch sleeve (4). Install lower copper washer (8) so gray coated side is next to thick thrust washer (7). Worm gear end play should be 0.004-0.017 inch (0.10-0.43 mm). Be sure clip of washer (10) properly engages camshaft bearing boss.

FLYWHEEL BRAKE. The engine is equipped with a band type flywheel brake. The brake should stop the engine within three seconds when the operator releases mower safety control and the speed control is in high speed position. Stopping time can be checked using tool 19255.

To check brake band adjustment, remove starter and properly ground spark plug lead to prevent accidental starting. On electric start models, remove battery. Turn flywheel nut using a torque wrench with brake engaged. Rotating flywheel nut at a steady rate in a clockwise direction should require at least 45 in.-lbs. (5.08 N·m) torque. An insufficient torque reading may indicate misadjustment or damaged components. Renew brake band if friction material of band is damaged or less than 0.030 inch (0.76 mm) thick.

To adjust brake, unscrew brake cable retaining screw so hole (H—Fig. B114B)

is vacant. (If a pop rivet secures the cable, do not remove rivet; gage tool can be inserted through hole in rivet.) Loosen screws (S) securing brake control bracket. Place bayonet end of gage 19256 (G) in hole (L) of control lever (C). Push against control lever and insert opposite end of gage (G) in hole (H), or in hole of pop rivet if used to secure cable. Apply pressure against brake control bracket (Fig. B114B) until spring tension on gage is just removed. Then while holding pressure, tighten bracket screws (S) to 25-30 in.-lbs. (2.82-3.39 N·m). As gage is removed a slight friction should be felt and control lever should not move.

Brake band must be renewed if damaged or friction material thickness is less

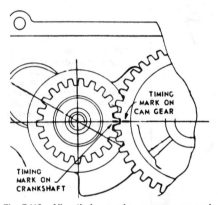

Fig. B113—Align timing marks on cam gear and crankshaft gear on plain bearing models.

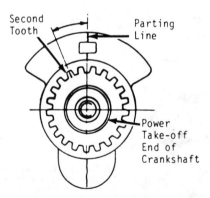

Fig. B114—Location of tooth to align with timing mark on cam gear if mark is not visible on crankshaft gear.

than 0.030 inch (0.76 mm). Use tool 19229 to bend retaining tang away from band end (B—Fig. B114B).

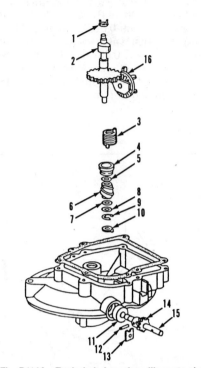

Fig. B114A—Exploded view of auxiliary pto shaft assembly used on Model 110980.

1. Clip washer	9. "E" ring
2. Camshaft assy.	10. Washer
3. Spring	11. Seal
4. Clutch sleeve	12. Pin
5. Thrust washer	13. Shaft stop
6. Worm gear	14. Worm gear
7. Thrust washer (thick)	15. Pto shaft
8. Copper washer	16. Governor & oil slinger assy.

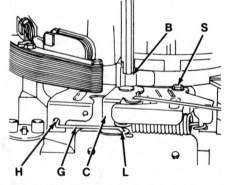

Fig. B114B—To adjust flywheel brake, loosen bracket screws (S) and position gage (G) as outlined in text.

BRIGGS & STRATTON

BRIGGS & STRATTON CORPORATION
Milwaukee, Wisconsin 53201

Model Series	No. Cyls.	Bore	Stroke	Displacement	Power Rating
170000, 171000	1	3.00 in. (76.2 mm)	2.375 in. (60.3 mm)	16.8 cu. in. (275 cc)	7 hp (5.2 kW)
190000, 191000, 192000, 193000, 194000, 195000, 196000	1	3.00 in. (76.2 mm)	2.750 in. (69.85 mm)	19.44 cu. in. (318 cc)	8 hp (6 kW)
220000, 221000, 222000	1	3.438 in. (87.3 mm)	2.375 in. (60.3 mm)	22.04 cu. in. (361 cc)	10 hp (7.5 kW)
250000, 251000, 252000, 253000, 254000, 255000, 256000, 257000, 258000, 259000	1	3.438 in. (87.3 mm)	2.625 in. (66.68 mm)	24.36 cu. in. (399 cc)	11 hp (8.2 kW)
280000, 281000, 282000, 283000	1	3.438 in. (87.3 mm)	3.06 in. (77.7 mm)	28.4 cu. in. (465 cc)	12 hp (9 kW)
285000, 286000, 289000	1	3.438 in. (87.3 mm)	3.06 in. (77.7 mm)	28.4 cu. in. (465 cc)	12.5 hp (9.4 kW)

Engines in this section are four-stroke, single-cylinder engines with either a horizontal or vertical crankshaft. The crankshaft may be supported by main bearings that are an integral part of crankcase and crankcase cover/oil pan or by ball bearings pressed on the crankshaft. All engines are constructed of aluminum. Cylinder bore may be either aluminum or a cast iron sleeve that is cast in the aluminum.

The connecting rod on all models rides directly on the crankpin journal. Horizontal crankshaft models are splash lubricated by an oil dipper attached to the connecting rod cap and vertical crankshaft models are lubricated by an oil slinger wheel located on the governor gear.

Early models are equipped with a magneto-type ignition system with points and condenser located underneath the flywheel. Later models are equipped with a breakerless (Magnetron) ignition system.

A float-type carburetor is used on all models. A fuel pump is available as optional equipment for some models.

Refer to BRIGGS & STRATTON ENGINE IDENTIFICATION INFORMATION section for engine identification. Engine model number as well as type number and serial number are necessary when ordering parts.

MAINTENANCE

LUBRICATION. Horizontal crankshaft engines have a splash lubrication system provided by an oil dipper attached to connecting rod. Refer to Fig. B501 for view of various types of dippers used.

Vertical crankshaft engines are lubricated by an oil slinger wheel on governor gear that is driven by the camshaft gear. See Fig. B502.

Engine oil should be changed after first eight hours of operation and after every 50 hours of operation or at least once each operating season. If equipment undergoes severe usage, change oil weekly or after every 25 hours of operation.

Manufacturer recommends using oil with an API service classification of SF or SG. Use SAE 30 oil for temperatures above 40° F (4° C); use SAE 10W-30 oil for temperatures between 0° F (–18° C) and 100° F (38° C); below 0° F (–18° C) use petroleum based SAE 5W-20 or a suitable synthetic oil.

Crankcase oil capacity for 16.8 and 19.44 cubic-inch engines is 2¼ pints (1.1 L) for vertical crankshaft models and 2¾ pints (1.3 L) for horizontal crankshaft models.

Crankcase oil capacity for 22.04, 24.36 and 28.4 cubic-inch engines is 3 pints (1.4 L) for vertical crankshaft models and 2½ pints (1.2 L) for horizontal crankshaft models.

SPARK PLUG. The original spark plug may be either 1½ inches or 2 inches long. Recommended spark plug is either Champion or Autolite.

If a Champion spark plug is used and spark plug is 1½ inches long, recom-

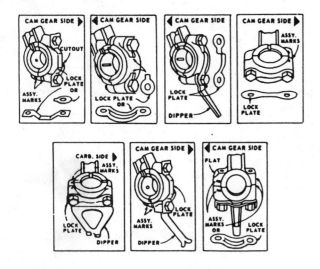

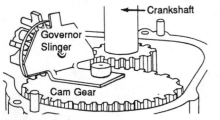

Fig. B502—View of governor weight assembly and oil slinger used on vertical crankshaft models.

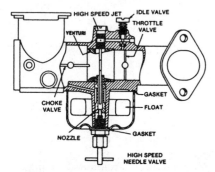

Fig. B503—Cross-sectional view of Flo-Jet I carburetor.

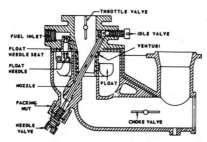

Fig. B501—Install connecting rod in engine as indicated according to type used. Note dipper installation on horizontal crankshaft engine connecting rod.

Fig. B504—Cross-sectional view of Flo-Jet II carburetor. Before separating upper and lower body section, remove packing nut and power needle valve as a unit and use special screwdriver (tool 19062) to remove nozzle.

Specified spark plug electrode gap is 0.030 inch (0.76 mm).

CAUTION: Briggs & Stratton does not recommend using abrasive blasting to clean spark plugs as this may introduce some abrasive material into the engine that could cause extensive damage.

CARBURETOR. Engines in this section may be equipped with one of three different Flo-Jet carburetors as well as a Walbro carburetor. The Flo-Jet carburetors are identified as either Flo-Jet I (Fig. B503), Flo-Jet II (Fig. B504) or Cross-Over Flo-Jet (Fig. B505). Refer to appropriate service section for model being serviced.

Flo-Jet I Carburetor. Initial setting of idle mixture screw is one turn out and high-speed needle valve is 1½ turns out. With engine at normal operating temperature and equipment control lever in "SLOW" position, adjust idle speed screw so engine idles at 1750 rpm. With engine running at idle speed, turn idle mixture screw clockwise until engine speed just starts to drop. Note screw position. Turn idle mixture screw counterclockwise until engine speed just starts to drop again. Note screw position, then turn screw to midpoint between the noted screw positions. Ad-

mended spark plug is CJ8 for normal operation. Champion J19LM may be used if fouling is encountered. Install Champion RCJ8 (RJ19LM for severe fouling) if a resistor-type spark plug is required. If spark plug is 2 inches long, recommended spark plug is J8C for normal operation. Champion J19LM may be used if fouling is encountered. Install Champion RJ8C (RJ19LM for severe fouling) if a resistor-type spark plug is required.

If an Autolite spark plug is used and spark plug is 1½ inches long, recommended spark plug is 235. Install Autolite 245 if a resistor-type spark plug is required. If spark plug is 2 inches long, recommended spark plug is 295. Install Autolite 306 if a resistor-type spark plug is required.

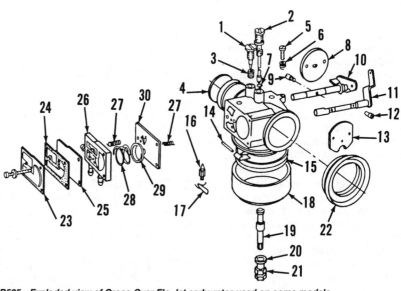

Fig. B505—Exploded view of Cross-Over Flo-Jet carburetor used on some models.

1. Idle mixture needle	9. Screw	23. Fuel pump cover
2. High-speed mixture needle	10. Throttle shaft	24. Gasket
3. Spring	11. Choke shaft	25. Diaphragm
4. "O" ring	12. Screw	26. Fuel pump body
5. Idle speed screw	13. Choke plate	27. Spring
6. Spring	14. Pin	28. Spring
7. Packing	15. Float	29. Spring cup
8. Throttle plate	16. Fuel inlet valve	30. Diaphragm
	17. Clip	
	18. Fuel bowl	
	19. Nozzle	
	20. Washer	
	21. Screw	
	22. Gasket	

just high-speed needle valve with control set to "FAST" using same procedure. If engine will not accelerate cleanly, slightly enrich mixture by turning idle mixture needle valve counterclockwise. If necessary, readjust idle speed screw.

To check float level, invert carburetor body and float assembly. Refer to Fig. B503 for proper float level dimensions. Adjust by bending float lever tang that contacts inlet valve.

Flo-Jet II Carburetor. Initial setting of idle mixture screw is 1¼ turns out and high-speed needle valve is 1½ turns out. With engine at normal operating temperature and equipment control lever in "SLOW" position, adjust idle speed screw so engine idles at 1750 rpm. With engine running at idle speed, turn idle mixture screw clockwise until engine speed just starts to drop. Note screw position. Turn idle mixture screw counterclockwise until engine speed just starts to drop again. Note screw position, then turn screw to midpoint between the noted screw positions. Adjust high-speed needle valve with control set to "FAST" using same procedure. If engine will not accelerate cleanly, slightly enrich mixture by turning idle mixture needle valve counterclockwise. If necessary, readjust idle speed screw.

To check float level, invert carburetor body and float assembly. Refer to Fig. B506 for proper float level dimensions. Adjust by bending float lever tang that contacts inlet valve. On Flo-Jet II carburetor, check upper body for distortion

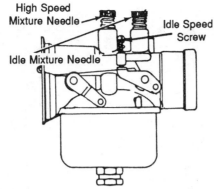

Fig. B508—View of adjustment screws on Cross-Over Flo-Jet carburetor.

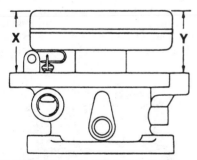

Fig. B506—Dimension (Y) must be the same as dimension (X) plus or minus 1/32 inch (0.8 mm).

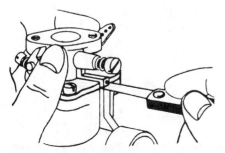

Fig. B507—Check upper body of Flo-Jet II carburetor for warping as outlined in text.

using a 0.002 inch (0.05 mm) feeler gauge as shown in Fig. B507. Upper body must be renewed if warped more than 0.002 inch (0.05 mm).

Cross-Over Flo-Jet Carburetor. The Cross-Over Flo-Jet shown in Fig. B505 is equipped with an integral diaphragm-type fuel pump.

Initial setting of idle mixture needle (Fig. B508) is one turn out and high-speed mixture needle is 1½ turns out. With engine at normal operating temperature and equipment control lever in "SLOW" position, adjust idle speed screw so engine idles at 1750 rpm. With engine running at idle speed, turn idle mixture needle clockwise until engine speed just starts to drop. Note needle position. Turn idle mixture needle counterclockwise until engine speed just starts to drop again. Note needle position, then turn needle to midpoint between the noted needle positions. If equipped with high-speed mixture needle, set control to "FAST" and adjust high-speed needle using same procedure. If engine will not accelerate cleanly, slightly enrich mixture by turning idle mixture needle counterclockwise. If necessary, readjust idle speed screw.

Overhaul of carburetor is evident after inspection of carburetor and referral to exploded view in Fig. B505. Clean and inspect components and discard

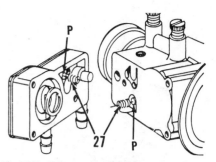

Fig. B510—When assembling fuel pump on Cross-Over Flo-Jet carburetor, install springs (27) on pegs (P) on pump body and carburetor body.

any parts that are damaged or excessively worn.

When reassembling carburetor, note the following: Install choke and throttle plates so indentations are located as shown in Fig. B509 when choke or throttle plate is in closed position. Fuel inlet seat is renewable using a suitable screw-type puller. Install inlet seat so it is flush with carburetor body surface. To check float level, invert carburetor body and float assembly. Float should be parallel to carburetor body as shown in Fig. B506. Adjust float level by bending float lever tang that contacts inlet valve. When assembling fuel pump, install springs (27—Fig. B510) on pegs (P) on pump body and carburetor body.

Walbro Carburetor. The Walbro carburetor may be equipped with a fixed main jet or the adjustable high-speed mixture needle shown in Fig. B511.

Initial setting of idle mixture needle (10) is one turn out and high-speed mixture needle (23), if so equipped, is 1½ turns out. With engine at normal operating temperature and equipment control lever in "SLOW" position, adjust idle speed screw (8) so engine idles at 1750 rpm. With engine running at idle speed, turn idle mixture needle clockwise until engine speed just starts to drop. Note needle position. Turn idle mixture needle counterclockwise until engine speed just starts to drop again. Note needle position, then turn needle to midpoint between the noted needle

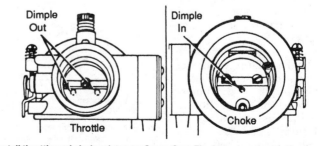

Fig. B509—Install throttle and choke plates on Cross-Over Flo-Jet carburetor so dimples are located as shown above when plates are closed.

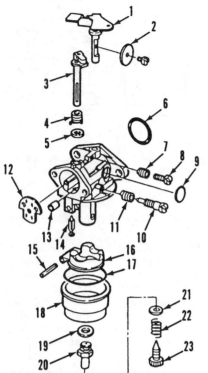

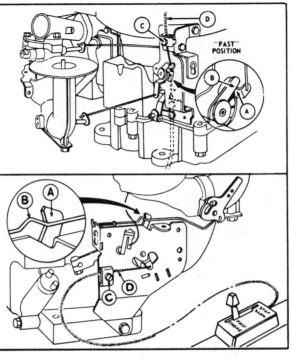

Fig. B512—On Choke-A-Matic controls shown, choke actuating lever (A) should just contact choke link or shaft (B) when control is at "FAST" position. If not, loosen screw (C) and move control wire housing (D) as required.

Fig. B511—Exploded view of Walbro-type float carburetor.

1. Throttle shaft	13. Air jet
2. Throttle plate	14. Fuel inlet valve
3. Choke shaft	15. Float pin
4. Spring	16. Float
5. Seal	17. Gasket
6. Gasket	18. Fuel bowl
7. Spring	19. Washer
8. Idle speed screw	20. Bowl retainer
9. Welch plug	21. "O" ring
10. Idle mixture needle	22. Spring
11. Spring	23. Main fuel
12. Choke plate	mixture needle

positions. If equipped with high-speed mixture needle, set control to "FAST" and adjust high-speed needle using same procedure. If engine will not accelerate cleanly, slightly enrich mixture by turning idle mixture needle counterclockwise. If necessary, readjust idle speed screw. If engine does not run properly at high altitude, remove main air jet (13) and repeat carburetor adjustment.

Overhaul of carburetor is evident after inspection of carburetor and referral to exploded view in Fig. B511. A 5/32-inch punch ground flat at the end makes a suitable tool for removing Welch plug (9). Clean and inspect components and discard any parts that are damaged or excessively worn.

When reassembling carburetor, note the following: Do not deform Welch plug (9) during installation; it should be flat. Seal outer edges of plug with nonhardening sealer. Install choke and throttle plates so numbers are on outer face when choke or throttle plate is in closed position. Install fuel inlet seat using B&S drive 19057 or a suitable tool so

grooved face of seat is down. Float height is not adjustable. Tighten fuel bowl retaining nut to 50 in.-lbs. (5.6 N•m). Tighten carburetor mounting nuts to 90 in.-lbs. (10.2 N•m).

CHOKE-A-MATIC CARBURETOR CONTROLS. Engines may be equipped with a control unit that operates the carburetor choke, throttle and magneto grounding switch from a single lever (Choke-A-Matic carburetors).

To check operation of Choke-A-Matic controls, move control lever to "CHOKE" position; carburetor choke slide or plate must be completely closed. Move control lever to "STOP" position; magneto grounding switch should be making contact. With control in "RUN," "FAST" or "SLOW" position, carburetor choke should be completely open. On units with remote controls, synchronize movement of remote lever to carburetor control lever by loosening screw (C—Fig. B512) and moving control wire housing (D) as required. Tighten screw to clamp housing

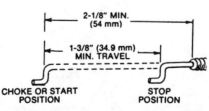

Fig. B513—For proper operation of Choke-A-Matic controls, remote control wire must extend to dimension shown and have a minimum travel of 1-3/8 inches (34.9 mm).

securely. Refer to Fig. B513 to check remote control wire movement.

AUTOMATIC CHOKE (THERMOSTAT-TYPE). A thermostat-operated choke is used on some models equipped with Flo-Jet II carburetor. To adjust choke linkage, hold choke shaft so thermostat lever is free. At room temperature, stop screw in thermostat collar should be located midway between thermostat stops. If not, loosen stop screw, adjust collar and tighten stop screw. Loosen set screw (S—Fig. B514) on thermostat lever. Slide lever on shaft

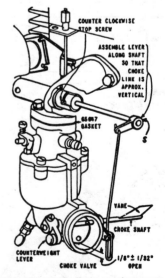

Fig. B514—Automatic choke used on some models equipped with Flo-Jet II carburetor showing unit in "HOT" position.

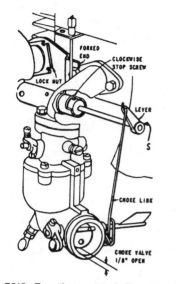

Fig. B515—Turn thermostat shaft counterclockwise until stop screw contacts thermostat stop as shown.

to ensure free movement of choke unit. Turn thermostat shaft clockwise until stop screw contacts thermostat stop. While holding shaft in this position, move shaft lever until choke is open exactly 1/8 inch (3 mm) and tighten lever set screw. Turn thermostat shaft counterclockwise until stop screw contacts thermostat stop as shown in Fig. B515. Manually open choke valve until it stops against top of choke link opening. At this time, choke should be open at least 3/32 inch (2.4 mm), but not more than 5/32 inch (4 mm). Hold choke valve in wide-open position and check position of counterweight lever. Lever should be in a horizontal position with free end toward right.

FUEL TANK OUTLET. Some models are equipped with a fuel tank outlet as shown in Fig. B516. Other models may be equipped with a fuel sediment bowl that is part of the fuel tank outlet shown in Fig. B517.

Clean any debris or dirt from tank outlet screens with a brush. Varnish or other gasoline deposits can be removed using a suitable solvent. Tighten packing nut or remove nut and shutoff valve,

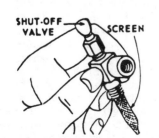

Fig. B516—Fuel tank outlet used on some B&S models.

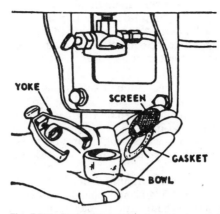

Fig. B517—Fuel sediment bowl and tank outlet used on some models.

then renew packing if leakage occurs around shutoff valve stem.

FUEL PUMP. A fuel pump is available as optional equipment on some models. Refer to BRIGGS & STRATTON ACCESSORIES section for service information.

GOVERNOR. All engines are equipped with a gear-driven mechanical-type governor attached to the crankcase cover or oil pan. The governor is driven by the camshaft gear. Governor and linkage must operate properly to prevent "hunting" or unsteady operation. The carburetor must be properly adjusted before performing governor adjustments.

To adjust governor linkage, loosen clamp bolt on governor lever shown in Figs. B518 or B519. Move link end of governor lever so carburetor throttle plate is in wide-open position. Using a screwdriver, rotate governor lever shaft clockwise as far as possible and tighten clamp bolt.

On models equipped with governed idle screw (I—Fig. B520), set remote

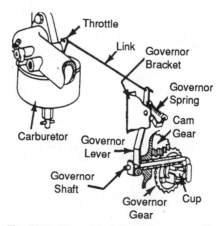

Fig. B518—View of typical governor assembly used on engines with vertical crankshaft.

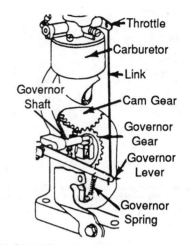

Fig. B519—View of typical governor assembly used on engines with horizontal crankshaft.

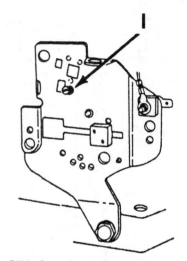

Fig. B520—On engines equipped with a governed idle adjustment screw (I), refer to text for adjustment procedure.

control to idle position, then adjust idle speed screw on carburetor so engine idles at 1550 rpm. Place remote control so engine idles at 1750 rpm, then rotate governed idle screw (I) so screw just contacts remote control lever.

On models equipped with a governed idle stop (P—Fig. B521), set remote control to idle position, then adjust idle speed screw on carburetor so engine idles at 1550 rpm. Loosen governed idle stop screw (W). Place remote control so engine idles at 1750 rpm, then position stop (P) so it contacts remote control lever and tighten screw (W).

On Models 253400 and 255400, set remote control to idle position, then adjust idle speed screw on carburetor so engine idles at 1550 rpm. Bend tang (G—Fig. B522) so engine idles at 1750 rpm.

IMPORTANT: Running an engine at a maximum speed other than the speed specified by the equipment

Engine Repair

RIDING LAWN MOWER

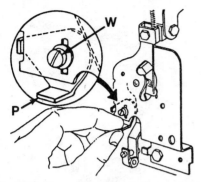

Fig. B521—On models equipped with a governed idle stop (P), refer to GOVERNOR section to adjust governed idle speed.

manufacturer can be dangerous to the operator, harmful to the equipment and inefficient. Adjust governed engine speed to specification stipulated by equipment manufacturer.

To set maximum no-load speed on all models except 253400 and 255400, move remote speed control to maximum speed position. With engine running, bend governor spring anchor tang (T—Fig. B523) to obtain desired maximum no-load speed.

To set maximum no-load speed on Models 253400 and 255400, move remote speed control to maximum speed

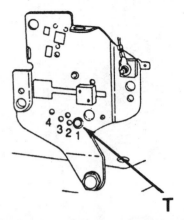

Fig. B525—Some engines may be equipped with a maximum governed speed limit screw (T). Location of screw in one of the numbered holes determines maximum governed speed. See text.

position. With engine running, turn screw (S—Fig. B524) to obtain desired maximum no-load speed.

Some models are equipped with a top speed screw (T—Fig. B525) that determines maximum no-load speed according to which hole the screw occupies. There may be one, two, three or four numbered holes. If a screw is not installed in one of the numbered holes, the maximum speed determined by adjusting the governor spring anchor tang will determine maximum no-load engine speed. If a screw is installed in a numbered hole, the maximum speed will be reduced. Installing the top speed screw (T) in a higher numbered hole will reduce top engine speed the most. For instance, installing the screw in hole "2" will reduce engine speed to 3300 rpm while installing the screw in hole "4" will reduce engine speed to 2400 rpm. An accurate tachometer should be used to determine engine speed for specific holes.

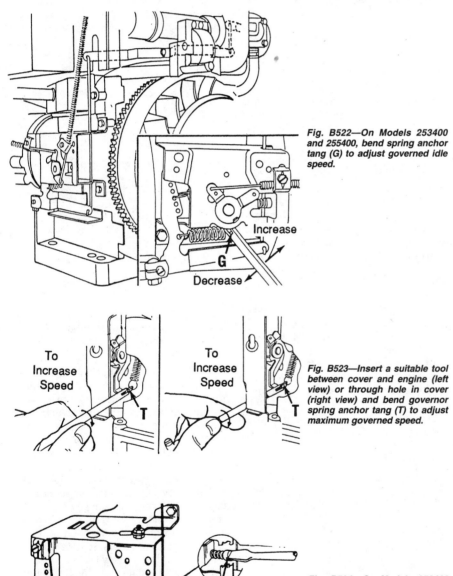

Fig. B522—On Models 253400 and 255400, bend spring anchor tang (G) to adjust governed idle speed.

Fig. B523—Insert a suitable tool between cover and engine (left view) or through hole in cover (right view) and bend governor spring anchor tang (T) to adjust maximum governed speed.

Fig. B524—On Models 253400 and 255400, rotate screw (S) to adjust maximum governor speed.

IGNITION SYSTEM. Early models are equipped with a magneto ignition system; later models are equipped with a Magnetron breakerless ignition system. Refer to appropriate section for model being serviced.

Magneto Ignition. All models are equipped with breaker points and condenser located under the flywheel.

One of two different types of ignition points, as shown in Figs. B526 and B527, are used. Breaker point gap is 0.020 inch (0.51 mm) for all models with magneto ignition.

On each type, breaker contact arm is actuated by a plunger in a bore in engine crankcase that rides against a cam on engine crankshaft. Plunger can be removed after removing breaker points. Renew plunger if worn to a length of 0.870 inch (22.10 mm) or less. If breaker point plunger bore in crankcase is worn, oil will leak past plunger. Check bore

376

Illustrations Courtesy Briggs & Stratton Corp.

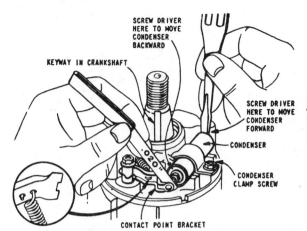

Fig. B526—View showing breaker point adjustment on models with breaker points that are integral with condenser. Move condenser to adjust point gap.

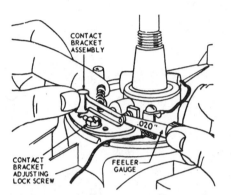

Fig. B527—View showing adjustment of breaker points that are separate from condenser.

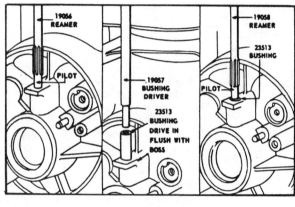

Fig. B529—Views showing reaming plunger bore to accept bushing (left view), installing bushing (center) and finish reaming bore of bushing (right).

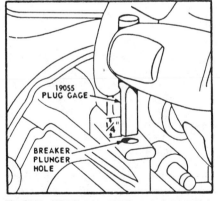

Fig. B528—If B&S gauge 19055 can be inserted into plunger bore 1/4 inch (6.4 mm) or more, bore is worn and must be rebushed.

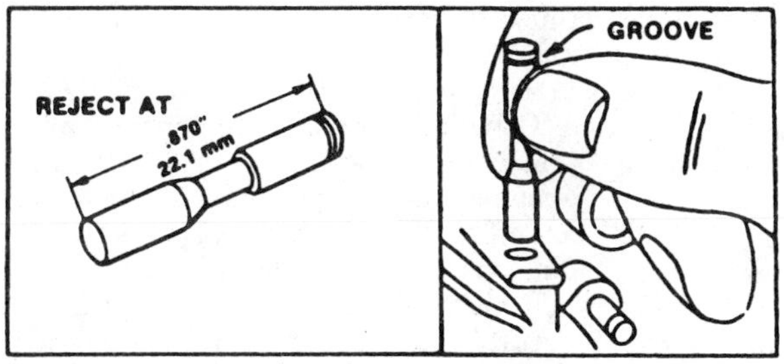

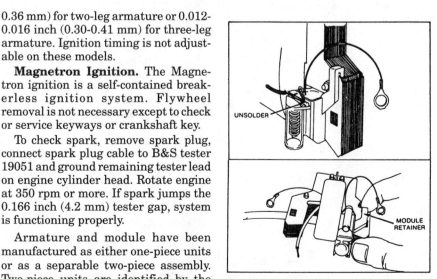

Fig. B530—Insert plunger into bore with groove toward top.

mature laminations. To remove armature and Magnetron module, remove flywheel shroud and armature retaining screws. On one-piece units, disconnect stop switch wire at spade connector. On two-piece units, use a 3/16 inch (4.8 mm) diameter pin punch to release stop switch wire from module. To remove module on two-piece units, unsolder wires, push module retainer away from laminations and remove module. See Fig. B531.

Resolder wires for reinstallation and use Permatex or equivalent to hold ground wires in position.

with B&S gauge 19055. If plug gauge will enter bore 1/4 inch (6.4 mm) or more, bore should be reamed and a bushing installed. Refer to Fig. B528. To ream bore and install bushing it will be necessary to remove breaker points, armature, ignition coil and crankshaft. Refer to Fig. B529 for steps in reaming bore and installation of bushing.

Plunger must be reinstalled with groove toward top (Fig. B530) to prevent oil contamination in breaker point box.

To reassemble, set armature-to-flywheel air gap at 0.010-0.014 inch (0.25-

0.36 mm) for two-leg armature or 0.012-0.016 inch (0.30-0.41 mm) for three-leg armature. Ignition timing is not adjustable on these models.

Magnetron Ignition. The Magnetron ignition is a self-contained breakerless ignition system. Flywheel removal is not necessary except to check or service keyways or crankshaft key.

To check spark, remove spark plug, connect spark plug cable to B&S tester 19051 and ground remaining tester lead on engine cylinder head. Rotate engine at 350 rpm or more. If spark jumps the 0.166 inch (4.2 mm) tester gap, system is functioning properly.

Armature and module have been manufactured as either one-piece units or as a separable two-piece assembly. Two-piece units are identified by the large rivet heads on one side of the ar-

Fig. B531—Wires must be unsoldered to remove Magnetron module.

Armature air gap should be 0.010-0.014 inch (0.25-0.36 mm) for two-leg armature or 0.012-0.016 inch (0.30-0.41 mm) for three-leg armature. Ignition timing is not adjustable on these models.

VALVE ADJUSTMENT. To correctly set tappet clearance, remove spark plug and, using a suitable measuring tool, rotate crankshaft in normal direction (clockwise at flywheel) so piston is at top dead center on compression stroke. Continue to rotate crankshaft so piston is ¼ inch (6.4 mm) down from top dead center. This position places the tappets away from the compression release devices on the cam lobes.

Exhaust valve tappet clearance (cold) for all models is 0.009-0.011 inch (0.23-0.28 mm). Intake valve tappet clearance (cold) for all models except Series 253400 and 255400 engines with electric start is 0.005-0.007 inch (0.13-0.18 mm). On Series 253400 and 255400 engines with electric start, intake valve tappet clearance for intake valve is 0.009-0.011 inch (0.23-0.28 mm). If a Series 253400 or 255400 engine is equipped with a manual starter and an electric starter, intake valve tappet clearance is 0.005-0.007 inch (0.13-0.18 mm).

Valve tappet clearance is adjusted on all models by carefully grinding end of valve stem to increase clearance or by grinding valve seats deeper and/or renewing valve or lifter to decrease clearance.

CRANKCASE BREATHER. A crankcase breather is built into engine valve cover. A partial vacuum must exist in crankcase to prevent oil seepage past oil seals, gaskets, breaker point plunger or piston rings. Air can flow out of crankcase through breather, but a one-way valve blocks return flow, maintaining necessary vacuum. Breather mounting holes are offset one way. A vent tube connects breather to carburetor air horn for extra protection against dusty conditions.

CYLINDER HEAD. After 100 to 300 hours of engine operation, the cylinder head should be removed and any carbon or deposits should be removed.

REPAIRS

CYLINDER HEAD. When removing cylinder head, note location and lengths of cylinder head retaining screws so they can be installed in their original positions.

Always install a new cylinder head gasket. Do not apply sealer to head gasket. Lubricate cylinder head retaining screws with graphite grease and tighten

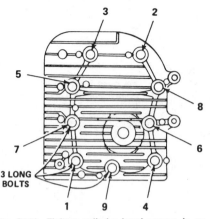

Fig. B532—Tighten cylinder head screws in sequence shown. Note location of three long screws.

screws in sequence shown in Fig. B532 to 165 in.-lbs. (19 N•m).

VALVE SYSTEM. Valve face and seat angle should be ground at 45°. Renew valve if margin is ⅟₆₄ inch (0.4 mm) or less. Seat width should be ³⁄₆₄ to ⅟₁₆ inch (1.2-1.6 mm). All models are equipped with seat inserts. Peen around insert after installing new insert.

Valve guides are renewable. Using tool 19204, press in bushing so bushing is flush with top of guide bore. Valve guide 230655 does not require reaming; however, other valve guides must be finish reamed using B&S reamer 19233 and reamer guide 19234.

Some engines may be equipped with a "Cobalite" exhaust valve and exhaust seat insert as well as a rotocoil on the exhaust valve stem. These components are offered as replacement parts for engines used in severe engine service.

If engine is operated on LP fuel or natural gas, rotocoil should not be used and valve stem and guide should be lubricated with B&S 93963 Valve Guide Lubricant during assembly.

CRANKCASE COVER/OIL PAN. Tighten crankcase cover or oil pan retaining screws to 140 in.-lbs. (15.8 N•m). On horizontal crankshaft models not equipped with a right-angle drive, apply nonhardening sealant to screw (S—Fig. B533).

CAMSHAFT. The camshaft is supported at both ends in bearing bores machined in crankcase and crankcase cover or oil pan. The camshaft gear is an integral part of camshaft.

Camshaft should be renewed if either journal is worn to a diameter of 0.498 inch (12.66 mm) or less, or if cam lobes are worn or damaged.

Crankcase, crankcase cover or oil pan must be renewed if bearing bores are

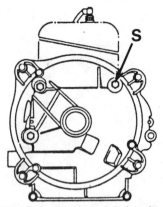

Fig. B533—On horizontal crankshaft engines without right-angle drive, apply nonhardening sealant to crankcase cover retaining screw (S).

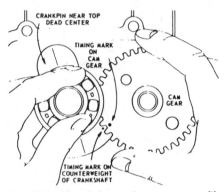

Fig. B534—Align timing mark on cam gear with mark on crankshaft counterweight on ball bearing equipped models.

0.506 inch (12.85 mm) or larger, or if tool 19164 enters bearing bore ¼ inch (6.4 mm) or more.

Compression release mechanism on camshaft gear holds exhaust valve slightly open at very low engine rpm as a starting aid. Mechanism should work freely and spring should hold actuator cam against pin.

When installing camshaft in engines with ball bearing main bearings, align timing marks on camshaft gear and crankshaft counterweight as shown in Fig. B534.

When installing camshaft in engines with integral-type main bearings, align timing marks on camshaft and crankshaft gears as shown in Fig. B535.

If timing mark is not visible on crankshaft gear, align camshaft gear timing mark with second tooth to the left of crankshaft counterweight parting line as shown in Fig. B536.

PISTON, PIN AND RINGS. Connecting rod and piston are removed from cylinder head end of block as an assembly.

Cylinder bore may be aluminum or a cast iron sleeve. Pistons are designed to

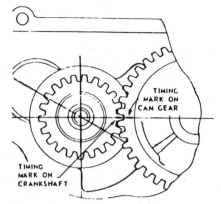

Fig. B535—Align timing marks on cam gear and crankshaft gear on plain bearing models.

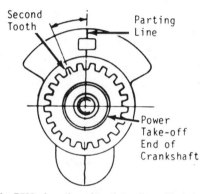

Fig. B536—Location of tooth to align with timing mark on cam gear if mark is not visible on crankshaft gear.

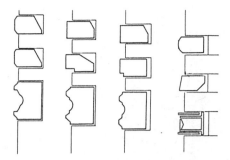

Fig. B537—Refer to above illustration for proper arrangement of piston rings used in engines with aluminum bore.

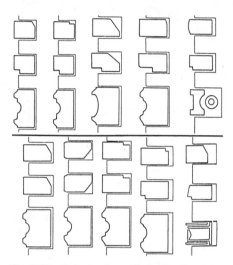

Fig. B538—Refer to above illustration for proper arrangement of piston rings used in engines with cast iron sleeve.

run in only one type of bore. Pistons designed for use in a cast iron bore have a dull finish and are stamped with an "L" on the piston's crown. Pistons designed for use in an aluminum cylinder bore are chrome plated (shiny finish). Pistons cannot be interchanged.

Reject piston showing visible signs of wear, scoring and scuffing. If, after cleaning carbon from top ring groove, a new top ring has a side clearance of 0.009 inch (0.23 mm), reject the piston. Reject piston or hone piston pin hole to 0.005 inch (0.13 mm) oversize if pin hole is 0.0005 inch (0.013 mm) or more out-of-round, or is worn to a diameter of 0.673 inch (17.09 mm) or more on 170000, 171000, 190000, 191000, 192000, 193000, 194000, 195000 and 196000 series engines, or 0.801 inch (20.34 mm) or more on all other engines.

If the piston pin is 0.0005 inch (0.013 mm) or more out-of-round, or is worn to a diameter of 0.671 inch (17.04 mm) or smaller on 170000, 171000, 190000, 191000, 192000, 193000, 194000, 195000 and 196000 series engines, or 0.799 inch (20.30 mm) or smaller on all other models, reject pin.

On aluminum bore engines, reject compression rings having an end gap of 0.035 inch (0.90 mm) or more and reject oil rings having an end gap of 0.045 inch (1.14 mm) or more. On cast iron bore engines, reject compression rings having an end gap of 0.030 inch (0.75 mm) or more and reject oil rings having an end gap of 0.035 inch (0.90 mm) or more.

Pistons and rings are available in several oversizes as well as standard. Refer to Figs. B537 and B538 for correct installation of piston rings.

A chrome piston ring set is available for slightly worn standard bore cylinders. No honing or cylinder deglazing is required for these rings. The cylinder bore can be a

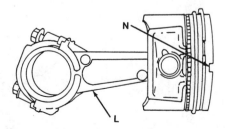

Fig. B539—If piston crown is notched (N), assemble connecting rod and piston as shown while noting relation of long side of rod (L) and notch (N) in piston crown.

maximum of 0.005 inch (0.13 mm) oversize when using chrome rings.

If piston has a notch (N—Fig. B539) in piston crown, assemble connecting rod and piston as shown in Fig. B539. Install piston and rod in engine so notch (N) is toward flywheel.

CONNECTING ROD. Connecting rod and piston are removed from cylinder head end of block as an assembly. The aluminum alloy connecting rod rides directly on an induction hardened crankshaft crankpin journal. Rod should be rejected if big end of rod is scored or out-of-round more than 0.0007 inch (0.018 mm) or if piston pin bore is scored or out-of-round more than 0.0005 inch (0.013 mm). Renew connecting rod if either crankpin bore or piston pin bore is worn to, or larger than, sizes given in following table:

REJECT SIZES FOR CONNECTING ROD

Model Series	Crankpin Bore	Pin Bore*
170000, 171000	1.095 in. (27.81 mm)	0.674 in. (17.12 mm)
190000, 191000, 192000, 193000, 194000, 195000, 196000	1.127 in. (28.61 mm)	0.674 in. (17.12 mm)
All other models	1.252 in. (31.8 mm)	0.802 in. (20.37 mm)

*Piston pins that are 0.005 inch (0.13 mm) oversize are available for service. Piston pin bore in rod can be reamed to this size if crankpin bore is within specifications.

Refer to Fig. B501, locate type of rod being serviced and note installation instructions. If piston has a notch (N—Fig. B539) in piston crown, assemble connecting rod and piston as shown in Fig. B539. Install piston and rod in engine so notch (N) is toward flywheel.

Tighten connecting rod screws to 165 in.-lbs. (19 N·m) on 170000 and 171000 series engines and to 190 in.-lbs. (22 N·m) on all other engines.

GOVERNOR. Governor gear and weight unit can be removed when engine is disassembled. Refer to exploded views of engines in Figs. B540, B541, B542 and B543. Governor weight unit on horizontal crankshaft models rides on a shaft in the crankcase cover. The governor weight unit along with the oil slinger on vertical crankshaft models rides on the end of the camshaft as shown in Fig. B502.

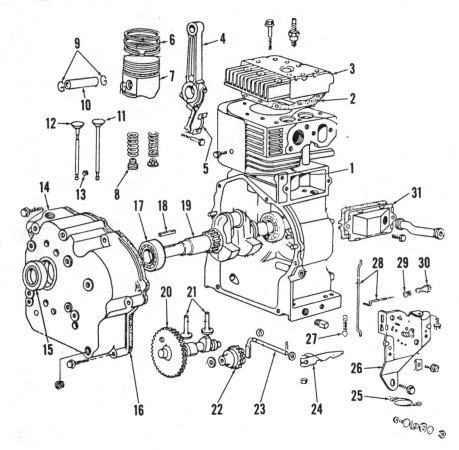

Fig. B540—Exploded view of Series 220000 or 221000 horizontal crankshaft engine assembly. Series 170000, 171000, 190000 and 195000 are similar. Series 222000 is similar, but ball bearings (17) are not used.

1. Cylinder block/crankcase
2. Head gasket
3. Cylinder head
4. Connecting rod
5. Rod bolt lock
6. Piston rings
7. Piston
8. Rotocoil (exhaust valve)
9. Retainer clips
10. Piston pin
11. Intake valve
12. Exhaust valve
13. Retainers
14. Crankcase cover
15. Oil seal
16. Crankcase gasket
17. Main bearing
18. Key
19. Crankshaft
20. Camshaft
21. Tappet
22. Governor gear
23. Governor crank
24. Governor lever
25. Ground wire
26. Governor control plate
27. Spring
28. Governor rod
29. Spring
30. Nut
31. Breather assy.

Fig. B541—Exploded view of Series 251000, 252000 or 254000 engine assembly. Series 253000 and 255000 are similar.

1. Cylinder head
2. Head gasket
3. Cylinder block/crankcase
4. Rod bolt lock
5. Connecting rod
6. Piston rings
7. Piston
8. Piston pin
9. Retainer clips
10. Dipstick
11. Crankcase cover
12. Crankcase gasket
13. Oil seal
14. Counterweight & bearing assy.
17. Crankshaft
18. Camshaft
19. Tappet
20. Governor gear
21. Governor crank
22. Governor lever
23. Governor nut & spring
24. Governor control rod
25. Ground wire
26. Governor control plate
27. Drain plug
28. Spring
29. Governor link
30. Choke link
31. Breather assy.
32. Rotocoil (exhaust valve)
33. Valve springs
34. Retainer
35. Exhaust valve
36. Intake valve

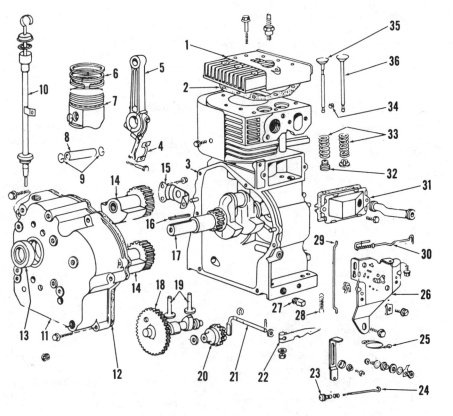

Illustrations Courtesy Briggs & Stratton Corp.

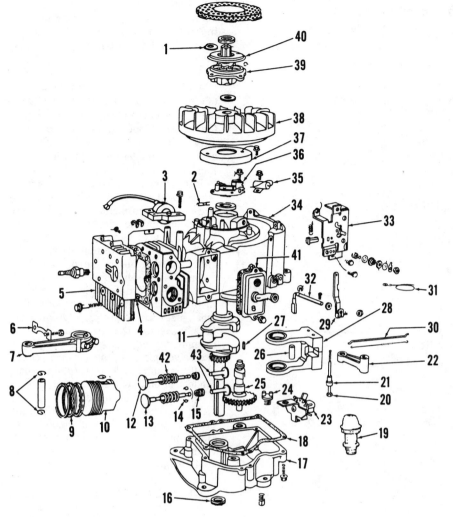

Fig. B542—Exploded view of typical vertical crankshaft engine equipped with Synchro-Balancer.

1. Thrust washer
2. Breaker point plunger
3. Armature assy.
4. Head gasket
5. Cylinder head
6. Rod bolt lock
7. Connecting rod
8. Piston pin & retaining clips
9. Piston rings
10. Piston
11. Crankshaft
12. Intake valve
13. Exhaust valve
14. Retainer
15. Rotocoil (exhaust valve)
16. Oil seal
17. Oil pan
18. Crankcase gasket
19. Oil minder
20. Cap screw (2)
21. Spacer (2)
22. Link
23. Governor & oil slinger
24. Plug
25. Camshaft
26. Dowel pin (2)
27. Key
28. Counterweight assy.
29. Governor lever
30. Governor link
31. Ground wire
32. Governor crank
33. Choke-A-Matic control
34. Cylinder block/crankcase
35. Condenser
36. Breaker points
37. Cover
38. Flywheel assy.
39. Clutch housing
40. Rewind starter clutch
41. Breather assy.
42. Valve springs
43. Tappet

Remove governor lever, cotter pin and washer from outer end of governor lever shaft. Slide governor lever out of bushing toward inside of engine. Governor gear and weight unit can now be removed. Renew governor lever shaft bushing in crankcase, if necessary, and ream new bushing after installation to 0.2385-0.2390 inch (6.058-6.071 mm). Briggs & Stratton tool 19333 can be used to ream bushing.

CRANKSHAFT AND MAIN BEARINGS. The crankshaft may be supported by bearing surfaces that are an integral part of crankcase, crankcase cover or oil pan, or by ball bearings at each end of crankshaft. The ball bearings are a press fit on the crankshaft and fit into machined bores in the crankcase, crankcase cover or oil pan.

The crankshaft used in models with integral bearings should be renewed or reground if main bearing journals exceed service limits specified in following table:

CRANKSHAFT REJECT SIZES

Model Series	Magneto End Journal	PTO End Journal
170000, 171000, 190000, 191000, 192000, 193000, 194000, 195000, 196000	0.997 in.* (25.32 mm)	1.179 in. (29.95 mm)
All other models	1.376 in. (34.95 mm)	1.376 in. (34.95 mm)

*Models equipped with Synchro-Balancer have a main bearing rejection size for main bearing at magneto side of 1.179 inch (29.95 mm).

Crankshaft for models with ball bearing main bearings should be renewed if new bearings are loose on journals. Bearings should be a press fit.

Crankshaft for all models should be renewed or reground if connecting rod crankpin journal diameter exceeds service limit listed in following table:

CRANKSHAFT REJECT SIZES

Model	Crankpin Journal
170000, 171000	1.090 in. (27.69 mm)
190000, 191000, 192000, 193000, 194000, 195000, 196000	1.122 in. (28.50 mm)
All other models	1.247 in. (31.67 mm)

A connecting rod with undersize big end diameter is available to fit crankshaft that has had crankpin journal reground to 0.020 inch (0.51 mm) undersize.

On models equipped with integral main bearings, crankcase, crankcase cover or oil pan must be renewed or reamed to accept service bushings if service limits in following table are exceeded:

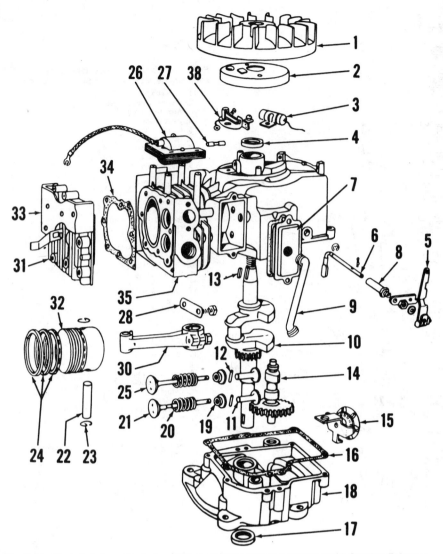

Fig. B543—Exploded view of typical vertical crankshaft engine not equipped with Synchro-Balancer.

1. Flywheel	10. Crankshaft	19. Valve spring retainer	27. Breaker point plunger
2. Cover	11. Tappet	20. Valve springs	28. Rod bolt lock
3. Condenser	12. Valve retaining pins	21. Exhaust valve	30. Connecting rod
4. Oil seal	13. Key	22. Piston pin	31. Cylinder head
5. Governor lever	14. Camshaft	23. Retainer clip	32. Piston
6. Governor crank	15. Governor & oil slinger	24. Piston rings	33. Air baffle
7. Breather assy.	16. Crankcase gasket	25. Intake valve	34. Head gasket
8. Bushing	17. Oil seal	26. Armature & coil assy.	35. Cylinder block/crankcase
9. Breather vent tube	18. Oil pan		38. Breaker points

MAIN BEARING REJECT SIZES

Model Series	Magneto End Bearing	PTO End Bearing
170000, 171000, 190000, 191000, 192000, 193000, 194000, 195000, 196000	1.004 in.* (25.50 mm)	1.185 in. (30.10 mm)
All other models	1.383 in. (35.13 mm)	1.383 in. (35.13 mm)

*Models equipped with Synchro-Balancer have a main bearing rejection size for main bearing at magneto side of 1.185 inch (30.10 mm).

Install steel-backed aluminum service bushing as follows. Use a suitable tool and, prior to bushing installation, make an indentation in bore of crankcase. Install bushing so oil notches are properly aligned and bushing is flush with bore. Oil hole must be clear after installation. Stake bushing into previously made indentation and finish ream bushing. Do not stake where bushing is split.

When installing "DU"-type bushing, stake bushing at oil notches in crankcase, but locate bushing so bushing split is not aligned with an oil notch. On Series 170000 and 190000 models,

bushing should be $\frac{3}{32}$ inch (2.4 mm) below face of crankcase bore and $\frac{1}{32}$ inch (0.8 mm) below face of crankcase cover or oil pan. On Series 171000, 191000, 192000, 193000, 194000, 195000 and 196000 models, bushing should be $\frac{1}{64}$ inch (0.4 mm) below face of crankcase bore and $\frac{1}{32}$ inch (0.8 mm) below face of crankcase cover or oil pan. On all other models, bushing should be $\frac{7}{64}$ inch (2.8 mm) below face of crankcase bore and $\frac{1}{8}$ inch (3.2 mm) below face of crankcase cover or oil pan.

Ball bearing mains are a press fit on the crankshaft and must be removed by pressing the crankshaft out of the bearing. Reject ball bearing if worn or rough. Expand new bearing by heating it in oil and install it on crankshaft with seal side toward crankpin journal.

Crankshaft end play is 0.002-0.008 inch (0.05-0.20 mm). At least one 0.015-inch crankcase gasket must be in place when measuring end play. Additional gaskets in several sizes are available to aid in end play adjustment. If end play is excessive, place shims between crankshaft gear and crankcase on plain bearing models, or on flywheel side of crankshaft if equipped with a ball bearing.

When reinstalling crankshaft, make certain timing marks are aligned (Figs. B534 or B535) and, if equipped with counterbalance weights, refer to Fig. B544 for proper alignment.

CYLINDER. If cylinder bore wear is 0.003 inch (0.08 mm) or more or is 0.0025 inch (0.06 mm) or more out-of-round, cylinder must be rebored to next larger oversize.

Standard cylinder bore diameter is 2.9990-3.0000 inches (76.175-76.230 mm) for Series 170000, 171000, 190000, 191000, 192000, 193000, 194000, 195000 and 196000 models. Standard cylinder bore diameter is 3.4365-3.4375 inches (87.287-87.313 mm) for all other models.

Special stones are required to hone aluminum cylinder bore on models so equipped. Follow recommendations and

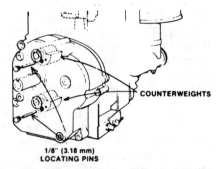

Fig. B544—To properly align counterweights, remove two small screws from crankcase cover and insert 1/8-inch (3.2 mm) diameter locating pins.

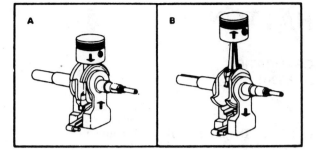

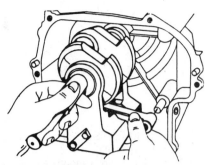

Fig. B545—View showing operating principle of Synchro-Balancer used on some vertical crankshaft engines. Counterweight oscillates in opposite direction of piston.

Fig. B548—When installing crankshaft and balancer assembly, place free end of link on anchor pin in crankcase.

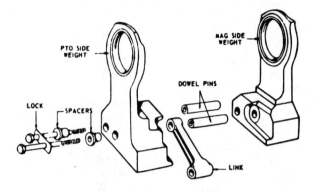

Fig. B546—Exploded view of Synchro-Balancer assembly. Counterweights ride on eccentric journals on crankshaft.

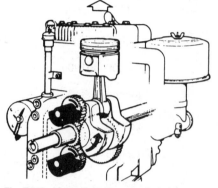

Fig. B549—View of rotating counterbalance system used on some models. Counterweight gears are driven by crankshaft.

procedures specified by hone manufacturer.

A chrome piston ring set is available for slightly worn standard bore cylinders. No honing or cylinder deglazing is required for these rings. The cylinder bore can be a maximum of 0.005 inch (0.13 mm) oversize when using chrome rings.

SYNCHRO-BALANCER. All vertical crankshaft engines, except Series 220000, 221000 and 222000 models, may be equipped with an oscillating Synchro-Balancer. Balance weight assembly rides on eccentric journals on the crankshaft and move in opposite direction of piston (Fig. B545).

To disassemble balancer unit, first remove flywheel, oil pan, cam gear, cylinder head and connecting rod and piston assembly. Carefully pry off crankshaft gear and key. Remove the two cap screws holding halves of counterweight together. Separate weights and remove link, dowel pins and spacers. Slide weights from crankshaft (Fig. B546).

To reassemble, install magneto side weight on magneto end of crankshaft. Place crankshaft (pto end up) in a vise (Fig. B547). Install both dowel pins and place link on pin as shown. Note rounded edge on free end of link must

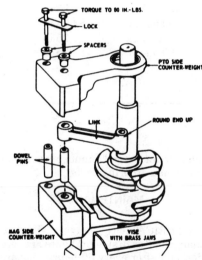

Fig. B547—Assemble balance units on crankshaft as shown. Install link with rounded edge on free end toward pto end of crankshaft.

be up. Install pto side weight, spacers, lock and cap screws. Tighten cap screws to 80 in.-lbs. (9 N·m) and secure with lock tabs. Install key and crankshaft gear with chamfer on inside of gear facing shoulder on crankshaft.

Install crankshaft and balancer assembly in crankcase, sliding free end of link on anchor pin as shown in Fig. B548. Reassemble engine.

ROTATING COUNTERBALANCE SYSTEM. All horizontal crankshaft engines, except Series 220000, 221000 and 222000 models, may be equipped with two gear-driven counterweights in constant mesh with crankshaft gear. Gears, mounted in crankcase cover, rotate in opposite direction of crankshaft (Fig. B549).

To properly align counterweights when installing cover, remove two small screws from cover and insert ⅛-inch (3.2 mm) diameter locating pins through holes and into holes in counterweights as shown in Fig. B544.

With piston at TDC, install cover assembly. Remove locating pins, coat threads of timing hole screws with nonhardening sealer and install screws with fiber sealing washers.

NOTE: If counterweights are removed from crankcase cover, exercise care in handling or cleaning to prevent loss of needle bearings.

BRIGGS & STRATTON

BRIGGS & STRATTON CORPORATION
Milwaukee, Wisconsin 53201

Model Series	No. Cyls.	Bore	Stroke	Displacement	Power Rating
19, 19D, 191000, 193000	1	3.00 in. (76.2 mm)	2.625 in. (66.68 mm)	18.56 cu. in. (304 cc)	7.25 hp (5.5 kW)
200000	1	3.00 in. (76.2 mm)	2.875 in. (73.02 mm)	20.32 cu. in. (333 cc)	8 hp (6 kW)
22, 23A, 23C, 23D 231000, 233000	1	3.00 in. (76.2 mm)	3.25 in. (82.55 mm)	22.97 cu. in. (376 cc)	9 hp (6.7 kW)
243000	1	3.0625 in. (77.79 mm)	3.25 in. (82.55 mm)	23.94 cu. in. (392 cc)	10 hp (7.5 kW)
300000, 301000	1	3.4375 in. (87.31 mm)	3.25 in. (82.55 mm)	30.16 cu. in. (494 cc)	12 hp (9 kW)
302000	1	3.4375 in. (87.31 mm)	3.25 in. (82.55 mm)	30.16 cu. in. (494 cc)	13 hp (9.7 kW)
320000	1	3.5625 in. (90.5 mm)	3.25 in. (82.55 mm)	32.4 cu. in. (531 cc)	14 hp (10.4 kW)
325000	1	3.5625 in. (90.5 mm)	3.25 in. (82.55 mm)	32.4 cu. in. (531 cc)	15 hp (11.2 kW)
326000	1	3.5625 in. (90.5 mm)	3.25 in. (82.55 mm)	32.4 cu. in. (531 cc)	16 hp (11.9 kW)

Engines in this section are four-stroke, single-cylinder engines with a horizontal crankshaft. The crankshaft may be supported by main bearings that are an integral part of main bearing support plate or by ball bearings pressed on the crankshaft. All engines are constructed of aluminum. Cylinder block and bore are a single casting.

The connecting rod on all models rides directly on the crankpin journal. The engine is splash lubricated by an oil dipper attached to the connecting rod cap.

Early models are equipped with a variety of magneto-type ignition systems with points and condenser either mounted externally or located underneath the flywheel. Later models are equipped with a breakerless (Magnetron) ignition system.

A float-type carburetor is used on all models. A fuel pump is available as optional equipment for some models.

Refer to BRIGGS & STRATTON ENGINE IDENTIFICATION INFORMATION section for engine identification. Engine model number as well as type number and serial number are necessary when ordering parts.

MAINTENANCE

LUBRICATION. Engine oil should be changed after first eight hours of operation and after every 50 hours of operation or at least once each operating season. If equipment undergoes severe usage, change oil weekly or after every 25 hours of operation.

Manufacturer recommends using oil with an API service classification of SF or SG. Use SAE 30 oil for temperatures above 40° F (4° C); use SAE 10W-30 oil for temperatures between 0° F (−18° C) and 100° F (38° C); below 0° F (−18° C) use petroleum based SAE 5W-20 or a suitable synthetic oil.

Crankcase oil capacity for 18.56 and 20.32 cubic-inch engines is 3 pints (1.4 L). Crankcase oil capacity for all other models is 4 pints (1.9 L).

SPARK PLUG. The original spark plug may be either 1½ inches or 2 inches long. Recommended spark plug is either Champion or Autolite.

If a Champion spark plug is used and spark plug is 1½ inches long, recommended spark plug is CJ8 for normal operation. Champion J19LM may be used if fouling is encountered. Install Champion RCJ8 (RJ19LM for severe fouling) if a resistor-type spark plug is required. If spark plug is 2 inches long, recommended spark plug is J8C for normal operation. Champion J19LM may be used if fouling is encountered. Install Champion RJ8C (RJ19LM for severe fouling) if a resistor-type spark plug is required.

If an Autolite spark plug is used and spark plug is 1½ inches long, recommended spark plug is 235. Install Autolite 245 if a resistor-type spark plug is required. If spark plug is 2 inches long, recommended spark plug is 295. Install Autolite 306 if a resistor-type spark plug is required.

Specified spark plug electrode gap is 0.030 inch (0.76 mm).

CAUTION: Briggs & Stratton does not recommend using abrasive blasting to clean spark plugs as this may introduce some abrasive material into

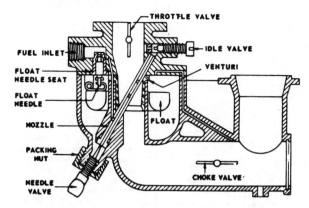

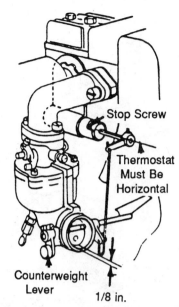

Fig. B601—Cross-sectional view of two-piece Flo-Jet II carburetor. Before separating upper and lower body section, remove packing nut and power needle valve as a unit and use special screwdriver (tool 19062) to remove nozzle.

the engine that could cause extensive damage.

CARBURETOR. All engines are equipped with a two-piece Flo-Jet carburetor. Refer to Fig. B601 for a cross-sectional view of carburetor and location of mixture adjustment needles.

Initial setting of idle mixture needle is 1¼ turns out and high-speed needle valve is 1½ turns out. With engine at normal operating temperature and equipment control lever in "SLOW" position, adjust idle speed screw so engine idles at 1750 rpm. With engine running at idle speed, turn idle mixture needle clockwise until engine speed just starts to drop. Note needle position. Turn idle mixture needle counterclockwise until engine speed just starts to drop again. Note needle position, then turn needle to midpoint between the noted positions. Adjust high-speed needle valve with control set to "FAST" using same procedure. If engine will not accelerate cleanly, slightly enrich mixture by turning idle mixture needle valve counterclockwise. If necessary, readjust idle speed screw.

To check float level, invert carburetor body and float assembly. Refer to Fig. B602 for proper float level dimensions. Adjust by bending float lever tang that contacts inlet valve. Check upper body for distortion using a 0.002 inch (0.05 mm) feeler gauge as shown in Fig. B603.

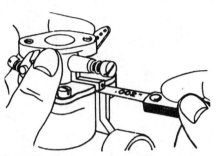

Fig. B603—Check upper body of Flo-Jet II carburetor for distortion as outlined in text.

Upper body must be renewed if warped more than 0.002 inch (0.05 mm).

AUTOMATIC CHOKE. A thermostat operated choke is used on some models. To adjust choke linkage, hold choke shaft so thermostat lever is free. At room temperature, stop screw in thermostat collar should be located midway between thermostat stops. If not, loosen stop screw, adjust collar and tighten stop screw. Loosen set screw

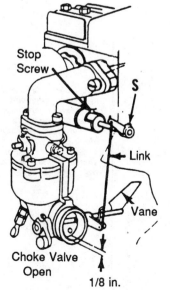

Fig. B604—Typical automatic choke unit in "HOT" position.

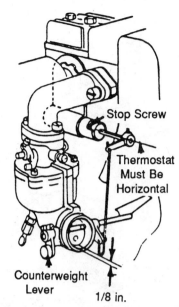

Fig. B605—Turn thermostat shaft counterclockwise until stop screw contacts thermostat stop as shown.

(S—Fig. B604) on thermostat lever. Slide lever on shaft to ensure free movement of choke unit. Turn thermostat shaft clockwise until stop screw contacts thermostat stop. While holding shaft in this position, move shaft lever until choke is open exactly ⅛ inch (3 mm) and tighten lever set screw. Turn thermostat shaft counterclockwise until stop screw contacts thermostat stop as shown in Fig. B605. Manually open choke valve until it stops against top of choke link opening. At this time choke should be open at least ³⁄₃₂ inch (2.4 mm), but not more than ⁵⁄₃₂ inch (4 mm). Hold choke valve in wide-open position and check position of counterweight lever. Lever should be in a horizontal position with free end toward the right.

FUEL PUMP. A fuel pump is available as optional equipment on some models. Refer to BRIGGS & STRATTON ACCESSORIES section for service information.

GOVERNOR. All engines are equipped with a gear-driven mechanical-type governor attached to the crankcase cover or oil pan. The governor is driven by the camshaft gear. Governor and linkage must operate properly to prevent "hunting" or unsteady operation. The carburetor must be properly adjusted before performing governor adjustments.

To adjust governor linkage, loosen clamp bolt nut (N—Fig. B606) on governor lever. Move link end of governor lever so carburetor throttle plate is in wide-open position. Using a screw-

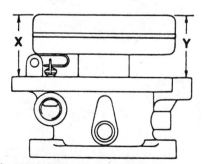

Fig. B602—Dimension (Y) must be the same as dimension (X) plus or minus 1/32 inch (0.8 mm).

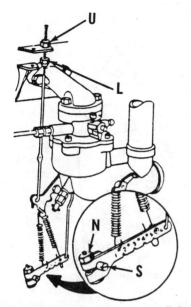

Fig. B606—View showing governor linkage, springs and levers properly installed on 243000, 300000, 301000, 302000, 320000, 325000 and 326000 series engines. Refer to Fig. B609 for remote control hook-up.

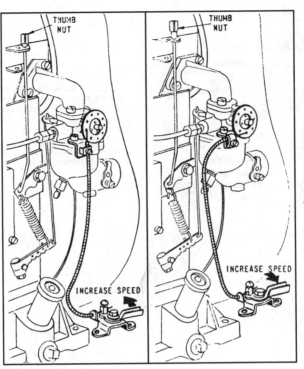

Fig. B608—Views showing methods of connecting remote throttle controls. When control lever is in high-speed position, governor controls speed of engines and governed speed is adjusted by turning thumb nut. Moving control lever to slow speed position moves carburetor throttle shaft stop to decrease engine speed.

driver, rotate governor lever shaft (S) counterclockwise as far as possible and tighten clamp bolt to 35-45 in.-lbs. (4.0-5.1 N•m).

Refer to Figs. B606 through B609 for governor control and carburetor linkage hook-up and adjustments.

IGNITION SYSTEM. Early models use a variety of magneto-type ignition systems and late production models use Briggs & Stratton Magnetron ignition

system. Refer to appropriate section for model being serviced.

Model 23C Magneto. Refer to Fig. B610 for exploded view of magneto used on 23C model engine. Condenser and breaker points are mounted on crankshaft bearing support plate (17) and are accessible after removing flywheel and magneto cover (7).

Breaker point gap is 0.020 inch (0.51 mm) and condenser capacity is 0.18-0.24 mfd.

Breaker point plunger can be removed from bore in crankshaft bearing support when breaker points are removed. Plunger should be renewed if worn to a length of 0.870 inch (22.10 mm) or less. Plunger bore diameter can be checked using B&S plunger bore gauge 19055. If gauge enters plunger bore ¼ inch (6.4 mm) or more, install service bushing 23513. To install bush-

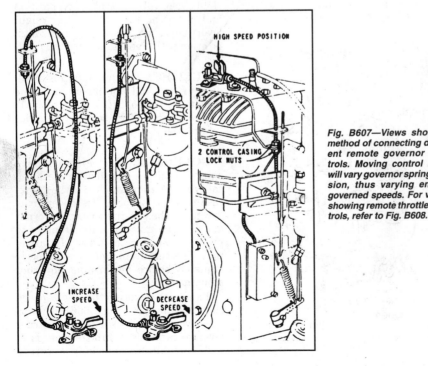

Fig. B607—Views showing method of connecting different remote governor controls. Moving control lever will vary governor spring tension, thus varying engine governed speeds. For views showing remote throttle controls, refer to Fig. B608.

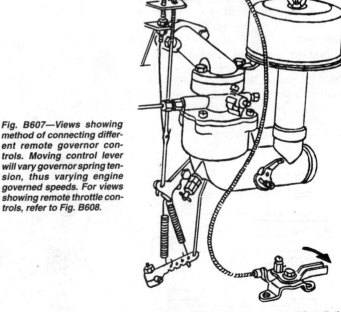

Fig. B609—Remote governor control installation on 243000, 300000, 301000, 302000, 320000, 325000 and 326000 series engines.

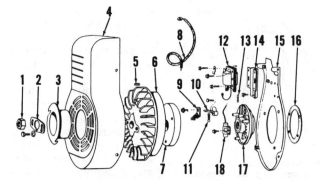

Fig. B610—Exploded view of magneto ignition system used on 23C model engines. Breaker points and condenser are mounted on bearing support (17) and are enclosed by cover (7) and flywheel. Points are actuated by plunger (13) which rides against breaker cam machined on engine crankshaft.

1. Flywheel nut
2. Nut retainer
3. Starter pulley
4. Blower housing
5. Flywheel key
6. Flywheel
7. Breaker cover
8. Spark plug wire
9. Breaker point base
10. Breaker point arm
11. Breaker spring
12. Coil & armature
13. Plunger
14. Armature support
15. Back plate
16. Shim gasket
17. Bearing support
18. Condenser

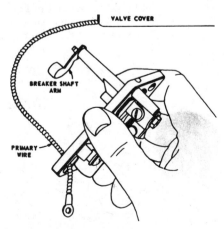

Fig. B612—When installing breaker points on 19, 23 and 23A models and 191000 and 231000 series engines, be sure dowel on breaker point base enters hole in insulator. Place sides of base and insulating plate parallel with edge of breaker box.

ing, remove bearing support from engine, then ream bore using B&S reamer 19056, drive bushing in flush with outer end of plunger bore with B&S driver 19057 and use B&S reamer 19058 to finish ream inside of bushing.

When reinstalling flywheel, inspect the soft metal key and renew if damaged in any way.

NOTE: Renew key with correct B&S part. DO NOT substitute a steel key.

After flywheel is installed and retaining nut tightened, check armature air gap and adjust as necessary to 0.022-0.026 inch (0.56-0.66 mm).

Series or Models 19, 23, 23A, 191000 and 231000 Magneto. Refer to Fig. B611 for exploded view of magneto used on these models.

Condenser and breaker points are mounted externally in a breaker box located on carburetor side of engine and are accessible after removing breaker box cover (18—Fig. B611).

Breaker point gap is 0.020 inch (0.51 mm) and condenser capacity is 0.18-0.24 mfd.

When renewing breaker points, or if oil leak is noted, breaker shaft oil seal (16) should be renewed. To renew points and/or seal, turn engine so breaker point gap is at maximum. Remove ter-

minal and breaker spring screws and loosen breaker arm retaining nut (19) so it is flush with end of shaft (29). Tap loosened nut lightly to free breaker arm (21) from taper on shaft, then remove breaker arm, breaker plate (22), pivot (23), insulating plate (24) and eccentric (17). Pry oil seal out and press new oil seal in with metal side out. Place breaker plate on insulating plate with dowel on breaker plate entering hole in insulator. Then install unit with edges of plates parallel with breaker box as shown in Fig. B612. Turn breaker shaft clockwise as far as possible and install breaker arm while holding shaft in this position.

Breaker box can be removed without removing points or condenser. Refer to Fig. B613. Disassembly of unit is evident after removal from engine.

To renew ignition coil, engine flywheel must be removed. Disconnect coil ground and primary wires and pull spark plug wire from hole in back plate. Disengage clips (8—Fig. B611) retaining coil core (9) to armature (14) and push core from coil. Insert core in new

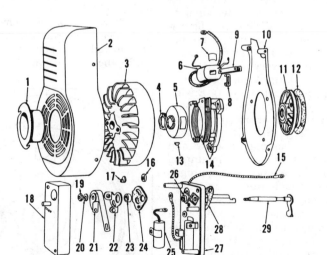

Fig. B611—Exploded view of magneto ignition system used on 19, 23 and 23A models and 191000 and 231000 series engines. Flywheel is not keyed to crankshaft and can be installed in any position; however, on crank start models, flywheel should be installed as shown in Fig. B618. Breaker arm (21) is mounted on shaft (29) which is actuated by a cam on engine cam gear. See Fig. B619. Two different methods of attaching magneto rotor (5) to engine crankshaft have been used. Refer to Figs. B614 and B615.

1. Starter pulley
2. Blower housing
3. Flywheel
4. Rotor clamp
5. Magneto rotor
6. Ignition coil
7. Coil retainer
8. Core clip
9. Coil core
10. Back plate
11. Bearing support
12. Shim gasket
13. Rotor key
14. Armature
15. Primary coil lead
16. Shaft seal
17. Eccentric
18. Breaker box cover
19. Nut
20. Washer
21. Breaker point cam
22. Breaker point base
23. Pivot
24. Insulator
25. Condenser
26. Seal retainer
27. Breaker box
28. Gasket
29. Shaft

Fig. B613—To remove breaker box on 19, 23 and 23A models and 191000 and 231000 series engines it is not necessary to remove points and condenser as unit can be removed as an assembly.

Illustrations Courtesy Briggs & Stratton Corp.

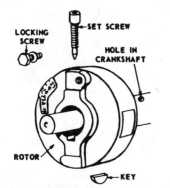

Fig. B614—On some models, magneto rotor is fastened to crankshaft by a set screw that enters hole in shaft. Set screw is locked in place by a second screw. Refer to Fig. B615 also.

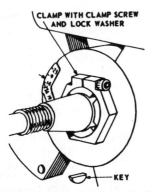

Fig. B615—View showing magneto rotor fastened to crankshaft with clamp. Make certain split in clamp is between two slots in rotor as shown and check clearance between rotor and shoulder on crankshaft as shown in Fig. B616.

coil with rounded side of core toward spark plug wire. Place coil and core on armature with retainer (7) between coil and armature. Reinstall core retaining clips, connect coil ground and primary wires and insert spark plug wire through hole in back plate.

Two-types of magnetic rotors have been used. Refer to Fig. B614 for view of rotor retained by set screw and to Fig. B615 for rotor retained by clamp ring. If rotor is as shown in Fig. B615, refer to

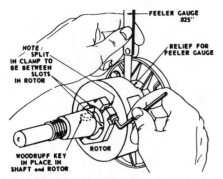

Fig. B616—On models having magneto rotor clamped to crankshaft, position rotor 0.025 inch (6.4 mm) from shoulder on shaft, then tighten clamping screw.

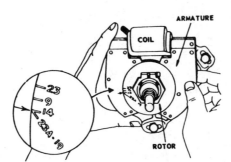

Fig. B617—With engine turned so breaker points are just starting to open, align model number line on rotor with arrow on armature by rotating armature in slotted mounting holes.

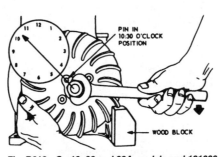

Fig. B618—On 19, 23 and 23A models and 191000 and 231000 series engines equipped with crank starter, mount flywheel with pin in position shown with armature timing marks aligned.

Fig. B616 when installing rotor on crankshaft.

If armature coil has been loosened or removed, rotor timing must be readjusted. With point gap adjusted to 0.020 inch (0.51 mm), connect a static timing light from breaker point terminal to ground (coil primary wire must be disconnected) and turn engine in normal direction of rotation until light goes on. Then turn engine very slowly in same direction until light just goes out (breaker points start to open). Engine model number on magneto rotor should now be aligned with arrow on armature as shown in Fig. B617. If not, loosen armature core retaining cap screws and turn armature in slotted mounting holes so arrow is aligned with appropriate engine model number on rotor. Tighten armature mounting screws.

To install flywheel on models with crank starter, place flywheel on crankshaft as shown in Fig. B618 with magneto timing marks aligned as in previous paragraph. On models not having a crank starter, flywheel can be installed in any position.

Magneto breaker points are actuated by a cam on a centrifugal weight mounted on engine camshaft (Fig. B619). When engine is being overhauled, or cam gear is removed, check action of advance spring and centrifugal weight unit by holding cam gear in po-

sition shown and pressing weight down. When weight is released, spring should return weight to its original position. If weight does not return to its original position, check weight for binding and renew spring.

Models 19D and 23D Magneto. Refer to Fig. B620 for exploded view of magneto system.

Condenser and breaker points are mounted externally in a breaker box located on carburetor side of engine and are accessible after removing breaker box cover (8—Fig. B620).

Breaker point gap is 0.020 inch (0.51 mm) and condenser capacity is 0.18-0.24 mfd.

Installation of new breaker points is made easier by turning engine so points are open to their widest gap before removing old points. For method of adjusting breaker point gap, refer to Fig. B621.

NOTE: When installing points, apply Permatex or equivalent sealer to retaining screw threads to prevent engine oil from leaking into breaker box.

Breaker points are actuated by a plunger that rides against breaker cam on engine cam gear. Plunger and plunger bushing in crankcase are renewable after removing cam gear and breaker points.

Magneto armature and ignition coil are mounted outside engine flywheel. Adjust armature air gap to 0.022-0.026 inch (0.56-0.66 mm).

If flywheel has been removed, magneto edge gap (armature timing) must be adjusted. With point gap adjusted to 0.020 inch (0.51 mm) and flywheel

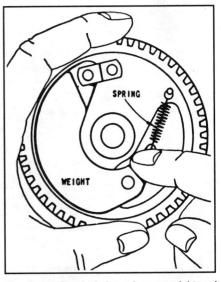

Fig. B619—Check timing advance weight and spring on 19, 23 and 23A models and 191000 and 231000 series engines. Refer to text.

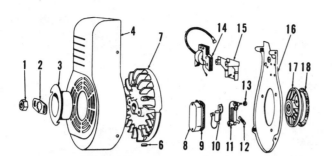

Fig. B620—Exploded view of magneto ignition system used on 19D and 23D models. Magneto rotor (flywheel) to armature timing is adjustable as shown in Figs. B622 and B623. Adjust breaker points as in Fig. B621.

1. Flywheel nut		14. Coil & armature assy.
2. Nut retainer	6. Flywheel key	15. Armature mounting bracket
3. Starter pulley	7. Flywheel	10. Condenser	16. Back plate
4. Blower housing	8. Breaker box cover	11. Breaker points	17. Bearing support
5. Key cap screw	9. Gasket	12. Breaker spring	18. Shim gasket
		13. locknut	

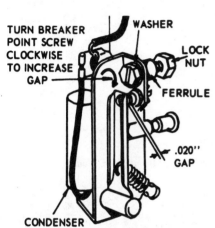

Fig. B621—On all models equipped with this-type of breaker points, loosen locknut and turn adjusting screw to obtain 0.020 inch (0.51 mm) gap.

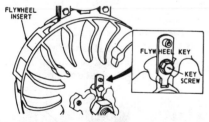

Fig. B622—On 19D and 23D models, magneto timing is adjusted by reposition flywheel on crankshaft. Flywheel is then locked into proper position by tightening key screw and flywheel retaining nut. Refer also to Figs. B623 and B624.

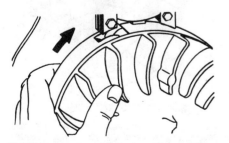

Fig. B623—Turning engine in normal direction of rotation with flywheel and flywheel key loose. Turn engine slowly until breaker points are just starting to open. Refer to text and Figs. B622 and B624.

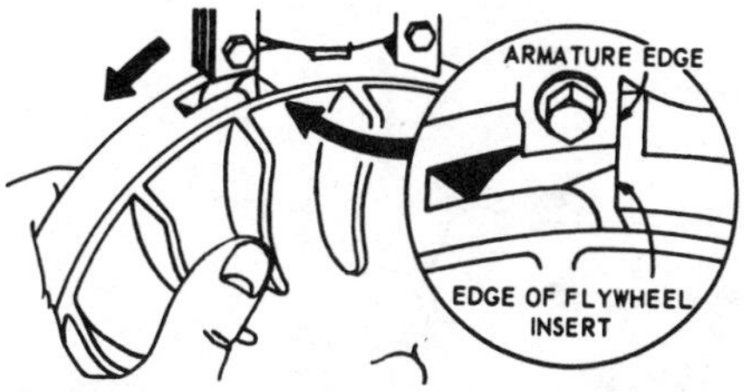

Fig. B624—Turn flywheel counterclockwise on crankshaft until edge of flywheel insert is aligned with edge of armature as shown in insert. Then, tighten flywheel key screw and retaining nut.

loosely installed on crankshaft, install flywheel key (Fig. B622) leaving retaining cap screw loose. Disconnect magneto primary wire and connect test light across breaker points. Turn flywheel in clockwise direction (Fig. B623) until breaker points just start to open (timing light goes out). While making sure engine crankshaft does not turn, rotate flywheel back slightly in counterclockwise direction so edge of flywheel insert lines up with edge of armature as shown in Fig. B624. Tighten flywheel key screw, then tighten flywheel retaining

nut to 110-118 ft.-lbs. (149-160 N·m) for 19D model and to 138-150 ft.-lbs. (187-203 N·m) for 23D model. Readjust armature air gap as needed.

Series 193000, 200000, 233000, 243000, 300000, 301000, 302000, 320000, 325000 and 326000 Magneto. Refer to Fig. B625 for exploded view of magneto system.

Condenser and breaker points are mounted externally in a breaker box located on carburetor side of engine and are accessible after removing breaker box cover (8—Fig. B625).

Breaker point gap is 0.020 inch (0.51 mm) and condenser capacity is 0.18-0.24 mfd.

Installation of new breaker points is made easier by turning engine so points are open to their widest gap before removing old points. For method of adjusting breaker point gap, refer to Fig. B621.

NOTE: When installing points, apply Permatex or equivalent sealer to retaining screw threads to prevent engine oil from leaking into breaker box.

Breaker points are actuated by a plunger that rides against breaker cam on engine cam gear. Plunger (43—Fig. B626) and plunger bushing (PB) are renewable after removing engine cam gear and breaker points. On 300000, 301000, 302000, 320000, 325000 and 326000 series engines breaker plunger and plunger bushing are similar to those shown in Fig. B626.

Magneto armature and ignition coil are mounted outside engine flywheel. Adjust armature air gap to 0.010-0.014 inch (0.25-0.36 mm) as shown in Fig. B627.

If flywheel has been removed, magneto edge gap (armature timing) must be adjusted. With point gap adjusted to

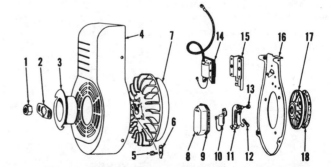

Fig. B625—Exploded view of 193000, 200000, 233000 and 243000 series magneto ignition system. Magneto used on 300000, 301000, 302000, 320000, 325000 and 326000 series is similar. Position of armature is adjustable to time armature with magneto rotor (flywheel) by moving armature mounting bracket (15) on slotted mounting holes. Refer to text and Figs. B627 and B628.

1. Flywheel nut				15. Armature mounting bracket
2. Nut retainer		11. Breaker points		
3. Starter pulley	7. Flywheel	12. Breaker spring		16. Back plate
4. Blower housing	8. Breaker box cover	13. locknut		17. Bearing support
6. Flywheel key	9. Gasket	14. Coil & armature assy.		18. Shim gasket
	10. Condenser			

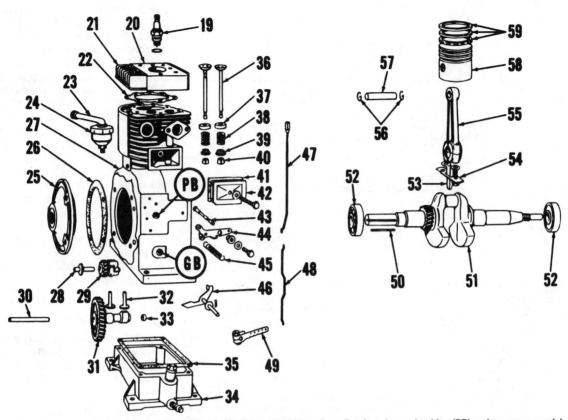

Fig. B626—Exploded view of typical 19D, 23D, 193000, 200000, 233000 and 243000 engines. Breaker plunger bushing (PB) and governor crank bushing (GB) in engine crankcase (27) are renewable. Breaker plunger (43) rides against a lobe on cam gear (31).

19. Spark plug	32. Tappets	39. Spring retainers or "Roto-Caps"
20. Air baffle	33. Camshaft plug	40. Keepers
21. Cylinder head	34. Engine base	41. Gasket
22. Gasket	35. Gasket	42. Tappet chamber cover
23. Breather tube	36. Valves	43. Breaker point plunger
24. Breather	37. Valve spring	44. Governor control lever
25. Main bearing plate	washers	45. Governor spring
26. Gasket	38. Valve springs	46. Governor crank
27. Engine crankcase		
& cylinder block		
28. Governor shaft		
29. Governor gear		
& weight unit		
30. Camshaft		
31. Cam gear		

47. Governor control rod	53. Oil dipper
48. Governor link	54. Rod bolt lock
49. Governor lever	55. Connecting rod
50. Output drive key	56. Piston pin
51. Crankshaft	retaining rings
52. Ball bearings	57. Piston pin
(on models so equipped)	58. Piston
	59. Piston rings

0.020 inch (0.51 mm) and armature ignition coil assembly removed from bracket connect a test light across breaker points. Disconnect coil primary wire and slowly turn flywheel in a clockwise direction until light just goes out (breaker points start to open). At this time, arrow on flywheel should be exactly aligned with arrow on armature mounting bracket (Fig. B628). If not, mark position of bracket, remove flywheel and shift bracket on slotted

mounting holes (Fig. B629) to bring arrows into alignment.

Reinstall flywheel, make certain arrows are aligned and tighten flywheel retaining nut to 110-118 ft.-lbs. (149-160 N·m) on 193000 and 200000 series

engines and to 138-150 ft.-lbs. (187-203 N·m) on all other models. Readjust armature air gap as needed.

Magnetron Ignition. The Magnetron ignition is a self-contained breakerless ignition system. Flywheel

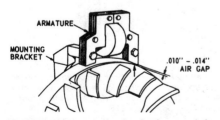

Fig. B627—After mounting bracket is properly installed (Fig. B628), install armature and coil assembly so there is a 0.010-0.014 inch (0.25-0.36 mm) air gap between armature and flywheel.

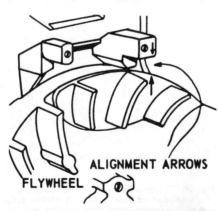

Fig. B628—On 193000, 200000, 233000, 243000, 300000, 301000, 302000, 320000, 325000 and 326000 series, time magneto by aligning armature core support so arrow on support is aligned with arrow on flywheel when breaker points are just starting to open. Refer to text for procedure.

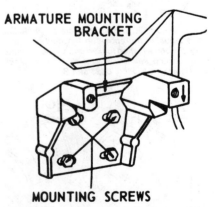

Fig. B629—View with flywheel removed on 193000, 200000, 233000, 243000, 300000, 301000, 302000, 320000, 325000 and 326000 series engines. Magneto is timed by shifting armature mounting bracket on slotted mounting holes. Refer to Fig. B627 also.

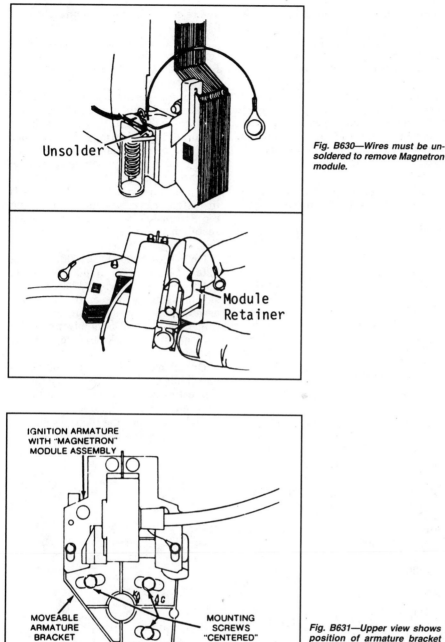

Fig. B630—Wires must be un-soldered to remove Magnetron module.

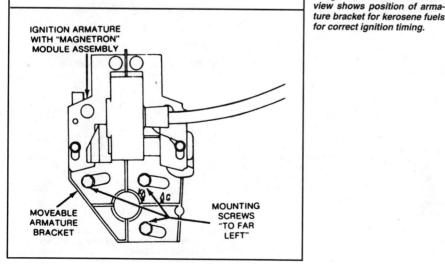

Fig. B631—Upper view shows position of armature bracket for gasoline fuels and lower view shows position of armature bracket for kerosene fuels for correct ignition timing.

removal is not necessary except to change timing by moving armature bracket or to service crankshaft key or keyway.

To check spark, remove spark plug, connect spark plug cable to B&S tester 19051 and ground remaining tester lead on engine cylinder head. Rotate engine at 350 rpm or more. If spark jumps the 0.166 inch (4.2 mm) tester gap, system is functioning properly.

Armature and module have been manufactured as either one-piece units or as a separable two-piece assembly. Two-piece units are identified by the large rivet heads on one side of the armature laminations. To remove armature and Magnetron module, remove flywheel shroud and armature retaining screws. On one-piece units, disconnect stop switch wire at spade connector. On two-piece units, use a 3/16-inch (4.8 mm) diameter pin punch to release stop switch wire from module. To remove module on two-piece units, unsolder wires, push module retainer away from laminations and remove module. See Fig. B630.

Resolder wires for reinstallation and use Permatex or equivalent to hold ground wires in position.

To set timing for gasoline fuel operation, install armature bracket so mounting screws are centered in slots (Fig. B631).

To set timing for kerosene fuel operation, install armature bracket as far to left as possible (Fig. B631).

Armature air gap should be 0.010-0.014 inch (0.25-0.36 mm) for two-leg armature or 0.012-0.016 inch (0.30-0.41 mm) for three-leg armature.

VALVE ADJUSTMENT. Valve tappet clearance (cold) for 19, 19D, 191000, 193000 or 200000 series or models is 0.007-0.009 inch (0.18-0.23 mm) for intake valve and 0.014-0.016 inch (0.36-0.41 mm) for exhaust valve.

Valve tappet clearance (cold) for all other models is 0.007-0.009 inch (0.18-0.23 mm) for intake valve and 0.017-0.019 inch (0.43-0.48 mm) for exhaust valve.

To correctly set tappet clearance, remove spark plug and using a suitable measuring tool, rotate crankshaft in normal direction (clockwise at flywheel) so piston is at top dead center on compression stroke. Continue to rotate crankshaft so piston is 1/4 inch (6.4 mm) down from top dead center. This position places the tappets away from the compression release devices on the cam lobes.

Valve tappet clearance is adjusted on all models by carefully grinding end of valve stem to increase clearance or by grinding valve seats deeper and/or renewing valve or lifter to decrease clearance.

CYLINDER HEAD. After 100 to 300 hours of engine operation, the cylinder head should be removed and any carbon or deposits should be removed.

REPAIRS

CYLINDER HEAD. When removing cylinder head note location and lengths of cylinder head retaining screws so they can be installed in their original positions.

Always install a new cylinder head gasket. Do not apply sealer to head gasket. Lubricate cylinder head retaining screws with graphite grease and tighten screws in sequence shown in Fig. B632 to 190 in.-lbs. (22 N•m).

VALVE SYSTEM. The intake valve seat is machined directly in the cylinder block. A renewable insert is used as the exhaust valve seat. Valve face and seat angle should be ground at 45°. Renew valve if margin is 1/64 inch (0.4 mm) or less. Seat width should be 3/64 to 1/16 inch (1.2-1.6 mm).

Valve guides are renewable. Check valve guides using valve guide gauge 19151. If gauge enters valve guide 5/16 inch (7.9 mm) or more, guide should be reamed using reamer 19233 and reamer bushing 19234 (part of valve guide repair kit 19232).

Some engines may be equipped with a "Cobalite" exhaust valve and exhaust seat insert as well as a rotocoil on the exhaust valve stem. These components are offered as replacement parts for engines used in severe engine service.

If engine is operated on LP fuel or natural gas, rotocoil should not be used and valve stem and guide should be lubricated with B&S 93963 Valve Guide Lubricant during assembly.

PISTON, PIN AND RINGS. Connecting rod and piston are removed from cylinder head end of block as an assembly.

Reject pistons showing visible signs of wear, scoring and scuffing. If, after cleaning carbon from top ring groove, a new top ring has a side clearance of 0.009 inch (0.23 mm), reject the piston. Reject piston or hone piston pin hole to 0.005 inch (0.13 mm) oversize if pin hole is 0.0005 inch (0.013 mm) or more out-of-round, or if wear exceeds service limit listed in following table:

PISTON PIN BORE REJECTION SIZES

Model Series	Pin Bore
19, 19D, 191000 193000, 200000, 243000	0.673 in. (17.09 mm)
23, 23A, 23C, 23D, 231000, 233000	0.736 in. (18.69 mm)
300000, 301000, 302000, 320000, 325000, 326000	0.801 in. (20.34 mm)

If the piston pin is 0.0005 inch (0.013 mm) or more out-of-round, or if wear exceeds service limit listed in following table, renew piston pin:

PISTON PIN REJECTION SIZES

Model Series	Pin Diameter
19, 19D, 191000 193000, 200000, 243000	0.671 in. (17.04 mm)
23, 23A, 23C, 23D, 231000, 233000	0.734 in. (18.64 mm)
300000, 301000, 302000, 320000, 325000, 326000	0.799 in. (20.30 mm)

Reject compression rings having an end gap of 0.030 inch (0.75 mm) or more

and reject oil rings having an end gap of 0.035 inch (0.90 mm) or more.

Pistons and rings are available in several oversizes as well as standard. Refer to Fig. B633 for correct installation of piston rings.

A chrome piston ring set is available for slightly worn standard bore cylinders. No honing or cylinder deglazing is required for these rings. The cylinder bore can be a maximum of 0.005 inch (0.13 mm) oversize when using chrome rings.

If piston has a notch (N—Fig. B634) in piston crown, assemble connecting rod and piston as shown in Fig. B634. Install piston and rod in engine so notch (N) is toward flywheel.

On Series 300000, 301000, 302000, 320000, 325000 or 326000 engines, notch on piston crown and letter "F" on side of piston must be on the same side as assembly marks on connecting rod (Fig. B635). Install assembly in cylinder with assembly marks toward flywheel side of engine.

On all other models, install piston and connecting rod assembly so flat on connecting rod shoulder is toward camshaft as shown in Fig. B636.

Tighten connecting rod screws on all models to 190 in.-lbs. (22 N•m).

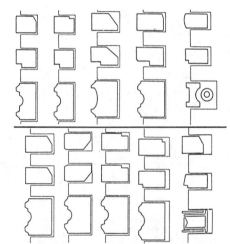

Fig. B633—Refer to above illustration for proper arrangement of piston rings.

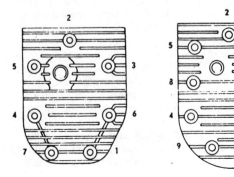

Fig. B632—View of two different cylinder heads used. Tighten cylinder head cap screws in sequence shown to 190 in.-lbs. (22 N•m). Refer to text for tightening procedure.

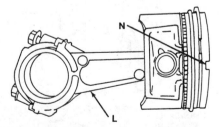

Fig. B634—If piston crown is notched (N), assemble connecting rod and piston as shown while noting relation of long side of rod (L) and notch (N) in piston crown.

Illustrations Courtesy Briggs & Stratton Corp.

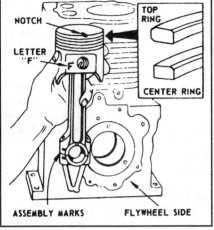

Fig. B635—On 300000, 301000, 302000, 320000, 325000 and 326000 series, assemble piston to connecting rod with notch and stamped letter "F" on piston to same side as assembly marks on rod. Install assembly in cylinder with assembly marks to flywheel side of crankcase.

CONNECTING ROD. Connecting rod and piston are removed from cylinder head end of block as an assembly. The aluminum alloy connecting rod rides directly on an induction hardened crankshaft crankpin journal. Rod should be rejected if big end of rod is scored or out-of-round more than 0.0007 inch (0.018 mm) or if piston pin bore is scored or out-of-round more than 0.0005 inch (0.013 mm). Renew connecting rod if either crankpin bore or piston pin bore is worn to, or larger than, sizes given in following table:

REJECT SIZES FOR CONNECTING ROD

Model Series	Crankpin Bore	Pin Bore*
19, 19D, 191000, 193000	1.001 in. (25.43 mm)	0.674 in. (17.12 mm)

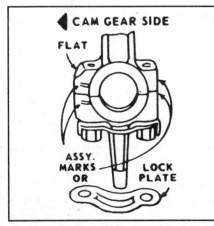

Fig. B636—Drawing of lower end of connecting rod showing clearance flat and assembly marks.

200000	1.127 in. (28.61 mm)	0.674 in. (17.12 mm)
23, 23A, 23C, 23D, 231000, 233000	1.189 in. (30.20 mm)	0.736 in. (18.69 mm)
243000	1.314 in. (23.38 mm)	0.674 in. (17.12 mm)
300000, 301000 302000, 320000, 325000, 326000	1.314 in. (23.38 mm)	0.802 in. (20.37 mm)

*Piston pins that are 0.005 inch (0.13 mm) oversize are available for service. Piston pin bore in rod can be reamed to this size if crankpin bore is within specifications.

Refer to previous section for assembly of connecting rod and piston. Tighten connecting rod screws on all models to 190 in.-lbs. (22 N•m).

CAM GEAR AND CAMSHAFT. On Model 19, 19D, 23, 23A, 23C and 23D engines and Series 191000, 193000, 200000, 233000 and 243000 engines, the timing gear and camshaft lobes are cast as an integral part and are referred to as a "cam gear." Cam gear (31—Fig. B637) turns on a stationary shaft (30) referred to as a "camshaft." Reject camshaft if it is worn to, or less than, a diameter of 0.4968 inch (12.619 mm).

On all remaining models, cam gear and lobes are an integral part referred to as a "cam gear." Camshaft (53—Fig. B638) rotates with cam gear (52). Camshaft rides in a bearing in cylinder block on pto end of engine and journal on cam gear rides in renewable cam bearing (21) on magneto end of engine.

Renew camshaft if worn to 0.6145 inch (15.608 mm) or less and renew cam gear (52) if journal diameter is 0.8105 inch (20.587 mm) or less, or if lobes are worn to a diameter of 1.184 inches (30.07 mm) or less for Series 300000, 301000 and 302000 engines, or 1.215 inches (30.86 mm) or less for Series 320000, 325000 and 326000 engines.

When installing cam gear in Series 300000, 301000, 302000, 320000, 325000 and 326000 engines, cam gear end play should be 0.002-0.008 inch (0.05-0.20 mm) and is controlled by installing different thickness shims (20) between cam gear bearing (21) and crankcase. Shims are available in a variety of thicknesses. Tighten cam gear bearing cap screws to 85 in.-lbs. (10 N•m).

On engines with "Magna-Matic" ignition system, cam gear is equipped with an ignition advance weight (AW—Fig. B637). A tang on the advance weight contacts breaker shaft lever (29—Fig. B611) each camshaft revolution. On all other models, breaker plunger rides against a lobe on cam gear.

On models with "Easy-Spin" starting intake cam lobe is machined to hold intake valve slightly open during part of compression stroke, thereby relieving compression and making engine easier to start due to increased cranking speed.

NOTE: To check compression on models with "Easy-Spin" starting, engine must be turned backwards.

"Easy-Spin" cam gears can be identified by two holes drilled in web of gear. If part number of older cam gear and "Easy-Spin" cam gear are the same except for an "E" following new part number, gears are interchangeable.

On all models, align timing marks on crankshaft gear and cam gear when reassembling engine.

CRANKSHAFT AND MAIN BEARINGS. Crankshaft may be supported at each end in main bearings that are an integral part of crankcase and sump or ball bearing mains that are a press fit on crankshaft and fit into machined bores in main bearing support plates.

Crankshaft for models with main bearings as an integral part of main bearing support plates should be renewed or reground if journals are out-of-round 0.0007 inch (0.018 mm) or more. Reject or regrind crankshaft on 19, 19D, 191000, 193000 and 200000 series engines if main bearing journals are worn to a diameter of 1.179 inch (29.95 mm) or less. Reject or regrind crankshaft on 23, 23A, 23C, 23D, 231000 and 233000 series engines if main bearing journals are worn to a diameter of 1.3759 inch (34.948 mm) or less.

Crankshaft for models with ball bearing main bearings should be renewed if new bearings are loose on journals. Bearings should be a press fit.

Crankshaft for all models should be renewed or reground if connecting rod crankpin journal diameter exceeds service limit listed in following table:

CRANKSHAFT REJECT SIZES

Model Series	Crankpin Journal
19, 19D, 190000, 193000	1.090 in. (27.69 mm)
200000	1.122 in. (28.50 mm)
23, 23A, 23C, 23D, 230000	1.247 in. (31.67 mm)

243000, 300000,
 301000, 302000,
 320000, 325000,
 326000 . . . . 1.309 in.
 (33.25 mm)

A connecting rod with undersize big end diameter is available to fit crankshaft that has had crankpin journal reground to 0.020 inch (0.51 mm) undersize.

Crankshaft main bearing support plates should be renewed if integral-type main bearing bores are 0.0007 inch (0.018 mm) or more out-of-round. Renew bearing support plates on 19, 19D, 191000, 193000 and 200000 series engines if main bearing bores are worn to a diameter of 1.185 inch (30.10 mm) or more. Renew bearing support plates on 23, 23A, 23C, 23D, 231000 and 233000 series engines if main bearing bores are worn to a diameter of 1.382 inch (34.10 mm) or less. Service bushings for main bearings are not available.

Ball bearing mains are a press fit on the crankshaft and must be removed by pressing the crankshaft out of the bearing. Reject ball bearing if worn or rough. Expand new bearing by heating it in oil and install it on crankshaft with seal side toward crankpin journal.

Crankshaft end play is 0.002-0.008 inch (0.05-0.20 mm). End Play is adjusted by varying thickness of gaskets between flywheel main bearing support plate and crankcase as shown in Fig. B639. Gaskets are available in a variety of thicknesses.

When reinstalling crankshaft, make certain timing marks are aligned (Fig. B640 or B641).

CYLINDER. If cylinder bore wear is 0.003 inch (0.08 mm) or more or is 0.0025 inch (0.06 mm) or more out-of-round, cylinder must be rebored to next larger oversize.

Refer to following table for standard cylinder bore sizes:

STANDARD CYLINDER BORE SIZES

Model Series	Std. Bore Size
19, 19D, 22, 23A, 23C, 23D,191000, 193000, 200000, 231000, 233000	2.999-3.000 in. (76.18-76.20 mm)
243000	3.0615-3.0625 in. (77.76-77.79 mm)
300000, 301000, 302000	3.4365-3.4375 in. (87.287-87.313 mm)
320000, 325000, 326000	3.5615-3.5625 in. (90.462-90.488 mm)

A chrome piston ring set is available for slightly worn standard bore cylinders. No honing or cylinder deglazing is required for these rings. The cylinder bore can be a maximum of 0.005 inch

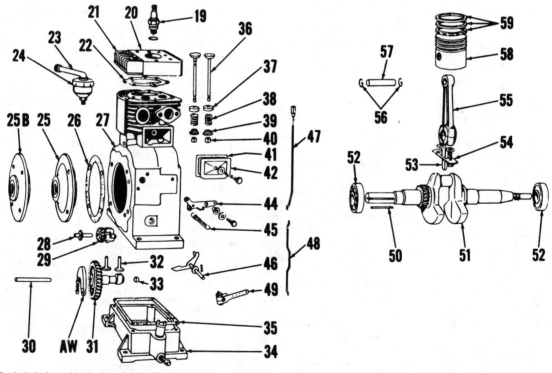

Fig. B637—Exploded view of typical model 19, 23, 23A, 191000 and 231000 engines equipped with "Magna-Matic" ignition system; note ignition advance weight (AW). Refer to Fig. B611 for ignition system.

AW. Advance weight	25B. Bearing plate (ball bearing)	31. Cam gear	38. Valve springs	46. Governor crank	53. Oil dipper
19. Spark plug	26. Gasket	32. Tappets	39. Spring retainers or "Roto-Caps"	47. Governor control rod	54. Rod bolt lock
20. Air baffle	27. Engine crankcase & cylinder block	33. Camshaft plug	40. Keepers	48. Governor link	55. Connecting rod
21. Cylinder head	28. Governor shaft	34. Engine base	41. Gasket	49. Governor lever	56. Piston pin retaining rings
22. Gasket	29. Governor gear & weight unit	35. Gasket	42. Tappet chamber cover	50. Output drive key	57. Piston pin
23. Breather tube	30. Camshaft	36. Valves	43. Governor control lever	51. Crankshaft	58. Piston
24. Breather		37. Valve spring washers	44. Governor control lever	52. Ball bearings (on models so equipped)	59. Piston rings
25. Main bearing plate (plain bushing)			45. Governor spring		

Illustrations Courtesy Briggs & Stratton Corp.

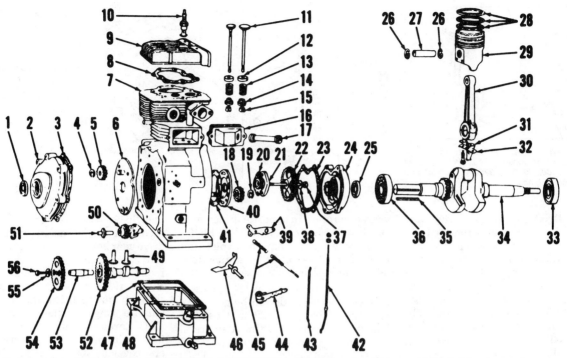

Fig. B638—Exploded view of typical 300000, 301000, 302000, 320000, 325000 and 326000 engines. Balance weights, ball bearings and cover assemblies (2 and 24) are serviced only as assemblies.

1. Oil seal
2. Cover & balance assy. (pto end)
3. Gasket
4. "E" ring
5. Idler gear
6. Bearing support plate
7. Engine crankcase & cylinder block
8. Gasket
9. Cylinder head
10. Spark plug
11. Valves
12. Spring caps
13. Valve springs
14. Spring retainers or "Roto-Caps"
15. Keepers
16. Breather
17. Breather tube
18. Idler gear
19. "E" ring
20. Shim
21. Cam bearing
22. Balancer drive gear
23. Gasket
24. Cover & balance assy. (magneto end)
25. Oil seal
26. Piston pin retaining rings
27. Piston pin
28. Piston rings
29. Piston
30. Connecting rod
31. Oil dipper
32. Rod bolt lock
33. Ball bearing
34. Crankshaft
35. Key
36. Ball bearing
37. Drive gear bolt
38. Belleville washer
39. Governor control lever
40. Bearing support plate
41. Shim
42. Governor control rod
43. Governor link
44. Governor lever
45. Governor springs
46. Governor crank
47. Gasket
48. Engine base
49. Tappets
50. Governor gear & weight unit
51. Governor shaft
52. Cam gear
53. Camshaft
54. Balancer drive gear
55. Belleville washer
56. Drive gear bolt

(0.13 mm) oversize when using chrome rings.

GOVERNOR WEIGHT UNIT. Tangs on governor weights should be square and smooth and weights should operate freely. If not, renew gear and weight assembly (29—Figs. B626 and B637) or (50—Fig. B638). Renew governor shaft if worn or scored.

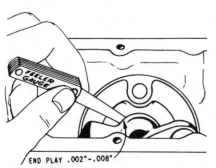

Fig. B639—Crankshaft end play can be checked as shown on models with main bearings that are an integral part of bearing support plates.

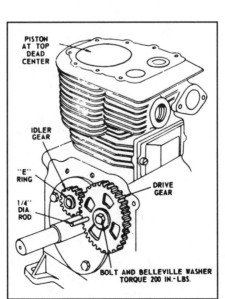

Fig. B640—View showing balancer drive gear (magneto end) being timed. With piston at TDC, insert 1/4-inch (6.4 mm) rod through timing hole in crankshaft bearing support plate.

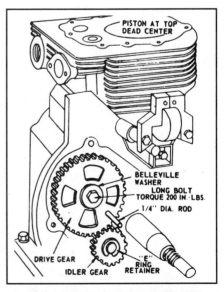

Fig. B641—View showing balancer drive gear on pto end of crankshaft being timed. With piston at TDC, insert 1/4-inch (6.4 mm) rod through timing hole in gear and into locating hole in crankshaft bearing support plate.

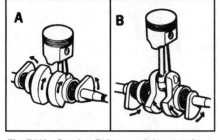

Fig. B642—Synchro-Balance weight rotate in opposite direction of crankshaft counterweights on 300000, 301000, 302000, 320000, 325000 and 326000 series engines.

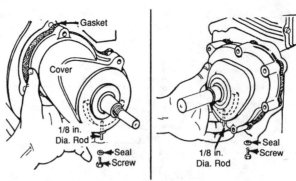

Fig. B643—Insert 1/8-inch (3.2 mm) rod through timing hole in covers and into hole in balance weights when installing cover assemblies. Piston must be at TDC.

GOVERNOR CRANK. With governor weight and gear unit removed, remove and inspect governor crank (46—Fig. B637 or B638); renew if worn. Governor crank should be a free fit in bushing in engine crankcase with minimum bushing-to-crank clearance. Renew bushing if new crank fits loosely. Bushing should be finish reamed to 0.2385-0.2390 inch (6.058-6.071 mm) after installation.

SYNCHRO-BALANCER. Series 300000, 301000, 302000, 320000, 325000 and 326000 engines are equipped with rotating balance weights at each end of crankshaft. Balancers are geared to rotate in opposite direction of crankshaft counterweights (Fig. B642). Balance weights, ball bearings and cover (2 and 24—Fig. B638) are serviced as assemblies only.

Balancers are driven by idler gears (5 and 18) which are driven by gears (22 and 54). Drive gear (22 and 54) are bolted to camshaft. To time balancers, first remove cover and balancer assemblies (2 and 24). Position piston at TDC. Loosen bolts (37 and 56) until drive gears will rotate on cam gear and camshaft. Insert a 1/4-inch (6.4 mm) rod through timing hole in each drive gear and into locating holes in main bearing support plates as shown in Figs. B640 and B641. With piston at TDC and 1/4-inch (6.4 mm) rods in place, tighten drive gear bolts to a torque of 200 in.-lbs. (23 N•m). Remove 1/4-inch (6.4 mm) rods. Remove timing hole screws (Fig. B643) and insert 1/8-inch (3.2 mm) rods through timing holes and into hole in balance weights. Then, with piston at TDC, carefully slide cover assemblies into position. Tighten cap screws in pto end cover to 200 in.-lbs. (23 N•m) and tighten magneto end cover cap screws to 120 in.-lbs. (14 N•m). Remove 1/8-inch (3.2 mm) rods. Coat threads of timing hole screws with Permatex or equivalent and install screws with fiber sealing washers.

Illustrations Courtesy Briggs & Stratton Corp.

BRIGGS & STRATTON

BRIGGS & STRATTON CORPORATION
Milwaukee, Wisconsin 53201

VANGUARD SINGLE-CYLINDER ENGINES

Model Series	No. Cyls.	Bore	Stroke	Displacement	Power Rating
161400	1	76.2 mm (3.00 in.)	59.3 mm (2.33 in.)	270 cc (16.5 cu.in.)	6.8 kW (9 hp)
260700, 261700	1	87 mm (3.43 in.)	73 mm (2.86 in.)	435 cc (26.5 cu.in.)	10.5 kW (14 hp)

NOTE: Metric fasteners are used throughout engine except threaded hole in pto end of crankshaft, flange mounting holes and flywheel puller holes, which are US threads.

The Vanguard models covered in this section are air-cooled, four-stroke, single-cylinder engines. The engine uses an overhead valve system.

Refer to BRIGGS & STRATTON ENGINE IDENTIFICATION INFORMATION section for engine identification. Engine model number as well as type number and serial number are necessary when ordering parts.

MAINTENANCE

LUBRICATION. Vertical crankshaft engines are lubricated by oil supplied by a rotor-type oil pump located in the bottom of the crankcase. Horizontal crankshaft engines have a splash lubrication system provided by an oil dipper attached to the connecting rod.

Periodically check oil level; do not overfill. Oil dipstick should be screwed in until bottomed for correct oil level reading. Check oil level after first eight hours of operation and every 50 hours thereafter under normal operating conditions. Recommended oil change interval is 25 hours if severe service is encountered.

Series 260700 and 261700 engines may be equipped with a spin-on-type oil filter. If so equipped, manufacturer recommends changing oil filter after every 100 hours of operation. Filter should be changed more frequently if engine is operated in a severe environment.

Manufacturer recommends using oil with an API service classification of SF or SG. Use SAE 30 oil for temperatures above 40° F (4° C), use SAE 10W-30 oil for temperatures between 0° F (–18° C) and 100° F (38° C) and, below 0° F (–18° C), use petroleum based SAE 5W-20 or a suitable synthetic oil.

Crankcase capacity for Series 161400 engines is 1.2 liters (2.5 pints). Crankcase capacity for Series 260700 and 261700 engines is 2.1 liters (4.4 pints) if equipped with an oil filter, 1.9 liters (4.0 pints) if not equipped with a filter.

Series 161400 engines may be equipped with a low-oil system that uses a float to detect a low oil level in the engine. A switch is connected to the float and, when the oil level is low, a warning light is activated and the engine stops. Unscrew float mounting flange (F—Fig. B701) to check float and switch.

Series 260700 and 261700 engines may be equipped with low oil pressure switch shown in Fig. B702. Switch should be closed at zero pressure and open at 49.0-68.6 kPa (7.1-9.9 psi).

FUEL FILTER. The fuel tank is equipped with a filter at the outlet and an inline filter may be installed. Check filters annually and periodically during operating season.

CRANKCASE BREATHER. The engine is equipped with a crankcase breather that provides a vacuum for the crankcase. Vapor from the crankcase is evacuated to the intake manifold. A fiber disk acts as a one-way valve to maintain crankcase vacuum. The breather system must operate properly or excessive oil consumption can result.

The breather valve is located in the top of the rocker arm cover on Series 161400 or in the side of the crankcase on Series 260700 and 261700 as shown in Fig. B703. The fiber disk valve should be renewed if warped, damaged or excessively worn. It should be possible to insert a 1.27 mm (0.050 in.) wire between disk and breather body (Fig.

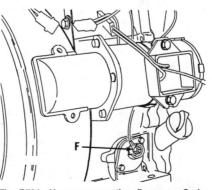

Fig. B701—Unscrew mounting flange on Series 161400 engines to remove low-oil level float assembly.

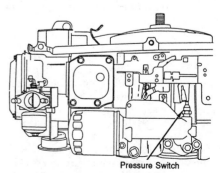

Pressure Switch

Fig. B702—View showing location of oil pressure switch on Series 260700 and 261700 engines.

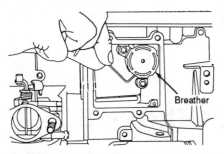

Fig. B703—Crankcase breather on Series 260700 and 261700 engines is located behind cover on side of crankcase.

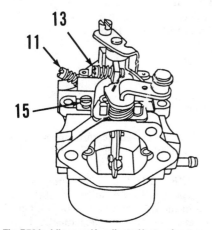

Fig. B704—Idle speed is adjusted by turning screw (13) and idle mixture is adjusted by turning idle mixture screw (11). Idle mixture jet (15) is not adjustable.

B703); do not use excessive force when measuring gap. Inspect breather tube for cracks and damage that can cause leakage.

SPARK PLUG. Recommended spark plug is either an Autolite 3924 or Champion RC12YC. Specified spark plug electrode gap is 0.76 mm (0.030 in.). Tighten spark plug to 19 N•m (165 in.-lbs.).

CAUTION: Briggs & Stratton does not recommend using abrasive blasting to clean spark plugs as this may introduce some abrasive material into the engine that could cause extensive damage.

CARBURETOR. Adjustment. Adjust idle speed at normal operating temperature to 1200 rpm. Then, after carburetor adjustments are completed, adjust governed idle speed as outlined in GOVERNOR section. Adjust idle speed by turning idle speed screw (13—Fig. B704). Idle mixture is controlled by idle jet (15) and idle mixture screw (11). Initial setting of idle mixture screw (11) is 1¼ turns out. To adjust idle mixture,

turn idle mixture screw clockwise and lean mixture until engine speed just starts to slow, then turn screw counterclockwise and enrich mixture just until engine speed begins to slow. Turn idle mixture screw to halfway point between lean and rich positions. Turn idle mixture screw counterclockwise in small increments to enrich mixture if engine will not accelerate without stumbling. Idle mixture jet is not adjustable. High-speed operation is controlled by main jet (22 or 24—Fig. B705). An optional main jet is available for high altitude operation.

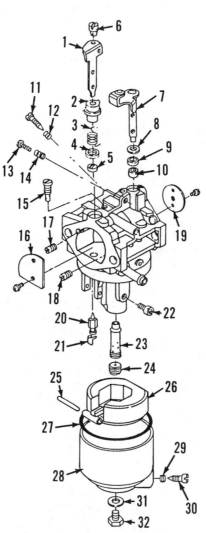

Fig. B705—Exploded view of carburetor.

1. Choke shaft & lever	17. Idle air bleed
2. Bushing	18. Main air bleed
3. Spring	19. Throttle plate
4. Seal	20. Fuel inlet valve
5. Bushing	21. Clip
6. Link retainer	22. Main jet
7. Throttle shaft & lever	23. Main fuel nozzle
8. Washer	24. Main jet
9. Seal	25. Float pin
10. Bushing	26. Float
11. Idle mixture screw	27. Gasket
12. Spring	28. Fuel bowl
13. Idle speed screw	29. Spring
14. Spring	30. Drain screw
15. Idle mixture jet	31. Washer
16. Choke plate	32. Screw

Overhaul. To disassemble carburetor, remove fuel bowl retaining screw (32—Fig. B705), gasket (31) and fuel bowl (28). Remove float pin (25) by pushing against round end of pin toward the square end of pin. Remove float and fuel inlet needle. Remove throttle and choke shaft assemblies after unscrewing throttle and choke plate retaining screws. Remove idle mixture screw (11), idle mixture jet (15), main jet (22 or 24), main fuel nozzle (23) and air bleeds (17 and 18).

When assembling the carburetor, note the following: Place a small drop of nonhardening sealant, such as Permatex #2 or equivalent, on throttle and choke plate retaining screws. Numbers on choke plate must face out and be on fuel inlet side of carburetor. Install throttle shaft seal with flat side toward carburetor. Numbers on throttle plate must face out and be on fuel inlet side of carburetor. Be sure groove of fuel inlet valve engages slot in float tab. Float should be parallel with body when carburetor is inverted, as shown in Fig. B706. Float height is not adjustable; replace components necessary so float is parallel.

On Series 161400, tighten carburetor mounting nuts to 6 N•m (53 in.-lbs.).

On Series 260700 and 261700 engines, if removed, install spacer between carburetor and manifold so large, irregular opening is toward engine. Tighten carburetor mounting nuts to 14 N•m (124 in.-lbs.).

On all engines with remote control, the control wire must travel at least 35 mm (1⅜ in.) for proper operation. See Fig. B707.

On engines with remote control, synchronize movement of remote lever to carburetor control lever by moving remote control lever to "FAST" position. Loosen cable clamp screw shown in Fig. B708 and move cable so holes in governor lever and bracket are aligned. Retighten clamp screw. On Series

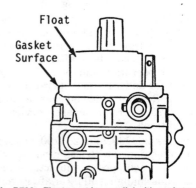

Fig. B706—Float must be parallel with gasket surface when carburetor is inverted. Float height is not adjustable so components must be replaced if not parallel.

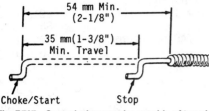

Fig. B707—Control wire must be capable of travel shown above for proper operation.

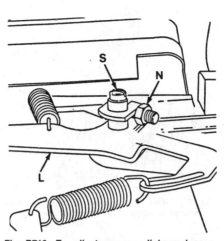

Fig. B710—To adjust governor linkage, loosen governor lever clamp nut (N), rotate governor lever (L) so throttle plate is fully open and hold lever in place. Turn governor shaft (S) clockwise as far as possible, then tighten nut (N) to 4 N•m (35 in.-lbs.).

161400 equipped with Choke-A-Matic, place control lever in "FAST" position. End of choke link shown in Fig. B709 should just touch choke lever slot end. Bend loop in choke link as needed. With control lever in "CHOKE" position, carburetor choke plate should be closed. Bend loop in choke link as needed.

GOVERNOR. The engine is equipped with a mechanical, flyweight-type governor. To adjust governor linkage, proceed as follows: Loosen governor lever clamp nut (N—Fig. B710), rotate governor lever (L) so throttle plate is fully open and hold lever in place. Turn governor shaft (S) clockwise as far as possible, then tighten nut (N) to 4 N•m (35 in.-lbs.).

If internal governor assembly must be serviced, refer to REPAIRS section.

To adjust governed idle speed, set remote control to "SLOW" position. Insert a ⅛-inch (3.2 mm) pin in alignment holes of governor control lever and bracket as shown in Figs. B711 and B712. Bend tang (T) so engine idle speed is 1400 rpm.

To adjust maximum no-load governed speed, set remote control to "FAST" position. Insert a ⅛-inch (3.2 mm) pin in alignment holes of governor control lever and bracket as shown in Figs. B713 and B714. Bend tang (T—Fig. B713) or rotate screw as shown in Fig. B714 so engine runs at desired maximum no-load speed.

IGNITION SYSTEM. All models are equipped with a Magnetron ignition system.

To check spark, remove spark plug and connect spark plug cable to B&S tester 19051, then ground remaining tester lead to engine. Spin engine at 350 rpm or more. If spark jumps the 4.2 mm (0.166 in.) tester gap, system is functioning properly.

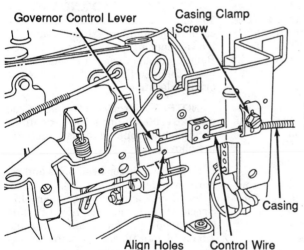

Fig. B708—Refer to text to adjust remote control on Series 260700 and 261700 engines.

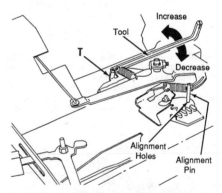

Fig. B711—To adjust governed idle speed on Series 161400 engines, set remote control to "SLOW" position. Insert a 1/8-inch (3.2 mm) pin in alignment holes of governor control lever and bracket as shown and bend tang (T) so engine idle speed is 1400 rpm.

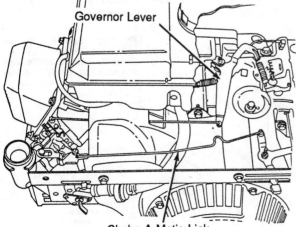

Fig. B709—On Series 161400 equipped with Choke-A-Matic, bend loop in Choke-A-Matic link so end of choke link just touches choke lever slot end with control in "FAST" position. Bend loop so carburetor choke plate is closed with control in "CHOKE" position.

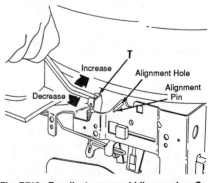

Fig. B712—To adjust governed idle speed on Series 260700 and 261700 engines, set remote control to "SLOW" position. Insert a 1/8-inch (3.2 mm) pin in alignment holes of governor control lever and bracket as shown and bend tang (T) so engine idle speed is 1400 rpm.

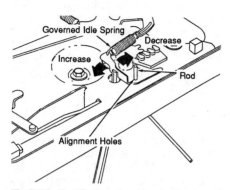

Fig. B713—To adjust maximum no-load governed speed on Series 161400 engines, set remote control to "FAST" position. Insert a 1/8-inch (3.2 mm) pin in alignment holes of governor control lever and bracket, then bend tang (T) so engine runs at desired maximum no-load speed.

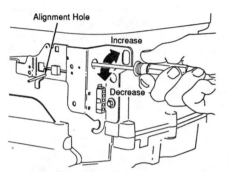

Fig. B714—To adjust maximum no-load governed speed on Series 260700 and 261700 engines, set remote control to "FAST" position. Insert a 1/8-inch (3.2 mm) pin in alignment holes of governor control lever and bracket, then rotate screw as shown so engine runs at desired maximum no-load speed.

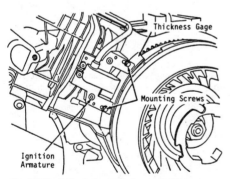

Fig. B715—Adjust air gap between ignition armature and flywheel to 0.20-0.30 mm (0.008-0.012 in.)

To remove armature and Magnetron module, remove flywheel shroud and armature retaining screws. disconnect stop switch wire from module. Position armature so air gap between armature legs and flywheel surface is 0.20-0.30 mm (0.008-0.012 in.) as shown in Fig. B715.

VALVE ADJUSTMENT. Remove rocker arm cover. Remove spark plug. Rotate crankshaft so piston is at top

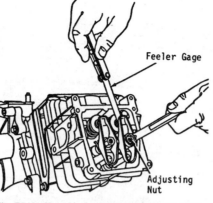

Fig. B716—Use a feeler gauge to measure clearance between valve stem and rocker arm.

dead center on compression stroke. Using a suitable measuring device inserted through spark plug hole, rotate crankshaft clockwise as viewed at flywheel end so piston is 6.35 mm (0.250 in.) below TDC to prevent interference by the compression release mechanism with the exhaust valve. Use a feeler gauge to measure clearance between valve stem or wear button and rocker arm. Valve clearance should be 0.08-0.12 mm (0.003-0.005 in.). Loosen lock screw and turn adjusting nut (Fig. B716) to obtain desired clearance. Tighten lock screw to 6.2 N·m (55 in.-lbs.). Tighten valve cover screws to 6.2 N·m (55 in.-lbs.).

CYLINDER HEAD. Manufacturer recommends that the cylinder head be removed and cleaned of deposits after every 500 hours of operation.

REPAIRS

TIGHTENING TORQUES. Recommended tightening torque specifications are as follows:

Carburetor mounting nuts:
161400 . . . . 6 N·m
(53 in.-lbs.)
260700, 261700 . . . . 14 N·m
(124 in.-lbs.)

Connecting rod:
161400 . . . . 21.8 N·m
(185 in.-lbs.)
260700, 261700 . . . . 23.5 N·m
(200 in.-lbs.)
Crankcase cover/oil pan:
161400 . . . . 16 N·m
(140 in.-lbs.)
260700, 261700 . . . . 28.2 N·m
(250 in.-lbs.)
Cylinder head:
161400 . . . . 19 N·m
(165 in.-lbs.)
260700, 261700 . . . . 25.4 N·m
(225 in.-lbs.)
Flywheel nut:
161400 . . . . 88 N·m
(65 ft.-lbs.)
260700, 261700 . . . . 170 N·m
(125 ft.-lbs.)
Oil pump cover. . . . . 6.2 N·m
(55 in.-lbs.)
Rocker arm cover. . . . . 6.2 N·m
(55 in.-lbs.)
Rocker arm lock screw 6.2 N·m
(55 in.-lbs.)
Rocker arm stud . . . . 15.8 N·m
(140 in.-lbs.)
Spark plug . . . . 19 N·m
(165 in.-lbs.)

CYLINDER HEAD AND VALVES. To remove cylinder head, first remove carburetor, muffler, exhaust manifold, blower housing and rocker arm cover. Remove rocker arms and push rods; mark them so they can be returned to original location.

NOTE: Push rods on Series 260700 and 261700 engines are not interchangeable; upper (exhaust) push rod is hollow.

Unscrew cylinder head bolts and remove cylinder head.

Valve face and seat angles are 45°. Specified seat width is 1.09-1.65 mm (0.043-0.065 in.) for intake valve and 1.58-2.16 mm (0.062-0.085 in.) for exhaust valve. Minimum allowable valve margin is 0.38 mm (0.015 in.).

The cylinder head (4—Fig. B717) is equipped with renewable valve guides

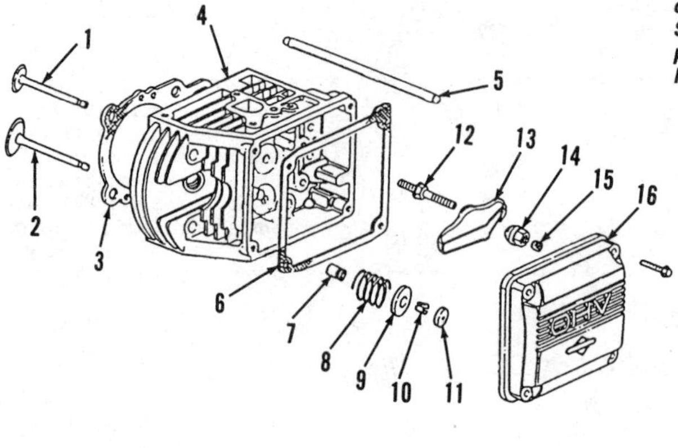

Fig. B717—Exploded view of cylinder head assembly used on Series 260700 and 261700. Upper push rod (exhaust) is hollow. Series 161400 is similar.

1. Exhaust valve
2. Intake valve
3. Head gasket
4. Cylinder head
5. Push rod
6. Gasket
7. Valve seal
8. Valve spring
9. Valve spring retainer
10. Keepers
11. Valve cap
12. Stud
13. Rocker arm
14. Adjusting nut
15. Lock screw
16. Rocker cover

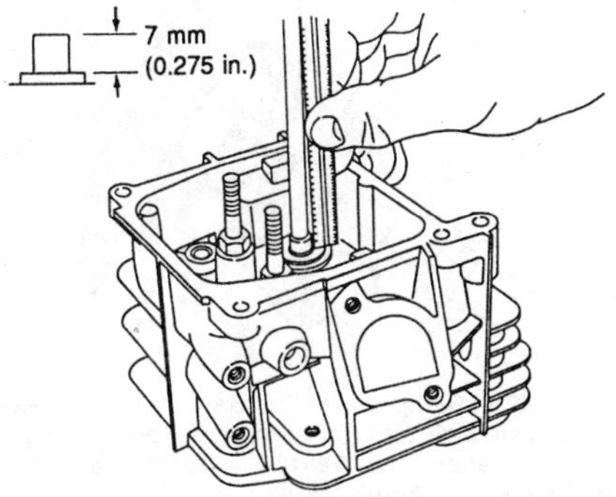

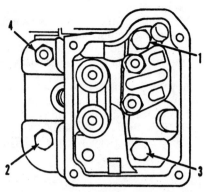

Fig. B718—Valve guides should protrude 7.0 mm (0.275 in.) as shown above.

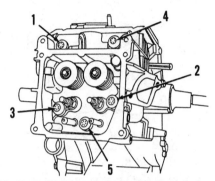

Fig. B720—Tighten cylinder head bolts on Series 260700 and 261700 engines in sequence shown above.

Fig. B719—Tighten cylinder head bolts on Series 161400 engines in sequence shown above.

cylinder head gasket. Tighten cylinder head bolts in steps using sequence shown in Figs. B719 or B720. Final tightening torque is 19 N·m (165 in.-lbs.) on Series 161400 and 25.4 N·m (225 in.-lbs.) on Series 260700 and 261700.

CAMSHAFT. Camshaft and camshaft gear (22—Fig. B721 or B722) are an integral casting that is equipped with a compression release mechanism. The compression release lobe (L—Fig. B723) extends at cranking speed to hold the exhaust valve open slightly, thereby reducing compression pressure.

To remove camshaft, proceed as follows: Remove engine from equipment and drain crankcase oil. Clean pto end of crankshaft and remove any burrs or rust. Remove rocker arm push rods and mark them so they can be returned to original position. Unscrew fasteners and remove crankcase cover or oil pan. Rotate crankshaft so timing marks shown in Fig. B724 on crankshaft and camshaft gears are aligned (this will position valve tappets out of the way). Remove camshaft and tappets.

Reject size for bearing journal at both ends of camshaft is 15.82 mm (0.623 in.). Reject size for camshaft lobes is

for both valves. Maximum allowable inside diameter of guide is 6.10 mm (0.240 in.). Use B&S tool 19274 to remove and install guides. Guides can be installed either way. Top of guide should protrude 7.0 mm (0.275 in.) as shown in Fig. B718. Use B&S tools 19345 and 19346 to ream valve guide to correct size.

Rocker arm studs are threaded into cylinder head. When installing studs, tighten to 15.8 N·m (140 in.-lbs.).

Note the following when reinstalling cylinder head: Do not apply sealer to

Fig. B721—Exploded view of crankcase and cylinder block assembly on Series 161400 engine.

1. Oil seal
2. Crankcase cover
3. Gasket
4. Governor weight assy.
5. Retainer
6. Idler gear
7. Snap ring
8. Ball bearing
9. Crankshaft gear
10. Piston rings
11. Piston
12. Snap rings
13. Piston pin
14. Screw
15. Oil dipper
16. Connecting rod
17. Key
18. Crankshaft
19. Balance shaft
20. Dowel pin
21. Dowel pin
22. Camshaft
23. Tappet
24. Crankcase/cylinder block
25. Washers
26. Cotter pin
27. Oil seal
28. Governor shaft

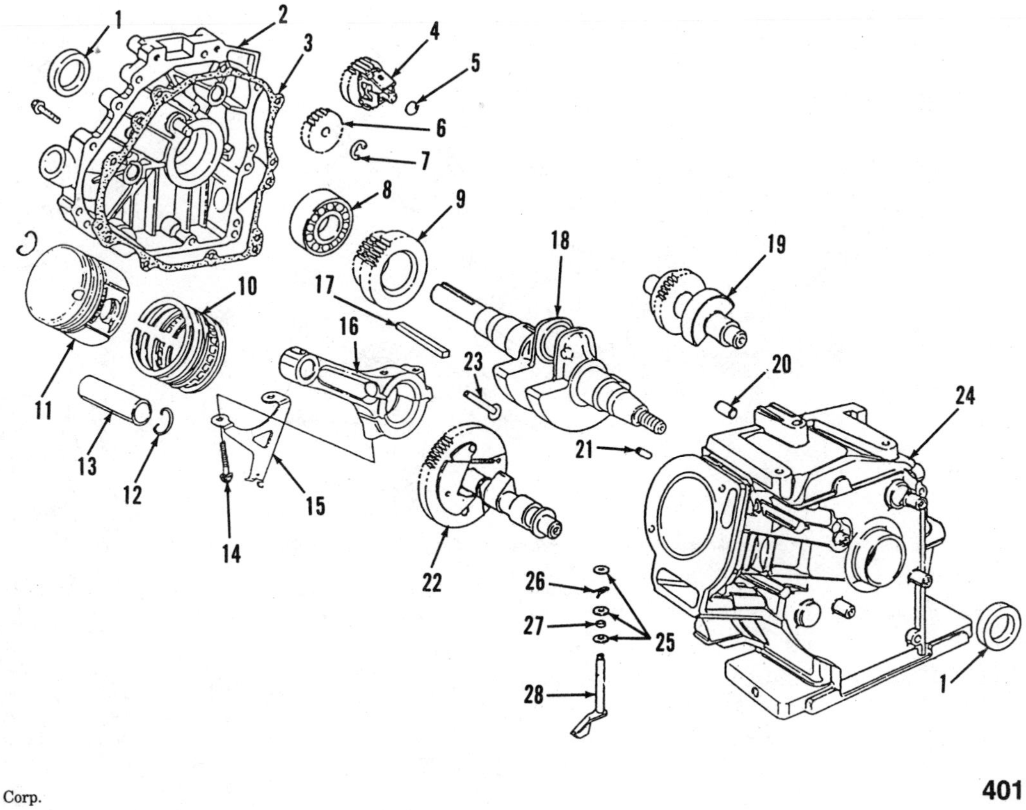

30.94 mm (1.218 in.) for Series 161400 and 34.92 mm (1.375 in.) for Series 260700 and 261700. With compression release lobe (L—Fig. B723) fully extended, lobe protrusion should be 0.56-0.71 mm (0.022-0.028 in.) for Series 161400 and 0.64-0.76 mm (0.025-0.030 in.) for Series 260700 and 261700. If not, renew camshaft. Compression release mechanism must operate freely without binding.

Reverse removal procedure to reassemble components. Install camshaft while aligning timing marks (Fig. B724) on crankshaft and camshaft gears. Be sure governor arm is in proper position to contact governor as shown in Fig. B725 or B726. Install crankcase cover or oil pan. Tighten screws to 16 N•m (140 in.-lbs.) on Series 161400 and to 28.2 N•m (250 in.-lbs.) on Series 260700 and 261700 in sequence shown in Fig. B727

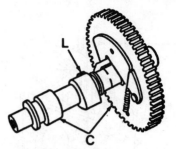

Fig. B723—Compression release lobe (L) on exhaust cam protrudes at cranking speed to slightly open exhaust valve thereby reducing compression pressure during starting.

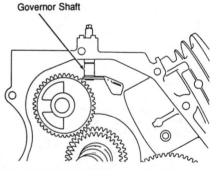

Fig. B724—Install camshaft so timing marks on camshaft and crankshaft gears are aligned.

Fig. B725—When installing crankcase cover on Series 161400 engines, the governor shaft arm must be positioned as shown.

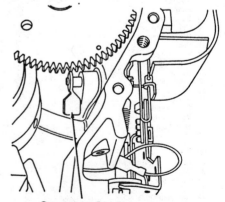

Fig. B726—When installing oil pan on Series 260700 and 261700 engines, the governor shaft arm must be positioned as shown.

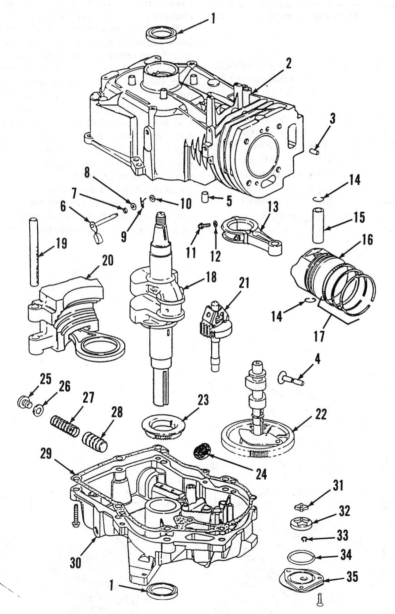

Fig. B722—Exploded view of crankcase and cylinder block assembly on Series 260700 and 261700 engines.

1. Oil seal
2. Crankcase/cylinder block
3. Dowel pin
4. Tappet
5. Dowel pin
6. Governor shaft
7. Oil seal
8. Washer
9. Cotter pin
10. Washer
11. Screw
12. Washer
13. Connecting rod
14. Snap rings
15. Piston pin
16. Piston
17. Piston rings
18. Crankshaft
19. Balancer shaft
20. Balancer assy.
21. Governor weight assy.
22. Camshaft
23. Crankshaft gear
24. Oil inlet screen
25. Screw
26. Washer
27. Oil pressure relief spring
28. Oil pressure relief valve
29. Gasket
30. Oil pan
31. Oil pump inner rotor
32. Oil pump outer rotor
33. Snap ring
34. "O" ring
35. Oil pump cover

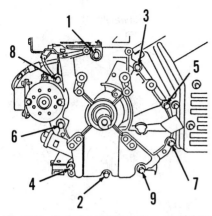

Fig. B727—On Series 161400 engines, use tightening sequence shown above when tightening crankcase cover screws.

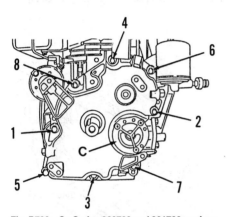

Fig. B728—On Series 260700 and 261700 engines, use tightening sequence shown above when tightening crankcase cover screws. Remove cover (C) for access to oil pump.

or B728. Do not force mating of cover or oil pan with crankcase. Reassemble remainder of components.

PISTON, PIN, RINGS AND CONNECTING ROD. To remove piston and rod assembly, drain engine oil and remove engine from equipment. Remove cylinder head as previously outlined. Clean pto end of crankshaft and remove any burrs or rust. Unscrew fasteners and remove crankcase cover or oil pan. Rotate crankshaft so timing marks shown in Fig. B724 on crankshaft and camshaft gears are aligned (this will position valve tappets out of the way). Remove camshaft. Unscrew connecting rod screws and remove piston and rod.

Reject size for piston ring end gap is 0.76 mm (0.030 in.) for compression rings on all models, 1.65 mm (0.065 in.) for oil ring on Series 161400, and 0.76 mm (0.030 in.) for oil ring on Series 260700 and 261700. Reject piston if piston ring side clearance equals or exceeds 0.10 mm (0.004 in.) for

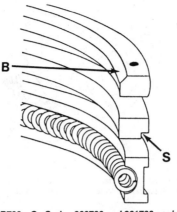

Fig. B729—On Series 260700 and 261700 engines, install top piston ring so bevel (B) is toward piston crown and install second ring so step (S) is toward piston skirt.

compression rings and 0.20 mm (0.008 in.) for oil ring.

Pistons and rings are available in several oversizes as well as standard.

Piston pin is a slip fit in piston and rod. Reject size for piston pin bore is 20.35 mm (0.801 in.). Reject size for piston pin diameter is 20.32 mm (0.800 in.).

The connecting rod rides directly on crankpin. Reject size for rod big end diameter is 36.40 mm (1.433 in.) for Series 161400 and 41.33 mm (1.627 in.) for Series 260700 and 261700. Reject size for small end diameter is 20.35 mm (0.801 in.). A connecting rod with 0.51 mm (0.020 in.) undersize big end diameter is available to accommodate a worn crankpin (machining instructions are included with new rod).

When assembling piston and connecting rod, be sure notch in piston crown is on flywheel side of rod (some rods have "MAG" marked on flywheel side of rod). On Series 161400 engines, install compression rings so marked side is toward piston crown. On Series 260700 and 261700, refer to Fig. B729 and install top ring so bevel (B) is toward piston crown and install second ring so step (S) is toward piston skirt. Install piston and rod assembly in engine with notch on piston crown toward

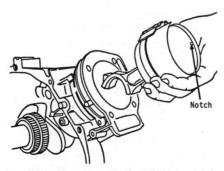

Fig. B730—Piston must be installed so notch in piston crown is toward flywheel side of engine.

flywheel (Fig. B730). Be sure match marks are aligned on rod and rod cap. Install oil dipper on rod cap of Series 161400 engines. On Series 161400 engines, tighten connecting rod screw to 21.8 N·m (185 in.-lbs.). On Series 260700 and 261700 engines, tighten connecting rod screw to 23.5 N·m (200 in.-lbs.).

Install camshaft while aligning timing marks (Fig. B724) on crankshaft and camshaft gears. Be sure governor arm is in proper position to contact governor as shown in Figs. B725 or B726. Install crankcase cover or oil pan. Tighten screws to 16 N·m (140 in.-lbs.) on Series 161400 and to 28.2 N·m (250 in.-lbs.) on Series 260700 and 261700 in sequence shown in Figs. B727 or B728. Do not force mating of cover or oil pan with crankcase. Reassemble remainder of components.

GOVERNOR. The governor gear and flyweight assembly is located on the inside of the crankcase cover or oil pan. The plunger in the gear assembly contacts the governor arm and shaft in the crankcase. The governor shaft and arm transfer governor action to the external governor linkage.

To gain access to the governor gear assembly, remove engine from equipment and drain crankcase oil. Clean pto end of crankshaft and remove any burrs or rust. Unscrew fasteners and remove crankcase cover or oil pan. Flyweight assembly must operate freely for proper governor action. On Series 161400 engines, the governor gear is driven by idler gear (6—Fig. B721), which can be removed after detaching snap ring (7).

The governor shaft and arm ride in a bushing in the crankcase. The bushing should be renewed if worn excessively. B&S reamer 19333 will size bushing to desired diameter.

To reassemble, position governor gear assembly in crankcase cover. Be sure governor arm is in proper position to contact governor as shown in Figs. B725 or B726. Install crankcase cover or oil pan. Tighten screws to 16 N·m (140 in.-lbs.) on Series 161400 and to 28.2 N·m (250 in.-lbs.) on Series 260700 and 261700 in sequence shown in Figs. B727 or B728. Do not force mating of cover or oil pan with crankcase. Reassemble remainder of components.

CRANKSHAFT AND MAIN BEARINGS. On all models, the flywheel end of the crankshaft rides in a bushing in the crankcase (Fig. B731). On Series 161400 engines, the pto end of the crankshaft is supported by a ball bearing. On Series 260700 and 261700 engines, the pto end of the crankshaft

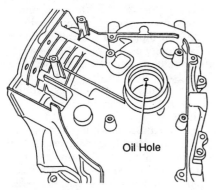

Fig. B731—Oil hole in bushing and crankcase must be open.

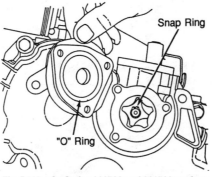

Fig. B732—On Series 260700 and 261700 engines, detach snap ring to remove inner oil pump rotor.

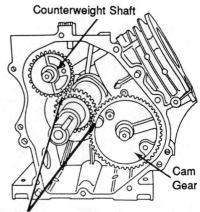

Fig. B734—On Series 161400 engines, timing marks on camshaft gear, crankshaft gear and balancer gear must be aligned during assembly.

rides directly in the oil pan and a service bushing is not available.

To remove crankshaft, first remove flywheel and camshaft. Rotate crankshaft so piston is at top dead center and remove connecting rod cap. Rotate crankshaft so it will clear connecting rod and withdraw crankshaft from crankcase.

Renew crankshaft on Series 161400 engines if main bearing journal at flywheel end is 38.02 mm (1.497 in.) or less. Renew crankshaft on Series 260700 and 261700 engines if either main bearing journal is 41.20 mm (1.622 in.) or less.

Reject size for crankpin is 36.30 mm (1.429 in.) on Series 161400 engines and 41.20 mm (1.622 in.) on Series 260700 and 261700 engines. A connecting rod with 0.51 mm (0.020 in.) undersize big end diameter is available to accommodate a worn crankpin (machining instructions are included with new rod).

Renew crankcase if bushing diameter is 38.13 mm (1.501 in.) or less on Series 161400 engines or 41.35 mm (1.628 in.) or less on Series 260700 and 261700 engines. Renew oil pan on Series 260700 and 261700 engines if bearing bore diameter is 41.35 mm (1.628 in.) or less. A service bushing is not available.

The ball bearing main bearing at pto end of Series 161400 engines is a press fit in crankcase cover. To remove bearing, press bearing toward inside of crankcase cover. Install bearing by pressing toward outside of crankcase cover until bearing is flush with inside face of crankcase cover.

CYLINDER. If cylinder bore wear exceeds 0.076 mm (0.003 in.) or if out-of-round of bore exceeds 0.038 mm (0.0015 in.), then cylinder should be bored to the next oversize.

Standard cylinder bore diameter is 76.18-76.20 mm (2.999-3.000 in.) for Series 161400 and 87.29-87.31 mm

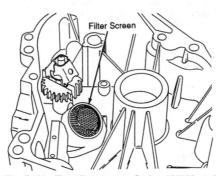

Fig. B733—The oil pump on Series 260700 and 261700 engines is located adjacent to governor assembly.

(3.4365-3.4375 in.) for Series 260700 and 261700.

OIL PUMP. Series 260700 and 261700 engines are equipped with a rotor-type oil pump located in the oil pan and driven by the governor shaft. A relief valve (28—Fig. B722) is located in the side of the oil pan.

Remove engine from equipment for access to oil pump cover (C—Fig. B728). Remove cover, detach snap ring on shaft (Fig. B732) and extract pump rotors. Mark rotors so they can be reinstalled in their original position. Renew any components that are damaged or excessively worn. Be sure "O" ring (Fig. B732) is installed in cover before installing cover. Tighten oil pump cover screws to 6.2 N•m (55 in.-lbs.).

The oil pump filter screen shown in Fig. B733 is removable after removing oil pan. Install screen so hole is away from governor and notch is toward governor.

SYNCHRO-BALANCER. All models are equipped with a balancing system. Series 161400 engines are equipped with a counterweight gear (19—Fig. B721) that rides directly in bores in the crankcase and crankcase cover. Series 260700 and 261700 engines are equipped with an oscillating

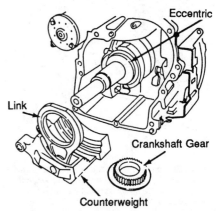

Fig. B735—View of Synchro-Balancer used on Series 260700 and 261700 engines. The balancer link fits around the eccentric on the crankshaft.

weight-type system that is actuated by an eccentric journal on the crankshaft.

Remove crankcase cover for access to counterweight shaft on Series 161400 engines. Renew counterweight if either bearing journal is 15.82 mm (0.623 in.) or less. Renew crankcase or crankcase cover if bearing bore is 15.95 mm (0.628 in.) or more. When installing counterweight, align timing marks on crankshaft gear and cam gear as shown in Fig. B734, then install counterweight so timing marks on crankshaft gear and counterweight gear are aligned.

To service Synchro-Balancer unit on Series 260700 and 261700 engines, remove oil pan. Rotate crankshaft so timing marks on crankshaft gear and camshaft gear are aligned. Remove crankshaft gear and camshaft, then withdraw balancer unit as shown in Fig. B735. Note reject sizes in following table:

REJECT SIZE

Counterweight
    pivot shaft . . . . 12.65 mm
                    (0.498 in.)
Counterweight
    pivot shaft bore . . . . 12.78 mm
                    (0.503 in.)
Counterweight
    link pin bore . . . . 15.82 mm
                    (0.623 in.)
Link pin . . . . 15.72 mm
                    (0.619 in.)

Connector link
    pin bore . . . . 15.80 mm
                    (0.622 in.)
Connector link
    eccentric bore . . . . 68.17 mm
                    (2.684 in.)

Reassemble Synchro-Balancer unit by reversing disassembly procedure while being sure to align timing marks on crankshaft gear and camshaft gear (Fig. B724).

REDUCTION GEAR. Series 161400 engines may be equipped with the reduction gear unit shown in Fig. B736. Maintain oil level even with opening for oil level plug (P). Fill unit with oil recommended for engine through opening for fill plug (F). Note that fill plug has a vent hole that must be open. Drain oil by removing drain plug (D).

Overhaul is evident after inspection of unit and referral to Fig. B737. Output shaft end play should be 0.05-0.76 mm (0.002-0.030 in.). Tighten housing (2) retaining screws to 15.8 N•m (140 in.-lbs.) and bend ear of lock plate against screw head. Tighten cover (5) retaining screws to 20.9 N•m (185 in.-lbs.).

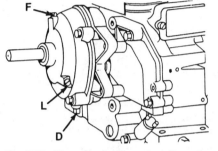

Fig. B736—View of reduction gear unit used on some Series 161400 engines showing location of oil level plug (L), oil fill plug (F) and drain plug (D).

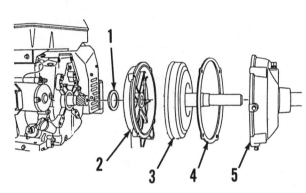

Fig. B737—Exploded view of reduction gear unit used on some Series 161400 engines.

1. Gasket
2. Housing
3. Ring gear
4. Gasket
5. Cover

BRIGGS & STRATTON

BRIGGS & STRATTON CORPORATION
Milwaukee, Wisconsin 53201

Models	No. Cyls.	Bore	Stroke	Displacement	Power Rating
400400	2	3.44 in. (87.3 mm)	2.16 in. (54.8 mm)	40 cu. in. (656 cc)	14 hp. (10.4 kW)
400700	2	3.44 in. (87.3 mm)	2.16 in. (54.8 mm)	40 cu. in. (656 cc)	14 hp. (10.4 kW)
401400	2	3.44 in. (87.3 mm)	2.16 in. (54.8 mm)	40 cu. in. (656 cc)	16 hp. (11.9 kW)
401700	2	3.44 in. (87.3 mm)	2.16 in. (54.8 mm)	40 cu. in. (656 cc)	16 hp. (11.9 kW)
402400	2	3.44 in. (87.3 mm)	2.16 in. (54.8 mm)	40 cu. in. (656 cc)	16 hp. (11.9 kW)
402700	2	3.44 in. (87.3 mm)	2.16 in. (54.8 mm)	40 cu. in. (656 cc)	16 hp. (11.9 kW)
404400	2	3.44 in. (87.3 mm)	2.16 in. (54.8 mm)	40 cu. in. (656 cc)	16 hp. (11.9 kW)
404700	2	3.44 in. (87.3 mm)	2.16 in. (54.8 mm)	40 cu. in. (656 cc)	16 hp. (11.9 kW)
421400	2	3.44 in. (87.3 mm)	2.28 in. (57.9 mm)	42.33 cu. in. (694 cc)	18 hp. (13.4 kW)
421700	2	3.44 in. (87.3 mm)	2.28 in. (57.9 mm)	42.33 cu. in. (694 cc)	18 hp. (13.4 kW)
422400	2	3.44 in. (87.3 mm)	2.28 in. (57.9 mm)	42.33 cu. in. (694 cc)	18 hp. (13.4 kW)
422700	2	3.44 in. (87.3 mm)	2.28 in. (57.9 mm)	42.33 cu. in. (694 cc)	18 hp. (13.4 kW)

Engines in this section are four-stroke, two-cylinder, air-cooled engines. The crankshaft is supported at each end either with ball bearings or plain bearings. The plain bearings are either integral with crankcase, cover or engine base, or renewable DU-type bearings. Cylinder block and crankcase are a single aluminum casting. Some models are equipped with integral cast iron cylinder liners.

Connecting rods for all models ride directly on crankpin journals. Models 402440, 402770, 422440 and 422770 are pressure lubricated by a rotor-type oil pump. All other models are splash lubricated. Vertical crankshaft models that are splash lubricated are equipped with a gear-driven oil slinger and horizontal crankshaft models use an oil dipper attached to number one cylinder connecting rod cap.

Early models are equipped with a flywheel magneto ignition with breaker points, condenser and coil mounted externally on engine. Later models are equipped with a Magnetron breakerless ignition.

All models use a float-type carburetor with an integral fuel pump.

Always provide engine model and serial number when ordering parts or special tools.

MAINTENANCE

LUBRICATION. Models 402440, 402770, 422440 and 422770 are equipped with a pressure lubrication system and an oil filter. Oil is routed from an oil pump driven by the camshaft to the crankshaft. All other models are splash lubricated using a gear-driven oil slinger (5—Fig. B901) on vertical crankshaft models or an oil dipper attached to number one connecting rod (27—Fig. B902) on horizontal crankshaft models.

Manufacturer recommends using oil with an API service classification of SF or SG. Use SAE 30 oil for temperatures above 40° F (4° C), SAE 10W-30 oil for temperatures between 0° F (–18° C) and 100° F (38° C), and, below 20° F (–7° C), use petroleum-based SAE 5W-20 or a suitable synthetic oil.

Check oil at regular intervals and maintain at "FULL" mark on dipstick. Dipstick should be pushed or screwed in completely for accurate measurement. DO NOT overfill.

Change oil after first 5 hours of operation. Thereafter, recommended oil change interval is every 25 hours on splash lubricated models, or every 50 hours on models 402440, 402770, 422440 and 422770. Decrease oil change interval if usage is severe.

Crankcase oil capacity for early production engines is 3.5 pints (1.65 L). Oil capacity for late production engines is 3 pints (1.42 L). Check oil level with dipstick.

On Models 402440, 402770, 422440 and 422770, a low oil pressure switch

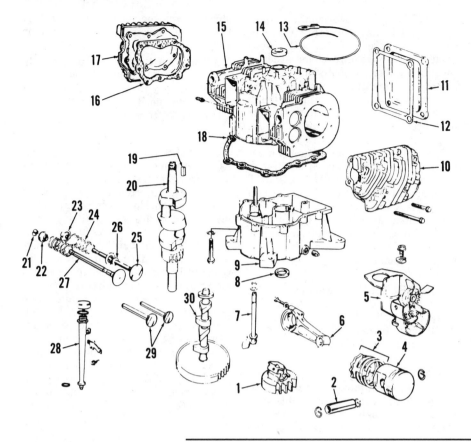

Fig. B901—Exploded view of vertical crankshaft engine assembly.

1. Governor gear
2. Piston pin & clips
3. Piston rings
4. Piston
5. Oil slinger assy.
6. Connecting rod
7. Governor shaft assy.
8. Oil seal
9. Engine base
10. Cylinder head
11. Crankcase cover
12. Crankcase gasket
13. Ground wire
14. Oil seal
15. Cylinder/crankcase assy.
16. Head gasket
17. Cylinder head
18. Gasket
19. Key
20. Crankshaft
21. Retainer
22. Rotocoil (exhaust valve)
23. Retainer (intake valve)
24. Valve spring (2)
25. Intake valve
26. Seal & retainer assy.
27. Exhaust valve
28. Oil dipstick assy.
29. Valve tappet (2)
30. Camshaft assy.

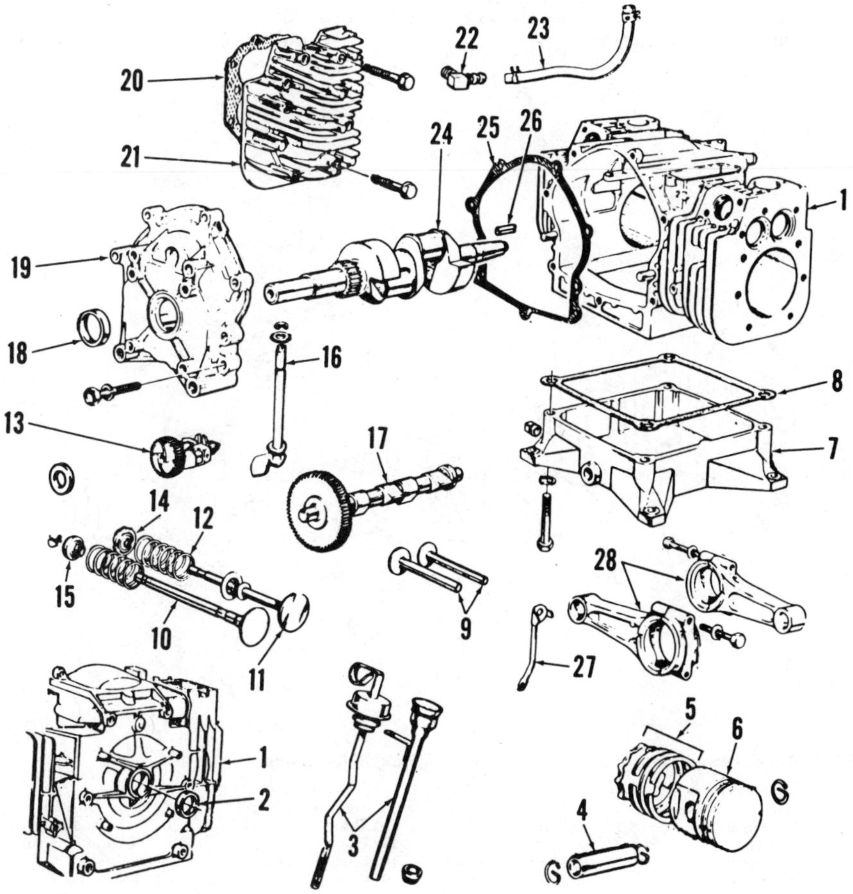

Fig. B902—Exploded view of horizontal crankshaft assembly.

1. Cylinder/crankcase assy.
2. Oil seal
3. Dipstick assy.
4. Piston pin & retainer clips
5. Piston rings
6. Piston
7. Engine base
8. Gasket
9. Valve tappets
10. Exhaust valve
11. Intake valve
12. Valve spring
13. Governor gear assy.
14. Intake valve retainer
15. Rotocoil (exhaust valve)
16. Governor shaft
17. Camshaft
18. Oil seal
19. Crankcase cover
20. Head gasket
21. Cylinder head
22. Elbow connector
23. Fuel line
24. Crankshaft
25. Gasket
26. Key
27. Oil dipper
28. Connecting rods

may be located on the oil filter adapter. Switch should be closed at zero pressure and open at 5 psi (34.5 kpa). Switch may be connected to a warning device or into the ignition circuit.

Splash lubricated models may be equipped with a low oil level warning system called Oil Gard. A sensor is screwed into the engine base and monitors oil level. If the oil level falls below a certain level, the sensor activates a warning device or disables the ignition circuit, depending on the equipment. To check sensor, disconnect sensor lead, then connect ohmmeter leads to sensor lead and engine base. Ohmmeter should indicate 50-80 ohms. If not, check condition of connections and sensor wire, and if found satisfactory, renew sensor.

CRANKCASE BREATHER.

Crankcase breathers are built into engine valve covers. Horizontal crankshaft models have breather valve in each cover assembly. Vertical crankshaft models have only one breather in cover of number one cylinder.

Breathers maintain a partial vacuum in crankcase to prevent oil from being forced out past oil seals and gaskets or past breaker point plunger or piston rings.

Fiber disc of breather assembly must not be stuck or binding. A 0.045-inch (1.14 mm) wire gauge SHOULD NOT enter space between fiber disc valve and body. Check with gauge at 90° intervals around fiber disc (Fig. B903).

When installing breathers, make certain side of gasket with notches is toward crankshaft.

SPARK PLUG.

Recommended spark plug for all models is Champion RJ12 or Autolite 308. Electrode gap is 0.030 inch (0.76 mm). Tighten spark plug to 200 in.-lbs. (22.6 N•m).

CAUTION: Briggs & Stratton does not recommend using abrasive blasting to clean spark plugs as this may introduce abrasive material into the engine that could cause extensive damage.

CARBURETOR.

A downdraft float-type carburetor is used. The carburetor is equipped with an integral diaphragm-type fuel pump. Refer to Fig. B904 for an exploded view of carburetor and fuel pump.

Adjustment. Initial setting of idle mixture screw (11-Fig. B904) for all models is 1½ turns out. If equipped with a high-speed mixture screw, initial setting is 1½ turns out.

MODELS PRIOR TO TYPE 1100. Run engine until engine operating temperature is reached. To adjust idle mixture screw, place remote speed control in idle position. Hold carburetor throttle lever against idle speed adjusting screw and adjust idle speed to 1200 rpm. With throttle lever against idle speed adjusting screw, turn idle mixture screw clockwise until a reduction in engine speed is noted. Back out idle mixture screw ½ turn. With throttle lever against idle speed screw, readjust idle speed to 900 rpm. Release throttle lever. Move remote speed control to a position where a ⅛-inch diameter pin can be inserted through two holes in governor control plate (Fig. B905). With remote control in governed idle position, bend tab "A," Fig. B906, to obtain 1200 rpm. Remove pin.

If equipped with a high-speed mixture screw, place remote speed control in fast position and adjust high-speed mixture screw for leanest setting that will allow satisfactory acceleration and steady governor operation.

NOTE: Some early models are equipped with a fixed main jet that appears the same as the adjustable high-speed mixture screw and is located in the same position. The fixed main jet is identified by a small hole in the tip. The fixed main jet must be seated fully in the carburetor; backing out main jet screw will result in an overly rich mixture.

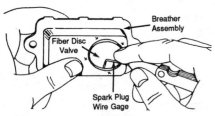

Fig. B903—Clearance between fiber disc valve and crankcase breather housing must be less than 0.045 inch (1.15 mm). A spark plug gauge can be used to check clearance as shown, but do not apply pressure against disc valve.

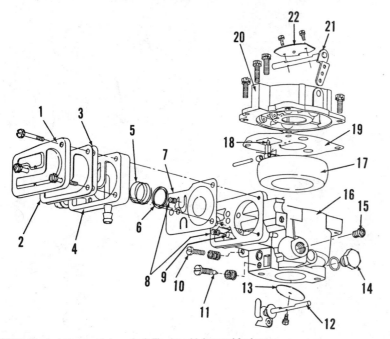

Fig. B904—Exploded view of downdraft Flo-Jet with integral fuel pump.

1. Diaphragm cover	
2. Gasket	
3. Damping diaphragm	7. Diaphragm
4. Pump body	8. Springs
5. Pump spring	9. Spring boss
6. Spring cap	10. Idle speed screw
	11. Idle mixture screw

12. Throttle shaft
13. Throttle plate
14. Plug
15. Fixed main jet
16. Carburetor lower body

17. Float
18. Fuel inlet valve
19. Carburetor body gasket
20. Carburetor upper body
21. Choke shaft
22. Choke valve

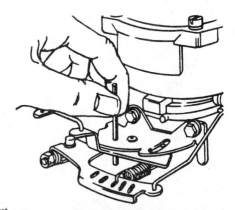

Fig. B905—Insert a 1/8-inch (3.2 mm) diameter pin through the two holes in governor control plate to correctly set governed idle position.

Illustrations Courtesy Briggs & Stratton Corp.

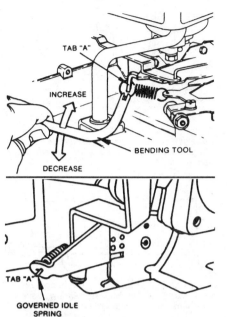

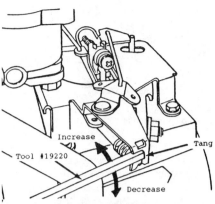

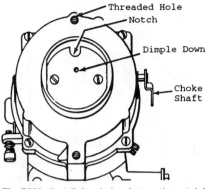

Fig. B908—With remote control in governed idle position, bend tab "A" to obtain 1200 rpm.

Fig. B909—Install the choke plate so the notch is toward the threaded hole.

Fig. B906—With governor plate locked with a 1/8-inch (3.2 mm) pin (Fig. B905), bend tab "A" to obtain 1200 rpm. Upper view is for a horizontal crankshaft engine and lower view is for vertical crankshaft engines.

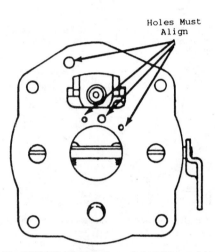

Fig. B910—Holes in body gasket of late models must be properly aligned with holes in upper carburetor body.

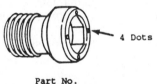

Part No. 231500

Fig. B907—Optional high-speed jet to provide a richer fuel mixture is identified by four dots on the jet face.

readjust idle speed to 900 rpm. Release throttle lever. With remote control in governed idle position, bend tang (Fig. B908) to obtain 1200 rpm.

If equipped with a high-speed mixture screw, place remote speed control in fast position and adjust high-speed mixture screw for leanest setting that will allow satisfactory acceleration and steady governor operation. The fixed main jet is not adjustable. If throttle response is poor or if engine hesitates when it is accelerated or placed under load due to a lean fuel mixture, a richer jet may be required. The optional richer main jet is identified by four dots on the jet face (Fig. B907).

An optional jet for high altitude operation is offered.

Overhaul. To disassemble carburetor, remove idle and main fuel mixture screws. Remove anti-afterfire solenoid from carburetor, if so equipped. Remove fuel pump body (4—Fig. B904) and upper carburetor body (20). Remove float assembly (17) and fuel inlet valve (18). Inlet valve seat is a press fit in upper carburetor body. Use a self-threading screw to remove seat. New seat should be pressed into upper body until flush with body. Remove retaining screws from throttle plate (13) and choke plate (22) and withdraw throttle shaft (12) and choke shaft (21).

If necessary to renew throttle shaft bushings, use a ¼ × 20 tap to remove old bushings.

NOTE: If carburetor body has a plug in the side of throttle shaft bore, bushing on that side is not renewable and plug should not be removed.

Press new bushings in using a vise and ream with B&S tool 19056. Align-ream bushings with a 7/32-inch drill if throttle shaft binds.

When assembling the carburetor, note the following: Install the choke

Some models are equipped with a fixed high-speed jet (15). The jet is located behind a plug (14) in the same location as the high-speed mixture adjusting screw of other models. An optional jet for high altitude operation is offered. The high altitude jet is identified by four dots on the jet face (Fig. B907).

MODELS TYPE 1100 AND ABOVE. Run engine until engine operating temperature is reached. To adjust idle mixture screw, place remote speed control in idle position. Hold carburetor throttle lever against idle speed adjusting screw and adjust idle speed to 1200 rpm. With throttle lever against idle speed adjusting screw, turn idle mixture screw clockwise until a reduction in engine speed is noted and mark screw position. Back out idle mixture screw until engine speed lessens again and mark screw position. Rotate screw so it is halfway between the two marked positions. With throttle lever against idle speed screw,

plate so the notch is toward the threaded hole in upper body as shown in Fig. B909 and the dimple on the plate is down. Be sure holes in body gasket are properly aligned with holes in upper carburetor body as shown in Figs. B910 and B911. Note proper installation of fuel inlet valve clip in Fig. B912. To check float level, invert carburetor body and float assembly. Float should be parallel to body as shown in Fig. B913. Adjust float by bending float lever tang that contacts inlet valve. Install throttle plate so that, with throttle closed, dimples will be on opposite side of shaft from idle port, and convex sides of dimples are toward carburetor base surface (see Fig. B914). When installing fixed jet plug or anti-afterfire solenoid, tighten plug or solenoid to 100 in.-lbs. (11.3 N·m). Be sure springs (8—Fig. B904) fit onto spring bosses shown in Fig. B915.

ANTI-AFTERFIRE SYSTEM. Some models are equipped with an anti-afterfire system that stops fuel flow through the carburetor when the igni-

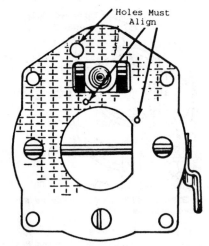

Fig. B911—Holes in body gasket of older models must be properly aligned with holes in upper carburetor body.

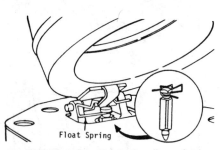

Fig. B912—Install fuel inlet valve clip as shown.

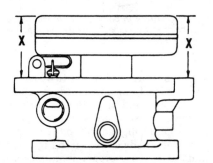

Fig. B913—Check carburetor float setting as shown. Bend tang, if necessary, to adjust float level.

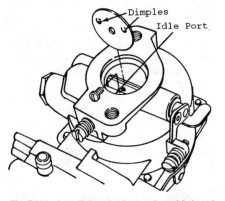

Fig. B914—Install throttle plate so that with throttle closed dimples will be on opposite side of shaft from idle port, and convex sides of dimples are toward carburetor base surface.

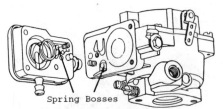

Fig. B915—Fuel pump check valve springs must fit onto spring bosses.

tion switch is in off position. Two different systems have been used. Early systems use a vacuum solenoid that blocks vacuum to the fuel bowl, thereby stopping fuel flow through fuel passages. Later systems are found on carburetors with a fixed main fuel jet. A solenoid inserts a plunger into the jet to stop fuel flow.

A view of the vacuum-type anti-afterfire system is shown in Fig. B916. The solenoid is controlled electrically by the ignition switch. The solenoid blocks the fuel bowl vent circuit and allows crankcase vacuum to enter the circuit when the ignition switch is off. Solenoid should "click" if operating properly. All hoses must be clamped tight, without kinks and undamaged. Vacuum block in air cleaner must fit properly.

Refer to Fig. B917 for drawing of anti-afterfire system used on carburetor with fixed jet. Solenoid can be removed and tested by connecting a 9-volt battery to solenoid. Solenoid plunger should retract when energized and should extend freely when battery is disconnected. A faulty solenoid will affect engine performance.

FUEL PUMP. All parts of the vacuum diaphragm-type pump are serviced separately. When disassembling pump, take care to prevent damage to pump body (plastic housing) and diaphragm. Inspect diaphragm for punctures, wrinkles or wear. All mounting surfaces must be free of nicks, burrs and debris.

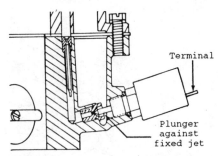

Fig. B917—Carburetors with fixed main jet may be equipped with the anti-afterfire system shown above.

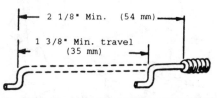

Fig. B918—For proper operation, remote control wire must extend to dimension shown above and have minimum travel of 1-3/8 inches (35 mm).

To assemble pump, position diaphragm on carburetor. Place spring and cup on top of diaphragm. Install flapper valve springs. Carefully place pump body, remaining diaphragm, gasket and cover plate over carburetor casting and install mounting screws. Tighten screws in a staggered sequence to avoid distortion.

CARBURETOR CONTROL MECHANISM. To assure proper speed control, measure travel of remote control wire with remote control unit installed. Minimum wire travel is $1\frac{3}{8}$ inches (35 mm) as shown in Fig. B918.

To adjust speed control cable on engines with a type number below 1100, move remote control lever to idle position. Carburetor throttle lever should contact idle speed screw. If not, loosen cable housing clamp and reposition cable housing.

To adjust speed control cable on engines with type number 1100 and above,

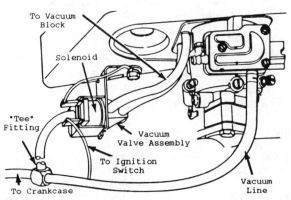

Fig. B916—A view of the vacuum-type anti-afterfire system.

Illustrations Courtesy Briggs & Stratton Corp.

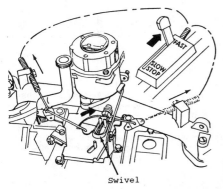

Fig. B919—On engines with type number 1100 and above, swivel should be against side of quarter circle when remote control lever is in FAST position.

move remote control lever to FAST position. Swivel shown in Fig. B919 should be against side of quarter circle. If not, loosen cable housing clamp and reposition cable housing.

Remote choke control should completely close carburetor choke plate when remote control is in "CHOKE" position. If necessary, loosen cable clamp and reposition cable to synchronize carburetor choke and remote control.

GOVERNOR. All models are equipped with a gear-driven mechanical governor. Governor gear and weight assembly is enclosed within the engine and is driven by the camshaft gear.

To adjust governor, loosen nut (N—Fig. B920) securing governor lever to governor shaft (S). Push governor lever counterclockwise until throttle is wide open. Hold lever in this position while rotating governor shaft (S) counterclockwise as far as it will go. Tighten governor lever nut to 100 in.-lbs. (11.3 N•m).

To adjust top governed speed on engines with a type number below 1100, first adjust carburetor and governed idle as outlined in CARBURETOR section. Install governor spring end loop in appropriate hole in governor lever for desired engine rpm as shown in Fig.

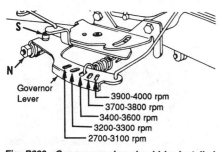

Fig. B920—Governor spring should be installed with end loops as shown. Install loop in appropriate governor lever hole for engine speed (rpm) desired.

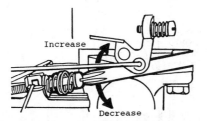

Fig. B921—Turn top governed speed adjusting screw to obtain desired engine rpm.

B920. Check engine top governed speed using an accurate tachometer.

To adjust top governed speed on engines with type number 1100 and above, first adjust carburetor and governed idle as outlined in CARBURETOR section. Turn top governed speed adjusting screw shown in Fig. B921 until desired engine rpm is obtained. Check engine rpm using an accurate tachometer.

IGNITION SYSTEM. Early production engines were equipped with a flywheel-type magneto ignition with points, condenser and coil located externally on engine. Late production engines are equipped with a "Magnetron" breakerless ignition system.

Refer to appropriate paragraph for model being serviced.

Flywheel Magneto Ignition. The flywheel magneto system consists of a permanent magnet cast into flywheel, armature and coil assembly, breaker points and condenser.

Breaker points and condenser are located under or behind intake manifold and are protected by a metal cover that must be sealed around edges and at wire entry location to prevent entry of dirt or moisture.

Breaker point gap should be 0.020 inch (0.52 mm) for all models.

Breaker points are actuated by a plunger (Fig. B922) that is installed with the smaller diameter end toward breaker points. Renew plunger if length is 1.115 inch (28.32 mm) or less. Renew plunger seal by installing seal on plunger (make certain it is securely at-

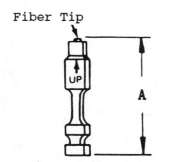

Fiber Tip

UP

A

Fig. B922—Plunger must be renewed if plunger length (A) is worn to 1.115 inch (28.32 mm) or less.

tached) and installing seal and plunger assembly into plunger bore. Slide seal over plunger bore. Slide seal over plunger boss until seated against casting at base of boss.

Armature air gap should be 0.010-0.014 inch (0.25-0.36 mm) and is adjusted by loosening armature retaining bolts and moving armature as necessary on slotted holes. Tighten armature retaining bolts.

Magnetron Ignition. "Magnetron" ignition consists of permanent magnets cast in flywheel and a self-contained transistor module mounted on the ignition armature.

To check ignition, attach B&S tester number 19051 to each spark plug lead and ground tester to engine. Spin flywheel at least 350 rpm. If spark jumps the 0.166 inch (4.2 mm) tester gap, ignition system is operating satisfactorily.

Armature air gap should be 0.008-0.012 inch (0.20-0.30 mm) and is adjusted by loosening armature retaining bolts and moving armature as necessary on slotted holes. Tighten armature bolts.

Flywheel does not need to be removed to service Magnetron ignition except to check condition of flywheel key or keyway.

To remove Magnetron module from armature, remove stop switch wire, module primary wire and armature primary wire from module by using a $\frac{3}{16}$-inch (5 mm) rod to release spring and retainer (Fig. B923). Remove spring and retainer clip. Unsolder wires. Remove module by pulling out on module retainer while pushing down on module until free of armature laminations.

During reinstallation, use 60/40 rosin core solder and make certain all wires are held firmly against coil body with tape, Permatex No. 2 or equivalent gasket sealer.

VALVE ADJUSTMENT. To correctly set tappet clearance, remove spark plug and insert a suitable meas-

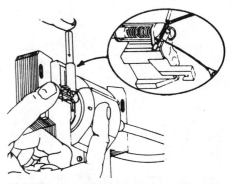

Fig. B923—Use a 3/16-inch (5 mm) diameter rod to release wires from Magnetron module. Refer to text.

uring tool through spark plug hole. Rotate crankshaft in normal direction (clockwise at flywheel) so piston is at top dead center on compression stroke, then continue to rotate crankshaft so piston is ¼ inch (6.4 mm) down from top dead center. This position places the tappets away from the compression release devices on the cam lobes.

If valve springs are installed, valve stem-to-tappet end clearance should be 0.007-0.009 inch (0.18-0.23 mm) for exhaust valves and 0.004-0.006 inch (0.10-0.15 mm) for intake valves. Without springs, valve stem-to-tappet end clearance should be 0.009-0.011 inch (0.23-0.28 mm) for exhaust valves and 0.006-0.008 inch (0.15-0.23 mm) for intake valves. If clearance is less than specified, grind end of stem as necessary. If clearance is excessive, grind valve seat deeper or renew valve as necessary.

COMPRESSION PRESSURE. Compression pressure measured at cranking speed should not vary more than 25 percent between cylinders.

CYLINDER HEAD. Carbon and lead deposits should be removed at 100- to 300-hour intervals, or whenever cylinder head is removed.

REPAIRS

TIGHTENING TORQUES. Recommended tightening torque specifications are as follows:

Carburetor mounting
  screws . . . . 100 in.-lbs.
                                         (11.3 N·m)
Connecting rod . . . . 190 in.-lbs.
                                         (22 N·m)
Crankcase cover:
  Horizontal crank . . . . . . 225 in.-lbs.
                                         (25.4 N·m)
  Vertical crank—
    Aluminum . . . . 27 ft.-lbs.
                                         (36.7 N·m)
    Steel . . . . 250 in.-lbs.
                                         (28.2 N·m)

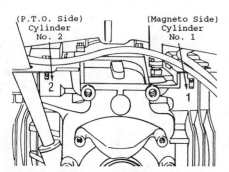

Fig. B924—Cylinder numbers are cast on the tappet chambers on flywheel side of engine. Cylinder heads are also identified (Fig. B925) and must be installed on the corresponding cylinder.

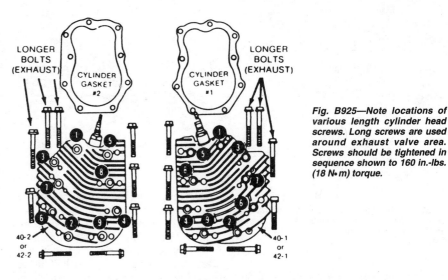

Fig. B925—Note locations of various length cylinder head screws. Long screws are used around exhaust valve area. Screws should be tightened in sequence shown to 160 in.-lbs. (18 N·m) torque.

Cylinder head . . . . 160 in.-lbs.
                                         (18 N·m)
Engine base:
  Horizontal crank . . . . 27 ft.-lbs.
                                         (36.7 N·m)
  Vertical crank . . . . 225 in.-lbs.
                                         (25.4 N·m)
Flywheel nut . . . . 150 ft.-lbs.
                                         (204 N·m)
Intake manifold . . . . 90 in.-lbs.
                                         (10.2 N·m)
Spark plug . . . . 200 in.-lbs.
                                         (22.6 N·m)

CYLINDER HEADS. When removing cylinder heads, note locations from which different length retaining screws are removed as they must be reinstalled in their original positions. Also note that cylinder heads and cylinders are numbered and heads must be reinstalled on corresponding cylinders. See Figs. B924 and B925.

Always use a new gasket when reinstalling cylinder head. Do not use sealer on gasket. Lubricate cylinder head retaining screw threads with graphite grease. Install cylinder head retaining screws in correct locations and tighten evenly in several steps in sequence shown in Fig. B925 to 160 in.-lbs. (18 N·m).

VALVE SYSTEM. Valves seat in renewable inserts pressed into cylinder head surfaces of block. Valve seat width should be 3/64 to 1/16 inch (1.17 to 1.57 mm). Seat angle is 45° for exhaust seat and 30° for intake seat. If seats are loose, check clearance between seat and cylinder block counterbore using a 0.005 inch (0.13 mm) feeler gauge. If feeler gauge cannot be inserted between seat and cylinder block, peen seat as shown in Fig. B926. If feeler gauge can be inserted between seat and cylinder block, renew seat. Use a suitable puller such as B&S tool 19138 to remove valve seat insert. Drive new seat into cylinder

block until it bottoms, peen seat as shown in Fig. B926 and grind to correct angle.

Valves should be refaced at a 45-degree angle for exhaust valves and at a 30-degree angle for intake valves. Valves should be rejected if margin is less than 1/64 inch (0.10 mm). See Fig. B927.

Valve guides should be checked for wear using valve guide gauge (B&S tool 19151). If gauge enters guide 5/16 inch (7.9 mm) or more, guide should be reconditioned or renewed.

To recondition aluminum valve guides, use B&S tool kit 19232. Place reamer 19231 and guide 19234 in worn guide and center with valve seat. Mark reamer 1/16 inch (1.57 mm) above top edge of service bushing (Fig. B928). Ream worn guide until mark on reamer is flush with top of guide bushing. DO NOT ream completely through guide. Place service bushing, part 231218, on driver 19204 so grooved end of bushing will enter guide bore first. Press bushing into guide until it bottoms. Finish ream completely through guide using

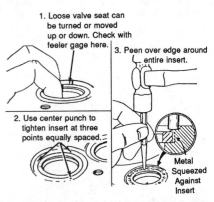

Fig. B926—Loose valve seat inserts can be tightened or renewed as shown. If a 0.005 inch (0.13 mm) feeler gauge can be inserted between seat and seat bore, insert oversize insert or renew cylinder.

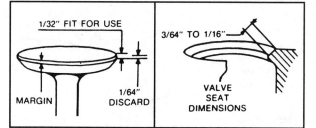

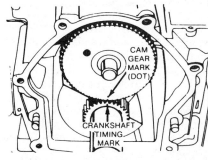

Fig. B927—Drawing showing correct valve face and seat dimensions. Refer to text.

Fig. B930—Align timing marks as shown on models having main bearings as an integral part of crankcase, cover or engine base. Refer to text.

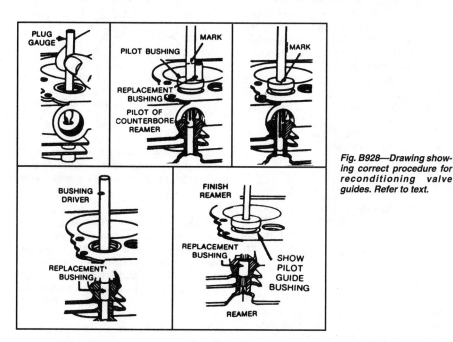

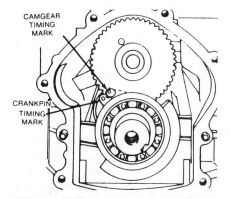

Fig. B928—Drawing showing correct procedure for reconditioning valve guides. Refer to text.

Fig. B931—Align timing marks as shown on models having ball bearing-type main bearings. Refer to text.

Fig. B929—Use correct bushing when renewing valve guide bushings. Refer to adjacent illustration to identify bushing.

CAMSHAFT. Camshaft and camshaft gear are an integral part that ride on journals at each end of camshaft. Camshaft on pressure lubricated models has an oil passage that extends through the center of the camshaft. Note that camshafts cannot be interchanged between pressure lubricated and splash lubricated models.

To remove camshaft, refer to appropriate paragraph in CRANKSHAFT section for model being serviced.

Camshaft should be renewed if gear teeth or lobes are worn or damaged. Reject camshaft if either bearing journal diameter is 0.623 inch (15.82 mm) or less. Reject dimensions for cam lobes are 1.150 inch (29.21 mm) for intake and 1.120 inches (28.45 mm) for exhaust.

Be sure oil passage in camshaft on pressure lubricated models is open and clean. When installing camshaft, be sure that timing marks are aligned as shown in Figs. B930 or B931.

PISTONS, PINS AND RINGS. Pistons used in engines with cast iron cylinder liners (Series 400400, 400700, 402400, 402440, 402700, 402770, 422400, 422440, 422700 and 422770) have a shiny finish, and on early models, were marked with an "L" on piston

reamer 19233 and guide 19234. Lubricate reamer with kerosene during reaming procedure.

To renew brass or sintered iron guides, use tap 19264 to thread worn guide bushing approximately ½ inch (12.7 mm) deep. DO NOT thread more than 1 inch (25.4 mm) deep. Install puller washer 19240 on puller screw 19238 and thread screw and washer assembly into worn guide. Center washer on valve seat and tighten puller nut 19239 against washer, continue to tighten while keeping threaded screw from turning until guide has been removed. Identify guide using Fig. B929

and find appropriate replacement. Place correct service bushing on driver 19204 so the two grooves on service bushings 231218 are down. Remaining bushing types can be installed either way. Press bushing in until it bottoms. Finish ream with reamer 19233 and reamer guide 19234. Lubricate reamer with kerosene and ream completely through new service bushing.

When reinstalling valves, note exhaust valve spring is shorter, has heavier diameter coils and is usually painted red. Intake valve has a stem seal that should be renewed if valve has been removed.

crown. A chrome-plated aluminum piston is used in aluminum bore (Kool-Bore) cylinders. Due to the two different cylinder bore materials, pistons and piston rings WILL NOT interchange.

Pistons for all models should be renewed if they are scored or damaged, or if a 0.009 inch (0.23 mm) feeler gauge can be inserted between a new top ring and ring groove. Refer to the following table for piston ring end gap rejection sizes:

Model Series	Compression Ring	Oil Ring
401400, 401700, 421400, 421700	0.035 in. (0.89 mm)	0.045 in. (1.14 mm)
All Other Models	0.030 in. (0.76 mm)	0.035 in. (0.89 mm)

Pistons and rings are available in several oversizes as well as standard bore size.

Piston pin is a slip fit in both piston and connecting rod bores. If piston pin bore measures 0.801 inch (20.35 mm) or more, piston should be renewed or pin bore reamed for 0.005 inch (0.127 mm) oversize pin. Standard piston pin diameter is 0.799 inch (20.30 mm) and should be renewed if worn or out-of-round more than 0.0005 inch (0.0127

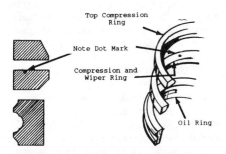

Fig. B932—Drawing of piston rings showing correct installation. Be sure dot mark on second compression ring is toward piston crown.

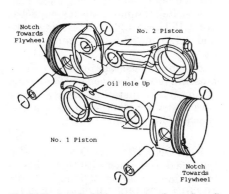

Fig. B933—Install piston on connecting rod so oil hole in connecting rod is toward cam gear side of engine when notch on top of piston is toward flywheel.

mm). A 0.005 inch (0.127 mm) oversize pin is available for all models.

Install piston rings on piston as shown in Fig. B932. Arrange piston rings so end gaps are staggered around piston. Install pistons so notch in piston crown is toward flywheel side of engine as shown in Fig. B933.

CONNECTING RODS. Connecting rods and pistons are removed from cylinder head end of block as an assembly after first removing cylinder head, crankcase cover or engine base. Identify pistons and connecting rods so they can be reinstalled in original cylinder.

Aluminum alloy connecting rods ride directly on crankpin journals. Connecting rod should be renewed if crankpin bearing bore measures 1.627 inches (41.33 mm) or more, if bearing surfaces are scored or damaged, or if pin bore measures 0.802 inch (20.37 mm) or more. A 0.005 inch (0.127 mm) oversize piston pin is available.

NOTE: Connecting rods of Models 402440, 402770, 422440 and 422770 (pressure lubricated) are not interchangeable with other models (splash lubricated).

Connecting rod should be installed on piston so oil hole in connecting rod is toward cam gear side of engine when notch on top of piston is toward flywheel with piston and rod assembly installed. See Fig. B933. Make certain match marks on connecting rod and cap are aligned, and if so equipped, install oil dipper on number one rod. Install special washers and nuts and tighten to 190 in.-lbs. (22 N•m) for all models.

NOTE: Some horizontal crankshaft models that operate at slow speeds

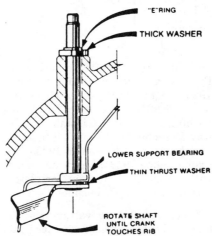

Fig. B934—Cross-sectional view of early governor shaft assembly. To disassemble, remove "E" ring and washer. Carefully guide shaft down past crankshaft.

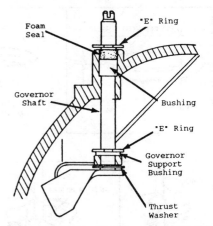

Fig. B935—Drawing of governor shaft assembly used on models below type number 1100 equipped with two "E" rings.

and under high load are equipped with an oil dipper attached to number two connecting rod as well as number one rod.

GOVERNOR. To remove governor shaft, loosen nut and remove governor lever. Remove crankcase cover or engine base. To obtain maximum clearance, rotate crankshaft until timing mark on crankshaft gear is at approximately 10 o'clock position. If equipped with ball bearings, rotate crankshaft to obtain clearance with crankshaft counterweight. On early models (see Fig. B934), remove "E" ring and thick washer on outer end of governor shaft and slide shaft out. On models equipped with two "E" rings (see Fig. B935), detach the two rings and slide out shaft. On models with type number 1100 and above (shown in Fig. B936), detach "E" ring and slide out shaft. On all models, it may be necessary to rotate crankshaft to gain clearance for governor shaft removal. DO NOT force shaft against crankshaft when removing.

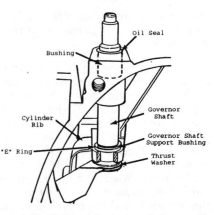

Fig. B936—Drawing of governor shaft assembly used on models with type number 1100 and above.

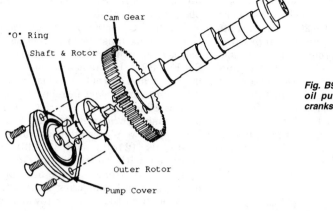

Fig. B937—Exploded view of oil pump used on vertical crankshaft engines.

Later models (Figs. B935 and B936) use a renewable governor shaft bushing. Use suitable tools for removal and installation of bushing. Drive or pull bushing out toward outside of crankcase. Bushing should bottom against shoulder in bore during installation.

After installation, rotate governor shaft so governor arm is against cylinder rib.

Governor gear assembly is available only as a unit assembly. Be sure assembly rotates and operates freely without binding. Note that there is a thrust washer located between gear assembly and boss. Refer to MAINTENANCE section for governor adjustment.

OIL PUMP. Pressure lubricated engines are equipped with rotor-type oil pump. The pump is driven by the end of the camshaft on vertical crankshaft engines (see Fig. B937) or by a separate gear that is driven by the camshaft gear on horizontal engines (see Fig. B938).

The oil pump on vertical crankshaft models is accessible by removing pump cover on bottom of sump. On horizontal crankshaft models it is necessary to remove crankcase cover for access to oil pump. Inspect pump components and renew if damaged.

The pump relief valve is located in the oil filter adapter shown in Fig. B939. Remove adapter from crankcase while being careful not to drop spring and ball. Spring length must be 1.091-1.159

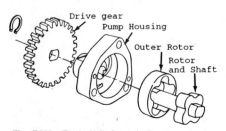

Fig. B938—Exploded view of oil pump used on horizontal crankshaft engines.

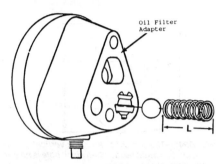

Fig. B939—Relief valve spring length (L) must be 1.091-1.159 inches (27.71-29.44 mm), otherwise reject spring.

inches (27.71-29.44 mm), otherwise reject spring.

CRANKSHAFT. Crankshaft and camshaft used on pressure lubricated engines are dissimilar and not interchangeable with crankshaft and camshaft of splash lubricated engines.

To remove crankshaft from engines with integral-type or DU-type bearings, remove necessary air shrouds. Remove flywheel and front gear cover or sump. Remove connecting rod caps. Remove cam gear making certain valve tappets clear camshaft lobes. Remove crankshaft.

To reinstall crankshaft, reverse removal procedure making certain timing marks are aligned as shown in Fig. B930.

To remove crankshaft from engines with ball bearing main bearing, remove all necessary air shrouds and remove flywheel. Remove front gear cover or sump. Remove connecting rod caps. Compress exhaust and intake valve springs on number two cylinder to provide clearance for camshaft lobes. Remove crankshaft and camshaft together.

To reinstall crankshaft, reverse removal procedure making certain timing marks are aligned as shown in Fig. B931.

Renew crankshaft if main bearing journal at either end is 1.376 inches (34.95 mm) or less. Renew or regrind crankshaft if crankpin journal diameter is 1.622 inches (41.15 mm) or less. A 0.020 inch (0.51 mm) undersize connecting rod is available.

Crankshaft end play for all models should be 0.002-0.008 inch (0.05-0.20 mm). At least one 0.015 inch cover or sump gasket must be installed. Additional gaskets of 0.005 and 0.009 inch thickness are available if end play is less than 0.002 inch (0.05 mm). If end play is over 0.008 inch (0.20 mm), metal shims are available for installation between crankshaft gear and cover or sump. Do not use shims on engines with double ball bearings.

CYLINDERS. Cylinder bores may be either aluminum or a cast iron liner that is an integral part of the cylinder block casting. Pistons and piston rings are not interchangeable between the two types. Series 400400, 400700, 402400, 402440, 402700, 402770, 422400, 422440, 422700 and 422770 have cast iron cylinder liners as an integral part of cylinder block casting. Series 401400, 401700, 421400 and 421700 have aluminum cylinder bores (Kool-Bore).

Standard cylinder bore diameter for all models is 3.4365-3.4375 inches (87.29-87.31 mm). Cylinder should be resized if more than 0.003 inch (0.076 mm) oversize or 0.0015 inch (0.038 mm) out-of-round for cast iron bore, or 0.003 inch (0.076 mm) oversize or 0.0025 inch (0.064 mm) out-of-round for aluminum bore. Use a suitable hone such as B&S tool 19205 for aluminum bore or B&S tool 19211 for cast iron bore. Resize to nearest oversize for which piston and rings are available.

CRANKCASE AND MAIN BEARINGS. Crankshaft may be supported at each end in main bearings that are an integral part of crankcase, cover or engine base. Crankshaft on some models may be supported by DU-type bearings. Some models may use ball bearings in the crankcase, engine base or cover to support the crankshaft.

Ball bearing main bearing is a press fit on crankshaft and must be removed by pressing crankshaft out of bearing. Renew ball bearing if worn or rough. Expand new bearing by heating in oil and install with shield side toward crankpin. If ball bearing is loose in crankcase, cover or engine base bores, renew crankcase, cover or engine base.

Integral-type main bearings should be reamed out and service bushings installed if bearings are 0.0007 inch

(0.018 mm) or more out-of-round or if diameter is 1.382 inches (35.10 mm) or more. Special reamers are available from Briggs & Stratton.

DU-type main bearings should be renewed if bearings are 0.0007 inch (0.0178 mm) or more out-of-round or if diameter is 1.382 inches (35.10 mm) or more.

Worn DU-type bearings are pressed out of bores using B&S cylinder support 19227 and driver 19226. Note that pto main bearing of pressure lubricated models has an oil groove in inner diameter. Make certain oil holes in bearings align with oil holes in block and cover or sump. Press bearings in until they are 1/8 inch (3.2 mm) below thrust face, except on pto main bearing of vertical crankshaft models discussed in follow-

ing paragraph. Stake bearings into place. See Fig. B940.

The pto DU bearing on vertical crankshaft models must be installed so oil hole is nearer thrust face of engine base. See Fig. B941. Install bearing so oil hole is aligned and end of bearing is 1/32 inch (0.8 mm) from thrust face on pressure lubricated models, or 5/32 inch (4.0 mm) on splash lubricated models. Stake bearing in two places after installation.

Models 421400 and 422400 are equipped with an oil trough in the crankcase that encloses the oil dipper on number one connecting rod. Install the trough so the notch is toward the flywheel side of engine.

Tighten crankcase cover screws on horizontal crankshaft engines to 225 in.-lbs. (25.4 N•m). Tighten crankcase cover screws on vertical crankshaft engines with an aluminum cover to 27 ft.-lbs. (36.7 N•m), or if equipped with a steel cover, to 250 in.-lbs. (28.2 N•m). Tighten engine base retaining screws on horizontal crankshaft engines to 27 ft.-lbs. (36.7 N•m). Tighten engine base retaining screws on vertical crankshaft engines to 225 in.-lbs. (25.4 N•m).

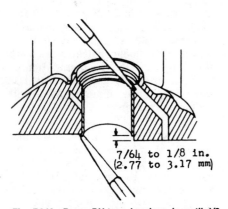

Fig. B940—Press DU-type bearings in until 1/8 inch (3.2 mm) from thrust surface. Make certain oil holes are aligned. Stake bearing as shown. Refer to text.

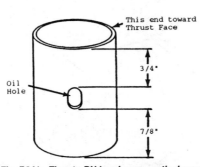

Fig. B941—The pto DU bearing on vertical crankshaft models must be installed so oil hole is nearer thrust face of engine base.

SERVICING BRIGGS & STRATTON ACCESSORIES

REWIND STARTER

Single-Cylinder Models
Except Vanguard

To renew broken rewind spring, proceed as follows: Grasp free outer end of spring (S—Fig. BS101) and pull broken end from starter housing. With blower housing removed, remove tangs (T) and remove starter pulley from housing. Untie knot in rope (R) and remove rope and inner end of broken spring from pulley. Apply a small amount of grease on inner face of pulley, thread inner end of spring through notch in starter housing, engage inner end of spring in pulley hub and place bar in pulley hub. Turn pulley approximately 13½ turns counterclockwise as shown in Fig. BS102. Tie wrench to blower housing with wire to hold pulley so hole (H) in pulley is aligned with rope guide (G) in housing as shown in Fig. BS103. Hook a wire in inner end of rope and thread rope through guide and hole in pulley; then, tie a knot in rope and release the pulley

allowing spring to wind rope into pulley groove.

To renew starter rope only, it is not generally necessary to remove starter pulley and spring. Wind up spring and install new rope as outlined in preceding paragraph.

Two different types of starter clutches have been used; refer to exploded view of early production unit in Fig. BS104 and exploded view of late production unit in Fig. BS105. Outer end of late production ratchet (refer to cut away view in Fig. BS106) is sealed with a felt and a retaining plug and a rubber ring is used to seal ratchet to ratchet cover.

To disassemble early type starter clutch unit, refer to Fig. BS104 and proceed as follows: Remove snap ring (3) and lift ratchet (5) and cover (4) from starter housing (7) and crankshaft. Be

careful not to lose steel balls (6). Starter housing (7) is also flywheel retaining nut; to remove housing, first remove screen (2) and using B&S flywheel wrench 19114, unscrew housing from crankshaft in counterclockwise direction. When reinstalling housing, be sure spring washer (8) is placed on crankshaft with cup (hollow) side toward flywheel, then install starter housing and tighten securely. Reinstall rotating screen. Place ratchet on crankshaft and into housing and insert the steel balls. Reinstall cover and retaining snap ring.

To disassemble late starter clutch unit, refer to Fig. BS105 and proceed as follows: Remove rotating screen (2) and starter ratchet cover (4). Lift ratchet (5) from housing and crankshaft and extract the steel balls (6). If necessary to remove housing (7), hold flywheel and unscrew housing in counterclockwise direction using B&S tool 19114. When

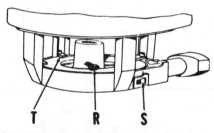

Fig. BS101—View of rewind starter used on single-cylinder engines, except Vanguard models, showing rope (R), spring end (S) and retaining tangs (T).

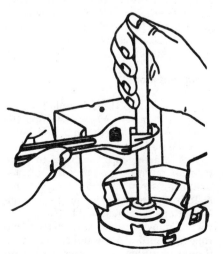

Fig. BS102—Using square shaft and wrench to wind up the rewind starter spring. Refer to text.

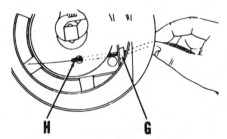

Fig. BS103—Thread rope through guide (G) in housing and hole (H) in starter pulley with wire hooked in end of rope.

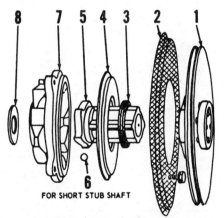

Fig. BS104—Exploded view of early production starter clutch unit; refer to Fig. BS107 for "long stub shaft." A late-type unit (Fig. BS105) should be installed when renewing "long" crankshaft with "short" (late production) shaft.

1. Starter rope pulley
2. Rotating screen
3. Snap ring
4. Ratchet cover
5. Starter ratchet
6. Steel balls
7. Clutch housing (flywheel nut)
8. Spring washer

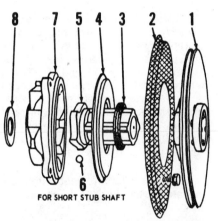

FOR SHORT STUB SHAFT

Fig. BS105—Exploded view of late production, sealed starter, clutch unit. Late unit can be used with "short stub shaft" only. Refer to Fig. BS107.

1. Starter rope pulley
2. Rotating screen
3. Rubber seal
4. Ratchet cover
5. Starter ratchet
6. Steel balls
7. Clutch housing (flywheel nut)
8. Spring washer

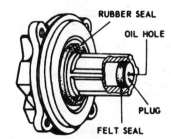

Fig. BS106—Cutaway showing felt seal and plug in end of late production starter ratchet (5—Fig. BS105).

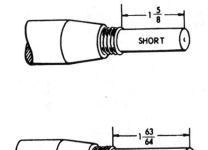

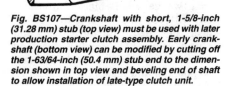

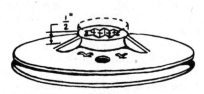

Fig. BS107—Crankshaft with short, 1-5/8-inch (31.28 mm) stub (top view) must be used with later production starter clutch assembly. Early crankshaft (bottom view) can be modified by cutting off the 1-63/64-inch (50.4 mm) stub end to the dimension shown in top view and beveling end of shaft to allow installation of late-type clutch unit.

Fig. BS108—When installing late-type starter clutch unit as a replacement for early-type, either install new starter rope pulley or cut hub of old pulley to 1/2 inch (12.7 mm) as shown.

installing housing, be sure spring washer (8) is in place on crankshaft with cup (hollow) side toward flywheel; then, tighten housing securely. Inspect felt seal and plug in outer end of ratchet. Renew ratchet if seal or plug is damaged as these parts are not serviced separately. Lubricate the felt with oil and place ratchet on crankshaft. Insert the steel balls and install ratchet cover, rubber seal and rotating screen.

NOTE: Crankshafts used with early and late starter clutches differ. See Fig. BS107.

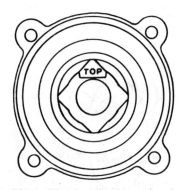

Fig. BS109—When installing blower housing and starter assembly, turn starter ratchet so word "TOP" stamped on outer end of ratchet is toward engine cylinder head.

If renewing early (long) crankshaft with late (short) shaft, also install late-type starter clutch unit. If renewing early starter clutch with late-type unit, crankshaft must be shortened to dimension shown for short shaft in Fig. BS107. Hub or starter rope pulley must also be shortened to ½ inch (12.7 mm) dimension shown in Fig. BS108. Bevel end of crankshaft after removing approximately ⅜ inch (9.5 mm) from shaft.

When installing blower housing and starter assembly, turn starter ratchet so word "TOP" on ratchet is toward engine cylinder head (Fig. BS109).

Twin-Cylinder Models Except Vanguard

To remove rewind starter shown in Fig. BS110, remove the four nuts and lockwashers from studs in blower housing. Separate starter assembly from blower housing, then separate assembly from blower housing and starter clutch assembly. To disassemble, remove handle and pin, and allow rope to rewind into housing. Grip end of rope in knot cavity and remove rope. Grip outer end of spring with pliers (Fig. BS110) and pull spring out of housing as far as possible. Turn spring ¼ turn and remove from pulley or bend one of the tangs with B&S tool 19229. Remove starter pulley and detach spring.

Clean spring and housing and oil spring sparingly before reinstallation. If pulley was removed, place a small amount of multipurpose grease on pulley, ratchet spring and ratchet spring adapter (Fig. BS111). Place ratchet

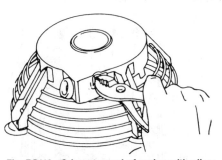

Fig. BS110—Grip outer end of spring with pliers and pull spring out of housing as far as possible. Refer to text.

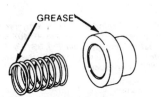

Fig. BS111—Lubricate pulley, spring and adapter with multipurpose grease. Refer to text.

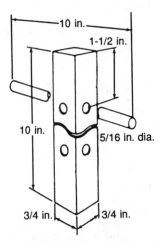

Fig. BS112—Use 3/4-inch square stock to fabricate a spring rewind tool to the dimensions shown.

spring, spring adapter and pulley into rewind housing and bend tang using B&S tool 19229 to bend and adjust tang gap to ¹⁄₁₆ inch (1.6 mm) minimum.

Fabricate a rewind tool (Fig. BS112) and wind pulley counterclockwise until spring is wound tight. Unwind one turn or until hole in pulley for rope knot and eyelet in blower housing are aligned. Lock spring securely in smaller portion of tapered hole. Reinstall rope.

To disassemble starter clutch unit, refer to Fig. BS105 and proceed as follows: Remove rotating screen (2) and starter ratchet cover (4). Lift ratchet (5) from housing and crankshaft and extract the steel balls (6). If necessary to remove housing (7), hold flywheel and unscrew housing in counterclockwise direction. When installing housing, be sure spring washer (8) is in place on crankshaft with cup (hollow) side toward flywheel; then, tighten housing securely. Inspect felt seal and plug in outer end of ratchet. Renew ratchet if seal or plug is damaged as these parts are not serviced separately. Lubricate the felt with oil and place ratchet on crankshaft. Insert the steel balls and install ratchet cover, rubber seal and rotating screen.

Vanguard Models

Refer to Fig. BS113 for exploded view of rewind starter. When installing the starter, position starter on blower housing then pull out starter rope until dogs engage starter cup. Continue to place tension on rope and tighten starter mounting screws to 60 in.-lbs. (7 N·m).

To install a new rope, proceed as follows. Rope length should be 70 in. (178 cm). Remove starter and extract old rope from pulley. Allow pulley to unwind then turn pulley counterclockwise until spring is tightly wound. Rotate pulley

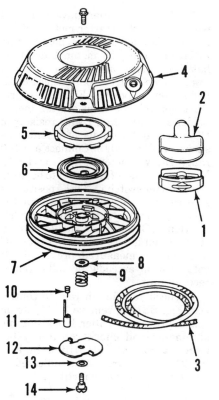

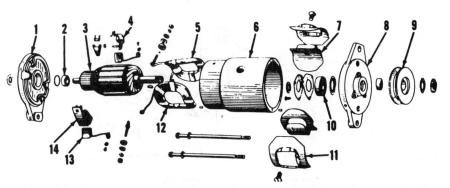

Fig. BS115—Exploded view of Delco-Remy starter-generator used on some engines.

1. Commutator end frame	5. Field coil (left)	8. Drive end frame	11. Field coil insulator
2. Bearing	6. Frame	9. Pulley	12. Field coil (right)
3. Armature	7. Pole shoe	10. Bearing	13. Brush
4. Ground brush holder			14. Insulated brush holder

Fig. BS113—Exploded view of rewind starter used on Vanguard models.

1. Insert	8. Washer
2. Rope handle	9. Brake spring
3. Rope	10. Spring
4. Housing	11. Dog
5. Spring cup	12. Retainer
6. Rewind spring	13. Washer
7. Pulley	14. Screw

clockwise until rope hole in pulley is aligned with rope outlet in housing. Pass rope through pulley hole and housing outlet and tie a temporary knot near handle end of rope. Release pulley and allow rope to wind onto pulley. Install rope handle, release temporary knot and allow rope to enter starter.

To disassemble starter, remove rope handle and allow pulley to totally unwind. Unscrew pulley retaining screw. Remove retainer (12—Fig. BS113), dogs (11), springs (10) and brake spring (9). Wear appropriate safety eyewear and

gloves before disengaging pulley from starter as spring may uncoil uncontrolled. Place shop towel around pulley and lift pulley out of housing; spring should remain with pulley. Do not attempt to separate spring from cup as they are a unit assembly.

Inspect components for damage and excessive wear. Reverse disassembly procedure to install components. Be sure inner end of rewind spring engages spring retainer adjacent to housing center post. Tighten screw (13) to 70 in.-lbs. (8 N•m). Install rope as previously outlined.

12-VOLT STARTER-GENERATOR UNITS

The combination starter-generator functions as a cranking motor when the starting switch is closed. When engine is operating and with the starting switch open, unit operates as a generator. Generator output and circuit voltage for battery and various operating requirements are controlled by a current-voltage regulator. On units where voltage regulator is mounted separately from generator unit, do not mount regulator with cover down as regulator will not function in this position.

To adjust belt tension, apply approximately 30 pounds (13.6 kg) pull on generator adjusting flange and tighten

mounting bolts. Belt tension is correct when a pressure of 10 pounds (44.5 N) applied midway between pulleys will deflect belt ¼ inch (6.4 mm). See Fig. BS114. On units equipped with two drive belts, always renew belts in pairs. A 50-ampere capacity battery is recommended. Starter-generator units are intended for use in temperatures above 0° F (−18° C). Refer to Fig. BS115 for exploded view of starter-generator. Parts and service on starter-generator are available at authorized Delco-Remy service stations.

GEAR DRIVE STARTERS

Gear drive starters manufactured by Briggs & Stratton, American Bosch or Mitsubishi may be used, either as a 110-volt AC starter or a 12-volt DC starter. Refer to Figs. BS116 and BS117 for exploded views of starter motors. A properly grounded receptacle should be used with power cord connected to 110-volt AC starter motor. A 32-ampere hour capacity battery is recommended for use with 12-volt starter motor.

CAUTION: Do not clamp starter motor housing in a vise or strike housing as some motors have ceramic field magnets that may be damaged.

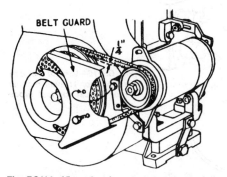

Fig. BS114—View showing starter-generator belt adjustment on models so equipped. Refer to text.

Fig. BS116—Exploded view of 110-volt AC starter motor. A 12-volt version is similar. Rectifier and switch unit (8) is used on 110-volt starter motor only.

1. Pinion gear
2. Helix
3. Armature shaft
4. Drive cap
5. Thrust washer
6. Housing
7. End cap
8. Rectifier & switch unit
9. Bolt
10. Nut

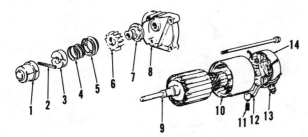

Fig. BS117—Exploded view of 12-volt starter motor used on some models.

1. Cap
2. Roll pin
3. Retainer
4. Pinion spring
5. Spring cup
6. Starter gear
7. Clutch assy.
8. Drive end cap assy.
9. Armature
10. Housing
11. Spring
12. Brush assy.
13. Battery wire terminal
14. Commutator end cap assy.

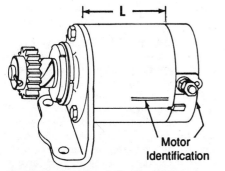

Fig.BS118—On Briggs & Stratton starters, measure length (L) of starter housing to determine correct test specifications. See text.

To renew a worn or damaged flywheel ring gear, drill out retaining rivets using a ³⁄₁₆-inch drill bit. Attach the new ring gear using screws provided with new ring gear.

To check for correct operation of starter motor, remove starter motor from engine and place motor in a vise or other holding fixture. Install a 0-5 amp ammeter in power cord to 110-volt AC starter motor. On 12-volt DC motor, connect a 12-volt battery to motor with a 0-50 amp ammeter in series with positive line from battery to starter motor. Connect a tachometer to drive end of starter motor. Determine manufacturer of starter motor and refer to following table for test specifications (note that some motors are tested using a 6-volt battery). If Briggs & Stratton manufactured the 12-volt starter motor, measure housing length (except on Vanguard models) as shown in Fig. BS118.

12-Volt Starter Motor

Starter Motor	Minimum Rpm	Maximum Amps
B&S		
3 in.	6500	18
3¹⁄₁₆ in.	6500	18
3⁵⁄₈ in.	6500	18
3¹³⁄₁₆ in.	6900	19
3²¹⁄₃₂ in.	6500	18
3³⁄₄ in.	6900	19
4³⁄₈ in.	6500	20
4½ in.	6500	35
Vanguard	6500	35
Bosch		
SME-12A-8*	5000	25
SMH-12A-11	4800	16
1965-23-		
MO-30-SM	5500	16
Mitsubishi		
MMO-4FL*,		
MMO-5ML*,		
MOO1TO2271*	6700	16

*Use 6 volt battery for tests.

110-Volt Starter Motor

Starter Motor	Minimum Rpm	Maximum Amps
B&S	6500	2.7
Bosch		
SME-110-C3,		
SME-110-C6,		
SME-110-C8	7400	3.5
06026-28-		
M030SM	7400	3
Mitsubishi		
J282188	7800	3.5

If starter motor does not operate satisfactorily, check operation of rectifier in starter control box. If rectifier and starter switch are good, disassemble and inspect starter motor.

Two types of rectifiers have been used with 110-volt AC starter motors. Early type is contained in control box (8—Fig. BS116) mounted on motor. Later type has four prongs and can be removed from remote control box. To check rectifier in control box (8—Fig. BS116), remove control box from starter motor. Solder a 10,000 ohm, 1 watt resistor to DC internal terminals of rectifier as shown in Fig. BS119. Connect a 0-100 range DC voltmeter to resistor leads. Measure voltage of AC outlet to be used. With starter switch in "OFF" position, a zero reading should be shown on DC voltmeter. With starter switch in "ON" position, DC voltmeter should show a reading that is 0-14 volts lower than AC line voltage measured previously. If voltage drop exceeds 14 volts, renew rectifier unit.

To check rectifier in remote control box (Fig. BS120), remove backplate on box and remove rectifier. Use a suitable ohmmeter and check continuity between terminals identified in Fig. BS121. If tests are not as indicated in following table, renew rectifier.

(+) Tester Lead	(−) Tester Lead	Tester Reading
A	B	Infinity
B	A	Continuity
B	C	Infinity
C	B	Continuity
C	D	Continuity
D	C	Infinity
D	A	Continuity
A	D	Infinity

There should be no continuity between any terminal and rectifier case, otherwise, renew rectifier.

Disassembly of starter motor is self-evident after inspection of unit and referral to Figs. BS116, BS117, BS122 and BS123. Mark housing and end caps before disassembly and note position of bolts during disassembly so they can be installed in their original positions during reassembly. On Briggs & Stratton

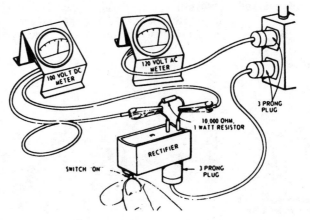

Fig. BS119—View of test connections for 110-volt rectifier. Refer to text for test procedure.

motors, minimum brush length is 1/8 inch (3.2 mm) and minimum commutator diameter is 1.23 inches (31.24 mm) for 12-volt starter and 1.32 inches (33.53 mm) for 120-volt starter. Lubricate bearings with SAE 20 oil. If so equipped, be sure to match drive cap keyway to stamped key in housing when sliding armature into motor housing. Note installation of brushes in Figs.

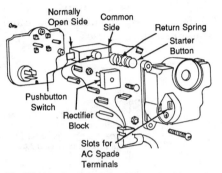

Fig. BS120—Exploded view of control unit for 110-volt AC starter motor used on some engines.

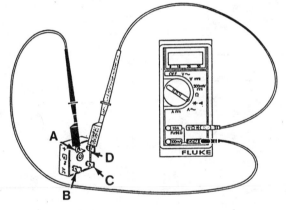

Fig. BS121—Identify terminals on rectifier as shown and refer to text for test procedure. Note that "A" is adjacent to "+" on rectifier case.

BS124, BS125, BS126 and BS127. If helix (2—Fig. BS116) is separate, splined end must be toward end of armature shaft as shown in Fig. BS128. Some early starters are equipped with shim washers to limit armature shaft end play to 0.006-0.038 inch (0.15-0.96 mm). Tighten armature shaft nut on models so equipped to 170 in.-lbs. (19 N m). Tighten through-bolts if 10-24 to 40-45 in.-lbs. (4.5-5.1 N•m), or if 1/4-20 to 45-55 in.-lbs. (5.1-6.2 N•m). On models equipped with a retaining pin (Figs. BS122 or BS123), install pin so split is toward end of armature shaft. Note position of drive components in Figs. BS122 and BS123.

ALTERNATOR

Type of alternator used can be identified by noting configuration, color of stator leads and wire connector. Refer to Figs. BS129 through BS158. Identify type to be serviced and refer to appropriate following section.

3-Amp DC Alternator

The 3-amp DC alternator (Fig. BS129) is regulated only by engine speed and provides 2- to 3-amp charging current to maintain battery state of charge.

To check output, connect an ammeter in series with red lead, start engine and run at 2400 rpm. Ammeter should show

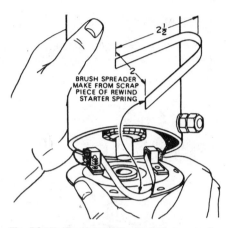

Fig. BS124—Brush retaining tool shown can be fabricated to hold type of brushes shown when installing motor end cap.

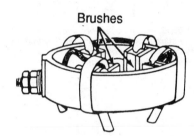

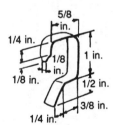

Fig. BS125—To hold brushes shown while assembling starter motor, a brush retainer tool can be fabricated from a piece of rewind starter spring using the dimensions shown.

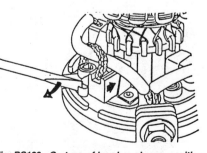

Fig. BS126—On type of brushes shown, position end of retaining spring against rear of brush as shown to hold brush in guide.

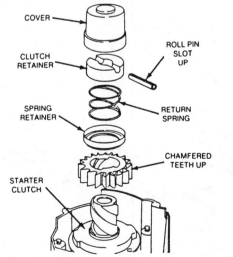

Fig. BS122—Exploded view of starter drive used on some early production starters.

Fig. BS123—Exploded view of starter drive used on some current production starters.

2-amp charging current. Increase engine speed to 3600 rpm. Ammeter should show 3-amp charging current. If charging current is not as specified, stop engine and connect an ohmmeter lead to laminations of stator and connect remaining ohmmeter lead to red stator lead. Ohmmeter should indicate continuity. If not, renew stator. If continuity is indicated, but system fails to produce charging current, inspect magnets in flywheel.

4-Amp Alternator

Some engines are equipped with the 4-amp alternator shown in Fig. BS130

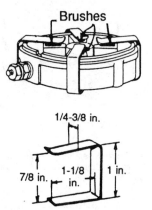

Fig. BS127—To hold brushes shown while assembling starter motor, a brush retainer tool can be fabricated from a piece of rewind starter spring using the dimensions shown.

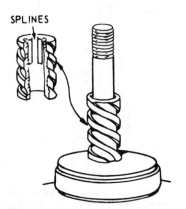

Fig. BS128—Install helix on armature so splines of helix are toward outer end of shaft as shown.

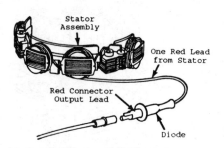

Fig. BS129—Drawing of 3-amp direct current alternator used on some models.

that is regulated only by engine speed. A solid-state rectifier and 7½-amp fuse are used with this alternator.

If the battery is run down and no output from alternator is suspected, first check the 7½-amp fuse. If the fuse is good, clean and tighten all connections. Disconnect charging lead and connect an ammeter as shown in Fig. BS131. Start engine and check for alternator output. If ammeter shows no charge, stop engine, remove ammeter and install a test lamp as shown in Fig. BS132. Test lamp should not light. If it

does light, stator or rectifier is defective. Unplug rectifier plug under blower housing. If test lamp does not go out, stator is shorted.

If shorted stator is indicated, use an ohmmeter and check continuity as follows: Touch one test lead to lead inside of fuse holder as shown in Fig. BS133. Touch remaining test lead to each of the four pins in rectifier connector. Unless ohmmeter shows continuity at each of the four pins, stator winding is open and stator must be renewed.

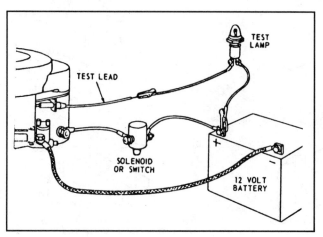

Fig. BS130—Stator and rectifier assemblies used on the 4-amp alternator. Fuse is 71/2 amp AGC or 3AG.

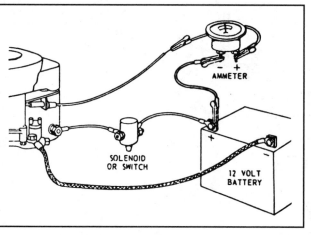

Fig. BS131—Connect ammeter as shown for output test.

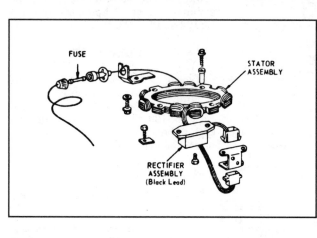

Fig. BS132—Connect a test lamp as shown to test for shorted stator or defective rectifier. Refer to text.

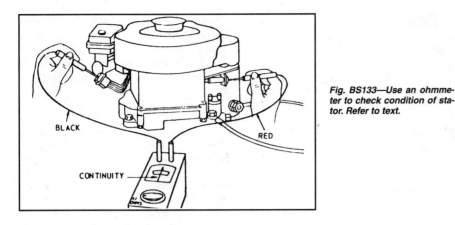

Fig. BS133—Use an ohmmeter to check condition of stator. Refer to text.

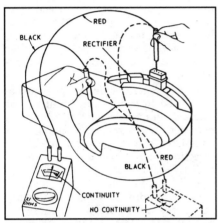

Fig. BS134—If ohmmeter shows continuity in both directions or in neither direction, rectifier is defective.

If defective rectifier is indicated, unbolt and remove flywheel blower housing with rectifier. Connect one ohmmeter test lead to blower housing and remaining test lead to the single pin connector in rectifier connector. See Fig. BS134. Check for continuity, then reverse leads and again test for continuity. If tests show no continuity in either direction or continuity in both directions, rectifier is faulty and must be renewed.

5-Amp AC Alternator

The 5-amp alternator shown in Fig. BS135 provides alternating current that is regulated only by engine speed.

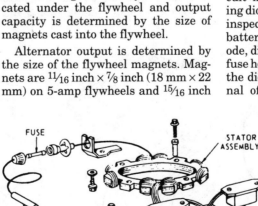

Fig. BS136—Drawing of 5-amp or 9-amp alternator and regulator used on some models.

To check alternator, connect a voltmeter to black stator lead and check voltage reading with engine running at 3600 rpm. Voltage reading should be at least 14 volts. If not, renew stator.

5-Amp And 9-Amp Regulated Alternator

The 5-amp and 9-amp alternators (Fig. BS136) provide regulated charging current. Charging rate is determined by state of charge in battery. Stator is located under the flywheel and output capacity is determined by the size of magnets cast into the flywheel.

Alternator output is determined by the size of the flywheel magnets. Magnets are $11/16$ inch $\times$ $7/8$ inch (18 mm $\times$ 22 mm) on 5-amp flywheels and $15/16$ inch

$\times$ $1^{1}/16$ inch (24 mm $\times$ 27 mm) on 16-amp flywheels.

To check stator output, disconnect green connector and connect voltmeter leads to stator lead. With engine running at 3600 rpm, voltmeter should indicate at least 28 VAC for 5-amp systems and 40 Vac for 9-amp systems. If not, renew stator.

To test regulator, the 12-volt battery must have a minimum charge of 5 volts. Connect an ammeter in series with charging circuit positive (red) lead and run engine at normal operating rpm. Test leads must be connected before starting engine and must not be disconnected while engine is running as regulator may be damaged. Ammeter should indicate a charge that will vary according to battery state of charge and capacity of alternator. If no charging current is indicated, check that wires are connected properly and regulator is grounded. Retest and renew regulator if charge current remains unsatisfactory.

7-Amp Alternator

The 7-amp regulated alternator (Fig. BS137) is equipped with a solid state rectifier and regulator. An isolation diode is also used on most models.

If engine will not start using the electric starter motor and starter motor is good, install an ammeter in circuit as shown in Fig. BS138. Start engine manually. Ammeter should indicate charge. If ammeter does not show battery charging taking place, check for defective wiring and, if necessary, proceed with troubleshooting.

If battery charging occurs with engine running, but battery does not retain charge, then isolation diode may be defective. The isolation diode is used to prevent battery drain if alternator circuit malfunctions. After troubleshooting diode, remainder of circuit should be inspected to find reason for excessive battery drain. To check operation of diode, disconnect white lead of diode from fuse holder and connect a test lamp from the diode white lead to negative terminal of battery. Test lamp should not

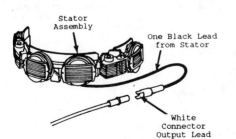

Fig. BS135—Drawing of 5-amp alternating current alternator used on some models.

Fig. BS137—Stator, rectifier and regulator assemblies used on 7-amp alternator.

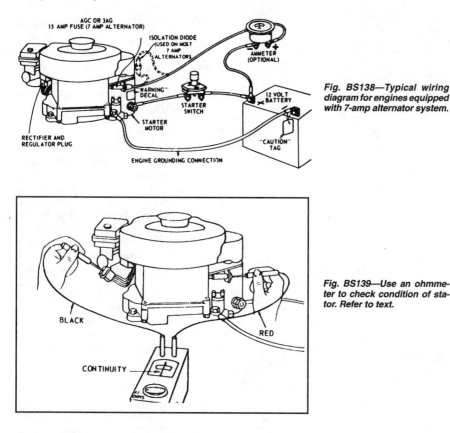

Fig. BS138—Typical wiring diagram for engines equipped with 7-amp alternator system.

Fig. BS139—Use an ohmmeter to check condition of stator. Refer to text.

negative lead to one of the pins in rectifier and regulator connector. Check each of the four pins in connector. Ohmmeter should show continuity at each pin. If not, there is an open in stator and stator must be renewed.

To test rectifier, unplug rectifier and regulator connector plug and remove blower housing from engine. Using an ohmmeter, check for continuity between connector pins connected to black wires and blower housing as shown in Fig. BS140. Be sure good contact is made with metal of blower housing. Reverse ohmmeter leads and check continuity again. Ohmmeter should show a continuity reading for only one direction on each plug. If either pin shows a continuity reading for both directions, or if either pin shows no continuity for either direction, then rectifier must be renewed.

To test regulator unit, repeat procedure used to test rectifier unit except connect ohmmeter lead to pins connected to red wire and white wire. If ohmmeter shows continuity in either direction for red lead pin, regulator is defective and must be renewed. White lead pin should read as an open on ohmmeter in one direction and a weak reading in the other direction. Otherwise, regulator is defective and must be renewed.

Early 10-Amp Alternator

Early engines may be equipped with a 10-amp regulated alternator that uses a solid state rectifier-regulator. The early 10-amp system is identified by a fuse in the system (see Fig. BS141). To check charging system, disconnect charging lead from battery. Connect a DC voltmeter between charging lead and ground as shown in Fig. BS142. Start engine and run at 3600 rpm. A voltmeter reading of 14 volts or above

light. If test lamp lights, diode is defective. Disconnect test lamp and disconnect red lead of diode. Test continuity of diode with ohmmeter by connecting leads of ohmmeter to leads of diode then reverse lead connection. Ohmmeter should show continuity in one direction and an open circuit in the other direction. If readings are incorrect, then diode is defective and must be renewed.

To troubleshoot alternator assembly, proceed as follows: Disconnect white lead of isolation diode from fuse holder and connect a test lamp between positive terminal of battery and fuse holder on engine. Engine must not be started. With connections made, test lamp should not light. If test lamp does light, stator, regulator or rectifier is defective. Unplug rectifier-regulator plug under blower housing. If lamp remains lighted, stator is grounded. If lamp goes out, regulator or rectifier is shorted.

If previous test indicated stator is grounded, check stator leads for defects and repair if necessary. If shorted leads are not found, renew stator. Check stator for an open circuit as follows: Using an ohmmeter, connect positive lead to fuse holder as shown in Fig. BS139 and

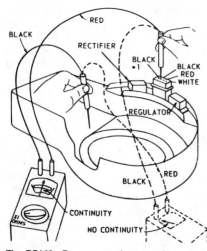

Fig. BS140—Be sure good contact is made between ohmmeter test lead and metal cover when checking rectifier and regulator.

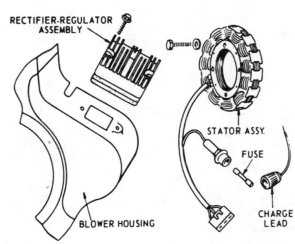

Fig. BS141—Drawing of early 10-amp alternator stator and rectifier-regulator used on some engines.

indicates alternator is functioning. If reading is less than 14 volts, stator or rectifier-regulator is defective.

To test stator, disconnect stator plug from rectifier-regulator. Run engine at 3600 rpm and connect AC voltmeter leads to AC terminals in stator plug as shown in Fig. BS143. Voltmeter reading above 20 volts indicates stator is good. A reading less than 20 volts indicates stator is defective.

To test rectifier-regulator, make certain charging lead is connected to battery and stator plug is connected to rectifier-regulator. Check voltage across battery terminals with DC voltmeter (Fig. BS144). If voltmeter reading is 13.8 volts or higher, reduce battery voltage by connecting a 12-volt load lamp across battery terminals. When battery voltage is below 13.5 volts, start engine and operate at 3600 rpm. Voltmeter reading should rise. If battery is fully charged, reading should rise above 13.8 volts. If voltage does not increase or if voltage reading rises above 14.7 volts, rectifier-regulator is defective and must be renewed.

Later 10, 13 And 16-Amp Alternator

The 10, 13 and 16-amp alternators (Fig. BS145) provide regulated charging current. Charging rate is determined by state of charge in battery. Stator is located under the flywheel and output capacity is determined by the size of magnets cast into the flywheel.

Alternator output is determined by the size of the flywheel magnets. Magnets are $11/16$ inch $\times$ $7/8$ inch (18 mm $\times$ 22 mm) on 10-amp flywheels, $11/16$ inch $\times$ $11/16$ inch (18 mm $\times$ 27 mm) on 13-amp flywheels, and $15/16$ inch $\times$ $11/16$ inch (24 mm $\times$ 27 mm) on 16-amp flywheels.

To check stator output, disconnect yellow connector and connect voltmeter leads to pins for stator leads. With engine running at 3600 rpm, voltmeter should indicate at least 20 VAC for 10-amp and 13-amp systems, and 30 VAC for 16-amp systems. If not, renew stator.

To test regulator, the 12-volt battery must have a minimum of 5-volt charge. Connect an ammeter in series with charging circuit positive (red) lead and run engine at normal operating rpm. Test leads must be connected before starting engine and must not be disconnected while engine is running as regulator may be damaged. Ammeter should indicate a charge that will vary according to battery state of charge and capacity of alternator. If no charging current is indicated, check that wires are connected properly and regulator is grounded. Retest and renew regulator if charge current remains unsatisfactory.

Early Dual Circuit Alternator

A dual circuit alternator may be used on some early engines. The early dual circuit system is identified by a fuse in the system (see Figs. BS146 or BS147). The dual circuit alternator has one circuit to provide charging current to maintain battery state of charge and a separate circuit to provide alternating current for lights. The amount of current produced is regulated only by engine speed.

The charging circuit supplies alternating current through a solid state rectifier that converts the alternating

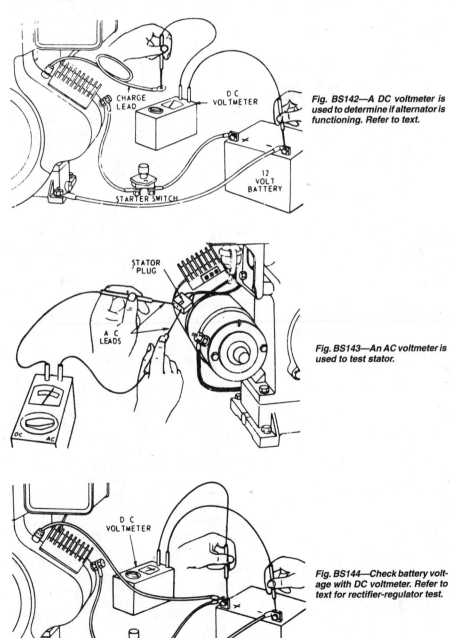

Fig. BS142—A DC voltmeter is used to determine if alternator is functioning. Refer to text.

Fig. BS143—An AC voltmeter is used to test stator.

Fig. BS144—Check battery voltage with DC voltmeter. Refer to text for rectifier-regulator test.

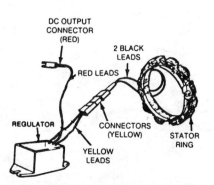

Fig. BS145—Drawing of 10, 13 or 16-amp alternator used on some later models.

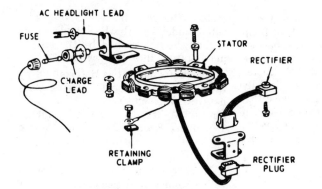

Fig. BS146—Drawing of stator and rectifier assemblies used on early dual circuit alternator system. Fuse is 7 1/2 amp AGC or 3AG.

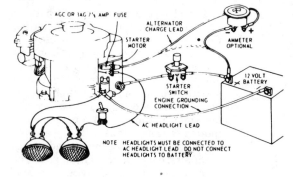

Fig. BS147—Typical wiring diagram for engines equipped with a dual circuit alternator system.

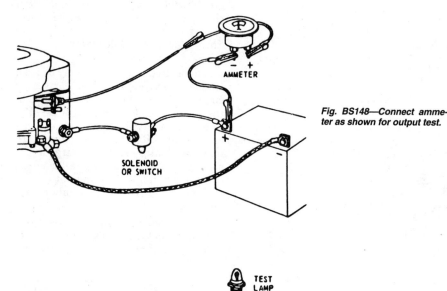

Fig. BS148—Connect ammeter as shown for output test.

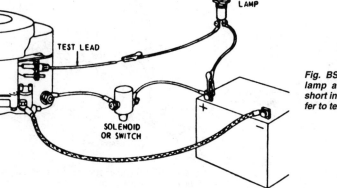

Fig. BS149—Connect a test lamp as shown to test for short in stator or rectifier. Refer to text.

current to direct current to maintain battery state of charge.

The lighting circuit provides alternating current to the lights.

The stator is located under the flywheel. A single ring of magnets cast into the flywheel creates the magnetic field for both circuits.

Current for lights is available only when engine is operating. Twelve-volt lights with a total rating of 60 to 100 watts may be used. With a rating of 70 watts, voltage rises from 8 volts at 2400 rpm to 12 volts at 3600 rpm.

Battery charging current connection is made through a 7 1/2-amp fuse mounted in a fuse holder. Current for lights is available at plastic connector below fuse holder. The 7 1/2-amp fuse protects the 3-amp charging alternator and rectifier from burn-out due to reverse polarity battery connections. The 5-amp lighting alternator does not require a fuse.

To check charging alternator output, install ammeter in circuit as shown in Fig. BS148. Start engine and operate it at 3000 rpm. Ammeter should indicate charging. If not, and fuse is known to be good, test for short in stator or rectifier as follows: Disconnect charging lead from battery and connect a small test lamp between battery positive terminal and fuse cap as shown in Fig. BS149. DO NOT start engine. Test lamp should not light. If it does light, stator's charging lead is grounded or rectifier is defective. Unplug rectifier plug under blower housing. If test lamp goes out, rectifier is defective. If test lamp does not go out, stator charging lead is grounded.

If test indicates stator charging lead is grounded, remove blower housing, flywheel, starter motor and retaining clamp, then examine length of red lead for damaged insulation or obvious shorts in lead. If bare spots are found, repair with electrical tape and shellac. If short cannot be repaired, renew stator. Charging lead should also be checked for continuity as follows: Touch one lead of ohmmeter to lead at fuse holder and other ohmmeter lead to red lead pin in connector as shown in Fig. BS150. If ohmmeter does not show continuity, charging lead is open and stator must be renewed. Charging coils should be checked for continuity as follows: Touch ohmmeter test leads to the two black lead pins as shown in Fig. BS151. If ohmmeter does not show continuity, charging coils are defective and stator must be renewed. Test for grounded charging coils by touching one test lead of ohmmeter to a clean ground surface on the engine and the other test lead to each of the black lead pins as shown in Fig. BS152. If ohmmeter shows continu-

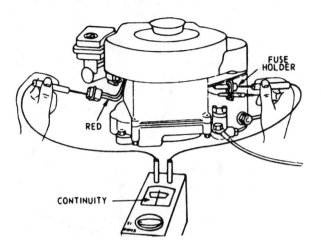

Fig. BS150—Use an ohmmeter to check charging lead for continuity. Refer to text.

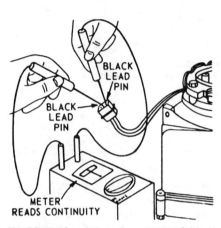

Fig. BS151—Connect an ohmmeter as shown to check charging coils for an open circuit. Meter should show continuity.

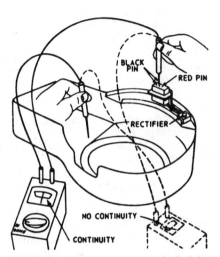

Fig. BS153—If ohmmeter shows continuity in both directions or neither direction, rectifier is defective.

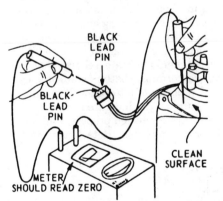

Fig. BS152—Connect an ohmmeter as shown to check charging coils for a grounded circuit. Refer to text.

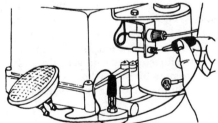

Fig. BS154—A load lamp (GE 4001 or equivalent) is used to test AC lighting circuit output.

ity, charging coils are grounded and stator must be renewed.

To test rectifier, use an ohmmeter and check for continuity between each of the three lead pin sockets and blower housing. See Fig. BS153. Reverse ohmmeter leads and check continuity again. Ohmmeter should show a continuity reading for one direction only on each lead socket. If any pin socket shows continu-

ity reading in both directions or neither direction, rectifier is defective and must be renewed.

To test AC lighting alternator circuit, connect a load lamp to AC output plug and ground as shown in Fig. BS154. Load lamp should light at full brilliance at medium engine speed. If lamp does not light or is very dim at medium speeds, remove blower housing and flywheel. Disconnect ground end of AC coil from retaining clamp screw (Fig. BS155). Connect ohmmeter between

ground lead of AC coil and AC output terminal as shown in Fig. BS155. Ohmmeter should show continuity. If not, stator must be renewed. Be sure AC ground lead is not touching a grounded surface, then check continuity from AC output terminal to engine ground. If ohmmeter indicates continuity, lighting coils are grounded and stator must be renewed.

Later Dual Circuit Alternator

Dual circuit alternator (Fig. BS156) has one circuit to provide charging current to maintain battery state of charge and a separate circuit to provide alternating current for lights. The amount of current produced is regulated only by engine speed.

The charging circuit supplies alternating current through a solid-state rectifier that converts the alternating current to direct current to maintain battery state of charge.

The lighting circuit provides alternating current to the lights.

The stator is located under the flywheel. A single ring of magnets cast into the flywheel creates the magnetic field for both circuits.

To test charging circuit output, connect an ammeter in series with the charging circuit lead (red wire). Start and run engine at 2400 rpm. Ammeter should indicate 2-amp charging current. Increase engine speed to 3600 rpm. Ammeter should indicate 3-amp charging current. If no charging current is indicated, check the diode in the connector. Attach ohmmeter lead to charging circuit connector pin in plug (a bump on the plug identifies the diode). Stick a pin through the red charging circuit wire just behind the plug and connect remaining ohmmeter lead to pin. Note reading then reverse leads. Ohmmeter should indicate continuity in only one position. If not, renew plug assembly. If diode is good, but system still does not show a charge, renew stator.

To test lighting circuit, connect an AC voltmeter in series with stator lighting circuit lead (black wire) and ground. Run engine at 3600 rpm. Voltmeter reading should be at least 14 volts. Renew stator if there is insufficient voltage.

Tri-Circuit Alternator

The tri-circuit alternator (Fig. BS157) consists of a single ring of magnets cast into the flywheel that provides a magnetic field for the stator located under the flywheel. The stator produces alternating current and has a single output lead. Circuit separation is

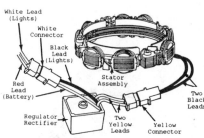

Fig. BS155—Connect an ohm-meter as shown to check AC lighting circuit for continuity. Refer to text.

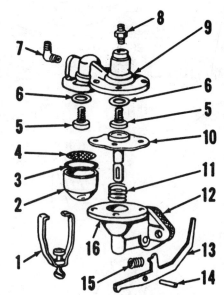

Fig. BS160—Exploded view of diaphragm-type fuel pump used on some engines.

1. Yoke assy.	9. Fuel pump head
2. Filter bowl	10. Pump diaphragm
3. Gasket	11. Diaphragm spring
4. Filter screen	12. Gasket
5. Pump valves	13. Pump lever
6. Gaskets	14. Lever pin
7. Elbow fitting	15. Spring
8. Connector	16. Fuel pump body

Fig. BS156—Drawing of later dual circuit alternator used on some models with lights.

Fig. BS158—Drawing of quad circuit alternator used on some models.

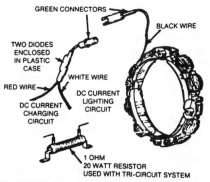

Fig. BS157—Drawing of tri-circuit alternator used on some models with lights and electric pto clutches.

achieved by the use of a positive (+) diode and a negative (-) diode. The charging lead diode rectifies negative (-) 12 VDC (5 amps at 3600 rpm) for lighting. This same charge lead contains a second diode that rectifies positive (+) 12 VDC (5 amps at 3600 rpm) for battery charging and external loads. Some equipment manufacturers incorporate one or both diodes in wiring harness. Check wiring diagram for models being serviced for diode location.

To test alternator output, connect an AC voltmeter in series between stator output lead and ground. Start and run engine at 3600 rpm. Voltmeter should register 28 volts AC or more. Voltage will vary with engine rpm. If charge current is not indicated, renew stator.

To check diodes, disconnect charge lead from stator output lead. Connect ohmmeter lead to connector pin and connect remaining lead to the white (lighting circuit) wire. Reverse connec-

tions. Ohmmeter should indicate continuity in one position only. If not, renew diode. Repeat the procedure on red wire (charging circuit).

Quad Circuit Alternator

The quad circuit alternator (Fig. BS158) provides 8-amp positive (+) DC from the red regulator lead and 8-amp negative (-) DC from the black regulator lead. Note that the black regulator wire changes to a white wire at white connector. Charging rate is determined by state of charge in battery. Stator is located under the flywheel and output capacity is determined by the size of magnets cast into the flywheel.

To check stator output, disconnect yellow connector and connect voltmeter leads to pins for stator leads. With engine running at 3600 rpm, voltmeter

should indicate at least 30 VAC. If not, renew stator.

To test regulator output, the 12-volt battery must have a minimum of 5 volt charge. Connect an ammeter in series with charging circuit positive (red) lead and start and run engine at normal operating rpm. Test leads must be connected before starting engine and must not be disconnected while engine is running as regulator may be damaged. Ammeter should indicate a charge that will vary according to battery state of charge and capacity of alternator. If no charging current is indicated, check that wires are connected properly and regulator is grounded. Retest and renew

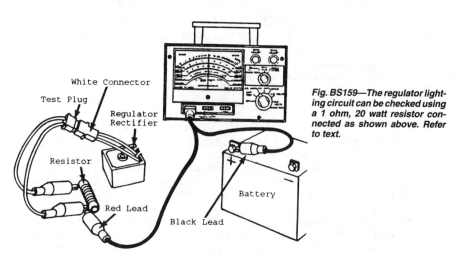

Fig. BS159—The regulator lighting circuit can be checked using a 1 ohm, 20 watt resistor connected as shown above. Refer to text.

regulator if charge current remains unsatisfactory.

To check lighting circuit of regulator, obtain a 1 ohm, 20 watt resistor. Use a suitable jumper wire and connect to white connector of regulator as shown in Fig. BS159. Connect an ammeter between resistor and battery as shown. Run engine at 3600 rpm just long enough to produce test reading. Ammeter should indicate approximately 8 amp, if not renew regulator.

FUEL PUMP

A diaphragm-type fuel pump is available on many models as optional equipment. Refer to Fig. BS160 for exploded view of pump.

To disassemble pump, refer to Figs. BS160 and BS161; then, proceed as follows: Remove clamp (1), fuel bowl (2), gasket (3) and screen (4). Remove screws retaining upper body (9) to lower body (16). Pump valves (5) and gaskets (6) can now be removed. Drive pin (14) out to either side of body (16), then press diaphragm (10) against spring (11) as shown in view A, Fig. BS161, and remove lever (13). Diaphragm and spring (11—Fig. BS160) can now be removed.

To reassemble, place diaphragm spring in lower body and place diaphragm on spring, being sure spring enters cup on bottom side of diaphragm and slot in shaft is at right angle to pump lever. Then, compressing diaphragm against spring as in view A, Fig. BS161, insert hooked end of lever with hole in lower body and drive pin into place. Then, insert lever spring (15) into body and push outer end of spring into place over hook on arm of lever as shown in view B. Hold lever downward as shown in view C while tightening screws holding upper body to lower body. When installing pump on engine, apply a liberal amount of grease on lever (13) at point where it contacts groove in crankshaft.

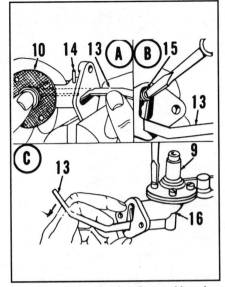

Fig. BS161—Views showing disassembly and reassembly of diaphragm-type fuel pump. Refer to text for procedure and to Fig. BS160 for exploded view of pump and parts identification.

BRIGGS & STRATTON SPECIAL TOOLS

The following special tools are available from Briggs & Stratton
Central Parts Distributors.

TOOL KITS

19138—Valve seat insert puller for all models and series so equipped.

19184—Main bearing service kit for Series 170000 and 190000.

19205—Cylinder hone kit for all aluminum bore (Kool-Bore) engines.

19211—Cylinder hone kit for all cast iron cylinder engines.

19228—Main bearing tool kit for all twin-cylinder engines with integral and DU-type main bearings, except Vanguard.

19232—Valve guide puller/reamer kit for Series 170000, 190000, 220000, 250000, 280000, 300000, 320000 and twin-cylinder engines, except Vanguard.

19237—Valve seat cutter kit for all models and series.

PLUG GAUGES

19055—Check breaker plunger bore on Model 23C and Series 170000, 190000 and 220000.

19117—Check main bearing bore on Models 19, 19D, 23, 23A, 23C, 23D and Series 190000, 200000 and 230000.

19151—Check valve guide bores on Models 19, 19D, 23, 23A, 23C, 23D and Series 170000, 190000, 200000, 230000, 240000, 250000, 300000, 320000 and twin-cylinder engines, except Vanguard.

19164—Check camshaft bearings on Series 170000, 190000, 220000 and 250000.

19219—Check integral or DU-type main bearing bore on twin-cylinder engines.

19380—Check main bearing bores on Vanguard.

19381—Check valve guide bores on Vanguard.

19384—Check camshaft bearings on Vanguard.

REAMERS

19056—Breaker plunger bushing reamer for 170000, 190000, 220000 and 250000.

19058—Finish reamer for breaker plunger bushing for Series 170000, 190000, 220000 and 250000.

19173—Finish reamer for main bearings for Series 170000 and 190000.

19174—Counterbore reamer for main bearings for Series 170000, 171000, 190000 and 191000.

19175—Finish reamer for main bearings for Series 170000, 171000, 190000 and 191000.

19183—Valve guide reamer for bushing installation for Models 19, 19D, 23, 23A, 23C, 23D and Series 170000, 190000, 200000, 220000, 230000, 240000, 251000, 300000 and 320000.

19231—Valve guide bushing reamer for Models 19 and 23 and Series 170000, 190000, 200000, 220000, 230000, 240000, 250000, 300000, 320000 and twin-cylinder engines.

19281—Counterbore reamer for main bearings for Series 170000 and 190000.

19333—Valve guide bushing finish reamer for Series 170000, 190000, 200000, 230000, 240000, 250000, 280000, 300000, 320000 and twin-cylinder engines, except Vanguard.

19346—Valve guide bushing reamer for Vanguard.

PILOTS

19096—Pilot for main bearing reamer for Series 170000, 171000, 190000 and 191000.

19127—Expansion pilot for valve seat counterbore cutter for Models 19 and 23 and Series 170000, 190000, 200000, 220000, 230000, 240000, 300000, 320000 and twin-cylinder engines.

19130—"T" handle for 19127 pilot.

REAMER GUIDE BUSHING

19192—Guide bushing for valve guide reaming for Models 19 and 23 and Series 170000, 190000, 200000,

220000, 230000, 240000, 251000, 300000 and 320000.

19201—Guide bushing for main bearing reaming for Series 171000 and 191000.

19222—Guide bushing for main bearing reaming for tool kit 19228 for twin-cylinder engines.

19234—Guide bushing for main bearing reaming for tool kit 19232 for twin-cylinder engines.

19282—Guide bushing for main bearing reaming for Series 170000 and 190000.

19301—Guide bushing for main bearing reaming for Series 170000 and 190000.

19367—Guide bushing for valve guide reaming for Vanguard.

PILOT GUIDE BUSHINGS

19168—Pilot guide bushing for main bearing reaming for Series 170000 and 190000.

19169—Pilot guide bushing for main bearing reaming for Series 170000 and 190000.

19220—Pilot guide bushing for main bearing reaming for tool lit 19228 for twin-cylinder engines.

COUNTERBORE CUTTERS

19131—Counterbore valve seat cutter for Models 19, 19D, 23, 23A, 23D and Series 190000, 200000, 230000 and 240000.

CRANKCASE SUPPORT JACK

19123—To support crankcase when removing or installing main bearings on Series 170000 and 190000.

19227—To support crankcase when removing or installing DU-type main bearings on twin-cylinder engines.

DRIVERS

19057—To install breaker plunger bushing on Series 170000, 190000, 220000 and 250000.

19136—To install valve seat inserts on all engines.

19179—To install main bearing on Series 170000 and 190000.

19344—To install main bearing retaining pin on Vanguard.

19349—To install main bearing on Vanguard.

19367—To install valve guides on Vanguard.

FLYWHEEL PULLERS

19068—Flywheel removal on Models 19, 19D, 23, 23A, 23C, 23D and Series 190000, 200000, 230000, 240000 300000 and 320000.

19165—Flywheel removal on Series 170000, 190000 and 250000.

19203—Flywheel removal on Models 19 and 23 and Series 190000, 200000, 220000, 230000, 240000, 250000, 280000, 300000, 320000 and twin-cylinder engines.

VALVE SPRING COMPRESSOR

19063—Valve spring compressor for all models and series, except Vanguard.

19347—Valve spring compressor for Vanguard.

PISTON RING COMPRESSOR

19070—Piston ring compressor for Vanguard.

19230—Piston ring compressor for all models and series, except Vanguard.

STARTER WRENCH

19114—All models and series with rewind starter.

19161—All models and series with rewind starter (to be used with ½-inch torque wrench).

19244—To remove, install and torque rewind starter clutches.

BENDING TOOL

19229—Governor tang bending tool, except Vanguard.

19352—Governor tang bending tool for Vanguard.

IGNITION SPARK TESTER

19051—Test ignition spark for all engines (except Magnamatic).

19368—Test ignition spark for Vanguard.

KAWASAKI

KAWASAKI MOTORS
P.O. Box 504
Shakopee, Minnesota 55379

Model	Bore	Stroke	Displacement
FA210V	72 mm	51 mm	207 cc
	(2.83 in.)	(2.01 in.)	(12.7 cu. in.)

ENGINE IDENTIFICATION

Kawasaki FA210V engine is four-stroke, single-cylinder, air-cooled engine. The engine model number and serial number may be located on the blower shroud or on the crankcase. The model number and serial number may be needed to order parts.

MAINTENANCE

LUBRICATION. The engine is splash lubricated. Check engine oil level prior to operation. Maintain oil level between reference marks on dipstick attached to oil fill plug. Do not screw in oil plug when checking oil level (Fig. KW21), but insert plug so it just contacts oil filler neck.

Manufacturer recommends oil with an API service classification of SF. Use SAE 5W20 oil in winter and SAE 30 oil in summer.

Oil should be changed after first 20 hours of operation and after every 100 hours of operation thereafter. Crankcase capacity is 0.6 L (1.25 pt.).

AIR FILTER. Engine is equipped with a paper (dry)-type air cleaner (Fig. KW22). The air cleaner should be removed and cleaned after every 25 hours of operation under normal operating conditions. Remove air cleaner cover and separate foam precleaner from paper element. Tap paper element lightly to dislodge dirt from element. Renew paper element if it is oily or very dirty. Wash foam precleaner in water and detergent and rinse in clean water. Allow to air dry. Soak foam precleaner in clean engine oil and carefully squeeze out excess oil. Slide precleaner over paper element and reinstall elements in air cleaner case.

SPARK PLUG. Recommended spark plug is a Champion RN11YC or equivalent. Specified spark plug electrode gap for all models is 0.7-0.8 mm (0.028-0.031 in.). Tighten spark plug to 24 N·m (212 in.-lbs.).

CARBURETOR. Engine is equipped with a float-type carburetor.

Adjust throttle control on Model FA210V as follows: Place engine throttle lever in fast position. Loosen clamp (W—Fig. KW23) and align holes in throttle control lever (T) and bracket (B) Insert a 15/64-inch drill bit through the hole (H) to prevent throttle lever from moving. Pull throttle cable housing tight and retighten cable clamp screw. Rotate choke lever screw (C) on back side of bracket so there is a gap between screw and choke control lever, then turn back in until screw just touches lever. Remove drill bit. With throttle control lever in choke position, carburetor choke plate should be closed, if not, repeat procedure.

To adjust the carburetor, turn idle mixture screw (7—Fig. KW24) clockwise until lightly seated, then turn mixture screw counterclockwise 1⅛ turns. Carburetor is equipped with a fixed main jet (13) and no high speed

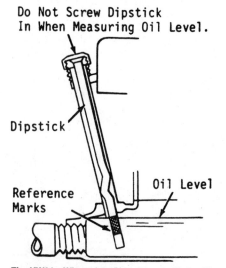

Fig. KW21—When checking oil level, oil plug/dipstick should not be screwed in, but should just touch threads.

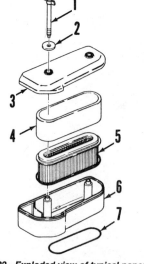

Fig. KW22—Exploded view of typical paper (dry)-type air cleaner.

1. Bolt
2. Washer
3. Cover
4. Precleaner (foam)
5. Paper element (filter)
6. Element case
7. Gasket

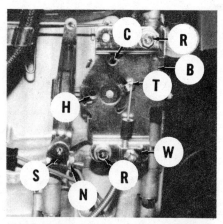

Fig. KW23—View of external governor linkage on Model FA210V. Choke control lever screw is visible through hole (C) in bracket. Refer to text for adjustment.

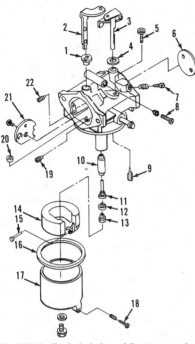

Fig. KW24—Exploded view of float-type carburetor used Model FA210V.

1. Collar
2. Choke shaft
3. Throttle shaft
4. Seal
5. Pilot jet
6. Throttle plate
7. Idle mixture screw
8. Idle speed screw
9. Fuel inlet needle
10. Main nozzle
11. Bleed pipe
12. Main jet holder
13. Main jet
14. Float
15. Pin
16. Gasket
17. Float bowl
18. Drain screw
19. Air jet
20. Collar
21. Choke plate
22. Air jet

mixture adjustment is necessary. Make final adjustment with engine running and at normal operating temperature. Adjust idle speed screw (8) so engine runs at 1500 rpm. Adjust idle mixture screw (7) so engine runs at highest idle speed, then turn mixture screw out ¼ turn. Readjust idle speed screw (8) so idle speed is 1550 rpm.

Disassembly of carburetor is evident after inspection of carburetor and referral to exploded view in Fig. KW24. Clean all parts (except plastic) with carburetor cleaning solvent. Do not use drill bits or wires to clean holes or passages as calibration of carburetor could be affected if the passages are enlarged. Rinse carburetor in warm water and dry with compressed air. Inspect all parts for wear or damage and replace as necessary.

To check float level, invert carburetor throttle body and float assembly. Float surface should be parallel to carburetor throttle body. The float level is not adjustable and float must be renewed if float level is incorrect.

GOVERNOR. A gear-driven flyweight governor assembly is located in-side engine crankcase on crankcase cover.

CAUTION: Maximum engine speed must not exceed 4000 rpm even during adjustment procedure. Engine damage may occur if engine speed exceeds 4000 rpm.

To adjust external linkage on Model FA210V, place throttle control lever in fast position. Loosen governor lever clamp nut (N—Fig. KW23), hold lever and turn governor shaft (S) as far as possible clockwise. Retighten nut. Maximum no-load engine speed should be 3350 rpm and is adjusted as follows: Run engine until normal operating temperature is reached. Align holes in throttle lever (T) and bracket (B) and insert a ¹⁵⁄₆₄ inch drill bit. Run engine under no load and determine engine speed using an accurate tachometer. If engine speed is not 3350 rpm, loosen bracket retaining screws (R) and reposition bracket to obtain desired engine speed. Retighten screws and recheck engine speed. Check choke operation as outlined in CARBURETOR section.

IGNITION SYSTEM. The engine is equipped with a breakerless electronic-type ignition system. The breakerless ignition system requires no regular maintenance. Ignition coil unit is mounted outside the flywheel. Air gap between flywheel and coil should be 0.3 mm (0.012 in.). Loosen ignition coil mounting screws and reposition coil unit as necessary to obtain desired air gap, then tighten screws.

To check ignition coil primary side, connect one ohmmeter lead to primary wire terminal on coil and touch iron coil laminations with remaining lead. Ohmmeter should register 0.4-0.8 ohm.

To check ignition coil secondary side, connect one ohmmeter lead to the spark plug lead wire (with spark plug boot removed) and remaining lead to the iron core laminations. Ohmmeter should read 10k-18k ohms. If ohmmeter readings are not as specified, renew ignition coil.

VALVE ADJUSTMENT. Valve tappet gap (engine cold) should be 0.12-0.18 mm (0.005-0.007 in.) for intake valve and 0.12-0.34 mm (0.005-0.013 in.) for exhaust valve. To check tappet gap, remove tappet chamber cover. Turn crankshaft until piston is at highest position on compression stroke. Use a feeler gauge to measure clearance between each tappet and end of valve stem.

To increase clearance, grind off end of valve stem. To reduce clearance, grind valve seat deeper or renew valve and/or valve tappet. Refer also to VALVE SYSTEM paragraphs in REPAIRS section.

When installing tappet chamber cover, position the cover so oil drain hole is down.

CYLINDER HEAD AND COMBUSTION CHAMBER. The cylinder head, combustion chamber and piston should be cleaned of carbon and other deposits after every 300 hours of operation. Refer to REPAIRS section for service procedure.

REPAIRS

TIGHTENING TORQUES. Recommended tightening torques are as follows:

Drain plug . . . . 13 N•m
(115 in.-lbs.)
Connecting rod. . . . . 19 N•m
(168 in.-lbs.)
Crankcase cover/oil
pan FA210V . . . . 21 N•m
(185 in.-lbs.)
Cylinder head. . . . . 19 N•m
(168 in.-lbs.)
Flywheel nut . . . . 60 Nm
(44 ft.-lbs.)
Spark plug . . . . 24 Nm
(212 in.-lbs.)

CYLINDER HEAD. To remove cylinder head, first remove blower housing and cylinder head shroud. Clean engine to prevent entrance of foreign material. Loosen cylinder head screws in sequence shown in Fig. KW25 and remove cylinder head.

Unscrew spark plug and clean carbon and other deposits from cylinder head. Place cylinder head on a flat surface and check entire sealing surface for distortion. If cylinder head is warped in excess of 0.40 mm (0.015 in.), cylinder head must be renewed. Slight distortion can be repaired by lapping cylinder head.

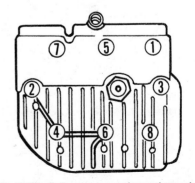

Fig. KW25—Follow sequence shown above when loosening or tightening cylinder head screws.

Engine Repair

Using a figure eight pattern, lap head against 200 grit and then 400 grit emery paper on a flat surface.

Reinstall cylinder head with a new gasket. Lubricate threads of cylinder head screws with light film of oil, then tighten screws in sequence shown in Fig. KW25 as follows: Tighten screws to initial torque of 10 N•m (89 in.-lbs.). Then continue to tighten in sequence 4 N•m (35 in.-lbs.) at a time until final torque of 21 N•m (186 in.-lbs.) is reached.

VALVE SYSTEM. To remove valves, first remove cylinder head and tappet chamber cover. Use a spring compressor to compress valve spring and remove spring retainer. Remove compressor, valve, spring and retainer. Identify valve components so they can be installed in their original positions. Tappet chamber cover should be installed with the oil drain hole positioned downward.

The valve face and seat angles should be 45° for intake and exhaust. Correct valve seat width is 1.0-1.6 mm (0.039-0.063 in.). Maximum allowable valve stem runout is 0.03 mm (0.001 in.). Minimum valve stem diameter is 5.95 mm (0.234 in.). Maximum valve guide inner diameter is 6.10 mm (0.240 in.) for intake valve and 6.13 mm (0.242 in.) for exhaust valve. Renew valves if valve head margin is less than 0.6 mm (0.020 in.). Valve spring minimum free length is 23.50 mm (0.930 in.).

CAMSHAFT. The camshaft (24—Fig. KW26) rides in bores in crankcase (4) and crankcase cover/oil pan (33). To remove camshaft, first drain engine oil and remove crankcase cover. Rotate crankshaft until timing marks on crankshaft gear and camshaft gear are aligned (Fig. KW27). Position engine so tappets (20—Fig. KW26) will not fall out, then withdraw camshaft. If valve tappets are removed, they should be marked so they can be returned to their original positions.

The camshaft is equipped with a compression release mechanism. The compression release arm (A—Fig. KW28) extends at cranking speed to hold the exhaust valve open slightly thereby reducing compression pressure. When weight (W—Fig. KW29) is extended to running position, release arm (A) must be beneath surface of cam lobe (B).

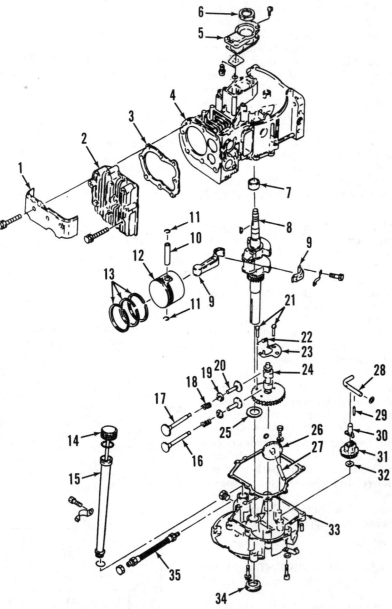

Fig. KW26—Exploded view of Model FA210V engine assembly.

1. Cover	10. Piston pin	19. Spring retainer	27. Shaft
2. Cylinder head	11. Retaining rings	20. Tappet	28. Governor arm
3. Gasket	12. Piston	21. Pins	29. Pin
4. Crankcase/cylinder block	13. Piston rings	22. Spring	30. Sleeve
5. Cover	14. Dipstick	23. Compression	31. Governor assy.
6. Oil seal	15. Oil filler tube	release plate	32. Thrust washer
7. Bushing	16. Exhaust valve	24. Camshaft	33. Crankcase cover/oil pan
8. Crankshaft	17. Intake valve	25. Spacer	34. Oil seal
9. Connecting rod	18. Valve spring	26. Oil slinger	35. Oil drain hose

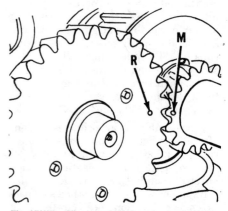

Fig. KW27—Align crankshaft and camshaft gear timing marks (R & M) as shown during assembly.

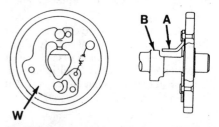

Fig. KW28—Compression release arm (A) should protrude above cam lobe (B) when weight (W) is in innermost (starting) position.

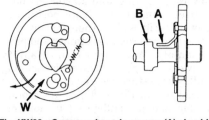

Fig. KW29—Compression release arm (A) should be beneath surface of cam lobe (B) when weight (W) is extended to running position.

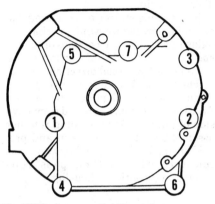

Fig. KW30—Loosen or tighten crankcase cover or oil pan screws in sequence shown.

Maximum allowable clearance between camshaft journal and crankcase cover/oil pan bore is 0.1 mm (0.004 in.). Minimum allowable camshaft journal diameter is 12.94 mm (0.509 in.). Maximum allowable crankcase cover/oil pan bore is 13.05 mm (0.514 in.). Minimum camshaft lobe height is 26.45 mm (1.041 in.) for intake valve lobe and 26.35 mm (1.037 in.) for exhaust valve lobe.

Install camshaft while aligning timing marks (Fig. KW27) on crankshaft and camshaft gears. Be sure governor weights are closed and governor gear will align with camshaft gear. Tighten crankcase cover/oil pan screws to 21 N•m (185 in.-lbs.) following sequence shown in Fig. KW30.

PISTON, PIN AND RINGS. Piston (12—Fig. KW26) and connecting rod (9) are removed as an assembly. To remove piston and connecting rod, drain oil, then clean crankshaft and remove any rust or burrs. Remove cylinder head. Unscrew crankcase cover/oil pan retaining screws and remove crankcase cover/oil pan (33). Remove connecting rod cap screws and cap. Remove ring ridge (if present) from top of cylinder bore, then push connecting rod and piston assembly out of cylinder. Remove piston pin retaining rings (11) and piston pin (10), then separate piston from connecting rod.

Maximum allowable piston-to-cylinder bore clearance is 0.25 mm (0.010 in.). Insert new second ring and oil control ring in piston ring grooves and use a feeler gauge to measure side clearance between rings and grooves. (Top ring is tapered and side clearance cannot be measured.) Renew piston if ring side clearance exceeds 0.13 mm (0.005 in.) for compression ring and 0.17 mm (0.007 in.) for oil control ring. Maximum piston ring end gap for all compression rings is 1.00 mm (0.039 in.) 1.40 mm (0.055 in.) for oil control ring.

Maximum allowable piston pin-to-piston clearance is 0.07 mm (0.0027 in.).

Install piston rings so marked side is toward piston crown. Install piston on connecting rod so the side of connecting rod that is marked "MADE IN JAPAN" is toward the "M" stamped on piston pin boss. Lubricate piston and cylinder bore with engine oil, then install piston and connecting rod so side of connecting rod marked "MADE IN JAPAN" is toward flywheel side of engine. Notch on piston crown must be toward flywheel side of engine after installation. Tighten connecting rod screws to 19 N•m (168 in.-lbs.).

CONNECTING ROD. Connecting rod rides directly on crankshaft journal on all models. Piston and connecting rod are removed as a unit. Refer to PISTON, PIN AND RINGS section for removal and installation procedures.

Inspect connecting rod and renew if piston pin bore or crankpin bearing bore are excessively worn or damaged. Renew connecting rod if clearance between piston pin and connecting rod piston pin bore exceeds 0.06 mm (0.0024 in.). Maximum allowable clearance between crankshaft crankpin and connecting rod big end is 0.11 mm (0.0043 in.).

CRANKSHAFT, MAIN BEARINGS AND SEALS. The crankshaft (8—Fig. KW26) is supported at flywheel end by bushing-type main bearing (7) that is pressed into crankcase. Pto end of crankshaft is supported directly in crankcase cover/oil pan bearing bore.

To remove crankshaft, remove all metal shrouds, flywheel, cylinder head and crankcase cover/oil pan. Remove camshaft, piston and connecting rod assembly and crankshaft.

Minimum allowable crankpin diameter is 26.95 mm (1.061 in.). Maximum allowable clearance between crankpin and connecting rod bearing bore is 0.11 mm (0.004 in.). Maximum allowable clearance between crankshaft main journals and main bearing bores is 0.13 mm (0.005 in.). When renewing bushing-type main bearing, install bushing

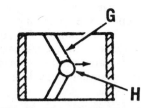

Fig. KW31—If crankcase bushing has oil grooves (G), install bushing so grooves point in direction that is opposite crankshaft rotation. Oil hole (H) must be aligned with hole in crankcase.

so oil grooves (G—Fig. KW31) point in direction that is opposite to crankshaft rotation. Make sure oil hole (H) in bushing is aligned with oil hole in crankcase. Press bushing in 1 mm (0.039 in.) below inside edge of bushing bore.

Crankcase cover/oil pan oil seal (34—Fig. KW26) should be pressed into seal bore until it is 4 mm (0.158 in.) below outer edge of seal bore. Crankcase crankshaft seal (6) should be pressed into seal bore until flush with outer edge of seal bore.

When installing crankshaft, make certain timing marks on crankshaft gear and camshaft gear are aligned as shown in Fig. KW27. Crankshaft end play should be 0.00-0.30 mm (0.000-0.012 in.). Install shims as needed on pto end of crankshaft to obtain desired end play. Tighten crankcase cover/oil pan screws to 21 N•m (185 in.-lbs.) following sequence shown in Fig. KW30.

CYLINDER AND CRANKCASE. Cylinder and crankcase are an integral casting (4—Fig. KW26). Standard cylinder bore size is 72.00 mm (2.835 in.) and wear limit is 72.06 mm (2.837 mm). If cylinder bore is excessively worn or damaged, cylinder may be bored for installation of oversize piston and rings.

GOVERNOR. The internal centrifugal flyweight governor is gear-driven off of the camshaft gear. Refer to GOVERNOR paragraph in MAINTENANCE section for external governor adjustments.

To remove governor assembly (items 28 through 32—Fig. KW26), remove external linkage, metal cooling shrouds and crankcase cover/oil pan (33). Governor gear (31) and flyweights are attached to crankcase cover/oil pan. Remove governor sleeve (30), gear (31) and flyweight assembly only if renewal is necessary. Use a screwdriver to press lock tabs in to remove sleeve (30).

NOTE: Removing governor assembly from shaft will damage governor and require installation of a new governor assembly.

Remove governor assembly by prying or pulling off shaft. Shaft must protrude above boss 32.2-32.8 mm (1.27-1.29 in.). Be sure to install thrust washer (32) between gear and crankcase cover/oil pan. Install governor by pushing down until it snaps onto the locating groove. Adjust external linkage as outlined in MAINTENANCE section.

REWIND STARTER. To disassemble starter, remove rope handle and allow rope to wind into starter. Remove starter from engine. Note position of pawl (4—Fig. KW32), then unscrew center screw and remove retainer and pawl assembly. Wear appropriate safety eyewear and gloves before disengaging pulley from starter as spring may uncoil uncontrolled. Place shop towel around pulley and lift pulley out of housing; spring should remain with pulley. If spring must be removed from pulley, position pulley so spring side is down and against floor, then tap pulley to dislodge spring.

Reassemble starter by reversing disassembly procedure while noting the following: Lightly grease sides of rewind spring and pulley. Install rewind spring (7) in pulley (6) so coil direction is counterclockwise from outer spring end. Wind rope around pulley in counterclockwise direction as viewed from pawl side of pulley. After installing retainer assembly, hold rope in notch and preload spring by turning pulley two turns counterclockwise then pass rope through rope outlet in housing.

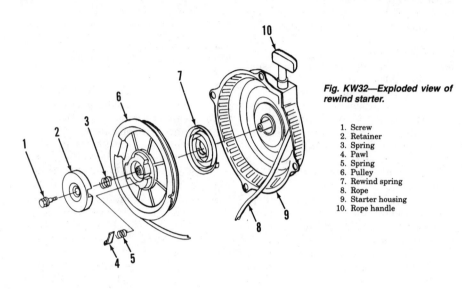

Fig. KW32—Exploded view of rewind starter.

1. Screw
2. Retainer
3. Spring
4. Pawl
5. Spring
6. Pulley
7. Rewind spring
8. Rope
9. Starter housing
10. Rope handle

KAWASAKI

KAWASAKI MOTORS CORP. USA
P.O. Box 504
Shakopee, Minnesota 55379

Model	No. Cyls.	Bore	Stroke	Displacement	Power Rating
FB460V-AS, FB460V-BS	1	89 mm (3.5 in.)	74 mm (2.9 in.)	460 cc (28.1 cu. in.)	9.3 kW (12.5 hp.)

ENGINE IDENTIFICATION

Model FB460V is a four-stroke, single-cylinder air-cooled engine with a vertical crankshaft, pressurized lubrication and reciprocating balancer. Engine develops 9.3 kW (12.5 hp.) at 3600 rpm.

MAINTENANCE

SPARK PLUG. Recommended spark plug is a Champion RCJ8 or equivalent.

Spark plug should be removed, cleaned and electrode gap set to 0.6-0.7 mm (0.024-0.028 in.) after every 100 hours of operation. Renew spark plug if electrode is severely burnt or damaged.

NOTE: Caution should be exercised if abrasive type spark plug cleaner is used. Inadequate cleaning procedure may allow the abrasive cleaner to be deposited in engine cylinder causing rapid wear and premature failure of engine components.

CARBURETOR. All models are equipped with a float type side draft carburetor. Carburetor adjustment should be checked after every 50 hours of operation or whenever poor or erratic performance is noted.

Engine idle speed (no-load rpm) should be 1350-1450 rpm. Adjust idle speed by turning throttle stop screw (1–Fig. KW110) clockwise to increase idle speed or counterclockwise to decrease idle speed. Initial adjustment of pilot screw (2) from a lightly seated position is 1⅛ turns open.

Make final adjustments with engine at operating temperature and running. Adjust pilot screw (2) to obtain maximum engine rpm, then turn pilot screw out (counterclockwise) ¼ turn more. Adjust throttle stop screw (1) so engine idles at 1350-1450 rpm. Main fuel mixture is controlled by a fixed jet.

Standard pilot jet (3) size is number 47.5 for all models. Standard main fuel jet (13) is number 112.5 for Model

FB460V-AS and number 115 for Model FB460V-BS.

Float should be parallel to carburetor float bowl mating surface when float tab just touches inlet needle valve. Carefully bend float tab to adjust.

AIR FILTER. The air filter element should be removed and cleaned after the first 10 hours of operation and every 25 hours of operation thereafter. Paper element (5–Fig. KW111) should be renewed after 300 hours of operation.

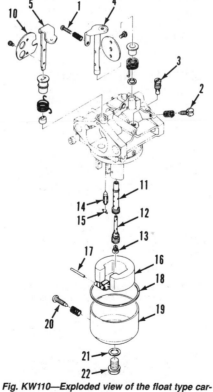

Fig. KW110—Exploded view of the float type carburetor used on all models.

1. Throttle stop screw	14. Fuel inlet needle
2. Pilot screw	15. Clip
3. Pilot jet	16. Float
4. Throttle plate shaft	17. Float pin
5. Choke plate shaft	18. Gasket
10. Choke plate	19. Float bowl
11. Main nozzle	20. Drain screw
12. Bleed pipe	21. Washer
13. Main jet	22. Plug

To remove filter elements (4 and 5), remove the two wing bolts (1) and washers (2). Remove cover (3) and elements (4 and 5). Separate foam element (4) from paper element (5). Clean foam element in solution of warm water and detergent, then squeeze out water and allow to air dry. Soak element in SAE 30 motor oil and squeeze out excess oil. Clean paper element (5) by tapping element gently to remove dust. DO NOT use compressed air to clean element. DO NOT wash paper element. Inspect for holes or damage. Reinstall by reversing removal procedure.

GOVERNOR. A gear driven flyweight governor assembly is located inside engine crankcase. To adjust external linkage, place engine throttle control in "FAST" position. Make certain all linkage is in good condition and that tension spring (4–Fig. KW112) is not stretched. Spring (2) around governor-

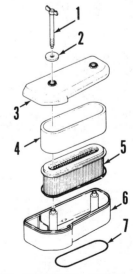

Fig. KW111—Exploded view of air filter assembly.

1. Wing bolt	
2. Washer	5. Paper element
3. Cover	6. Housing
4. Foam element	7. "O" ring

to-carburetor rod must pull governor lever (3) and throttle lever toward each other. Loosen clamp bolt (5) nut on governor lever (3). Turn governor shaft (6) clockwise as far as possible. Tighten clamp bolt (5) nut. Speed control lever (7) should be at wide open position, but choke should not be activated. Adjusting choke setting screw (9) controls choke action.

IGNITION SYSTEM. All models are equipped with a transistor ignition system and regular maintenance is not required. Ignition timing is nonadjustable. Ignition coil is located outside flywheel. Ignition coil edge air gap should be 0.3 mm (0.01 in.).

To test ignition coil, remove cooling shrouds and ignition coil and refer to Fig. KW113. Connect one ohmmeter lead to coil core and remaining lead to high tension (spark plug) terminal. Secondary coil resistance should be 10,000-18,000 ohms. Remove the lead connected to high tension (spark plug) terminal and reconnect lead to primary terminal. Primary coil resistance should be 0.4-0.5 ohms. If readings are not as specified, renew ignition coil.

To test control unit, refer to Fig. KW114 and disconnect all electrical leads. Connect positive ohmmeter lead to terminal (T) and negative ohmmeter lead to ground lead or control unit case (G) according to model being serviced. Ohmmeter reading should be 10-40 ohms. Reverse leads. Ohmmeter reading should be 3-4 ohms. If ohmmeter readings are not as specified, renew control unit.

VALVE ADJUSTMENT. Valves and seats should be refaced and stem clearance adjusted after every 300 hours of operation. Refer to VALVE SYSTEM in REPAIRS section for service procedure and specifications.

CYLINDER HEAD AND COMBUSTION CHAMBER. Standard compression reading should be 380 kPa (55 psi). Excessive carbon build up on piston and cylinder head is indicated by higher than standard compression reading. A

leaking cylinder head gasket, worn piston rings and cylinder bore or poorly seated valves are indicated by lower than standard compression reading. Cylinder head, combustion chamber and piston should be cleaned and carbon and other deposits removed after every 300 hours of operation. Refer to CYLINDER HEAD in REPAIRS section for service procedure.

LUBRICATION. Engine oil level should be checked prior to each operating interval. Oil should be maintained between reference marks on dipstick with dipstick just touching first threads. Do not screw dipstick in to check oil level (Fig. KW115).

Manufacturer recommends oil with an API service classification SF, SE/CC, SE or SD. Use SAE 5W-20 oil when temperature is below 0° C(32° F) and SAE 30 oil when temperature is above 0° C (32° F).

Oil should be changed after 25 hours of operation if engine is not equipped with an oil filter or after 50 hours of operation if engine is equipped with an oil filter. Crankcase capacity is 1.4 L (2.96 pt.) for all models.

Oil pressure is regulated by an oil pressure relief valve located inside crankcase beside oil pump. Oil pressure should be 29.4 kPa (4.26 psi) at 3000 rpm. Oil pressure sensor (as equipped) should light when oil pressure falls below 29.4 kPa (4.26 psi).

GENERAL MAINTENANCE. Check and tighten all loose bolts, nuts or clamps prior to each day of operation.

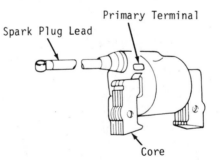

Fig. KW113—View of ignition coil showing location of primary terminal, spark plug lead and iron core.

Check for fuel or oil leakage and repair if necessary.

Clean dust, dirt, grease or any foreign material from cylinder head and cylinder block cooling fins after every 100 hours of operation. Inspect fins for damage and repair if necessary.

REPAIRS

TIGHTENING TORQUES. Recommended tightening torques are as follows:

Spark plug	28 N·m (20 ft.-lbs.)
Head bolts	34-39 N·m (25-29 ft.-lbs.)
Connecting rod bolts	19-20 N·m (14-15 ft.lbs.)

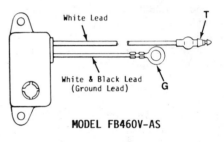

MODEL FB460V-AS

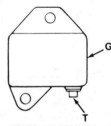

MODEL FB460V-BS

Fig. KW114—Model FB460V-AS is equipped with the control unit shown in upper view and Model FB460V-BS is equipped with the control unit shown in lower view.

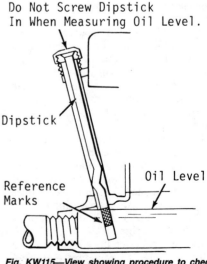

Fig. KW115—View showing procedure to check crankcase oil level. Refer to text.

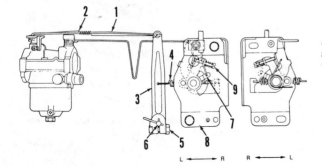

Fig. KW112—View of external governor linkage used on all models.
1. Governor-to-carburetor rod
2. Spring
3. Governor lever
4. Tension spring
5. Clamp bolt
6. Governor shaft
7. Speed control lever
8. Control plate
9. Choke setting screw

Crankcase

cover bolts . . . . 17-23 N·m
(12-17 ft.-lbs.)

Oil pump cover . . . . 17-23 N·m
(12-17 ft.-lbs.)

Flywheel . . . . 83-88 N·m
(62-65 ft.-lbs.)

CYLINDER HEAD. To remove cylinder head, first remove cylinder head shroud. Clean engine to prevent entrance of foreign material. Loosen the six cylinder head bolts and the three cylinder head stud nuts in ¼-turn increments following sequence shown in Fig. KW116 until all bolts are loose enough to remove by hand.

Remove spark splug and clean carbon and other deposits from cylinder head. Place cylinder head on a flat surface and check entire sealing surface for warpage. If warpage exceeds 0.4 mm (0.015

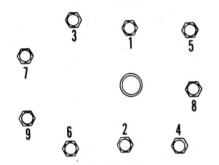

Fig. KW116—Cylinder head bolts and nuts must be tightened evenly to the recommended torque following the sequence shown.

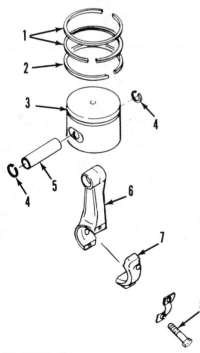

Fig. KW117—Exploded view of piston and connecting rod assembly.

1. Compression rings
2. Oil control ring
3. Piston
4. Retaining rings
5. Piston pin
6. Connecting rod
7. Connecting rod cap
8. Bolts

in.), cylinder head must be renewed. Slight warpage may be repaired by lapping cylinder head. In a figure eight pattern, lap head on a flat surface against 200 grit and then 400 grit emery paper.

Reinstall cylinder head and tighten bolts and nuts evenly to specified torque following sequence shown in Fig. KW116.

CONNECTING ROD. Connecting rod rides directly on crankshaft journal. Piston and connecting rod are removed as an assembly after removing cylinder head and splitting crankcase. Remove the two connecting rod bolts (8 – Fig. KW117) and connecting rod cap (7). Push piston and connecting rod assembly out through the top of cylinder block. Remove retaining rings (4) and push piston pin (5) out of piston to separate piston (3) from connecting rod (6). Use new retaining rings (4) during reassembly.

Maximum inside diameter for connecting rod small end is 21.039 mm (0.8283 in.) and maximum inside diameter for standard connecting rod big end bearing surface is 37.066 mm (1.4593 in.). A connecting rod is available for an undersize crankshaft journal. Inside diameter for undersize connecting rod big end bearing surface should be 36.5 mm (1.437 in.). Refer to CRANKSHAFT AND BALANCER section.

PISTON, PIN AND RINGS. Piston and connecting rod are removed as an assembly. Refer to CONNECTING ROD for removal and installation procedure.

After separating piston and connecting rod, carefully remove piston rings and clean carbon and other deposits from piston surface and piston ring lands.

CAUTION: Extreme care should be exercised when cleaning piston ring lands. Do not damage squared edges or widen piston ring grooves. If piston ring lands are damaged, piston must be renewed.

If piston pin bore in piston exceeds 21.028 mm (0.8279 in.), renew piston. Piston pin outside diameter is 20.978 mm (0.8259 in.). If piston pin diameter is less than specified, renew piston pin.

If ring groove exceeds 2.120 mm (0.0835 in.) for top ring groove, 2.095 mm (0.0825 in.) for second ring groove or 4.055 mm (0.1596 in.) for oil ring groove, renew piston.

Piston ring thickness is 1.945 mm (0.0766 in.) for top ring and 1.941 mm (0.0764 in.) for second ring. Renew ring if thickness is less than specified.

Piston ring end gap is measured by placing piston ring into cylinder bore and using the top of the piston to press

piston ring squarely into cylinder bore. Piston ring end gap should be 0.7 mm (0.028 in.) for top and second ring. If piston ring gap is greater than specified, check cylinder bore for wear. If cylinder bore is within limits, then renew piston ring.

During reassembly, install piston on connecting rod so arrow on top of piston is toward the "MADE IN JAPAN" side of connecting rod. Install piston in cylinder so arrow on top of piston is toward flywheel side of engine.

Oversize pistons are available in 0.25 mm (0.010 in.), 0.50 mm (0.020 in.) and 0.75 mm (0.030 in.) sizes and cylinder can be bored or honed to 89.230-89.250 mm (3.51299-3.51378 in.) for the 0.25 mm (0.010 in.) oversize piston, 89.480-89.500 mm (3.52283-3.52362 in.) for the 0.50 mm (0.020 in.) oversize piston and to 89.730-89.750 mm (3.53268-3.53346 in.) for the 0.75 mm (0.030 in.) oversize piston.

CYLINDER, CRANKCASE, MAIN BEARINGS AND SEALS. Cylinder and crankcase are an integral casting. Standard cylinder bore diameter is 88.980-89.000 mm (3.5031-3.5039 in.). Maximum bore out-of-round is 0.063 mm (0.0025 in.). Cylinder may be bored or honed to fit oversize pistons.

The main bearing on pto side is an integral part of cylinder and crankcase assembly. Main bearing on flywheel side is a ball bearing. Inside diameter for the integral bearing on pto side is 35.061 mm (1.3804 in.). Ball bearing on flywheel side should be a press fit on crankshaft and in bearing bore of crankcase cover.

Renew crankcase seals if removed. Pack seals with high temperature grease prior to installation. Press flywheel side crankshaft oil seal into seal bore in crankcase cover until flush with housing. Press pto side crankshaft oil seal into cylinder and crankcase assembly seal bore so outside edge of seal is 0.5 mm (0.02 in.) below seal bore surface.

When installing crankcase cover, tighten crankcase cover bolts to specified torque following sequence shown in Fig. KW118.

CRANKSHAFT AND BALANCER. Crankshaft is supported on flywheel side by a ball bearing type main bearing and on pto side by a plain type bearing which is an integral casting with cylinder and crankcase assembly. To remove crankshaft, remove all metal shrouds, flywheel, fan housing and cylinder head. Remove crankcase cover. Remove piston and connecting rod assembly. Remove governor shaft retaining pin and remove governor shaft.

Rotate crankshaft until timing marks on crankshaft gear and camshaft gear are aligned. Remove camshaft. Mark locations and remove valve tappets. Rotate crankshaft carefully until crankpin is down toward balancer weight. Remove balancer guide (16 – Fig. KW120). Remove crankshaft and balancer weight.

Clean and inspect crankshaft and balancer link rods. Crankshaft main journal diameter on flywheel side should be 34.945 mm (1.3757 in.). Crankshaft main journal diameter on pto side should be 34.914 mm (1.3746 in.).

Standard connecting rod bearing journal diameter should be 36.934 mm (1.4541 in.). Connecting rod bearing journal may be reground to a diameter of 36.47-36.48 mm (1.4357-1.4362 in.) and a special undersize connecting rod must be used. Refer to Fig. KW119 and CONNECTING ROD.

Diameter of crankshaft balancer link rod journals should be 53.951 mm (2.12406 in.). Maximum inside diameters of balancer link rod big end bushings is 54.121 mm (2.13074 in.). If diameters are greater than specified, press old bushings out of balancer link rods and press new bushings in until bushings are 0.5 mm (0.02 in.) below flange surface of balancer link rods. Maximum small end inside diameter of balancer link rods is 12.059 mm (0.4748 in.). If diameters are

greater than specified, balancer link rods must be renewed.

Balancer weight bushing inside diameter should be 26.097 mm (1.02744 in.). If bushing diameter is greater than specified, press old bushing out, align oil hole in new bushing with oil hole in balancer weight and press new bushing into bushing bore until 0.5 mm (0.02 in.) below balancer weight. Make certain oil holes are aligned.

Balancer guide (16 – Fig. KW120) outside diameter should be 25.927 mm (1.0208 in.). If diameter is less than specified, renew balancer guide.

To reinstall crankshaft, install link rods, collars, gear, bearing and balancer weight. Oil grooves in link rods must

face toward connecting rod after installation and oil hole in balancer weight must face flywheel side of engine. Install crankshaft with connecting rod journal at bottom dead center (BDC). Align center hole of balancer weight and support shaft hole in crankcase. Install "O" ring (15 – Fig. KW120) on balancer guide (16) and install balancer guide. Install piston and connecting rod assembly making certain the arrow on top of piston is toward flywheel side of engine. Install connecting rod cap with match marks aligned and tighten connecting rod bolts to specified torque. Install valve tappets in the tappet bores from which they were removed. Install governor shaft (10). Carefully rotate

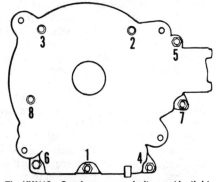

Fig. KW118—Crankcase cover bolts must be tightened evenly to the recommended torque following the sequence shown.

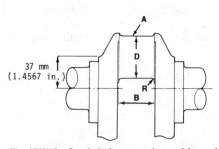

Fig. KW119—Crankshaft connecting rod journal (A) may be reground tot he dimensions shown and a special undersized connecting rod must be used.

D. 36.467-36.480 mm (1.4357-1.4362 in.)
R. 2.30-2.70 mm (0.09-0.11 in.)
B. 32.3 mm (1.272 in.)

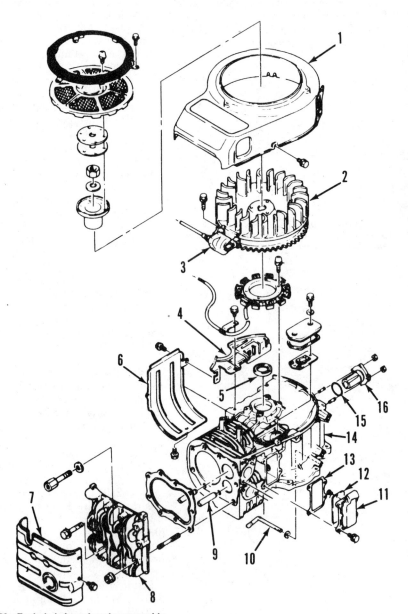

Fig. KW120—Exploded view of engine assembly.

1. Blower housing	6. Cooling shroud	10. Governor shaft	14. Cylinder block &
2. Flywheel	7. Cooling shroud	11. Valve chamber cover	crankcase
3. Coil	8. Cylinder head	12. Cover	15. "O" ring
4. Shroud	9. Valve guide	13. Gasket	16. Balancer guide
5. Oil seal			

crankshaft until piston is at top dead center (TDC).

Align crankshaft and camshaft gear timing marks and install camshaft. Measure distance from crankcase cover mounting surface to pto shaft bearing edge as shown at (A – Fig. KW121) and note dimension. Measure distance from crankgear end of crankshaft to crankcase gasket surface (with gasket installed) as shown at (B) and note dimension. Subtract dimension (B) from dimension (A) and refer to chart shown in Fig. KW122 to determine shim thickness needed to provide 0.09-0.2 mm (0.0035-0.0078 in.) crankshaft end play after assembly. Make certain governor weights are closed, align oil pump shaft convex with camshaft end groove, align governor gear teeth with cam gear teeth and install crankcase cover. Tighten crankcase cover to specified torque following sequence shown in Fig. KW118.

CAMSHAFT AND BEARINGS. Camshaft is supported at each end in bearings which are an integral part of crankcase or oil pump cover. Refer to CRANKSHAFT AND BALANCER for camshaft removal. Camshaft lobe height for intake and exhaust lobes should be 35.40 mm (1.3937 in.). Outside diameter of camshaft bearing journal on pto side should be 19.907 mm (0.7837 in.). Outside diameter of camshaft bearing journal on flywheel side should be 15.907 mm (0.6263 in.). If bearing diameters are less than specified, camshaft must be renewed. Inside diameter of camshaft bearing in crankcase should be 16.068

mm (0.6326 in.). Inside diameter of camshaft bearing in oil pump cover should be 20.071 mm (0.7902 in.). If diameters are greater than specified, renew crankcase or oil pump cover as required.

GOVERNOR. The internal centrifugal flyweight governor is gear driven off of the camshaft gear. Refer to GOVERNOR under MAINTENANCE section for external governor adjustments.

To remove governor assembly, remove external linkage, metal cooling shrouds, flywheel and crankcase cover. Use two screwdrivers to snap governor gear and flyweight assembly off governor stud shaft. Remove the thrust washer located between governor gear assembly and crankcase cover. To reinstall, place thrust washer over governor stud shaft. Place governor gear and flyweight assembly over governor stud shaft and push down on governor assembly to snap into place.

LOW OIL SENSOR. The low oil sensor is located as shown in Fig. KW123. Oil sensor activates low oil pressure warning light if oil pressure falls below 29.4 kPa (4.26 psi).

OIL PUMP AND RELIEF VALVE. The trochoid type oil pump mounted on crankcase cover draws oil through a filtering screen and inlet into pump chamber. Pressurized oil is pumped to the pto main journal, into and through crankshaft to lubricate connecting rod bearing, lower balancer link rods and

crankpins. Oil at the crankpin is passed through a metered orifice in the connecting rod and is sprayed onto the piston to cool the piston and prevent ring sticking. Return oil mists and then lubricates the flywheel side ball bearing and all other bearings.

To remove oil pump, remove crankcase cover. Refer to CAMSHAFT AND BEARINGS section and check camshaft bearing diameter in oil pump cover. Remove oil pump cover and inspect oil screen. Inspect seating of ball in relief valve. Inspect relief valve spring free length. Free length should be 19.5 mm (0.768 in.). If spring free length is less

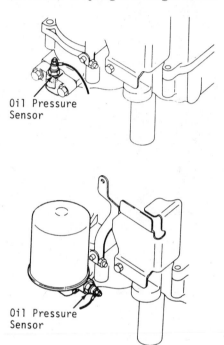

Fig. KW123—View showing locations of the low oil pressure sensing unit.

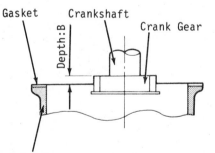

Fig. KW121—Refer to text to determine shim thickness for correct crankshaft end play.

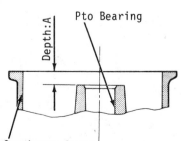

Fig. KW122—Chart showing recommend shim for correct crankshaft end play.

Difference in depth : A−B	Part Number of Shim	Thickness of Shim
1.92 to 1.99 mm (0.0755 to 0.0748 in.)	92025-2153	1.74 mm (0.0685 in.)
1.85 to 1.92 mm (0.0728 to 0.0755 in.)	92025-2152	1.67 mm (0.0657 in.)
1.78 to 1.85 mm (0.0700 to 0.0728 in.)	92025-2151	1.60 mm (0.0629 in.)
1.71 to 1.78 mm (0.0673 to 0.0700 in.)	92025-2150	1.53 mm (0.0602 in.)
1.64 to 1.71 mm (0.0645 to 0.0673 in.)	92025-2149	1.46 mm (0.0574 in.)
1.57 to 1.64 mm (0.0618 to 0.0645 in.)	92025-2148	1.39 mm (0.0547 in.)
1.50 to 1.57 mm (0.0590 to 0.0618 in.)	92025-2147	1.32 mm (0.0519 in.)
1.43 to 1.50 mm (0.0562 to 0.0590 in.)	92025-2146	1.25 mm (0.0492 in.)
1.36 to 1.43 mm (0.0535 to 0.0562 in.)	92025-2145	1.18 mm (0.0464 in.)

than specified, renew spring. Cap screws retaining oil pressure relief valve cover and oil induction guide plate are treated with thread locking compound. Remove only as required.

Reinstall by reversing removal procedure. Tighten oil pump cover to specified torque. Tighten crankcase cover to specified torque following sequence shown in Fig. KW118.

VALVE SYSTEM. Clearance between valve stem and valve tappet (cold) should be 0.10-0.16 mm (0.0039-0.0063 in.) for intake and exhaust valves. If clearance is not as specified, valves must be removed and end of stems ground off to increase clearance or seats ground deeper to reduce clearance.

Valve face and seat angles are 45 degrees and maximum valve seat width is 1.0-1.6 mm (0.039-0.063 in.). Minimum valve margin is 0.6 mm (0.02 in.).

Minimum valve stem diameter is 7.912 mm (0.3115 in.) for intake valve and 7.919 mm (0.3118 in.) for exhaust valve. Maximum valve stem bend is 0.03 mm (0.0012 in.). If valve stem bend exceeds specification, renew valve.

Valve spring free length should be 43.3 mm (1.705 in.) for intake valve spring and 39.0 mm (1.535 in.) for exhaust valve spring.

Maximum valve guide inside diameter for the renewable type valve guides is 8.062 mm (0.3174 in.). If guide inside diameter is greater than specified, use a suitable valve guide puller to remove guide. Press new guides into guide bore until top surface of guide is 30 mm (1.18 in.) from cylinder head mating surface on cylinder.

KAWASAKI

KAWASAKI MOTORS
P.O. Box 504
Shakopee, Minnesota 55379

Model	No. Cyls.	Bore	Stroke	Displacement	Power Rating
FC290V	1	78 mm (3.07 in.)	60 mm (2.36 in.)	286 cc (17.4 cu. in.)	6.7 kW (9 hp)
FC420V	1	89 mm (3.50 in.)	68 mm (2.68 in.)	423 cc (25.8 cu. in.)	10.5 kW (14 hp)
FC540V	1	89 mm (3.50 in.)	86 mm (3.38 in.)	535 cc (32.6 cu. in.)	12.8 kW (17 hp)

All models are four-stroke, single-cylinder, air-cooled engines with a vertical crankshaft. Splash lubrication is used on Model FC290V and lubrication on Models FC420V and FC540V is provided by an oil pump. Engine serial number plate is located on the flywheel blower housing.

MAINTENANCE

LUBRICATION. Engine oil level should be checked prior to each operating interval. Oil should be maintained between reference marks on dipstick with dipstick just touching first threads. Do not screw dipstick in to check oil level (Fig. KW201).

Manufacturer recommends using oil with an API service classification of SF or SG. Use oil of suitable viscosity for the expected air temperature range during the period between oil changes. Refer to temperature/viscosity chart shown in Fig. KW202.

On models without an oil filter, engine oil should be changed after every 50 hours of operation or yearly, whichever comes first. On models equipped with an oil filter, oil and filter should be changed after every 100 hours of operation or yearly, whichever comes first. Oil should be drained while engine is warm. Crankcase oil capacity for FC290V is approximately 1.1 L (2.3 pt.). Crankcase oil capacity for FC420V is approximately 1.3 L (2.75 pt.) without filter and 1.5 L (3.17 pt.) with filter. Crankcase oil capacity for FC540V is approximately 1.6 L (3.4 pt.) without filter and 1.9 L (4.0 pt.) with filter.

Models FC420V and FC540V may be equipped with an oil pressure sensor located on the oil filter adapter if equipped with an oil filter, or on the oil passage cover if not equipped with an oil filter. Switch should be closed at zero pressure and open at 29.4 kPa (4.3 psi). Switch is connected to a warning device.

AIR FILTER. The air filter element should be removed and cleaned after every 25 hours of operation, or more often if operating in extremely dusty conditions. Paper element (5—Figs. KW203 and KW204) should be renewed after every 300 hours of operation. Element should also be renewed if it is very dirty or if it is damaged in any way.

To remove filter elements (4 and 5), remove the retaining knob or wing bolts (1) and washers (2). Remove cover (3), foam precleaner element and paper element. Clean foam element in solution of warm water and liquid detergent, then squeeze out water and allow to air dry. DO NOT wash paper element. Apply light coat of engine oil to foam element and squeeze out excess oil. Clean paper element by tapping gently to remove dust. DO NOT use compressed air to clean element. Inspect paper element for holes or other damage. Reinstall by reversing removal procedure.

CRANKCASE BREATHER. Crankcase pressure is vented to the cylinder head. A reed valve is located on the top of the cylinder on Model FC290V or in the rocker arm chamber on Models FC420V and FC540V. Renew reed valve if tip of reed stands up more than 0.2 mm (0.008 in.) on Model FC290V or 2.0

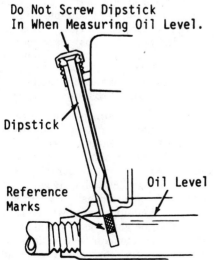

Fig. KW201—View showing procedure to check crankcase oil level. Refer to text.

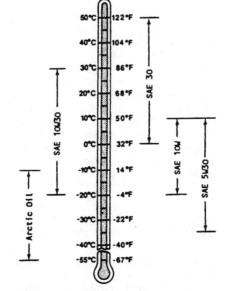

Fig. KW202—Engine oil viscosity should be based on expected air temperature as indicated in chart above.

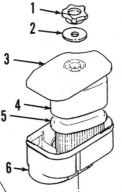

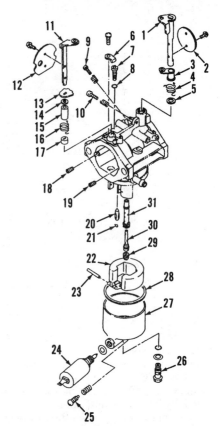

Fig. KW203—Exploded view of air filter assembly used on Model FC290V.

1. Knob
2. Washer
3. Cover
4. Foam element
5. Paper element
6. Housing
7. Stud
8. Gasket
9. Base
10. Breather hose

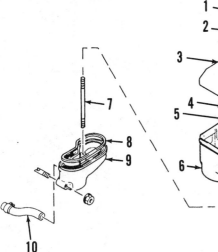

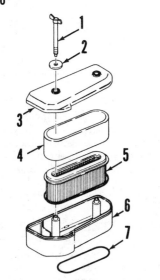

Fig. KW204—Exploded view of air filter assembly used on Models FC420V and FC540V.

1. Wing bolt
2. Washer
3. Cover
4. Foam element
5. Paper element
6. Housing
7. "O" ring

mm (0.080 in.) on Models FC420V and FC540V, or if reed is damaged or worn excessively.

SPARK PLUG. Recommended spark plug is NGK BPR5ES or Champion RN11YC for Model FC290V and NGK BMR4A or Champion RCJ8 for Models FC420V and FC540V.

Spark plug should be removed, cleaned and electrode gap set after every 100 hours of operation. Specified spark plug gap is 0.76 mm (0.030 in.) for Model FC290V and 0.7 mm (0.028 in.) for Models FC420V and FC540V. Renew spark plug if electrode is severely burned or damaged.

CARBURETOR. All models are equipped with a float-type, side draft carburetor. Carburetor should be

checked whenever poor or erratic performance is noted.

Recommended engine idle speed is 1550 rpm on Model FC290V and 1350-1450 rpm on Models FC420V and FC540V. Adjust idle speed by turning throttle stop screw (10—Fig. KW205) clockwise to increase idle speed or counterclockwise to decrease idle speed.

Adjust throttle control as follows: Place engine throttle lever in fast position. Using a $^{15}/_{64}$-inch drill bit, insert bit through hole (H—Fig. KW206) in speed control lever (7) and bracket (8). Loosen throttle cable housing clamp screw (10), pull cable housing tight and retighten cable clamp screw. Rotate choke lever screw (9) on back side of bracket so there is a gap between screw and choke control lever, then turn back in until screw just touches lever. Remove drill bit. With throttle control lever in choke position, carburetor choke plate should be closed. If not, repeat procedure.

Initial adjustment of pilot air screw (7—Fig. KW205) is 1½ turns open from a lightly seated position. Turning pilot air screw clockwise leans the fuel/air mixture. Make final adjustment with engine at operating temperature and running. Adjust pilot screw to obtain maximum engine idle speed, then turn pilot screw out (counterclockwise) an additional ¼ turn. Adjust throttle stop screw (10) so engine idles at 1550 rpm on Model FC290V and 1350-1450 rpm on Models FC420V and FC540V.

Main fuel mixture is controlled by a fixed jet (29). Different size main jets are available for high altitude operation.

Disassembly of carburetor is self-evident upon examination of unit and reference to Fig. KW205. Note that pilot jet (7) is pressed into carburetor body on some FC540V engines.

Fig. KW205—Exploded view of typical float-type carburetor used on all models. Fuel shut-off solenoid (24) is not used on some engines.

1. Throttle shaft
2. Throttle plate
3. Ring
4. Spring
5. Seal
6. Retainer plate
7. Pilot jet
8. "O" ring
9. Pilot screw
10. Idle speed screw
11. Choke shaft
12. Choke plate
13. Plate
14. Seal
15. Ring
16. Spring
17. Ring
18. Pilot air jet
19. Main air jet
20. Fuel inlet needle
21. Clip
22. Float
23. Pin
24. Fuel shut-off solenoid
25. Drain screw
26. Special bolt
27. Float bowl
28. Gasket
29. Main jet
30. Bleed pipe
31. Main nozzle

Clean carburetor parts (except plastic components) using suitable carburetor cleaner. Do not clean jets or passages with drill bits or wire as enlargement of passages could affect calibration of carburetor. Rinse parts in warm water to neutralize corrosive action of carburetor cleaner and dry with compressed air.

When assembling the carburetor, note the following: Place a small drop of nonhardening sealant, such as Permatex #2 or equivalent, on throttle and choke plate retaining screws. Float should be parallel with body when carburetor is inverted as shown in Fig. KW207. If equipped with white plastic float, float height is not adjustable. Replace any components that are damaged or excessively worn that would adversely affect float position. On models with an adjustable float, bend float tab

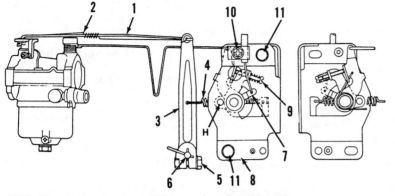

Fig. KW206—View of external governor linkage used on all models.

1. Governor-to-carburetor rod
2. Spring
3. Governor lever
4. Tension spring
5. Clamp bolt
6. Governor shaft
7. Speed control lever
8. Control plate
9. Choke setting screw
10. Clamp screw
11. Retaining screws

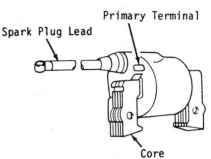

Fig. KW209—View of ignition coil showing location of primary terminal, spark plug lead and iron core.

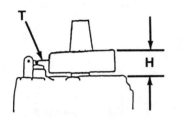

Fig. KW207—Float height (H) should be parallel with fuel bowl mounting surface of carburetor body. If float height is adjustable, bend float tab (T) to adjust float height.

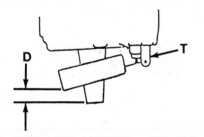

Fig. KW208—On Models FC290V and FC540V, float drop (D) should be 10.5-12.5 mm (0.413-0.492 in.). Bend tab on back of float arm to adjust float drop.

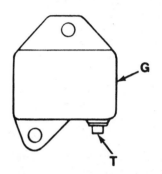

Fig. KW210—All models are equipped with the ignition control unit shown. Refer to text for test procedure.

mum no-load engine speed should be 3350 rpm and is adjusted as follows: Run engine until normal operating temperature is reached. Align holes in speed control lever (7) and bracket (8) and insert a $^{15}/_{64}$-inch drill bit. Run engine under no load and determine engine speed using an accurate tachometer. If engine speed is not 3350 rpm, loosen bracket retaining screws (11) and reposition bracket to obtain desired engine speed. Retighten screws and recheck engine speed. Check choke operation as outlined in CARBURETOR section.

IGNITION SYSTEM. All models are equipped with a transistor ignition system and regular maintenance is not required. Ignition timing is not adjustable. Ignition coil is located outside flywheel. Air gap between ignition coil and flywheel should be 0.30 mm (0.012 in.).

To test ignition coil, remove cooling shrouds and disconnect spark plug cable and primary lead wire (Fig. KW209). Connect ohmmeter test leads between coil core (ground) and high-tension (spark plug) terminal. Secondary coil resistance should be 10.9k-16.3k ohms. Remove test lead connected to high-tension terminal and connect lead to coil primary terminal. Primary coil resistance should be 0.48-0.72 ohms. If readings vary significantly from specifications, renew ignition coil.

To test control unit, refer to Fig. KW210 and disconnect all electrical leads. Connect positive ohmmeter lead to terminal (T) and negative ohmmeter lead to ground lead or control unit case (G) according to model being serviced. Ohmmeter reading should be 400-600 ohms. Reverse leads. Ohmmeter reading should be 60-100 ohms. If ohmmeter readings are not as specified, renew control unit.

VALVE ADJUSTMENT. Clearance between valve stem ends and rocker arms should be checked and adjusted after every 300 hours of operation. Engine must be cold for valve adjustment. Rotate crankshaft so piston is at top dead center on compression stroke. Remove rocker arm cover. Valve clearance gap (G—Fig. KW211) for both valves should be 0.15 mm (0.006 in.). Loosen nut (N) and turn adjusting screw (S) to obtain desired clearance. Tighten nut to 20 N·m (177 in.-lbs.) and recheck adjustment.

CYLINDER HEAD AND COMBUSTION CHAMBER. Standard compression reading should be 483 kPa (71 psi).

NOTE: When checking compression pressure, spark plug high-tension

to adjust float height. On Models FC290V and FC540V, measure float drop (D—Fig. KW208). Float drop should be 10.5-12.5 mm (0.413-0.492 in.). Bend tab on back of float arm to adjust float drop.

GOVERNOR. A gear-driven flyweight-type governor is located inside engine crankcase. Before adjusting governor linkage, make certain all linkage is in good condition and that tension spring (4—Fig. KW206) is not stretched.

To adjust external linkage, place engine throttle control in "FAST" position. Spring (2) around governor-to-carburetor rod must pull governor lever (3) and throttle lever toward each other. Loosen governor lever clamp bolt (5) and turn governor shaft (6) clockwise as far as possible. Tighten clamp bolt nut. Maxi-

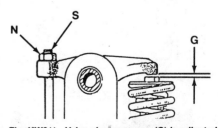

Fig. KW211—Valve clearance gap (G) is adjusted by loosening nut (N) and rotating adjusting screw (S). Valve clearance should be 0.15 mm (0.006 in.).

lead must be grounded or electronic ignition could be damaged.

Excessive carbon buildup on piston and cylinder head is indicated by a higher than standard compression reading. A leaking cylinder head gasket, worn piston rings and cylinder bore or poorly seated valves are indicated by lower than standard compression readings.

REPAIRS

TIGHTENING TORQUES. Recommended tightening torques are as follows:

Connecting rod . . . . 20 N·m
　　　　　　　　　　　(177 in.-lbs.)
Crankshaft
　(pto end) . . . . 38 N·m
　　　　　　　　　　　(28 ft.-lbs.)
Cylinder head:
　FC290V . . . . 24 N·m
　　　　　　　　　　　(212 in.-lbs.)
　FC420V, FC540V . . . . 52 N·m
　　　　　　　　　　　(38 ft.-lbs.)
Flywheel:
　FC290V . . . . 86 N·m
　　　　　　　　　　　(63 ft.-lbs.)
　FC420V . . . . 137 N·m
　　　　　　　　　　　(101 ft.-lbs.)
　FC540V . . . . 172 N·m
　　　　　　　　　　　(126 ft.-lbs.)
Oil drain plug . . . . 23 N·m
　　　　　　　　　　　(204 in.-lbs.)
Oil pan . . . . 26 N·m
　　　　　　　　　　　(19 ft.-lbs.)

CYLINDER HEAD. To remove cylinder head, remove cylinder head shroud and blower housing. Remove carburetor and muffler. Remove rocker arm cover, loosen cylinder head mounting bolts evenly and remove cylinder head and gasket.

Remove carbon deposits from combustion chamber, being careful not to damage gasket sealing surface. Inspect cylinder head for cracks, nicks or other damage. Place cylinder head on a flat surface and check entire sealing surface for distortion using a feeler gauge. Renew cylinder head if sealing surface is warped more than 0.05 mm (0.002 in.).

To reinstall cylinder head, reverse removal procedure. Surfaces of cylinder head gasket are coated with a sealant and do not require additional sealant. Push rods should be installed in their original positions. Tighten cylinder head screws in sequence shown in Fig. KW212 to initial torque of 18 N·m (159 in.-lbs.) on Model FC290V and 32 N·m (24 ft.-lbs.) on Models FC420V and FC540V. On Model FC290V, tighten screws 3 N·m (27 in.-lbs.) at a time following sequence in Fig. KW212. On Models FC420V and FC540V, tighten screws 7 N·m (5 ft.-lbs.) at a time following sequence in Fig. KW212. Final torque is 24 N·m (18 ft.-lbs.) on Model FC290V and 52 N·m (38 ft.-lbs.) on Models FC420V and FC540V. Adjust valve clearance as outlined in MAINTENANCE section.

VALVE SYSTEM. Remove cylinder head as outlined above. Remove rocker arm shaft (21—Fig. KW213) and rocker arms (6 and 7). Use suitable valve spring compressor to compress valve springs and remove collet halves (8).

Remove retainers (9), springs (10) and valves (19 and 20). Remove valve stem seals (11) from top of valve guides.

NOTE: Removal of valve stem seal will damage the seal. Renew seals whenever they are removed.

Check all parts for wear or damage. Refer to the following specifications:

Rocker arm shaft OD—
　Wear limit . . . . 12.94 mm
　　　　　　　　　　　(0.509 in.)
Rocker arm ID—
　Wear limit . . . . 13.07 mm
　　　　　　　　　　　(0.515 in.)
Valve spring free length—
　Minimum allowable:
　　FC290V . . . . 31.00 mm
　　　　　　　　　　　(1.220 in.)
　　FC420V, FC540V . . . . . 37.50 mm
　　　　　　　　　　　(1.476 in.)
Valve guide ID—
　Wear limit . . . . 7.07 mm
　　　　　　　　　　　(0.278 in.)

Renew valves if stem is warped more than 0.03 mm (0.001 in.) or if valve margin is less than 0.60 mm (0.020 in.). Valve stem ends should be ground square. Valve face and seat angles are 45° for intake and exhaust.

NOTE: Grinding face of exhaust valve is not recommended as life of valve will be shortened.

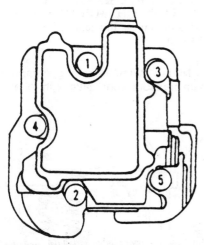

Fig. KW212—Tighten cylinder head bolts in sequence shown.

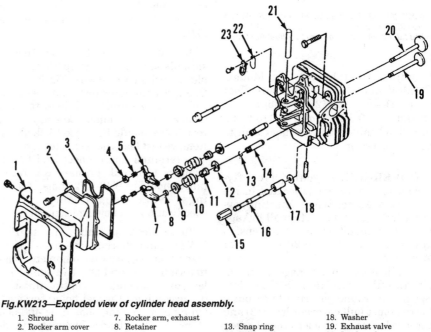

Fig. KW213—Exploded view of cylinder head assembly.

1. Shroud	7. Rocker arm, exhaust	13. Snap ring
2. Rocker arm cover	8. Retainer	14. Valve guide
3. Gasket	9. Retainer	15. Nut
4. Locknut	10. Valve spring	16. Stud
5. Adjusting screw	11. Seal	17. Bushing
6. Rocker arm, intake	12. Plate	

18. Washer
19. Exhaust valve
20. Intake valve
21. Rocker arm shaft
22. Breather valve
23. Retainer plate

Valve seating surface should be 0.80 mm (0.031 in.) for Model FC290V, 1.00-1.46 mm (0.039-0.057 in.) for Model FC420V and 1.20 mm (0.048 in.) for Model FC540V. Seats can be narrowed using a 30° stone or cutter. Valves should be lapped into the seats to ensure proper contact. Seats should contact center of valve face.

Valve guides (14) can be renewed using suitable valve guide driver. Guides should be pressed into cylinder head until snap ring (13) just seats against cylinder head. Ream new guides with a 7 mm valve guide reamer. Valve guide finished inside diameter should be 7.0-7.02 mm (0.2756-0.2763 in.).

CONNECTING ROD. Connecting rod (16—Fig. KW214 or KW215) and piston are removed as an assembly after removing cylinder head and oil pan. Remove carbon and ring ridge (if present) from top of cylinder before removing piston. Remove connecting rod bolts and connecting rod cap, then push connecting rod and piston out through top of cylinder. Remove retaining rings (18) and push piston pin (17) out of piston to separate piston from connecting rod.

Connecting rod rides directly on crankshaft journal. Maximum allowable inside diameter for connecting rod big end bearing surface is 35.57 mm (1.400 in.) for Model FC290V and 41.07 mm (1.617 in.) for Models FC420V and FC540V. Maximum connecting rod-to-crankpin clearance is 0.14 mm (0.006 in.). A connecting rod is available with 0.50 mm (0.020 in.) undersize big end for use with undersize crankshaft crankpin. Refer to CRANKSHAFT AND BALANCER section.

Maximum inside diameter of connecting rod small end is 19.06 mm (0.750 in.) for Model FC290V and 22.06 mm (0.868 in.) for Models FC420V and FC540V. Maximum allowable connecting rod-to-piston pin clearance is 0.08 mm (0.003 in.).

When reassembling, install piston on connecting rod so arrow on top of piston is toward the "MADE IN JAPAN" side of connecting rod. Install piston and connecting rod in cylinder so arrow on top of piston is toward flywheel side of engine. Tighten connecting rod cap bolts to 20 N•m (15 ft.-lbs.).

PISTON, PIN AND RINGS. Piston and connecting rod are removed as an assembly after removing cylinder head and oil pan. Refer to CONNECTING ROD section for removal and installation procedure.

After separating piston and connecting rod, carefully remove piston rings and clean carbon and other deposits from piston surface and piston ring lands.

CAUTION: Exercise extreme care when cleaning piston ring lands. Do not damage squared edges or widen piston ring grooves. If piston ring lands are damaged, piston must be renewed.

Maximum inside diameter of pin bore in piston is 19.03 mm (0.749 in.) for Model FC290V and 22.04 mm (0.868 in.) for Models FC420V and FC540V. Minimum piston pin outside diameter is 18.98 mm (0.747 in.) for Model FC290V and 21.98 mm (0.827 in.) for Models FC420V and FC540V. Maximum piston-to-pin clearance is 0.05 mm (0.0020 in.) for Model FC290V and 0.06 mm (0.0024 in.) for Models FC420V and FC540V.

To check piston ring grooves for wear, insert a new ring in ring groove and use a feeler gauge to measure ring side clearance in groove. On Model FC290V, renew piston if side clearance exceeds 0.16 mm (0.006 in.) for top ring, 0.14 mm (0.005 in.) for second ring or 0.19 mm (0.007 in.) for oil ring. On Models FC420V and FC540V, renew piston if side clearance exceeds 0.17 mm (0.007 in.) for top ring, 0.15 mm (0.006 in.) for second ring or 0.20 mm (0.008 in.) for oil ring.

Insert each ring squarely in cylinder bore about 25 mm (1 in.) below top of cylinder and measure ring end gap. On Model FC290V, maximum allowable end gap is 0.80 mm (0.031 in.) for compression rings and 1.20 mm (0.047 in.) for oil control ring. On Models FC420V and FC540V, maximum allowable end gap is 0.90 mm (0.035 in.) for compression rings and 1.30 mm (0.051 in.) for oil control ring. If piston ring gap is greater than specified, check cylinder bore for wear.

During reassembly, install piston on connecting rod so arrow on top of piston is toward "MADE IN JAPAN" side of connecting rod. Use new snap rings to retain piston pin in piston. Install oil ring spacer (3—Fig. KW216) first, then install side rails (4). Position side rail end gaps 180° apart. Install second ring (2) and first ring (1) on piston with "N" or "NPR" mark on ring facing up. Stagger piston ring end gaps 180° apart, but do not align with side rail end gaps. Lubricate piston and cylinder with engine oil. Use a suitable ring compressor to compress rings when installing piston in cylinder. Be sure that arrow on top of piston faces flywheel side of engine.

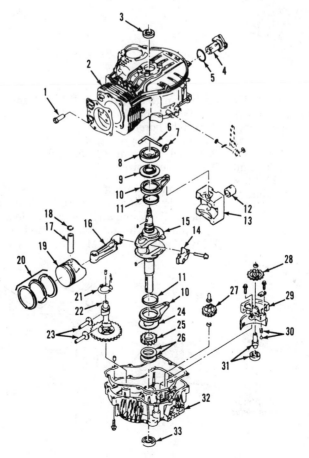

Fig. KW214—Exploded view of FC420V and FC540V engines.

1. Check valve
2. Cylinder block & crankcase
3. Oil seal
4. Counterweight support shaft
5. "O" ring
6. Governor shaft
7. Washer
8. Main bearing
9. Spacer
10. Link rod
11. Bushing
12. Bushing
13. Balancer counterweight
14. Rod cap
15. Crankshaft
16. Connecting rod
17. Piston pin
18. Snap ring
19. Piston
20. Piston rings
21. Compression release mechanism
22. Camshaft assy.
23. Valve tappets
24. Spacer
25. Gear
26. Shims
27. Governor flyweight assy.
28. Gear
29. Oil pump housing
30. Oil pressure relief valve
31. Oil pump rotors
32. Oil pan
33. Oil seal

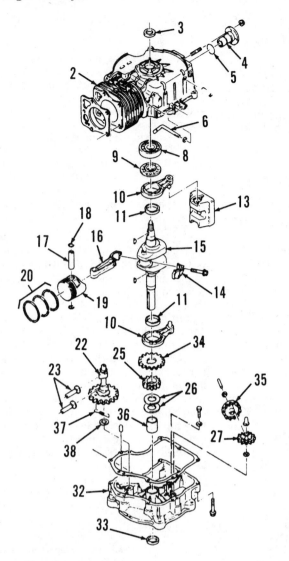

Fig. KW215—Exploded view of Model FC290V.

2. Cylinder block & crankcase
3. Oil seal
4. Counterweight support shaft
5. "O" ring
6. Governor shaft
8. Main bearing
9. Spacer
10. Link rod
14. Rod cap
15. Crankshaft
16. Connecting rod
17. Piston pin
18. Snap ring
19. Piston
20. Piston rings
22. Camshaft assy.
23. Valve tappets
25. Gear
26. Shims
27. Governor flyweight assy.
32. Oil pan
33. Oil seal
34. Governor drive gear
35. Oil slinger gear
36. Bushing
37. Compression release spring
38. Shim

flywheel side of all models is a ball bearing.

On Model FC290V, maximum outside diameter of bushing in oil pan is 30.13 mm (1.186 in.). If bushing renewal is required, use a suitable tool and press out old bushing. Install new bushing so grooves (G—Fig. KW217) point toward inside of oil pan and split (T) in bushing is located as shown in Fig. KW217. Bearing on flywheel side should be a press fit on crankshaft and in bearing bore of crankcase.

On Models FC420V and FC540V, maximum inside diameter for integral bearing bore in oil pan is 35.07 mm (1.381 in.) for FC420V and 38.06 mm (1.498 in.) for FC540V. Bearing on flywheel side should be a press fit on crankshaft and in bearing bore of crankcase.

Renew crankshaft seals (3 and 33—Fig. KW214 or KW215) if worn or damaged. Pack seals with lithium-base grease prior to installation. Install seals with lip facing inside of engine, and press in until flush with crankcase and oil pan (Model FC420V). On Model FC540V, press seal into oil pan until 0.50 mm (0.020 in.) below oil pan flange surface.

When installing oil pan, tighten cover mounting screws to 20 N•m (15 ft.-lbs.) on Models FC290V and FC540V and 26 N•m (19 ft.-lbs.) on Model FC420V. On all models, tighten mounting screws in sequence shown in Fig. KW218 or Fig. KW219.

CRANKSHAFT AND BALANCER. The crankshaft is supported on flywheel side by a ball-type main bearing and on pto side by a plain-type bearing in the oil pan. A reciprocating balancer is used on all models.

To remove crankshaft, remove shrouds, fan housing, flywheel, cylinder head and oil pan. Rotate crankshaft until timing marks on camshaft gear and crankshaft gear are aligned, then remove camshaft and gear. Remove valve tappets (23—Fig. KW214 or KW215); identify tappets so they can be reinstalled in original position. Remove con-

CYLINDER, CRANKCASE, MAIN BEARINGS AND SEALS. Cylinder and crankcase are an integral casting. Standard cylinder bore diameter is 77.98-78.00 mm (3.070-3.071 in.) for Model FC290V and 88.90-89.00 mm (3.500-3.504 in.) for Models FC420V and FC540V. Cylinder bore wear limit is 78.05 mm (3.073 in.) for Model FC290V,

89.08 mm (3.507 in.) for FC420V and 89.06 mm (3.506 in.) for FC540V. Cylinder can be bored or honed to fit oversize pistons. Pistons are available in 0.25, 0.50 and 0.75 mm (0.010, 0.020 and 0.030 in.) oversizes.

The main bearing on pto side is a renewable bushing in the oil pan on Model FC290V and an integral bushing is a part of the oil pan on Models FC420V and FC540V. Main bearing on

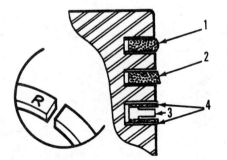

Fig. KW216—Cross-sectional view of piston showing correct installation of piston rings. Refer to text.

1. Top ring
2. Second ring
3. Spacer
4. Side rails

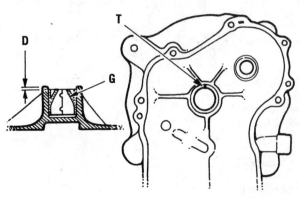

Fig. KW217—Install new bushing on FC290V engine so grooves (G) point toward inside of oil pan and split (T) in bushing is located as shown. Bushing depth (D) must be 1 mm (0.030 in.) below surface.

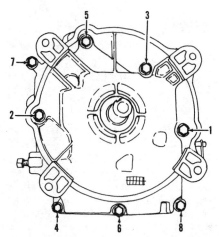

Fig. KW218—Oil pan screws on FC290V engines must be tightened evenly to specified torque following sequence shown.

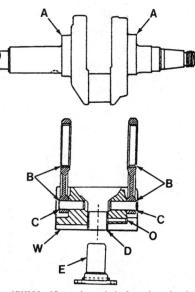

Fig. KW220—View of crankshaft and engine balancer wear check points. Refer to text.

A. Crankshaft journals
B. Link rod bearings
C. Wrist pins
D. Support shaft bushing
E. Support shaft
O. Oil hole
W. Balance weight

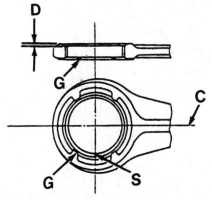

Fig. KW221—Bushing in big end of balancer link rod is renewable. Refer to text for special installation instructions.

C. Link rod centerline
D. Bushing depth
G. Oil grooves
S. Bushing seam

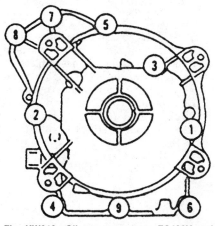

Fig. KW219—Oil pan screws on FC420V and FC540V engines must be tightened evenly to specified torque following sequence shown.

necting rod and piston. Unbolt and remove counterweight support shaft (4). Remove crankshaft and balancer assembly from crankcase.

To disassemble balancer, remove collar (9), gear (25), spacer (24) and link rods (10) from crankshaft (15) and balancer (13) wrist pins.

Clean and inspect all parts for wear or damage. Crankshaft main journal minimum diameter on pto side is 29.92 mm (1.178 in.) for Model FC290V, 34.91 mm (1.374 in.) for Model FC420V and 37.90 mm (1.492 in.) for Model FC540V. Main journals cannot be resized. Refer to CYLINDER, CRANKCASE, MAIN BEARINGS AND SEALS section for main bearing dimensions. Measure crankshaft runout at the main journals. Crankshaft should be renewed if runout exceeds 0.05 mm (0.002 in.). Crankshaft cannot be straightened.

Crankpin journal minimum diameter is 35.43 mm (1.395 in.) for Model FC290V and 40.93 mm (1.611 in.) for

Models FC420V and FC540V. Crankpin can be reground to accept undersize connecting rod. Refer to CONNECTING ROD section.

Measure outside diameter of crankshaft balancer link rod journals (A—Fig. KW220), inside diameter of big end and small end of balancer link rods (B), inside diameter of support shaft bushing (D) and outside diameter of support shaft (E). Refer to the following table for wear limit specifications and renew parts as necessary.

Link rod journal OD—
  FC290V . . . . 46.86 mm
                  (1.845 in.)
  FC420V . . . . 53.95 mm
                  (2.124 in.)
  FC540V . . . . 57.94 mm
                  (2.281 in.)
Link rod big end ID—
  FC290V . . . . 47.12 mm
                  (1.855 in.)
  FC420V . . . . 54.12 mm
                  (2.132 in.)
  FC540V . . . . 58.19 mm
                  (2.291 in.)
Link rod small end ID—
  All models . . . . 12.06 mm
                  (0.475 in.)
Support shaft bushing ID—
  All models . . . . 26.10 mm
                  (1.027 in.)
Support shaft OD—
  All models . . . . 25.93 mm
                  (1.021 in.)

Balancer link rod bushing (11—Figs. KW214 and KW215) is renewable on all models. When installing new link rod

bushing, press bushing into link rod from side opposite oil grooves (G—Fig. KW221). Position seam (S) of bushing 90° from centerline (C) of link rod. Install bushing so depth (D) below machined surface of rod is 1.0 mm (0.040 in.) for FC290V and FC540V engines or 0.50 mm (0.020 in.) for FC420V engine.

Support shaft bushing (12) is renewable on all models except Model FC290V. When installing new support shaft bushing, make sure that oil hole in bushing is aligned with oil passage in balancer. On FC420V engine, install support shaft bushing flush with surface of balancer. On FC540V engine, install bushing so it is 0.50 mm (0.020 in.) below surface of balancer.

To assemble crankshaft and balancer, install balance weight (W—Fig. KW220) with oil hole (O) toward flywheel side of crankshaft. Install link rods (B) with oil grooves facing away from crankwebs. Install spacer (24—Fig. KW214) on Models FC42V and FC540V with chamfered face toward link rod. On all models, install balancer assembly with crankshaft in crankcase being careful not to damage crankshaft oil seal. Align balancer weight with hole in crankcase and insert support shaft (4). Install connecting rod and piston. Rotate crankshaft until piston is at top dead center.

Install valve tappets in their original bores. Align timing marks on crankshaft gear and camshaft gear, and install camshaft. Install oil pan with original shims (26), then use a dial indicator to measure crankshaft end play. Add or remove shims as necessary to obtain specified end play of 0.09-0.22 mm (0.004-0.009 in.).

CAMSHAFT AND BEARINGS.
Camshaft is supported at each end in

bearings that are an integral part of crankcase or oil pan. Refer to CRANK-SHAFT AND BALANCER section for camshaft and valve tappet removal. Mark tappets so they can be installed in their original guides if reused.

Camshaft minimum lobe height for intake and exhaust lobes is 27.08 mm (1.066 in.) for FC290V engine, 36.75 mm (1.446 in.) for FC420V engine or 37.10 mm (1.461 in.) for FC540V engine.

Bearing journal minimum diameter for FC290V engine is 13.92 mm (0.548 in.) for pto side of camshaft and 15.92 mm (0.627 in.) for magneto side. Bearing journal minimum diameter for FC420V engine is 20.91 mm (0.823 in.) for pto side of camshaft and 19.91 mm (0.784 in.) for magneto side. Bearing journal minimum diameter for FC540V engine is 20.91 mm (0.823 in.) for both sides of camshaft.

Camshaft bearing bore maximum inside diameter for FC290V engine is 14.05 mm (0.553 in.) for oil pan bearing and 16.06 mm (0.632 in.) for crankcase bearing. Camshaft bearing bore maximum inside diameter for FC420V engine is 21.08 mm (0.830 in.) for oil pan bearing and 20.08 mm (0.790 in.) for crankcase bearing. Camshaft bearing bore maximum inside diameter for FC540V engine is 21.08 mm (0.830 in.) for both crankcase and oil pan bearings.

Camshaft end play must be adjusted on all FC290V engines and FC540V engines prior to serial number 014455 whenever camshaft, oil pan or crankcase is renewed. Correct end play is 0.20 mm (0.008 in.). End play is adjusted by changing the thickness of shim located between oil pan and camshaft. To calculate correct shim thickness, position camshaft and oil pan gasket on crankcase as shown in Fig. KW222. Measure distance (B) from gasket (A) to thrust face (C) on camshaft. Measure distance (D) from oil pan face to top of camshaft bearing boss (E). For FC290V engine, **subtract** measurement (B) from measurement (D). For FC540V engine, **add** measurement (B) to measurement (D). For either engine, subtract 0.20 mm (0.008 in.) from the result of the above calculation to determine required shim thickness. Install shim (38—Fig. KW215) on camshaft thrust face (C—Fig. KW222).

When reinstalling camshaft and tappets, be sure that tappets are installed in their original position. If camshaft is renewed, tappets should also be renewed. Make sure that timing marks on

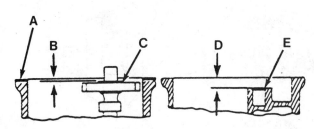

Fig. KW222—Refer to text to determine shim thickness to adjust camshaft end play on all FC290V engines and FC540 engines prior to serial number 014455.

camshaft gear and crankshaft gear are aligned.

GOVERNOR. The internal centrifugal flyweight governor (27—Figs. KW214 and KW215) is mounted in oil pan. On Model FC290V, the governor is gear driven by gear (34—Fig. KW215) on the crankshaft and the governor on Models FC420V and FC540V is driven by the camshaft gear. The governor gear on Model FC290V also drives the oil slinger gear (25—Fig. KW215).

To remove governor assembly, split oil pan from crankcase. Use two screwdrivers to snap governor gear and flyweight assembly off governor stub shaft. Governor unit will be damaged when removed and must be renewed if removed. Shaft must protrude above boss 32.2-32.8 mm (1.27-1.29 in.). Be sure to install thrust washer between gear and oil pan. Install governor by pushing down until it snaps onto the locating groove.

If removed, install governor shaft and arm in side of crankcase and attach cotter pin.

Refer to MAINTENANCE section for external governor linkage adjustment.

OIL PUMP AND RELIEF VALVE. Models FC420V and FC540V are equipped with an oil pump and Model 290V is equipped with an oil slinger gear.

The trochoid-type oil pump (Fig. KW223) used on Models FC420V and FC540V is mounted on oil pan (11). To remove oil pump, first separate oil pan from cylinder block. Remove pump drive gear (2). Remove pump housing mounting cap screws and withdraw pump housing (4) and inner rotor shaft (6) together from oil pan. Remove retainer plate (3) and relief valve ball and spring (5).

Inspect seating of relief valve ball. Measure relief valve spring free length. Renew spring if free length is less than 19.00 mm (0.748 in.) on Model FC420V or 19.50 mm (0.768 in.) on Model FC540V.

Measure diameter of outer rotor shaft (6); wear limit is 12.63 mm (0.497 in.). Measure inside diameter of rotor shaft bearing surface in pump housing; wear limit is 12.76 mm (0.502 in.). Measure inside diameter of outer rotor bearing surface in oil pan; wear limit is 29.20 mm (1.149 in.) for Model FC420V or 40.77 mm (1.605 in.) for Model FC540V.

To reinstall pump, reverse removal procedure. Lubricate parts with engine oil.

ELECTRIC STARTER. Place alignment marks on pinion housing, frame and end cover before disassembling so they can be reinstalled in original position. Renew brushes if length is less than 8.5 mm (0.33 in.) on Model FC290V, 6 mm (0.24 in.) on Model FC420V, or 10.5 mm (0.41 in.) on Model FC540V.

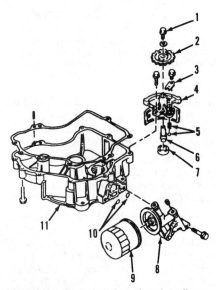

Fig. KW226—Exploded view of engine oil pump assembly used on FC420V and FC540V engines.

1. Cap screw
2. Drive gear
3. Retainer plate
4. Pump housing
5. Pressure relief valve assy.
6. Pump inner rotor
7. Pump outer rotor
8. Filter base
9. Oil filter
10. "O" rings
11. Oil pan

KOHLER

KOHLER COMPANY
Kohler, Wisconsin 53044

Models	No. Cyls.	Bore	Stroke	Displacement	Power Rating
CH11, CV11	1	87 mm (3.43 in.)	67 mm (2.64 in.)	398 cc (24.3 cu. in.)	10.5 kW (14 hp)
CH12.5, CV12.5	1	87 mm (3.43 in.)	67 mm (2.64 in.)	398 cc (24.3 cu. in.)	9.33 kW (12.5 hp)
CH14, CV14	1	87 mm (3.43 in.)	67 mm (2.64 in.)	398 cc (24.3 cu. in.)	10.5 kW (14 hp)

NOTE: Metric fasteners are used throughout engine.

The Kohler engines covered in this section are four-stroke, air-cooled, single-cylinder engines using an overhead valve system. Engine identification numbers are located on a decal affixed to flywheel fan shroud. Refer to preceding Kohler section for engine identification information.

MAINTENANCE

LUBRICATION. Periodically check oil level; do not overfill. Oil dipstick should be resting on tube to check oil level; do not screw in dipstick. Change oil after first 5 hours of operation. Thereafter, change oil after every 100 hours of operation. Oil should be drained while engine is warm. Oil capacity is approximately 1.9 liters (2.0 qt.). It is recommended that a new oil filter be installed at each oil change.

Manufacturer recommends using oil with an API service classification of SF or SG. Use 10W-30 or 10W-40 oil for temperatures above 0° F (-18° C). When operating in temperatures below 32° F (0° C), SAE 5W-20 or 5W-30 may be used. Manufacturer recommends use of SAE 10W-30 API SF oil for first 5 hours of operation of overhauled engines or new short blocks, then change oil according to ambient temperature requirements.

The engine may be equipped with a low-oil sensor. The sensor circuit may be designed to stop engine or trigger a warning device if oil level is low.

AIR FILTER. The engine is equipped with a foam precleaner element and paper-type air filter. Service the precleaner after every 25 hours of operation and the air filter after every 100 hours of operation. Service more frequently if engine is operated in severe conditions.

Clean precleaner element by washing in soapy water. Allow to dry then apply clean engine oil. Squeeze out excess oil.

The air filter should be renewed rather than cleaned. Do not wash or direct pressurized air at filter.

FUEL FILTER. If so equipped, periodically inspect fuel filter. If dirty or damaged, renew filter.

CRANKCASE BREATHER. A breather valve is attached to the top of the cylinder head under the rocker cover. A tube connects valve cover to the air cleaner base to allow crankcase vapors to be burned by the engine. Inspect and clean breather valve as needed to prevent or remove restrictions.

SPARK PLUG. Recommended spark plug is Champion RC12YC or equivalent. Specified electrode gap is 1.0 mm (0.040 in.). Tighten spark plug to 38-43 N•m (28-32 ft.-lbs.).

NOTE: Manufacturer does not recommend spark plug cleaning using abrasive grit as grit may enter engine.

CARBURETOR. Initial setting of idle mixture screw (Fig. KO201) is 1¼ turns out on Models CH11 and CH12.5, 1¾ turns out on Model CH14, and one turn out on all CV models. Initial setting of high-speed mixture screw is 1½ turns out on Models CH11 and CH12.5, and 1¼ turns out on Model CH14 (there is no high-speed mixture screw on CV models). Final adjustment of mixture screws should be made with engine at normal operating temperature. Adjust idle speed screw so engine idles at 1500 rpm on CH models and at 1200 rpm on CV models, or at speed specified by equipment manufacturer. Turn idle mixture screw counterclockwise until engine rpm decreases and note screw position. Turn screw clockwise until engine rpm decreases again and note screw position. Turn screw to midpoint between the two noted positions. Reset idle speed screw if necessary to obtain desired idle speed.

To adjust high-speed mixture screw (Fig. KO201) on CH models, run engine at maximum speed under load. Slowly rotate high-speed mixture screw in until engine speed decreases, then turn screw out ¼ turn.

The high-speed mixture on CV models is controlled by a fixed main jet. No optional jets are offered, although a high altitude kit is available.

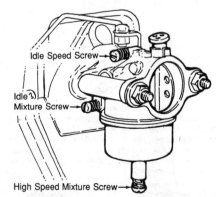

Fig. KO201—View of carburetor showing adjustment points. High-speed mixture screw is not used on CV models. Some models may be equipped with a fuel shut-off solenoid valve on bottom of fuel bowl.

Engine Repair

To disassemble carburetor, refer to Fig. KO202. The edges of throttle and choke plates (3 and 8) are beveled and must be reinstalled in their original positions. Mark choke and throttle plates before removal to ensure correct reassembly. Use a suitably sized screw to pull out the fuel inlet seat if seat is to be renewed. Do not reinstall a seat that has been removed. Use a sharp punch to pierce Welch plug and pry plug from carburetor body. Be careful to prevent punch from contacting and damaging carburetor body.

Clean all parts in suitable carburetor cleaner and blow out all passages with compressed air. Be careful not to enlarge any fuel passages or jets as calibration of carburetor may be altered.

Press new fuel inlet seat into carburetor body so seat is bottomed. Apply Loctite 609 to throttle plate retaining screw. Be sure throttle plate is properly seated against carburetor bore before

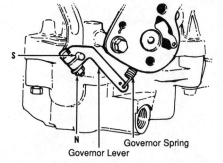

Fig. KO203—View of governor external linkage. Refer to text for adjustment procedure.

tightening screw. Be sure choke shaft properly engages detent spring on carburetor. Locking tabs on choke plate must straddle choke shaft. Use a suitable sealant on Welch plug.

IGNITION. The engine is equipped with a breakerless, electronic magneto ignition system. The electronic ignition module is mounted outside the flywheel. The ignition switch grounds the module to stop the engine. There is no periodic maintenance or adjustment required with this ignition system.

Air gap between module and flywheel should be 0.20-0.30 mm (0.008-0.012 in.). Loosen module retaining screws and position module to obtain desired gap. Tighten screws to 4 N·m (35 in.-lbs.) for used engines or to 6.2 N·m (55 in.-lbs.) on a new engine cylinder block.

If ignition module fails to produce a spark, check for faulty kill switch or grounded wires. Measure resistance of ignition module secondary using suitable ohmmeter. Connect one test lead to spark plug terminal of high-tension wire and other test lead to module core laminations. Resistance should be 7900-10,850 ohms. If resistance is low or infinite, renew module.

GOVERNOR. A flyweight-type governor is located in the crankcase. The governor gear is driven by the camshaft

gear. Refer to REPAIRS section for overhaul information.

To adjust governor linkage, proceed as follows: Loosen governor lever clamp nut (N—Fig. KO203) and push governor lever so throttle is wide open. Turn governor cross shaft (S) counterclockwise as far as possible and tighten clamp nut.

The engine should never run at speeds exceeding 3750 rpm. Maximum high-speed setting depends on engine application. Use a tachometer to check engine speed.

To adjust high idle speed setting on CV models, first loosen throttle control cable clamp (Fig. KO204). Move the equipment speed control lever to "Fast" position. Align the hole in throttle lever with hole in speed control bracket by inserting a pencil or drill bit through the holes. Pull up on throttle control cable shield to remove slack and tighten cable clamp. Start engine and allow to reach operating temperature. Align hole in throttle lever with hole in speed control bracket as previously outlined. Loosen speed control bracket mounting screws and move bracket up (toward flywheel) to decrease high idle speed or down (toward pto) to increase high idle speed. When desired speed is obtained, tighten control bracket screws to 10.7 N·m (95 in.-lbs.) on a new short block or to 7.3 N·m (65 in.-lbs.) on all other engines.

On CH models, governor spring end should be located in following specified hole from end of governor lever for specified high idle speed: outer hole for 3800 rpm, second hole for 3600 rpm, third hole for 3400 rpm, fifth hole for 3200, sixth hole for 3000 rpm. Note that throttle end of governor spring is attached to third hole from top of throttle lever for 3800 rpm and first hole for all other speeds.

Governor sensitivity is adjusted by positioning governor spring in different holes in governor lever arm. On CV models, it is recommended that spring be installed in the hole closest to governor shaft if high idle speed is 3600 rpm

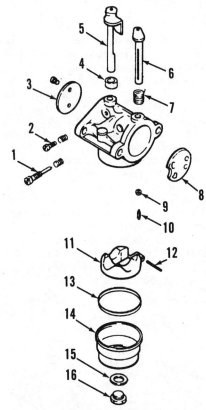

Fig. KO202—Exploded view of float-type carburetor used on all engines. A high-speed mixture screw is located in bottom of fuel bowl in place of retaining screw (16) on CH models. Some engines may be equipped with an electric fuel shut-off solenoid located in bottom of fuel bowl in place of retaining screw (16).

1. Idle mixture screw
2. Idle speed screw
3. Throttle plate
4. Throttle shaft dust seal
5. Throttle shaft
6. Choke shaft
7. Return spring
8. Choke plate
9. Fuel inlet valve seat
10. Fuel inlet valve
11. Float
12. Float shaft
13. Gasket
14. Fuel bowl
15. Gasket
16. Retaining screw

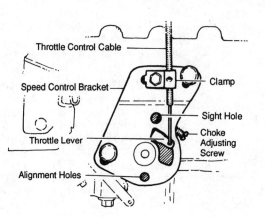

Fig. KO204—View of typical speed control linkage on CV models. Refer to text for adjustment procedure.

Illustrations Courtesy Kohler Co.

or less. If high idle speed is greater than 3600 rpm, use the second hole that is farthest from governor cross shaft. On CH models, governor sensitivity is adjusted by reattaching governor spring to another hole in governor arm. Move spring to an outer hole on arm to decrease governor sensitivity.

VALVE CLEARANCE. All models are equipped with hydraulic valve lifters that automatically maintain proper valve clearance. No periodic adjustment is required.

REPAIRS

TIGHTENING TORQUES. Recommended tightening torques are as follows:

Connecting rod . . . . 22.6 N•m
(200 in.-lbs.)

Crankcase cover/ oil pan. . . . 24.4 N•m
(216 in.-lbs.)

Cylinder head . . . . 41 N•m
(30 ft.-lbs.)

Flywheel . . . . 66 N•m
(49 ft.-lbs.)

Spark plug. . . . . 38-43 N•m
(28-32 ft.-lbs.)

FUEL PUMP. Some engines may be equipped with a mechanically operated diaphragm-type fuel pump. The fuel pump is actuated by an eccentric on engine camshaft. Individual compo-

nents are not available; pump must be renewed as a unit assembly.

When installing fuel pump assembly, make certain that fuel pump lever is positioned to the right side of camshaft. Damage to fuel pump and engine may result if lever is positioned on left side of camshaft. Tighten fuel pump mounting screws to 9.0 N•m (80 in.-lbs.) for first-time installation on new short block. On all other engines, tighten mounting screws to 7.3 N•m (65 in.-lbs.).

CYLINDER HEAD. To remove cylinder head, remove air cleaner assembly and base. Detach speed control linkage and fuel line. Unbolt and remove carburetor and muffler. Remove recoil starter, blower housing and cylinder head air baffles and shields. Remove rocker arm cover. Rotate crankshaft so piston is at top dead center on compression stroke. Push rods and rocker arms should be marked so they can be reinstalled in their original position. Unscrew cylinder head bolts and remove cylinder head and gasket.

To disassemble, remove spark plug. Remove breather retainer (14—Fig. KO205) and reed (15). Push rocker shaft (13) out breather side of rocker arm bridge (12) and remove rocker arms (11). Use a valve spring compressor tool to compress valve springs. Remove split retainers (2), release spring tension and remove valves from cylinder head.

Clean combustion deposits from cylinder head and inspect for cracks or other damage. Check cylinder head surface for flatness; renew head if warped more than 0.076 mm (0.003 in.).

To reassemble cylinder head components, reverse disassembly procedure. Be sure rocker pedestal (12) is installed with small counterbored hole toward exhaust port side of cylinder head. Tighten rocker pedestal mounting screws to 9.9 N•m (88 in.-lbs.). Install a new stem seal (6) on intake valve; do not reuse old seal.

Reverse removal procedure to reinstall head. Tighten cylinder head screws in increments of 14 N•m (10 ft.-lbs.) following sequence shown in Fig. KO206 until final torque of 41 N•m (30 ft.-lbs.) is reached. Install push rods in their original position, compress valve springs and snap push rods underneath rocker arms. Silicone sealant is used as a gasket between valve cover and cylinder head. GE Silmate-type RTV-1473 or RTV-108 sealant (or equivalent) is recommended. The use of a silicone removing solvent is recommended to remove old silicone gasket, as scraping the mating surfaces may damage them and could cause leaks. Apply a 1.6 mm (1/16 in.) bead of sealant to gasket surface of cylinder head. Follow tightening sequence shown in Fig. KO207 and tighten valve cover screws to 10.7 N•m (95 in.-lbs.) if a new cylinder head is installed, or to 7.3 N•m (65 in.-lbs.) if original head is installed.

VALVE SYSTEM. Clean valve heads and stems with a wire brush. Inspect each valve for warped or burned head, pitting or worn stem and renew as required.

Valve face and seat angles are 45° for intake and exhaust. Renew valve if valve margin is less than 1.5 mm (0.060 in.) after grinding valve face.

Specified valve stem-to-guide clearance is 0.038-0.076 mm (0.0015-0.0030

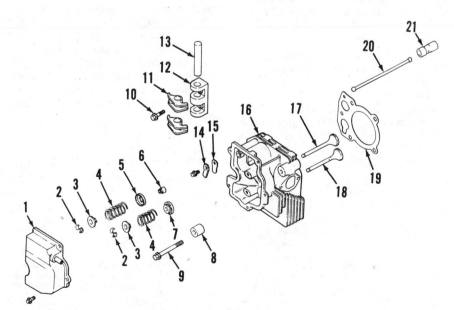

Fig. KO205—Exploded view of cylinder head and valve components. Exhaust valve rotator (7) is used on early production CV model engines before S.N. 1933593554.

1. Valve cover
2. Split retainer
3. Spring retainer
4. Valve spring
5. Spring seat
6. Valve seal (intake)
7. Valve rotator (exhaust)
8. Spacer
9. Head bolt
10. Screw
11. Rocker arm
12. Rocker bridge
13. Rocker shaft
14. Retainer plate
15. Breather reed
16. Cylinder head
17. Intake valve
18. Exhaust valve
19. Head gasket
20. Push rod
21. Valve lifter

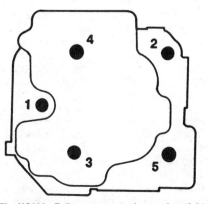

Fig. KO206—Follow sequence shown when tightening cylinder head bolts. Refer to text.

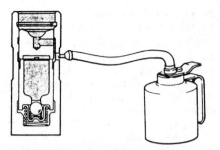

Fig. KO207—Follow sequence shown when tightening valve cover mounting screws. Refer to text.

in.) for intake valve and 0.050-0.088 mm (0.0020-0.0035 in.) for exhaust valve. Specified new valve stem diameter is 6.982-7.000 mm (0.2749-0.2756 in.) for intake and 6.970-6.988 mm (0.2744-0.2751 in.) for exhaust. Specified new valve guide inside diameter for either valve is 7.033-7.058 mm (0.2769-0.2779 in.). Maximum allowable valve guide inside diameter is 7.134 mm (0.2809 in.) for intake guide and 7.159 mm (0.2819 in.) for exhaust guide. Valve guides are not renewable; however, guides can be reamed to accept valves with 0.25 mm oversize stem.

On late production CV engines, starting with serial number 1933503554, the exhaust valve rotator (7—Fig. KO205) has been eliminated and a new spring seat with different length valve spring is used in its place. Free length of the new valve spring is 55.8 mm (2.197 in.), and spring is color coded green for identification. Free length of early production exhaust valve spring is 48.69 mm (1.917 in.).

CAMSHAFT AND HYDRAULIC LIFTERS. To remove camshaft, first rotate crankshaft so piston is at top dead center on compression stroke. Remove rocker cover, compress valve springs and disengage push rods from rocker arms. Remove push rods while marking them so they can be returned to original position. Remove crankcase cover or oil pan mounting screws, then pry cover or oil pan from crankcase at prying lugs located on cover or oil pan. Rotate crankshaft so timing marks on crankshaft and camshaft gears are aligned. Remove camshaft from crankcase. Identify the valve lifters as either intake or exhaust so they can be returned to original position, then remove lifters from crankcase.

Fig. KO208—Whenever hydraulic lifters are removed, they should be primed with oil prior to reassembly. Refer to text.

The camshaft is equipped with a compression reduction device to aid starting. The lever and weight mechanism on the camshaft gear moves a pin inside the exhaust cam lobe. During starting the pin protrudes above the cam lobe and forces the exhaust valve to stay open longer thereby reducing compression. At running speeds the pin remains below the surface of the cam lobe. Inspect mechanism for proper operation.

Inspect camshaft and lifters for scoring, pitting and excessive wear. Minimum cam lobe height is 8.96 mm (0.353 in.) for intake lobe and 9.14 mm (0.360 in.) for exhaust lobe. If camshaft is renewed, new valve lifters should also be installed.

If the hydraulic valve lifters are noisy after engine has run for several minutes and reached operating temperature, it is probably an indication that contamination is preventing the lifter check ball from seating or there is internal wear in the lifter. Individual parts are not available for the hydraulic lifters. Lifters should be renewed if faulty.

Before reassembling engine, the hydraulic lifters should be primed as follows: Use a lever-operated oil can filled with SAE 10W-30 oil. Insert oil can nozzle into oil feed hole in side of lifter body as shown in Fig. KO208. Pump oil into lifter until body is full and oil is level with top of lifter body. Use a push rod to push down on lifter socket; lifter should

feel solid. If socket can be pushed down into lifter body, repeat priming procedure and retest. If lifter will not become solid (pump up), renew lifter assembly.

Lubricate lifter bores with oil and install hydraulic lifters in their original position. The exhaust lifter bore is closest to crankcase gasket surface.

Install camshaft, aligning timing marks (Fig. KO209) on crankshaft and camshaft gears as shown. Camshaft end play is adjusted with shims (19—Fig. KO210 or KO211), which are installed between camshaft and oil pan. To determine camshaft end play, install camshaft with original thickness shim in crankcase. Attach end play checking tool KO-1031 to crankcase and use a feeler gauge to measure clearance between the shim and checking tool. Camshaft end play should be 0.076-0.127 mm (0.003-0.005 in.). Install different thickness shim as necessary to obtain desired end play.

No gasket is used with crankcase cover or oil pan. Apply a 1.6 mm ($\frac{1}{16}$ in.) bead of silicone gasket sealant (GE Silmate RTV-108, RTV-1473 or equivalent) around crankcase cover or oil pan mating surface as shown in Fig. KO212. apply silicone gasket compound to mating surface of pan. Tighten crankcase cover or oil pan screws to 24.4 N•m (216 in.-lbs.) using sequence shown in Fig. KO213.

CAUTION: Hydraulic lifter high-pressure cavity will be filled with oil and lifter extended to maximum open position during the priming procedure. A waiting period is required after assembling engine before starting the engine. This allows valve spring pressure to return the hydraulic lifter socket to its proper position and seat the valve. Failure to wait may result in bent push rods or other engine damage.

After completing assembly of engine, wait ten minutes before attempting to

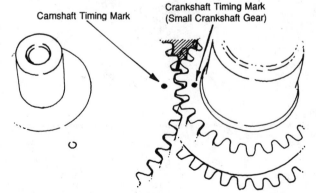

Camshaft Timing Mark

Crankshaft Timing Mark (Small Crankshaft Gear)

Fig. KO209—Align timing mark on small crankshaft gear with timing mark on camshaft gear.

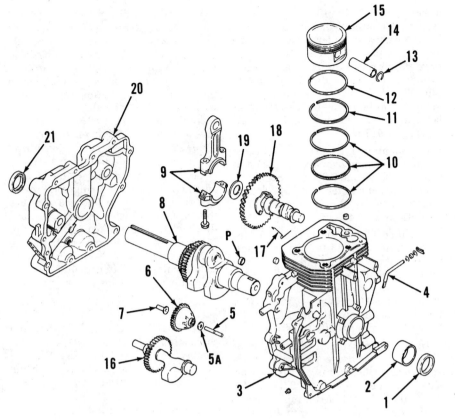

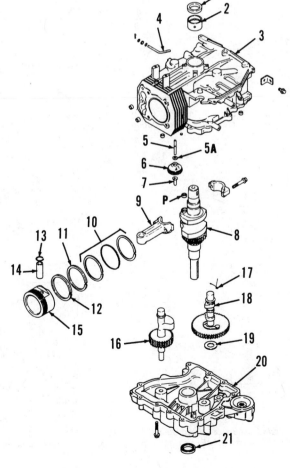

Fig. KO210—Exploded view of crankcase/cylinder block assembly of CH models.

1. Oil seal
2. Main bearing
3. Crankcase/cylinder block
4. Governor cross shaft
5. Governor gear shaft
5A. Thrust washer
6. Governor gear assy.
7. Governor pin
8. Crankshaft
9. Connecting rod
10. Oil control ring
11. Second compression ring
12. Top compression ring
13. Snap ring
14. Piston pin
15. Piston
16. Balance shaft & gear assy.
17. Compression release spring
18. Camshaft & gear assy.
19. Shim
20. Crankcase cover
21. Oil seal

Fig. KO211—Exploded view of crankcase/cylinder block assembly of CV models.

1. Oil seal
2. Main bearing
3. Crankcase/cylinder block
4. Governor cross shaft
5. Governor gear shaft
5A. Thrust washer
6. Governor gear assy.
7. Governor pin
8. Crankshaft
9. Connecting rod
10. Oil control ring
11. Second compression ring
12. Top compression ring
13. Snap ring
14. Piston pin
15. Piston
16. Balance shaft & gear assy.
17. Compression release spring
18. Camshaft & gear assy.
19. Shim
20. Oil pan
21. Oil seal

start engine. Then, rotate engine slowly and check for compression. If there is compression, valves are seating and engine may be started.

PISTON, PIN AND RINGS. The piston and connecting rod are removed as an assembly. Remove cylinder head and camshaft as previously outlined. Remove balance shaft from crankcase. Remove carbon deposits and ring ridge (if present) from top of cylinder before removing piston and rod assembly. Remove connecting rod cap and push connecting rod and piston out of cylinder. Remove piston pin retaining rings and separate piston and rod.

To determine piston clearance in cylinder, measure piston skirt diameter at

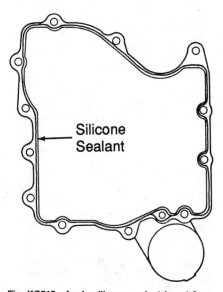

Fig. KO212—Apply silicone sealant in a 1.6 mm (1/16 in.) bead around crankcase cover mating surface as shown.

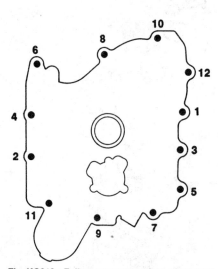

Fig. KO213—Follow sequence shown when tightening crankcase cover or oil pan mounting screws.

a point 6 mm (0.24 in.) from bottom of skirt and perpendicular to piston pin bore. Measure cylinder bore inside diameter at point of greatest wear, approximately 63 mm (2.5 in.) below top of cylinder and perpendicular to piston pin. The difference between the two measurements is piston clearance in bore, which should be 0.041-0.044 mm (0.0016-0.0017 in.).

Piston and rings are available in standard size and oversizes of 0.25 and 0.50 mm (0.010 and 0.020 in.). Standard piston skirt diameter is 86.941-86.959 mm (3.4229-3.4236 in.), and wear limit is 86.814 mm (3.418 in.).

Specified piston pin bore is 19.006-19.012 mm (0.7483-0.7485 in.), and wear limit is 19.025 mm (0.749 in.). Specified piston pin diameter 18.995-19.000 mm (0.7478-0.7480 in.), and wear limit is 18.994 mm (0.7478 in.). Piston-to-piston pin clearance should be 0.006-0.017 mm (0.0002-0.0007 in.).

Insert new rings in piston ring grooves and measure ring side clearance using a feeler gauge. Piston ring side clearance should be 0.040-0.105 mm (0.0016-0.0041 in.) for top compression ring; 0.040-0.072 mm (0.0016-0.0028 in.) for second compression ring; 0.551-0.675 mm (0.0217-0.0266 in.) for oil control ring. Renew piston if side clearance is excessive.

Specified piston ring end gap for compression rings is 0.30-0.50 mm (0.012-0.020 in.). Maximum allowable ring end gap in a used cylinder is 0.77 mm (0.030 in.).

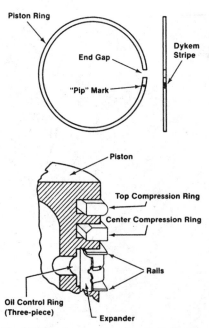

Fig. KO214—Cross-sectional view of piston showing correct installation of piston rings. Refer to text for details.

When assembling piston rings on piston, install oil control ring expander (Fig. KO214) first and then the side rails. Install compression rings so side marked with "pip" mark is toward piston crown and stripe on face of ring is to the left of end gap. Second compression ring has a bevel on inside of ring and has a pink stripe on face of ring. Top compression ring has a barrel face and has a blue stripe on face of ring. Stagger ring end gaps evenly around the piston.

Lubricate piston and cylinder with oil, then use suitable ring compressor tool to install piston and rod. Be sure that arrow on piston crown is toward flywheel side of crankcase as shown in Fig. KO215. Tighten connecting rod cap bolts evenly to 22.6 N•m (200 in.-lbs.). Install balance shaft, camshaft and cylinder head as outlined in appropriate sections.

CONNECTING ROD. Piston and connecting rod are removed as an assembly as outlined in PISTON, PIN AND RINGS section. Remove piston pin retaining rings and separate piston and rod.

Renew connecting rod if bearing surfaces are scored or excessively worn. Specified connecting rod small end diameter is 19.015-19.023 mm (0.7486-0.7489 in.), and wear limit is 19.036 mm (0.7495 in.). Specified connecting rod-to-piston pin running clearance is 0.015-0.028 mm (0.0006-0.0011 in.).

Specified connecting rod-to-crankpin bearing clearance is 0.030-0.055 mm (0.0011-0.0022 in.), and maximum allowable clearance is 0.07 mm (0.0025 in.). A connecting rod with 0.25 mm (0.010 in.) undersize big end is available. The undersized rod can be identified by the drilled hole located in lower end of the rod.

Specified rod side clearance on crankpin is 0.18-0.41 mm (0.007-0.016 in.).

To reinstall connecting rod and piston assembly, reverse the removal procedure. Be sure that arrow mark on top of piston is toward flywheel side of crankcase (Fig. KO215). Tighten connecting rod cap bolts evenly to 22.6 N•m (200

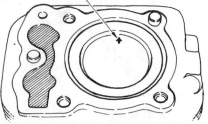

Fig. KO215—Piston must be installed with arrow pointing toward flywheel side of engine.

in.-lbs.). Refer to PISTON, PIN AND RINGS section and reverse removal procedure to install remainder of components.

GOVERNOR. The engine is equipped with a flyweight mechanism mounted on governor gear (6—Figs. KO210 or KO211). Remove crankcase cover or oil pan (20) for access to governor gear. Inspect gear assembly for excess wear and damage. The governor gear is held onto governor shaft (5) by molded tabs on the gear. When gear is removed, the tabs are damaged and replacement of governor gear will be required. Gear and flyweight assembly are available only as a unit assembly. If governor gear shaft (5) requires renewal, tap new shaft into crankcase so it protrudes 32.64-32.84 mm (1.285-1.293 in.) above crankcase boss. Remove cotter pin to remove governor lever shaft (4). Inspect shaft oil seal in crankcase bore and renew if necessary.

No gasket is used with crankcase cover or oil pan. Apply a 1.6 mm ($\frac{1}{16}$ in.) bead of silicone gasket sealant (GE Silmate RTV-108, RTV-1473 or equivalent) around crankcase cover or oil pan mating surface as shown in Fig. KO212. apply silicone gasket compound to mating surface of pan. Tighten crankcase cover or oil pan screws to 24.4 N•m (216 in.-lbs.) using sequence shown in Fig. KO213. Adjust governor as previously outlined in MAINTENANCE section.

CRANKSHAFT. To remove crankshaft, remove starter and flywheel. Remove crankcase cover or oil pan, piston, connecting rod and camshaft as previously outlined. Remove balance shaft. Remove crankshaft from crankcase. The crankshaft rides in a renewable bushing (2—Fig. KO210 or KO211) in the crankcase and in an integral bearing in the crankcase cover or oil pan.

Specified main journal diameter at flywheel end is 44.913-44.935 mm (1.7682-1.7691 in.), and wear limit is 44.84 mm (1.765 in.). Bearing inside diameter at flywheel end is 44.965-45.003 mm (1.7703-1.7718 in.), and wear limit is 45.016 mm (1.7723 in.). Crankshaft-to-bearing running clearance should be 0.03-0.09 mm (0.0012-0.0035 in.). When renewing main bearing, make certain that oil hole in bearing aligns with oil passage in crankcase.

Specified main journal diameter at pto end is 41.915-41.935 mm (1.6502-1.6510 in.), and wear limit is 41.86 mm (1.648 in.). Crankshaft-to-oil pan bore running clearance should be 0.03-0.09 mm (0.0012-0.0035 in.).

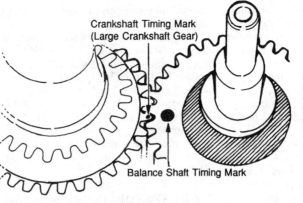

Fig. KO216—When assembling engine, align timing mark on large crankshaft gear with timing mark on balance shaft gear.

Maximum allowable main journal taper is 0.020 mm (0.0008 in.) and maximum allowable out-of-round is 0.025 mm (0.0010 in.). Main journals cannot be machined undersize.

Specified standard crankpin diameter is 38.958-38.970 mm (1.5338-1.5343 in.). Minimum allowable crankpin diameter is 38.94 mm (1.533 in.). Maximum allowable crankpin taper is 0.012 mm (0.0005 in.) and maximum allowable out-of-round is 0.025 mm (0.0010 in.). Crankpin can be ground to accept a connecting rod that is 0.25 mm (0.010 in.) undersize. Plug (P—Fig. KO210 or KO211) should be removed after machining operation so oil passages can be cleaned thoroughly. Use a suitable screw-type puller to extract plug. Be sure new plug does not leak.

Maximum allowable crankshaft runout is 0.15 mm (0.006 in.) measured at pto end of crankshaft with crankshaft supported in engine. Maximum allowable crankshaft runout is 0.10 mm (0.004 in.) measured at any point on crankshaft with crankshaft supported in V-blocks.

To install crankshaft, reverse the removal procedure. Install balance shaft, aligning timing marks on large crankshaft gear and balance shaft gear as shown in Fig. KO216. Install camshaft, aligning timing marks on small crankshaft gear and camshaft gear as shown in Fig. KO209. No gasket is used with crankcase cover or oil pan. Apply a 1.6 mm ($\frac{1}{16}$ in.) bead of silicone gasket sealant (GE Silmate RTV-108, RTV-1473 or equivalent) around crankcase cover or oil pan mating surface as shown in Fig. KO212. apply silicone gasket compound to mating surface of pan. Tighten crankcase cover or oil pan screws to 24.4 N•m (216 in.-lbs.) using sequence shown in Fig. KO213. Tighten flywheel retaining nut to 66 N•m (90 ft.-lbs.).

CYLINDER/CRANKCASE. Cylinder bore standard diameter is 87.000-

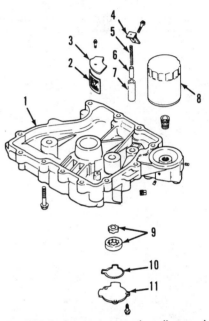

Fig. KO217—Gerotor-type engine oil pump is mounted in crankcase cover on CH models or in oil pan on CV models. Oil pickup screen (2) and cover (3) are used on CV models. Not shown is oil pickup tube assembly used on CH models.

1. Crankcase cover/oil pan
2. Oil pick-up screen
3. Cover
4. Relief valve bracket
5. Relief valve spring
6. Relief valve piston
7. Relief valve body
8. Oil filter
9. Inner & outer rotors
10. "O" ring
11. Pump cover

87.025 (3.4252-3.4262 in.), and wear limit is 87.063 mm (3.4277 in.). Maximum bore out-of-round is 0.12 mm (0.005 in.). Maximum bore taper is 0.05 mm (0.002 in.). Cylinder can be bored to accept an oversize piston.

Install crankshaft oil seals in crankcase and oil pan using seal driver KO-1036. Force seal into crankcase or oil pan until tool bottoms.

OIL PUMP. A gerotor-type oil pump is located in crankcase cover of CH models or oil pan of CV models. The oil pump is driven by the engine balance shaft. Oil pump rotors (9—Fig. KO217) can be removed for inspection after removing pump cover (11) from bottom of crankcase cover or oil pan. The crankcase cover or oil pan must be removed for access to oil pick-up or oil pressure regulator valve (5 through 7).

Check oil pump rotors and oil pan cavity for scoring or excessive wear. Pressure relief valve body (7) and piston (6) must be free of scratches or burrs. Relief valve spring (5) free length should be approximately 25.20 mm (0.992 in.).

Lubricate oil pump cavity and pump rotors with oil during reassembly. Install new "O" ring (10) in groove in crankcase cover or oil pan. Install pump cover (11) and tighten mounting screws to 6.2 N·m (55 in.-lbs.) on a new crankcase cover or oil pan or 4.0 N·m (35 in.-lbs.) on a used crankcase cover or oil pan.

No gasket is used with crankcase cover or oil pan. Apply a 1.6 mm ($\frac{1}{16}$ in.) bead of silicone gasket sealant (GE Silmate RTV-108, RTV-1473 or equivalent) around crankcase cover or oil pan mating surface as shown in Fig. KO212. Apply silicone gasket compound to mating surface of pan. Tighten crankcase cover or oil pan screws to 24.4 N·m (216 in.-lbs.) using sequence shown in Fig. KO213.

OIL SENSOR. Some engines are equipped with an Oil Sentry oil pressure monitor. The system uses a pressure switch installed in one of the main oil galleries of the crankcase cover or oil pan, or on the oil filter adapter. The pressure switch is designed to break contact as oil pressure increases to normal pressure, and to make contact when oil pressure decreases within the range of 20-35 kPa (3-5 psi). When switch contacts close, either the engine will stop or a "Low Oil" warning light will be activated, depending on engine application.

To check sensor pressure switch, a regulated supply of compressed air and a continuity tester are required. With zero pressure applied to switch, tester should indicate continuity across switch terminal and ground. When pressure is increased through range of 20-35 kPa (3-5 psi), switch should open and tester should indicate no continuity. If switch fails test, install new switch.

KOHLER

KOHLER COMPANY
Kohler, Wisconsin 53044

Model	No. Cyls.	Bore	Stroke	Displacement	Power Rating
K-482	2	3.250 in. (82.55 mm)	2.875 in. (73.03 mm)	47.8 cu. in. (781.73 cc)	18 hp. (13.4 kW)
K-532	2	3.375 in. (85.73 mm)	3.0 in. (76.2 mm)	53.67 cu. in. (879.7 cc)	20 hp. (14.9 kW)
K-582	2	3.5 in. (88.9 mm)	3.0 in. (76.2 mm)	57.7 cu. in. (946 cc)	23 hp. (17.2 kW)
K-662	2	3.625 in. (92.08 mm)	3.250 in. (82.55 mm)	67.2 cu. in. (1099.4 cc)	24 hp. (17.9 kW)

All engines in this section are four-stroke, two cylinder opposed, horizontal crankshaft engines. Crankshaft for K-482, K-532 and K-582 models is supported by a ball bearing at output end and a sleeve type bearing at flywheel end of crankshaft. Crankshaft for K-662 model is supported at each end by tapered roller bearings.

Connecting rod for K-482, K-532 and K-582 models rides directly on crankpin journal and K-662 model connecting rod is equipped with a renewable type precision bearing insert. Pressure lubrication is provided by a gear type oil pump driven by crankshaft gear.

Either a battery type or magneto type ignition system is used according to model and application.

A side draft, float type carburetor is used for K-482, K-532 and K-582 models and a down draft, float type carburetor is used on K-662 model.

Engine model, serial and specification numbers must be given when ordering parts.

MAINTENANCE

SPARK PLUG. Recommended spark plug is Champion H10 or equivalent for K-482, K-532 and K-582 models or Champion J8C or equivalent for K-662 model. Electrode gap is 0.025 inch (0.635 mm) for all models except K-582. Electrode gap for K-582 is 0.035 inch (0.889 mm).

CARBURETOR. Refer to Fig. KO61 for exploded view of Kohler side draft carburetor used on Models K-482, K-532 and K-582 engines and to Figs. KO62 or KO63 for Carter or Zenith downdraft carburetors used on Model K-662 engines. For initial adjustment on all models, open idle fuel needle 1-1/4 turns and open main fuel needle 2 turns. Make final adjustment with engine at operating temperature and running. Operate engine under load and adjust main fuel needle for leanest mixture that will allow satisfactory acceleration and steady governor operation.

Adjust idle speed stop screw to maintain a low idle speed of 1000 rpm. Then, adjust idle mixture needle for smoothest idle operation.

Since main fuel and idle fuel adjustments affect each other, recheck

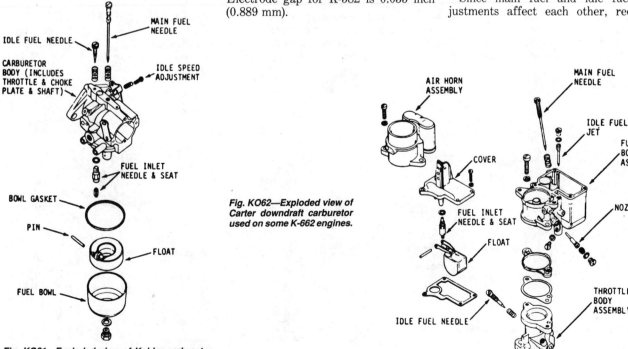

Fig. KO61—Exploded view of Kohler carburetor used on K-482, K-532 and K-582 models.

Fig. KO62—Exploded view of Carter downdraft carburetor used on some K-662 engines.

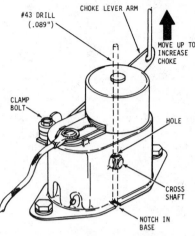

Fig. KO63—Exploded view of Zenith downdraft carburetor used on some K-662 engines.

Fig. KO63B—To adjust choke, remove air cleaner and insert a small round rod through cross shaft until it engages notch in base. Loosen clamp bolt on choke lever and adjust choke plate to desired setting. Tighten clamp bolt.

engine operation and readjust fuel needles as necessary.

To check float level, invert carburetor body and float assembly. There should be 11/64-inch (4.366 mm) clearance between machined surface of body casting and free end of float on Kohler carburetor used on Models K-482, K-532 and K-582. On Carter or Zenith carburetors used on Model K-662, there should be a distance of 1 1/2 inches (38.1 mm) between machined surface of casting and top of float. Adjust as necessary by bending float lever tang that contacts inlet valve.

AUTOMATIC CHOKE. One of two different types automatic choke may be used according to model and application. One is an integral part of the downdraft

carburetor while the other is mounted on exhaust manifold and choke plate is controlled through external linkage.

To adjust type which is integral with carburetor, loosen the three screws (Fig. KO63A) and rotate housing in clockwise direction to close, or counterclockwise to open.

To adjust exhaust manifold mounted type, remove air cleaner and move choke arm (Fig. KO63B) until hole in brass shaft aligns with slot in bearing and insert a small round rod as shown. Loosen clamp bolt on choke lever and adjust choke plate to desired position. Tighten clamp bolt and remove rod.

The electrical lead on this choke is connected so current flows to thermostatic element when ignition is switched on. Tension of thermostatic spring should

be set to allow full choke at starting. Current through heating element controls tension of thermostatic spring, which gradually opens choke as engine warms up.

Choke on all models should be fully open when engine has reached operating temperature.

GOVERNOR. An externally mounted centrifugal flyweight type governor is used on all engines. Governor is driven by the camshaft gear and is lubricated by an external oil line connected to engine lubrication system.

GOVERNOR INSTALLATION AND TIMING (K-482, K-532 and K-582). Ignition breaker points are mounted on governor housing on Models K-482,

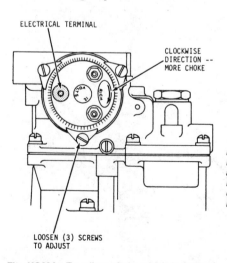

Fig. KO63A—To adjust choke which is integral part of carburetor, loosen the three screws and rotate housing clockwise to increase or counterclockwise to decrease choke action.

Fig. KO64—Top view showing location of sight holes and timing marks used when installing governor assembly on K-482, K-532 or K-582 models.

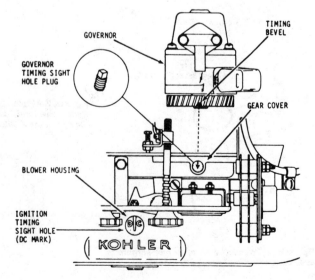

Illustrations Courtesy Kohler Co.

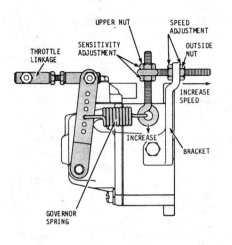

Fig. KO65—View of governor linkage, maximum speed stop set screw and governor spring used on K-482, K-532 and K-582 models. Governor sensitivity is adjusted by moving governor spring to alternate holes.

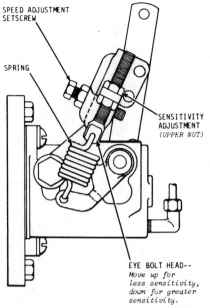

Fig. KO66—View of governor spring, maximum speed adjustment set screw and sensitivity adjustment on K-662 model governor.

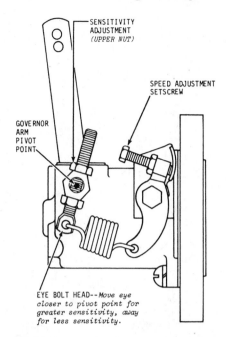

Fig. KO66A—View of K-662 governor linkage showing various adjustment points.

K-532 and K-582 and are activated by a push rod which rides on a cam on governor drive shaft. Therefore, governor must be timed to engine.

To install governor assembly, first uncover ignition timing sight hole in top center of blower housing. See Fig. KO64. Rotate engine crankshaft until "DC" mark on flywheel is centered in sight hole. Remove governor timing sight hole plug from engine gear cover. Install governor assembly so tooth with special timing bevel on governor gear is centered in governor timing sight hole. Install governor retaining cap screws. Recheck to make certain both the "DC" mark on flywheel and beveled tooth on governor gear are centered in sight holes, then install sight hole plug and cover.

After governor is installed, readjust ignition timing as outlined in **IGNITION TIMING** paragraph.

GOVERNOR INSTALLATON (K-662). Since breaker points are not mounted on or driven off governor on Model K-662, governor does not have to be timed to the engine. Installation of governor assembly is obvious.

GOVERNOR ADJUSTMENT. Different governor adjustment procedures must be followed for models running at constant speed than for models running at variable speed. Model K-662 has a slightly different adjustment procedure due to the use of a different governor assembly. Make certain correct procedure is followed for model being serviced and set idle and high speed adjustments to manufacturers recommendation for application for which engine is used.

To adjust governor on all models with variable speed application use the following procedure: First move governor arm forward to high idle position and check to see that throttle linkage moves carburetor throttle shaft to wide open position. If not, adjust length of throttle linkage as necessary. Make certain throttle linkage moves freely.

Start engine and move speed control lever to high idle position. Using a tachometer, check engine speed. Loosen locknuts and adjust high speed stop set screw on speed control bracket (Fig. KO65 or KO66) to obtain maximum no-load speed shown in operators manual and make certain allowable maximum speed for each different engine application is not exceeded, varying applications require varying maximum speeds. Retighten locknuts.

Refer to Fig. KO65 for proper place-

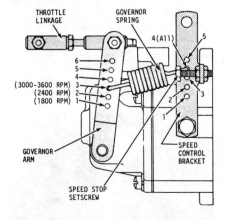

Fig. KO65A—View of governor linkage on constant speed governor for K-482, K-532 and K-582 models.

Fig. KO67—Breaker points are externally mounted on K-482, K-532 and K-582 models governor housings. "SP" (27° BTDC) mark should be centered in sight hole at 1200 rpm or above. Refer to text.

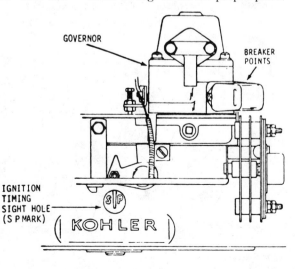

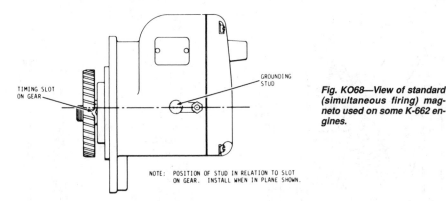

Fig. KO68—View of standard (simultaneous firing) magneto used on some K-662 engines.

ment of governor spring in hole of governor arm and control bracket. If governor surging or hunting occurs, governor is too sensitive and governor spring should be moved to a set of holes closer together. If a big drop in speed occurs when normal load is applied, governor should be set for greater sensitivity. Increase spring tension by placing spring in holes spaced further apart. Move spring one hole at a time and recheck engine operation and high idle rpm after each adjustment.

On Model K-662, governor sensitivity is adjusted by loosening one nut and tightening opposite nut on spring eye bolt. See Fig. KO66. If governor hunting or surging occurs, governor is too sensitive. To correct, loosen bottom nut and tighten top nut. To increase sensitivity, loosen top nut and tighten bottom nut. After adjustment, recheck engine high idle rpm as changing sensitivity will affect high idle speed.

To adjust governor on all models except K-662, constant speed application, use the following procedure: Remove air cleaner and note throttle shaft must be a certain length to maintain a fixed operating speed such as 1800 rpm for 60 cycle electric generators. Any changes in length will result in changes in generator output, therefore only slight readjustment of speed is recommended and always check generator for correct output after adjustments. To increase speed, loosen speed adjusting nuts (Fig. KO65A) and draw eye of bolt closer to the bracket. Reverse procedure to decrease speed. Make certain all adjusting nuts are tight after final adjustments.

Sensitivity is varied by changing length of sensitivity eye bolt. Move bolt downward to increase sensitivity and upward to decrease sensitivity.

On K-662 models, refer to Fig. KO66A. To increase sensitivity draw eye of bolt closer to pivot point and to decrease sensitivity move eye of bolt away from pivot point.

On all models recheck speeds and check output of generators if applicable.

IGNITION TIMING (K-482, K-532 and K-582). Ignition points are externally mounted on governor housing and are activiated by a push rod which rides on a cam on governor drive shaft. An automatic spark advance-retard mechanism is incorporated in the governor which allows engine to start at 8° BTDC and run (1200 rpm or above) at 27° BTDC.

To adjust ignition timing, first remove breaker point cover and adjust breaker

contact gap to 0.020 inch (0.508 mm). Install breaker point cover, then remove cover from ignition timing sight hole in top center of blower housing. Attach timing light to number "1" spark plug (cylinder nearest to flywheel). Start engine and operate at 1200 rpm or above. Aim timing light at ignition timing sight hole. The "SP" mark on flywheel should be centered in sight hole when light flashes. See Fig. KO67. If "SP" mark is not centered in sight hole, loosen governor mounting cap screws and rotate governor assembly until the "SP" (27° BTDC) mark is centered as light flashes. Retighten governor mounting cap screws.

If slotted holes in governor flange will not allow enough rotation to center the timing mark, check governor timing as outlined in **GOVERNOR INSTALLATION** and **TIMING** paragraph.

IGNITION TIMING (K-662). Two types of external, self-contained magnetos have been used on Model K-662 engines. Standard magneto (Fig. KO68) is referred to as a simultaneous firing magneto. This type fires both spark plugs at the same time. Ignition occurs only in cylinder in which piston is on compression stroke. At this time, piston in opposite cylinder is on exhaust stroke and that spark is ineffective.

The other magneto (Fig. KO69) is classified as a distributor type magneto. This magneto is equipped with a distributor rotor which directs ignition voltage to the proper spark plug at appropriate time.

Breaker point gap on either type magneto is 0.015 inch (0.381 mm).

To install and time standard type magneto, first crank engine over slowly by hand until "DC" mark on flywheel is centered in timing sight hole (A – Fig. KO70). Rotate magneto drive gear until impulse coupling trips. Then turn gear backwards until timing slot in gear is aligned with grounding stud on case as shown in Fig. KO68. Using a new flange gasket, carefully install magneto assembly. Tighten retaining cap screws securely. Slowly crank engine one revolution until impulse coupling trips. At this time, "DC" mark on flywheel should be just past center of timing sight hole. To

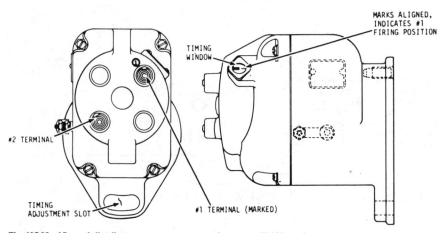

Fig. KO69—View of distributor type magneto used on some K-662 engines.

Fig. KO70—Location of ignition timing sight hole (A) on K-662 model engine.

Illustrations Courtesy Kohler Co.

check and adjust running timing, attach a timing light, start engine and operate at 1200 rpm or above. Aim timing light at timing sight hole (A – Fig. KO70). The "SP" mark on flywheel should be centered in sight hole when timing light flashes. If not, loosen magneto mounting cap screws and rotate magneto assembly until the "SP" (22° BTDC) mark is centered in sight hole. Tighten mounting cap screws.

To install and time distributor type magneto (Fig. KO69), first remove spark plug from No. 1 cylinder (cylinder closest to flywheel). Slowly crank engine over until No. 1 piston is on compression stroke and "M" mark on engine flywheel is centered in ignition sight hole (A – Fig. KO70). Turn magneto drive gear counter-clockwise (facing gear) until white mark is centered in timing window on magneto. See Fig. KO69. Using a new flange gasket, carefully install magneto assembly. Tighten retaining cap screws securely. Slowly crank engine in normal direction of rotation until impulse coupling trips. At this time, "DC" mark on flywheel should be just in center of timing sight hole. To check and adjust running timing, attach a timing light, start engine and operate at 1200 rpm or above. Aim timing light at timing sight hole (A-Fig. KO70). The "SP" (22° BTDC) mark should be centered in sight hole. Tighten mounting cap screws.

COMPRESSION TEST. Results of a compression test can be used to partially determine the condition of the engine. To check compression, remove spark plugs, make certain air cleaner is clean and set throttle and choke in wide open position. Crank engine with starting motor to a speed of about 1000 rpm. Insert gage in spark plug hole and take several readings on both cylinders. Consistent readings in the 110-120 psi (758-827 kPa) range indicate good compression. When compression falls below 100 psi (690 kPa) on either cylinder, valve leakage or excessive wear in cylinder, or ring wear is indicated.

If compression reading is higher than 120 psi (827 kPa), it indicates excessive carbon deposits have built up in combustion chamber. Remove cylinder heads and clean carbon from heads.

LUBRICATION. A gear type oil pump supplies oil through internal galleries to front main bearing, camshaft bearings, connecting rods and other wear areas. A full flow, spin-on type oil filter, located on crankcase in front of number "2" cylinder on Models K-482, K-532 and K-582, or just to the rear of number "1" cylinder on Model K-662, or a remote mounted cannister

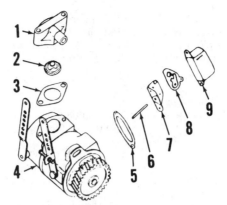

Fig. KO71—View showing location of breather valve assembly and breaker points on K-482, K-532 or K-582 models governor assembly. Breather valve (2) and valve housing (1) are available as an assembly.

1. Valve housing	6. Breaker push rod
2. Breather valve	7. Bracket
3. Gasket	8. Breaker points
4. Governor assy.	9. Cover
5. Gasket	

type oil filter connected to engine via two pressure hoses located on left side of engine block, are used in the oil pressure system. Normal oil pressure for all models when operating at normal temperature should be 25 psi (172 kPa) at 1200 rpm, 30-50 psi (207-345 kPa) at 1800 rpm, 35-55 psi (241-379 kPa) at 2200 rpm and 45-65 psi (310-448 kPa) at 3200-3600 rpm. On Models K-482, K-532 and K-582, an oil pressure relief valve is located on crankcase just forward of number "1" cylinder (cylinder nearest to flywheel). To adjust oil pressure, loosen locknut and turn adjusting screw clockwise to increase pressure or counter-clockwise to decrease pressure. Retighten locknut.

High quality detergent type oil having API classification "SC", "SD", "SE" or "SF" are recommended for use in Kohler engines. Use SAE 30 oil if temperature is above 32° F. (0° C) and use SAE 5W-20 or 5W-30 if temperature is below 32° F. (0° C).

Maintain crankcase oil level at full mark on dipstick, but do not overfill.

Recommended oil change interval is every 50 hours of normal operation. Oil capacity is 3.0 qts. (2.8 L). Add an extra 0.5 qt. (0.47 L) when filter on K-482, K-532 and K-582 is changed and an extra 1.0 qt. (0.95 L) to K-662 when filter is changed.

CRANKCASE BREATHER (K-482, K-532 and K-582). A one-way breather valve (2 – Fig. KO71) located on top of governor housing is connected by a hose to air inlet side of carburetor. The breather system maintains a slight vacuum within the crankcase. Vacuum should be approximately 12 inches on a water manometer with engine operating at 3600 rpm. If manometer shows crankcase pressure, breather valve is faulty, oil seals or gaskets are worn or damaged or engine has excessive blow-by due to worn rings.

Breather valve is pressed into valve housing (1) and is available only as an assembly with the housing.

CRANKCASE BREATHER (K-662). A reed type breather valve (Fig. KO72) located on top of gear cover maintains a partial vacuum within engine crankcase. Vacuum should be approximately 16 inches on a water manometer with engine operating at 3200 rpm. If manometer shows crankcase pressure, breather valve is faulty, oil seals or gaskets are worn or damaged, or engine has excessive blow-by due to worn rings.

Breather components must be correctly installed to function properly. See Fig. KO72. Reed must be free of rust, dents or cracks and must lay flat on breather ports in gear cover. Tabs on reed stop must be 0.020 inch (0.508 mm) above reed.

A closed system was also used on some K-662 models and all parts are the same except for a special housing which is connected to air inlet side of carburetor by a tube and provides a positive draw on breather whenever engine is in operation.

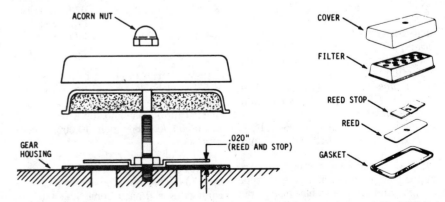

Fig. KO72—Reed type crankcase breather used on K-662 model. Tabs on reed stop must be 0.020 inch (0.508 mm) above reed as shown.

REPAIRS

TIGHTENING TORQUES. Recommended tightening torques with lightly lubricated threads are as follows:

Spark plug ....22 ft.-lbs.
(30 N·m)
Camshaft nut—
K-482, K-532 & K-582.....40 ft.-lbs.
(54 N·m)
K-662 ....25 ft.-lbs.
(34 N·m)
Connecting rod cap screws—
K-482, K-532 & K-582.....25 ft.-lbs.
(34 N·m)
K-662 ....35 ft.-lbs.
(48 N·m)
Cylinder head cap screws—
K-482, K-532 & K-582.....35 ft.-lbs.
(48 N·m)
K-662 ....40 ft.-lbs.
(54 N·m)
Closure plate cap screws—
K-482, K-532 & K-582.....30 ft.-lbs.
(40 N·m)
K-662 ....50 ft.-lbs.
(68 N·m)
Flywheel nut—
K-482, K-532 & K-582.....115 ft.-lbs.
(156 N·m)
K-662 ....130 ft.-lbs.
(176 N·m)
Oil pan cap screws—
K-482, K-532 & K-582.....30 ft.-lbs.
(40 N·m)
K-662 ....45 ft.-lbs.
(61 N·m)

CONNECTING RODS. Connecting rod and piston assemblies can be removed after removing oil pan (engine base) and cylinder heads. Identify each rod and piston assembly so they can be reinstalled in their original cylinders and do not intermix connecting rod caps.

On Models K-482, K-532 and K-582, connecting rods ride directly on the crankpins. Connecting rods 0.010 inch (0.254 mm) oversize are available for undersize reground crankshafts. Standard crankpin diameter is 1.6245-1.6250 inches (41.262-41.275 mm). Desired running clearances are as follows:

Connecting rods to
crankpins ....0.001-0.0035 in.
(0.0254-0.0889 mm)
Connecting rods to
piston pins ....0.0003-0.0008 in.
(0.0076-0.0203 mm)
Rod side play on
crankpins ....0.005-0.014 in.
(0.1270-0.3556 mm)

On K-662 model connecting rods are equipped with renewable insert type bearings and a renewable piston pin bushing. Bearings are available for 0.002, 0.010 and 0.020 inch (0.0508,

0.254 and 0.508 mm) undersize crankshafts. Standard crankpin diameter is 1.8745-1.8750 inches (47.612-47.625 mm). Desired running clearances are as follows:

Connecting rods to
crankpins ....0.0003-0.0035 in.
(0.0076-0.0889 mm)
Connecting rods to
piston pins ....0.0001-0.0006 in.
(0.0025-0.0152 mm)
Rod side play on
crankpins ....0.007-0.011 in.
(0.1778-0.2794 mm)

On all models, when installing connecting rod and piston units, make certain raised match marks on rods and rod caps are aligned and are towards flywheel side of engine. Kohler recommends connecting rod cap screws of K-482, K-532 and K-582 be tightened evenly to a torque of 30 ft.-lbs. (40 N·m), then loosened and retorqued to 25 ft.-lbs. (34 N·m). Kohler recommends connecting rod cap screws on K-662 engines be tightened to 40 ft.-lbs. (54 N·m), then loosened and retorqued to 35 ft.-lbs. (48 N·m).

On all models connecting rod cap screw threads should be lightly lubricated before installation.

PISTONS, PINS AND RINGS. Aluminum alloy pistons are fitted with two compression rings and one oil control ring. Renew pistons if scored or if side clearance of new ring in piston top ring groove exceeds 0.006 inch (0.1524 mm). Pistons are available in oversizes of 0.010, 0.020 and 0.030 inch (0.254, 0.508 and 0.762 mm) as well as standard size. Recommended piston to cylinder bore clearance when measured just below oil ring at right angle to pin is as follows:

K-482 ....0.007-0.009 in.
(0.1778-0.2286 mm)
K-532 ....0.0065-0.0095 in.
(0.1651-0.2413 mm)
K-582 ....0.007-0.010 in.
(0.178-0.254 mm)
K-662 ....0.001-0.003 in.
(0.0254-0.0762 mm)

Piston pin fit in piston boss on K-482, K-532 and K-582 should be from 0.000 (light interference) to 0.0005 inch (0.0127 mm) loose and for K-662 should be 0.0001-0.0003 inch (0.0025-0.0076 mm) loose.

Piston pin fit in rod on K-482, K-532 and K-582 should be 0.0003-0.0008 inch (0.0076-0.0203 mm) loose. Model K-662 connecting rod has a renewable bushing for piston pin and piston fit should be 0.0001-0.0006 inch (0.0025-0.0152 mm)

loose. Always renew piston pin retaining rings.

Kohler recommends piston rings should always be renewed when they are removed.

Piston ring end gap for all models should be 0.010-0.020 inch (0.254-0.508 mm) for new bores and a maximum of 0.030 inch (0.762 mm) for used bores.

Piston ring specifications are as follows:

Ring width
Compression rings ....0.093 in.
(2.36 mm)
Oil ring ....0.187 in.
(4.750 mm)
Ring side clearance (K-482, K-532 and K-582)
Top ring ....0.002-0.004 in.
(0.0508-0.1016 mm)
2nd ring.........0.0015-0.0035 in.
(0.0381-0.0889 mm)
Oil ring ....0.001-0.003 in.
(0.0254-0.0762 mm)
Ring side clearance (K-662)
Top ring ....0.0025-0.0045 in.
(0.0635-0.1143 mm)
2nd ring ....0.0025-0.0045 in.
(0.0635-0.1143 mm)
Oil ring ....0.002-0.0035 in.
(0.0508-0.0889 mm)

Piston rings are available in standard size and oversizes of 0.010, 0.020 and 0.030 inch (0.254, 0.508 and 0.762 mm).

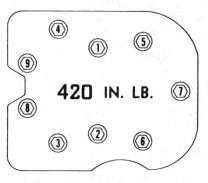

Fig. KO73—Tighten cylinder head cap screws on K-482, K-532 and K-582 models to 35 ft.-lbs. (48 N·m) torque using sequence shown.

Fig. KO74—Tighten cylinder head cap screws on K-662 model to 50 ft.-lbs. (68 N·m) torque using sequence shown.

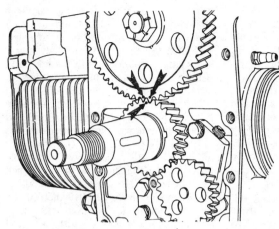

Fig. KO75—View showing timing marks on camshaft gear and crankshaft gear on K-482, K-532 and K-582 models. Model K-662 is similar.

Fig. KO76—Front crankshaft seal on K-662 model rotates with crankshaft and seals against gear cover.

CYLINDERS. If cylinder walls are scored or bores are tapered or out-of-round more than 0.005 inch (0.127 mm) cylinders should be bored to nearest suitable oversize of 0.010, 0.020 or 0.030 inch (0.254, 0.508 or 0.762 mm). Standard cylinder bore for K-482 is 3.250 inches (82.55 mm), for K-532 is 3.375 inches (85.73 mm), for K-582 is 3.5 inches (88.9 mm) and for K-662 is 3.625 inches (92.08 mm).

CYLINDER HEADS. Always use new head gaskets when installing cylinder heads. Tighten cylinder head cap screws evenly to a torque of 35 ft.-lbs. (48 N·m) on Models K-482, K-532 and K-582 using sequence shown in Fig. KO73 or 50 ft.-lbs. (68 N·m) on Model K-662 using sequence shown in Fig. KO74.

CRANKSHAFT AND MAIN BEARINGS (K-482, K-532 and K-582). Crankshaft is supported by a ball bearing at pto end of crankshaft and a sleeve type bearing at flywheel end of shaft.

The sleeve bearing is pressed into front of crankcase with an interference fit of 0.0015-0.0045 inch (0.038-0.114 mm). Standard front crankshaft journal diameter is 1.7490-1.750 inches (44.44-44.45 mm) and normal running clearance is 0.002-0.0035 inch (0.0508-0.0889 mm) in sleeve bearing.

The rear main (ball bearing) is secured to crankshaft and closure plate with retaining rings. If retaining rings, grooves and bearing are in good condition, crankshaft end play will be within recommended range of 0.004-0.010 inch (0.1016-0.254 mm).

Standard crankpin diameter is 1.6245-1.6250 inches (41.26-41.28 mm). If crankpin journals are scored or out-of-round more than 0.0005 inch (0.0127 mm) they may be reground 0.010 inch (0.254 mm) undersize for use with connecting rod for undersize shaft.

Renewable crankshaft gear is a light press fit on crankshaft. When installing crankshaft gear, align single punch mark on crankshaft gear with two punch marks on camshaft gear as shown in Fig. KO75.

Crankshaft oil seals can be installed after gear cover and closure plate are installed. Carefully work oil seals over crankshaft and drive seals into place

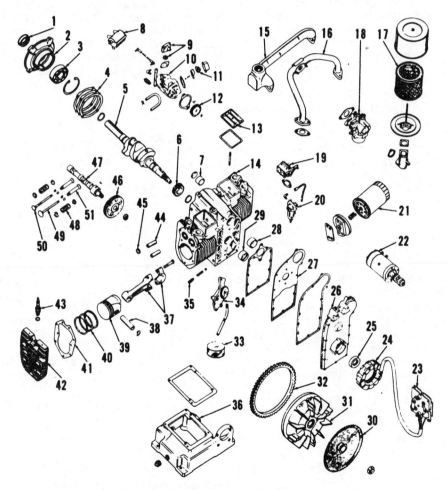

Fig. KO77—Exploded view of K-482, K-532 and K-582 model basic engine assembly.

1. Oil seal	13. Valve cover
2. Closure plate	14. Crankcase & cylinder block
3. Rear main (ball) bearing	15. Exhaust manifold
4. Gaskets	16. Intake manifold
5. Crankshaft	17. Air cleaner element
6. Crankshaft gear	18. Carburetor
7. Camshaft rear bushing	19. Fuel pump
8. Ignition coil	20. Fuel filter
9. Breather valve assy.	21. Oil filter
10. Governor assy.	22. Starting motor
11. Breaker points	23. Rectifier-regulator
12. Governor gear	24. Alternator stator
	25. Oil seal

26. Gear cover	38. Piston pin
27. Gear cover plate	39. Piston
28. Camshaft front bushing	40. Piston rings
29. Front main (sleeve)	41. Head gasket
30. Flywheel screen	42. Cylinder head
31. Flywheel	43. Spark plug
32. Starter ring gear	44. Valve guides
33. Oil strainer	45. Exhaust valve seat
34. Oil pump	46. Camshaft gear
35. Oil pressure adjusting screw	47. Camshaft
36. Oil pan	48. Valve spring
37. Connecting rod	49. Intake valve
	50. Exhaust valve
	51. Valve tappets

with hollow driver that contacts outer edge of seals.

CRANKSHAFT AND MAIN BEARINGS (K-662). Crankshaft is supported by tapered roller bearings at each end. Crankshaft end play should be 0.0035-0.0055 inch (0.0889-0.1397 mm) and is controlled by varying thickness of shim gaskets between crankcase and closure (bearing) plate. Shim gaskets are available in a variety of thicknesses.

Oil transfer sleeves which are pressed into flywheel end of crankcase and closure convey oil to connecting rod bearings. When installing oil sleeves, make certain oil holes in sleeves are aligned with oil holes in closure plate and crankcase.

Standard crankpin diameter is 1.8745-1.8750 inches (47.61-47.63 mm). Connecting rod bearings of 0.002 inch (0.0508 mm) oversize are available for use with moderately worn crankpin. Rod bearings of 0.010 inch (0.254 mm) and 0.020 inch (0.508 mm) oversize are available for use with reground crankpins.

Renewable crankshaft gear is a light press fit on crankshaft. When installing crankshaft gear, align single punch mark on crankshaft gear with two punch marks on camshaft gear as shown in Fig. KO75.

To install rear (pto end) oil seal, carefully work seal, with lip inward, over end of shaft. Use a close fitting seal driver and tap seal into closure plate. Front oil seal (Fig. KO76) is a compression type seal which rotates with crankshaft and seals against gear cover.

CAMSHAFT. Camshaft is supported in two renewable bushings. To remove camshaft first remove flywheel, gear cover, governor assembly and fuel pump. On Model K-662, remove magneto assembly. On all models, remove valve covers, valve spring keepers, spring retainers and valve springs. Wedge a piece of wood between camshaft gear and crankshaft gear and remove gear retaining nut and washer. Attach a suitable puller and remove camshaft gear and Woodruff key. Unbolt and remove gear cover plate from crankcase. Move tappets away from camshaft and carefully withdraw camshaft.

NOTE: To prevent tappets from sliding into crankcase, tie a wire around adjusting nuts on each set of tappets.

Camshaft bushings can now be renewed. Camshaft bushings are presized and if carefully installed need no final sizing. Normal camshaft to bushing clearance is 0.0005-0.0035 inch (0.0127-0.0889 mm). Install new expansion plug behind rear

camshaft bushing. Align two punch marked teeth on camshaft gear with single punch marked tooth on crankshaft gear (Fig. KO75) and reassemble engine by reversing disassembly procedure.

Camshaft end play for K-582 models is 0.004-0.010 inch (0.1016-0.254 mm) and end play for all other models is 0.017-0.038 inch (0.432-0.965 mm). End play is controlled by gear cover plate and gasket. If end play is excessive check plate for excessive wear and renew as necessary.

Tighten camshaft gear retaining nut and flywheel retaining nut to torque specified in **TIGHTENING TORQUES** paragraph for model being serviced.

Adjust valves as outlined in **VALVE SYSTEM** paragraph.

VALVE SYSTEM. Exhaust valve seats are renewable hardened valve seat inserts on all models. Intake valves in K-662 models seat on renewable inserts but intake valves in K-482, K-532 and K-582 models may seat on renewable inserts or seat may be machined directly

into block casting. Seating surfaces should be 1/32-inch (0.794 mm) in width and must be reconditioned if over 1/16-inch (1.588 mm) wide. Valves and seats are ground to 45° angle and Kohler recommends lapping valves to assure proper valve to seat seal.

Maximum intake valve stem clearance in guide is 0.0045 inch (0.1143 mm) and maximum exhaust valve stem clearance in guide is 0.0065 inch (0.1651 mm) for all models. All models have renewable intake and exhaust valve guides which must be reamed to size after installation. K-662 models have a 0.010 inch (0.254 mm) oversize outside diameter guide available for crankcases with damaged guide bores.

Remove guides by driving them into valve stem chamber and breaking the end off until guide is completely removed. Use care not to damage engine block. Press new guides of K-482, K-532 and K-582 models in to a depth of 1-11/32 inch (34.131 mm) measured from cylinder head surface of block to end of guide. Press new guides of K-662 model

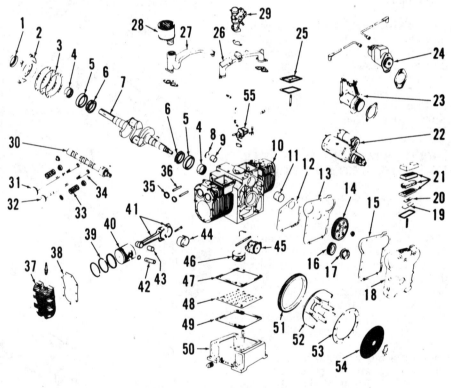

Fig. KO78—Exploded view of K-662 model basic engine assembly.

1. Rear oil seal	13. Gear cover plate	28. Muffler
2. Closure plate	14. Camshaft gear	29. Carburetor
3. Shim gaskets	15. Gasket	30. Camshaft
4. Oil transfer sleeve	16. Crankshaft gear	31. Intake valve
5. Bearing cup	17. Front oil seal	32. Exhaust valve
6. Bearing cone	18. Gear cover	33. Valve springs
7. Crankshaft	19. Breather reed	34. Valve tappets
8. Expansion plug	20. Reed stop	35. Valve seat inserts
9. Camshaft bushing (rear)	21. Breather filter	36. Valve guides
10. Crankcase and cylinder block	22. Starting motor	37. Cylinder head
11. Camshaft bushing (front)	23. Governor assy.	38. Head gasket
12. Gasket	24. Magneto	39. Piston rings
	25. Valve cover	40. Piston
	26. Intake manifold	41. Connecting rod
	27. Exhaust manifold	42. Piston pin
		43. Pin bushing
		44. Connecting rod bearing
		45. Oil pump
		46. Oil strainer
		47. Gasket
		48. Baffle
		49. Gasket
		50. Oil pan
		51. Starter ring gear
		52. Flywheel
		53. Flywheel plate
		54. Flywheel screen
		55. Fuel pump

in to a depth of 1-7/16 inch (35.513 mm) measured from cylinder head surface of block to end of guide.

Ream new guides installed in K-482, K-532 and K-582 models to 0.312-0.313 inch (7.8248-7.9502 mm) and ream new guides installed in K-662 model to 0.3430-0.3445 inch (8.7122-8.7503 mm).

Valve spring free length for K-482, K-532 and K-582 models should be 1.793 inches (45.54 mm) and for K-662 model should be 2.250 inches (57.15 mm). If rotator is used on exhaust valve, exhaust valve spring free length for K-482, K-532 and K-582 models should be 1.531 inches (38.8874 mm) and for K-662 model should be 1.812 inches (46.03 mm).

Valve tappet gap (clearance) for K-482, K-532 and K-582 models should be adjusted so intake valves have 0.008-0.010 inch (0.203-0.254 mm) clearance and exhaust valves have 0.017-0.020 inch (0.432-0.508 mm) clearance when cold. Valve tappet gap (clearance) for K-662 model should be adjusted so intake valves have 0.006-0.008 inch (0.152-0.203 mm) clearance and exhaust valves have 0.015-0.017 inch (0.381-0.432 mm) clearance when cold.

OIL PUMP. A gear type oil pump supplies oil via internal galleries to front main bearing, camshaft bearings, connecting rods and other wear areas.

Model K-662 uses transfer sleeves to direct oil to the tapered roller main bearings.

Oil pressure on Models K-482, K-532 and K-582 is controlled by an adjustable pressure valve. Refer to **LUBRICATION** paragraph for operating pressures.

If faulty, oil pump must be renewed as it is serviced as an assembly only.

FUEL PUMP. A mechanically operated diaphragm type fuel pump is used. Pump is actuated by a lever which rides on an eccentric on camshaft. A priming lever is provided on the pump and repair kit is available for reconditioning pump.

SERVICING KOHLER ACCESSORIES

REWIND STARTERS

Fairbanks-Morse or Eaton rewind starters are used on some Kohler engines. When servicing starters, refer to appropriate following paragraph.

Fairbanks-Morse

OVERHAUL. To disassemble starter, remove retainer ring, retainer washer, brake spring, friction washer, friction shoe assembly and second friction washer as shown in Fig. KA101. Hold rope handle in one hand and cover in the other hand and allow rotor to rotate to unwind recoil spring. Note winding direction of recoil spring and rope for aid in reassembly. Remove recoil spring from cover and unwind rope from rotor.

When reassembling unit, lubricate recoil spring, cover shaft and its bore in rotor with Lubriplate or equivalent. Install rope on rotor and rotor to shaft, then engage recoil spring inner end hook. Preload recoil spring four turns, then install middle flange and mounting flange. Check friction shoe shaft ends and renew if necessary. Install friction washers, friction shoe assembly, brake spring, retainer washer and retainer ring. Make certain friction shoe assembly is installed properly for correct starter rotation. If properly installed, sharp ends of friction shoe plates will extend when rope is pulled.

Starter operation can be reversed by winding rope and recoil spring in opposite direction and turning friction shoe assembly upside down. See Fig. KA102 for counterclockwise assembly.

Eaton

OVERHAUL. To disassemble starter, first release tension of rewind spring as follows: Hold starter assembly with pulley facing up. Pull starter rope until notch in pulley is aligned with rope hole in cover. Use thumb pressure to prevent pulley from rotating. engage rope in notch of pulley and slowly release thumb pressure to allow spring to unwind until all tension is released.

When removing rope pulley, use extreme care to keep starter spring confined in housing. Check starter spring for breaks, cracks or distortion. If starter spring is to be renewed, carefully remove it from housing, noting direction of rotation of spring before removing. Exploded view of clockwise starter is shown in Fig. KA103.

Check pawl, brake, spring, retainer and hub for wear and renew as necessary. If starter rope is worn or frayed, remove from pulley, noting direction it is wrapped on pulley. Renew rope and install pulley in housing, aligning notch in pulley assembly in housing, align notch in pulley hub with hook in end of spring. Use a wire bent to form a hook to aid in positioning spring in hub.

After securing pulley assembly in housing, engage rope in notch and rotate pulley at least two full turns in same direction it is pulled to properly preload starter spring. Pull rope to fully extended position. Release handle and if spring is properly preloaded, rope will fully rewind.

Before installing starter on engine, check teeth in starter driven hub (165—Fig. KA104) for wear and renew hub if necessary.

Command And Later Magnum Models

OVERHAUL. Command models may be equipped with the rewind starter shown in Fig. KA105. To disassemble starter, remove rope handle and allow rope to wind into starter. Unscrew center retaining screw and separate starter components. To disengage rewind spring from starter housing, rotate pulley two turns clockwise. Wear appropriate safety eyewear and gloves to prevent injury should rewind spring uncoil uncontrolled. The rewind spring is contained in cup (9) and manufacturer recommends installation of a new spring and cup if spring uncoils from cup.

Assemble starter before installing rope. Lubricate rewind spring before in-

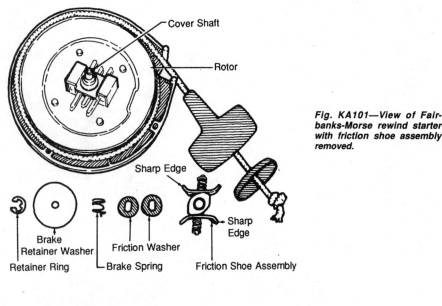

Fig. KA101—View of Fairbanks-Morse rewind starter with friction shoe assembly removed.

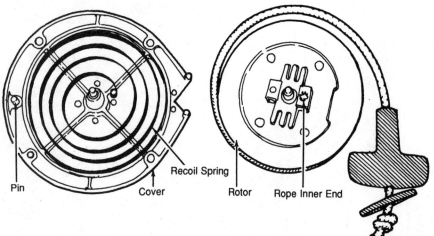

Fig. KA102—View showing recoil spring and rope installed for counterclockwise starter operation.

Illustrations Courtesy Kohler Co.

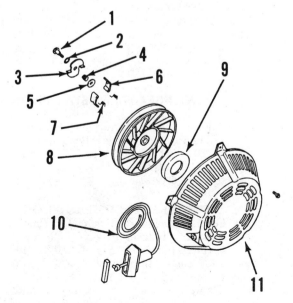

Fig. KA103—Exploded view of Eaton rewind starter.

1. Retainer screw	5. Pawl
2. Brake washer	6. Spring
3. Spacer	7. Brake
4. Retainer	8. Thrust washer

9. Pulley hub	12. Recoil spring
10. Pulley	13. Rope
11. Screw	14. Handle
	15. Starter housing

Fig. KA104—View showing rewind starter and starter hub.

165. Starter hub
166. Screen
170. Bracket
171. Air director
203. Rewind starter

stallation. Apply a small amount of grease on brake spring (4) ends. Apply Loctite 271 to threads of center screw (1) and tighten to 7.4-8.5 N m (65-75 in.-lbs.). Use following procedure to install rope. With starter assembled except for rope, rotate pulley six turns counterclockwise and stop when rope hole on

pulley is aligned with rope outlet on starter housing. Hold pulley so it cannot rotate and insert rope through rope outlet and attach rope end to pulley. Attach rope handle and release pulley. Check starter operation.

12-VOLT STARTER-GENERATOR

A combination 12-volt starter-generator, manufactured by Delco-Remy, is used on some Kohler engines. Starter-generator functions as a cranking motor when starting switch is closed. When engine is operating and with starting switch open, unit operates as a generator. Generator output and circuit voltage for battery and various operating requirements are controlled by a current-voltage regulator.

Kohler recommends starter-generator belt tension be adjusted until about 10 pounds (4.5 kg) pulley pressure ap-

Fig. KA105—Exploded view of rewind starter used on Command and later Magnum models.

1. Screw
2. Washer
3. Pawl retainer
4. Brake spring
5. Washer
6. Pawls
7. Pawl springs
8. Pulley
9. Rewind spring & cup
10. Rope
11. Starter housing

plied midway between pulleys will deflect belt ½ inch (12.7 mm).

To determine cause of abnormal operation, starter-generator should be given a no-load test or a generator output test. Generator output test can be performed with starter-generator on or off engine. No-load test must be made with starter-generator removed from engine. Refer to Fig. KA106 for exploded view of starter-generator assembly. Parts are available from Kohler as well as authorized Delco-Remy service stations.

Starter-generator brush spring tension for all models should be 24-32 oz. (0.68-0.91 kg).

Starter-generator and regulator service test specifications are as follows:

Starter-Generators 1101940, 1101970, 1101973 and 1101980

Field draw:
Amperes 1.52-1.62
Volts 12
Cold output:
Amperes 12
Volts 12
Rpm 4950
No-load test:
Volts 11
Amperes (max.) 18
Rpm (min.)................ 2500
Rpm (max.)............... 2900

Starter-Generators 1101932, 1101948, 1101968, 1101972 and 1101974

Field draw:
Amperes 1.45-1.57
Volts 12
Cold output:
Amperes 10
Volts 14
Rpm 5450
No-load test:
Volts 11
Amperes (max.) 17
Rpm (min.)................ 2500
Rpm (max.)............... 2900

Starter-Generators 1101951 and 1101967

Field draw:
Amperes 1.52-1.62
Volts 12
Cold output:
Amperes 15
Volts 14
Rpm 3400
No-load test:
Volts 11
Amperes (max.) 14
Rpm (min.)................ 1650
Rpm (max.)............... 1950

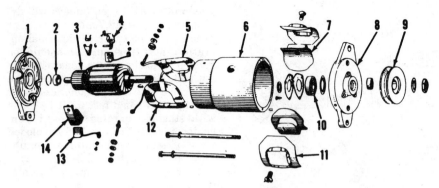

Fig. KA106—Exploded view of typical Delco-Remy starter-generator assembly.

1. Commutator end frame				11. Field coil insulator
2. Bearing	5. Field coil (L.H.)	8. Drive end frame		12. Field coil (R.H.)
3. Armature	6. Frame	9. Pulley		13. Brush
4. Ground brush holder	7. Pole shoe	10. Bearing		14. Insulated brush holder

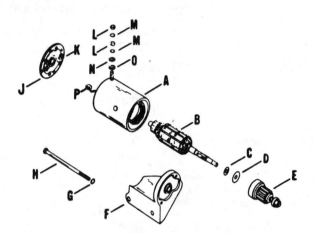

Fig. KA107—Exploded view of two-brush compact gear drive starting motor.

A. Frame & field coil assy.	E. Bendix drive assy.	H. Through-bolt	M. Lockwashers
B. Armature	F. Drive end plate &	J. Commutator end plate	N. Flat washer
C. Spacer	mounting bracket	K. Ground brush	O. Insulating washer
D. Thrust washer	G. Lockwasher	L. Terminal nuts	P. Field brush

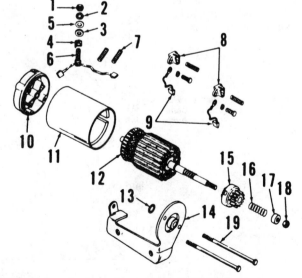

Fig. KA108—Exploded view of permanent magnet-type starting motor.

	10. Commutator end cap	
1. Terminal nut	6. Terminal stud &	11. Frame & permanent magnets
2. Lockwasher	input brushes	12. Armature
3. Insulating washer	7. Brush springs (4)	13. Thrust washer
4. Terminal insulator	8. Brush holders	14. Drive end plate &
5. Flat washer	9. Brushes	mounting bracket
		15. Drive assy.
		16. Anti-drift spring
		17. Spacer
		18. Nut
		19. Through-bolts

Starter-Generator 1101996

Field draw:	
Amperes	1.52-1.62
Volts	12
Cold output:	
Amperes	12
Volts	14
Rpm	4950
No-load test:	
Volts	11
Amperes (max.)	18
Rpm (min.)	2500
Rpm (max.)	2900

Regulators 1118984, 1118988 and 1118999

Ground polarity	Negative
Cut-out relay:	
Air gap	0.020 in. (0.51 mm)
Point gap	0.020 in. (0.51 mm)
Closing voltage:	
Range	11.8-14.0
Adjust to	12.8
Voltage regulator:	
Air gap	0.075 in. (1.90 mm)
Setting voltage:	
Range	13.6-14.5
Adjust to	14.0

Regulator 1118985

Ground polarity	Positive
Cut-out relay:	
Air gap	0.020 in. (0.51 mm)
Point gap	0.020 in. (0.51 mm)
Closing voltage:	
Range	11.8-14.0
Adjust to	12.8
Voltage regulator:	
Air gap	0.075 in. (1.90 mm)
Setting voltage:	
Range	13.6-14.5
Adjust to	14.0

12-VOLT GEAR DRIVE STARTERS

Four types of gear drive starters are used on Kohler engines. Refer to Figs. KA107, KA108, KA109, KA110 and KA111 for exploded views of starter motors and drives.

TWO-BRUSH COMPACT-TYPE. To disassemble starting motor, clamp mounting bracket in a vise. Remove through-bolts (H—Fig. KA107) and slide commutator end plate (J) and frame assembly (A) off armature. Clamp steel armature core in a vise and

Illustrations Courtesy Kohler Co.

remove Bendix drive (E), drive end plate (F), thrust washer (D) and spacer (C) from armature (B).

Renew brushes if unevenly worn or worn to a length of $^5/_{16}$ inch (7.9 mm) or less. To renew ground brush (K), drill out rivet, then rivet new brush lead to end plate. Field brush (P) is soldered to field coil lead.

Reassemble by reversing disassembly procedure. Lubricate bushings with a light coat of SAE 10 oil. Inspect Bendix drive pinion and splined sleeve for damage. If Bendix is in good condition, wipe clean and install completely dry. Tighten Bendix drive retaining nut to a torque of 130-150 in.-lbs. (15-18 N·m). Tighten through-bolts (H) to a torque of 40-55 in.-lbs. (4-7 N·m).

PERMANENT MAGNET-TYPE.

To disassemble starting motor, clamp mounting bracket in a vise and remove through-bolts (19—Fig. KA108).

CAUTION: Do not clamp frame (11) in a vise or strike frame as it has ceramic field magnets that may be damaged.

Carefully slide end cap (10) and frame (11) off armature. Clamp steel armature core in a vise and remove nut (18), spacer (17), anti-drift spring (16), drive assembly (15), end plate (14) and thrust washer (13) from armature (12).

The two input brushes are part of terminal stud (6). Remaining two brushes (9) are secured with cap screws. When reassembling, lubricate bushings with American Bosch lubricant LU3001 or equivalent. Do not lubricate starter drive. Use rubber band or clip shown in Fig. KA112 to hold brushes in position until started in commutator. Cut and remove rubber band after assembly. Tighten through-bolts to 80-95 in.-lbs. (8-10 N·m). Apply Loctite to nut (18) and tighten to 135 in.-lbs. (15.2 N·m).

FOUR-BRUSH BENDIX DRIVE-TYPE.

To disassemble starting motor, remove screws securing drive end plate (K—Fig. KA109) to frame (I). Carefully withdraw armature and drive assembly from frame assembly. Clamp steel armature core in a vise and remove Bendix drive retaining nut, then remove drive unit (A), end plate (K) and thrust washer from armature (J). Remove cover (H) and screws securing end plate (E) to frame. Pull field brushes (C) from brush holders and remove end plate assembly.

The two ground brush leads are secured to end plate (E) and the two field

brush leads are soldered to field coils. Renew brush set if excessively worn.

Inspect bushing (L) in end plate (K) and renew bushing if necessary. When reassembling, lubricate bushings with light coat of SAE 10 oil. Do not lubricate Bendix drive assembly.

Note starter can be reinstalled with Bendix in engaged or disengaged position. Do not attempt to disengage Bendix if it is in the engaged position.

SOLENOID SHIFT-TYPE (K-Series).

To disassemble starting motor, refer to Fig. KA110, then unbolt and remove solenoid switch assembly (items 1 through 6). Remove through-bolts (23), end plate (24) and frame (30) with brushes (26), brush holders (27 and 29) and field coil assembly (33). Remove screws retaining center bearing (21) to drive housing (12), remove shift lever pivot bolt, raise shift lever (9) and care-

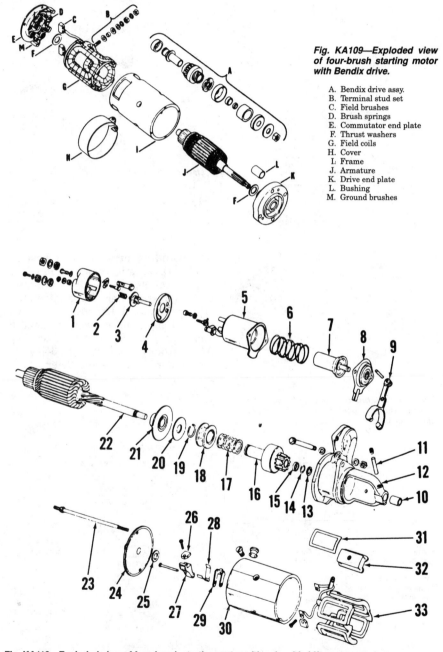

Fig. KA109—Exploded view of four-brush starting motor with Bendix drive.

A. Bendix drive assy.
B. Terminal stud set
C. Field brushes
D. Brush springs
E. Commutator end plate
F. Thrust washers
G. Field coils
H. Cover
I. Frame
J. Armature
K. Drive end plate
L. Bushing
M. Ground brushes

Fig. KA110—Exploded view of four-brush starting motor with solenoid shift engagement.

1. Switch cover
2. Spring
3. Contact disc
4. Gasket
5. Coil assy.
6. Return spring
7. Plunger
8. Seal
9. Shift lever
10. Bushing
11. Lubrication wick
12. Drive housing
13. Drive end thrust washer
14. Snap ring
15. Retainer
16. Drive unit
17. Spring
18. Shift collar
19. Snap ring
20. Brake washer
21. Center bearing
22. Armature
23. Through-bolt
24. End plate
25. Thrust washer
26. Brushes (4)
27. Insulated brush holder
28. Brush spring
29. Ground brush
30. Frame
31. Field coil insulator
32. Pole shoe
33. Field coil assy.

Illustrations Courtesy Kohler Co.

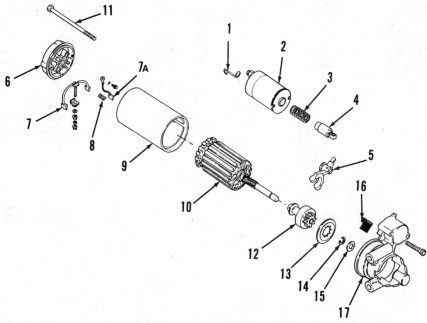

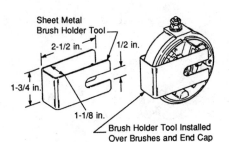

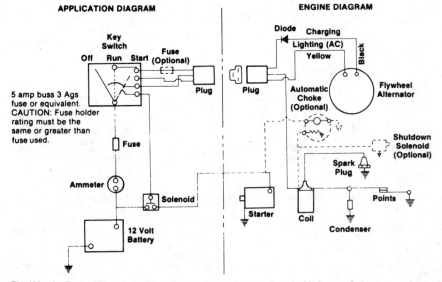

Fig. KA111—Exploded view of permanent magnet-type starter with solenoid shift engagement.

1. Clip	6. Commutator end cap	9. Frame & permanent	13. Seal
2. Solenoid	7. Terminal stud &	magnets	14. Retainer
3. Spring	input brushes	10. Armature	15. Thrust washer
4. Plunger	7A. Brush	11. Through-bolts	16. Dust cover
5. Shift lever	8. Brush springs (4)	12. Drive assy.	17. Drive housing

Fig. KA112—A brush retaining clip can be fabricated as shown to hold brushes in end cap during starter assembly.

Fig. KA113—Typical electrical wiring diagram for engines equipped with 3-amp alternator.

bearing (21) and bushings in end plate (24) and drive housing (12) as needed.

SOLENOID SHIFT-TYPE (Magnum And Command Series). Refer to Fig. KA111 for an exploded view of starter.

CAUTION: Do not clamp frame (9) in a vise or strike frame as it has ceramic field magnets that may be damaged.

To disassemble starter, detach clip (1) then unscrew and remove solenoid. Mark frame (9), end cap (6) and drive housing (17) so they can be assembled in original position. Unscrew through-bolts and separate starter components. Detach retainer (14) from armature to remove drive unit (12) from shaft.

The two input brushes are part of terminal stud (7). Remaining two brushes (7A) are secured with cap screws. Renew brushes as needed. The clip shown in Fig. KA112 can be fabricated to hold brushes in end cap during assembly.

FLYWHEEL ALTERNATORS

3-AMP ALTERNATOR. The 3-amp alternator consists of a permanent magnet ring with five or six magnets on flywheel rim, a stator assembly attached to crankcase and a diode in charging output lead. See Fig. KA113.

To avoid damage to the charging system, the following precautions must be observed:

1. Negative post of battery must be connected to engine ground and correct battery polarity must be observed at all times.

2. Prevent alternator leads (AC) from touching or shorting.

3. Remove battery or disconnect battery cables when recharging battery with battery charger.

4. Do not operate engine without a battery in the system.

5. Disconnect plug before electric welding is done on equipment powered by, and in common ground with, the engine.

Troubleshooting. Defective conditions and possible causes are as follows:

1. No output. Could be caused by:
   A. Faulty windings in stator.
   B. Defective diode.
   C. Broken lead wire.

2. No lighting. Could be caused by:
   A. Shorted stator wiring.
   B. Broken lead.

fully withdraw armature and drive assembly. Drive unit (16) and center bearing (21) can be removed from armature (22) after snap ring (14) and retainer (15) are removed. Drive out shift lever pin and separate plunger (7), seal (8) and shift lever (9) from drive housing. Any further disassembly is obvious after examination of unit. Refer to Fig. KA110. Renew brushes (26), center

If "no output" condition is the trouble, run following tests:

1. Connect ammeter in series with charging lead. Start engine and run at 2400 rpm. Ammeter should register 2 amp charge. Run engine at 3600 rpm. Ammeter should register 3 amp charge.

2. Disconnect battery charge lead from battery, measure resistance of lead to ground with an ohmmeter. Reverse ohmmeter leads and take another reading. One reading should be about mid-scale with meter set at R × 1. If both readings are high, diode or stator is open.

3. Expose diode connections on battery charge lead. Check resistance on stator side to ground. Reading should be 1 ohm. If zero ohms, winding is shorted. If infinity ohms, stator winding is open or lead wire is broken.

If "no lighting" condition is the trouble, use an AC voltmeter and measure open circuit voltage from lighting lead to ground with engine running at 3000 rpm. If 15 volts, wiring may be shorted.

Check resistance of lighting lead to ground. If 0.5 ohms, stator is good, zero ohms indicates shorted stator and a reading of infinity indicates stator is open or lead is broken.

3/6 AMP ALTERNATOR. The 3/6 amp alternator consists of a permanent magnet ring with six magnets on flywheel rim, a stator assembly attached to crankcase and two diodes in battery charging lead and auxiliary load lead. See Fig. KA114.

To avoid damage to the charging system, the following precautions must be observed:

1. Negative post of battery must be connected to engine ground and correct battery polarity must be observed at all times.

2. Prevent alternator leads (AC) from touching or shorting.

3. Remove battery or disconnect battery cables when recharging battery with battery charger.

4. Do not operate engine without a battery in the system.

5. Disconnect plug before electric welding is done on equipment powered by, and in common ground with, the engine.

Troubleshooting. Defective conditions and possible causes are as follows:

1. No output. Could be caused by:
   A. Faulty windings in stator.
   B. Defective diode.
   C. Broken lead wire.

2. No lighting. Could be caused by:
   A. Shorted stator wiring.
   B. Broken lead.

If "no output" condition is the trouble, run following tests:

1. Disconnect auxiliary load lead and measure voltage from lead to ground with engine running 3000 rpm. If 17 volts or more, stator is good.

2. Disconnect battery charging lead from battery. Measure voltage from charging lead to ground with engine running at 3000 rpm. If 17 volts or more, stator is good.

3. Disconnect battery charge lead from battery and auxiliary load lead from switch. Measure resistance of both leads to ground. Reverse ohmmeter

leads and take another reading. One reading should be about mid-scale with meter set at R × 1. If both readings are low, diode is shorted. If both readings are high, diode or stator is open.

4. Expose diode connections on battery charge lead and auxiliary load lead. Check resistance on stator side of diodes to ground. Reading should be 0.5 ohm. If zero ohms, winding is shorted. If infinity ohms, stator winding is open or lead wire is broken.

If "no lighting" condition is the trouble, disconnect lighting lead and measure open circuit voltage with an AC voltmeter from lighting lead to ground with engine running at 3000 rpm. If 22 volts or more, stator is good. If less than 22 volts, wiring may be shorted.

Check resistance of lighting lead to ground. If 0.5 ohms, stator is good, zero ohms indicates shorted stator and a reading of infinity indicates stator is open or lead is broken.

10-, 15- AND 25-AMP ALTERNATOR. Some engines may be equipped with a 10-, 15- or 25-amp alternator. Alternator output is controlled by a solid state rectifier-regulator.

To avoid damage to charging system, the following precautions must be observed:

1. Negative post of battery must be connected to engine ground and correct battery polarity must be observed at all times.

2. Rectifier-regulator must be connected in common ground with engine and battery.

3. Disconnect leads at rectifier-regulator if electric welding is to be done on equipment in common ground with engine.

4. Remove battery or disconnect battery cables when recharging battery with battery charger.

5. Do not operate engine with battery disconnected.

6. Prevent possible grounding of AC leads.

Operation. Alternating current (AC) produced by alternator is changed to direct current (DC) in rectifier-regulator. See Figs. KA115, KA116 or KA117. Current regulation is provided by electronic devices that "sense" counter-voltage created by battery to control or limit charging rate. No adjustments are possible on alternator charging system. Faulty components must be renewed. Refer to the following troubleshooting paragraph to help locate possible defective parts.

Troubleshooting. Defective conditions and possible causes are as follows:

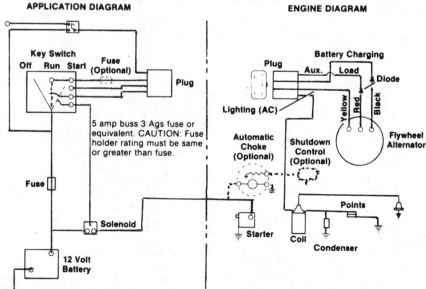

APPLICATION DIAGRAM

ENGINE DIAGRAM

Fig. KA114—Typical electrical wiring diagram for engine equipped with 3/6-amp alternator.

APPLICATION DIAGRAM   **ENGINE DIAGRAM**

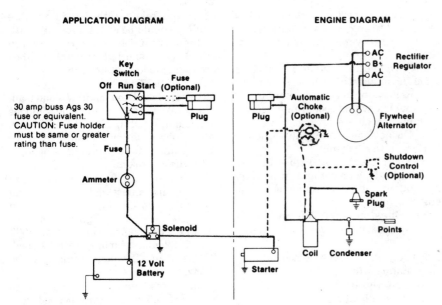

Fig. KA115—Typical electrical wiring diagram for engines equipped with 15-amp alternator and breaker point ignition. The 10-amp alternator is similar.

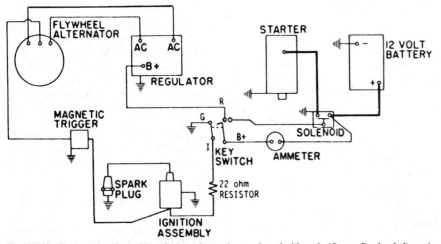

Fig. KA116—Typical electrical wiring diagram for engine equipped with early 15-amp flywheel alternator and breakerless ignition system. The 10-amp alternator is similar. Note differences of rectifier-regulators in Fig. KA117.

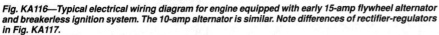
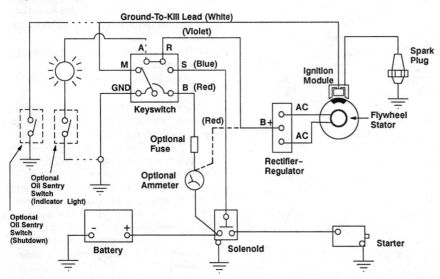

Fig. KA117—View of rectifier-regulator used on 10-amp and early 15-amp alternators. Although similar in appearance, units must not be interchanged.

1. No output. Could be caused by:
   A. Faulty windings in stator.
   B. Defective diode(s) in rectifier.
   C. Rectifier-regulator not properly grounded.

2. Full charge-no regulation. Could be caused by:
   A. Defective rectifier-regulator.
   B. Defective battery.

If "no output" condition is the trouble, disconnect B+ cable from rectifier-regulator (Fig. KA118). Connect a DC voltmeter between B+ terminal on rectifier-regulator and engine ground. Start engine and operate at 3600 rpm. Voltage should be above 13.8 volts. If reading is above zero volts but less than 13.8 volts, check for defective rectifier-regulator. If reading is zero volts, check for defective rectifier-regulator or defective stator by disconnecting AC leads from rectifier-regulator and connecting an AC voltmeter to the two AC leads.

Check AC voltage with engine running at 3600 rpm. If reading is less than 20 volts (10-amp alternator) or 28 volts (15-amp alternator), stator is defective. If reading is more than 20 volts (10-amp alternator) or 28 volts (15-amp alternator), rectifier-regulator is defective.

If "full charge-no regulation" is the condition, use a DC voltmeter and check

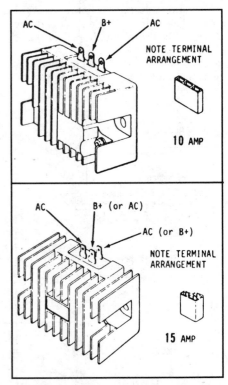

Fig. KA118—Typical electrical wiring diagram for later 15-amp and 25-amp flywheel alternator. Note that B+ wire (dashed line) from rectifier-regulator on 25-amp system is routed to ammeter rather than keyswitch.

Illustrations Courtesy Kohler Co.

B+ to ground with engine operating at 3600 rpm. If reading is over 14.7 volts, rectifier-regulator is defective. If reading is under 14.7 volts but over 14.0 volts, alternator and rectifier-regulator are satisfactory and battery is probably defective (unable to hold a charge).

30-AMP ALTERNATOR. A 30-amp flywheel alternator, consisting of a permanent field magnet ring (on flywheel) and an alternator stator (on bearing plate on single-cylinder engines or gear cover on two-cylinder engines), is used on some models. Alternator output is controlled by a solid-state rectifier-regulator.

To avoid damage to charging system, the following precautions must be observed:

1. Negative post of battery must be connected to engine ground and correct battery polarity must be observed at all times.

2. Rectifier-regulator must be connected in common ground with engine and battery.

3. Disconnect wire from rectifier-regulator terminal marked "BATT. NEG" if electric welding is to be done on equipment in common ground with engine.

4. Remove battery or disconnect battery cables when recharging battery with battery charger.

5. Do not operate engine with battery disconnected.

6. Prevent possible grounding of AC leads.

Operation. Alternating current (AC) produced by alternator is carried by two black wires to a full wave bridge rectifier where it is changed to direct current (DC). Two red stator wires serve to complete a circuit from regulator to secondary winding in stator. A zener diode is used to sense battery voltage and it controls a silicone controller rectifier (SCR). SCR functions as a switch to allow current to flow in secondary winding in stator when battery voltage exceeds a specific level.

An increase in battery voltage increases current flow in secondary winding in stator. This increased current flow in secondary winding brings about a corresponding decrease in AC current in primary winding, thus controlling output.

When battery voltage decreases, zener diode shuts off SCR and no current flows to secondary winding. At this time, maximum AC current is produced by primary winding.

Troubleshooting. Refer to Figs. KA119 or KA120 for wiring diagram. Defective conditions and possible causes are as follows:

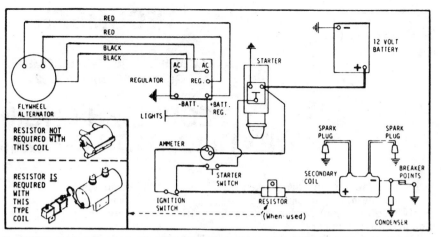

Fig. KA119—Typical electrical wiring diagram for two-cylinder engine equipped with 30-amp alternator charging system. The 30-amp alternator on single-cylinder engines is similar.

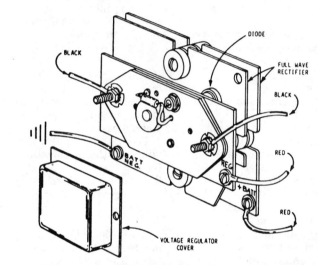

Fig. KA120—Rectifier-regulator used with 30-amp flywheel alternator, showing stator wire connections. Refer also to Fig. KA119.

1. No output. Could be caused by:
   A. Faulty windings in stator.
   B. Defective diode(s) in rectifier.

2. No charge (when normal load is applied to battery). Could be caused by:
   A. Faulty secondary winding in stator.

3. Full charge-no regulation. Could be caused by:
   A. Faulty secondary winding in stator.
   B. Defective regulator.

If "no ouput" is the trouble, check stator windings by disconnecting all four stator wires from rectifier-regulator. Check resistance on R × 1 scale of ohmmeter. Connect ohmmeter leads to the two red stator wires. About 2.0 ohms should be indicated. Connect ohmmeter leads to the two black stator wires. Approximately 0.1 ohm should be indicated. If readings are not at specified values, renew stator. If ohmmeter readings are correct, stator is good and trouble is in rectifier-regulator. Renew rectifier-regulator.

If "no charge when normal load is applied to battery" is the trouble, check stator secondary winding by disconnecting red wire from "REG" terminal on rectifier-regulator. Operate engine at 3600 rpm. Alternator should now charge at full output. If full output of at least 30 amps is not attained, renew stator.

If "full charge-no regulation" is the trouble, check stator secondary winding by removing both red wires from rectifier-regulator and connecting ends of these two wires together. Operate engine at 3600 rpm. A maximum 4-amp charge should be noted. If not, stator secondary winding is faulty. Renew stator. If maximum 4-amp charge is indicated, stator is good and trouble is in rectifier-regulator. Renew rectifier-regulator.

TECUMSEH

TECUMSEH PRODUCTS COMPANY
Grafton, Wisconsin 53024

TECUMSEH ENGINE IDENTIFICATION INFORMATION

In order to obtain correct service parts it is necessary to locate and correctly identify engine model, specification and serial numbers.

Model and serial numbers can be stamped into blower housing at cylinder head end or on a nameplate or tag located on the side of the blower housing. Refer to Fig. T1.

Letters at the beginning of the model number indicates the basic engine type.

V – Vertical shaft
VM – Vertical shaft, medium frame
LAV – Lightweight aluminum, vertical shaft
VH – Vertical shaft, heavy duty (cast iron)
TVS – Tecumseh vertical styled
TNT – Toro N' Tecumseh
ECV – Exclusive Craftsman vertical
OVM – Overhead valve, vertical medium frame
OVRM – Overhead valve vertical rotary mower
H – Horizontal shaft

HS – Horizontal shaft, small frame
HM – Horizontal shaft, small frame
HHM – Horizontal shaft heavy duty, medium frame
HH – Horizontal shaft heavy duty (cast iron)
ECH – Exclusive Craftsman horizontal
OH – Overhead valve heavy duty (cast iron)
OHM – Overhead valve horizontal medium frame

The number following the letters indicate horsepower or cubic inch displacement.

The number following the model number is the specification number and the last three numbers of the specification number indicate a variation to the basic engine specification.

The serial number indicates the production date.

Using Model OVM120-202008, serial number 8234C as an example, interpretation is as follows:

OVM120-202008 is the model and specification number;

OVM indicates overhead valve medium frame;

120 indicates 12 horsepower;

202008 is the specification number required for correct parts identification;

8234C is the serial number;

8 indicates the year manufactured (1988);

234 indicates calendar day of the year (234th day of 1988);

C indicates the line and shift on which the engine was built at the factory.

Small frame engines have aluminum blocks and cylinder bores. Medium frame engines have aluminum blocks with cast iron cylinder sleeves. Heavy frame engines have caset iron cylinder and block assemblies.

Early Models VH70 and HH70 were identified as Models V70 and H70.

It is necessary to have the correct model, specification and serial numbers to obtain parts.

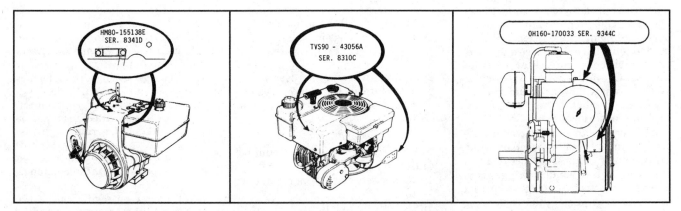

Fig. T1—View showing locations of engine model, specification and serial numbers on a variety of engines.

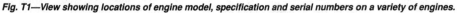

TECUMSEH 4-STROKE

Model	Bore	Stroke	Displacement
LAV25, LAV30, TVS75, H25, H30 prior to 1983	2.313 in. (58.74 mm)	1.844 in. (46.84 mm)	7.75 cu. in. (127 cc)
H30 after 1982, LV35, LAV35, TVS90, H35 prior to 1983, ECH90	2.500 in. (63.50 mm)	1.844 in. (46.84 mm)	9.05 cu. in. (148 cc)
H35 after 1982	2.500 in. (63.50 mm)	1.938 in. (49.23 mm)	9.51 cu. in. (156 cc)
LAV40, V40 external ignition, TVS105, HS40, ECV105	2.625 in. (66.68 mm)	1.938 in. (49.23 mm)	10.49 cu. in. (172 cc)
TNT100, TVS100, ECV100	2.625 in. (66.68 mm)	1.844 in. (46.84 mm)	9.98 cu. in. (164 cc)
V40, VH40, H40, HH40	2.500 in. (63.50 mm)	2.250 in. (57.15 mm)	11.04 cu. in. (181 cc)
ECV110	2.750 in. (69.85 mm)	1.938 in. (49.23 mm)	11.50 cu. in. (189 cc)
LAV50, ECV120, TNT120, TVS120, HS50	2.812 in. (71.43 mm)	1.938 in. (49.23 mm)	12.04 cu. in. (197 cc)
H50, HH50, V50, VH50, TVM125	2.625 in. (66.68 mm)	2.250 in. (57.15 mm)	12.18 cu. in. (229 cc)
H60, HH60, V60, VH60, TVM140	2.625 in. (66.68 mm)	2.500 in. (63.50 mm)	13.53 cu. in. (222 cc)

ENGINE IDENTIFICATION

Engines must be identified by the complete model number, including the specification number in order to obtain correct repair parts. These numbers are located on the name plate and/or tags that are positioned as shown in Fig. T1 or Fig. T1A. It is important to transfer identification tags from the original engine to replacement short block assemblies so unit can be identified when servicing.

If selecting a replacement engine and model or type number of the old engine is not known, refer to chart in Fig. T1B and proceed as follows:

1. List the corresponding number which indicates the crankshaft position.

2. Determine the horsepower needed.

3. Determine the primary features needed. (Refer to the Tecumseh Engines Specification Book No. 692531 for specific engine variations.)

4. Refer to Fig. T1C for Tecumseh engine model number and serial number interpretation.

The number following the letter code is the horsepower or cubic inch displacement. The number following the model number is the specification number. The last three digits of the specification number indicate a variation to the basic engine specification.

MAINTENANCE

SPARK PLUG. Spark plug recommendations are shown in the following chart.

14 mm—³/₈ inch
   reach..............Champion J8
18 mm—¹/₂ inch
   reach ....Champion D16
                       or MD16
All ⁷/₈ inch reach ....Champion W18

CARBURETOR. Several different carburetors are used on these engines. Refer to the appropriate paragraph for model being serviced.

Tecumseh Diaphragm Carburetor. Refer to model number stamped on the carburetor mounting flange and to Fig.

T2 for exploded view of Tecumseh diaphragm type carburetor.

Initial adjustment of idle mixture and main fuel mixture screws from a lightly seated position is one turn open. Clockwise rotation leans mixture and counterclockwise rotation richens mixture.

Final adjustments are made with engine at operating temperature and running. Operate engine at rated speed and adjust main fuel mixture screw (14) for smoothest engine operation. Operate engine at idle speed and adjust idle mixture screw (10) for smoothest engine idle. If engine does not accelerate smoothly, slight adjustment of main fuel mixture screw may be required. Engine idle speed should be approximately 1800 rpm.

The fuel strainer in the fuel inlet fitting can be cleaned by reverse flushing with compressed air after the inlet needle and seat (19—Fig. T2) are removed. The inlet needle seat fitting is metal with a neoprene seat, so the fitting (and enclosed seat) should be removed before

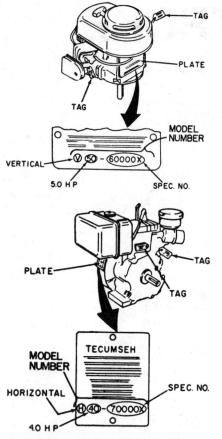

Fig. T1—Tags and plates used to identify engine model will most often be located in one of the positions shown.

carburetor is cleaned with a commercial solvent. The stamped line on carburetor throttle plate should be toward top of carburetor, parallel with throttle shaft and facing outward as shown in Fig. T3. Flat side of choke plate should

TECUMSEH SERVICE NUMBER SYSTEM

(EXAMPLE) 8 0 4 1 0 1 A

1st DIGIT	2nd & 3rd DIGIT	4th DIGIT	5th & 6th DIGIT	7th DIGIT
CRANKSHAFT POSITION	HORSEPOWER OR 2 CYCLE	PRIMARY FEATURES	ENGINE VARIATION NUMBER	REVISION LETTER
8 - Vertical 9 - Horizontal	00 = 2 Cycle 02 = 3 H.P. 03 = 3.5 H.P. 04 = 4 H.P. 05 = 5 H.P. 06 = 6 H.P. 07 = 7 H.P. 08 = 8 H.P. 10 = 10 H.P. 12 = 12 H.P. 14 = 14 H.P. 16 = 16 H.P. 18 = 18 H.P.	1 = Rotary Mower 2 = Industrial 3 = Snow King 4 = Mini Bike 5 = Tractor 6 = Tiller 7 = Rider 8 = Rotary Mower	00 thru 99 00 thru 99 00 thru 99 00 thru 99 00 thru 99 00 thru 99 00 thru 99 00 thru 99	

Fig. T1B—Reference chart used to select or identify replacement engines.

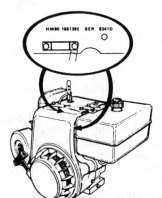

Fig. T1A—Locations of tags and plates used to identify later model engines.

Fig. T1C—Chart showing engine model number and serial number interpretation.

V	- Vertical Shaft
LAV	- Lightweight Aluminum Vertical
VM	- Vertical Medium Frame
TVM	- Tecumseh Vertical (Medium Frame)
VH	- Vertical Heavy Duty (Cast Iron)
TVS	- Tecumseh Vertical Styled
TNT	- Toro N' Tecumseh
ECV	- Exclusive Craftsman Vertical
OVM	- Overhead Valve Vertical Medium Frame
H	- Horizontal Shaft
HS	- Horizontal Small Frame
HM	- Horizontal Medium Frame
HHM	- Horizontal Heavy Duty (Cast Iron) Medium Frame
HH	- Horizontal Heavy Duty (Cast Iron)
ECH	- Exclusive Craftsman Horizontal

(EXAMPLE)

TVS90-43056A is the model and specification number

TVS	- Tecumseh Vertical Styled
90	- Indicates a 9 cubic inch displacement
43056A	- is the specification number used for properly identifying the parts of the engine

8310C is the serial number

8	- first digit is the year of manufacture (1978)
310	- indicates calendar day of that year (310th day or November 6, 1978)
C	- represents the line and shift on which the engine was built at the factory.

SHORT BLOCKS. New short blocks are identified by a tag marked SBH (Short Block Horizontal) or SBV (Short Block Vertical). Original model tags of an engine should always be transferred to a new short block for correct parts identification.

Illustrations Courtesy Tecumseh Products Co.

be toward the fuel inlet fitting side of carburetor. Mark on choke plate should be parallel to shaft and should face IN-WARD when choke is closed. Diaphragm (21—Fig. T2) should be installed with rounded head of center rivet up toward the inlet needle (19) regardless of size or placement of washers around the rivet.

On carburetor Models 0234-252, 265, 266, 269, 270, 271, 282, 293, 303, 322, 327, 333, 334, 344, 345, 348, 349, 350, 351, 352, 356, 368, 371, 374, 378, 379, 380, 404 and 405, or carburetors marked with a "F" as shown in Fig. T2A, gasket (20—Fig. T2) must be installed between diaphragm (21) and cover (22). All other models are assembled as shown, with gasket (20) between diaphragm (21) and carburetor body (6).

Tecumseh Standard Float Carburetor. Refer to Fig. T4 for exploded view of Tecumseh standard float type carburetor.

Initial adjustment of idle mixture and main fuel mixture screws from a lightly seated position is one turn open. Clockwise rotation leans mixture and counterclockwise rotation richens mixture.

Fuel adjustments are made with engine at operating temperature and running. Operate engine at rated speed and adjust main fuel mixture screw (34) for

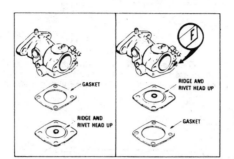

Fig. T2A—Illustration showing correct position of diaphragm on carburetors unmarked and marked with a "F."

smoothest engine operation. Operate engine at idle speed and adjust idle mixture screws for smoothest engine idle. If engine does not accelerate smoothly, slight adjustment of main fuel mixture screw may be required.

Carburetor must be disassembled and all neoprene or Viton rubber parts removed before carburetor is immersed in cleaning solvent. Do not attempt to reuse any expansion plugs. Install new plugs if any are removed for cleaning.

A resilient tip on fuel inlet needle is used on some carburetors (Fig. T5). The soft tip contacts the seating surface machined into the carburetor body.

On some carburetors, the fuel inlet valve needle seats against a Viton seat which must be removed before cleaning. The seat can be removed by blowing compressed air in from the fuel inlet fitting or by using a hooked wire. The grooved face of valve seat should be IN toward bottom of bore and the valve

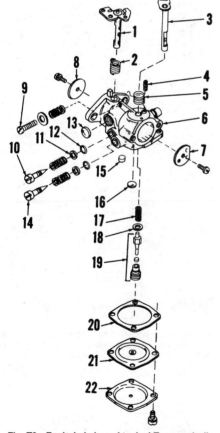

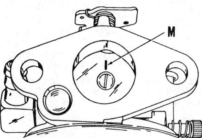

Fig. T3—The mark (M) on throttle plate should be parallel to the throttle shaft and outward as shown. Some models may also have mark at 3 o'clock position.

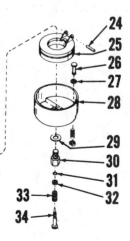

Fig. T5—View of float and fuel inlet valve needle. The valve needle shown is equipped with a resilient tip and a clip. Bend tab shown to adjust float height.

Fig. T4—Exploded view of standard Tecumseh float type carburetor.

1. Idle speed screw
2. Throttle plate
3. Return spring
4. Throttle shaft
5. Choke stop spring
6. Choke shaft
7. Return spring
8. Fuel inlet fitting
9. Carburetor body
10. Choke plate
11. Welch plug
12. Idle mixture needle
13. Spring
14. Washer
15. "O" ring
16. Ball plug
17. Welch plug
18. Pin
19. Cup plugs
20. Bowl gasket
21. Inlet needle seat
22. Inlet needle
23. Clip
24. Float shaft
25. Float
26. Drain stem
27. Gasket
28. Bowl
29. Gasket
30. Bowl retainer
31. "O" ring
32. Washer
33. Spring
34. Main fuel needle

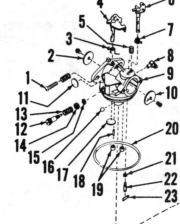

Fig. T2—Exploded view of typical Tecumseh diaphragm carburetor.

1. Throttle shaft
2. Return spring
3. Choke shaft
4. Choke stop spring
5. Return spring
6. Carburetor body
7. Choke plate
8. Throttle plate
9. Idle speed screw
10. Idle mixture screw
11. Washers
12. "O" ring
13. Welch plug
14. Main fuel mixture screw
15. Cup plug
16. Welch plug
17. Inlet needle spring
18. Gasket
19. Inlet needle & seat
20. Gasket
21. Diaphragm
22. Cover

needle should seat on smooth side of the Viton seat (Fig. T7).

A Viton seat contained in a brass seat fitting is used on some models. Use a 10-24 or 10-32 tap to pull the seat and fitting from carburetor bore as shown in Fig. T6. Use a flat, close fitting punch to install new seat and fitting.

Install the throttle plate (2—Fig. T4) with the two stamped marks out and at 12 and 3 o'clock positions. The 12 o'clock line should be parallel with the throttle shaft and toward top of carburetor. Install choke plate (10) with flat side down toward bottom of carburetor. Float height should be 0.200-0.220 inch (5.1-5.6 mm), measured from surface of carburetor body to float with carburetor body inverted as shown in Fig. T8. Float height may also be set using Tecumseh float gage 670253A as shown in Fig. T8A. Remove float and bend tab at float hinge to change float setting. The fuel inlet fitting (8—Fig. T4) is pressed into body on some models. Start fitting into body, then apply a light coat of Loctite sealant to shank and press fitting into position. The flat on fuel bowl should be under the fuel inlet fitting. Refer to Fig. T9.

Be sure to use correct parts when servicing the carburetor. Some fuel bowl gaskets are square section, while others are round. The bowl retainer screw (30—Fig. T4) contains a drilled passage for fuel to the high speed metering needle (34). A diagonal port through one side of the bowl retainer is used on carburetors with external vent. The port is through both sides on models with internal vent (Fig. T10).

Tecumseh "Automagic" Float Carburetor. Refer to Fig. T11 and note carburetor can be identified by the absence of the idle mixture screw, choke and main mixture screw. Refer to Fig. T12 for operating principles.

Float height setting is 0.210 inch (5.33 mm) measured from rim of carburetor body to surface of float as shown in Fig. T8. Float may also be set using Tecumseh float gage 670253 as shown in Fig.

T8A. Bend float tab to adjust float height.

Service procedures for "Automagic" carburetor are the same as for standard Tecumseh float carburetors.

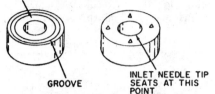

Fig. T7—The Viton seat used on some Tecumseh carburetors must be installed correctly to operate properly. All-metal needle is used with the Viton seat.

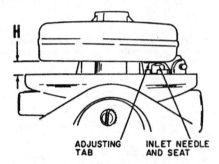

Fig. T8—Distance (H) between carburetor body and float with body inverted should be 0.200-0.220 inch (5.1-5.6 mm).

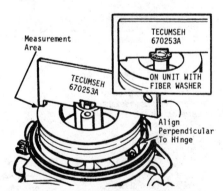

Fig. T8A—Float height can be set using Tecumseh float tool 670253A as shown.

Carter Carburetor. Refer to Fig. T13 for identification and exploded view of Carter carburetor.

Initial adjustment of idle mixture screw and main fuel mixture screws from a lightly seated position is $1\frac{1}{2}$ turns open for idle mixture screw and $1\frac{3}{4}$ turns open for main fuel mixture screw. Clockwise rotation leans mixture and counterclockwise rotation richens mixture.

Final adjustments are made with engine at operating temperature and running. Operate engine at rated speed and adjust main fuel mixture screw (4) for smoothest engine operation. Operate engine at idle speed and adjust idle mixture screw (9) for smoothest engine idle.

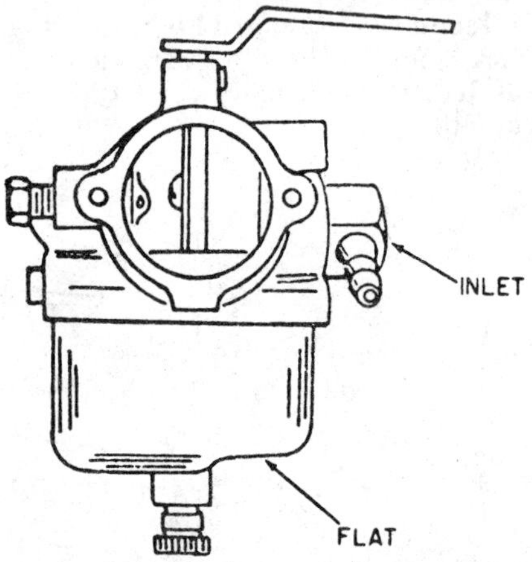

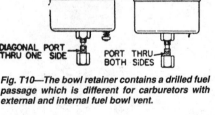

Fig. T9—Flat part of float bowl should be located under the fuel inlet fitting.

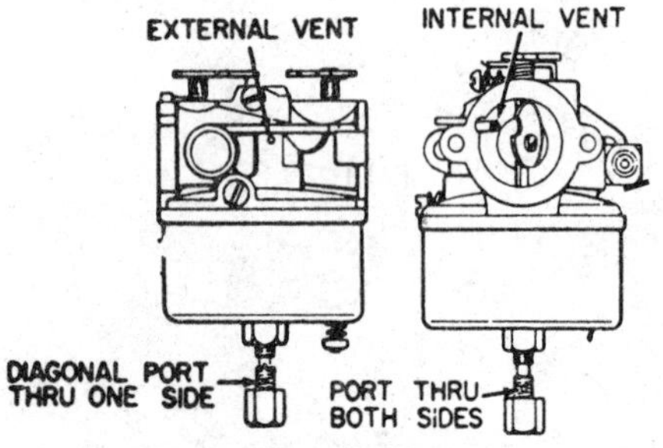

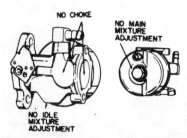

Fig. T10—The bowl retainer contains a drilled fuel passage which is different for carburetors with external and internal fuel bowl vent.

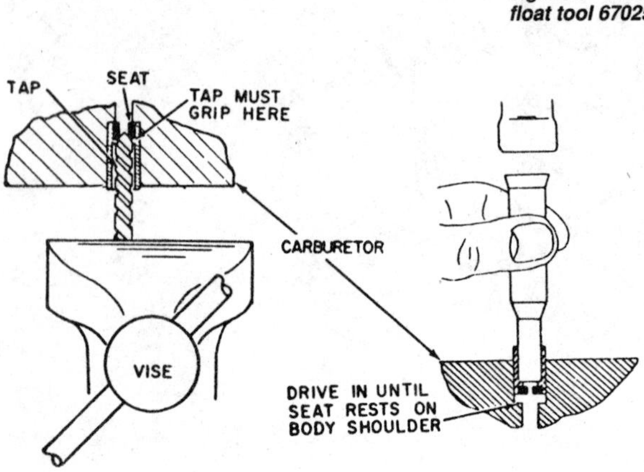

Fig. T6—A 10-24 or 10-32 tap is used to pull the brass seat fitting and fuel inlet valve seat from some carburetors. Use a close fitting flat punch to install new seat and fitting.

Fig. T11—Tecumseh "Automagic" carburetor is similar to standard float models, but can be identified by absence of choke and adjusting needles.

If engine acceleration is not smooth, main fuel mixture screw may have to be adjusted slightly.

To check float level, invert carburetor body and float assembly. There should be $^{11}/_{64}$ inch (4.37 mm) clearance between free side of float and machined surface of body casting. Bend float lever tang to provide correct measurement.

Marvel-Schebler. Refer to Fig. T14 for identification and exploded view of Marvel-Schebler Series AH carburetor.

Initial adjustment of idle mixture screw and main fuel mixture screw from a lightly seated position is one turn open for idle mixture screw and $1^{1}/_{4}$ turns open for main fuel mixture screw. Clockwise rotation leans mixture and counterclockwise rotation richens mixture.

Final adjustments are made with engine at operating temperature and running. Operate engine at rated speed and adjust main fuel mixture screw (13) for smoothest engine operation. Operate engine at idle speed and adjust idle fuel mixture needle (18) for smoothest engine idle. Adjust idle speed screw (1) to obtain 1800 rpm.

To adjust float level, invert carburetor throttle body and float assembly. Float clearance should be $^{3}/_{32}$ inch (2.38 mm) between free end of float and machined surface of carburetor body. Bend tang on float which contacts fuel inlet needle as necessary to obtain correct float level.

Tillotson Type "MT" Carburetor. Refer to Fig. T15 for identification and exploded view of Tillotson type MT carburetor.

Initial adjustment of idle mixture screw and main fuel mixture screw from a lightly seated position is $^{3}/_{4}$ turn open for idle mixture screw (21) and one turn open for main fuel mixture screw (20). Clockwise rotation leans fuel mixture

and counterclockwise rotation richens fuel mixture. Final adjustments are made with engine at operating temperature and running. Operate engine at rated speed and adjust main fuel mix-

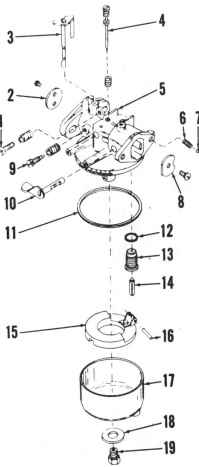

Fig. T13—Exploded view of typical Carter N carburetor.

1. Idle speed screw	10. Choke shaft
2. Throttle plate	11. Bowl gasket
3. Throttle shaft	12. Gasket
4. Main adjusting screw	13. Inlet valve seat
5. Carburetor body	14. Inlet valve
6. Choke detent spring	15. Float
7. Ball	16. Float shaft
8. Choke plate	17. Fuel bowl
9. Idle mixture screw	18. Gasket
	19. Bowl retainer

ture screw for smoothest engine operation. Operate engine at idle speed and adjust idle mixture screw for smoothest engine idle. Adjust throttle stop screw (1) to obtain 1800 rpm. If engine acceleration is not smooth, main fuel mixture screw may have to be adjusted slightly.

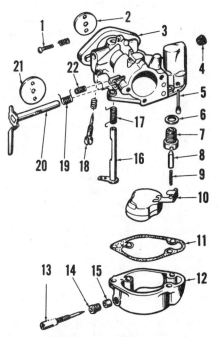

Fig. T14—Exploded view of Marvel-Schebler carburetor.

1. Idle speed screw	13. Main adjusting screw
2. Throttle plate	14. Retainer
3. Carburetor body	15. Packing
4. Fuel screen	16. Throttle shaft
5. Float	17. Throttle spring
6. Gasket	18. Idle mixture screw
7. Inlet valve seat	19. Choke spring
8. Inlet valve	20. Choke shaft
9. Spring	21. Choke plate
10. Float	22. Choke ratchet spring
11. Gasket	
12. Fuel bowl	

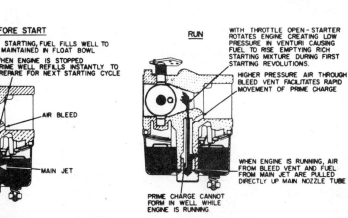

Fig. T12—The "Automagic" carburetor provides a rich starting mixture without using a choke plate. Mixture will be changed by operating with a dirty air filter or by incorrect float setting.

Fig. T15—Exploded view of typical Tillotson MT carburetor.

1. Idle speed screw	12. Inlet needle & seat
2. Throttle plate	13. Float
3. Throttle spring	14. Choke plate
4. Throttle shaft	15. Friction pin
5. Idle tube	16. Choke shaft spring
6. Main nozzle	17. Carburetor body
7. Choke shaft	18. Packing
8. Gasket	19. Retainer
9. Bowl cover	20. Main adjusting screw
10. Float shaft	21. Idle mixture screw
11. Gasket	

To check float setting, invert carburetor throttle body and measure distance from top of float to carburetor body float bowl mating surface. Distance should be 1¹³/₃₂ inch (35.72 mm). Carefully bend float tang which contacts fuel inlet needle as necessary to obtain correct float level.

Tillotson Type "E" Carburetor. Refer to Fig. T16 for identification and exploded view of Tillotson type E carburetor.

Initial adjustment of idle mixture screw and main fuel mixture screw from a lightly seated position, is ¾ turn open for idle mixture screw (18) and 1 turn open for main fuel mixture screw (14). Clockwise rotation leans mixture and counterclockwise rotation richens mixture.

Final adjustments are made with engine at operating temperature and running. Operate engine at rated speed and adjust main fuel mixture screw for smoothest engine operation. Operate engine at idle speed and adjust idle mixture screw for smoothest engine idle. Adjust throttle stop screw (8) to obtain desired idle speed. If engine does not accelerate smoothly, it may be necessary to adjust main fuel mixture screw slightly.

To check float setting, invert carburetor throttle body and measure distance from top of float at free end to float bowl mating surface on carburetor as shown in Fig. T17. Distance should be 1⁵/₁₆ inch (27.38 mm). Gasket should not be installed when measuring float height. Carefully bend float tang which contacts fuel inlet needle as necessary to obtain correct float level.

Walbro Carburetor. Refer to Fig. T18 for identification and exploded view of Walbro carburetor.

Initial adjustment of idle mixture and main fuel mixture screws from a lightly seated position is one turn open. Clockwise rotation leans fuel mixture and counterclockwise rotation richens fuel mixture.

Final adjustments are made with engine at operating temperature and running. Operate engine at rated speed and adjust main fuel mixture screw (33) for smoothest engine operation. Operate engine at idle speed and adjust idle mixture screw for smoothest engine idle. Adjust throttle stop screw (7) so engine idles at 1800 rpm.

To check float level, invert carburetor throttle body and measure clearance between free end of float and machined surface of carburetor. Clearance should be ⅛ inch (3.18 mm). Refer to Fig. T19. Carefully bend float tang which contacts fuel inlet needle as necessary to obtain correct float setting.

NOTE: If carburetor has been disassembled and main nozzle (19—Fig. T18) removed, do not reinstall the original equipment nozzle. Install a new service nozzle. Refer to Fig. T20 for differences between original and service nozzles.

PNEUMATIC GOVERNOR. Some engines are equipped with a pneumatic (air vane) type governor. On fixed linkage hookups, the recommended idle speed is 1800 rpm. Standard no-load speed is 3300 rpm. On engines not equipped with slide control (Fig. T23), obtain desired speed by varying the tension on governor speed regulating spring by moving speed adjusting lever (Fig. T21) in or out as required. If engine speed fluctuates due to governor hunting or surging, move carburetor end of governor spring into next outer hole on carburetor throttle arm shown in Fig. T22.

A too-lean mixture or friction in governor linkage will also cause hunting or unsteady operation.

On engines with slide control carburetors, speed adjustment is made with engine running. Remove slide control cover (Fig. T23) marked "choke, fast, slow, etc." Lock the carburetor in high speed "Run" position by matching the hole in slide control member (A) with hole (B) closest to choke end of brack-

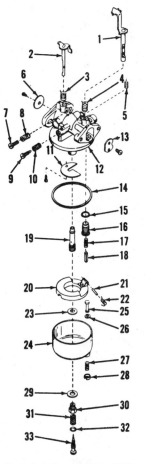

Fig. T18—Exploded view of Walbro LMG carburetor.

1.	Choke shaft	17.	Spring
2.	Throttle shaft	18.	Inlet valve
3.	Throttle return	19.	Main nozzle
	spring	20.	Float
4.	Choke return spring	21.	Float shaft
5.	Choke stop spring	22.	Spring
6.	Throttle plate	23.	Gasket
7.	Idle speed stop	24.	Bowl
	screw	25.	Drain stem
8.	Spring	26.	Gasket
9.	Idle mixture screw	27.	Spring
10.	Spring	28.	Retainer
11.	Baffle	29.	Gasket
12.	Carburetor body	30.	Bowl retainer
13.	Choke plate	31.	Spring
14.	Bowl gasket	32.	"O" ring
15.	Gasket	33.	Main fuel screw
16.	Inlet valve seat		

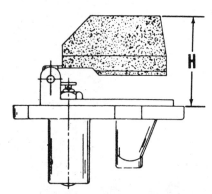

Fig. T17—Float height (H) should be measured as shown for Tillotson type "E" carburetors. Gasket should not be installed when measuring.

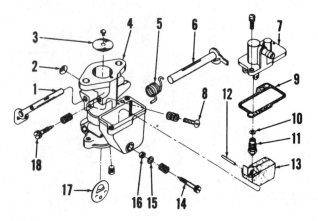

Fig. T16—Exploded view of typical Tillotson E carburetor.

1.	Throttle shaft
2.	Welch plug
3.	Throttle plate
4.	Carburetor body
5.	Return spring
6.	Choke shaft
7.	Bowl cover
8.	Idle speed stop screw
9.	Bowl gasket
10.	Gasket
11.	Inlet needle & seat
12.	Float shaft
13.	Float
14.	Main fuel needle
15.	Washer
16.	Packing
17.	Choke plate
18.	Idle mixture screw

et. Temporarily hold in this position by inserting a tapered punch or pin of suitable size into the hole.

At this time the choke should be wide open and the choke activating arm (E) should be clear of choke lever (F) by $\frac{1}{64}$ inch (0.40 mm). Obtain clearance gap by bending arm (E). To increase engine speed, bend slide arm at point (D) outward from engine. To decrease speed, bend arm inward toward engine.

Make certain on models equipped with wiper grounding switch that wiper (G) touches slide (A) when control is moved to "Stop" position.

Refer to Figs. T24, T25, T26 and T27 for assembled views of pneumatic governor systems.

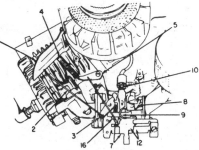

Fig. T21A—Exploded view of Light Frame vertical crankshaft engine. Model shown has plunger type oil pump (P) and air vane (V) governor.

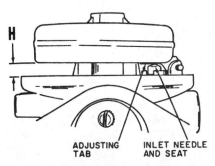

Fig. T19—Float height (H) should be measured as shown on Walbro float carburetors. Bend the adjusting tab to adjust height.

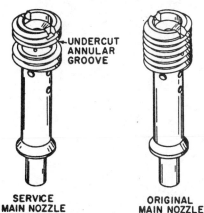

Fig. T20—The main nozzle originally installed is drilled after installation through hole in body. Service main nozzles are grooved so alignment is not necessary.

Fig. T22—Outer spring anchorage holes in carburetor throttle lever may be used to reduce speed fluctuations or surging.

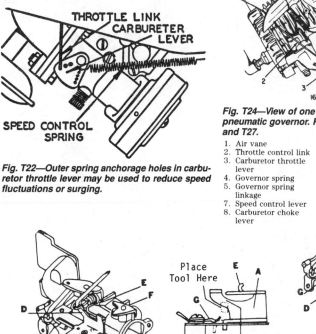

Fig. T24—View of one type of speed control with pneumatic governor. Refer also to Figs. T25, T26 and T27.

1. Air vane
2. Throttle control link
3. Carburetor throttle lever
4. Governor spring
5. Governor spring linkage
7. Speed control lever
8. Carburetor choke lever
9. Choke control
10. Stop switch
12. Alignment holes
16. Idle speed stop screw
18. High speed stop screw (Fig. T27)

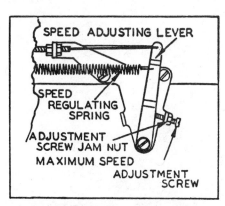

Fig. T21—Speed adjusting screw and lever. The no-load speed should not exceed 3300 rpm.

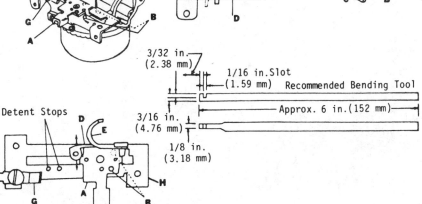

Fig. T23—When carburetor is equipped with slide control, governed speed is adjusted by bending slide arm at point "D." Bend arm outward from engine to increase speed.

MECHANICAL GOVERNOR. Some engines are equipped with a mechanical (flyweight) type governor. To adjust the governor linkage, refer to Fig. T28 and loosen governor lever screw. Twist protruding end of governor shaft counterclockwise as far as possible on vertical crankshaft engines; clockwise on horizontal crankshaft engines. On all models, move the governor lever until carburetor throttle shaft is in wide open position, then tighten governor lever clamp screw.

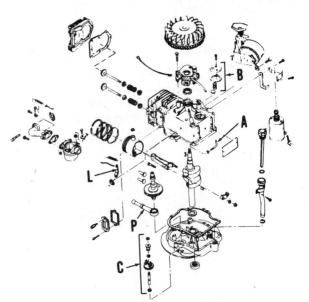

Fig. T27A—View of Light Frame vertical crankshaft engine typical of Models ECV100, ECV105, ECV110 and ECV120.

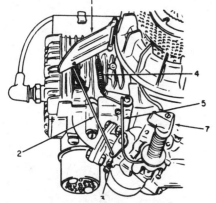

Fig. T25—Pneumatic governor linkage.

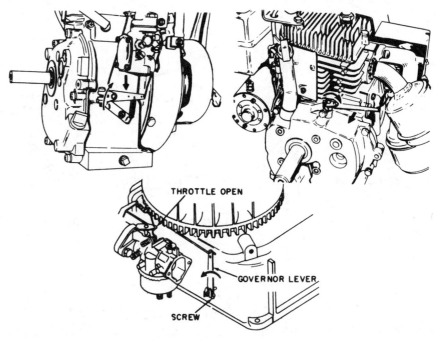

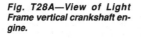

Fig. T28—Views showing location of mechanical governor lever and direction to turn when adjusting position of governor shaft.

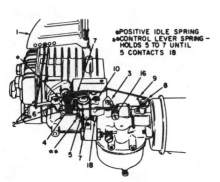

Fig. T26—Pneumatic governor linkage.

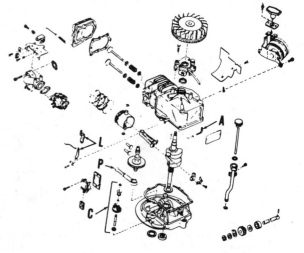

Fig. T28A—View of Light Frame vertical crankshaft engine.

Fig. T27—Pneumatic governor linkage.

Illustrations Courtesy Tecumseh Products Co.

Binding or worn governor linkage will result in hunting or unsteady engine operation. An improperly adjusted carburetor will also cause a surging or hunting condition.

Refer to Figs. T29 through T47 for views of typical mechanical governor speed control linkage installations. On some models the governor gear shaft is renewable. New governor gear shaft must be pressed into bore in cover until the correct amount of the shaft protrudes. Refer to illustration in Fig. T50.

IGNITION SYSTEM. A magneto ignition system with breaker points or capacitor-discharge ignition (CDI) may have been used according to model and application. Refer to appropriate paragraph for model being serviced.

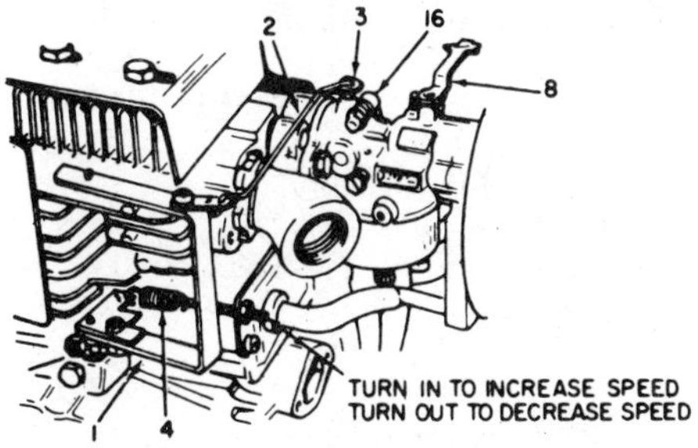

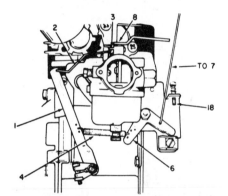

Fig. T29—View of mechanical governor with one type of constant speed control. Refer also to Fig. T30 through T43 for other mechanical governor installations.

1. Governor lever
2. Throttle control
3. Carburetor throttle lever
4. Governor spring
8. Choke lever
16. Idle speed stop screw

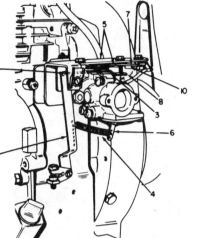

Fig. T32—Mechanical governor linkage. Refer to Fig. T31 for legend. Bellcrank is shown at (6).

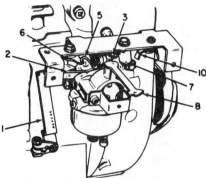

Fig. T35—Mechanical governor linkage. Governed speed of engine is increased by closing loop in linkage (5); decrease speed by spreading loop. Refer to Fig. T33 for legend.

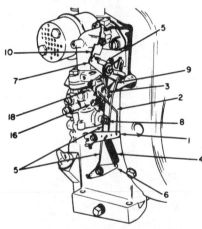

Fig. T30—Mechanical governor linkage. Refer to Fig. T29 for legend except for the following.

6. Bellcrank
7. Speed control lever
18. High speed stop screw

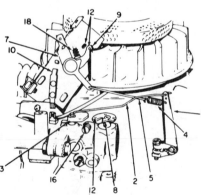

Fig. T33—Mechanical governor linkage. Control cover is raised to view underside.

1. Governor lever
2. Throttle control link
3. Carburetor throttle lever
4. Governor spring
5. Governor spring linkage
7. Speed control lever
8. Choke lever
9. Choke control
10. Stop switch
12. Alignment holes
16. Idle speed stop screw
18. High speed stop screw

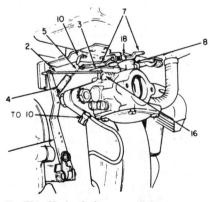

Fig. T36—Mechanical governor linkage.

1. Governor lever
2. Throttle control link
3. Throttle lever
4. Governor spring
5. Governor spring linkage
6. Bellcrank
7. Speed control lever
8. Choke lever
9. Choke control link
10. Stop switch
16. Idle speed stop screw
18. High speed stop screw

Fig. T31—Mechanical governor linkage.

1. Governor lever
2. Throttle control link
3. Carburetor throttle
4. Governor spring
5. Governor spring linkage
7. Speed control lever
8. Choke lever
10. Stop switch
16. Idle speed stop screw
18. High speed stop screw

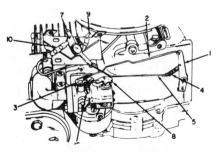

Fig. T34—Mechanical governor linkage with control cover raised. Refer to Fig. T33 for legend.

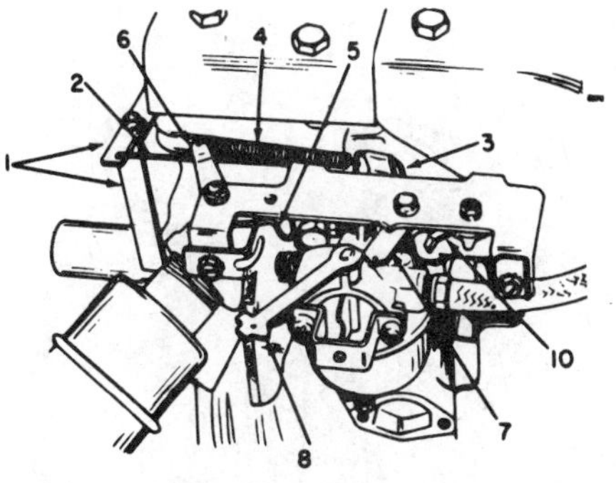

Fig. T37—View of control linkage used on some engines. To increase governed engine speed, close loop (5); to decrease speed, spread loop. Refer to Fig. T36 for legend.

Illustrations Courtesy Tecumseh Products Co.

Engine Repair

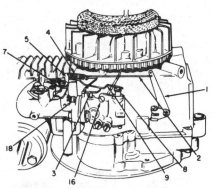

Fig. T38—View of mechanical governor control linkage. Governor spring (4) is hooked onto loop in link (2).

1. Governor lever
2. Throttle control link
3. Throttle lever
4. Governor spring
5. Governor spring linkage
7. Speed control lever
8. Choke lever
9. Choke control link
16. Idle speed stop screw
18. High speed stop screw

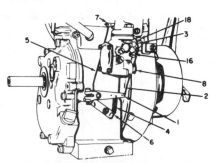

Fig. T39—Linkage for mechanical governor. Refer to Fig. T38 for legend. Bellcrank is shown at (6).

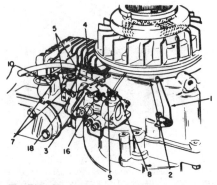

Fig. T40—Mechanical governor linkage. Refer to Fig. T38 for legend.

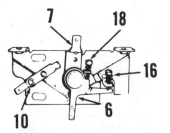

Fig. T42—Models with "Automagic" carburetor use control shown.

6. Governor spring
7. Control lever
10. Idle speed stop screw
16. Idle speed stop screw
18. High speed stop screw

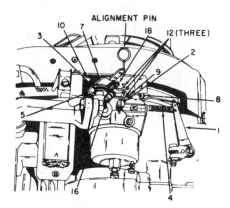

Fig. T43—On model shown, adjust location of cover so control lever is aligned with high speed slot and holes (12) are aligned.

1. Governor lever
2. Throttle control link
3. Throttle lever
4. Governor spring
5. Governor spring linkage
7. Control lever
8. Choke lever
9. Choke linkage
10. Stop switch
12. Alignment holes
16. Idle speed stop screw
18. High speed stop screw

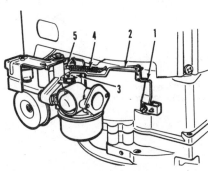

Fig. T44—View of governor linkage on TNT100 engines. TNT120 engines are similar. Refer also to Fig. T45 for models with primer carburetor.

1. Governor lever
2. Throttle link
3. Throttle lever
4. Governor spring
5. Control lever

Fig. T45—View of governor linkage on TNT100 engine with primer carburetor. Refer to Fig. T44 for parts identification.

RIDING LAWN MOWER

Breaker-Point Ignition System. Breaker-point gap at maximum opening should be 0.020 inch (0.51 mm) for all models. Marks are usually located on stator and mounting post to facilitate timing (Fig. T51).

Ignition timing can be checked and adjusted to occur when piston is at specific location (BTDC) if marks are missing. Refer to the following specifications for recommended timing.

Models	Piston Position BTDC
HS40, LAV40, TVS105, ECV100, ECV105, ECV110, ECV120, TNT100, TNT120	0.035 in. (0.89 mm)

Fig. T46—View of governor linkage on TVS engines with adjustable carburetor.

1. Governor lever
2. Throttle link
4. Governor spring
6. Idle mixture screw
7. Main mixture screw
8. Idle speed screw

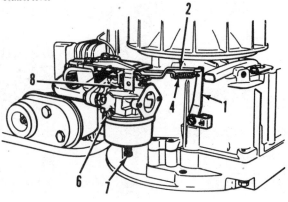

Fig. T41—Mechanical governor linkage. Refer to Fig. T38 for legend.

486

Illustrations Courtesy Tecumseh Products Co.

V40, VH40, LAV50,
TVS120, H40, HH40, HS50 . .0.050 in.
(1.27 mm)
LAV25, LAV30, LV35,
LAV35, TVS90, H25, H30,
H35, TVS75, ECH90 . . . . .0.065 in.
(1.65 mm)
V50, VH50, V60, VH60,
H50, HH50, H60, HH60,
TVM125, TVM140 . . . . .0.080 in.
(2.03 mm)

Some models may be equipped with the coil and laminations mounted outside the flywheel. Engines equipped with breaker-point ignition have the ignition points and condenser mounted under the flywheel, and the coil and laminations mounted outside the flywheel. This system is identified by the round shape of the coil and a stamping "Gray Key" in the coil to identify the correct flywheel key.

The correct air gap setting between the flywheel magnets and the coil laminations is 0.0125 inch (0.32 mm). Use Tecumseh gage 670297 or equivalent thickness plastic strip to set gap as shown in Fig. T54.

Solid-State Ignition System. The Tecumseh solid-state ignition system does not use ignition breaker points. The only moving part of the system is the rotating flywheel with the charging magnets. As the flywheel magnet passes the input coil (2—Fig. T52), a low voltage ac current is induced into input coil. Ac current passes through the rectifier (3), which converts this current to dc current. It then travels to the capacitor (4) where it is stored. The flywheel rotates approximately 180 degrees to position (1B). As it passes trigger coil (5), it induces a very small electric charge into the coil. This charge passes through resistor (6) and turns on the SCR (silicon controlled rectifier) switch (7). With the SCR switch closed, low voltage cur-

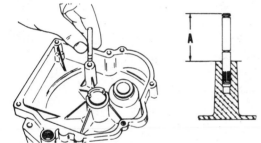

Fig. T47—View of governor linkage on TVS engines with primer carburetor.

1. Governor lever
2. Throttle link
3. Throttle lever
4. Governor spring

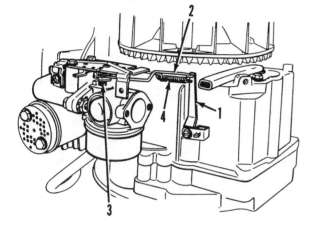

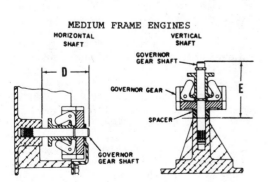

LIGHT FRAME ENGINES

HORIZONTAL SHAFT / VERTICAL SHAFT

GOVERNOR SPOOL
GOVERNOR GEAR SHAFT
GOVERNOR GEAR
BASE PLATE

MEDIUM FRAME ENGINES

HORIZONTAL SHAFT / VERTICAL SHAFT

GOVERNOR GEAR SHAFT
GOVERNOR GEAR
SPACER
GOVERNOR GEAR SHAFT

Fig. T50—The governor gear shaft must be pressed into bore until the correct amount of shaft protrudes (A, B, C, D or E). Refer also to illustrations for correct assembly of governor gear and associated parts.

B. 1-5/16 inches (33.34 mm)
C. 1-5/16 inches (33.34 mm)
D. 1-3/8 inches (34.92 mm)
E. 1-19/32 inches (40.48 mm)

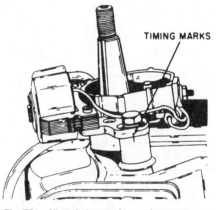

Fig. T51—Align timing marks as shown on magneto ignition system.

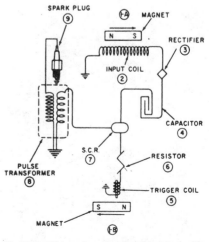

Fig. T52—Wiring diagram of solid-state ignition system for models using ignition components shown in Fig. T53.

REPAIRS

rent stored in capacitor (4) travels to pulse transformer (8). Voltage is stepped up instantaneously and current is discharged across the electrodes of spark plug (9), producing a spark.

Some units are equipped with a second trigger coil and resistor set to turn the SCR switch on at a lower rpm. This second trigger pin is closer to the flywheel and produces a spark at TDC for easier starting. As engine rpm increases, the first (shorter) trigger pin picks up the small electric charge and turns the SCR switch on, firing the spark plug earlier (before TDC).

If system fails to produce a spark to the spark plug, first check high tension lead (Fig. T53). If condition of high tension lead is questionable, renew pulse transformer and high tension lead assembly. Check low tension lead and renew if insulation is faulty. The magneto charging coil, electronic triggering system and mounting plate are available only as an assembly. If necessary to renew this assembly, place unit in position on engine. Start retaining screws, turn mounting plate counterclockwise as far as possible, then tighten retaining screws to 5-7 ft.-lbs. (7-10 N·m).

Engines with solid-state (CDI) ignition have all the ignition components sealed in a module and located outside the flywheel. There are no components under the flywheel except a spring clip to hold the flywheel key in position. This system is identified by the square shape module and a stamping "Gold Key" to identify the correct flywheel key.

The correct air gap setting between the flywheel magnets and the laminations on ignition module is 0.0125 inch (0.32 mm). Use Tecumseh gage 670297 or equivalent thickness plastic strip to set gap as shown in Fig. T54.

LUBRICATION. Vertical crankshaft engines may be equipped with a barrel and plunger type oil pump or a gear-driven rotor type oil pump. Horizontal crankshaft engines may be equipped with a gear-driven rotor type pump or with a dipper type oil slinger attached to the connecting rod.

Oil level should be checked after every five hours of operation. Maintain oil level at lower edge of filler plug or at "FULL" mark on dipstick.

Manufacturer recommends oil with an API service classification SE or SF. Use SAE 30 or SAE 10W-30 motor oil for temperatures above 32° F (0° C). Use SAE 5W-30 or SAE 10W for temperatures below 32° F (0° C). Manufacturer explicitly states: DO NOT USE SAE 10W-40 motor oil.

Oil should be changed after the first two hours of engine operation (new or rebuilt engine) and after every 25 hours of operation thereafter.

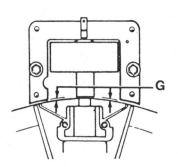

Fig. T54—Set coil lamination air gap (G) at 0.0125 inch (0.32 mm) at locations shown.

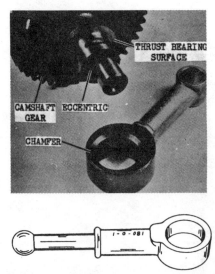

Fig. T55—Various types of barrel and plunger oil pumps have been used. Chamfered face of collar should be toward camshaft if drive collar has only one chamfered side. If drive collar has a flat boss, the boss should be next to the engine crankcase cover (mounting flange), away from camshaft gear.

TIGHTENING TORQUES. Recommended tightening torque specifications are as follows:

Carburetor to intake
  pipe . . . . .48-72 in.-lbs.
                                 (5-8 N·m)
Connecting rod nuts
(except Durlok nuts):
  1.7 hp, 2.5 hp, 3.0 hp,
  ECH90, ECV100 . . . . . .65-75 in.-lbs.
                                 (7-9 N·m)
  4 hp & 5 hp light frame
  models, ECV105, ECV110,
  ECV120 . . . . .80-95 in.-lbs.
                                 (9-11 N·m)
  5 hp medium frame,
  6 hp . . . . .86-110 in.-lbs.
                                 (10-12 N·m)
Connecting rod screws
(Durlok):
  5 hp light frame . . . .110-130 in.-lbs.
                                 (12-15 N·m)
  5 hp medium
  frame, 6hp . . . . .130-150 in.-lbs.
                                 (15-17 N·m)
  All other models . . . . .95-110 in.-lbs.
                                 (11-12 N·m)
Cylinder head . . . . . . .160-200 in.-lbs.
                                 (18-23 N·m)
Flywheel:
  Light frame . . . . .30-33 ft.-lbs.
                                 (41-45 N·m)
  Medium frame . . . . . . .36-40 ft.-lbs.
                                 (49-54 N·m)
  External ignition . . . . .33-36 ft.-lbs.
                                 (45-50 N·m)
Gear reduction cover . .75-110 in.-lbs.
                                 (9-12 N·m)
Gear reduction
  housing . . . . .100-144 in.-lbs.
                                 (11-16 N·m)
Intake pipe to cylinder . .72-96 in.-lbs.
                                 (8-11 N·m)
Magneto stator . . . . .40-90 in.-lbs.
                                 (5-10 N·m)
Mounting flange . . . . . . .75-110 in.-lbs.
                                 (9-12 N·m)
Spark plug . . . . .21-30 ft.-lbs.
                                 (28-41 N·m)

FLYWHEEL. On models so equipped, disengage flywheel brake as outlined in FLYWHEEL BRAKE section. If flywheel has tapped holes, use a suitable puller to remove flywheel. If no holes are present, screw a knock-off nut onto crankshaft so there is a small gap between nut and flywheel. Gently pry against bottom of flywheel while tapping sharply on nut.

After installing flywheel, tighten flywheel nut to torque listed in TIGHTENING TORQUE table.

CONNECTING ROD. Piston and connecting rod assembly is removed from cylinder head end of engine. Before

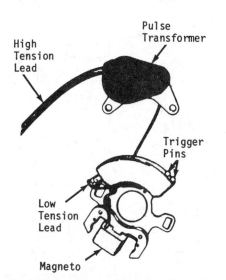

Fig. T53—Drawing of solid-state ignition system components used on some models.

removing piston, remove any carbon or ring ridge from top of cylinder to prevent ring breakage. The aluminum alloy connecting rod rides directly on crankshaft crankpin.

Refer to the following table for standard crankpin journal diameter (if engine has external ignition, check list for a different specification than engines not so equipped):

Model	Diameter
LAV25, LAV30, TVS75, H25, H30, LV35, LAV35, TVS90, H35 (prior 1983), ECH90, TNT100, ECV100, TVS100	0.8610-0.8615 in. (21.869-21.882 mm)
H35 (after 1982), LAV40, TVS105, V40 (external ignition), HS40, ECV105, ECV110, ECV120, TNT120, LAV50, HS50, TVS120	0.9995-1.0000 in. (25.390-25.400 mm)
V40, VH40, H40, HH40, H50, HH50, V50, VH50, TVM125, TVM140, V60, VH60, H60, HH60	1.0615-1.0620 in. (26.962-26.975 mm)

Standard inside diameter for connecting rod crankpin bearing is listed in the following table (if engine has external ignition, check list for a different specification than engines not so equipped):

Model	Diameter
LAV25, LAV30, TVS75, H25, H30, LV35, LAV35, TVS90, H35 (prior 1983), ECH90, TNT100, ECV100, TVS100	0.8620-0.8625 in. (21.895-21.908 mm)
H35 (after 1982), LAV40, TVS105, V40 (external ignition), HS40, ECV105, ECV110, ECV120, TNT120, LAV50, HS50, TVS120	1.0005-1.0010 in. (25.413-25.425 mm)
V40, VH40, H40, HH40, H50, HH50, V50, VH50, TVM125, TVM140, V60, VH60, H60, HH60	1.0630-1.0636 in. (27.000-27.013 mm)

Connecting rod bearing-to-crankpin journal clearance should be 0.0005-0.0015 inch (0.013-0.038 mm) for all models.

When installing connecting rod and piston assembly, align the match marks on connecting rod and cap as shown in Fig. T58. On some models, the piston pin hole is offset in piston and arrow on top of piston should be toward valves. On all engines, the match marks on connect-

ing rod and cap must be toward power takeoff (pto) end of crankshaft. Lock plates, if so equipped, for connecting rod cap retaining screws should be renewed each time cap is removed.

PISTON, PIN AND RINGS. Aluminum alloy pistons are equipped with two compression rings and one oil control ring.

Piston ring end gap is 0.007-0.017 inch (0.18-0.43 mm) on models without external ignition and displacement of 12.04 cu. in. (197 cc) or less. If engine is equipped with an external ignition, or displacement is 12.18 cu. in. (229 cc) or greater, piston ring end gap should be 0.010-0.020 inch (0.25-0.50 mm).

Piston skirt-to-cylinder clearances are listed in the following table (if engine has external ignition, check list for a different specification than engines not so equipped):

Model	Clearance
H25, H30 (prior 1983), LAV25, LAV30, TVS75	0.0025-0.0043 in. (0.064-0.110 mm)

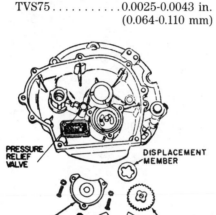

Fig. T56—View of typical gear-driven rotor type oil pump disassembled.

Model	Clearance
V40, VH40, H40, HH40	0.0055-0.0070 in. (0.140-0.178 mm)
ECV110	0.0045-0.0060 in. (0.114-0.152 mm)
H50, H60, HH50, HH60, TVM125, TVM140, V50, V60	0.0035-0.0050 in. (0.089-0.127 mm)
H50 (external ignition), H60 (external ignition), TVM125 (external ignition), TVM140 (external ignition)	0.0030-0.0048 in. (0.076-0.123 mm)
HH50, VH50, HH60, VH60	0.0015-0.0055 in. (0.038-0.140 mm)

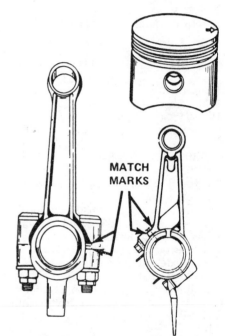

Fig. T58—Match marks on connecting rod and cap should be aligned and should be toward pto end of crankshaft.

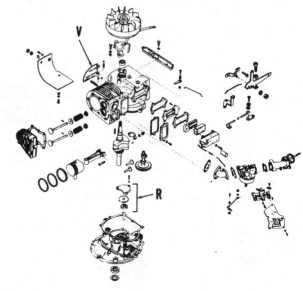

Fig. T57—View of vertical crankshaft engine. Rotor type oil pump is shown at (R); governor air vane at (V).

ECH90, ECV100, ECV105,
ECV120, H30 (after 1982)
H35 (prior 1983),
HS40, HS50, LAV35,
LAV40, LAV50, LV35,
TNT100, TNT120, TVS90
TVS100, TVS105, TVS120,
V40 (external
  ignition) . . . . 0.0040-0.0058 in.
        (0.102-0.147 mm)

Standard piston diameters measured at piston skirt 90 degrees from piston pin bore are listed in the following table (if engine has external ignition, check list for a different specification than engines not so equipped):

Model	Diameter
LAV25, LAV30, TVS75, H25, H30 (prior 1983)	2.3092-2.3100 in. (58.654-58.674 mm)
H40, HH40, V40, VH40	2.4945-2.4950 in. (63.360-63.373 mm)
LV35, LAV35, H30 (after 1982), H35, TVS90, ECH90	2.4952-2.4960 in. (63.378-63.398 mm)
ECV100, ECV105, HS40, LAV40, TNT100, TVS100, TVS105, V40 (external ignition)	2.6202-2.6210 in. (66.553-66.573 mm)
HH50 (external ignition), HH60 (external ignition), VH50 (external ignition), VH60 (external ignition)	2.6205-2.6235 in. (66.561-66.637 mm)
H50, HH50, V50, VH50, TVM125, TVM140, H60, HH60, V60, VH60	2.6210-2.6215 in. (66.573-66.586 mm)
TVM125 (external ignition), TVM140 (external ignition)	2.6212-2.6220 in. (66.578-66.599 mm)
ECV110	2.7450-2.7455 in. (69.723-69.736 mm)
HS50, LAV50, TVS120, ECV120, TNT120	2.8072-2.8080 in. (71.303-71.323 mm)

Standard ring side clearance in ring grooves is listed in the following table (if engine has external ignition, check list for a different specification than engines not so equipped):

Model	Clearance
ECH90, H25, H30 H35, LAV25, LAV30, LAV35, LV35, TVS75, TVS90:	

Compression rings . . . 0.002-0.005 in.
        (0.05-0.13 mm)
Oil control ring . . . 0.0005-0.0035 in.
        (0.013-0.089 mm)
ECV100, ECV105, ECV120,
H40, H50 (external ignition),
H60 (external ignition),
HH40, HH50 (external ignition),
HH60 (external ignition),
HS40, HS50,
HS50 (external ignition),
LAV40, LAV50,
LAV50 (external ignition),
TNT100, TNT120,
TVM125 (external ignition),
TVM140 (external ignition),
TVS100, TVS105, TVS120,
TVS120 (external ignition),
V40, V40 (external ignition),
VH40, VH50 (external ignition),
VH60 (external ignition):
  Compression rings . . . 0.002-0.005 in.
        (0.05-0.13 mm)
  Oil control ring . . . . . 0.001-0.004 in.
        (0.03-0.10 mm)
ECV110:
  Compression rings . . . 0.002-0.004 in.
        (0.05-0.10 mm)
  Oil control ring . . . . . 0.001-0.002 in.
        (0.03-0.05 mm)
H50, H60, HH50,
HH60, TVM125, TVM140,
V50, V60, VH50,
VH60:
  Compression rings . . . 0.002-0.004 in.
        (0.05-0.10 mm)
  Oil control ring . . . . . 0.002-0.004 in.
        (0.05-0.10 mm)

Refer to CONNECTING ROD section for correct piston to connecting rod assembly and correct piston installation procedure. Piston pin should be a tight push fit in piston pin bore and connecting rod pin bore and is retained by snap rings at each end of piston pin bore. Install marked side of piston rings up. Stagger ring end gaps equally around circumference of piston during installation, however, on models with a "trenched" cylinder (see Fig. T60), position ring end gaps so they are not in trenched area. This will lessen the possibility of the ring end snagging during installation of piston.

CYLINDER AND CRANKCASE. Cylinder and crankcase are an integral casting on all models. Cylinder should be honed and fitted to nearest oversize for

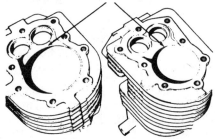

Fig. T60—Cylinder block on models H50, HH50, V50, VH50, TVM125 and TVM140 has been "trenched" to improve fuel flow and power.

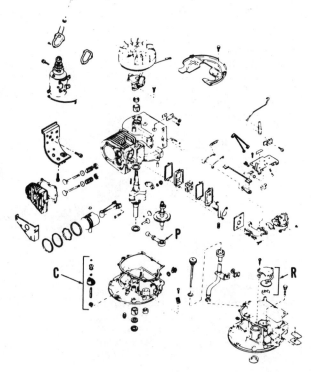

Fig. T59—View of Medium Frame engine with vertical crankshaft. Some models use plunger type oil pump (P); others are equipped with rotor type oil pump (R).

which piston and ring set are available if cylinder is scored, tapered or out-of-round more than 0.005 inch (0.13 mm).

Standard cylinder bore diameters are listed in the following table (if engine has external ignition, check list for a different specification than engines not so equipped):

Model	Diameter
LAV25, LAV30, TVS75, H25, H30 (prior 1983)	2.3125-2.3135 in. (58.738-58.763 mm)
ECH90, H30 (after 1982), H35, H40, HH40, LAV35, LV35, TVS90, V40, VH40	2.5000-2.5010 in. (63.500-63.525 mm)
ECV100, ECV105, H50, H60, HH50, HH60, HS40, LAV40, TNT100, TVM125, TVS100, TVS105, V40 (external ignition), V50, VH50	2.6250-2.6260 in. (66.675-66.700 mm)
ECV110	2.7500-2.7510 in. (69.850-69.875 mm)
LAV50, TVS120, HS50, ECV120, TNT120	2.8120-2.8130 in. (71.425-71.450 mm)

Refer to PISTON, PIN AND RINGS section for correct piston-to-cylinder block clearance. Note also that cylinder block used on Models H50, HH50, V50, VH50, TVM125 and TVM140 has been "trenched" to improve fuel flow and power (Fig. T60).

CRANKSHAFT, MAIN BEARINGS AND SEALS. Refer to CONNECTING ROD section for standard crankshaft crankpin journal diameters.

Crankshaft main bearing journals on some models ride directly in the aluminum alloy bores in the cylinder block and the crankcase cover (mounting flange). Other engines were originally equipped with renewable steel backed bronze bushings and some were originally equipped with a ball type main bearing at the pto end of crankshaft.

Standard main bearing bore diameters for main bearings are listed in the following table (if engine has external ignition, check list for a different specification than engines not so equipped):

Model	Diameter
LAV25, LAV30 TVS75, LV35, LAV35, TVS90, ECV100, H25, H30 (prior 1983), ECH90	0.8755-0.8760 in. (22.238-22.250 mm)

Model	Diameter
ECV105, ECV110, ECV120, H35 (after 1982), H40, H50, H60, HH40, HH50, HH60, HS40, HS50, LAV40, LAV50, TNT120, TVM125, TVM140, TVS105, TVS120, V40, V50, V60, VH40, VH50, VH60	1.0005-1.0010 in. (25.413-25.425 mm)

ECV100 (external ignition), H30 (after 1982), TVS75 (external ignition), TVS90 (external ignition), TNT100, TVS100:

Crankcase side....1.0005-1.0010 in. (25.413-25.425 mm)

Cover (flange) side ....0.8755-0.8760 in. (22.238-22.250 mm)

Standard diameters for crankshaft main bearing journals are shown in the following table (if engine has external ignition, check list for a different specification than engines not so equipped):

Model	Diameter
LAV25, LAV30 TVS75, LV35, LAV35, TVS90, ECV100, H25, H30 (prior 1983), ECH90	0.8735-0.8740 in. (22.187-22.200 mm)

Model	Diameter
ECV105, ECV110, ECV120, H35 (after 1982), H40, H50, H60, HH40, HH50, HH60, HS40, HS50, LAV40, LAV50, TNT120, TVM125, TVM140, TVS105, TVS120, V40, V50, V60, VH40, VH50, VH60	0.9985-0.9990 in. (25.362-25.375 mm)

ECV100 (external ignition), H30 (after 1982), TVS75 (external ignition), TVS90 (external ignition), TNT100, TVS100:

Crankcase side ...0.9985-0.9990 in. (25.362-25.375 mm)

Cover (flange) side...........0.8735-0.8740 in. (22.187-22.200 mm)

Main bearing clearance should be 0.0015-0.0025 inch (0.038-0.064 mm). Crankshaft end play should be 0.005-0.027 inch (0.13-0.69 mm) for all models.

On Models H30 through HS50, it is necessary to remove a snap ring (Fig. T61) which is located under oil seal. Note oil seal depth before removal of seal, then remove seal and snap ring.

Crankcase cover may now be removed. When installing cover, press new seal in to same depth as old seal before removal.

Ball bearing should be inspected and renewed if rough, loose or damaged. Bearing must be pressed on or off of crankshaft journal using a suitable press or puller.

Always note oil seal depth and direction before removing oil seal from crankcase or cover. New seals must be pressed into seal bores to the same depth as old seal before removal on all models.

When installing crankshaft, align crankshaft and camshaft gear timing marks as shown in Fig. T65 except on certain engines manufactured for Craftsman. Refer to CRAFTSMAN engine section of this manual.

CAMSHAFT. The camshaft and camshaft gear are an integral part which rides on journals at each end of camshaft. Camshaft on some models also has a compression release mechanism mounted on camshaft gear which lifts exhaust valve at low cranking rpm to reduce compression and aid starting (Fig. T63).

When removing camshaft, align timing marks on camshaft gear and crankshaft gear to relieve valve spring pressure on camshaft lobes. On models with compression release, it is necessary to rotate crankshaft three teeth past the aligned position to allow compression release mechanism to clear the exhaust valve tappet.

Renew camshaft if lobes or journals are worn or scored. Spring on compression release mechanism should snap weight against camshaft. Compression release mechanism and camshaft are serviced as an assembly only.

Standard camshaft journal diameter is 0.6230-0.6235 inch (15.824-15.837 mm) for Models V40, VH40, H40, HH40, H50, HH50, V50, VH50, H60, HH60, V60, VH60, TVM125 and TVM140, and

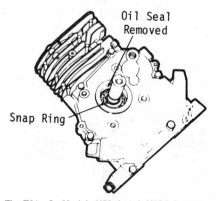

Fig. T61—On Models H30 through H50 it is necessary to remove snap ring under oil seal before removing crankcase cover.

0.4975-0.4980 inch (12.637-12.649 mm) for all other models.

On models equipped with the barrel and plunger type oil pump, the pump is operated by an eccentric on the camshaft. Refer to OIL PUMP paragraph.

When installing camshaft, align crankshaft and camshaft timing marks as shown in Fig. T65 except on certain engines manufactured for Craftsman. Refer to CRAFTSMAN engine section of this manual.

OIL PUMP. Vertical crankshaft engines may be equipped with a barrel and plunger type oil pump or a gear-driven rotor type oil pump. Horizontal crankshaft engines may be equipped with a gear-driven rotor type pump or with a

dipper type oil slinger attached to the connecting rod.

The barrel and plunger type oil pump is driven by an eccentric on the camshaft. Chamfered side of drive collar (Fig. T55) should be toward engine lower cover. Oil pumps may be equipped with two chamfered sides, one chamfered side or with flat boss as shown. Be sure installation is correct.

On engines equipped with gear-driven rotor oil pump (Fig. T56), check drive gear and rotor for excessive wear and other damage. End clearance of rotor in pump body should be within limits of 0.006-0.007 inch (0.15-0.18 mm) and is controlled by cover gasket. Gaskets are available in a variety of thicknesses.

On all models with oil pump, be sure to prime pump during assembly to ensure immediate lubrication of engine.

VALVE SYSTEM. Clearance between valve tappet and valve stem (engine cold) is 0.010 inch (0.25 mm) for intake and exhaust valves for Models V50, VH50, H50, HH50, V60, VH60, H60, HH60, TVM125 and TVM140. Valve tappet clearance for all other models is 0.008 inch (0.20 mm) for intake and exhaust valves. Check clearance with piston at TDC on compression stroke. Grind valve stem end as necessary to obtain specified clearance.

Valve face angle is 45 degrees and valve seat angle is 46 degrees except on very early production 2.25 horsepower models which have 30 degree valve face and seat angles.

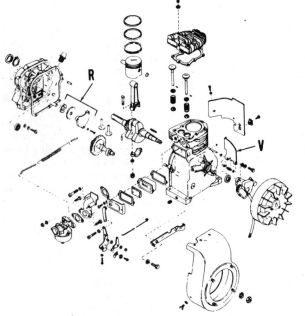

Fig. T62—View of Light Frame engine with horizontal crankshaft. Air vane (V) type governor and rotor type oil pump (R) are used on models shown.

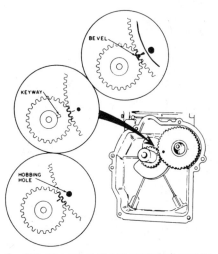

Fig. T65—The camshaft and crankshaft must be correctly timed to ensure valves open at correct time. Different types of marks have been used, but marks should be aligned when assembling.

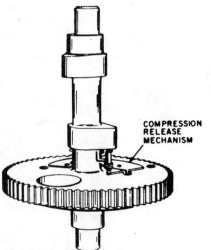

Fig. T63—View of Instamatic Ezee-Start compression release camshaft.

Fig. T64—View of Light Frame horizontal crankshaft engine with mechanical governor and splash lubrication. Governor centrifugal weights are shown at (C) and lubrication dipper at (D).

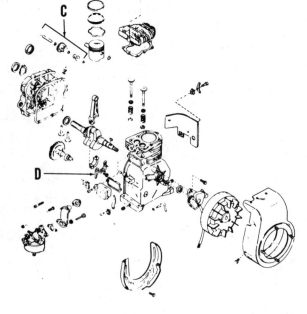

Valve seat width should be 0.042-0.052 inch (1.07-1.32 mm) for Models V40, VH40, H40, HH40, H50, HH50, V50,

VH50, H60, HH60, V60, VH60, TVM125 and TVM140; and 0.035-0.045 inch (0.89-1.14 mm) for all other models.

Valve stem guides are cast into cylinder block and are not renewable. If excessive clearance exists between valve stem and guide, guide should be reamed and a new valve with an oversize stem installed.

REDUCED SPEED PTO SHAFTS. A pto (power takeoff) shaft which rotates at half the speed of the crankshaft is available by extending the camshaft through the cover (lower mounting flange). Refer to Fig. T68. Except for the seal around the extended camshaft, service is similar to standard models.

A slow speed (8.5:1) auxiliary pto shaft is used on some vertical shaft engines (Fig. T69). A worm gear (W) on the

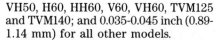

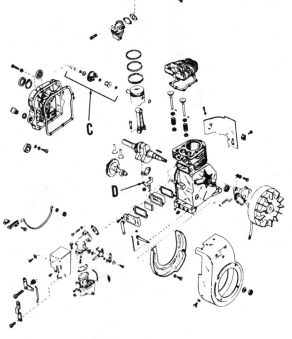

Fig. T66—View of Medium Frame horizontal crankshaft engine with mechanical governor (C). An oil dipper for splash lubrication is cast onto the connecting rod cap instead of using the rotor type oil pump (R).

Fig. T67—View of Light Frame horizontal crankshaft engine with mechanical governor and splash lubrication.

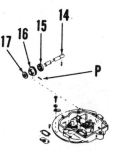

Fig. T68—An auxiliary pto shaft that turns at 1/2 the speed of the crankshaft is available by using a special extended camshaft. The hole in lower cover is sealed using lip type seal (8).

Fig. T69—Three different 8.5:1 auxiliary pto drives have been used. Early units are shown at right. Pin (P) attaches gear (16) to the pto shaft (14). On later units, the shaft is held in position by snap ring (4) or (13). Worm gear (W) on crankshaft drives the gear (5, 10 or 16) on all models.

1. Pto shaft
2. Seal
3. Washers (2)
4. Snap ring
5. Gear
6. Tang washer
7. Pto shaft
8. Seal
9. Thick washer
10. Gear
11. Tang washer
12. Washer
13. Snap ring
14. Pto shaft
15. Seal
16. Gear
17. Washer

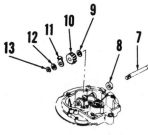

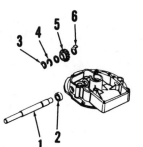

crankshaft turns the pto gear and pto shaft. Several different versions of this unit have been used. A roll pin (Fig. T70) is used to hold the gear on the shaft on early models. A pipe plug and a threaded boss are located as shown in center and lower views of some of these early models. The roll pin can be driven out of the gear and shaft through the threaded hole of models so equipped.

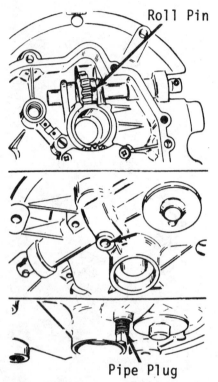

Fig. T70—The roll pin must be removed from early 8.5:1 auxiliary pto before the shaft and gear can be withdrawn. On some models (center), the boss is closed. The boss can be drilled and tapped to accept a 7-28 NPT 1/8 inch pipe plug as shown in lower view.

Refer to Fig. T69 for order of assembly.

Disassembly and repair procedure for the 6:1 reduction will be evident after examination of the unit and reference to Fig. T71.

FLYWHEEL BRAKE. A flywheel brake is used on some engines that will stop the engine within three seconds when the mower safety handle is released. The ignition circuit is grounded also when the brake is actuated. On electric start models, an interlock switch prevents energizing the starter motor if the brake is engaged.

Two configurations have been used. The brake shown in Fig. T72 contacts the bottom surface of the flywheel while the brake shown in Fig. T73 contacts the inside of the flywheel. Before the flywheel can be removed for either type, the brake must be disengaged from the flywheel. On bottom surface type, unhook brake spring (B—Fig. T72). On inside surface type, push lever (L—Fig. T73) toward spark plug so brake pad moves away from flywheel, then insert Tecumseh tool 670298 or a suitable pin in hole (H) to hold lever.

Inspect mechanism for excessive wear and damage. Tighten mounting screws

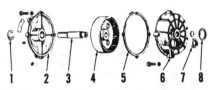

Fig. T71—Exploded view of the 6:1 gear reduction assembly. Housing (6) is bolted to cylinder block and the pinion gear is made onto end of crankshaft.

1. Seal
2. Cover
3. Output shaft
4. Gear
5. Gasket
6. Housing
7. Seal
8. Cork gasket

on bottom surface type brake to 60-70 in.-lbs. (6.8-7.9 N·m). On inside surface type, minimum allowable thickness of brake pad at narrowest point is 0.060 inch (1.52 mm). Install brake mechanism and push up on bracket so bracket mounting screws are at bottom of slotted holes (M) in bracket. Tighten mounting screws to 90 in.-lbs. (10.2 N·m).

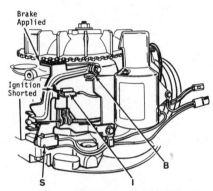

Fig. T72—View of bottom-surface type flywheel brake showing location of brake spring (B), ignition cut-out switch (I) and interlock switch (S) for electric starter.

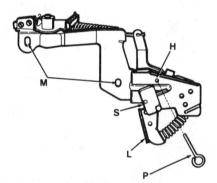

Fig. T73—Push against lever (L) and insert pin (P) through holes (H) to hold brake pad away from flywheel. Interlock switch (S) is used on engines with an electric starter.

Illustrations Courtesy Tecumseh Products Co.

TECUMSEH

TECUMSEH PRODUCTS COMPANY
Grafton, Wisconsin 53204

Model	No. Cyls.	Bore	Stroke	Displacement	Power Rating
H70	1	2.75 in. (69.9 mm)	2.531 in. (64.3 mm)	15 cu. in. (246.8 cc)	7 hp (5.2 kW)
V70	1	2.75 in. (69.9 mm)	2.531 in. (64.3 mm)	15 cu. in. (246.8 cc)	7 hp (5.2 kW)
HM70*	1	2.94 in. (74.61 mm)	2.531 in. (64.3 mm)	17.16 cu. in. (281 cc)	7 hp (5.2 kW)
HM70†	1	3.125 in. (79.38 mm)	2.531 in. (64.3 mm)	19.4 cu. in. (318 cc)	8 hp (6 kW)
HMXL70	1	3.125 in. (79.38 mm)	2.531 in. (64.3 mm)	19.4 cu. in. (318 cc)	8 hp (6 kW)
VM70	1	2.75 in. (69.9 mm)	2.531 in. (64.3 mm)	15 cu. in. (246.8 cc)	7 hp (5.2 kW)
TVM170	1	2.94 in. (74.61 mm)	2.531 in. (64.3 mm)	17.16 cu. in. (281 cc)	7 hp (5.2 kW)
H80	1	3.062 in. (77.8 mm)	2.531 in. (64.3 mm)	18.65 cu. in. (305.7 cc)	8 hp (6 kW)
V80	1	3.062 in. (77.8 mm)	2.531 in. (64.3 mm)	18.65 cu. in. (305.7 cc)	8 hp (6 kW)
HM80*	1	3.062 in. (77.8 mm)	2.531 in. (64.3 mm)	18.65 cu. in. (305.7 cc)	8 hp (6 kW)
HM80†	1	3.125 in. (79.38 mm)	2.531 in. (64.3 mm)	19.4 cu. in. (318 cc)	8 hp (6 kW)
HHM80	1	3.125 in. (79.38 mm)	2.531 in. (64.3 mm)	19.4 cu. in. (318 cc)	8 hp (6 kW)
VM80*	1	3.062 in. (77.8 mm)	2.531 in. (64.3 mm)	18.65 cu. in. (305.7 cc)	8 hp (6 kW)
VM80†	1	3.125 in. (79.38 mm)	2.531 in. (64.3 mm)	19.4 cu. in. (318 cc)	8 hp (6 kW)
TVM195, TVXL195	1	3.125 in. (79.38 mm)	2.531 in. (64.3 mm)	19.4 cu. in. (318 cc)	8 hp (6 kW)
HM100‡	1	3.187 in. (80.95 mm)	2.531 in. (64.3 mm)	20.2 cu. in. (330.9 cc)	10 hp (7.5 kW)
HM100**	1	3.313 in. (84.15 mm)	2.531 in. (64.3 mm)	21.82 cu. in. (357.6 cc)	10 hp (7.5 kW)
VM100	1	3.187 in. (80.95 mm)	2.531 in. (64.3 mm)	20.2 cu. in. (330.9 cc)	10 hp (7.5 kW)
TVM220, TVXL220	1	3.313 in. (84.15 mm)	2.531 in. (64.3 mm)	21.82 cu. in. (357.6 cc)	10 hp (7.5 kW)

*HM70, HM80 or VM80 models prior to type letter E.
†HM70, HM80 or VM80 models type letter E and after.
‡Early HM100 models.
**Later HM100 models.

All models are small or medium frame, four-stroke, single-cylinder engines, except Model HHM80. Small frame engines have an aluminum block and cylinder bore. Medium frame engines have an aluminum block with a cast iron cylinder sleeve liner that is an integral part of the cylinder casting, except Model HHM80, which has a cast iron cylinder block. Refer to the TECUMSEH ENGINE IDENTIFICATION INFORMATION section to correctly identify engine to be serviced.

The connecting rod for all models rides directly on the crankshaft crankpin journal. Lubrication for all horizontal crankshaft engines is provided by splash lubrication. An oil dipper is either bolted to the connecting rod cap or is an integral part of the connecting rod cap casting. Lubrication for all vertical crankshaft engines is provided by a positive displacement plunger-type oil pump that is operated by an eccentric on the camshaft.

MAINTENANCE

LUBRICATION. Vertical crankshaft models are equipped with a positive displacement barrel and plunger-type oil pump driven by an eccentric on the camshaft. Oil from the pump lubricates the upper main bearing and the connecting rod journal.

All horizontal crankshaft models are splash lubricated. On some models, the dipper is an integral part of connecting rod cap and, on other models, the dipper is retained on connecting rod by the connecting rod bolts.

Manufacturer recommends oil with an API service classification of SF or SG.

Use an SAE 30 oil for temperatures above 32° F (0° C) and SAE 5W-20 or 5W-30 oil for temperatures below 32° F (0° C).

Check oil level after every 5 hours of operation or before initial start up of engine. As equipped, maintain oil level at edge of filler hole or at "FULL" mark on dipstick.

Oil should be changed after 25 hours of normal operation; more frequently if operation is severe.

SPARK PLUG. Recommended spark plug for all models is Champion J8C or equivalent. Electrode gap should be 0.030 inch (0.76 mm).

CARBURETOR. Engine may be equipped with a Tecumseh or Walbro float-type carburetor. Refer to appropriate following section for carburetor service information.

Tecumseh Carburetor. Refer to Fig. T501 for an exploded view of Tecumseh carburetor and location of fuel mixture screws.

For initial carburetor adjustment on all models, open idle mixture screw (12)

and main fuel mixture screw (34) 1½ turns from a lightly seated position.

Make final adjustments with engine at normal operating temperature and running. Place engine under load and adjust main fuel mixture screw (34) for leanest mixture that will allow satisfactory acceleration and steady governor operation. Set engine at idle speed (no load) and adjust idle mixture screw (12) to obtain smoothest idle operation.

As each adjustment affects the other, adjustment procedure may have to be repeated.

To check float height, invert carburetor throttle body and float assembly. Float setting should be 7/32 inch (5.6 mm) measured between free end of float and rim on carburetor body. Adjust float by carefully bending float lever tab that contacts inlet valve (Fig. T502).

Refer to Fig. T501 for exploded view of carburetor during disassembly. When reinstalling Viton inlet valve seat, grooved side of seat must be installed in bore first so inlet valve will seat against smooth side (Fig. T503). Some later models have a Viton tipped inlet needle (Fig. T502) and a brass seat.

Install throttle plate (2—Fig. T501) with the two stamped lines facing out and at 12- and 3-o'clock positions. The 12-o'clock line should be parallel with

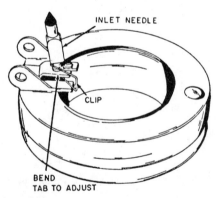

Fig. T502—Fuel inlet valve needle shown is equipped with a resilient tip and a clip. Bend tab on float arm to adjust float level.

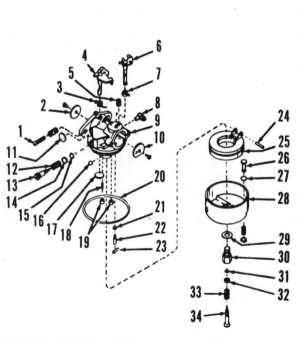

Fig. T501—Exploded view of Tecumseh carburetor.

1. Idle speed screw		26. Drain stem
2. Throttle plate	10. Choke plate	27. Gasket
3. Return spring	11. Welch plug	28. Fuel bowl
4. Throttle shaft	12. Idle mixture screw	29. Gasket
5. Choke stop spring	13. Spring	30. Bowl retainer
6. Choke shaft	14. Washer	31. "O" ring
7. Return spring	15. "O" ring	32. Washer
8. Fuel inlet spring	16. Ball plug	33. Spring
9. Carburetor body	17. Welch plug	34. Main fuel screw
	18. Pin	
	19. Cup plugs	
	20. Gasket	
	21. Fuel inlet valve seat	
	22. Fuel inlet valve	
	23. Clip	
	24. Pin	
	25. Float	

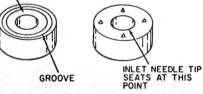

Fig. T503—Viton fuel inlet valve seat used on some Tecumseh carburetors must be installed correctly to operate properly. An all-metal needle valve is used with seat shown.

Illustrations Courtesy Tecumseh Products Co.

throttle shaft and facing toward top of carburetor.

Install choke plate (10) with float side toward bottom of carburetor.

Fuel fitting (8) is pressed into body. When installing fuel inlet fitting, start fitting into bore, then apply a light coat of Loctite grade A on shank and press fitting into place.

Walbro Carburetor. Refer to Fig. T504 for an exploded view of the Walbro float-type carburetor and location of fuel mixture adjustment screws.

For initial carburetor adjustment on Models VM80, HHM80 and HM80, open idle mixture screw (9) 1¾ turns and main mixture screw (33) 2 turns from a lightly seated position.

For initial carburetor adjustment on all remaining models, open idle mixture screw (9) and main mixture screw (33) one turn from a lightly seated position.

Make final adjustments with engine at normal operating temperature and running. Place engine under load and adjust main fuel mixture screw (33) for leanest mixture that will allow satisfactory acceleration and steady governor operation. Set engine at idle speed (no load) and adjust idle mixture screw (9) to obtain smoothest idle operation.

As each adjustment affects the other, adjustment procedure may have to be repeated.

To check float height, invert carburetor throttle body and float assembly (Fig. T505). Float setting (dimension H) should be ⅛ inch (3.2 mm) for horizontal crankshaft engines and 3/32 inch (2.4 mm) for vertical crankshaft engines. Adjust float height by carefully bending float lever tab.

Float drop (travel) for all models should be 9/16 inch (14.3 mm) and is adjusted by carefully bending limiting tab on float.

GOVERNOR. A mechanical flyweight-type governor is used on all models.

To adjust governor lever position on vertical crankshaft models, refer to Fig. T506. Loosen clamp screw on governor lever and rotate governor lever shaft counterclockwise as far as possible. Move governor lever to left until throttle is fully open, then tighten clamp screw.

On horizontal crankshaft models, loosen clamp screw on lever and rotate governor lever shaft clockwise as far as possible. See Fig. T507. Move governor lever clockwise until throttle is wide open, then tighten clamp screw.

On Snow King engines equipped with a loop (L—Fig. T508) in speed control link, open or close link to adjust engine speed.

On some engines, the governed idle speed is adjusted by bending tab (T—Fig. T509) rather than by adjusting idle speed screw on carburetor.

On some TVM170, TVM195 and TVM200 engines, a governor override system is used. Linkage is shown in Fig. T510. On these engines, high-speed setting is adjusted by turning top screw (H) of override lever and low idle speed is adjusted by turning bottom screw (L).

IGNITION SYSTEM. Engines may be equipped with either a magneto-type ignition system or a solid-state electronic ignition system. Note that the type of ignition system used determines the type of flywheel key to be installed. Refer to the appropriate service information for type of ignition being serviced.

Magneto Ignition System. Tecumseh flywheel-type magnetos are used on some H70, V70, HM70, VM70, H80,

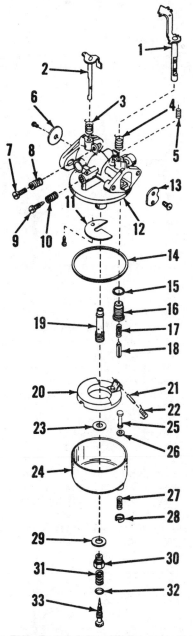

Fig. T504—Exploded view of Walbro carburetor.

1. Choke shaft
2. Throttle shaft
3. Throttle return spring
4. Choke return spring
5. Choke stop spring
6. Throttle plate
7. Idle speed screw
8. Spring
9. Idle mixture screw
10. Spring
11. Baffle
12. Carburetor body
13. Choke plate
14. Gasket
15. Gasket
16. Fuel inlet valve seat
17. Spring
18. Fuel inlet valve
19. Main nozzle
20. Float
21. Pin
22. Spring
23. Gasket
24. Fuel bowl
25. Drain stem
26. Gasket
27. Spring
28. Retainer
29. Gasket
30. Bowl retainer
31. Spring
32. "O" ring
33. Main mixture screw

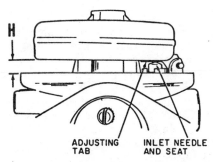

Fig. T505—Float height (H) on Walbro carburetor should be measured as shown. Bend adjusting tab to adjust height.

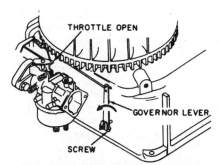

Fig. T506—When adjusting governor linkage on Models V70, VM70, V80, VM80, VM100, TVM170, TVM195 or TVM220, loosen clamp screw and rotate governor lever shaft and lever counterclockwise as far as possible.

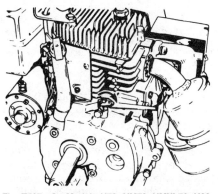

Fig. T507—On Models H70, HM70, HMXL70, H80, HHM80, HM80 and HM100, rotate governor lever shaft and lever clockwise when adjusting linkage.

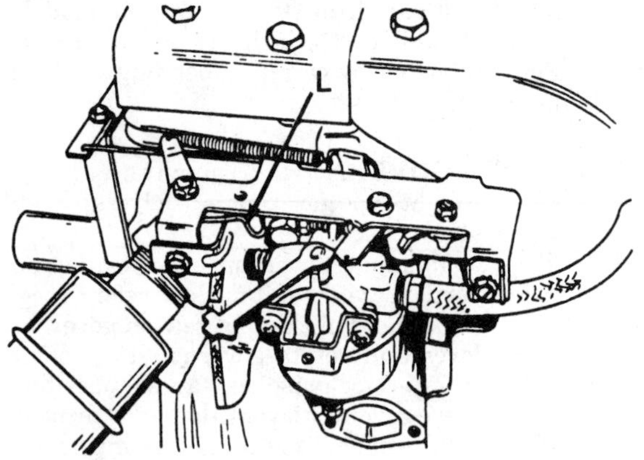

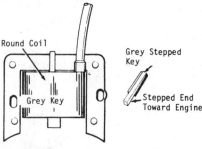

Fig. T508—On some Snow King engines, open or close loop (L) in speed control link to adjust engine speed.

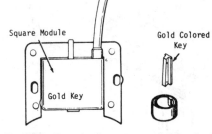

Fig. T512—View showing round breaker-point ignition coil that uses a gray flywheel key. Refer to text.

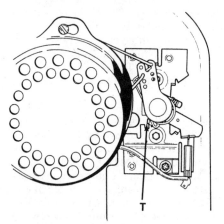

Fig. T509—On horizontal shaft engines with governed idle speed, bend tab (T) to adjust idle speed.

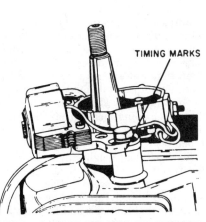

Fig. T511—On Models H70, HM70, V70, VM70, H80, HHM80, HM80, V80, VM80, HM100 and VM100 equipped with magneto ignition, adjust breaker-point gap to 0.020 inch (0.51 mm) and align timing marks as shown.

Fig. T513—View showing square solid-state ignition module that uses a gold flywheel key. Refer to text.

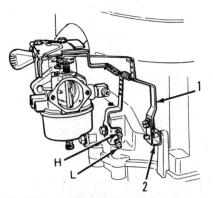

Fig. T510—Drawing of governor external linkage typical of engines equipped with governor override system. Refer to text for adjustment procedure.

V80, HHM80, HM80, VM80, HM100 and VM100 models. This ignition system is identified by the round shape of the coil and the stamping "GRAY KEY" in the coil to identify the correct flywheel key to be used. Breaker points are located behind the flywheel. Breaker-point gap should be adjusted to 0.020 inch (0.51 mm). Timing is correct when timing mark on magneto base plate is in line with mark on bearing plate as shown in Fig. T511. To verify timing if timing marks are defaced, points should start to open when piston is 0.085-0.095 inch (2.16-2.41 mm) BTDC.

Coil edge gap at flywheel should be 0.0125 inch (0.32 mm) on all models. To adjust air gap, turn flywheel magnet into position under coil core. Loosen retaining screws and place shim stock or feeler gauge of specified thickness between coil and magnet. Press coil against gauge and tighten screws.

Original magneto ignition coil must be installed using the gray flywheel key. The original magneto ignition coil is no longer available and, if ordered, the solid-state module and key assembly will be substituted. Make certain the gray flywheel key is used with the magneto (round) ignition coil and that the gold flywheel key is used with the solid-state (square) module (Figs. T512 and T513).

Solid-State Ignition System. Tecumseh solid-state ignition module has no moving parts except the flywheel. Some ignition modules are equipped with charging (alternator) coils. Test all solid-state ignition systems by holding high-tension lead 1/8 inch (3.2 mm) from spark plug (Fig. T514). Crank engine and check for a good blue spark. If no spark is present, check high-tension lead and coil lead for loose connections or faulty insulation. Check air gap between flywheel and ignition unit as shown in Fig. T515. Air gap should be 0.0125 inch (0.32 mm). To adjust air gap, loosen the two retaining screws and move ignition unit as necessary, then tighten retaining screws.

To test ignition charging (alternator) coil, remove coil lead from ignition terminal and connect an ohmmeter as shown in Fig. T516. If series resistance is below 400 ohms, renew stator and coil

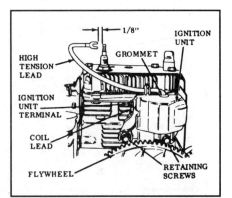

Fig. T514—View of solid-state ignition unit used on some models equipped with a flywheel alternator. System should produce a good blue spark that is 1/8 inch (3.2 mm) long at cranking speed.

Illustrations Courtesy Tecumseh Products Co.

assembly (Fig. T517). If resistance is above 400 ohms, renew ignition unit.

VALVE ADJUSTMENT. Valve tappet gap (cold) on all models should be 0.010 inch (0.25 mm) with piston at TDC on compression stroke.

To increase clearance, grind off end of valve stem. To reduce clearance, grind valve seat deeper or renew valve and/or valve tappet. Refer also to VALVE SYSTEM paragraphs in REPAIRS section.

REPAIRS

TIGHTENING TORQUES. Recommended tightening torque specifications are as follows:

Ball bearing retainer nut:
 All models so equipped . 15-22 in.-lbs.
  (1.7-3 N•m)
Connecting rod:
 Standard-type
  screws . . . . 106-130 in.-lbs.
   (12-14.7 N•m)
 Durlock-type
  screws . . . . 200-220 in.-lbs.
   (22.6-24.8 N•m)
Crankcase cover . . . . . . 65-110 in.-lbs.
   (7.3-12 N•m)
Cylinder head . . . . 200 in.-lbs.
   (22.6 N•m)
Flywheel nut:
 Light frame . . . . 34-37 ft.-lbs.
   (45-50 N•m)

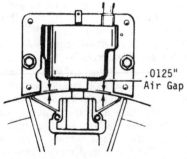

Fig. T515—Air gap between flywheel and ignition coil or module should be 0.0125 inch (0.32 mm).

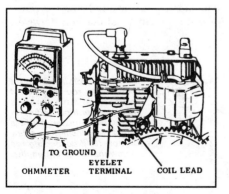

Fig. T516—View showing an ohmmeter connected for resistance test of ignition charging (alternator) coil.

Medium frame:
 (Internal coil) . . . . . . 36-42 ft.-lbs.
   (49-57 N•m)
 (External coil) . . . . . . 50-55 ft.-lbs.
   (68-75 N•m)

CYLINDER HEAD. When removing cylinder head, note location of different length cap screws to aid in reassembly. Always install new head gasket and tighten cap screws evenly following sequence shown in Figs. T518 and T519. Tighten cylinder head screws to 200 in.-lbs. (22.6 N•m).

VALVE SYSTEM. Valve seats are machined directly into cylinder block assembly. Seats are ground at a 45-degree angle and should not exceed 3/64 inch (1.19 mm) in width.

Valve face angle should be 45°. Valve margin should not be less than 1/32 inch (0.79 mm). See Fig. T520. Valves are available with 1/32 inch (0.79 mm) over-

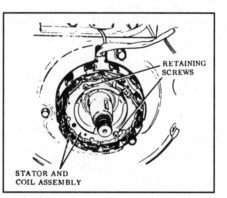

Fig. T517—Ignition charging (alternator) coil and stator are serviced only as an assembly.

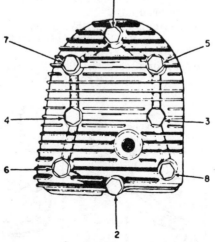

Fig. T518—On H70, V70, H80 and V80 models, tighten cylinder head cap screws evenly to 200 in.-lbs. (22.6 N•m) following tightening sequence shown.

size stem for use with oversize valve guide bore.

Valve guides are not renewable. If guides are excessively worn, ream to 0.3432-0.3442 inch (8.72-8.74 mm) and install a valve with 1/32 inch (0.794 mm) oversize valve stem. Drill upper and lower valve spring caps as necessary to fit oversize valve stem.

OIL PUMP. Vertical crankshaft models are equipped with a positive displacement barrel and plunger-type oil pump (Figs. T521 and T522) driven by an eccentric on the camshaft. Oil from the pump lubricates the upper main bearing and the connecting rod journal.

When installing early-type pump (Fig. T521), chamfered side of drive collar must be against thrust bearing surface on camshaft gear. When installing late-type pump, place side of drive collar with large flat surface (shown in Fig. T522) away from camshaft gear.

CAMSHAFT. The camshaft and camshaft gear are an integral part that

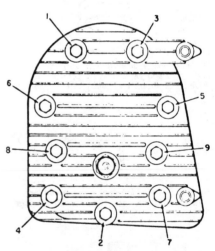

Fig. T519—On HHM80, HM80, VM80, HM100, VM100, TVM170, TVM195, TVXL195, TVM220 and TVXL220 models, tighten cylinder head cap screws evenly to 200 in.-lbs. (22.6 N•m) following tightening sequence shown.

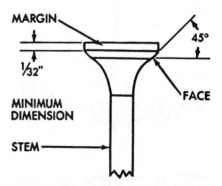

Fig. T520—Valve face angle should be 45°. Minimum valve head margin is 1/32 inch (0.79 mm).

rides on journals at each end of camshaft.

Some engines have a camshaft equipped with a compression release mechanism (Fig. T523). A camshaft equipped with a compression release mechanism is easier to remove and install if the crankshaft is rotated three teeth past aligned position that allows compression release mechanism to clear exhaust valve lifter. Compression release mechanism parts should operate freely with no binding or sticking. Parts are not serviced separately from camshaft assembly.

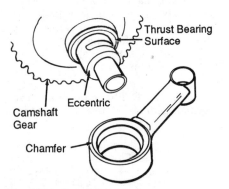

Fig. T521—View of early-type oil pump used on V70, VM70 and VM80 models. Chamfered face of drive collar should be toward camshaft gear.

Fig. T522—Install late-type oil pump so large flat surface on drive collar is away from camshaft gear.

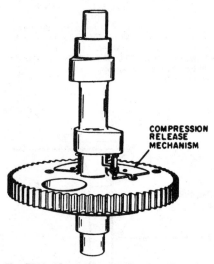

Fig. T523—View of Insta-matic Ezee-Start compression release camshaft assembly used on all models.

Valve lifters should be identified before removal so they can be reinstalled in their original positions. Some models use lifters of different length. Short lifter is installed at intake position and longer lifter is installed at exhaust position.

Camshaft journal diameter should be 0.6230-0.6235 inch (15.82-15.84 mm) and journal-to-bearing running clearance should be 0.003 inch (0.08 mm). Renew camshaft if gear teeth are worn or if journal or lobe surfaces are worn or damaged.

Make certain timing marks on camshaft gear and crankshaft gear are aligned during assembly.

PISTON, PIN AND RINGS. The engine is fitted with an aluminum piston that has two compression rings and an oil control ring. Piston and connecting rod are removed as an assembly from cylinder head end of engine.

Measure piston skirt diameter at bottom edge of skirt at a right angle to piston pin for all models. Refer to following list of standard piston diameter sizes:

Model	Piston Diameter
H70, V70, VM70	2.7450-2.7455 in. (69.723-69.736 mm)
HM70 prior to type letter E	2.9325-2.9335 in. (74.486-74.511 mm)
HM70 with type letter E or after	3.1195-3.1205 in. (79.235-79.261 mm)
HMXL70	3.1195-3.1205 in. (79.235-79.261 mm)
H80, V80, VM80	3.0575-3.0585 in. (77.660-77.686 mm)
HHM80	3.1195-3.1205 in. (79.235-79.261 mm)
HM80 prior to type letter E	3.0575-3.0585 in. (77.660-77.686 mm)
HM80 with type letter E or after	3.1195-3.1205 in. (79.235-79.261 mm)

VM80	3.1195-3.1205 in. (79.235-79.261 mm)
HM100 (early production), VM100	3.1817-3.1842 in. (80.815-80.879 mm)
HM100 (late production), TVM220	3.308-3.310 in. (84.023-84.074 mm)
TVM170	2.9325-2.9335 in. (74.486-74.511 mm)
TVM195, TVXL195	3.1195-3.1205 in. (79.235-79.261 mm)

Measure piston skirt-to-cylinder wall clearance at bottom edge of skirt at a right angle to piston pin for all models. Refer to following list for specified piston clearance:

Model	Piston Clearance
H70, V70, VM70	0.0045-0.0060 in. (0.114-0.152 mm)
H80, V80, VM80	0.0035-0.0055 in. (0.089-0.140 mm)
HM80 prior to type letter E	0.0035-0.0055 in. (0.089-0.140 mm)
HM100 (early production), VM100	0.0028-0.0063 in. (0.071-0.160 mm)
HM100 (late production), TVM220	0.002-0.005 in. (0.05-0.13 mm)
All other models	0.004-0.006 in. (0.10-0.15 mm)

Side clearance of top ring in piston groove should be 0.002-0.003 inch (0.05-0.08 mm) on Models H70, V70 and VM70, and 0.002-0.005 inch (0.05-0.13 mm) for all other models.

If piston crown has an arrow, install piston on connecting rod so arrow on piston crown will point toward carburetor side of engine after installation. If an arrow is located below piston pin hole on piston, or there is no arrow on piston, refer to Fig. T524 and note proper assembly of piston and connecting rod.

Note location and arrangement of piston rings in Fig. T525. Stagger ring end gaps equally around circumference of piston during installation; however,

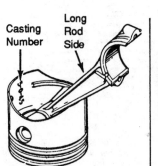

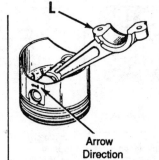

Fig. T524—Note installation of connecting rod in piston if piston does not have an arrow (left view) or if piston has an arrow below piston pin hole (right view). Install long screw in hole (L) if connecting rod screws have different lengths.

Illustrations Courtesy Tecumseh Products Co.

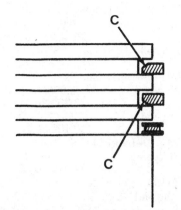

Fig. T525—Chamfer (C) on top piston ring must be up. If second ring on Models HM100 and TVM220 has a chamfer (C), chamfer must be down. On all other engines, chamfer, if so equipped, on second ring must be up. If outside diameter of ring is notched, notch must be down.

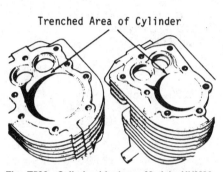

Fig. T526—Cylinder block on Models HHM80, HM80, HM100 and TVM220 has been "trenched" to improve fuel flow and power.

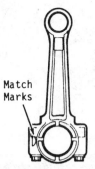

Fig. T527—Match marks on connecting rod and cap must be aligned and face pto end of crankshaft after installation. Connecting rod used on horizontal crankshaft engines is equipped with an oil dipper on connecting rod cap.

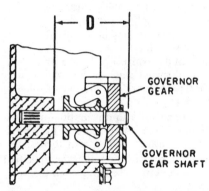

Fig. T258—Correct installation of governor shaft, gear and weight assembly on Models H70, HM70, HMXL70, H80, HHM80, HM80 and HM100. Dimension (D) should be 1-3/8 inches (34.92 mm) on all models.

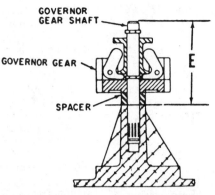

Fig. T529—Governor gear and shaft installation on Models V70, VM70, V80, VM80, VM100, TVM170, TVM195, TVXL195, TVM220 and TVXL220. Dimension (E) should be 1-19/32 inches (40.48 mm).

on models with a "trenched" cylinder (see Fig. T526), position ring end gaps so they are not in trenched area. This will lessen the possibility of the ring ends snagging during installation of piston.

Piston and rings are available in standard size and oversizes.

CONNECTING ROD. Piston and connecting rod are removed as an assembly from cylinder head end of engine. Connecting rod rides directly on crankpin journal of crankshaft. On horizontal crankshaft models, an oil dipper is an integral part of connecting rod cap, or a separate oil dipper is attached to the rod by the connecting rod bolts.

Standard connecting rod big end diameter may be either 1.3760-1.3765 inch (34.950-34.963 mm) or 1.1880-1.1885 inch (30.175-30.188 mm). Check unworn portion of crankpin to determine original specification.

Connecting rod-to-crankpin journal running clearance should be 0.002 inch (0.05 mm) for all models.

Connecting rods are equipped with match marks that must be aligned and face pto end of crankshaft after installation. See Fig. T527. If equipped with connecting rod screws with different lengths, long screw must be installed in hole (L—Fig. T524) nearer piston pin hole.

GOVERNOR. Governor weight and gear assembly is driven by camshaft gear and rides on a renewable shaft that is pressed into engine crankcase or crankcase cover.

If renewal of governor shaft is necessary, press governor shaft in until shaft end is located, as shown in Figs. T528 or T529.

Adjust external linkage as outlined in MAINTENANCE section.

CRANKSHAFT AND MAIN BEARINGS. On vertical crankshaft engines, crankshaft main journals ride directly in aluminum alloy bearings in crankcase and oil pan (engine base). On horizontal crankshaft engines, crankshaft main journals ride in two renewable steel-backed bronze bushings, or a renewable sleeve bushing at flywheel

end and a ball bearing or bushing at pto end.

Refer to following list for main bearing bushing inner diameters:

Model	Main Bearing Bushing Dia.
H70—Both bearings	1.0005-1.0010 inch (25.413-25.425 mm)
HM70—Early Models: Cylinder bearing	1.0005-1.0010 in. (25.413-25.425 mm)
Pto bearing	1.1890-1.1895 in. (30.201-30.213 mm)
HM70—Later Models: Both bearings	1.3765-1.3770 in. (34.963-34.976 mm)
HMXL70: Both bearings	1.3765-1.3770 in. (34.963-34.976 mm)
H80: Cylinder bearing	1.0005-1.0010 in. (25.413-25.425 mm)
Pto bearing	1.1890-1.1895 in. (30.201-30.213 mm)
HHM80: Cylinder bearing	1.0005-1.0010 in. (25.413-25.425 mm)
Pto bearing	1.1890-1.1895 in. (30.201-30.213 mm)
HM80, HM100—Early Models: Cylinder bearing	1.0005-1.0010 in. (25.413-25.425 mm)
Pto bearing	1.1890-1.1895 in. (30.201-30.213 mm)
HM80, HM100—Later Models: Both bearings	1.3765-1.3770 in. (34.963-34.976 mm)
V70, VM70: Both bearings	1.0005-1.0010 in. (25.413-25.425 mm)
V80, VM80, VM100: Cylinder bearing	1.0005-1.0010 in. (25.413-25.425 mm)
Pto bearing	1.1890-1.1895 in. (30.201-30.213 mm)
TVM170—Early Models: Cylinder bearing	1.0005-1.0010 in. (25.413-25.425 mm)

Pto bearing . . . . . 1.1890-1.1895 in.
(30.201-30.213 mm)
TVM170—Later Models:
Both bearings . . . 1.3765-1.3770 in.
(34.963-34.976 mm)
TVM195—Early Models:
Cylinder bearing . 1.0005-1.0010 in.
(25.413-25.425 mm)
Pto bearing . . . . . 1.1890-1.1895 in.
(30.201-30.213 mm)
TVM195—Later Models:
Both bearings . . . 1.3765-1.3770 in.
(34.963-34.976 mm)
TVXL195:
Both bearings . . . 1.3765-1.3770 in.
(34.963-34.976 mm)
TVM220—Early Models:
Cylinder bearing . 1.0005-1.0010 in.
(25.413-25.425 mm)
Pto bearing . . . . 1.1890-1.1895 in.
(30.201-30.213 mm)
TVM220—Later Models:
Both bearings . . . 1.3765-1.3770 in.
(34.963-34.976 mm)
TVXL220:
Both bearings . . . 1.3765-1.3770 in.
(34.963-34.976 mm)

Normal running clearance of crankshaft journals in aluminum bearings or bronze bushings is 0.0015-0.0025 inch (0.038-0.064 mm). Renew crankshaft if main journals are more than 0.001 inch (0.025 mm) out-of-round; renew or regrind crankshaft if connecting rod journal is more than 0.0005 inch (0.013 mm) out-of-round.

Check crankshaft gear for wear, broken teeth or loose fit on crankshaft. If crankshaft gear is damaged, remove gear from crankshaft with an arbor press. Renew gear pin and press new gear on shaft making certain timing mark is facing pto end of shaft.

On models equipped with a ball bearing at pto end of shaft, refer to Figs. T530 and T531 before removing crankcase cover. Loosen locknuts and rotate protruding ends of lock pins counterclockwise to release bearing and remove

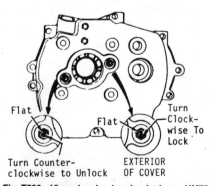

Fig. T530—View showing bearing locks on HM70, HM80 and HM100 models equipped with ball bearing main bearings. Locks must be released before removing crankcase cover. Refer to Fig. T531 for interior view of cover and locks.

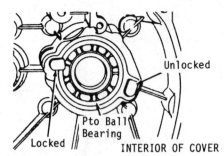

Fig. T531—Interior view of crankcase cover and ball bearing locks used on HM70, HM80 and HM100 models.

cover. Ball bearing will remain on crankshaft. When reassembling, turn lock pins clockwise until flats on pins face each other, then tighten locknuts to 15-22 in.-lbs. (2-3 N•m).

Crankshaft end play for all models should be 0.005-0.027 inch (0.13-0.69 mm) and is controlled by varying thickness of thrust washers between crankshaft and cylinder block or crankcase cover.

Bronze or aluminum bushing-type main bearings are renewable and finish reamers are available from Tecumseh.

Refer to following list for specified crankshaft main bearing journal diameters:

**Main Bearing
Journal Diameter**

H70, V70, VM70
Both ends . . . . . . 0.9985-0.9990 in.
(25.362-25.375 mm)
HM70—Early Models:
Mag end . . . . 0.9985-0.9990 in.
(25.362-25.375 mm)
Pto end . . . . 1.1870-1.1875 in.
(30.150-30.162 mm)
HM70—Later Models:
Both ends . . . . . . 1.3745-1.3750 in.
(34.912-34.925 mm)
HMXL70
Both ends . . . . . . 1.3745-1.3750 in.
(34.912-34.925 mm)
H80
Mag end . . . . 0.9985-0.9990 in.
(25.362-25.375 mm)
Pto end . . . . 1.1870-1.1875 in.
(30.150-30.162 mm)
HHM80
Mag end . . . . 0.9985-0.9990 in.
(25.362-25.375 mm)
Pto end . . . . 1.1870-1.1875 in.
(30.150-30.162 mm)
HM80, HM100—
Early Models:
Mag end . . . . . . 0.9985-0.9990 in.
(25.362-25.375 mm)
Pto end . . . . . . 1.1870-1.1875 in.
(30.150-30.162 mm)
HM80, HM100—
Later Models
Both ends . . . . . . 1.3745-1.3750 in.
(34.912-34.925 mm)

V80, VM80, VM100
Mag end . . . . 0.9985-0.9990 in.
(25.362-25.375 mm)
Pto end . . . . 1.1870-1.1875 in.
(30.150-30.162 mm)
TVM170—Early Models
Mag end . . . . 0.9985-0.9990 in.
(25.362-25.375 mm)
Pto end . . . . 1.1870-1.1875 in.
(30.150-30.162 mm)
TVM170—Later Models
Both ends . . . . 1.3745-1.3750 in.
(34.912-34.925 mm)
TVM195—Early Models
Mag end . . . . 0.9985-0.9990 in.
(25.362-25.375 mm)
Pto end . . . . 1.1870-1.1875 in.
(30.150-30.162 mm)
TVM195—Later Models
Both ends . . . . 1.3745-1.3750 in.
(34.912-34.925 mm)
TVXL195
Both ends . . . . 1.3745-1.3750 in.
(34.912-34.925 mm)
TVM220—Early Models
Mag end . . . . 0.9985-0.9990 in.
(25.362-25.375 mm)
Pto end . . . . 1.1870-1.1875 in.
(30.150-30.162 mm)
TVM220—Later Models
Both ends . . . . 1.3745-1.3750 in.
(34.912-34.925 mm)
TVXL220
Both ends . . . . 1.3745-1.3750 in.
(34.912-34.925 mm)

Crankshaft crankpin diameter may be either 1.3740-1.3745 inch (34.900-34.912 mm) or 1.1860-1.1865 inch (30.124-30.137 mm). Check unworn portion of crankpin to determine original specification.

Make certain timing marks on camshaft gear and crankshaft gear are aligned during assembly.

CYLINDER. If cylinder is scored or excessively worn, or if taper or out-of-round exceeds 0.004 inch (0.10 mm), cylinder should be bored to next oversize for which piston and rings are available. Refer to following list of standard bore diameters:

Model	Std. Bore Diameter
H70, V70, VM70	2.750-2.751 in. (69.85-69.88 mm)
HM70, HMXL70, TVM170	2.9375-2.9385 in. (74.612-74.638 mm)
H80, V80, VM80	3.062-3.063 in. (77.77-77.80 mm)
HHM80	3.125-3.126 in. (79.38-79.40 mm)

Illustrations Courtesy Tecumseh Products Co.

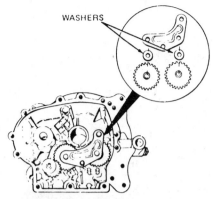

Fig. T532—View showing Dyna-Static balancer gears installed in models so equipped. Note location of washers between gears retaining bracket.

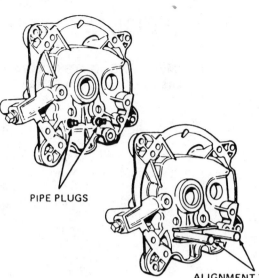

Fig. T534—To time engine balancer gears, remove pipe plugs and insert Tecumseh alignment tool 670240 through oil pan and into slots in balancer gears. Refer also to Fig. T535.

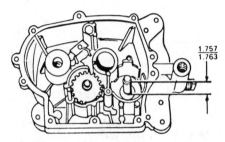

Fig. T533—On VM80 and VM100 models, press balancer gear shafts into cover or oil pan so height between boss on crankcase cover or oil pan and step on shafts is 1.757-1.763 inches (44.63-44.78 mm).

HM80 prior to
  type letter E . . . .   3.062-3.063 in.
                                (77.77-77.80 mm)

HM80 with type
  letter E or after . . . .   3.125-3.126 in.
                                  (79.38-79.40 mm)

VM80, TVM195,
  TVXL195 . . . .   3.125-3.126 in.
                                  (79.38-79.40 mm)

HM100 (early pro-
  duction), VM100 . . .   3.187-3.188 in.
                                  (80.95-80.98 mm)

HM100 (late pro-
  duction) . . . .   3.312-3.313 in.
                                  (84.12-84.15 mm)

TVM220, TVXL220 . . .   3.312-3.313 in.
                                  (84.12-84.15 mm)

DYNA-STATIC BALANCER. The Dyna-Static engine balancer, used on medium frame models, consists of counterweighted gears driven by the crankshaft gear to counteract unbalance caused by the counterweights on the crankshaft.

Counterweight gears are held in position on shafts by a bracket bolted to crankcase or oil pan (Fig. T532).

Renewable balancer gear shafts are pressed into crankcase cover or oil pan. Press shafts into cover or oil pan so height between boss on crankcase cover or oil pan and step on shafts is 1.757-1.763 inches (44.63-44.78 mm) as shown in Fig. T533.

Balancer gears are equipped with renewable caged needle bearings. Using Tecumseh tool 670210, press new bearings into gears until cage is flush to 0.015 inch (0.38 mm) below edge of bore.

When reassembling engine, balancer gears must be timed with crankshaft for correct operation. Refer to Fig. T534 and remove pipe plugs. Insert Tecumseh alignment tool 670240 through crankcase cover or engine base and into timing slots in balancer gears. Rotate

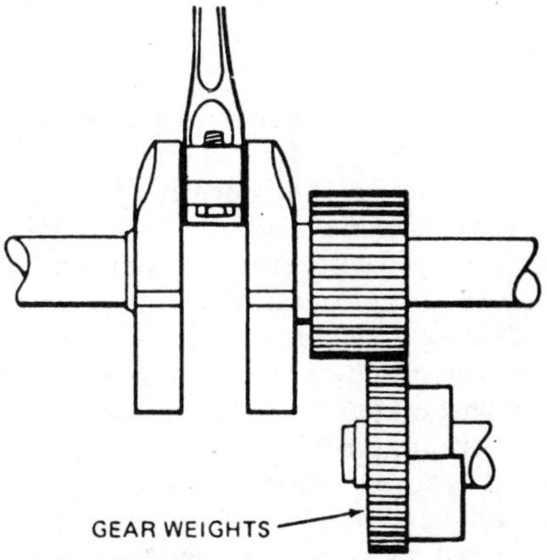

Fig. T535—View showing correct balancer gear timing to crankshaft gear on VM80 and VM100 models. With piston at TDC, weights should be directly opposite.

engine until piston is at TDC on compression stroke and install cover and gear assembly while tools retain gears in correct position. See Fig. T534.

When correctly assembled, piston should be at TDC and weights on balancer gear should be directly opposite. See Fig. T535.

TECUMSEH

TECUMSEH PRODUCTS COMPANY
Grafton, Wisconsin 53204

Model	No. Cyls.	Bore	Stroke	Displacement	Power Rating
OHM120	1	3.31 in. (84.2 mm)	2.53 in. (64.3 mm)	21.82 cu. in. (357 cc)	12 hp (8.9 kW)
OVM120	1	3.31 in. (84.2 mm)	2.53 in. (64.3 mm)	21.82 cu. in. (357 cc)	12 hp (8.9 kW)
OVXL120	1	3.31 in. (84.2 mm)	2.53 in. (64.3 mm)	21.82 cu. in. (357 cc)	12 hp (8.9 kW)
OVXL125, OVXL/C125	1	3.31 in. (84.2 mm)	2.53 in. (64.3 mm)	21.82 cu. in. (357 cc)	12.5 hp (9.3 kW)

All models are four-stroke, overhead valve, single-cylinder gasoline engines. Model OHM120 is equipped with a horizontal crankshaft and all other models are equipped with a vertical crankshaft. The aluminum alloy cylinder and crankcase assembly is equipped with a cast iron cylinder sleeve that is an integral part of the cylinder. Lubrication for all horizontal crankshaft engines is provided by splash lubrication. Lubrication for all vertical crankshaft engines is provided by a positive displacement plunger-type oil pump that is operated by an eccentric on the camshaft.

Engine model number, serial number and specification number are stamped into the cooling shroud just above the rocker arm cover as shown. Always furnish correct engine model, serial and specification numbers when ordering parts.

MAINTENANCE

LUBRICATION. Vertical crankshaft models are equipped with a positive displacement plunger-type oil pump that is located in the bottom of the oil pan. An eccentric on camshaft works the oil pump plunger back and forth in the barrel to force oil up the center of the camshaft. The pressurized oil lubricates top main bearing and top camshaft bearing. Oil is sprayed out of a hole between camshaft and main bearings to lubricate connecting rod and other internal parts.

All horizontal crankshaft models are splash lubricated by a dipper on the connecting rod cap.

Oil level should be checked before initial start-up and at five-hour intervals. Maintain oil level at "FULL" mark on dipstick.

Recommended oil change interval is every 25 hours of normal operation. Oil should be drained when engine is warm. Manufacturer recommends using oil with API service classification SE, SF or SG. Use SAE 30 oil for temperatures above 32° F (0° C) and SAE 5W-20 or 10W-30 for temperatures below 32° F (0° C).

SPARK PLUG. Recommended spark plug is a Champion L86C or equivalent. Recommended electrode gap is 0.030 in. (0.76 mm).

CARBURETOR. All models are equipped with a float-type carburetor.

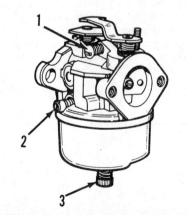

Fig. T701—View of carburetor showing idle speed screw (1), idle mixture adjusting screw (2) and high-speed fuel mixture adjusting screw (3). Some models may not be equipped with adjustable high-speed fuel mixture screw (3).

Some models are equipped with a carburetor that has both an idle and a high-speed fuel mixture adjustment screw. However, some models are equipped with just an idle speed fuel mixture screw; the high-speed mixture is controlled by a fixed main jet. Other than adjustment, service procedure is similar for either type carburetor.

Initial adjustment of idle mixture screw (2—Fig. T701) for all models is one turn open from a lightly seated position. Initial adjustment of high-speed adjustment screw (3), if so equipped, is one turn open from a lightly seated position for Model OVM120 and 1½ turns open for Models OHM120, OVXL120 and OVXL125.

Make final adjustments on all models with engine at normal operating temperature. On models with high-speed adjustment screw, set engine speed at full throttle and turn adjusting screw to find the lean drop-off point and the rich drop-off point. Then, set adjusting screw midway between the two extremes. When correctly set, engine should accelerate smoothly and run under load with steady governor operation. On all models, turn idle speed adjustment screw (1) to obtain desired idle speed as specified by the equipment manufacturer. Adjust idle mixture adjustment screw (2) to obtain smoothest idle operation using the same procedure as outlined for high-speed adjustment screw.

As each adjustment affects the other, adjustment procedure may have to be repeated.

To clean carburetor, disassemble and clean all metallic parts with solvent or carburetor cleaner. Welch plugs should be removed from carburetor body to expose drilled passages to thoroughly clean carburetor. Use a small, sharp pointed chisel to pierce the Welch plug and pry plug out of carburetor body. When installing new plugs, use a flat punch equal to or greater than the size of the plug and just flatten the plug. Do not drive the center of plug below surface of carburetor body.

NOTE: Do not remove main nozzle tube in carburetor body. Tube is installed to a predetermined depth, and altering its position in carburetor body will affect metering characteristics of the carburetor.

Use compressed air and solvent to clean drilled passages and jets. Do not use drill bits or wire to clean jets or passages as carburetor calibration may be affected if openings are enlarged.

There are two different types of bowl nuts (33—Fig. T702) that are used on carburetors equipped with adjustable main jets. One type has one fuel inlet port at bottom of the nut and the other type has two fuel inlet ports at bottom of the nut (Fig. T703). The difference between the nuts has to do with calibration changes of the carburetor, depending on engine application. DO NOT interchange bowl nuts. Fuel inlet port(s) and idle fuel transfer port, located in annular groove at top of nut, must be open and free of any debris to ensure proper fuel flow to high and low-speed circuits.

When reassembling carburetor, it is important that throttle plate is installed with line on the plate facing outward and positioned at the 3 o'clock position. Choke plate must be installed with cut-out section facing downward. Be sure that throttle and choke plates open and close without binding.

Fuel inlet needle (23—Fig. T702) and seat (22) are renewable. If needle tip or seat is worn or deformed, new needle and seat should be installed. Make certain when installing new seat that grooved side of seat is installed in bore first so the inlet needle will seat against the smooth side of seat (Fig. T704).

Assemble float, inlet needle and needle clip as shown in Fig. T705. To prevent binding, the long end of clip should face choke end of carburetor body.

To check float height, invert carburetor body and use float setting tool 670253A as shown in Fig. T706. Float height is correct if float does not touch step portion of tool (1) and contacts step (2) as tool is pulled toward float hinge

pin as shown. If tool is not available, measure distance from top of main nozzle boss to surface of float. Distance should be 0.275-0.315 inch (7.0-8.0 mm). If adjustment is required, bend float tab that contacts fuel inlet needle, being careful not to force inlet needle onto its seat.

GOVERNOR. All models are equipped with a mechanical flyweight-type governor located inside the crankcase.

To adjust external governor linkage, stop engine and loosen the screw securing governor lever (1—Fig. T707 or Fig. T708) and governor clamp (2). Push governor lever to fully open carburetor throttle. On vertical crankshaft models, turn governor clamp counterclockwise as far as it will go. On horizontal crankshaft models, rotate governor lever shaft clockwise as far as possible. While holding clamp and lever in this position, tighten screw.

On 1985 and later production OVM120 and OVXL120 engines, a governor override system is used. Linkage is shown in Fig. T708. On these engines, high-speed setting is adjusted by turning top screw (H) of override lever and low idle speed is adjusted by turning bottom screw (L).

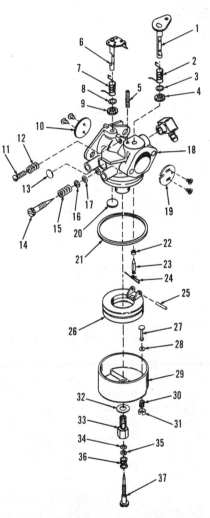

Fig. T702—Exploded view of carburetor. Some models are not equipped with high-speed mixture adjusting screw (37), choke spring (5) or drain pin (27).

1. Choke shaft
2. Choke return spring
3. Washer
4. Dust seal
5. Choke stop spring
6. Throttle shaft
7. Throttle return spring
8. Washer
9. Dust seal
10. Throttle plate
11. Idle speed screw
12. Spring
13. Welch plug
14. Idle mixture needle
15. Spring
16. Washer
17. "O" ring
18. Carburetor body
19. Choke plate
20. Welch plug
21. Bowl gasket
22. Inlet valve seat
23. Fuel inlet valve
24. Clip
25. Float pin
26. Float
27. Drain stem
28. Gasket
29. Fuel bowl
30. Spring
31. Retainer
32. Washer
33. Bowl retainer
34. "O" ring
35. Washer
36. Spring
37. High-speed mixture screw

Fig. T703—Two different types of fuel bowl retaining nuts are used on adjustable main jet-type carburetors. Different type nuts must not be interchanged. Refer to text.

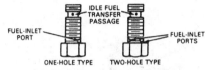

Fig. T704—Fuel inlet needle seat must be installed with grooved side against carburetor body. Refer to text.

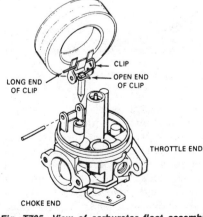

Fig. T705—View of carburetor float assembly showing correct installation of fuel inlet needle clip.

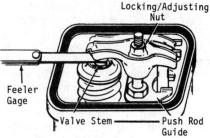

Fig. T710—Use a feeler gauge to correctly set valve clearance.

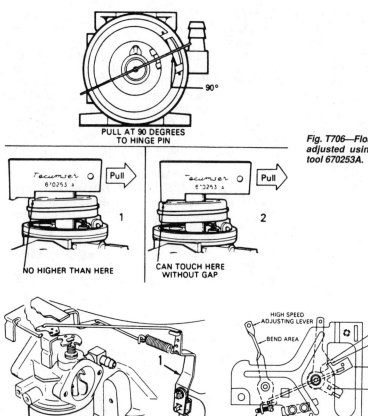

Fig. T706—Float height can be adjusted using float setting tool 670253A.

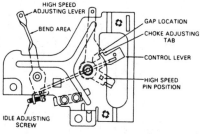

Fig. T707—Drawing of governor external linkage typical of standard engines without governor override system. Refer to text for adjustment procedure.

Fig. T709—Drawing of typical speed control plate used on engines equipped with remote control linkage.

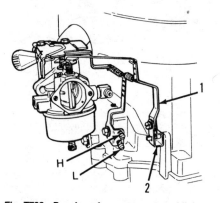

Fig. T708—Drawing of governor external linkage typical of engines equipped with governor override system. Refer to text for adjustment procedure.

Various types of speed controls are used. A typical panel used on vertical crankshaft models with remote control lever is shown in Fig. T709. To adjust speed control panel, loosen panel mounting screws. Move speed control lever to full speed position and insert a wire through hole in panel, hole in choke actuating lever and hole in choke shaft arm. With components aligned in this manner, tighten panel mounting

screws. Move control linkage to choke position, and check for 0.040-0.070 inch (1.0-1.8 mm) gap at control lever as shown in Fig. T709. Bend choke adjusting tab if necessary. Engine idle speed can be set by turning idle speed adjusting screw. Maximum governed speed is adjusted by bending high-speed adjusting lever. Bend lever away from panel to increase speed and in the opposite direction to decrease speed.

IGNITION SYSTEM. A solid-state ignition system is used on all models. Ignition system has no moving parts and is considered satisfactory if a spark will jump a 1/8-inch (3.2 mm) air gap when engine is cranked at 125 rpm.

Air gap setting between ignition module and flywheel magnets is 0.0125 inch (0.32 mm). To set air gap, loosen module mounting screws, move module as necessary and retighten screws.

VALVE ADJUSTMENT. Clearance between rocker arms and valve stem ends should be checked and adjusted with engine cold. Specified clearance is 0.002 inch (0.05 mm) for intake valve

and 0.004 inch (0.10 mm) for exhaust valve.

To adjust clearance, remove rocker arm cover and rotate crankshaft to position piston at top dead center (TDC) of compression stroke. Both valves should be closed and the push rods loose at this point. Use a feeler gauge to measure clearance between rocker arm and valve stem as shown in Fig. T710. Turn rocker arm locking/adjusting nut to obtain specified clearance.

REPAIRS

TIGHTENING TORQUES. Recommended tightening torques are as follows:

Connecting rod bolts .. 200-220 in.-lbs. (22.6-24.8 N•m)
Crankcase cover/oil pan....... 100-130 in.-lbs. (11.3-14.7 N•m)
Cylinder head bolts ... 180-240 in.-lbs. (20.4-27.1 N•m)
Flywheel nut .... 50-55 ft.-lbs. (68-74 N•m)
Intake pipe........... 72-96 in.-lbs. (8.2-10.8 N•m)
Rocker arm studs..... 170-210 in.-lbs. (19.2-23.7 N•m)
Rocker cover.......... 15-20 in.-lbs. (1.7-2.2 N•m)
Spark plug .... 220-280 in.-lbs. (24.9-31.6 N•m)

CYLINDER HEAD. Always allow engine to cool completely before loosening cylinder head bolts. To remove cylinder head, first locate piston at top dead center of compression stroke. Remove rocker arm adjusting nuts (1—Fig. T711), bearing (2) and rocker arms (3). Depress valve spring caps (14) and remove split retainers (13), caps, springs (15), spring seats (16) and "O" rings (17) and (18). Note that a white Teflon "O" ring (17) is used on exhaust valve guide and a black rubber "O" ring (18) is used on intake valve guide. Remove rocker arm studs (4), push rod guide (5) and rocker arm housing retaining screw (10) and withdraw rocker arm housing (7). Remove cylinder head mounting bolts and remove cylinder head (22) and valves. Remove valves from cylinder head.

Thoroughly clean cylinder head and inspect for cracks or other damage. Position cylinder head on a flat plate and use a feeler gauge to check flatness of head gasket sealing surface. Renew cylinder head if necessary.

Use a new head gasket when installing cylinder head. Install Belleville washer on cylinder head bolt with crown up toward bolt head, then install flat washer (Fig. T712). The two 1⅜-inch (34.9 mm) long head bolts go in positions marked "1" and "5" in Fig. T713. Tighten head bolts in 60 in.-lbs. (6.8 N•m) increments following sequence shown in Fig. T713 until specified torque is obtained.

When installing valve guide seals, be sure that white Teflon "O" ring (17—Fig. T711) is installed on exhaust valve guide (guide is bronze in color) and black "O" ring (18) is installed on intake valve guide (guide is silver in color). Switching the position of "O" rings may result in improper sealing and possible engine damage. Be sure to install new "O" rings on push rod tube (9) and underneath push rod guide (5) and retaining screw (10).

To install valve springs, valves must be raised and held on their seats. One way to do this is to insert a piece of rubber fuel line through intake and exhaust ports and wedge each end of the hose on opposite sides of the valve stem. Install valve springs with dampening coils (coils closer together) toward cylinder head. Place spring retainer on spring, use suitable tool to compress valve spring and install split retainer.

NOTE: Anytime rocker arm housing assembly is removed from engine, new rocker arm locking/adjusting nuts and rocker arm cover screws should be installed.

Tighten rocker arm studs (4) to 170-210 in.-lbs. (19.2-23.7 N•m). Install rocker arms and adjust valve clearance as outlined in MAINTENANCE section.

VALVE SYSTEM. Valve seats are machined directly in the cylinder head. Seats should be cut at a 46° angle and valve faces cut or ground at a 45° angle. Valve seat width should be ³⁄₆₄ inch (1.2 mm). The recommended procedure to cut the valve seats is as follows: First, use a 60-degree cutter to narrow seat from bottom toward the center. Second, use a 30-degree cutter to narrow seat from top toward the center. Then, use

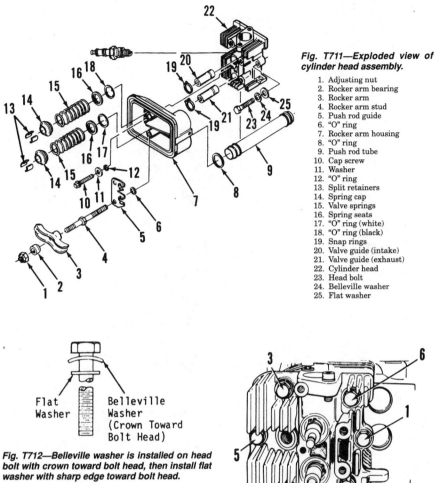

Fig. T711—Exploded view of cylinder head assembly.

1. Adjusting nut
2. Rocker arm bearing
3. Rocker arm
4. Rocker arm stud
5. Push rod guide
6. "O" ring
7. Rocker arm housing
8. "O" ring
9. Push rod tube
10. Cap screw
11. Washer
12. "O" ring
13. Split retainers
14. Spring cap
15. Valve springs
16. Spring seats
17. "O" ring (white)
18. "O" ring (black)
19. Snap rings
20. Valve guide (intake)
21. Valve guide (exhaust)
22. Cylinder head
23. Head bolt
24. Belleville washer
25. Flat washer

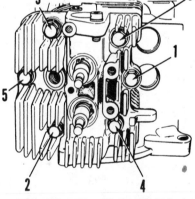

Fig. T712—Belleville washer is installed on head bolt with crown toward bolt head, then install flat washer with sharp edge toward bolt head.

46-degree cutter to cut seat to desired width.

Clean all combustion deposits from valves. Renew valves that are burned, excessively pitted, warped, or if valve head margin after grinding is less than ¹⁄₃₂ inch (0.8 mm). Valves should be lapped to their seats using fine lapping compound.

Valve spring free length should be 1.980 inches (50.29 mm). It is recommended that valve springs be renewed when engine is overhauled. The valve spring dampening coils are coils wound closer together at one end than the other. The end with closer coils should be installed against cylinder head.

Standard valve guide inside diameter is 0.312-0.313 inch (7.93-7.95 mm). Guides can be reamed to 0.343-0.344 inch (8.71-8.74 mm) for use with oversize valve stems.

To renew valve guides, submerge cylinder head in a large pan of oil. Heat on a hot plate to temperature of 375° F to 400° F (190° C to 205° C) for about 20 minutes. Remove cylinder head from the oil and use an arbor press and ½-inch (13 mm) driver to push valve guides out top side of cylinder head.

Fig. T713—Cylinder head bolts should be loosened and tightened following the sequence shown. The two 1-3/8-inch (34.9 mm) long bolts are installed in positions "1" and "5."

Make certain that driver does not contact and damage head as guide is removed.

To install new guides, place replacement guides in a freezer or on ice for minimum of 30 minutes prior to installation. Heat head in a pan of oil as previously outlined. Install locating snap rings on new guides, then press guides into cylinder head from the top until snap rings contact surface of head. Make certain that silver colored guide is installed in intake side and brass colored guide is installed in exhaust side. Allow cylinder head to cool, then reface both valve seats to ensure that they are concentric with valve guides.

OIL PUMP. Models with a vertical crankshaft are equipped with a positive displacement oil pump (33—Fig. T714).

Oil pump is located in oil pan and is driven by an eccentric on camshaft.

When installing oil pump, be sure that chamfered side of pump faces the camshaft, and that plunger ball seats in recess in oil pan.

CAMSHAFT. Camshaft and camshaft gear are an integral part that can be removed from engine after removing the rocker arms, push rods and oil pan or crankcase cover. Identify position of tappets as they are removed so they can be reinstalled in original position if reused.

Camshaft bearings are an integral part of crankcase and oil pan or crankcase cover. Camshaft journal diameter should be 0.6235-0.6240 inch (15.84-15.85 mm). Camshaft bearing inside diameter should be 0.6245-0.6255 inch (15.86-15.89 mm). Clearance between camshaft journal and camshaft bearing should not exceed 0.003 inch (0.08 mm). Inspect camshaft lobes for pitting, scratches or excessive wear and renew as necessary. Tappets should be renewed whenever a new camshaft is installed.

Camshaft is equipped with a compression release mechanism (Fig. T715) to aid starting. Compression release mechanism parts should work freely with no binding or sticking. Parts are not serviced separately from camshaft.

When installing camshaft, be sure that timing marks on camshaft gear and crankshaft gear are aligned as shown in Fig. T716.

PISTON, PIN AND RINGS. Piston and connecting rod are removed as an assembly. Refer to CONNECTING ROD section for removal procedure.

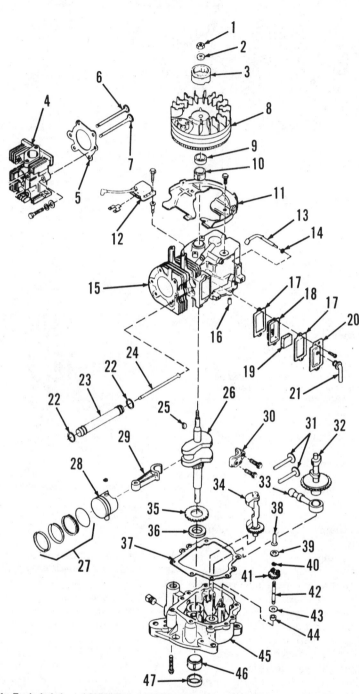

Fig. T714—Exploded view of OVM120 and OVMXL120 engines. Other vertical and horizontal crankshaft models are similar. Push rod tubes (23) and bushings (10 and 46) are not used on all models. Oil pump (33) and spacer (44) are not used on horizontal crankshaft engines.

1. Nut	13. Governor shaft	25. Key	37. Gasket
2. Lockwasher	14. Washer	26. Crankshaft	38. Thrust spool
3. Starter cup	15. Cylinder block	27. Piston rings	39. Washer
4. Cylinder head	16. Dowel pin	28. Piston	40. Snap ring
5. Gasket	17. Gasket	29. Connecting rod	41. Governor gear
6. Intake valve	18. Breather	30. Rod cap	& weight assy.
7. Exhaust valve	19. Breather element	31. Tappets	42. Governor shaft
8. Flywheel	20. Cover	32. Camshaft	43. Washer
9. Oil seal	21. Breather tube	33. Oil pump	44. Spacer
10. Bushing	22. "O" ring	34. Balancer	45. Oil pan
11. Baffle	23. Push rod tube	35. Gear	46. Bushing
12. Ignition module	24. Push rod	36. Shim	47. Oil seal

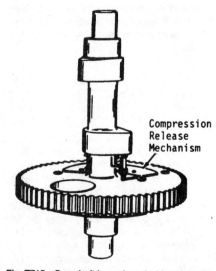

Fig. T715—Camshaft is equipped with a compression release mechanism.

Illustrations Courtesy Tecumseh Products Co.

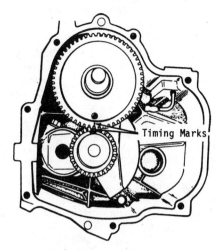

Fig. T716—Camshaft and crankshaft timing marks must be aligned after installation for proper valve timing.

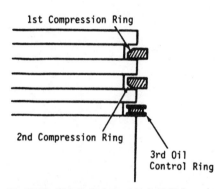

Fig. T717—Piston rings must be installed on piston so chamfered edge of top ring is facing up and chamfered edge of second ring is facing down.

Standard piston skirt diameter, measured at bottom of skirt 90° from piston pin bore, is 3.309-3.311 inches (84.05-84.09 mm) for all models. Specified clearance between piston skirt and cylinder wall is 0.0012-0.0032 inch (0.031-0.081 mm). Oversize pistons are available. Oversize piston size should be stamped on top of piston.

To check piston ring grooves for wear, clean carbon from ring grooves and install new rings in grooves. Use a feeler gauge to measure side clearance between ring land and ring. Specified side clearance is 0.0015-0.0035 inch (0.038-0.089 mm) for compression rings and 0.001-0.004 inch (0.025-0.102 mm) for oil control ring. Renew piston if ring side clearance is excessive.

Ring end gap should be 0.010-0.020 inch (0.25-0.51 mm) for all rings.

Rings must be installed on piston as shown in Fig. T717. Stagger ring end gaps around piston. Lubricate piston and cylinder with engine oil prior to installing piston. Be sure that arrow on top of piston points toward push rod side

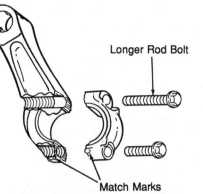

Fig. T718—Match marks on sides of connecting rod and cap must be aligned. Install rod and piston so match marks are toward pto end of crankshaft. On models with connecting rod cap screws of different lengths, long screw must be installed in hole nearer piston pin.

of engine and match marks on connecting rod and cap are toward open side of crankcase after installation.

CONNECTING ROD. Piston and connecting rod are removed as an assembly as follows: Remove all cooling shrouds. Remove rocker arm cover and cylinder head as previously outlined. Drain oil and remove oil pan or crankcase cover. Remove connecting rod cap. Remove carbon or ring ridge (if present) from top of cylinder before removing piston. Push the connecting rod and piston out top of cylinder.

Connecting rod rides directly on crankshaft crankpin. Inside diameter of connecting rod bearing bore at crankshaft end should be 1.3775-1.3780 inches (34.950-34.963 mm).

Piston must be assembled on connecting rod so arrow on top of piston will be pointing toward push rod side of engine. Connecting rods are equipped with match marks that must be aligned and face pto end of crankshaft after installation. See Fig. T718. If equipped with connecting rod screws with different lengths, long screw must be installed in hole nearer piston pin hole as shown in Fig. T718.

GOVERNOR. Governor weight and gear assembly is driven by camshaft gear and rides on a renewable shaft that is pressed into engine crankcase or crankcase cover.

Governor gear, flyweights and shaft are serviced only as an assembly. If governor gear shaft is renewed, new shaft should be pressed into oil pan or crankcase cover boss until exposed shaft length is 1³⁄₃₂ inches (27.8 mm) on Model OHM120 and 1²³⁄₆₄ inches (34.5 mm) on all other models.

Adjust external linkage as outlined in MAINTENANCE section.

CRANKSHAFT, MAIN BEARINGS AND SEALS. To remove crankshaft, first remove all shrouds. Remove flywheel. Remove connecting rod and piston as previously outlined. Remove balancer gear and shaft assembly. Remove balancer drive gear from crankshaft. Position engine so tappets fall away from camshaft, then withdraw camshaft from cylinder block and remove crankshaft.

Crankshaft is supported at each end in renewable bushing-type main bearings on Models OVM120 and OVXL120. On Model OHM120, the bushing in the crankcase cover is renewable, but the bushing in the crankcase is not renewable. On other models, main bearings are integral part of crankcase and oil pan or crankcase cover. On all models, main bearing inside diameter should be 1.3765-1.3770 inches (34.963-34.976 mm).

Standard crankshaft main journal diameter is 1.3745-1.3750 inches (34.912-34.925 mm) for each end. Standard crankpin journal diameter is 1.3740-1.3745 inches (34.900-34.912 mm).

Crankshaft end play should be 0.001-0.004 inch (0.025-0.10 mm) and is controlled by varying thickness of thrust washers between crankshaft and oil pan or crankcase cover.

When renewing crankshaft oil seals, note if old seal is raised or flush with outer surface of crankcase and oil pan or crankcase cover and install new seal to same dimension. Attempting to install seal too far into casting bore may damage seal or engine. Use suitable installing tool to install new seal until it is lightly seated in casting bore.

When installing crankshaft, align timing mark on crankshaft gear with timing mark on camshaft gear to ensure correct valve timing. See Fig. T716. With piston at top dead center, install counterbalance gear assembly and crankshaft balancer drive gear with timing marks (arrow) on gears facing each other as shown in Fig. T719. Install oil pump and oil pan or crankcase cover. Apply Loctite 242 to threads of oil pan or crankcase cover cap screws and tighten to 100-130 in.-lbs. (11.3-14.7 N•m).

CYLINDER AND CRANKCASE. A cast iron liner is permanently cast into the aluminum alloy cylinder and crankcase assembly. Standard piston bore inside diameter is 3.312-3.313 inches (84.125-84.150 mm). If cylinder taper or out-of-round exceeds 0.004 inch (0.10 mm), cylinder should be bored to near-

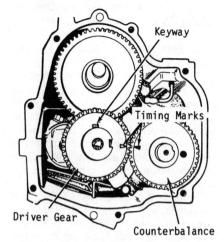

Fig. T719—Counterbalance gear and drive gear timing marks must be aligned after installation.

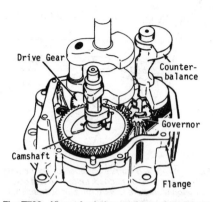

Fig. T720—View of relative position of camshaft, crankshaft and counterbalance shaft in oil pan or crankcase cover.

est oversize for which piston and rings are available.

ULTRA-BALANCE SYSTEM. All models are equipped with Tecumseh's Ultra-Balance system, which consists of a single counterbalance shaft driven by a gear on the crankshaft (Fig. T720).

To correctly time the balancer shaft and the crankshaft during installation, position piston at top dead center and insert the counterbalance shaft into its boss in the crankcase with arrow on counterbalance gear pointing toward crankshaft. Slide drive gear onto the crankshaft, making certain the drive gear is secured in its keyway and that the arrow on the drive gear is aligned with the arrow on counterbalance shaft gear (Fig. T719).

SERVICING TECUMSEH ACCESSORIES

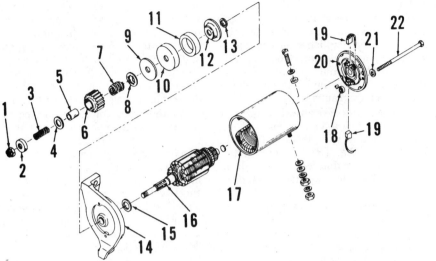

Fig. TRL101—Exploded view of 12-volt electric starter used on early model engines.

1. Nut
2. Pinion stop
3. Spring
4. Washer
5. Antidrift sleeve
6. Pinion gear
7. Screw shaft
8. Stop washer
9. Thrust washer
10. Cushion
11. Rubber cushion
12. Thrust washer
13. Thrust bushing
14. Drive end cap
15. Spacer washer
16. Armature
17. Frame & field coil assy.
18. Brush spring
19. Brush
20. End cap
21. Washer
22. Bolt

12-VOLT STARTING AND CHARGING SYSTEMS

Some Tecumseh engines may be equipped with 12-volt electrical systems. Refer to the following paragraphs for servicing of Tecumseh electrical units and 12-volt Delco-Remy starter-generator used on some models.

12-VOLT STARTER MOTOR (BENDIX DRIVE TYPE). Refer to Figs. TRL101 or TRL102 for an exploded view of 12-volt starter motor and Bendix drive unit used on some engines. To identify starter, refer to service number stamped on end cap.

When assembling starter motor in Fig. TRL101, use spacers (15) of varying thicknesses to obtain an armature end play of 0.005-0.015 inch (0.13-0.38 mm). Note following tightening torque specifications:

Armature nut (1):
  Starters 29965, 32468,
    32468A, 32468B,
    33202 . . . . 100 in.-lbs.
                           (11.3 N·m)
  Starter 32510 . . . . . . 130-150 in.-lbs.
                           (14.7-16.9 N·m)
  Starter 32817 . . . . . . 170-220 in.-lbs.
                           (19.2-24.8 N·m)

Through-bolts (22):
  Starters 29965, 32468,
    32468A, 32468B,
    33202 . . . . 30-35 in.-lbs.
                           (3.4-3.9 N·m)
  Starter 32510 . . . . 45-50 in.-lbs.
                           (5.0-5.6 N·m)
  Starter 32817 . . . . 35-44 in.-lbs.
                           (3.9-5.0 N·m)

To perform no-load test for starter motors 29965, 32468 and 32468A, use a fully charged 6-volt battery. Maximum current draw should not exceed 25 amps at 6 volts. Minimum rpm is 6500.

No-load test for Models 32468B and 33202 requires a fully charged 12-volt battery. Maximum current draw should

Fig. TRL102—Exploded view of 12-volt starter motor used on later models. Drive components in inset are used on opposite direction starters.

1. Dust cover
2. Clip
3. Spring retainer
4. Spring
5. Pinion
6. Retainer
7. Drive end cap
8. Armature
9. Housing
10. Brush card
11. Brush spring
12. Brush
13. Thrust washer
14. End cap

not exceed 25 amps at 11.8 volts. Minimum rpm is 8000.

No-load test for starter motors 32510 and 32817 must be performed with a 12-volt battery. Maximum current draw should not exceed 25 amps at 11.5 volts. Minimum rpm is 8000.

Disassembly and reassembly of starter motors 33605, 33606 and 33835 is evident after inspection of unit and referral to Fig. TRL102. Note that stops on through-bolts (14) are used to secure brush card (10) in housing (9).

Through-bolts must be installed with stops toward end cover (15).

Maximum current draw with starter on engine should not exceed 55 amps at a minimum of 850 rpm for starters 33605 and 33606 or 70 amps at a minimum of 600 rpm for starter 33835. Cranking test should not exceed 10 seconds.

ALTERNATOR CHARGING SYSTEMS. The engine may be equipped with an alternator to provide battery charging direct current, or provide electricity for accessories, or both. The alternator coils may be located under the flywheel, or on some models with an external ignition module, the alternator coils are attached to the legs of the ignition coil. Rectification of alternating current is accomplished either with a rectifier panel, regulator-rectifier unit, external or internal, or by an inline diode contained in the harness. Refer to following paragraphs.

Inline Diode System. The inline diode system has a diode connected into the alternator wire leading from the engine. See Fig. TRL103. The system produces approximately 3 amps direct current. The diode rectifies alternator alternating current into direct current. A 6-amp fuse provides overload protection.

To check system, disconnect harness connector and using a DC voltmeter connect tester positive lead to red wire connector terminal and ground tester negative lead to engine. At 3600 rpm engine speed, voltmeter reading should be at least 11.5 volts. If engine speed is less, the voltmeter reading will be less. If voltage reading is unsatisfactory, check alternator coils by taking an AC voltage reading. Connect one tester lead between diode and engine, and ground other tester lead to engine. At engine speed of 3600 rpm, voltage reading should be 26 volts, otherwise alternator is defective. If engine cannot attain 3600 rpm, voltage reading will be less.

Another type inline diode-type system provides 3 amps direct current and 5 amps alternating current. This system has a two-wire pigtail consisting of a red wire and a black wire; the diode is inline with the red wire. To test system, check voltage at pigtail connector. At engine speed of 3600 rpm (less engine speed will produce less voltage), voltage at red wire terminal should be 13 volts DC, while voltage at black wire terminal should be 13 volts AC. If voltage reading is unsatisfactory, check alternator coils by taking an AC voltage reading. Connect one tester lead to red wire between diode and engine, and ground other tester lead to engine. At engine speed of 3600 rpm, voltage reading should be 29 volts, otherwise alternator is defective. If engine cannot attain 3600 rpm, voltage reading will be less.

Rectifier Panel Systems. The system shown in Fig. TRL104 has a maximum charging output of about 3 amperes at 3600 rpm. No current regulator is used on this low output system. The rectifier panel includes two diodes (rectifiers) and a 6 ampere fuse for overload protection.

The system shown in Fig. TRL105 has a maximum output of 7 amperes. To prevent overcharging the battery, a double-pole switch is used in low-output position to reduce the output to 3 amperes for charging the battery. Move switch to high-output position (7 amperes) when using accessories.

To test systems, remove rectifiers and test them with either a continuity light or an ohmmeter. Rectifiers should show current flow in one direction only. Alternator output can be checked using an induction ammeter over the positive lead wire to battery.

External Regulator-Rectifier System. The system shown in (Fig. TRL106) may produce 7, 10 or 20 amperes and uses a solid-state regulator-rectifier outside the flywheel that converts the generated alternating current to direct current for charging the battery. The regulator-rectifier also allows only the required amount of current flow for existing battery conditions. When battery is fully charged, current

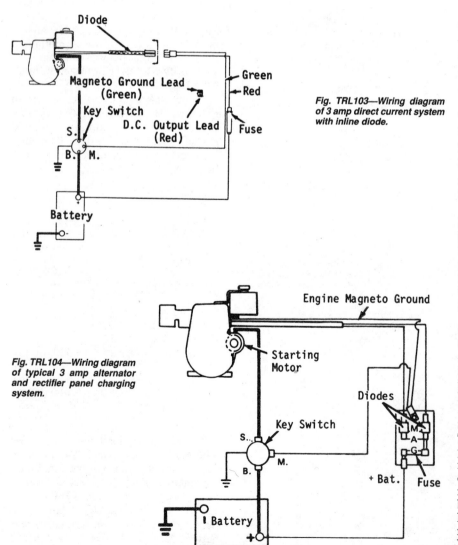

Fig. TRL103—Wiring diagram of 3 amp direct current system with inline diode.

Fig. TRL104—Wiring diagram of typical 3 amp alternator and rectifier panel charging system.

Illustrations Courtesy Tecumseh Products Co.

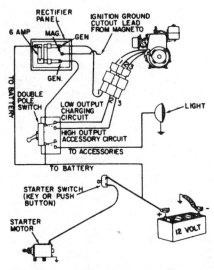

Fig. TRL105—Wiring diagram of typical 7 amp alternator and rectifier panel charging system. The double pole switch in one position reduces output to 3 amps for charging or increases output to 7 amps in other position to operate accessories.

output is decreased to prevent overcharging the battery.

To test 7 or 10 amp system, disconnect B+ lead and connect a DC voltmeter as shown in Fig. TRL107. With engine running at 3000 rpm, voltage should be at least 14 volts on 7 amp system and 16 volts on 10 amp system. If reading is excessively high or low, regulator-rectifier unit may be defective. To check alternator coils, connect an AC voltmeter to the AC leads as shown in Fig. TRL108. With engine running at 3000 rpm check AC voltage. Alternator is defective if voltage is less than 18 volts on 7 amp system or 19 volts on 10 amp system.

To test 20 amp system, disconnect B+ lead and connect a DC voltmeter as shown in Fig. TRL107. With headlights on or another load on system so battery voltage is less than 12.5 volts, run engine from 2500 rpm to full throttle. If

voltmeter indicates a voltage rise, system is good. To check alternator coils, connect an AC voltmeter to the AC leads as shown in Fig. TRL108. With engine running at 3000 rpm check AC voltage. Alternator is defective if voltage is less than 38 volts. With B+ wire connected in series with a DC ammeter as shown in Fig. TRL109, alternator is defective if meter indicates less than 13 amps at 2500 rpm, 15 amps at 3000 rpm and 17 amps at 3600 rpm. Regulator-rectifier is defective if battery voltage exceeds 14.8 volts with battery fully charged.

Internal Regulator-Rectifier System. The regulator-rectifier unit is epoxy covered or epoxied in an aluminum box and mounted under the blower housing. Units are not interchangeable. Two systems may be used that produce either 7 or 20 amps at full throttle. A schematic is shown in Fig. TRL110.

It is not possible to perform an open-circuit DC test. To check alternator, remove regulator-rectifier unit from blower housing, then reinstall blower housing. Do not run engine without blower housing installed. Connect AC voltmeter leads to "AC" terminals of regulator-rectifier unit as shown in Fig. TRL111. At engine speed of 3600 rpm (less engine speed will produce less voltage), voltage should be at least 23 volts

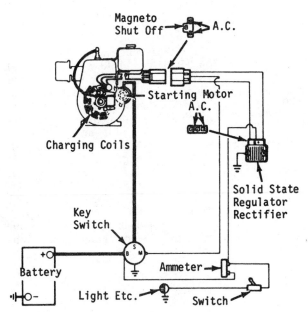

Fig. TRL106—Wiring diagram of typical 7, 10 or 20 amp alternator and regulator-rectifier charging system.

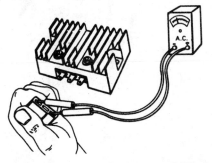

Fig. TRL108—Connect AC voltmeter to AC leads as shown when checking alternator coils.

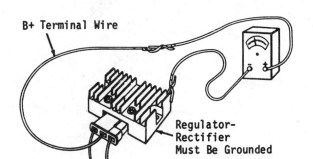

Regulator-Rectifier Must Be Grounded

Fig. TRL107—Connect DC voltmeter as shown when checking the regulator-rectifier.

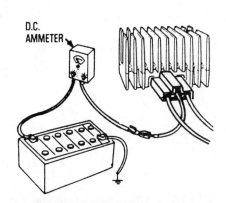

Fig. TRL109—On 20 amp system, connect a DC ammeter as shown when checking regulator-rectifier as outlined in text.

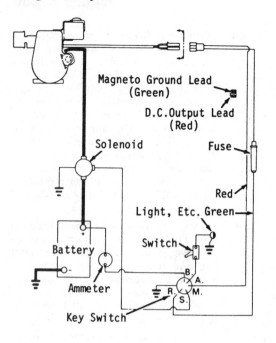

Fig. TRL110—Wiring diagram of charging system using an internal regulator-rectifier unit.

AC for 7 amp system and at least 45 volts for 20 amp system. If voltage reading is less than 23 volts (7 amp system) or 45 volts (20 amp system), alternator is defective. If voltage reading is satisfactory and a known to be good battery is not charged by the system, then the regulator-rectifier unit is defective. On 20 amp systems, regulator-rectifier is defective if battery voltage exceeds 14.8 volts with battery fully charged.

External Ignition Module Alternator. Engines with an external ignition may have an alternator coil attached to the ignition module. The alternator produces approximately 350 milliamperes for battery charging. To check alternator output, connect a DC voltmeter to battery (battery must be in normal circuit) as shown in Fig. TRL112 and note voltage reading. Run engine and again note voltage reading. Voltage should be higher when engine is running, or alternator is defective.

REWIND STARTERS

Friction Shoe-Type

To disassemble the starter refer to Fig. TRL113 and hold starter rotor (12) securely with thumb and remove the four screws securing flanges (1 and 2) to cover (15). Remove flanges and release thumb pressure enough to allow spring to rotate pulley until spring (13) is unwound. Remove retaining ring (3), washer (4), spring (5), slotted washer (6) and fiber washer (7). Lift out friction shoe assembly (8, 9, 10 and 11), then remove second fiber washer and slotted washer. Withdraw rotor (12) with rope from cover and spring. Remove rewind spring from cover and unwind rope from rotor.

Fig. TRL111—Connect AC voltmeter to AC leads of regulator-rectifier to check alternator output. Note that three types of internal regulator-rectifier units have been used.

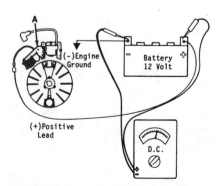

Fig. TRL112—Connect a DC voltmeter to battery as shown to test output of alternator (A) on engines equipped with an external ignition system.

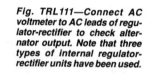

Fig. TRL113—Exploded view of typical friction shoe rewind starter.

1. Mounting flange	6. Slotted washer	10. Friction shoe	14. Centering spring
2. Flange	7. Fiber washer	11. Actuating lever	15. Cover
3. Retaining ring	8. Spring retainer	12. Rotor	16. Rope
4. Washer	9. Spring	13. Rewind spring	17. Roller
5. Spring			

Illustrations Courtesy Tecumseh Products Co.

When reassembling, lubricate rewind spring, cover shaft and center bore in rotor with a light coat of Lubriplate or equivalent. Install rewind spring so windings are in same direction as removed spring. Install rope on rotor, then place rotor on cover shaft. Make certain inner and outer ends of spring are correctly hooked on cover and rotor. Preload the rewind spring by rotating the rotor two full turns. Hold rotor in preload position and install flanges (1 and 2). Check sharp end of friction shoes (10)

and sharpen or renew as necessary. Install washers (6 and 7), friction shoe assembly, spring (5), washer (4) and retaining ring (3). Make certain friction shoe assembly is installed properly for correct starter rotation. If properly installed, sharp ends of friction shoes will extend when rope is pulled.

Remove brass centering pin (14) from cover shaft, straighten pin if necessary, then reinsert pin ⅓ of its length into cover shaft. When installing starter on engine, centering pin will align starter with center hole in end of crankshaft.

Dog-Type

TEARDROP HOUSING. Note shape of starter housing in Fig. TRL114, TRL115 or TRL116. The pulley may be secured with either a retainer screw (9-Fig. TRL114 or 11—Fig. TRL115) or retainer pin (10-Fig. TRL116). Refer to following paragraphs for service.

To disassemble starter shown in Fig. TRL114 and equipped with retainer screw (9), release preload tension of rewind spring by removing rope handle and allowing rope to wind into starter. Remove retainer screw (9), retainer (8) and spring (7). Remove dog (6) and spring (5). Remove pulley with spring. Wear appropriate safety eyewear and gloves before disengaging keeper (2) and rewind spring (3) from pulley as spring may uncoil uncontrolled. To reassemble, reverse the disassembly procedure. Spring (3) should be lightly greased. Assemble starter but install rope last as follows: Turn pulley counterclockwise until tight, then allow to unwind so hole in pulley aligns with rope outlet as shown in Fig. TRL117. Insert rope through starter housing and pulley hole, tie a knot in rope end, allow

rope to wind onto pulley and install rope handle. Some models use centering pin (10) to align starter with starter cup. Place nylon bushing (11) on pin (10), then bottom pin in hole in retainer screw (9). Pin and bushing should index in end of crankshaft when installing starter on engine.

To disassemble starter shown in Fig. TRL115 and equipped with retainer screw (11), pull starter rope until notch in pulley half (5) is aligned with rope hole in housing (1). Hold pulley and prevent from rotating. Engage rope in notch and allow pulley to slowly rotate so rewind spring will unwind. Remove components as shown in Fig. TRL115. Note direction rewind spring is wound. Wear appropriate safety eyewear and gloves when working with rewind spring as spring may uncoil uncontrolled. Reassemble by reversing disassembly procedure. Preload rewind spring by turning pulley two turns with rope.

To disassemble starter equipped with retainer pin (Fig. TRL116), release preload tension of rewind spring by removing rope handle and allowing rope to wind into starter. Remove retainer pin (11) by supporting pulley and driving out pin using a ¼-inch punch.

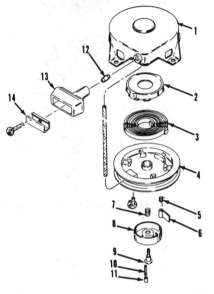

Fig. TRL114—Exploded view of typical dog-type rewind starter with teardrop shaped housing (1) using retainer screw (9). Some starters may have three starter dogs (6).

1. Housing
2. Spring keeper
3. Rewind spring
4. Pulley
5. Spring
6. Dog
7. Brake spring
8. Retainer
9. Screw
10. Centering pin
11. Nylon bushing
12. Rope coupler
13. Handle
14. Insert

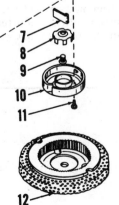

Fig. TRL115—Exploded view of dog-type rewind starter assembly used on some models. Some units are equipped with three starter dogs (7).

1. Housing
2. Rope
3. Rewind spring
4. Pulley half
5. Pulley half & hub
6. Retainer spring
7. Starter dog
8. Brake
9. Brake screw
10. Retainer
11. Retainer screw
12. Hub & screen assy.

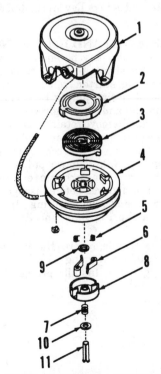

Fig. TRL116—Exploded view of typical dog-type rewind starter with teardrop shaped housing (1) using retainer pin (11).

1. Housing		
2. Spring keeper		7. Brake spring
3. Rewind spring		8. Retainer
4. Pulley		9. Washer
5. Spring		10. Washer
6. Dog		11. Pin

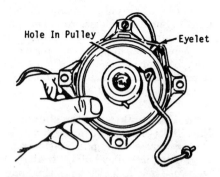

Fig. TRL117—Insert rope through starter housing eyelet and hole in pulley then tie knot in rope end.

Remove spring (7) and retainer (8). Remove dog (6) and spring (5). Remove pulley with spring. Wear appropriate safety eyewear and gloves before disengaging keeper (2) and rewind spring (3) from pulley as spring may uncoil uncontrolled. To reassemble, reverse the disassembly procedure. Spring (3) should be lightly greased. Assemble starter but install rope last. Drive in retainer pin (11) until seated against shoulder of housing. To install rope, rotate pulley counterclockwise until tight, then allow to unwind so hole in pulley aligns with rope outlet as shown in Fig. TRL117. Insert rope through starter housing and pulley hole, tie a knot in rope end, allow rope to wind onto pulley and install rope handle.

SERIES VM AND HM ENGINES. These engines may be equipped with the starter shown in Fig. TRL118. To disassemble starter, release preload tension of rewind spring by removing rope handle and allowing rope to wind into starter. Remove retainer screw (11), dog cam (10), spring (9), and washer (8). Detach "E" rings (7) and remove dogs (6) and springs (5). Remove pulley with spring. Wear appropriate safety eyewear and gloves before disengaging keeper (2) and rewind spring (3) from pulley as spring may uncoil uncontrolled.

To reassemble, reverse the disassembly procedure. Spring (3) should be lightly greased. Install springs (5) so

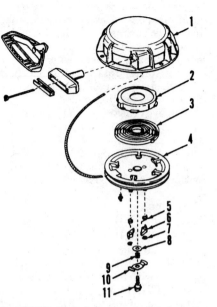

Fig. TRL118—Exploded view of rewind starter used on VM and HM engines.

1. Housing
2. Spring keeper
3. Rewind spring
4. Pulley
5. Spring
6. Dog
7. "E" ring
8. Washer
9. Spring
10. Dog cam
11. Screw

dogs are held in against pulley. Assemble starter but install rope last as follows: Turn pulley counterclockwise until tight, then allow to unwind so hole in pulley aligns with rope outlet as shown in Fig. TRL117. Insert rope through starter housing and pulley hole, tie a knot in rope end, allow rope to wind onto pulley and install rope handle.

STYLIZED STARTER. The "stylized" starter is shown in Fig. TRL119. To disassemble starter, remove rope handle and allow rope to wind into starter. Position a suitable sleeve support under retainer pawl (8) and using a 5/16-inch punch, drive pin (11) free of starter. Remove brake spring (9), retainer (8), dogs (6) and springs (5). Wear appropriate safety eyewear and gloves before disengaging pulley from starter as spring may uncoil uncontrolled. Place rags around pulley and lift pulley

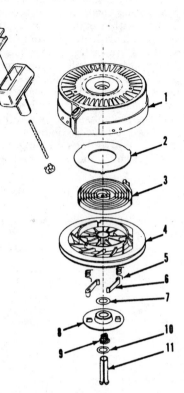

Fig. TRL119—Exploded view of "stylized" rewind starter.

1. Starter housing
2. Cover
3. Rewind spring
4. Pulley
5. Springs (2)
6. Dogs (2)
7. Plastic washers (2)
8. Retainer pawl
9. Brake spring
10. Metal washer
11. Pin

out of housing; spring should remain with pulley.

Inspect components for damage and excessive wear. Reverse disassembly procedure to install components. Rewind spring coils wind in clockwise direction from outer end. Wind rope around pulley in counterclockwise direction as viewed from retainer side of pulley. Be sure inner end of rewind spring engages spring retainer adjacent to housing center post. Use two plastic washers (7). Install a new pin (11) so top of pin is 1/8 inch (3.2 mm) below top of starter. Driving pin in too far may damage retainer pawl.

WISCONSIN ROBIN

TELEDYNE TOTAL POWER
P.O. Box 181160
Memphis, Tennessee 38181

Model	No. Cyls.	Bore	Stroke	Displacement	Power Rating
W1-450V	1	90 mm (3.54 in.)	70 mm (2.76 in.)	445 cc (27.17 cu. in.)	9 kW (12 hp)

Model W1-450V is a four-stroke, air-cooled, single-cylinder gasoline engine with a vertical crankshaft. The engine is pressure-lubricated by an oil pump located in the oil pan. The engine model and specification numbers are located on the nameplate on flywheel shroud. The serial number is stamped on the crankcase base. Always furnish engine model, specification and serial numbers when ordering parts.

MAINTENANCE

LUBRICATION. Check engine oil level daily and maintain oil level at full mark on dipstick.

Manufacturer recommends oil with an API service classification of SF or SG. Use SAE 30 oil when temperature is above 40° F (4° C), SAE 20 oil when temperature is between 15° F (–9° C) and 40° F (4° C), and SAE 10W-30 oil when temperature is below 15° F (–9° C).

Oil should be changed after every 50 hours of operation. Crankcase capacity is 1.3 liters (2.7 pt.).

SPARK PLUG. Recommended spark plug is a NGK BM6A or equivalent. Specified spark plug electrode gap is 0.6-0.7 mm (0.024-0.028 in.). Tighten spark plug to 12-16 N•m (106-142 in.-lbs.).

CARBURETOR. A Mikuni float-type carburetor is used. Refer to Fig. WR701 for exploded view of carburetor. Carburetor has a fixed high-speed jet.

Initial adjustment of low-speed mixture screw (8) is 1½ turns open from a lightly seated position. Make final carburetor adjustment with engine at normal operating temperature and running. Adjust low-speed mixture screw to obtain smoothest idle operation and acceleration.

Adjust idle speed screw to obtain an idle speed of 1200 rpm at normal operating temperature.

To check or adjust float level, remove fuel bowl and place carburetor body on end (on manifold flange) so float pin is in vertical position. Position float so float arm just contacts fuel inlet valve.

NOTE: Needle valve is spring loaded. Float tab should just contact needle valve pin but should not compress spring.

Float should be parallel with fuel bowl mating surface as shown in Fig. WR702. Carefully bend tab on float arm to obtain correct setting.

Refer to Fig. WR703 for correct installation of gaskets used with carburetor and intake manifold.

GOVERNOR. The engine is equipped with a centrifugal flyweight-type governor. To adjust external governor linkage, loosen clamp screw (R—Fig. WR704) on governor lever (L). Move governor lever so throttle valve in carburetor is wide open. Hold lever in this position and rotate governor shaft (S) clockwise as far as possible. Tighten clamp screw. Run engine under no load and rotate speed control lever (D) until it contacts speed adjusting screw. Rotate screw so desired no-load engine speed is obtained; this also establishes

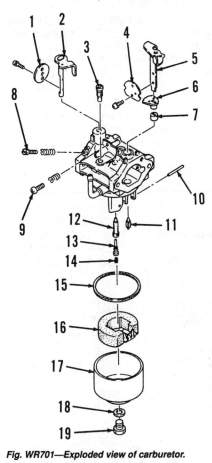

Fig. WR701—Exploded view of carburetor.

1. Throttle plate
2. Throttle shaft
3. Idle mixture jet
4. Choke plate
5. Choke shaft
6. Detent plate
7. Bushing
8. Idle mixture screw
9. Idle speed screw
10. Pin
11. Fuel inlet valve
12. Main nozzle
13. Nozzle
14. Main jet
15. Gasket
16. Float
17. Fuel bowl
18. Gasket
19. Plug

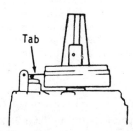

Fig. WR702—Float should be parallel with fuel bowl mating surface.

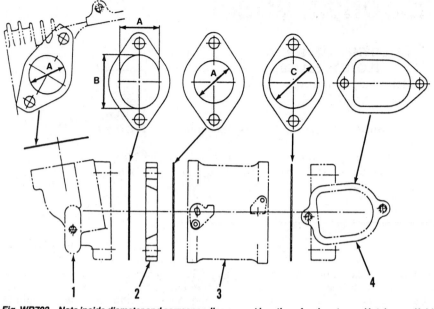

Fig. WR703—Note inside diameter and corresponding correct location of carburetor and intake manifold gaskets.

A. 32 mm (1.26 in.)
B. 41 mm (1.61 in.)
C. 39 mm (1.53 in.)
1. Intake manifold
2. Insulator
3. Carburetor
4. Elbow

guide clearance for both valves is 0.300 mm (0.0118 in.).

Specified valve stem diameter is 7.945-7.970 mm (0.3128-0.3138 in.) for intake valve and 7.904-7.930 mm (0.3112-0.3122 in.) for exhaust valve. Minimum diameter for both valves is 7.85 mm (0.309 in.).

Valve guides are renewable. Specified valve guide inside diameter for both valves is 7.964-8.000 mm (0.3135-0.3150 in.) with a wear limit of 8.150 mm (0.3209 in.).

Specified valve spring length is 46.0 mm (1.81 in.) with a minimum spring length of 44.5 mm (1.75 in.).

PISTON, PIN AND RINGS. To remove piston and rod assembly, drain engine oil and remove engine from equipment. Remove cylinder head. Clean pto end of crankshaft and remove any burrs or rust. Unscrew fasteners and remove oil pan. Remove balancer shafts. Unscrew connecting rod screws and remove piston and rod.

The piston is equipped with one compression ring, one scraper ring and one oil control ring. Install rings as shown in Fig. WR705. Stagger ring end gaps at 90-degree intervals around piston.

Piston and rings are available in standard and oversizes.

Piston ring end gap for the top two rings should be 0.10-0.30 mm (0.004-0.012 in.); maximum allowable gap is 1.5 mm (0.059 in.).

Specified piston ring side clearance is listed below:

Top ring . . . . 0.110-0.150 mm
(0.0043-0.0059 in.)
Second ring . . . . 0.060-0.100 mm
(0.0024-0.0039 in.)
Oil ring . . . . 0.010-0.050 mm
(0.0004-0.0020 in.)

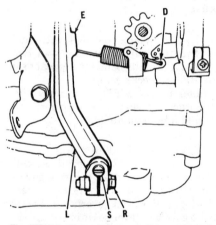

Fig. WR704—View of governor linkage. Refer to text for adjustment.

clearance, grind valve seat deeper or renew valve and/or valve tappet.

REPAIRS

TIGHTENING TORQUES. Recommended tightening torque specifications are as follows:

Connecting rod . . . . 25-30 N•m
(18.4-22 ft.-lbs.)
Cylinder head . . . . 34-39 N•m
(25-29 ft-lbs.)
Flywheel nut . . . . 80-100 N•m
(59-74 ft-lbs.)
Oil pan . . . . 17-19 N•m
(150-168 in.-lbs.)
Spark plug . . . . 12-16 N•m
(106-142 in.-lbs.)

CYLINDER HEAD. Renew cylinder head if it is warped more than 0.15 mm (0.006 in.). Always use a new head gasket when installing cylinder head. Tighten cylinder head bolts or nuts evenly and in stages until reaching final torque of 34-39 N•m (25-29 ft-lbs.).

VALVE SYSTEM. On all models, valve face and seat angles should be 45°. Standard seat width is 1.2-1.5 mm (0.047-0.059 in.). Maximum allowable seat width is 2.5 mm (0.098 in.).

Valve stem-to-guide clearance should be 0.030-0.091 mm (0.0012-0.0036 in.) for intake valve and 0.070-0.126 mm (0.0028-0.0050 in.) for exhaust valve. Maximum allowable valve stem-to-

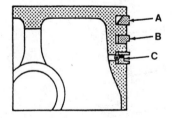

Fig. WR705—Install piston rings as shown. Note that bevel on top compression ring (A) and slot in oil control ring (C) is toward piston crown. Bevel in second compression ring (B) is toward piston skirt.

A. Top compression ring
B. Second compression ring
C. Oil control ring
D. Expander

choke operating point. Governor sensitivity is adjusted by relocating governor spring end (E) in holes in governor lever (L).

IGNITION SYSTEM. The engine is equipped with a breakerless, solid-state ignition system. There is no scheduled maintenance. Specified air gap between ignition coil and flywheel is 0.5 mm (0.020 in.).

VALVE ADJUSTMENT. Valve tappet gap (cold) should be 0.08-0.12 mm (0.003-0.005 in.). To increase clearance, grind off end of valve stem. To reduce

Illustrations Courtesy Teledyne Total Power

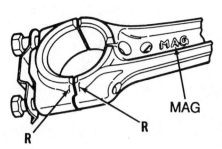

Fig. WR706—Install rod cap on rod so ribs are adjacent. Install piston and rod so "MAG" on rod is toward flywheel.

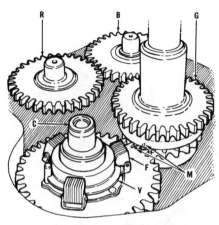

Fig. WR707—Align timing marks (M) on crankshaft and camshaft gears when installing camshaft. Timing marks on large crankshaft gear (G) and balancer gear (B) must be aligned, as well as timing marks on balancer gears (B and R).

Renew piston rings and/or piston if ring side clearance exceeds 0.15 mm (0.006 in.).

Specified piston-to-cylinder clearance is 0.011-0.053 mm (0.0004-0.0021 in.) with a maximum clearance of 0.28 mm (0.011 in.).

Specified piston diameter is 89.950-89.970 mm (3.5413-3.5421 in.) with a wear limit of 89.87 mm (3.538 in.). Measure piston diameter on skirt perpendicular to pin hole.

Specified piston pin diameter is 19.991-20.000 mm (0.7870-0.7874 in.); minimum allowable diameter is 19.965 mm (0.7860 in.). Specified piston bore diameter for pin is 19.989-20.002 mm (0.7870-0.7875 in.); maximum allowable diameter is 19.960 mm (0.7858 in.). Piston pin clearance in piston should be 0.011 mm (0.0004 in.).

Install piston and rod so "MAG" on side of rod (see Fig. WR706) is toward flywheel. Align match marks (cast ribs) on connecting rod and cap as shown in Fig. WR706. Tighten connecting rod cap screws to 25-30 N•m (18.4-22 ft.-lbs.).

When installing oil pan, be sure drive pin in end of camshaft is properly aligned with slot in oil pump shaft. Do not force oil pan on crankcase. Light tapping only should be required if all components are properly aligned.

CONNECTING ROD. Connecting rod and piston are removed as a unit as outlined in previous section. Connecting rod rides directly on crankpin.

Connecting rod-to-crankpin clearance should be 0.050-0.082 mm (0.0020-0.0032 in.). If clearance exceeds 0.20 mm (0.008 in.), renew rod and/or crankshaft.

Connecting rod side clearance should be 0.1-0.3 mm (0.004-0.012 in.). If side clearance exceeds 1.0 mm (0.039 in.), renew connecting rod and/or crankshaft.

GOVERNOR. The governor flyweight assembly is mounted on the camshaft gear and is not available separately from camshaft. Components must move freely without binding. When installing thrust sleeve (V—Fig. WR707) on camshaft (C), be sure sleeve flange properly engages slots in flyweights (F).

CRANKSHAFT. The crankshaft is supported by a ball bearing at both ends. Renew bearings if rough, noisy, excessively worn or otherwise damaged.

Specified crankpin diameter is 37.934-37.950 mm (1.4935-1.4941 in.) with a wear limit of 37.85 mm (1.490 in.). Specified main bearing journal diameter at flywheel end is 34.986-35.000 mm (1.3774-1.3780 in.) with a wear limit of 34.95 mm (1.376 in.). Specified main bearing journal diameter at pto end is 34.997-35.000 mm (1.3778-1.3780 in.) with a wear limit of 34.95 mm (1.376 in.).

Connecting rod-to-crankpin clearance should be 0.050-0.082 mm (0.0020-0.0032 in.). If clearance exceeds 0.20 mm (0.008 in.), renew rod and/or crankshaft. Maximum allowable crankpin taper and out-of-round is 0.005 mm (0.0002 in.).

Install crankshaft seals with lips toward ball bearings.

Crankshaft end play should be 0.03-0.25 mm (0.001-0.009 in.). End play is controlled by a shim (16—Fig. WR708) located between crankshaft gear and main bearing. Several thicknesses are available, but only one shim is installed.

To determine shim thickness, measure from inner race of bearing (D—Fig. WR709) to machined surface on oil pan and add compressed thickness (C) of gasket, which is 0.22 mm (0.0087 in.). From total, subtract distance from thrust surface (B) of large crankshaft gear to surface of crankcase machined surface (A). Calculation establishes end play without shim. Select shim so crankshaft end play is 0.03-0.25 mm (0.001-0.009 in.).

When reassembling engine, make certain timing marks (M—Fig. WR707) on crankshaft and camshaft gears are aligned. Align timing marks on large crankshaft gear (G) and balancer gear (B).

When installing oil pan, be sure drive pin in end of camshaft is properly aligned with slot in oil pump shaft. Do not force oil pan on crankcase. Light tapping only should be required if all components are properly aligned.

CAMSHAFT. The camshaft drives the oil pump and rides in bores in crankcase and oil pan.

When removing camshaft, position engine so tappets will not fall out. If valve tappets are removed, they should be marked so they can be returned to their original positions.

Specified camshaft journal diameter at both ends is 19.967-19.980 mm (0.7861-0.7866 in.) with a wear limit of 19.75 mm (0.7776 in.). Specified intake lobe height is 35.90-36.10 mm (1.413-1.421 in.) with a wear limit of 35.75 mm (1.407 in.). Specified exhaust lobe height is 35.40-35.60 mm (1.394-1.402 in.) with a wear limit of 35.25 mm (1.388 in.).

When reinstalling camshaft, align timing marks (M—Fig. WR707) on camshaft and crankshaft gears.

Camshaft end play should be 0.03-0.25 mm (0.001-0.009 in.) and is controlled by a shim (26—Fig. WR708). Several thicknesses are available, but only one shim is installed.

To determine shim thickness, measure from thrust surface (F—Fig. WR709) on oil pan to machined surface on oil pan and add compressed thickness (C) of gasket, which is 0.22 mm (0.0087 in.). From total, subtract distance from camshaft thrust surface (E) to surface of crankcase machined surface (A). Calculation establishes end play without shim. Select shim so camshaft end play is 0.03-0.25 mm (0.001-0.009 in.).

When installing oil pan, be sure drive pin in end of camshaft is properly aligned with slot in oil pump shaft. Do not force oil pan on crankcase. Light tapping only should be required if all components are properly aligned.

BALANCER SHAFTS. The engine is equipped with two balancer shafts (35 and 36—Fig. WR708) that ride in ball bearings in the crankcase and oil pan. During installation, align timing mark

Fig. WR708—Exploded view of engine.

1. Cylinder head
2. Head gasket
3. Exhaust valve
4. Intake valve
5. Valve guide
6. Oil seal
7. Piston rings
8. Piston
9. Snap ring
10. Piston pin
11. Connecting rod
12. Oil pan
13. Gasket
14. Dowel pin
15. Ball bearing
16. Shim
17. Crankshaft gear (large)
18. Spacer
19. Crankshaft gear (small)
20. Crankshaft
21. Key
22. Rod cap
23. Valve spring
24. Valve spring retainer
25. Valve retainer
26. Shim
27. Camshaft
28. Tappet
29. Outer rotor
30. Inner rotor
31. Oil pump housing
32. Cover
33. Ball bearings
34. Washers
35. Balancer
36. Balancer
37. Crankcase

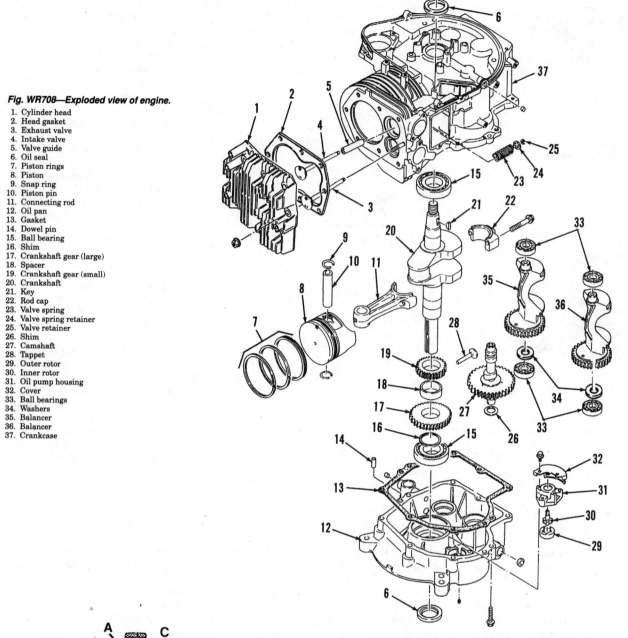

Fig. WR709—View showing location of measuring points to determine correct shim thickness for obtaining correct camshaft and crankshaft end play. Refer to text.

on balancer gear (B—Fig. WR707) with timing mark on crankshaft gear (G). Align timing marks on balancer gears (B) and (R).

OIL PUMP. Engine lubrication is provided by an oil pump located in the oil pan. The oil pan must be removed for access to oil pump components (29 through 32—Fig. WR708). The oil pump is driven by a pin in the end of the camshaft. Inspect oil pump housing and rotors for damage and excessive wear.

When installing oil pan, be sure drive pin in end of camshaft is properly aligned with slot in oil pump shaft. Do not force oil pan on crankcase. Light tapping only should be required if all components are properly aligned.

METRIC CONVERSION TABLE

INCHES FRACT.	INCHES DECIMALS	MM		INCHES FRACT.	INCHES DECIMALS	MM		INCHES FRACT.	INCHES DECIMALS	MM		INCHES FRACT.	INCHES DECIMALS	MM
	.000 04	.001			.066 93	1.7		11/64	.171 88	4.3656			.287 40	7.3
	.000 39	.01			.07	1.778			.173 23	4.4			.29	7.366
	.001	.025			.07087	1.8			.177 17	4.5			.291 34	7.4
	.000 78	.02			.075	1.905			.18	4.572			.295 28	7.5
	.001 18	.03		5/64	.078 13	1.9844			.181 10	4.6		19/64	.296 88	7.5406
	.001 57	.04			.078 74	2.0			.185 04	4.7			.299 21	7.66
	.00197	.05			.08	2.032		3/16	.187 5	4.7625			.30	7.62
	.002	.051			.082 68	2.1			.188 98	4.8			.303 15	7.7
	.002 36	.06			.086 61	2.2			.19	4.826			.307 09	7.8
	.002 5	.0635			.088 58	2.25			.192 91	4.9			.31	7.874
	.002 76	.07			.09	2.286			.196 85	5.0			.311 02	7.9
	.002 95	.075			.090 55	2.3			.2	5.08		5/16	.312 5	7.9375
	.003	.0762		3/32	.093 75	2.3812			.200 79	5.1			.314 96	8.0
	.003 15	.08			.094 49	2.4		13/64	.203 13	5.1594			.318 90	8.1
	.003 54	.09			.098 43	2.5			.204 72	5.2			.32	8.128
	.003 94	.1			.1	2.54			.208 66	5.3			.322 83	8.2
	.004	.1016			.102 36	2.6			.21	5.334			.326 77	8.3
	.005	.1270			.106 30	2.7			.216 60	5.4		21/64	.328 13	8.3344
	.007 87	.2			.108 27	2.75			.216 54	5.5			.33	8.382
	.009 84	.25		7/64	.109 37	2.7781		7/32	.218 75	5.5562			.330 71	8.4
	.01	.254			.11	2.794			.22	5.588			.334 65	8.5
	.011 81	.3			.110 24	2.8			.220 47	5.6			.338 58	8.6
1/64	.015 63	.3969			.114 17	2.9			.224 41	5.7			.34	8.636
	.015 75	.4			.118 11	3.0			.228 35	5.8			.342 52	8.7
	.019 69	.5			.12	3.048			.23	5.842		11/32	.343 75	8.7312
	.02	.508			.122 05	3.1			.232 28	5.9			.346 46	8.8
	.023 62	.6		1/8	.125	3.175		15/64	.234 38	5.9531			.35	8.89
	.025	.635			.125 98	3.2			.236 22	6.0			.350 39	8.9
	.027 56	.7			.127 96	3.25			.24	6.096			.354 33	9.0
	.029 5	.75			.129 92	3.3			.240 16	6.1			.358 27	9.1
	.03	.762			.13	3.302			.244 09	6.2		23/64	.359 38	9.1281
1/32	.031 25	.7938			.133 86	3.4			.248 03	6.3			.36	9.144
	.031 5	.8			.137 80	3.5		1/4	.25	6.35			.362 20	9.2
	.035 43	.9			.14	3.556			.251 97	6.4			.366 14	9.3
	.039 37	1.0		9/64	.140 63	3.5719			.255 91	6.5			.37	9.398
	.04	1.016			.141 73	3.6			.259 84	6.6			.370 08	9.4
	.043 31	1.1			.145 67	3.7			.26	6.604			.374 02	9.5
3/64	.046 87	1.191			.149 61	3.8			.263 78	6.7		3/8	.375	9.525
	.047 24	1.2			.15	3.810		17/64	.265 63	6.7469			.377 95	9.6
	.049 21	1.25			.153 54	3.9			.267 72	6.8			.38	9.652
	.05	1.27		5/32	.156 25	3.9688			.27	6.858			.381 89	9.7
	.051 18	1.3			.157 48	4.0			.271 65	6.9			.385 83	9.8
	.055 12	1.4			.16	4.064			.275 59	7.0			.389 76	9.9
	.059 06	1.5			.161 42	4.1			.279 53	7.1			.39	9.906
	.06	1.524			.165 35	4.2			.28	7.112		25/64	.390 63	9.9219
1/16	.062 5	1.5875			.169 29	4.3		9/32	.281 25	7.1438			.393 70	10.0
	.062 99	1.6			.17	4.318			.283 46	7.2			.397 64	10.1

Group 1

INCHES FRACT.	INCHES DECIMALS	MM
	.40	10.16
	.401 57	10.2
	.405 51	10.3
13/32	.406 25	10.3188
	.409 45	10.4
	.41	10.414
	.413 39	10.5
	.417 32	10.6
	.42	10.668
	.421 26	10.7
27/64	.421 88	10.7156
	.425 20	10.8
	.429 13	10.9
	.43	10.992
	.433 07	11.0
	.437 01	11.1
7/16	.437 5	11.1125
	.44	11.176
	.440 94	11.2
	.444 88	11.3
	.448 82	11.4
	.45	11.430
	.452 76	11.5
29/64	.453 13	11.5094
	.456 69	11.6
	.46	11.684
	.460 63	11.7
	.464 57	11.8
	.468 50	11.9
15/32	.468 75	11.9062
	.47	11.938
	.472 44	12.0
	.476 38	12.1
	.48	12.192
	.480 31	12.2
	.484 25	12.3
31/64	.484 38	12.3031
	.488 19	12.4
	.49	12.446
	.492 13	12.5
	.496 06	12.6
1/2	.50	12.7
	.503 94	12.8
	.507 87	12.9
	.51	12.954
	.511 81	13.0
33/64	.515 63	13.0969
	.515 75	13.1
	.519 68	13.2
	.52	13.208
	.523 62	13.3
	.527 56	13.4
	.53	13.462
17/32	.531 25	13.4938
	.531 50	13.5
	.535 43	13.6
	.539 37	13.7
	.54	13.716
	.543 31	13.8
35/64	.546 88	13.8906
	.547 24	13.9
	.55	13.970
	.551 18	14.0
	.555 12	14.1
	.559 05	14.2
	.56	14.224
9/16	.562 50	14.2875
	.562 99	14.3

Group 2

INCHES FRACT.	INCHES DECIMALS	MM
	.566 93	14.4
	.57	14.478
	.570 87	14.5
	.574 80	14.6
37/64	.578 13	14.6844
	.578 74	14.7
	.58	14.732
	.582 68	14.8
	.586 61	14.9
	.59	14.986
	.590 55	15.0
19/32	.593 75	15.0812
	.594 49	15.1
	.598 42	15.2
	.60	15.24
	.602 36	15.3
	.606 30	15.4
39/64	.609 38	15.4781
	.61	15.494
	.610 24	15.5
	.614 17	15.6
	.618 11	15.7
	.62	15.748
	.622 05	15.8
5/8	.625	15.875
	.625 98	15.9
	.629 92	16.0
	.63	16.002
	.633 86	16.1
	.637 79	16.2
	.64	16.256
41/64	.640 63	16.2719
	.641 73	16.3
	.645 67	16.4
	.649 61	16.5
	.65	16.510
	.653 54	16.6
21/32	.656 25	16.6688
	.657 48	16.7
	.66	16.764
	.661 42	16.8
	.665 35	16.9
	.669 29	17.0
	.67	17.018
43/64	.671 88	17.0656
	.673 23	17.1
	.677 16	17.2
	.68	17.272
	.681 10	17.3
	.684 05	17.4
11/16	.687 50	17.4625
	.688 98	17.5
	.69	17.526
	.692 91	17.6
	.696 85	17.7
	.70	17.78
	.700 79	17.8
45/64	.703 13	17.8594
	.704 72	17.9
	.708 66	18.0
	.71	18.034
	.712 60	18.1
	.716 53	18.2
23/32	.718 75	18.2562
	.72	18.288
	.720 47	18.3
	.724 41	18.4
	.728 35	18.5

Group 3

INCHES FRACT.	INCHES DECIMALS	MM
	.73	18.542
	.732 28	18.6
47/64	.734 38	18.6531
	.736 22	18.7
	.74	18.796
	.740 16	18.8
	.744 09	18.9
	.748 03	19.0
3/4	.75	19.050
	.751 97	19.1
	.755 90	19.2
	.759 84	19.3
	.76	19.307
	.763 78	19.4
49/64	.765 63	19.4469
	.767 72	19.5
	.77	19.558
	.771 65	19.6
	.775 59	19.7
	.779 53	19.8
	.78	19.812
25/32	.781 25	19.8438
	.783 46	19.9
	.787 40	20.0
	.79	20.066
	.791 34	20.1
	.795 27	20.2
51/64	.796 88	20.2406
	.799 21	20.3
	.80	20.320
	.803 15	20.4
	.807 09	20.5
	.81	20.574
	.811 02	20.6
13/16	.812 50	20.6375
	.814 96	20.7
	.818 90	20.8
	.82	20.828
	.822 83	20.9
	.826 77	21.0
53/64	.828 13	21.0344
	.83	21.082
	.830 71	21.1
	.834 64	21.2
	.838 58	21.3
	.84	21.336
	.842 52	21.4
27/32	.843 75	21.4312
	.846 46	21.5
	.85	21.590
	.850 39	21.6
	.854 33	21.7
	.858 27	21.8
55/64	.859 38	21.8281
	.86	21.844
	.862 20	21.9
	.866 14	22.0
	.87	22.098
	.870 08	22.1
	.874 01	22.2
7/8	.875	22.225
	.877 95	22.3
	.88	22.352
	.881 89	22.4
	.885 83	22.5
	.889 76	22.6
	.89	22.606
57/64	.890 63	22.6219

Group 4

INCHES FRACT.	INCHES DECIMALS	MM
	.893 70	22.7
	.897 64	22.8
	.90	22.860
	.901 57	22.9
	.905 51	23.0
29/32	.906 25	23.0188
	.909 49	23.1
	.91	23.114
	.913 38	23.2
	.917 32	23.3
	.92	23.368
	.921 26	23.4
59/64	.921 88	23.4156
	.925 20	23.5
	.929 13	23.6
	.93	23.622
	.933 07	23.7
	.937 01	23.8
15/16	.937 50	23.8125
	.94	23.876
	.940 94	23.9
	.944 88	24.0
	.948 82	24.1
	.95	24.130
	.952 75	24.2
61/64	.953 13	24.2094
	.956 69	24.3
	.96	24.384
	.960 63	24.4
	.964 57	24.5
	.968 50	24.6
31/32	.968 75	24.6062
	.97	24.638
	.972 44	24.7
	.976 38	24.8
	.98	24.892
	.980 31	24.9
	.984 25	25.0
63/64	.984 38	25.0031
	.988 19	25.1
	.99	25.146
	.992 12	25.2
	.996 06	25.3
1"	1.000 00	25.4000
1-1/4	1.25	31.75
1-1/2	1.50	38.1
1-3/4	1.75	44.45
2"	2.000	50.8
2-1/2	2.5	63.5
3"	3.000	76.2
3-1/2	3.5	88.9
	3.937	100.00
4"	4.000	101.6
4-1/2	4.5	114.3
5"	5.000	127.0
5-1/2	5.5	139.7
6"	6.000	152.4
6-1/2	6.5	165.1
7"	7.000	177.8
7-1/2	7.5	190.5
8"	8.000	203.2
8-1/2	8.5	215.9
9"	9.000	228.6
9-1/2	9.5	241.3
10"	10.000	254.00
10-1/2	10.5	266.7
11"	11.000	279.4
12"	12.000	304.8

NOTES

NOTES

NOTES

NOTES

NOTES

Genuine John Deere Service Literature

For ordering information, call John Deere at 1-800-522-7448.
All major credit cards accepted.

PARTS CATALOG

The parts catalog lists service parts available for your machine with exploded view illustrations to help you identify the correct parts. It is also useful in assembling and disassembling.

OPERATOR'S MANUAL

The operator's manual provides safety, operating, maintenance, and service information about John Deere machines.

The operator's manual and safety signs on your machine may also be available in other languages.

TECHNICAL AND SERVICE MANUALS

Technical and service manuals are service guides for your machine. Included in the manual are specifications, diagnosis, and adjustments. Also illustrations of assembly and disassembly procedures, hydraulic oil flows, and wiring diagrams.

Component technical manuals are required for some products. These supplemental manuals cover specific components.

FUNDAMENTALS OF SERVICE MANUALS

These basic manuals cover most makes and types of machines. FOS manuals tell you how to SERVICE machine systems. Each manual starts with basic theory and is fully illustrated with colorful diagrams and photographs. Both the "whys" and "hows" of adjustments and repairs are covered in this reference library.